MEET Math
School of Engineering

Sheridan College

NELSON
EDUCATION

This textbook is a Nelson custom publication. Because your instructor has chosen to produce a custom publication, you pay only for material that you will use in your course.

ISBN-13: 978-0-17-674333-8
ISBN-10: 0-17-674333-2

Consists of Selections from:

Technical Mathematics, 4th Edition
John C. Peterson
ISBN 10: 1-111-54046-2, © 2013

Algebra and Trigonometry, 7th Edition
Ron Larson
ISBN 10: 1-305-07173-5, © 2016

Mathematical Excursions, Enhanced Edition, 3rd Edition
Richard N. Aufmann
Joanne S. Lockwood
Richard D. Nation
Daniel K. Clegg
ISBN 10: 1-285-45422-7, © 2015

Introductory Technical Mathematics, 6th Edition
John Peterson
Robert D. Smith
ISBN 10: 1-111-54200-7, © 2013

Math for Electricity and Electronics, 4th Edition
Dr. Arthur Kramer
ISBN 10: 1-111-54507-3, © 2012

Cover Credit:

Maksim Toome/Shutterstock

Table of Contents

UNIT 7

PRECISION, ACCURACY, AND TOLERANCE

OBJECTIVES

After studying this unit you should be able to

- determine the degree of precision of any measurement number.
- round sums and differences of measurement numbers to proper degrees of precision.
- determine the number of significant digits of measurement numbers.
- round products and quotients of measurement numbers to proper degrees of accuracy.
- compute absolute and relative error between true and measured values.
- compute maximum and minimum clearances and interferences of bilateral and unilateral tolerance-dimensioned parts (customary and metric).
- compute total tolerance, maximum limits, and minimum limits of customary and metric unit lengths.
- solve practical applied problems involving tolerances and limits (customary and metric).

Measurement is used to communicate size, quantity, position, and time. Without measurement, a building could not be built nor a product manufactured.

The ability to measure with tools and instruments and to compute with measurements is required in almost all occupations. In the construction field, measurements are calculated and measurements are made with tape measures, carpenters squares, and transits. The manufacturing industry uses a great variety of measuring instruments, such as micrometers, calipers, and gauge blocks. Measurement calculations from engineering drawings are requirements. Electricians and electronics technicians compute circuit measurements and read measurements on electrical meters. Environmental systems occupations require heat load and pressure calculations and make measurements with instruments such as manometers and pressure gauges.

7–1 EXACT AND APPROXIMATE (MEASUREMENT) NUMBERS

If a board is cut into 6 pieces, 6 is an exact number; exactly 6 pieces are cut. If 150 bolts are counted, 150 bolts is an exact number; exactly 150 bolts are counted. These are examples of counting numbers and are exact.

However, if the length of a board is measured as $7\frac{3}{8}$ inches, $7\frac{3}{8}$ inches is not exact. If the diameter of a bolt is measured as 12.5 millimeters, 12.5 millimeters is not exact. The $7\frac{3}{8}$ inches and 12.5 millimeters are approximate values. Measured values are always approximate.

Measurement is the comparison of a quantity with a standard unit. For example, a linear measurement is a means of expressing the distance between two points; it is the measurement of lengths. A linear measurement has two parts: a unit of length and a multiplier.

multiplier —↑ 2.5 inches ↑— *unit of length*   *multiplier* —↑ $15\frac{1}{4}$ miles ↑— *unit of length*

The measurements 2.5 inches and $15\frac{1}{4}$ miles are examples of denominate numbers. A **denominate number** is a number that refers to a special unit of measure. A **compound denominate number** consists of more than one unit of measure, such as 7 feet 2 inches.

7–2 DEGREE OF PRECISION OF MEASURING INSTRUMENTS

The exact length of an object cannot be measured. All measurements are approximations. By increasing the number of graduations on a measuring instrument, the degree of precision is increased. Increasing the number of graduations enables the user to get closer to the exact length. The precision of a measurement depends on the measuring instrument used. The **degree of precision** of a measuring instrument depends on the smallest graduated unit of the instrument.

The degree of precision necessary in different trades varies. In building construction, generally $\frac{1}{16}$-inch or 2-millimeter precision is adequate. Sheet metal technicians often work to $\frac{1}{32}$-inch or 1-millimeter precision. Machinists and automobile mechanics usually work to 0.001-inch or 0.02-millimeter precision. In the manufacture of some products, very precise measurements to 0.00001 inch or 0.0003 millimeter and 0.000001 inch or 0.00003 millimeter are sometimes required. For example, the dial indicator in Figure 7–1 can be used to measure to the nearest 0.001″ while the one in Figure 7–2 measures to the nearest 0.0005″.

Courtesy of S-T Industries

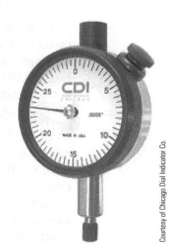

Courtesy of Chicago Dial Indicator Co.

FIGURE 7–1   FIGURE 7–2

Various measuring instruments have different limitations on the degree of precision possible. The accuracy achieved in measurement does not depend only on the limitations of the measuring instrument. Accuracy can also be affected by errors of measurement. Errors can be caused by defects in the measuring instruments and by environmental changes such as differences in temperature. Perhaps the greatest cause of error is the inaccuracy of the person using the measuring instrument.

7–3 COMMON LINEAR MEASURING INSTRUMENTS

Tape Measure. Tape measures are commonly used by garment makers and tailors. Customary tape measures are generally 5 feet long with $\frac{1}{8}$ inch the smallest graduation. Therefore, the degree of precision is $\frac{1}{8}$ inch. Metric tape measures are generally 2 meters long with 1 millimeter the smallest graduation. The degree of precision for a metric tape measure is 1 millimeter.

Folding Rule. Folding rules are used by construction workers such as carpenters, cabinetmakers, electricians, and masons. Customary rules are generally 6 feet long and fold to 6 inches. The smallest graduation is usually $\frac{1}{16}$ inch. The smallest graduation on metric rules is generally 1 millimeter. Customary units and metric units are available on the same rule. The customary units are on one side of the rule, and the metric units are on the opposite side.

Steel Tape. Steel tapes are used by contractors, construction workers, and surveyors. Customary steel tapes are available in 25-foot, 50-foot, and 100-foot lengths. Generally, the smallest graduation is $\frac{1}{8}$ inch. Metric tapes are available in 10-meter, 15-meter, 20-meter, and 30-meter lengths. Generally, the smallest graduation is 1 millimeter. Customary units and metric units are also available on the same tape. Customary units are on one side of the tape, and metric units are on the opposite side.

Steel Rules. Steel rules are widely used in manufacturing industries by machine operators, machinists, and sheet metal technicians. Customary steel rules are available in sizes from 1 inch to 144 inches; 6 inches is the most common length. Customary rules are available in both fractional and decimal-inch graduations. The smallest graduation on fractional rules is $\frac{1}{64}$ inch; the smallest graduation on a decimal-inch is 0.01 inch. Metric measure steel rules are available in a range from 150 millimeters to 1000 millimeters (1 meter) in length. The smallest graduation is 0.5 millimeter.

Vernier and Dial Calipers. Vernier calipers and dial calipers are widely used in the metal trades. The most common customary unit lengths are 6 inches and 12 inches, although calipers are available in up to 72-inch lengths. The smallest unit that can be read is 0.001 inch. Metric measure rules are available in lengths from 150 millimeters to 600 millimeters. The smallest unit that can be read is 0.02 millimeter. Some vernier calipers are designed with both customary and metric unit scales on the same instrument.

Micrometers. Micrometers are used by tool and die makers, automobile mechanics, and inspectors. Micrometers are used when relatively high precision measurements are required. There are many different types and sizes of micrometers. Customary outside micrometers are available in sizes from 0.5 inch to 60 inches. The smallest graduation is 0.0001 inch with a vernier attachment. Metric outside micrometers are available in sizes up to 600 millimeters. The smallest graduation is 0.002 millimeter with a vernier attachment.

Digital Calipers and Micrometers. Used by the same people who use vernier and dial calipers and micrometers, these digital instruments are battery-operated versions of these measuring instruments. Not only do they provide faster and more accurate readings, the same instrument can be used for metric and customary measures. More expensive versions of these instruments can transmit data through wireless connections or a USB (Universal Serial Bus) port. They can also provide SPC (Statistical Process Control) analysis and documentation. SPC will be briefly studied in Unit 32.

7–4 DEGREE OF PRECISION OF A MEASUREMENT NUMBER

The degree of precision of a measurement number depends on the number of decimal places used. The number becomes more precise as the number of decimal places increases. For example, 4.923 inches is more precise than 4.92 inches. The range includes all of the values that are represented by the number.

EXAMPLES

1. What is the degree of precision and the range for 2 inches?

   The degree of precision of 2 inches is to the nearest inch as shown in Figure 7–3. The range of values includes all numbers equal to or greater than 1.5 inches or less than 2.5 inches.

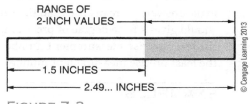

   FIGURE 7–3

2. What is the degree of precision and the range for 2.0 inches?

   The degree of precision of 2.0 inches is to the nearest 0.1 inch as shown in Figure 7–4. The range of values includes all numbers equal to or greater than 1.95 inches and less than 2.05 inches.

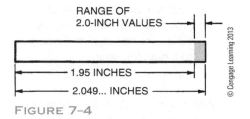

   FIGURE 7–4

3. What is the degree of precision and the range for 2.00 inches?

   The degree of precision of 2.00 inches is to the nearest 0.01 inch as shown in Figure 7–5. The range of values includes all numbers equal to or greater than 1.995 inches and less than 2.005 inches.

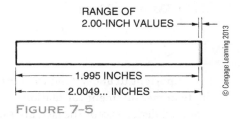

   FIGURE 7–5

4. What is the degree of precision and the range for 2.000 inches?

   The degree of precision of 2.000 inches is to the nearest 0.001 inch. The range of values includes all numbers equal to or greater than 1.9995 inches and less than 2.0005 inches.

EXERCISE 7–4   For each measurement find:
a. the degree of precision
b. the range

1. 3.6 in.	4. 7.08 mm	7. 12.002 in.	10. 23.00 in.
2. 1.62 in.	5. 15.885 in.	8. 36.0 mm	11. 9.1 mm
3. 4.3 mm	6. 9.1837 in.	9. 7.01 mm	12. 14.01070 in.

7–5   DEGREES OF PRECISION IN ADDING AND SUBTRACTING MEASUREMENT NUMBERS

When adding or subtracting measurements, all measurements must be expressed in the same kind of units. Often measurement numbers of different degrees of precision are added or subtracted. When adding and subtracting numbers, there is a tendency to make answers more precise than they are. An answer that has more decimal places than it should gives a false degree of precision. A sum or difference cannot be more precise than the least precise measurement number used in the computations. Round the answer to the least precise measurement number used in the computations.

EXAMPLES

1. 15.63 in. + 2.7 in. + 0.348 in. = 18.678 in., 18.7 in. ANS
   Since the least precise number is 2.7 in., round the answer to 1 decimal place.
2. 3.0928 cm − 0.532 cm = 2.5608 cm, 2.561 cm ANS
   Since the least precise number is 0.532 cm, round the answer to 3 decimal places.
3. 73 ft + 34.21 ft = 107.21 ft, 107 ft ANS
   Since the least precise number is 73 ft, round the answer to the nearest whole number.
4. 73.0 ft + 34.21 ft = 107.21 ft, 107.2 ft ANS
   Notice that this example is identical to Example 3, except the first measurement is 73.0 ft instead of 73 ft. Since the least precise measurement is 73.0 ft, round the answer to 1 decimal place.

EXERCISE 7–5   Add or subtract the following measurement numbers. Round answers to the degree of precision of the least precise number.

1. 2.69 in. + 7.871 in.	7. 18.005 in. − 10.00362 in.
2. 14.863 mm − 5.0943 mm	8. 0.0187 cm^3 + 0.70 cm^3
3. 80.0 ft + 7.34 ft	9. 33.92 gal + 27 gal
4. 0.0009 in. + 0.001 in.	10. 6.01 lb + 15.93 lb + 18.0 lb
5. 2256 mi − 783.7 mi	11. 26.50 sq in. − 26.49275 sq in.
6. 31.708 cm^2 − 27.69 cm^2	12. 84.987 mm + 39.01 mm − 77 mm

7–6   SIGNIFICANT DIGITS

It is important to understand what is meant by significant digits and to apply significant digits in measurement calculations. A measurement number has all of its digits significant if all digits, except the last, are exact and the last digit has an error of no more than half the unit of measurement in the last digit. For example, 6.28 inches has 3 significant digits when measured to the nearest hundredth of an inch.

The following rules are used for determining significant digits:

1. All nonzero digits are significant.
2. Zeros between nonzero digits are significant.
3. Final zeros in a decimal or mixed decimal are significant.
4. Zeros used as placeholders are *not* significant unless they are identified as significant. Usually a zero is identified as significant by tagging it with a bar above it.

EXAMPLES

The next seven items are examples of significant digits. They represent measurement (approximate) numbers.

1. 812   3 significant digits, all nonzero digits are significant
2. 7.139   4 significant digits, all nonzero digits are significant
3. 14.3005   6 significant digits, zeros between nonzero digits are significant
4. 9.300   4 significant digits, final zeros of a decimal are significant
5. 0.008   1 significant digit, zeros used as placeholders are *not* significant
6. 23,000   2 significant digits, zeros used as placeholders are *not* significant
7. 23,$\overline{0}$00   3 significant digits, a zero tagged is significant

In addition to the previous examples, study the following examples. The number of significant digits, shown in parentheses, is given for each number.

1. 3.905 (4)   5. 147.500 (6)   9. 1.00187 (6)   13. 8600 (2)
2. 3.950 (4)   6. 7.004 (4)   10. 8.020 (4)   14. 0.01040 (4)
3. 83.693 (5)   7. 0.004 (1)   11. 0.020 (2)   15. 95,080.7 (6)
4. 147.005 (6)   8. 0.00187 (3)   12. 8603.0 (5)   16. 90,00$\overline{0}$ (5)

EXERCISE 7–6   Determine the number of significant digits for the following measurement (approximate) numbers.

1. 2.0378   6. 9700   11. 0.00095   16. 87,195
2. 0.0378   7. 12.090   12. 385.007   17. 66,08$\overline{0}$
3. 126.10   8. 137.000   13. 4353.0   18. 87,200.00
4. 0.020   9. 137,0$\overline{0}$0   14. 1.040   19. 6.010
5. 9709.3   10. 8.005   15. 0.0370   20. 4,000,100

7–7 ACCURACY

The number of significant digits in a measurement number determines its accuracy. The greater the number of significant digits, the more accurate the number. For example, consider the measurements of 8 millimeters and 126 millimeters. Both measurements are equally precise; they are both measured to the nearest millimeter. The two measurements are not equally accurate. The greatest error in both measurements is 0.5 millimeter. However, the error in the 8 millimeter measurement is more serious than the error in the 126 millimeter measurement. The 126 millimeter measurement (3 significant digits) is more accurate than the 8 millimeter measurement (1 significant digit).

Examples of the Accuracy of Measurement Numbers

1. 2.09 is accurate to 3 significant digits
2. 0.1250 is accurate to 4 significant digits
3. 0.0087 is accurate to 2 significant digits
4. 50,000 is accurate to 1 significant digit
5. 68.9520 is accurate to 6 significant digits

When measurement numbers have the same number of significant digits, the number that begins with the largest digit is the most accurate. For example, consider the measurement numbers 3700, 4100, and 2900. Although all 3 numbers have 2 significant digits, 4100 is the most accurate.

EXERCISE 7–7   For each of the following groups of measurement numbers, identify the number that is most accurate.

1. 5.05; 4.9; 0.002
2. 18.6; 1.860; 0.186
3. 1000; 29; 173
4. 0.0009; 0.004; 0.44
5. 123.0; 9460; 36.7
6. 0.27; 50,720; 52.6
7. 4.16; 5.16; 8.92
8. 39.03; 436; 0.0235
9. 70,108; 69.07; 8.09
10. 0.930; 0.0086; 5.31
11. 917; 43.08; 0.0936
12. 86,000; 9300; 435
13. 0.0002; 0.0200; 0.0020
14. 5.0003; 5.030; 5.003
15. 636.0; 818.0; 727.0
16. 0.1229; 7.063; 20.125

7–8 ACCURACY IN MULTIPLYING AND DIVIDING MEASUREMENT NUMBERS

Care must be taken to maintain proper accuracy when multiplying and dividing measurement numbers. There is a tendency to make answers more accurate than they actually are. An answer that has more significant digits than it should gives a false impression of accuracy. A product or quotient cannot be more accurate than the least accurate measurement number used in the computations.

Examples of Multiplying and Dividing Measurement Number

1. 3.896 in. × 63.6 = 247.7856 in., 248 in. ANS
   Since the least accurate number is 63.6, round the answer to 3 significant digits.
2. 7500 mi × 2.250 = 16,875 mi, 17,000 mi ANS
   Since the least accurate number is 7500, round the answer to 2 significant digits.
3. 0.009 mm ÷ 0.4876 = 0.018457752 mm, 0.02 mm ANS
   Since the least accurate number is 0.009, round the answer to 1 significant digit.
4. 802,000 lb ÷ 430.78 × 1.494 = 2,781.438321 lb, 2780 lb ANS
   Since the least accurate number is 802,000, round the answer to 3 significant digits.
5. If a machined part weighs 0.1386 kilogram, what is the weight of 8 parts? Since 8 is a counting number and is exact, only the number of significant digits in the measurement number, 0.1386, is considered.
   8 × 0.1386 kg = 1.1088 kg, 1.109 kg ANS, rounded to 4 significant digits.

EXERCISE 7–8   Multiply or divide the following measurement numbers. Round answers to the same number of significant digits as the least accurate number.

1. 18.9 mm × 2.373
2. 1.85 in. × 3.7
3. 8900 ÷ 52.861
4. 9.085 cm ÷ 1.07
5. 33.08 mi × 0.23
6. 51.9 ÷ 0.97623
7. 0.007 × 0.852
8. 830.367 × 9.455

9. 6.80 ÷ 9.765 × 0.007
10. 71,200 × 19.470 × 0.168
11. 5.00017 × 16.874 × 0.12300
12. 30,000 ÷ 154.9 ÷ 80.03
13. 0.00956 × 34.3 × 0.75
14. 15.635 × 0.415 × 10.07
15. 270.001 ÷ 7.100 × 19.853
16. 52.3 × 6.890 × 0.0073

7–9   ABSOLUTE AND RELATIVE ERROR

Absolute error and relative error are commonly used to express the amount of error between an actual or true value and a measured value.

Absolute error is the difference between a true value and a measured value. Since the measured value can be either a smaller or larger value than the true value, subtract the smaller value from the larger value.

$$\text{Absolute Error} = \text{True Value} - \text{Measured Value}$$

or

$$\text{Absolute Error} = \text{Measured Value} - \text{True Value}$$

Relative error is the ratio of the absolute error to the true value.

$$\text{Relative Error} = \frac{\text{Absolute Error}}{\text{True Value}}$$

Percent error is relative error expressed as a percent.

$$\text{Percent error} = \text{Relative error} \times 100\%$$

or

$$\text{Percent error} = \frac{\text{Absolute error}}{\text{True error}} \times 100\%$$

NOTE: *100 is an exact number*

Examples of Absolute, Relative, and Percent Error

1. The actual or true value of the diameter of a shaft is 1.7056 inches. The shaft is measured as 1.7040 inches. Compute the absolute error and the relative error.

The true value is larger than the measured value, therefore:

Absolute Error = True Value − Measured Value
Absolute Error = 1.7056 in. − 1.7040 in. = 0.0016 in. Ans

$$\text{Relative Error} = \frac{\text{Absolute Error}}{\text{True Value}}$$

$$\text{Relative Error} = \frac{0.0016 \text{ in.}}{1.7056 \text{ in.}} \approx 0.00094 \text{ Ans, rounded to 2 significant digits.}$$

Percent error = Relative error × 100%
Percent error = 0.00094 × 100% = 0.094% Ans

Calculator Application

.0016 $\div$ 1.7056 $\times$ 100 = 0.09380863, 0.094% Ans, rounded

2. In an electrical circuit, a calculated or measured value calls for a resistance of 98 ohms. What are the absolute, relative, and percent error in using a resistor that has an actual or true value of 91 ohms?

The measured value is larger than the true value, therefore:

Absolute Error = Measured Value − True Value

Absolute error = 98 ohms − 91 ohms = 7 ohms Ans

Relative error = $\dfrac{7 \text{ ohms}}{91 \text{ ohms}}$ ≈ 0.08 Ans, rounded to 1 significant digit

Percent error = 0.08 × 100% = 8% Ans

EXERCISE 7–9   Compute the absolute error, relative error, and percent error of each of the values given in the table in Figure 7–6. Round answers to the proper number of significant digits.

	Actual or True Value	Measured Value			Actual or True Value	Measured Value
1.	3.872 in.	3.870 in.		7.	105 ohms	102 ohms
2.	0.53 mm	0.52 mm		8.	0.9347 in.	0.9341 in.
3.	12.7 lb	12.9 lb		9.	1.005 m^2	1.015 m^2
4.	485 mi	482 mi		10.	27.2 ft	26.9 ft
5.	23.86 cm	24.00 cm		11.	1827.6 m	1830.2 m
6.	6056 kg	6100 kg		12.	0.983 cu ft	1.000 cu ft

© Cengage Learning 2013

FIGURE 7–6

7–10 TOLERANCE (LINEAR)

Tolerance (linear) is the amount of variation permitted for a given length. Tolerance is equal to the difference between the maximum and minimum limits of a given length.

EXAMPLES

1. The maximum permitted length (limit) of the tapered shaft shown in Figure 7–7 is 134.2 millimeters. The minimum permitted length (limit) is 133.4 millimeters. Find the tolerance.

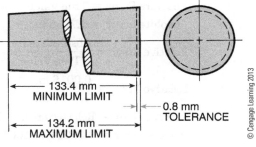

© Cengage Learning 2013

FIGURE 7–7

The tolerance equals the maximum limit minus the minimum limit.

134.2 mm − 133.4 mm = 0.8 mm Ans

2. The maximum permitted depth (limit) of the dado joint shown in Figure 7–8 is $\frac{21}{32}$ inch. The tolerance is $\frac{1}{16}$ inch. Find the minimum permitted depth (limit).

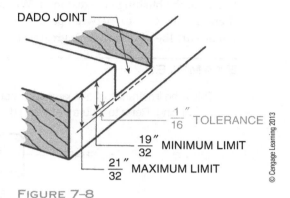

FIGURE 7–8

The minimum limit equals the maximum limit minus the tolerance.

$$\frac{21''}{32} - \frac{1''}{16} = \frac{19''}{32} \quad \text{ANS}$$

EXERCISE 7–10   Refer to the tables in Figures 7–9 and 7–10 and determine the tolerance, maximum limit, or minimum limit as required for each problem.

	Tolerance	Maximum Limit	Minimum Limit
1.		$5\frac{7}{16}''$	$5\frac{13}{32}''$
2.		$7'\text{-}9\frac{1}{16}''$	$7'\text{-}8\frac{15}{16}''$
3.	0.02″	16.76″	
4.	0.007″		0.904″
5.		1.7001″	1.6998″
6.	0.0025″		3.069″

FIGURE 7–9

	Tolerance	Maximum Limit	Minimum Limit
7.		50.7 mm	49.8 mm
8.		26.8 cm	26.6 cm
9.	0.04 mm		258.03 mm
10.	0.12 mm	80.09 mm	
11.	0.006 cm		12.731 cm
12.		4.01 mm	3.98 mm

FIGURE 7–10

7–11 UNILATERAL AND BILATERAL TOLERANCE WITH CLEARANCE AND INTERFERENCE FITS

A **basic dimension** is the standard size from which the maximum and minimum limits are made.

Unilateral tolerance means that the total tolerance is taken in only one direction from the basic dimension, such as:

$$+ 0.0000$$
$$2.6856$$
$$- 0.0020$$

Bilateral tolerance means that the tolerance is divided partly above ($+$) and partly below ($-$) the basic dimension, such as 2.6846 $\pm$ 0.0010.

When one part is to move within another there is a clearance between the parts. A shaft made to turn in a bushing is an example of a clearance fit. The shaft diameter is less than the bushing hole diameter. When one part is made to be forced into the other, there is interference between parts. A pin pressed into a hole is an example of an interference fit. The pin diameter is greater than the hole diameter.

EXAMPLES

1. This is an illustration of a clearance fit between a shaft and a hole using unilateral tolerancing. Refer to Figure 7–11 and determine the following:

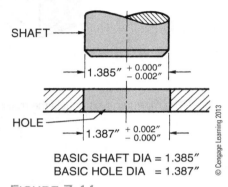

BASIC SHAFT DIA = 1.385″
BASIC HOLE DIA = 1.387″

FIGURE 7–11

a. Maximum shaft diameter
   1.385″ + 0.000″ = 1.385″ ANS
b. Minimum shaft diameter
   1.385″ − 0.002″ = 1.383″ ANS
c. Maximum hole diameter
   1.387″ + 0.002″ = 1.389″ ANS
d. Minimum hole diameter
   1.387″ − 0.000″ = 1.387″ ANS
e. Maximum clearance equals maximum hole diameter minus minimum shaft diameter
   1.389″ − 1.383″ = 0.006″ ANS
f. Minimum clearance equals minimum hole diameter minus maximum shaft diameter
   1.387″ − 1.385″ = 0.002″ ANS

2. This is an illustration of an interference fit between a pin and a hole using bilateral tolerancing. Refer to Figure 7–12 and determine the following:

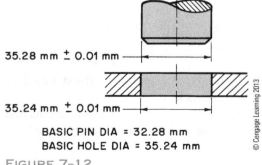

35.28 mm ± 0.01 mm

35.24 mm ± 0.01 mm

BASIC PIN DIA = 32.28 mm
BASIC HOLE DIA = 35.24 mm

FIGURE 7–12

    a. Maximum pin diameter
       35.28 mm + 0.01 mm = 35.29 mm Ans
    b. Minimum pin diameter
       35.28 mm − 0.01 mm = 35.27 mm Ans
    c. Maximum hole diameter
       35.24 mm + 0.01 mm = 35.25 mm Ans
    d. Minimum hole diameter
       35.24 mm − 0.01 mm = 35.23 mm Ans
    e. Maximum interference equals maximum pin diameter minus minimum hole diameter
       35.29 mm − 35.23 mm = 0.06 mm Ans
    f. Minimum interference equals minimum pin diameter minus maximum hole diameter
       35.27 mm − 35.25 mm = 0.02 mm Ans

EXERCISE 7–11   Problems 1 through 5 involve clearance fits between a shaft and hole using unilateral tolerancing. Given diameters *A* and *B*, compute the missing values in the table.

    Refer to Figure 7–13 to determine the table values in Figure 7–14. The values for problem 1 are given.

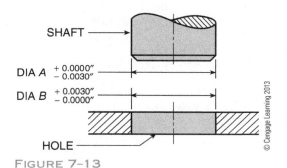

FIGURE 7–13

		Basic Dimension (inches)	Maximum Diameter (inches)	Minimum Diameter (inches)	Maximum Clearance (inches)	Minimum Clearance (inches)
1.	DIA *A*	1.4580	1.4580	1.4550	0.0090	0.0030
	DIA *B*	1.4610	1.4640	1.4610		
2.	DIA *A*	0.9345				
	DIA *B*	0.9365				
3.	DIA *A*	2.1053				
	DIA *B*	2.1078				
4.	DIA *A*	0.4961				
	DIA *B*	0.4970				
5.	DIA *A*	0.9996				
	DIA *B*	1.0007				

FIGURE 7–14

Problems 6 through 10 involve interference fits between a pin and hole using bilateral tolerancing. Given diameters *A* and *B*, compute the missing values in the table.

Refer to Figure 7–15 to determine the table values in Figure 7–16. The values for problem 6 are given.

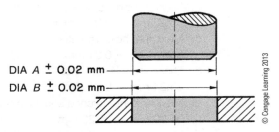

DIA *A* ± 0.02 mm

DIA *B* ± 0.02 mm

© Cengage Learning 2013

FIGURE 7-15

		Basic Dimension (millimeters)	Maximum Diameter (millimeters)	Minimum Diameter (millimeters)	Maximum Clearance (millimeters)	Minimum Clearance (millimeters)
6.	DIA *A*	20.73	20.75	20.71	0.09	0.01
	DIA *B*	20.68	20.70	20.66		
7.	DIA *A*	32.07				
	DIA *B*	32.01				
8.	DIA *A*	10.82				
	DIA *B*	10.75				
9.	DIA *A*	41.91				
	DIA *B*	41.85				
10.	DIA *A*	26.73				
	DIA *B*	26.65				

© Cengage Learning 2013

FIGURE 7-16

UNIT EXERCISE AND PROBLEM REVIEW

DEGREE OF PRECISION OF NUMBERS

For each measurement find:

    a. the degree of precision

    b. the range

1. 5.3 in.
2. 2.78 mm
3. 1.834 in.
4. 12.9 mm
5. 19.001 in.
6. 28.35 mm
7. 29.0 mm
8. 6.1088 in.

DEGREES OF PRECISION IN ADDING AND SUBTRACTING MEASUREMENT NUMBERS

Add or subtract the following measurement numbers. Round answers to the degree of precision of the least precise number.

9. 26.954 mm − 6.0374 mm
10. 0.0008 in. + 0.003 in.
11. 3343 mi − 894.5 mi
12. 28.609 cm + 19.73 cm
13. 27.004 in. − 13.00727 in.
14. $0.0263 \text{ cm}^2 + 0.80 \text{ cm}^2$
15. 16 in. + 6.93 in. + 18.0 in.
16. 96.823 mm + 43.06 mm + 52 mm

SIGNIFICANT DIGITS

Determine the number of significant digits for the following measurement numbers.

17. 9.8350
18. 0.0463
19. 8604.3
20. 0.00086
21. 27.005
22. 89,100
23. 94,126.0
24. 70,000

ACCURACY

For each of the following groups of measurement numbers, identify the number which is most accurate.

25. 6.07; 3.2; 0.005
26. 0.0004; 0.006; 0.56
27. 16.3; 13.0; 48,070
28. 41.02; 364; 0.0384

29. 0.870; 0.0091; 4.22
30. 71,000; 4200; 593
31. 3.0006; 2.070; 9.001
32. 0.0007; 0.0600; 0.0030

ACCURACY IN MULTIPLYING AND DIVIDING MEASUREMENT NUMBERS

Multiply or divide the following measurement numbers. Round answers to the same number of significant digits as the least accurate number.

33. 2.76×4.9
34. 9.043×1.02
35. 0.005×0.973
36. $55,000 \div 767$

37. $82,400 \times 21.503 \times 0.203$
38. $30,000 \div 127.8 \div 86.07$
39. $0.00827 \times 43.2 \times 0.66$
40. $360.002 \div 8.200 \times 15.107$

ABSOLUTE, RELATIVE, AND PERCENT ERROR

Compute the absolute error, relative error, and percent error of each of the values in the table in Figure 7–17. Round answers to the proper number of significant digits.

	Actual or True Value	Measured Value		Actual or True Value	Measured Value
41.	5.963 in.	5.960 in.	44.	107 ohms	99 ohms
42.	392 mm	388 mm	45.	0.8639 cm	0.8634 cm
43.	5056 lb	4998 lb	46.	71.3 ft	70.6 ft

FIGURE 7–17

© Cengage Learning 2013

TOLERANCE

Refer to the tables in Figures 7–18 and 7–19 and determine the tolerance, maximum limit, or minimum limit as required for each exercise.

	Tolerance	Maximum Limit	Minimum Limit
47.		$7\frac{3}{16}''$	$7\frac{1}{8}''$
48.	$\frac{1}{64}''$	$18\frac{1}{4}''$	
49.	$0.006''$		$2.775''$
50.		$0.3064''$	$0.3051''$

FIGURE 7–18

© Cengage Learning 2013

	Tolerance	Maximum Limit	Minimum Limit
51.		40.3 mm	39.7 mm
52.	0.008 cm		6.502 cm
53.	0.18 cm	78.84 mm	
54.		34.02 mm	33.95 cm

FIGURE 7–19

© Cengage Learning 2013

UNILATERAL TOLERANCE

These exercises require computation with unilateral tolerance clearance fits between mating parts. Given dimensions *A* and *B*, compute the missing values in the tables.

Refer to Figure 7–20 to determine the table values in Figure 7–21.

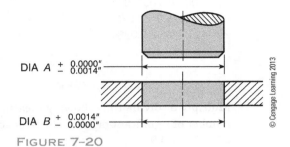

DIA *A* $\pm$ $^{0.0000''}_{0.0014''}$

DIA *B* $\pm$ $^{0.0014''}_{0.0000''}$

© Cengage Learning 2013

FIGURE 7–20

		Basic Dimension (inches)	Maximum Diameter (inches)	Minimum Diameter (inches)	Maximum Clearance (inches)	Minimum Clearance (inches)
55.	DIA *A*	1.7120				
	DIA *B*	1.7136				
56.	DIA *A*	0.2962				
	DIA *B*	0.2970				
57.	DIA *A*	2.8064				
	DIA *B*	2.8075				

© Cengage Learning 2013

FIGURE 7–21

BILATERAL TOLERANCE

These exercises require computations with bilateral tolerances of mating parts with interference fits. Given dimensions *A* and *B*, compute the missing values in the tables.

Refer to Figure 7–22 to determine the table values in Figure 7–23.

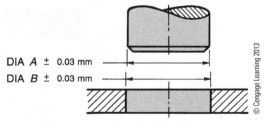

DIA *A* $\pm$ 0.03 mm

DIA *B* $\pm$ 0.03 mm

© Cengage Learning 2013

FIGURE 7–22

		Basic Dimension (Millimeters)	Maximum Diameter (Millimeters)	Minimum Diameter (Millimeters)	Maximum Clearance (Millimeters)	Minimum Clearance (Millimeters)
58.	DIA *A*	78.78				
	DIA *B*	78.70				
59.	DIA *A*	9.94				
	DIA *B*	9.85				
60.	DIA *A*	130.03				
	DIA *B*	129.96				

© Cengage Learning 2013

FIGURE 7–23

PRACTICAL APPLIED PROBLEMS

61. A cabinetmaker saws a board as shown in Figure 7–24. What are the maximum and minimum permissible values of length *A*?

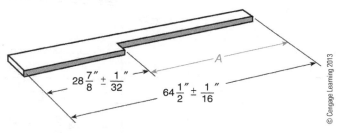

FIGURE 7–24

62. A sheet metal technician lays out a job to the dimensions and tolerances shown in Figure 7–25. Determine the maximum permissible value of length *A*.

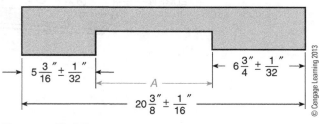

FIGURE 7–25

63. Determine the maximum and minimum permissible wall thickness of the steel sleeve shown in Figure 7–26.

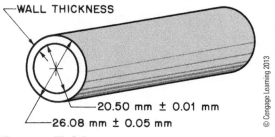

FIGURE 7–26

17

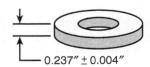

64. Spacers are manufactured to the dimension and tolerance shown in Figure 7-27. An inspector measures 10 bushings and records the following thicknesses:

0.243″   0.239″   0.236″   0.242″   0.234″
0.231″   0.241″   0.238″   0.240″   0.232″

Which spacers are defective (above the maximum limit or below the minimum limit)?

65. The drawing in Figure 7-28 gives the locations with tolerances of 6 holes that are to be drilled in a length of angle iron. An ironworker drills the holes, then checks them for proper locations from edge A. The actual locations of the drilled holes are shown in Figure 7-29. Which holes are drilled out of tolerance (located incorrectly)?

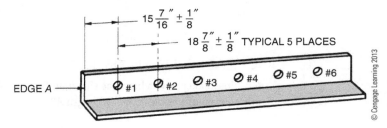

FIGURE 7-28

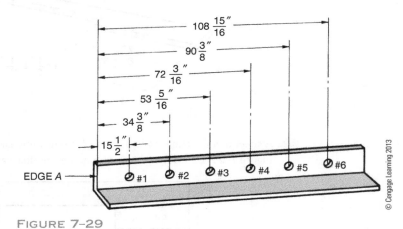

FIGURE 7-29

UNIT 8

CUSTOMARY MEASUREMENT UNITS

OBJECTIVES

After studying this unit you should be able to

- express lengths as smaller or larger customary linear compound numbers.
- perform arithmetic operations with customary linear units and compound numbers.
- express given customary length, area, and volume measures in larger and smaller units.
- express given customary capacity and weight units as larger and smaller units.
- solve practical applied customary length, area, volume, capacity, and weight problems.
- express customary compound unit measures as equivalent compound unit measures.
- solve practical applied compound unit measures problems.

The United States uses two systems of weights and measures, the American customary system and the SI metric system. The American or U.S. customary system is based on the English system of weights and measures. The International System of Units called the SI metric system is used by all but a few nations.

Although the American customary units are based on the English system, they are now defined in terms of metric units.

The American customary length unit, yard, is defined in terms of the metric length base unit, meter. The American customary mass (weight) unit, pound, is defined in terms of the SI metric mass base unit, kilogram.

Throughout this book, the American customary units are called "customary" units and the SI metric units called "metric" units. It is important that you have the ability to measure and compute with both the customary and metric systems. This chapter will examine the customary measurement system, and the next chapter will look the metric system.

Linear Measure

A linear measurement is a means of expressing the distance between two points; it is the measurement of lengths. Most occupations require the ability to compute linear measurements and to make direct length measurements.

A drafter computes length measurements when drawing a machined part or an architectural floor plan, an electrician determines the amount of cable required for a job, a welder calculates the length of material needed for a weldment, a printer "figures" the number of pieces that can be cut from a sheet of stock, a carpenter calculates the total length of baseboard required for a building, and an automobile technician computes the amount of metal to be removed for a cylinder re-bore.

8–1   CUSTOMARY LINEAR UNITS

The yard is the standard unit of linear measure in the customary system. From the yard, other units such as the inch and foot are established. The smallest unit is the inch. Customary units of linear measure are shown in Figure 8–1.

Customary Units of Linear Measure
1 foot (ft) = 12 inches (in.)
1 yard (yd) = 3 feet (ft)
1 yard (yd) = 36 inches (in.)
1 rod (rd) = 16.5 feet (ft)
1 rod (rd) = 5.5 yards (yd)
1 furlong = 220 yards (yd)
1 mile (mi) = 5280 feet (ft)
1 mile (mi) = 1760 yards (yd)
1 mile (mi) = 320 rod (rd)
1 mile (mi) = 8 furlongs

© Cengage Learning 2013

FIGURE 8–1

Notice that most of the symbols, ft for foot, mi for mile, yd for yard, do not have periods at the end. That is because they are symbols and not abbreviations. The one exception is in. for inch. Many people prefer in. because the period helps you know that they do not mean the word "in."

8–2 EXPRESSING EQUIVALENT UNITS OF MEASURE

When expressing equivalent units of measure, either of two methods can be used. Throughout Unit 8, examples are given using either of the two methods. Many examples show how both methods are used in expressing equivalent units of measure.

METHOD 1

In this method you multiply or divide by a known conversion amount.

This is a practical method used for many on-the-job applications. It is useful when simple unit conversions are made.

METHOD 2

This method is called the **unity fraction method**. The unity fraction method eliminates the problem of incorrectly expressing equivalent units of measure. Using this method removes any doubt as to whether to multiply or divide when making a conversion. The unity fraction method is particularly useful in solving problems that involve a number of unit conversions.

In this method, the given unit of measure is multiplied by a fraction equal to one, called a unity fraction. The unity fraction contains the given unit of measure and the unit of measure to which the given unit is to be converted. The unity fraction is set up in such a way that the original unit cancels out and the unit you are converting to remains. Recall that cancelling is the common term used when a numerator and a denominator are divided by a common factor.

Expressing Smaller Customary Units of Linear Measure as Larger Units

To express a smaller unit of length as a larger unit of length using Method 1, divide the given length by the number of smaller units contained in one of the larger units.

EXAMPLE

Express 76.53 inches as feet.

METHOD 1

Since 12 inches equal 1 foot, divide 76.53 by 12.

$76.53 \div 12 = 6.3775$
76.53 inches ≈ 6.378 feet ANS

20

METHOD 2

Since 76.53 inches is to be expressed as feet,

multiplying by the unity fraction $\dfrac{1\ ft}{12\ in.}$

permits the inch unit to be canceled and the foot unit to remain.

In the numerator and denominator, divide by the common factor, 1 inch.

Divide 76.53 ft by 12.

$$76.53\ \cancel{in.} \times \frac{1\ ft}{12\ \cancel{in.}} = \frac{76.53\ ft}{12} \approx 6.378\ ft\ \text{ANS}$$

Calculator Application

76.53 $\boxed{\div}$ 12 $\boxed{=}$ 6.3775

6.378 ft ANS rounded to 4 significant digits

EXERCISE 8–2A   Express each length as indicated. Round each answer to the same number of significant digits as in the original quantity. Customary units of linear measure are given in the table in Figure 8–1.

1. 51.0 inches as feet
2. 272.5 inches as feet
3. 21.25 feet as yards
4. 67.8 feet as yards
5. 6300 feet as miles
6. 404.6 inches as yards

7. 44.4 inches as feet
8. 4928 yards as miles
9. 56.8 feet as yards
10. 53.25 feet as yards
11. 216 rods as miles
12. 6.05 furlongs as miles

Expressing Smaller Units as a Combination of Units

For actual on-the-job applications, smaller units are often expressed as a combination of larger and smaller units (compound denominate numbers).

EXAMPLE

A carpenter wants to express $134\frac{7}{8}$ inches as feet and inches as shown in Figure 8–2.

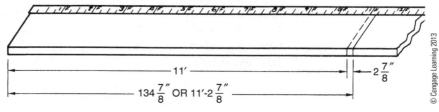

© Cengage Learning 2013

FIGURE 8–2

Since 12 inches equal 1 foot, divide $134\frac{7}{8}$ by 12. There are 11 feet plus a remainder of $2\frac{7}{8}$ inches in $134\frac{7}{8}$ inches.

The carpenter uses 11 feet $2\frac{7}{8}$ inches as an actual on-the-job measurement. ANS

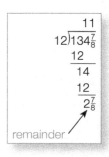

remainder

EXERCISE 8–2B   Express each length as indicated. Customary units of linear measure are given in the table in Figure 8–1.

1. 75 inches as feet and inches
2. 40 inches as feet and inches
3. 2420 yards as miles and yards
4. 15,000 feet as miles and feet
5. $127\frac{1}{2}$ inches as feet and inches

6. 63.2 feet as yards and feet
7. $1925\frac{1}{3}$ yards as miles and yards
8. $678\frac{3}{4}$ rods as miles and rods

Expressing Larger Customary Units of Linear Measure as Smaller Units

To express a larger unit of length as a smaller unit of length, multiply the given length by the number of smaller units contained in one of the larger units.

EXAMPLE

Express 2.28 yards as inches.

METHOD 1

Since 36 inches equal 1 yard, multiply 2.28 by 36.

$2.28 \times 36 = 82.08$
2.28 yards ≈ 82.1 in. Ans

METHOD 2

Multiply 2.28 yards by the unity fraction.

$\dfrac{36 \text{ in.}}{1 \text{ yd}}$

$2.28 \text{ yd} \times \dfrac{36 \text{ in.}}{1 \text{ yd}} = 2.28 \times 36 \text{ in.} \approx 82.1 \text{ in.}$ Ans

Divide the numerator and denominator by the common factor, 1 yard

EXERCISE 8–2C   Express each length as indicated. Round each answer to the same number of significant digits as in the original quantity. Customary units of linear measure are given in the table in Figure 8–1.

1. 6.0 feet as inches
2. 0.75 yard as inches
3. 16.30 yards as feet
4. 0.122 mile as yards
5. 1.350 miles as feet
6. 9.046 feet as inches

7. 4.25 yards as feet
8. 2.309 miles as yards
9. 0.250 mile as feet
10. 3.20 yards as inches
11. 1.45 miles as rods
12. 3.6 miles as furlongs

Expressing Larger Units as a Combination of Units

Larger units are often expressed as a combination of two different smaller units.

EXAMPLE

Express 2.3 yards as feet and inches.

METHOD 1

Express 2.3 yards as feet.
Multiply 2.3 by 3.

Express 0.9 foot as inches.
Multiply 0.9 by 12.

Combine feet and inches.

$2.3 \times 3 = 6.9$
2.3 yd $= 6.9$ ft
$0.9 \times 12 = 10.8$
0.9 ft $= 10.8$ in.
2.3 yd $= 6$ ft 10.8 in. Ans

METHOD 2

Multiply 2.3 yards by the unity fraction $\dfrac{3 \text{ ft}}{1 \text{ yd}}$.

Multiply 0.9 feet by the unity fraction $\dfrac{12 \text{ in.}}{1 \text{ ft}}$.

Combine feet and inches.

$$2.3 \text{ yd} \times \dfrac{3 \text{ ft}}{1 \text{ yd}} = 2.3 \times 3 \text{ ft} = 6.9 \text{ ft}$$

$$0.9 \text{ ft} \times \dfrac{12 \text{ in.}}{1 \text{ ft}} = 0.9 \times 12 \text{ in.} = 10.8 \text{ in.}$$

2.3 yd = 6 ft 10.8 in. ANS

EXERCISE 8–2D Express each length as indicated.

1. $6\dfrac{1}{2}$ yards as feet and inches

2. 8.250 yards as feet and inches

3. 0.0900 mile as yards and feet

4. $\dfrac{5}{12}$ mile as yards and feet

5. 2.180 miles as rods and yards

6. $8\dfrac{7}{32}$ yards as feet and inches

7. 0.90 yard as feet and inches

8. 0.3700 mile as yards and feet

8–3 ARITHMETIC OPERATIONS WITH COMPOUND NUMBERS

Basic arithmetic operations with compound numbers are often required for on-the-job applications. For example, a material estimator may compute the stock requirements of a certain job by adding 16 feet $7\frac{1}{2}$ inches and 9 feet 10 inches. An ironworker may be required to divide a 14-foot 10-inch beam in three equal parts.

The method generally used for occupational problems is given for each basic operation.

Addition of Compound Numbers

To add compound numbers, arrange like units in the same column, then add each column. When necessary, simplify the sum.

EXAMPLE

Determine the amount of stock, in feet and inches, required to make the welded angle bracket shown in Figure 8–3.

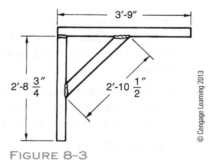

FIGURE 8–3

Arrange like units in the same column.

Add each column.

$$
\begin{array}{r}
3 \text{ ft }\ 9 \text{ in.} \\
2 \text{ ft } 10\frac{1}{2} \text{ in.} \\
2 \text{ ft }\ 8\frac{3}{4} \text{ in.} \\
\hline
7 \text{ ft } 28\frac{1}{4} \text{ in.}
\end{array}
$$

Simplify the sum. Divide $28\frac{1}{4}$ by 12 to express $28\frac{1}{4}$ inches as 2 feet $4\frac{1}{4}$ inches.

$28\frac{1}{4}$ inches $= 2$ feet $4\frac{1}{4}$ inches

Add. 7 feet $+ 2$ feet $4\frac{1}{4}$ inches $= 9$ feet $4\frac{1}{4}$ inches ANS

Subtraction of Compound Numbers

To subtract compound numbers, arrange like units in the same column, then subtract each column starting from the right. Regroup as necessary.

EXAMPLES

1. Determine length A of the pipe shown in Figure 8–4.

   Arrange like units in the same column.

	15 ft $8\frac{1}{2}$ in.
	7 ft $3\frac{1}{4}$ in.
	8 ft $5\frac{1}{4}$ in. ANS

   Subtract each column.

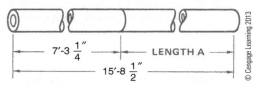

   $7'\text{-}3\frac{1}{4}''$ LENGTH A

   $15'\text{-}8\frac{1}{2}''$

   FIGURE 8–4

2. Subtract 8 yards 2 feet 7 inches from 12 yards 1 foot 3 inches.

   Arrange like units in the same column.

   Subtract each column.

   Since 7 inches cannot be subtracted from 3 inches, subtract 1 foot from the foot column (leaving 0 feet). Express 1 foot as 12 inches; then add 12 inches to 3 inches.

   Since 2 feet cannot be subtracted from 0 feet, subtract 1 yard from the yard column (leaving 11 yards). Express 1 yard as 3 feet; then add 3 feet to 0 feet.

   Subtract each column.

12 yd 1 ft 3 in.
−8 yd 2 ft 7 in.
12 yd 0 ft 15 in.
−8 yd 2 ft   7 in.
11 yd 3 ft 15 in.
−8 yd 2 ft   7 in.
3 yd 1 ft   8 in. ANS

EXERCISE 8–3A Add. Express each answer in the same units as those given in the exercise. Regroup the answer when necessary.

1. 5 ft 6 in. + 7 ft 3 in.
2. 3 ft 9 in. + 4 ft 8 in.
3. 6 ft $3\frac{3}{8}$ in. + 4 ft $1\frac{1}{2}$ in. + 8 ft $10\frac{1}{4}$ in.

4. $5 \text{ yd } 2 \text{ ft} + 2 \text{ yd } \frac{1}{2} \text{ ft} + 7 \text{ yd } \frac{1}{4} \text{ ft}$

5. $3 \text{ yd } 2 \text{ ft} + 5 \text{ yd } \frac{1}{4} \text{ ft} + 9 \text{ yd } 2 \frac{3}{4} \text{ ft}$

6. 9 yd 2 ft 3 in. + 2 yd 0 ft 6 in.

7. 12 yd 2 ft 8 in. + 10 yd 2 ft 7 in.

8. $4 \text{ yd } 1 \text{ ft } 3 \frac{1}{2} \text{ in.} + 7 \text{ yd } 0 \text{ ft } 9 \text{ in.} + 4 \text{ yd } 2 \text{ ft } 0 \text{ in.}$

9. 3 rd 4 yd + 2 rd 1 yd

10. $6 \text{ rd } 3 \frac{1}{4} \text{ yd} + 8 \text{ rd} + 4 \text{ yd}$

11. 1 mi 150 rd + 1 mi 285 rd

12. $3 \text{ mi } 75 \text{ rd } 2 \text{ yd} + 2 \text{ mi } 150 \text{ rd } 3 \frac{1}{4} \text{ yd} + 1 \text{ mi } 200 \text{ rd } 5 \text{ yd}$

Subtract. Express each answer in the same units as those given in the exercise. Regroup the answer when necessary.

13. 6 ft 7 in. − 2 ft 4 in.

14. 15 ft 3 in. − 12 ft 9 in.

15. $10 \text{ ft } 1 \frac{3}{8} \text{ in.} - 7 \text{ ft } 8 \frac{7}{16} \text{ in.}$

16. $8 \text{ yd } 1 \frac{1}{2} \text{ ft} - 4 \text{ yd } 2 \frac{3}{4} \text{ ft}$

17. 14 yd 2 ft − 11 yd 1.5 ft

18. 7 yd 1 ft 9 in. − 2 yd 2 ft 11 in.

19. 16 yd 2 ft 2.15 in. − 14 yd 2 ft 4.25 in.

20. $23 \text{ yd } 1 \text{ ft } 0 \text{ in.} - 3 \text{ yd } 0 \text{ ft } 6 \frac{5}{8} \text{ in.}$

21. 5 rd 3 yd 2 ft − 4 rd 2 yd 1 ft

22. $2 \text{ rd } 5 \text{ yd } 1 \frac{1}{3} \text{ ft} - 1 \text{ rd } 0 \text{ yd } 1 \frac{2}{3} \text{ ft}$

23. 7 mi 240 rd − 3 mi 310 rd

24. 4 mi 150 rd 4 yd − 1 mi 175 rd 5 yd

Multiplication of Compound Numbers

To multiply compound numbers, multiply each unit of the compound number by the multiplier. When necessary, simplify the product.

EXAMPLE

A plumber cuts 5 pieces of copper tubing. Each piece is 8 feet $9\frac{3}{4}$ inches long. Determine the total length of tubing required.

Multiply each unit by 5.

$$\begin{array}{r} 8 \text{ ft } 9\frac{3}{4} \text{ in.} \\ \times\ 5 \\ \hline 40 \text{ ft } 48\frac{3}{4} \text{ in.} \end{array}$$

Simplify the product.

Divide $48\frac{3}{4}$ by 12 to express

$48\frac{3}{4}$ inches as 4 feet $\frac{3}{4}$ inch.

$48\frac{3}{4}$ inches = 4 feet $\frac{3}{4}$ inch

Add.

40 feet + 4 feet $\frac{3}{4}$ inch = 44 feet $\frac{3}{4}$ inch Ans

Division of Compound Numbers

To divide compound numbers, divide each unit by the divisor starting at the left. If a unit is not exactly divisible, express the remainder as the next smaller unit and add it to the given number of smaller units. Continue the process until all units are divided.

EXAMPLE

The 4 holes in the I beam shown in Figure 8–5 are equally spaced. Determine the distance between 2 consecutive holes.

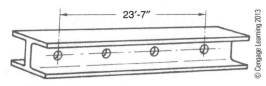

FIGURE 8–5

© Cengage Learning 2013

Since there are 3 spaces between holes, divide 23 feet 7 inches by 3.

Divide 23 feet by 3.

Express the 2-foot remainder as 24 inches.
Add 24 inches to the 7 inches given in the problem.
Divide 31 inches by 3.

Collect quotients.

> 23 ft ÷ 3 = 7 ft (quotient) and a 2 ft remainder
>
> 2 ft = 2 × 12 in. = 24 in.
>
> 24 in. + 7 in. = 31 in.
>
> 31 in. ÷ 3 = $10\frac{1}{3}$ in. (quotient)
>
> 7 ft $10\frac{1}{3}$ in. ANS

EXERCISE 8–3B   Multiply. Express each answer in the same units as those given in the exercise. Regroup the answer when necessary.

1. 7 ft 3 in. × 2
2. 4 ft 5 in. × 3
3. 12 ft 3 in. × 5.5
4. 6 yd $\frac{1}{2}$ ft × 4

5. 16 yd 2 ft × 8
6. 5 yd 1.25 ft × 4.8
7. 9 yd 2 ft 3 in. × 2
8. 11 yd 1 ft $7\frac{3}{4}$ in. × 3

9. 10 yd 2 ft 9 in. × $\frac{1}{2}$
10. 6 rd 4 yd × 5
11. 5 mi 210 rd × 1.4
12. 3 mi 180 rd 5 yd × 2

Divide. Express each answer in the same units as those given in the exercise.

13. 9 ft 6 in. ÷ 3
14. 7 ft 4 in. ÷ 2
15. 18 ft 3.9 in. ÷ 4
16. 16 yd 2 ft ÷ 8
17. 21 yd 1 ft ÷ $1\frac{1}{2}$

18. 4 yd 3.75 ft ÷ 3
19. 14 yd 2 ft 6 in. ÷ 2
20. 17 yd 1 ft 10 in. ÷ 5
21. 6 yd 2 ft $3\frac{1}{4}$ in. ÷ 0.5

22. 5 rd 2 yd ÷ 4
23. 3 mi 150 rd ÷ $1\frac{1}{2}$
24. 4 mi 310 rd 4 yd ÷ 3

8–4 CUSTOMARY LINEAR MEASURE PRACTICAL APPLICATIONS

EXAMPLE

The electrical conduit in Figure 8–6 is made from $\frac{5}{8}$-inch diameter tubing. What is the total length of the straight tubing used for the conduit? Give the answer in feet and inches.

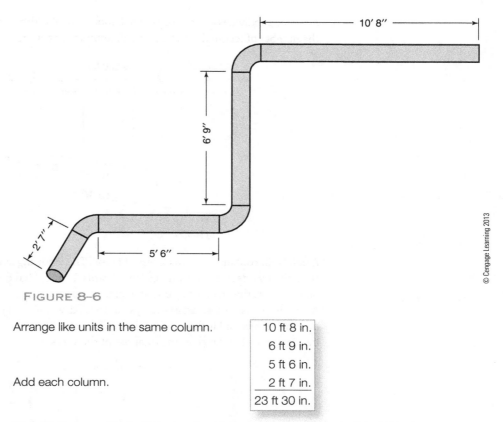

FIGURE 8-6

Arrange like units in the same column.

10 ft 8 in.
6 ft 9 in.
5 ft 6 in.
2 ft 7 in.
23 ft 30 in.

Add each column.

Simplify the sum. Divide 30 inches by 12 to change 30 inches to 2 feet 6 inches.
Add 23 ft + 2 ft 6 in. = 25 ft 6 in. ANS

EXERCISE 8-4   Solve the following problems.

1. The first-floor plan of a house is shown in Figure 8–7. Find distances A, B, C, and D in feet and inches.

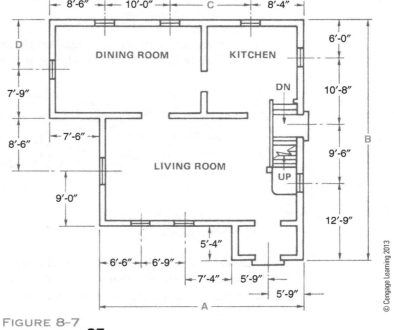

FIGURE 8-7

27

2. A survey subdivides a parcel of land in 5 lots of equal width as shown in Figure 8–8. Find the number of feet in distances A and B. Round the answers to 3 significant digits.

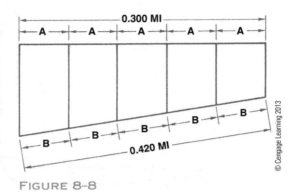

FIGURE 8–8

3. A bolt (roll) contains 70 yards 2 feet of fabric. The following lengths of fabric are sold from the bolt: 4 yards 2 feet, 5 yards $1\frac{1}{4}$ feet, 7 yards $2\frac{1}{2}$ feet. Find the length of fabric left on the bolt. Express the answer in yards and feet.

4. A building construction assistant lays out the stairway shown in Figure 8–9.
   a. Find, in feet and inches, the total run of the stairs.
   b. Find, in feet and inches, the total rise of the stairs.

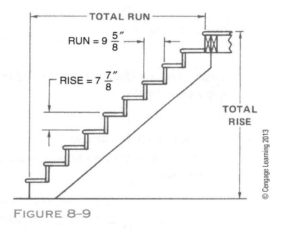

FIGURE 8–9

5. A structural steel fabricator cuts 4 equal lengths from a channel iron shown in Figure 8–10. Allow $\frac{1}{8}''$ waste for each cut. Find the length, in feet and inches, of the remaining piece.

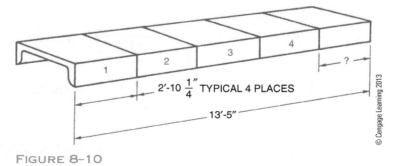

FIGURE 8–10

6. The floor of a room shown in Figure 8–11 is to be covered with oak flooring. The flooring is $2\frac{1}{4}$ inches wide. Allow 320 linear feet for waste. Find the total number of linear feet of oak flooring, including waste, needed for the floor.

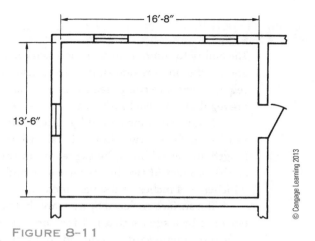

FIGURE 8-11

7. A concrete beam shown in Figure 8–12 is $12\frac{1}{3}$ yards long. Find distances A, B, and C in feet and inches.

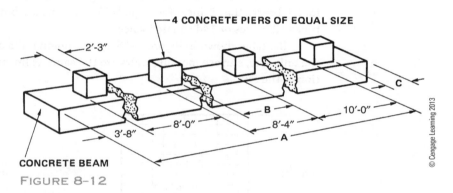

FIGURE 8-12

8. A carpet installer contracts to supply and install carpeting in the hallways of an office building. The locations of the hallways are shown in Figure 8–13. The hallways are $4\frac{1}{2}$ feet wide. The price charged for both carpet cost and installation is $38.75 per running (linear) yard. Find the total cost of the installation job.

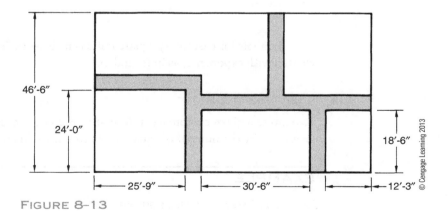

FIGURE 8-13

9. An apparel maker must know the fabric cost per garment. Find the material cost of a garment that requires 68 inches of fabric at $4.75 per yard and 52 inches of lining at $2.20 per yard.

8–5 CUSTOMARY UNITS OF SURFACE MEASURE (AREA)

The ability to compute areas is necessary in many occupations. In agriculture, crop yields and production are determined in relation to land area. Fertilizers and other chemical requirements are computed in terms of land area. In the construction field, carpenters are regularly involved with surface measure, such as floor and roof areas.

A surface is measured by determining the number of surface units contained in it. A surface is two-dimensional. It has length and width, but no thickness. Both length and width must be expressed in the same unit of measure. Area is computed as the product of two linear measures and is expressed in square units. For example, 2 inches × 4 inches = 8 square inches.

The surface enclosed by a square that is 1 foot on a side is 1 square foot. The surface enclosed by a square that is 1 inch on a side is 1 square inch. Similar meanings are attached to square yard, square rod, and square mile. For our uses, the statement "area of the surface enclosed by a figure" is shortened to "area of a figure." Therefore, areas will be referred to as the area of a rectangle, area of a triangle, area of a circle, and so forth.

Look at the reduced drawing in Figure 8–14 showing a square inch and a square foot. Observe that 1 linear foot equals 12 linear inches, but 1 square foot equals 12 inches times 12 inches or 144 square inches.

The table shown in Figure 8–15 lists common units of surface measure. Other than the unit acre, surface measure units are the same as linear measure units with the addition of the term square.

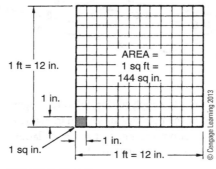

FIGURE 8–14

Customary Units of Area Measure	
1 square foot (sq ft)	= 144 square inches (sq in.)
1 square yard (sq yd)	= 9 square feet (sq ft)
1 square rod (sq rd)	= 30.25 square yards (sq yd)
1 acre (ac)	= 160 square rods (sq rd)
1 acre (ac)	= 43,560 square feet (sq ft)
1 square mile (sq mi)	= 640 acres (ac)

FIGURE 8–15

Symbols for customary square units can either be "spelled," as in sq ft and sq in., or written with exponents, as in ft^2 and $in.^2$

Expressing Customary Area Measure Equivalents

To express a given customary unit of area as a larger customary unit of area, divide the given area by the number of square units contained in one of the larger units.

EXAMPLE

Express 728 square inches as square feet.

METHOD 1

    Since 144 sq in. = 1 sq ft, divide 728 by 144.

    728 ÷ 144 ≈ 5.06; 728 sq in. ≈ 5.06 sq ft ANS

METHOD 2

$$728 \text{ sq in.} \times \frac{1 \text{ sq ft}}{144 \text{ sq in.}} = \frac{728 \text{ sq ft}}{144} \approx 5.06 \text{ sq ft } \text{ANS}$$

To express a given customary unit of area as a smaller customary unit of area, multiply the given area by the number of square units contained in one of the larger units.

EXAMPLE

Express 0.612 square yard as square inches.

Multiply 0.612 square yard by the unity fractions $\frac{9 \text{ sq ft}}{1 \text{ sq yd}}$ and $\frac{144 \text{ sq in.}}{1 \text{ sq ft}}$.

$$0.612 \text{ sq yd} \times \frac{9 \text{ sq ft}}{1 \text{ sq yd}} \times \frac{144 \text{ sq in.}}{1 \text{ sq ft}} \approx 793 \text{ sq in. } \text{ANS}$$

Calculator Application

.612 $\boxed{\times}$ 9 $\boxed{\times}$ 144 $\boxed{=}$ 793.152

793 sq in. (rounded to 3 significant digits) ANS

EXERCISE 8-5   Express each areas as indicated. Round each answer to the same number of significant digits as in the original quantity. Customary units of area measure are given in the table in Figure 8–15.

1. 196 square inches as square feet
2. 1085 square inches as square feet
3. 45.8 square feet as square yards
4. 2.02 square feet as square yards
5. 1600 acres as square miles
6. 192 acres as square miles
7. 120,000 square feet as acres
8. 122.5 square yards as square rods
9. 17,400 square feet as acres
10. 2300 square inches as square yards
11. 871,000 square feet as square miles
12. 2600 square feet as square rods

13. 2.35 square feet as square inches
14. 0.624 square foot as square inches
15. 4.30 square yards as square feet
16. 0.59 square yard as square feet
17. 3.8075 square miles as acres
18. 0.462 square mile as acres
19. 2.150 acres as square feet
20. 0.25 acre as square feet
21. 5.45 square rods as square yards
22. 0.612 square yard as square inches
23. 0.0250 square mile as square feet
24. 1.75 square rods as square feet

8–6 CUSTOMARY AREA MEASURE PRACTICAL APPLICATIONS

EXAMPLE

A sheet of aluminum that contains 18.00 square feet is sheared into 38 strips of equal size. What is the area of each strip in square inches?

Since 1 square foot equals 144 square inches, multiply 18.00 by 144. Divide 2592 square inches by the number of strips (38).

18.00 × 144 = 2592
18.00 square feet = 2592 square inches
2592 ÷ 38 ≈ 68.21 rounded to 4 significant digits
The area of each strip is 68.21 square inches. ANS

Calculator Application

18 $\boxed{\times}$ 144 $\boxed{÷}$ 38 $\boxed{=}$ 68.21052632

68.21 square inches (rounded to 4 significant digits) ANS

EXERCISE 8-6   Solve the following problems.

1. How many strips, each having an area of 48.00 square inches, can be sheared from a sheet of steel that measures 18.00 square feet?

2. A contractor estimates the cost of developing a 0.3000-square-mile parcel of land at $1200 per acre. What is the total cost of developing this parcel?

3. A painter and decorator compute the total interior wall surface of a building as 220 square yards after allowing for windows and doors. Two coats of paint are required for the job. If 1 gallon of paint covers 500 square feet, how many gallons of paint are required? Give the answer to the nearest gallon.

4. A bag of lawn food sells for $16.50 and covers 12,500 square feet. What is the cost to the nearest dollar to cover $1\frac{1}{2}$ acres of lawn?

5. A basement floor that measures 875 square feet is to be covered with floor tiles. Each tile measures 100 square inches. Make an allowance of 5% for waste. How many tiles are needed? Give answer to the nearest 10 tiles.

6. A land developer purchased 0.200 square mile of land. The land was subdivided into 256 building lots of approximately the same area. What is the average number of square feet per building lot? Give answer to the nearest 100 square feet.

7. A total of 180 square yards of the interior walls of a building are to be paneled. Each panel is 32 square feet. Allowing for 15% waste, how many whole panels are required?

8-7 CUSTOMARY UNITS OF VOLUME (CUBIC MEASURE)

A solid is measured by determining the number of cubic units contained in it. A solid is three-dimensional; it has length, width, and thickness or height. Length, width, and thickness must be expressed in the same unit of measure. Volume is the product of three linear measures and is expressed in cubic units. For example, 2 inches × 3 inches × 5 inches = 30 cubic inches.

The volume of a cube having sides 1 foot long is 1 cubic foot. The volume of a cube having sides 1 inch long is 1 cubic inch. A similar meaning is attached to the cubic yard.

A reduced illustration of a cubic foot and a cubic inch is shown in Figure 8–16. Observe that 1 linear foot equals 12 linear inches, but 1 cubic foot equals 12 inches × 12 inches × 12 inches, or 1728 cubic inches.

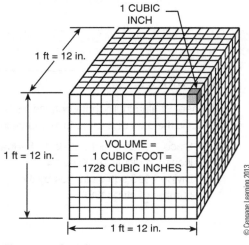

FIGURE 8-16

The table in Figure 8–17 lists common units of volume measure with their abbreviations. Volume measure units are the same as linear unit measures with the addition of the term **cubic**.

32

Customary Units of Volume Measure
1 cubic foot (cu ft) = 1728 cubic inches (cu in.)
1 cubic yard (cu yd) = 27 cubic feet (cu ft)

FIGURE 8-17

© Cengage Learning 2013

As with square units, customary cubic units can be written as cu ft or ft^3 and cu in. or in.^{3}

Expressing Customary Volume Measure Equivalents

To express a given unit of volume as a larger unit, divide the given volume by the number of cubic units contained in one of the larger units.

EXAMPLE

Express 4300 cubic inches as cubic feet.

METHOD 1

Since 1728 cu in. = 1 cu ft, divide 4300 by 1728.

4300 ÷ 1728 ≈ 2.5; 4320 cu in. ≈ 2.5 cu ft ANS

METHOD 2

$4300 \text{ cu in.} \times \dfrac{1 \text{ cu ft}}{1728 \text{ cu in.}} \approx 2.5 \text{ cu ft}$ ANS

To express a given unit of volume as a smaller unit, multiply the given volume by the number of cubic units contained in one of the larger units.

EXAMPLE

Express 0.0197 cubic yards as cubic inches.

Multiply 0.0197 cubic yard by the unity fractions $\dfrac{27 \text{ cu ft}}{1 \text{ cu yd}}$ and $\dfrac{1728 \text{ cu in.}}{1 \text{ cu ft}}$.

$0.0197 \text{ cu yd} \times \dfrac{27 \text{ cu ft}}{1 \text{ cu yd}} \times \dfrac{1728 \text{ cu in.}}{1 \text{ cu ft}} \approx 919 \text{ cu in.}$ ANS

Calculator Application

.0197 ☒ 27 ☒ 1728 ☐ 919.1212; 919 cu in. (rounded to 3 significant digits) ANS

EXERCISE 8-7 Express each volume as indicated. Round each answer to the same number of significant digits as the original quantity. Customary units of volume measure are given in the table in Figure 8–17.

1. 4320 cu in. = ? cu ft
2. 860 cu in. = ? cu ft
3. 117 cu ft = ? cu yd
4. 187 cu ft = ? cu yd
5. 12,900 cu in. = ? cu ft
6. 18,000 cu in. = ? cu yd
7. 73 cu ft = ? cu yd
8. 124.7 cu ft = ? cu yd
9. 562 cu in. = ? cu ft
10. 51,000 cu in. = ? cu yd

11. 1.650 cu ft = ? cu in.
12. 0.325 cu ft = ? cu in.
13. 16.4 cu yd = ? cu ft
14. 243.0 cu yd = ? cu ft
15. 0.273 cu ft = ? cu in.
16. 0.09 cu yd = ? cu in.
17. 113.4 cu yd = ? cu ft
18. 0.36 cu yd = ? cu ft
19. 0.55 cu ft = ? cu in.
20. 0.1300 cu yd = ? cu in.

8–8 CUSTOMARY VOLUME PRACTICAL APPLICATIONS

EXAMPLE

Castings are to be made from 2.250 cubic feet of molten metal. If each casting requires 15.8 cubic inches of metal, how many castings can be made?

METHOD 1

Since 1728 cubic inches equal 1 cubic foot, multiply 1728 by 2.250.

$$1728 \times 2.250 = 3888$$

Therefore, 2.250 cubic feet = 3888 cubic inches.

Divide.

$$3888 \div 15.8 \approx 246$$
246 castings can be made. ANS

METHOD 2

$$2.250 \ \text{cu ft} \times \frac{1728 \ \text{cu in.}}{1 \ \text{cu ft}} \times \frac{1 \ \text{casting}}{15.8 \ \text{cu in.}} \approx 246 \ \text{castings} \ \text{ANS}$$

Calculator Application

$1728 \boxed{\times} 2.25 \boxed{\div} 15.8 \boxed{=} 246.0759494$; 246 castings ANS

EXERCISE 8–8   Solve the following problems.

1. Each casting requires 8.500 cubic inches of bronze. How many cubic feet of molten bronze are required to make 2500 castings?

2. A cord is a unit of measure of cut and stacked fuel wood equal to 128 cubic feet. Wood is burned at the rate of $\frac{1}{2}$ cord per week. How many weeks will a stack of wood measuring $21\frac{1}{3}$ cubic yards last?

3. Common brick weighs 112.0 pounds per cubic foot. How many cubic yards of brick can be carried by a truck whose maximum carrying load is rated as 8 gross tons? One gross ton = 2240 pounds.

4. Hot air passes through a duct at the rate of 550 cubic inches per second. Find the number of cubic feet of hot air passing through the duct in 1 minute. Give the answer to the nearest cubic foot.

5. For lumber that is 1 inch thick, 1 board foot of lumber has a volume of $\frac{1}{12}$ cubic foot. Seasoned white pine weighs $31\frac{1}{2}$ pounds per cubic foot. Find the weight of 1400 board feet of seasoned white pine.

6. Concrete is poured for a building foundation at the rate of $8\frac{1}{2}$ cubic feet per minute. How many cubic yards are pumped in $\frac{3}{4}$ hour? Give the answer to the nearest cubic yard.

8–9 CUSTOMARY UNITS OF CAPACITY

Capacity is a measure of volume. The capacity of a container is the number of units of material that the container can hold.

In the customary system, there are three different kinds of measures of capacity. **Liquid measure** is for measuring liquids. For example, it is used for measuring water and gasoline and for stating the capacity of fuel tanks and reservoirs. **Dry measure** is for measuring fruit, vegetables, grain, and the like. **Apothecaries' fluid measure** is for measuring drugs and prescriptions.

The most common units of customary liquid and fluid measure are listed in the table shown in Figure 8–18. Also listed are common capacity–cubic measure equivalents.

Customary Units of Capacity Measure		
16 ounces (oz)	=	1 pint (pt)
2 pints (pt)	=	1 quart (qt)
4 quarts (qt)	=	1 gallon (gal)
Commonly Used Capacity–Cubic Measure Equivalents		
1 gallon (gal)	=	231 cubic inches (cu in.)
7.5 gallons (gal)	=	1 cubic foot (cu ft)

© Cengage Learning 2013

FIGURE 8–18

Expressing Equivalent Customary Capacity Measures

It is often necessary to express given capacity units as either larger or smaller units. The procedure is the same as used with linear, square, and cubic units of measure.

EXAMPLE

1. Express 20.5 ounces as pints.

   METHOD 1

   Since 16 ounces = 1 pint, divide 20.5 by 16.

   $20.5 \div 16 = 1.28125$
   $20.5 \text{ oz} \approx 1.28 \text{ pt}$ (rounded to 3 significant digits) ANS

   METHOD 2

   Multiply 20.5 oz by the unity fraction $\frac{1 \text{ pt}}{16 \text{ oz}}$.

   $20.5 \text{ oz} \times \frac{1 \text{ pt}}{16 \text{ oz}} = \frac{20.5 \text{ pt}}{16} \approx 1.28 \text{ pt}$ (rounded to 3 significant digits) ANS

EXERCISE 8–9   Express each unit of measure as indicated. Round each answer to the same number of significant digits as in the original quantity. Customary and metric units of capacity measure are given in the table in Figure 8–17.

1. 6.52 pt = ? qt
2. 38 oz = ? pt
3. 9.25 gal = ? qt
4. 0.35 pt = ? oz
5. 35 qt = ? gal
6. 17.75 qt = ? pt
7. 3.07 gal = ? cu in.

8. 53.8 gal = ? cu ft
9. 46 cu in. = ? gal
10. 0.90 cu ft = ? gal
11. 62 oz = ? qt
12. 0.22 gal = ? pt
13. 1.6 qt = ? oz
14. 43 pt = ? gal

8–10 CUSTOMARY CAPACITY PRACTICAL APPLICATIONS

EXAMPLE

How many ounces of solution are contained in a $\frac{3}{4}$-quart container when full?

METHOD 1

Since 16 oz = 1 pt and 2 pt = 1 qt, there are 16 × 2 or 32 oz in 1 qt.

Multiply 32 by $\frac{3}{4}$.

$32 \times \frac{3}{4} = 24; \frac{3}{4} \text{ qt} = 24 \text{ oz ANS}$

METHOD 2

Multiply $\frac{3}{4}$ quart by unity fractions $\frac{2 \text{ pt}}{1 \text{ qt}}$

and $\frac{16 \text{ oz}}{1 \text{ pt}}$.

$$\frac{3}{\underset{1}{\cancel{4}}} \cancel{\text{qt}} \times \frac{2 \text{ } \cancel{\text{pt}}}{1 \text{ } \cancel{\text{qt}}} \times \frac{\overset{4}{\cancel{16}} \text{ oz}}{1 \text{ } \cancel{\text{pt}}} = 24 \text{ oz ANS}$$

EXERCISE 8–10   Solve the following problems.

1. In planning for a reception, a chef estimates that eighty 4-ounce servings of tomato juice are required. How many quarts of juice must be ordered?

2. When mixing oil with gasoline for an outboard engine, 1 part of oil is added to 10 parts of gasoline. How many pints of oil are added to 4.5 gal of gasoline?

3. A water tank has a volume of 4550 cubic feet. The tank is $\frac{9}{10}$ full. How many gallons of water are contained in the tank? Round answer to the nearest hundred gallons.

4. Automotive cooling systems require 4 qt of coolant for each 10 qt of capacity to provide protection to $-13°$F. A cooling system has a capacity of 17 qt. How many quarts and pints of coolant are required?

5. An empty fuel oil tank has a volume of 575 cubic feet. Oil is pumped into the tank at the rate of 132 gallons per minute. How long does it take to fill the tank? Round answer to the nearest minute.

6. A small oil can holds $\frac{1}{5}$ pt. How many times can it be refilled from a 1.25 gal can of oil?

7. A cutting lubricant requires 8.75 oz of concentrate for 1 qt of water. How much concentrate will be required for 3.6 gal of water?

8. A solution contains 12.5% acid and 87.5% water. How many gallons of solution are made with 27 ounces of acid? Round answer to the nearest tenth gallon.

9. A water storage tank has a volume of 165 cubic yards. When the tank is $\frac{1}{4}$ full of water, how many gallons of water are required to fill the tank? Round the answer to the nearest one hundred gallons.

8–11 CUSTOMARY UNITS OF WEIGHT (MASS)

Weight is a measure of the force of attraction of the earth on an object. **Mass** is a measure of the amount of matter contained in an object. The weight of an object varies with its distance from the earth's center. The mass of an object remains the same regardless of its location in the universe.

Scientific applications dealing with objects located other than on the earth's surface are *not* considered in this book. Therefore, the terms *weight* and *mass* are used interchangeably.

As with capacity measures, the customary system has three types of weight measures. **Troy weights** are used in weighing jewels and precious metals such as gold and silver. **Apothecaries' weights** are for measuring drugs and prescriptions. **Avoirdupois** or **commercial weights** are used for all commodities except precious metals, jewels, and drugs.

The most common units of customary weight measure are listed in the table shown in Figure 8–19.

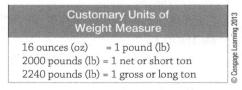

Customary Units of Weight Measure	
16 ounces (oz)	= 1 pound (lb)
2000 pounds (lb)	= 1 net or short ton
2240 pounds (lb)	= 1 gross or long ton

© Cengage Learning 2013

FIGURE 8–19

The long ton is seldom used. Originally, it was used to measure the weight of anthracite coal in Pennsylvania, bulk amounts of certain iron and steel products, and the deadweight tonnage of ships.

Expressing Equivalent Customary Weight Measures

In the customary system, apply the same procedures that are used with other measures. The following example shows the method of expressing given weight units as larger or smaller units.

EXAMPLE

Express 0.28 pound as ounces.

METHOD 1

Since 16 oz = 1 lb, multiply 0.28 by 16.

$$0.28 \times 16 = 4.48$$
$$0.28 \text{ lb} \approx 4.5 \text{ oz Ans}$$

METHOD 2

Multiply 0.28 by the unity fraction $\dfrac{16 \text{ oz}}{1 \text{ lb}}$.

$$0.28 \, \cancel{\text{lb}} \times \frac{16 \text{ oz}}{1 \, \cancel{\text{lb}}} \approx 4.5 \text{ oz Ans}$$

EXERCISE 8–11 Express each unit of weight as indicated. Round each answer to the same number of significant digits as in the original quantity. Customary and metric units of weight are given in the table in Figure 8–18.

1. 35 oz = ? lb
2. 0.6 lb = ? oz
3. 2.4 long tons = ? lb
4. 3.1 short tons = ? lb
5. 5300 lb = ? short tons

6. 7850 lb = ? long tons
7. 43.5 oz = ? lb
8. 0.120 lb = ? oz
9. 0.12 short ton = ? lb
10. 720 lb = ? short tons

8–12 CUSTOMARY WEIGHT PRACTICAL APPLICATIONS

EXAMPLE

A truck delivers 4 prefabricated concrete wall sections to a job site. Each wall section has a volume of 1.65 cubic yards. One cubic yard of concrete weighs 4040 pounds. How many tons are carried on this delivery?

Find the volume of 4 wall sections.
Find the weight of 6.6 cubic yards.
Find the number of tons.

$$4 \times 1.65 \text{ yd}^3 = 6.6 \text{ yd}^3$$
$$6.6 \times 4040 \text{ lb} = 25{,}664 \text{ lb}$$
$$25{,}664 \text{ lb} \div 2000 \text{ lb/ton} \approx 13.3 \text{ tons Ans}$$

Calculator Application

4 $\boxed{\times}$ 1.65 $\boxed{\times}$ 4040 $\boxed{\div}$ 2000 $\boxed{=}$ 13.332,
13.3 tons Ans (rounded to 3 significant digits)

EXERCISE 8-12   Solve each problem.

1. What is the total weight, in pounds, of 1 gross (144) 12.0-ounce cans of fruit?

2. 250 identical strips are sheared from a sheet of steel that weighs 42.25 lb. Find the weight, in ounces, of each strip.

3. One cubic foot of stainless steel weighs 486.9 pounds. How many pounds and ounces does 0.175 cubic foot of stainless steel weigh? Give answer to the nearest whole ounce.

4. A technician measures the weights of some objects as 12.3 oz, 9.6 oz, 7.4 oz, 11.6 oz, 9.2 oz, 13.8 oz, and 8.4 oz. Find the total weight in pounds and ounces.

5. A force of 760 tons (short tons) is exerted on the base of a steel support column. The base has a cross-sectional area of 160 square inches. How many pounds of force are exerted per square inch of cross-sectional area?

6. An assembly housing weighs 8.25 pounds. The weight of the housing is reduced to 6.50 pounds by drilling holes in the housing. Each drilled hole removes 0.80 ounce of material. How many holes are drilled?

7. A cubic foot of water weighs 62.42 pounds at 40 degrees Fahrenheit and 61.21 pounds at 120 degrees Fahrenheit. Over this temperature change, what is the average decrease in weight in ounces per cubic foot for each degree increase in temperature? Give answer to the nearest hundredth ounce.

8-13 COMPOUND UNITS

In this unit, you have worked with basic units of length, area, volume, capacity, and weight. Methods of expressing equivalent measures between smaller and larger basic units of measure have been presented.

In actual practice, it is often required to use a combination of the basic units in solving problems. Compound units are the products or quotients of two or more basic units. Many quantities or rates are expressed as compound units. Following are examples of compound units.

EXAMPLES

1. Speed can be expressed as miles per hour. *Per* indicates division. Miles per hour can be written as mi/hr, $\dfrac{\text{mi}}{\text{hr}}$, or mph.

2. Pressure can be expressed as pounds per square inch. Pounds per square inch can be written as lb/sq in., $\dfrac{\text{lb}}{\text{sq in.}}$, or psi. Since square inch may be written as in.^{2}, pounds per square inch may be written as lb/in.^{2}

Expressing Simple Compound Unit Equivalents

Compound unit measures are converted to smaller or larger equivalent compound unit measures using unity fractions. Following are examples of simple equivalent compound unit conversions.

EXAMPLE

Express 2870 pounds per square foot as pounds per square inch.

Multiply 2870 lb/sq ft by unity fraction $\dfrac{1 \text{ sq ft}}{144 \text{ sq in.}}$.

$$\dfrac{2870 \text{ lb}}{\cancel{\text{sq ft}}} \times \dfrac{1 \cancel{\text{ sq ft}}}{144 \text{ sq in.}} \approx 19.9 \text{ lb/sq in. ANS}$$

EXERCISE 8–13A   Express each simple compound unit measure as indicated. Round each answer to the same number of significant digits as in the original quantity.

1. 61.3 mi/hr = ? mi/min
2. 7.025 lb/sq in. = ? lb/sq ft
3. 2150 rev/min = ? rev/sec
4. $1.69/gal = ? $/qt

5. 0.260 ft/sec = ? ft/hr
6. 0.500 lb/cu in. = ? lb/cu ft
7. 0.16 short ton/sq in. = ? lb/sq in.
8. 538 cu in./sec = ? cu ft/sec

Expressing Complex Compound Unit Equivalents

Exercise 8–13A involves the conversion of simple compound units. The conversion of only one unit is required; the other unit remains the same. In problem 1, the hour unit is converted to a minute unit; the mile unit remains the same. In problem 2, the square inch unit is converted to a square foot unit; the pound unit remains the same.

Problems often involve the conversion of more than one unit in their solutions. It is necessary to convert both units of a compound unit quantity to smaller or larger units. Following is an example of complex compound unit conversions in which both units are converted.

EXAMPLE

Express 0.283 short tons per square foot as pounds per square inch.

Multiply 0.283 ton by unity fractions

$$\frac{2000\ lb}{1\ ton}\ \text{and}\ \frac{1\ sq\ ft}{144\ sq\ in.}.$$

$$\frac{0.283\ \cancel{ton}}{1\ \cancel{sq\ ft}} \times \frac{2000\ lb}{1\ \cancel{ton}} \times \frac{1\ \cancel{sq\ ft}}{144\ sq\ in.} \approx 3.93\ lb/sq\ in.\ \text{ANS}$$

Calculator Application

.283 ☒ 2000 ☐ 144 ☐ 3.930555556,

3.93 lb/sq in. (rounded to 3 significant digits) ANS

EXERCISE 8–13B   Express each complex compound unit measure as indicated. Round each answer to the same number of significant digits as in the original quantity.

1. 73.9 lb/sq in. = ? short tons/sq ft
2. 4870 ft/min = ? mi/hr
3. $2.32/gal = ? cents/pt

4. 3.5 short ton/sq ft = ? lb/sq in.
5. 63.8 cu in./sec = ? cu ft/hr
6. 53.6 mi/hr = ? ft/sec

8–14 COMPOUND UNITS PRACTICAL APPLICATIONS

EXAMPLE

Aluminum weighs 0.0975 pound per cubic inch. What is the weight, in short tons, of 26.8 cubic feet of aluminum?

Find the weight in tons per 1 cubic foot. Multiply 0.0975 lb/cu in. by unity fractions

$$\frac{1728\ cu\ in.}{1\ cu\ ft}\ \text{and}\ \frac{1\ ton}{2000\ lb}.$$

$$\frac{0.0975\ \cancel{lb}}{\cancel{cu\ in.}} \times \frac{1728\ \cancel{cu\ in.}}{1\ cu\ ft} \times \frac{1\ ton}{2000\ \cancel{lb}} = 0.08424\ \frac{ton}{cu\ ft}$$

Find the weight of 26.8 cubic feet. Multiply 0.08424 ton/cu ft by 26.8 cu ft.

$$\frac{0.08424\ ton}{\cancel{cu\ ft}} \times 26.8\ \cancel{cu\ ft} \approx 2.26\ tons\ \text{ANS}$$

Calculator Application

.0975 $\boxed{\times}$ 1728 $\boxed{\div}$ 2000 $\boxed{\times}$ 26.8 $\boxed{=}$ 2.257632,

2.26 tons (rounded to 3 significant digits) Ans

EXERCISE 8–14

Solve the following problems.

1. Unbroken anthracite coal weighs 93.6 lb/ft³. Find the weight of 3.5 cubic yards of coal in
   a. short tons and
   b. long tons.
      Round each answer to 2 significant digits.

2. A British thermal unit (Btu) is the amount of heat required to raise the temperature of one pound of water one degree Fahrenheit. A building has 12 air-conditioning units. Each unit removes 24,000 British thermal units of heat per hour (Btu/hr). How many Btu are removed from the building in 10 minutes?

3. With a concrete curb machine, a two-person crew can install 47.5 linear feet of edging per hour. Each linear foot takes 0.25 ft³ of concrete.
   a. How many cubic feet of concrete will be needed to edge 1217 linear feet of land?
   b. If each cubic foot of wet concrete weighs 194.8 lb, what is the total weight of the wet concrete used for this curbing? Round the answer to the nearest hundred pounds.
   c. How long will it take the two-person crew to complete the job?
   d. If the price for natural gray curb is $3.50/lf with an average cost of $0.40/lf for materials, how much will this curbing cost?

4. An oil spill needs to be treated with a bacterium culture at the rate of 1 oz of culture per 100 cubic feet of oil. If the spill is 786,000 barrels, how much culture will be needed? 1 barrel is 31.5 gal. Give the answer in pounds rounded to three decimal places.

5. Hot air passes through a duct at the rate of 675 cubic inches per second. Find the number of cubic feet of hot air passing through the duct in 18.5 minutes. Round the answer to the nearest cubic foot.

6. The speed of sound in air is 1090 feet per second at 32°F. How many miles does sound travel in 0.225 hour? Round the answer to the nearest mile.

7. Materials expand when heated. Different materials expand at different rates. Mechanical and construction technicians must often consider material rates of expansion. The amount of expansion for short lengths of material is very small. Expansion is computed if a product is made to a high degree of precision and is subjected to a large temperature change. Also, expansion is computed for large structures because of the long lengths of structural members used. The table in Figure 8–20 lists the expansion per inch for each Fahrenheit degree rise in temperature for a 1-inch length of material. For example, the

   expansion of a 1-inch length of aluminum is expressed as 0.00001244 $\dfrac{\text{in./in.}}{1°\text{F}}$.

Material	Expansion of One Inch of Material in One Fahrenheit Degree Temperature Increase
Aluminum	0.00001244 inch
Copper	0.00000900 inch
Structural Steel	0.00000722 inch
Brick	0.00000300 inch
Concrete	0.00000800 inch

© Cengage Learning 2013

FIGURE 8–20

Find the total expansion for each of the materials listed in the table in Figure 8–21. Express the answer to 3 significant digits.

	Material	Length Before Temperature Increase	Fahrenheit Temperature Change	Total Expansion in Inches
a.	Copper Cable	315.2 ft	From 35.3°F to 92.5°F	
b.	Steel I Beam	50.7 ft	From 5.27°F to 90.3°F	
c.	Brick Wall	224.4 ft	From 20.8°F to 81.6°F	
d.	Aluminum Wire	415.0 ft	From 43.2°F to 105.7°F	
e.	Concrete	120.5 ft	From 15.3°F to 89.2°F	

FIGURE 8-21

© Cengage Learning 2013

UNIT EXERCISE AND PROBLEM REVIEW

EQUIVALENT CUSTOMARY UNITS OF LINEAR MEASURE

Express each length as indicated. Round the answers to 3 decimal places when necessary.

1. $25\frac{1}{2}$ inches as feet
2. 16.25 feet as yards
3. 3960 feet as miles
4. 78 inches as feet and inches
5. 47 feet as yards and feet
6. $7\frac{1}{4}$ feet as inches
7. $8\frac{1}{6}$ yards as feet

8. 0.6 mile as feet
9. $2\frac{1}{4}$ yards as inches
10. $5\frac{1}{2}$ yards as feet and inches
11. $\frac{1}{12}$ mile as yards and feet
12. 6.2 yards as feet and inches

ARITHMETIC OPERATIONS WITH CUSTOMARY COMPOUND NUMBERS

Perform the indicated arithmetic operation. Express the answer in the same units as those given in the exercise. Regroup the answer when necessary.

13. 5 ft 7 in. + 6 ft 8 in.
14. 4 yd 2 ft + 5 yd 2 ft
15. 6 ft $9\frac{1}{2}$ in. + 3 ft $4\frac{1}{4}$ in.
16. 10 ft 7 in. − 3 ft 4 in.
17. 14 yd $\frac{1}{2}$ ft − 11 yd 2 ft
18. 6 ft $1\frac{3}{4}$ in. − 4 ft $8\frac{1}{4}$ in.

19. 5 ft 3 in. × 5
20. 6 ft $8\frac{1}{2}$ in. × 3
21. 3 yd 2 ft 7 in. × 4
22. 20 ft 10 in. ÷ 5
23. 11 yd 2 ft ÷ 3
24. 3 yd 2 ft 4 in. ÷ 2

EQUIVALENT CUSTOMARY UNITS OF AREA MEASURE

Express each customary area measure in the indicated unit. Round each answer to the same number of significant digits as in the original quantity.

25. 504 sq in. as sq ft
26. 128 sq ft as sq yd
27. 4.08 sq ft as sq in.
28. 2480 acres as sq mi
29. 217,800 sq ft as acres

30. 0.2600 acres as sq ft
31. 5.33 sq yd as sq ft
32. 0.275 sq mi as acres
33. 0.080 sq yd as sq in.
34. 0.0108 sq mi as sq ft

EQUIVALENT CUSTOMARY UNITS OF VOLUME MEASURE

Express each volume in the unit indicated. Round each answer to the same number of significant digits as in the original quantity.

35. 4700 cu in. as cu ft
36. 215 cu ft as cu yd
37. 0.712 cu ft as cu in.
38. 12.34 cu yd as cu ft
39. 0.5935 cu ft as cu in.
40. 19.80 cu ft as cu yd
41. 20,000 cu in. as cu yd
42. 0.030 cu yd as cu in.

EQUIVALENT CUSTOMARY UNITS OF CAPACITY MEASURE

Express each capacity in the unit indicated. Round each answer to the same number of significant digits as in the original quantity.

43. 15.3 gal as qt
44. 31 oz as pt
45. 6.5 pt as qt
46. 6.2 qt as gal
47. 1.04 gal as cu in.
48. 84 cu ft as gal
49. 0.20 gal as pt
50. 1.40 qt as oz

EQUIVALENT CUSTOMARY UNITS OF WEIGHT MEASURE

Express each weight in the unit indicated. Round each answer to the same number of significant digits as in the original quantity.

51. 34 oz as lb
52. 0.060 lb as oz
53. 48,400 lb as long tons
54. 7800 lb as short tons
55. 0.660 short tons as lb
56. 1.087 long tons as lb

SIMPLE COMPOUND UNIT MEASURES

Express each simple compound unit measure as indicated. Round each answer to the same number of significant digits as in the original quantity.

57. 8.123 lb/sq in. = ? lb/sq ft
58. 50.7 mi/hr = ? mi/min
59. 618 cu ft/sec = ? cu ft/hr
60. 2090 rev/min = ? rev/sec

COMPLEX COMPOUND UNIT MEASURES

Express each complex compound unit measure as indicated. Round each answer to the same number of significant digits as in the original quantity.

61. 5190 ft/min = ? mi/hr
62. $3.81/gal = ? cents/pt
63. 57.2 cu in./sec = ? cu ft/hr
64. 62.9 mi/hr = ? ft/sec

PRACTICAL APPLICATIONS PROBLEMS

Solve the following problems.

65. The first-floor plan of a ranch house is shown in Figure 8–22. Determine distances A, B, C, and D in feet and inches.

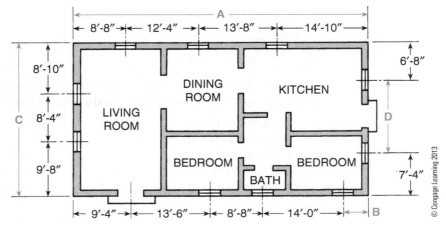

FIGURE 8–22

42

66. A bolt of fabric contains $80\frac{1}{2}$ yards of fabric. The following lengths of fabric are sold: 2 lengths each 5 yards 2 feet long, 3 lengths each 8 yards $1\frac{1}{2}$ feet long, and 5 lengths each 6 yards 2 feet long. What length of fabric does the bolt now contain? Express the answer in yards and feet.

67. How many strips, each having an area of 36 square inches, can be sheared from a sheet of aluminum that measures 6 square feet?

68. A painter computes the total interior wall surface of a building as 330 square yards after allowing for windows and doors. Two coats of paint are required for the job. One gallon of paint covers 500 square feet. How many gallons of paint are required? Round answer to the nearest gallon.

69. Hot air passes through a duct at the rate of 830 cubic inches per second. Compute the number of cubic feet of hot air that passes through the duct in 2.5 minutes. Round answer to 2 significant digits.

70. A cord is a unit of measure of cut fuel wood equal to 128 cubic feet. If wood is burned at the rate of $\frac{1}{2}$ cord per week, how many weeks would a stack of wood measuring 12 cubic yards last? Round answer to one decimal place.

71. Common brick weighs 112 pounds per cubic foot. How many cubic yards of brick can be carried by a truck whose maximum carrying load is rated at 12 short tons? Round answer to 2 significant digits.

72. A solution contains 5% acid and 95% water. How many quarts of the solution can be made with 3.8 ounces of acid? Round answer to 1 decimal place.

73. A water tank that has a volume of 4550 cubic feet is $\frac{3}{4}$ full. How many gallons of water are contained in the tank? Round answer to the nearest hundred gallons.

74. Carpet is installed in the hallways of a building. The cost of carpet and installation is $32.50 per square yard. A total length of 432.0 feet of carpet 5.0 feet wide is required. What is the total cost of carpet and installation? (Number of square feet = length in feet × width in feet)

75. The interior walls of a building are to be covered with plasterboard. After making allowances for windows and doors, a contractor estimates that 438 square yards of wall area are to be covered. One sheet of plasterboard has a surface area of 24.0 square feet. Allowing 15% for waste, how many sheets of plasterboard are required for this job? Round answer to the nearest whole sheet.

METRIC MEASUREMENT UNITS

After studying this unit you should be able to

- express lengths as smaller or larger metric linear numbers.
- perform arithmetic operations with metric linear units.
- select appropriate linear metric units in various applications.
- express given metric length, area, and volume measures in larger and smaller units.
- express given metric capacity and weight units as larger and smaller units.
- solve practical applied metric length, area, volume, capacity, and weight problems.
- express metric compound unit measures as equivalent compound unit measures.
- solve practical applied compound unit measures.
- convert between customary measures and metric measures.

The International System of Units, called the SI metric system, is the primary measurement system used by all countries except the United States, Liberia, and Myanmar. In the United States, the customary units tend to be used in areas such as construction, real estate transactions, and retail trade. Other areas, such as automotive maintenance, nursing, other health care areas, and biotechnology use the metric system.

Linear Measure

A linear measurement is a means of expressing the distance between two points; it is the measurement of lengths. Most occupations require the ability to compute linear measurements and to make direct length measurements.

A drafter computes length measurements when drawing a machined part or an architectural floor plan, an electrician determines the amount of cable required for a job, a welder calculates the length of material needed for a weldment, a printer "figures" the number of pieces that can be cut from a sheet of stock, a carpenter calculates the total length of baseboard required for a building, and an automobile technician computes the amount of metal to be removed for a cylinder re-bore.

9–1 METRIC UNITS OF LINEAR MEASURE

An advantage of the metric system is that it allows easy, fast computations. Since metric system units are based on powers of 10, figuring is simplified. To express a certain metric unit as a larger or smaller metric unit, all that is required is to move the decimal point a proper number of places to the left or right. Metric system units are also easy to learn.

The metric system does not require difficult conversions as in the customary system. It is easier to remember that 1000 meters equal 1 kilometer than to remember that 1760 yards equal 1 mile.

Many occupations require working with metric units of linear measure. A manufacturing technician may measure and compute using millimeters. An architectural drafter and a construction technician may use meters and centimeters. Kilometers are used to measure relatively long distances such as those traveled by a vehicle per unit of time, such as kilometers per hour.

Millimeters are used to measure small lengths often requiring a high degree of precision. The thickness of a spoon, fork, and compact disc are approximately 1 millimeter. The thickness of your pen or pencil is a little less than 1 centimeter; this book is about 3 centimeters thick. Most home kitchen counters are roughly 1 meter high and doors are 2 meters high. The length of 10 football fields is about 1 kilometer.

EXAMPLES

For each of the following, an estimate of length with the appropriate unit is given.
1. The length of your pen is about 15 centimeters.
2. The thickness of each of your fingernails is less than 1 millimeter.
3. The length of most automobiles is approximately 5 meters.
4. The thickness of a saw blade is about 1 millimeter.
5. The thickness of a brick is about 6 centimeters.
6. The room ceiling height in a typical house is between 2 and 2.5 meters.
7. Most automobiles are capable of exceeding 160 kilometers per hour.

EXERCISE 9–1A   Select the linear measurement unit most appropriate for each of the following. Identify as millimeter, centimeter, meter, or kilometer.

1. The height of a drinking glass.
2. The distance from New York City to Chicago.
3. The length of a bus.
4. The thickness of a photographic print.
5. The length of your index finger.
6. The thickness of a blade of grass.
7. The length of the Mississippi River.
8. The width of a house.

EXERCISE 9–1B   For each of the following, write the most appropriate metric unit; identify it as millimeter, centimeter, meter, or kilometer.

1. Most handheld calculators are about 15 ? long.
2. The Empire State Building is approximately 442 ? high.
3. The thickness of a hardcover book is about 3 ? thick.
4. Many young men have an 80 ? waist.
5. The diameter of a large safety pin is approximately 0.5 ?.
6. The speed of light is roughly 300 000 ? per second.
7. My driveway is about 45 ? long.
8. Computer monitor screens are often about 28 ? wide.
9. Most kitchen counter tops are about 30 ? thick.
10. The handle of a hammer is about 20 ? long.

Prefixes and Symbols for Metric Units of Length

The following metric power-of-10 prefixes are based on the meter:

milli means one thousandth (0.001)   **deka** means ten (10)

centi means one hundredth (0.01)   **hecto** means hundred (100)

deci means one tenth (0.1)   **kilo** means thousand (1000)

The table shown in Figure 9–1 lists the metric units of length with their symbols. These units are based on the meter. Observe that each unit is 10 times greater than the unit directly above it.

Metric Units of Linear Measure	
1 millimeter (mm) = 0.001 meter (m)	1000 millimeter (mm) = 1 meter (m)
1 centimeter (cm) = 0.01 meter (m)	100 centimeter (cm) = 1 meter (m)
1 decimeter (dm) = 0.1 meter (m)	10 decimeter (dm) = 1 meter (m)
1 meter (m) = 1 meter (m)	1 meter (m) = 1 meter (m)
1 dekameter (dam) = 10 meters (m)	0.1 dekameter (dam) = 1 meter (m)
1 hectometer (hm) = 100 meters (m)	0.01 hectometer (hm) = 1 meter (m)
1 kilometer (km) = 1000 meters (m)	0.001 kilometer (km) = 1 meter (m)

© Cengage Learning 2013

FIGURE 9–1

The most frequently used metric units of length are the kilometer (km), meter (m), centimeter (cm), and millimeter (mm). In actual applications, the dekameter (dam) and hectometer (hm) are not used. The decimeter (dm) is seldom used. The metric prefixes for very large and very small numbers will be studied in Unit 9–17.

To make numbers easier to read they may be divided into groups of three, separated by spaces (or thin spaces), as in 12 345, but not commas or points. This applies to digits on both sides of the decimal marker (0.901 234 56). Numbers with four digits may be written either with the space (5 678) or without it (5678).

This practice not only makes large numbers easier to read, but also allows all countries to keep their custom of using either a point or a comma as decimal marker. For example, engine size in the United States is written as 3.2 L and in Germany as 3,2 L. The space prevents possible confusion and sources of error.

9–2 EXPRESSING EQUIVALENT UNITS WITHIN THE METRIC SYSTEM

To express a given unit of length as a larger unit, move the decimal point a certain number of places to the left. To express a given unit of length as a smaller unit, move the decimal point a certain number of places to the right. The exact procedure of moving decimal points is shown in the following examples. Refer to the metric units of linear measure table shown in Figure 9–1.

EXAMPLES

1. Express 65 decimeters as meters.

   Since a meter is the next larger unit to a decimeter, move the decimal point 1 place to the left.   65.

   In moving the decimal point 1 place to the left, you are actually dividing by 10.

                                                    65 dm = 6.5 m Ans

2. Express 0.28 decimeter as centimeters.

Since a centimeter is the next smaller unit to a decimeter, move the decimal point 1
place to the right.   0.28
                                                                                      ↰

In moving the decimal point 1 place to the right, you are actually multiplying by 10.
                                                                          0.28 dm = 2.8 cm ANS

3. Express 0.378 meter (m) as millimeters (mm).

Expressing meters as millimeters involves 3 steps.

$$0.378 \text{ m} = \underbrace{3.78 \text{ dm}}_{①} = \underbrace{37.8 \text{ cm}}_{②} = \underbrace{378}_{③} \text{ mm}$$

Since a millimeter is 3 smaller units from a meter, move the decimal point 3 places to the
right. In moving the decimal point 3 places to the right, you are actually multiplying by
10^3 ($10 \times 10 \times 10$), or 1000.

> 0.378
> 0.378 m = 378 mm ANS

4. Express 2 700 centimeters as meters.

Since a meter is 2 larger units from a centimeter,
move the decimal point 2 places to the left

> 2700.
> ↰
> 2 700 cm = 27 m ANS

Notice the answer is 27 meters, not 27.00 meters.
Because 2 700 centimeters has 2 significant digits,
the answer is rounded to 2 significant digits.

Moving the decimal point a certain number of places to the left or right is the most
practical way of expressing equivalent metric units. However, the unity fraction method
can also be used in expressing equivalent metric units.

EXAMPLES

1. Express 0.378 kilometer as meters.

   Multiply 0.378 kilometer by the unity
   fraction $\dfrac{1000 \text{ m}}{1 \text{ km}}$.

   > $0.378 \text{ km} \times \dfrac{1000 \text{ m}}{1 \text{ km}} = 378 \text{ m}$ ANS

2. Express 237 millimeters as decimeters.

   Since a decimeter is 10×10 or 100 times
   greater than a millimeter, multiply 237
   millimeters by the unity fraction $\dfrac{1 \text{ dm}}{100 \text{ mm}}$.

   > $237 \text{ mm} \times \dfrac{1 \text{ dm}}{100 \text{ mm}} = 2.37 \text{ dm}$ ANS

EXERCISE 9–2   Express these lengths in meters. Metric units of linear measure are given in the table in
Figure 9–1.

1. 34 decimeters
2. 4 320 millimeters
3. 0.05 kilometers
4. 2.58 dekameters

5. 335 millimeters
6. 95.6 centimeters
7. 0.84 hectometers
8. 402 decimeters

9. 1.05 kilometers
10. 56.9 millimeters
11. 14.8 dekameters
12. 2 070 centimeters

47

Express each value as indicated.

13. 7 decimeters as centimeters

14. 28 millimeters as centimeters

15. 5 centimeters as millimeters

16. 0.38 meter as dekameters

17. 2.4 kilometers as hectometers

18. 27 dekameters as meters

19. 310.6 decimeters as meters

20. 3.9 hectometers as kilometers

21. 735 millimeters as decimeters

22. 8.5 meters as centimeters

23. 616 meters as kilometers

24. 404 dekameters as decimeters

25. 0.08 kilometers as decimeters

26. 8975 millimeters as dekameters

27. 0.06 hectometers as centimeters

28. 302 decimeters as kilometers

9–3 ARITHMETIC OPERATIONS WITH METRIC LENGTHS

Arithmetic operations are performed with metric denominate numbers the same as with customary denominate numbers. Compute the arithmetic operations, then write the proper metric unit of measure.

EXAMPLES

1. 3.2 m + 5.3 m = 8.5 m
2. 20.65 mm − 16.32 mm = 4.33 mm
3. 7.225 cm × 10.60 = 76.59 cm, rounded to 4 significant digits
4. 24.8 km ÷ 4.625 = 5.36 km, rounded to 3 significant digits

As with the customary system, only like units can be added or subtracted.

9–4 METRIC LINEAR MEASURE PRACTICAL APPLICATIONS

EXAMPLE

A structural steel fabricator cuts 25 pieces each 16.2 centimeters long from a 6.35-meter length of channel iron. Allowing 4 millimeters waste for each piece, find the length in meters of channel iron left after all 25 pieces have been cut.

Express each 16.2-centimeter piece as meters.	16.2 cm = 0.162 m
Find the total length of 25 pieces.	25 × 0.162 m = 4.05 m
Express each 4 millimeters of waste as meters.	4 mm = 0.004 m
Find the total amount of waste.	25 × 0.004 m = 0.1 m
Find the amount of channel iron left.	6.35 m − (4.05 m + 0.1 m) = 2.2 m ANS

Calculator Application

6.35 $\boxed{-}$ $\boxed{(}$ 25 $\boxed{\times}$ .162 $\boxed{+}$ 25 $\boxed{\times}$ .004 $\boxed{)}$ $\boxed{=}$ 2.2

2.2 m of channel iron are left ANS

EXERCISE 9–4   Solve the following problems.

1. Three pieces of stock measuring 3.2 decimeters, 9 centimeters, and 7 centimeters in length are cut from a piece of fabric 0.6 meter long. How many centimeters long is the remaining piece?

2. Find, in meters, the total length of the wall section shown in Figure 9–2.

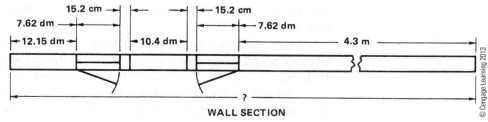

FIGURE 9–2

3. Preshrunk fabric is shrunk by the manufacturer. A length of fabric measures 150 meters before shrinking. If the shrinkage is 7 millimeters per meter of length, what is the total length of fabric after shrinking?

4. Find dimensions A and B, in centimeters, of the pattern shown in Figure 9–3.

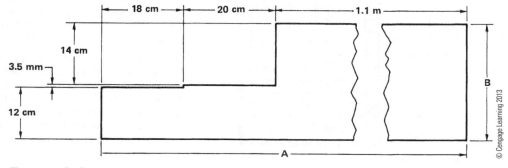

FIGURE 9–3

5. Three different parts, each of a different material, are made in a manufacturing plant. Refer to the table in Figure 9–4. Compute the cost of material per piece and the cost of a production run of 2500 pieces of each part including a 15% waste and scrap allowance.

Part Number	Length of Each Piece in Millimeters	Cost per Meter of Material	Cost per Piece	Cost per 2500 Pieces Including 15% Allowance (Round to Nearer Dollar)
105-AD	86.00	$2.20		
106-AD	51.00	$2.80		
107-AD	90.00	$3.03		

FIGURE 9–4

9–5 METRIC UNITS OF SURFACE MEASURE (AREA)

The method of computing surface measure is the same in the metric system as in the customary system. The product of two linear measures produces square measure. The only difference is in the use of metric rather than customary units. For example, 2 centimeters × 4 centimeters = 8 square centimeters.

Surface measure symbols are expressed as linear measure symbols with an exponent of 2. For example, 4 square meters is written as 4 m^2, and 25 square centimeters is written as 25 cm^2. The hectare (ha) is one area measure that does not use an exponent of 2. A hectare is another name for a square hectometer.

The basic unit of area is the square meter. The surface enclosed by a square that is 1 meter on a side is 1 square meter. The surface enclosed by a square that is 1 centimeter on a side is 1 square centimeter. Similar meanings are attached to the other square units of measure.

A reduced drawing of a square decimeter and a square meter is shown in Figure 9–5. Observe that 1 linear meter equals 10 linear decimeters, but 1 square meter equals 10 decimeters $\times$ 10 decimeters or 100 square decimeters.

The table in Figure 9–6 shows the units of surface measure with their symbols. These units are based on the square meter. Notice that each unit in the table is 100 times greater than the unit directly above it.

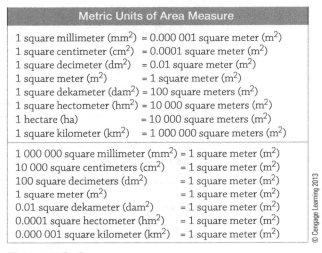

Metric Units of Area Measure
1 square millimeter (mm^2) = 0.000 001 square meter (m^2)
1 square centimeter (cm^2) = 0.0001 square meter (m^2)
1 square decimeter (dm^2) = 0.01 square meter (m^2)
1 square meter (m^2) = 1 square meter (m^2)
1 square dekameter (dam^2) = 100 square meters (m^2)
1 square hectometer (hm^2) = 10 000 square meters (m^2)
1 hectare (ha) = 10 000 square meters (m^2)
1 square kilometer (km^2) = 1 000 000 square meters (m^2)
1 000 000 square millimeter (mm^2) = 1 square meter (m^2)
10 000 square centimeters (cm^2) = 1 square meter (m^2)
100 square decimeters (dm^2) = 1 square meter (m^2)
1 square meter (m^2) = 1 square meter (m^2)
0.01 square dekameter (dam^2) = 1 square meter (m^2)
0.0001 square hectometer (hm^2) = 1 square meter (m^2)
0.000 001 square kilometer (km^2) = 1 square meter (m^2)

© Cengage Learning 2013

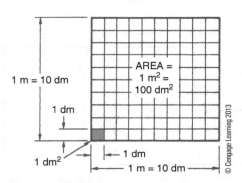

FIGURE 9–5

FIGURE 9–6

Expressing Metric Area Measure Equivalents

To express a given metric unit of area as the next larger metric unit of area, move the decimal point two places to the left. Moving the decimal point two places to the left is actually a shortcut method of dividing by 100.

EXAMPLE

Express 840.5 square decimeters (dm^2) as square meters (m^2).

Since a square meter is the next larger unit to a square decimeter, move the decimal point 2 places to the left: 840.5

840.5 dm^2 = 8.405 m^2 ANS

In moving the decimal point 2 places to the left, you are actually dividing by 100.

To express a given metric unit of area as the next smaller metric unit of area, move the decimal point two places to the right. Moving the decimal point two places to the right is actually a shortcut method of multiplying by 100.

EXAMPLES

1. Express 46 square centimeters (cm^2) as square millimeters (mm^2).

   Since a square millimeter is the next smaller unit to a square centimeter, move the decimal point 2 places to the right.

   46.00

   46 cm^2 = 4600 mm^2 ANS

   In moving the decimal point 2 places to the right, you are actually multiplying by 100.

2. Express 0.08 square kilometer (km^2) as square meters (m^2).

   Since a square meter is 3 units smaller than a square kilometer, the decimal point is moved 3 × 2 or 6 places to the right.

   0.080 000

   0.08 km^2 = 80 000 m^2 ANS

   In moving the decimal point 6 places to the right, you are actually multiplying by 100 × 100 × 100 or 1 000 000.

EXERCISE 9–5   Express each area as indicated. Metric units of area measure are given in the table in Figure 9–6 on page 268.

1. 500 square millimeters as square centimeters
2. 82 square decimeters as square meters
3. 4900 square centimeters as square decimeters
4. 15.6 square hectometers as square kilometers
5. 10 000 square millimeters as square decimeters
6. 7 300 square centimeters as square meters
7. 350 000 square millimeters as square meters
8. 2 700 000 square meters as square kilometers
9. 8 square meters as square decimeters
10. 23 square centimeters as square millimeters
11. 0.48 square meter as square centimeters
12. 0.06 square meter as square millimeters
13. 2.08 square decimeters as square centimeters
14. 0.009 square kilometer as square meters
15. 0.044 square kilometer as square decimeters

9–6 ARITHMETIC OPERATIONS WITH METRIC AREA UNITS

Arithmetic operations are performed with metric area denominate numbers the same as with customary area denominate numbers. Compute the arithmetic operations, then write the proper metric unit of surface measure.

EXAMPLES

1. 42.87 cm^2 + 16.05 cm^2 = 58.92 cm^2 ANS
2. 7.62 m^2 − 4.06 m^2 = 3.56 m^2 ANS
3. 6.15 × 30.8 mm^2 ≈ 189 mm^2 ANS
4. 12.95 km^2 ÷ 4.233 ≈ 3.059 km^2 ANS

As with the customary system, only like units can be added or subtracted.

9–7 METRIC AREA MEASURE PRACTICAL APPLICATIONS

EXAMPLE

A flooring contractor measures the floor of a room and calculates the area as 42.2 square meters. The floor is to be covered with tiles. Each tile measures 680.0 square centimeters. Allowing 5% for waste, determine the number of tiles needed.

Express each 680.0 square centimeter tile as square meters.

Find the number of tiles needed to cover 42.2 m².

Find the number of tiles needed allowing 5% for waste.

$$680.0 \text{ cm}^2 = 0.0680 \text{ m}^2$$

$$42.2 \text{ m}^2 \div 0.0680 \text{ m}^2 \approx 621$$
621 tiles

$$1.05 \times 621 \text{ tiles} \approx 652 \text{ tiles ANS}$$

Calculator Application

42.2 ÷ .068 × 1.05 = 651.6176471, 652 tiles ANS

EXERCISE 9–7   Solve the following problems.

1. How many pieces, each having an area of 450 square centimeters, can be cut from an aluminum sheet that measures 2.7 square meters?

2. A state purchases 3 parcels of land that are to be developed into a park. The respective areas of the parcels are 16 000 square meters, 21 000 square meters, and 23 000 square meters. How many square kilometers are purchased for the park?

3. Acidic soil is corrected (neutralized) by liming. A soil sample shows that 0.4 metric ton of lime per 1 000 square meters of a certain soil is required to correct an acidic condition. How many metric tons of lime are needed to neutralize 0.3 square kilometer of soil?

4. An assembly consists of 4 metal plates. The respective areas of the plates are 500 square centimeters, 700 square centimeters, 18 square decimeters, and 0.15 square meter. Find the total surface measure of the 4 plates in square meters.

5. A roll of gasket material has a surface measure of 2.25 square meters. Gaskets, each requiring 1 200 square centimeters of material, are cut from the roll. Allow 20% for waste. Find the number of gaskets that can be cut from the roll.

9–8 METRIC UNITS OF VOLUME (CUBIC MEASURE)

The method of computing volume measure is the same in the metric system as in the customary system. The product of three linear measures produces cubic measure. The only difference is in the use of metric rather than customary units. For example, 2 centimeters × 3 centimeters × 5 centimeters = 30 cubic centimeters.

Volume measure symbols are expressed as linear measure symbols with an exponent of 3. For example, 6 cubic meters is written as 6 m³, and 45 cubic decimeters is written as 45 dm³.

The basic unit of volume is the cubic meter. The volume of a cube having sides 1 meter long is 1 cubic meter. The volume of a cube having sides 1 decimeter long is 1 cubic decimeter. Similar meanings are attached to the cubic centimeter and cubic millimeter.

A reduced illustration of a cubic meter and a cubic decimeter is shown in Figure 9–7. Observe that 1 linear meter equals 10 linear decimeters, but 1 cubic meter equals 10 decimeters × 10 decimeters × 10 decimeters or 1 000 cubic decimeters.

The table in Figure 9–8 shows the units of volume measure with their symbols. These units are based on the cubic meter. Notice that each unit in the table is 1 000 times greater than the unit directly above it.

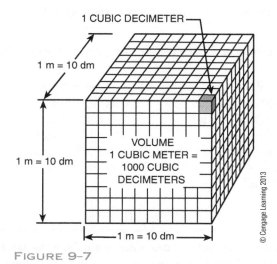

FIGURE 9–7

Metric Units of Volume Measure	
1 cubic millimeter (mm^3) = 0.000 000 001 cubic meter (m^3)	
1 cubic centimeter (cm^3) = 0.000 001 cubic meter (m^3)	
1 cubic decimeter (dm^3) = 0.001 cubic meter (m^3)	
1 cubic meter (m^3) = 1 cubic meter (m^3)	
1 000 000 000 cubic millimeter (mm^3)	= 1 cubic meter (m^3)
1 000 000 cubic centimeters (cm^3)	= 1 cubic meter (m^3)
1000 square decimeters (dm^3)	= 1 cubic meter (m^3)
1 cubic meter (m^3)	= 1 cubic meter (m^3)

FIGURE 9–8

Expressing Metric Volume Measure Equivalents

To express a given unit of volume as the next larger unit, move the decimal point three places to the left. Moving the decimal point three places to the left is actually a shortcut method of dividing by 1 000.

EXAMPLES

1. Express 1 450 cubic millimeters (mm^3) as cubic centimeters (cm^3).

   Since a cubic centimeter is the next larger unit to a cubic millimeter, move the decimal point 3 places to the left.   1 450.

   $$1\,450\ mm^3 = 1.45\ cm^3\ \text{ANS}$$

   In moving the decimal point 3 places to the left, you are actually dividing by 1000.

2. Express 27 000 cubic centimeters (cm^3) as cubic meters (m^3).

   Since a cubic meter is 2 units larger than a cubic centimeter, the decimal point is moved 2 × 3 or 6 places to the left.   027 000.

   $$27\,000\ cm^3 = 0.027\ m^3\ \text{ANS}$$

   In moving the decimal point 6 places to the left, you are actually dividing by 1000 × 1000 or 1 000 000.

To express a given unit of volume as the next smaller unit, move the decimal point three places to the right. Moving the decimal point three places to the right is actually a shortcut method of multiplying by 1000.

EXAMPLE

Express 12.6 cubic meters (m³) as cubic decimeters (dm³).

Since a cubic decimeter is the next smaller unit to a cubic meter, move the decimal point 3 places to the right.

$$12.600$$

$$12.6 \text{ m}^3 = 12\,600 \text{ dm}^3 \text{ Ans}$$

In moving the decimal point 3 places to the right, you are actually multiplying by 1000.

EXERCISE 9–8   Express each volume as indicated. Metric units of volume measure are given in the table in Figure 9–8 (on page 271).

1. $2700 \text{ mm}^3 = ? \text{ cm}^3$
2. $4320 \text{ cm}^3 = ? \text{ dm}^3$
3. $940 \text{ dm}^3 = ? \text{ m}^3$
4. $80 \text{ cm}^3 = ? \text{ dm}^3$
5. $48\,000 \text{ mm}^3 = ? \text{ dm}^3$
6. $650 \text{ cm}^3 = ? \text{ dm}^3$
7. $150\,000 \text{ dm}^3 = ? \text{ m}^3$

8. $20 \text{ mm}^3 = ? \text{ cm}^3$
9. $70\,000 \text{ mm}^3 = ? \text{ dm}^3$
10. $120\,000 \text{ cm}^3 = ? \text{ m}^3$
11. $5 \text{ dm}^3 = ? \text{ cm}^3$
12. $38 \text{ cm}^3 = ? \text{ mm}^3$
13. $0.8 \text{ m}^3 = ? \text{ cm}^3$
14. $0.075 \text{ dm}^3 = ? \text{ cm}^3$

15. $5.23 \text{ cm}^3 = ? \text{ mm}^3$
16. $0.94 \text{ m}^3 = ? \text{ dm}^3$
17. $1.03 \text{ dm}^3 = ? \text{ cm}^3$
18. $0.096 \text{ m}^3 = ? \text{ cm}^3$
19. $0.106 \text{ dm}^3 = ? \text{ mm}^3$
20. $0.006 \text{ m}^3 = ? \text{ cm}^3$

9–9 ARITHMETIC OPERATIONS WITH METRIC VOLUME UNITS

Arithmetic operations are performed with metric volume denominate numbers the same as with customary volume denominate numbers. Compute using the arithmetic operations, and then write the proper metric unit of volume. As with the customary system, only like units can be added or subtracted.

EXAMPLES

1. $4.37 \text{ m}^3 + 11.52 \text{ m}^3 = 15.89 \text{ m}^3$ Ans
2. $280.6 \text{ cm}^3 - 102.9 \text{ cm}^3 = 177.7 \text{ cm}^3$ Ans
3. $0.590 \times 1400 \text{ mm}^3 \approx 830 \text{ mm}^3$ Ans
4. $126 \text{ dm}^3 \div 6.515 \approx 19.3 \text{ dm}^3$ Ans

9–10 METRIC VOLUME PRACTICAL APPLICATIONS

EXAMPLE

A total of 340 pieces are punched from a strip of stock that has a volume of 12.8 cubic centimeters. Each piece has a volume of 22.5 cubic millimeters. What percent of the volume of stock is wasted?

Express each 22.5 cubic millimeter piece as cubic centimeters.	$22.5 \text{ mm}^3 = 0.0225 \text{ cm}^3$
Find the total volume of 340 pieces.	$0.0225 \text{ cm}^3 \times 340 = 7.65 \text{ cm}^3$
Find the amount of stock wasted.	$12.8 \text{ cm}^3 - 7.65 \text{ cm}^3 = 5.15 \text{ cm}^3$
Find the percent of stock wasted.	$\dfrac{5.15 \text{ cm}^3}{12.8 \text{ cm}^3} \approx 0.402$
	$0.402 = 40.2\%$, 40.2% waste Ans

Calculator Application

.0225 ☒ 340 ☐ 7.65

(12.8 ☐ 7.65) ☐ 12.8 ☐ 0.402 343 75, 0.402 rounded 40.2% waste Ans

EXERCISE 9–10   Solve each volume exercise.

1. Thirty concrete support bases are required for a construction job. Eighty-two cubic decimeters of concrete are used for each base. Find the total number of cubic meters of concrete needed for the bases. Round answer to 2 significant digits.

2. Before machining, an aluminum piece has a volume of 3.75 cubic decimeters. Machining operations remove 50.0 cubic centimeters from the top. There are 6 holes drilled. Each hole removes 30.0 cubic centimeters. There are 4 grooves milled. Each groove removes 2 500 cubic millimeters of stock. Find the volume of the piece, in cubic decimeters, after the machining operations.

3. Anthracite coal weighs 1.50 kilograms per cubic decimeter. Find the weight of a 5.60 cubic meter load of coal.

4. A total of 620 pieces are punched from a strip of stock that has a volume of 38.6 cubic centimeters. Each piece has a volume of 45.0 cubic millimeters. How many cubic centimeters of strip stock are wasted after the pieces are punched?

5. A magnesium alloy contains the following volumes of each element: 426.5 cubic decimeters of magnesium, 38.7 cubic decimeters of aluminum, 610 cubic centimeters of manganese, and 840 cubic centimeters of zinc. Find the percent composition by volume of each element in the alloy. Round answers to the nearest hundredth percent.

9–11 METRIC UNITS OF CAPACITY

Capacity is a measure of volume. The capacity of a container is the number of units of material that the container can hold.

The metric system uses only one kind of capacity measure; the units are standardized for all types of measure.

In the metric system, the liter is the standard unit of capacity. Measures made in gallons in the customary system are measured in liters in the metric system. In addition to the liter, the milliliter is used as a unit of capacity measure. Liters and milliliters are used for fluids (gases and liquids) and for dry ingredients in recipes.

The relationship between the liter and milliliter is shown in the table in Figure 9–9. Also listed are common metric capacity–cubic measure equivalents.

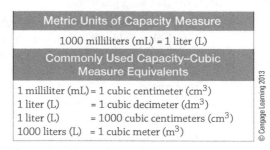

Metric Units of Capacity Measure
1000 milliliters (mL) = 1 liter (L)
Commonly Used Capacity–Cubic Measure Equivalents
1 milliliter (mL) = 1 cubic centimeter (cm^3)
1 liter (L) = 1 cubic decimeter (dm^3)
1 liter (L) = 1000 cubic centimeters (cm^3)
1000 liters (L) = 1 cubic meter (m^3)

© Cengage Learning 2013

FIGURE 9–9

Expressing Equivalent Metric Capacity Measures

It is often necessary to express given capacity units as either larger or smaller units. The procedure is the same as used with linear, square, and cubic units of measure.

EXAMPLE

Express 0.714 liters as milliliters.

Since 1 liter = 1000 milliliters, multiply 1000 by 0.714.

1000 × 0.714 = 714; 0.714 L = 714 mL ANS

EXERCISE 9–11   Express each unit of measure as indicated. Round each answer to the same number of significant digits as in the original quantity. Customary and metric units of capacity measure are given in the table in Figure 9–9 on page 273.

1. $3\,670$ mL $= ?$ L
2. 1.2 L $= ?$ mL
3. 23.6 mL $= ?$ cm^3
4. 3.9 L $= ?$ cm^3
5. $5\,300$ cm^3 $= ?$ L
6. 218 cm^3 $= ?$ mL
7. 0.08 m^3 $= ?$ L
8. 650 L $= ?$ m^3
9. 83 dm^3 $= ?$ L
10. 0.63 L $= ?$ mL
11. 7.3 dm^3 $= ?$ L
12. 478 mL $= ?$ L
13. $29\,000$ mL $= ?$ L
14. 0.75 m^3 $= ?$ L

9–12 METRIC CAPACITY PRACTICAL APPLICATIONS

EXAMPLE

An automobile gasoline tank holds 72 liters. Gasoline weighs 0.803 g/cm^3. What is the weight of the gasoline in a full tank? Give the answer in kilograms rounded off to the nearest tenth kilogram.

$$72\,\cancel{L} \times \frac{1000\ \cancel{mL}}{1\ \cancel{L}} \times \frac{1\ \cancel{cm^3}}{1\ \cancel{mL}} \times \frac{0.803\ \cancel{g}}{1\ \cancel{cm^3}} \times \frac{1\ kg}{1000\ \cancel{g}} = 57.816\ kg,\ 57.8\ kg\ \text{ANS}$$

EXERCISE 9–12   Solve the following problems.

1. In planning for a banquet, the chef estimates that 150 glasses of orange juice will be needed. If each glass holds 120 mL of juice, how many liters of orange juice should be ordered?
2. The liquid intake of a hospital patient during a specified period of time is 300 mL, 250 mL, 125 mL, 275 mL, 350 mL, 150 mL, and 200 mL. Find the total liter intake of liquid for this time period.
3. An oil-storage tank has a volume of 300,000 barrels (bbl). (1 bbl is 119.25 L.) However, there are 30,000 bbl of sludge at the bottom of the tank. The rest of the tank is full of usable oil. How many liters of oil are in the tank? Round answer to the nearest thousand liters.
4. An automobile engine originally has a displacement of 2.300 liters. The engine is rebored an additional 150.0 cubic centimeters. What is the engine displacement in liters after it is rebored?
5. An empty underground storage tank for unleaded gasoline has a volume of 37.85 m^3. The tank is being filled at the rate of 500 liters per minute. How long will it take to fill the tank? Round the answer to the nearest minute.
6. A bottle contains 2.250 liters of solution. A laboratory technician takes 28 samples from the bottle. Each sample contains 35.0 milliliters of solution. How many liters of solution remain in the bottle?

7. An engine running at a constant speed uses 120 milliliters of gasoline in one minute. How many liters of gasoline are used in 5 hours?
8. A solution contains 17.5% acid and 82.5% water. How many liters of the solution can be made with 750 mL of acid? Round the answer to the nearest tenth liter.
9. A water-storage tank has a volume of 135 cubic meters. When the tank is $\frac{1}{3}$ full of water, how many liters of water are required to fill the tank?

9–13   METRIC UNITS OF WEIGHT (MASS)

Weight is a measure of the force of attraction of the earth on an object. **Mass** is a measure of the amount of matter contained in an object. The weight of an object varies with its distance from the earth's center. The mass of an object remains the same regardless of its location in the universe.

Scientific applications dealing with objects located other than on the earth's surface are *not* considered in this book. Therefore, the terms *weight* and *mass* are used interchangeably.

In the metric system, the kilogram is the standard unit of mass. Objects that are measured in pounds in the customary system are measured in kilograms in the metric system.

The most common units of metric weight (mass) are listed in the table shown in Figure 9–10.

Metric Units of Weight (Mass) Measure
1000 milligrams (mg) = 1 gram (g)
1000 grams (g)   = 1 kilogram (kg)
1000 kilograms (kg)   = 1 metric ton (t)

FIGURE 9–10
© Cengage Learning 2013

Expressing Equivalent Metric Weight Measures

In both the customary and metric systems, apply the same procedures that are used with other measures. The following examples show the method of expressing given weight units as larger or smaller units.

EXAMPLE

Express 657 grams as kilograms.
Since 1 000 g = 1 kg, divide 657 by 1000.
Move the decimal point 3 places to the left.   657 g = 0.657 kg ANS

EXERCISE 9–13   Express each unit of weight as indicated. Round each answer to the same number of significant digits as in the original quantity. Metric units of weight are given in the table in Figure 9–10.

1. 1.72 g = ? mg
2. 890 mg = ? g
3. 2.6 metric tons = ? kg
4. 1230 g = ? kg
5. 2700 kg = ? metric tons
6. 0.6 kg = ? g
7. 0.04 g = ? mg
8. 900 kg = ? metric tons
9. 23 000 mg = ? g
10. 95 g = ? kg

9–14 METRIC WEIGHT PRACTICAL APPLICATIONS

EXAMPLE

A truck delivers 4 prefabricated concrete wall sections to a job site. Each wall section has a volume of 1.28 cubic meters. One cubic meter of concrete weighs 2 350 kilograms. How many metric tons are carried on this delivery?

Find the volume of 4 wall sections.	$4 \times 1.28 \text{ m}^3 = 5.12 \text{ m}^3$
Find the weight of 5.12 cubic meters.	$5.12 \times 2350 \text{ kg} = 12\,032 \text{ kg}$
Find the number of metric tons.	$12\,032 \text{ kg} \div 1000 \approx 12.0$ metric tons ANS

Calculator Application

4 ✕ 1.28 ✕ 2350 ÷ 1000 = 12.037 12,
12.0 metric tons (rounded to 3 significant digits) ANS

EXERCISE 9–14   Solve each problem.

1. What is the total weight, in kilograms, of 3 cases of 425-g cans of peas if each case has 48 cans?
2. An analytical balance is used by laboratory technicians in measuring the following weights: 750 mg, 600 mg, 920 mg, 550 mg, and 870 mg. Find the total measured weight in grams.
3. Three hundred identical strips are sheared from a sheet of steel. The sheet weighs 16.5 kilograms. Find the weight, in grams, of each strip.
4. One cubic meter of aluminum weighs 2.707 metric tons. How many kilograms does 0.155 cubic meter of aluminum weigh? Give answer to the nearest whole kilogram.
5. A force of 760 metric tons is exerted on the base of a steel support column. The base has a cross-sectional area of 12 100 cm². How many kilograms of force are exerted per square centimeter of cross-sectional area?
6. A piece of steel weighed 3.75 kg. Its weight was reduced to 3.07 kg by drilling holes in the steel. Each drilled hole removed 42.5 g of steel. How many holes were drilled?
7. A liter of water weighs 1.032 kg at 4°C and 0.988 kg at 50°C. Over this temperature change, what is the average weight decrease in grams per liter for each degree increase in temperature? Give answers to the nearest hundredth gram.

9–15 COMPOUND UNITS

In this unit, you have worked with basic units of length, area, volume, capacity, and weight. Methods of expressing equivalent measures between smaller and larger basic units of measure have been presented.

In actual practice, it is often required to use a combination of the basic units in solving problems. **Compound units** are the products or quotients of two or more basic units. Many quantities or rates are expressed as compound units. Following are examples of compound units.

EXAMPLES

1. Speed can be expressed as miles per hour. *Per* indicates division. Kilometers per hour can be written as km/h, $\frac{\text{km}}{\text{h}}$, or kph.

58

2. A bending force or torque is expressed as a newton·meter, which can be written as N·m.

3. Volume flow can be expressed as cubic centimeters per second. Cubic centimeters per second is written as cm^3/s.

Expressing Simple Compound Unit Equivalents

Compound unit measures are converted to smaller or larger equivalent compound unit measures using unity fractions. Following are examples of simple equivalent compound unit conversions.

EXAMPLE

Express 4700 liters per hour as liters per second.

Multiply 4700 L/h by unity fraction $\dfrac{1\ hr}{3600\ s}$.

$$\frac{4700\ L}{\cancel{h}} \times \frac{1\ \cancel{h}}{3600\ s} \approx 1.3\ \text{L/s} \ \text{ANS}$$

EXERCISE 9–15A Express each simple compound unit measure as indicated. Round each answer to the same number of significant digits as in the original quantity.

1. $129\ g/cm^2 = ?\ g/mm^2$
2. $53\ km/hr = ?\ km·min$
3. $0.128\ dm^3/sec = ?\ m^3/sec$
4. $31520\ kg/m^2 = ?\ kg/dm^2$

5. $87.0\ hp/L = ?\ hp/cm^3$
6. $930\ mg/mm^2 = ?\ g/mm^2$
7. $\$9.03/kg = ?\ \$/g$
8. $510\ cm/sec = ?\ m/sec$

Expressing Complex Compound Unit Equivalents

Exercise 9–15A involves the conversion of simple compound units. The conversion of only one unit is required; the other unit remains the same. In problem 1, the square centimeter unit is converted to a square millimeter unit; the gram unit remains the same. In problem 2, the hour unit is converted to a minute unit; the kilometer unit remains the same.

Problems often involve the conversion of more than one unit in their solutions. It is necessary to convert both units of a compound unit quantity to smaller or larger units. Following is an example of complex compound unit conversions in which both units are converted.

EXAMPLE

Express 62.35 kilometers per hour as meters per minute.

Multiply 62.35 km/hr by unity fractions $\dfrac{1000\ m}{1\ km}$ and $\dfrac{1\ hr}{60\ min}$.

$$\frac{62.35\ \cancel{km}}{\cancel{hr}} \times \frac{1000\ m}{1\ \cancel{km}} \times \frac{1\ \cancel{hr}}{60\ min} \approx 1039\ \text{m/min}\ \text{ANS}$$

Calculator Application

62.35 $\boxed{\times}$ 1000 $\boxed{\div}$ 60 $\boxed{=}$ 1039.166667,

1039 m/min (rounded to 4 significant digits) ANS

EXERCISE 9–15B   Express each complex compound unit measure as indicated. Round each answer to the same number of significant digits as in the original quantity.

1. $67 \text{ km/hr} = ? \text{ m/sec}$
2. $0.43 \text{ kg/cm}^2 = ? \text{ g/mm}^2$
3. $12.66 \text{ m/sec} = ? \text{ km/min}$
4. $0.88 \text{ g/mm}^2 = ? \text{ mg/cm}^2$
5. $\$4.77/\text{L} = ? \text{ cents/mL}$
6. $0.06 \text{ kg/cm}^3 = ? \text{ metric tons/m}^3$

9–16 COMPOUND UNITS PRACTICAL APPLICATIONS

EXAMPLE

A heating installation consists of 5 air ducts of equal size. Hot air passes through each duct at the rate of 12.8 cubic decimeters per second. Compute the total number of cubic meters of hot air that passes through the 5 ducts in 3.25 minutes.

Find the number of cubic meters per minute of air flowing through 1 duct. Multiply 12.8 dm³/sec by unity fractions $\dfrac{1 \text{ m}^3}{1000 \text{ dm}^3}$ and $\dfrac{60 \text{ sec}}{1 \text{ min}}$.

$$12.8 \frac{\text{dm}^3}{\text{sec}} \times \frac{1 \text{ m}^3}{1000 \text{ dm}^3} \times \frac{60 \text{ sec}}{1 \text{ min}} = 0.768 \text{ m}^3/\text{min}$$

Find the total volume of air passing through 5 ducts in 3.25 minutes. Multiply 0.768 m³/min by 5 and by 3.25 min.

$$0.768 \frac{\text{m}^3}{\text{min}} \times 5 \times 3.25 \text{ min} \approx 12.5 \text{ m}^3 \text{ ANS}$$

Calculator Application

12.8 ÷ 1000 × 60 × 5 × 3.25 = 12.48,

12.5 m³ (rounded to 3 significant digits) ANS

EXERCISE 9–16   Solve the following problems.

1. Anthracite coal weighs 1.5 kilograms per cubic decimeter. Find the weight, in metric tons, of a 3.5 cubic meter load of coal. Round the answer to 2 significant digits.

2. A joule (J) is the amount of energy required to raise the temperature of 0.24 g of water from 0°C to 1°C. A building has 18 air-conditioning units. Each unit removes 25 300 000 J per hour (J/h). How many joules are removed from the building in 20 minutes?

3. A 0.15-square-kilometer tract of land is to be seeded with Kentucky Bluegrass. At a seeding rate of 7.5 grams per square meter of land, how many kilograms of seed are required for the complete tract? Round the answer to 2 significant digits.

4. In drilling a piece of stock, a drill makes 360 revolutions per minute with a feed of 0.50 millimeter. Feed is the distance the drill advances per revolution. How many seconds are required to cut through a steel plate which is 3.5 centimeters thick? Round the answer to the nearest second.

5. Air passes through a duct at the rate of 12 000 cm³/s. Find the number of cubic meters of air passing through the duct in 27.75 minutes. Round the answer to the nearest cubic meter.

6. The speed of sound in air is 332 meters per second (mps) at 0 degrees Celsius. At this speed, how many kilometers does sound travel in 0.345 hour? Round the answer to the nearest kilometer.

7. Materials expand when heated. Different materials expand at different rates. Mechanical and construction technicians must often consider material rates of expansion. The amount

of expansion for short lengths of material is very small. Expansion is computed if a product is made to a high degree of precision and is subjected to a large temperature change. Also, expansion is computed for large structures because of the long lengths of structural member used. The table in Figure 9–11 lists the expansion per millimeter for each Celsius degree rise in temperature for a 1-mm length of material. For example, the expansion of a 1-mm length of aluminum is expressed as $0.000\,024\,\dfrac{mm/mm}{1°C}$ or $0.000\,024\,\dfrac{mm}{mm \cdot 1°C}$.

Material	Expansion of One Millimeter of Material in One Celsius Degree Temperature Increase
Aluminum	0.000 024 mm
Copper	0.000 019 8 mm
Structural Steel	0.000 015 8 mm
Brick	0.000 006 6 mm
Concrete	0.000 017 5 mm

© Cengage Learning 2013

FIGURE 9–11

Find the total expansion for each of the materials listed in the table in Figure 9–12. Express the answer to 3 significant digits.

	Material	Length Before Temperature Increase	Celsius Temperature Change	Total Expansion in mm
a.	Copper Cable	107.5 m	From 2.3°C to 25.4°C	
b.	Steel I-Beam	17.25 m	From −23.6°C to 26.4°C	
c.	Brick Wall	87.25 m	From −7.2°C to 21.9°C	
d.	Aluminum Wire	143.6 m	From 4.6°C to 41.2°C	
e.	Concrete Foundation	38.5 m	From −15.7°C to 23.5°C	

© Cengage Learning 2013

FIGURE 9–12

9–17 METRIC PREFIXES APPLIED TO VERY LARGE AND VERY SMALL NUMBERS

Electronics and physics often involve applications and computations with very large and very small numbers. Biotechnology uses very small numbers. Computers process data in the central processing unit (CPU). Small silicon wafers called chips contain integrated circuits and other processing circuitry. A single chip possesses an enormous amount of computing power. Data transformation operation takes place at extremely high speeds. Some computers can process millions of functions in a fraction of a second.

Data transmission can be measured by the number of bits per second. A bit is the on or off state of a single circuit represented by the binary digits 1 and 0. Coaxial cables can transmit data at the rate of 10 million bits per second for short distances. Transmission speeds using high-frequency radio waves (microwaves) can send signals at 50 million bits per second. Optical fibers using laser technologies can transmit with speeds of 1 billion bits per second.

NOTE: *The binary system is presented on pages 352 through 355.*

The prefixes most commonly used with very large and very small numbers and their corresponding values are listed in the table in Figure 9–13. Notice that each value is 1000 or 10^3 times larger or smaller than the value it directly precedes.

PREFIXES USED FOR LARGE AND SMALL VALUES				
	Symbol	Meaning	Factor Value	Power of 10
tera	T	one trillion	1 000 000 000 000	10^{12}
giga	G	one billion	1 000 000 000	10^9
mega	M	one million	1 000 000	10^6
kilo	k	one thousand	1000	10^3
—	—	—	1	10^0
milli	m	one-thousandth	0.001	10^{-3}
micro	μ	one-millionth	0.000 001	10^{-6}
nano	n	one-billionth	0.000 000 001	10^{-9}
pico	p	one-trillionth	0.000 000 000 001	10^{-12}

© Cengage Learning 2013

FIGURE 9–13

Some quantities with their definitions and units, which are commonly used in electronics/computer technology, are listed in the table in Figure 9–14.

SOME COMMONLY USED ELECTRONICS/COMPUTER QUANTITIES		
Quantity and (Symbol)	Definition	Unit and (Symbol)
Current (I)	The transfer of electrical charge through materials.	ampere (A)
Frequency (F)	The number of complete cycles in a unit of time.	hertz (Hz)
Resistance (R)	The opposition a material has to current flow.	ohm (Ω)
Power (P)	The rate at which energy is generated or dissipated.	watt (W)
Voltage (E)	Electromotive force or electrical pressure.	volt (V)
Capacitance (C)	The property of a capacitor that permits the storage of electrostatic energy.	farad (F)

© Cengage Learning 2013

FIGURE 9–14

Expressing Electrical/Computer Measure Unit Equivalents

In expressing equivalent units either of the following two methods can be used.

Method 1. The decimal point is moved to the proper number of decimal places to the left or right.

Method 2. The unity fraction method multiplies the given unit of measure by a fraction equal to one.

EXAMPLES

Refer to Figure 9–13 for the following three examples.

1. Express 5 300 000 bits (b) as megabits (Mb).

   METHOD 1. Move the decimal   5 300 000.   5 300 000 b = 5.3 Mb ᴀɴꜱ
   point 6 places to the left.

   METHOD 2. Multiply 5 300 000 b

   by the unity fraction $\dfrac{1\ \text{Mb}}{1\,000\,000\ \text{b}}$ $5\,300\,000\ \text{b} \times \dfrac{1\ \text{Mb}}{1\,000\,000\ \text{b}} = 5.3\ \text{Mb}$ ᴀɴꜱ

2. Express 4.6 amperes (A) as milliamperes (mA)

   METHOD 1. Move the decimal   4.600   4.6 A = 4600 mA ᴀɴꜱ
   point 3 places to the right.

   METHOD 2. Multiply 4.6 A by the

   unity fraction $\dfrac{1000\ \text{mA}}{1\ \text{A}}$ $4.6\ \text{A} \times \dfrac{1000\ \text{mA}}{1\ \text{A}} = 4600\ \text{mA}$ ᴀɴꜱ

3. Express 6 500 microseconds (μs) as milliseconds (ms)

   6 500 μs = 6.5 ms ᴀɴꜱ

   or $6\,500\ \mu\text{s} \times \dfrac{1\ \text{ms}}{1000\ \mu\text{s}} = 6.5\ \text{ms}$ ᴀɴꜱ

EXERCISE 9–17A   Express each of the following values as the indicated unit value.

1. 15 200 milliamperes (mA) as amperes (A)
2. 0.26 second (s) as microseconds (μs)
3. 750 watts (W) as kilowatts (kW)
4. 0.097 megaohm (MΩ) as ohms (Ω)
5. 8.2×10^9 bits (b) as gigabits (Gb)
6. 414 kilohertz (kHz) as hertz (Hz)
7. 380 milliseconds (ms) as seconds (s)
8. 4.4×10^6 microamperes (μA) as amperes (A)
9. 1.68 terabits per second (Tbps) as bits per second (bps)
10. 350 000 microfarads (μF) as farads (F)
11. 270 watts (W) as milliwatts (mW)
12. 0.03 second (s) as nano seconds (ns)
13. 5.8×10^5 hertz (Hz) as megahertz (MHz)
14. 120 picofarads (pF) as farads (F)
15. 2 600 milliamperes (mA) as microamperes (μA)
16. 97 000 kilobits (kb) as gigabits (Gb)

Expressing Biotechnology Measure Unit Equivalents

The unity fraction method is the most useful procedure to use when converting these metric units in biotechnology.

EXAMPLES

1. Express 4 500 pmol as nmol.

   Multiply 4 500 pmol by the unity fraction $\dfrac{1\ \text{nmol}}{1000\ \text{pmol}}$.

   $4\,500\ \text{pmol} \times \dfrac{1\ \text{nmol}}{1000\ \text{pmol}} = 4.5\ \text{nmol}$ ᴀɴꜱ

2. Express 27.5 micrograms as picograms.

Since one microgram is 10^{-6} g and one picogram is 10^{-12} g the unity fraction is $\dfrac{10^6 \text{ pg}}{1 \text{ } \mu g}$.

Thus, $27.5 \text{ } \mu g \times \dfrac{10^6 \text{ pg}}{1 \mu g} = 27.5 \times 10^6 \text{ pg} = 27\,500\,000 \text{ pg}$ ANS

EXERCISE 9–17B Express each of the following values as the indicated unit value. Express the answer to 3 significant digits.

1. 25.3 centimeters as nanometers
2. 595 nanometers as picometers
3. 172.5 nanograms as micrograms
4. 38.75 picograms as micrograms
5. 23.6 microliters as nanoliters
6. 2.4 picomoles as nanomoles

Arithmetic Operations

Arithmetic operations are performed the same way as with any other metric value. Compute the arithmetic operations, then write the appropriate unit of measure. Remember, when values are added or subtracted they must be in the same units.

EXAMPLES

1. Express answer as V: 18.60 V + 410.0 mV = 18.60 V + 0.4100 V = 19.01 V ANS
2. Express answer as μs: 510 μs − 12 000 ns = 510 μs − 12 μs = 498 μs ANS
3. Express answer as A: $(2.4 \times 10^4) \text{ } \mu A \times 375 = (9 \times 10^6) \text{ } \mu A = 9 \text{ A}$ ANS
4. Express answer as Hz: 0.75 MHz ÷ 970 ≈ 0.000 773 MHz ≈ 773 Hz ANS

EXERCISE 9–17C Compute each of the following values. Express each answer as the indicated unit value.

1. 13.0 V + 810 mV = ? V
2. 0.35 MW + 6500 W = ? kW
3. 0.04 A − 1400 μA = ? mA
4. 15.8 × 0.018 W = ? mW
5. 3.96 MHz ÷ 1.32 = ? kHz
6. 870 pF + 0.002 μF = ? pF
7. 96.5 Ω − 0.025 kΩ = ? Ω
8. (1.2×10^4) ns × (3×10^6) = ? s
9. 5 400 b × (2.5×10^7) = ? Gb
10. 0.93 MHz ÷ 31 = ? Hz
11. 440 mA + 260 000 μA = ? A
12. (8.42×10^3) mF − (7.15×10^5) μF = ? F
13. 8 000 ks + 360 Ms = ? Gs
14. (1.7×10^6) W × (5×10^4) = ? GW
15. 20 ns ÷ (5×10^{-10}) = ? s
16. (3.6×10^5) μA + (5.0×10^2) mA = ? A
17. 52 000 nF − 14 μF = ? mF

9–18 CONVERSION BETWEEN METRIC AND CUSTOMARY SYSTEMS

In technical work it is sometimes necessary to change from one measurement system to the other. Use the following metric–customary conversions for the length of an object. Because the length of an inch is defined in terms of a centimeter, some of these conversions are exact.

Metric–Customary Length Conversions

1 in. = 2.54 cm

1 ft = 30.48 cm

1 yd = 0.9144 m

1 mi ≈ 1.6093 km

To convert from one system to the other, you can either use unity fractions or multiply by the conversion factor given in the table.

EXAMPLES

1. Convert 3.7 ft to centimeters.

   METHOD 1
   Since 1 ft = 30.48 cm, multiply 3.7 by 30.48.

   $$3.7 \times 30.48 = 112.8$$
   $$3.7 \text{ ft} = 112.8 \text{ cm Ans}$$

   METHOD 2
   Since 3.7 ft is to be expressed in centimeters, multiply by the unity fraction $\dfrac{30.48 \text{ cm}}{1 \text{ ft}}$.

   $$3.7 \text{ ft} = 3.7 \text{ ft} \times \frac{30.48 \text{ cm}}{1 \text{ ft}} = 112.8 \text{ cm Ans}$$

2. Convert 5.4 km to miles.

   METHOD 1
   Since 1 mi ≈ 1.6093 km, divide 5.4 by 1.6093.

   $$5.4 \div 1.6093 = 3.4$$
   $$5.4 \text{ km} \approx 3.4 \text{ mi Ans}$$

   METHOD 2
   Since 5.4 km is to be expressed in miles, multiply by the unity fraction $\dfrac{1 \text{ mi}}{1.6093 \text{ km}}$.

   $$3.7 \text{ ft} = 5.4 \text{ km} \times \frac{1 \text{ mi}}{1.6093 \text{ km}} \approx 3.4 \text{ mi Ans}$$

   There will be times when more than one unity fraction will have to be used.

3. Convert 7.36 in. to millimeters.
   There is no inch–millimeter conversion in the table. So, we must use two conversions. First, convert inches to centimeters and then convert centimeters to millimeters. The unity fractions are $\dfrac{2.54 \text{ cm}}{1 \text{ in.}}$ and $\dfrac{10 \text{ mm}}{1 \text{ cm}}$.

   $$7.36 \text{ in.} = 7.36 \text{ in} \times \frac{2.54 \text{ cm}}{1 \text{ in.}} \times \frac{10 \text{ mm}}{1 \text{ cm}} = 187 \text{ mm Ans}$$

EXERCISE 9–18A   Express each length as indicated. Round each answer to the same number of significant digits as in the original quantity.

1. 12.0 in. as centimeters
2. 25.3 in. as millimeters
3. 3.25 ft as millimeters
4. 12.65 ft as centimeters
5. 1.20 m as feet
6. 4.2 m as yards
7. 36.75 mi as kilometers
8. 152.6 km as miles
9. 115.2 yd as centimeters
10. 8 ft $7\frac{1}{2}$ in. as meters

Dual Dimensions

Companies involved in international trade may use "dual dimensioning" on technical drawings and specifications. Dual dimensioning means that both metric and customary dimensions are given, as shown in Figure 9–15.

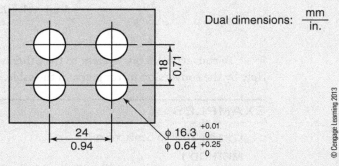

Dual dimensions: $\dfrac{mm}{in.}$

© Cengage Learning 2013

FIGURE 9–15

The metric measurements are supposed to be written on top of the fraction bar, but it is a good idea to look for a key. Diameter dimensions are marked with a ϕ.

Metric–Customary Area Conversions

$$1 \text{ square inch (sq in. or in.}^2) = 6.4516 \text{ cm}^2$$

$$1 \text{ square foot (sq ft or ft}^2) \approx 0.0929 \text{ m}^2$$

$$1 \text{ square yard (sq yd or yd}^2) \approx 0.8361 \text{ m}^2$$

$$1 \text{ acre} \approx 0.4047 \text{ ha}$$

$$1 \text{ square mile (sq mi or mi}^2) \approx 2.59 \text{ km}^2$$

EXAMPLE

Convert 12.75 ft^2 to square centimeters.

Since 12.75 ft^2 is to be expressed in square centimeters, multiply by the unity fractions $\dfrac{0.0929 \text{ m}^2}{1 \text{ ft}^2}$ and $\dfrac{10\,000 \text{ cm}^2}{1 \text{ m}^2}$.

$$12.75 \text{ ft}^2 = 12.75 \text{ ft}^2 \times \frac{0.0929 \text{ m}^2}{1 \text{ ft}^2} \times \frac{10\,000 \text{ cm}^2}{1 \text{ m}^2} = 11\,844.75 \text{ cm}^2, \; 11\,840 \text{ cm}^2 \text{ ANS}$$

EXERCISE 9–18B   Express each area as indicated. Round each answer to the same number of significant digits as in the original quantity.

1. 18.5 ft^2 as square centimeters
2. 47.75 in.^{2} as square millimeters
3. 3.9 yd^2 as square meters
4. 12$\overline{0}$ ft^2 as square meters

5. 65 ha as acres
6. 50$\overline{0}$ ha as square miles
7. 18.75 m^2 as square feet
8. 18.75 m^2 as square yards

Metric–Customary Volume Conversions

1 cubic inch (cu in. or in.^{3}) = 16.387 cm^3

1 fluid ounce (fl oz) ≈ 29.574 cm^3

1 teaspoon (tsp) ≈ 4.929 mL

1 tablespoon (tbsp) ≈ 14.787 mL

1 cup ≈ 236.6 mL

1 quart (qt) ≈ 0.9464 L

1 gallon (gl) ≈ 3.785 L

EXAMPLES

1. Convert 2.5 gal to liters.

$$2.5 \text{ gal} = 2.5 \text{ gal} \times \frac{3.785 \text{ L}}{1 \text{ gal}} = 9.4625 \text{ L, } 9.5 \text{ L ANS}$$

2. Convert 17.25 liters to quarts.

$$17.25 \text{ L} = 17.25 \text{ L} \times \frac{1 \text{ qt}}{0.9464 \text{ L}} \approx 18.226965, \text{ } 18.23 \text{ qt ANS}$$

EXERCISE 9–18C Express each volume as indicated. Round each answer to the same number of significant digits as in the original quantity.

1. 278.5 cubic inches as
   a. cubic centimeters and
   b. liters
2. $1\frac{1}{2}$ cups as milliliters
3. 25.75 fluid ounces as milliliters
4. 6.5 quarts as liters
5. 42.75 liters as gallons
6. 2.4 liters as quarts
7. 15.8 milliliters as fluid ounces
8. 135.4 milliliters as cubic inches

Metric–Customary Weight Conversions

1 ounce (oz) = 28.35 g

1 pound (lb) ≈ 0.4536 kg

1 (short) ton ≈ 907.2 kg

EXAMPLE

Convert 75.2 grams to pounds.

$$75.2 \text{ g} = 75.2 \text{ g} \times \frac{1 \text{ oz}}{28.35 \text{ g}} \times \frac{1 \text{ lb}}{16 \text{ oz}} = 0.165784 \text{ lb, } 0.166 \text{ lb ANS}$$

EXERCISE 9–18D   Express each weight as indicated. Round each answer to the same number of significant digits as in the original quantity.

1. 165 pounds as kilograms
2. 5.25 tons as metric tons
3. 43.76 ounces as grams
4. 70.5 grams as ounces
5. 23.8 kilograms as pounds
6. 2 759 kilograms as (short) tons

UNIT EXERCISE AND PROBLEM REVIEW

METRIC UNITS OF LINEAR MEASURE

For each of the following write the most appropriate metric unit.

1. Most audio compact discs are about 12 ? in diameter.
2. Some large trees grow over 30 ? high.
3. Slices of cheese are usually between 1 and 2?
4. Many home refrigerators are about 0.8 ? wide.
5. My desktop computer keyboard is 48 ? long.

EQUIVALENT METRIC UNITS OF LINEAR MEASURE

Express each value in the unit indicated.

6. 30 mm as cm	9. 23 m as cm	12. 0.014 m as mm
7. 8 cm as mm	10. 650 m as km	13. 12.2 cm as mm
8. 2460 mm as m	11. 0.8 km as m	14. 372.5 m as km

ARITHMETIC OPERATIONS WITH METRIC LENGTHS

Solve each exercise. Express the answers in the unit indicated.

15. 6.3 cm + 13.6 mm = ? mm
16. 1.7 m − 92 cm = ? cm
17. 20.8 × 31.0 m = ? m
18. 8.46 dm ÷ 6.27 = ? dm
19. 0.264 km + 37.9 m + 21 hm = ? m
20. 723.2 cm − 5.1 m = ? cm
21. 70.6 dm + 127 mm + 4.7 m = ? dm
22. 41.8 cm + 4.3 dm + 77.7 mm + 0.03 m = ? cm

EQUIVALENT METRIC UNITS OF AREA MEASURE

Express each metric area measure in the indicated unit.

23. 532 mm^2 as cm^2	28. 1.96 m^2 as cm^2
24. 23.6 dm^2 as m^2	29. 0.009 km^2 as m^2
25. 14 660 cm^2 as m^2	30. 173 000 m^2 as km^2
26. 53 cm^2 as mm^2	31. 28 000 mm^2 as m^2
27. 6 m^2 as dm^2	32. 0.7 dm^2 as mm^2

EQUIVALENT METRIC UNITS OF VOLUME MEASURE

Express each volume in the unit indicated.

33. 2 400 mm^3 as cm^3	37. 4.6 m^3 as dm^3
34. 1 700 cm^3 as dm^3	38. 420 dm^3 as m^3
35. 7 dm^3 as cm^3	39. 60 000 cm^3 as m^3
36. 15 cm^3 as mm^3	40. 0.0048 dm^3 as mm^3

EQUIVALENT METRIC UNITS OF CAPACITY MEASURE

Express each metric capacity in the unit indicated.

41. 1.3 L as mL
42. 2 100 mL as L
43. 93.4 mL as cm^3
44. 5 210 cm^3 as L
45. 618 L as m^3
46. 3.17 dm^3 as L
47. 0.06 L as mL
48. 19 000 mL as L

EQUIVALENT METRIC UNITS OF WEIGHT MEASURE

Express each metric weight in the unit indicated.

49. 1 880 g as kg
50. 730 mg as g
51. 2.7 metric tons as kg
52. 4.75 g as mg
53. 0.21 kg as g
54. 310 000 kg as metric tons

SIMPLE COMPOUND UNIT MEASURES

Express each simple compound unit measure as indicated. Round each answer to the same number of significant digits as in the original quantity.

55. 58 km/h = ? km/min
56. 148 g/cm^2 = ? g/mm^2
57. 32 040 kg/m^2 = ? kg/dm^2
58. 94.0 hp/L = ? hp/cm^3

COMPLEX COMPOUND UNIT MEASURES

Express each complex compound unit measure as indicated. Round each answer to the same number of significant digits as in the original quantity.

59. 10.58 m/sec = ? km/min
60. 42 km/hr = ? m/sec
61. 0.39 kg/cm^2 = ? g/mm^2
62. 0.90 g/mm^2 = ? mg/cm^2

METRIC PREFIXES

Express each of the following values as the indicated unit value.

63. 940 watts (W) as kilowatts (kW)
64. 7.3×10^8 bits (b) as gigabits (Gb)
65. 0.005 second (s) as nanoseconds (ns)
66. 4.9×10^5 hertz (Hz) as megahertz (MHz)
67. 1780 milliamperes (mA) as microamperes (μA)
68. 63×10^{-11} farads (F) as picofarads (pF)
69. 1294 picometers as nanometers
70. 95.73 microliters as nanoliters

CONVERSION BETWEEN METRIC AND CUSTOMARY SYSTEMS

Convert each unit to the indicated unit. Round each answer to the same number of significant digits as in the original quantity.

71. Convert 147.4 in. to meters
72. Convert 6.75 ft to centimeters
73. Convert 47.35 mm to inches
74. Convert 853.25 kilometers to miles
75. Convert 23.6 square yards to square meters
76. Convert 125 hectars to acres
77. Convert 47.25 cubic feet to cubic meters
78. Convert 17.6 gallons to liters

79. Convert 482.3 milliliters to quarts
80. Convert 369.5 cubic centimeters to fluid ounces
81. Convert 621.8 pounds to kilograms
82. Convert 16 ounces to fluid grams

PRACTICAL APPLICATIONS PROBLEMS

Solve the following problems.

83. A car travels from Town A to Town C by way of Town B. The car travels 135 kilometers. The trip takes 2.25 hours. It takes 0.8 hour to get from Town A to Town B. Assuming the same speed is maintained for the entire trip, how many kilometers apart are Town A and Town B?

84. Determine the total length, in meters, of the wall section shown in Figure 9–16.

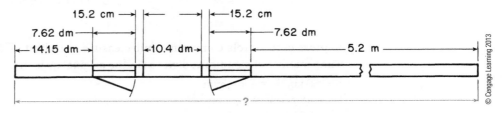

FIGURE 9–16

85. An assembly consists of 5 metal plates. The respective areas of the plates are 650 cm^2, 800 cm^2, 16.3 dm^2, 12 dm^2, and 0.12 m^2. Determine the total surface measure, in square meters, of the 5 plates.

86. A roll of fabric has a surface measure of 12.0 square meters. How many pieces, each requiring 1800 square centimeters of fabric, can be cut from the roll? Make an allowance of 10% for waste.

87. A total of 325 pieces are punched from a strip of stock that has a volume of 11.6 cubic centimeters. Each piece has a volume of 22.4 cubic millimeters. How many cubic centimeters of strip stock are wasted after the pieces are punched? Round answer to 3 significant digits.

88. Twenty concrete support bases are required for a construction job. Ninety-five cubic decimeters of concrete are used for each base. Compute the total number of cubic meters of concrete required for the 20 bases.

89. A truck is to deliver 8 prefabricated concrete wall sections to a job site. Each wall section has a volume of 0.620 cubic meter. One cubic meter of concrete weighs 2 350 kilograms. How many metric tons are carried on this delivery? Round answer to 3 significant digits.

90. The liquid intake of a hospital patient during a specified period of time is as follows: 275 mL, 150 mL, 325 mL, 275 mL, 175 mL, 200 mL, and 300 mL. What is the total liter intake of liquid for the time period?

SYSTEMS OF MEASUREMENT

The metric system, also called the International System (SI), is very important in engineering and technology. Every component in an electrical or electronic system is identified by its measurement: a 1.5-volt battery, a 1.1-megohm resistor, a 60-milliamp current, a 10-microfarad capacitor, etc. This chapter will help you develop a clear understanding of the metric system and the electrical measurements that are used. It explains the basic units and shows you how to change between different metric prefixes. Two types of notation are studied, engineering notation and scientific notation. Engineering notation uses powers of ten that correspond to the metric prefixes used in electronics. Scientific notation uses powers of ten to express large and small numbers that occur in electrical applications. In addition to the metric system, the U.S. customary system is still used to a great extent in the United States. It is important to understand its relation to the metric system and to know how to convert between metric units and U.S. units. A special calculator section at the end provides additional instruction on scientific notation, engineering notation, changing metric units, and converting between metric units and U.S. units.

4.1 SCIENTIFIC AND ENGINEERING NOTATION

Consider the following distance problem. The brightest star in the sky, Sirius, is 8.7 light-years away. This means it takes 8.7 years for light to travel from this star to the earth. If light travels at 186,000 mi/s (miles per second), how far away is Sirius? The distance, rounded to two significant digits, is calculated as follows:

(186,000 mi/sec) (60 sec/min) (60 min/hr) (24 hr/day) (365 day/yr) (8.7 yr)

$\quad = 51,031,500,000,000 \approx 51,000,000,000,000$ miles

The answer is more than 50 trillion miles. It is rounded to two significant digits because the data, 8.7 yr, is only accurate to two significant digits. Try this multiplication on the calculator. It automatically switches to *scientific notation* because the result is too large for ordinary notation:

$\quad$ 186000 $\boxed{\times}$ 60 $\boxed{\times}$ 60 $\boxed{\times}$ 24 $\boxed{\times}$ 365 $\boxed{\times}$ 8.7 $\boxed{=}$ $\rightarrow$ 5.10315 E13

97

The number on the right side of the display is the power of ten (E = exponent), and the answer to the distance problem in scientific notation to two significant digits is:

$$51{,}000{,}000{,}000{,}000 \text{ miles} = 5.1 \times 10^{13} \text{ miles}$$

Any digits after 5.1 shown on the display are not considered significant.

Definition | **Scientific Notation**

A number between 1 and 10 (including 1 but not 10) times a power of ten:

$$5.05 \times 10^7, \quad 6.23 \times 10^{-6}, \quad 9.99 \times 10^0, \quad 4.12 \times 10^{-2}, \quad 1.00 \times 10^{12}$$

The rule for changing from ordinary notation to scientific notation is:

Rule | **Changing Ordinary Notation to Scientific Notation**

Move the decimal point to the right of the first significant digit, called the *zero position*. The number of places from the zero position to the original decimal point equals the power of ten: positive if the decimal point is to the right of the zero position, negative if it is to the left.

EXAMPLE 4.1

Change to scientific notation:

(a) 532,000   **(b)** 6790   **(c)** 9.68   **(d)** 0.0702   **(e)** 0.00000410

Solution

(a) $532{,}000. = 5.32 \times 10^5$

(b) $6790. = 6.79 \times 10^3$

(c) $9.68 = 9.68 \times 10^0$

(d) $0.0702 = 7.02 \times 10^{-2}$

(e) $0.00000410 = 4.10 \times 10^{-6}$

The arrows show the movement of the decimal point to the zero position. A number greater than 10 has a positive exponent such as (a) and (b) above. A number between 1 and 10 has a zero exponent, such as (c) above, and a number less than 1 has a negative exponent such as (d) and (e) above. Note that *only significant digits are shown in scientific notation.*

Engineering notation also expresses numbers with powers of ten where the powers correspond to metric units:

Definition | **Engineering Notation**

A number between 1 and 1000 (including 1 but not 1000) times a power of ten, which *is a multiple of three:*

$$2.22 \times 10^{-3}, \quad 65.4 \times 10^9, \quad 1.00 \times 10^{-6}, \quad 329 \times 10^0, \quad 23 \times 10^3$$

The answer to the distance problem above in engineering notation is:

$$51,000,000,000,000 \text{ miles} = 51 \times 10^{12} \text{ miles}$$

Powers of ten that are multiples of three correspond to the units used in electronics and in the metric system. For example, 10^6 corresponds to mega, 10^3 corresponds to kilo, 10^{-3} to milli, and 10^{-6} to micro. Table 4-2 in Section 4.2, page 109 shows these engineering prefixes. The rule for changing to engineering notation is:

Rule **Changing Ordinary Notation to Engineering Notation**

Move the decimal point a multiple of three places: 3, 6, 9, etc., to change to a number from 1 to less than 1000. The number of places from the new position to the original decimal point equals the power of ten: positive if the original decimal point is to the right of the new position, negative if it is to the left.

EXAMPLE 4.2 Change to engineering notation:

(a) 208,000   (b) 92,300   (c) 509   (d) 0.0615   (e) 0.0000544

Solution

(a) $208,000. = 208 \times 10^3$

(b) $92,300. = 92.3 \times 10^3$

(c) $509. = 509 \times 10^0$

Note in (a), (b), and (c) that a number greater than 1 has a zero or positive exponent.

(d) $0.0615 = 61.5 \times 10^{-3}$

(e) $0.0000544 = 54.4 \times 10^{-6}$

Note in (d) and (e) that a number less than 1 has a negative exponent.

EXAMPLE 4.3 Change each number to both scientific and engineering notation:

(a) 48,900,000   (b) 63,500   (c) 77.1   (d) 0.0123   (e) 0.00655

Solution

	Scientific Notation	Engineering Notation
(a) 48,900,000	4.89×10^7	48.9×10^6
(b) 63,500	6.35×10^4	63.5×10^3
(c) 77.1	7.71×10^1	77.1×10^0
(d) 0.0123	1.23×10^{-2}	12.3×10^{-3}
(e) 0.00655	6.55×10^{-3}	6.55×10^{-3}

Note that the last number, 0.00655, is the same in scientific and engineering notation.

Rule   **Changing to Ordinary Notation**

Move the decimal point, to the right if the exponent is positive and to the left if it is negative, by the number of places equal to the power of ten.

EXAMPLE 4.4   Change to ordinary notation:

(a) 3.40×10^3 (b) 663×10^{-3} (c) 8.23×10^{-1}
(d) 0.768×10^6 (e) 55.2×10^{-6}

Solution

(a) $3.40 \times 10^3 = 3400$

(b) $663 \times 10^{-3} = 0.663$

(c) $8.23 \times 10^{-1} = 0.823$

(d) $0.768 \times 10^6 = 768,000$

(e) $55.2 \times 10^{-6} = 0.0000552$

EXAMPLE 4.5   Given:
$$(4,800)(56,000)(0.0390)$$

(a) Express the numbers in scientific notation, then calculate and express the answer in scientific notation to three significant digits.
(b) Express the answer in ordinary and engineering notation to three significant digits.

Solution

(a) The numbers in scientific notation are:

$$(4.8 \times 10^3)(5.6 \times 10^4)(3.90 \times 10^{-2})$$

Scientific notation is useful for calculation because all the numbers are between 1 and 10. Now apply the rules for multiplying with powers of ten from Chapter 3:

$$(4.8 \times 10^3)(5.6 \times 10^4)(3.9 \times 10^{-2})$$
$$= (4.8)(5.6)(3.9) \times 10^{3+4-2} \approx 105 \times 10^5$$

Note that the answer is *not* in scientific notation because the decimal point is not to the right of the first significant digit. Move the decimal point two places to the left to the zero position and balance the number by increasing the power of ten by 2:

$$105 \times 10^5 = 1.05 \times 10^7$$

(b) Write the number in ordinary notation by applying the power of ten and moving the decimal point seven places to the right, then change to engineering notation:

$$1.05 \times 10^7 = 10,500,000 = 10.5 \times 10^6$$

Error Box

To avoid making an error with the different notations, you should be able to quickly recognize whether a number is in ordinary, scientific, or engineering notation. When a number is written in ordinary notation, the power of ten is actually zero: $0.345 = 0.345 \times 10^0$. When this number is written in scientific notation, the decimal point is to the right of the first digit: 3.45×10^{-1}. When this number is written in engineering notation, the power of ten is a multiple of 3 and the number is between 1 and 1000: 345×10^{-3}. It is possible for a number to be written in more than one notation, such as 5.98×10^0, which is in ordinary, scientific, *and* engineering notation.

Practice Problems: Tell which notation or notations each number is written in, or if it is not written in any notation.

1. 1339
2. 56.7×10^9
3. 2.0×10^2
4. 126
5. 6.91×10^{-3}
6. 1.00×10^0
7. 0.555×10^5
8. 99.9×10^{-9}
9. 7.87×10^{-4}
10. 10×10^{-2}
11. 5.55
12. 0.872
13. 3.23×10^{-1}
14. 999×10^9
15. 0.292×10^3

The mode of the calculator can be set to scientific notation or engineering notation by using the [MODE], [FSE], or a similar key. To enter any number times a power of ten on the calculator use the [EE] or [EXP] key. For example, 3.9×10^{-2} is entered as follows:

DAL: 3.9 [EE] [(−)] 2 → 3.9   E −2
Not DAL: 3.9 [EXP] 2 [+/−] → 3.9   E −2

The factor of 10 does not appear on the display. It is understood. Only the significant digits and the exponent are shown. The calculator solution for Example 4.5 is, in scientific notation:

DAL: 4.8 [EE] 3 [×] 5.6 [EE] 4 [×] 3.9 [EXP] [(−)] 2 [=] → 1.05   E −7
Not DAL: 4.8 [EXP] 3 [×] 5.6 [EXP] 4 [×] 3.9 [EXP] 2 [+/−] [=] → 1.05   E −7

Depending on how you set your calculator, this result could be in ordinary, scientific, or engineering notation.

EXAMPLE 4.6

(a) Express the numbers in scientific notation, then calculate and express the answer in scientific notation to three significant digits.

(b) Express the answer in ordinary and engineering notation to three significant digits.

$$\frac{(328{,}000)(0.0850)}{0.00569}$$

Solution

(a) The numbers in scientific notation are:

$$\frac{(328{,}000)(0.0850)}{0.00569} = \frac{(3.28 \times 10^5)(8.50 \times 10^{-2})}{5.69 \times 10^{-3}}$$

Apply the rules for multiplying and dividing with powers of ten. Multiply the numerator first, then divide:

$$\frac{(3.28 \times 10^5)(8.50 \times 10^{-2})}{5.69 \times 10^{-3}} = \frac{(3.28)(8.50) \times 10^{5-2}}{5.69 \times 10^{-3}}$$

$$= \frac{27.88 \times 10^3}{5.69 \times 10^{-3}} = \frac{27.88}{5.69} \times 10^{3+3}$$

$$= 4.8998 \times 10^6 \approx 4.90 \times 10^6$$

(b) The answer to (a) is also in engineering notation. Change to ordinary notation by applying the power of ten:

$$4.90 \times 10^6 = 4{,}900{,}000$$

The calculator solution using powers of ten and scientific notation is:

DAL: 3.28 [EE] 5 [×] 8.5 [EE] [(−)] 2 [÷] 5.69 [EE] [(−)] 3
              [=] → 4.90   E6

Not DAL: 3.28 [EXP] 5 [×] 8.5 [EXP] 2 [+/−] [÷] 5.69 [EXP] 3 [+/−]
              [=] → 4.90   E6

EXAMPLE 4.7   Given:

$$\frac{(7{,}610{,}000)}{(0.00542)(183)}$$

(a) Write the numbers in scientific notation and estimate the answer without the calculator by rounding the numbers to one digit.

(b) Do the example on the calculator and express the answer in scientific notation to three significant digits.

Solution

(a) Scientific notation makes estimation easier because all the numbers can be rounded to a number between 1 and 10 and the calculations can be done without a calculator or even mentally:

$$\frac{7,610,000}{(0.00542)(183)} = \frac{7.61 \times 10^6}{(5.42 \times 10^{-3})(1.83 \times 10^2)}$$

$$\approx \frac{8 \times 10^6}{(5 \times 10^{-3})(2 \times 10^2)}$$

Apply the rules for powers of ten to get the estimate:

$$\frac{8 \times 10^6}{(5 \times 10^{-3})(2 \times 10^2)} = \frac{8 \times 10^6}{(2)(5) \times 10^{-(3-2)}} = \frac{8 \times 10^6}{10 \times 10^{-1}} = \frac{8}{10} \times 10^{6+1}$$

$$= 0.8 \times 10^7$$

The estimate of 0.8×10^7, when changed to scientific notation, is:

$$0.8 \times 10^7 = 8 \times 10^6$$

(b) The calculator solution is:

DAL: 7.61 ⎡EE⎤ 6 ⎡÷⎤ ⎡(⎤ 5.42 ⎡EE⎤ ⎡(−)⎤ 3 ⎡x⎤ 1.83 ⎡EE⎤ 2 ⎡)⎤
⎡=⎤ → 7.67   E6

Not DAL: 7.61 ⎡EXP⎤ 6 ⎡÷⎤ ⎡(⎤ 5.42 ⎡EXP⎤ 3 ⎡+/−⎤ ⎡x⎤ 1.83 ⎡EXP⎤ 2 ⎡)⎤
⎡=⎤ → 7.67   E6

This answer, 7.67×10^6, agrees closely with the estimate, 8×10^6, thereby verifying the calculation.

CLOSE THE

CIRCUIT

EXAMPLE 4.8

The voltage, in volts, of a circuit is given by:

$$V = (0.000133)(470,000)$$

Write the numbers in engineering notation and calculate V, in volts. Express the answer in engineering notation to three significant digits.

Solution

Write the numbers in engineering notation and multiply, applying the rules for powers of ten:

$$(133 \times 10^{-6})(470 \times 10^3) = (133)(470) \times 10^{-(6-3)} = 62,510 \times 10^{-3}$$

Change the answer to engineering notation by moving the decimal point and changing the power of ten:

$$62510 \times 10^{-3} = 62.51 \times 10^0 \approx 62.5 \times 10^0 \text{ or } 62.5 \text{ V}$$

The calculator solution is:

DAL: 133 $\boxed{\text{EE}}$ $\boxed{(-)}$ 6 $\boxed{\times}$ 470 $\boxed{\text{EE}}$ 3 $\boxed{=}$ → 62.5   E0

Not DAL: 133 $\boxed{\text{EXP}}$ 6 $\boxed{+/-}$ $\boxed{\times}$ 470 $\boxed{\text{EXP}}$ 3 $\boxed{=}$ → 62.5   E0

The size of numbers written with powers of ten can be misleading. The increase from 10^2 to 10^3 is only 900, but the increase from 10^6 to 10^7 is 9,000,000! Figure 4-1 gives you an idea of how powers of ten relate to some of the world's important (and not so important) scientific phenomena. For example, if you could add all the words ever spoken since people first started babbling, the number would still be less than 10^{18}!

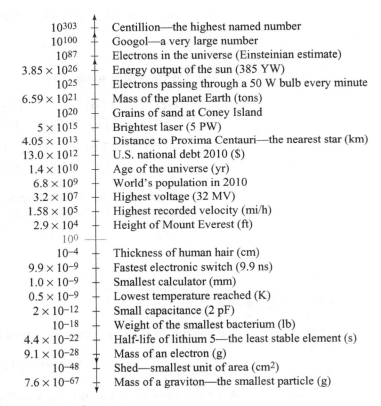

10^{303}	Centillion—the highest named number
10^{100}	Googol—a very large number
10^{87}	Electrons in the universe (Einsteinian estimate)
3.85×10^{26}	Energy output of the sun (385 YW)
10^{25}	Electrons passing through a 50 W bulb every minute
6.59×10^{21}	Mass of the planet Earth (tons)
10^{20}	Grains of sand at Coney Island
5×10^{15}	Brightest laser (5 PW)
4.05×10^{13}	Distance to Proxima Centauri—the nearest star (km)
13.0×10^{12}	U.S. national debt 2010 ($)
1.4×10^{10}	Age of the universe (yr)
6.8×10^9	World's population in 2010
3.2×10^7	Highest voltage (32 MV)
1.58×10^5	Highest recorded velocity (mi/h)
2.9×10^4	Height of Mount Everest (ft)
10^0	
10^{-4}	Thickness of human hair (cm)
9.9×10^{-9}	Fastest electronic switch (9.9 ns)
1.0×10^{-9}	Smallest calculator (mm)
0.5×10^{-9}	Lowest temperature reached (K)
2×10^{-12}	Small capacitance (2 pF)
10^{-18}	Weight of the smallest bacterium (lb)
4.4×10^{-22}	Half-life of lithium 5—the least stable element (s)
9.1×10^{-28}	Mass of an electron (g)
10^{-48}	Shed—smallest unit of area (cm²)
7.6×10^{-67}	Mass of a graviton—the smallest particle (g)

FIGURE 4-1 Scientific notation.

Answers to Error Box Problems, page 101:

1. Ord.   **2.** Eng.   **3.** Sci.   **4.** Eng., Ord.   **5.** Sci. Eng.   **6.** All three   **7.** None

8. Eng.   **9.** Sci.   **10.** None   **11.** All three   **12.** Ord.   **13.** Sci.   **14.** Eng.   **15.** None

EXERCISE 4.1

In exercises 1 through 20 express each number in scientific notation and engineering notation.

1. 42,600,000,000
2. 11,700,000
3. 0.000930
4. 0.0000301
5. 10,500,000
6. 44,900
7. 45.6
8. 27.0
9. 2.35
10. 8.73
11. 0.00117
12. 0.0981
13. 334
14. 69,900
15. 0.112
16. 0.409
17. 1000
18. 10
19. 162,000
20. 7760

In exercises 21 through 54 express each number in ordinary, scientific, and engineering notation.

21. 564×10^5
22. 3.36×10^2
23. 1200×10^3
24. 14×10^6
25. 11.4×10^{-8}
26. 345×10^{-4}
27. 0.0528×10^3
28. 0.00384×10^2
29. 5690×10^{-6}
30. 1560×10^{-3}
31. 5.66×10^6
32. 9.90×10^9
33. 552×10^{-6}
34. 89.1×10^{-3}
35. 2.64×10^7
36. 4.33×10^5
37. 3.90×10^{-6}

38. 9.31×10^{-5}
39. 1.45×10^0
40. 46.7×10^0
41. 0.101×10^{-1}
42. 634×10^{-4}
43. 112×10^3
44. 87.0×10^3
45. 10.5×10^{-6}
46. 717×10^{-3}
47. 0.871×10^9
48. 4.44×10^6
49. 1230×10^{-3}
50. 1005×10^{-9}
51. 125×10^3
52. 10.1×10^{-6}
53. 5.03×10^{-1}
54. 5.50×10^{-2}

In exercises 55 through 64:

(a) Express the numbers in scientific notation, then calculate and express the answer in scientific notation to three significant digits.

(b) Express the answer in ordinary and engineering notation to three significant digits.

55. (8400)(28,000)(0.0550)
56. (0.00444)(12,800)(100,000)
57. $\dfrac{4510}{0.000334}$
58. $\dfrac{4,660,000}{0.0198}$
59. $\dfrac{8670}{(0.0139)(0.183)}$
60. $\dfrac{(0.00677)}{(0.298)(12,900)}$
61. $\dfrac{(0.1530)(0.00183)}{3900}$
62. $\dfrac{(1,560,000)(0.0124)}{(0.00345)}$
63. $\dfrac{(254,000)(2.74)}{(0.000881)(5,300)}$
64. $\dfrac{(0.000122)(3.34)}{(665)(0.113)}$

79

In exercises 65 through 84.

(a) If indicated by the instructor, estimate each answer without the calculator by writing the numbers in scientific notation and rounding off to one digit. Based on the estimate, choose the correct answer in engineering notation to three significant digits. See Example 4.7 for estimation procedure.

(b) Calculate the answer in engineering notation to three significant digits.

65. $(0.00000101)(9,330)$ $[9.42 \times 10^{-6}, 9.42 \times 10^{-3}, 9.42 \times 10^{-2}, 9.42 \times 10^{0}]$

66. $(4,780,000)(0.000767)$ $[3.66 \times 10^{2}, 3.66 \times 10^{3}, 3.67 \times 10^{3}, 36.7 \times 10^{3}]$

67. $(32,200)(86,500)(2830)$ $[7.88 \times 10^{9}, 78.8 \times 10^{9}, 78.8 \times 10^{12}, 7.88 \times 10^{12}]$

68. $(52,100)(54,500)(0.156)$ $[44.3 \times 10^{6}, 443 \times 10^{6}, 44.3 \times 10^{9}, 443 \times 10^{9}]$

69. $\dfrac{0.00000656}{0.000123}$ $[5.33 \times 10^{0}, 53.3 \times 10^{-6}, 533 \times 10^{-3}, 53.3 \times 10^{-3}]$

70. $\dfrac{303,000}{4,050,000}$ $[748 \times 10^{0}, 748 \times 10^{-3}, 7.48 \times 10^{-3}, 74.8 \times 10^{-3}]$

71. $\dfrac{(449,000)(0.00776)}{(0.0659)}$ $[5.29 \times 10^{4}, 5.29 \times 10^{3}, 52.9 \times 10^{3}, 52.9 \times 10^{6}]$

72. $\dfrac{3200}{(0.129)(0.00450)}$ $[5.51 \times 10^{6}, 55.1 \times 10^{3}, 55.1 \times 10^{6}, 5.51 \times 10^{3}]$

73. $\dfrac{0.877}{(45,100)(2670)}$ $[7.28 \times 10^{-9}, 0.728 \times 10^{-9}, 72.8 \times 10^{-9}, 728 \times 10^{-9}]$

74. $\dfrac{(0.0000210)(0.00349)}{451}$ $[163 \times 10^{-12}, 16.3 \times 10^{-9}, 1.63 \times 10^{-9}, 0.163 \times 10^{-9}]$

75. $\dfrac{(123,000)(0.0356)}{(1770)(0.0434)}$ $[57.0 \times 10^{0}, 570 \times 10^{-3}, 5.70 \times 10^{0}, 510 \times 10^{0}]$

76. $\dfrac{(0.00909)(0.0117)}{(0.000100)(0.514)}$ $[2.07 \times 10^{0}, 20.7 \times 10^{0}, 207 \times 10^{0}, 207 \times 10^{-3}]$

77. $\dfrac{8.89 \times 10^{12}}{9.89 \times 10^{6}}$ $[0.899 \times 10^{6}, 8.99 \times 10^{6}, 89.9 \times 10^{6}, 899 \times 10^{3}]$

78. $\dfrac{5.96 \times 10^{9}}{8.01 \times 10^{3}}$ $[74.4 \times 10^{6}, 7.44 \times 10^{6}, 74.4 \times 10^{3}, 744 \times 10^{3}]$

79. $\dfrac{3.03 \times 10^{-3}}{6.06 \times 10^{2}}$ $[5.00 \times 10^{-6}, 5.00 \times 10^{-3}, 50.0 \times 10^{-6}, 500 \times 10^{-3}]$

80. $\dfrac{92.3 \times 10^{-6}}{2.54 \times 10^{-3}}$ $[363 \times 10^{-6}, 0.363 \times 10^{-3}, 36.3 \times 10^{-3}, 3.63 \times 10^{-3}]$

81. $\dfrac{1.26 \times 10^{12}}{(35.0 \times 10^{-3})(0.900 \times 10^{6})}$ $[4.00 \times 10^{6}, 40.0 \times 10^{6}, 0.400 \times 10^{6}, 400 \times 10^{6}]$

82. $\dfrac{81.2 \times 10^{3}}{(366 \times 10^{-3})(45.5 \times 10^{3})}$ $[4.88 \times 10^{0}, 4.88 \times 10^{3}, 48.8 \times 10^{0}, 0.488 \times 10^{3}]$

83. $\dfrac{(116 \times 10^{3})(0.203 \times 10^{6})}{94.1 \times 10^{-3}}$ $[0.250 \times 10^{12}, 2.50 \times 10^{12}, 25.0 \times 10^{12}, 250 \times 10^{9}]$

84. $\dfrac{(26.5 \times 10^{-3})(69.3 \times 10^{6})}{0.0860 \times 10^{12}}$ $[21.3 \times 10^{-6}, 21.4 \times 10^{-6}, 2.13 \times 10^{-6}, 213 \times 10^{-6}]$

Applied Problems

In problems 85 through 90 solve each applied problem to three significant digits.

85. The North American Free Trade Agreement (NAFTA) requires that the United States spend $1,500,000,000 on environmental cleanup. Express this amount in scientific and engineering notation.

86. It is estimated that policies enacted during President George W. Bush's administration will increase the U.S. national debt by $10,350,000,000,000. Express this amount in scientific and engineering notation.

87. Parker Bros. Inc., manufacturer of the board game Monopoly, printed $18,500,000,000,000 of toy money in 1990 for all its games, which is more than all the real money in circulation in the world. If all this "money" were distributed equally among the world's population, equal to 5.3 billion (5.3×10^9) in 1990, how much would each person get to the nearest cent?

88. In 2009, British Petroleum (BP) made one of the greatest profits achieved by an industrial company. Worldwide revenue totaled $246,100,000,000, with its total assets valued at $236,000,000,000. What percentage of the assets does the revenue represent?

89. One of the shortest blips of light produced at the AT&T laboratories in New Jersey lasted 8.0×10^{-15} seconds. If the speed of light is 300×10^6 meters per second, how many meters does light travel in that time? Give the answer in engineering notation.

    Note: (Rate)(Time) = (Distance)

90. The most massive living thing on earth is the giant sequoia, named the General Sherman, in Sequoia National Park, California. Its weight is estimated at 5.51×10^6 lb. The seed of such a tree weighs only 1.67×10^{-4} oz. Calculate the ratio of the weight of the mature tree to the weight of the seed. Give the answer in scientific notation.

    Note: 1 lb = 16 oz.

Applications to Electronics

In problems 91 through 98 solve each applied problem. Give the answer in engineering notation to three significant digits.

91. The world's most expensive pipeline is the Alaska pipeline, which is built to carry 2,000,000 barrels a day of crude oil. If 6.65×10^6 barrels of oil (1 million tons) can generate 4.00×10^9 kWh (kilowatt-hours) of electricity, how many kilowatt-hours could be generated in one year from the Alaska pipeline oil?

92. A CRAY scientific computer can do a simple addition in 130×10^{-12} seconds (130 picoseconds). How many additions can the CRAY computer do in 1 minute?

93. Find the voltage, in volts, of a circuit given by:

$$V = (0.00021)(870)$$

94. Find the power, in watts, of a circuit given by:

$$P = (0.550)(0.0670)$$

95. Find the current, in amps, in a circuit given by:

$$I = \frac{120 \times 10^0}{1.3 \times 10^3}$$

96. Find the current, in amps, in a circuit given by:

$$I = \frac{350 \times 10^{-3}}{3.30 \times 10^3}$$

97. The total resistance R_T of a series circuit, in ohms, is given by:

$$R_T = (3.30 \times 10^3) + (910 \times 10^0) + (1.20 \times 10^3)$$

Find R_T in ohms.

Note: You cannot add powers of ten unless they are the same.

98. The total voltage V_T across a series circuit is given by:

$$V_T = (1.20 \times 10^0) + (430 \times 10^{-3}) + (550 \times 10^{-3})$$

Find V_T in volts.

Note: You cannot add powers of ten unless they are the same.

ADDITION AND SUBTRACTION

One of the first things that everyone notices about algebra is that it uses letters and other symbols to represent numbers. Algebra also uses letters and other symbols to represent unknown amounts in equations and inequalities. In the first chapter we used letters to help present some of the rules. For example, we said that

$$b^{-n} = \frac{1}{b^n}, \text{ if } b \neq 0.$$

VARIABLES

When a letter or other symbol is used to indicate something that can be assigned any value from a given or implied set of numbers, it is called a variable. We have already used letters as variables in this book. For example, we used a, b, and c as variables when we said that $a(b + c) = ab + ac$. We used b and n as variables when we said that $b^{-n} = \frac{1}{b^n}$, if $b \neq 0$. Another place where variables are used is on a calculator. For example, the x^2 , $\sqrt{x}$, $1/x$, and y^x keys on a calculator all use the letter x as a variable and one uses the letter y.

CONSTANTS

Letters or other symbols may also be used to designate fixed, but unspecified, numbers called constants. One constant that you are already familiar with is π, which represents the number $3.14159265\ldots$. (The $\ldots$ at the end of this number

83

means that there are more digits after the 5.) Another constant that we will use a lot is $e = 2.7182818284.\ldots$ Usually letters near the beginning of the alphabet, like a, b, c, d, are used to represent constants. Letters near the end of the alphabet, such as w, x, y, and z, are used to indicate variables. Thus, in the expression $ax + b$, a and b represent constants and x is a variable.

ALGEBRAIC EXPRESSIONS

The term **algebraic expression** is used for any combination of variables and constants that is formed using a finite number of operations. Examples of algebraic expressions include ax^2, $ax^2 + bx + c$, $\dfrac{x^3 + \sqrt{y}}{ax^2 - by}$, $\dfrac{4x^{-3} + 7x^2}{2x - 3w}$, and $1.8C + 32$.

ALGEBRAIC TERMS

If an algebraic expression consists of parts connected by plus or minus signs, it is called an **algebraic sum**. Each of the parts of an algebraic sum, together with the sign preceding it, is called an **algebraic term**.

EXAMPLE 2.1	What are the algebraic terms of the algebraic sum $5x^7 + 2x^3y - \dfrac{4x}{y^2}$?

SOLUTION This algebraic sum has three algebraic terms: $5x^7$, $2x^3y$, and $-\dfrac{4x}{y^2}$.

An algebraic term may consist of several **factors**. The term $5xy$ has the individual factors of 5, x, and y. Other factors are products of two or more of the individual factors. Thus, $5x$, $5y$, xy, and $5xy$ are also factors of $5xy$.

EXAMPLE 2.2	What are the factors of $\dfrac{6x^2}{y}$?

SOLUTION The individual factors are 2, 3, x, and $\dfrac{1}{y}$. Other factors are 6, $2x$, $3x$, $6x$, x^2, $2x^2$, $3x^2$, $6x^2$, $\dfrac{2}{y}$, $\dfrac{3}{y}$, $\dfrac{6}{y}$, $\dfrac{x}{y}$, $\dfrac{2x}{y}$, $\dfrac{3x}{y}$, $\dfrac{6x}{y}$, $\dfrac{x^2}{y}$, $\dfrac{2x^2}{y}$, $\dfrac{3x^2}{y}$, and $\dfrac{6x^2}{y}$.

EXAMPLE 2.3	What are the factors of $\dfrac{-10(x + y)}{z}$?

SOLUTION The individual factors are -1, 2, 5, $x + y$, and $\dfrac{1}{z}$. The other factors are products of these factors. Notice that the negative sign was treated by using -1 as a factor.

Each term has two parts. One part is the coefficient and the other part contains the variables. The coefficient is the product of all of the constants. Normally the coefficient is written at the front of the term. A variable with no visible coefficient, such as x or y, is understood to have a coefficient of 1. The coefficient of the term $4x^2$ is 4; of $18y^3z$ is 18; of $\frac{w^2}{3}$ is $\frac{1}{3}$; and of yx^2 is 1. The coefficient of $4\pi bx$ is $4\pi b$ if we assume that b is a constant.

Terms that involve exactly the same variables raised to exactly the same power are called like terms. For example, $7x^2y$ and $4x^2y$ are like terms because both contain the same variables (x and y), the variable x is raised to the second power in each term and the y is raised to the first power. $4xyz^3$ and $5xyz^2$ are not like terms even though they both contain the variables x, y, and z, because one term has the variable z raised to the third power and in the other term it is raised to the second power.

MONOMIALS AND MULTINOMIALS

An algebraic expression with only one term is a monomial. An algebraic sum with exactly two terms is a binomial; an algebraic sum with three terms is a trinomial; and an algebraic sum with two or more terms is a multinomial. As you can see, binomials and trinomials are special kinds of multinomials.

EXAMPLE 2.4

$4x^2$, $\frac{7}{5}xy$, and $-8xz^3 \sqrt{w}$ are all monomials.
$ax^2 + by$, $\sqrt{3}x^3z - 2w$, and $4x^2 + 2$ are binomials.
$3x^3 - 2x + 1$ and $2xy + 3yz - 4\sqrt{2y}$ are trinomials.
$16x^3 - 7\sqrt{2}y^2 + \frac{2}{3}xy - 7^5x^3y$ is a multinomial with four terms. In this last expression the coefficient of the first term is 16, the second term has a coefficient of $-7\sqrt{2}$, the third $\frac{2}{3}$, and the fourth -7^5 (or $-16,807$).

ADDING AND SUBTRACTING MULTINOMIALS

In order to add or subtract monomials, we add or subtract the coefficients of like terms. So, $3x^2 + 5x^2 = 8x^2$. We can justify this with the distributive property, since $3x^2 + 5x^2 = (3 + 5)x^2 = 8x^2$.

NOTE Remember, you can only add or subtract like terms.

So,

$$3x^2 + 2xy - y^3 - 8xy = 3x^2 - 6xy - y^3$$

because the only like terms are $2xy$ and $-8xy$. When these are added, we get $-6xy$. None of the other terms can be combined because they are not like terms.

EXAMPLE 2.5

$(3x^2 + 2yx - 5y) + (-6xy + 6x^2 - 7y)$
$$= (3x^2 + 6x^2) + (2yx - 6xy) + (-5y - 7y)$$
$$= 9x^2 - 4yx - 12y$$

Notice that $2yx$ and $-6xy$ are like terms even though the variables are written in a different order. This is an application of the commutative law introduced in Section 1.1.

EXAMPLE 2.6

$(4y - 3z + 4xy) - (7y - 3z - 6xy)$
$$= 4y - 3z + 4xy - 7y + 3z + 6xy$$
$$= (4y - 7y) + (-3z + 3z) + (4xy + 6xy)$$
$$= -3y + 10xy$$

Notice that when you have a negative sign in front of a parenthesis it means to multiply *each* term inside the parentheses by -1. So,

$$-(7y - 3z - 6xy) = -7y + 3z + 6xy$$

As mentioned in Section 1.2, there are several different symbols for grouping. These symbols are parentheses ( ), brackets [ ], and braces { }. When it is necessary to simplify an expression, you should start removing grouping symbols from the inside. For example, the expression

$$5\{2x - [3x + (4x - 5) + 2] - 3x\}$$

would be simplified by first removing the parentheses and combining any like terms that are within the brackets.

$$5\{2x - [3x + (4x - 5) + 2] - 3x\} = 5\{2x - [3x + 4x - 5 + 2] - 3x\}$$
$$= 5\{2x - [7x - 3] - 3x\}$$

Next, remove the brackets. Do not forget the negative sign in front of the left bracket [. This indicates that each term inside the brackets is to be multiplied by -1 when the brackets are removed.

$$= 5\{2x - [7x - 3] - 3x\}$$
$$= 5\{2x - 7x + 3 - 3x\}$$
$$= 5\{-8x + 3\}$$

Now, remove the braces. The 5 in front of the left brace { means that each term within the braces should be multiplied by 5.

$$= 5\{-8x + 3\}$$
$$= -40x + 15$$

APPLICATION ELECTRONICS

EXAMPLE 2.7

The total resistance, R, in a parallel circuit with two resistances, R_1 and R_2, is given by the formula $\dfrac{1}{R} = \dfrac{1}{R_1} + \dfrac{1}{R_2}$. Simplify the right-hand side of this equation.

SOLUTION In order to simplify these two fractions, we need to have a common denominator. For this fraction, the common denominator is R_1R_2.

$$\frac{1}{R} = \frac{R_2}{R_1R_2} + \frac{R_1}{R_1R_2} = \frac{R_2 + R_1}{R_1R_2}$$

EXERCISE SET 2.1

In Exercises 1–4, identify the variables and constants in each expression.

1. $4xy$

2. $\dfrac{5x^2}{3tw}$

3. $8\pi r^2$

4. $\sqrt{7}ax + by$

In Exercises 5–8, identify the algebraic terms in each expression.

5. $3x^3 + 4x$

6. $47x^4 - 9y^5$

7. $(2x^3)(5y) + \sqrt{3}ab - \dfrac{7a}{b}$

8. $-3x^5 - (4a)\left(\dfrac{b}{5}\right) + 9\sqrt{y}$

Solve Exercises 9 and 10.

9. What are the individual factors of $\dfrac{-5x^3}{y^2}$?

10. What are the individual factors of $\dfrac{15(x - y)}{x^2 + 3y}$?

In Exercises 11–14, identify the coefficient of each expression.

11. $47xy^5$

12. $\dfrac{2\sqrt{3}y}{x^5}$

13. $\dfrac{\pi ax}{4y}$

14. $\dfrac{\sqrt{17}byz}{\sqrt{5}at}$

In Exercises 15–20, identify the like terms in each exercise.

15. $3x^2y$, $17x^2y$, and $12xy^2$

16. $\sqrt{5}xy, \dfrac{2}{3}ax^5y$, and $\dfrac{2}{3}bxy$

17. $(x + y)^2$, $2(x + y)$, $4(x + y)^3$, and $5(x + y)^2$

18. $3x^2y$, $-9xy^2$, $5(xy^2)$, and $6(x^2 + y)$

19. $5(a + b + c)$, $a + b - c$, and $-2(a + b - c)$

20. ax^2, a^2x, $5x^2$, and $5a^5x$

In Exercises 21–70, simplify each algebraic expression.

21. $4x + 7x$

22. $5y - 2y$

23. $3z - z$

24. $7w + 4w - w$

25. $8x + 9x^2 - 2x$

26. $11y - 7y + 6y^2$

27. $10w + w^2 - 8w^2$

28. $y^2 - 6y^2 + 4y$

29. $ax^2 + a^2x + ax^2$

30. $by - by^2 + by$

31. $7xy^2 - 5x^2y + 4xy^2$

32. $12wz - 8w^2z + 6w^2z$

33. $(a + 6b) - (a - 6b)$

34. $(x - 7y) - (7y - x)$

35. $(2a^2 + 3b) + (2b + 4a)$

36. $(7c^2 - 8d) + (6d - 8c)$

37. $(4x^2 + 3x) - (2x^2 - 3x)$

38. $(3y^2 - 4x) - (4y + 2x)$

39. $2(6y^2 + 7x)$

40. $5(3a + 4b)$

41. $-3(4b - 2c)$

42. $-2(-6b + 3a)$

43. $4(a + b) + 3(b + a)$

44. $2(c + d) + 8(d + c)$

45. $3(x + y) - 2(x + y)$

46. $3(x^2 - y) - 2(y + x^2)$

47. $2(a + b + c) + 3(a + b - c)$

48. $4(x - y + z) + 2(x + y - z)$

49. $3[2(x + y)]$

50. $4[3(x - y)]$

51. $3(a + b) + 4(a + b) - 2(a + b)$

52. $2(x + y) - 3(x + y) - 4(x + y)$

53. $2(a + b + c) + 3(a - b + c) + (a - b - c)$

54. $3(x - y + z) - 2(x + y - z) + 4(-x - y + z)$

55. $2(x + 3y) - 3(x - 2y) + 5(2x - y)$

56. $3(y - 2a) - (a + 3y) + 4(a - 3y)$

57. $3(x + y - z) - 2(3x + 2y - z) - 3(x - y + 4z)$

58. $5(x - y + z) - (y - x + z) + 2(x - 2y + z)$

59. $(x + y) - 3(x - z) + 4(y + 4z) - 2(x + y - 3z)$

60. $(a + b) - 2(b - c) + 4(c + 2d) - 5(d + 2c - 3b - a)$

61. $x + [3x + 2(x + y)]$

62. $x + [5y + 3(y - x)]$

63. $y - [2z - 3(y + z) + y]$

64. $2w - [4z - 5(z + w) + 2w]$

65. $[2x + 3(x + y) - 2(x - y) + y] - 2x$

66. $[4a - 8(a + b) + 2(a - b) + 3a] - 3b$

67. $-\{-[2a - (3b + a)]\}$

68. $-\{-3[4x - (5x - 4y)]\}$

69. $5a - 2\{4[a + 2(4a + b) - b] + a\} - a$

70. $7x - 3\{-[x + 2(x - y) - y] + 2x\} - 3y$

Solve the word problems in Exercises 71–76.

71. **Civil engineering** In order to determine the cost of widening a highway, several cost comparisons were used. These led to the following expression for determining the total cost: $p + \frac{1}{2}p + \frac{2}{3}p$. Simplify by combining like terms.

72. **Construction** A concrete mix has the following ingredients by volume: 1 part cement, 2 parts water, 3 parts aggregate, and 3 parts sand. These are used to produce the expression $x + 2x + 3x + 3x$. This expression is then used to determine the amount of each ingredient for a specific amount of concrete. Simplify by combining like terms.

73. **Electronics** The total capacitance, C_T, in a series circuit with two capacitors, C_1 and C_2, is given by the formula

$$\frac{1}{C_T} = \frac{1}{C_1} + \frac{1}{C_2}$$

Simplify the right-hand side of this equation.

74. **Electronics** The total inductance, L_T, in a parallel circuit with three inductors, L_1, L_2, and L_3, is given by

$$\frac{1}{L_T} = \frac{1}{L_1} + \frac{1}{L_2} + \frac{1}{L_3}$$

Simplify the right-hand side of this equation.

75. **Business** A employee earns a gross wage W. The employee's payroll deductions are shown in Table 2.1. The employee's net wage N is the difference between the gross wage and the total deductions.

    (a) Write an equation that shows how to determine the net wage from the information in the table.

    (b) Simplify the equation.

76. **Manufacturing** The part in Figure 2.1 is used in several different-sized assemblies. What is the total length, L, of the part?

TABLE 2.1							
Type of deduction	Federal income tax	Social Security (FICA)	FICA medical	Company retirement	Health insurance	Life insurance	401(k)
Deduction amount	$0.134W$	$0.046W$	$0.011W$	$0.075W$	$0.010W$	$0.002W$	$0.085W$

© Cengage Learning 2013

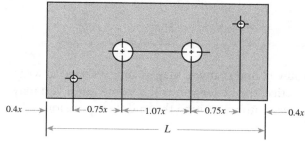

© Cengage Learning 2013

Figure 2.1

77. Electronics The total power in two circuits is given by $14(3I_a^2 + 5I_b^2)$. Use the distributive property to rewrite this expression.

78. Electronics The current in a circuit is given by $5t^2 + 7t + 3t^2 - 6t + 2$, where t is time. Simplify this expression.

▶ [IN YOUR WORDS]

79. Explain how an algebraic term and an algebraic expression are alike and how they are different.

80. Describe what is meant by "like terms."

2.2   MULTIPLICATION

In Section 1.3 we learned some rules for exponents. The very first rule stated that $b^m b^n = b^{m+n}$. We will use this rule as a foundation for learning how to multiply multinomials. We will also use the rule for multiplying real numbers from Section 1.2.

MULTIPLYING MONOMIALS

First, we will find the product of two or more monomials. When multiplying monomials, first multiply the numerical coefficients to get the numerical coefficient of the product. Then, multiply the remaining factors using the rules of exponents.

EXAMPLE 2.8

$$(3x^3)(-7bx^4) = -21bx^{3+4} = -21bx^7$$
$$(4ax^2)(7bx^3) = 28abx^{2+3} = 28abx^5$$
$$(-5xy^2z^3)(3x^2y^2) = -15x^3y^4z^3$$
$$(\sqrt{2}x^3y)(\sqrt{3}xy^4) = \sqrt{6}x^4y^5$$

To multiply a monomial and a multinomial, use the distributive property. Distribute the monomial over the multinomial. Thus, by the distributive property $a(b + c) = ab + ac$. Each term of the multinomial will be multiplied by the monomial.

EXAMPLE 2.9

$$-7ab^2(2ax^3 - 5abx + 3b^3) = (-7ab^2)(2ax^3) + (-7ab^2)(-5abx)$$
$$+ (-7ab^2)(3b^3)$$
$$= -14a^2b^2x^3 + 35a^2b^3x - 21ab^5$$

As you gain experience, you will find that you may not always need to write all the steps. The more you practice, the better you will become, until you may be able to write the correct answer without writing the middle expression.

MULTIPLYING MULTINOMIALS

To multiply one multinomial by another, multiply each term in one multinomial by each term in the other multinomial. Again, use the distributive property to help in the multiplication.

EXAMPLE 2.10

$$(x^2 + b)(x + c) = x^2(x + c) + b(x + c)$$
$$= x^3 + cx^2 + bx + bc$$

EXAMPLE 2.11

$$(y^2 + 2f)(y^2 - 3f) = y^2(y^2 - 3f) + 2f(y^2 - 3f)$$
$$= y^4 - 3y^2f + 2y^2f - 6f^2$$
$$= y^4 - y^2f - 6f^2$$

The preceding two examples show multiplication of two binomials. The same procedure is used for multiplying any two multinomials. The next example shows how to multiply two trinomials. This example uses an extended version of the distributive property, where $a(b + c + d) = ab + ac + ad$.

EXAMPLE 2.12

$$(2x + 3y + z)(4x - 3y - z) = 2x(4x - 3y - z) + 3y(4x - 3y - z)$$
$$+ z(4x - 3y - z)$$
$$= (8x^2 - 6xy - 2xz) + (12xy - 9y^2 - 3yz)$$
$$+ (4xz - 3yz - z^2)$$
$$= 8x^2 + 6xy + 2xz - 9y^2 - 6yz - z^2$$

Another method is to multiply in the same manner that you used with real numbers. This is shown in Example 2.13. When using this method, like terms are put in the same column.

EXAMPLE 2.13

$(x^3 + 2x^2 - 3x + 7)(5x^2 - 4x + 2)$

SOLUTION

$$
\begin{array}{r}
x^3 + 2x^2 - 3x + 7 \\
\times \quad 5x^2 - 4x + 2 \\
\hline
2x^3 + 4x^2 - 6x + 14 \\
- 4x^4 - 8x^3 + 12x^2 - 28x \\
5x^5 + 10x^4 - 15x^3 + 35x^2 \\
\hline
5x^5 + 6x^4 - 21x^3 + 51x^2 - 34x + 14
\end{array}
$$

THE FOIL METHOD FOR MULTIPLYING BINOMIALS

There will be many times when you will need to multiply two binomials. Because this happens so often, there are a few patterns that we should notice. The first pattern, called the FOIL method, is one that many people use to remember how to multiply two binomials. The letters for FOIL come from the first letters for the words First, Outside, Inside, and Last.

 HINT Use the FOIL method to help you remember how to multiply binomials. FOIL indicates the order in which terms of two binomials could be multiplied.

F suggests the product of the **F**irst terms.

O suggests the product of the **O**utside terms.

I suggests the product of the **I**nside terms.

L suggests the product of the **L**ast terms.

EXAMPLE 2.14

Use the FOIL method to multiply $(x + 4)(x + 3)$.

SOLUTION

$\underbrace{(x + 4)(x}_{F} + 3)$ x^2 the product of the **F**irst terms

$\underbrace{(x + 4)(x + 3)}_{O}$ $3x$ the **O**utside terms

$(x + \underbrace{4)(x}_{I} + 3)$ $4x$ the **I**nside terms

$(x + \underbrace{4)(x + 3)}_{L}$ 12 81 the **L**ast terms

Adding and combining the terms in the right-hand column

$$x^2 + 3x + 4x + 12 = x^2 + 7x + 12$$

gives the correct answer.

This example looks much longer than it really is. Try it! You will find that this will help "foil" errors caused by not multiplying all the terms.

THE SPECIAL PRODUCT $(a + b)(a - b)$

One special product is shown by this example:

$$(x + 4)(x - 4) = x^2 - 4x + 4x - 16 = x^2 - 16$$

Notice that the two middle terms are additive inverses of each other and their sum is zero.

Let's look at the general case of this type of problem.

$$(a + b)(a - b) = a^2 - ab + ab - b^2$$
$$= a^2 - b^2$$

What is so special about this problem? Look at the two factors in the original problem. One factor is $a + b$ and the other is $a - b$. Notice that each factor has the same first term, a, and that the second terms are additive inverses of each other, b and $-b$. Whenever you have a product of two binomials in the form $a + b$ and $a - b$, the answer is $a^2 - b^2$.

DIFFERENCE OF SQUARES

$$(a + b)(a - b) = a^2 - b^2$$

EXAMPLE 2.15

$$(x + 7)(x - 7) = x^2 - 49 \qquad \text{Note that } 49 = 7^2.$$

$$(3a + b)(3a - b) = 9a^2 - b^2 \qquad \text{Note that } (3a)^2 = 9a^2.$$

$$\left(\frac{4}{3}x - 2y\right)\left(\frac{4}{3}x + 2y\right) = \frac{16}{9}x^2 - 4y^2$$

THE SPECIAL PRODUCT $(a + b)^2$

The final special product of binomials is a perfect square: $(a + b)^2$. Remember that $(a + b)^2 = (a + b)(a + b)$. If we multiply these we get

$$(a + b)^2 = (a + b)(a + b) = a^2 + ab + ab + b^2$$
$$= a^2 + 2ab + b^2$$

The answer contains the squares of the first and last terms. The middle term in the answer is twice the product of the two terms, a and b. So, when you have a square of a binomial you get $(a + b)^2 = a^2 + 2ab + b^2$ or $(a - b)^2 = a^2 - 2ab + b^2$.

SQUARE OF A BINOMIAL

$$(a + b)^2 = a^2 + 2ab + b^2$$

$$(a - b)^2 = a^2 - 2ab + b^2$$

EXAMPLE 2.16

$$(x + 3y)^2 = x^2 + 6xy + 9y^2$$
$$(t + 7)^2 = t^2 + 14t + 49$$
$$(4a - b)^2 = 16a^2 - 8ab + b^2$$
$$\left(\frac{ax}{2} - \frac{3c}{4}\right)^2 = \frac{a^2x^2}{4} - \frac{3}{4}acx + \frac{9c^2}{16}$$ Note that $2\left(\frac{ax}{2}\right)\left(\frac{3c}{4}\right) = \frac{3}{4}acx.$

 CAUTION Remember: $(a + b)^2 \neq a^2 + b^2$ and $(a - b)^2 \neq a^2 - b^2$.

 APPLICATION GENERAL TECHNOLOGY

EXAMPLE 2.17

A physics equation that describes an elastic collision is $m_1(v_a - v_b)(v_a + v_b) = m_2(v_c - v_d)(v_c + v_d)$. Perform the indicated multiplications.

SOLUTION We will begin by multiplying the expressions in parentheses.

$$m_1(v_a - v_b)(v_a + v_b) = m_2(v_c - v_d)(v_c + v_d)$$
$$m_1(v_a^2 - v_b^2) = m_2(v_c^2 - v_d^2)$$

Next, we shall multiply through the left-hand side by m_1 and the right-hand side by m_2, producing

$$m_1{v_a}^2 - m_1{v_b}^2 = m_2{v_c}^2 - m_2{v_d}^2$$

We cannot simplify this equation any more, because none of the remaining terms are like terms.

EXERCISE SET 2.2

In Exercises 1–62, perform the indicated multiplication.

1. $(a^2x)(ax^2)$
2. $(by^2)(b^2y)$
3. $(3ax)(2ax^2)$
4. $(5by)(3b^2y)$
5. $(2xw^2z)(-3x^2w)$
6. $(-4ya^2b)(6y^2b)$
7. $(3x)(4ax)(-2x^2b)$
8. $(4y)(3y^2b)(-5by^2)$
9. $2(5y - 6)$
10. $4(3x - 5)$
11. $-5(4w - 7)$
12. $-3(8 + 5p)$

13. $3x(7y + 4)$
14. $6x(8y - 7)$
15. $-5t(-3 + t)$
16. $-3n(2n - 5)$
17. $\frac{1}{2}a(4a - 2)$
18. $\frac{1}{3}x(-21x - 15)$
19. $2x(3x^2 - x + 4)$
20. $3y(4y^2 - 5y - 7)$
21. $4y^2(-5y^2 + 2y - 5 + 3y^{-1} - 6y^{-2})$

22. $5p^2(-4p^3 - 3p + 2 + p^{-1} - 7p^{-2})$
23. $(a + b)(a + c)$
24. $(s + t)(s + 2t)$
25. $(x + 5)(x^2 + 6)$
26. $(y + 3)(y^2 + 7)$
27. $(2x + y)(3x - y)$
28. $(4a + b)(8a - b)$
29. $(2a - b)(3a - 2b)$
30. $(4p + q)(3p - 2q)$
31. $(b - 1)(2b + 5)$
32. $(4x - 1)(3x - 2)$

33. $(7a^2b + 3c)(8a^2b - 3c)$

34. $(6p^2r + 2t)(5p^2r + 4t)$

35. $(x + 4)(x - 4)$

36. $(a + 8)(a - 8)$

37. $(p - 6)(p + 6)$

38. $(b - 10)(b + 10)$

39. $(ax + 2)(ax - 2)$

40. $(xy - 3)(xy + 3)$

41. $(2r^2 + 3x)(2r^2 - 3x)$

42. $(4p^3 - 7d)(4p^3 + 7d)$

43. $(5a^2x^3 - 4d)(5a^2x^3 + 4d)$

44. $\left(3p^2st - \frac{11}{3}w^3\right)\left(3p^2st + \frac{11}{3}w^3\right)$

45. $\left(\frac{2}{3}pa^2f + \frac{3}{4}tb^3\right)$
$\times \left(-\frac{2}{3}pa^2f + \frac{3}{4}tb^3\right)$

46. $\left(\frac{\sqrt{3}}{2} + \frac{7}{5}t^2u\right)$
$\times \left(-\frac{\sqrt{3}}{2} + \frac{7}{5}t^2u\right)$

47. $(x + y)^2$

48. $(p + r)^2$

49. $(x - 5)^2$

50. $(b - 7)^2$

51. $(a + 3)^2$

52. $(w + 5)^2$

53. $(2a + b)^2$

54. $(3c + d)^2$

55. $(3x - 2y)^2$

56. $(5a - 6f)^2$

57. $4x(x + 4)(3x - 2)$

58. $5y(y - 6)(2y + 3)$

59. $(x + y - z)(x - y + z)$

60. $(a + b + c)(a - b - c)$

61. $(a + 2)^3$

62. $(m - n)^3$

Solve Exercises 63–68.

63. **Computer science** The amount of time required to test a computer "chip" with n cells is given by the expression $2[n(n + 2) + n]$. Simplify this expression. (In this problem, asking you to simplify means that you are to perform the indicated multiplications and add the like terms.)

64. **Aeronautical engineering** An aircraft uses its radar to measure the direct echo range R to another object. If x represents the distance to the ground echo point, then the following expression results:

$$(2R - x)^2 - x^2 - R^2$$

Simplify this expression.

65. **Construction** In computing the center of mass of a plate of uniform density, the expression $\frac{1}{2}(y_2 - y_1)(y_2 + y_1)$ is used. Simplify this expression.

66. **Business** After 3 years, an investment of $500 at an interest rate r compounded annually (once a year) is worth $500(1 + r)^3$. Perform the indicated multiplications.

67. **Automotive technology** Under certain conditions, position x of a motorcycle at time t is given by

$$x = 3(t + 4)(t + 1)$$

Simplify the right-hand side of this equation by multiplying the terms.

68. **Electronics** Electric power P in watts, W, is the product of the voltage E in volts, V, and the current I in amperes, A. If the current is increased to $4I - 5$, what is the electrical power in watts?

69. **Landscaping** A planter is in the shape of a trapezoid with bases $b_1 = 6'$ and $b_2 = 8'$ and height $h = 4'$. The area of a trapezoid is $A = \frac{1}{2}h(b_1 + b_2)$ so this planter has an area of $A = \frac{1}{2}(4)(6 + 8) = 28\,\text{ft}^2$. If the height and both bases are each lengthened by x ft, what is the new area?

70. **Thermal science** The quantity of heat, Q, transferred by radiation between two parallel equal areas, A, in time t is

$$Q = \bar{e}A\left\{\left(\frac{T_1}{100} - \frac{T_2}{100}\right)\left(\frac{T_1}{100} + \frac{T_2}{100}\right) \times \left[\left(\frac{T_1}{100}\right)^2 + \left(\frac{T_2}{100}\right)^2\right]\right\}10^8 t$$

where $\bar{e}$ is a radiation constant and T_1 and T_2 are absolute temperatures of the areas. Simplify this equation by multiplying the terms in the braces.

[IN YOUR WORDS]

71. Explain how to use the FOIL method for multiplying two binomials. (Do not look at the explanation in the book.)

72. Describe how you would multiply a binomial and a trinomial.

2.3 DIVISION

To find the quotient when one multinomial is divided by another, we will again need to use the rules of exponents. Rule 5 in Section 1.4 states that $\frac{b^m}{b^n} = b^{m-n}$, if $b \neq 0$. This is a very helpful rule in the division of algebraic expressions.

Remember that division can be indicated by $x \div y, \frac{x}{y}$, or x/y. You must be very careful, when reading algebra problems and writing your answers, to watch how terms are grouped. For example, in $a^2 + b/c + 3$ the only division is b divided by c. Thus, $a^2 + b/c + 3$ is equivalent to $a^2 + \frac{b}{c} + 3$. Now, consider $(a^2 + b)/c + 3$. The parentheses indicate that the entire expression $a^2 + b$ is being divided by c. So $(a^2 + b)/c + 3 = \left(\frac{a^2 + b}{c}\right) + 3$. This could be written without parentheses as $\frac{a^2 + b}{c} + 3$. Finally, $(a^2 + b)/(c + 3)$ means that the expression $a^2 + b$ is being divided by the expression $c + 3$. So, $(a^2 + b)/(c + 3) = \frac{a^2 + b}{c + 3}$.

DIVIDING A MONOMIAL BY A MONOMIAL

We begin by dividing a monomial by a monomial. Consider $16x^5 \div 8x^2$. Using the laws of exponents, we have $x^5 \div x^2 = x^{5-2} = x^3$. If there are numerical coefficients, they are divided separately. So, $16x^5 \div 8x^2 = \frac{16}{8} \frac{x^5}{x^2} = 2x^{5-2} = 2x^3$.

Each variable should be treated separately. For example, $24x^3y^2 \div 8xy^2 = \frac{24}{8} \frac{x^3}{x} \frac{y^2}{y^2} = 3x^{3-1}y^{2-2} = 3x^2y^0 = 3x^2$.

EXAMPLE 2.18

Divide $6w^2xy^4z$ by $9wx^3y^2z$.

SOLUTION $6w^2xy^4z \div 9wx^3y^2z = \dfrac{6w^2xy^4z}{9wx^3y^2z}$

$$= \frac{6}{9}w^{2-1}x^{1-3}y^{4-2}z^{1-1}$$

$$= \frac{2}{3}wx^{-2}y^2z^0$$

$$= \frac{2wy^2}{3x^2}$$

EXAMPLE 2.19

Divide $35a^2b^3c^{-2}$ by $-7a^{-3}bc^2$.

SOLUTION $35a^2b^3c^{-2} \div -7a^{-3}bc^2 = \dfrac{35a^2b^3c^{-2}}{-7a^{-3}bc^2}$

$$= \frac{35}{-7}a^{2-(-3)}b^{3-1}c^{-2-2}$$

$$= -5a^5b^2c^{-4}$$

$$= \frac{-5a^5b^2}{c^4}$$

 CAUTION Be careful! A typical error here is cancelling noncommon factors. Do not make either of the following mistakes:

$$\frac{x + y}{x} = 1 + y$$

or $\dfrac{x + \cancel{y}}{\cancel{y}} = x + 1$

These are *not correct*, as you can see by substituting some numerical values for *x* or *y*.

DIVIDING A MULTINOMIAL BY A MONOMIAL

In order to divide a multinomial by a monomial, you should divide each term of the multinomial by the monomial. You may remember that $\dfrac{a + b}{c} = \dfrac{a}{c} + \dfrac{b}{c}$. (This is part of Rule 6 in Section 1.2.)

EXAMPLE 2.20

Divide $(4r^2st^3 - 8rs^3)$ by $-2rst^2$.

SOLUTION $(4r^2st^3 - 8rs^3) \div -2rst^2 = \dfrac{4r^2st^3 - 8rs^3}{-2rst^2}$

$$= \frac{4r^2st^3}{-2rst^2} + \frac{-8rs^3}{-2rst^2}$$

$$= -2rt + 4\frac{s^2}{t^2}$$

Remember to divide each term in the multinomial by the monomial.

EXAMPLE 2.21

Divide $(6xy - 4xy^2 + 9x^2y - 12x^2y^2)$ by $3xy$.

SOLUTION $\dfrac{6xy - 4xy^2 + 9x^2y - 12x^2y^2}{3xy} = \dfrac{6xy}{3xy} - \dfrac{4xy^2}{3xy} + \dfrac{9x^2y}{3xy} - \dfrac{12x^2y^2}{3xy}$

$$= 2 - \frac{4}{3}y + 3x - 4xy$$

DIVIDING A MULTINOMIAL BY A MULTINOMIAL

The next step in the division process is to divide a multinomial by a multinomial. This is not as easy as dividing by a monomial, so we will learn it in two stages. In the first stage we will learn to divide a polynomial by a polynomial. In stage two we will apply what we learned in stage one.

Before we can learn to divide a polynomial by a polynomial we need to have a definition of a polynomial. A polynomial is a special type of multinomial. An algebraic sum is a **polynomial** in x if each term is of the form ax^n, where n is a non negative integer. One example of a polynomial in x is $7x^3 - \sqrt{3}x^2 + \frac{1}{2}x - 2$. (Remember that -2 can be written as $-2x^0$.) Another polynomial in x is $7x^{15} + 2x^3 - 5x$.

Not every polynomial is a polynomial in x. For example, $4y^3 - y^2$ is a polynomial in y and $\dfrac{-\sqrt{3}}{2}$ is a polynomial that is a constant. The multinomial $4x^3 + 5x^2 - 3 + x^{-3}$ is *not* a polynomial because the exponent on the last term is -3, which is not a non negative integer. The multinomial $6x + \sqrt{7x} = 6x + \sqrt{7}x^{1/2}$ is not a polynomial in x because the exponent on the variable in the last term is $\frac{1}{2}$, which is not an integer.

We will now examine how to divide one polynomial by another. Study Example 2.22. Make sure you read the comments in Example 2.22, because they explain the method we use to divide polynomials.

EXAMPLE 2.22

Divide $6x^2 - 4 - 4x + 8x^4$ by $2x + 1$.

SOLUTION

1. **Write both the dividend and the divisor in decreasing order of powers.**

   The dividend is $6x^2 - 4 - 4x + 8x^4$. The largest power is 4, the next largest is 2, and so the dividend should be written as $8x^4 + 6x^2 - 4x - 4$. The divisor, $2x + 1$, is already in descending order of the powers.

2. **Are there any missing terms in the dividend? If so, write them with a coefficient of 0.**

   Here the dividend does not have an x^3 term. Rewrite the dividend as $8x^4 + 0x^3 + 6x^2 - 4x - 4$.

3. **Set up the problem just as you would any long division problem.**

$$2x + 1 \overline{\smash{)}8x^4 + 0x^3 + 6x^2 - 4x - 4}$$

4. **Divide the first term in the dividend by the first term in the divisor.**

   In this example the first term in the dividend is $8x^4$ and the first term in the divisor is $2x$. The result of this division, $4x^3$, is written above the dividend directly over the term with the same power.

$$\begin{array}{r} 4x^3 \\ 2x + 1 \overline{\smash{)}8x^4 + 0x^3 + 6x^2 - 4x - 4} \end{array}$$

EXAMPLE 2.22 (Cont.)

5. **Multiply the divisor by this first term of the quotient. Write the product below the dividend with like terms under the like terms in the dividend. Subtract this product from the dividend.** We will call this difference the "new dividend."

$$
\begin{array}{r}
4x^3 \\
2x + 1 \overline{)8x^4 + 0x^3 + 6x^2 - 4x - 4} \\
\underline{8x^4 + 4x^3} \\
-4x^3 + 6x^2 - 4x - 4 \quad \text{new dividend}
\end{array}
$$

CAUTION Be careful doing the subtraction. A common error would be to get $+4x^3$ for the x^3 term instead of $-4x^3$.

6. **Repeat the last two steps until the power of the new dividend is less than the power of the divisor.** Each time the last two steps are repeated, you should divide the first term of the new dividend by the first term of the divisor as shown here.

A.
$$
\begin{array}{r}
4x^3 - 2x^2 \\
2x + 1 \overline{)8x^4 + 0x^3 + 6x^2 - 4x - 4} \\
\underline{8x^4 + 4x^3} \\
-4x^3 + 6x^2 - 4x - 4 \\
\underline{-4x^3 - 2x^2} \\
8x^2 - 4x - 4 \quad \text{new dividend}
\end{array}
$$

B.
$$
\begin{array}{r}
4x^3 - 2x^2 + 4x \\
2x + 1 \overline{)8x^4 + 0x^3 + 6x^2 - 4x - 4} \\
\underline{8x^4 + 4x^3} \\
-4x^3 + 6x^2 - 4x - 4 \\
\underline{-4x^3 - 2x^2} \\
8x^2 - 4x - 4 \\
\underline{8x^2 + 4x} \\
-8x - 4 \quad \text{new dividend}
\end{array}
$$

C.
$$
\begin{array}{r}
4x^3 - 2x^2 + 4x - 4 \\
2x + 1 \overline{)8x^4 + 0x^3 + 6x^2 - 4x - 4} \\
\underline{8x^4 + 4x^3} \\
-4x^3 + 6x^2 - 4x - 4 \\
\underline{-4x^3 - 2x^2} \\
8x^2 - 4x - 4 \\
\underline{8x^2 + 4x} \\
-8x - 4 \\
\underline{-8x - 4} \\
0
\end{array}
$$

Stop! This is really $0x^0$ and its power, 0, is less than the power of the first term in the divisor, 1. So,

$$(8x^4 + 6x^2 - 4x - 4) \div (2x + 1) = 4x^3 - 2x^2 + 4x - 4$$

When you divide one polynomial by another, your work should look like the final step, C. The other steps were given to help you see what we were doing. In the next example we will show it all in one step.

EXAMPLE 2.23

Divide $4x^5 - 2x^3 + 6x^2 - 8$ by $4x^2 + 2$.

SOLUTION The dividend and divisor are already in descending order. The dividend, $4x^5 - 2x^3 + 6x^2 - 8$, does not have an x^4 or an x^1 term. We should include those terms with coefficients of zero. The dividend now becomes $4x^5 + 0x^4 - 2x^3 + 6x^2 + 0x - 8$. We will now set the problem up in the standard long division format and divide.

$$
\begin{array}{r}
x^3 + 0x^2 - x + \frac{3}{2} \\
4x^2 + 2 \overline{)4x^5 + 0x^4 - 2x^3 + 6x^2 + 0x - 8} \\
\underline{4x^5 \qquad\quad + 2x^3} \\
0x^4 - 4x^3 + 6x^2 + 0x - 8 \\
\underline{0x^4 \qquad\quad + 0x^2} \\
-4x^3 + 6x^2 + 0x - 8 \\
\underline{-4x^3 \qquad\quad - 2x} \\
6x^2 + 2x - 8 \\
\underline{6x^2 \qquad + 3} \\
2x - 11
\end{array}
$$

The power of the $2x$ term, 1, is less than the power of the x^2 term of the divisor, 2. This expression, $2x - 11$, is the remainder.

The remainder is written as $\dfrac{2x - 11}{4x^2 + 2}$. So,

$$(4x^5 - 2x^3 + 6x^2 - 8) \div (4x^2 + 2) = x^3 + 0x^2 - x + \frac{3}{2} + \frac{2x - 11}{4x^2 + 2}$$

$$= x^3 - x + \frac{3}{2} + \frac{2x - 11}{4x^2 + 2}$$

There is a faster method of division that can be used with some polynomials. This method is known as synthetic division. We will learn about synthetic division in Chapter 17.

In the next example, we will look at a division problem in which both the dividend and the divisor have more than one variable. The method used will be very similar to the method for dividing one polynomial by another.

EXAMPLE 2.24

Divide $27x^6 - 8y^6$ by $3x^2 - 2y^2$.

SOLUTION

$$
\begin{array}{r}
9x^4 + 6x^2y^2 + 4y^4 \\
3x^2 + 2y^2\overline{)27x^6 \qquad\qquad\qquad - 8y^6} \\
\underline{27x^6 - 18x^4y^2} \\
18x^4y^2 \qquad\qquad - 8y^6 \\
\underline{18x^4y^2 - 12x^2y^4} \\
12x^2y^4 - 8y^6 \\
\underline{12x^2y^4 - 8y^6} \\
0
\end{array}
$$

So, $(27x^6 - 8y^6) \div (3x^2 - 2y^2) = 9x^4 + 6x^2y^2 + 4y^4$.

EXERCISE SET 2.3

In Exercises 1—86, perform the indicated division.

1. x^7 by x^3
2. y^8 by y^6
3. $2x^6$ by x^4
4. $3w^4$ by w^2
5. $12y^5$ by $4y^3$
6. $15a^7$ by $3a^4$
7. $-45ab^2$ by $15ab$
8. $-55xy^3$ by $-11xy$
9. $33xy^2z$ by $3xyz$
10. $65x^2yz$ by $5xyz$
11. $96a^2xy^3$ by $-16axy^2$
12. $105b^3yw^2$ by $-15b^2yw$
13. $144c^3d^2f$ by $8cf$
14. $162x^2yz^3$ by $9x^2z^2$
15. $9np^3$ by $-15n^3p^2$
16. $15rs^2t$ by $-27r^2st^3$
17. $8abcdx^2y$ by $14adxy^2$
18. $9efg^2hr$ by $24e^2fh^3r$
19. $2a^3 + a^2$ by a
20. $4x^4 - x^3$ by x^2
21. $36b^4 - 18b^2$ by $9b$
22. $49y^5 + 35y^3$ by $7y^2$
23. $42x^2 + 28x$ by 7
24. $56z^6 - 48z^3$ by 8

25. $34x^5 - 51x^2$ by $17x^2$
26. $105w^6 + 63w^4$ by $21w^2$
27. $24x^6 - 8x^4$ by $-4x^3$
28. $42y^7 - 24y^5$ by $6y^4$
29. $5x^2y + 5xy^2$ by xy
30. $7a^2b - 7ab^2$ by ab
31. $10x^2y + 15xy^2$ by $5xy$
32. $25p^2q - 15pq^2$ by $5pq$
33. $ap^2q - 2pq$ by pq
34. $bx^2w + 3xw$ by xw
35. $a^2bc + abc$ by abc
36. $x^3yz - xyz$ by xyz
37. $9x^2y^2z - 3xyz^2$ by $-3xyz$
38. $12a^2b^2c + 4abc^2$ by $-4abc$
39. $b^3x^2 + b^3$ by $-b$
40. $c^5y^3 - cy^2$ by $-c$
41. $x^2y + xy - xy^2$ by xy
42. $ab^2 - ab + a^2b$ by ab
43. $18x^3y^2z - 24x^2y^3z$ by $-12x^2yz$
44. $36a^4b^2c - 27a^2b^4c^2$ by $-27a^2bc$
45. $x^2 + 7x + 12$ by $x + 3$
46. $x^2 + x - 12$ by $x + 4$

47. $x^2 - 3x + 2$ by $x - 2$
48. $x^2 - 2x - 15$ by $x - 5$
49. $x^2 + x - 2$ by $x + 2$
50. $x^2 + x - 6$ by $x + 3$
51. $6a^2 + 17a + 7$ by $3a + 7$
52. $4b^2 + 10b - 6$ by $4b - 2$
53. $8y^2 - 8y - 6$ by $2y - 3$
54. $12t^2 + t - 6$ by $4t + 3$
55. $x^3 - 5x + 2$ by $x^2 + 2x - 1$
56. $d^3 + d^2 - 3d + 2$ by $d^2 + d + 2$
57. $6a^3 - 7a^2 + 10a - 4$ by $3a^2 - 2a + 4$
58. $9y^3 - 16y + 8$ by $3y^2 + 3y - 4$
59. $4x^3 - 3x + 4$ by $2x - 1$
60. $7p^3 + 2p - 5$ by $3p + 2$
61. $r^3 - r^2 - 6r + 5$ by $r + 2$
62. $2c^3 - 3c^2 + c - 4$ by $c - 2$
63. $x^4 - 81$ by $x - 3$
64. $y^4 - 81$ by $y + 3$
65. $23x^2 - 5x^4 + 12x^5 - 12 - 14x^3 + 8x$ by $3x^2 - 2 + x$
66. $10a + 21a^3 - 35 + 6a^5 - 25a^4 + 21a^7 - 14a^6$ by $2a + 7a^3 - 7$

67. $x^2 - y^2$ by $x - y$
68. $a^2 - b^2$ by $a + b$
69. $w^3 - z^3$ by $w - z$
70. $x^3 + y^3$ by $x + y$
71. $x^3 + xy^2 + x^2y + y^3$ by $x + y$
72. $a^3 - a^2b + ab^2 - b^3$ by $a - b$
73. $c^3d^3 - 8$ by $cd - 2$
74. $e^3f^3 + 27$ by $ef + 3$
75. $x^2 - 2xy + y^2$ by $x - y$

76. $a^2 + 6ab + 9b^2$ by $a + 3b$
77. $5p^3r - 10p^2 + 15pr^2 - p^2r^2 +$
    $2pr - 3r^3$ by $5p - r$
78. $8x^3 - 12x^2y + 6xy^2 - y^3$ by
    $2x - y$
79. $a^2 - 2ad - 3d^2 + 3a - 13d$
    $- 8$ by $a - 3d - 1$
80. $2x^2 - xy - 6y^2 + x + 19y$
    $- 15$ by $2x + 3y - 5$
81. $a^2f - af^2$ by $a - f$

82. $d^3 - 2dm^2 + 2m^3 - d^2m$
    by $d - m$
83. $a^2 - b^2 + 2bc - c^2$
    by $a - b + c$
84. $e^2 + 2eh - f^2 + h^2$
    by $e + f + h$
85. $a^4 + 2a^2 - a + 2$ by $a^2 + a$
    $+ 2$
86. $x^6 - x^4 + 2x^2 - 1$ by $x^3 - x$
    $+ 1$

Solve Exercises 87–92.

87. **Electronics** The expression for the total resistance of three resistances in a parallel electrical circuit is

$$\frac{R_1R_2R_3}{R_2R_3 + R_1R_3 + R_1R_2}$$

Determine the reciprocal of this expression, and then perform the indicated division.

88. **Thermal science** The radiation constant, $\bar{e}$ (see Section 2.2, Exercise 70, page 82), is defined as

$$\bar{e} = \frac{\sigma}{\dfrac{e_1 + e_2 - e_1e_2}{e_1e_2}}$$

where e_1 and e_2 are radiation emissives of the respective areas and σ is the Stefan–Boltzmann constant. Find an equivalent formula by writing the denominator as three separate terms and simplifying those terms.

89. **Thermal science** One reference book gives the formula for the volume change of a gas under a constant pressure due to the changes in temperature from T_1 to T_2 as

$$V_2 = V_1\left(1 + \frac{T_2 - T_1}{T_1}\right)$$

where V_1 is the volume at T_1 and V_2 is the volume at T_2. Simplify the right-hand side of this equation.

90. The area of a certain rectangle is given by $x^3 + 6x^2 - 7x$, and the length of one side of the rectangle is $x + 7$.

    (a) If the area of a rectangle is the product of the length and the width, what algebraic expression describes the width of this rectangle?

    (b) If $x = 4$ ft, what are the length, width, and area of this rectangle?

91. **Electronics** Resistance R in ohms, Ω, is the quotient of the voltage V divided by the current I. That is, $R = \dfrac{V}{I}$. If the voltage is $24r^2 - 15r$ and the current is $3r$, what is the resistance?

92. **Mechanics** The tension T on a wire rope basket is given by the formula $T = \dfrac{WL}{NV}$, where W is the weight being lifted, L is the length of the chocker, N is the number of chockers, and V is the vertical distance from the load to the hook. Determine the tension if $W = 4x^2 + 2x - 2$, $L = 15x + 75$, $N = 4x + 20$, and $V = 2x^2 + x - 1$.

▶ **[IN YOUR WORDS]**

93. Describe how to divide a multinomial by a monomial.

94. Describe how to divide a multinomial by a multinomial.

2.4   SOLVING EQUATIONS

Until now we have worked with real numbers and learned how to add, subtract, multiply, and divide algebraic expressions. In these next two sections we are going to begin learning how to use these skills to solve problems.

The ability to solve a problem often depends on the ability to write an equation for a problem and then solve that equation. We will use this section to learn how to solve an equation. In the next section we will start to learn how to write an equation for a problem.

EQUATIONS

An **equation** is an algebraic statement. It asserts that two algebraic expressions are equal. The two algebraic expressions are called the left-hand side (or left side) of the equation and the right-hand side (or right side) of the equation. As the name indicates, the left-hand side is to the left of the equal sign and the right-hand side is to the right of the equal sign.

$$\underbrace{4x^3 + 2x - \sqrt{3}}_{\text{left-hand side}} = \underbrace{7x^2 - 5x}_{\text{right-hand side}}$$

Some equations are true for all values of their variables. These equations are called **identities**. For example, $(x + 2)(x - 2) = x^2 - 4$ is an identity. An equation that is true for only some values of the variables and not true for the other values is a **conditional equation**. Examples of conditional equations are $4x = -24$ and $y^2 = 25$. The first is true only when $x = -6$. The second is true only when $y = 5$ or $y = -5$.

Any value that can be substituted for the variable and that makes an equation true is called a **solution** or **root** of the equation. So, 5 is a solution of $2x^2 - 5x - 5 = 20$, since $2(5^2) - 5(5) - 5 = 20$. The root of $x + 7 = 10$ is 3, and this is often indicated by the phrase, "3 satisfies the equation $x + 7 = 10$." To solve an equation means to find all of its solutions or roots.

EQUIVALENT EQUATIONS

The purpose of this section is to help you learn how to find the solutions or roots of an equation. The techniques you learn here will be used whenever you need to solve an equation. Two equations are **equivalent** if they have exactly the same roots. There is a series of five operations that will allow you to change an equation into an equivalent equation.

To change an equation into an equivalent equation you can use any of the following five operations.

OPERATIONS FOR CHANGING EQUATIONS INTO EQUIVALENT EQUATIONS

1. Add or subtract the same algebraic expression or amount to/from both sides of the equation.
2. Multiply or divide both sides of the equation by the same algebraic expression, provided the expression does not equal zero.
3. Combine like terms on either side of the equation.
4. Replace one side (or both sides) with an identity.
5. Interchange the two sides of the equation.

In order to solve an equation you will generally have to use a combination of these five operations. You may have to use the same operation more than once. The following examples show how these operations are used. The first four examples use one operation and the other examples use a combination of operations.

EXAMPLE 2.25

Solve $x + 7 = 15$.

SOLUTION $x + 7 = 15$

$$(x + 7) - 7 = 15 - 7 \qquad \text{Subtract 7 from both sides (Operation #1).}$$
$$x = 8$$

Substituting this value in the original equation verifies that 8 is the solution, since $8 + 7 = 15$.

EXAMPLE 2.26

Solve $3x = -15$.

SOLUTION $3x = -15$

$$\frac{1}{3}(3x) = \frac{1}{3}(-15) \qquad \text{Multiply both sides by } \tfrac{1}{3}, \text{ the reciprocal of 3 (Operation #2).}$$
$$x = -5$$

Checking the solution in the original equation, we see that -5 satisfies the equation, since $3(-5) = -15$.

EXAMPLE 2.27

Solve $5x - 3x - x = 20 - 12$.

SOLUTION $5x - 3x - x = 20 - 12$

$$x = 8 \qquad \text{Combine like terms (Operation #3).}$$

Checking the root in the original, we see that $5 \times 8 - 3 \times 8 - 8 = 40 - 24 - 8 = 8$. This satisfies the original equation.

EXAMPLE 2.28

Solve $x^2 + 6x + 9 = 0$.

SOLUTION

$x^2 + 6x + 9 = 0$

$(x + 3)^2 = 0$ Replace $x^2 + 6x + 9$ with $(x + 3)^2$ (Operation #4).

We will stop this example here. To continue solving this problem takes some more mathematics, which we will learn later. The important thing to notice is that we used an identity to rewrite one side of the equation.

The next four examples use combinations of the operations.

EXAMPLE 2.29

Solve $3x + 27 = 6x$.

SOLUTION

$$3x + 27 = 6x$$
$$(3x + 27) - 3x = 6x - 3x \quad \text{Subtract } 3x \text{ (Operation #1).}$$
$$27 = 3x \quad \text{Combine like terms (Operation #3).}$$
$$3x = 27 \quad \text{Switch sides (Operation #5).}$$
$$\frac{1}{3}(3x) = \frac{1}{3}(27) \quad \text{Multiply by } \tfrac{1}{3} \text{ (Operation #2).}$$
$$x = 9$$

To check, replace the x in the original equation with the value we found, 9. The left-hand side is $3(9) + 27 = 27 + 27 = 54$ and the right-hand side is $6(9) = 54$. Since both sides give the same value, 9 is a solution.

EXAMPLE 2.30

Solve $7y + 6 = 216 - 3y$.

SOLUTION

$$7y + 6 = 216 - 3y$$
$$7y + 6 + 3y = 216 - 3y + 3y \quad \text{Add } 3y \text{ (Operation #1).}$$
$$10y + 6 = 216 \quad \text{Combine terms (Operation #3).}$$
$$10y + 6 - 6 = 216 - 6 \quad \text{Subtract 6 (Operation #1).}$$
$$10y = 210 \quad \text{Combine terms.}$$
$$\frac{10y}{10} = \frac{210}{10} \quad \text{Divide by 10 (Operation #2).}$$
$$y = 21$$

Check this answer in the original equation. When you replace y with 21 do you get the same value on both the left-hand and right-hand sides of the equation? You should.

Notice that in the next-to-last step we divided both sides by 10. We could have multiplied both sides by $\frac{1}{10}$ and arrived at the same result. Do you understand why? Both approaches are correct because division by 10 is the same as multiplication by $\frac{1}{10}$.

EXAMPLE 2.31

Solve $3(4z-8) + 2(3z + 5) = 4(z + 7)$.

SOLUTION

$$3(4z - 8) + 2(3z + 5) = 4(z + 7)$$

$$12z - 24 + 6z + 10 = 4z + 28 \qquad \text{Remove parentheses by distribution.}$$

$$18z - 14 = 4z + 28 \qquad \text{Combine terms.}$$

$$14z - 14 = 28 \qquad \text{Subtract } 4z.$$

$$14z = 42 \qquad \text{Add } 14.$$

$$z = 3 \qquad \text{Divide by 14 (or multiply by } \tfrac{1}{14}).$$

Check this in the original equation. You should get 40 on each side of the equation.

EXAMPLE 2.32

Solve $\dfrac{n}{2} + 5 = \dfrac{2n}{3}$.

SOLUTION

$$\frac{n}{2} + 5 = \frac{2n}{3}$$

$$6\left(\frac{n}{2} + 5\right) = 6\left(\frac{2n}{3}\right) \qquad \text{Multiply by 6. (6 is a common denominator of } \frac{n}{2} \text{ and } \frac{2n}{3}.)$$

$$3n + 30 = 4n$$

$$30 = n \qquad \text{Subtract } 3n.$$

Because most people like to give the variable first and then the value of that variable, you could now use Operation #5 and rewrite this as $n = 30$.

Check by substituting 30 for n in the original equation. The left side is $\dfrac{30}{2} + 5 = 15 + 5 = 20$. The right side is $\dfrac{2(30)}{3} = \dfrac{60}{3} = 20$. So, $n = 30$ satisfies the original equation.

Ratios and proportions are useful methods for solving equations.

RATIO

A **ratio** is a comparison of two quantities. If these quantities are represented by the values a and b, then the ratio comparing a to b is written $\dfrac{a}{b}$ or $a : b$. A **pure ratio** compares two quantities that have the same units. A pure ratio is written without units.

EXAMPLE 2.33

What is the ratio of (a) 4 m to 3 m, (b) 5 ft to 4 yards, and (c) 2 m to 35 cm?

SOLUTION We will write each of these as a pure ratio.

(a) $\dfrac{4\text{ m}}{3\text{ m}} = \dfrac{4}{3}$ or $4 : 3$

(b) $\dfrac{5\text{ ft}}{4\text{ yards}} = \dfrac{5\text{ ft}}{12\text{ ft}} = \dfrac{5}{12}$ or $5 : 12$

(c) $\dfrac{2\text{ m}}{35\text{ cm}} = \dfrac{200\text{ cm}}{35\text{ cm}} = \dfrac{200}{35} = \dfrac{40}{7}$ or $40 : 7$

NOTE The rational numbers got their name because they indicate a ratio of two numbers.

Some ratios are always expressed as a quantity compared to 1, as shown in the next example.

APPLICATION **MECHANICAL**

EXAMPLE 2.34

A driven gear has 26 teeth and the driving gear has 8 teeth. What is the gear ratio of the driven gear to the driving gear?

SOLUTION

$$\frac{\text{driven gear}}{\text{driving gear}} = \frac{26\text{ teeth}}{8\text{ teeth}} = \frac{26}{8} = \frac{13}{4} = \frac{3.25}{1} \text{ or } 3.25 : 1$$

RATE

A **rate** is a ratio that compares different kinds of units. Common rates include miles and gallons, revolutions and minutes, and miles and hours.

APPLICATION **AUTOMOTIVE**

EXAMPLE 2.35

An automobile travels 243 km in 3 h. What is its rate of speed?

SOLUTION $\dfrac{243\text{ km}}{3\text{ h}} = \dfrac{81\text{ km}}{1\text{ h}} = 81\text{ km/h}$

The car is traveling at the rate of 81 km/h.

PROPORTION

A statement that says two ratios are equal is called a **proportion**. If the ratio $a : b$ is equal to the ratio $c : d$, then we have the proportion $a : b = c : d$ or

$$\frac{a}{b} = \frac{c}{d}$$

which is read, "a is to b as c is to d."

Two ratios are equal, and hence form a proportion, when the cross-products are equal. This is stated algebraically as shown in the box.

EQUAL RATIOS

Two ratios $a : b$ and $c : d$ are equal, if $ad = bc$.

Stated using the "fractional notation" for ratios, this says that

$$\frac{a}{b} = \frac{c}{d}, \text{ if and only if } ad = bc$$

The following diagram may help you to remember which terms to multiply and also to explain why this is called a cross-product.

$$\frac{a}{b} \bowtie \frac{c}{d}$$

EXAMPLE 2.36

What is the missing number in the proportion $5 : 7 = x : 42$?

SOLUTION We are given $\dfrac{5}{7} = \dfrac{x}{42}$. Cross multiplying, we get

$$7x = 5 \cdot 42$$
$$= 210$$
$$x = 30$$

We have determined that $5 : 7 = 30 : 42$.

APPLICATION AUTOMOTIVE

EXAMPLE 2.37

If 74.5 L of fuel are used to drive 760 km, how many liters are needed to drive 3 754 km?

SOLUTION We have the rates of 74.5 L to 760 km and x L to 3 754 km. We will form a proportion where the left-hand side equals the ratio $\dfrac{\text{L}}{\text{km}}$. We must then have $\dfrac{\text{L}}{\text{km}}$ on the right-hand side. If we set these two rates equal, we have

$$\frac{74.5 \text{ L}}{760 \text{ km}} = \frac{x \text{ L}}{3754 \text{ km}}$$

EXAMPLE 2.37 (Cont.)

The cross-product is

$$760x = (74.5)(3\,754)$$
$$= 279\,673$$
$$x = 367.99079$$

So, it would require about 368 L of fuel to travel 3 754 km.

HINTS FOR SOLVING EQUATIONS

Several of the examples we have worked used a combination of the five operations used to make equivalent equations. Each of the examples showed how to use one or more of the hints for solving problems. As you continue through this book, you will get some more hints to help you become a better problem-solver.

HINTS FOR SOLVING EQUATIONS

1. Eliminate fractions. Multiply both sides of the equation by a common denominator.
2. Remove grouping symbols. Perform the indicated multiplications and then combine terms to remove parentheses, brackets, and braces.
3. Combine like terms whenever possible.
4. Get all terms containing the variable on one side of the equation. All other terms should be placed on the other side of the equation.
5. Check your answer in the original equation.

Here are two more examples. See if you can work each problem before studying the solution given.

EXAMPLE 2.38

Solve $\dfrac{3p + 7}{4} - \dfrac{2(p - 5)}{3} = \dfrac{p - 3}{2} + 6$.

SOLUTION

$$\frac{3p + 7}{4} - \frac{2(p - 5)}{3} = \frac{p - 3}{2} + 6$$

$$12\left[\frac{3p + 7}{4} - \frac{2(p - 5)}{3}\right] = 12\left[\frac{p - 3}{2} + 6\right]$$
Multiply both sides by 12, a common denominator of 2, 3, and 4.

$$12\left[\frac{3p + 7}{4}\right] - 12\left[\frac{2(p - 5)}{3}\right] = 12\left[\frac{p - 3}{2}\right] + 12(6)$$
Distribute the 12.

$$3[3p + 7] - 4[2(p - 5)] = 6[p - 3] + 12(6)$$
$$9p + 21 - 4[2p - 10] = 6p - 18 + 72$$
Remove grouping symbols.

$$9p + 21 - 8p + 40 = 6p - 18 + 72$$

$$p + 61 = 6p + 54 \qquad \text{Combine terms.}$$

$$7 = 5p \qquad \text{Use hint \#4.}$$

$$\frac{7}{5} = p \qquad \text{Divide by 5.}$$

The solution is $\frac{7}{5}$, or 1.4. Check. You should get 5.2 on both sides of the equation when you evaluate each side with $p = 1.4$. This would be a good time to practice using your calculator to see if you get 5.2 on each side of the equation.

EXAMPLE 2.39

Solve $\dfrac{3w + a}{2b} - \dfrac{4(w + a)}{b} = \dfrac{2w - 6}{3b} + \dfrac{2 + 6a}{b}$ for w.

SOLUTION There are several letters in this equation, a, b, and w, but you are asked to solve for w. This means that w is the variable and that a and b should be treated as constants.

$$\frac{3w + a}{2b} - \frac{4(w + a)}{b} = \frac{2w - 6}{3b} + \frac{2 + 6a}{b}$$

$$6b\left[\frac{3w + a}{2b} - \frac{4(w + a)}{b}\right] = 6b\left[\frac{2w - 6}{3b} + \frac{2 + 6a}{b}\right]$$

Multiply both sides by a common denominator $6b$.

$$6b\left[\frac{3w + a}{2b}\right] - 6b\left[\frac{4(w + a)}{b}\right] = 6b\left[\frac{2w - 6}{3b}\right] + 6b\left[\frac{2 + 6a}{b}\right]$$

$$3[3w + a] - 6[4(w + a)] = 2[2w - 6] + 6[2 + 6a]$$

$$9w + 3a - 24w - 24a = 4w - 12 + 12 + 36a \quad \text{Remove grouping.}$$

$$-15w - 21a = 4w + 36a \qquad \text{Combine like terms.}$$

$$-15w - 4w = 36a + 21a \qquad \text{Hint \#4.}$$

$$-19w = 57a \qquad \text{Combine like terms.}$$

$$w = \frac{57a}{-19} \qquad \text{Divide both sides by } -19.$$

$$w = -3a$$

Check. Substitute $-3a$ for w in the original equation. When you simplify each side, you get $\frac{4a}{b}$. Although it is easier to substitute for w at a later step, you might have made a mistake getting to that step. Sometimes you will even make an error when you copy the problem onto your paper. Always go back to the original problem to check your work.

EXERCISE SET 2.4

Solve the equations in Exercises 1–72.

1. $x - 7 = 32$
2. $y - 8 = 41$
3. $a + 13 = 25$
4. $b + 21 = 34$
5. $25 + c = 10$
6. $28 + d = 12$
7. $4x = 18$
8. $5y = 12$
9. $-3w = 24$
10. $6z = -42$
11. $21c = -14$
12. $24d = 16$
13. $\dfrac{p}{3} = 5$
14. $\dfrac{r}{5} = 4$
15. $\dfrac{t}{4} = -6$
16. $\dfrac{s}{-3} = -5$
17. $4a + 3 = 11$
18. $3b + 4 = 16$
19. $7 - 8d = 39$
20. $9 - 7c = 44$
21. $2.3w + 4.1 = 13.3$
22. $3.5z + 5.2 = 22.7$
23. $2x + 5x = 28$
24. $3y + 8y = 121$
25. $3a + 2(a + 5) = 45$
26. $4b + 3(7 + b) = 56$
27. $4(6 + c) - 5 = 21$
28. $5(7 + d) + 4 = 31$
29. $2(p - 4) + 3p = 16$
30. $7(n - 5) + 4n = 16$
31. $3x = 2x + 5$
32. $4y = 3y + 7$
33. $4w = 6w + 12$

34. $7z = 10z + 42$
35. $9a = 54 + 3a$
36. $8b = 55 + 3b$
37. $\dfrac{5x}{2} = \dfrac{4x}{3} - 7$
38. $\dfrac{3y}{7} = \dfrac{2y}{3} + 4$
39. $\dfrac{6p}{5} = \dfrac{3p}{2} + 4$
40. $\dfrac{5z}{3} = \dfrac{4z}{5} - 3$
41. $8n - 4 = 5n + 14$
42. $9p - 5 = 6p + 37$
43. $7r + 3 = 11r - 21$
44. $8s + 7 = 15s - 56$
45. $\dfrac{6x - 3}{2} = \dfrac{7x + 2}{3}$
46. $\dfrac{4r - 3}{3} = \dfrac{5r + 2}{2}$
47. $\dfrac{3t + 4}{4} = \dfrac{2t - 5}{2}$
48. $\dfrac{6a - 5}{3} = \dfrac{7a + 5}{6}$
49. $3(x + 5) = 2x - 3$
50. $2(y - 3) = 4 + 3y$
51. $\dfrac{x}{2} + \dfrac{x}{3} - \dfrac{x}{4} = 2$
52. $\dfrac{p}{2} - \dfrac{p}{3} - \dfrac{p}{4} = 3$
53. $\dfrac{4(a - 3)}{5} = \dfrac{3(a + 2)}{4}$
54. $\dfrac{5(b + 4)}{3} = \dfrac{4(b - 5)}{5}$
55. Solve $ax + b = 3ax$ for x
56. Solve $2by = 6 + 4by$ for y
57. Solve $ax - 3a + x = 5a$ for a

58. Solve $2(by - c) = 3\left(\dfrac{y}{2} - c\right)$ for y
59. $\dfrac{3}{x} + \dfrac{4}{x} = 3$
60. $\dfrac{5}{y} - \dfrac{3}{y} = 6$
61. $\dfrac{3}{4p} + \dfrac{1}{p} = \dfrac{7}{4}$
62. $\dfrac{6}{5q} - \dfrac{2}{q} = \dfrac{6}{5}$
63. $\dfrac{1}{x + 1} - \dfrac{2}{x - 1} = 0$
64. $\dfrac{3}{x + 2} - \dfrac{4}{x - 2} = 0$
65. $\dfrac{3}{2x} = \dfrac{1}{x + 5}$
66. $\dfrac{4}{3x} = \dfrac{2}{x + 1}$
67. $\dfrac{2x + 1}{2x - 1} = \dfrac{x - 1}{x - 3}$
68. $\dfrac{2x + 3}{2x + 5} = \dfrac{5x + 4}{5x + 2}$
69. Solve $\dfrac{6b - 5a}{3} + \dfrac{5a + b}{2}$
   $= \dfrac{5(a + 2b)}{4} + 5$ for a
70. Solve $\dfrac{3r + t}{5t} - \dfrac{r + 5t}{3t}$
   $= \dfrac{2(r - 4)}{15t} + 2$ for r
71. Solve $\dfrac{2z + a}{3x} - \dfrac{9z + a}{6x}$
   $= \dfrac{z - a}{2x} + \dfrac{4a}{3x}$ for a
72. Solve $\dfrac{3p + 2x}{2y} - \dfrac{5p - 3x}{3y}$
   $= \dfrac{x - 2p}{y} + \dfrac{3x + p}{6y}$ for x

110

Express each of the rates in Exercises 73–76 as a ratio.

73. $1.38 for 16 bolts   **74.** 725 rpm   **75.** 86 L/km   **76.** 236 mi in 4 h

Write each of the ratios in Exercises 77–80 as a ratio compared to 1.

77. $9:2$ **78.** $\dfrac{7}{5}$ **79.** $\dfrac{23}{7}$ **80.** $37:4$

Solve each of the proportions in Exercises 81–88.

81. $\dfrac{7}{8} = \dfrac{c}{32}$ **83.** $\dfrac{124}{62} = \dfrac{158}{d}$ **85.** $\dfrac{a}{4} = \dfrac{0.16}{0.15}$ **87.** $\dfrac{20}{b} = \dfrac{8}{5.6}$

82. $\dfrac{3}{b} = \dfrac{9}{24}$ **84.** $\dfrac{a}{3.5} = \dfrac{8}{20}$ **86.** $\dfrac{7.5}{10.5} = \dfrac{x}{6.3}$ **88.** $\dfrac{2.4}{10.8} = \dfrac{1.6}{d}$

Solve Exercises 89–90.

89. *Meteorology* The formula for converting Celsius temperatures to Fahrenheit temperatures is $F = \frac{9}{5}C + 32$, where F represents the Fahrenheit temperature and C, the Celsius temperature. Find the formula for converting Fahrenheit temperatures to Celsius by solving this equation for C.

90. *Physics* The velocity v of a falling object after t seconds is given by the formula $v = v_0 + at$, where v_0 represents the initial velocity and a is the acceleration due to gravity.

(a) Solve this equation for t in order to determine the length of time that it takes the object to reach some velocity v.

(b) Use your answer to part (a) to determine how long it takes an object to strike the ground, if its initial velocity is 12 m/s, its final velocity is 97 m/s, and the acceleration is 9.8 m/s².

 [IN YOUR WORDS]

91. Without looking in the text, write a summary of the operations you can use for solving equations.

92. Without looking in the text, write a summary of the hints for solving equations.

93. Explain the difference between a rate and a ratio.

2.6 APPLICATIONS OF EQUATIONS

In Section 2.4 we learned how to solve some equations. But, the ability to solve equations is helpful only if you are able to take a problem and write it in the form of one or more equations. Then, once you have the equations, you can solve them to find the answer to your original problem.

Most problems you have to solve at work will be verbal problems. Someone will tell you about a problem they want you to solve or they will write part, or all, of the problem. You will have to first take this verbal problem and organize it so that it is easier to understand. Then, you will look at the problem and decide what information is important and what is not. You should then take the important information and express it in one or more equations. Once you have written the equations, the most difficult part is over. All that is left is to solve the equations and check your answers. In this section, we will focus on taking written information and writing it as an equation.

SEVEN SUGGESTIONS TO HELP SOLVE WORD PROBLEMS

Verbal, or word problems, give several numerical relationships and then ask some questions about them. You must be able to translate the word problem into equations. The fewer equations you need, the easier it will be to solve the problem. Here are some suggestions and examples to help you.

SUGGESTIONS FOR SOLVING WORD PROBLEMS

1. Read the problem carefully. Make sure you understand what the problem is asking. You may need to read the problem several times to fully understand it.

2. Clearly identify the unknown quantities. Identify each unknown quantity with a letter (or variable). Write down what each letter stands for. Use a letter for an unknown quantity that makes sense to you. For example, you might use d for distance or t for time.

3. If possible, represent all the unknowns in terms of just one variable.

4. Make a sketch (if possible) if it makes the problem clearer.

5. Analyze the problem carefully. Try to write one equation that shows how all the unknowns and knowns are related. If it is not possible to write one equation, use more. (Later we will learn how to solve several equations that show the relationship between the unknowns.)

6. Solve the equation and indicate appropriate units.

7. Check your answer in the original problem.

Once you have found an answer and checked to see that it is correct, write your solution clearly and legibly indicating the correct units. You should try to write your answer in a complete sentence using proper grammar.

EXAMPLE 2.44

In order to get an A in a word processing class, one teacher requires that you type an average of 85 words per minute for 5 different timings. Bill had speeds of 77, 78, 87, and 91 words per minute on his first 4 timings. How fast must he type on the next test in order to get an A?

SOLUTION The unknown quantity is the typing speed on the next timed typing. We will let s represent the unknown typing speed. The average for the 5 timings is the sum of these 5 timings divided by 5 or $\dfrac{77 + 78 + 87 + 91 + s}{5}$. This average must be 85, and so we have the equation

$$\frac{77 + 78 + 87 + 91 + s}{5} = 85$$

$$\frac{333 + s}{5} = 85 \qquad \text{Combine terms.}$$

$$5\left(\frac{333 + s}{5}\right) = 5 \times 85 \qquad \text{Multiply by 5.}$$

$$333 + s = 425$$

$$333 + s - 333 = 425 - 333 \qquad \text{Subtract 333.}$$

$$s = 92$$

Bill must type 92 words per minute to have an average of 85 words per minute for the 5 timings, in order to get an A in the class.

APPLICATION BUSINESS

EXAMPLE 2.45

At the end of a model year, a dealer advertises that the list prices of last year's truck models are 15% off. What was the original price of a truck that is on sale for $14,416?

SOLUTION Suppose the original price of the truck was p dollars. The discounted amount is 15% of the original price, or $0.15p$. The sale price of $14,416 is the original price p less the discounted amount, $0.15\,p$. This can be written as

$$\text{original price} - \text{discounted amount} = \text{sale price}$$

$$p - 0.15p = 14{,}416$$

$$0.85p = 14{,}416 \qquad \text{Combine terms.}$$

$$p = \frac{14{,}416}{0.85} \qquad \text{Divide by 0.85.}$$

$$p = 16{,}960$$

The original price of the truck was $16,960.

You can check your answer by taking 15% of $16,960 ($0.15 \times 16{,}960 = 2{,}544$) and subtracting this from the original price ($16{,}960 - 2{,}544 = 14{,}416$). Is this the sale price?

We will now look at some types of problems that have applications to technology. The problems selected provide a variety of examples.

UNIFORM MOTION PROBLEMS

The distance an object travels is governed by the rate it is traveling and the time that it travels. This is often expressed with the formula

$$d = rt$$

where d is the distance traveled, r is the uniform or average rate of travel, and t is the time spent traveling.

APPLICATION GENERAL TECHNOLOGY

EXAMPLE 2.46

If an airplane flies 785 km/h for 4.5 h, how far does it travel?

SOLUTION We use the formula $d = rt$. We are given the rate r as 785 km/h and the time t as 4.5 h. So,

$$d = rt$$
$$= 785(4.5)$$
$$= 3532.5 \text{ km}$$

The plane will travel 3 532.5 km in 4.5 h.

It often helps to include the units as part of your work. In Example 2.46, we could have written

$$d = rt$$

$$= 785 \frac{\text{km}}{\text{h}} \times 4.5 \text{ h}$$

$$= 3\,532.5 \frac{\text{km} \cdot \cancel{\text{h}}}{\cancel{\text{h}}}$$

$$= 3\,532.5 \text{ km}$$

This same formula, $d = rt$, can be used to find any one of the three values, distance, rate, or time, provided that we know the other two.

APPLICATION **GENERAL TECHNOLOGY**

EXAMPLE 2.47

If a plane travels 1,150 mi in 2.5 h, what is its average rate of speed?

SOLUTION Again, we use the formula $d = rt$. This time we have the distance d as 1,150 mi and the time t as 2.5 h.

We will show two ways you can solve this problem. One does not show the units and the second method does.

Without Units	With Units
$d = rt$	$d = rt$
$1{,}150 = r(2.5)$	$1{,}150 \text{ mi} = r(2.5\,\text{h})$
$\dfrac{1{,}150}{2.5} = r$	$\dfrac{1{,}150 \text{ mi}}{2.5 \text{ h}} = r$
$460 = r$	$460 \text{ mph} = r$

The plane averaged 460 mph.

Sometimes it is helpful to use a table to organize the information. This often makes is easier to determine the necessary equations. This is demonstrated in the next example.

APPLICATION **GENERAL TECHNOLOGY**

EXAMPLE 2.48

The cruising air-speed in still air of a small airplane is 295 km/h. If the wind is blowing from the east at 75 km/h, how far to the east can a pilot fly and return in 4 h?

SOLUTION This problem again uses the formula $d = rt$. We begin by determining the speed of the plane as it flies east (into the wind) and then as it returns flying west (with the wind).

EXAMPLE 2.48 (Cont.)

$$295 \text{ km/h} = \text{speed of plane in still air}$$

$$75 \text{ km/h} = \text{speed of wind}$$

$$295 \text{ km/h} - 75 \text{ km/h} = 220 \text{ km/h} = \text{speed of plane flying east}$$

$$295 \text{ km/h} + 75 \text{ km/h} = 370 \text{ km/h} = \text{speed of plane flying west}$$

Next, we place the information in a table.

	Distance (d)	Rate (r)	Time (t)
Flying east	$220t$	220	t
Flying west	$370(4 - t)$	370	$4 - t$

Since the distance the pilot flies to the east is the same distance as the return flight, we know that the two quantities in the first column of the table must be the same. Thus, we have

$$220t = 370(4 - t)$$

$$= 1480 - 370t$$

$$590t = 1480$$

$$t = \frac{1480}{590} \approx 2.508$$

Thus, the plane should fly about 2.50 h to the east. Notice that this was rounded *down* to 2.50 h even though we would normally have rounded 2.508 *up* to 2.51 h. The reason is because using 2.51 h would not leave the plane enough time to return.

But, the question asked for the distance the plane should fly before turning around. Since it is traveling at 220 km/h when it flies to the east, it should travel $220 \times 2.50 \approx 550$ km.

Another motion problem is demonstrated in Example 2.49.

 APPLICATION GENERAL TECHNOLOGY

EXAMPLE 2.49

A car traveling on an interstate highway leaves a rest stop at 3 p.m., traveling at 75 km/h. Another car leaves the same rest stop 15 min later, headed in the same direction. If the second car travels at 100 km/h, how long will it be before it overtakes the first car?

SOLUTION Notice that the problem asks how long it will be before the cars meet, but does not say if this should be how much time or how many km. Let's find both.

The distance formula says that $d = rt$. If t is the amount of time (in hours) since the first car left, then for the first car the distance it has traveled, d, is $d = 75t$.

The distance traveled by the second car will be the same. The rate 100 km/h and the time will be different from those of the first car. The second car left

15 min or $\frac{1}{4}$h later. (Notice that we had to give this time in hours.) So, the time the second car traveled is $t - \frac{1}{4}$h. Thus, we have $d = 100(t - \frac{1}{4})$.

Both cars traveled the same distance, which means that

$$75t = 100\left(t - \frac{1}{4}\right)$$

$$75t = 100t - 25$$

$$75t - 100t = 100t - 25 - 100t \qquad \text{Subtract } 100t.$$

$$-25t = -25 \qquad \text{Combine terms.}$$

$$t = 1 \qquad \text{Divide by } -25.$$

The second car will catch the first 1 h after the first car left. This will be at 4 p.m., or 45 min after the second car leaves. The distance traveled by each car is $75(1) = 75$ km.

WORK PROBLEMS

Work problems provide a different type of challenge. In these problems, we want to determine the amount of work each person or machine can do in a given amount of time.

APPLICATION BUSINESS

EXAMPLE 2.50

One printer can complete a certain job in 3 h. Another printer can do the same job in 2 h. How long would it take if both printers work on the job?

SOLUTION We will let h stand for the hours it takes both machines to complete the job. In 1 h the two machines can complete $\frac{1}{h}$ of the job. The first printer does $\frac{1}{3}$ of the job in 1 h when it works alone. The second printer does $\frac{1}{2}$ of the job in 1 h when it works alone, but together they complete $\frac{1}{h}$ of the job in 1 h. So, $\frac{1}{h} = \frac{1}{3} + \frac{1}{2}$. A common denominator is $6h$. Multiplying by $6h$ we get

$$6 = 2h + 3h$$

$$6 = 5h$$

$$\frac{6}{5} = h$$

They can complete the job together in $\frac{6}{5}$ h or in 1 h 12 min.

A slightly different work problem is shown in Example 2.51.

APPLICATION GENERAL TECHNOLOGY

EXAMPLE 2.51

An oil tanker can be emptied by the main pump in 5 h. An auxiliary pump can empty the tank in 11 h. In the main pump is started at 8 a.m. and the auxiliary pump is started 1 h later, at what time will the tanker be empty?

EXAMPLE 2.51 (Cont.)

SOLUTION We will let t represent the time in hours it takes for the main pump to complete the job. Since the auxiliary pump is turned on 1 h after the main pump it completes the job in $t - 1$ hours. From the information we know that the main pump does $\frac{1}{5}$ of the job in 1 h and the auxiliary pump does $\frac{1}{11}$ of the job in the same amount of time. Thus, we see that the main pump completes $\frac{1}{5}t$ of the job during the time it works and the auxiliary pump finishes $\frac{1}{11}(t - 1)$ of the job while it is operating. Writing this as an equation we get

Part of job done by main pump	+	Part of job done by auxiliary pump	=	Total job
$\frac{1}{5}t$	+	$\frac{1}{11}(t - 1)$	=	1
$11t$	+	$5(t - 1)$	=	55
		$16t - 5$	=	55
		$16t$	=	60
		t	=	$\frac{60}{16}$
		t	=	3.75

It takes 3.75 h (or 3 h 45 min) to empty the tanker, so it is empty at 11:45 a.m.

MIXTURE PROBLEMS

In a mixture problem, two quantities are combined, or mixed, to produce a third quantity. Each quantity has a different percentage of some ingredient. The problems often ask for the percent of the ingredient in the third quantity.

APPLICATION GENERAL TECHNOLOGY

EXAMPLE 2.52

If 100 L of gasohol containing 12% alcohol is mixed with 300 L that contain 6% alcohol, how much alcohol is in the final mixture? What is the percent of alcohol in the final mixture?

SOLUTION Figure 2.3a shows the two given quantities on the left and the final mixture on the right. The first quantity has $0.12 \times 100 = 12$ L of alcohol. The second quantity has $0.06 \times 300 = 18$ L of alcohol.

The total amount of gasohol is $100 + 300 = 400$ L. The total amount of alcohol is $12 + 18 = 30$ L. The alcohol is $\frac{30}{400} = 7.5\%$ of the gasohol. (See Figure 2.3b.)

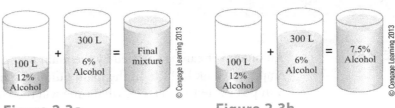

Figure 2.3a   Figure 2.3b

APPLICATION AUTOMOTIVE

EXAMPLE 2.53

A 15-L cooling system contains a solution of 20% antifreeze and 80% water. In order to get the most protection, the solution should contain 60% antifreeze and 40% water. How much of the 20% solution must be replaced with pure antifreeze to get the best protection?

SOLUTION Let n = the number of liters of the original solution that will be replaced with antifreeze. The amount of original solution that is not replaced is $(15 - n)$ L. You know that you will end up with 60% of 15 L, or 9 L of antifreeze. Thus, you can write

$$\text{antifreeze left} + \text{antifreeze added} = 9 \text{ L}$$

The antifreeze that is left is 20% of $15 - n$, so we can rewrite this equation as

$$20\%(15 - n) + n = 9$$
$$0.2(15 - n) + n = 5$$
$$3 - 0.2n + n = 9$$
$$3 + 0.8n = 9$$
$$0.8n = 6$$
$$n = \frac{6}{0.8}$$
$$n = 7.5$$

So, 7.5 L of the 20% solution must be replaced with pure antifreeze.

STATICS PROBLEMS

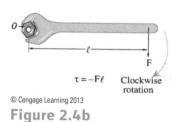

Counterclockwise
rotation

$\tau = +F\ell$

© Cengage Learning 2013

Figure 2.4a

$\tau = -F\ell$ Clockwise
rotation

© Cengage Learning 2013

Figure 2.4b

The **moment of force**, or **torque**, about a point O is the product of the force F and the perpendicular distance ℓ from the force to the point. The distance ℓ is also called the **moment arm** of the force about a point. The Greek letter tau, τ, is used to represent torque. Thus, we have the equation

$$\tau = F\ell$$

A torque that produces a counterclockwise rotation is considered positive, as shown in Figure 2.4a. A torque that produces a clockwise rotation is considered negative. (See Figure 2.4b.)

An object is in rotational equilibrium when the sum of all the torques acting on the object about any point is zero.

The **center of gravity** of an object is the point where the object's entire weight is regarded as being concentrated. If an object is hung from its center of gravity, it will not rotate. An object can also be balanced on its center of gravity without rotating. But, what is perhaps most important in studying the equilibrium of an object, is that its weight is considered to be a downward force from its center of gravity.

APPLICATION **GENERAL TECHNOLOGY**

EXAMPLE 2.54

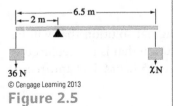

© Cengage Learning 2013

Figure 2.5

A 6.5-m rigid rod of negligible weight has a 36-N (newton) weight hung from one end. An unknown weight is hung from the other end. If the rod is balanced at a point 2 m from the end with the 36-N weight, how much is the unknown weight? (See Figure 2.5.)

SOLUTION Since the rod and weights are balanced, the torques of the two weights must be equal. On the left side the moment arm is 2 m and the force is 36 N. The torque on the left-hand side, τ_1, is $\tau_1 = 36$ N $\times$ 2 m $= 72$ N·m. The moment arm on the right is 6.5 m $-$ 2 m $= 4.5$ m. We are to find the force, x. So, the torque on the right-hand side is $\tau_2 = (x$ N)(4.5 m) $= 4.5x$ N·m. Since $\tau_1 = \tau_2$ then 72 N·m $= 4.5x$ N·m or $72 = 4.5x$. Solving this, we get

$$x = \frac{72}{4.5} = 16 \text{N}.$$ The unknown weight is 16 N.

APPLICATION **AUTOMOTIVE**

EXAMPLE 2.55

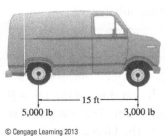

© Cengage Learning 2013

Figure 2.6

The front wheels of a truck together support 3,000 lb. Its rear wheels together support 5,000 lb. If the axles are 15 ft apart, where is the center of gravity? (See Figure 2.6.)

SOLUTION Let d represent the distance from the front axle to the center of gravity. Then $15 - d$ is the distance from the center of gravity to the rear axle. The torque on the right is $\tau_1 = 3,000d$ ft·lb. The torque on the left is $\tau_2 = -5,000(15 - d)$ ft·lb. (Notice that τ_2 is a counterclockwise rotation around the center of gravity and so it is positive. τ_1 is a clockwise rotation around the center of gravity and so it is negative.) Since the truck is in rotational equilibrium,

$$\tau_1 + \tau_2 = 0$$
$$3,000d - 5,000(15 - d) = 0$$
$$3,000d - 75,000 + 5,000d = 0$$
$$-75,000 + 8,000d = 0$$
$$8,000d = 75,000$$
$$d = \frac{75,000}{8,000}$$
$$d = 9.375$$

The center of gravity is 9.375 ft or 9 ft 4.5 in. behind the front axle.

EXERCISE SET 2.6

Solve Exercises 1–35.

1. On your first 3 mathematics exams you received scores of 79, 85, and 74. What do you need to get on the next exam in order to have an 80 average?

2. There are three parts to a state certification exam. You must pass all 3 parts with an average of 75 and you cannot get below 60 on any one part. Judy's first 2 scores were 65 and 72. What must she get on the last part in order to pass?

3. If Raphael got scores of 85 and 82 on the first 2 parts of the exam described in Exercise 2, what, must he get on the third part in order to pass the exam?

4. *Business* A resort promised that the temperature would average 72°F during your 4-day vacation or you would get your money back. The first 3 days the average temperatures were 69°, 73°, and 68°. How warm does it have to get today for the resort to be able to keep your money?

5. *Business* A discount store sells personal computers for $920. This price is 80% of the price at a wholesale store. What is the wholesale price? How much will you save at the discount store?

6. *Business* The personal computer discount store makes a profit of 15% based on its cost for the computer in Exercise 5. What does the computer cost the discount store?

7. An insurance company gives you $1,839 to replace a stolen car. At the time the company tells you that the car was only worth 30% of its original cost. What was the original cost?

8. *Automotive* Because of inflation, the price of automotive parts increased by 3% in January and by another 4% in May. What was last year's price of parts that cost $227.63 after the May increase?

9. *Finance* Sally invested $4,500. Part of it was invested at 3.5% and part of it at 5%. After 1 year her interest was $201. How much was invested at each rate?

10. *Finance* To help pay for his education, Jośe worked and invested his money. Altogether he was able to invest $8,200. Some money he invested at 4.2% and the rest at 3.25%. He was able to earn $320.65 in interest during the year. How much did he invest at each rate?

11. *Business* A factory pays time and a half for all hours over 40 h per week. Juannita makes $8.50 an hour and 1 wk brought home $429.25. How many hours of overtime did she work?

12. *Business* Mladen is paid $8.20 an hour. He also gets paid time-and-a-half overtime when he works more than 40 h a week if it is during the week. He gets double time if the extra hours are on the weekend. One week Mladen brought home $524.80 for 54 h of work. How many hours did he work on the weekend?

13. *Transportation* A freight train leaves Chicago traveling at an average rate of 38 mph. How far will it travel in 7 h?

14. *Transportation* How long does it take the train in Exercise 13 to travel 475 mi?

15. *Environmental science* An oil tanker has hit a reef and a hole has been knocked in the side of the tanker. Oil is leaking out of the tanker and forming an oil slick. The oil slick is moving toward a beach 380 km away at a rate of 12 km/d (kilometers per day). The day after the oil spill, cleanup ships leave a dock at the beach and head directly toward the oil slick at a rate of 80 km/d. How far will the ships be from the beach when they reach the oil slick?

16. A school group is traveling together on a school bus. The bus leaves a rest stop on an interstate highway at 1:00 p.m. and travels at a rate of 60 mph. One of the students did not get back on the bus before it left. A highway patrol car leaves the rest stop with the student at 1:30 p.m. and tries to catch the bus. If the patrol car averages 80 mph, at what time will it catch the bus? How far from the rest stop will the bus have traveled?

17. **Machine technology** The worker on machine *A* can complete a certain job in 6 h. The worker on machine *B* can do the same job in 4 h. In a rush situation, how long would it take both machines to do the job?

18. **Construction** Manuel can build a house in 45 days. With Errol's help they can build the house in 30 days. How long would it take Errol to build the same house by himself?

19. A tank can be filled by Pipe *A* in 4 h. Pipe *B* fills the same tank in 2 h. How long will it take to fill the tank if both pipes are used at the same time?

20. **Energy** A solar collector can generate 70 kJ (kilojoules) in 12 min. A second solar collector can generate the same amount of kJ in 4 min. How long will it take the two of them working together to generate 70 kJ?

21. **Chemistry** To generate hydrogen in a chemistry laboratory, a 40% solution of sulfuric acid is needed. You have 50 mL of an 86% solution of sulfuric acid. How many mL of water should be added to dilute the solution to the required level of sulfuric acid?

22. **Petroleum engineering** A petroleum distributor has two gasohol storage tanks. One tank contains 8% alcohol and the other 14% alcohol. An order is received for 1 000 000 L of gasohol containing 9% alcohol. How many liters from each tank should be used to fill this order?

23. **Chemistry** A copper alloy that is 35% copper is to be combined with an alloy that is 75% copper. The result will be 750 kg of an alloy that is 60% copper. How many kg of each alloy should be used?

24. **Chemistry** How many pounds of an alloy of 20% silver must be melted with 50 lb of an alloy with 30% silver in order to get an alloy of 27% silver?

25. **Civil engineering** A horizontal beam of negligible weight is 20 ft long and supported by columns at each end. A weight of 850 lb is placed at one spot on the beam. The force on one end is 500 lb. What is the force on the other end? Where is the weight located?

26. **Transportation engineering** A loaded truck weighs 140 000 N. The front wheels of the truck support 60 000 N and the rear wheels support the rest. Where is the center of gravity if the axles are 4.2 m apart?

27. **Physics** Locate the center of gravity of the beam in Figure 2.7 if the beam is 12 ft long.

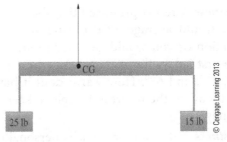

Figure 2.7

28. **Machine technology** Locate the center of gravity of the machine part in Figure 2.8 if it is all constructed from the same material.

29. **Machine technology** Locate the center of gravity of the machine part in Figure 2.9 if it is all made of the same metal. (Hint: The volume of a cylinder is $\pi r^2 h$ or $\frac{\pi}{4} d^2 h$, where *r* is the

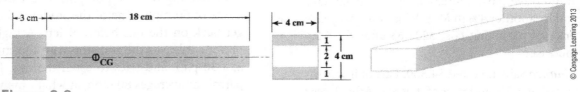

Figure 2.8

radius, d is the diameter of the circular bottom, and h is the height. This machine part is made of two circular cylinders.)

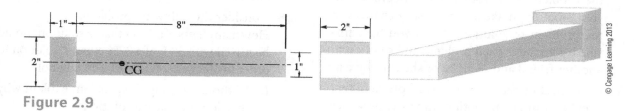

Figure 2.9

30. **Physics** The center of gravity of the object in Figure 2.10 is 10 cm from the left side. What is the thickness of the right side?

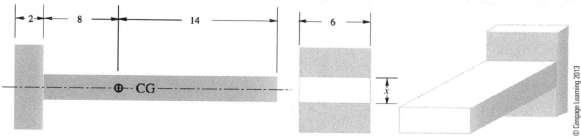

Figure 2.10

31. **Medical technology** How much pure alcohol must a nurse add to 10 cc (cm^3) of a 60% alcohol solution to strengthen it to a 90% solution?

32. **Chemistry** A chemist has 300 g of a 20% hydrochloric acid solution. She wishes to drain some off and replace it with an 80% solution in order to obtain 300 g of a 25% solution. How many grams of the 20% solution must she drain and replace with the 80% solution?

33. **Electronics** The voltage of V, in volts, in a circuit is the square root of the product of the power P, in watts, and the resistance R, in ohms.

(a) Write the statement as an equation.

(b) If the voltage is 240 V and the power is 2500 W, solve this equation for the resistance, R, in ohms. Round your answer to the nearest ohm.

34. **Electronics** The power P, in watts, of a certain circuit is the quotient of the square of the voltage V, in volts, and the resistance R, in ohms.

(a) Write this statement as an equation.

(b) If the power is 4.25 W and the resistance is 2850 Ω, solve this equation for the voltage, V. Round your answer to the nearest volt.

35. The impedance of Z is a certain circuit is the square root of the sum of the square of the resistance of R and the square of the reactance X in ohms.

(a) Write this statement as an equation.

(b) Solve this equation for the reactance X in ohms if $Z = 10\ \Omega$ and $R = 4:5\ \Omega$. Round your answer to the nearest tenth ohm.

 [IN YOUR WORDS]

36. On a sheet of paper write a word problem. On the back of the sheet of paper, write your name and explain how to solve the problem. Give the problem you wrote to a friend and let

him or her try to solve it. If your friend has difficulty understanding the problem or solving the problem, or if your friend disagrees with your solution, make any necessary changes in the problem or solution. When you have finished, give the revised problem and solution to another friend and see if he or she can solve it.

37. On a sheet of paper write a word problem that is either a uniform motion, mixture, or statics problem. (If your problem in Exercise 36 was from one of these three areas, then select a different area for this problem.) On the back of the sheet of paper, write your name and explain

how to solve the problem. Give the problem you wrote to a friend and let him or her try to solve it, and follow the suggestions given in Exercise 36.

38. Consider the following problem:
How many liters of a 25% ethanol solution should be mixed with 30 L of a 37% ethanol solution in order to obtain a solution of 62% ethanol?

(a) Without working the problem explain why this does not have a solution.

(b) Use algebra to solve the problem. Explain how you can tell from the algebraic solution that this problem does not have a solution.

7 FACTORING AND ALGEBRAIC FRACTIONS

Heavy rains often bring flooding. The height of the flood water depends on the volume of surface runoff. In Section 7.6, we will learn some of the basic algebra for estimating the volume of surface runoff.

This chapter uses the algebraic foundations established in Chapter 2. In Chapter 2, we learned how to multiply and divide algebraic expressions. In this chapter we will learn how to find the factors that, when multiplied together, give the original expression. Once we have the ability to factor algebraic expressions, we will use it to help solve second-degree or quadratic equations.

We will also use factoring to help add, subtract, multiply, divide, and simplify algebraic fractions. In spite of all the scientific and technical examples we have used that involve linear equations, many scientific and technical situations must be described with quadratic equations or with algebraic fractions.

343

OBJECTIVES

AFTER COMPLETING THIS CHAPTER, YOU WILL BE ABLE TO:

▼ Multiply polynomials.

▼ Factor polynomials using algebraic and graphical techniques.

▼ Simplify, multiply, divide, add, and subtract algebraic fractions.

▼ Simplify complex fractions.

▼ Use graphical techniques as a tool for checking.

▼ Use rational and polynomial functions in problem solving.

7.1   SPECIAL PRODUCTS

In mathematics we use certain products so often that we need to take the time to learn them. Success in factoring depends on your ability to recognize patterns in any form that they appear. All of these special products were developed in Section 2.2, but most were not stated in the general form. We will present each special product, give some examples of how it is used, and then summarize all of the special products at the end of this section.

The first special product is the distributive law of multiplication over addition, which we saw in Chapter 1.

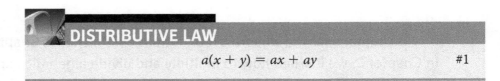

DISTRIBUTIVE LAW

$$a(x + y) = ax + ay \qquad\qquad \#1$$

EXAMPLE 7.1

$$8(4m + 3n) = 8(4m) + 8(3n)$$
$$= 32m + 24n$$

Here $a = 8$, $x = 4m$, and $y = 3n$. As you can see, the variable x can represent a product of a constant and a variable.

EXAMPLE 7.2

$$3x(2y + 5ax) = (3x)(2y) + (3x)(5ax)$$
$$= 6xy + 15ax^2$$

The term a in the distributive law can represent a constant, a variable, or the product of a constant and a variable.

The next special product is formed by multiplying the sum and difference of two terms. It is equal to the square of the first term minus the square of the second term.

DIFFERENCE OF TWO SQUARES

$$(x + y)(x - y) = x^2 - y^2 \qquad \#2$$

EXAMPLE 7.3

$$(x + 6)(x - 6) = x^2 - 6^2$$
$$= x^2 - 36$$

Notice that each term to the right of the equal sign is a perfect square.

EXAMPLE 7.4

$$(2a + 3\sqrt{y})(2a - 3\sqrt{y}) = (2a)^2 - (3\sqrt{y})^2$$
$$= 4a^2 - 9y$$

Again, once you realize that $y = (\sqrt{y})^2$, you can see that each term to the right of the equal sign is a perfect square. As you gain practice, you will be able to omit the middle step.

The third and fourth special products will be considered together.

PERFECT SQUARE TRINOMIALS

$$(x + y)^2 = x^2 + 2xy + y^2 \qquad \#3$$
$$(x - y)^2 = x^2 - 2xy + y^2 \qquad \#4$$

Note that both of these demonstrate that the square of a binomial is a trinomial.

 CAUTION Be careful, many students make the mistake of thinking that $(x + y)^2 = x^2 + y^2$. This is not true, as you can easily verify by using the FOIL method from Chapter 2.

EXAMPLE 7.5

$$(p + 7)^2 = p^2 + 2(7)p + 7^2$$
$$= p^2 + 14p + 49$$

Here $x = p$ and $y = 7$.

EXAMPLE 7.6

$$(2a - 5t^3)^2 = (2a)^2 - 2(2a)(5t^3) + (5t^3)^2$$
$$= 4a^2 - 20at^3 + 25t^6$$

Here $x = 2a$ and $y = 5t^3$.

The next special product is the product of two binomials that have the same first term. It can be verified by using the FOIL method.

TWO BINOMIALS, SAME FIRST TERM

$$(x + a)(x + b) = x^2 + (a + b)x + ab \qquad \#5$$

EXAMPLE 7.7

$$(p + 3)(p + 7) = p^2 + (3 + 7)p + (3)(7)$$
$$= p^2 + 10p + 21$$

EXAMPLE 7.8

$$(r + 2)(r - 8) = r^2 + (2 - 8)r + (2)(-8)$$
$$= r^2 - 6r - 16$$

In this example, $a = 2$ and $b = -8$. Remember that $r - 8$ can be written as $r + (-8)$.

The next special product is a general version of the last one. Again, this special product can be checked by using the FOIL method.

GENERAL QUADRATIC TRINOMIAL

$$(ax + b)(cx + d) = acx^2 + (ad + bc)x + bd \qquad \#6$$

EXAMPLE 7.9

Use Special Product 6 to multiply $(4x + 2)(3x + 5)$.

SOLUTION Here $a = 4$, $b = 2$, $c = 3$, and $d = 5$, so

$$(4x + 2)(3x + 5) = 4 \cdot 3x^2 + (4 \cdot 5 + 2 \cdot 3)x + 2 \cdot 5$$
$$= 12x^2 + (20 + 6)x + 10$$
$$= 12x^2 + 26x + 10$$

EXAMPLE 7.10

Multiply $(2x - 5)(2x + 9)$.

SOLUTION Here both a and c have the same value. That is, $a = c = 2$. Also, $b = -5$, and $d = 9$. The General Quadratic Trinomial formula (Special Product 6) produces

$$(2x - 5)(2x + 9) = (2x)^2 + [(2)(9) + (-5)(2)]x + (-5)(9)$$
$$= 4x^2 + [18 - 10]x + (-45)$$
$$= 4x^2 + 8x - 45$$

EXAMPLE 7.11

Multiply $(7x + 3y)(5x - 2y)$.

SOLUTION Here $a = 7$, $b = 3y$, $c = 5$, and $d = -2y$. Using Special Product 6 produces

$$(7x + 3y)(5x - 2y) = (7 \cdot 5x^2) + [7(-2y) + (3y)5]x + (3y)(-2y)$$
$$= 35x^2 + (-14y + 15y)x + (-6y^2)$$
$$= 35x^2 + xy - 6y^2$$

Of course, there is nothing to prevent the combination of two or more of these special products.

 NOTE Remember the order of operations in Chapter 1. Powers are executed before multiplication or division. So, in the following example, we first square $(3x - 5)$ and then multiply that result by $4x$.

EXAMPLE 7.12

$$4x(3x - 5)^2 = 4x(9x^2 - 30x + 25)$$
$$= 36x^3 - 120x^2 + 100x$$

EXAMPLE 7.13

$$(x^2 + 9)(x + 3)(x - 3) = (x^2 + 9)(x^2 - 9)$$
$$= x^4 - 81$$

In this example, the left-hand side has the special product $(x + 3)(x - 3) = x^2 - 9$. When these are multiplied, we get another special product: $(x^2 + 9)(x^2 - 9)$. The time spent looking at a problem for special products can save some computation and time. It can also reduce errors.

There are four other special products that you will use less often than the ones already listed. They will be presented in pairs. The first two are the cubes of a sum or difference.

PERFECT CUBES

$$(x + y)^3 = x^3 + 3x^2y + 3xy^2 + y^3 \qquad \#7$$

$$(x - y)^3 = x^3 - 3x^2y + 3xy^2 - y^3 \qquad \#8$$

EXAMPLE 7.14

$$(x + 5)^3 = x^3 + 3x^2(5) + 3x(5^2) + 5^3$$
$$= x^3 + 15x^2 + 75x + 125$$

EXAMPLE 7.15

$$(2a - 4)^3 = (2a)^3 - 3(2a)^2(4) + 3(2a)(4^2) - (4^3)$$
$$= 8a^3 - 48a^2 + 96a - 64$$

The last two special products also deal with cubes.

SUM AND DIFFERENCE OF TWO CUBES

$$(x + y)(x^2 - xy + y^2) = x^3 + y^3 \qquad \#9$$

$$(x - y)(x^2 + xy + y^2) = x^3 - y^3 \qquad \#10$$

EXAMPLE 7.16

$$(x - 3)(x^2 + 3x + 9) = x^3 - (3)^3$$
$$= x^3 - 27$$

EXAMPLE 7.17

$$(2d + 5)(4d^2 - 10d + 25) = (2d)^3 + (5)^3$$
$$= 8d^3 + 125$$

APPLICATION BUSINESS

EXAMPLE 7.18

An open box is going to be formed by cutting a square out of each corner of a rectangular piece of cardboard and folding up the sides as shown in Figure 7.1a. Suppose the piece of cardboard measures 10 cm × 12 cm. (a) Determine a

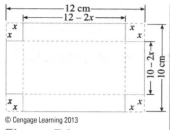

© Cengage Learning 2013

Figure 7.1a

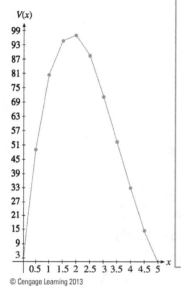

© Cengage Learning 2013

Figure 7.1b

function for the volume of the box. (b) What is the domain of this function? (c) Set up a partial table of values and sketch the graph of this function. (d) What size square seems to produce a box with the largest volume?

SOLUTIONS

(a) If the square measures x cm $\times$ x cm, then the lengths of the sides that will be folded up are $10 - 2x$ cm and $12 - 2x$ cm. So, the volume of the box is given by

$$V(x) = x(10 - 2x)(12 - 2x)$$
$$= 120x - 44x^2 + 4x^3$$

(b) The domain of the function is all real numbers. But, we cannot cut out a square that measures 0 cm or less and we cannot cut out a square that measures 5 cm or more. So, the "realistic" domain is represented by $\{x : 0 < x < 5\}$. Notice how the factored form helped us determine the domain. The expanded form will be more useful later in this book when we get to calculus.

(c) We have the following *partial* table of values.

x	0.5	1.0	1.5	2.0	2.5	3.0	3.5	4.0	4.5
$V(x)$	49.5	80.0	94.5	96.0	87.5	72.0	52.5	32.0	13.5

© Cengage Learning 2013

A graph formed from this table is shown in Figure 7.1b.

(d) From looking at the table, or the graph, it *seems* as if a 2 cm $\times$ 2 cm square will produce a box with the largest volume. Calculus can be used to show that $x \approx 1.8$ cm will produce the largest volume: 96.768 cm^3.

Thus, we have a total of 10 special products. Study them. Become familiar with them. Learn to recognize them and to use them to help simplify your work. The 10 special products are listed here together.

THE SPECIAL PRODUCTS

$a(x + y) = ax + ay$	#1
$(x + y)(x - y) = x^2 - y^2$	#2
$(x + y)^2 = x^2 + 2xy + y^2$	#3
$(x - y)^2 = x^2 - 2xy + y^2$	#4
$(x + a)(x + b) = x^2 + (a + b)x + ab$	#5
$(ax + b)(cx + d) = acx^2 + (ad + bc)x + bd$	#6
$(x + y)^3 = x^3 + 3x^2y + 3xy^2 + y^3$	#7
$(x - y)^3 = x^3 - 3x^2y + 3xy^2 - y^3$	#8
$(x + y)(x^2 - xy + y^2) = x^3 + y^3$	#9
$(x - y)(x^2 + xy + y^2) = x^3 - y^3$	#10

EXERCISE SET 7.1

In Exercises 1–44, find the indicated products by direct use of one of the 10 special products. It should not be necessary to write intermediate steps.

1. $3(p + q)$

2. $7(2 + x)$

3. $3x(5 - y)$

4. $2a(4 + a^2)$

5. $(p + q)(p - q)$

6. $(3a + b)(3a - b)$

7. $(2x - 6p)(2x + 6p)$

8. $\left(\dfrac{y}{2} + \dfrac{2p}{3}\right)\left(\dfrac{y}{2} - \dfrac{2p}{3}\right)$

9. $(r + w)^2$

10. $(q - f)^2$

11. $(2x + y)^2$

12. $(\tfrac{1}{2}a + b)^2$

13. $(\tfrac{2}{3}x + 4b)^2$

14. $(a - \tfrac{1}{2}y)^2$

15. $(2p - \tfrac{3}{4}r)^2$

16. $(\tfrac{2}{3}r - 5t)^2$

17. $(a + 2)(a + 3)$

18. $(x + 5)(x + 7)$

19. $(x - 5)(x + 2)$

20. $(a + 9)(x - 12)$

21. $(2a + b)(3a + b)$

22. $(4x + 2)(3x + 5)$

23. $(3x + 4)(2x - 5)$

24. $(3m - n)(4m + 2n)$

25. $(a + b)^3$

26. $(r - s)^3$

27. $(x + 4)^3$

28. $(2a + b)^3$

29. $(2a - b)^3$

30. $(3x + 2y)^3$

31. $(3x - 2y)^3$

32. $(4r - s)^3$

33. $(m + n)(m^2 - mn + n^2)$

34. $(a + 2)(a^2 - 2a + 4)$

35. $(r - t)(r^2 + rt + t^2)$

36. $(h - 3)(h^2 + 3h + 9)$

37. $(2x + b)(4x^2 - 2xb + b^2)$

38. $(3a + \tfrac{2}{3}c)(9a^2 - 2ac + \tfrac{4}{9}c^2)$

39. $(3a - d)(9a^2 + 3da + d^2)$

40. $\left(\dfrac{2e}{5} - \dfrac{5r}{4}\right)\left(\dfrac{4e^2}{25} + \dfrac{er}{2} + \dfrac{25r^2}{16}\right)$

41. $3(a + 2)^2$

42. $5(2a - 4)^2$

43. $\dfrac{5r}{t}\left(t + \dfrac{r}{5}\right)^2$

44. $(x^2 + 4)(x + 2)(x - 2)$

In Exercises 45–60, perform the indicated operations.

45. $(x^2 - 6)(x^2 + 6)$

46. $\left(\dfrac{2a}{b} + \dfrac{b}{2}\right)^2$

47. $\left(\dfrac{3x}{y} - \dfrac{y}{x}\right)\left(\dfrac{3x}{y} + \dfrac{y}{x}\right)x^2y^2$

48. $(x + 1)(x + 2)(x + 3)$

49. $(x - y)^2 - (y - x)^2$

50. $(x + y)^2 - (y - x)^2$

51. $(x + 3)(x - 3)^2$

52. $(y - 4)(y + 4)^2$

53. $r(r - t)^2 - t(t - r)^2$

54. $5(x + 4)(x - 4)(x^2 + 16)$

55. $(5 + 3x)(25 - 15x + 9x^2)$

56. $(2 - \sqrt{x})(2 + \sqrt{x})(4 + x)$

57. $[(x + y) - (w + z)]^2$

58. $[(r + s) + (t + u)]^2$

59. $(x + y - z)(x + y + z)$

60. $(a + b + 2)(a - b + 2)$

Solve Exercises 61–68.

61. Electronics The impedance, z, of an ac circuit at frequency f is given by the formula $z^2 = R^2 + (x_L - x_C)^2$, where R is the resistance, x_L is the inductive resistance, and x_C is the capacitive resistance at the frequency f. Use a special product to expand the equation.

62. Physics The kinetic energy, KE, of an object is given by the formula $KE = \frac{1}{2}mv^2$, where m is the mass of the object and v its velocity. If the velocity of an object at any time, t, is given by the equation $v = 3t + 1$, find an equation for the kinetic energy in terms of m and t and expand your result using a special formula.

63. Physics The magnitude of the centripetal acceleration of a body in uniform circular motion is given by the formula $a_c = \dfrac{v^2}{r}$, where v is the velocity of the body and r is the radius of the circular path. If the velocity at any given time t is expressed as $v = 2t^2 - t$, find an equation for the centripetal acceleration in terms of r and t, and expand your result.

64. Energy The work, W, done by a steam turbine in a certain period of time is given by the formula $W = \frac{1}{2}m(v_1 - v_2)(v_1 + v_2)$, where m is the mass of the steam that passes through the turbine during that period, v_1 is the velocity of the steam when it enters, and v_2 the velocity when it leaves. Simplify this formula by multiplying the factors together.

65. Architectural technology When the maximum deflections of two similar cantilever beams bearing the load at the ends are compared, the difference in deflection is given by

$$d = \left(\frac{P}{3EI}\right)(l_1 - l_2)(l_1^2 + l_1 l_2 + l_2^2)$$

Simplify this formula by multiplying the two factors containing l_1.

66. Architectural technology When the maximum deflections of two similar cantilever beams bearing distributed loads are compared, the difference in deflection is given by

$$d = \left(\frac{w}{8EI}\right)(l_1 - l_2)(l_1 + l_2)(l_1^2 + l_2^2)$$

Simplify this formula by multiplying the three factors containing l_1.

67. Metallurgy When the temperature of a bar of length L_0 is changed by $T°$ its new length is given by the formula $L = L_0(1 + \alpha T)$, where α is the coefficient of thermal expansion. Multiply this expression.

68. Metallurgy The object in Figure 7.2 is a cube with a cube removed from the inside. The volume of the material used to construct the object is given by

$$V = (s_2 - s_1)(s_2^2 + s_1 s_2 + s_1^2)$$

Rewrite this formula by multiplying these two factors.

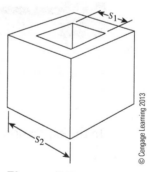

© Cengage Learning 2013

Figure 7.2

 [IN YOUR WORDS]

69. Describe how you can remember the expansions of the perfect square trinomials.

70. Describe how you can remember the expansions of the perfect cubes.

7.2 FACTORING

Sometimes it is important to determine what expressions were multiplied together to form a product, instead of multiplying quantities together as we did in the special products. Recall from Section 2.1 that an algebraic term consists of several factors. For example, the term $5xy$ has factors of 1, 5, x, y, $5x$, $5y$, xy, and $5xy$. In Section 7.1, we learned to multiply several factors together to form the special products. In this section, we will begin to learn how to factor an algebraic expression. Once we know how to factor we will be able to solve more complicated problems. Determining the factors of an algebraic expression is called *factoring*.

When factoring a polynomial, we will use only those factors that are also polynomials. Further, we will continue factoring a polynomial until the only remaining factors are 1 and -1. When this has been completed, we will be able to say that the polynomial has been factored completely and all of the factors will be *prime factors*.

COMMON FACTORS

The simplest type of factoring is the reverse of the distributive law of multiplication. This type of factoring is called removing a common factor. If each term in an expression contains the same factor, then this is a common factor and it can be factored out using the distributive law.

COMMON FACTOR

$$ax + ay = a(x + y)$$

EXAMPLE 7.19

In the expression $6a + 3a^2$, each term contains a factor of $3a$.

$$6a + 3a^2 = 2(3a) + a(3a)$$
$$= (2 + a)3a$$
$$= 3a(2 + a)$$

EXAMPLE 7.20

$8y^2 + 2y = 2y(4y + 1)$

Remember that $2y = (2y)(1)$. When you factor $2y$, you are left with a factor of 1.

EXAMPLE 7.21

$12x^5y + 8x^3y^2 = 4x^3y(3x^2 + 2y)$

You could have factored this in several other ways, such as $2xy(6x^4 + 4x^2y)$. This would not have been considered completely factored, since $6x^4 + 4x^2y$ can be factored further.

You may not see how to completely factor out all of the common factors in one step. For instance, in the last example you might have first written

$$12x^5y + 8x^3y^2 = 2xy(6x^4 + 4x^2y)$$

and then noticed that you could factor $6x^4 + 4x^2y$ as $2x^2(3x^2 + 2y)$. Then you would have had

$$12x^5y + 8x^3y^2 = 2xy(6x^4 + 4x^2y)$$
$$= 2xy(2x^2)(3x^2 + 2y)$$
$$= 4x^3y(3x^2 + 2y)$$

Notice that in the last step the two monomials were combined.

EXAMPLE 7.22

Factor $6x^2y + 9xy^2z - 3xyz$.

SOLUTION We can see that each term contains a multiple of 3, as well as an x and y factor. If we factor $3xy$ out of each term, we have $(3xy)(2x) + (3xy)(3yz) + (3xy)(-z) = 3xy(2x + 3yz - z)$. So, $6x^2y + 9xy^2z - 3xyz = 3xy(2x + 3yz - z)$.

The easiest factors to locate (and sometimes the easiest to overlook) are the monomials or common factors.

 HINT You should always begin factoring an algebraic expression by looking for common factors. Once you have factored out all common factors, the remaining expression is easier to factor.

USING THE SPECIAL PRODUCTS

Special product #2 gives us our second important form of factoring. Since $(x + y)(x - y) = x^2 - y^2$, we can reverse this to get

DIFFERENCE OF TWO SQUARES

$$x^2 - y^2 = (x + y)(x - y)$$

As you can see, to factor the difference between two squares you get factors that are the sum and difference of the quantities.

EXAMPLE 7.23

Factor $x^2 - 25$.

SOLUTION $x^2 - 25 = x^2 - 5^2$

$$= (x + 5)(x - 5)$$

You would have had to notice that 25 was 5^2 before you could recognize that this was the difference of two squares.

EXAMPLE 7.24

Factor $9a^2 - 49b^4$.

SOLUTION $9a^2 - 49b^4 = (3a)^2 - (7b^2)^2$

$$= (3a + 7b^2)(3a - 7b^2)$$

Again, you have to recognize the perfect squares: $9a^2 = (3a)^2$ and $49b^4 = (7b^2)^2$.

EXAMPLE 7.25

Factor $27x^3 - 75xy^2$.

SOLUTION $27x^3 - 75xy^2 = 3x(9x^2 - 25y^2)$

$$= 3x(3x + 5y)(3x - 5y)$$

This example demonstrates the value of first looking for common factors. There is a common factor of $3x$. When the common factor is factored out, it is easier to see that the remaining factor is the difference of two squares.

EXAMPLE 7.26

Factor $5x^4 - 80y^4$.

SOLUTION $5x^4 - 80y^4 = 5(x^4 - 16y^4)$

$$= 5[(x^2)^2 - (4y^2)^2]$$
$$= 5(x^2 + 4y^2)(x^2 - 4y^2)$$
$$= 5(x^2 + 4y^2)(x + 2y)(x - 2y)$$

Again, you should have noticed that there was a common factor of 5 and that each of the remaining terms was a perfect square. After factoring out $x^4 - 16y^4$ you were not finished, because $x^2 - 4y^2$ is also the difference of two squares. The other factor $x^2 + 4y^2$ cannot be factored further.

 NOTE Remember: $x^2 + y^2 \neq (x + y)^2$. In fact, $x^2 + y^2$ cannot be factored using real numbers.

 APPLICATION **ELECTRONICS**

EXAMPLE 7.27

In order to shield it from stray electromagnetic radiation, an electronic device is housed in a metal canister that is shaped like a right circular cylinder. The surface area of the cylinder is given by $A = 2\pi r^2 + 2\pi rh$, where r is the radius of the base and h is the height of the cylinder. Factor the right-hand side of this formula.

SOLUTION This formula has common factors of 2π and r. Factoring, we obtain
$$A = 2\pi r^2 + 2\pi rh$$
$$= 2\pi r(r + h)$$

EXERCISE SET 7.2

Completely factor each of the expressions in Exercises 1–40.

1. $6x + 6$
2. $12x + 12$
3. $12a - 6$
4. $15d - 5$
5. $4x - 2y + 8$
6. $6a + 9b - 3c$
7. $5x^2 + 10x + 15$
8. $16a^2 + 8b - 24$
9. $10x^2 - 15$
10. $14x^4 + 21$
11. $4x^2 + 6x$

12. $8a - 4a^2$
13. $7b^2y + 28b$
14. $9ax^2 + 27bx$
15. $3ax + 6ax^2 - 2ax$
16. $6by - 12b^2y + 7by^2$
17. $4ap^2 + 6a^2pq + 8apq^2$
18. $12p^2r^2 - 8p^3r + 24pr^2$
19. $a^2 - b^2$

20. $p^2 - r^2$
21. $x^2 - 4$
22. $a^2 - 16$
23. $y^2 - 81$
24. $m^2 - 49$
25. $4x^2 - 9$
26. $49y^2 - 64$
27. $9a^4 - b^2$
28. $16t^6 - a^2$
29. $25a^2 - 49b^2$
30. $121r^2 - 81t^2$

31. $144 - 25b^4$
32. $81 - 49r^4$
33. $5a^2 - 125$
34. $7x^2 - 63$
35. $28a^2 - 63b^4$
36. $81x^2 - 36t^6$
37. $a^4 - 81$
38. $b^4 - 256$
39. $16x^4 - 256y^4$
40. $25a^5 - 400ab^8$

Solve Exercises 41–50.

41. The total surface area of a cone is given by the formula $\pi r^2 + \pi r\sqrt{h^2 + r^2}$, where r is the radius of the base and h is the height of the cone. Factor this expression.

42. **Thermodynamics** The amount of heat that must be added to a metal object in order for it to melt is given by the formula $Q = mc\Delta t + mL_f$. Factor the right side of this equation.

43. **Wastewater technology** According to Bernoulli's equation, if a fluid of density d is flowing horizontally in a pipe and its pressure and velocity at one location are p_1 and v_1, respectively, and at a second location, they are p_2 and v_2, then the difference in their pressures is given by $p_1 - p_2 = \frac{1}{2}dv_2^2 - \frac{1}{2}dv_1^2$. Factor the right-hand side of this equation.

44. The cross-sectional area A of a tube can be determined from the formula $A = \pi R^2 - \pi r^2$, where R is the outside radius and r is the inside radius of the tube. Factor the right-hand side of this equation.

45. **Acoustical engineering** The angular acceleration α of a stereo turntable during a time period can be determined using the formula
$$\alpha = \frac{\omega_f^2 - \omega_0^2}{2\theta}$$
where ω_0 is the angular velocity at the beginning of the time interval, ω_f is the angular velocity at the end of the time interval, and θ is the number of radians the turntable rotated during the interval. Factor the right-hand side of this equation.

46. *Thermodynamics* A black body is a hypothetical body that absorbs, without reflection, all of the electromagnetic radiation that strikes its surface. The energy E radiated by a black body is given by $E = e\sigma T^4 - e\sigma T_0{}^4$, where T and T_0 are the absolute temperatures of the body and the surroundings, respectively, σ is the Stefan-Boltzmann constant, and e is the emissivity of the body. Factor the right-hand side of this equation.

47. *Energy* The work-energy equation for rotational motion is

$$W = \tfrac{1}{2}I\omega_2{}^2 - \tfrac{1}{2}I\omega_1{}^2$$

Factor the right-hand side of this equation.

48. *Optics* The *lensmaker's equation*

$$f^{-1} = nr_1{}^{-1} - nr_2{}^{-1} - r_1{}^{-1} + r_2{}^{-1}$$

gives the focal length f of a very thin lens.

(a) Rewrite the lensmaker's equation by factoring the right-hand side.

(b) Write your answer in (a) using only positive exponents.

49. *Environmental technology* At a certain time a circular oil spill has a radius of r meters. Some time later the radius has increased by 45 m. The change in the area of this spill is given by

$$\Delta A = \pi(r + 45)^2 - \pi r^2$$

Simplify and factor this expression.

50. *Metallurgy* The volume of the washer in Figure 7.3 is given by the formula

$$V = \pi r_2{}^2 h - \pi r_1{}^2 h$$

Factor this expression.

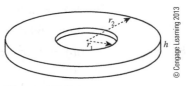

© Cengage Learning 2013

Figure 7.3

 [IN YOUR WORDS]

51. Explain how you recognize when an expression is a difference of two squares and then how you would factor it.

52. Describe what you look for when removing a common factor.

7.3 FACTORING TRINOMIALS

In Section 7.2, we introduced the idea of factoring and learned how to factor two types of problems. These problems were based on the first two special products that we learned in Section 7.1.

An algebraic expression that has three terms is called a **trinomial**. Special products #3 through #6 all resulted in quadratic trinomials. In this section we will focus on factoring quadratic trinomials with the purpose of reversing one of these four special products.

Not all quadratic trinomials can be factored using real numbers. The general quadratic trinomial is of the form $ax^2 + bx + c$, where a, b, and c represent constants.

NOTE You can determine if a quadratic trinomial can be factored by examining the discriminant $b^2 - 4ac$. If the discriminant is a perfect square, then it is possible to factor the quadratic using rational numbers.

DISCRIMINANT

The **discriminant** of the trinomial $ax^2 + bx + c$ is $b^2 - 4ac$.

If $b^2 - 4ac > 0$, then $ax^2 + bx + c$ can be factored using real numbers.

If $b^2 - 4ac$ is a perfect square, then $ax^2 + bx + c$ can be factored using rational numbers.

If $b^2 - 4ac < 0$, then $ax^2 + bx + c$ cannot be factored using real numbers.

EXAMPLE 7.28

Can the trinomial $4x^2 + 3x - 7$ be factored?

SOLUTION In this quadratic trinomial $a = 4$, $b = 3$, and $c = -7$, so
$$\begin{aligned} b^2 - 4ac &= (3)^2 - 4(4)(-7) \\ &= 9 - (-112) \\ &= 121 \end{aligned}$$

Using our knowledge (or a calculator) we see that $\sqrt{121} = 11$, so this trinomial can be factored using rational numbers. Later in this section, our job will be to find its factors.

EXAMPLE 7.29

Can the quadratic trinomial $5x^2 - 3x - 7$ be factored?

SOLUTION Here $a = 5$, $b = -3$, and $c = -7$, so
$$\begin{aligned} b^2 - 4ac &= (-3)^2 - 4(5)(-7) \\ &= 9 - (-140) \\ &= 149 \end{aligned}$$

Using a calculator, we find that $\sqrt{149} \approx 12.207$ and is not a perfect square. Thus, it is possible to factor this quadratic equation with real numbers.

We will skip special products #3 and #4 and consider special product #5: $(x + a)(x + b) = x^2 + (a + b)x + ab$. If you examine special products #3 and #4 you can see that they are just special cases of #5. In the special product where $(x + a)(x + b) = x^2 + (a + b)x + ab$, the leading coefficient (the coefficient of the x^2 term) is 1. This makes the job of factoring somewhat easier, because all we need to do is determine a and b. Notice that $a + b$ is the coefficient of the x-term and ab is the constant. Thus, we have the reverse of special product #5.

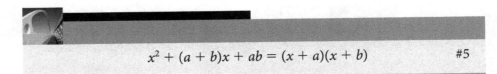

$$x^2 + (a + b)x + ab = (x + a)(x + b) \qquad \#5$$

Of course, the difficulty is determining the values of a and b.

EXAMPLE 7.30

Factor $x^2 - 3x - 10$.

SOLUTION Since the value of the discriminant is $49 = 7^2$, we know that this can be factored using rational numbers. From the formula in special product #5, we know that it factors into $(x + a)(x + b)$, where $a + b = -3$ and $ab = -10$.

What possible choices are there for a and b? From the factors of -10 we have the following four possible pairs.

Possible pairs of factors that satisfy $ab = -10$		Sum $(a + b)$
-10	and 1	-9
10	and -1	9
-5	and 2	-3
5	and -2	3

© Cengage Learning 2013

As you can see, only one of these pairs adds to -3, the pair of -5 and 2. So, if we let $a = -5$ and $b = 2$, then we have

$$x^2 - 3x - 10 = (x - 5)(x + 2)$$
$$= (x + 2)(x - 5)$$

EXAMPLE 7.31

Factor $x^2 + 10x + 16$.

SOLUTION The discriminant is 36, a perfect square, so this can be factored using rational numbers into the form $(x + a)(x + b)$. We want to find a and b so that $a + b = 10$ and $ab = 16$. Again, we will begin with the factors of the product $ab = 16$.

Possible pairs of factors that satisfy $ab = 16$		Sum $(a + b)$
16	and 1	17
-16	and -1	-17
8	and 2	10
-8	and -2	
4	and 4	
-4	and -4	

© Cengage Learning 2013

We stopped once we saw that the pairs of 8 and 2 added to 10, because we had found the pair that worked. If we let $a = 8$ and $b = 2$, we have factored the trinomial as

$$x^2 + 10x + 16 = (x + 8)(x + 2)$$
$$= (x + 2)(x + 8)$$

A check to see if the constant is positive or negative will give you some help in factoring. If the constant is positive, then the factors will have the same sign—both will be positive or both negative. If the constant term is negative, then the two factors will have different or unlike signs—one will be positive and the other negative.

EXAMPLE 7.32

Factor each trinomial completely.
  Here the constant term is positive.

(a) $x^2 + 7x + 12 = (x + 4)(x + 3)$ Both factors have positive signs.
(b) $x^2 - 7x + 12 = (x - 4)(x - 3)$ Both factors have negative signs.

© Cengage Learning 2013

Here the constant term is negative.

(c) $x^2 + x - 12 = (x + 4)(x - 3)$ } Factors have unlike signs—one
(d) $x^2 - x - 12 = (x - 4)(x + 3)$ } is positive and one is negative.

© Cengage Learning 2013

Factoring a quadratic trinomial with a leading coefficient that is not 1 is not as easy. Here we are looking at the reverse of special product #6, or

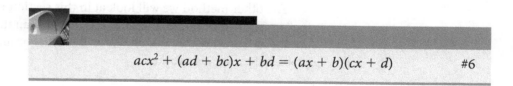

$$acx^2 + (ad + bc)x + bd = (ax + b)(cx + d) \qquad \#6$$

There are three techniques used to factor these quadratic trinomials. We will look at two of them in this section and examine the third in Section 7.4.

The first technique is called trial and error. In using the trial-and-error method, we make use of the fact that ac is the leading coefficient, bd is the constant term, and $ad + bc$ is the middle coefficient. We can also use our knowledge of signs to help find the signs of the factors.

EXAMPLE 7.33

Factor $3x^2 - 8x + 4$.

SOLUTION The discriminant is $16 = 4^2$, so this equation will factor using rational numbers. Since 3 is a prime number, we know that its only factors are 3 and 1. Also, since the constant is positive, both factors have the same sign. Thus, we know that the factors are $(3x + b)(x + d)$. Now, all we need to find are b and d.

Since $bd = 4$, the possible pairs of factors are -4, -1; 4, 1; 2, 2; and -2, -2. Next, we know that $3d + b = -8$ and the only choices from the pairs of factors that satisfy this are $b = -2$ and $d = -2$. Thus, the factors of $3x^2 - 8x + 4$ are $(3x - 2)(x - 2)$. You should multiply these factors together to check that their product is the original trinomial.

EXAMPLE 7.34

Factor $6x^2 + 7x - 20$.

SOLUTION The discriminant is $529 = 23^2$, so this equation will factor using rational numbers. The leading coefficient, 6, has factors of 6 and 1, and 2 and 3. We will try 6 and 1.

Since the constant term is negative, the factors will have unlike signs. Thus, we have $(6x + b)(x + d)$, where either b or d is negative, $bd = -20$, and $6d + b = 7$. The possible choices for the pairs b and d are 1, 20; 2, 10; and 4, 5, where one is positive and the other is negative.

If we try $b = 4$ and $d = -5$, we get $6(-5) + 4 = -26$. Since this is not 7, this is not the correct solution. All other possible combinations for b and d also fail. Thus, we must make another choice for a and c.

If $a = 2$ and $c = 3$, we have $(2x + b)(3x + d)$. If $b = 5$ and $d = -4$, we get $ad + bc = 2(-4) + (5)(3) = -8 + 15 = 7$. This is the correct coefficient for the x-term, so the factors of $6x^2 + 7x - 20$ are $(2x + 5)$ and $(3x - 4)$.

As you can see, the trial-and-error method can be very long and frustrating, but some people learn to factor a quadratic trinomial quickly by using this method.

The other method we will look at in this section is called either the "grouping" or "split-the-middle" method. It is longer than the trial-and-error method, but it is a "sure-fire" technique. We will use the grouping method on the same problem that we just worked.

EXAMPLE 7.35

Factor $6x^2 + 7x - 20$ using the grouping method.

SOLUTION

Step 1: Multiply the leading coefficient and the constant term: $(6)(-20) = -120$.

Step 2: Find two factors of this product whose sum is the coefficient of the middle term of the trinomial. For this problem we want to find factors p and q, where $pq = -120$ and $p + q = 7$. We get $p = 15$ and $q = -8$.

Step 3: Rewrite the trinomial by splitting the middle term into $px + qx$ and grouping the first two terms and the last two terms. In this problem, $7x = 15x - 8x$ and the trinomial becomes $(6x^2 + 15x) + (-8x - 20)$.

Step 4: Distribute the common factors from each grouping.
$$(6x^2 + 15x) + (-8x - 20) = 3x(2x + 5) - 4(2x + 5)$$

Step 5: Distribute the common factor $2x + 5$ from the entire expression.
$$3x(2x + 5) - 4(2x + 5) = (3x - 4)(2x + 5)$$

These are the required factors. Thus, we have factored $6x^2 + 7x - 20$ as $(3x - 4)(2x + 5)$.

EXAMPLE 7.36

Factor $21x^2 - 41x + 10$ using the grouping method.

SOLUTION

Step 1: $(21)(10) = 210$

Step 2: $210 = (-35)(-6)$ and $-35 - 6 = -41$

Step 3: $(21x^2 - 35x) + (-6x + 10)$

Step 4: $7x(3x - 5) - 2(3x - 5)$

Step 5: $(7x - 2)(3x - 5)$

 NOTE Remember to look for any common factors before you start to use either the trial-and-error or the grouping method.

EXAMPLE 7.37

Factor $20x^3 + 22x^2 - 12x$.

SOLUTION There is a common factor of $2x$, so
$$20x^3 + 22x^2 - 12x = 2x(10x^2 + 11x - 6)$$
$$= 2x(5x - 2)(2x + 3)$$

Not all trinomials have just one variable. The grouping method is the best method to use when factoring trinomials that have more than one variable. For example, as shown in the next example, $2x^2 - 17xy + 36y^2$ can be factored using the grouping method.

EXAMPLE 7.38

Factor $2x^2 - 17xy + 36y^2$ completely.

SOLUTION

Step 1: $2x^2(36y^2) = 72x^2y^2$

Step 2: $72x^2y^2 = (-9xy)(-8xy)$ and $-9xy - 8xy = -17xy$

Step 3: $(2x^2 - 9xy) + (-8xy + 36y^2)$

EXAMPLE 7.38 (Cont.)

Step 4: $x(2x - 9y) - 4y(2x - 9y)$

Step 5: $(x - 4y)(2x - 9y)$

As a check, multiplying the two factors in Step 5 gives the original expression, and so we can say that $2x^2 - 17xy + 36y^2 = (x - 4y)(2x - 9y)$.

It is also possible to factor trinomials with powers greater than 2 if one exponent is twice the other.

EXAMPLE 7.39

Factor $x^8 + 5x^4 + 6$.

SOLUTION $x^8 + 5x^4 + 6 = (x^4)^2 + 5x^4 + 6$
$$= (x^4 + 3)(x^4 + 2)$$

Two other useful methods are based on special products #9 and #10. These are the sum and difference of two cubes.

SUM OF TWO CUBES
$$(x + y)(x^2 - xy + y^2) = x^3 + y^3 \qquad \text{\#9}$$

DIFFERENCE OF TWO CUBES
$$(x - y)(x^2 + xy + y^2) = x^3 - y^3 \qquad \text{\#10}$$

EXAMPLE 7.40

Factor $8x^3 + 125$.

SOLUTION $8x^3 = (2x)^3$ and $125 = 5^3$, so this is the sum of two cubes, and $8x^3 + 125 = (2x)^3 + 5^3 = (2x + 5)(4x^2 - 10x + 25)$.

 APPLICATION MECHANICAL

EXAMPLE 7.41

The volume V of a box of height x can be given by $V(x) = 4x^3 - 64x^2 + 252x$. Factor the right-hand side of this equation to determine the "realistic" domain for the height x.

SOLUTION First, we notice that each term on the right-hand side of $V(x) = 4x^3 - 64x^2 + 252x$ has a common factor of $4x$. So, $V(x) = 4x(x^2 - 16x + 63)$. The quadratic expression factors as $x^2 - 16x + 63 = (x - 9)(x - 7)$. So, the completely factored form is

$$V(x) = 4x(x - 9)(x - 7)$$

From this, we see that the domain is $0 < x < 7$ or $x > 9$. We will see later that $x > 9$ will not satisfy many methods used to make such a box.

The six special factors are listed here. Study them, and learn to recognize them either as factors or as one of the special factors.

THE SPECIAL FACTORS

$ax + ay = a(x + y)$	#1
$x^2 - y^2 = (x + y)(x - y)$	#2
$x^2 + (a + b)x + ab = (x + a)(x + b)$	#5
$acx^2 + (ad + bc)x + bd = (ax + b)(cx + d)$	#6
$x^3 + y^3 = (x + y)(x^2 - xy + y^2)$	#9
$x^3 - y^3 = (x - y)(x^2 + xy + y^2)$	#10

EXERCISE SET 7.3

Determine if each of the trinomials in Exercises 1–6 can be factored.

1. $x^2 + 9x - 8$
2. $x^2 + 7x - 8$
3. $3x^2 - 10x - 8$
4. $2x^2 + 16x + 14$
5. $5x^2 + 23x + 18$
6. $7x^2 - 5x + 16$

Factor each of the following trinomials completely.

7. $x^2 + 7x + 10$
8. $x^2 + 8x + 15$
9. $x^2 - 12x + 27$
10. $x^2 - 14x + 33$
11. $x^2 - 27x + 50$
12. $x^2 + 19x + 48$
13. $x^2 - x - 2$
14. $x^2 - 4x - 5$
15. $x^2 - 3x - 10$

16. $p^2 - 16p + 64$
17. $r^2 + 10r + 25$
18. $v^2 - 14v + 49$
19. $a^2 + 22a + 121$
20. $e^2 + 26e + 169$
21. $f^2 - 30f + 225$
22. $3x^2 + 4x + 1$
23. $6y^2 - 7y + 1$
24. $3p^2 + 5p + 2$

25. $7t^2 + 9t + 2$
26. $5a^2 + 14a - 3$
27. $7b^2 - 34b - 5$
28. $2y^2 + y - 6$
29. $4e^2 + 19e - 5$
30. $6m^2 - 19m + 3$
31. $3u^2 + 10u + 8$
32. $7r^2 + 13r - 2$
33. $9t^2 - 25t - 6$

34. $4x^2 + 8x + 3$

35. $6x^2 + 13x - 5$

36. $8y^2 - 8y - 6$

37. $15a^2 - 16a - 15$

38. $15d^2 + 16d - 15$

39. $15e^2 + 34e + 15$

40. $14a^2 - 39a + 10$

41. $10x^2 - 19x + 6$

42. $3x^2 + 18x + 27$

43. $3r^2 - 18r - 21$

44. $15x^2 + 50x + 35$

45. $49t^4 - 105t^3 + 14t^2$

46. $2y^4 - 9y^2 + 7$

47. $6x^2 - 11xy - 10y^2$

48. $4p^2 + 20pq + 25q^2$

49. $8a^2 - 14ab - 9b^2$

50. $6d^9 + 15d^5e^2 + 6de^4$

51. $a^3 - b^3$

52. $y^3 - 8$

53. $8x^3 - 27$

54. $64p^3 + 125t^6$

Solve Exercises 55–62.

55. *Electronics* The current i, in amperes, in a certain circuit varies with time, in seconds, according to the equation

$$i = 0.7t^2 - 2.1t - 2.8$$

Factor the right-hand side of this equation.

56. *Sheet metal technology* A box with an open top is made from a rectangular sheet of metal by cutting equal-sized squares from the corners and folding up the sides. If the length of the side of a square that is removed is x, then the volume of this box is given by $V = 180x - 58x^2 + 4x^3$. Factor this expression.

57. *Business* The cost C for a certain company to produce n items is given by the equation $C(n) = 0.0001n^3 - 0.2n^2 - 3n + 6{,}000$. Factor the right-hand side of this equation.

58. *Dynamics* A ball is thrown upward with a speed of 48 ft/s from the edge of a cliff 448 ft above the ground. The distance s of this ball above the ground at any time t is given by $s(t) = -16t^2 + 48t + 448$. Factor the right-hand side of this equation.

59. *Ecology* An ecology center wants to make an experimental garden. A gravel border of uniform width will be placed around the rectangular garden. The garden is 10 m long and 6 m wide. The builder has only enough gravel to cover 36 m² to the desired depth. In order to determine the width of the border, the equation

$$(6 + 2x)(10 + 2x) - 60 = 36$$

must be solved. **(a)** Simplify this equation and **(b)** factor your answer.

60. *Fire science* The flow rate, Q, in a certain hose can be found by solving the equation $2Q^2 + Q - 21 = 0$. Factor the left-hand side of this equation.

61. *Industrial design* A pizza box is to be made from a rectangular piece of cardboard that measures $18'' \times 36''$. In order for the cardboard to fold into a box with a lid, six squares are cut from the cardboard as shown in Figure 7.4. The volume of the box depends on the size of the six squares and is given by

$$V = 324x - 63.0x^2 + 3.0x^3$$

Factor the right-hand side of this equation.

62. *Civil engineering* The deflection, Δ, of a certain beam is given by the equation

$$\delta = 9x^2 - 30xL + 24L^2$$

Factor the right-hand side of this equation.

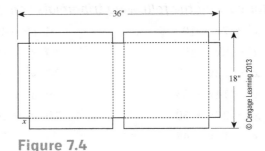

Figure 7.4

[IN YOUR WORDS]

63. Explain how to use the discriminant to find if a trinomial can be factored by **(a)** rational numbers and **(b)** real numbers.

64. Explain how you recognize when an expression is a difference of two cubes and then how you would factor it.

 7.4 **FRACTIONS**

Working with algebraic expressions in technical situations often requires work with algebraic fractions. Working with algebraic fractions is very similar to working with fractions based on real numbers. In this section, we will work with some fundamental properties of fractions, and in Sections 7.5 and 7.6 we will use these properties on the basic operations of addition, subtraction, multiplication, and division with fractions. We begin by stating the Fundamental Principle of Fractions.

FUNDAMENTAL PRINCIPLE OF FRACTIONS

Multiplying or dividing both the numerator and denominator of a fraction by the same number, except zero, results in a fraction that is equivalent to the original fraction. Two fractions are equivalent if their cross-products are equal.

EXAMPLE 7.42

Since $\frac{3}{4} = \frac{3 \cdot 5}{4 \cdot 5} = \frac{15}{20}$ then the fractions $\frac{15}{20}$ and $\frac{3}{4}$ are equivalent by the Fundamental Principle of Fractions.

You can check their cross-products to verify that $\frac{3}{4}$ and $\frac{15}{20}$ are equivalent. Since $(3)(20) = 60$ and $(4)(15) = 60$, their cross-products are equal and the fractions are equivalent.

EXAMPLE 7.43

$$\frac{a}{x} = \frac{a(xy)}{x(xy)} = \frac{axy}{x^2y}$$

SOLUTION We can verify that $\dfrac{a}{x} = \dfrac{axy}{x^2y}$ by comparing their cross-products:

$$a(x^2y) = ax^2y \qquad \text{and} \qquad x(axy) = ax^2y$$

Since the cross-products are equal, the fractions are equivalent as well.

EXAMPLE 7.44

$$\frac{x + 3}{x - 2} = \frac{(x + 3)(x - 3)}{(x - 2)(x - 3)} = \frac{x^2 - 9}{x^2 - 5x + 6}$$

As long as $x \neq 3$, we can say that $\dfrac{x + 3}{x - 2} = \dfrac{x^2 - 9}{x^2 - 5x + 6}$.

Saying that two fractions are equivalent is another way of saying that they represent the same number. Remembering the rules for signed numbers in Section 1.2, we stated that the number of negative signs can be reduced (or increased) by twos without changing the value of the expression. The Fundamental Principle of Fractions says essentially the same thing:

EXAMPLE 7.45

$$\frac{-a}{b} = \frac{-a(-1)}{b(-1)} = \frac{a}{-b}$$

One of the most important applications of the Fundamental Principle of Fractions is in reducing a fraction to *lowest terms* or *simplest form*. A fraction is in lowest terms when the numerator and denominator have no factors in common other than $+1$.

EXAMPLE 7.46

Reduce $\dfrac{14\,ab^2x}{7ax^3}$ to simplest form.

SOLUTION The numerator and denominator have a common factor of $7ax$. We can then write $\dfrac{14ab^2x}{7ax^3} = \dfrac{7ax(2b^2)}{7ax(x^2)} = \dfrac{2b^2}{x^2}$. Notice that we used a part of the Fundamental Principle of Fractions that we had not used before. We *divided* both the numerator and the denominator by $7ax$, the common factor.

EXAMPLE 7.47

Reduce $\dfrac{x^2(x - 3)}{x^2 - 9}$ to lowest terms.

SOLUTION We need to find a common factor of both the numerator and the denominator; x^2 is *not* that common factor. While x^2 is a factor of the numerator, it is not a factor of the denominator. However, the denominator will factor into $(x - 3)(x + 3)$, so

$$\frac{x^2(x - 3)}{x^2 - 9} = \frac{x^2(x - 3)}{(x - 3)(x + 3)} = \frac{x^2}{x + 3}$$

Again, we used the Fundamental Principle of Fractions and divided both the numerator and denominator by $x - 3$.

NOTE Some factors differ only in sign. Although this difference may not seem like much, it is often overlooked. In particular, you should note that

$$x - y = (-1)(-x + y) = -(-x + y) = -(y - x)$$

Of these four, the first and last are the ones you will use the most. Remember, $x - y$ and $y - x$ differ only in sign.

EXAMPLE 7.48

Reduce $\dfrac{5x - xy}{3y - 15}$ to lowest terms.

SOLUTION First, factor the numerator and the denominator:

$$\frac{5x - xy}{3y - 15} = \frac{x(5 - y)}{3(y - 5)}$$

Since $5 - y = -(y - 5)$, replace $5 - y$ with $-(y - 5)$:

$$\frac{x(5 - y)}{3(y - 5)} = \frac{-x(y - 5)}{3(y - 5)} = \frac{-x}{3}$$

Is $\dfrac{-x}{3}$ equal to $\dfrac{5x - xy}{3y - 15}$? You can always verify your answer by checking the cross-products. In this case, the cross-products are equal.

EXAMPLE 7.49

Reduce $\dfrac{2x^3 + 4x^2 - 30x}{15x^2 + x^3 - 2x^4}$ to simplest form.

SOLUTION First remove the common factors:

$$\frac{2x^3 + 4x^2 - 30x}{15x^2 + x^3 - 2x^4} = \frac{2x(x^2 + 2x - 15)}{x^2(15 + x - 2x^2)}$$

Factor each of the expressions in parentheses:

$$\frac{2x(x^2 + 2x - 15)}{x^2(15 + x - 2x^2)} = \frac{2x(x + 5)(x - 3)}{x^2(5 + 2x)(3 - x)}$$

Notice that $x - 3 = -(3 - x)$ and rewrite the numerator:

$$\frac{-2x(x + 5)(3 - x)}{x^2(5 + 2x)(3 - x)}$$

Divide both numerator and denominator by $x(3 - x)$, obtaining

$$\frac{-2x(x + 5)(3 - x)}{x^2(5 + 2x)(3 - x)} = \frac{-2(x + 5)}{x(5 + 2x)}$$

and we have the final result:

$$\frac{2x^3 + 4x^2 - 30x}{15x^2 + x^3 - 2x^4} = \frac{-2(x + 5)}{x(5 + 2x)}$$

EXERCISE SET 7.4

In Exercises 1–10, multiply the numerator and denominator of each fraction by the given factor. Check the cross-products to verify that your answer is equivalent to the given fraction.

1. $\frac{7}{8}$ (by 5)

2. $\frac{-5}{9}$ (by −4)

3. $\frac{x}{y}$ (by a)

4. $\frac{r}{t}$ (by z)

5. $\frac{x^2 y}{a}$ (by $3ax$)

6. $\frac{a^3 b}{ca}$ (by $3ab$)

7. $\frac{4}{x - y}$ (by $x + y$)

8. $\frac{a + b}{4}$ (by $a - 4$)

9. $\frac{a + b}{a - b}$ (by $a + b$)

10. $\frac{x - 2}{x + 3}$ (by $x - 3$)

In Exercises 11–18, divide the numerator and denominator of each of the fractions by the given factor. Check the cross-products to verify that your answer is equivalent to the given fraction.

11. $\frac{38}{24}$ (by 2)

12. $\frac{51}{119}$ (by 17)

13. $\frac{3x^2}{12x}$ (by $3x$)

14. $\frac{15a^3 x^2}{3a^4 x}$ (by $3a^3 x$)

15. $\frac{4(x + 2)}{(x + 2)(x - 3)}$ (by $x + 2$)

16. $\frac{7(x - 3)(x + 5)}{14(x + 5)(x - 1)}$ [by $7(x + 5)$]

17. $\frac{x^2 - 16}{x^2 + 8x + 16}$ (by $x + 4$)

18. $\frac{(x - a)(x - b)(x - c)}{(x - c)(x - b)(x - d)}$ [by $(x - c)(x - b)$]

In Exercises 19–40, reduce each fraction to lowest terms.

19. $\frac{4x^2}{12x}$

20. $\frac{9y}{3y^2}$

21. $\frac{x^2 + 3x}{x^3 + 5x}$

22. $\frac{y^2 - 4y}{2y + y^3}$

23. $\frac{6m^2 - 3m^3}{9m + 18m^3}$

24. $\frac{4r^2 + 12r^3}{8r + 12r^2}$

25. $\frac{x^2 + 3x}{x^2 - 9}$

26. $\frac{a^2 - 9a}{a^2 - 81}$

27. $\frac{2b^2 - 10b}{3b^2 - 75}$

28. $\frac{4e^2 - 196}{14e - 2e^2}$

29. $\frac{z^2 - 9}{z^2 - 6z + 9}$

30. $\frac{x^2 - 16}{x^2 + 8x + 16}$

31. $\frac{x^2 + 4x + 3}{x^2 + 7x + 12}$

32. $\frac{a^2 - 5a + 6}{a^2 + 5a - 14}$

33. $\frac{2x^2 + 9x + 4}{x^2 + 9x + 20}$

34. $\frac{15m^2 - 22m - 5}{3m^2 + 4m - 15}$

35. $\frac{12y^3 + 12y^2 + 3y}{6y^2 - 3y - 3}$

36. $\frac{45x^2 - 60x + 20}{6x^2 + 5x - 6}$

37. $\frac{x^3 y^6 - y^3 x^6}{2x^3 y^4 - 2x^4 y^3}$

38. $\frac{x^3 - y^3}{y^2 - x^2}$

39. $\frac{x^2 - y^2}{x + y}$

40. $\frac{y - x}{x^2 - y^2}$

Solve Exercises 41–44.

41. Construction The safe load, p (in pounds), when using a drop hammer pile driver, can be determined by the formula:

$$p = \frac{6whs + 6wh}{3s^2 + 6s + 3}$$

Simplify this expression.

42. Construction The safe load, p (in pounds), when using a steam pile driver, can be determined by the formula:

$$p = \frac{2whs + 2whk + 2amhs + 2amhk - 2bhs - 2bhk}{s^2 + 2sk + k^2}$$

Simplify this expression.

43. Physics The change in volume, ΔV, of a gas under constant pressure involves the equation:

$$\Delta V = V_1\left(1 + \frac{T_2 - T_1}{T_1}\right) - V_2\left(\frac{T_2 - T_1}{T_2} - 1\right)$$

Simplify the right-hand side of this equation.

44. Physics Suppose that two elastic bodies with masses m and m_0, respectively, collide. If each body was moving at velocity v toward the other before the collision, then the rebound velocity of the body with mass m_0 is given by

$$\left(\frac{m}{m + m_0} - \frac{m_0}{m + m_0}\right)v + \frac{2vm_0}{m + m_0}$$

Simplify this expression.

 [IN YOUR WORDS]

45. Explain the Fundamental Principle of Fractions.

46. Describe how to use the Fundamental Principle of Fractions to simplify a fraction.

7.5 MULTIPLICATION AND DIVISION OF FRACTIONS

The ability to simplify fractions is a skill that will be helpful in this section and the next, as we learn to operate with fractions. After that, it is a skill that will be required throughout this book.

In Section 1.2, we learned the basic operations with real numbers. Among those were Rules 7 and 8, which dealt with multiplying and dividing rational numbers. To refresh your memory, they are repeated here.

RULE 7

To multiply two rational numbers, multiply the numerators and multiply the denominators.

EXAMPLE 7.50

$$\frac{3}{4} \times \frac{-5}{8} = \frac{3 \times (-5)}{4 \times 8} = \frac{-15}{32}$$

RULE 8

To divide one rational number by another, multiply the first by the reciprocal of the second.

EXAMPLE 7.51

Compute $\dfrac{-5}{8} \div \dfrac{2}{3}$.

SOLUTION The reciprocal of $\frac{2}{3}$ is $\frac{3}{2}$, so

$$\frac{-5}{8} \div \frac{2}{3} = \frac{-5}{8} \times \frac{3}{2} = \frac{(-5)(3)}{(8)(2)} = \frac{-15}{16}$$

NOTE You do not need common denominators when multiplying or dividing two rational numbers.

If we express these two rules symbolically, we will have the rules for multiplying or dividing any two fractions, whether they are rational numbers or algebraic fractions. The rule for multiplying two rational numbers can be restated as the following.

MULTIPLYING FRACTIONS

If $\dfrac{a}{b}$ and $\dfrac{c}{d}$ are fractions, then their product is

$$\frac{a}{b} \cdot \frac{c}{d} = \frac{ac}{bd}$$

Similarly, we can state the following rule for dividing one rational number by another.

DIVIDING FRACTIONS

If $\dfrac{a}{b}$ and $\dfrac{c}{d}$ are fractions, then their quotient is

$$\frac{a}{b} \div \frac{c}{d} = \frac{a}{b} \times \frac{d}{c} = \frac{ad}{bc}$$

EXAMPLE 7.52

Find the product of $\dfrac{3a^2}{x}$ and $\dfrac{7y}{5p^3}$.

SOLUTION $\dfrac{3a^2}{x} \cdot \dfrac{7y}{5p^3} = \dfrac{(3a^2)(7y)}{(x)(5p^3)} = \dfrac{21a^2y}{5xp^3}$

EXAMPLE 7.53

Find the product of $\dfrac{x-2}{x+3}$ and $\dfrac{x+2}{x-5}$.

SOLUTION $\dfrac{x-2}{x+3} \cdot \dfrac{x+2}{x-5} = \dfrac{(x-2)(x+2)}{(x+3)(x-5)}$

$= \dfrac{x^2-4}{x^2-2x-15}$

EXAMPLE 7.54

Find the quotient when $\dfrac{7x^2}{3a}$ is divided by $\dfrac{5y}{4x}$.

SOLUTION $\dfrac{7x^2}{3a} \div \dfrac{5y}{4x} = \dfrac{7x^2}{3a} \cdot \dfrac{4x}{5y}$

$= \dfrac{(7x^2)(4x)}{(3a)(5y)}$

$= \dfrac{28x^3}{15ay}$

EXAMPLE 7.55

Find $\dfrac{x-2}{x+3} \div \dfrac{x-4}{x-3}$.

SOLUTION $\dfrac{x-2}{x+3} \div \dfrac{x-4}{x-3} = \dfrac{x-2}{x+3} \cdot \dfrac{x-3}{x-4} = \dfrac{(x-2)(x-3)}{(x+3)(x-4)}$

$= \dfrac{x^2-5x+6}{x^2-x-12}$

 NOTE It is often beneficial to leave the answer in factored form. For example, in Example 7.55, you might have wanted to leave the answer as $\dfrac{(x-2)(x-3)}{(x+3)(x-4)}$. This version has two multiplication operations, one division operation, three subtraction operations, and one addition operation, for a total of seven operations. The answer $\dfrac{x^2-5x+6}{x^2-x-12}$ has 3 multiplication operations, one division operation, three subtractions, and one addition, for a total of eight operations. In computer programming, more operations require more computer time, which costs more money.

CAUTION When you divide, make sure that you multiply by the reciprocal of the *divisor*. Do not invert the dividend.

The following examples use all of the skills we have learned for simplifying fractions.

EXAMPLE 7.56

Multiply $\dfrac{x^2 - 9}{4x - 8}$ and $\dfrac{2x + 8}{x + 3}$.

SOLUTION If we proceed as before, we get

$$\frac{x^2 - 9}{4x - 8} \cdot \frac{2x + 8}{x + 3} = \frac{(x^2 - 9)(2x + 8)}{(4x - 8)(x + 3)} = \frac{2x^3 + 8x^2 - 18x - 72}{4x^2 + 4x - 24}$$

Although this is correct, it is not the easiest approach. It is a good idea to study a problem for a few seconds before you start to work it. If we had stopped to factor these fractions we could have saved some work:

$$\frac{x^2 - 9}{4x - 8} \cdot \frac{2x + 8}{x + 3} = \frac{(x + 3)(x - 3)}{4(x - 2)} \cdot \frac{2(x + 4)}{(x + 3)}$$

$$= \frac{2(x + 3)(x - 3)(x + 4)}{4(x - 2)(x + 3)}$$

$$= \frac{(x - 3)(x + 4)}{2(x - 2)}$$

or $\qquad\qquad = \dfrac{x^2 + x - 12}{2x - 4}$

EXAMPLE 7.57

Compute $\dfrac{2x^2 + 9x - 5}{3x^2 - 3x - 60} \cdot \dfrac{3x + 12}{2x + 10}$.

SOLUTION $\dfrac{2x^2 + 9x - 5}{3x^2 - 3x - 60} \cdot \dfrac{3x + 12}{2x + 10} = \dfrac{(2x - 1)(x + 5)(3)(x + 4)}{3(x - 5)(x + 4)(2)(x + 5)}$

$$= \frac{2x - 1}{2(x - 5)}$$

The common factor $3(x + 5)(x + 4)$ is easily seen using this procedure.

 CAUTION Be sure to factor the numerator and denominator first. Only common factors can be "canceled."

 HINT When a polynomial is factored, all the $+$ and $-$ signs are inside parentheses.

EXAMPLE 7.58

Compute $\dfrac{x^2 - 9}{6x^2 - 21x} \div \dfrac{(x + 3)^2}{2x - 7}$.

SOLUTION $\dfrac{x^2 - 9}{6x^2 - 21x} \div \dfrac{(x + 3)^2}{2x - 7} = \dfrac{x^2 - 9}{6x^2 - 21x} \cdot \dfrac{2x - 7}{(x + 3)^2}$

$= \dfrac{(x - 3)(x + 3)(2x - 7)}{3x(2x - 7)(x + 3)(x + 3)}$

$= \dfrac{x - 3}{3x(x + 3)} = \dfrac{x - 3}{3x^2 + 9x}$

There are times when it is just as useful to leave the final answer in the factored form rather than multiplying the factors together. Thus, we could have left the last answer in the form $\dfrac{x - 3}{3x(x + 3)}$.

EXAMPLE 7.59

Simplify $\dfrac{\dfrac{6x}{x^2 - 4}}{\dfrac{2x^2 + 10x}{x + 2}}$.

SOLUTION We have to remember that $\frac{a}{b}$ means $a \div b$. So, this is the division problem:

$\dfrac{6x}{x^2 - 4} \div \dfrac{2x^2 + 10x}{x + 2} = \dfrac{6x}{x^2 - 4} \cdot \dfrac{x + 2}{2x^2 + 10x}$

$= \dfrac{6x}{(x - 2)(x + 2)} \cdot \dfrac{x + 2}{2x(x + 5)}$

$= \dfrac{6x(x + 2)}{(x - 2)(x + 2)2x(x + 5)}$

$= \dfrac{3}{(x - 2)(x + 5)}$

EXERCISE SET 7.5

In Exercises 1–46, perform the indicated operation and simplify.

1. $\dfrac{2}{x} \cdot \dfrac{5}{y}$

2. $\dfrac{4}{y} \cdot \dfrac{x}{3}$

3. $\dfrac{4x^2}{5} \cdot \dfrac{3}{y^3}$

4. $\dfrac{7x}{6} \cdot \dfrac{5y}{2t}$

5. $\dfrac{3}{x} \div \dfrac{7}{y}$

6. $\dfrac{a}{3} \div \dfrac{b}{4}$

7. $\dfrac{2x^2}{3} \div \dfrac{7y}{4x}$

8. $\dfrac{9x}{2y} \div \dfrac{4y}{3a}$

9. $\dfrac{2x}{3y} \cdot \dfrac{5}{4x^2}$

10. $\dfrac{3xy}{7} \cdot \dfrac{14x}{5y^2}$

11. $\dfrac{3a^2b}{5d} \cdot \dfrac{25ad^2}{6b^2}$

12. $\dfrac{x^2y^2t}{abc} \cdot \dfrac{b^2c}{y^3t}$

13. $\dfrac{3y}{5x} \div \dfrac{15x^2}{8xy}$

14. $\dfrac{4y^2}{7x} \div \dfrac{8y^3}{21x}$

15. $\dfrac{3x^2y}{7p} \div \dfrac{15x^2p}{7y^2}$

16. $\dfrac{9xyz}{7a} \div \dfrac{3ayz}{14z}$

17. $\dfrac{4y + 16}{5} \cdot \dfrac{15y}{3y + 12}$

18. $\dfrac{x^2 + 3x}{6a} \cdot \dfrac{a^2}{x^2 - 9}$

19. $\dfrac{a^2 - b^2}{a + 3b} \cdot \dfrac{5a + 15b}{a + b}$

20. $(x + y)\dfrac{x^2 + 2x}{x^2 - y^2}$

21. $\dfrac{x^2 - 100}{10} \div \dfrac{2x + 10}{15}$

22. $\dfrac{5a^2}{x^2 - 49} \div \dfrac{25ax - 25a}{x^2 + 7x}$

23. $\dfrac{4x^2 - 1}{9x - 3x^2} \div \dfrac{2x + 1}{x^2 - 9}$

24. $\dfrac{x + y}{3x - 3y} \div \dfrac{(x + y)^2}{x^2 - y^2}$

25. $\dfrac{a^2 - 8a}{a - 8} \cdot \dfrac{a + 2}{a}$

26. $\dfrac{49 - x^2}{x + y} \cdot \dfrac{x}{7 - x}$

27. $\dfrac{2a - b}{4a} \cdot \dfrac{2a - b}{4a^2 - 4ab + b^2}$

28. $\dfrac{x^4 - 81}{(x - 3)^2} \cdot \dfrac{x - 3}{4 - x^2}$

29. $\dfrac{y^2}{x^2 - 1} \div \dfrac{y^2}{x - 1}$

30. $\dfrac{m^2 - 49}{m^2 - 5m - 14} \div \dfrac{m + 7}{2m^2 - 13m - 7}$

31. $\dfrac{2y^2 - y}{4y^2 - 4y + 1} \div \dfrac{y^2}{8y - 4}$

32. $\dfrac{a - 1}{a^2 - 1} \div \dfrac{(a - 1)^2}{a^2 - 1}$

33. $\dfrac{x^2 - 3x + 2}{x^2 + 5x + 6} \cdot \dfrac{x + 3}{3x - 6}$

34. $\dfrac{2x + 2}{x^2 + 2x - 8} \cdot \dfrac{x^2 - 4}{x^2 + 4x + 4}$

35. $\dfrac{x^2 + xy - 6y^2}{x^2 + 6xy + 8y^2} \cdot \dfrac{x^2 - 9xy + 20y^2}{x^2 - 4xy - 21y^2}$

36. $\dfrac{y^2 + 14xy + 49x^2}{y^2 - 7xy - 30x^2} \cdot \dfrac{y^2 - 100x^2}{y^3 + 7xy^2}$

37. $\dfrac{9x^2 - 25}{x^2 + 6x + 9} \div \dfrac{3x + 5}{x + 3}$

38. $\dfrac{x^2 - 16}{x^2 - 6x + 8} \div \dfrac{x^3 + 4x^2}{x^2 - 9x + 14}$

39. $\dfrac{x^2 + 4xy + 4y^2}{x^2 - 4y^2} \div \dfrac{x^2 + xy - 2y^2}{x^2 - xy - 2y^2}$

40. $\dfrac{p^3 - 27q^3}{3p^2 + 9pq + 27q^2} \div \dfrac{9q^2 - p^2}{6p + 18q}$

41. $\dfrac{x + y}{4x - 4y} \div \left[\dfrac{(x + y)^2}{x^2 - y^2} \cdot \dfrac{x^3 - y^3}{x^3 + y^3} \right]$

42. $\dfrac{2.4m^2n}{0.8mn^2} \div \left[\dfrac{0.6m}{0.3n} \cdot \dfrac{3.6m}{2.4n} \right]$

43. $\dfrac{x^2 - 25}{5x^2 - 24x - 5} \cdot \dfrac{2x^2 + 12x + 2}{6x^2 - 12x} \div \dfrac{x^2 + 6x + 1}{5x^2 - 9x - 2}$

44. $\dfrac{a - b}{a^3 - b^3} \cdot \dfrac{a^3 + ab^2}{4a + 4b} \div \dfrac{a^4 - b^4}{8a^2 - 8b^2}$

45. $\left(\dfrac{2x^2 - 5x - 3}{x^2 - x - 12} \div \dfrac{2x^2 + 5x + 2}{3x + 9} \right) \div \dfrac{x^2 - 9}{x^2 - 2x - 8}$

46. $\dfrac{a^2 + 4a - 5}{a^2 - 3a - 4} \cdot \dfrac{a^2 + 3a - 28}{(a - 3)^2} \div \dfrac{a^2 + 12a + 35}{a^2 - 2a - 3}$

Solve Exercises 47–50.

47. Construction The volume strain of a beam is given by the expression:

$$\frac{(a^3 - a'^3)/a^3}{(a^2 - a'^2)/a^2}$$

Simplify this expression.

48. Electronics The charge on a capacitor is given by $Q = CV$. The energy stored in the capacitor is given by $E = \dfrac{1Q^2}{2V}$. Find the ratio of charge to energy.

49. Physics The quotient

$$\frac{8\pi ne^2 w}{mv^2 - mvw^2} \div \frac{2mv^2 - 2\pi ne^2}{mv^2}$$

is used in the study of electromagnetic processes in space. Divide and simplify the expression.

50. Physics In a mass spectrometer the radius of curvature of a charged particle depends on its mass. If the instrument is properly calibrated, then measuring the radius allows the mass of small particles to be measured. The mass spectrometer uses the equation $R = \dfrac{my}{qB}$ and the frequency of oscillation is given by $f = \dfrac{v}{2\pi R}$. Substitute the value of R from the first equation into the second equation, and then divide and simplify the expression.

 [IN YOUR WORDS]

51. (a) Explain how to divide two fractions: $\dfrac{a}{b} \div \dfrac{c}{d}$.

(b) What do you think is the most common mistake people make when they divide two fractions?

52. (a) Explain how to multiply two fractions: $\dfrac{a}{b} \times \dfrac{c}{d}$.

(b) What do you think is the most common mistake people make when they multiply two fractions?

 **7.6   ADDITION AND SUBTRACTION OF FRACTIONS**

In Section 7.5, we learned how to multiply and divide two fractions. In this section, we will look at two other operations with fractions—addition and subtraction.

As we mentioned earlier, much of this work with algebraic fractions is patterned after our work with rational numbers from Section 1.2. Rule 6 dealt with the addition and subtraction of rational numbers. This rule is repeated here.

> ### RULE 6
>
> To add (or subtract) two rational numbers, change both denominators to the same positive integer (the common denominator), add (or subtract) the numerators, and place the result over the common denominator.

EXAMPLE 7.60

Perform the indicated operations and simplify (a) $\dfrac{2}{3} + \dfrac{-5}{6}$ and (b) $\dfrac{-5}{7} - \dfrac{-8}{3}$.

SOLUTIONS

(a) A common denominator of 3 and 6 is 6, so

$$\frac{2}{3} + \frac{-5}{6} = \frac{4}{6} + \frac{-5}{6} = \frac{4 + (-5)}{6} = \frac{-1}{6}$$

(b) A common denominator of 7 and 3 is 21, so

$$\frac{-5}{7} = \frac{-15}{21} \quad \text{and} \quad \frac{-8}{3} = \frac{-56}{21}$$

As a result, we obtain

$$\frac{-5}{7} - \frac{-8}{3} = \frac{-15}{21} - \frac{-56}{21} = \frac{-15 - (-56)}{21} = \frac{41}{21}$$

Before we restate Rule 6 in symbols, we will consider a special case of adding or subtracting fractions. If two fractions have the same denominator, then you need only add or subtract the numerators. Symbolically, this is represented as

$$\frac{a}{c} + \frac{b}{c} = \frac{a + b}{c} \quad \text{and} \quad \frac{a}{c} - \frac{b}{c} = \frac{a - b}{c}$$

EXAMPLE 7.61

Simplify (a) $\dfrac{7}{2x} + \dfrac{9y}{2x}$ and (b) $\dfrac{x}{x + 5} - \dfrac{2x - y}{x + 5}$.

SOLUTIONS

(a) $\dfrac{7}{2x} + \dfrac{9y}{2x} = \dfrac{7 + 9y}{2x}$

(b) $\dfrac{x}{x + 5} - \dfrac{2x - y}{x + 5} = \dfrac{x - (2x - y)}{x + 5} = \dfrac{x - 2x + y}{x + 5}$

$$= \frac{-x + y}{x + 5}$$

If the denominators are not the same, then addition and subtraction become somewhat more complicated. As Rule 6 indicates, you need to find a common denominator and rewrite each fraction as an equivalent fraction with this common denominator. The quickest way to find a common denominator is to multiply the denominators together. This method is demonstrated next.

 CAUTION When adding or subtracting fractions, remember to multiply both the numerator and denominator of a fraction by the same quantity.

ADDING AND SUBTRACTING FRACTIONS

The sum of two fractions $\dfrac{a}{b}$ and $\dfrac{c}{d}$ is

$$\frac{a}{b} + \frac{c}{d} = \frac{ad}{bd} + \frac{bc}{bd} = \frac{ad + bc}{bd}$$

The difference of two fractions $\dfrac{a}{b}$ and $\dfrac{c}{d}$ is

$$\frac{a}{b} - \frac{c}{d} = \frac{ad}{bd} - \frac{bc}{bd} = \frac{ad - bc}{bd}$$

As you will see in Examples 7.63 and 7.66, this may not produce the lowest common denominator. You must also remember that both the numerator and denominator must be multiplied by the same quantity.

EXAMPLE 7.62

Simplify $\dfrac{3}{x + 5} + \dfrac{x}{x - 5}$.

SOLUTION

$$\frac{3}{x + 5} + \frac{x}{x - 5} = \frac{3}{x + 5} \cdot \frac{x - 5}{x - 5} + \frac{x}{x - 5} \cdot \frac{x + 5}{x + 5}$$

$$= \frac{3(x - 5)}{(x + 5)(x - 5)} + \frac{x(x + 5)}{(x + 5)(x - 5)}$$

$$= \frac{3(x - 5) + (x^2 + 5x)}{(x + 5)(x - 5)}$$

$$= \frac{3x - 15 + x^2 + 5x}{(x + 5)(x - 5)}$$

$$= \frac{x^2 + 8x - 15}{x^2 - 25}$$

EXAMPLE 7.63

Simplify $\dfrac{2x}{x + 3} - \dfrac{x - 4}{x^2 - 9}$.

SOLUTION A common denominator of these fractions is $(x + 3)(x^2 - 9)$. We begin by rewriting each fraction with this common denominator and then subtract the two fractions:

$$\frac{2x}{x + 3} - \frac{x - 4}{x^2 - 9} = \frac{2x}{x + 3} \cdot \frac{x^2 - 9}{x^2 - 9} - \frac{x - 4}{x^2 - 9} \cdot \frac{x + 3}{x + 3}$$

$$= \frac{2x(x^2 - 9)}{(x + 3)(x^2 - 9)} - \frac{(x - 4)(x + 3)}{(x + 3)(x^2 - 9)}$$

EXAMPLE 7.63 (Cont.)

$$= \frac{(2x^3 - 18x) - (x^2 - x - 12)}{(x + 3)(x^2 - 9)}$$

$$= \frac{2x^3 - x^2 - 17x + 12}{x^3 + 3x^2 - 9x - 27}$$

We will see this same problem later in Example 7.66. At that time you will not only see an easier way to work the problem but that it simplifies to $\dfrac{2x^2 - 7x + 4}{x^2 - 9}$.

LEAST COMMON DENOMINATOR

Perhaps you wondered if the last answer was in simplest form. It is not, since

$$\frac{2x^3 - x^2 - 17x + 12}{x^3 + 3x^2 - 9x - 27} = \frac{(x + 3)(2x^2 - 7x + 4)}{(x + 3)(x^2 - 9)} = \frac{2x^2 - 7x + 4}{x^2 - 9}$$

If we want our answers in the simplest form, then simply multiplying the denominators together is not the best method to use. What we need to do is determine the **least common denominator**, or LCD, of the fractions to be added or subtracted.

There are three steps to determining the LCD:

HOW TO FIND THE LEAST COMMON DENOMINATOR

(1) Factor the denominator of each of the fractions in the problem.

(2) Determine the different factors and the highest power of each factor that occurs in any denominator.

(3) Multiply the distinct factors from Step 2 after each has been raised to its highest power.

EXAMPLE 7.64

Find the LCD of the fractions $\dfrac{7x + 1}{x^4 + x^3}$, $\dfrac{14}{x^3 - 4x^2 + 4x}$, and $\dfrac{9}{2x^2 - 2x - 4}$.

SOLUTION

Step 1: Factor the denominator of each of the fractions: $\dfrac{7x + 1}{x^3(x + 1)}$, $\dfrac{14}{x(x - 2)^2}$, and $\dfrac{9}{2(x + 1)(x - 2)}$.

Step 2: List each factor and the highest exponent of each.

Factor	Highest exponent	Final factors
2	1	2^1
x	3	x^3
$x + 1$	1	$(x + 1)^1$
$x - 2$	2	$(x - 2)^2$

Step 3: The LCD is $2x^3(x + 1)(x - 2)^2$.

EXAMPLE 7.65

Find the least common denominator of $\dfrac{2x}{x^2 + 5x + 6}$, $\dfrac{x - 3}{x^3 + 2x^2}$, and $\dfrac{x^2 + x}{x^3 + 6x^2 + 9x}$.

SOLUTION

Step 1: Factor each denominator: $\dfrac{2x}{(x + 2)(x + 3)}$, $\dfrac{x - 3}{x^2(x + 2)}$, and $\dfrac{x^2 + x}{x(x + 3)^2}$.

Step 2: List each factor and the highest exponent of each.

Factor	Highest exponent	Final factors
$x + 2$	1	$x + 2$
$x + 3$	2	$(x + 3)^2$
x	2	x^2

Step 3: The LCD is $x^2(x + 2)(x + 3)^2$.

Now we have the foundation for a much better way to add or subtract algebraic fractions, or any fractions. For each fraction, multiply both the numerator and denominator by a quantity that makes the denominator equal to the LCD of the fractions being added or subtracted. Then, add or subtract the numerators; place the result over the common denominator; and, if possible, simplify.

EXAMPLE 7.66

Calculate $\dfrac{2x}{x + 3} - \dfrac{x - 4}{x^2 - 9}$.

SOLUTION This is the same difference we were asked to compute in Example 7.63. First we find the LCD, which is $(x + 3)(x - 3)$.

We rewrite the first fraction as $\dfrac{2x}{x + 3} = \dfrac{2x(x - 3)}{(x + 3)(x - 3)}$. The second fraction, $\dfrac{x - 4}{x^2 - 9}$, is already written with the common denominator. So,

$$\frac{2x}{x + 3} - \frac{x - 4}{x^2 - 9} = \frac{2x(x - 3)}{(x + 3)(x - 3)} - \frac{x - 4}{x^2 - 9}$$

$$= \frac{2x(x - 3) - (x - 4)}{x^2 - 9}$$

EXAMPLE 7.66 (Cont.)

$$= \frac{(2x^2 - 6x) - (x - 4)}{x^2 - 9}$$

$$= \frac{2x^2 - 7x + 4}{x^2 - 9}$$

This was the same problem we worked in Example 7.63. Notice how much simpler this answer looks compared to the answer we found before.

EXAMPLE 7.67

Calculate $\dfrac{2x}{x + 2} + \dfrac{x}{x - 2} - \dfrac{1}{x^2 - 4}$.

SOLUTION The LCD of these fractions is $(x + 2)(x - 2)$. So,

$$\frac{2x}{x + 2} = \frac{2x(x - 2)}{(x + 2)(x - 2)},$$

$$\frac{x}{x - 2} = \frac{x(x + 2)}{(x - 2)(x + 2)},$$

$$\text{and } \frac{1}{x^2 - 4} = \frac{1}{(x - 2)(x + 2)}.$$

Thus, we get

$$\frac{2x}{x + 2} + \frac{x}{x - 2} - \frac{1}{x^2 - 4} = \frac{2x(x - 2)}{(x + 2)(x - 2)} + \frac{x(x + 2)}{(x - 2)(x + 2)} - \frac{1}{x^2 - 4}$$

$$= \frac{(2x^2 - 4x) + (x^2 + 2x) - 1}{x^2 - 4}$$

$$= \frac{3x^2 - 2x - 1}{x^2 - 4}$$

 APPLICATION ENVIRONMENTAL SCIENCE

EXAMPLE 7.68

In order to estimate the runoff from a rainstorm, the formula

$$Q = P - I_a - s + \frac{s^2}{P - I_a + s}$$

is used, where Q is the amount of runoff, P is the rainfall, s is the potential maximum retention after runoff begins, and I_a is the initial abstraction and all values are in inches. Rewrite the right-hand side of this formula as a single fraction.

SOLUTION If we represent $P - I_a$ with x then this formula can be written as

$$Q = x - s + \frac{s^2}{x + s}$$

Writing $x - s$ as a fraction with a denominator of $x + s$ will require the use of the difference of two squares in the numerator:

$$Q = \frac{(x - s)(x + s)}{x + s} + \frac{s^2}{x + s}$$

$$= \frac{x^2 - s^2}{x + s} + \frac{s^2}{x + s}$$

$$= \frac{x^2}{x + s}$$

Replacing x with $P - I_a$ we obtain the final simplification:

$$Q = \frac{(P - I_a)^2}{P - I_a + s}$$

COMPLEX FRACTIONS

A **complex fraction** is a fraction in which the numerator, the denominator, or both contain a fraction. There are two methods that are commonly used to simplify complex fractions.

Method 1: Find the LCD of all the fractions that appear in the numerator and denominator. Multiply both the numerator and denominator by the LCD.

Method 2: Combine the terms in the numerator into a single fraction. Combine the terms in the denominator into a single fraction. Divide the numerator by the denominator.

We will work each of the next two examples using both methods. Then you will be better able to select the method you prefer.

EXAMPLE 7.69

Simplify $\dfrac{2 + \dfrac{1}{x}}{x - \dfrac{2}{x^2}}$.

SOLUTION

Method 1: The LCD of 2, $\dfrac{1}{x}$, x, and $\dfrac{2}{x^2}$ is x^2, so

$$\frac{2 + \dfrac{1}{x}}{x - \dfrac{2}{x^2}} = \frac{2 + \dfrac{1}{x}}{x - \dfrac{2}{x^2}} \cdot \frac{x^2}{x^2}$$

$$= \frac{2x^2 + x}{x^3 - 2}$$

$$= \frac{x(2x + 1)}{x^3 - 2}$$

EXAMPLE 7.69 (Cont.) | **Method 2:**

$$2 + \frac{1}{x} = \frac{2x}{x} + \frac{1}{x} = \frac{2x + 1}{x}$$

$$x - \frac{2}{x^2} = \frac{x^3}{x^2} - \frac{2}{x^2} = \frac{x^3 - 2}{x^2}$$

$$\frac{2 + \dfrac{1}{x}}{x - \dfrac{2}{x^2}} = \frac{\dfrac{2x + 1}{x}}{\dfrac{x^3 - 2}{x^2}} = \frac{2x + 1}{x} \div \frac{x^3 - 2}{x^2}$$

$$= \frac{2x + 1}{x} \cdot \frac{x^2}{x^3 - 2} = \frac{x(2x + 1)}{x^3 - 2}$$

EXAMPLE 7.70

Simplify $\dfrac{\dfrac{1}{2x} - \dfrac{6}{y}}{\dfrac{1}{x} + \dfrac{2}{3y}}$.

SOLUTION

Method 1: The LCD of $\dfrac{1}{2x}, \dfrac{6}{y}, \dfrac{1}{x}$, and $\dfrac{2}{3y}$ is 6xy, so

$$\frac{\dfrac{1}{2x} - \dfrac{6}{y}}{\dfrac{1}{x} + \dfrac{2}{3y}} = \frac{\left(\dfrac{1}{2x} - \dfrac{6}{y}\right)}{\left(\dfrac{1}{x} + \dfrac{2}{3y}\right)} \cdot \frac{6xy}{6xy}$$

$$= \frac{3y - 36x}{6y + 4x} = \frac{3(y - 12x)}{2(3y + 2x)}$$

Method 2:

$$\frac{1}{2x} - \frac{6}{y} = \frac{y}{2xy} - \frac{12x}{2xy} = \frac{y - 12x}{2xy}$$

$$\frac{1}{x} + \frac{2}{3y} = \frac{3y}{3xy} + \frac{2x}{3xy} = \frac{3y + 2x}{3xy}$$

$$\frac{\dfrac{1}{2x} - \dfrac{6}{y}}{\dfrac{1}{x} + \dfrac{2}{3y}} = \frac{\dfrac{y - 12x}{2xy}}{\dfrac{3y + 2x}{3xy}}$$

$$= \frac{y - 12x}{2xy} \div \frac{3y + 2x}{3xy}$$

$$= \frac{y - 12x}{2xy} \cdot \frac{3xy}{3y + 2x}$$

$$= \frac{3(y - 12x)}{2(3y + 2x)}$$

APPLICATION ELECTRONICS

EXAMPLE 7.71

If four resistances are connected in a series-parallel circuit, the total resistance R is given by the equation

$$R = \frac{1}{R_1 + R_2} + \frac{1}{R_3 + R_4}$$

where R_1, R_2, R_3, and R_4 represent four resistances. Simplify this equation by adding the right-hand side.

SOLUTION We find that the LCD of the right-hand side of the given equation is $(R_1 + R_2)(R_3 + R_4)$. So,

$$R = \frac{1}{R_1 + R_2} \cdot \frac{R_3 + R_4}{R_3 + R_4} + \frac{1}{R_3 + R_4} \cdot \frac{R_1 + R_2}{R_1 + R_2}$$

$$= \frac{R_3 + R_4}{(R_1 + R_2)(R_3 + R_4)} + \frac{R_1 + R_2}{(R_1 + R_2)(R_3 + R_4)}$$

$$= \frac{R_1 + R_2 + R_3 + R_4}{(R_1 + R_2)(R_3 + R_4)}$$

EXERCISE SET 7.6

In Exercises 1–44, perform the indicated operations and simplify.

1. $\frac{2}{7} + \frac{5}{7}$

2. $\frac{4}{5} + \frac{-11}{5}$

3. $\frac{7}{3} - \frac{5}{3}$

4. $\frac{-2}{9} - \frac{8}{9}$

5. $\frac{1}{2} + \frac{1}{3}$

6. $\frac{3}{4} + \frac{-2}{3}$

7. $\frac{4}{5} - \frac{2}{3}$

8. $-\frac{5}{7} - \frac{3}{5}$

9. $\frac{1}{x} + \frac{5}{x}$

10. $\frac{2}{y} + \frac{-5}{y}$

11. $\frac{4}{a} - \frac{3}{a}$

12. $\frac{-5}{p} - \frac{-7}{p}$

13. $\frac{2x}{y} + \frac{3x}{y}$

14. $\frac{4p}{q} - \frac{6p}{q}$

15. $\frac{3r}{2t} + \frac{-r}{2t} - \frac{5r}{2t}$

16. $\frac{3x}{2y} - \frac{5x}{2y} + \frac{x}{2y}$

17. $\frac{3}{x + 2} + \frac{x}{x + 2}$

18. $\frac{5}{y - 3} + \frac{y}{y - 3}$

19. $\frac{t}{t + 1} - \frac{2}{t + 1}$

20. $\frac{a}{b - 3} - \frac{4}{3 - b}$

21. $\frac{y - 3}{x + 2} + \frac{3 + y}{x + 2}$

22. $\frac{x + 4}{x - 2} + \frac{x - 5}{x - 2}$

23. $\frac{x + 2}{a + b} - \frac{x - 5}{a + b}$

24. $\frac{x + 4}{y - 5} - \frac{2 - x}{y - 5}$

25. $\dfrac{2}{x} + \dfrac{3}{y}$

26. $\dfrac{x}{y} + \dfrac{5}{x}$

27. $\dfrac{a}{b} - \dfrac{4}{d}$

28. $\dfrac{2x}{y} - \dfrac{3y}{x}$

29. $\dfrac{3}{x(x+1)} + \dfrac{4}{x^2-1}$

30. $\dfrac{5}{y(x+1)} + \dfrac{x}{y(x+2)}$

31. $\dfrac{2}{x^2-1} - \dfrac{4}{(x+1)^2}$

32. $\dfrac{6}{y-2} - \dfrac{3}{y+2}$

33. $\dfrac{x}{x^2-11x+30} + \dfrac{2}{x^2-36}$

34. $\dfrac{a}{a^2-9a+18} + \dfrac{a}{a^2-9}$

35. $\dfrac{2}{x^2-x-6} - \dfrac{5}{x^2-4}$

36. $\dfrac{b}{b^2-10b+21} - \dfrac{b}{b^2-9}$

37. $\dfrac{x-1}{3x^2-13x+4} + \dfrac{3x+1}{4x-x^2}$

38. $\dfrac{x-3}{x^2+3x+2} + \dfrac{2x-5}{x^2+x-2}$

39. $\dfrac{x-3}{x^2-1} + \dfrac{2x-7}{x^2+5x+4}$

40. $\dfrac{x+4}{x^2-9} - \dfrac{x-3}{x^2+6x+9}$

41. $\dfrac{y+3}{y^2-y-2} - \dfrac{2y-1}{y^2+2y-8}$

42. $\dfrac{\dfrac{1}{(a-b)(a-c)} + \dfrac{1}{(b-a)(b-c)}}{(b-c)(a-c)}$

43. $\dfrac{x}{(x^2+3)(x-1)} + \dfrac{3x^2}{(x-1)^2(x+2)} - \dfrac{x+2}{x^2+3}$

44. $\dfrac{2x-1}{x^2+5x+6} - \dfrac{x-2}{x^2+4x+3} + \dfrac{x-4}{x^2+3x+2}$

Use Method 1 to simplify each of the complex fractions in Exercises 45–50.

45. $\dfrac{1+\dfrac{2}{x}}{1-\dfrac{3}{x}}$

46. $\dfrac{x+\dfrac{1}{x}}{2-\dfrac{1}{x}}$

47. $\dfrac{x-1}{1+\dfrac{1}{x}}$

48. $\dfrac{x^2-25}{\dfrac{1}{x}-\dfrac{1}{5}}$

49. $\dfrac{\dfrac{x}{x+y} - \dfrac{y}{x-y}}{\dfrac{x}{x+y} + \dfrac{y}{x-y}}$

50. $\dfrac{x+3-\dfrac{16}{x+3}}{x-6+\dfrac{20}{x+6}}$

Use Method 2 to simplify each of the complex fractions in Exercises 51–56.

51. $\dfrac{1+\dfrac{3}{x}}{1+\dfrac{2}{x}}$

52. $\dfrac{y+\dfrac{1}{y}}{3+\dfrac{2}{y}}$

53. $\dfrac{t-1}{t+\dfrac{1}{t}}$

54. $\dfrac{x^2-36}{\dfrac{1}{6}-\dfrac{1}{x}}$

55. $\dfrac{\dfrac{x}{x-y} - \dfrac{y}{x+y}}{\dfrac{1}{x-y} + \dfrac{1}{x+y}}$

56. $\dfrac{t-5+\dfrac{25}{t-5}}{t+3+\dfrac{10}{t-3}}$

Solve Exercises 57–64.

57. Electronics If two resistors, R_1 and R_2, are connected in parallel, the equivalent resistance of the combination can be found using $\dfrac{1}{R} = \dfrac{1}{R_1} + \dfrac{1}{R_2}$. Add the right-hand side of the equation.

58. Optics The lensmaker's equation states that if p is the object distance, q the image distance, and f the focal length of a lens, then $\dfrac{1}{p} + \dfrac{1}{q} = \dfrac{1}{f}$. Simplify the left-hand side of this equation.

59. Electronics If three capacitors with capacitance C_1, C_2, and C_3 are connected together in series, then they can be replaced by a single capacitor of capacitance C. The value of C can be determined from the equation $\dfrac{1}{C} = \dfrac{1}{C_1} + \dfrac{1}{C_2} + \dfrac{1}{C_3}$. Simplify the right-hand side of the equation.

60. Transportation A car travels the first part of a trip for a distance d_1 at velocity v_1, and the second part of the trip it travels d_2 at the velocity v_2. The average speed for these two parts of the trip is given by $\dfrac{d_1 + d_2}{\dfrac{d_1}{v_1} + \dfrac{d_2}{v_2}}$. Simplify this fraction.

61. Civil engineering The Gordon-Rankine formula for intermediate steel columns is

$$P = A\left(\frac{k}{1 + \dfrac{L^2}{kr^2}} \right)$$

Simplify the right-hand side of this formula.

62. Electrical engineering In calculating the electric intensity of a field set up by a dipole, the following expression is used.

$$\frac{1}{\left(r - \dfrac{d}{2}\right)^2} - \frac{1}{\left(r + \dfrac{d}{2}\right)^2}$$

Simplify this expression.

63. Electrical engineering Millman's theorem provides a shortcut for finding the common voltage, V, across any number of parallel branches with different voltage sources. If there are three branches, then the common voltage is

$$V = \frac{\dfrac{V_1}{R_1} + \dfrac{V_2}{R_2} + \dfrac{V_3}{R_3}}{\dfrac{1}{R_1} + \dfrac{1}{R_2} + \dfrac{1}{R_3}}$$

Simplify the right-hand side of this equation.

64. Electronics The expression

$$\frac{1}{\left(r - \dfrac{d}{2}\right)^2} - \frac{1}{\left(r + \dfrac{d}{2}\right)^2}$$

is used to calculate the electric intensity in a field set up by a dipole. Combine the two terms and simplify the resulting expression.

 [IN YOUR WORDS]

65. (a) What is a common denominator?

(b) Explain how to find the least common denominator.

66. Describe a complex algebraic fraction. Give examples of fractions that are complex algebraic fractions, and give examples of some that are not. How are they different?

CHAPTER 7 REVIEW

IMPORTANT TERMS AND CONCEPTS

Binomial	Addition	Subtraction
Common factor	Complex	Least common denominator (LCD)
Denominator	Division	
Discriminant	Equivalent	Numerator
Factor	Multiplication	Trinomial
Fractions	Reducing	

REVIEW EXERCISES

In Exercises 1–10, find the indicated products by direct use of one of the special products.

1. $5x(x - y)$

2. $(3 + x)^2$

3. $(x - 2y)^3$

4. $(x + y)(x - 6)$

5. $(2x + 3)(x - 6)$

6. $(x + 7)(x - 7)$

7. $(x^2 - 5)(x^2 + 5)$

8. $(7x - 1)(x + 5)$

9. $(2 + x)^3$

10. $(x - 7)^2$

Completely factor each of the expressions in Exercises 11–20.

11. $9 + 9y$

12. $x^2 - 4$

13. $7x^2 - 63$

14. $x^2 - 12x + 36$

15. $x^2 - 11x + 30$

16. $x^2 + 15x + 36$

17. $x^2 + 6x - 16$

18. $x^2 - 4x - 45$

19. $2x^2 - 3x - 9$

20. $8x^3 + 6x^2 - 20x$

In Exercises 21–26, reduce each fraction to lowest terms.

21. $\dfrac{2x}{6y}$

22. $\dfrac{7x^2y}{9xy^2}$

23. $\dfrac{x^2 - 9}{(x + 3)^2}$

24. $\dfrac{x^2 - 4x - 45}{x^2 - 81}$

25. $\dfrac{x^3 + y^3}{x^2 + 2xy + y^2}$

26. $\dfrac{x^3 - 16x}{x^2 + 2x - 8}$

In Exercises 27–40, perform the indicated operations and simplify.

27. $\dfrac{x^2}{y} \cdot \dfrac{3y^2}{7x}$

28. $\dfrac{x^2 - 9}{x + 4} \cdot \dfrac{x^3 - 16x}{x - 3}$

29. $\dfrac{4x}{3y} \div \dfrac{2x^2}{6y}$

30. $\dfrac{x^2 - 25}{x^2 - 4x} \div \dfrac{2x^2 + 2x - 40}{x^3 - x}$

31. $\dfrac{4x}{y} + \dfrac{3x}{y}$

32. $\dfrac{4}{x-y} + \dfrac{6}{x+y}$

33. $\dfrac{3(x-3)}{(x+2)(x-5)^2} + \dfrac{4(x-1)}{(x+2)^2(x-5)}$

34. $\dfrac{8a}{b} - \dfrac{3}{b}$

35. $\dfrac{x}{y+x} - \dfrac{x}{y-x}$

36. $\dfrac{2(x+3)}{(x+1)^2(x+2)} - \dfrac{3(x-1)}{(x+1)(x+2)^2}$

37. $\dfrac{x^2-5x-6}{x^2+8x+12} + \dfrac{x^2+7x+6}{x^2-4x-12}$

38. $\dfrac{2x-1}{4x^2-12x+5} - \dfrac{x+1}{4x^2-4x-15}$

39. $\dfrac{x^2-5x-6}{x^2+8x+12} \div \dfrac{x^2+7x+6}{x^2-4x-12}$

40. $\dfrac{x^2+x-2}{7a^2x^2-14a^2x+7a^2} \cdot \dfrac{14ax-28a}{1-2x+x^2}$

Simplify each of the complex fractions in Exercises 41–46.

41. $\dfrac{\dfrac{1}{x} - \dfrac{1}{y}}{\dfrac{1}{x} + \dfrac{1}{y}}$

42. $\dfrac{\dfrac{1}{x} + \dfrac{1}{y}}{x+y}$

43. $\dfrac{\dfrac{1}{x} - \dfrac{1}{y}}{\dfrac{x-y}{xy}}$

44. $\dfrac{1 - \dfrac{1}{x}}{x - 2 + \dfrac{1}{x}}$

45. $\dfrac{\dfrac{x}{1+x} - \dfrac{1-x}{x}}{\dfrac{x}{1+x} + \dfrac{1-x}{x}}$

46. $\dfrac{x - \dfrac{xy}{x-y}}{\dfrac{x^2}{x^2-y^2} - 1}$

CHAPTER 7 TEST

1. Multiply $(x+5)(x-3)$.
2. Multiply $(2x-3)(2x+3)$.
3. Multiply $(3x^2-4)(2-5x)$.
4. Multiply $(x-4)^3$.
5. Completely factor $2x^2 - 128$.
6. Completely factor $x^2 - 12x + 32$.
7. Completely factor $10x^2 + x - 21$.
8. Completely factor $x^3 - 125$.
9. Reduce $\dfrac{x^2-25}{x^2+6x+5}$ to lowest terms.
10. Simplify $\dfrac{3(a+b)^3 - x(a+b)}{a^2-b^2}$.
11. Calculate $\dfrac{3x}{x+2} \cdot \dfrac{x-1}{x+2}$.

12. Calculate $\dfrac{2x+6}{x-2} \div \dfrac{3x+9}{x^2-4}$.

13. Calculate $\dfrac{6}{x-5} + \dfrac{x^2-2x}{x-5}$.

14. Calculate $\dfrac{2x}{x+3} - \dfrac{x+4}{x-2}$.

15. Simplify $\dfrac{x - \dfrac{1}{x}}{x - \dfrac{2}{x+1}}$.

16. Reduce $\dfrac{1}{2x+1} - \dfrac{2}{4x^2+4x+1}$.

17. The average rate, r, for a round trip with a one-way distance d is

$$r = \frac{2d}{\dfrac{d}{r_1} + \dfrac{d}{r_2}}$$

Simplify this complex fraction.

18. The total resistance, R, in a parallel electrical circuit with three resistances is given by

$$\frac{1}{R} = \frac{1}{R_1} + \frac{1}{R_2} + \frac{1}{R_3}$$

Express the sum on the right-hand side as a single fraction.

9.1   FRACTIONAL EQUATIONS

An equation in which one or more terms is a fraction is called a *fractional equation*. Solving a fractional equation requires a technique that we used in solving systems of linear equations. In order to add or subtract two linear equations in Section 6.2, you often had to multiply one or both equations by a nonzero number. To solve fractional equations, we will use that same technique—we will multiply the equation by a nonzero quantity. In particular, we will multiply the equation by the LCD, the lowest common denominator. This is often referred to as *clearing the equation.*

The easiest type of fractional equations to solve are those in which the variables occur only in the numerator.

EXAMPLE 9.1

Solve $\dfrac{2x}{3} - \dfrac{3x}{5} = \dfrac{1}{10}$ for x.

SOLUTION The LCD of $\dfrac{2x}{3}$, $\dfrac{3x}{5}$, and $\dfrac{1}{10}$ is 30, so we will multiply both sides of the equation by 30.

$$30\left(\frac{2x}{3} - \frac{3x}{5}\right) = 30\left(\frac{1}{10}\right)$$

$$30\left(\frac{2x}{3}\right) - 30\left(\frac{3x}{5}\right) = 30\left(\frac{1}{10}\right)$$

$$20x - 18x = 3$$

$$2x = 3$$

$$x = \frac{3}{2} = 1.5$$

If we check our answer in the original problem, we see that $\dfrac{2(1.5)}{3} - \dfrac{3(1.5)}{5} = \dfrac{3}{3} - \dfrac{4.5}{5} = 1 - \dfrac{9}{10} = \dfrac{1}{10}$. The answer checks.

If the variables are in the denominator, we then need to use more caution.

 CAUTION The original equation will not be defined for any values of the variable that give any of the denominators a value of 0. If you forget this, you may get an answer that does not satisfy the original problem. This type of answer is called an **extraneous solution** because it seems to be a solution but is not a valid one. For this reason, it is a good idea to study the equation first and to note any values that make the denominator 0.

In these next examples, we multiply the equation by the least common denominator for the fractions. Notice that we begin each solution by finding out which values make a denominator 0.

EXAMPLE 9.2

Solve $\dfrac{2}{x-5} = \dfrac{1}{4x-12}$ for x.

SOLUTION The LCD of $\dfrac{2}{x-5}$ and $\dfrac{1}{4x-12}$ is $4(x-5)(x-3)$. Since the LCD has a value of 0 when $x = 5$ or $x = 3$, neither of these values is a possible solution for this equation.

If we multiply both sides of the equation by the LCD, we obtain

$$4(x-5)(x-3)\left(\frac{2}{x-5}\right) = 4(x-5)(x-3)\left(\frac{1}{4x-12}\right)$$
$$4(x-3)(2) = x-5$$
$$8(x-3) = x-5$$
$$8x-24 = x-5$$
$$7x = 19$$
$$x = \frac{19}{7}$$

Thus, $x = \frac{19}{7}$ appears to be the solution. But, we should check our work to ensure that we have made no errors.

Check: The left-hand side of the equation becomes

$$\frac{2}{\dfrac{19}{7}-5} = \frac{2}{\dfrac{19}{7}-\dfrac{35}{7}} = \frac{2}{\dfrac{-16}{7}} = -\frac{7}{8}$$

The value of the right-hand side is

$$\frac{1}{4\left(\dfrac{19}{7}\right)-12} = \frac{1}{\dfrac{76}{7}-12} = \frac{1}{\dfrac{76}{7}-\dfrac{84}{7}} = \frac{1}{\dfrac{-8}{7}} = -\frac{7}{8}$$

Both sides of the equation have a value of $-\frac{7}{8}$ when $x = \frac{19}{7}$, so $x = \frac{19}{7}$ must be the correct solution.

We could have used cross-multiplication to solve the equation in the last example. But, cross-multiplication can only be used when there is one term on each side of the equation. The next three examples show what to do when you cannot use cross-multiplication.

EXAMPLE 9.3

Solve $\dfrac{4}{x^2 - 1} = \dfrac{2}{x - 1} - \dfrac{3}{x + 1}$.

SOLUTION The LCD of $\dfrac{4}{x^2 - 1}, \dfrac{2}{x - 1}$, and $\dfrac{3}{x + 1}$ is $(x + 1)(x - 1) = x^2 - 1$. Notice that $x \neq 1$ and $x \neq -1$, because each of these values makes two of the denominators 0. Multiplying both sides of the given equation by $x^2 - 1$, we obtain

$$(x^2 - 1)\left(\frac{4}{x^2 - 1}\right) = (x^2 - 1)\left(\frac{2}{x - 1}\right) - (x^2 - 1)\left(\frac{3}{x + 1}\right)$$
$$4 = (x + 1)2 - (x - 1)3$$
$$4 = 2x + 2 - (3x - 3)$$
$$4 = 2x + 2 - 3x + 3$$
$$4 = -x + 5$$
$$-1 = -x$$

or $x = 1$

Since $x = 1$ is not an allowable solution, the "solution" $x = 1$ is extraneous. *This equation has no solution.*

EXAMPLE 9.4

Solve $\dfrac{3x}{x - 2} + 5 = \dfrac{7x}{x - 2}$.

SOLUTION The LCD is $x - 2$, so $x \neq 2$. Multiplying both sides by $x - 2$, we get

$$(x - 2)\left(\frac{3x}{x - 2} + 5\right) = (x - 2)\left(\frac{7x}{x - 2}\right)$$
$$(x - 2)\left(\frac{3x}{x - 2}\right) + (x - 2)5 = (x - 2)\left(\frac{7x}{x - 2}\right)$$
$$3x + 5x - 10 = 7x$$
$$8x - 10 = 7x$$
$$x = 10$$

Substituting $x = 10$ into the original equation shows that it satisfies the equation.

 APPLICATION GENERAL TECHNOLOGY

EXAMPLE 9.5

In a lens, if the object distance is p, the image distance is q, and the focal length is f, then the relation exists where $\dfrac{1}{f} = \dfrac{1}{p} + \dfrac{1}{q}$. Solve this equation for q.

EXAMPLE 9.5 (Cont.)

SOLUTION The LCD of $\frac{1}{f}$, $\frac{1}{p}$, and $\frac{1}{q}$ is fpq. Multiplying both sides of the equation by fpq, we obtain

$$fpq\left(\frac{1}{f}\right) = fpq\left(\frac{1}{p} + \frac{1}{q}\right)$$

$$pq = fpq\left(\frac{1}{p}\right) + fpq\left(\frac{1}{q}\right)$$

Multiplying further, we obtain

$$pq = fq + fp$$

To solve for q, we put the terms containing q on the left-hand side with all other terms on the right-hand side of the equation.

$$pq - fq = fp$$

At this point, we need to determine the coefficient of q. We do this by factoring.

$$q(p - f) = fp$$

We see that $p - f$ acts as the coefficient of q. Dividing by this coefficient, we obtain the desired solution.

$$q = \frac{fp}{p - f}$$

 APPLICATION BUSINESS

EXAMPLE 9.6

A technician can assemble an instrument in 12.5 h. After working for 3 h on a job, the technician is joined by another technician, who is able to assemble the instrument alone in 9.5 h. How long does it take to assemble this instrument?

SOLUTION The problem is similar to the work problem we solved in Chapter 2. To solve this example, let h represent the number of hours that the technicians worked together on the instrument. The time to assemble the instrument will be $h + 3$ h because the first technician worked alone for 3 h.

The first technician, working alone, can complete the job in 12.5 h. So, each hour this technician works, $\frac{1}{12.5}$ of the instrument is assembled. Similarly, the second technician will assemble $\frac{1}{9.5}$ of the instrument for each hour worked. The first technician works $h + 3$ h and is able to complete $\frac{1}{12.5}(h + 3)$ of the work. The second technician works h hours and completes $\frac{1}{9.5}(h)$ of the work. Together, they assemble the entire instrument, so we get the equation

$$\frac{1}{12.5}(h + 3) + \frac{1}{9.5}(h) = 1$$

Multiplying by the common denominator $(12.5)(9.5)$, we obtain

$$9.5(h + 3) + 12.5(h) = (9.5)(12.5)$$
$$9.5h + 28.5 + 12.5h = 118.75$$
$$22h = 90.25$$
$$h \approx 4.1$$

Thus, the two technicians will be able to completely assemble the instrument in about 7.1 h or 7 h 6 min. (Remember, the total time of 7.1 is $h + 3$ h.)

EXERCISE SET 9.1

In Exercises 1–30, solve the given equations and check the results.

1. $\dfrac{x}{2} + \dfrac{x}{3} = \dfrac{1}{4}$

2. $\dfrac{x}{3} - \dfrac{x}{4} = \dfrac{1}{2}$

3. $\dfrac{y}{2} + 3 = \dfrac{4y}{5}$

4. $\dfrac{y}{5} - 5\dfrac{1}{2} = \dfrac{3y}{4}$

5. $\dfrac{x - 1}{2} + \dfrac{x + 1}{3} = \dfrac{x - 1}{4}$

6. $\dfrac{x + 2}{3} - \dfrac{x + 4}{2} = \dfrac{x - 1}{6}$

7. $\dfrac{1}{x} + \dfrac{2}{x} = \dfrac{1}{3}$

8. $\dfrac{3}{x} - \dfrac{4}{x} = \dfrac{2}{5}$

9. $\dfrac{7}{w - 4} = \dfrac{1}{2w + 5}$

10. $\dfrac{5}{y + 1} = \dfrac{3}{y - 3}$

11. $\dfrac{2}{2x - 1} = \dfrac{5}{x + 5}$

12. $\dfrac{3}{4x + 2} = \dfrac{1}{x + 2}$

13. $\dfrac{4x}{x - 3} - 1 = \dfrac{3x}{x - 3}$

14. $7 - \dfrac{3x}{x + 2} = \dfrac{4x}{x + 2}$

15. $\dfrac{4}{x + 2} - \dfrac{3}{x - 1} = \dfrac{5}{(x - 1)(x + 2)}$

16. $\dfrac{3}{x - 3} + \dfrac{2}{2 - x} = \dfrac{5}{(x - 3)(x - 2)}$

17. $\dfrac{x + 1}{x + 2} + \dfrac{x + 3}{x - 2} = \dfrac{2x^2 + 3x - 5}{x^2 - 4}$

18. $\dfrac{x + 2}{x + 3} - \dfrac{x + 5}{x - 3} = \dfrac{2x - 1}{x^2 - 9}$

19. $\dfrac{3}{a + 1} + \dfrac{a + 1}{a - 1} = \dfrac{a^2}{a^2 - 1}$

20. $\dfrac{5}{x - 4} - \dfrac{x + 2}{x + 4} = \dfrac{x^2}{16 - x^2}$

21. $\dfrac{2}{x - 1} + \dfrac{5}{x + 1} = \dfrac{4}{x^2 - 1}$

22. $\dfrac{3x + 4}{x + 2} - \dfrac{3x - 5}{x - 4} = \dfrac{12}{x^2 - 2x - 8}$

23. $\dfrac{5x - 2}{x - 3} + \dfrac{4 - 5x}{x + 4} = \dfrac{10}{x^2 + x - 12}$

24. $\dfrac{2x}{x - 1} - \dfrac{3}{x + 2} = \dfrac{4x}{x^2 + x - 2} + 2$

25. $\dfrac{5}{x} + \dfrac{3}{x + 1} = \dfrac{x}{x + 1} - \dfrac{x + 1}{x}$

26. $\dfrac{y}{y + 2} + \dfrac{5}{y - 1} = \dfrac{3}{y + 2} + \dfrac{y}{y - 1}$

27. $\dfrac{2t - 4}{2t + 4} = \dfrac{t + 2}{t + 4}$

28. $\dfrac{3x + 5}{x - 5} = \dfrac{3x - 1}{x + 3}$

29. $\dfrac{3x + 1}{x - 1} - \dfrac{x - 2}{x + 3} = \dfrac{2x - 3}{x + 3} + \dfrac{4}{x - 1}$

30. $\dfrac{7x + 2}{x + 2} + \dfrac{3x - 1}{x + 3} = \dfrac{6x + 1}{x + 3} + \dfrac{4x - 3}{x + 2}$

Solve each of Exercises 31–38 for the indicated variable.

31. $\dfrac{1}{r} + \dfrac{1}{s} = \dfrac{1}{t}$ for s

32. $\dfrac{P_1 V_1}{T_1} = \dfrac{P_2 V_2}{T_2}$ for T_1

33. $\dfrac{1}{R} = \dfrac{1}{R_1} + \dfrac{1}{R_2} + \dfrac{1}{R_3}$ for R

34. $P = \dfrac{E^2}{R + r} - \dfrac{E^2}{(R + r)^2}$ for E^2

35. $V = 2\pi rh + 2\pi r^2$ for h

36. $\frac{5}{9}(F - 32) = C$ for F

37. $\dfrac{1}{f} = (n - 1)\left(\dfrac{1}{R_1} + \dfrac{1}{R_2}\right)$ for R_2

38. $\dfrac{P_1}{g} + \dfrac{V_1^2}{2g} + h_1 = \dfrac{P_2}{dg} + \dfrac{V_2^2}{2g} + h_2$ for g

Solve Exercises 39–56.

39. Electrical engineering The capacitance, C, of a spherical capacitor is given by the formula

$$\frac{d}{(9 \times 10^9)C} = \frac{1}{R_2} - \frac{1}{R_1}$$

where R_2 is the outside radius of the sphere, R_1 is the inside radius, and d is the dielectric constant. Solve this equation for C.

40. Electrical engineering The capacitance, C, of a circuit containing three capacitances C_1, C_2, and C_3 in series is given by

$$\frac{1}{C} = \frac{1}{C_1} + \frac{1}{C_2} + \frac{1}{C_3}$$

Solve this equation for C.

41. Optics The *lensmaker's equation*

$$\frac{1}{f} = (n - 1)\left(\frac{1}{r_1} - \frac{1}{r_2}\right)$$

gives the focal length, f, of a very thin lens. Solve this equation for f.

42. Optics An important equation in optics is

$$\frac{1}{f} = \frac{1}{p} + \frac{1}{q}$$

where f is the focal length of the lens, p is the distance to the object from the lens, and q is the distance to the image from the lens. Solve this equation for p.

43. Mechanical engineering A formula relating the depth, h, of a gear tooth to the major diameter, D, of the gear and the minor diameter, d, of the gear may be expressed as

$$\frac{h}{D - d} = 2$$

Solve this equation for D.

44. Automotive engineering The formula for the efficiency of a diesel engine is given by

$$\text{Eff} = 1 - \frac{T_4 - T_1}{\alpha(T_3 - T_2)}$$

Solve this equation for T_1.

45. Business One computer can process a company's payroll in 10 h, while a newer computer can do the same job in 6 h. Working together at these rates, how long would it take to complete the payroll?

46. Wastewater technology Working alone, one pipe can fill a tank in 12 h, while a second pipe can fill the tank in 15 h. If both pipes are opened at the same time, how long does it take to fill the tank?

47. Wastewater technology Pipe A can fill a tank in 6 h and Pipe B can fill it in 4 h. If Pipe A is opened 1 h before Pipe B is opened, how long does it take to fill the tank?

48. **Computer technology** One microprocessor can process a set of data in 5 μs (microseconds) and a second microprocessor can process the same amount of data in 8 μs. If they process the data together, how many microseconds should it take?

49. **Electricity** A generator can charge a group of batteries in 18 h. It begins charging the batteries, and 4 h later a second generator starts charging the same set of batteries. If the second generator alone could charge the batteries in 12 h, how long will it take both to charge the batteries?

50. **Transportation** An airplane traveling against the wind travels 500 km in the same time it takes it to travel 650 km with the wind. If the wind speed is 20 km/h, find the speed of the airplane in still air.

51. **Wastewater technology** Working alone, it takes one large pipe 3 h to fill a tank. Two smaller pipes are used to drain the tank. Each of the smaller pipes requires 4 h to drain the tank. By mistake, one of the small pipes is left open when the tank is being filled. Assuming that no one notices the mistake, how long does it take to fill the tank?

52. **Solar energy** Solar collector A can absorb 12,000 Btu in 8 h. A second collector, B, is added. Together collectors A and B collect 45,000 Btu in 6 h. How long would it take collector B alone to collect 45,000 Btu?

53. **Acoustics** The apparent frequency f_a of sound when the source and listener are moving toward each other can be determined by solving the equation

$$\frac{V - V_s}{f} = \frac{V + V_L}{f_a}$$

for f_a. Solve the equation for f_a.

54. **Automotive technology** UH3D (UnderHood 3 Dimensional) is a computational fluid dynamics code used primarily in the application of prediction cooling system performance based on geometric data and performance maps of fans and heat exchangers. The volume flow coefficient ϕ used by UH3D is defined as the volumetric airflow, $\dot{Q}$, divided by the product of the fan area, A_{fan}, and the fan tip velocity, U_{tip}. That is,

$$\phi = \frac{\dot{Q}}{A_{fan} U_{tip}}$$

The fan tip velocity is defined as $U_{tip} = \pi d_{tip} \dfrac{N}{60}$, where d_{tip} is the diameter of the fan and N is the fan speed in rpm. Substitute this value of U_{tip} into the equation for ϕ and solve the resulting equation for d_{tip}.

55. **Electronics** Millman's theorem is used to determine the common voltage V across any network. It is written as

$$V = \frac{\dfrac{V_1}{R_1} + \dfrac{V_2}{R_2} + \dfrac{V_3}{R_3}}{\dfrac{1}{R_1} + \dfrac{1}{R_2} + \dfrac{1}{R_3}}$$

Solve this equation for R_1.

56. **Optics** Most of the discrepancy in focal points arises from approximations of the equivalency of sine and tangent values of respective angles made to the Gaussian lens equation for a spherical refracting surface:

$$\frac{n}{s} + \frac{n'}{s'} = \frac{n' - n}{r}$$

Solve this equation for r and simplify the answer.

 [IN YOUR WORDS]

57. **(a)** What is an extraneous solution? **(b)** Are they good or bad? **(c)** How can you tell if you have an extraneous solution? **(d)** What should you do if you get an extraneous solution?

58. Describe what is meant by clearing an equation.

9.4 QUADRATIC EQUATIONS AND FACTORING

Until now, all the equations we have solved have been first-degree, or linear, equations and systems of linear equations. Many technical problems require the ability to solve more complicated equations. In the remainder of this chapter, we will focus on second-degree, or quadratic, equations. As we continue through the book, we will learn how to solve more types of equations.

QUADRATIC EQUATIONS

We worked with quadratics, binomials, and trinomials in Chapter 7. A polynomial equation of the second degree is a quadratic equation.

QUADRATIC EQUATION

If a, b, and c are constants and $a \neq 0$, then

$$ax^2 + bx + c = 0$$

is the **standard quadratic equation**.

EXAMPLE 9.29

The following are all quadratic equations written in the standard form:

(a) $2x^2 - 3x + 5 = 0$ $a = 2, b = -3, c = 5$

(b) $4x^2 + 7x = 0$ $a = 4, b = 7, c = 0$

(c) $5x^2 - 125 = 0$ $a = 5, b = 0, c = -125$

(d) $(p + 3)x^2 + px - p + 2 = 0$ $a = p + 3, b = p, c = 2 - p$

EXAMPLE 9.30

The following are also quadratic equations, but are not in the standard form:

(a) $x^2 = 49$ $a = 1, b = 0, c = -49$

(b) $8 + 2x = \dfrac{7x^2}{2}$ $a = \dfrac{7}{2}, b = -2, c = -8$

NOTE Quadratic equations that contain fractions are often simplified by writing them without fractions and with $a > 0$. This simplification is achieved by multiplying the equation by the LCD of the coefficients. (We could write the equation in Example 9.30[b] as $-\frac{7}{2}x^2 + 2x + 8 = 0$, but it would be better to multiply the equation by -2 and obtain the equivalent equation $7x^2 - 4x - 16 = 0$, since integer coefficients are usually easier to use.)

EXAMPLE 9.31

The following are not quadratic equations:

(a) $2x^3 - x^2 + 5 = 0$ This equation has a term of degree 3. The highest degree of any term in a quadratic equation is 2.

(b) $4x + 5 = 0$ This does not have a term of degree 2. This means that $a = 0$, which contradicts part of the definition of a quadratic equation.

In order to solve a quadratic equation, we need another property for the real numbers. We have not needed the **zero-product rule** until now.

ZERO-PRODUCT RULE FOR REAL NUMBERS

If a and b are numbers and $ab = 0$, then $a = 0$, $b = 0$, or both a and b are 0.

This is a very simple but powerful statement, as shown by the next example.

EXAMPLE 9.32

Use the zero-product rule to solve $(x - 1)(x + 5) = 0$.

SOLUTION Here a has the value $x - 1$ and b has the value $x + 5$. According to the zero-product rule, either $x - 1 = 0$ or $x + 5 = 0$ (or both). If $x - 1 = 0$, then $x = 1$. If $x + 5 = 0$, then $x = -5$. These are the roots (also called solutions or zeros) of the equation.

Substitute 1 into the original equation. Did you get 0? Now substitute -5 and you will get 0 again. So, both of these answers check. The solutions are $x = -5$ and $x = 1$.

ROOTS OF QUADRATIC EQUATIONS

The zero-product rule indicates that if we can factor a quadratic equation, then we can find its roots or solutions. A quadratic equation will never have more than two roots. Normally, all quadratic equations are considered to have two roots. But, there are times when both of these roots are the same number. In this case, the roots are referred to as *double roots*. There are also times when there will be no real numbers that are roots of a quadratic equation. In this case, the roots will be imaginary numbers. (We will talk more about this later in this chapter and again in Chapter 14.)

FINDING ROOTS BY FACTORING

Let's begin by looking at the general idea behind the method of factoring to find roots of a quadratic equation. Suppose we have a general quadratic equation $ax^2 + bx + c = 0$ and that this equation can be factored as follows:

$$ax^2 + bx + c = (rx + t)(sx + v) = 0$$

From the zero-product rule, we know that $rx + t = 0$ or $sx + v = 0$. Solving each of these linear equations, we get $x = \dfrac{-t}{r}$ and $x = \dfrac{-v}{s}$, which are the roots of the quadratic equation. Now, let's look at some examples showing how to use this method.

EXAMPLE 9.33

Find the roots of $x^2 - x - 6 = 0$.

SOLUTION This quadratic equation factors to $(x - 3)(x + 2)$. So, from the zero-product rule, we have

$$x^2 - x - 6 = 0$$
$$(x - 3)(x + 2) = 0$$
$$x - 3 = 0 \text{ and } x = 3$$
$$\text{or} \quad x + 2 = 0 \text{ and } x = -2$$

EXAMPLE 9.34

Find the roots of $-x^2 + 6x - 9 = 0$.

SOLUTION Begin by factoring a -1 out of the left-hand side of the equation. The result is $-1(x^2 - 6x + 9) = 0$ or $-(x^2 - 6x + 9) = 0$. Factoring $x^2 - 6x + 9 = 0$, we get $(x - 3)^2$, so

$$-x^2 + 6x - 9 = 0$$
$$-(x^2 - 6x + 9) = 0$$
$$-(x - 3)(x - 3) = 0$$
$$x - 3 = 0 \text{ and } x = 3$$

This is a double root. Both roots are the same: 3.

EXAMPLE 9.35

Find the roots of $6x^2 - 11x - 35 = 0$.

SOLUTION
$$6x^2 - 11x - 35 = 0$$
$$(3x + 5)(2x - 7) = 0$$
$$3x + 5 = 0 \text{ and } x = -\frac{5}{3}$$
$$\text{or} \qquad 2x - 7 = 0 \text{ and } x = \frac{7}{2}$$

It is very important that one side of the equation is equal to 0.

 CAUTION The property that we are using, the zero-product rule, says that if $ab = 0$, then $a = 0$ or $b = 0$ (or both). It is guaranteed to work *only* if the right-hand side of the equation is 0. For example, $ab = 1$ does *not* imply that $a = 1$ or $b = 1$.

Suppose you had a problem such as $(x - 2)(x + 4) = 16$, where the right-hand side of the equation is not 0, and you try to use the zero-product rule to solve the equation. If $(x - 2)(x + 4) = 16$, you might incorrectly say $x - 2 = 16$ or $x + 4 = 16$. In the first case, $x - 2 = 16$, we get a possible solution of $x = 18$. In the second case, $x + 4 = 16$, we obtain an answer of $x = 12$.

Now check these answers.

If $x = 18$, then $(x - 2)(x + 4) = (18 - 2)(18 + 4) = (16)(22) = 352$, which is certainly not 16. This answer does not check. Let's try the other solution.

If $x = 12$, then $(x - 2)(x + 4) = (12 - 2)(12 + 4) = (10)(16) = 160$. Again, we do not get an answer of 16.

This was intended to show you that it is important to make sure that the right-hand side of the equation is 0 before applying the zero-product rule. The next example will show how you should have solved a problem such as this one when the right-hand side of the equation is not 0.

EXAMPLE 9.36

Solve $(x - 2)(x + 4) = 16$ for x.

SOLUTION Begin by expanding the left-hand side of the equation and then subtracting 16 from both sides.

$$(x - 2)(x + 4) = 16$$
$$x^2 + 2x - 8 = 16$$
$$x^2 + 2x - 24 = 0$$
$$(x - 4)(x + 6) = 0$$
$$x - 4 = 0 \text{ and } x = 4$$
$$\text{or} \qquad x + 6 = 0 \text{ and } x = -6$$

Now check these answers.

If $x = 4$, then $(x - 2)(x + 4) = (4 - 2)(4 + 4) = (2)(8) = 16$. So, 4 is a solution.

If $x = -6$, then $(x - 2)(x + 4) = (-6 - 2)(-6 + 4) = (-8)(-2) = 16$. Again, we get a correct answer.

EXAMPLE 9.37

Find the roots of $4x^2 - 10 = 3x$.

SOLUTION Before we can factor this problem, we have to get all the terms on the left-hand side of the equation; then the right-hand side will be 0.

$$4x^2 - 10 = 3x$$
$$4x^2 - 3x - 10 = 0$$
$$(4x + 5)(x - 2) = 0$$
$$4x + 5 = 0 \text{ and } x = -\frac{5}{4}$$
$$\text{or} \qquad x - 2 = 0 \text{ and } x = 2$$

So, the two roots of this equation are $x = -\frac{5}{4}$ and $x = 2$.

It is also possible to solve some fractional equations by factoring. You will need to first multiply the equation by the LCD, and then put all the nonzero terms on the left-hand side of the equation before you begin to factor the equation. The next example shows how to do this.

EXAMPLE 9.38

Find the roots of $\dfrac{6}{x(3 - 2x)} - \dfrac{4}{3 - 2x} = 1$.

SOLUTION The LCD is $x(3 - 2x)$, so $x \neq 0$ and $x \neq \frac{3}{2}$. Multiplying both sides of the equation by $x(3 - 2x)$ provides

454   CHAPTER 9   Fractional and Quadratic Equations

EXAMPLE 9.38 (Cont.)

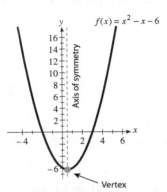

$f(x) = x^2 - x - 6$

© Cengage Learning 2013

Figure 9.1

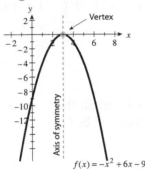

$f(x) = -x^2 + 6x - 9$

© Cengage Learning 2013

Figure 9.2

$$6 - 4x = x(3 - 2x)$$
$$6 - 4x - x(3 - 2x) = 0$$
$$6 - 4x - 3x + 2x^2 = 0$$
$$2x^2 - 7x + 6 = 0$$
$$(2x - 3)(x - 2) = 0$$
$$2x - 3 = 0 \text{ and } x = \frac{3}{2}$$
or $$x - 2 = 0 \text{ and } x = 2$$

Since $x \neq \frac{3}{2}$, the only root is $x = 2$.

This section will not place much emphasis on graphing. But, you should realize that a quadratic function and its roots can be graphically represented. Figures 9.1 and 9.2 show the graphs for the quadratic functions $f(x) = x^2 - x - 6$ and $f(x) = x^2 + 6x + 9$, formed by the quadratic equations in Examples 9.33 and 9.34. As we will learn in Chapter 15, these are both examples of graphs called "parabolas."

Every **parabola** is symmetric about a line called the *axis of symmetry*. In Figure 9.1 the axis of symmetry is the line $x = 0.5$. In Figure 9.2 the axis of symmetry is the line $x = 3$. The point where the parabola crosses the axis of symmetry is the *vertex*. The x-coordinate of the vertex of a quadratic function $f(x) = ax^2 + bx + c$ is $x = \dfrac{-b}{2a}$. So, for the quadratic function in Figure 9.1, the vertex is when $x = \dfrac{-(-1)}{2(1)} = 0.5$. The y-coordinate of the vertex is $f(0.5) = -6.25$.

In Example 9.33, we found that the roots of $x^2 - x - 6 = 0$ were -2 and 3 and that these are the points where the graph crosses the x-axis as shown in Figure 9.1. In Example 9.34, the quadratic equation $-x^2 + 6x - 9 = 0$ had a double root, $x = 3$. The graph of the quadratic function for Example 9.34, $f(x) = -x^2 + 6x - 9$ as shown in Figure 9.2, intersects the x-axis at exactly one point, and that one point is $x = 3$.

EXAMPLE 9.39

Find the roots of $x^2 = 16$.

SOLUTION This equation is equivalent to $x^2 - 16 = 0$. Factoring, we obtain $(x - 4)(x + 4) = 0$ and $x = 4$ or $x = -4$. We could have solved this problem with less work if we had taken the square root of both sides.

$$x^2 = 16$$
$$x = \pm \sqrt{16}$$
$$x = \pm 4$$

In general, if $c \geq 0$ and $x^2 = c$, then $x = \pm \sqrt{c}$.

184

EXAMPLE 9.40

Find the roots of $9x^2 = 25$.

SOLUTION $9x^2 = 25$

$$x^2 = \frac{25}{9}$$

$$x = \pm\sqrt{\frac{25}{9}} = \pm\frac{5}{3}$$

EXAMPLE 9.41

Find the roots of $(x - 4)^2 = 25$.

SOLUTION There are two ways to work this problem.

Method 1: First, we will square the left-hand side of the equation and collect like terms.

$$(x - 4)^2 = 25$$
$$x^2 - 8x + 16 = 25$$
$$x^2 - 8x + 16 - 25 = 0$$
$$x^2 - 8x - 9 = 0$$
$$(x - 9)(x + 1) = 0$$
$$x = 9 \text{ or } x = -1$$

Method 2: This is a shortcut. It will save time, but you have to be careful that you do not make errors. We will first take the square root of both sides. Once this is done, we will solve the linear equation for both values of x.

$$(x - 4)^2 = 25$$
$$\sqrt{(x - 4)^2} = \pm\sqrt{25}$$
$$x - 4 = \pm 5$$
$$x = 4 + 5 = 9$$
or
$$x = 4 - 5 = -1$$

This is the same answer we got using the first method.

APPLICATION **MECHANICAL**

EXAMPLE 9.42

A rectangular piece of aluminum is to be used to form a box. (See Figure 9.3a.) A 2-in. square is to be cut from each corner and the ends are to be folded up to form an open box. (See Figure 9.3b.) If the original piece of aluminum was twice as long as it was wide, and the volume of the box is 672 in.³, what were the dimensions of the original rectangle?

SOLUTION If the width of the original rectangle is w, then the length is $2w$. The width of the box is $w - 4$ and the length of the box is $2w - 4$. The volume of the box is the product of the width, length, and height or

EXAMPLE 9.42 (Cont.)

$$wlh = V$$
$$(w - 4)(2w - 4)2 = 672$$
$$4w^2 - 24w + 32 = 672 \qquad \text{Multiply.}$$
$$4w^2 - 24w - 640 = 0 \qquad \text{Put equation in standard form.}$$
$$w^2 - 6w - 160 = 0 \qquad \text{Divide both sides by 4.}$$
$$(w - 16)(w + 10) = 0 \qquad \text{Factor.}$$

If $w - 16 = 0$, then $w = 16$, and if $w + 10 = 0$, then $w = -10$. The last answer does not make sense. We cannot have a rectangle with a width of -10 in. So, the width of the original rectangle is 16 in. and the length is 32 in.

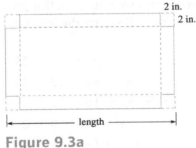

Figure 9.3a   Figure 9.3b

© Cengage Learning 2013

EXERCISE SET 9.4

In Exercises 1–44, solve the quadratic equations by factoring.

1. $x^2 - 9 = 0$
2. $x^2 - 100 = 0$
3. $x^2 + x - 6 = 0$
4. $x^2 - 6x - 7 = 0$
5. $x^2 - 11x - 12 = 0$
6. $x^2 - 5x + 4 = 0$
7. $x^2 + 2x - 8 = 0$
8. $x^2 + 2x - 15 = 0$
9. $x^2 - 5x = 0$
10. $x^2 + 10x = 0$
11. $x^2 + 12 = 7x$
12. $x^2 = 7x - 10$
13. $2x^2 - 3x - 14 = 0$
14. $2x^2 + x - 15 = 0$
15. $2x^2 + 12 = 11x$
16. $2x^2 + 18 = 15x$
17. $3x^2 - 8x - 3 = 0$
18. $3x^2 - 4x - 4 = 0$

19. $4x^2 - 24x + 35 = 0$
20. $6x^2 - 13x + 6 = 0$
21. $6x^2 + 11x - 35 = 0$
22. $10x^2 + 9x - 9 = 0$
23. $10x^2 - 17x + 3 = 0$
24. $14x^2 - 29x - 15 = 0$
25. $6x^2 = 31x + 60$
26. $15x^2 = 23x - 4$
27. $(x - 1)^2 = 4$
28. $(x + 2)^2 = 9$
29. $(5x - 2)^2 = 16$
30. $(3x + 2)^2 = 64$
31. $\dfrac{x}{x + 1} = \dfrac{x + 2}{3x}$
32. $\dfrac{4x}{x - 1} = \dfrac{7x + 2}{x}$
33. $(x + 5)^3 = x^3 + 1385$
34. $(x - 3)^3 = x^3 - 63$

35. $(x - 4)^3 - x^3 = -316$
36. $(x + 2)^3 - x^3 = 56$
37. $\dfrac{1}{x - 3} + \dfrac{1}{x + 4} = \dfrac{1}{12}$
38. $\dfrac{1}{x - 5} + \dfrac{1}{x + 3} = \dfrac{1}{3}$
39. $\dfrac{1}{x - 1} + \dfrac{1}{x - 2} = \dfrac{7}{12}$
40. $\dfrac{1}{x + 1} - \dfrac{1}{x + 2} = \dfrac{1}{20}$
41. $\dfrac{2}{x - 4} + \dfrac{1}{x - 9} = \dfrac{1}{6}$
42. $\dfrac{x}{x + 1} + \dfrac{1}{x} = \dfrac{13}{12}$
43. $\dfrac{x}{x + 1} - \dfrac{2x}{x + 3} = -\dfrac{1}{15}$
44. $\dfrac{3x}{x - 1} - \dfrac{9x}{x + 2} = 8.4$

Solve Exercises 45–58.

45. Dynamics A ball is thrown vertically upward into the air from the roof of a building 192 ft high. The height of the ball above the ground is a function of the time in seconds and the initial velocity of the ball. If the initial velocity is 64 ft/s, then the height is given by $h(t) = -16t^2 + 64t + 192$. How many seconds will it take for the ball to return to the roof? (That is, when will $h(t) = 192$?)

46. Dynamics If the ball in Exercise 45 misses the building when it comes down, how long will it take for the ball to hit the ground? (When will $h(t) = 0$?)

47. The length of a rectangle is 5 cm more than its width. Find the length and width, if the area is 104 cm².

48. Dynamics Figure 9.4 is a drawing of the Burj Khalifa in Dubai. At 828 m (2,716.5 ft), this is the tallest building in the world. Suppose that a ball is dropped from the top of the building and it can fall without hitting anything until it strikes the ground. Neglecting air resistance, the ball falls at 4.9 m/s². How long will it take for the ball to strike the ground? (Hint: Solve $4.9t^2 = 828$.)

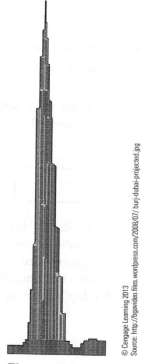

© Cengage Learning 2013
Source: http://hgavideo.files.wordpress.com/2008/07/burj-dubai-projected.jpg

Figure 9.4

49. Solar Energy In order to support a solar collector at the correct angle, the roof trusses for a building are designed as right triangles, as shown in Figure 9.5. The rafter on the same side as the solar collector is 7 m shorter than the other rafter and the base of each truss is 13 m long. What are the lengths of the rafters?

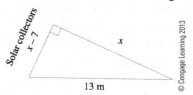

Solar collectors
$x - 7$
x
13 m
© Cengage Learning 2013

Figure 9.5

50. Computer technology Working alone, computer A can complete a data-processing job in 6 h less than computer B working alone. Together the two computers can complete the job in 4 h. How long would it take each computer by itself?

51. Construction A rectangular concrete pipe is constructed with a 10.00 in. by 16.00 in. interior channel, as shown in Figure 9.6. What uniform width w of concrete must be formed on all sides if the total cross-sectional area of the concrete must be 192 in.²?

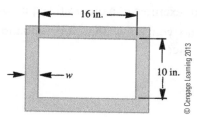

16 in.
10 in.
w
© Cengage Learning 2013

Figure 9.6

52. Construction A rectangular parking lot at a shopping mall is 50.0 m wide and 80.0 m long. The developers of the mall want to expand the parking area to 18 000 m². They plan to do this by adding an equal length, in meters, to the length and to the width. What are the dimensions of the new parking lot?

53. Recreation A swim club has a circular swimming pool with a diameter of 24 m. The club wants to build a deck of uniform width around the pool. Because of the financial condition of the club and the cost of materials, the club members can only afford to build a deck of area 432π m² around the pool. How wide should they build the deck?

54. *Recreation* A swim club has a rectangular swimming pool 30.0 ft long and 22 ft wide. The club wants to build a deck of uniform width around the pool. Because of the financial condition of the club and the cost of materials, the club members can only afford to build a deck of 480 ft² around the pool. How wide should they build the deck?

55. *Wastewater technology* Working together, two pipes, A and B, can fill a tank in 4 h. It takes pipe A 6 h longer than pipe B to fill the tank alone. How long would it take each pipe alone to fill the tank?

56. *Electronics* In a certain circuit, the power (in watts) is measured using current, I (in amperes, A), voltage E (in volts, V), and resistance, R (in ohms, Ω), by $RI^2 + EI = 18\,000$. If the resistance is 10.0 Ω and the voltage is 510 V, find the current in amperes.

57. *Forestry* Volume estimates, V, in ft³, for shortleaf pine trees are based on D, the d.b.h. (diameter at breast height) in inches; top d.i.b. (the diameter inside the bark at the top of the tree) in inches; and H (the height of the tree in ft). One formula for trees with a 3-in. top d.i.b. is

$$V = 0.002837D^2H - 0.127248$$

Determine D for a 75-ft-high tree that has a volume estimate of 47.75 ft³. (Note: This formula does not require any unit conversions.)

58. *Forestry* Volume estimates, V, in ft³, for shortleaf pine trees are based on D, the d.b.h. (diameter at breast height) in inches; top d.i.b. (the diameter inside the bark at the top of the tree) in inches; and H (the height of the tree in ft). One formula for trees with a 4-in. top d.i.b. is

$$V = 0.002835D^2H - 0.337655$$

Determine D for an 85-ft-high tree that has a volume estimate of 61.35 ft³.

 [IN YOUR WORDS]

59. (a) Give an example of a quadratic equation.

   (b) How do you know that your equation is quadratic?

60. (a) What is a root of a quadratic equation?

   (b) What is the zero-product rule for real numbers?

   (c) How does the zero-product rule help to find roots of a quadratic equation?

9.5   COMPLETING THE SQUARE AND THE QUADRATIC FORMULA

Factoring is one method that can be used to solve quadratic equations. However, it is very difficult to factor some equations. In fact, most equations cannot be factored using integers or rational numbers. We are going to introduce a technique called **completing the square**, which we can use to solve these quadratic equations. We will then use completing the square to develop a formula that will allow us to solve any quadratic equation.

COMPLETING THE SQUARE

Let's look at some special products—those that are perfect squares. The general form is $(x + k)^2 = x^2 + 2kx + k^2$. Notice that the constant, k^2, is the square of one-half of $2k$, the coefficient of x. If we combine the method for solving quadratic equations and the special product for perfect squares, we can develop the method of completing the square.

Suppose you had the equation $x^2 + 6x - 10 = 0$. A quick check of the discriminant ($b^2 - 4ac$) shows that it is $6^2 - 4(1)(-10) = 36 + 40 = 76$. Since 76 is not a perfect square, we cannot factor this equation. Rewrite the equation so that the variables are on the left-hand side and the constant term is on the right-hand side. We want to add something to the left-hand side so that side is a perfect square. (We have placed an empty box on each side of the equation to show that we will add something to both sides when we complete the square.)

$$x^2 + 6x + \boxed{} = 10 + \boxed{}$$

Complete the square on the left-hand side by taking one-half of the coefficient of the x-term, squaring it, and adding this number to both sides of the equation. The coefficient of x is 6, half of that is 3, and $3^2 = 9$. This is added to both sides of the equation and placed inside the empty boxes.

$$x^2 + 6x + \boxed{9} = 10 + \boxed{9}$$

or $\qquad x^2 + 6x + 9 = 19$

The left-hand side is now a perfect square.

$$(x + 3)^2 = 19$$

We can solve this equation by using the second method from Example 9.41.

$$\sqrt{(x + 3)^2} = \pm\sqrt{19}$$

$$x + 3 = \pm\sqrt{19}$$

$$x = -3 \pm\sqrt{19}$$

$$x = -3 + \sqrt{19} \text{ or } = -3 - \sqrt{19}$$

Check these answers. (The easiest way is to use your calculator.) You should see that they check when they are substituted in the original equation $x^2 + 6x - 10 = 0$.

EXAMPLE 9.43

Find the roots of $x^2 - 9x - 5 = 0$.

SOLUTION

$$x^2 - 9x - 5 = 0$$

$$x^2 - 9x + \boxed{} = 5 + \boxed{}$$

$$x^2 - 9x + \boxed{\left(\frac{9}{2}\right)^2} = 5 + \boxed{\left(\frac{9}{2}\right)^2}$$

$$= 5 + \frac{81}{4}$$

$$= \frac{101}{4}$$

$$\left(x - \frac{9}{2}\right)^2 = \frac{101}{4}$$

$$\sqrt{\left(x - \frac{9}{2}\right)^2} = \pm\sqrt{\frac{101}{4}} = \pm\frac{\sqrt{101}}{2}$$

$$x - \frac{9}{2} = \pm\frac{\sqrt{101}}{2}$$

$$x = \frac{9}{2} \pm \frac{\sqrt{101}}{2}$$

$$x = \frac{9 + \sqrt{101}}{2} \text{ or } x = \frac{9 - \sqrt{101}}{2}$$

Before you complete the square, the coefficient on the x^2-term must be 1. One way to do this is shown in the next example.

EXAMPLE 9.44

Find the roots of $2x^2 - 8x + 3 = 0$.

SOLUTION This is slightly complicated by the fact the coefficient of $2x^2$ is not 1. Our first step will be to divide the equation by 2 and then proceed as we have before.

$$2x^2 - 8x + 3 = 0$$

$$x^2 - 4x + \frac{3}{2} = 0$$

$$x^2 - 4x + \boxed{} = -\frac{3}{2} + \boxed{}$$

$$x^2 - 4x + \boxed{2^2} = -\frac{3}{2} + \boxed{2^2}$$

$$(x - 2)^2 = -\frac{3}{2} + 4 = \frac{5}{2}$$

$$x - 2 = \pm\sqrt{\frac{5}{2}}$$

$$x = 2 \pm \sqrt{\frac{5}{2}}$$

THE QUADRATIC FORMULA

We will now use completing the square to develop a general formula that can be used to find the roots of any quadratic equation.

Suppose we have a standard quadratic equation

$$ax^2 + bx + c = 0, \text{ with } a \neq 0$$

What are the roots of this quadratic equation? If we complete the square, we can find out.

$$ax^2 + bx + c = 0$$

$$x^2 + \frac{b}{a}x + \frac{c}{a} = 0 \qquad \text{Divide both sides by } a.$$

$$x^2 + \frac{b}{a}x = -\frac{c}{a} \qquad \text{Add } -\frac{c}{a} \text{ to both sides.}$$

$$x^2 + \frac{b}{a}x + \left(\frac{b}{2a}\right)^2 = -\frac{c}{a} + \left(\frac{b}{2a}\right)^2 \qquad \text{Complete the square by adding to } \left(\frac{b}{2a}\right)^2 \text{ both sides.}$$

$$\left(x + \frac{b}{2a}\right)^2 = \frac{b^2}{4a^2} - \frac{4ac}{4a^2} \qquad \text{Factor the left-hand side; reverse terms on the right-hand side.}$$

$$= \frac{b^2 - 4ac}{4a^2} \qquad \text{Collect terms on the right-hand side.}$$

$$x + \frac{b}{2a} = \pm\sqrt{\frac{b^2 - 4ac}{4a^2}} \qquad \text{Take the square root of both sides.}$$

$$= \pm\frac{\sqrt{b^2 - 4ac}}{2a}$$

$$x = \frac{-b}{2a} \pm \frac{\sqrt{b^2 - 4ac}}{2a} \qquad \text{Solve for } x.$$

$$= \frac{-b \pm \sqrt{b^2 - 4ac}}{2a}$$

This is the **quadratic formula**.

QUADRATIC FORMULA

The solutions of the equation $ax^2 + bx + c = 0$, $(a \neq 0)$ are given by

$$x = \frac{-b \pm \sqrt{b^2 - 4ac}}{2a}$$

The expression $b^2 - 4ac$ is called the **discriminant**.

To solve a quadratic equation by using the quadratic formula, write the equation in the standard form, identify a, b, and c, and substitute these numbers into the equation. The quadratic formula is a very useful tool, but many equations are easier to solve by factoring.

You may recognize something we have used before in part of the quadratic formula. The quantity $b^2 - 4ac$ is the discriminant. We used it to help tell us when a quadratic equation can be factored. Now we can use it to tell us something else. Since the quadratic formula takes the square root of the discriminant, a quadratic equation will have only real numbers as roots when $b^2 - 4ac \geq 0$. In Chapter 14, when we study complex numbers, we will consider quadratic equations in which the discriminant is negative.

EXAMPLE 9.45

Solve $x^2 + 7x - 8 = 0$.

SOLUTION In this equation, $a = 1$, $b = 7$, and $c = -8$. Putting these values in the quadratic formula we get

$$x = \frac{-7 \pm \sqrt{7^2 - 4(1)(-8)}}{2(1)}$$

$$= \frac{-7 \pm \sqrt{49 + 32}}{2}$$

$$= \frac{-7 \pm \sqrt{81}}{2}$$

$$= \frac{-7 \pm 9}{2}$$

$$x = \frac{-7 + 9}{2} = \frac{2}{2} = 1$$

or

$$x = \frac{-7 - 9}{2} = \frac{-16}{2} = -8$$

The roots are 1 and -8. This is an equation that we could have solved by factoring.

EXAMPLE 9.46

Solve $2x^2 + 5x - 3 = 0$.

SOLUTION In this equation $a = 2$, $b = 5$, and $c = -3$. Putting these values in the quadratic formula we get

$$x = \frac{-5 \pm \sqrt{5^2 - 4(2)(-3)}}{2(2)}$$

$$= \frac{-5 \pm \sqrt{25 + 24}}{4}$$

$$= \frac{-5 \pm \sqrt{49}}{4}$$

$$= \frac{-5 \pm 7}{4}$$

So,

$$x = \frac{-5 + 7}{4} = \frac{2}{4} = \frac{1}{2} \text{ or } x = \frac{-5 - 7}{4} = \frac{-12}{4} = -3$$

The roots are $\frac{1}{2}$ and -3.

EXAMPLE 9.47

Solve $9x^2 + 49 = 42x$.

SOLUTION This equation is not in the standard form. If we subtract $42x$ from both sides, we get $9x^2 - 42x + 49 = 0$, with $a = 9$, $b = -42$, and $c = 49$. Substituting these values for a, b, and c in the quadratic formula, we obtain

$$x = \frac{42 \pm \sqrt{(-42)^2 - 4(9)(49)}}{2(9)}$$

$$= \frac{42 \pm \sqrt{1764 - 1764}}{18}$$

$$= \frac{42 \pm 0}{18}$$

$$= \frac{7}{3}$$

This is a double root; in this case both roots are $\frac{7}{3}$.

EXAMPLE 9.48

Find the roots of $3x^2 + 7x + 3 = 0$.

SOLUTION In this equation, $a = 3$, $b = 7$, and $c = 3$, so

$$x = \frac{-7 \pm \sqrt{7^2 - 4(3)(3)}}{2(3)}$$

$$= \frac{-7 \pm \sqrt{49 - 36}}{6}$$

$$= \frac{-7 \pm \sqrt{13}}{6}$$

So, $x = \dfrac{-7 + \sqrt{13}}{6}$ or $x = \dfrac{-7 - \sqrt{13}}{6}$

Notice that we really needed the quadratic formula to find the factors.

 HINT Unless you quickly see that an equation can be factored, it may be best to use the quadratic formula.

APPLICATION MECHANICAL

EXAMPLE 9.49

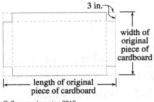

© Cengage Learning 2013

Figure 9.7

The length of a rectangular piece of cardboard is 4 in. more than its width. A 3-in. square is removed from each corner as shown in Figure 9.7. The remaining cardboard is bent to form an open box. If the volume of the box is 420 in.³, what are the dimensions of the original piece of cardboard?

SOLUTION We will begin by letting x be the width, in inches, of the original piece of cardboard. The length of this cardboard is $x + 4$ in. After the squares are removed and the sides have been folded up, the dimensions of the box are

$$\text{length} = (x + 4) - 2 \cdot 3 = x - 2$$
$$\text{width} = x - 6$$
$$\text{height} = 3$$

The volume, 420 in.³, is: length × width × height, or $V = lwh$, and so we obtain

$$(x - 2)(x - 6)3 = 420$$
$$(x - 2)(x - 6) = 140$$
$$x^2 - 8x + 12 = 140$$
$$x^2 - 8x - 128 = 0$$
$$(x - 16)(x + 8) = 0$$
$$x = 16 \text{ or } x = -8$$

It would make no sense for the width of a piece of cardboard to be -8 in., so we reject $x = -8$ as an answer.

Thus, the piece of cardboard must have a width of 16 in. and a length of $16 + 4 = 20$ in.

APPLICATION GENERAL TECHNOLOGY

EXAMPLE 9.50

A ball is thrown upward from the top of a building that is 555 ft high with an initial velocity of 64 ft/s. The height of the ball in feet above the ground at any time t is given by the formula $s(t) = 555 + 64t - 16t^2$. When will the ball hit the ground?

SOLUTION When the ball hits the ground, its height will be 0. So, we want to solve the equation

$$0 = 555 + 64t - 16t^2$$

for t. First write the equation in standard form and then use the quadratic formula to solve it. Multiplying the equation by -1 produces

$$16t^2 - 64t - 555 = 0$$

Here $a = 16$, $b = -64$, and $c = -555$. Substituting these into the quadratic formula we get

$$t = \frac{-b \pm \sqrt{b^2 - 4ac}}{2a}$$

$$= \frac{-(-64) \pm \sqrt{(-64)^2 - 4(16)(-555)}}{2(16)}$$

$$= \frac{64 \pm \sqrt{4096 + 35{,}520}}{32}$$

$$= \frac{64 \pm \sqrt{39{,}616}}{32}$$

$$\approx \frac{64 \pm 199.03768}{32}$$

$$\approx 2 \pm 6.22$$

Thus, $t \approx 8.22$ s or $t \approx -4.22$ s. The second answer makes no sense, because this would mean that the ball struck the ground before it was thrown. The first answer, about 8.22 s, checks when it is substituted into the original equation, and so it is the correct answer.

APPLICATION **ENVIRONMENTAL SCIENCE**

EXAMPLE 9.51

The photograph in Figure 9.8a shows a solar collector. The roof trusses for a solar collector are often designed as right triangles, so the solar collector will be supported at the correct angle. Rafters form the legs of the right triangle and the base of the truss forms the hypotenuse. Suppose the rafter along the back of the solar collector is 3.5 m shorter than the other rafter and that the base of each truss is 6.5 m long. What is the length of each rafter?

SOLUTION A triangle has been drawn over the photograph of the solar collector in Figure 9.8a. The triangle is labeled with the given information and shown by itself in Figure 9.8b. Since this is a right triangle, we can use the Pythagorean theorem. Thus, we have

$$x^2 + (x - 3.5)^2 = 6.5^2$$

Squaring both sides produces

$$x^2 + (x^2 - 7x + 12.25) = 42.25$$

$$\text{or} \qquad 2x^2 - 7x - 30 = 0$$

EXAMPLE 9.51 (Cont.)

Figure 9.8a

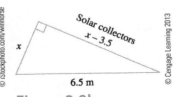

Figure 9.8b

Using the quadratic formula we get

$$x = \frac{-(-7) \pm \sqrt{(-7)^2 - 4(2)(-30)}}{2 \cdot 2}$$

$$= \frac{7 \pm \sqrt{49 + 240}}{4}$$

$$= \frac{7 \pm 17}{4}$$

Thus, $x = 6$ or $x = -2.5$.

It would not make sense for a rafter to be -2.5 m long. The lengths of the rafters must be 6 m and $6 - 3.5 = 2.5$ m long.

EXERCISE SET 9.5

Find the roots of each of the quadratic equations in Exercises 1–8 by completing the square.

1. $x^2 + 6x + 8 = 0$ **3.** $2x^2 - 3x = 14$ **5.** $4x^2 - 12x - 18 = 0$ **7.** $x^2 + 2kx + c = 0$

2. $x^2 - 7x - 8 = 0$ **4.** $3x^2 + 12x - 18 = 0$ **6.** $3x^2 - 9x = 33$ **8.** $px^2 + 2qx + r = 0$

In Exercises 9–46, use the quadratic formula to find the roots of each equation.

9. $x^2 + 3x - 4 = 0$ **17.** $3x^2 + 2x - 8 = 0$ **25.** $2x^2 + 6x - 3 = 0$ **33.** $\frac{2}{3}x^2 - \frac{1}{9}x + 3 = 0$

10. $x^2 - 8x - 33 = 0$ **18.** $9x^2 - 6x + 1 = 0$ **26.** $5x^2 + 2x - 1 = 0$ **34.** $\frac{1}{2}x^2 - 2x + \frac{1}{3} = 0$

11. $3x^2 - 5x - 2 = 0$ **19.** $9x^2 + 12x + 4 = 0$ **27.** $x^2 - 2x - 7 = 0$ **35.** $0.01x^2 + 0.2x = 0.6$

12. $7x^2 + 5x - 2 = 0$ **20.** $3x^2 + 3x - 7 = 0$ **28.** $x^2 + 3 = 0$ **36.** $0.16x^2 = 0.8x - 1$

13. $7x^2 + 6x - 1 = 0$ **21.** $2x^2 - 3x - 1 = 0$ **29.** $2x^2 - 3 = 0$ **37.** $\frac{1}{4}x^2 + 3 = \frac{5}{2}x$

14. $2x^2 - 3x - 20 = 0$ **22.** $2x^2 - 5x + 1 = 0$ **30.** $2x^2 = 5$ **38.** $\frac{3}{2}x^2 + 2x = \frac{7}{2}$

15. $2x^2 - 5x - 7 = 0$ **23.** $x^2 + 5x + 2 = 0$ **31.** $3x^2 + 4 = 0$ **39.** $1.2x^2 = 2x - 0.5$

16. $3x^2 + 4x - 7 = 0$ **24.** $3x^2 - 6x - 2 = 0$ **32.** $3x^2 + 1 = 5x$

40. $1.4x^2 + 0.2x = 2.3$

41. $3x^2 + \sqrt{3}x - 7 = 0$

42. $2x^2 - \sqrt{89}x + 5 = 0$

43. $\dfrac{x - 3}{7} = 2x^2$

44. $\dfrac{x - 5}{3} = 5x^2$

45. $\dfrac{2}{x - 1} + 3 = \dfrac{-2}{x + 1}$

46. $\dfrac{3x}{x + 2} + 2x = \dfrac{2x^2 - 1}{x + 1}$

Solve Exercises 47–68.

47. Dynamics The Petronas Towers are 452 m high. If a ball is dropped from the top of one of the towers, its height at time t is given by the formula $h(t) = -4.9t^2 + 452$. The ball will hit the ground when $h(t) = 0$. How long does it take for the ball to fall to the ground?

48. Dynamics If the ball in the previous problem is thrown downward with an initial velocity of 20 m/s, its height at time t is given by $h(t) = -4.9t^2 - 20t + 452$. When does it hit the ground?

49. Dynamics If the ball in the previous problem is thrown upward with an initial velocity of 20 m/s, its height at time t is given by $h(t) = -4.9t^2 + 20t + 452$. How long will it take to hit the ground?

50. Sheet metal technology An open box is to be made from a square piece of aluminum by cutting out a 4-cm square from each corner and folding up the sides. If the box is to have a volume of 100 cm³, find the dimensions of the piece of aluminum that is needed.

51. Sheet metal technology An open box is to be made from a rectangular piece of aluminum. A 3-cm square is to be cut from each corner and the sides will be folded up. If the original piece of aluminum was 1.5 times as long as its width and the volume of the box is 578 cm³, what were the dimensions of the original rectangle?

52. Construction An angle beam is to be constructed as shown in Figure 9.9. If the cross-sectional area of the angle beam is 81.25 cm², what is the thickness of the beam?

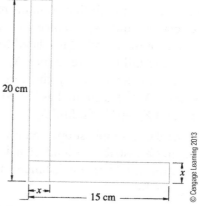

Figure 9.9

53. Sheet metal technology A gutter is to be made by folding up the edges of a strip of metal as shown in Figure 9.10. If the metal is 12 in. wide and the cross-sectional area of the gutter is to be $16\frac{7}{8}$ in.², what are the width and depth of the gutter?

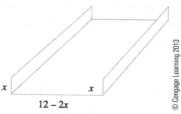

Figure 9.10

54. Package design A cylindrical container is to be made with a height of 10 cm. If the total surface area of the container is to be 245 cm², what is the radius of the base?

55. Business An oil distributor has 1,000 commercial customers who each pay a base rate of $30 per month for oil. The distributor figures that for each $1-per-month increase in the base rate, 5 customers will convert to coal. The distributor needs to increase its monthly income to $45,000 and lose as few customers as possible. How much should the base rate be increased?

56. **Electricity** In an ac circuit that contains resistance, inductance, and capacitance in series, the applied voltage V can be found by solving $V^2 = V_R^2 + (V_L - V_C)^2$. If $V = 5.8$ V, $V_R = 5$ V, and $V_C = 10$ V, find V_L.

57. **Electricity** In an ac circuit that contains resistance, inductance, and capacitance in series, the impedance of the circuit Z is related to the resistance R, the inductive reactance X_L, and the capacitive reactance X_C, by the formula, $Z^2 = R^2 + (X_L - X_C)^2$. If a circuit has $Z = 610\,\Omega$, $R = 300\,\Omega$, and $X_C = 531\,\Omega$, find X_L.

58. **Construction** For a simply supported beam of length l having a distributed load of w kg/m, the binding moment M at any distance x from one end is given by

$$M = \frac{1}{2}wlx - \frac{1}{2}wx^2$$

At which locations is the binding moment zero?

59. **Construction** A rectangular concrete pipe is constructed with a 10.00 in. by 16.00 in. interior channel, as shown in Figure 9.11. What uniform width w of concrete must be formed on all sides if the total cross-sectional area of the concrete must be 245in.^{2}?

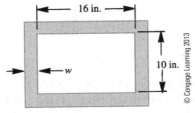

16 in.

10 in.

w

© Cengage Learning 2013

Figure 9.11

60. **Construction** A rectangular parking lot at a shopping mall is 50.0 m wide and 80.0 m long. The developers of the mall want to double the parking area. They plan to do this by adding an equal distance, in meters, to the length and to the width of the lot. What are the dimensions of the new parking lot?

61. **Forestry** The Scribner log-rule equation for 16-ft logs is $V = 0.79D^2 - 2D - 4$, where V is the volume, in board ft, of the log and D is the diameter, in in., of the small end of a log inside the bark. If a certain 16-ft log has a volume of 926.0 board ft, what is the diameter of the small end of the log inside the bark?

62. **Forestry** Use the Scribner log-rule equation (see Exercise 61), to determine the diameter of the small end of the log inside the bark of a 16.0-ft log that has a volume of 1078.0 board ft.

63. **Physics** When an object is dropped from a building that is 196 ft tall, its height h at any time t after it was dropped is given by the function $h(t) = 196 - 16t^2$. Find the time it takes for the object to strike the ground.

64. **Business** Total revenue from selling a certain object is the product of the price and the quantity of the object sold. If q represents the quantity sold and the price is $\$2{,}520 - 3q$, find the quantity that produces a total revenue of $\$140{,}400$.

65. **Business** Total revenue from selling a certain object is the product of the price and the quantity of the object sold. If q represents the quantity sold and the price of the object is $\$1{,}560 - 4q$, find the quantity that produces a total revenue of $\$29{,}600$.

66. **Agriculture** A farmer has 1,500 ft of fencing to enclose a rectangular field. Find the dimensions of the field so that the enclosed area will be 137,600 ft^2.

67. **Agriculture** A farmer has 2,700 ft of fencing to enclose two adjacent rectangular fields. Find the dimensions of the fields, so that the enclosed area will be 270,000 ft^2.

68. **Electronics** When two resistors, R_1 and R_2, are connected in parallel, their combined resistance, R, is given by $\dfrac{1}{R} = \dfrac{1}{R_1} + \dfrac{1}{R_2}$. Two certain resistors that are connected in parallel have a combined resistance of 6 Ω, and the resistance of one of them is 5 Ω more than that of the other. What is the resistance of each resistor?

[IN YOUR WORDS]

69. Without looking at the definition in the book, describe the technique called "completing the square."

70. Write a word problem in your technology area of interest that requires you to use a quadratic equation. On the back of the sheet of paper, write your name and explain how to solve the problem by using factoring or completing the square. Give the problem you wrote to a friend and let him or her try to solve it. If your friend has difficulty understanding the problem or solving the problem, or disagrees with your solution, make any necessary changes in the problem or solution. When you have finished, give the revised problem and solution to another friend and see if he or she can solve it.

71. (a) Use factoring to solve $3x^2 + 5x - 2 = 0$.

(b) Use the quadratic formula to solve $3x^2 + 5x - 2 = 0$. You should get the same answers you got in (a).

(c) Explain to a classmate how to use the quadratic formula. Check to see how well your classmate understands your explanation by asking him or her to solve $3x^2 + 5x - 2 = 0$.

(d) Under what conditions is the quadratic formula easier to use than factoring?

72. (a) What is the discriminant?

(b) What does the discriminant tell you if it is nonnegative?

11.1 FRACTIONAL EXPONENTS

The basic rules for exponents were given in Section 1.3. They are repeated here to refresh your memory.

BASIC RULES FOR EXPONENTS

Rule 1: $b^m b^n = b^{m+n}$

Rule 2: $(b^m)^n = b^{mn}$

Rule 3: $(ab)^n = a^n b^n$

Rule 4: $\left(\dfrac{a}{b}\right)^m = \dfrac{a^m}{b^m}, b \neq 0$

Rule 5: $\dfrac{b^m}{b^n} = b^{m-n}, b \neq 0$

Rule 6: $b^0 = 1, b \neq 0$

Rule 7: $b^{-n} = \dfrac{1}{b^n}, b \neq 0$

When we studied these rules in Section 1.3, m and n had to be integers. In Section 1.5, we examined the meaning of $b^{1/n}$ and found that it meant $\sqrt[n]{b}$. This makes sense, since $(b^{1/n})^n = b^{n/n} = b$. This gives us a new rule:

RULE 8 FOR EXPONENTS

$$b^{1/n} = \sqrt[n]{b}$$

EXAMPLE 11.1

Evaluate (a) $27^{1/3}$, (b) $16^{1/2}$, and (c) $625^{1/4}$.

SOLUTIONS   (a) $27^{1/3} = \sqrt[3]{27} = 3$

(b) $16^{1/2} = \sqrt{16} = 4$

(c) $625^{1/4} = \sqrt[4]{625} = 5$

If we combine Rules 2 and 8, we obtain the following new rule.

RULE 9 FOR EXPONENTS

$$b^{m/n} = (b^m)^{1/n} = \sqrt[n]{b^m}$$

EXAMPLE 11.2

Evaluate (a) $8^{2/3}$, (b) $64^{5/2}$, (c) $81^{5/4}$, and (d) $9^{-3/2}$.

SOLUTIONS   (a) $8^{2/3} = \sqrt[3]{8^2} = \sqrt[3]{64} = 4$

(b) $64^{5/2} = \sqrt{64^5} = \sqrt{1,073,741,824} = 32,768$

(c) $81^{5/4} = \sqrt[4]{81^5} = \sqrt[4]{3,486,784,401} = 243$

(d) $9^{-3/2} = \dfrac{1}{\sqrt{9^3}} = \dfrac{1}{\sqrt{729}} = \dfrac{1}{27}$

It is often easier to find the root before raising the number to a power. Thus, we could rewrite Rule 9.

RULE 9 FOR EXPONENTS

$$b^{m/n} = (b^{1/n})^m = (\sqrt[n]{b})^m$$

We will rework the problems in Example 11.2 using this variation of Rule 9.

EXAMPLE 11.3

Evaluate (a) $8^{2/3}$, (b) $64^{5/2}$, (c) $81^{5/4}$, (d) $9^{-3/2}$, (e) $(-8)^{2/3}$, (f) $\left(\frac{8}{27}\right)^{-1/3}$, (g) $\left(\frac{1}{16}\right)^{-5/4}$, and (h) $\left(-\frac{64}{125}\right)^{-2/3}$.

SOLUTIONS

(a) $8^{2/3} = (\sqrt[3]{8})^2 = 2^2 = 4$

(b) $64^{5/2} = (\sqrt{64})^5 = 8^5 = 32,768$

(c) $81^{5/4} = (\sqrt[4]{81})^5 = 3^5 = 243$

(d) $9^{-3/2} = \dfrac{1}{(\sqrt{9})^3} = \dfrac{1}{3^3} = \dfrac{1}{27}$

(e) $(-8)^{2/3} = \left(\sqrt[3]{-8}\right)^2 = (-2)^2 = 4$

(f) $\left(\dfrac{8}{27}\right)^{-1/3} = \left(\dfrac{27}{8}\right)^{1/3} = \sqrt[3]{\dfrac{27}{8}} = \dfrac{3}{2}$

(g) $\left(\dfrac{1}{16}\right)^{-5/4} = 16^{5/4} = \left(\sqrt[4]{16}\right)^5 = 2^5 = 32$

(h) $\left(-\dfrac{64}{125}\right)^{-2/3} = \left(-\dfrac{125}{64}\right)^{2/3} = \left(\sqrt[3]{-\dfrac{125}{64}}\right)^2 = \left(-\dfrac{5}{4}\right)^2 = \dfrac{25}{16}$

All of the rules for integer exponents apply to fractional exponents. This is demonstrated in the following example.

EXAMPLE 11.4

(a) $x^{1/2} x^{2/3} = x^{1/2 + 2/3} = x^{7/6}$

(b) $(y^{2/3})^{4/5} = y^{2/3 \cdot 4/5} = y^{8/15}$

(c) $\left(\dfrac{x}{y}\right)^{4/5} = \dfrac{x^{4/5}}{y^{4/5}}$

(d) $\dfrac{x^{3/4}}{x^{5/3}} = x^{3/4 - 5/3} = x^{-11/12} = \dfrac{1}{x^{11/12}}$

(e) $\dfrac{4x^2}{x^{2/3}} = 4x^{2 - 2/3} = 4x^{4/3}$

(f) $(8y^3)^{5/3} = 8^{5/3} (y^3)^{5/3} = 32y^5$

(g) $\left(\dfrac{x^{15}}{y^9}\right)^{-1/3} = \left(\dfrac{y^9}{x^{15}}\right)^{1/3} = \dfrac{y^3}{x^5}$

(h) $\left(\dfrac{x^{1/3} y^{2/5}}{z^{3/5}}\right)^{15} = \dfrac{(x^{1/3})^{15} (y^{2/5})^{15}}{(z^{3/5})^{15}} = \dfrac{x^5 y^6}{z^9}$

(i) $x^{2/5} x^{-1/3} = x^{2/5 - 1/3} = x^{1/15}$

EVALUATING EXPONENTS USING A CALCULATOR

You can use the x^2 key to calculate the square, or second power, of a number and the $\wedge$ key for the value of any power.

EXAMPLE 11.5

Evaluate $4.7^{3.42}$.

SOLUTION

PRESS	DISPLAY
4.7 $\wedge$ 3.42 **ENTER**	198.8724729

Some calculators have a $\sqrt[x]{}$ key that you access through a menu. To use this key to evaluate $\sqrt[3]{8}$ you press 3 $\sqrt[x]{}$ 8 ENTER. Check the manual for your calculator to see if it has such an option and which menu you use to access it.

EXAMPLE 11.6

Evaluate $\sqrt[7]{943.2}$.

SOLUTION

PRESS	DISPLAY
943.2 ∧ (1 ÷ 7) ENTER	2.660378313
or 7 $\sqrt[x]{}$ 943.2 ENTER	2.660378313

 HINT To evaluate $b^{m/n}$, where n is odd and b is a negative number, your calculator must "think" of this as $(b^m)^{1/n}$ or, equivalently as $(b^{1/n})^m$.

EXAMPLE 11.7

Evaluate $12^{5/3}$.

SOLUTION

PRESS	DISPLAY
12 ∧ (5 ÷ 3) ENTER	62.89779351
or 3 $\sqrt[x]{}$ 12 ∧ 5 ENTER	62.89779351

EXAMPLE 11.8

Evaluate $(-8)^{5/3}$.

SOLUTION You have to treat $(-8)^{5/3}$ as $[(-8)^5]^{1/3}$ or as $[(-8)^{1/3}]^5$.

PRESS	DISPLAY
((−) 8) ∧ (1 ÷ 3) ∧ 5 ENTER	−32
or ((−) 8) ∧ 5 ∧ (1 ÷ 3) ENTER	−32
or (3 $\sqrt[x]{}$ (−) 8) ∧ 5 ENTER	−32

 NOTE Remember, you cannot take an even root of a negative number. That is, you cannot take the square root of a negative number, you cannot take the fourth root of a negative number, you cannot take the sixth root of a negative number, and so on.

 APPLICATION **ENVIRONMENTAL SCIENCE**

EXAMPLE 11.9

One study of a lake found that the light intensity was reduced 15% through a depth of 25 cm. The formula $I = (0.85)^{d/25}$ gives the approximate fraction of surface light intensity at a depth d, in centimeters. Find I at a depth of 60 cm.

SOLUTION Since $d = 60$ cm, we want to evaluate $I = (0.85)^{60/25}$. Using a calculator, we enter

$$0.85 \;\boxed{\wedge}\; \boxed{(} \; 60 \; \boxed{\div} \; 25 \; \boxed{)} \; \boxed{\text{ENTER}}$$

and obtain 0.677026115965. So, the light intensity at 60 cm is about 67.7% of the surface light intensity.

EXERCISE SET 11.1

In Exercises 1–20, evaluate the given expression without the use of a calculator.

1. $25^{1/2}$

2. $27^{1/3}$

3. $64^{1/3}$

4. $125^{1/3}$

5. $25^{-1/2}$

6. $81^{-1/4}$

7. $32^{-1/5}$

8. $64^{-1/3}$

9. $27^{2/3}$

10. $81^{3/4}$

11. $125^{2/3}$

12. $32^{3/5}$

13. $16^{-3/4}$

14. $(-8)^{2/3}$

15. $(-8)^{-1/3}$

16. $(-27)^{-2/3}$

17. $\left(\dfrac{1}{8}\right)^{1/3}$

18. $\left(\dfrac{1}{25}\right)^{3/2}$

19. $\left(\dfrac{1}{16}\right)^{-5/4}$

20. $\left(\dfrac{-1}{27}\right)^{4/3}$

In Exercises 21–70, express each of the given expressions in the simplest form containing only positive exponents.

21. $3^2 \cdot 3^5$

22. $5^9 5^8$

23. $7^6 7^{-2}$

24. $11^9 11^{-6}$

25. $x^4 x^6$

26. $y^7 y^9$

27. $y^6 y^{-4}$

28. $x^8 x^{-2}$

29. $(9^5)^2$

30. $(11^8)^{-5}$

31. $(x^7)^3$

32. $(p^9)^{-5}$

33. $(xy)^5$

34. $(yt)^3$

35. $(ab)^{-5}$

36. $(xyz)^{-9}$

37. $\dfrac{x^{10}}{x^2}$

38. $\dfrac{p^9}{p^3}$

39. $\dfrac{x^2}{x^8}$

40. $\dfrac{a^3}{a^{12}}$

41. $x^{1/2} x^{3/2}$

42. $a^{1/3} a^{4/3}$

43. $r^{3/4} r$

44. $a^2 a^{2/3}$

45. $a^{1/2} a^{1/3}$

46. $b^{2/3} b^{1/4}$

47. $d^{2/3} d^{-1/4}$

48. $x^{3/5} y^{-2/3}$

49. $\dfrac{a^2 b^5}{a^5 b^2}$

50. $\dfrac{x^3 y^2}{x^7 y}$

51. $\dfrac{r^5 s^2 t}{t r^3 s^5}$

52. $\dfrac{a^2 b c^3}{(abc)^3}$

53. $\dfrac{(xy^2 z)^4}{x^4 (yz^2)^2}$

54. $\dfrac{m^6 n^7}{(m^2 n)^3}$

55. $\left(\dfrac{a}{b^2}\right)^3 \left(\dfrac{a}{b^3}\right)^2$

56. $\left(\dfrac{x^2}{y}\right)^4 \left(\dfrac{x}{y^2}\right)^2$

57. $\dfrac{(xy^2 b^3)^{1/2}}{(x^{1/4} b^4 y)^2}$

58. $\dfrac{(x^{1/3} y^3)^3}{(y^{10} x^5)^{1/5}}$

59. $\left(\dfrac{2x}{p^2}\right)^{-2} \left(\dfrac{p}{4}\right)^{-1}$

60. $\left(\dfrac{5a^2}{6b}\right)^{-2} \left(\dfrac{6}{a}\right)^{-4}$

61. $\dfrac{(x^2 y^{-1} z)^{-2}}{(xy)^{-4}}$

62. $\left\{\left[(2x^2)^3\right]^{-4}\right\}^{-1}$

63. $\dfrac{(27x^6 y^3)^{-1/3}}{(16x^4 y^{12})^{-1/4}}$

64. $\dfrac{(64x^6 y^{12})^{-5/6}}{(9x^4 y^2)^{-3/2}}$

65. $\left(\dfrac{x^2}{y^3}\right)^{-1/5} \left(\dfrac{y^2}{x^5}\right)^{1/3}$

66. $\left(\dfrac{a^2 x^3}{b^5 y}\right)^{-4/3} \left(\dfrac{axy^{-2}}{b}\right)^{5/3}$

67. $\left(\dfrac{9x^3}{t^5}\right)^{-1/2} \left(\dfrac{8t^2}{x^5}\right)^{-1/3}$

68. $\left(\dfrac{125a^6}{8b^3}\right)^{-2/3} \left(\dfrac{8b}{5a^2}\right)^{-1/2}$

69. $\dfrac{(9x^4 y^{-6})^{-3/2}}{(8x^{-6} y^3)^{-2/3}}$

70. $\dfrac{(81x^5 y^{-8} z)^{-3/4}}{(64xy^{-3} z^2)^{-5/3}}$

Use a calculator or computer to determine the value of each of the numbers in Exercises 71–80.

71. $8.3^{2/3}$

72. $7.3^{2/5}$

73. $92.47^{5/7}$

74. $81.94^{3/5}$

75. $(-81.52)^{2/7}$

76. $(-78.64)^{1/3}$

77. $432.61^{1/4}$

78. $(-537.15)^{2/3}$

79. $(-32.35)^{-3/7}$

80. $(-0.1439074804)^{-3/5}$

Solve Exercises 81–86.

81. *Physics* The distance in meters traveled by a falling body starting from rest is $9.8t^2$, where t is the time, in seconds, the object has been falling. In 4.75 s, the distance fallen will be $9.8(4.75)^2$ m. Evaluate this quantity.

82. The volume of a sphere is $\frac{4}{3}\pi r^3$. If the radius r of a sphere is 19.25 in., what is the volume?

83. *Physics* When 5 m³ of helium at a temperature of 315 K and a pressure of 15 N/m² is adiabatically compressed to 0.5 m³, its new pressure p and temperature T are given by

$$p = (5)^5 \left(\frac{15}{0.5}\right)^{5/3}$$

$$\text{and } T = 315\left(\frac{15}{0.5}\right)^{5/3}$$

Evaluate p and T.

84. *Nuclear technology* Radium has a half-life of approximately 1,600 years. It decays according to the formula $q(t) = q_0 2^{-t/1,600}$, where q_0 is the original quantity of radium and $q(t)$ is the amount left at time t. In this problem, t is given

in years. If you begin with 75 mg of pure radium, how much will remain after 2,000 years?

85. *Aeronautical engineering* The efficiency of a turbojet engine is given by the expression

$$E = 1 - \left(\frac{p_1}{p_2}\right)^{\alpha/(1-\alpha)}$$

where $\dfrac{p_1}{p_2}$ is the compression ratio. Simplify the expression for $\alpha = 1.4$.

86. *Finance* The periodic payment, R, for a debt, A, at the annual interest rate, r, with n payments per year for t years is given by

$$R = A\left[\frac{\dfrac{r}{n}}{1 - \left(1 + \dfrac{r}{n}\right)^{-nt}}\right]$$

A person borrowed \$15,000 for an automobile at an annual rate of 9%. How much is each monthly payment if she borrowed the money for 5 years?

 [IN YOUR WORDS]

87. Describe how to use your calculator to evaluate $(1.44)^{3/2}$.

88. (a) Use your calculator to evaluate $\left(-\frac{1}{8}\right)^{-2/3}$, $-\dfrac{1}{8^{-2/3}}$, $-8^{2/3}$, $(-8)^{2/3}$, and $(-8)^{-2/3}$.

(b) Explain why some answers in (a) are the same and some are different.

11.2 **LAWS OF RADICALS**

In Section 1.3, we introduced the concept of roots. We used them in Section 11.1 for the discussion of fractional exponents. The more general name for roots is radicals. Fractional exponents can be used for any operation that requires radicals.

LAWS OF RADICALS

A *radical* is any number of the form $\sqrt[n]{b}$. The number under the radical b is called the radicand. The number indicating the root n is called the *order* or index.

In Section 1.3, we introduced four basic rules or laws of radicals. These rules are listed in the following box.

BASIC RULES FOR RADICALS

$$\text{Rule 1: } \sqrt[n]{ab} = \sqrt[n]{a}\,\sqrt[n]{b}$$

$$\text{Rule 2: } \sqrt[n]{\frac{a}{b}} = \frac{\sqrt[n]{a}}{\sqrt[n]{b}}, b \neq 0$$

$$\text{Rule 3: } \left(\sqrt[n]{b}\right)^n = b^{n/n} = b$$

$$\text{Rule 4: } \sqrt[n]{b} = b^{1/n}$$

We assume in each of these rules that if n is even, neither a nor b is a negative real number.

EXAMPLE 11.10

Simplify (a) $\sqrt[6]{27}$, (b) $\sqrt[5]{96}$, (c) $\sqrt{x^6 y^8}$, (d) $\sqrt[3]{\dfrac{125y^6}{x^9}}$, and (e) $\sqrt[3]{54x^8}$.

SOLUTIONS

(a) $\sqrt[6]{27} = \sqrt[6]{3^3} = 3^{3/6} = 3^{1/2} = \sqrt{3}$

(b) $\sqrt[5]{96} = \sqrt[5]{32 \cdot 3} = \sqrt[5]{32}\,\sqrt[5]{3} = \sqrt[5]{2^5}\,\sqrt[5]{3} = 2\sqrt[5]{3}$

(c) $\sqrt{x^6 y^8} = (x^6 y^8)^{1/2} = x^{6/2} y^{8/2} = x^3 y^4$

(d) $\sqrt[3]{\dfrac{125y^6}{x^9}} = \sqrt[3]{\dfrac{5^3 y^6}{x^9}} = \dfrac{5^{3/3} y^{6/3}}{x^{9/3}} = \dfrac{5y^2}{x^3}$

EXAMPLE 11.10 (Cont.)

(e) $\sqrt[3]{54x^8} = \sqrt[3]{2 \cdot 3^3 x^6 x^2}$

$= 2^{1/3} 3^{3/3} x^{6/3} x^{2/3}$

$= 2^{1/3} \cdot 3 \cdot x^2 x^{2/3}$

$= 3x^2 2^{1/3} x^{2/3}$

$= 3x^2 (2x^2)^{1/3}$

$= 3x^2 \sqrt[3]{2x^2}$

Notice that several examples started with as many factors as possible with nth roots that could be easily found. Thus, in Example 11.10(b), we used $\sqrt[n]{ab} = \sqrt[n]{a}\sqrt[n]{b}$, when we wrote $\sqrt[5]{96} = \sqrt[5]{32} \cdot \sqrt[5]{3}$.

 HINT In general, we try to express a radical so that the exponent of any factor in the radicand is less than the index of the radical. Thus, in Example 11.10(e), we wrote $\sqrt[3]{x^8}$ as $x^2\sqrt[3]{x^2}$.

RATIONALIZING DENOMINATORS

When a radicand is a fraction, a variation of Rule 2, $\sqrt[n]{\dfrac{a}{b}} = \dfrac{\sqrt[n]{a}}{\sqrt[n]{b}}$, is used to eliminate the radical in the denominator. This technique is called rationalizing the denominator.

RATIONALIZING THE DENOMINATOR

To rationalize a denominator of the form $\sqrt[n]{x^r}$, multiply the denominator by another radical with the same radicand and the same index, $\sqrt[n]{x^s}$, where $r + s$ is a multiple of n.

The process of rationalizing the denominator makes the denominator a perfect power of x and eliminates the radical in the denominator.

 NOTE Remember that whenever you multiply the denominator by something other than 1, you must also multiply the numerator by the same quantity.

EXAMPLE 11.11

Rationalize the denominators of **(a)** $\sqrt{\dfrac{3}{5}}$, **(b)** $\dfrac{1}{\sqrt[3]{2}}$, and **(c)** $\sqrt[5]{\dfrac{3}{8x^2}}$.

SOLUTIONS

(a) Rewrite $\sqrt{\dfrac{3}{5}}$ as $\dfrac{\sqrt{3}}{\sqrt{5}}$.

Multiply both the numerator and denominator by $\sqrt{5}$ because $5 \cdot 5 = 5^2$.

$$\sqrt{\frac{3}{5}} = \frac{\sqrt{3}}{\sqrt{5}} = \frac{\sqrt{3}}{\sqrt{5}} \cdot \frac{\sqrt{5}}{\sqrt{5}}$$

$$= \frac{\sqrt{3 \cdot 5}}{\sqrt{5 \cdot 5}} = \frac{\sqrt{15}}{\sqrt{5^2}} = \frac{\sqrt{15}}{5}$$

(b) Multiply both the numerator and denominator by $\sqrt[3]{2^2}$ because $2 \cdot 2^2 = 2^3$, a perfect cube.

$$\frac{1}{\sqrt[3]{2}} = \frac{1}{\sqrt[3]{2}} \cdot \frac{\sqrt[3]{2^2}}{\sqrt[3]{2^2}}$$

$$= \frac{\sqrt[3]{2^2}}{\sqrt[3]{2^3}} = \frac{\sqrt[3]{4}}{2}$$

(c) Rewrite $\sqrt[5]{\frac{3}{8x^2}}$ as $\frac{\sqrt[5]{3}}{\sqrt[5]{8x^2}}$.

$\sqrt[5]{8x^2} = \sqrt[5]{2^3 x^2}$, so we will multiply both the numerator and denominator by $\sqrt[5]{2^2 x^3}$ because $(2^3 x^2)(2^2 x^3) = 2^5 x^5$.

$$\sqrt[5]{\frac{3}{8x^2}} = \frac{\sqrt[5]{3}}{\sqrt[5]{8x^2}} = \frac{\sqrt[5]{3}}{\sqrt[5]{8x^2}} \cdot \frac{\sqrt[5]{2^2 x^3}}{\sqrt[5]{2^2 x^3}}$$

$$= \frac{\sqrt[5]{3 \cdot 2^2 x^3}}{\sqrt[5]{8x^2 2^2 x^3}} = \frac{\sqrt[5]{3 \cdot 2^2 x^3}}{\sqrt[5]{2^5 x^5}}$$

$$= \frac{\sqrt[5]{12x^3}}{2x}$$

Rationalizing the denominator was originally developed as a way to help computations, but the increased use of calculators and computers reduces its importance in calculations. Rationalizing the denominator, however, is often a useful way to write numbers.

Another helpful rule is used with radicals.

RULE 5 FOR RADICALS

$$\sqrt[m]{\sqrt[n]{b}} = \sqrt[mn]{b}$$

EXAMPLE 11.12

(a) $\sqrt[3]{\sqrt{27}} = \sqrt[6]{27}$, (b) $\sqrt[4]{\sqrt[5]{914}} = \sqrt[20]{914}$, (c) $\sqrt[5]{\sqrt[3]{-82}} = \sqrt[15]{-82}$, and (d) $\sqrt[4]{\sqrt[3]{x}} = \sqrt[12]{x}$

Sometimes it is possible to reduce the index of a radical. For example,

$$\sqrt[6]{y^2} = y^{2/6} = y^{1/3} = \sqrt[3]{y}$$

Here the index was reduced from 6 to 3. Another example can be seen from Example 11.12(a).

$$\sqrt[3]{\sqrt{27}} = \sqrt[3]{\sqrt{3^3}} = \sqrt[6]{3^3} = 3^{3/6} = 3^{1/2} = \sqrt{3}$$

The last version, $\sqrt{3}$, is a simpler version with which to work.

EXAMPLE 11.13

Reduce the index of **(a)** $\sqrt[8]{16}$, **(b)** $\sqrt[6]{16x^2}$, and **(c)** $\sqrt[12]{27x^6y^3}$.

SOLUTIONS

(a) $\sqrt[8]{16} = \sqrt[8]{2^4} = 2^{4/8} = 2^{1/2} = \sqrt{2}$

(b) $\sqrt[6]{16x^2} = \sqrt[6]{2^4x^2} = 2^{4/6}x^{2/6} = 2^{2/3}x^{1/3} = \sqrt[3]{4x}$

(c) $\sqrt[12]{27x^6y^3} = \sqrt[12]{3^3x^6y^3} = 3^{3/12}x^{6/12}y^{3/12} = 3^{1/4}x^{2/4}y^{1/4} = \sqrt[4]{3x^2y}$

Notice that, in the last example, we could have factored the x^2 out of the radical using Rule 1 and written $\sqrt[4]{3x^2y} = \sqrt[4]{3y}\sqrt[4]{x^2} = \sqrt[4]{3y}\sqrt{x}$.

SIMPLIFYING RADICALS

Simplifying a radical makes it easier to work with. The following three steps are used to simplify a radical.

STEPS FOR SIMPLIFYING RADICALS

A radical is simplified when all of the following steps are finished.

Step 1. All possible factors have been removed from the radicand.

Step 2. All denominators are rationalized.

Step 3. The index has been reduced as much as possible.

EXAMPLE 11.14

Simplify the following: (a) $\sqrt{\dfrac{x^3}{y}}$, (b) $\sqrt[4]{x^5y^{11}}$, (c) $\sqrt[5]{x^3y^{-7}}$, and (d) $\sqrt[3]{\dfrac{x}{y^2} + \dfrac{5y^2}{x}}$.

SOLUTIONS

(a) $\sqrt{\dfrac{x^3}{y}} = \sqrt{\dfrac{x^3}{y}}\sqrt{\dfrac{y}{y}} = \dfrac{\sqrt{x^3y}}{\sqrt{y^2}} = \dfrac{\sqrt{x^3y}}{|y|} = \dfrac{|x|\sqrt{xy}}{|y|}$

(b) $\sqrt[4]{x^5y^{11}} = \sqrt[4]{x^4xy^8y^3} = \sqrt[4]{x^4y^8} \cdot \sqrt[4]{xy^3} = |x|y^2\sqrt[4]{xy^3}$

(c) $\sqrt[5]{x^3y^{-7}} = \sqrt[5]{\dfrac{x^3}{y^7}} = \sqrt[5]{\dfrac{x^3}{y^7}} \cdot \sqrt[5]{\dfrac{y^3}{y^3}} = \dfrac{\sqrt[5]{x^3y^3}}{\sqrt[5]{y^{10}}} = \dfrac{\sqrt[5]{x^3y^3}}{y^2}$

(d) $\sqrt[3]{\dfrac{x}{y^2} + \dfrac{5y^2}{x}} = \sqrt[3]{\dfrac{x \cdot x}{y^2 x} + \dfrac{5y^2 y^2}{xy^2}} = \sqrt[3]{\dfrac{x^2 + 5y^4}{xy^2}}$

$\qquad = \sqrt[3]{\dfrac{(x^2 + 5y^4)x^2 y}{(xy^2)x^2 y}} = \dfrac{\sqrt[3]{x^4 y + 5x^2 y^5}}{\sqrt[3]{x^3 y^3}}$

$\qquad = \dfrac{\sqrt[3]{x^4 y + 5x^2 y^5}}{xy}$

In Examples 11.14(a) and (b) we needed to use the absolute value symbol to denote the principal square root of an even root. Remember, $\sqrt{(-4)^2} = |-4| = 4$. Thus, $\sqrt{x^2} = |x|$ and $\sqrt[4]{x^{12}} = |x^3|$ because we do not know if x is positive or negative.

You do not need to use absolute values when finding odd roots. Thus, just as $\sqrt[3]{-64} = \sqrt[3]{-4^3} = -4$, we can write $\sqrt[3]{x^3} = x$.

 NOTE $\sqrt{a^2 b} = |a|\sqrt{b}$ but $\sqrt{a^2 + b} \neq |a|\sqrt{1 + b}$ and also $\sqrt{a^2 + b} \neq |a| + \sqrt{b}$.

Notice also that in Example 11.14(d) we had to find a common denominator before we could add the fractions. After the fractions were added, we were able to rationalize the denominator.

 APPLICATION **GENERAL TECHNOLOGY**

EXAMPLE 11.15

The frequency of oscillation f of a simple pendulum is given by

$$f = \dfrac{1}{2\pi}\sqrt{\dfrac{g}{L}}$$

where $g \approx 9.8$ m/s^2 is the acceleration due to gravity in the metric system and L is the length of the pendulum in meters. (a) Express f in simplest form, when $L = 0.35$ m. (b) Evaluate f to the nearest hundredth.

SOLUTIONS

(a) Given $g \approx 9.8$ m/s^2 and $L = 0.35$ m,

$$f = \dfrac{1}{2\pi}\sqrt{\dfrac{g}{L}}$$

$$= \dfrac{1}{2\pi}\sqrt{\dfrac{9.8}{0.35}}$$

$$= \dfrac{1}{2\pi}\sqrt{28}$$

$$= \dfrac{\sqrt{7}}{\pi}$$

EXAMPLE 11.15 (Cont.)

(b) Evaluating $\dfrac{\sqrt{7}}{\pi}$ with a calculator, we press `2nd` `√` `7` `÷` `2nd` `π` `ENTER` and obtain 0.842168798696. Thus, the pendulum oscillates about once every 0.84 sec.

EXERCISE SET 11.2

Use the rules for radicals to express each of Exercises 1–60 in simplest radical form.

1. $\sqrt[3]{16}$

2. $\sqrt[3]{81}$

3. $\sqrt{45}$

4. $\sqrt[3]{40}$

5. $\sqrt[3]{y^{12}}$

6. $\sqrt[4]{p^8}$

7. $\sqrt[5]{a^7}$

8. $\sqrt[7]{b^{10}}$

9. $\sqrt{x^2 y^7}$

10. $\sqrt[3]{x^5 y^3}$

11. $\sqrt[4]{a^5 b^3}$

12. $\sqrt[5]{p^{12} y^8}$

13. $\sqrt[3]{8x^4}$

14. $\sqrt[4]{81 y^9}$

15. $\sqrt{27 x^3 y}$

16. $\sqrt[3]{32 a^5 b^2}$

17. $\sqrt[3]{-8}$

18. $\sqrt[5]{-243}$

19. $\sqrt[3]{a^2 b^4}\sqrt[3]{ab^5}$

20. $\sqrt[5]{x^3 y^2 z^4}\sqrt[5]{x^2 y^8 z}$

21. $\sqrt[4]{p^3 q^2 r^6}\sqrt[4]{pq^6 r}$

22. $\sqrt[6]{m^3 n^2 e^7}\sqrt[6]{m^2 n^4 e^5}$

23. $\sqrt[3]{\dfrac{8x^3}{27}}$

24. $\sqrt[4]{\dfrac{81 y^8}{16}}$

25. $\sqrt[5]{\dfrac{x^5 y^{10}}{z^5}}$

26. $\sqrt[3]{\dfrac{a^3 b^9}{c^6}}$

27. $\sqrt[3]{\dfrac{16 x^3 y^2}{z^6}}$

28. $\sqrt{\dfrac{125 a^5 b^2}{c^4}}$

29. $\sqrt{\dfrac{64 x^3 y^4}{9 z^4 p^2}}$

30. $\sqrt[3]{\dfrac{8 a^5 b^3}{27 r^6 s^9}}$

31. $\sqrt{\dfrac{16}{3}}$

32. $\sqrt{\dfrac{4}{5}}$

33. $\sqrt[3]{\dfrac{27}{4}}$

34. $\sqrt[3]{\dfrac{16}{25}}$

35. $\sqrt{\dfrac{25}{2x}}$

36. $\sqrt[3]{\dfrac{8}{5y^2}}$

37. $\sqrt[4]{\dfrac{81}{32 z^2}}$

38. $\sqrt[3]{\dfrac{-2}{25 r^2}}$

39. $\sqrt[3]{\dfrac{16 x^2 y}{x^5}}$

40. $\sqrt[4]{\dfrac{25 a^3 b^5}{a^7 b}}$

41. $\sqrt[3]{\dfrac{-8 x^3 yz}{27 b^2 z^4}}$

42. $\sqrt[4]{\dfrac{25 a^2 b^3}{16 c^3 b^6}}$

43. $\sqrt{4 \times 10^4}$

44. $\sqrt{9 \times 10^6}$

45. $\sqrt{25 \times 10^3}$

46. $\sqrt{16 \times 10^7}$

47. $\sqrt{4 \times 10^7}$

48. $\sqrt{9 \times 10^9}$

49. $\sqrt[3]{1.25 \times 10^{10}}$

50. $\sqrt[5]{3.2 \times 10^{14}}$

51. $\sqrt{\dfrac{x}{y} + \dfrac{y}{x}}$

52. $\sqrt{\dfrac{a}{b} - \dfrac{b}{a}}$

53. $\sqrt{a^2 + 2ab + b^2}$

54. $\sqrt{x^2 - 2xy + y^2}$

55. $\sqrt{\dfrac{1}{a^2} + \dfrac{1}{b}}$

56. $\sqrt{\dfrac{x}{y^2} + \dfrac{y}{x^2}}$

57. $\sqrt[6]{\sqrt[3]{27 x^2}}$

58. $\sqrt[4]{\sqrt[6]{125 x^3 y^5}}$

59. $\sqrt[3]{\sqrt[7]{-624.2 x^{15} y^{10} z}}$

60. $\sqrt{\sqrt[4]{9 x^8 y^3}}$

Solve Exercises 61–66.

61. **Music** Many musical instruments contain strings, which vibrate to produce music. The frequency of vibration f of a string of length L fixed at both ends and vibrating in its fundamental mode is given by

$$f = \frac{1}{2L}\sqrt{\frac{T}{\mu}}$$

where μ is the mass per unit length and T is the tension in the string. Rationalize the right-hand side of this equation.

62. **Music** In the equation in Exercise 61, what happens to the frequency when the tension is quadrupled?

63. **Electricity** The impedance Z of a certain circuit is given by the equation

$$Z = \frac{1}{\sqrt{\dfrac{1}{x^2} + \dfrac{1}{R^2}}}$$

Rationalize the denominator in order to simplify this equation.

64. **Chemistry** The distance between ion layers of a sodium chloride crystal is given by the expression

$$\sqrt[3]{\dfrac{M}{2\rho N}}$$

where M is the molecular weight, N is Avogadro's number, and ρ is the density. Express this in simplest form.

65. **Mechanical engineering** The formula

$$k = 1 + \sqrt{1 + \dfrac{2h}{m}}$$

is used to calculate the impact factor for dynamic loading. Rewrite the right-hand side in simplest radical form. Make sure you rationalize the denominator.

66. **Civil engineering** The frequency f, in Hz, of an object attached to the end of a cantilever beam of length l is given by

$$f = \frac{1}{2\pi}\sqrt{\dfrac{3EI}{ml^3}}$$

Express the formula in simplest radical form.

 [IN YOUR WORDS]

67. Without looking in the text, explain the meaning of each of the following terms: **(a)** radical, **(b)** radicand, and **(c)** index.

68. Explain how to rationalize the denominator of the form $\sqrt[n]{x^r}$.

11.3   BASIC OPERATIONS WITH RADICALS

In this section, we will study the basic operations of addition, subtraction, multiplication, and division of radicals. Adding and subtracting radicals are similar to adding and subtracting algebraic expressions. However, there are two cases to consider when multiplying or dividing radicals. The first case is when the radicals have the same index; the second case is when they have different indices. Each of these cases will be considered in this section.

ADDITION AND SUBTRACTION OF RADICALS

When we learned how to add and subtract algebraic expressions, we found that only like terms can be added or subtracted. Addition and subtraction of radicals are very similar.

 NOTE Radicals can only be added or subtracted if the radicands are identical and the indices are the same.

Trying to add or subtract two radicals such as $\sqrt{2}$ and $\sqrt{5}$ is similar to adding and subtracting x and y. Example 11.16 shows the similarity between combining radicals and combining algebraic expressions.

EXAMPLE 11.16

| Combining Radicals | Combining Algebraic Expressions |

(a) $\sqrt{2} + \sqrt{5} + \sqrt{2}$
   $= 2\sqrt{2} + \sqrt{5}$

$x + y + x = 2x + y$, where
$x = \sqrt{2}$ and $y = \sqrt{5}$

(b) $2\sqrt{3} + 4\sqrt{7} + 6\sqrt{3}$
   $= 8\sqrt{3} + 4\sqrt{7}$

$2a + 4b + 6a = 8a + 4b$, where
$a = \sqrt{3}$ and $b = \sqrt{7}$

(c) $3\sqrt[3]{6} - 7\sqrt[3]{6} = -4\sqrt[3]{6}$

$3p - 7p = -4p$, where $p = \sqrt[3]{6}$

(d) $\dfrac{5\sqrt{3}}{2} - \dfrac{\sqrt{3}}{2} = \dfrac{4\sqrt{3}}{2} = 2\sqrt{3}$

$\dfrac{5x}{2} - \dfrac{x}{2} = \dfrac{4x}{2} = 2x$, where $x = \sqrt{3}$

In each case, only the similar radicals are combined. Radicals that are not similar remain as separate terms and the addition or subtraction is only indicated. Sometimes it is possible to combine radicals that do not appear to be similar by first simplifying the radicals. For example $\sqrt{8}$ and $\sqrt{2}$ can be combined, since $\sqrt{8} = \sqrt{4}\sqrt{2} = 2\sqrt{2}$.

EXAMPLE 11.17

Simplify and combine similar radicals.

(a) $\sqrt{2} + \sqrt{8} = \sqrt{2} + 2\sqrt{2} = 3\sqrt{2}$

(b) $3\sqrt{8} + 5\sqrt{18} = 6\sqrt{2} + 15\sqrt{2} = 21\sqrt{2}$
   Note that $\sqrt{18} = \sqrt{9}\sqrt{2} = 3\sqrt{2}$ and $5\sqrt{18} = 5\sqrt{9}\sqrt{2} = 5 \cdot 3\sqrt{2}$
   $= 15\sqrt{2}$.

(c) $\sqrt{98x} + \sqrt{32x} = 7\sqrt{2x} + 4\sqrt{2x} = 11\sqrt{2x}$

(d) $\sqrt{20x^3} + \sqrt{8x^2} - \sqrt{45x} = 2x\sqrt{5x} + 2x\sqrt{2} - 3\sqrt{5x}$
   $= (2x - 3)\sqrt{5x} + 2x\sqrt{2}$
   Note that the difference $2x\sqrt{5x} - 3\sqrt{5x}$ can only be simplified as $(2x - 3)\sqrt{5x}$. We factored $\sqrt{5x}$ out of each term.

(e) $\sqrt{\dfrac{5}{3}} + \dfrac{\sqrt{3}}{\sqrt{125}} = \dfrac{\sqrt{5}}{\sqrt{3}} + \dfrac{\sqrt{3}}{5\sqrt{5}} = \dfrac{\sqrt{5}\sqrt{3}}{\sqrt{3}\sqrt{3}} + \dfrac{\sqrt{3}\sqrt{5}}{5\sqrt{5}\sqrt{5}}$

   $= \dfrac{\sqrt{15}}{3} + \dfrac{\sqrt{15}}{25} = \dfrac{25\sqrt{15}}{75} + \dfrac{3\sqrt{15}}{75}$

   $= \dfrac{28\sqrt{15}}{75}$

Here, we rationalized the denominators and then added the fractions by finding the common denominator. We could have rationalized the second fraction by multiplying by $\sqrt{125}$, but it was easier to first simplify the denominator to $5\sqrt{5}$ then multiply by $\sqrt{5}$.

MULTIPLYING RADICALS WITH THE SAME INDEX

Multiplying and dividing radicals that have the same index use two of the rules we have discussed.

$$\sqrt[n]{a}\,\sqrt[n]{b} = \sqrt[n]{ab}$$

and

$$\frac{\sqrt[n]{a}}{\sqrt[n]{b}} = \sqrt[n]{\frac{a}{b}}, b \neq 0$$

EXAMPLE 11.18

Multiply the following radical expressions: **(a)** $\sqrt{2}\sqrt{5}$, **(b)** $\sqrt[3]{5}\sqrt[3]{10}$, **(c)** $\sqrt{xy}\sqrt{2x}$, **(d)** $\sqrt[3]{\frac{3}{2}}\sqrt[3]{\frac{5x}{4}}$, **(e)** $\sqrt{5x}(\sqrt{5x} + \sqrt{10x^3})$, and **(f)** $(\sqrt{x} + \sqrt{y})(\sqrt{x} - \sqrt{y})$.

SOLUTIONS

(a)
$$\sqrt{2}\sqrt{5} = \sqrt{2 \cdot 5} = \sqrt{10}$$

(b)
$$\sqrt[3]{5}\sqrt[3]{10} = \sqrt[3]{5 \cdot 10} = \sqrt[3]{50}$$

(c)
$$\sqrt{xy}\sqrt{2x} = \sqrt{(xy)(2x)} = \sqrt{2x^2y} = x\sqrt{2y}$$

(d)
$$\sqrt[3]{\frac{3}{2}}\sqrt[3]{\frac{5x}{4}} = \sqrt[3]{\left(\frac{3}{2}\right)\left(\frac{5x}{4}\right)} = \sqrt[3]{\frac{15x}{8}} = \frac{\sqrt[3]{15x}}{2}$$

(e)
$$\sqrt{5x}(\sqrt{5x} + \sqrt{10x^3}) = \sqrt{5x}\sqrt{5x} + \sqrt{5x}\sqrt{10x^3}$$
$$= \sqrt{25x^2} + \sqrt{50x^4}$$
$$= 5x + 5x^2\sqrt{2}$$

(f) $(\sqrt{x} + \sqrt{y})(\sqrt{x} - \sqrt{y}) = (\sqrt{x})^2 - (\sqrt{y})^2 = x - y$ using the special product for the difference of two squares.

MULTIPLYING RADICALS WITH DIFFERENT INDICES

Radicals with different indices can be multiplied if they are rewritten so that they have the same index. The easiest way to do this is with fractional exponents.

EXAMPLE 11.19

Multiply the following: (a) $\sqrt[3]{2}\sqrt{7}$, (b) $\sqrt[4]{5x^2}\sqrt[3]{2x}$, and (c) $\sqrt[3]{4ab^2}\sqrt[5]{16a^4b^2}$.

SOLUTIONS In each of these solutions, we first rewrite the radical expressions using fractional exponents. Then, if they need to be added as in Examples 11.19(b) and (c), we next find the common denominator.

(a) $\sqrt[3]{2}\sqrt{7} = 2^{1/3}7^{1/2} = 2^{2/6}7^{3/6} = (2^2 7^3)^{1/6}$
$$= \sqrt[6]{2^2 7^3}$$
$$= \sqrt[6]{1,372}$$

EXAMPLE 11.19 (Cont.)

(b) $\sqrt[4]{5x^2}\sqrt[3]{2x} = (5x^2)^{1/4}(2x)^{1/3} = (5x^2)^{3/12}(2x)^{4/12}$

$$= \sqrt[12]{(5x^2)^3}\,\sqrt[12]{(2x)^4}$$

$$= \sqrt[12]{(5x^2)^3(2x)^4}$$

$$= \sqrt[12]{5^3 x^6 2^4 x^4}$$

$$= \sqrt[12]{2{,}000 x^{10}}$$

(c) $\sqrt[3]{4ab^2}\sqrt[5]{16a^4b^2} = (4ab^2)^{1/3}(16a^4b^2)^{1/5}$

$$= (4ab^2)^{5/15}(16a^4b^2)^{3/15}$$

$$= \sqrt[15]{(4ab^2)^5}\,\sqrt[15]{(16a^4b^2)^3}$$

$$= \sqrt[15]{(2^2 ab^2)^5}\,\sqrt[15]{(2^4 a^4 b^2)^3}$$

$$= \sqrt[15]{2^{10} a^5 b^{10}}\,\sqrt[15]{2^{12} a^{12} b^6}$$

$$= \sqrt[15]{2^{22} a^{17} b^{16}}$$

$$= 2ab\,\sqrt[15]{2^7 a^2 b}$$

$$= 2ab\,\sqrt[15]{128 a^2 b}$$

DIVISION OF RADICALS

Division of radicals with the same index is done using Rule 2 for radicals. The result is usually simplified by rationalizing the denominator.

EXAMPLE 11.20

Divide each of the following: (a) $\dfrac{\sqrt{10}}{\sqrt{3}}$, (b) $\dfrac{\sqrt[3]{4x}}{\sqrt[3]{2x}}$, (c) $\dfrac{\sqrt[3]{x^2 y}}{\sqrt[3]{z}}$, and (d) $\dfrac{\sqrt{3xy}}{\sqrt{7x^5 y}}$.

SOLUTIONS

(a) $\dfrac{\sqrt{10}}{\sqrt{3}} = \dfrac{\sqrt{10}}{\sqrt{3}} \cdot \dfrac{\sqrt{3}}{\sqrt{3}} = \dfrac{\sqrt{30}}{3}$

(b) $\dfrac{\sqrt[3]{4x}}{\sqrt[3]{2x}} = \sqrt[3]{\dfrac{4x}{2x}} = \sqrt[3]{2}$

(c) $\dfrac{\sqrt[3]{x^2 y}}{\sqrt[3]{z}} = \dfrac{\sqrt[3]{x^2 y}\,\sqrt[3]{z^2}}{\sqrt[3]{z}\,\sqrt[3]{z^2}} = \dfrac{\sqrt[3]{x^2 y z^2}}{z}$

(d) $\dfrac{\sqrt{3xy}}{\sqrt{7x^5 y}} = \dfrac{\sqrt{3xy}}{x^2 \sqrt{7xy}} = \dfrac{1}{x^2} \cdot \sqrt{\dfrac{3xy}{7xy}} = \dfrac{1}{x^2}\sqrt{\dfrac{3}{7}}$

We now rationalize the denominator.

$$= \dfrac{1}{x^2}\sqrt{\dfrac{3}{7}}\sqrt{\dfrac{7}{7}} = \dfrac{\sqrt{21}}{7x^2}$$

CONJUGATE OF A RADICAL EXPRESSION

If a, b, $\sqrt{m}$, and $\sqrt{n}$ are real numbers, then radical expressions of the form $a\sqrt{m} + b\sqrt{n}$ and $a\sqrt{m} - b\sqrt{n}$ are **conjugates** of each other.

Sometimes the denominator of a fraction is the sum of the difference of two square roots. Examples of this are $\sqrt{2} + \sqrt{5}$ and $\sqrt{x} - \sqrt{y}$. In this case, the numerator and denominator can be multiplied by the conjugate in order to make the denominator the difference of two squares. For example, if the denominator is $\sqrt{2} + \sqrt{5}$, then multiply the numerator and denominator by $\sqrt{2} - \sqrt{5}$. If the denominator is $\sqrt{x} - \sqrt{y}$, then multiply both numerator and denominator by $\sqrt{x} + \sqrt{y}$. Notice that in each case the denominator is then in the form $a^2 - b^2$, where a or b is a radical.

EXAMPLE 11.21

Rationalize each of these denominators: (a) $\dfrac{1}{\sqrt{2} + \sqrt{5}}$, (b) $\dfrac{a}{\sqrt{x} - \sqrt{y}}$, and (c) $\dfrac{\sqrt{x+y}}{1 + \sqrt{x+y}}$.

SOLUTIONS (a) The conjugate of $\sqrt{2} + \sqrt{5}$ is $\sqrt{2} - \sqrt{5}$.

$$\frac{1}{\sqrt{2} + \sqrt{5}} = \frac{1}{\sqrt{2} + \sqrt{5}} \cdot \frac{\sqrt{2} - \sqrt{5}}{\sqrt{2} - \sqrt{5}}$$

$$= \frac{\sqrt{2} - \sqrt{5}}{(\sqrt{2})^2 - (\sqrt{5})^2}$$

$$= \frac{\sqrt{2} - \sqrt{5}}{2 - 5}$$

$$= \frac{\sqrt{2} - \sqrt{5}}{-3} = \frac{\sqrt{5} - \sqrt{2}}{3}$$

(b) The conjugate of $\sqrt{x} - \sqrt{y}$ is $\sqrt{x} + \sqrt{y}$.

$$\frac{a}{\sqrt{x} - \sqrt{y}} = \frac{a}{\sqrt{x} - \sqrt{y}} \cdot \frac{\sqrt{x} + \sqrt{y}}{\sqrt{x} + \sqrt{y}}$$

$$= \frac{a(\sqrt{x} + \sqrt{y})}{(\sqrt{x})^2 - (\sqrt{y})^2}$$

$$= \frac{a\sqrt{x} + a\sqrt{y}}{x - y}, x \neq y$$

217

EXAMPLE 11.21 (Cont.)

(c) The conjugate of $1 + \sqrt{x + y}$ is $1 - \sqrt{x + y}$.

$$\frac{\sqrt{x + y}}{1 + \sqrt{x + y}} = \frac{\sqrt{x + y}}{1 + \sqrt{x + y}} \cdot \frac{1 - \sqrt{x + y}}{1 - \sqrt{x + y}}$$

$$= \frac{\sqrt{x + y}(1 - \sqrt{x + y})}{(1)^2 - (\sqrt{x + y})^2}$$

$$= \frac{\sqrt{x + y} - (\sqrt{x + y})^2}{1 - (x + y)}$$

$$= \frac{\sqrt{x + y} - x - y}{1 - x - y}, x + y \neq 1$$

Finally, to find the quotient of two radicals with different indices, we use fractional exponents in the same manner as when we multiplied radicals with different indices.

EXAMPLE 11.22

Find the following quotients: (a) $\dfrac{\sqrt[3]{15}}{\sqrt{15}}$ and (b) $\dfrac{\sqrt{2x}}{\sqrt[4]{8x^3}}$.

SOLUTIONS

(a) $\dfrac{\sqrt[3]{15}}{\sqrt{15}} = \dfrac{(15)^{1/3}}{(15)^{1/2}} = \dfrac{(15)^{2/6}}{(15)^{3/6}} = \dfrac{\sqrt[6]{15^2}}{\sqrt[6]{15^3}} = \dfrac{\sqrt[6]{15^2}}{\sqrt[6]{15^3}} \cdot \dfrac{\sqrt[6]{15^3}}{\sqrt[6]{15^3}}$

$$= \frac{\sqrt[6]{15^5}}{15}$$

(b) $\dfrac{\sqrt{2x}}{\sqrt[4]{8x^3}} = \dfrac{(2x)^{1/2}}{(8x^3)^{1/4}} = \dfrac{(2x)^{2/4}}{(8x^3)^{1/4}} = \dfrac{\sqrt[4]{(2x)^2}}{\sqrt[4]{8x^3}} = \dfrac{\sqrt[4]{4x^2}}{\sqrt[4]{8x^3}} \cdot \dfrac{\sqrt[4]{2x}}{\sqrt[4]{2x}}$

$$= \frac{\sqrt[4]{8x^3}}{2x}$$

EXERCISE SET 11.3

In Exercises 1–60, perform the indicated operations and express the answers in simplest form.

1. $2\sqrt{3} + 5\sqrt{3}$

2. $5\sqrt{6} - 3\sqrt{6}$

3. $\sqrt[3]{9} + 4\sqrt[3]{9}$

4. $\sqrt[4]{8} + 3\sqrt[4]{8}$

5. $2\sqrt{3} + 4\sqrt{2} + 6\sqrt{3}$

6. $5\sqrt{3} - 6\sqrt{5} - 9\sqrt{3}$

7. $\sqrt{5} + \sqrt{20}$

8. $\sqrt{8} + \sqrt{2}$

9. $\sqrt{7} - \sqrt{28}$

10. $\sqrt{8} - \sqrt{32}$

11. $\sqrt{60} - \sqrt{\frac{5}{3}}$

12. $\sqrt{84} + \sqrt{\frac{3}{7}}$

13. $\sqrt{\frac{1}{2}} - \sqrt{\frac{9}{2}}$

14. $\sqrt{\frac{4}{3}} - \sqrt{\frac{25}{3}}$

15. $\sqrt{x^3 y} + 2x\sqrt{xy}$

16. $\sqrt{a^5 b^3} - 3ab\sqrt{a^3 b}$

17. $\sqrt[3]{24p^2 q^4} + \sqrt[3]{3p^8 q}$

18. $\sqrt[4]{16a^2 b} - \sqrt[4]{81a^6 b}$

19. $\sqrt{\dfrac{x}{y^3}} - \sqrt{\dfrac{y}{x^3}}$

20. $\sqrt{\dfrac{a^3}{b^3}} + \sqrt{\dfrac{b}{a^5}}$

21. $a\sqrt{\dfrac{b}{3a}} + b\sqrt{\dfrac{a}{3b}}$

22. $x\sqrt{\dfrac{y}{5x}} - y\sqrt{\dfrac{x}{5y}}$

23. $\sqrt{5}\sqrt{8}$

24. $\sqrt[5]{-7}\sqrt[5]{11}$

25. $\sqrt{3x}\sqrt{5x}$

26. $\sqrt[3]{7x^2}\sqrt[3]{3x}$

27. $(\sqrt{4x})^3$

28. $(\sqrt[3]{2x^2y})^4$

29. $\sqrt[5]{\frac{5}{8}}\sqrt[5]{\frac{9}{10}}$

30. $\sqrt[7]{\frac{7}{6}}\sqrt[7]{\frac{12}{3}}$

31. $\sqrt{2}(\sqrt{x} + \sqrt{2})$

32. $\sqrt{3}(\sqrt{12} - \sqrt{y})$

33. $(\sqrt{x} + \sqrt{y})^2$

34. $(\sqrt{a} + 3\sqrt{b})^2$

35. $\sqrt[3]{\frac{5}{2}}\sqrt[3]{\frac{2}{7}}$

36. $\sqrt{\frac{ab}{5c}}\sqrt{\frac{abc}{5}}$

37. $(\sqrt{a} + \sqrt{b})$ $(\sqrt{a} - \sqrt{b})$

38. $(\sqrt{x} - 2\sqrt{y})$ $(\sqrt{x} + 5\sqrt{y})$

39. $\sqrt[3]{x}\sqrt{x}$

40. $\sqrt{5x}\sqrt[3]{2x^2}$

41. $\sqrt[3]{49x^2}\sqrt[4]{3x}$

42. $\sqrt[3]{9y}\sqrt[5]{-8x^2}$

43. $\frac{\sqrt{32}}{\sqrt{2}}$

44. $\frac{\sqrt[3]{a^2}}{\sqrt[3]{4a}}$

45. $\frac{\sqrt[3]{4b^2}}{\sqrt[3]{16b}}$

46. $\frac{\sqrt{5a^3b}}{\sqrt{15ab^3}}$

47. $\frac{\sqrt{3x^2}}{\sqrt[3]{9x}}$

48. $\frac{\sqrt[3]{15x}}{\sqrt{5x}}$

49. $\frac{\sqrt[3]{16a^2b}}{\sqrt[4]{2ab^3}}$

50. $\frac{\sqrt[5]{75a^3x^2}}{\sqrt[3]{-15ax^2}}$

51. $\frac{\sqrt[3]{4}}{\sqrt{2}}$

52. $\frac{\sqrt[5]{-8}}{\sqrt[3]{4}}$

53. $\frac{1}{x + \sqrt{5}}$

54. $\frac{1}{x + \sqrt{3}}$

55. $\frac{\sqrt{5} - \sqrt{3}}{\sqrt{5} + \sqrt{3}}$

56. $\frac{\sqrt{5} + \sqrt{7}}{\sqrt{7} - \sqrt{5}}$

57. $\frac{\sqrt{x} + 1}{\sqrt{x} - 1} + \frac{\sqrt{x} - 1}{\sqrt{x} + 1}$

58. $\frac{\sqrt{x} + 3}{\sqrt{x} - 3} - \frac{\sqrt{x} - 3}{\sqrt{x} + 3}$

59. $\frac{\sqrt{x + y}}{\sqrt{x - y} - \sqrt{x}}$

60. $\frac{\sqrt{1 + y}}{\sqrt{1 - y} + \sqrt{y}}$

Solve Exercises 61–66.

61. Use the quadratic equation to find the roots of $ax^2 + bx + c = 0$. What is the sum of the two roots?

62. **Oceanography** The velocity v of a small water wave is given by

$$v = \sqrt{\frac{\pi}{4\lambda d}} + \sqrt{\frac{4\pi}{\lambda d}}$$

Simplify and combine this equation.

63. **Electronics** The equivalent resistance R of two resistors, R_1 and R_2, connected in parallel is expressed

$$R = \frac{R_1 R_2}{R_1 + R_2}$$

In a given circuit, $R_1 = x^{3/2}$ and $R_2 = \sqrt{x}$. (a) Express R in terms of x. Make sure you simplify the answer. (b) If $x = 20\ \Omega$, what is R?

64. **Sound** The theory of waves in wires uses the equation

$$\frac{\sqrt{d_1} - \sqrt{d_2}}{\sqrt{d_1} + \sqrt{d_2}}$$

Simplify this expression.

65. What is the product of the two roots of the quadratic equation $ax^2 + bx + c = 0$?

66. **Civil Engineering** The potential energy in a truss is given by

$$C = \frac{3}{8\sqrt[3]{2}} \cdot \frac{KA}{\sqrt[3]{L}}$$

Simplify this expression.

▶ [IN YOUR WORDS]

67. Explain how to add two radicals. What precautions do you need to take regarding the radicands and the indices?

68. Describe how to multiply two radicals
    (a) With the same index.
    (b) With different indices.

| 3.1 |
LINES, ANGLES, AND TRIANGLES

Let's begin by discussing lines, segments, and rays. They are the building blocks for the remainder of this section. We will then look at two ways in which angles are measured. Finally, we will give a few areas in which angles and their measures are used.

LINES, SEGMENTS, AND RAYS

The basic parts of geometry are lines, angles, planes, surfaces, and the figures that they form. In this section, we will focus on the first two: lines and angles. A **line segment**, or *segment*, is a portion of a straight line between two endpoints. It is named by its endpoints, and a bar is placed over the endpoints names. For example, the segment joining the points A and B, written $\overline{AB}$, is shown in Figure 3.1a. This segment could also be named $\overline{BA}$. A *ray* or *half-line* is the portion of a line that lies on one side of a point and includes the point. For example, in Figure 3.1b, ray $\overrightarrow{CD}$ begins at point C, the *endpoint*, and passes through D. The second point used to name the ray can be any point on the ray other than the endpoint. Thus, in Figure 3.1b, $\overrightarrow{CD} = \overrightarrow{CE}$.

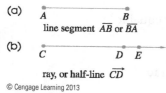

(a) A ———————— B
line segment $\overline{AB}$ or $\overline{BA}$

(b) C ———————— D E

ray, or half-line $\overrightarrow{CD}$

© Cengage Learning 2013

Figure 3.1

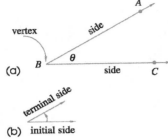

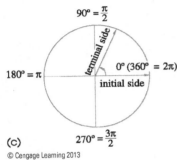

(c)

© Cengage Learning 2013

Figure 3.2

ANGLES

An **angle** is formed by two rays that have the same endpoint. This common endpoint is called the **vertex**, and the two rays are called the *sides* of the angle. The angle in Figure 3.2a has its vertex at B. This angle has several possible names, including $\angle B$, $\angle ABC$, $\angle CBA$, and $\angle \theta$, where the symbol $\angle$ means angle.

Another way to think of an angle is to think of it as generated by moving a ray from an initial position to a terminal position as in Figure 3.2b. If this generated angle was placed inside a circle with its vertex at the center of the circle, then you would have a figure something like the one shown in Figure 3.2c.

DEGREES AND RADIANS

Angles are measured using several different systems. The two most common units are **degrees** and **radians**. We will use both in this book. Look again at Figure 3.2c. The end of the initial side is marked $0°$ ($360° = 2\pi$). This indicates that if the terminal side were to rotate completely around the circle and stop at the initial side, the size of the angle would be 360 degrees ($360°$) or 2π radians (2π rad). Later we will see a relationship between the radian and the distance around a circle.

Other important angle measures are given in relation to the distance around the circle. One-fourth of the way around the circle is $90°$ or $\frac{\pi}{2}$ rad. Halfway around the circle is $180°$ or π rad and three-fourths of the way is $270°$ or $\frac{3\pi}{2}$ rad.

> **NOTE** If there is no degree symbol (°) after an angle measure, then assume that it is a radian measure.

Each degree is divided into 60 minutes and each minute into 60 seconds. There are 3,600 seconds in a degree. The symbol $'$ is used for minutes and $''$ for seconds. So, $60' = 1°$ and $60'' = 1'$. The use of calculators has caused decimal values for degrees to become more popular. Thus, in decimal degrees, $15' = \left(\frac{15}{60}\right)° = 0.25°$ and $27'' = \left(\frac{27}{3600}\right)° = 0.0075°$.

Some widely used angles besides those shown in Figure 3.2c are the $30° = \frac{\pi}{6}$, $45° = \frac{\pi}{4}$, and $60° = \frac{\pi}{3}$ angles.

There are times when you will need to convert from degrees to radians or from radians to degrees. Since $180° = \pi$ rad, then

$$1\,\text{rad} = \frac{180°}{\pi} \approx \frac{180°}{3.1416} \approx 57.296°$$

(The symbol $\approx$ means "is approximately equal to.") and you also have

$$1° = \frac{\pi}{180°} \approx \frac{3.1416}{180°} \approx 0.01745\,\text{rad}$$

Therefore, we have the following conversion formulas.

CONVERSION BETWEEN DEGREES AND RADIANS

To change from radians to degrees multiply the number of radians by $\frac{180°}{\pi}$.

To change from degrees to radians multiply by $\frac{\pi}{180°}$.

EXAMPLE 3.1

Change (a) 1.89 and (b) $\frac{5\pi}{6}$ to degrees.

SOLUTIONS Since there is no degree symbol, these must be in radians.

(a) $1.89 \, \text{rad} \approx 1.89 \, \text{rad} \times \frac{180°}{\pi \, \text{rad}} \approx 108.29°$

(b) $\frac{5\pi}{6} = \frac{5\pi}{6} \times \frac{180°}{\pi} = 150°$

EXAMPLE 3.2

Change (a) 120° and (b) 82.5° to radians.

SOLUTIONS

(a) $120° = 120° \times \frac{\pi}{180°} \text{rad} = \frac{2\pi}{3} \text{rad}$

Notice here that the answer is left in terms of π and we have $120° = \frac{2\pi}{3}$, the exact answer. You may leave the answer in terms of π or compute a decimal approximation and see that $120° \approx 2.094$ rad.

(b) $82.5° = 82.5° \times \frac{\pi}{180°} = \frac{11\pi}{24} \approx 1.440 \, \text{rad}$

HINT Some people find that it is easier to convert between degrees and radians by using the proportion

$$\frac{D}{180°} = \frac{R}{\pi}$$

where D represents a known or unknown number of degrees and R represents a known or unknown number of radians.

EXAMPLE 3.3

Use the proportion $\frac{D}{180°} = \frac{R}{\pi}$ to change (a) 120° to radians and (b) $\frac{5\pi}{6}$ to degrees.

SOLUTIONS

(a) Since we are asked to convert 120° to radians, we substitute 120° for D in the proportion and solve it for R as follows:

$$\frac{120°}{180°} = \frac{R}{\pi}$$

EXAMPLE 3.3 (Cont.)

$$R = \frac{120°}{180°}\pi$$

$$= \frac{2}{3}\pi$$

Thus, $120° = \frac{2}{3}\pi = \frac{2\pi}{3}$ radians.

(b) To convert $\frac{5\pi}{6}$ to degrees substitute $\frac{5\pi}{6}$ for R in the proportion.

$$\frac{D}{180°} = \frac{R}{\pi}$$

$$\frac{D}{180°} = \frac{5\pi/6}{\pi}$$

$$D = \frac{5\pi}{6} \cdot \frac{180°}{\pi}$$

$$= 150°$$

As in Example 3.1(b), we obtain $\frac{5\pi}{6} = 150°$.

TYPES OF ANGLES

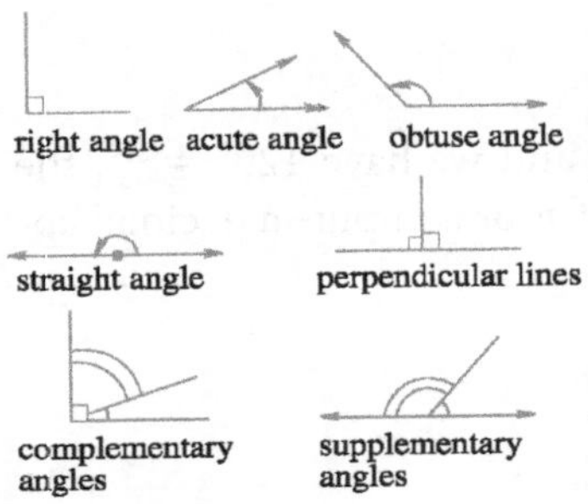

right angle   acute angle   obtuse angle

straight angle   perpendicular lines

complementary   supplementary
angles   angles

© Cengage Learning 2013

Figure 3.3

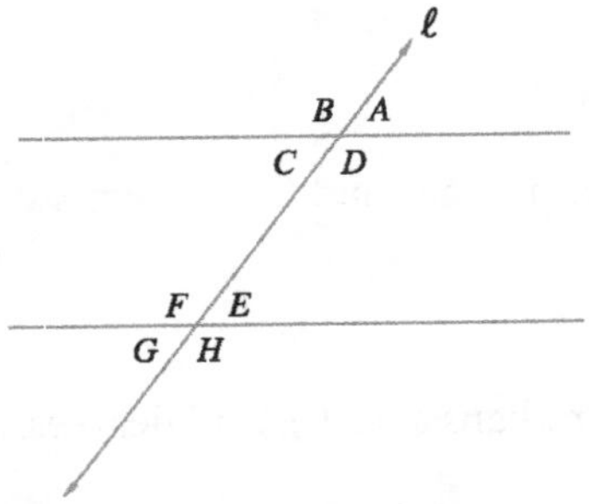

Figure 3.3 shows four basic types of angles. A right angle has a measure of 90° or $\frac{\pi}{2}$ rad. It is usually indicated by placing a small square at the vertex of the angle. An acute angle measures between 0° and 90° (0 and $\frac{\pi}{2}$ rad) and an obtuse angle measures between 90° and 180° ($\frac{\pi}{2}$ and π rad). A straight angle has a measure of 180° or π rad. If two lines meet and form a right angle, then the lines are perpendicular. Two angles are supplementary if their sum is a straight angle (180° or π rad) and are complementary if their sum is a right angle (90° or $\frac{\pi}{2}$ rad).

In geometry, when two objects are the same size we say that they are congruent. Two 37° angles are said to be congruent. Two segments that are 3 cm long are congruent.

Two angles that have the same vertex and a common side are called adjacent angles. In Figure 3.4, $\angle A$ and $\angle B$ are adjacent angles. They are also supplementary angles. A transversal is a line that intersects, or crosses, two or more lines. In Figure 3.4, line ℓ is a transversal of the other two lines.

© Cengage Learning 2013

Figure 3.4

If parallel lines are intersected by two transversals, then the corresponding segments are proportional. *Corresponding segments* are the parts of the transversals between the same parallel lines. In Figure 3.5, lines P_1, P_2, and P_3 are parallel lines intersected by transversals ℓ_1 and ℓ_2. The points of intersection have been marked with capital letters. Segments $\overline{AB}$ and $\overline{DE}$ are corresponding segments, as are $\overline{BC}$ and $\overline{EF}$. Likewise, $\overline{AC}$ and $\overline{DF}$ are corresponding segments. Therefore, we have the proportion

$$\frac{AB}{DE} = \frac{BC}{EF} = \frac{AC}{DF}$$

APPLICATION CIVIL ENGINEERING

EXAMPLE 3.4

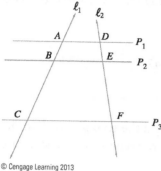

© Cengage Learning 2013

Figure 3.5

Find the distance across the lake in Figure 3.6.

SOLUTION You carefully use stakes to mark off the segments $\overline{AF}$, $\overline{BE}$, and $\overline{CD}$ so that the segments are parallel. We also make sure that A, B, C are in a line, as are D, E, and F. We know that corresponding segments are proportional, so $\dfrac{AB}{EF} = \dfrac{BC}{DE}$. Using the lengths in Figure 3.6, $\dfrac{100}{75} = \dfrac{BC}{168}$. Solving this, we get $BC = \dfrac{100 \times 168}{75} = 224$. It is 224 m across the lake.

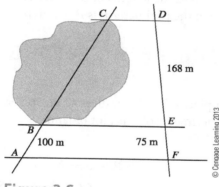

Figure 3.6

POLYGONS

A **polygon** is a figure in a plane that is formed by three or more line segments, called *sides*, joined at their endpoints. The endpoints are called *vertices* and a single endpoint is called a **vertex**.

TRIANGLES

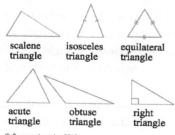

© Cengage Learning 2013

Figure 3.7

A **triangle** is a polygon that has exactly three sides. (See Figure 3.7.) Triangles are named according to a property of their sides or their angles. When classified according to its sides, a triangle is **scalene** if none of the sides are the same length, **isosceles** if two sides are the same length, and **equilateral** if all three sides are the same length. When sides are the same length, single, double, or triple marks are used to show which sides are congruent.

An **acute triangle** has three acute angles, an **obtuse triangle** has one obtuse angle, and a **right triangle** has one right angle. (See Figure 3.7.) In an equilateral triangle, all three angles are congruent, and some people called it an equiangular triangle. In an isosceles triangle the angles opposite the congruent sides are congruent.

The sum of the three angles of a triangle is 180°, or π rad. Since all three angles in an equilateral triangle are congruent, the size of each angle must be $\dfrac{180°}{3} = 60°$ or $\dfrac{\pi}{3}$ rad. Since a right angle is 90°, a right triangle must have two acute angles, because the other two angles, when added together, can have only a total of 90°. This means that each of the angles must be less than 90°. In a similar manner, an obtuse triangle must have two acute angles.

EXAMPLE 3.5

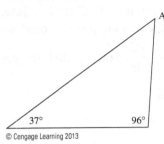

37°   96°

© Cengage Learning 2013

Figure 3.8

Find the size of the third angle of the triangle in Figure 3.8 if the other two angles measure 37° and 96°.

SOLUTION If we call the unknown angle $\angle A$, then
$$\angle A = 180° - 37° - 96° = 47°$$
The third angle of this triangle is 47°.

The **perimeter** of a triangle is the distance around the triangle. To find the perimeter, you add the lengths of the three sides. If the lengths of the sides are a, b, and c, then the perimeter P is $P = a + b + c$.

APPLICATION **ARCHITECTURE**

EXAMPLE 3.6

A triangular piece of land measures 42 m, 36.2 m, and 58.7 m on the three sides. What is the perimeter of this plot of land?

SOLUTION

$$P = a + b + c$$
$$= 42 + 36.2 + 58.7$$
$$= 136.9$$

The perimeter is 136.9 m.

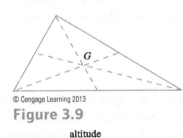

© Cengage Learning 2013

Figure 3.9

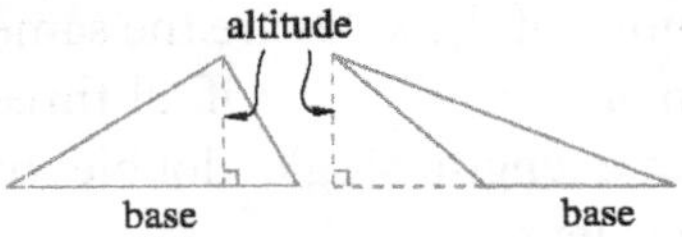

altitude

base   base

© Cengage Learning 2013

Figure 3.10

A segment drawn from a vertex to the middle (or midpoint) of the opposite side is called a *median*. If you draw all three medians of a triangle, they meet in a common point, G, called the *centroid*, as shown in Figure 3.9. The centroid is the *center of gravity* of a triangle.

A segment drawn from a vertex and perpendicular to the opposite side is an **altitude** of a triangle. The opposite side is called the *base*. (See Figure 3.10.) When solving some problems, it is sometimes necessary to extend the base so that it will intersect the altitude. The altitudes of an equilateral triangle bisect the sides of the triangle. The altitude of an isosceles triangle from the vertex of the equal sides bisects the third side of the triangle.

The area of a triangle is found by the product of $\frac{1}{2}$ and the lengths of the base and the altitude. If b is the length of the base and h the length of the altitude, then the area A is given by the formula

$$A = \frac{1}{2}bh$$

If the base and altitude are in the same units, then the area is in square units.

EXAMPLE 3.7

Find the area of a triangle with a base of 1.2 m and an altitude of 4.5 m.

SOLUTION $A = \dfrac{1}{2}bh$

$$= \dfrac{1}{2}(1.2)(4.5)$$

$$= 2.7$$

The area is 2.7 m².

NOTE You may have noticed that m² was used to indicate square meters. Similar notation is used for other area units. For example, cm² is used for square centimeters, and ft² for square feet.

Sometimes the length of the altitude is not known. It is possible to find the area using *Hero's formula*, also referred to as *Heron's formula*. Instead of the altitude, you will need the lengths of the three sides and the semiperimeter. If we let *a*, *b*, and *c* represent the lengths of the sides, then the *semiperimeter*, *s*, is found using the formula $s = \dfrac{a + b + c}{2}$. We can find the area from Hero's formula:

$$A = \sqrt{s(s - a)(s - b)(s - c)}$$

APPLICATION CIVIL ENGINEERING

EXAMPLE 3.8

A triangular piece of land measures 51′9″, 47′3″, and 82′6″ on the three sides. What is the area of the lot of land?

SOLUTION We will let $a = 51′9″ = 51.75$ ft, $b = 47′3″ = 47.25$ ft, and $c = 82′6″ = 82.5$ ft.

$$s = \frac{a + b + c}{2} = \frac{51.75 + 47.25 + 82.5}{2} = \frac{181.5}{2} = 90.75$$

$$A = \sqrt{s(s - a)(s - b)(s - c)}$$

$$= \sqrt{90.75(90.75 - 51.75)(90.75 - 47.25)(90.75 - 82.5)}$$

$$= \sqrt{90.75(39)(43.5)(8.25)}$$

$$= \sqrt{1,270,148.3}$$

$$\approx 1,127.0086$$

The area is about 1,127 ft².

Two triangles are congruent if the corresponding angles and sides of each triangle are congruent. For example, in Figure 3.11, sides $\overline{AB}$ and $\overline{EF}$ are both

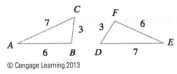

© Cengage Learning 2013

Figure 3.11

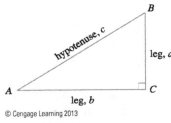

© Cengage Learning 2013

Figure 3.12

6 units long, $\overline{BC}$ and $\overline{DF}$ are both 3 units long, and $\overline{AC}$ and $\overline{DE}$ are 7 units long. If you measure the angles you will find that $\angle A \cong \angle E$, $\angle B \cong \angle F$, and $\angle C \cong \angle D$. As you can see, *congruent triangles* have the same size and shape.

We indicate that the triangles in Figure 3.11 are congruent by writing $\triangle ABC \cong \triangle EFD$. When we show that two triangles are congruent, we write it so the corresponding vertices are in the same order. Thus, writing $\triangle ABC \cong \triangle EFD$ indicates that $\angle A \cong \angle E$, $\angle B \cong \angle F$, and $\angle C \cong \angle D$.

One of the most valuable theorems in geometry involves the right triangle. In a right triangle, the side opposite the right angle is called the hypotenuse, as shown in Figure 3.12. The other two sides are the *legs*. The hypotenuse is the longest side of a right triangle. If the lengths of the two legs are a and b and the length of the hypotenuse is c, then the Pythagorean theorem is stated as follows.

PYTHAGOREAN THEOREM

$\triangle ABC$ is a right triangle with a hypotenuse of length c and legs of lengths a and b, if and only if

$$a^2 + b^2 = c^2$$

EXAMPLE 3.9

A right triangle has legs of length 6 in. and 8 in. What is the length of the hypotenuse?

SOLUTION If we let $a = 6$ and $b = 8$, then, by using the Pythagorean theorem, we have

$$c^2 = a^2 + b^2$$
$$= 6^2 + 8^2$$
$$= 36 + 64$$
$$= 100$$
$$c = \sqrt{100} = 10$$

The hypotenuse is 10 in. long.

EXAMPLE 3.10

The hypotenuse of a right triangle is 7.3 cm long. One leg is 4.8 cm long. What is the length of the other leg?

SOLUTION We are given $c = 7.3$ and $a = 4.8$, and so, by using the Pythagorean theorem, we obtain

$$c^2 = a^2 + b^2$$
$$(7.3)^2 = (4.8)^2 + b^2$$
$$(7.3)^2 - (4.8)^2 = b^2$$

or

$$b^2 = (7.3)^2 - (4.8)^2$$
$$= 53.29 - 23.04$$
$$= 30.25$$
$$b = \sqrt{30.25} = 5.5$$

The length of the remaining side is 5.5 cm.

APPLICATION CONSTRUCTION

EXAMPLE 3.11

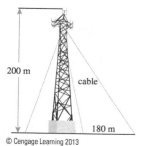

200 m

cable

180 m

© Cengage Learning 2013

Figure 3.13

A television tower is 208 ft tall. If a cable could be strung in a straight line from the top of the tower to a point on the ground $13\overline{0}$ m from the base of the tower, how long would the cable have to be? (See Figure 3.13.)

SOLUTION The cable, tower, and ground form a right triangle. We know that the height of the tower is 200 m. This is one leg of the triangle. The other leg is 130 m. The cable will form the hypotenuse. So,

$$c^2 = a^2 + b^2$$
$$c^2 = 130^2 + 200^2$$
$$= 16\,900 + 40\,000$$
$$= 56\,900$$
$$c = \sqrt{56\,900} \approx 238.54$$

Since the given data, $20\overline{0}$ m and $13\overline{0}$ m, have three significant digits, the cable would be about 239 m long.

The last example might not have been exactly realistic. It failed to account for any sag in the cable or any additional cable that would be needed to fasten it at each end. Later, we will find some methods to get more accurate answers to this problem.

Remember that the Pythagorean theorem can be used only with right triangles. The following exercises provide some additional examples that use the Pythagorean theorem.

EXERCISE SET 3.1

Convert each of the angle measures in Exercises 1–14 from degrees to radians or from radians to degrees without using a calculator. (You may leave your answers in terms of π.)

1. 15°

2. 75°

3. 210°

4. 10°45′

5. 85.4°

6. 48.6°

7. 163.5°

8. 242° 35′

9. $\frac{4\pi}{3}$

10. $\frac{\pi}{6}$

11. 1.3π

12. 2.15

13. 0.25

14. 1.1

Solve Exercises 15 and 16.

15. Find the supplement of a 35° angle in **(a)** degrees and **(b)** radians.

16. Find the complement of a 65° angle in **(a)** degrees and **(b)** radians.

Find the indicated variables in Exercises 17–24. Identical marks on segments or angles indicate that they are congruent.

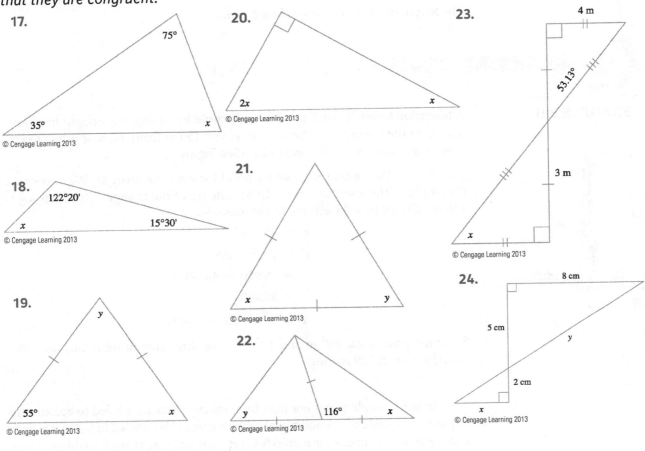

17.

75°

35°

© Cengage Learning 2013

18.

122°20'

x   15°30'

© Cengage Learning 2013

19.

y

55°   x

© Cengage Learning 2013

20.

2x   x

© Cengage Learning 2013

21.

x   y

© Cengage Learning 2013

22.

y   116°   x

© Cengage Learning 2013

23.

4 m

53.13°

3 m

x

© Cengage Learning 2013

24.

8 cm

5 cm

y

2 cm

x

© Cengage Learning 2013

Find the area and perimeter of ABC in Exercises 25–28.

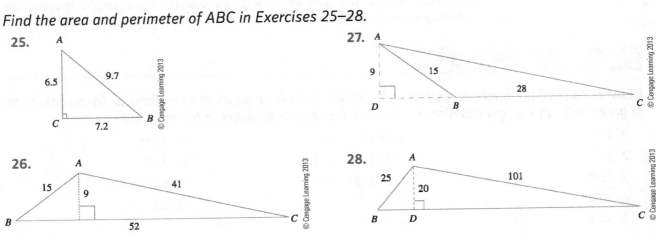

25.

A

6.5   9.7

C   7.2   B

© Cengage Learning 2013

26.

A

15   41
       9

B   52   C

© Cengage Learning 2013

27.

A

9   15
                28
D   B   C

© Cengage Learning 2013

28.

A

25   101
       20
B   D   C

© Cengage Learning 2013

Solve Exercises 29–54.

29. What is the distance from A to B in Figure 3.14 if lines ℓ_1, ℓ_2, and ℓ_3 are parallel?

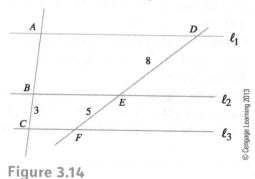

Figure 3.14

30. In Figure 3.15, if the lines ℓ_1, ℓ_2, and ℓ_3 are parallel, what is the distance from A to B?

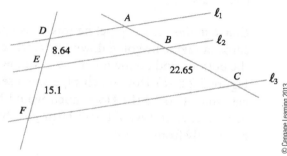

Figure 3.15

31. In Figure 3.16, angles A and B are the same size. Find the sizes of angles A and B.

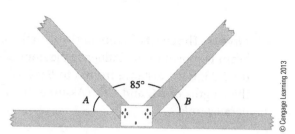

Figure 3.16

32. *Civil engineering* Figure 3.17 shows part of a bridge that is made of suspended cables hung from a girder to the deck of the bridge. What is the length from A to B?

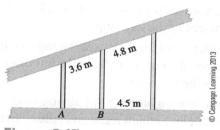

Figure 3.17

33. *Electronics* The angular frequency ω of an ac current is $\omega = 2\pi f$ rad/s, where f is the frequency. If $f = 60$ Hz for ordinary house current, what is the angular frequency?

34. *Mechanical technology* An angular velocity ω of a rigid object, such as a drive shaft, pulley, or wheel, is related to the angle θ through which the body rotates in a period of time t by the formula $\theta = \omega t$ or $\omega = \dfrac{\theta}{t}$.

  (a) Find the angular velocity of a gear wheel that rotates 285° in 0.6 s.

  (b) Find the angular velocity of a wheel that rotates $\frac{11\pi}{16}$ rad in 0.9 s.

35. *Metalworking* A machinist needs to weld a piece of pipe to two existing parallel pipes, as shown in Figure 3.18. What is the size of angle x?

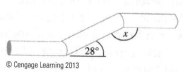

Figure 3.18

36. *Programming* Use the conversion factors at the beginning of this section to write a program for, your graphing calculator that will **(a)** convert degrees to radians and **(b)** convert radians to degrees.

37. *Landscape architecture* A triangular piece of land measures 23.2 m, 47.6 m, and 62.5 m. **(a)** How much fencing is needed to enclose this land? **(b)** How many square meters of sod would be needed to sod the entire piece of land?

38. The shadow of a building is 123'6". At the same time, the shadow of a yard stick is 2'3". What is the height of the building?

39. A ladder 15 m long reaches the top of a building when its foot is 5 m from the building. How high is the building?

40. *Mechanical engineering* A triangular metal plate was made by cutting a rectangular plate along a diagonal. If the rectangular piece was 23 cm long and 16 cm high, what is the area of the plate?

41. *Transportation engineering* A traffic light support is to be suspended parallel to the ground. It reaches diagonally across the intersection of two perpendicular streets. One street is 45 ft wide and the other is 62 ft wide. Determine the length of the support.

42. *Construction* A house is 8 m wide and the ridge is 3 m higher than the side walls. If the rafters, *r*, extend 0.5 m beyond the sides of the house, how long are the rafters? (See Figure 3.19.)

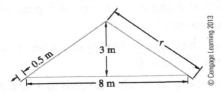

Figure 3.19

43. *Construction* Several cross beams are placed across an A-frame house. The highest beam is placed 2 600 mm from the ridge and the top of this beam is 2 400 mm long. The top of the next beam is placed 2 800 mm below the bottom of the top beam and the top of the third is 2 800 mm below the bottom of the second. The bottom of the third beam is 900 mm above the ground. Each beam is 300 mm thick. **(a)** How long are the tops of the second and third beams? **(b)** How far apart is the base of the A-frame? (See Figure 3.20.)

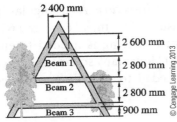

Figure 3.20

44. *Construction* An antenna 175 m high is supported by cables positioned around the antenna. One cable is 50 m from the base of the antenna, one is 75 m, and the third is 100 m. How long is each cable?

45. *Electrical engineering* A 30 m length of conduit is bent as shown in Figure 3.21. What is the length of the offset, *x*?

46. *Electrical engineering* If it were possible to run a straight conduit from *A* to *B* in Figure 3.21, how much conduit would be saved?

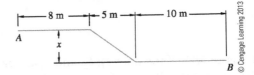

Figure 3.21

47. *Construction* A gas pipeline was constructed across a ravine by going down one side, across the bottom, and up the other side, as shown in Figure 3.22. **(a)** How much pipe was used to get from *A* to *B*? **(b)** How much would have been needed if it would have been possible to go directly from *A* to *B*?

Figure 3.22

48. *Physics* The effect of a moving load on the stress beam is shown in the influence diagram of Figure 3.23. If the distance from *A* to *B* is 24 ft, find the lengths of $\overline{BC}$ and $\overline{CD}$. (Assume that $\overline{AF}$ is parallel to $\overline{EG}$.)

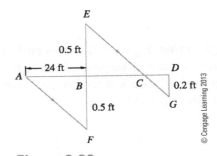

Figure 3.23

49. *Civil engineering* A building, located on level ground, casts a shadow of 128.45 m. At the same time, a meter stick casts a shadow of 1.75 m. What is the height of the building?

50. *Construction* Find the length of the brace in Figure 3.24.

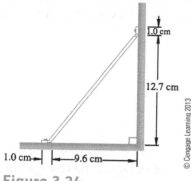

Figure 3.24

51. *Construction* Maria has a can of paint. Each can will cover about 425 ft². She needs to paint four walls. Two of the walls are 8 ft high and 10 ft long and the other two walls are 8 ft high and 14 ft long.

(a) Does Maria have enough paint?

(b) If not, how much more does she need? If she has enough, about how many more square feet could she paint?

52. *Electronics* Olé and Hilkka are going to install solar roof tiles on their house. Each tile measures 59″ × 17″ and weighs 5 lb/ft². Their roof is rectangular and measures 39 ft-4 in long and 18 ft-5 wide.

(a) What is the area of their roof to the nearest tenth of a square foot?

(b) How many solar roof tiles will it take to completely cover the roof?

(c) What is the total weight of these solar roof tiles?

53. *Construction* A ramp at a loading dock has the dimensions shown in Figure 3.25. To the nearest tenth of a foot, what is the horizontal distance x that the ramp covers?

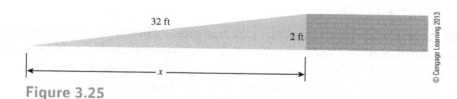

Figure 3.25

54. *Metalworking* Three holes are drilled in a metal plate as shown in Figure 3.26. Determine the dimensions of A and B to one decimal point.

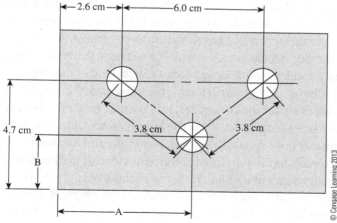

Figure 3.26

[IN YOUR WORDS]

55. (a) Without looking in the text, describe the relationship between degrees and radians.

(b) Explain how you can use the relationship between degrees and radians to convert between the units.

56. (a) Draw a diagram that shows parallel lines intersected by two transversals.

(b) Explain how you can use parallel lines and transversals to find some distances that are difficult to measure directly.

57. Describe an acute, obtuse, and right triangle. How are they alike? How are they different?

3.2   OTHER POLYGONS

In Section 3.1 we looked at the simplest type of polygon, the triangle. In this section, we will look at polygons that have more than three sides.

After the triangle, the most commonly used polygons are those with four sides. A polygon with exactly four sides is a quadrilateral. Other polygons that we will use are the pentagon, which has exactly five sides, the hexagon with six sides, and the octagon with eight sides. Any polygon that has all congruent sides and congruent angles is a *regular polygon*. For example, equilateral is another name for a regular triangle.

QUADRILATERALS

All quadrilaterals have four sides. Like triangles, different names are given to the quadrilaterals with special properties. The properties deal with the lengths of the sides, if the sides are parallel, and the sizes of the angles. Among the special types of quadrilaterals are the ones shown in Figure 3.27.

The **kite** has two pairs of adjacent sides congruent. A trapezoid has at least one pair of opposite sides parallel. If a trapezoid also has a pair of congruent sides that are not parallel, it is an *isosceles trapezoid* and has the congruent angles indicated in Figure 3.27. A parallelogram is a quadrilateral with both pairs of opposite sides parallel. As a result, the opposite sides are also congruent.

A rhombus is a parallelogram that has all four sides congruent. A rectangle is a parallelogram that has four right angles. A square is a rectangle that has four congruent sides. As you can see in Figure 3.27, a square is a special kind of rhombus.

To find the perimeter of a quadrilateral, you must add the lengths of the four sides. In the case of a rhombus or square, this is made easier by the fact that all four sides are the same length. So, if s is the length of one side of a rhombus or square, the perimeter is $4s$. A parallelogram, rectangle, and kite are not much more difficult, since each has two pairs of congruent sides. If the lengths of the sides that are not congruent are a and b, then the perimeter is $2(a + b)$.

In most cases, the area of a quadrilateral depends on the length of one or more sides and the distance between this side and its opposite side. If the height h is

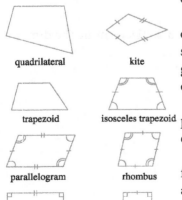

quadrilateral   kite

trapezoid   isosceles trapezoid

parallelogram   rhombus

rectangle   square

© Cengage Learning 2013

Figure 3.27

the distance between the sides and the length of the base is b, then the area of a rectangle, square, rhombus, or parallelogram can all be expressed as $A = bh$. In a trapezoid you must use the average length of the two parallel sides, $\frac{1}{2}(b_1 + b_2)$, and the height, h. So, for a trapezoid, $A = \frac{1}{2}h(b_1 + b_2)$. A kite is an exception, since its area can be found by multiplying $\frac{1}{2}$ by the lengths of the diagonals, d_1 and d_2. So, the area of a kite is $\frac{1}{2}d_1 d_2$. All of this is summarized in Figure 3.28, where the parts of each figure are labeled and the formulas for the perimeter and area of each polygon are given.

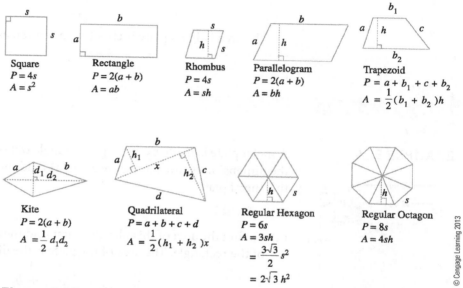

Figure 3.28

AREA AND PERIMETER OF OTHER POLYGONS

Figure 3.28 shows the formulas for the perimeter and area of a general quadrilateral. Also included are the area and perimeter for a regular hexagon and a regular octagon. In general, with a regular polygon of n sides, you can divide it into n congruent triangles, each with height h and base with length s. The perimeter of the polygon is ns and the area is $\frac{1}{2}nsh$. In Figure 3.28, two additional formulas for the area of a regular hexagon are given. These come from the fact that it is divided into six equilateral triangles and by using the Pythagorean theorem.

EXAMPLE 3.12

Find the perimeter and area of a rectangle with a length of 16 m and a width of 9 m.

SOLUTION

$$P = 2(a + b) \qquad\qquad A = ab$$
$$= 2(16 + 9) \qquad\qquad\; = 16 \cdot 9$$
$$= 2(25) = 50 \qquad\qquad = 144$$

The perimeter is 50 meters and the area is 144 square meters. These answers are usually written as 50 m and 144 m².

EXAMPLE 3.13

A trapezoid has bases of 14 and 18 in. and a height of 7 in. What is its area?

SOLUTION

$$A = \frac{1}{2}h(b_1 + b_2)$$

$$= \frac{1}{2}(7)(14 + 18)$$

$$= \frac{1}{2}(7)(32)$$

$$= 112$$

The area is 112 square inches (often written as 112 in.^{2}).

APPLICATION MECHANICAL

EXAMPLE 3.14

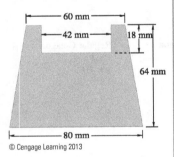

© Cengage Learning 2013

Figure 3.29

A metal plate is made by cutting a rectangle out of an isosceles trapezoid, using the dimensions shown in Figure 3.29. (a) Find the area and (b) the perimeter of this metal plate.

SOLUTIONS

(a) To find the area of this plate, we first find the area of the trapezoid and then of the rectangle. The area of the plate is the difference between the two.

$$A_{\text{trapezoid}} = \frac{1}{2}h(b_1 + b_2)$$

$$= \frac{1}{2}(64)(60 + 80)$$

$$= 4480$$

$$A_{\text{rectangle}} = bh$$

$$= (42)(18)$$

$$= 756$$

$$A_{\text{plate}} = A_{\text{trapezoid}} - A_{\text{rectangle}}$$

$$= 4480 - 756$$

$$= 3724$$

The area of this plate is 3724 mm^2.

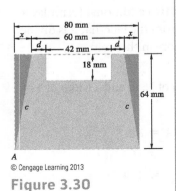

© Cengage Learning 2013

Figure 3.30

(b) We have all the measurements we need to find the perimeter except for the lengths of the two slanted sides of the trapezoid. For this we will use the Pythagorean theorem. Look at Figure 3.30. The plate has been drawn inside a rectangle. Because the plate is an isosceles trapezoid, we know that the two lengths marked x are the same length. We also know that 2x 1 60 5 80, so x 5 10 mm.

The slanted sides of the trapezoid are the hypotenuse c of the two shaded triangles in Figure 3.30. The legs of these triangles are 10 and 64 so

$$c^2 = 10^2 + 64^2$$
$$= 100 + 4\,096$$
$$= 4\,196$$
$$c = \sqrt{4\,196} \approx 64.78$$

If we assume that the rectangular cutout is centered, then

$$d = \left(\frac{60 - 42}{2}\right) = 9\,\text{mm}$$

The perimeter can be found by starting at point A and adding the lengths of the sides in a clockwise direction:

$$P = 64.78 + 9 + 18 + 42 + 18 + 9 + 64.78 + 80$$
$$= 305.56$$

The perimeter of this plate is approximately 305.56 mm.

EXERCISE SET 3.2

Find the perimeter and area of each polygon in Exercises 1–10. Use the formulas in Figure 3.28.

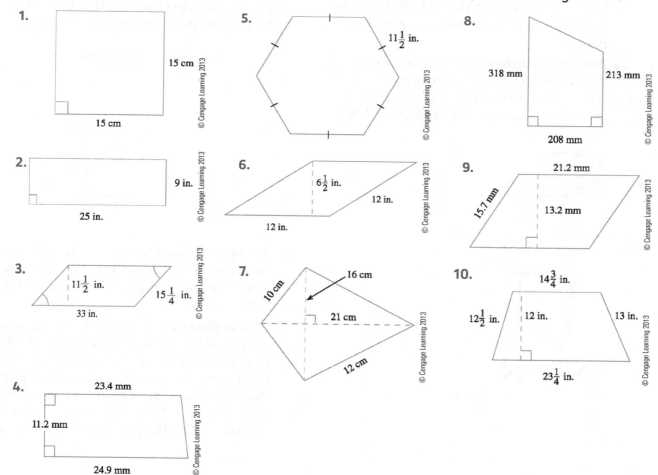

1.
15 cm
15 cm

2.
9 in.
25 in.

3.
$11\frac{1}{2}$ in.
$15\frac{1}{4}$ in.
33 in.

4.
23.4 mm
11.2 mm
24.9 mm

5.
$11\frac{1}{2}$ in.

6.
$6\frac{1}{2}$ in.
12 in.
12 in.

7.
10 cm
16 cm
21 cm
12 cm

8.
318 mm
213 mm
208 mm

9.
21.2 mm
15.7 mm
13.2 mm

10.
$14\frac{3}{4}$ in.
$12\frac{1}{2}$ in.
12 in.
13 in.
$23\frac{1}{4}$ in.

© Cengage Learning 2013

Solve Exercises 11–22.

11. Construction Find the area of the L-shaped patio in Figure 3.31.

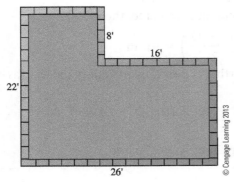

Figure 3.31

12. Construction You plan to put a brick border around the patio in Figure 3.31. Each brick is 8 in. long and 4 in. wide. If the bricks are placed end to end, how many bricks are needed?

13. Mechanical engineering What is the area of the cross-section of the I-beam in Figure 3.32a? (Hint: Think of it as a rectangle and subtract the areas of the two trapezoids. See Figure 3.32b.)

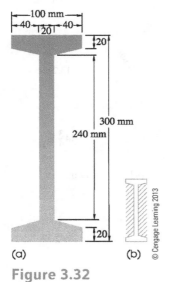

(a)   (b)

Figure 3.32

14. Civil engineering Find the area of the concrete highway support shown in Figure 3.33.

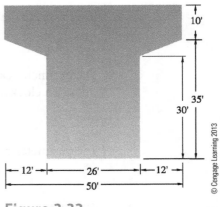

Figure 3.33

15. Machine technology A hexagonal bolt measures $\frac{7}{8}''$ across the short distance. (See Figure 3.34.) What are the perimeter and area of this bolt?

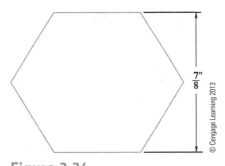

Figure 3.34

16. Machine technology A hexagonal bolt measures 15 mm across the short distance. What are the perimeter and area of this bolt?

17. Civil engineering A river bed is going to be constructed in the shape of a trapezoid. The height of the trapezoid is designed to contain flood waters between the dykes, which form the walls. The trapezoid has the dimensions given in Figure 3.35. **(a)** What is the cross-sectional area? **(b)** How many linear feet of

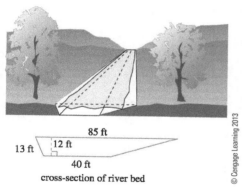

85 ft

13 ft 12 ft

40 ft

cross-section of river bed

Figure 3.35

concrete are needed to surface the walls and the bottom?

18. *Interior design* What will it cost to carpet the floor of a rectangular room that is 20′6″ by 15′3″ at $6.75 a square yard? (There are 9 ft² in 1 yd².)

19. *Civil engineering* A structural supporting member is made in the shape of an angle as shown in Figure 3.36. What is the cross-sectional area?

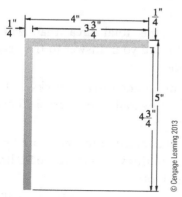

$\frac{1}{4}$″   4″ $\frac{1}{4}$″

$3\frac{3}{4}$″

5″

$4\frac{3}{4}$″

Figure 3.36

20. *Architecture* How many 9″ square tiles will cover a floor 12′ by 17′3″?

21. *Civil engineering* Find the area of the cross-section of the structural tee in Figure 3.37.

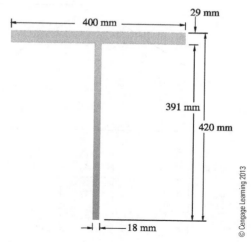

400 mm   29 mm

391 mm

420 mm

18 mm

Figure 3.37

22. *Architecture* Find the area of the side of the house in Figure 3.38.

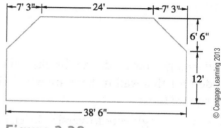

7′ 3″   24′   7′ 3″

6′ 6″

12′

38′ 6″

Figure 3.38

23. *Construction* The estimation of the quantity of brick to complete a wall with a thickness of a single brick is derived from multiplying the square feet of wall area by the number of bricks required per square foot. The number of bricks per square foot depends on the size of the brick. Wall openings such as doors and windows must be factored in the calculations or material estimates can be too high. For the house in Figure 3.39, the entire wall will be bricked except for the windows and the door.

(a) Determine the total area that will be bricked. Round your answer to the nearest square foot.

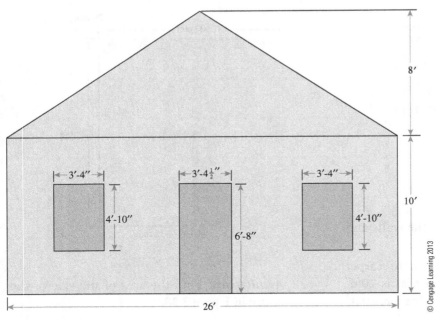

Figure 3.39

(b) How many standard-size bricks will be needed for this wall if there are 6.75 bricks per square foot?

(c) How many engineered/oversize bricks will be needed for this wall if there are 5.8 bricks per square foot?

(d) How many economy-size bricks will be needed for this wall if there are 4.5 bricks per square foot?

24. Construction Since brick must be cut at openings and waste occurs, estimations can be simplified if wall opening dimensions exclude inches and fractions, using only the foot measurements. For example, a door opening measuring $3'$–$4\frac{1}{2}''$ wide and $6'$–$8''$ high can be

considered as $3' \times 6'$ for estimating purposes. Use this estimation method for the house in Figure 3.39 and

(a) Determine the total area that will be bricked. Round your answer to the nearest square foot.

(b) How many standard-size bricks will be needed for this wall if there are 6.75 bricks per square foot?

(c) How many engineered/oversize bricks will be needed for this wall if there are 5.8 bricks per square foot?

(d) How many economy-size bricks will be needed for this wall if there are 4.5 bricks per square foot?

 [IN YOUR WORDS]

25. (a) Describe how a trapezoid and a parallelogram are different.

(b) Can a trapezoid ever be a parallelogram? Explain your answer.

26. Describe what is meant by area and perimeter.

5 AN INTRODUCTION TO TRIGONOMETRY AND VARIATION

The angle an access ramp makes with the ground must be 4.8° or less. Trigonometry allows you to determine how much room is needed for such a ramp.

Until now, we have studied only linear functions. But much of the mathematics used by people working in technical areas involves triangles.

In this chapter, we will learn about a new type of function—the trigonometric function. Trigonometric functions were originally developed to describe the relationship between the sides and angles of triangles. But, as so often happens in mathematics, other uses were discovered for these functions. Technical and scientific areas rely a great deal on trigonometric functions.

We will begin our study of trigonometry with the study of angles and angular measurements. We will then define the six trigonometric functions and their inverse functions, and study how we can use trigonometry to solve problems involving right triangles. (Chapter 8 will expand the applications to all types of triangles.) This chapter also provides some good opportunities to use our calculators and computers in new ways.

OBJECTIVES

AFTER COMPLETING THIS CHAPTER, YOU WILL BE ABLE TO:

▼ Convert angles between decimal degrees, radians, and degrees, minutes, and seconds.

▼ Draw (sketch by hand) an angle in standard position using either the measure of the angle in degrees or in radians or using the coordinates of a point on the terminal side of the angle.

▼ Find the trigonometric functions of an angle using a point on the terminal side of the angle and using a calculator or a spreadsheet.

▼ Find the acute angle (the reference angle) that produces a given value of a trigonometric function and use that angle to find the other angle (within one revolution) that has the same value of that trigonometric function (evaluate inverse trigonometric functions).

▼ Find the missing sides and angles of a right triangle.

▼ Find the algebraic sign of a given trigonometric function for an angle in any quadrant.

▼ Find the value of a trigonometric function, given any angle, using a calculator or spreadsheet.

▼ Find the value of inverse trigonometric functions.

▼ Convert between angular velocity measured in radians per second or in degrees per second and revolutions per second.

▼ Apply the trigonometric functions to applications of circular motion and to mechanics.

5.1 ANGLES, ANGLE MEASURE, AND TRIGONOMETRIC FUNCTIONS

At the beginning of this section, we will review our knowledge of angles and how they are measured. From this introduction we will quickly move into a study of the trigonometric functions.

POSITIVE AND NEGATIVE ANGLES

In Chapter 3, we gave two definitions of an angle. One of these was to think of generating a ray from an initial position to a terminal position. One revolution is the amount a ray would turn to return to its original position. As can be seen in Figure 5.1, if the rotation of the terminal side from the initial side is counterclockwise, the angle is a positive angle, but if the rotation is clockwise, the angle is a negative angle.

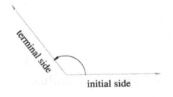

Positive Angle
(counterclockwise rotation)

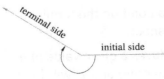

Negative Angle
(clockwise rotation)

© Cengage Learning 2013

Figure 5.1

DEGREES AND RADIANS

Angles are measured using several different systems. The two most common are degrees and radians. In Chapter 3, we discussed how to change from degrees to radians and from radians to degrees. This is an important skill. We will briefly review this technique, but for more details you should refer to Section 3.1.

A degree is $\frac{1}{360}$ of a circle and the symbol ° is used to indicate degree(s). A radian is $\frac{1}{2\pi}$ of a circle. An entire circle contains 360° or 2π rad.

DEGREE-RADIAN CONVERSIONS

To convert from degrees to radians, multiply the number of degrees by $\frac{\pi}{180°}$.

To convert from radians to degrees, multiply the number of radians by $\frac{180°}{\pi}$.

Some scientific calculators have a key that will allow you to convert between degrees and radians. (Consult your owner's manual to see if your calculator can do this.)

EXAMPLE 5.1

Convert 72° to radians.

SOLUTION
$$72° = 72°\left(\frac{\pi}{180°}\right)$$
$$= \frac{72\pi}{180}$$
$$= \frac{2\pi}{5}\text{ rad} \approx 1.25664\text{ rad}$$

EXAMPLE 5.2

Convert 0.62 rad to degrees.

SOLUTION
$$0.62\text{ rad} = 0.62 \times \frac{180°}{\pi}$$
$$\approx 35.52352°$$

EXAMPLE 5.3

Convert $\frac{3\pi}{4}$ rad to degrees.

SOLUTION We multiply by $\frac{180°}{\pi}$.
$$\frac{3\pi}{4} = \frac{3\pi}{4} \times \frac{180°}{\pi}$$

$$= \frac{3}{4} \times 180°$$

$$= 135°$$

If you cannot remember these conversion values and if your calculator is not handy, use your knowledge of proportions. Since $180° = \pi$ rad, we can use the proportion given in the box.

CONVERTING BETWEEN DEGREES AND RADIANS

To convert d degrees to r radians (or vice versa), use the proportion

$$\frac{d}{180°} = \frac{r}{\pi}$$

When you use this ratio, you will know the value of either d or r and want to find the other.

EXAMPLE 5.4

Use this ratio to convert 72° to radians.

SOLUTION Here $d = 72°$, so

$$\frac{72°}{180°} = \frac{r}{\pi}$$

and $\frac{72°}{180°}\pi = \frac{2}{5}\pi \approx 1.25664$ gives you the same answer we got in Example 5.1. Notice that 72° is exactly $\frac{2}{5}\pi$, whereas 1.25664 is an approximation.

EXAMPLE 5.5

Use the ratio method to convert $\frac{3\pi}{4}$ to degrees.

SOLUTION

This is the same problem we worked in Example 5.3. Here $r = \frac{3\pi}{4}$, so

$$\frac{d}{180°} = \frac{3\pi/4}{\pi}$$

and

$$d = \frac{3\pi/4}{\pi} \cdot 180°$$

$$= \frac{3\pi}{4} \cdot \frac{1}{\pi} \cdot 180°$$

$$= \frac{3\cancel{\pi}}{4} \cdot \frac{1}{\cancel{\pi}} \cdot 180°$$

EXAMPLE 5.5 (Cont.)

$$= \frac{3}{4} \cdot 180°$$

$$= 135°.$$

Thus, we see that $\frac{3\pi}{4} = 135°$.

COTERMINAL ANGLES

If two angles have the same initial side and the same terminal side, they are coterminal angles. An example of coterminal angles is given in Figure 5.2. One way to find a coterminal angle of a given angle is to add 360° to the original angle. In Figure 5.2, the original angle is 50° and one coterminal angle is 50° + 360° = 410°. In fact, you could add any integer multiple of 360° to the original angle to find a coterminal angle. So, 50° + 4(360°) = 50° + 1,440° = 1,490° is another coterminal angle of a 50° angle.

In the same way, you could subtract an integer multiple of 360° from the original angle to get a coterminal angle. Thus, 50° − 360° = −310° is a coterminal angle of a 50° angle, and so is 50° − 2(360°) = 50° − 720° = −670°.

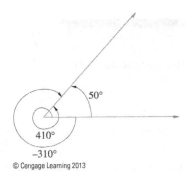

© Cengage Learning 2013

Figure 5.2

An angle is in standard position if its vertex is at the origin of a rectangular coordinate system and its initial side coincides with the positive x-axis. The angle is determined by the position of the terminal side. The angle is said to be in a certain quadrant if its terminal side lies in that quadrant. If the terminal side coincides with one of the coordinate axes, the angle is a quadrantal angle.

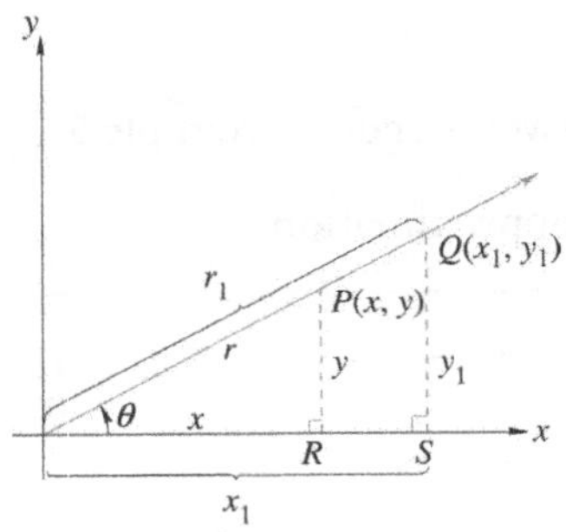

Consider an angle θ in a standard position and let $P(x, y)$ be a fixed point on the terminal side of θ, as in Figure 5.3. We will call r the distance from O to P. From the Pythagorean theorem we know $r = \sqrt{x^2 + y^2}$. The length r is also called the *radius vector*. Suppose $Q(x_1, y_1)$ is any other point on the terminal side θ. If PR and QS are both perpendicular to the x-axis, then ΔPOR and ΔQOS are similar. As you remember from our discussion on proportions (Section 2.4), the corresponding sides of similar triangles are proportional. So, the ratios of the corresponding sides are equal. For example, $\frac{y}{r} = \frac{y_1}{r_1}$ and $\frac{x}{y} = \frac{x_1}{y_1}$. As long as θ does not change, these ratios will not change.

© Cengage Learning 2013

Figure 5.3

THE TRIGONOMETRIC FUNCTIONS

There are six possible ratios of two sides of a triangle. Each of these ratios has been given a name. These names (and their abbreviations) are sine (sin), cosine (cos), tangent (tan), cosecant (csc), secant (sec), and cotangent (cot). Because these ratios depend on the size of angle θ, they are written sin θ, cos θ, and so on. So, what you have are ratios that are functions of θ—the trigonometric functions. The six trigonometric, or trig, functions are defined using the triangle in Figure 5.4.

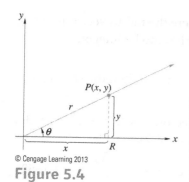

© Cengage Learning 2013

Figure 5.4

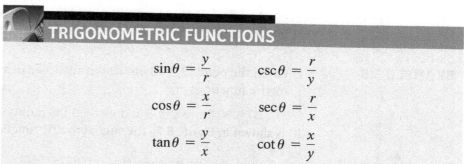

TRIGONOMETRIC FUNCTIONS

$$\sin\theta = \frac{y}{r} \qquad \csc\theta = \frac{r}{y}$$

$$\cos\theta = \frac{x}{r} \qquad \sec\theta = \frac{r}{x}$$

$$\tan\theta = \frac{y}{x} \qquad \cot\theta = \frac{x}{y}$$

EXAMPLE 5.6

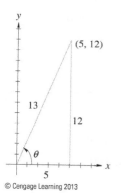

© Cengage Learning 2013

Figure 5.5

Given the point (5, 12) on the terminal side of an angle θ, find the six trigonometric functions of θ.

SOLUTION A sketch of the angle is in Figure 5.5. Since $x = 5$ and $y = 12$, we can find the radius vector r by using the Pythagorean theorem.

$$r = \sqrt{x^2 + y^2} = \sqrt{5^2 + 12^2} = \sqrt{25 + 144} = \sqrt{169} = 13$$

$$\sin\theta = \frac{y}{r} = \frac{12}{13} \qquad \csc\theta = \frac{r}{y} = \frac{13}{12}$$

$$\cos\theta = \frac{x}{r} = \frac{5}{13} \qquad \sec\theta = \frac{r}{x} = \frac{13}{5}$$

$$\tan\theta = \frac{y}{x} = \frac{12}{5} \qquad \cot\theta = \frac{x}{y} = \frac{5}{12}$$

NOTE The values of x and y may be positive, negative, or zero; but r is always positive or zero. Remember, r is never negative because $r = \sqrt{x^2 + y^2}$ and the expression $\sqrt{x^2 + y^2}$ is never negative.

Of course, there is nothing to restrict the terminal side to the first quadrant. In the next two examples, the terminal side is in Quadrants II and IV, respectively.

EXAMPLE 5.7

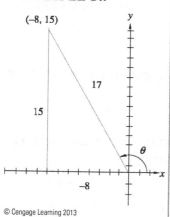

© Cengage Learning 2013

Figure 5.6

Given the point $(-8, 15)$ on the terminal side of an angle θ, find the six trigonometric functions of θ.

SOLUTION Here we have $x = -8$ and $y = 15$, so the radius vector r is given by $\sqrt{(-8)^2 + (15)^2} = \sqrt{64 + 225} = \sqrt{289} = 17$ as shown in Figure 5.6. The six trigonometric functions are

$$\sin\theta = \frac{15}{17} \qquad \csc\theta = \frac{17}{15}$$

$$\cos\theta = \frac{-8}{17} \qquad \sec\theta = \frac{-17}{8}$$

$$\tan\theta = -\frac{15}{8} \qquad \cot\theta = -\frac{8}{15}$$

As a final example, we will consider a case where the radius vector is not an integer. Note that none of the sides of the triangle have to be integers.

EXAMPLE 5.8

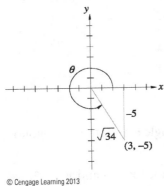

© Cengage Learning 2013

Figure 5.7

Given the point $(3, -5)$ on the terminal side of an angle θ, find the six trigonometric functions of θ.

SOLUTION Since $x = 3$ and $y = -5$ the radius vector, r, is $\sqrt{9 + 25} = \sqrt{34}$, as shown in Figure 5.7. The trigonometric functions of θ are

$$\sin\theta = \frac{-5}{\sqrt{34}} \approx -0.8575 \qquad \csc\theta = -\frac{\sqrt{34}}{5} \approx -1.1662$$

$$\cos\theta = \frac{3}{\sqrt{34}} \approx 0.5145 \qquad \sec\theta = \frac{\sqrt{34}}{3} \approx 1.9437$$

$$\tan\theta = -\frac{5}{3} \approx -1.6667 \qquad \cot\theta = -\frac{3}{5} = -0.6$$

EXERCISE SET 5.1

Convert each of the angle measures in Exercises 1–8 from degrees to radians.

1. 90°

2. 45°

3. 80°

4. −15°

5. 155°

6. −235°

7. 215°

8. 180°

Convert each of the angle measures in Exercises 9–16 from radians to degrees.

9. 2

10. 3

11. 1.5

12. π

13. $\frac{\pi}{3}$

14. $\frac{5\pi}{6}$

15. $-\frac{\pi}{4}$

16. −1.3

In Exercises 17–20, (a) draw each of the angles in standard position; (b) draw an arrow to indicate the rotation; (c) for each angle, find two other angles, one positive and one negative, that are coterminal with the given angle. (Note: There are many possible correct answers.)

17. 150°

18. 315°

19. −135°

20. −30°

Each point in Exercises 21–30 is on the terminal side of angle θ in standard position. Find the six trigonometric functions of the angle θ associated with each of these points.

21. $(4, 3)$

22. $(-6, -8)$

23. $(8, -15)$

24. $(-20, 21)$

25. $(1, 2)$

26. $(-2, 4)$

27. $(10, -8)$

28. $(-5, -2)$

29. $(\sqrt{11}, 5)$

30. $(-6, \sqrt{13})$

Find the trigonometric functions that exist for each of the quadrantral angles θ when drawn in standard position for each of the points in Exercises 31–34.

31. $(3, 0)$

32. $(0, -4)$

33. $(-5, 0)$

34. $(0, 6)$

For each of Exercises 35–40, there is a point P on the terminal side of an angle θ in standard position. From the information given, determine the six trigonometric functions of θ.

35. $x = 6, r = 10, y > 0$

36. $y = -9, r = 15, x > 0$

37. $x = -20, r = 29, y > 0$

38. $y = 5, r = 13, x < 0$

39. $x = -7, r = 8, y < 0$

40. $y = 5, r = 30, x < 0$

[IN YOUR WORDS]

41. (a) Write an explanation of how to convert from degrees to radians.

(b) Ask a classmate to use your written explanation to convert 50° to radians.

(c) Did your classmate get 50° ≈ 0.87266? If not, either your classmate did not follow your directions or your explanation needs to be rewritten. Decide where the error was made and make the necessary corrections.

42. (a) Draw a right triangle on the *xy*-coordinate system with an acute angle at the origin, one leg on the positive *x*-axis, and the other leg vertical. Label the angle at the origin *θ*, the hypotenuse *r*, the horizontal leg *x*, and the vertical leg *y*.

(b) Define each of the trigonometric functions of *θ* in terms of *x*, *y*, and *r*.

(c) Compare your drawing in (a) with Figure 5.4. Compare your definitions in (b) with those in the "Trigonometric Functions" box near Figure 5.4.

5.2   VALUES OF THE TRIGONOMETRIC FUNCTIONS

We have learned how to calculate the values of the trigonometric functions for an angle *θ* in standard position when we are given a point on the terminal side of *θ*. This is not always the most convenient way to find the values of the trigonometric functions for *θ*.

If we have an angle *θ* in the standard position and draw the triangle as we did in Figure 5.4, we get a picture that helps us to determine the values of the trigonometric functions for *θ*. If we look at just △*POR*, we get a figure much like the one in Figure 5.8. The length of the hypotenuse is *r*, the length *y* is for the side opposite angle *θ*, and the other side *x* is the side adjacent to angle *θ*. We can use these descriptions of the sides to rephrase our definitions for the trigonometric function.

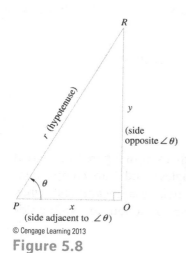

© Cengage Learning 2013

Figure 5.8

TRIGONOMETRIC FUNCTIONS

$$\sin\theta = \frac{y}{r} = \frac{\text{side opposite } \theta}{\text{hypotenuse}}$$

$$\csc\theta = \frac{r}{y} = \frac{\text{hypotenuse}}{\text{side opposite } \theta}$$

$$\cos\theta = \frac{x}{r} = \frac{\text{side adjacent to } \theta}{\text{hypotenuse}}$$

$$\sec\theta = \frac{r}{x} = \frac{\text{hypotenuse}}{\text{side adjacent to } \theta}$$

$$\tan\theta = \frac{y}{x} = \frac{\text{side opposite } \theta}{\text{side adjacent to } \theta}$$

$$\cot\theta = \frac{x}{y} = \frac{\text{side adjacent to } \theta}{\text{side opposite } \theta}$$

With these relationships, we can find the trigonometric functions of any angle of a right triangle.

EXAMPLE 5.9

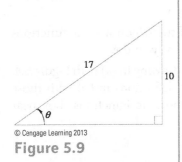

© Cengage Learning 2013
Figure 5.9

Determine the values of the trigonometric functions for an angle of a triangle with a hypotenuse of 17 and the opposite side of length 10, as shown in Figure 5.9.

SOLUTION The length of the adjacent side x is missing. Use the Pythagorean theorem, $x = \sqrt{r^2 - y^2}$. Since $r = 17$ and $y = 10$, $x = \sqrt{17^2 - 10^2} = \sqrt{189} = 3\sqrt{21}$. The trigonometric functions are

$$\sin\theta = \frac{\text{side opposite}}{\text{hypotenuse}} = \frac{10}{17} \qquad \csc\theta = \frac{\text{hypotenuse}}{\text{side opposite}} = \frac{17}{10}$$

$$\cos\theta = \frac{\text{side adjacent}}{\text{hypotenuse}} = \frac{3\sqrt{21}}{17} \qquad \sec\theta = \frac{\text{hypotenuse}}{\text{side adjacent}} = \frac{17}{3\sqrt{21}}$$

$$\tan\theta = \frac{\text{side opposite}}{\text{side adjacent}} = \frac{10}{3\sqrt{21}} \qquad \cot\theta = \frac{\text{side adjacent}}{\text{side opposite}} = \frac{3\sqrt{21}}{10}$$

We could have worked the problem had we been given the value of one of the trigonometric functions rather than the lengths of two of the sides.

EXAMPLE 5.10

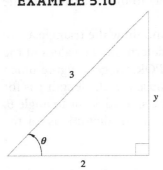

© Cengage Learning 2013
Figure 5.10

In Figure 5.10, if θ is an angle of a triangle and $\cos\theta = \frac{2}{3}$, what are the values of the other trigonometric functions?

SOLUTION The length y of the side opposite θ is $\sqrt{3^2 - 2^2} = \sqrt{5}$. Thus, we have the values for the other functions

$$\sin\theta = \frac{\sqrt{5}}{3} \qquad \csc\theta = \frac{3}{\sqrt{5}} \qquad \sec\theta = \frac{3}{2}$$

$$\tan\theta = \frac{\sqrt{5}}{2} \qquad \cot\theta = \frac{2}{\sqrt{5}}$$

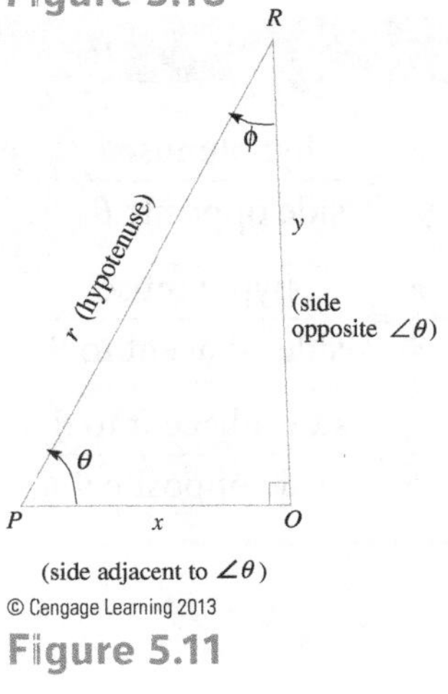

Look at Figure 5.11. This is the same triangle that was in Figure 5.8. There is another acute angle in that triangle, labeled ϕ. Angles θ and ϕ are complementary. Remember, complementary angles are two angles that measure 90° when added. So, $\theta + \phi = 90°$. What are the trigonometric functions for ϕ? The side opposite ϕ is x and the side adjacent to ϕ is y, so

$$\sin\phi = \frac{x}{r} \qquad \csc\phi = \frac{r}{x}$$

$$\cos\phi = \frac{y}{r} \qquad \sec\phi = \frac{r}{y}$$

$$\tan\phi = \frac{x}{y} \qquad \cot\phi = \frac{y}{x}$$

From this, we get the principle of cofunctions of complementary angles.

© Cengage Learning 2013
Figure 5.11

TRIGONOMETRIC FUNCTIONS OF COMPLEMENTARY ANGLES

If θ and ϕ are complementary angles, then

$$\sin \theta = \cos \phi \qquad \tan \theta = \cot \phi \qquad \csc \theta = \sec \phi$$

You may have begun to notice a pattern with the trigonometric functions. The values of some of the trig functions are the reciprocals of other functions. These are known as the **reciprocal identities**. There are three reciprocal identities. (An identity is an equation that is true for every value in the domain of its variables.)

RECIPROCAL IDENTITIES

$$\csc \theta = \frac{1}{\sin \theta} \qquad \sec \theta = \frac{1}{\cos \theta} \qquad \cot \theta = \frac{1}{\tan \theta}$$

There is also a relationship between the $\sin \theta$, $\cos \theta$, and the $\tan \theta$. This relationship, and its reciprocal, are known as the **quotient identities**.

QUOTIENT IDENTITIES

$$\tan \theta = \frac{\sin \theta}{\cos \theta} \qquad \cot \theta = \frac{\cos \theta}{\sin \theta}$$

None of these identities is true when the denominator is zero.

EXAMPLE 5.11

If $\sin \theta = \frac{1}{2}$ and $\cos \theta = \frac{\sqrt{3}}{2}$, find the values of the other four trigonometric functions.

SOLUTION Using the reciprocal and quotient identities we have

$$\tan \theta = \frac{\sin \theta}{\cos \theta} = \frac{\frac{1}{2}}{\frac{\sqrt{3}}{2}} = \frac{1}{\sqrt{3}}$$

EXAMPLE 5.11 (Cont.)

$$\cot\theta = \frac{1}{\tan\theta} = \frac{1}{\dfrac{1}{\sqrt{3}}} = \frac{\sqrt{3}}{1} = \sqrt{3}$$

$$\csc\theta = \frac{1}{\sin\theta} = \frac{1}{\dfrac{1}{2}} = \frac{2}{1} = 2$$

$$\sec\theta = \frac{1}{\cos\theta} = \frac{1}{\dfrac{\sqrt{3}}{2}} = \frac{2}{\sqrt{3}}$$

TRIGONOMETRIC VALUES

Until now, we have been finding the values of trigonometric functions without knowing the size of the angle θ. But, many times we are given the value of θ and are asked to determine the values of the trigonometric functions for that angle.

There are two basic methods used to find values of trigonometric functions. By far, the easiest way is with a calculator or a computer. The other basic method is with a table of trigonometric values. There are some trigonometric angles that seem to be used quite frequently. Some people learn the values of these basic angles so they can readily use these values when they are needed. We will concentrate on calculators and computers for determining the value of a trigonometric function.

Before you use a calculator or a computer, you need to decide if the angle is measured in degrees or radians. Most calculators can compute the trigonometric functions of an angle whether it is in degrees or radians, as long as the calculator is set to work in that mode.

GRAPHING CALCULATORS

© Cengage Learning 2013

Figure 5.12

Different models of calculators have different symbols or different locations for the symbols that let you know which mode the calculator is in. For example, on a graphing calculator, such as the Texas Instruments TI-83 or TI-84, press MODE . The TI-83 or TI-84 will display a screen like that in Figure 5.12. (The calculator displayed in Figure 5.12 is in degree mode.)

Use the cursor keys ▲, ▼, ◄, and ► to darken the appropriate degree or radian mode. Press ENTER to set the calculator in that mode. If your calculator is not a TI-83 or TI-84, make sure that you consult the owner's manual for your calculator.

TRIGONOMETRIC VALUES ON A CALCULATOR

Some calculators have three trigonometric function keys— SIN , COS , and TAN . If you want one of the other trigonometric functions, you will have to use one of these keys and the 1/x or x^{-1} key. Here you need to know the reciprocal identities discussed earlier in this section. You must press the 1/x or x^{-1} key *after* you have pressed the trigonometric function key.

CAUTION Make sure that your calculator is set in the correct degree or radian mode before you begin to work the problem.

EXAMPLE 5.12

Determine the trigonometric functions of 48.9°.

SOLUTION Put the calculator in degree mode, and then proceed as follows.

Function	ENTER	DISPLAY
sin 48.9°	SIN 48.9 ENTER	0.753563
cos 48.9°	COS 48.9 ENTER	0.6573752
tan 48.9°	TAN 48.9 ENTER	1.1463215
csc 48.9°	(SIN 48.9) x^{-1} ENTER	1.3270284
sec 48.9°	(COS 48.9) x^{-1} ENTER	1.5212012
cot 48.9°	(TAN 48.9) x^{-1} ENTER	0.8723556

 HINT You do not need to change modes to find the trigonometric function of an angle measured in degrees. There is a degree symbol on the ANGLE menu of a TI-83 or TI-84 graphics calculator. You can use the calculator's degree symbol to get the correct answer from either degree or radian mode. To get sin 48.9° on a TI-83/84, press SIN 48.9 2ND APPS [ANGLE] 1) ENTER . The calculator should display the result .7535633923.

To find the values of the trigonometric functions for an angle in radians, put the calculator in the radian mode. Then proceed as in Example 5.13.

EXAMPLE 5.13

Use a calculator to determine the trigonometric functions of 0.65 rad.

SOLUTION Put the calculator in radian mode and then proceed as follows.

Function	ENTER	DISPLAY
sin 0.65	SIN 0.65 ENTER	0.6051864
cos 0.65	COS 0.65 ENTER	0.7960838
tan 0.65	TAN 0.65 ENTER	0.7602044
csc 0.65	(SIN 0.65) x^{-1} ENTER	1.6523834
sec 0.65	(COS 0.65) x^{-1} ENTER	1.2561492
cot 0.65	(TAN 0.65) x^{-1} ENTER	1.3154357

 HINT Just as you do not need to change modes to find the trigonometric function of an angle measured in degrees, you also do not need to change modes to find the trigonometric function of an angle measured in radians. The radian symbol on the TI-83 or TI-84 calculator is an *r*. You can use the calculator's radian symbol to get the correct answer from either degree or radian mode. To get sin 0.65 on a

TI-83/84, press SIN .65 2ND APPS [ANGLE] 3) ENTER . The calculator should display sin .65' on one line, with the result, .6051864057, on the next line.

SPREADSHEETS AND THE TRIGONOMETRIC FUNCTIONS

When performing calculations with trigonometric functions, it is important to know that the spreadsheet is always in radian "mode," using the terminology of the graphing calculator. There is no way to switch modes but it is fairly easy to convert degrees to radians.

To find $\sin\left(\frac{\pi}{3}\right)$ enter the expression almost as it is written. Remember to enter π as either PI( ) or pi( ) (See Figure 5.13a.) You can enter the expression in upper case letters as shown in Figure 5.13a or in lower case letters: sin (pi ( ) /3).

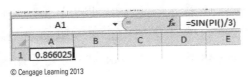

© Cengage Learning 2013

Figure 5.13a

To find the sin (60°), you must convert 60° to radians by entering RADIANS (60) either within the expression (see Figure 5.13b) or separately (see Figure 5.13c).

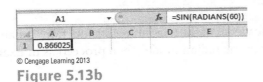

© Cengage Learning 2013

Figure 5.13b

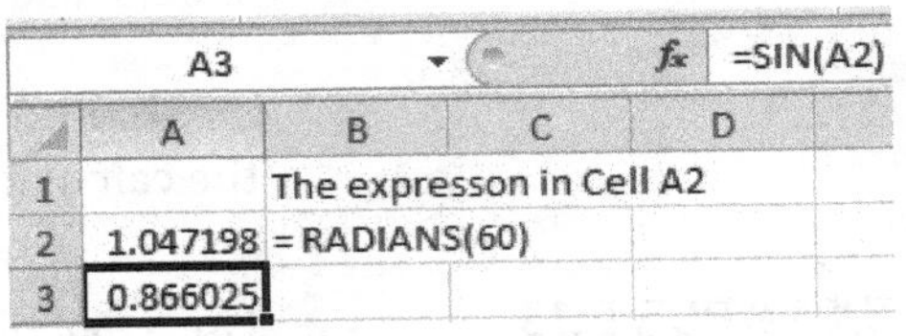

Figure 5.13c

We will rework Examples 5.12 and 5.13 using a spreadsheet rather than a calculator.

EXAMPLE 5.14

Use a spreadsheet to determine the trigonometric functions of 48.9°.

SOLUTION Remember that a spreadsheet is automatically in radian mode, so you must tell the program that you want answers for degrees. The input and the results are shown in Figure 5.14.

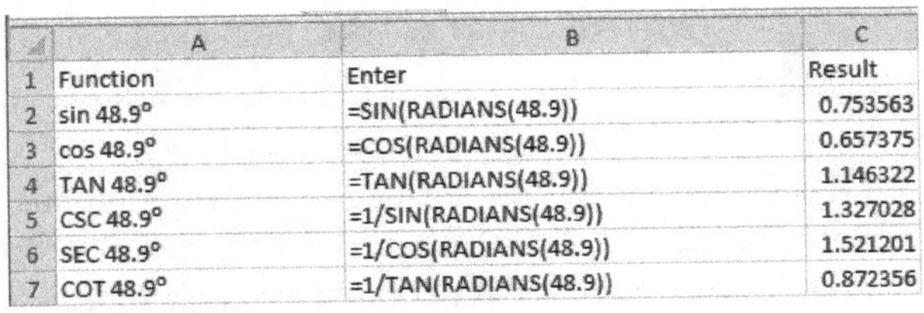

	A	B	C
1	Function	Enter	Result
2	sin 48.9°	=SIN(RADIANS(48.9))	0.753563
3	cos 48.9°	=COS(RADIANS(48.9))	0.657375
4	TAN 48.9°	=TAN(RADIANS(48.9))	1.146322
5	CSC 48.9°	=1/SIN(RADIANS(48.9))	1.327028
6	SEC 48.9°	=1/COS(RADIANS(48.9))	1.521201
7	COT 48.9°	=1/TAN(RADIANS(48.9))	0.872356

© Cengage Learning 2013

Figure 5.14

EXAMPLE 5.15

Use a spreadsheet to determine the trigonometric functions of 0.65 rad.

SOLUTION Remember that a spreadsheet is automatically in radian mode. The input and the results are shown in Figure 5.15.

	A	B	C
1	Function	Enter	Result
2	sin 0.65	=SIN(0.65)	0.605186
3	cos 0.65	=COS(0.65)	0.796084
4	TAN 0.65	=TAN(0.65)	0.760204
5	CSC 0.65	=1/SIN(0.65)	1.652383
6	SEC 0.65	=1/COS(0.65)	1.256149
7	COT 0.65	=1/TAN(0.65)	1.315436

© Cengage Learning 2013

Figure 5.15

EXERCISE SET 5.2

In Exercises 1–6, find the six trigonometric functions for angle θ for the indicated sides of △ABC. (See Figure 5.16)

1. $a = 5, c = 13$

2. $a = 7, b = 8$

3. $a = 1.2, c = 2$

4. $a = 2.1, b = 2.8$

5. $a = 1.4, b = 2.3$

6. $c = 3.5, b = 2.1$

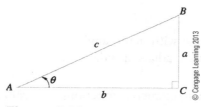

Figure 5.16

© Cengage Learning 2013

In Exercises 7–12, let θ be an angle of a right triangle with the given trigonometric function. Find the values of the other trigonometric functions.

7. $\cos \theta = \frac{8}{17}$

8. $\tan \theta = \frac{21}{20}$

9. $\sin \theta = \frac{3}{5}$

10. $\sec \theta = \frac{10}{6}$

11. $\csc \theta = \frac{29}{20}$

12. $\csc \theta = \frac{15}{12}$

In Exercises 13–16, the values of two of the trigonometric functions of angle θ are given. Use this information to determine the values of the other four trigonometric functions for θ.

13. $\sin \theta = 0.866, \cos \theta = 0.5$

14. $\sin \theta = 0.975, \cos \theta = 0.222$

15. $\sin \theta = 0.085, \sec \theta = 1.004$

16. $\csc \theta = 4.872, \cos \theta = 0.979$

Use a calculator or a spreadsheet to determine the values of each of the indicated trigonometric functions in Exercises 17–32.

17. $\sin 18.6°$

18. $\cos 38.4°$

19. $\tan 18.3°$

20. $\sin 20°15'$

21. $\tan 76°32'$

22. $\sec 24° 14'$

23. $\cot 82.6°$

24. $\csc 19°50'$

25. $\sin 0.25$ rad

26. $\cos 0.4$ rad

27. $\tan 0.63$ rad

28. $\sec 1.35$ rad

29. $\cot 1.43$ rad

30. $\sin 1.21$ rad

31. $\csc 0.21$ rad

32. $\tan 1.555$ rad

Solve Exercises 33–36.

33. **Dynamics** If there is no air resistance, a projectile fired at an angle θ above the horizontal with an initial velocity of v_0 has a range R of

$$R = \frac{v_0^2}{g}\sin 2\theta$$

A football is thrown with initial velocity of 15 m/s at an angle of 40° above the horizontal. If $g = 9.8$ m/s^2, how far will the football travel?

34. **Dynamics** If the football in Exercise 33 had been thrown at an angle of 45° above the horizontal, how much further, or shorter, would the ball have traveled? If the angle had been 48°, how would the results have differed?

35. **Electricity** In an ac circuit that contains resistance, inductance, and capacitance in series, the angle of the applied voltage v and the voltage drop across the resistance V_R is the *phase angle* ϕ, and $V_R = V\cos\phi$. If the phase angle is 32° and the applied voltage is 5.8 V, what is the effective voltage across the resistor V_R?

36. **Electricity** Consider an ac circuit that contains resistance, inductance, and capacitance in series, as in Exercise 35. If the phase angle is 71° and the applied voltage is 11.25 V, what is the effective voltage across the resistor, V_R?

 [IN YOUR WORDS]

37. (a) Draw a right triangle with acute angle θ. Label the hypotenuse, adjacent side, and opposite side.

(b) Define each of the trigonometric functions of θ in terms of the hypotenuse, the adjacent side, and the opposite side.

(c) Compare your drawing in (a) with Figure 5.8. Check your definitions in (b) with those in the box near Figure 5.8.

38. (a) What are the reciprocal identities?

(b) What are the quotient identities?

5.3   THE RIGHT TRIANGLE

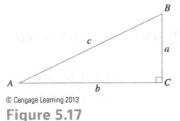

© Cengage Learning 2013

Figure 5.17

In Section 5.2, we learned how to determine trigonometric functions given the lengths of two sides of a right triangle. We are now ready to begin finding the unknown parts of a triangle if we know the length of one side and the size of one of the acute angles. Once we can do that, we will begin to apply our knowledge to solving some problems that involve triangles.

Look at the right triangle in Figure 5.17. The right angle is labeled C and the other two vertices A and B. The side opposite each of these vertices is labeled with the lowercase version of the same letter. Thus, side a is opposite $\angle A$, side b is opposite $\angle B$, and side c is opposite $\angle C$. Since this is a right triangle, angles A and B are complementary.

We now have the tools to solve right triangles. To solve a triangle means to find the sizes of all unknown sides and angles.

EXAMPLE 5.16

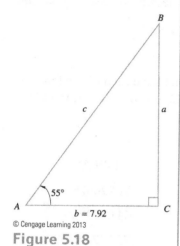

© Cengage Learning 2013

Figure 5.18

Given $A = 55°$ and $b = 7.92$, solve the right triangle ABC.

SOLUTION This data chart contains the information that we know and shows what we have left to find. Notice that, since this is a right triangle, we wrote that $C = 90°$.

sides	angles
$a =$ ____	$A = 55°$
$b = 7.92$	$B =$ ____
$c =$ ____	$C = 90°$

Since $A = 55°$, then $B = 90° - 55° = 35°$. If you look at Figure 5.18 you see that $\tan A = \dfrac{a}{b}$ or $a = b \tan A$. We know $A = 55°$ and $b = 7.92$, so $a = 7.92 \tan 55° \approx 11.310932$ or about 11.31. You could use $\sec A = \dfrac{c}{b}$, to determine c, since $c = b \sec A$. But, your calculator does not have a sec key so we will find c using $\cos A$.

$$\cos A = \frac{b}{c}$$

$$\text{so } c = \frac{b}{\cos A}$$

$$= \frac{7.92}{\cos 55°}$$

$$\approx 13.81$$

Look at the data chart again. This time all of the parts of the chart have been filled in, so we know that we have solved for all the missing parts of this triangle. From the completed chart, we can easily see the measures of any part of the triangle.

sides	angles
$a \approx 11.31$	$A = 55°$
$b = 7.92$	$B = 35°$
$c \approx 13.81$	$C = 90°$

We could have used our derived value of a and the Pythagorean theorem to find c, or we could have used a and one of the other trigonometric functions.

 HINT It is usually best not to use the derived values to calculate other values because of errors that can be introduced by rounding.

By the way, if you use the Pythagorean theorem to check the results in Example 5.16, you will see that $(7.92)^2 + (11.31)^2 \neq (13.81)^2$. The Pythagorean theorem says that these should be equal, but because we are using rounded-off values, they are not. However, they are equal to three significant digits.

USING THE 2ND OR INV KEY ON A CALCULATOR

Until now, we have calculated the values of a trigonometric function from the size of the angle. But, what if we know the value of a trigonometric function and want to know the size of the angle? Here you press the INV or 2nd key on the calculator before you enter the function key.

EXAMPLE 5.17

Use a graphing calculator to determine the angles that have each of the following values of trigonometric functions: $\sin A = 0.785$, $\cos B = 0.437$, $\tan C = 4.213$, and $\csc D = 8.915$.

SOLUTION

Function	ENTER				DISPLAY
$\sin A = 0.785$	2nd SIN	0.785			51.720678
$\cos B = 0.437$	2nd COS	0.437			64.087375
$\tan C = 4.213$	2nd TAN	4.213			75.547345
$\csc D = 8.915$	2nd SIN	8.915 x^{-1}			6.4404506
or	2nd SIN	(1 ÷ 8.915)			6.4404506

So, $A \approx 51.72°$, $B \approx 64.09°$, $C \approx 76.65°$, and $D \approx 6.44°$. Notice that to find angle D, we had to use the 2nd SIN keys with the reciprocal of 8.915. This is because $\csc D = 8.915$ is the same as $\dfrac{1}{\sin D} = 8.915$ or $\sin D = \dfrac{1}{8.915}$. Hence, $D = \sin^{-1}\dfrac{1}{8.915}$, which may be entered in your calculator as either

2nd SIN 8.915 x^{-1}

or   2nd SIN (1 ÷ 8.915)

EXAMPLE 5.18

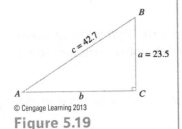

© Cengage Learning 2013

Figure 5.19

Solve right triangle ABC ($\triangle ABC$), if $a = 23.5$ and $c = 42.7$, as shown in Figure 5.19.

SOLUTION The following data chart shows the information we are starting with and what we have to find.

sides	angles
$a = 23.5$	$A = \underline{\quad}$
$b = \underline{\quad}$	$B = \underline{\quad}$
$c = 42.7$	$C = 90°$

From the Pythagorean theorem we know that $b^2 = c^2 - a^2 = (42.7)^2 - (23.5)^2 = 1271.04$, so $b = 35.7$. Now, $\sin A = \frac{23.5}{42.7} \approx 0.5503513$. Pressing 2nd SIN 0.5503513, we get 33.391116. Thus, $A \approx 33.4°$ and $B \approx 90° - 33.4° = 56.6°$. The completed data chart follows.

sides	angles
$a = 23.5$	$A \approx 33.4°$
$b \approx 35.7$	$B \approx 56.6°$
$c = 42.7$	$C = 90°$

 HINT Two possible shortcuts could have been taken in Example 5.18 when you determined the size of A.

1. After you calculated $\sin A = \frac{23.5}{42.7} \approx 0.5503513$, you could have used the ability of a graphing calculator to keep the last answer in memory. Thus, rather than press `2nd` `SIN` 0.5503513, you could have pressed

    `2nd` `SIN` `2nd` `ANS` `ENTER`

2. An even faster method would have performed the calculation in one step:

    `2nd` `SIN` `(` 23.5 ÷ 42.7 `)` `ENTER`

EXAMPLE 5.19

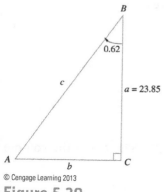

© Cengage Learning 2013

Figure 5.20

Solve for the right triangle ABC if $B = 0.62$ rad and $a = 23.85$, as shown in Figure 5.20.

SOLUTION The data chart for this triangle is

sides	angles
$a = 23.85$	$A = \underline{\quad}$
$b = \underline{\quad}$	$B = 0.62$
$c = \underline{\quad}$	$C = \dfrac{\pi}{2} \approx 1.57$

In this example, we can use angle B as our reference angle. So, $\tan B = \dfrac{b}{a}$ and $b = a \tan B = (23.85) \tan 0.62 = 17.02673$, or $b \approx 17.03$. (Did you remember to put your calculator in radian mode?)

Also, $\cos B = \dfrac{a}{c}$, so

$$c = \frac{a}{\cos B}$$

$$= \frac{23.85}{\cos 0.62}$$

$$\approx 29.30413$$

$$\text{or} \approx 29.30$$

Finally, we have $\tan A = \dfrac{23.85}{17.03} = 1.4004698$, and pressing `2nd` `TAN` 1.4004698, we get 0.9507055, or $A \approx 0.95$ rad.

EXAMPLE 5.19 (Cont.)

Remember from Exercise 1 in Exercise Set 5.1 that $90° \approx 1.57$ rad. If you used your calculator to convert $90°$ to radians, you could then have found A as $1.57 - 0.62 = 0.95$.

The completed data chart for this example is

sides	angles
$a = 23.85$	$A \approx 0.95$
$b \approx 17.03$	$B = 0.62$
$c \approx 29.30$	$C = \dfrac{\pi}{2} \approx 1.57$

APPLICATION CONSTRUCTION

EXAMPLE 5.20

A concrete access ramp to a building is being built. The ramp will be $48''$ wide and make a $4.8°$ angle with the ground. If it ends at a platform that is $23\frac{1}{4}''$ above the ground, how much concrete will be needed?

© Cengage Learning 2013

Figure 5.21

SOLUTION A side view of the ramp is in Figure 5.21. We are interested only in the concrete needed for the shaded part of the figure. The ramp is in the shape of a triangular prism. We want to first find the area of the triangle that forms the base of the prism. We know the height of the triangle is $23\frac{1}{4}''$. We need to find the length of the side that lies on the ground. Here we have

$$\tan 4.8° = \frac{23\frac{1}{4}''}{\text{bottom}}$$

$$\text{bottom} = \frac{23\frac{1}{4}''}{\tan 4.8°}$$

$$\approx 276.876 \text{ inches}$$

The area of the base of the prism is $A = \frac{1}{2}\left(23\frac{1}{4}''\right)(276.876'')$, and the volume of the prism is

$$V = 48''\ A = 48''\left[\frac{1}{2}\left(23\frac{1}{4}''\right)(276.876'')\right]$$

$$\approx 154{,}496.8 \text{ in.}^3$$

Concrete is sold in cubic yards, so we need to convert this answer to cubic yards. There are $36''$ in one yard, which gives the following conversion.

$$V = 154{,}496.8 \,\text{in.}^3$$

$$= \frac{154{,}496.8 \,\text{in.}^3}{1}\ \frac{1\,\text{yd}^3}{(36\,\text{in.})^3}$$

$$\approx 3.31 \,\text{yd}^3$$

It will take about 3.31 yd^3 of concrete to build this ramp.

ANGLES OF ELEVATION OR DEPRESSION

Frequently when solving problems involving trigonometry, we have to use the angle of elevation (see Figure 5.22), which is the angle, measured from the horizontal, through which an observer would have to elevate his or her line of sight in order to see an object. Similarly, the angle of depression is the angle, measured from the horizontal, through which an observer has to lower his or her line of sight in order to see an object. (See Figure 5.23.)

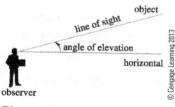

Figure 5.22

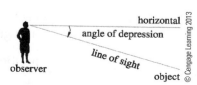

Figure 5.23

APPLICATION CIVIL ENGINEERING

EXAMPLE 5.21

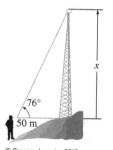

© Cengage Learning 2013

Figure 5.24

A person is standing 50 m from the base of a tower at eye level with the base of the tower. (See Figure 5.24.) The angle of elevation to the top of the tower is 76°. How high is the tower?

SOLUTION We have a right triangle as sketched in Figure 5.24. The height of the tower is labeled x, so we have $\tan 76° = \dfrac{x}{50}$, or

$$x = 50 \tan 76°$$
$$= 200.53905$$

The tower is about 200.5 m high.

APPLICATION CIVIL ENGINEERING

EXAMPLE 5.22

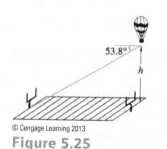

© Cengage Learning 2013

Figure 5.25

Two people are in a hot air balloon. One of them is able to get a sighting from the gondola of the balloon as it passes over one end of a football field, as shown in Figure 5.25. The angle of depression to the other end of the football field is 53.8°. This person knows that the length of the football field, including the end zones, is 120 yd. How high was the balloon when it went over the football field?

SOLUTION We want to determine the height of the right triangle. The height has been labeled h in Figure 5.25. So, we have $\tan 53.8° = \dfrac{h}{120}$, or

$$h = 120 \tan 53.8°$$
$$= 163.9592079$$

The balloon was about 164 yd high.

APPLICATION CONSTRUCTION

EXAMPLE 5.23

A surveyor marks off a right-angle corner of a rectangular house foundation. In sighting on the diagonally opposite corner of the foundation, the line of sight has to move through an angle of 35° as shown in Figure 5.26a. If the length of the short side of the foundation is 46.3 ft, what is the length of the long side?

SOLUTION We have the situation sketched in Figure 5.26b. (Notice that in Figure 5.26b, the right angle does not look like a right angle.) But, this is confusing; so in Figure 5.26c the triangle has been rotated to the more "typical" position with the right angle along the bottom. Since $\tan 35° = \dfrac{46.3}{x}$, we have

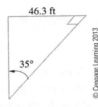

Figure 5.26a

Figure 5.26b

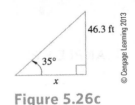

46.3 ft

35°

x

Figure 5.26c

© Cengage Learning 2013

$$x = \frac{46.3}{\tan 35°}$$
$$= 66.123253$$

So the long side is about 66.1 ft.

EXERCISE SET 5.3

Find the acute angles for the trigonometric functions given in Exercises 1–12. (Give answers to the nearest 0.01.)

1. $\sin A = 0.732$

2. $\cos B = 0.285$

3. $\tan C = 4.671$

4. $\sin D = 0.049$

5. $\cos E = 0.839$

6. $\tan F = 0.539$

7. $\sec G = 3.421$

8. $\csc H = 1.924$

9. $\cot I = 0.539$

10. $\sec J = 1.734$

11. $\csc K = 4.761$

12. $\cot L = 4.021$

In Exercises 13–30, sketch each right triangle and solve it. Use your knowledge of significant figures to round off appropriately.

13. $A = 16.5°, a = 7.3$

14. $B = 53°, b = 9.1$

15. $A = 72.6°, c = 20$

16. $B = 12.7°, a = 19.4$

17. $A = 43°, b = 34.6$

18. $B = 67°, c = 32.4$

19. $A = 0.92$ rad, $a = 6.5$

20. $B = 1.13$ rad, $b = 24$

21. $A = 0.15$ rad, $c = 18$

22. $B = 0.23$ rad, $a = 9.7$

23. $A = 1.41$ rad, $b = 40$

24. $A = 1.15$ rad, $c = 18$

25. $a = 9$, $b = 15$

26. $a = 19.3$, $c = 24.4$

27. $b = 9.3$, $c = 18$

28. $a = 14$, $b = 9.3$

29. $a = 20$, $c = 30$

30. $b = 15$, $c = 25$

Solve Exercises 31–44.

31. **Electricity** In an ac circuit that has inductance x_L and resistance R, the phase angle can be determined from the equation $\tan\phi = \dfrac{x_L}{R}$. If $x_L = 12.3\ \Omega$ and $R = 19.7\ \Omega$, what is the phase angle?

32. **Navigation** From the top of a lighthouse, the angle of depression to the waterline of a boat is 23.2°. If the lighthouse is 222 ft high, how far away is the ship from the bottom of the lighthouse?

33. **Navigation** An airplane is flying at an altitude of 700 m when the copilot spots a ship in distress at an angle of depression of 37.6°. How far is it from the plane to the ship?

34. **Construction** A bridge is to be constructed across a river. As shown in Figure 5.27, a piling is to be placed at point A and another at C. To find the distance between A and C a surveyor locates point B exactly 95 m from C so that $\angle C$ is a right angle. If $\angle B$ is 57.62°, how far apart are the pilings?

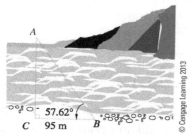

Figure 5.27

35. A vector is usually resolved into component vectors that are perpendicular to each other. Thus, you get a rectangle with one side F_x, the horizontal component, and the other F_y, the vertical component, as shown in Figure 5.28. The original vector F is the diagonal of the rectangle. If $F = 10\ \text{N}$ and $\theta = 30°$, what are the horizontal and vertical components of this force?

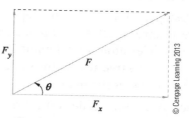

Figure 5.28

36. **Physics** Two forces, one of 20 lb and the other of 12 lb, act on a body in directions perpendicular to each other. The magnitude of the resultant is the length of the diagonal of the rectangle formed from the two perpendicular forces. What is the magnitude of the resultant of these forces? What is the size of the angle the resultant of these forces makes with the smaller force?

37. **Transportation engineering** Highway curves are usually banked at an angle ϕ. The proper banking angle for a car making a turn of radius r at velocity v is $\tan\phi = \dfrac{v}{gr}$, where $g = 32\ \text{ft/s}^2$ or $9.8\ \text{m/s}^2$. Find the proper banking angle for a car moving at 55 mph to go around a curve 1,200 ft in radius. (First, convert 55 mph to ft/s.)

38. **Transportation engineering** Find the proper banking angle for a car moving 88 km/h to go around a curve 500 m in radius. (First, convert 88 km/h to m/s.)

39. **Transportation engineering** Two straight highways A and B intersect at an angle 67°. A service station is located on highway A 300 m from the intersection. What is the location of the point on highway B that is closest to the service station? How near is it?

40. **Air traffic control** One way of measuring the ceiling, or height of the bottom of the clouds, at an airport is to focus a light beam straight up at the clouds at a known distance from an observation point. The angle of elevation from

the observation point to the light beam on the clouds is θ. Find the ceiling height if the observation point is 950 ft from the source of the light beam and $\theta = 58.6°$.

41. **Forestry** Using a clinometer and tape measure, a forest ranger locates the top of a tree at a 67.3° angle of elevation from a point 25.75 ft from the base of the tree and on the same level as the base. How tall is the tree?

42. **Fire science** A 32.0-m ladder on a fire truck can be extended at an angle of 65.0°. The base of the ladder is located at a point that is 2.7 m above the ground.

   (a) How close to the base of a building must the base of the ladder be located for the end of the ladder to reach the building?

   (b) A person needing to be rescued is located 35.85 m above the ground. Can a 1.92-m tall firefighter reach the person if the firefighter (foolishly) stands on the very top rung of the ladder?

43. **Construction** The roof in Figure 5.29 is 8 ft high at its apex. If the roof is 36 ft wide, what is the angle of incline of the roof?

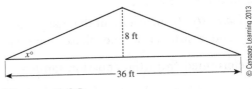

Figure 5.29

44. **Electricity** A furnace 4'0" wide and 3'8" high is placed in an attic with the front side 2 ft back from a line dropped from the apex. The gabled roof has an incline of 22° and covers a width span of 33 ft (Figure 5.30). What is the clearance between the top back edge of the furnace and the roof?

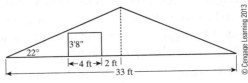

Figure 5.30

[IN YOUR WORDS]

45. Describe what it means to solve a triangle.

46. What is the difference between an angle of elevation and an angle of depression? How can you tell one from another?

5.4 TRIGONOMETRIC FUNCTIONS OF ANY ANGLE

In Sections 5.2 and 5.3, we have concentrated on the trigonometric functions for angles between 0° and 90° or 0 and $\frac{\pi}{2}$ rad. We will now examine other angles.

If you remember, we originally defined the trigonometric functions in terms of a point on the terminal side of an angle in standard position. We want to return to that definition as we look at angles that are not acute.

REFERENCE ANGLES

Consider angle θ in Figure 5.31. Point P is on the terminal side and is in the second quadrant. If a perpendicular line is dropped from P to the x-axis, a triangle is formed with an acute angle θ_{Ref}. If we use the definition of the trigonometric functions from Section 5.1, we seem to get the same values we got for angle θ of the triangle.

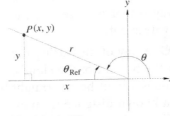

© Cengage Learning 2013

Figure 5.31

REFERENCE ANGLE

The acute angle, θ_{Ref}, between the terminal side of θ and the x-axis is called the **reference angle** for θ. Thus, we can see that the trigonometric functions of θ are numerically the same as those of its reference angle, θ_{Ref}. The reference angle θ_{Ref} for any angle θ in each of four quadrants is shown in Figures 5.32a–d.

EXAMPLE 5.24

Find the reference angle θ_{Ref} for each angle θ: **(a)** $\theta = 75°$, **(b)** $\theta = 218°$, **(c)** $\theta = 320°$, **(d)** $\theta = \frac{3\pi}{4}$, **(e)** $\theta = \frac{7\pi}{6}$.

SOLUTIONS The solutions will use the guidelines demonstrated in Figure 5.32.

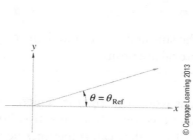

Figure 5.32a

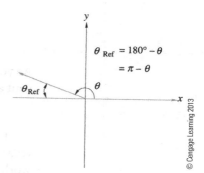

Figure 5.32b

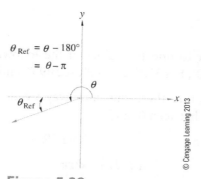

Figure 5.32c

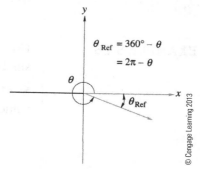

Figure 5.32d

(a) $75°$ is in Quadrant I, so $\theta_{Ref} = 75°$.

(b) $218°$ is Quadrant III, so $\theta_{Ref} = 218° - 180° = 38°$.

(c) $320°$ is in Quadrant IV, so $\theta_{Ref} = 360° - 320° = 40°$.

(d) $\frac{3\pi}{4}$ is in Quadrant II, so $\theta_{Ref} = \pi - \frac{3\pi}{4} = \frac{4\pi}{4} - \frac{3\pi}{4} = \frac{\pi}{4}$.

(e) $\frac{7\pi}{6}$ is in Quadrant III, so $\theta_{Ref} = \frac{7\pi}{6} - \pi = \frac{7\pi}{6} - \frac{6\pi}{6} = \frac{\pi}{6}$.

HINT The reference angle is always measured from the x-axis and never from the y-axis. The "bowtie" in Figure 5.33 may help you remember how to determine the reference angle.

EXAMPLE 5.25

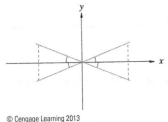

© Cengage Learning 2013
Figure 5.33

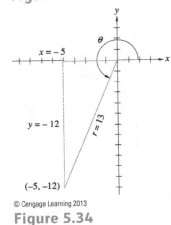

© Cengage Learning 2013
Figure 5.34

A point on the terminal side of an angle θ has the coordinates $(-5, -12)$. Write the six trigonometric functions of θ to three decimal places.

SOLUTION A sketch of the angle is in Figure 5.34. This angle is in the third quadrant. From the Pythagorean theorem we get

$$r = \sqrt{(-5)^2 + (-12)^2} = \sqrt{25 + 144} = \sqrt{169} = 13$$

So, the trigonometric functions of θ are

$$\sin\theta = \frac{y}{r} = \frac{-12}{13} \approx -0.923 \qquad \csc\theta = \frac{r}{y} = \frac{13}{-12} \approx -1.083$$

$$\cos\theta = \frac{x}{r} = \frac{-5}{13} \approx -0.385 \qquad \sec\theta = \frac{r}{x} = \frac{13}{-5} = -2.6$$

$$\tan\theta = \frac{y}{x} = \frac{-12}{-5} = 2.4 \qquad \cot\theta = \frac{x}{y} = \frac{-5}{-12} \approx 0.417$$

As you can see, the sine and cosine and their reciprocals are negative. The tangent and its reciprocal are positive.

In our previous work with right triangles, we found that the values of the trigonometric functions were always positive. You can see here and from our work in Section 5.1 that they can sometimes be negative. Whenever the angle is in the second, third, or fourth quadrant, some of the trigonometric functions will be negative.

EXAMPLE 5.26

Use a calculator to find the values of the following trigonometric functions: $\sin 215°$, $\cos 110°$, $\tan 332°$, $\csc 163°$, $\sec 493°$, and $\cot (-87°)$.

SOLUTION We find these the same way we used the calculator to find the values of angles between 0° and 90°:

Function	ENTER	DISPLAY
sin 215°	SIN 215 ENTER	−0.5735764
cos 110°	COS 110 ENTER	−0.3420201
tan 332°	TAN 332 ENTER	−0.5317094
csc 163°	(SIN 163) x⁻¹ ENTER	3.4203036
sec 493°	(COS 493) x⁻¹ ENTER	−1.4662792
cot (−87°)	(TAN (−) 87) x⁻¹ ENTER	−0.0524078

EXAMPLE 5.27

Use a spreadsheet to find the values of the following trigonometric functions: sin 215°, cos 110°, tan 332°, csc 163°, sec 493°, cot(−87°).

SOLUTION We find these the same way we used a spreadsheet to find the values of angles between 0° and 90°. These are the same values and functions that we evaluated with a calculator in the previous example. The input and the results are shown in Figure 5.35.

	A	B	C
1	Function	Enter	Result
2	sin 215°	=SIN(RADIANS(215))	-0.57358
3	cos 110°	=COS(RADIANS(110))	-0.34202
4	tan 332°	=TAN(RADIANS(332))	-0.53171
5	csc 163°	=1/SIN(RADIANS(163))	3.42030
6	sec 493°	=1/COS(RADIANS(493))	-1.46628
7	cot (-87°)	=1/TAN(RADIANS(-87))	-0.05241

© Cengage Learning 2013

Figure 5.35

There are times when we need to know the sign of an angle and we may not have a calculator or computer spreadsheet handy. One case might be if you are using the table of trigonometric functions. But you will need it more often when you have to find the size of an angle and you know the value of a trigonometric function. You will see in Section 5.5 that the calculator or spreadsheet will give you an answer, but it may not be the correct answer to the problem. You will have to determine the correct answer from the calculator's answer and from your knowledge of the signs of the trigonometric functions.

To find the sign of a trigonometric function, make a sketch of the angle. You do not need a very accurate sketch, but make sure you get the angle in the correct quadrant. Draw the triangle for the reference angle and note the signs of x and y. Remember that the radius vector r is always positive. Then set up the ratio using the two values from x, y, and r that are appropriate for this angle.

EXAMPLE 5.28

What is the sign of sec 215°?

SOLUTION Examine the sketch in Figure 5.36. We have drawn a right triangle for the reference triangle and labeled the sides with the sign in parentheses after the letter x, y, or r. Since sec 215° $= \dfrac{r}{x}$, where r is positive and x is negative, the sign of the sec 215° is negative.

Figure 5.37 summarizes the signs of the trigonometric functions in each quadrant. If a function is not mentioned in a quadrant, then the function is negative. Thus in Quadrant II, since they are not mentioned, the cos, tan, cot, and sec are all negative.

We will finish this section with a discussion of how to find the values of trigonometric functions from a table. If an angle is not an acute angle, you need to use the reference angle and the coterminal angle.

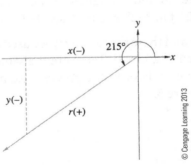

Figure 5.36

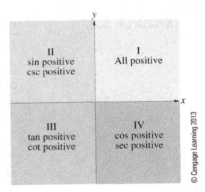

Figure 5.37

If an angle is negative, or if it is a positive angle with measure more than 360° or 2π rad, replace it with a coterminal angle that is between 0° and 360° or 0 and 2π rad. To do this, you will add or subtract multiples of 360° if the angle is in degrees, or 2π if it is in radians, until you have the desired coterminal angle.

EXAMPLE 5.29

For each angle find a coterminal angle between 0° and 360° or 0 and 2π rad:
(a) 1,292°, **(b)** $-683°$, **(c)** $\frac{17}{4}\pi$, **(d)** $-\frac{5\pi}{3}$, **(e)** -8.7 rad.

SOLUTIONS

(a) $1,292° - 3(360°) = 1,292° - 1,080° = 212°$

(b) $-683° + 2(360°) = -683° + 720° = 37°$

(c) $\frac{17}{4}\pi - 2(2\pi) = \frac{17}{4}\pi - 2\left(\frac{8\pi}{4}\right) = \frac{17\pi}{4} - \frac{16\pi}{4} = \frac{\pi}{4}$

(d) $-\frac{5\pi}{3} + 1(2\pi) = \frac{-5\pi}{3} + \frac{6\pi}{3} = \frac{\pi}{3}$

(e) $-8.7 + 2(2\pi) = -8.7 + 12.566371 = 3.8663706$ rad

The value of any trigonometric function of an angle θ is the same as the value of the function for the reference angle θ_{Ref}, except for an occasional change in the algebraic sign. If the angle is not between 0° and 360° or 0 and 2π rad, first find the coterminal angle in that interval and then find the reference angle of the coterminal angle.

INVERSE TRIGONOMETRIC FUNCTIONS

In our earlier work with inverse trigonometric functions, we were concerned with right triangles. Thus, all the angles we had to find were acute angles. As we just saw, simply knowing the value of a trigonometric function for an angle did not allow us to determine the size of the angle. For example, if $\sin\theta = 0.2437$, we know that θ must be in Quadrant I or II. These are the only quadrants where sine is positive. This means that $\theta = 14.105021°$ or

$\theta = 180° - 14.105021° = 165.894979°$. It is possible that θ could be any angle coterminal with either of these two angles.

In a similar manner, if $\tan \theta = -1.5$, then using a calculator you obtain $\theta = -56.309932°$. This is coterminal with $\theta = 303.690068°$. This angle is in Quadrant IV. The tangent is also negative for values in Quadrant II. In Quadrant II, the angle would be $123.69007°$.

USING CALCULATORS FOR INVERSE TRIGONOMETRIC FUNCTIONS

Using a calulator as we did in previous examples is certainly fast and accurate. But, it may not always give us the angle that we want. For example, it will never give an angle in Quadrant III. Why is this? It goes back to the basic idea of a function—the idea that for each different value of x there is exactly one value of y.

Because people wanted inverse trigonometric *functions* they had to restrict the answers to exactly one value of y for each value of x. That is why, when you use your calculator to determine inverse sin 0.5, you obtain 30° by pressing **2nd** **SIN** 0.5.

This is nothing new. At one time we studied a function $f(x) = x^2$ and its inverse $f^{-1}(x) = \sqrt{x}$. We knew that $f(-5) = f(5) = 5^2 = 25$, but that $f^{-1}(25) = \sqrt{25} = 5$. The inverse function of x^2, $\sqrt{x}$, only gave the principal value of the square root. In the same way, the inverse trigonometric functions have only the *principal value* of the angle defined for each value of x. Thus, we have the following inverse trigonometric functions.

INVERSE TRIGONOMETRIC FUNCTIONS

If $\sin \theta = x$, then arcsin $x = \theta$, where $\quad -90° \leq \theta \leq 90°$

$\quad\quad\quad\quad\quad\quad\quad\quad$ or $\quad -\frac{\pi}{2} \leq \theta \leq \frac{\pi}{2}$

If $\cos \theta = x$, then arccos $x = \theta$, where $\quad 0° \leq \theta \leq 180°$

$\quad\quad\quad\quad\quad\quad\quad\quad$ or $\quad 0 \leq \theta \leq \pi$

If $\tan \theta = x$, then arctan $x = \theta$, where $\quad -90° < \theta < 90°$

$\quad\quad\quad\quad\quad\quad\quad\quad$ or $\quad \frac{-\pi}{2} < \theta < \frac{\pi}{2}$

If $\csc \theta = x$, then arccsc $x = \theta$, where $\quad -90° \leq \theta \leq 90°, \theta \neq 0°$

$\quad\quad\quad\quad\quad\quad\quad\quad$ or $\quad -\frac{\pi}{2} \leq \theta \leq \frac{\pi}{2}, \theta \neq 0$

If $\sec \theta = x$, then arcsec $x = \theta$, where $\quad 0° \leq \theta \leq 180°, \theta \neq 90°$

$\quad\quad\quad\quad\quad\quad\quad\quad$ or $\quad 0 \leq \theta \leq \pi, \theta \neq \frac{\pi}{2}$

If $\cot \theta = x$, then arccot $x = \theta$, where $\quad 0° < \theta < 180°$

$\quad\quad\quad\quad\quad\quad\quad\quad$ or $\quad 0 < \theta < \pi$

As you can see, for positive values you always get an angle in the first quadrant. If you want the inverse value of a negative number, then you will get an angle in the fourth quadrant for INV SIN and INV TAN and an angle in the second quadrant for INV COS. Working with a calculator will also show you that the angles in the fourth quadrant are given as negative angles. Thus on a calculator, arcsin $(-0.5) = -30°$ and not $330°$.

In the previous list, we used the symbol arcsin x to represent the inverse of the sin θ. Arcsin is an accepted symbol for the inverse of the sine function. Another symbol that is often used is $\sin^{-1}x$. Just as we used $f^{-1}(x) = \sqrt{x}$, here we use $f^{-1}(x) = \sin^{-1}x$. Similarly, arccos $x = \cos^{-1}x$, arctan $x = \tan^{-1}x$, and so on. In fact, above the SIN, COS, and TAN keys on your calculator you should see $\sin^{-1}$, $\cos^{-1}$, and $\tan^{-1}$, respectively.

USING SPREADSHEETS FOR INVERSE TRIGONOMETRIC FUNCTIONS

The spreadsheet function for $\sin^{-1}$ (or arcsin) is ASIN. Similarly, ACOS and ATAN are used for $\cos^{-1}$ and $\tan^{-1}$, respectively. The returned angle is given in radians. If you want your answer in degrees, then multiply the result by 180/PI( ) or use the DEGREES function.

EXAMPLE 5.30

Use a spreadsheet to find $\sin^{-1} 0.5$ in **(a)** radians and **(b)** degrees.

SOLUTIONS

(a) Since we want this answer in radians all we need to do is enter ASIN(0.5) as shown in Figure 5.38a. From the figure we see that $\sin^{-1}0.5 \approx 0.52360$ radians.

	A	B
1	Enter	Result
2	=ASIN(0.5)	0.52360

© Cengage Learning 2013

Figure 5.38a

(b) This answer is to be in degrees. As noted, we have two options: multiply the result by 180/PI( ) or use the DEGREES. Each of these is shown in Figure 5.38b, where we see that $\sin^{-1} 0.5 = 30°$.

	A	B
1	Enter	Result
2	=ASIN(0.5)*180/PI()	30.0
3	=DEGREES(ASIN(0.5))	30.0

© Cengage Learning 2013

Figure 5.38b

FINDING ALL ANGLES FOR INVERSE TRIGONOMETRIC FUNCTIONS

Since inverse trigonometric functions only give one answer to problems like $\sin\theta = \frac{1}{2}$ where $\theta = \sin^{-1}\frac{1}{2}$, we must develop a method for finding other angles that satisfy this equation. We will use our knowledge of reference angles and the sign of the functions in the four quadrants to do this.

To find the reference angle of an equation of the form $\sin \theta = n$, where n is a number in the range of sine, we will use the absolute value of n, $|n|$. Then the desired answers can be found by adding or subtracting the reference angle from $180°$ (or π) or subtracting from $360°$ (or 2π).

EXAMPLE 5.31

Find all angles θ in the interval $(0°, 360°)$ where $\cos \theta = -0.42$.

SOLUTION Here, we have $n = -0.42$, so $|n| = |-0.42| = 0.42$ and $\theta_{\text{Ref}} = \cos^{-1} 0.42 = 65.2°$. Since n was negative, we have answers in Quadrants II and III, the quadrants where cosine is negative.

$$\theta_{\text{II}} = 180° - \theta_{\text{Ref}} = 180° - 65.2° = 114.8°$$
$$\theta_{\text{III}} = 180° + \theta_{\text{Ref}} = 180° + 65.2° = 245.2°$$

The answers are $114.8°$ and $245.2°$.

EXAMPLE 5.32

Find all angles θ in the interval $(0, 2\pi)$ where $\cot \theta = -1.73$.

SOLUTION Here, we have $n = -1.73$, so $|n| = |-1.73| = 1.73$ and $\theta_{\text{Ref}} = \cot^{-1} 1.73 = \tan^{-1} \frac{1}{1.73} = 0.5241$. Since n was negative, we have answers in Quadrants II and IV, the quadrants where cotangent is negative.

$$\theta_{\text{II}} = \pi - \theta_{\text{Ref}} = \pi - 0.5241 \approx 2.6175$$
$$\theta_{\text{IV}} = 2\pi - \theta_{\text{Ref}} = 2\pi - 0.5241 \approx 5.7591$$

The answers are 2.6175 rad and 5.7591 rad.

In the previous two examples, we only found two answers. There are, however, an infinite number of angles coterminal with these answers. If we want to represent all these answers, we proceed as follows.

For Example 5.31:

$$114.8° + 360° k \text{ and } 245.2° + 360° k \text{, where } k \text{ is an integer}$$

For Example 5.32:

$$2.6175 + 2\pi k \text{ rad and } 5.7591 + 2\pi k \text{ rad, where } k \text{ is an integer}$$

EXERCISE SET 5.4

Give the reference angle for each of the angles in Exercises 1–8.

1. $87°$

2. $200°$

3. $137°$

4. $298°$

5. $\frac{9\pi}{8}$ rad

6. 2.1 rad

7. 4.5 rad

8. 5.85 rad

Give the coterminal angle for each of the angles in Exercises 9–16.

9. 518°

10. 1,673°

11. −871°

12. −137°

13. 7.3 rad

14. $\frac{16\pi}{3}$ rad

15. −2.17 rad

16. −8.43 rad

State which quadrant or quadrants the terminal side of θ is in for each of the angles, expressions, or trigonometric functions in Exercises 17–38.

17. 165°

18. 285°

19. −47°

20. 312°

21. 250°

22. 197°

23. 98°

24. −177°

25. $\sin \theta = \frac{1}{2}$

26. $\tan \theta = \frac{3}{4}$

27. $\cot \theta = -2$

28. $\cos \theta = -0.25$

29. $\sec \theta = 4.3$

30. $\cos \theta = 0.8$

31. $\csc \theta = -6.1$

32. $\sin \theta = -\dfrac{\sqrt{3}}{2}$

33. $\sin \theta$ is positive.

34. $\tan \theta$ is negative.

35. $\cos \theta$ is positive.

36. $\sec \theta$ is negative.

37. $\csc \theta$ is negative and $\cos \theta$ is positive.

38. $\tan \theta$ and $\sec \theta$ are negative.

State whether each of the expressions in Exercises 39–46 is positive or negative.

39. sin 105°

40. sec 237°

41. tan 372°

42. cos (−53°)

43. cos 1.93 rad

44. cot 4.63 rad

45. sin 215°

46. csc 5.42 rad

Find the values of each of the trigonometric functions in Exercises 47–68.

47. sin 137°

48. cos 263°

49. tan 293°

50. sin 312°

51. tan 164.2°

52. csc 197.3°

53. sin 2.4 rad

54. cos 1.93 rad

55. tan 6.1 rad

56. sec 4.32 rad

57. tan 1.37 rad

58. sin 3.2 rad

59. sin 415.5°

60. tan 512.1°

61. cot −87.4°

62. cos 372.1°

63. cos 357.3°

64. sin 6.5 rad

65. tan 8.35 rad

66. sin 9.42 rad

67. cos − 0.43 rad

68. sec 9.34 rad

In Exercises 69–76, find, to the nearest tenth of a degree, all angles θ, where 0° ≤ θ < 360°, with the given trigonometric function.

69. $\sin \theta = \frac{1}{2}$

70. $\tan \theta = \frac{3}{4}$

71. $\cot \theta = -2$

72. $\cos \theta = -0.25$

73. $\sec \theta = 4.3$

74. $\cos \theta = 0.8$

75. $\csc \theta = -6.1$

76. $\sin \theta = -\dfrac{\sqrt{3}}{2}$

In Exercises 77–84, find, to the nearest hundredth of a radian, all angles θ, where 0 ≤ θ < 2π, with the given trigonometric function.

77. $\sin \theta = 0.75$

78. $\tan \theta = 1.6$

79. $\cot \theta = -0.4$

80. $\cos \theta = 0.25$

81. $\csc \theta = 4.3$

82. $\sin \theta = -0.08$

83. $\sec \theta = 2.7$

84. $\cos \theta = -0.95$

Evaluate each of the functions in Exercises 85–92. Write each answer to the nearest tenth of a degree.

85. arcsin 0.84

86. arccos(−0.21)

87. arctan 4.21

88. arccot(−0.25)

89. $\sin^{-1} 0.32$

90. $\cos^{-1} 0.47$

91. $\tan^{-1}(-0.64)$

92. $\csc^{-1}(-3.61)$

Evaluate each of the functions in Exercises 93–100. Write each answer to the nearest hundredth of a radian.

93. $\arccos(-0.33)$

94. $\arctan 1.55$

95. $\arccos 0.29$

96. $\operatorname{arcsec}(-3.15)$

97. $\sin^{-1} 0.95$

98. $\cos^{-1}(-0.67)$

99. $\tan^{-1} 0.25$

100. $\cot^{-1}(-0.75)$

Solve Exercises 101–110.

101. Electronics The intensity, I, of a sinusoidal current in an ac circuit is given by $I = I_{max} \sin \theta$, where I_{max} is the maximum intensity of the current. Find I when $I_{max} = 32.65$ mA and $\theta = 132.0°$.

102. Electronics The potential voltage, V, of a sinusoidal current in an ac circuit is given by $V = V_{max} \sin \theta$, where V_{max} is the maximum potential. Find V when $V_{max} = 115.2$ V and $\theta = 113.4°$.

103. Metalworking Find the length of the piece of metal ABC in Figure 5.39.

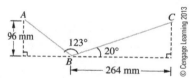

Figure 5.39

104. Metalworking Figure 5.40 shows the outline of an isosceles trapezoid that is to be cut from a metal sheet. Find the size of $\angle\theta$.

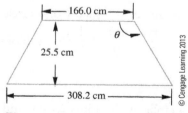

Figure 5.40

105. Landscape architecture Figure 5.41 shows the outline of some ground that needs to be sodded. How many square feet of sod are needed to completely cover the ground?

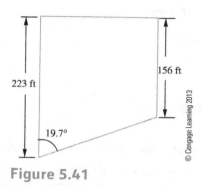

Figure 5.41

106. Metalworking Find the length of side AB on the metal sheet shown in Figure 5.42.

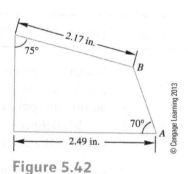

Figure 5.42

107. Electronics The phase angle, θ, in an RC circuit between the capacitive reactance, X_C, and the resistance, R, when resistance is in series with capacitive reactance, can be found by using $\theta = \tan^{-1}\left(-\dfrac{X_C}{R}\right)$. Find θ when $X_C = 33\ \Omega$ and $R = 40\ \Omega$.

108. Electronics The phase angle, θ, in an inductive circuit between the impedance, Z, and the resistance, R, can be found by using $\theta = \cos^{-1}\left(\dfrac{Z}{R}\right)$. Find θ when $Z = 30\ \Omega$ and $R = 50\ \Omega$.

109. *Automotive technology* Find the angle, θ, of the diesel engine valve face in Figure 5.43.

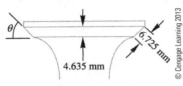

Figure 5.43

110. *Dynamics* The maximum height, h, of a projectile with initial velocity, v_0, at angle θ is given by

$$h = \frac{v_0^2 \sin^2 \theta}{2g}$$

where g is the acceleration due to gravity.

(a) Solve for θ.

(b) If $v_0 = 172.5$ m/s and $g = 9.8$ m/s^2, at what angle was the projectile shot if its maximum height was 431.1 m?

 [IN YOUR WORDS]

111. Explain what is meant by a reference angle?

112. Describe how you can tell the signs of the six trigonometric functions of a particular angle if you know the quadrant in which the angle lies.

113. Describe the difference between $\sin^{-1}\theta$ and $(\sin \theta)^{-1}$.

114. Describe the difference between $\cos^{-1}\theta$ and $(\sec \theta)^{-1}$.

5.5　APPLICATIONS OF TRIGONOMETRY

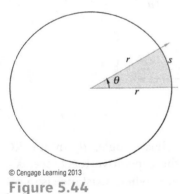

© Cengage Learning 2013

Figure 5.44

In earlier sections, we looked at some applications of trigonometry, particularly applications dealing with right triangles. In this section, we will look at some additional applications of trigonometry.

We defined a radian as $\frac{1}{2\pi}$ of a circle. Another way to look at a radian is to examine the circle in Figure 5.44. If r is the radius of the circle and s is the length of the arc opposite θ, then $\theta = \frac{s}{r}$ or $\theta r = s$, where θ is in radians.

We can use this relationship to find the area of the sector of a circle. For the shaded sector in Figure 5.44, the area $A = \frac{rs}{2} = \frac{r^2\theta}{2} = \frac{1}{2}r^2\theta$. Both of these formulas work if the angles are in radians.

EXAMPLE 5.33

Find the arc length and area of a sector of a circle, with radius 2.7 cm and central angle 1.3 rad.

SOLUTION To find the arc length we use $s = \theta r$ with $\theta = 1.3$ rad and $r = 2.7$ cm.

$$s = \theta r$$
$$= (1.3)(2.7)$$
$$= 3.51 \, \text{cm}$$

The area is found using $A = \frac{1}{2}r^2\theta$.

$$A = \frac{1}{2}r^2\theta$$

$$= \frac{1}{2}(2.7)^2(1.3)$$

$$= 4.7385 \text{ or } 4.74 \text{ cm}^2$$

Radian measure was developed with the aid of a circle and is used to measure angles. One application of radian measure involves rotational motion. When we work with motion in a straight line, we use the formula $d = vt$ or distance = velocity (or rate) × time. We assume that the rate is constant.

Suppose instead that we had an object moving around a circle at a constant rate of speed. If we let s represent the distance around the circle and v the velocity (or rate), then $s = vt$ or $v = \frac{s}{t}$. Since $s = \theta r$, where r is the radius of the circle, we have $v = \frac{\theta r}{t}$. The centripetal acceleration is $a_c = \frac{v^2}{r} = \frac{\theta^2 r}{t^2}$.

 APPLICATION **GENERAL TECHNOLOGY**

EXAMPLE 5.34

A ball is spun in a horizontal circle 60 cm in radius at the rate of one revolution every 3 s. What is the ball's velocity and centripetal acceleration?

SOLUTION The velocity $v = \frac{s}{t}$. We know that $t = 3$ s, but we have to find s. In one revolution, the ball covers one complete circle, so $\theta = 2\pi$, and since $r = 60$ cm, we have $s = \theta r = 120\pi$. Thus,

$$v = \frac{s}{t}$$

$$= \frac{120\pi \text{ cm}}{3 \text{ s}}$$

$$= 40\pi \text{ cm/s} = 125.66 \text{ cm/s}$$

The centripetal acceleration is

$$a_c = \frac{v^2}{r} = \frac{(40\pi \text{ cm/s})^2}{60 \text{ cm}}$$

$$= 263.19 \text{ cm/s}^2$$

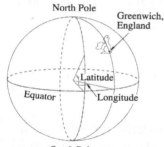

North Pole

Greenwich, England

Latitude

Equator   Longitude

South Pole

© Cengage Learning 2013

Figure 5.45

The angular distance D (measured at the earth's center) between two points P_1 and P_2 on the earth's surface is determined by

$$\cos D = \sin L_1 \sin L_2 + \cos L_1 \cos L_2 \cos (M_1 - M_2)$$

where L_1, L_2 and M_1, M_2 are the respective latitudes and longitudes of two points. The latitude is the angle measured at the earth's surface between a point on the earth and the equator on the same meridian. Meridians are imaginary lines on the surface of the earth, which pass through both the north and south poles. (See Figure 5.45.)

The longitude is the angle between the meridian passing through a point on the earth and the 0° meridian passing through Greenwich, England.

APPLICATION CIVIL ENGINEERING

EXAMPLE 5.35

If Knoxville, Tennessee, is at latitude 36° N and longitude 83°55′ W, and Denver, Colorado, is at latitude 39°44′ N and longitude 104°59′ W, and the radius of the earth is 3,960 mi, how far is it from Knoxville to Denver?

SOLUTION We have $L_1 = 36°$, $L_2 = 39°44′$, $M_1 = 83°55′$, and $M_2 = 104°59′$, so $M_1 - M_2 = -21°04′$.

$$\cos D = (\sin 36°)[\sin(39°44′)] + (\cos 36°)(\cos 39°44′)[\cos(-21°04′)]$$
$$= (0.5878)(0.6392) + (0.8090)(0.7690)(0.9332)$$
$$= 0.9563$$
$$D = \cos^{-1}(0.9563)$$
$$= 17.00$$
$$= 0.2967 \, \text{rad}$$

Notice that we had to convert our answer for D from degrees to radians. Since $r = 3,960$ mi, the distance from Knoxville to Denver is

$$s = \theta r = (0.2967)(3,960) = 1,174.93 \text{ mi}$$

This would, of course, be air miles and not the distance you would travel by automobile.

One use of radian measure involves rotational motion. Remember that for motion in a straight line, distance = velocity (or rate) × time or $d = vt$, where we assumed that the rate remains constant. Now, if the motion is in a circular direction instead of a straight line, we would have the formula $s = vt$. Since $s = \theta r$ and $v = \dfrac{s}{t}$, then $v = \dfrac{\theta r}{t} = r\left(\dfrac{\theta}{t}\right)$. This ratio, $\dfrac{\theta}{t}$, is called the *angular velocity* and is usually denoted by the Greek letter ω (omega). Thus it is known that angular velocity ω of an object that turns through the angle θ in time t is given by $\omega = \dfrac{\theta}{t}$. The linear velocity v of a point that moves in a circle of radius r with uniform angular velocity ω is $v = \omega r$. A rotating body with an angular velocity that changes from ω_0 to ω_f in the time interval t has an angular acceleration of $\alpha = \dfrac{\omega_f - \omega_0}{t}$.

APPLICATION MECHANICAL

EXAMPLE 5.36

A steel cylinder 8 cm in diameter is to be machined in a lathe. If the desired linear velocity of the cylinder's surface is to be 80.5 cm/s, how many rpm should it rotate?

SOLUTION We have $v = \omega r$. We want to find ω and $\omega = \dfrac{v}{r}$, where $v = 80.5$ cm/s and $r = 4$ cm.

$$\omega = \frac{80.5\,\text{cm/s}}{4\,\text{cm}}$$

$$= 20.125\,\text{rad/s}$$

Now, 1 rpm is 2π rad/60 s, so using dimensional analysis we have

$$\omega = \frac{20.125\,\text{rad}}{1\,\text{sec}} \cdot \frac{60\,\text{sec}}{1\,\text{min}} \cdot \frac{1\,\text{rev}}{2\pi\,\text{rad}}$$

$$= \frac{20.125 \times 60\,\text{rev}}{2\pi\,\text{min}}$$

$$\approx 192.22\,\text{rpm}$$

APPLICATION MECHANICAL

EXAMPLE 5.37

An engine requires 6 s to go from its idling speed of 600 rpm to 1500 rpm. What is its angular acceleration?

SOLUTION The initial velocity of the engine is

$$\omega_0 = 600\,\text{rpm}$$

$$= \frac{600\,\text{rev}}{1\,\text{min}} \cdot \frac{2\pi\,\text{rad}}{1\,\text{rev}} \cdot \frac{1\,\text{min}}{60\,\text{sec}}$$

$$\approx 62.83\,\text{rad/s}$$

and the final velocity is

$$\omega_f = 1500\,\text{rpm}$$

$$= \frac{1500\,\text{rev}}{1\,\text{min}} \cdot \frac{2\pi\,\text{rad}}{1\,\text{rev}} \cdot \frac{1\,\text{min}}{60\,\text{sec}}$$

$$\approx 157.058\,\text{rad/s}$$

The angular acceleration is

$$\alpha = \frac{\omega_f - \omega_0}{t}$$

$$= \frac{157.05 - 62.82}{6}$$

$$= \frac{94.23\,\text{rad/s}}{6\,\text{s}}$$

$$= 15.705\,\text{rad/s}^2$$

EXERCISE SET 5.5

Solve Exercises 1–30.

1. **Transportation engineering** A circular highway curve has a radius of 1050.250 m and a central angle of 47° measured to the center line of the road. What is the length of the curve?

2. **Physics** An object is moving around a circle of radius 8 in. with an angular velocity of 5 rad/s. What is the linear velocity?

3. **Physics** A flywheel rotates with an angular velocity of 30 rpm. If its radius is 12 in., what is the linear velocity of the rim?

4. **Industrial technology** A pulley belt 4 m long takes 2 s to complete one revolution. If the radius of the pulley is 180 mm, what is the angular velocity of a point on the rim of the pulley?

5. In a circle of radius 15 cm, what is the length of the arc intercepted by a central angle of $\frac{5\pi}{8}$?

6. In a circle of radius 235 mm, what is the length of the arc intercepted by a central angle of 85°?

7. What is the area of the sector in Exercise 5?

8. What is the area of the sector in Exercise 6?

9. **Physics** A clock pendulum 1.2 m long oscillates through an angle of 0.07 rad on each side of the vertical. What is the distance the end of the pendulum travels from one end to the other?

10. **Space technology** A communication satellite is in orbit at 22,300 mi above the surface of the earth. The satellite is in permanent orbit above a certain point on the equator. Thus, the satellite makes one revolution every 24 h. What is the angular velocity of the satellite? What is its linear velocity? (The radius of the earth at the equator is 3,963 mi.)

11. **Acoustical engineering** A phonograph record is 175.26 mm in diameter and rotates at 45 rpm. **(a)** What is the linear velocity of a point on the rim? **(b)** How far does this point travel in 1 min?

12. **Acoustical engineering** A phonograph turntable rotating at 4.2 rad/s makes 4 complete turns

before it stops after 11.92 s. What is its angular acceleration?

13. **Navigation** City A is at 35°30′ N, 78°40′ W and City B is at 40°40′ N, 88°50′ W. What is the angular distance between the two cities? How far is it between the cities?

14. **Mechanical engineering** A 1,200-rpm motor is directly connected to a 12-in.-diameter circular saw blade. What is the linear velocity of the saw's teeth in ft/min?

15. **Computer science** The outer track on a $5\frac{1}{4}''$ diameter diskette for a microcomputer is $2\frac{1}{2}''$ from the center of the diskette. If 8 bytes of data can be stored on $\frac{1}{4}''$ of track, how many bytes can be stored in the length of the track subtended by $\frac{\pi}{3}$ rad?

16. **Computer science** Some diskettes are divided into 16 sectors per track. What is the length of one sector of the track in Exercise 15?

17. **Mechanical engineering** A flywheel makes 850 rev in 1 min. How many degrees does it rotate in 1 s?

18. **Mechanical engineering** If the flywheel in Exercise 17 has a 15-in. diameter, what is the linear velocity of a point on its outer edge?

19. **Energy technology** A wind generator has blades 4.2 m long. What is the speed of a blade tip when the blades are rotating at 20 rpm?

20. **Physics** A 2,500-newton weight is resting on an inclined plane that makes an angle of 23° with the horizontal. Find the component F_x and F_y of the weight parallel to and perpendicular to the surface of the plane, as shown in Figure 5.46.

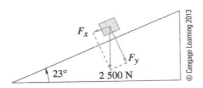

Figure 5.46

21. **Navigation** The arctic circle is approximately at latitude 66.5° N. If the radius of the earth is 6,370 km, how far is the arctic circle from the equator?

22. **Optics** When unpolarized light strikes an interface between two materials, *Brewster's law* states that the reflected light is completely polarized perpendicular to the plane of incidence if the angle of incidence, θ, is given by

$$\tan\theta = \frac{n_b}{n_a}$$

If sunlight is reflected off commercial plate glass, at what angle of reflection is the light completely polarized? Here, for air $n_a = 1.00$ and for commercial plate glass, $n_b = 1.516$.

23. **Optics** The intensity, I, of a light beam transmitted by a pair of polarizing filters is given by the equation

$$I = I_m \cos^2\theta$$

where I_m is the maximum intensity and θ is the angle between the filters. At what angle does the intensity drop to three-fourths of the maximum intensity?

24. **Construction** A roof that slopes at 23° to the horizontal is 14.5 m long and has a slant height of 9.2 m. How large an area does the roof actually cover? (Hint: Find the area of rectangle *ABCD* in Figure 5.47)

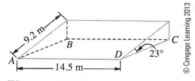

Figure 5.47

25. **Space technology** The global positioning system (GPS) consists of 24 satellites, each orbiting the earth in a circular orbit at an altitude of 11,000 mi. Each satellite orbits the earth once every 12 hr. If the earth's radius is 3,960 mi, determine:

(a) The angular speed of each GPS satellite in rad/s

(b) The linear speed of each GPS satellite in mi/s.

26. **Navigation** A nautical mile may be defined as the arc length intercepted on the surface of the earth by a central angle with measure 1′. Suppose that the radius of the earth is 3,960 (statute) miles and that one statute mile is 5,280 ft.

(a) Determine the number of feet in a nautical mile.

(b) How much longer (in ft) is a nautical mile than a statute mile?

27. **Construction** (a) Find the width L of the taper shown in Figure 5.48. (b) Determine the length of the slanted sides of the taper.

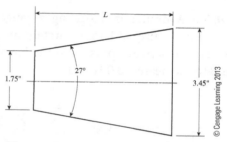

Figure 5.48

28. **Electricity** An electrician must bend a pipe to make a 1.8-ft rise in a 6.3-ft horizontal distance, as shown in Figure 5.49. (a) What is the angle at A? (b) What is the angle at B?

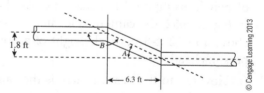

Figure 5.49

29. **Graphic design** A graphic artist is designing a Web page that will include the animation of a piston, crank, and wheel. The crank is attached to the wheel and piston as shown in Figures 5.50a and 5.50b. As the wheel rotates, the crank moves the piston. $\angle A$ will vary from 0 to 2π radians. To make the motion appear realistic, the artist needs to find an expression for $\angle B$. Express $\angle B$ in terms of the length of the crank, c, the radius of the wheel, r, and $\angle A$.

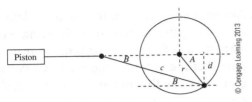

Figure 5.50a

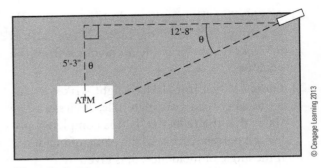

Figure 5.52

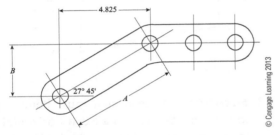

Figure 5.50b

30. *Drafting* A drafter is designing a gauge like the one in Figure 5.51 to accurately measure the distance between pins. Find the lengths *A* and *B* to the nearest 0.001 inch.

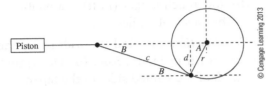

Figure 5.51

31. A security camera is is positioned to get a view of people using an ATM machine. As shown in Figure 5.52, the camera is located 5 ft-3 in. above and 12 ft-8 in. to the right of a normal person's head.

   (a) How far, to the nearest inch, is the camera from the person's head?

   (b) What is the angle θ to the nearest tenth degree that the camera is depressed below the horizontal?

32. Two utility poles are on opposite sides of an interstate highway, much like those in Figure 5.53. In order to find the distance between the poles, Ali paced off 90 ft along the highway and perpendicular to a line joining the two poles. The angle between the poles is measured at 68°. Determine the distance between the two poles to the nearest tenth foot.

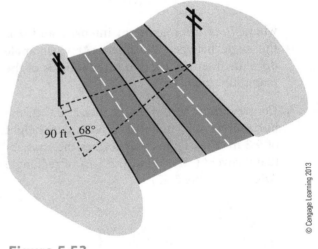

Figure 5.53

  [IN YOUR WORDS]

33. Write a word problem in your technology area of interest that requires you to use trigonometry. On the back of the sheet of paper, write your name and explain how to solve the problem by using trigonometry. Give the problem you wrote to a friend and let him or her try to solve it. If your friend has difficulty understanding the problem or solving the problem, or disagrees with your solution, make any necessary changes in the problem or solution. When you have finished, give the revised problem and solution to another friend and see if he or she can solve it.

34. As in Exercise 33, write a word problem in your technology area that requires you to use trigonometry. This problem should use a different trigonometric function from the one in Exercise 33.

CHAPTER 5 REVIEW

IMPORTANT TERMS AND CONCEPTS

Angle(s)
  Complementary
  Coterminal
  Negative
  Of depression
  Of elevation
  Positive
  Quadrantal
  Reference
  Standard position

Degrees
Inverse trigonometric functions
  Arccos or cos^{-1}
  Arccot or cot^{-1}
  Arccsc or csc^{-1}
  Arcsec or sec^{-1}
  Arcsin or sin^{-1}
  Arctan or tan^{-1}
Quotient identities
Radians

Reciprocal identities
Trigonometric functions
  Cosecant (csc)
  Cosine (cos)
  Cotangent (cot)
  Secant (sec)
  Sine (sin)
  Tangent (tan)

REVIEW EXERCISES

Convert each of the angle measures in Exercises 1–6 from degrees to radians.

1. 60°
2. 198°
3. 325°

4. 180°
5. −115°
6. 435°

Convert each of the angle measures in Exercises 7–12 from radians to degrees.

7. $\frac{3\pi}{4}$ rad
8. 1.10 rad
9. 2.15 rad

10. $\frac{7\pi}{3}$ rad
11. −4.31 rad
12. 5.92 rad

For Exercises 13–24, (a) tell which quadrant the angle is in, (b) give the reference angle for the given angle, and (c) give two coterminal angles, one positive and one negative.

13. 60°
14. 198°
15. 325°

16. 180°
17. −115°
18. 435°

19. $\frac{3\pi}{4}$ rad
20. 1.10 rad
21. 2.15 rad

22. $\frac{7\pi}{3}$ rad
23. −4.31 rad
24. 5.92 rad

Each point in Exercises 25–30 is on the terminal side of an angle θ in standard position. Find the six trigonometric functions of the angle θ associated with each of these points.

25. $(3, -4)$

26. $(5, 12)$

27. $(-20, 21)$

28. $(-4, -7)$

29. $(7, 1)$

30. $(-12, 8)$

In Exercises 31–36, find the trigonometric functions of angle θ at vertex A of triangle ABC for the indicated sides.

31. $a = 8, c = 17$

32. $a = 5, b = 12$

33. $b = 8, c = \frac{40}{3}$

34. $a = 6, c = 7.5$

35. $b = 7, c = 18.2$

36. $a = 42, b = 44.1$

In Exercises 37–39, let θ be an angle of a triangle with the given trigonometric function. Find the values of the other trigonometric functions.

37. $\sin \theta = \dfrac{12.8}{27.2}$

38. $\tan \theta = \dfrac{16}{16.8}$

39. $\sec \theta = \dfrac{4}{2.5}$

In Exercises 40–42, the values of two trigonometric functions of an angle θ are given. Use this information to determine the values of the other four trigonometric functions for θ.

40. $\sin \theta = 0.532, \tan \theta = 0.628$

41. $\sin \theta = 0.5, \cos \theta = 0.866$

42. $\cos \theta = 0.680, \csc \theta = 1.364$

Use a calculator or spreadsheet to determine the values of each of the indicated trigonometric functions in Exercises 43–50.

43. $\sin 45°$

44. $\cos 82.5°$

45. $\tan 213.5°$

46. $\sec (-81°)$

47. $\cos 2.3$ rad

48. $\sin 4.75$ rad

49. $\tan (-3.2)$ rad

50. $\csc 0.21$ rad

In Exercises 51–54, find, to the nearest tenth of a degree, all angles θ, where $0° \leq \theta < 360°$, with the given trigonometric function.

51. $\sin \theta = 0.5$

52. $\tan \theta = 2.5$

53. $\cos \theta = -0.75$

54. $\csc \theta = 3.0$

In Exercises 55–58, find, to the nearest hundredth of a radian, all angles θ, where $0 \leq \theta < 2\pi$, with the given trigonometric function.

55. $\cos \theta = -0.5$

56. $\sin \theta = 0.717$

57. $\tan \theta = -0.95$

58. $\sec \theta = 2.25$

Evaluate each of the functions in Exercises 59–64. Write each answer to the nearest tenth of a degree.

59. arcsin 0.866

60. arccos 0.5

61. arctan (-1)

62. $\cos^{-1}(-0.707)$

63. $\sin^{-1} 0.385$

64. $\cot^{-1}(3.5)$

Solve Exercises 65–80.

65. *Optics* The index of refraction n of a medium is the ratio of the speed of light c in air to the speed of light in the medium c_m. According to Snell's law, the angles of incidence i and refraction r (see Figure 5.54) of a light ray are related by the formula

$$n = \frac{\sin i}{\sin r}$$

The index of refraction for water is 1.33. If a light beam enters a lake at an angle of incidence of 30°, what is the angle of refraction?

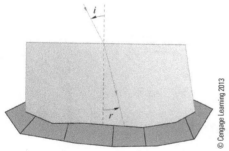

Figure 5.54

66. *Optics* A beam of light enters a pane of glass at an angle of incidence of 0.90 rad. If the angle of refraction is 0.55 rad, what is the index of refraction of the glass?

67. *Electronics* The current in an ac circuit varies with time t and the maximum value of the current I_m according to the formula

$$I = I_m \sin \omega t$$

where ω is the angular frequency of the alternating current. Find I, if $I_m = 12.6$ A and ωt is $\frac{\pi}{5}$ rad.

68. *Machine technology* An engine valve is shown in Figure 5.55. What is the angle θ of the valve face, in degrees?

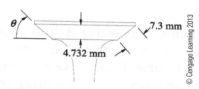

Figure 5.55

69. *Electronics* If resistor and capacitor are connected in series to an ac power source, the phase angle θ is given by the formula

$$\tan \theta = \frac{V_L}{V_R}$$

where θ is the phase angle between the total voltage V and the resistive voltage V_R. If V_L, the voltage across the inductor, is 44 V and $V_R = 50$ V, what is the phase angle θ? What is the total voltage V? (See Figure 5.56.)

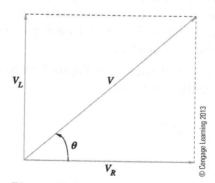

Figure 5.56

70. *Machine technology* A tapered shaft in the shape of an equilateral trapezoid is shown in Figure 5.57. What is the height of the shaft?

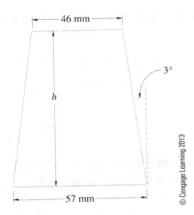

Figure 5.57

71. **Transportation engineering** A guard rail is going to be constructed around the outer edge of a highway curve. If the curve has a radius of 900 ft and an angle of 37°, how many feet of railing are needed?

72. **Computer technology** The drive speed of a disk drive for a microcomputer is 300 rpm. How many radians does it rotate in 1 s? What is the linear velocity of a point on the rim of a $5\frac{1}{4}''$ diskette?

73. **Space technology** Earth is approximately 93,000,000 mi from the sun and revolves around the sun in an almost circular orbit every 365 days. What is the approximate linear speed in miles per hour of Earth in its orbit?

74. **Construction** A guy wire for an electric pole is anchored to the ground at a point 15 ft from the base of the pole. The wire makes an angle of 68° with the level ground. How high up the pole is the wire attached?

75. Find the size of angle x in Figure 5.58 to the nearest tenth of a degree.

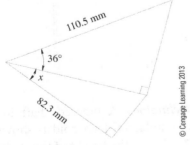

Figure 5.58

76. **Forestry** A tree 56 ft tall casts a shadow 43 ft long. What is the angle of the elevation of the sun at that moment?

77. **Construction** The light on the top of a tower is at an angle of elevation of 53.7°, when a person is 150 ft from the base of the tower. How high is the light?

78. Determine the size of angle θ in Figure 5.59 to the nearest tenth of a degree.

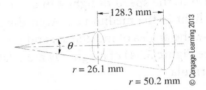

Figure 5.59

79. **Automotive technology** A 3,500-lb automobile rests on a ramp that makes an angle of 34.3° with the horizontal. Determine the components F_x and F_y, as shown in Figure 5.60.

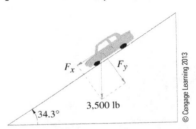

Figure 5.60

80. **Construction** Two guy wires from the top of a tower are anchored in the ground 35 m apart and in direct line with the tower. If the wires make angles of 36.4° and 23.7° with the top of the tower as shown in Figure 5.61, what is the height of the tower?

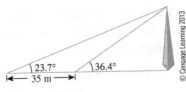

Figure 5.61

CHAPTER 5   TEST

1. Convert $50°$ to radians.

2. Convert $\frac{4\pi}{3}$ to degrees.

3. (a) In what quadrant is a $237°$ angle?

   (b) Give the reference angle for a $237°$ angle.

4. The point $(-5, 12)$ is on the terminal side of an angle θ in standard position. Give the six trigonometric functions of this angle.

5. If angle θ is at vertex A of right $\triangle ABC$ with sides $a = 9$ and $c = 23.4$, then determine

   (a) $\sin \theta$

   (b) $\tan \theta$

6. If $\cot \theta = \frac{6.75}{30}$, then determine

   (a) $\tan \theta$

   (b) $\sin \theta$

7. Determine each of the indicated values:

   (a) $\sin 53°$

   (b) $\tan (-112°)$

   (c) $\sec 127°$

   (d) $\cos 4.2$

8. Find, to the nearest tenth of a degree, all angles θ, where $0° \leq \theta < 360°$, with the given function.

   (a) $\tan \theta = 1.2$

   (b) $\sin \theta = -0.72$

9. A guy wire for a tower is anchored to the ground 135 ft from the base of the tower. The wire makes an angle of $53°$ with the level ground. How high up the tower is the wire attached?

10. The drive speed of a computer hard disk drive is 3,600 rpm. How many radians does it rotate in 1 s?

8 VECTORS AND TRIGONOMETRIC FUNCTIONS

An accident investigator might use a special wheel tape to measure skid marks at an accident. In Section 8.1, you will use vectors to determine the vertical and horizontal forces the investigator exerts on the wheel.

Many applications of mathematics involve quantities that have both a magnitude (or size) and a direction. The quantities include force, displacement, velocity, acceleration, torque, and magnetic flux density. In this chapter, we will focus on ways to represent these quantities and how they can be used in conjunction with trigonometry to solve problems. These methods will require that you learn about vectors and how to use them with trigonometry.

389

OBJECTIVES

AFTER COMPLETING THIS CHAPTER, YOU WILL BE ABLE TO:

▼ Resolve a vector into components.

▼ Combine the components of a vector into a resultant.

▼ Solve practical problems using vectors.

▼ Solve oblique triangles using the law of sines.

▼ Solve oblique triangles using the law of cosines.

▼ Solve applied problems requiring oblique triangles.

8.1   INTRODUCTION TO VECTORS

Our study will begin with the introduction of two quantities: scalars and vectors. After we finish this introductory material, you will be ready to learn some of the basic operations with scalars and vectors. We will use these operations to help solve some applied problems.

SCALARS

Quantities that have size or magnitude, but no direction are called scalars. Time, volume, mass, speed, distance, and temperature are some examples of scalars.

VECTORS

A vector is a quantity that has both magnitude and direction. The magnitude of the vector is indicated by its length. The direction of a vector is often given by an angle. A vector is usually pictured as an arrow with the arrowhead pointing in the direction of the vector. Force, velocity, acceleration, torque, and electric and magnetic fields are all examples of vectors.

Vectors are usually represented with boldface letters such as **a** or **A** or by letters with arrows over them, $\vec{a}$ or $\vec{A}$. If a vector extends from a point A, called the initial point, to a point B, called the terminal point, then the vector can be represented by $\overrightarrow{AB}$ with the arrowhead over the terminal point B. In written work, it is hard to write in boldface, so you should use $\vec{a}$ or $\vec{b}$ or $\overrightarrow{AB}$.

The magnitude of a vector **A** is usually denoted by $|\mathbf{A}|$ or A. The magnitude of a vector is never negative. Two vectors, $\overrightarrow{AB}$ and $\overrightarrow{CD}$, are *equal* or *equivalent*, if they have the same magnitude and direction, and we write $\overrightarrow{AB} = \overrightarrow{CD}$. In Figure 8.1, $\overrightarrow{AB} = \overrightarrow{CD}$ but $\overrightarrow{AB} \neq \overrightarrow{EF}$ because, although they have the same magnitude,

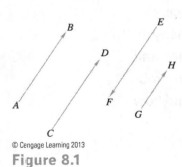

© Cengage Learning 2013

Figure 8.1

© Cengage Learning 2013

Figure 8.2a

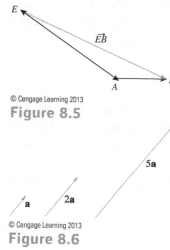

© Cengage Learning 2013

Figure 8.2b

they are not in the same direction. Also, $\overrightarrow{AB} \neq \overrightarrow{GH}$, because they do not have the same magnitude, even though they are in the same direction.

RESULTANT VECTORS

If $\overrightarrow{AB}$ is the vector from A to B and $\overrightarrow{BC}$ is the vector from B to C, then the vector $\overrightarrow{AC}$ is the **resultant vector** and represents the sum of $\overrightarrow{AB}$ and $\overrightarrow{BC}$.

$$\overrightarrow{AC} = \overrightarrow{AB} + \overrightarrow{BC}$$

The sum of two vectors is shown geometrically in Figure 8.2a. It is also possible to add vectors such as $\overrightarrow{AB} + \overrightarrow{AD}$, as shown in Figure 8.2b. Here $\overrightarrow{AC} = \overrightarrow{AB} + \overrightarrow{AD}$. As you can probably guess from the shape of Figure 8.2b, this method of adding vectors is called the **parallelogram method**.

The vectors that are being added do not need an endpoint in common. For example, to find $\overrightarrow{AB} + \overrightarrow{EF}$ in Figure 8.3a we would find the vector $\overrightarrow{BC}$, which is equivalent to $\overrightarrow{EF}$. That is, $\overrightarrow{BC} = \overrightarrow{EF}$. We are then back to the first method and $\overrightarrow{AB} + \overrightarrow{EF} = \overrightarrow{AB} + \overrightarrow{BC} = \overrightarrow{AC}$, as shown in Figure 8.3b.

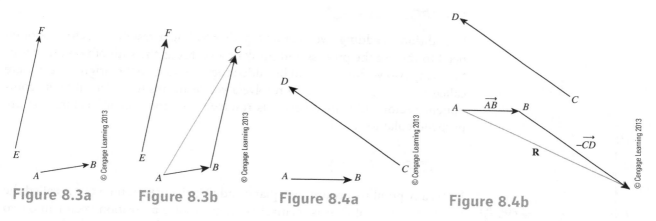

Figure 8.3a   **Figure 8.3b**   **Figure 8.4a**   **Figure 8.4b**

© Cengage Learning 2013

Figure 8.5

Vectors can also be subtracted. Here you need to realize that the vector $-\mathbf{V}$ has the opposite direction of the vector $\mathbf{V}$. An example of vector subtraction, $\overrightarrow{AB} - \overrightarrow{CD} = \overrightarrow{R}$, is shown in Figures 8.4a and 8.4b.

Another way to represent subtraction of vectors is shown in Figure 8.5. If we want to subtract $\overrightarrow{AB} - \overrightarrow{CD}$ as in Figure 8.4b, we could draw $\overrightarrow{AE}$, where $\overrightarrow{AE} = \overrightarrow{CD}$. Then $\overrightarrow{EB}$ would be the vector that represents $\overrightarrow{AB} - \overrightarrow{CD} = \overrightarrow{AB} - \overrightarrow{AE}$. Notice that in Figure 8.5, $\overrightarrow{EB}$ is drawn from the terminal point of the second vector in the difference ($\overrightarrow{AE}$) to the terminal point of the first vector ($\overrightarrow{AB}$).

A vector can be multiplied by a scalar. Thus, 2**a** has twice the magnitude but the same direction as **a** and 5**a** has five times the magnitude and the same direction as **a** (see Figure 8.6).

© Cengage Learning 2013

Figure 8.6

EXAMPLE 8.1

Use the vectors **A** and **B** in Figure 8.7a to determine vector 2**A** + **B**.

SOLUTION We begin by sketching **A** and placing it so that its initial point is at the terminal point of the original **A**. This new vector is 2**A** and is shown in Figure 8.7b.

Next, we move vector **B** so that its initial point is at the terminal point of vector 2**A** as shown in Figure 8.7c. The resultant vector, 2**A** + **B**, is drawn from the initial point of 2**A** to the terminal point of the moved vector **B**.

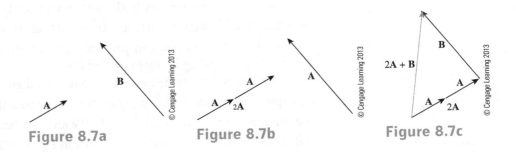

Figure 8.7a   Figure 8.7b   Figure 8.7c

COMPONENT VECTORS

In addition to adding two vectors together to find a resultant vector, we often need to reverse the process and think of a vector as the sum of two other vectors. Any two vectors that can be added together to give the original vector are called component vectors. To resolve a vector means to replace it by its component vectors. Usually a vector is resolved into component vectors that are perpendicular to each other.

POSITION VECTOR

If P is any point in a coordinate plane and O is the origin, then $\overrightarrow{OP}$ is called the position vector of P. It is relatively easy to resolve a position vector into two component vectors by using the x- and y-axis. These are called the *horizontal* (or x-) *component* and the *vertical* (or y-) *component*. In Figure 8.8, $\mathbf{P}_x$ is the horizontal component of $\overrightarrow{OP}$ and $\mathbf{P}_y$ is the vertical component.

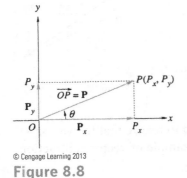

© Cengage Learning 2013

Figure 8.8

FINDING COMPONENT VECTORS

If you study Figure 8.8, you can see that the coordinates of P are (P_x, P_y). (Remember that P_x is the magnitude of vector $\mathbf{P}_x$.) Since every position vector has O as its initial point, it is easier to refer to a position vector by its terminal point. From now on we will refer to $\overrightarrow{OP}$ as **P**.

If the angle that a position vector **P** makes with the positive x-axis is θ, then the components of **P** are found as follows.

COMPONENTS OF A VECTOR

A position vector **P** that makes an angle θ with the positive x-axis can be resolved into component vectors $\mathbf{P}_x$ and $\mathbf{P}_y$ along the x- and y-axis, respectively, with magnitudes P_x and P_y, where

$$P_x = P \cos \theta$$

$$\text{and} \quad P_y = P \sin \theta$$

EXAMPLE 8.2

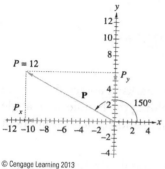

© Cengage Learning 2013

Figure 8.9

Resolve a vector 12.0 units long and at an angle of 150° into its horizontal and vertical components.

SOLUTION Consider this to be a position vector and put the initial point at the origin. The vector will look like vector **P** in Figure 8.9. We are told that $P = 12$ and $\theta = 150°$, so

$$P_x = 12 \cos 150°$$
$$= -10.392$$
$$\text{and} \quad P_y = 12 \sin 150°$$
$$= 6$$

We can resolve **P** into two component vectors. One component is along the negative x-axis and has an approximate magnitude of 10.4 units. The other component is along the positive y-axis and has a magnitude of 6.00 units.

EXAMPLE 8.3

Vector **P** is shown in Figure 8.10a. Resolve **P** into its horizontal and vertical components.

SOLUTION This vector is in Quadrant III, so both components will be negative. The reference angle is 67°. We want to know the angle that this vector makes with the positive x-axis. Since the vector is in Quadrant III, $\theta = 180° + 67° = 247°$. We see that $P = 130$, so we determine

$$P_x = 130 \cos 247°$$
$$\approx -50.7950$$
$$\approx -50.8$$
$$P_y = 130 \sin 247°$$
$$\approx -119.6656$$
$$\approx -120$$

Thus, **P** has been resolved into component vectors $\mathbf{P}_x$ of magnitude 50.8 units along the negative x-axis and $\mathbf{P}_y$ of magnitude 120 units along the negative y-axis, as shown in Figure 8.10b.

EXAMPLE 8.3 (Cont.)

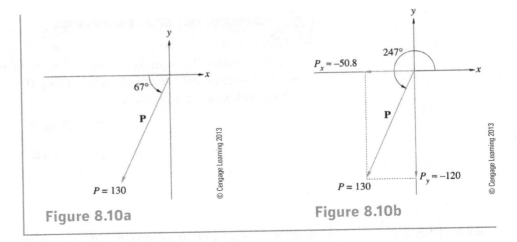

Figure 8.10a

Figure 8.10b

   APPLICATION   **GENERAL TECHNOLOGY**

EXAMPLE 8.4

The police officer in Figure 8.11a is measuring skid marks at an accident scene by pushing a wheel tape with a force of 10 lb and holding the handle at an angle of 46° with the ground. Resolve this into its horizontal and vertical component vectors.

SOLUTION   A vector diagram has been drawn over the illustration of the police officer operating the wheel tape. The vector diagram is shown alone in Figure 8.11b. The initial point of the vector is at the officer's hand and the terminal point is at the hub, or axle, of the wheel tape. We have placed the origin of our coordinate system at the initial point of the vector, and the horizontal or x-axis is parallel to the ground.

The vector makes an angle of $360° - 46° = 314°$ with the positive x-axis. Thus, we have $P = 10$ and $\theta = 314°$, so

Figure 8.11a

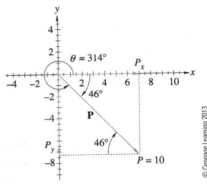

Figure 8.11b

$$P_x = 10 \cos 314°$$
$$\approx 6.9466$$
$$\text{and} \quad P_y = 10 \sin 314°$$
$$\approx -7.1934$$

The police officer exerts a horizontal force of about 6.9 lb and a vertical force of approximately 7.2 lb.

 APPLICATION **CONSTRUCTION**

EXAMPLE 8.5

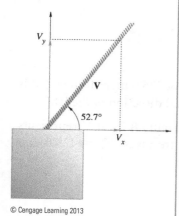

© Cengage Learning 2013

Figure 8.12

A cable supporting a television tower exerts a force of 723 N at an angle of 52.7° with the horizontal, as shown in Figure 8.12. Resolve this force into its vertical and horizontal components.

SOLUTION A vector diagram has been drawn in Figure 8.12. If the cable is represented by vector **V**, then the horizontal component is V_x and the vertical component is V_y. In this example, $\theta = 52.7°$, and so,

$$V_x = 723 \cos 52.7°$$
$$\approx 438.1296$$
$$\text{and} \quad V_y = 723 \sin 52.7°$$
$$\approx 575.1273$$

We see that this cable exerts a horizontal force of approximately 438 N and a vertical force of about 575 N.

FINDING THE MAGNITUDE AND DIRECTION OF VECTORS

If we have the horizontal and vertical components of a vector **P**, then we can use the components to determine the magnitude and direction of the resultant vector.

 MAGNITUDE AND DIRECTION OF A VECTOR

If P_x is the horizontal component of vector **P** and P_y is its vertical component, then

$$|\mathbf{P}| = P = \sqrt{P_x^2 + P_y^2}$$

$$\text{and} \quad \theta_{\text{Ref}} = \tan^{-1}\left|\frac{P_y}{P_x}\right|$$

EXAMPLE 8.6

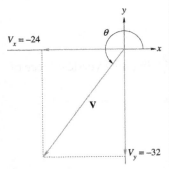

© Cengage Learning 2013
Figure 8.13

A position vector $\mathbf{V}$ has its horizontal component $V_x = -24$ and its vertical component $V_y = -32$. What are the direction and magnitude of $\mathbf{V}$?

SOLUTION A sketch of this problem in Figure 8.13 shows that $\mathbf{V}$ is in the third quadrant. Since $\theta_{\text{Ref}} = \tan^{-1}\left|\frac{-32}{-24}\right| \approx 53.13°$, we see that $\theta \approx 180° + 53.13° = 233.13°$.

We know that

$$\mathbf{V} = \sqrt{V_x^2 + V_y^2}$$
$$= \sqrt{(-24)^2 + (-32)^2} = \sqrt{1{,}600}$$
$$= 40$$

So, the magnitude of $\mathbf{V}$ is 40 and $\mathbf{V}$ is at an angle of 233.13°.

APPLICATION GENERAL TECHNOLOGY

EXAMPLE 8.7

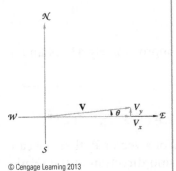

© Cengage Learning 2013
Figure 8.14

A pilot heads a jet plane due east at a ground speed of 425.0 mph. If the wind is blowing due north at 47 mph, find the true speed and direction of the jet.

SOLUTION A sketch of this situation is shown in Figure 8.14. If $\mathbf{V}$ represents the vector with components V_x and V_y, then we are given $V_x = 425.0$ and $V_y = 47$. Thus,

$$\mathbf{V} = \sqrt{V_x^2 + V_y^2}$$
$$= \sqrt{425.0^2 + 47^2}$$
$$\approx 427.59$$

and $\quad \theta = \tan^{-1}\left(\dfrac{47}{425}\right)$

$$= \tan^{-1} 0.110588$$

and so, $\quad \theta = 6.31°$

The jet is flying at a speed of approximately 427.6 mph in a direction 6.31° north of due east.

EXERCISE SET 8.1

In Exercises 1–4, add the given vectors by drawing the resultant vector.

1.

2.

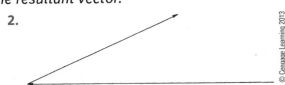

© Cengage Learning 2013

3.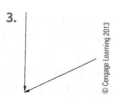

4.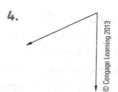

For Exercises 5–20, trace each of the vectors A–D in Figure 8.15. Use these vectors to find each of the indicated sums or differences.

    B   D

Figure 8.15
© Cengage Learning 2013

5. A + B

6. B + D

7. A + B + C

8. B + C + D

9. A − B

10. C − D

11. B − A

12. D − C

13. A + 3B

14. C + 2D

15. 2C − D

16. 3B − A

17. A + 2B − C

18. A + 3C − D

19. 2B − C + 2.5D

20. 4C − 3B − 2D

In Exercises 21–26, use trigonometric functions to find the horizontal and vertical components of the given vectors.

21. Magnitude 20, $\theta = 75°$

22. Magnitude 16, $\theta = 212°$

23. Magnitude 18.4, $\theta = 4.97$ rad

24. Magnitude 23.7, $\theta = 2.22$ rad

25. $V = 9.75$, $\theta = 16°$

26. $P = 24.6$, $\theta = 317°$

In Exercises 27–30, the horizontal and vertical components are given for a vector. Find the magnitude and direction of each resultant vector.

27. $A_x = -9$; $A_y = 12$

28. $B_x = 10$; $B_y = -24$

29. $C_x = 8$; $C_y = 15$

30. $D_x = -14$; $D_y = -20$

Solve Exercises 31–38.

31. *Navigation* A ship heads into port at 12.0 km/h. The current is perpendicular to the ship at 5 km/h. What is the resultant velocity of the ship?

32. *Navigation* A pilot heads a jet plane due east at a ground speed of 756.0 km/h. If the wind is blowing due north at 73 km/h, find the true speed and direction of the jet.

33. *Construction* A cable supporting a tower exerts a force of 976 N at an angle of 72.4° with the horizontal. Resolve this force into its vertical and horizontal components.

34. *Construction* A sign of mass 125.0 lb hangs from a cable. A worker is pulling the sign horizontally by a force of 26.50 lb. Find the force and the angle of the resultant force on the sign.

35. **Medical technology** A ramp for the physically challenged makes an angle of 4.8° with the horizontal. A woman and her wheelchair weigh 153 lb. What are the components of this weight parallel and perpendicular to the ramp?

36. **Electronics** If a resistor, a capacitor, and an inductor are connected in series to an ac power source, then the effective voltage of the source is given by the vector **V**, where **V** is the sum of the vector quantities V_R and $V_L - V_C$, as shown in Figure 8.16. The phase angle, ϕ, is the angle between **V** and V_R, where $\tan \phi = \dfrac{V_L - V_C}{V_R}$. If the effective voltages across the circuit components are $V_R = 12$ V, $V_C = 10$ V, and $V_L = 5$ V, determine the effective voltage and the phase angle.

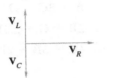
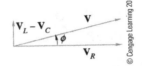

Figure 8.16

37. **Electronics** A resistor, capacitor, and inductor are connected in series to an ac power source. If the effective voltages across the circuit components are $V_R = 15.0$ V, $V_C = 17.0$ V, and $V_L = 8.0$ V, determine the effective voltage and the phase angle.

38. **Electronics** A resistor, capacitor, and inductor are connected in series to an ac power source. If the effective voltages across the circuit components are $V_R = 22.6$ V, $V_C = 15.2$ V, and $V_L = 28.3$ V, determine the effective voltage and phase angle.

39. **Navigation** A light airplane is flying due north at 145 mph. The plane is flying into a 45-mph headwind from the northwest at an angle of 35° as shown in Figure 8.17. **(a)** Draw the resultant vector for the plane's path. **(b)** Determine the magnitude for the resultant vector of the plane's path. This is the plane's actual velocity.

Figure 8.17

40. **Aeronautics** A passenger jet plane needs to change its altitude. The plane's speed (velocity) is 535.0 mph and it begins climbing at an angle of 13.5° with the horizontal. Find the horizontal, V_x, and vertical, V_y, components of the velocity vector **V**.

41. **Fire science** The water from a fire hose exerts a force of 200 lb on the person holding the hose. The nozzle of the hose weighs 20 pounds. **(a)** What force is needed to hold the hose horizontal? **(b)** At what angle to the horizontal will this force need to be applied?

42. **Navigation** A river 0.75 mi wide flows south with a current of 5 mph. What speed and heading should a motorboat assume to travel directly across the river from east to west in 10 min?

 [IN YOUR WORDS]

43. **(a)** Distinguish between scalars and vectors. How are they alike and how are they different?

   (b) What does it mean for two vectors to be equal?

44. **(a)** Describe how to use the components of a vector to determine the vector's magnitude and direction.

   (b) Explain how to use the magnitude and direction of a vector to determine its component vectors.

8.2 ADDING AND SUBTRACTING VECTORS

In Section 8.1, we learned how to use diagrams to add and subtract vectors. We also learned how to use trigonometry to determine the horizontal and vertical components of a vector. In this section, we will learn how to use trigonometry and the Pythagorean theorem to add and subtract vectors.

We will begin by looking at two special cases. In the first case, both vectors are on the same axis. In the second case, the vectors are on different axes.

EXAMPLE 8.8

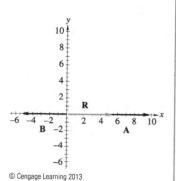

© Cengage Learning 2013

Figure 8.18

Add vectors **A** and **B**, where $A = 9.6$, $\theta_A = 0°$ and $B = 4.3$, $\theta_B = 180°$.

SOLUTION If we find the horizontal and vertical components of these two vectors we see that

$$A_x = 9.6 \cos 0° = 9.6$$
$$A_y = 9.6 \sin 0° = 0$$
$$B_x = 4.3 \cos 180° = -4.3$$
$$B_y = 4.3 \sin 180° = 0$$

The resultant vector **R** has horizontal component $R_x = A_x + B_x = 9.6 + -4.3 = 5.3$ and a vertical component $R_y = 0 + 0 = 0$. The angle of the resultant vector θ_R is found using $\tan \theta_R = \dfrac{R_y}{R_x} = \dfrac{0}{5.3} = 0$. Since $R_x > 0$, we know that θ_R is 0° rather than 180° (see Figure 8.18).

In this first case, the component method required a little extra work. But, the example gave us a foundation for the next example:

EXAMPLE 8.9

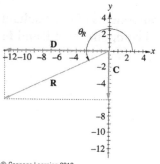

© Cengage Learning 2013

Figure 8.19

Find the resultant of **C** and **D**, when $C = 6.2$, $\theta_C = 270°$, $D = 12.4$, and $\theta_D = 180°$, as shown in Figure 8.19.

SOLUTION Since **C** and **D** are perpendicular, the length of the resultant vector can be found by using the Pythagorean theorem:

$$R = \sqrt{C^2 + D^2} = \sqrt{(6.2)^2 + (12.4)^2} \approx 13.9$$

We also know that $\tan \theta = \dfrac{C}{D} = \dfrac{6.2}{12.4} = \dfrac{1}{2}$ and that $\tan^{-1}\frac{1}{2} = 26.57°$. From Figure 8.19, we can see that **R** is in the third quadrant. So, $\theta_R = 206.57° \approx 207°$.

If we want to find the resultant of two vectors that are not at right angles, the method takes a bit longer. We first resolve each vector into its horizontal and vertical components and then add the horizontal and vertical components, as outlined in the following box.

ADDING VECTORS USING COMPONENTS

1. Resolve each vector into its horizontal and vertical components.
2. Add the horizontal components. This sum is R_x, the horizontal component of the resultant vector.
3. Add the vertical components. This sum is R_y, the vertical component of the resultant vector.
4. Use R_x and R_y to determine the magnitude R and direction θ of the resultant vector, where

$$R = \sqrt{R_x^2 + R_y^2} \quad \text{and} \quad \tan \theta = \frac{R_y}{R_x}$$

CAUTION Calculators yield the same answer for $\tan^{-1}\left(\dfrac{R_y}{R_x}\right)$ and $\tan^{-1}\left(\dfrac{-R_y}{-R_x}\right)$. Similarly, they also give the same answer to $\tan^{-1}\left(\dfrac{-R_y}{R_x}\right)$ and $\tan^{-1}\left(\dfrac{R_y}{-R_x}\right)$. You must be careful to check the quadrant in which **R** is located and then, if necessary, add π (or 180°) to the resultant angle.

EXAMPLE 8.10

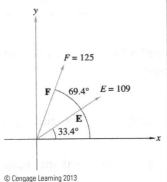

© Cengage Learning 2013

Figure 8.20a

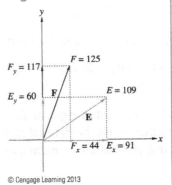

© Cengage Learning 2013

Figure 8.20b

Find the resultant of two vectors **E** and **F**, where $E = 109$, $\theta_E = 33.4°$, $F = 125$, and $\theta_F = 69.4°$ (see Figure 8.20a).

SOLUTION Resolving **E** into its horizontal and vertical components we get

$$E_x = 109 \cos 33.4° = 91$$
$$\text{and} \quad E_y = 109 \sin 33.4° = 60$$

The components for vector **F** are

$$F_x = 125 \cos 69.4° = 44$$
$$F_y = 125 \sin 69.4° = 117$$

These components are shown in Figure 8.20b. The components of the resultant vector are found by adding the horizontal and vertical components of **E** and **F**:

$$R_x = E_x + F_x$$
$$= 91 + 44$$
$$= 135$$
$$R_y = E_y + F_y$$
$$= 60 + 117$$
$$= 177$$

These two component vectors and their resultant vector are shown in Figure 8.20c.

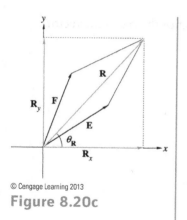

© Cengage Learning 2013

Figure 8.20c

$$R = \sqrt{R_x^2 + R_y^2}$$
$$= \sqrt{135^2 + 177^2}$$
$$\approx 222.61$$

$$\text{and} \quad \tan\theta_R = \frac{R_y}{R_x}$$

$$\tan\theta_R = \frac{177}{135}$$

$$\theta_R = \tan^{-1}\frac{177}{135}$$

$$\text{so } \theta_R = 52.7°$$

It is often helpful to use a table to help keep track of vectors and their components. It is an effective way to organize this information. A table for Example 8.10 follows. It lists the horizontal and vertical components of each vector and the resultant vector.

Vector	Horizontal component	Vertical component
E	$E_x = 109\cos 33.4° = 91$	$E_y = 109\sin 33.4° = 60$
F	$F_x = 125\cos 69.4° = \underline{44}$	$F_y = 125\sin 69.4° = \underline{117}$
R	$R_x \qquad\qquad\qquad 135$	$R_y \qquad\qquad\qquad 177$

© Cengage Learning 2013

From these values for R_x and R_y, we can determine $R \approx 223$ and $\theta_R = 52.7°$.

EXAMPLE 8.11

Find the resultant of two vectors **G** and **H**, where $G = 449$, $\theta_G = 128.6°$, $H = 521$, and $\theta_H = 327.6°$ (see Figure 8.21a).

SOLUTION Again, we will resolve each vector into its horizontal and vertical components.

$$G_x = 449\cos 128.6°$$
$$= -280.1$$
$$G_y = 449\sin 128.6°$$
$$= 350.9$$
$$H_x = 521\cos 327.6°$$
$$= 439.9$$
$$H_y = 521\sin 327.6°$$
$$= -279.2$$

© Cengage Learning 2013

Figure 8.21a

Figure 8.21b shows each vector and its horizontal and vertical components.

Adding the horizontal components gives the horizontal component of the resultant vector.

$$R_x = G_x + H_x$$
$$= -280.1 + 439.9$$
$$= 159.8$$

EXAMPLE 8.11 (Cont.)

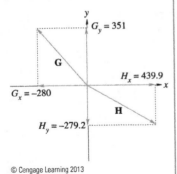

© Cengage Learning 2013

Figure 8.21b

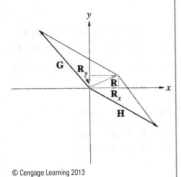

© Cengage Learning 2013

Figure 8.21c

Similarly, we can determine the vertical component of the resultant vector:

$$R_y = G_y + H_y$$
$$= 350.9 - 279.2$$
$$= 71.7$$

The resultant vector is shown in Figure 8.21c.
The magnitude of the resultant vector is

$$R = \sqrt{R_x^2 + R_y^2}$$
$$= \sqrt{159.8^2 + 71.7^2}$$
$$\approx 175.1$$

and the direction of the resultant vector is found from

$$\tan \theta_R = \frac{R_y}{R_x}$$
$$= \frac{71.7}{159.8}$$
$$= 0.4487$$

so

$$\theta_R = \tan^{-1} 0.4487$$
$$= 24.2°$$

The table method for Example 8.11 would appear as follows.

Vector	Horizontal component		Vertical component	
G	$G_x = 449 \cos 128.6° =$	-280.1	$G_y = 449 \sin 128.6° =$	350.9
H	$H_x = 521 \cos 327.6° =$	$\underline{439.9}$	$H_y = 521 \sin 327.6° =$	$\underline{-279.2}$
R	R_x	159.8	R_y	71.7

© Cengage Learning 2013

These values for R_x and R_y can be used as before to find $R = 175.1$ and $\theta_R = 24.2°$.

EXAMPLE 8.12

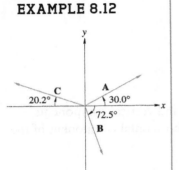

© Cengage Learning 2013

Figure 8.22

Find the resultant of the three vectors shown in Figure 8.22, if $A = 137$, $B = 89.4$, and $C = 164.6$.

SOLUTION The table that follows lists the horizontal and vertical components of each of the vectors and the resultant vector **R**.

Vector	Horizontal component		Vertical component	
A	$A_x = 137 \cos 30° =$	118.6	$A_y = 137 \sin 30° =$	68.5
B	$B_x = 89.4 \cos 287.5° =$	26.9	$B_y = 89.4 \sin 287.5° =$	-85.3
C	$C_x = 164.6 \cos 159.8° =$	$\underline{-154.5}$	$C_y = 164.6 \sin 159.8° =$	$\underline{56.8}$
R	R_x	-9.0	R_y	40.0

© Cengage Learning 2013

Once again, the values for R_x and R_y can be used to find

$$R = \sqrt{R_x^2 + R_y^2}$$
$$= \sqrt{(-9)^2 + 40^2}$$
$$= 41$$

and

$$\theta_R = \tan^{-1}\frac{40}{-9}$$
$$\theta_R = 102.7°$$

APPLICATION CONSTRUCTION

EXAMPLE 8.13

A sign has been lifted into position by two cranes, as shown in Figure 8.23a. If the sign weighs 420 lb, what is the tension in each of the three cables?

SOLUTION We will draw the coordinate axes and label the angles as shown in Figure 8.23b. The origin is placed at the ring where the three cables meet, because the tension on all three cables acts on this ring.

As usual, we make a table listing the horizontal and vertical components of each vector.

Vector	Horizontal component	Vertical component
A	$A_x = A\cos 145°$	$A_y = A\sin 145°$
B	$B_x = B\cos 40°$	$B_y = B\sin 40°$
C	$C_x = C\cos 270° = \underline{0}$	$C_y = C\sin 270° = -C = \underline{-420}$
R	R_x	R_y

© Cengage Learning 2013

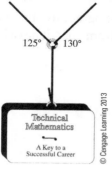

Figure 8.23a

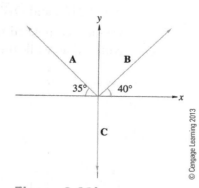

Figure 8.23b

The ring is at rest as a result of these three forces, so $R_x = 0$ and $R_y = 0$. Thus, we have

$$R_x = A\cos 145° + B\cos 40° = 0$$
$$R_y = A\sin 145° + B\sin 40° - 420 = 0$$

EXAMPLE 8.13 (Cont.)

Evaluating the trigonometric functions in these two equations, we are led to the following system of two equations in two variables:

$$\begin{cases} -0.81915A + 0.76604B = 0 \\ 0.57358A + 0.64279B = 420 \end{cases}$$

Solving this system of two equations in two variables (by Cramer's rule), we get

$$A \approx 333.0862 \text{ lb}$$

$$\text{and} \quad B \approx 356.1792 \text{ lb}$$

The tension in the cable on the left is about 333 lb and the tension in the cable on the right side is about 356 lb.

NOTE In flight terminology, the **heading** of an aircraft is the direction in which the aircraft is pointed. Usually the wind is pushing the aircraft so that it is actually moving in a different direction, called the **track** or **course**. The angle between the heading and the course is the **drift angle**. The **air speed** is the speed of the plane relative to the air. The **ground speed** is the speed of the aircraft relative to the ground.

NOTE In navigation, directions are usually given in terms of the size of the angle measured clockwise from true north. For example, the airplane in Figure 8.24 has a heading of 150°.

 APPLICATION   GENERAL TECHNOLOGY

EXAMPLE 8.14

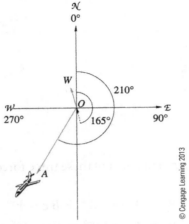

N
0°

150°

W
270°

E
90°

S
180°

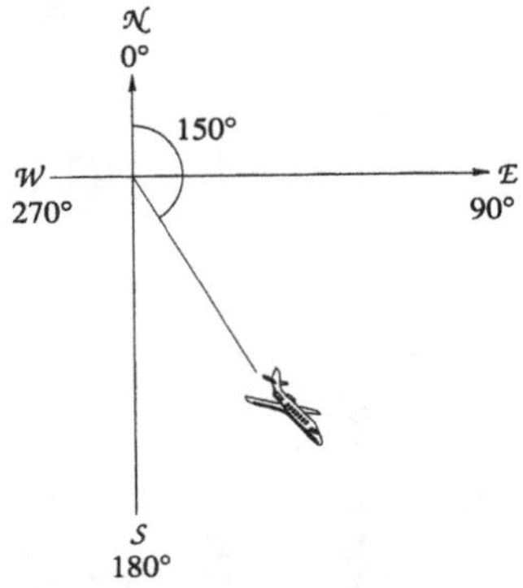

© Cengage Learning 2013

Figure 8.24

An airplane is flying at 340.0 mph with a heading of 210°. If a 50-mph wind is blowing from 165°, find the ground speed, drift angle, and course of the airplane.

SOLUTION In Figure 8.25a, $\overrightarrow{OA}$ represents the airspeed of 340 mph with a heading of 210°, and $\overrightarrow{OW}$ represents a wind of 50 mph from 165°. In Figure 8.25b, we have completed the parallelogram to obtain the vector $\overrightarrow{OR} = \overrightarrow{OA} + \overrightarrow{OW}$. Notice that, while the wind is from 165°, it has a heading of 180° + 165° = 345°.

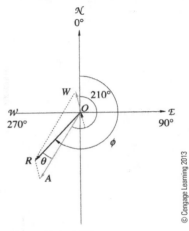

Figure 8.25a

Figure 8.25b

The length $\overrightarrow{OR}$ represents the ground speed, θ is the drift angle, and ϕ is the track or course. The following table lists the horizontal and vertical components of each vector $\overrightarrow{OA}$ and $\overrightarrow{OW}$ and the resultant vector $\overrightarrow{OR}$.

Vector	Horizontal component	Vertical component
$\overrightarrow{OA} = \mathbf{A}$	$A_x = 340 \cos 210° \approx -294.45$	$A_y = 340 \sin 210° = -170.00$
$\overrightarrow{OW} = \mathbf{W}$	$W_x = 50 \cos 345° \approx \quad 48.30$	$W_y = 50 \sin 345° \approx \underline{-12.94}$
$\overrightarrow{OR} = \mathbf{R}$	$R_x \qquad\qquad\qquad -246.15$	$R_y \qquad\qquad\qquad -182.94$

© Cengage Learning 2013

Using these values for R_x and R_y, we see that the length of the resultant vector is $\overrightarrow{OR} = \sqrt{(-246.15)^2 + (-182.94)^2} \approx 306.69$ and $\phi \approx \tan^{-1}\left(\frac{-182.94}{-246.15}\right) = 36.62°$. Since ϕ is in the third quadrant, $\phi = 180° + 36.62° = 216.62°$.

So, the plane has a ground speed of 306.69 mph, a drift angle of 6.62°, and a course of 216.62°.

EXERCISE SET 8.2

In Exercises 1–4, vectors **A** and **B** are both on the same axis. Find the magnitude and direction of the resultant vector.

1. $A = 20.0, \theta_A = 0°, B = 32.5, \theta_B = 180°$

2. $A = 14.3, \theta_A = 90°, B = 7.2, \theta_B = 90°$

3. $A = 121.7, \theta_A = 270°, B = 86.9, \theta_B = 90°$

4. $A = 63.1, \theta_A = 180°, B = 43.5, \theta_B = 180°$

In Exercises 5–8, vectors **C** and **D** are perpendicular. Find the magnitude and direction of the resultant vectors. It may help if you draw vectors **C**, **D**, and the resultant vector.

5. $C = 55, \theta_C = 90°, D = 48, \theta_D = 180°$

6. $C = 65, \theta_C = 270°, D = 72, \theta_C = 180°$

7. $C = 81.4, \theta_C = 0°, D = 37.6, \theta_D = 90°$

8. $C = 63.4, \theta_C = 270°, D = 9.4, \theta_D = 0°$

In Exercises 9–16, find the magnitude and direction of the vector with the given components.

9. $A_x = 33, A_y = 56$

10. $B_x = 231, B_y = 520$

11. $C_x = 11.7, C_y = 4.4$

12. $D_x = 31.9, D_y = 36.0$

13. $E_x = 6.3, E_y = 1.6$

14. $F_x = 5.1, F_y = 14.0$

15. $G_x = 8.4, G_y = 12.6$

16. $H_x = 15.3, H_y = 9.2$

In Exercises 17–30, add the given vectors by using the trigonometric functions and the Pythagorean theorem.

17. $A = 4, \theta_A = 60°, B = 9, \theta_B = 20°$

18. $C = 12, \theta_C = 75°, D = 15, \theta_D = 37°$

19. $C = 28, \theta_C = 120°, D = 45, \theta_D = 210°$

20. $E = 72, \theta_E = 287°, F = 65, \theta_F = 17°$

21. $A = 31.2, \theta_A = 197.5°, B = 62.1, \theta_B = 236.7°$

22. $C = 53.1, \theta_C = 324.3°, D = 68.9, \theta_D = 198.6°$

23. $E = 12.52, \theta_E = 46.4°, F = 18.93, \theta_F = 315°$

24. $G = 76.2, \theta_G = 15.7°, H = 89.4, \theta_H = 106.3°$

25. $A = 9.84, \theta_A = 215°30', B = 12.62, \theta_B = 105°15'$

26. $C = 79.63, \theta_C = 262°45', D = 43.72, \theta_D = 196°12'$

27. $E = 42.0, \theta_E = 3.4 \text{ rad}, F = 63.2, \theta_F = 5.3 \text{ rad}$

28. $G = 37.5, \theta_G = 0.25 \text{ rad}, H = 49.3, \theta_H = 1.92 \text{ rad}$

29.

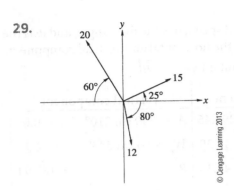

30.

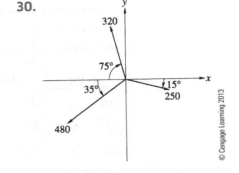

Solve Exercises 31–40.

31. Construction technology A sign is held in position by three cables, as shown in Figure 8.26. If the sign has a weight of 215 N, what is the tension in each of the three cables?

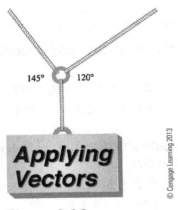

Figure 8.26

32. Construction technology A 175-lb sign is supported from a wall by a cable inclined 53° with the horizontal, and a brace perpendicular to the wall, as shown in Figure 8.27. Find the

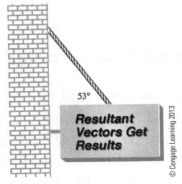

Figure 8.27

magnitudes of the forces in the cable and the brace that will keep the sign in equilibrium.

33. Construction technology A 235-lb sign is supported from a wall by a cable inclined 37° with the horizontal, and a brace perpendicular to the wall, similar to that shown in Figure 8.27. Find the tension in the cable and the compression in the boom.

34. Construction technology An 85-kg sign is held in position by three ropes, as shown in Figure 8.28. What is the tension in each of the three ropes?

Figure 8.28

35. Navigation An airplane is flying at 480 mph with a heading of 63°. A 45.0-mph wind is blowing from 325°. Find the ground speed, course, and drift angle of the airplane.

36. Navigation An airplane is flying at 320.0 mph with a heading of 172°. A 72.0-mph wind is blowing from 137°. Find the ground speed, course, and drift angle of the airplane.

37. **Electronics** A circuit has two ac voltages that are 68° out of phase. Each voltage is 196 V. What is the total voltage?

38. **Electronics** A two-phase generator produces two voltages that are 120° out of phase. The first voltage is 86 V. The second voltage is 110 V. What is the total voltage?

39. **Aeronautics** An airplane takes off from an airport with a velocity of 225 mph at an angle of 12°.

   (a) How fast is it rising?

   (b) What is its speed relative to the ground?

40. **Police science** The *momentum* of an object is equal to its mass, *m*, times its velocity, *v*. Thus, momentum is a vector, and momentum = *mv*. If friction forces are very small, we may assume that the momentum before a collision is the same as the momentum after the collision. Two cars collide at an icy intersection, as shown in Figure 8.29. Car *A* has a mass of 2450 kg and was traveling at 10 m/s before the cars hit, and car *B* has a mass of 2100 kg and was traveling

at 9 m/s. After the collision the cars are locked together and they slide on the flat icy road.

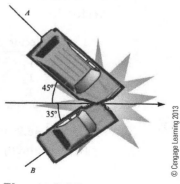

Figure 8.29

   (a) What are the resultant vectors for the momentum of car *A* before the collision?

   (b) What are the resultant vectors for the momentum of car *B* before the collision?

   (c) What are the resultant vectors for the momentum of the cars after the collision?

   (d) What was the speed and direction of the cars after the collision?

 [IN YOUR WORDS]

41. Without looking in the text, describe how you can use a vector's components to add vectors.

42. Flight terminology uses several technical terms. Write a brief definition of each of the following terms. Draw a figure to illustrate your explanations.

   (a) Heading

   (b) Drift angle

   (c) Course

   (d) Ground speed

   (e) Wind speed

 8.3   APPLICATIONS OF VECTORS

Vectors are used in science and technology, as well as in mathematics. In this section, we will look at some of those applications.

APPLICATION GENERAL TECHNOLOGY

EXAMPLE 8.15

Two forces, F_1 and F_2, act on an object. If F_1 is 40 lb, F_2 is 75 lb, and the angle θ between them is 50°, find the magnitude and direction of the resultant force.

EXAMPLE 8.15 (Cont.)

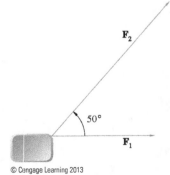

© Cengage Learning 2013
Figure 8.30

SOLUTION　We sketch the two forces as vectors and place the object at the origin with $\mathbf{F_1}$ along the positive x-axis as in Figure 8.30. We will use a table similar to the one in the last example to find the components of $\mathbf{F_1}$, $\mathbf{F_2}$, and the resultant vector.

Vector	Horizontal component		Vertical component	
$\mathbf{F_1}$		40.0		0.0
$\mathbf{F_2}$	$75 \cos 50° =$	48.2	$75 \sin 50° =$	57.5
$\mathbf{R}$	R_x	88.2	R_y	57.5

© Cengage Learning 2013

So, $R_x = 88.2$ and $R_y = 57.5$. The magnitude of $\mathbf{R}$ is $R = \sqrt{88.2^2 + 57.5^2} = 105.3$ lb and $\theta_R = \tan^{-1}\frac{57.5}{88.2} = 33.1°$.

 APPLICATION　**GENERAL TECHNOLOGY**

EXAMPLE 8.16

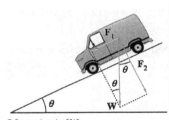

© Cengage Learning 2013
Figure 8.31

A truck weighing 22,500 lb is on a 25° hill. Find the components of the truck's weight parallel and perpendicular to the road.

SOLUTION　The weight of an object (truck, car, building, etc.) is the gravitational force with which earth attracts it. This force always acts vertically downward and is indicated by the vector $\mathbf{W}$ in Figure 8.31. The components of $\mathbf{W}$ have been labeled $\mathbf{F_1}$ and $\mathbf{F_2}$. Because $\mathbf{W}$ is vertical and $\mathbf{F_2}$ is perpendicular to the road, the angle θ between $\mathbf{W}$ and $\mathbf{F_2}$ is equal to the angle the road makes with the horizon. Using the trigonometric functions, we have

$$F_1 = W \sin \theta = 22{,}500 \sin 25° = 9{,}509 \text{ lb}$$
$$F_2 = W \cos \theta = 22{,}500 \cos 25° = 20{,}392 \text{ lb}$$

Thus, the components of the truck's weight are 9,509 lb parallel to the road and 20,392 lb perpendicular to the road.

 APPLICATION　**GENERAL TECHNOLOGY**

EXAMPLE 8.17

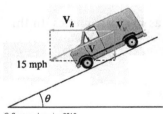

© Cengage Learning 2013
Figure 8.32

If the truck in Example 8.16 rolls down the hill at 15 mph, find the magnitudes of the horizontal and vertical components of the truck's velocity.

SOLUTION　The velocity vector $\mathbf{V}$ is shown in Figure 8.32. The horizontal and vertical components of $\mathbf{V}$ are marked $\mathbf{V}_h$ and $\mathbf{V}_v$:

$$V_v = V \sin 25° = 15 \sin 25° = 6.3 \text{ mph}$$
$$V_h = V \cos 25° = 15 \cos 25° = 13.6 \text{ mph}$$

APPLICATION GENERAL TECHNOLOGY

EXAMPLE 8.18

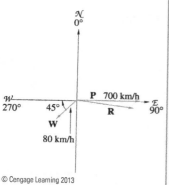

© Cengage Learning 2013

Figure 8.33

A jet plane is traveling due east at an airspeed of 700 km/h. If a wind of 80 km/h is blowing due southwest, find the magnitude and direction of the plane's resultant velocity (see Figure 8.33).

SOLUTION A table of the components for the wind's vector **W** and the plane's vector **P** allows us to quickly find the resultant vector **R**.

Vector	Horizontal component	Vertical component
W	$80 \cos 225° = -56.6$	$80 \sin 225° = -56.6$
P	$700 \cos 0° = \underline{700.0}$	$\underline{0.0}$
R	643.4	-56.6

© Cengage Learning 2013

The magnitude of **R** is $R = \sqrt{643.4^2 + (-56.6)^2} = 645.9$ km/h. This is the ground speed of the plane. The plane's direction is $\theta_R = \tan^{-1}\left(\frac{-56.6}{643.4}\right) = -5.03°$ or 5.03° south of east.

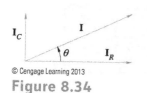

APPLICATION ELECTRONICS

EXAMPLE 8.19

© Cengage Learning 2013

Figure 8.34

In a parallel RC (resistance-capacitance) circuit, the current $\mathbf{I}_C$ through the capacitance leads the current $\mathbf{I}_R$ through the resistance by 90°, as shown in Figure 8.34. If $I_C = 0.5$ A and $I_R = 1.2$ A, find the total current **I** in the circuit and the phase angle θ of the circuit.

SOLUTION $I = \sqrt{I_R^2 + I_C^2} = \sqrt{(1.2)^2 + (0.5)^2} = 1.3$ A

$$\theta = \tan^{-1}\left(\frac{I_C}{I_R}\right)$$

$$\theta = \tan^{-1}\left(\frac{0.5}{1.2}\right) = 22.6°$$

APPLICATION GENERAL TECHNOLOGY

EXAMPLE 8.20

An airplane in level flight drops an object. The plane was traveling at 180 m/s at a height of 7 500 m. The vertical component of the dropped object is given by $V_y = -9.8t$ m/s. What is the magnitude of the velocity of the object after 8 s? At what angle with the ground is the object moving at this time?

SOLUTION The horizontal velocity of the object will have no effect on the vertical motion. Hence, V_x will remain at 180 m/s. We are told that $V_y = -9.8t$.

EXAMPLE 8.20 (Cont.)

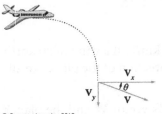

© Cengage Learning 2013

Figure 8.35

So, when $t = 8$, $V_y = -78.4$. The magnitude of the velocity of the object when $t = 8$ is

$$V = \sqrt{(-78.4)^2 + 180^2} = 196.3 \text{ m/s}$$

If θ is the angle that the object makes with the ground, then

$$\theta = \tan^{-1}\frac{V_y}{V_x} = \tan^{-1}\left(\frac{-78.4}{180}\right) \approx -23.5°$$

or 23.5° below the horizontal (see Figure 8.35).

EXERCISE SET 8.3

Solve Exercises 1–24.

1. **Physics** Two forces act on an object. One force is 70 lb and the other is 50 lb. If the angle between the two forces is 35°, find the magnitude and direction of the resultant force.

2. **Physics** A person pulling a cart exerts a force of 35 lb on the cart at an angle of 25° above the horizontal. Find the horizontal and vertical components of this force.

3. **Physics** A person pushes a lawn mower with a force of 25 lb. The handle of the lawn mower is 55° above the horizontal. **(a)** How much downward force is being exerted on the ground? **(b)** How much horizontal forward force is being exerted? **(c)** How do these forces change if the handle is lowered to 40° with the horizontal?

4. **Navigation** Two tugboats are pulling a ship. As shown in Figure 8.36, the first tug exerts a force of 1 500 N on a cable, making an angle of 37° with the axis of the ship. The second tug

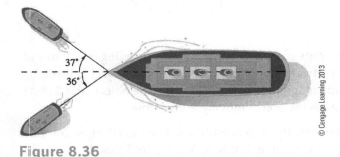

Figure 8.36

© Cengage Learning 2013

pulls on a cable, making an angle of 36° with the axis of the ship. The resultant force vector is in line with the axis of the ship. What is the force being exerted by the second tug?

5. **Navigation** A tugboat is turning a barge by pushing with a force of 1 700 N at an angle of 18° with the axis of the barge. What are the forward and sideward forces in newtons exerted by the tug on the barge? (See Figure 8.37)

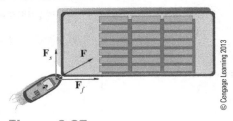

Figure 8.37

© Cengage Learning 2013

6. **Navigation** A ship heads due northwest at 15 km/h in a river that flows east at 7 km/h. What is the magnitude and direction of the ship's velocity relative to earth's surface?

7. **Navigation** A plane is heading due south at 370 mph with a wind from the west at 40 mph. What are the ground speed and the true direction of the plane?

8. **Navigation** On a compass, due north is 0°, east is 90°, south 180°, and so on. A plane has a compass heading of 115° and is traveling at 420 mph. The wind is at 62 mph and blowing at 32°.

What are the ground speed and true direction of the plane?

9. **Physics** A car with a mass of 1 200 kg is on a hill that makes an angle of 22° with the horizon. Which components of the car's mass are parallel and perpendicular to the road?

10. **Physics** Find the force necessary to push a 30-lb ball up a ramp that is inclined 15° with the horizon. (You want to find the component parallel to the ramp.)

11. **Construction** A guy wire runs from the top of a utility pole 35 ft high to a point on the ground 27 ft from the base of the pole. The tension in the wire is 195 lb. What are the horizontal and vertical components?

12. **Electronics** In a parallel RC circuit, the current I_C through the capacitance leads the current through the resistance I_R by 90°. If $I_C = 2.4$ A and $I_R = 1.6$ A, find the magnitude of the total current in the circuit and the phase angle.

13. **Electronics** If the total current I in a parallel RC circuit is 9.6 A and I_R is 7.5 A, what are I_C and the phase angle?

14. **Electronics** In a parallel RL (resistance-inductance) circuit, the current I_L through the inductance lags the current I_R through the resistance by 90°, as shown in Figure 8.38. Find the magnitude of the total current I and the negative phase angle θ, when $I_L = 6.2$ A and $I_R = 8.4$ A.

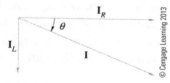

Figure 8.38

15. **Electronics** If the total current I in a parallel RL circuit is 12.4 A and I_R is 6.3 A, find I_L and the negative phase angle.

16. **Electronics** The total impedance Z of a series ac circuit is the resultant of the resistance R, the inductive reactance X_L, and the capacitive reactance X_C, as shown in Figure 8.39. Find Z and the phase angle, when $X_C = 50$ Ω, $X_L = 90$ Ω, and $R = 12$ Ω.

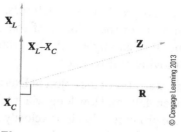

Figure 8.39

17. **Electronics** Find the total impedance Z and the phase angle of a series ac circuit, when $X_C = 60$ Ω, $X_L = 40$ Ω, and $R = 24$ Ω.

18. **Electronics** Find the total impedance and phase angle, when $X_L = 38$ Ω, $X_C = 265$ Ω, and $R = 75$ Ω.

19. **Electronics** In a synchronous ac motor, the current leads the applied voltage, and in an induction ac electric motor, the current lags the applied voltage. A circuit with a synchronous motor A connected in parallel with an induction motor B and a purely resistive load C has a current diagram as shown in Figure 8.40. If $I_A = 20$ A, $\theta_A = 35°$, $I_B = 15$ A, $\theta_B = -20°$, and $I_C = 25$ A, find the total current I and the phase angle between the total current and the applied voltage.

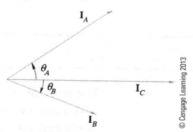

Figure 8.40

20. **Navigation** A ship is sailing at a speed of 12 km/h in the direction of 10°. A strong wind is exerting enough pressure on the ship's superstructure to move it in the direction of 270° at 2 km/h. A tidal current is flowing in the direction of 140° at the rate of 6 km/h. What is the ship's velocity and direction relative to the earth's surface?

21. **Navigation** An airplane in level flight drops an object. The plane was traveling at 120 m/s at a height of 5 000 m. The vertical component

of the dropped object is $V_y = -9.8t$ m/s. What is the magnitude of the velocity of the object after 4 s and at what angle with the ground is the object moving at this time?

22. *Navigation* At any time t the object in Exercise 21 will have fallen $4.9t^2$ m. How long will it take for it to strike the ground? What is its velocity at this time? At what angle will it strike the ground?

23. *Construction* A parallelogram with adjacent sides of lengths $1'9''$ and $2'3''$ is to be cut from

a rectangular piece of plywood. The parallelogram contains a 40° angle. What are the dimensions of the smallest piece of plywood from which this parallelogram can be cut?

24. *Construction* A parallelogram with adjacent sides of lengths 15 and 32 cm is to be cut from a rectangular piece of plywood. The parallelogram contains a 35° angle. What are the dimensions of the smallest piece of plywood from which this parallelogram can be cut?

[IN YOUR WORDS]

25. Write a word problem in your technology area of interest that requires you to use vectors. On the back of the sheet of paper, write your name and explain how to solve the problem by using vectors. Give the problem you wrote to a friend and let him or her try to solve it. If your friend has difficulty understanding the problem or solving the problem, or if he or she disagrees with your solution, make any necessary changes in the problem or solution. When you

have finished, give the revised problem and solution to another friend and see if he or she can solve it.

26. Write a word problem in your technology area of interest that requires you to use at least three vectors and their components in its solution. Follow the same procedures described in Exercise 25 for writing, sharing, and revising your problem.

8.4   OBLIQUE TRIANGLES: LAW OF SINES

The triangles we have examined until now have been right triangles. At first, trigonometry and the trigonometric functions dealt only with right triangles. Mathematicians quickly discovered that they needed to work with triangles that did not have a right angle. These triangles, the ones with no right angle, were named oblique triangles.

The trigonometric methods for solving right triangles do not work with oblique triangles. There are two methods that are usually used with oblique triangles. One of these, the Law of Sines, will be studied in this section. The other, the Law of Cosines, will be studied in Section 8.5.

The *Law of Sines* can be developed without too much difficulty. Consider the triangle in Figure 8.41. Select one of the vertices, in this case vertex C. Drop a perpendicular to the opposite side. From the resulting right triangles we have

$$\sin A = \frac{h}{b} \quad \text{and} \quad \sin B = \frac{h}{a}$$

or

$$h = b \sin A \quad \text{and} \quad h = a \sin B$$

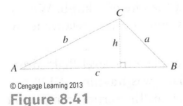

© Cengage Learning 2013
Figure 8.41

Since both of these are equal to h, then $b \sin A = a \sin B$ and $\dfrac{a}{\sin A} = \dfrac{b}{\sin B}$. If we dropped the perpendicular from vertex B we would get $\dfrac{a}{\sin A} = \dfrac{c}{\sin C}$.

Putting these together, we get the Law of Sines.

THE LAW OF SINES

The Law of Sines or Sine Law is a continued proportion and states that if $\triangle ABC$ is a triangle with sides of lengths a, b, and c and opposite angles A, B, and C, then

$$\frac{a}{\sin A} = \frac{b}{\sin B} = \frac{c}{\sin C}$$

You may recognize that this can also be written as the continued proportion $a : b : c = \sin A : \sin B : \sin C$.

The Law of Sines can be used to solve a triangle when the parts of a triangle are known in either of the following two cases:

Case 1 (SSA) The measure of two sides and the angle opposite one of them is known.

Case 2 (AAS) The measure of two angles and one side is known.

As is true with any continued proportion, you work with just two of the ratios at any one time. You should also remember that the angles of a triangle add up to 180° or π rad.

Let's look at an example that uses the Law of Sines. This example will fit the description of a Case 1 triangle or SSA.

EXAMPLE 8.21

In triangle $\triangle ABC$ as shown in Figure 8.42, $A = 33°$, $a = 14.3$, and $c = 9.4$. Solve the triangle.

SOLUTION To solve this triangle means that we are to find the length of the third side and the sizes of the other two angles. The following data chart shows the parts that we know and those we are to determine.

Sides	Angles
$a = 14.3$	$A = 33°$
$b = \underline{\quad}$	$B = \underline{\quad}$
$c = 9.4$	$C = \underline{\quad}$

© Cengage Learning 2013

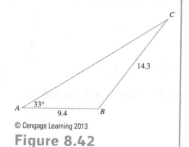

© Cengage Learning 2013

Figure 8.42

Since two of the known parts have the same letter, a, one of the ratios we should use is $\dfrac{a}{\sin A}$. The other known part has the letter c so the other ratio should be $\dfrac{c}{\sin C}$. By the Law of Sines

EXAMPLE 8.21 (Cont.)

$$\frac{a}{\sin A} = \frac{c}{\sin C}$$

$$\frac{14.3}{\sin 33°} = \frac{9.4}{\sin C}$$

$$\sin C = \frac{9.4(\sin 33°)}{14.3}$$

$$\approx 0.3580145$$

$$C \approx 20.98°$$

Since $C \approx 20.98°$ and $A = 33°$, then

$$B \approx 180 - 33° - 20.98°$$

$$= 126.02°$$

We can use this information to find the length of the third side of the triangle, b:

$$\frac{a}{\sin A} = \frac{b}{\sin B}$$

$$\frac{14.3}{\sin 33°} = \frac{b}{\sin 126.02°}$$

$$b = \frac{(14.3)(\sin 126.02°)}{\sin 33°}$$

$$\approx 21.24$$

We can now complete the data chart and show all the parts of this triangle:

Sides	Angles
$a = 14.3$	$A = 33°$
$b = 21.24$	$B = 126.02°$
$c = 9.4$	$C = 20.98°$

© Cengage Learning 2013

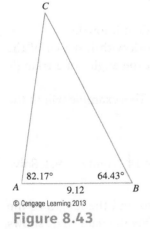

© Cengage Learning 2013

Figure 8.43

The last part of Example 8.21 was somewhat like the situation in Case 2. You knew two of the angles. Once you found the size of the third angle, you were ready to continue solving the problems.

EXAMPLE 8.22

Solve the triangle ABC, if $A = 82.17°$, $B = 64.43°$, and $c = 9.12$.

SOLUTION A sketch of the triangle using the given information is in Figure 8.43. The beginning data chart is

Sides	Angles
$a = $ ___	$A = 82.17°$
$b = $ ___	$B = 64.43°$
$c = 9.12$	$C = $ ___

© Cengage Learning 2013

This is a triangle that satisfies Case 2. (It is an AAS triangle.) Since we know that $A + B + C = 180°$ and are given that $A + B = 82.17° + 64.43° = 146.60°$, we know that $C = 180° - 146.60° = 33.40°$.

We can now use the Sine Law to find either a or b. We will first find a:

$$\frac{a}{\sin A} = \frac{c}{\sin C}$$

$$\frac{a}{\sin 82.17°} = \frac{9.12}{\sin 33.40°}$$

$$a = \frac{(9.12)(\sin 82.17°)}{\sin 33.40°}$$

$$\approx 16.41$$

Now we use the Sine Law to find b:

$$\frac{b}{\sin B} = \frac{c}{\sin C}$$

$$\frac{b}{\sin 64.43°} = \frac{9.12}{\sin 33.40°}$$

$$b = \frac{(9.12)(\sin 64.43°)}{\sin 33.40°}$$

$$\approx 14.94$$

The completed data chart is

Sides	Angles
$a = 16.41$	$A = 82.17°$
$b = 14.94$	$B = 64.43°$
$c = 9.12$	$C = 33.40°$

© Cengage Learning 2013

It is possible to find 0, 1, or 2 correct solutions to the triangle if the given information includes two sides and one angle. When this ambiguous case occurs, carefully consider the practical application of the solution. We will now examine two situations that produce ambiguous results.

EXAMPLE 8.23

Solve $\triangle ABC$, if $a = 20$, $b = 24$, and $A = 55.4°$.

SOLUTION As usual, we begin with the data chart showing the given and unknown measurements.

Sides	Angles
$a = 20$	$A = 55.4°$
$b = 24$	$B = \underline{\hspace{1cm}}$
$c = \underline{\hspace{1cm}}$	$C = \underline{\hspace{1cm}}$

© Cengage Learning 2013

EXAMPLE 8.23 (Cont.)

We will now find B.

$$\frac{a}{\sin A} = \frac{b}{\sin B}$$

$$\frac{20}{\sin 55.4°} = \frac{24}{\sin B}$$

$$\sin B = \frac{24(\sin 55.4°)}{20}$$

$$\approx 0.9877636$$

$$B = \sin^{-1}(0.9877636)$$

So, either $B = 81.03°$ or $B = 98.97°$. Remember, the sine is positive in both the first and second quadrants. Whenever you use the Sine Law and get an equation of the form $B = \sin^{-1}n$ or $\sin B = n$, where $0 < n < 1$, then there are two possible values for B.

Will both of these answers satisfy the given parts of the triangle? Let's call the two answers for angle B, B_1 and B_2. If $B_1 = 81.03°$, and since $A = 55.4°$, then $C_1 = 180° - 81.03° - 55.4° = 43.57°$. If $B_2 = 98.97°$, then $C_2 = 180° - 98.97° - 55.4° = 25.63°$.

We will now use these angles to find the length of side c. If $C_1 = 43.57°$, then

$$\frac{a}{\sin A} = \frac{c_1}{\sin C_1}$$

$$\frac{20}{\sin 55.4°} = \frac{c_1}{\sin 43.57°}$$

$$c_1 = \frac{20(\sin 43.57°)}{\sin 55.4°}$$

$$= 16.75$$

If we use $C_2 = 25.63°$, then we get

$$\frac{a}{\sin A} = \frac{c_2}{\sin C_2}$$

$$\frac{20}{\sin 55.4°} = \frac{c_2}{\sin 25.63°}$$

$$c_2 = \frac{20(\sin 25.63°)}{\sin 55.4°}$$

$$= 10.51$$

The data chart is now complete and written as two data charts.

Sides	Angles	Sides	Angles
$a = 20$	$A = 55.4°$	$a = 20$	$A = 55.4°$
$b = 24$	$B_1 = 81.03°$	$b = 24$	$B_2 = 98.97°$
$c_1 = 16.75$	$C_1 = 43.57°$	$c_2 = 10.51$	$C_2 = 25.63°$

© Cengage Learning 2013   © Cengage Learning 2013

The triangles formed with these two solutions are shown in Figure 8.44. Both are correct.

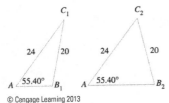

© Cengage Learning 2013

Figure 8.44

The other problem that can develop with the ambiguous case is that there may be no solution. Consider the situation in Example 8.24.

EXAMPLE 8.24

Solve for triangle ABC, when $a = 20$, $b = 27$, and $A = 70°$.

SOLUTION The beginning data chart is:

Aides	Angles
$a = 20$	$A = 70°$
$b = 27$	$B = $ ___
$c = $ ___	$C = $ ___

© Cengage Learning 2013

By the Sine Law $\dfrac{a}{\sin A} = \dfrac{b}{\sin B}$, so

$$\frac{20}{\sin 70°} = \frac{27}{\sin B}$$

$$\sin B = \frac{27(\sin 70°)}{20}$$

$$= 1.27$$

The sine of an angle is never larger than 1. This triangle is not possible. Perhaps if you look at Figure 8.45 you can get a better idea why this is not a legitimate triangle.

C

$70°$

A B

© Cengage Learning 2013

Figure 8.45

As with all trigonometry, there are many applications of the Law of Sines in technical areas. The problem of the technician is to recognize when the application requires trigonometry and then to select the appropriate method to solve it. The next example and the problems in the exercise set will help you make the correct selection.

 APPLICATION **AUTOMOTIVE**

EXAMPLE 8.25

The crankshaft $\overline{CA}$ of an engine is 5 cm long and the connecting rod $\overline{AB}$ is 21 cm long. Find the size of $\angle ACB$ when the size of $\angle ABC$ is 5°.

SOLUTION A sketch of this crankshaft is in Figure 8.46. This problem falls into the SSA case. We know the lengths of two sides, AC and AB, and of the angle opposite one of them, $\angle B$. Since $AC = b$ and $AB = c$, we can use the Sine Law with

$$\frac{b}{\sin B} = \frac{c}{\sin C}$$

$$\frac{5}{\sin 5°} = \frac{21}{\sin C}$$

A 21 cm

5 cm   5°

C B

© Cengage Learning 2013

Figure 8.46

EXAMPLE 8.25 (Cont.)

$$\sin C = \frac{21 \sin 5°}{5} = 0.3660541$$

$$C = 21.47° \quad \text{or} \quad 158.53°$$

There are two possible solutions. By looking at Figure 8.46, you can see that both are acceptable.

EXERCISE SET 8.4

In Exercises 1–20, solve each triangle with the given parts. Check for the ambiguous cases.

1. $A = 19.4°$, $B = 85.3°$, $c = 22.1$
2. $a = 12.4$, $B = 62.4°$, $C = 43.9°$
3. $a = 14.2$, $b = 15.3$, $B = 97°$
4. $A = 27.42°$, $a = 27.3$, $b = 35.49$
5. $A = 86.32°$, $a = 19.19$, $c = 18.42$
6. $B = 75.46°$, $b = 19.4$, $C = 44.95°$
7. $B = 39.4°$, $b = 19.4$, $c = 35.2$
8. $A = 84.3°$, $b = 9.7$, $C = 12.7°$
9. $A = 45°$, $a = 16.3$, $b = 19.4$
10. $a = 10.4$, $c = 5.2$, $C = 30°$

11. $a = 42.3$, $B = 14.3°$, $C = 16.9°$
12. $A = 105.4°$, $B = 68.2°$, $c = 4.91$
13. $b = 19.4$, $c = 12.5$, $C = 35.6°$
14. $a = 121.4$, $A = 19.7°$, $c = 63.4$
15. $a = 19.7$, $b = 8.5$, $B = 78.4°$
16. $b = 9.12$, $B = 1.3$ rad, $C = 0.67$ rad
17. $b = 8.5$, $c = 19.7$, $C = 1.37$ rad
18. $b = 19.7$, $c = 36.4$, $C = 0.45$ rad
19. $A = 0.47$ rad, $b = 195.4$, $C = 1.32$ rad
20. $a = 29.34$, $A = 1.23$ rad, $C = 1.67$ rad

Solve Exercises 21–30.

21. **Civil engineering** Two high-tension wires are to be strung across a river. There are two towers, A and B, on one side of the river. These two towers are 360 m apart. A third tower, C, is on the other side of the river. If $\angle ABC$ is 67.4° and $\angle BAC$ is 49.3°, what are the distances between towers A and C and towers B and C?

22. **Civil engineering** A tunnel is to be dug between points A and B on opposite sides of a hill. A point C is chosen 250 m from A and 275 m from B. If $\angle BAC$ measures 43.62°, find the length of the tunnel.

23. **Navigation** A plane leaves airport A with a heading of 313°. Several minutes later the plane is spotted from airport B at a heading of 27°. Airport B is due west of airport A and the two airports are 37 mi apart. How far had the airplane flown?

24. **Civil engineering** From a point on the top of one end of a football stadium, the angle of depression to the 40-yard marker is 10.45°. The angle of depression to the 50-yard marker is 11.36°. How high is that end of the stadium above the playing field?

25. **Civil engineering** Two technicians release a balloon containing a radio-controlled camera. In order for the camera's photographs to cover enough territory, they plan to start the camera when the balloon reaches a certain height. The technicians are 400 m apart. One technician triggers the balloon when the angle of elevation at that spot is 47°. At that instant, the angle of elevation for the other technician is 67°. If the balloon is directly above the line connecting the two technicians, what is its height?

26. *Automotive technology* The angles between the three holes in a seat bracket are shown in Figure 8.47. If $AB = 15.6$ cm, determine AC and BC.

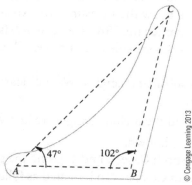

Figure 8.47

27. *Civil engineering* A 225.0-ft antenna mast stands on the edge of the roof of a building. A $6'0''$-tall observer on the ground at some point away from the building determines that the angles of elevation to the top and bottom of the mast are 67.4° and 57.8°, respectively. How high is the building? (The observer's eyes are $5'7''$ above the ground.)

28. *Machine technology* Holes are to be drilled in a metal plate at five equally spaced locations around a circle with a radius of 6.25 in. Find the distance between two adjacent holes.

29. *Machine technology* Holes are to be drilled in a metal plate at 12 equally spaced locations around a circle with a radius of 16.40 cm. Find the distance between two adjacent holes.

30. *Civil engineering* A guy wire to the top of a pole makes a 63.75° angle with level ground.

At a point 8.2 m farther from the pole than the guy wire, the angle of elevation to the top of the pole is 42.5°. How long is the guy wire?

31. *Industrial design* Figure 8.48 is a drawing of three holes in a tooling plate. Determine the length of $\overline{AC}$.

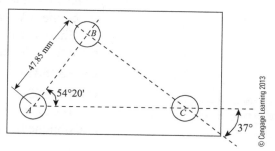

Figure 8.48

32. *Machine design* The side idler at C is used to maintain belt tightness in the bale drive shown in Figure 8.49. If $AC = 45.72$ cm, the distance from the center of the side idler to $\overline{AB}$ is 25.40 cm, and the size of $\angle A$ is twice the size of $\angle B$, find the lengths of $\overline{AB}$ and $\overline{BC}$.

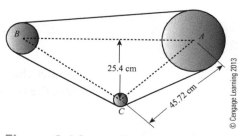

Figure 8.49

▶ [IN YOUR WORDS]

33. Without looking in the text, write the Sine Law and describe how to use it.

34. Describe how you can tell when to use the Sine Law.

35. When using the Sine Law you have to be careful of the ambiguous case.

   (a) Explain what is meant by the ambiguous case.

(b) How do you know that you might be working a problem that involves the ambiguous case?

(c) What should you do if you are working a problem that may include the ambiguous case?

8.5 OBLIQUE TRIANGLES: LAW OF COSINES

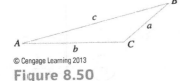

© Cengage Learning 2013

Figure 8.50

In Section 8.4, we learned the Law of Sines and when to use it. We were able to use the Sine Law in two cases. In Case 1, we knew the measures for two sides and the angle opposite one of them. This we named the SSA case. Case 2 existed when we knew the measures of two angles and one side of a triangle. This we called the AAS case.

There are two other cases that lead to solvable triangles. We will learn to solve the following two cases in this section:

Case 3 (SAS)   The measure of two sides and the included angle are known.

Case 4 (SSS)   The measure of three sides is known.

The Law of Cosines is used to help solve both Cases 3 and 4. Using the general oblique triangle in Figure 8.50, the Law of Cosines can be stated as follows.

THE LAW OF COSINES

If $\triangle ABC$ is a triangle with sides of lengths a, b, and c, and opposite angles A, B, C, then by the Law of Cosines or Cosine Law:

$$a^2 = b^2 + c^2 - 2bc \cos A$$

$$b^2 = a^2 + c^2 - 2ac \cos B$$

$$\text{or} \quad c^2 = a^2 + b^2 - 2ab \cos C$$

Notice that there are three versions of the Cosine Law. Each version simply restates the law so that different parts of the triangle are used.

HINT In the Cosine Law, the side on the left-hand side of the equation has the same letter as the angle on the right-hand side of the equation.

EXAMPLE 8.26

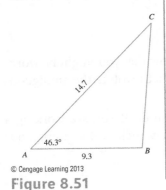

© Cengage Learning 2013

Figure 8.51

If $b = 14.7$, $c = 9.3$, and $A = 46.3°$, solve the triangle.

SOLUTION   A sketch of the triangle using the given information is in Figure 8.51. The data chart is

Sides	Angles
$a =$ ___	$A = 46.3°$
$b = 14.7$	$B =$ ___
$c = 9.3$	$C =$ ___

© Cengage Learning 2013

This is Case 3 or the SAS type of problem. Since we know the size of angle A, we first use the Law of Cosines to find the length of side a.

$$a^2 = b^2 + c^2 - 2bc \cos A$$
$$= (14.7)^2 + (9.3)^2 - 2(14.7)(9.3) \cos 46.3°$$
$$= 216.09 + 86.49 - 273.42(0.6908824)$$
$$= 216.09 + 86.49 - 188.90107$$
$$= 113.67893$$

So, $a = 10.662032$ or $a \approx 10.7$.

At this point, you have a choice as to which method to use to solve the remainder of the problem. You know the size of one angle so you could use the Sine Law. We will use an alternate version of the Cosine Law, which takes advantage of the fact that you know the lengths of all three sides. This alternate version of the Cosine Law is used for the SSS type of problem. It will be the next example, after we state the alternate version of the Cosine Law.

THE LAW OF COSINES (ALTERNATE VERSION)

If $\triangle ABC$ is a triangle with sides of lengths a, b, and c, and opposite angles A, B, C, then by the **Law of Cosines**:

$$\cos A = \frac{b^2 + c^2 - a^2}{2bc}$$
$$\cos B = \frac{a^2 + c^2 - b^2}{2ac}$$
$$\text{or } \cos C = \frac{a^2 + b^2 - c^2}{2ab}$$

You may notice that the alternate version of the Law of Cosines is just the original versions solved for $\cos A$, $\cos B$, and $\cos C$, respectively.

EXAMPLE 8.27

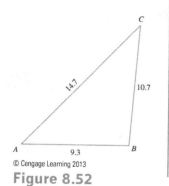

© Cengage Learning 2013

Figure 8.52

If $a = 10.7$, $b = 14.7$, and $c = 9.3$, find the sizes of the three angles.

SOLUTION A sketch of the triangle using the given information is in Figure 8.52. We will use the Cosine Law to find the size of angle B:

$$b^2 = a^2 + c^2 - 2ac \cos B$$
$$\cos B = \frac{(10.7)^2 + (9.3)^2 - (14.7)^2}{2(10.7)(9.3)}$$
$$\cos B = \frac{114.49 + 86.49 - 216.09}{199.02} \approx -0.07592201793$$
$$B = 94.354201 \approx 94.4°$$

EXAMPLE 8.27 (Cont.)   Since this is a continuation of Example 8.26, we know that $A = 46.3°$, so $C = 180° - 46.3° - 94.4° = 39.3°$. The completed data chart is

Sides	Angles
$a = 10.7$	$A = 46.3°$
$b = 14.7$	$B = 94.4°$
$c = 9.3$	$C = 39.3°$

© Cengage Learning 2013

APPLICATION ELECTRONICS

EXAMPLE 8.28

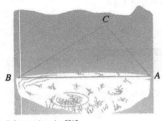

© Cengage Learning 2013

Figure 8.53

An electric transmission line is planned to go directly over a swamp. The power line will be supported by towers at points A and B in Figure 8.53. A surveyor measures the distance from B to C as 573 m, the distance from A to C as 347 m, and $\angle BCA$ as 106.63°. What is the distance from tower A to tower B?

SOLUTION $BC = a = 573$ m; $AC = b = 347$ m; $\angle BCA = \angle C = 106.63°$. This is an SAS type of problem. We want to find $AB = c$. Using the Cosine Law, we have

$$c^2 = a^2 + b^2 - 2ab \cos C$$
$$= (573)^2 + (347)^2 - 2(573)(347) \cos 106.63°$$
$$= 562\,544.93$$
$$c \approx 750$$

The distance between the towers will be about 750 m.

AREA OF TRIANGLES

Earlier, in Section 3.2, we saw that the area of a triangle is $A = \frac{1}{2}bh$, where b is the length of the base and h is the length of the altitude to that base.

There are situations in which you will need to compute the area of a triangle when you do not know the values of a base and a height. For example, in Figure 8.54, suppose you don't know h, but you do know the values of a, c, and angle B. You can use trigonometry to compute the height h as $h = a \sin B$. Therefore, we have the following formula for the area of a triangle if you know the lengths of two sides and the angle formed by those two sides.

© Cengage Learning 2013

Figure 8.54

AREA OF A TRIANGLE

$$A = \frac{1}{2}ac \sin B$$

Since the angles can be labeled in any order we also have the corresponding formulas:

$$A = \frac{1}{2}bc \sin A$$

$$A = \frac{1}{2}ab \sin C$$

The formula you use depends on which parts of the triangle are known.

EXAMPLE 8.29

If $\angle A = 37°$, $b = 1.2$ m, and $c = 2.5$ m, what is the area of $\triangle ABC$?

SOLUTION The area of the triangle is given by the formula:

$$A = \frac{1}{2}bc \sin A$$

$$= 0.5 \times 1.2 \times 2.5 \times \sin 37°$$

$$\approx 0.90$$

The answer should contain only two significant figures, and so the area of this triangle is about 0.90 m².

APPLICATION ARCHITECTURE

EXAMPLE 8.30

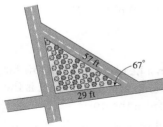

© Cengage Learning 2013
Figure 8.55

A landscape architect wants to plant flowers in a triangular section between two roads. The architect obtained the measures shown in Figure 8.55. **(a)** What is the area of the triangular region? **(b)** If each flower will eventually require a circle with a 4″ radius, how many flowers can be planted in this region?

SOLUTIONS

(a) Since we have the lengths, in feet, of two sides of the triangle and the size of the angle between these two sides, we can use the formula $A = \frac{1}{2}ac \sin B$ with $a = 29$, $c = 57$, and $B = 67°$. Thus,

$$A = \frac{1}{2}ac \sin B$$

$$\approx 760.797$$

The area is about 760.80 ft².

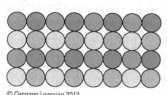

© Cengage Learning 2013
Figure 8.56a

(b) If each flower will need a circle with a 4″ $= \frac{1}{3}′$ radius, then each flower will need $\pi\left(\frac{1}{3}\right)^2 \approx 0.35$ ft². The number of flowers is determined by 760.80 ÷ 0.35 = 2173.71. You can plant 2174 flowers in this triangular region.

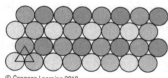

© Cengage Learning 2013
Figure 8.56b

Actually, the answer to Example 8.30(b) is too large. No matter how you arrange the flowers, there will have to be some unused space. One arrangement has all the flowers in rows and columns, as in Figure 8.56a. Another design puts three flowers at the vertices of an equilateral triangle as shown in the lower left-hand corner of Figure 8.56b. Which one will result in the most flowers for the triangular section in Example 8.30? We will leave that for you to answer in Exercise 40 of Exercise Set 8.5.

EXERCISE SET 8.5

In Exercises 1–20, solve each triangle with the given parts. The angles in Exercises 1–10 are in degrees and those in Exercises 11–20 are in radians.

1. $a = 9.3$, $b = 16.3$, $C = 42.3°$
2. $A = 16.25°$, $b = 29.43$, $c = 36.52$
3. $a = 47.85$, $B = 113.7°$, $c = 32.79$
4. $a = 19.52$, $b = 63.42$, $c = 56.53$
5. $a = 29.43$, $b = 16.37$, $c = 38.62$
6. $A = 121.37°$, $b = 112.37$, $c = 93.42$
7. $a = 63.92$, $B = 92.44°$, $c = 78.41$
8. $a = 19.53$, $b = 7.66$, $C = 32.56°$
9. $a = 4.527$, $b = 6.239$, $c = 8.635$
10. $A = 7.53°$, $b = 37.645$, $c = 42.635$

11. $a = 8.5$, $b = 15.8$, $C = 0.82$ rad
12. $A = 0.31$ rad, $b = 15.8$, $c = 38.47$
13. $a = 52.65$, $B = 1.98$ rad, $c = 35.8$
14. $a = 43.5$, $b = 63.4$, $c = 37.3$
15. $a = 36.27$, $b = 24.55$, $c = 44.26$
16. $A = 2.41$ rad, $b = 153.21$, $c = 87.49$
17. $a = 54.8$, $B = 1.625$ rad, $c = 38.33$
18. $a = 7.621$, $b = 3.429$, $C = 0.183$ rad
19. $a = 2.317$, $b = 1.713$, $c = 1.525$
20. $A = 0.09$ rad, $b = 40.75$, $c = 50.25$

In Exercises 21–24, find the area of each triangle.

21. $a = 3.7$ in., $b = 4.8$ in., $C = 39.2°$
22. $a = 9.72$ cm, $b = 3.84$ cm, $C = 117.5°$
23. $b = 34.7$ m, $c = 29.6$ m, $A = 87.5°$
24. $a = 12.875$ ft, $b = 15.250$ ft, $C = 17.2°$

Solve Exercises 25–36.

25. **Space technology** A tracking antenna is aimed 34.7° above the horizon. The distance from the antenna to a spacecraft is 12 325 km. If the radius of the earth is 6335 km, how high is the spacecraft above the surface of the earth? (See Figure 8.57) (Hint: Find the length of *BD*.)

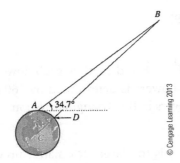

Figure 8.57

26. **Navigation** A ship leaves port at noon and travels due north at 21 km/h. At 3 p.m., the ship

changes direction to a heading of 37°. How far from the port is the ship at 7 p.m.? What is the bearing of the ship from the port?

27. **Construction** A hill makes an angle of 12.37° with the horizontal. A 75-ft antenna is erected on the top of the hill. A guy wire is to be strung from the top of the antenna to a point on the hill that is 40 ft from the base of the antenna. How long is the guy wire?

28. **Physics** Two forces are acting on an object. The magnitude of one force is 35 lb and the magnitude of the second force is 50 lb. If the angle between the two forces is 32.15°, what is the magnitude of the resultant force?

29. **Physics** Figure 8.58 shows two forces represented by vector $\overrightarrow{AB}$ and $\overrightarrow{BC}$. If $AB = 12$ N, $BC = 23$ N, and $\angle ABC = 121.27°$, find the magnitude of **R** and the size of θ.

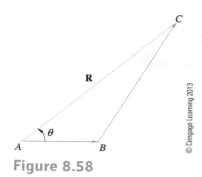

Figure 8.58

30. **Physics** Two forces of 15.5 and 36.4 lb are acting on an object. The resultant force is 30.1 lb. What is the size of the angle between the original two forces?

31. **Electronics** An inductive reactance, X_L, of 56 kΩ occurs in a circuit that has a resistance, R, of 38 kΩ. Power losses cause X_L to be 74° out of phase with R as shown in Figure 8.59. What is the impedance, Z, of the circuit?

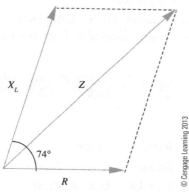

Figure 8.59

32. **Civil engineering** Find the length represented by x in the metal truss shown in Figure 8.60.

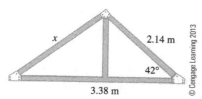

Figure 8.60

33. **Civil engineering** Figure 8.61 shows the drawing of a tower that is going to be erected vertically on sloping ground that is inclined 12.7° with the horizontal. Several cables will attach to a point 225 ft above the ground and be

fastened to the ground. Two of the cables are shown in the figure. The downhill cable will be fastened at a point 75 ft from the base of the tower and the uphill cable will be located 40 ft from the base. What is the length of each cable?

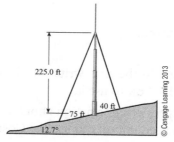

Figure 8.61

34. **Industrial design** Figure 8.62 is a drawing of three holes in a tooling plate. Determine the length of $\overline{BC}$.

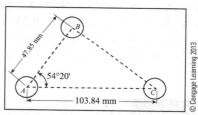

Figure 8.62

35. **Land management** A highway cuts a corner from a section of land, leaving the triangular piece shown in Figure 8.63. Determine the area in acres of the triangular lot. (1 acre = 43,560 ft²)

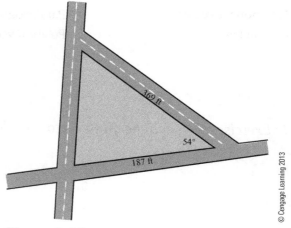

Figure 8.63

36. **Transportation engineering** Figure 8.64 shows a portion of a hill that must be removed in order to build a new highway. Determine the volume of the material that has to be removed.

Figure 8.64
© Cengage Learning 2013

 [IN YOUR WORDS]

37. Without looking in the text, write the Cosine Law and describe how to use it.

38. Describe the types of information about a triangle that you need in order to use the Cosine Law.

39. Explain how you decide whether to use the Sine Law or the Cosine Law.

40. The discussion following Example 8.30 showed two possible arrangements for placing flowers in the triangular section of Figure 8.55. Determine how many flowers can be planted in this section using each of the arrangements in

Figures 8.56a and 8.56b. Decide if there might be a third arrangement that would result in more flowers.

(a) Write a description that explains how you arrived at each answer.

(b) Describe any other arrangements that you tried and the number of flowers that could be planted using each arrangement.

(c) Which arrangement results in the most flowers being planted?

(d) How many flowers can be planted using the arrangement you selected in Exercise 40(c)?

CHAPTER 8 REVIEW

IMPORTANT TERMS AND CONCEPTS

Adding vectors
   By adding components
   By the parallelogram
   method
Component vectors
Cosine Law

Direction of a vector
Initial point
Magnitude of a vector
Oblique triangle
Parallelogram method
Position vector

Resultant vector
Scalar
Sine Law (Law of Sines)
   Ambiguous case
Terminal point
Vectors

REVIEW EXERCISES

In Exercises 1–4, add the given vectors by drawing the resultant vector.

1.

© Cengage Learning 2013

2.

© Cengage Learning 2013

3.

4.

In Exercises 5–8, find the horizontal and vertical components of the given vectors.

5. Magnitude 35, $\theta = 67°$

6. Magnitude 19.7, $\theta = 237°$

7. Magnitude 23.4, $\theta = 172.4°$

8. Magnitude 14.5, $\theta = 338°$

In Exercises 9 and 10, the horizontal and vertical components are given for a vector. Find each of the resultant vectors.

9. $A_x = 16, A_y = -8$

10. $B_x = -27, B_y = 32$

In Exercises 11–14, find the components of the indicated vectors.

11. $A = 38, \theta_A = 15°$

12. $B = 43.5, \theta_B = 127°$

13. $C = 19.4, \theta_C = 1.25$

14. $D = 62.7, \theta_D = 5.37$

In Exercises 15–18, add the given vectors by using the trigonometric functions and the Pythagorean theorem.

15. $A = 19, \theta_A = 32°, B = 32, \theta_B = 14°$

16. $C = 24, \theta_C = 57°, D = 35, \theta_D = 312°$

17. $E = 52.6, \theta_E = 2.53, F = 41.7, \theta_F = 3.92$

18. $G = 43.7, \theta_G = 4.73, H = 14.5, \theta_H = 4.42$

Solve each of the triangles in Exercises 19–26.

19. $a = 14, b = 32, c = 27$

20. $a = 43, b = 52, B = 86.4°$

21. $b = 87.4, B = 19.57°, c = 65.3$

22. $A = 121.3°, b = 42.5, c = 63.7$

23. $a = 127.35, A = 0.12, b = 132.6$

24. $b = 84.3, c = 95.4, C = 0.85$

25. $a = 67.9, b = 54.2, C = 2.21$

26. $a = 53.1, b = 63.2, c = 74.3$

Solve Exercises 27–32.

27. Physics Two tow trucks are attempting to right an overturned vehicle. One truck is exerting a force of 1650 kg. Its tow chain makes an angle of 68° with the axis of the vehicle. The other truck is exerting a force of 1325 kg. Its chain makes an angle of 76° with the axis of the vehicle. What is the magnitude and direction of the resultant force vector? (See Figure 8.65)

28. Civil engineering A highway engineer has to decide whether to go over or to cut through

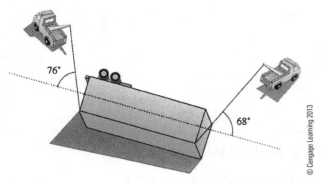

Figure 8.65

a hill. The top of the hill makes an angle of 72.4° with the sides. One side of the hill is 2,342 ft and the other side is 3,621 ft. It will cost 2.3 times as much per foot to cut through the hill and take the alternate route in Figure 8.66. How long is the alternate route? Which route is less expensive?

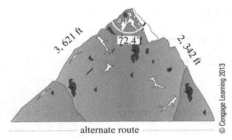

Figure 8.66

29. **Physics** A block is resting on a ramp that makes an angle of 31.7° with the horizontal. The block weighs 126.5 lb. Find the components of the block's weight that are parallel and perpendicular to the road. (See Figure 8.67)

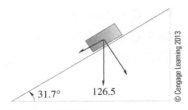

Figure 8.67

30. **Electronics** Find the total impedance Z and the phase angle of a series ac circuit when $X_C = 72\ \Omega$, $X_L = 52\ \Omega$, and $R = 35\ \Omega$.

31. **Civil engineering** A wire is to be strung across a valley. The wire will run from Tower A to Tower B. A surveyor is able to set up a position at a point C on the same side of the valley as Tower A, as shown in Figure 8.68. The distance from A to C is 73 m and $\angle BAC = 123.4°$ and $\angle ACB = 42.1°$. What is the distance from Tower A to Tower B?

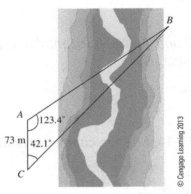

Figure 8.68

32. **Surveying** A surveyor needs to determine the distance across a swamp. From a point C in Figure 8.69, she locates a point B on one side of the swamp. The distance from B to C is 1235 m. Point A is directly across the swamp from B. The distance from A to C is 962 m and $\angle BCA$ is 52.57°. How far is it across the swamp from A to B?

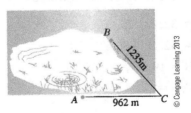

Figure 8.69

CHAPTER 8   TEST

1. Determine the horizontal and vertical components of a vector **V** of magnitude 47 and direction $\theta = 117°$.

2. If $A_x = 12.91$ and $A_y = -14.36$, determine the magnitude and direction of vector **A**.

3. Add the given vectors by using the trigonometric functions and the Pythagorean theorem: $A = 25$, $\theta_A = 64°$, $B = 40$, $\theta_B = 112°$.

4. Use the Sine Law to determine the length of side b in $\triangle ABC$, if $a = 9.42$, $\angle A = 35.6°$, and $\angle B = 67.5°$.

5. Use the Cosine Law to determine the length of side a of $\triangle ABC$, if $b = 4.95$, $c = 6.24$, and $\angle A = 113.4°$.

6. Solve $\triangle ABC$, if $A = 24°$, $b = 36.5$, and $C = 97°$.

7. Two walls meet at an angle of 97° to form the sides of a triangular corner cupboard. If the sides of the cupboard along each wall measure 30 and 36 in., what is the length of the front of the cupboard?

4.3   RECTANGULAR COORDINATES

In Chapter 1 we graphed some points on a number line. In this section we will expand our idea of graphing to a plane.

Why is a graph so important? A graph gives us a picture of an equation. By looking at a graph, we can often get a better idea of what we can expect an equation to do. The graphs will also help us find solutions to some of our problems.

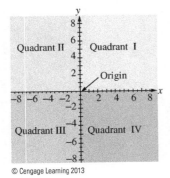

Figure 4.4

In Section 1.1 we learned that we could represent the numbers by points on a line. To get a graph in a plane, we need two number lines. The two number lines are usually drawn perpendicular to each other and intersect at the number zero as shown in Figure 4.4. The point of intersection is called the *origin*. If one of the lines is horizontal, then the other is vertical. The horizontal number line is called the *x*-axis and the vertical number line the *y*-axis. This is called the **rectangular coordinate system** or the **Cartesian coordinate system** in honor of the man who invented it, René Descartes.

On the *x*-axis, positive numbers are to the right of the origin and negative numbers to the left. On the *y*-axis, positive numbers are above the origin and negative values are below it. The two axes divide the plane into four regions called **quadrants**, with the first quadrant in the upper right section of the plane and the others numbered in a counterclockwise rotation around the origin. (See Figure 4.4.)

Suppose that *P* is a point in the plane. The coordinates of *P* can be determined by drawing a perpendicular line segment from *P* to the *x*-axis. If this perpendicular segment meets the *x*-axis at the value *a*, then the *x*-coordinate of the point *P* is *a*. Now draw a perpendicular segment from *P* to the *y*-axis. It meets the *y*-axis at *b*, so the *y*-coordinate of *P* is *b*. The coordinates of *P* are the ordered pair (a, b).

 NOTE The *x*-coordinate is always listed first. The order in which the coordinates are written is very important. In most cases, the point (a, b) is different than the point (b, a). (See Figure 4.5.)

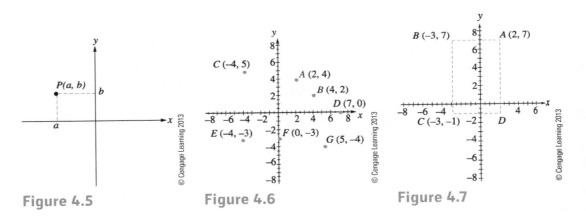

Figure 4.5   **Figure 4.6**   **Figure 4.7**

EXAMPLE 4.37   The positions of $A(2, 4)$, $B(4, 2)$, $C(-4, 5)$, $D(7, 0)$, $E(-4, -3)$, $F(0, -3)$, and $G(5, -4)$ are shown in Figure 4.6. Note that $A(2, 4)$ and $B(4, 2)$ are different points as are $C(-4, 5)$ and $G(5, -4)$.

EXAMPLE 4.38 $A(2, 7)$, $B(-3, 7)$, and $C(-3, -1)$ are three vertices of a rectangle as shown in Figure 4.7. What are the coordinates of the fourth vertex, *D*?

SOLUTION If we plot points *A*, *B*, and *C*, we can see that the missing vertex *D* will have the same *x*-coordinate as *A*, 2, and the same *y*-coordinate as *C*, −1. So, *D* has the coordinates $(2, -1)$.

EXAMPLE 4.39

Some ordered pairs for the equation $y = 2x + 7$ are $(-2,3), (-1,5), (0,7),$ $(\frac{1}{2},8), (1, 9),$ and $(2, 11)$. Plot these ordered pairs on a rectangular coordinate system.

SOLUTION The ordered pairs are plotted on the graph in Figure 4.8.

APPLICATION CONSTRUCTION

EXAMPLE 4.40

The following table shows the results of a series of drillings used to determine the depth of the bedrock at a building site. These drillings were taken along a straight line down the middle of the lot, from the front to the back, where the building will be placed. In the table, x is the distance from the front of the parking lot and y is the corresponding depth. Both x and y are given in feet.

x	0	20	40	60	80	100	120	140	160
y	33	35	40	45	42	38	46	40	48

© Cengage Learning 2013

Plot these ordered pairs on a rectangular coordinate system. Connect the points in order to get an estimate of the profile of the bedrock.

SOLUTION The ordered pairs are plotted on the graph in Figure 4.9. The points have been connected in order. Note that this graph is "upside down." That is, the top of the dirt is along the x-axis, while the bedrock, which is below ground, is above the x-axis.

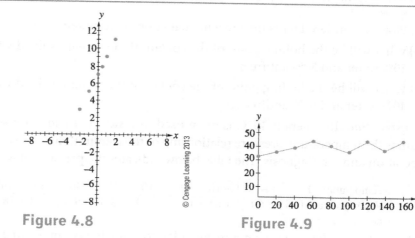

Figure 4.8

Figure 4.9

EXERCISE SET 4.3

In Exercises 1–10, plot the points on a rectangular coordinate system.

1. $(4, 5)$

2. $(1, 7)$

3. $(7, 1)$

4. $(-2, 4)$

5. $(-3, -5)$

6. $(6, -1)$

7. $(0, 0)$

8. $(-\frac{5}{2}, 3)$

9. $(2, -\frac{3}{2})$

10. $(4.5, -1.5)$

Solve Exercises 11–28.

11. If $A(2, 5)$, $B(-1, 5)$, and $C(2, -4)$ are three vertices of a rectangle, what are the coordinates of the fourth vertex?

12. The points $(-3, 6)$, $(-2, 1)$, $(-1, -2)$, $(0, -3)$, $(1, -2)$, $(2, 1)$, and $(3, 6)$ are some ordered pairs of the equation $y = x^2 - 3$. Plot these ordered pairs on the same rectangular coordinate system.

13. Plot the ordered pairs $(-5, 3)$, $(-3, 3)$, $(0, 3)$, $(1, 3)$, $(4, 3)$, and $(6, 3)$. What do all of these points have in common?

14. Plot the ordered pairs $(-2, 6)$, $(-2, 4)$, $(-2, 1)$, $(-2, -1)$, $(-2, -3)$, and $(-2, -4)$. What do all of these points have in common?

15. *Automotive technology* Graph these ordered pairs from the conversion formula 6.9 kPa = 1 psi: $(138, 20)$, $(172.5, 25)$, $(207, 30)$, $(241.5, 35)$, $(276, 40)$, $(345, 50)$, $(414, 60)$. Use a ruler and draw the segment connecting $(138, 20)$ and $(414, 60)$. What seems to happen?

16. Where are all the points whose x-coordinates are 0?

17. Where are all the points whose y-coordinates are -2?

18. Where are all the points whose y-coordinates are 7?

19. Where are all the points whose x-coordinates are -5?

20. Where are all the points whose y-coordinates are 0?

21. Where are all the points (x, y) for which $x > -3$?

22. Where are all the points (x, y) for which $x > 0$ and $y < 0$?

23. Where are all the points (x, y) for which $x > 1$ and $y < -2$?

24. *Automotive technology* If the antifreeze content of the coolant is increased, the boiling point of the coolant is also increased, as shown in the table below.

Percent antifreeze in coolant	0	10	20	30	40	50	60	70	80	90	100
Boiling temperature °F	210	212	214	218	222	228	236	246	258	271	330

© Cengage Learning 2013

(a) Plot these ordered pairs on a rectangular coordinate system.

(b) What will be the boiling point of the coolant if the system is filled with a recommended solution of 50% water and 50% antifreeze?

(c) What will be the boiling point of the coolant if the system is filled with a recommended solution of 40% water and 60% antifreeze?

25. *Construction* Refrigerant 407C is often used in residential and commercial air-conditioners and heat pumps the temperature-pressure relationship of refrigerant R-407C is very important to maintain proper operation and for diagnosis. The table below indicates the pressure of R-407C at various temperatures.

Temperature °F	−20	−10	0	10	20	30	40	50	60	70	80	90
Vapor pressure (psi)	6.6	12.5	19.6	28.0	38.0	49.6	63.1	78.7	96.8	117	140	166

© Cengage Learning 2013

(a) Plot these ordered pairs on a rectangular coordinate system. Connect the ordered pairs in order to help you answer (b) and (c).

(b) One day the early morning temperature was 45°F. What was the vapor pressure, in psi, when the temperature was 45°F?

(c) If a technician connected a pressure gauge to an air-conditioning system filled with R-407C on a 90°F summer day, what pressure, in psi, would the gauge indicate?

26. *Automotive technology* Recent automotive air-conditioning systems use R-134a rather than R-12. This action is based on evidence indicating that R-12 is causing depletion of the earth's protective

ozone layer. As with R-12, the temperature-pressure relationship of refrigerant R-134a is very important to maintain proper operation and diagnosis. The table below indicates the pressure of R-134a at
various temperatures.

Temperature (°C)	−20	−10	0	10	20	30
R-134a pressure (kPa)	31.4	99.4	191.4	312.9	469.5	666.7

© Cengage Learning 2013

(a) Plot these ordered pairs on a rectangular coordinate system. Connect the ordered pairs in order to
help you answer parts (b), (c), and (d).

(b) One day the early morning temperature was 5°C. What was the pressure, in kPa, when the temperature was 5°C?

(c) If a technician connected a pressure gauge to an air-conditioning system filled with R-134a on a 35°C
summer day, what pressure, in kPa, would the gauge indicate?

(d) Suppose a technician connected a pressure gauge to an air-conditioning system filled with R-134a and
got a reading of 500 kPa. What is the temperature in °C?

27. **Machine technology** The following table gives actual recording times and counter values as obtained on
one particular cassette tape deck.

Time (minutes)	1	2	3	4	5	10	15	20	25	30
Counter reading	30	60	88	115	141	262	369	466	556	640

© Cengage Learning 2013

(a) Plot these ordered pairs on a rectangular coordinate system. Connect the ordered pairs in order to
help you answer parts (b) and (c).

(b) What would you expect the counter to read after 12.5 min?

(c) How much time has passed if the counter has a value of 500?

28. **Forestry** The following table gives the girth of a pine tree measured in feet at shoulder height and the
amount of lumber in board feet that was finally obtained.

Girth (ft)	15	18	20	22	25	28	33	35	40	43
Lumber (bd ft)	9	27	42	60	90	126	198	231	324	387

© Cengage Learning 2013

(a) Plot these ordered pairs on a rectangular coordinate system. Connect the ordered pairs in order to
help you answer parts (b) and (c).

(b) How many board feet of lumber would you expect to obtain from a tree with a girth of 30 ft?

(c) What was the girth of a tree that produced 275 board feet of lumber?

[IN YOUR WORDS]

29. Look again at Example 4.40. Describe how you
would have changed the graph, or the way the
data was recorded, so that the graph would
appear rightside up instead of upside down.

30. Gather some data from your field of interest.
Write a problem that will require that data to
be graphed. Then write some questions that
are answered by reading the graph. Put your
answers on the back of the paper. Give your
problem to a classmate and ask him or her to
solve the problem. Rewrite your exercise or
solution to clarify places where your classmate
had difficulty.

1.2 Lines in the Plane

The Slope of a Line

In this section, you will study lines and their equations. The **slope** of a nonvertical line represents the number of units the line rises or falls vertically for each unit of horizontal change from left to right. For instance, consider the two points

$$(x_1, y_1) \quad \text{and} \quad (x_2, y_2)$$

on the line shown in Figure 1.11.

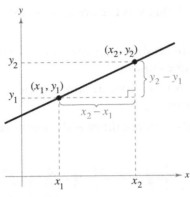

Figure 1.11

As you move from left to right along this line, a change of $(y_2 - y_1)$ units in the vertical direction corresponds to a change of $(x_2 - x_1)$ units in the horizontal direction. That is,

$$y_2 - y_1 = \text{the change in } y$$

and

$$x_2 - x_1 = \text{the change in } x.$$

The slope of the line is given by the ratio of these two changes.

Definition of the Slope of a Line

The **slope** m of the nonvertical line through (x_1, y_1) and (x_2, y_2) is

$$m = \frac{y_2 - y_1}{x_2 - x_1} = \frac{\text{change in } y}{\text{change in } x}$$

where $x_1 \neq x_2$.

When this formula for slope is used, the *order of subtraction* is important. Given two points on a line, you are free to label either one of them as (x_1, y_1) and the other as (x_2, y_2). Once you have done this, however, you must form the numerator and denominator using the same order of subtraction.

$$m = \frac{y_2 - y_1}{x_2 - x_1} \qquad m = \frac{y_1 - y_2}{x_1 - x_2} \qquad m = \frac{y_2 - y_1}{x_1 - x_2}$$

Correct · Correct · Incorrect

Throughout this text, the term *line* always means a *straight* line.

What you should learn
- ▶ Find the slopes of lines.
- ▶ Write linear equations given points on lines and their slopes.
- ▶ Use slope-intercept forms of linear equations to sketch lines.
- ▶ Use slope to identify parallel and perpendicular lines.

Why you should learn it

The slope of a line can be used to solve real-life problems. For instance, in Exercise 97 on page 95, you will use a linear equation to model student enrollment at Penn State University.

| EXAMPLE 1 | Finding the Slope of a Line |

Find the slope of the line passing through each pair of points.

a. $(-2, 0)$ and $(3, 1)$ **b.** $(-1, 2)$ and $(2, 2)$ **c.** $(0, 4)$ and $(1, -1)$

Solution

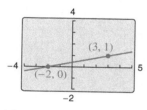

Difference in *y*-values

a. $m = \dfrac{y_2 - y_1}{x_2 - x_1} = \dfrac{1 - 0}{3 - (-2)} = \dfrac{1}{3 + 2} = \dfrac{1}{5}$

Difference in *x*-values

b. $m = \dfrac{2 - 2}{2 - (-1)} = \dfrac{0}{3} = 0$

c. $m = \dfrac{-1 - 4}{1 - 0} = \dfrac{-5}{1} = -5$

> **Explore the Concept**
> Use a graphing utility to compare the slopes of the lines $y = 0.5x$, $y = x$, $y = 2x$, and $y = 4x$. What do you observe about these lines? Compare the slopes of the lines $y = -0.5x$, $y = -x$, $y = -2x$, and $y = -4x$. What do you observe about these lines? (*Hint:* Use a *square setting* to obtain a true geometric perspective.)

The graphs of the three lines are shown in Figure 1.12. Note that the *square setting* gives the correct "steepness" of the lines.

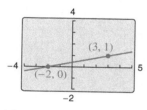
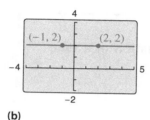
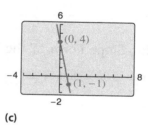

(a)   (b)   (c)

Figure 1.12

✓ *Checkpoint* ◀))) *Audio-video solution in English & Spanish at LarsonPrecalculus.com.*

Find the slope of the line passing through each pair of points.

a. $(-5, -6)$ and $(2, 8)$ **b.** $(4, 2)$ and $(2, 5)$ **c.** $(0, -1)$ and $(3, -1)$ ◼

The definition of slope does not apply to vertical lines. For instance, consider the points $(3, 4)$ and $(3, 1)$ on the vertical line shown in Figure 1.13. Applying the formula for slope, you obtain

$$m = \frac{4 - 1}{3 - 3} = \frac{3}{0}. \qquad \text{Undefined}$$

Because division by zero is undefined, the slope of a vertical line is undefined.

Figure 1.13

From the lines shown in Figures 1.12 and 1.13, you can make the following generalizations about the slope of a line.

> **The Slope of a Line**
>
> **1.** A line with positive slope ($m > 0$) *rises* from left to right.
>
> **2.** A line with negative slope ($m < 0$) *falls* from left to right.
>
> **3.** A line with zero slope ($m = 0$) is *horizontal*.
>
> **4.** A line with undefined slope is *vertical*.

The Point-Slope Form of the Equation of a Line

When you know the slope of a line *and* you also know the coordinates of one point on the line, you can find an equation of the line. For instance, in Figure 1.14, let (x_1, y_1) be a point on the line whose slope is m. When (x, y) is any *other* point on the line, it follows that

$$\frac{y - y_1}{x - x_1} = m.$$

This equation in the variables x and y can be rewritten in the **point-slope form** of the equation of a line.

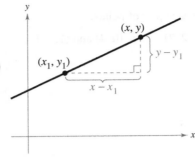

Figure 1.14

> **Point-Slope Form of the Equation of a Line**
>
> The **point-slope form** of the equation of the line that passes through the point (x_1, y_1) and has a slope of m is
>
> $$y - y_1 = m(x - x_1).$$

EXAMPLE 2   The Point-Slope Form of the Equation of a Line

Find an equation of the line that passes through the point

$$(1, -2)$$

and has a slope of 3.

Solution

$y - y_1 = m(x - x_1)$	Point-slope form
$y - (-2) = 3(x - 1)$	Substitute for y_1, m, and x_1.
$y + 2 = 3x - 3$	Simplify.
$y = 3x - 5$	Solve for y.

The line is shown in Figure 1.15.

$y = 3x - 5$

$(1, -2)$

Figure 1.15

✓ **Checkpoint** 🔊)) *Audio-video solution in English & Spanish at LarsonPrecalculus.com.*

Find an equation of the line that passes through the point $(3, -7)$ and has a slope of 2. ∎

The point-slope form can be used to find an equation of a nonvertical line passing through two points

$$(x_1, y_1) \quad \text{and} \quad (x_2, y_2).$$

First, find the slope of the line.

$$m = \frac{y_2 - y_1}{x_2 - x_1}, \quad x_1 \neq x_2$$

Then use the point-slope form to obtain the equation

$$y - y_1 = \frac{y_2 - y_1}{x_2 - x_1}(x - x_1).$$

This is sometimes called the **two-point form** of the equation of a line.

Remark

When you find an equation of the line that passes through two given points, you need to substitute the coordinates of only one of the points into the point-slope form. It does not matter which point you choose because both points will yield the same result.

EXAMPLE 3   A Linear Model for Profits Prediction

In 2011, Tyson Foods had sales of $32.266 billion, and in 2012, sales were $33.278 billion. Write a linear equation giving the sales y in terms of the year x. Then use the equation to predict the sales for 2013.   (Source: Tyson Foods, Inc.)

Solution

Let $x = 0$ represent 2000. In Figure 1.16, let (11, 32.266) and (12, 33.278) be two points on the line representing the sales. The slope of this line is

$$m = \frac{33.278 - 32.266}{12 - 11} = 1.012.$$

Next, use the point-slope form to find the equation of the line.

$$y - 32.266 = 1.012(x - 11)$$
$$y = 1.012x + 21.134$$

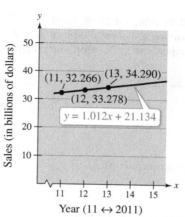

Now, using this equation, you can predict the 2013 sales ($x = 13$) to be

Figure 1.16

$$y = 1.012(13) + 21.134 = 13.156 + 21.134 = \$34.290 \text{ billion.}$$

(In this case, the prediction is quite good—the actual sales in 2013 were $34.374 billion.)

✓ **Checkpoint** ◆))) *Audio-video solution in English & Spanish at LarsonPrecalculus.com.*

In 2012, Apple had sales of $156.508 billion, and in 2013, sales were $170.910 billion. Write a linear equation giving the sales y in terms of the year x. Then use the equation to predict the sales for 2014.   (Source: Apple, Inc.)

Library of Parent Functions: Linear Function

In the next section, you will be introduced to the precise meaning of the term *function*. The simplest type of function is the *parent linear function*

$$f(x) = x.$$

As its name implies, the graph of the parent linear function is a line. The basic characteristics of the parent linear function are summarized below and on the inside cover of this text. (Note that some of the terms below will be defined later in the text.)

Graph of $f(x) = x$
Domain: $(-\infty, \infty)$
Range: $(-\infty, \infty)$
Intercept: $(0, 0)$
Increasing

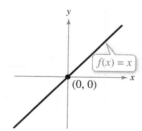

The function $f(x) = x$ is also referred to as the *identity function*. Later in this text, you will learn that the graph of the linear function $f(x) = mx + b$ is a line with slope m and y-intercept $(0, b)$. When $m = 0$, $f(x) = b$ is called a *constant function* and its graph is a horizontal line.

Sketching Graphs of Lines

Many problems in coordinate geometry can be classified in two categories.

1. Given a graph (or parts of it), find its equation.

2. Given an equation, sketch its graph.

For lines, the first problem can be solved by using the point-slope form. This formula, however, is not particularly useful for solving the second type of problem. The form that is better suited to graphing linear equations is the **slope-intercept form** of the equation of a line, $y = mx + b$.

Slope-Intercept Form of the Equation of a Line

The graph of the equation

$$y = mx + b$$

is a line whose slope is m and whose y-intercept is $(0, b)$.

EXAMPLE 4   Using the Slope-Intercept Form

See LarsonPrecalculus.com for an interactive version of this type of example.

Determine the slope and y-intercept of each linear equation. Then describe its graph.

a. $x + y = 2$ **b.** $y = 2$

Algebraic Solution

a. Begin by writing the equation in slope-intercept form.

$$x + y = 2 \qquad \text{Write original equation.}$$
$$y = 2 - x \qquad \text{Subtract } x \text{ from each side.}$$
$$y = -x + 2 \qquad \text{Write in slope-intercept form.}$$

From the slope-intercept form of the equation, the slope is -1 and the y-intercept is

$$(0, 2).$$

Because the slope is negative, you know that the graph of the equation is a line that falls one unit for every unit it moves to the right.

b. By writing the equation $y = 2$ in slope-intercept form

$$y = (0)x + 2$$

you can see that the slope is 0 and the y-intercept is

$$(0, 2).$$

A zero slope implies that the line is horizontal.

Graphical Solution

a.

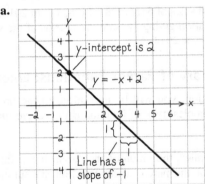

b.

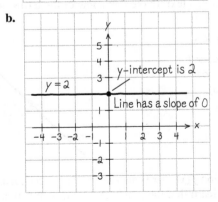

✓ *Checkpoint* 🔊))) *Audio-video solution in English & Spanish at LarsonPrecalculus.com.*

Determine the slope and y-intercept of $x - 2y = 4$. Then describe its graph.   ▪

From the slope-intercept form of the equation of a line, you can see that a horizontal line ($m = 0$) has an equation of the form $y = b$. This is consistent with the fact that each point on a horizontal line through $(0, b)$ has a y-coordinate of b. Similarly, each point on a vertical line through $(a, 0)$ has an x-coordinate of a. So, a vertical line has an equation of the form $x = a$. This equation cannot be written in slope-intercept form because the slope of a vertical line is undefined. However, every line has an equation that can be written in the **general form**

$$Ax + By + C = 0 \qquad \text{General form of the equation of a line}$$

where A and B are not *both* zero.

Summary of Equations of Lines

1. General form: $Ax + By + C = 0$
2. Vertical line: $x = a$
3. Horizontal line: $y = b$
4. Slope-intercept form: $y = mx + b$
5. Point-slope form: $y - y_1 = m(x - x_1)$

EXAMPLE 5   Different Viewing Windows

When a graphing utility is used to graph a line, it is important to realize that the line may not visually appear to have the slope indicated by its equation. This occurs because of the viewing window used for the graph. For instance, Figure 1.17 shows graphs of $y = 2x + 1$ produced on a graphing utility using three different viewing windows. Notice that the slopes in Figures 1.17(a) and (b) do not visually appear to be equal to 2. When you use a *square setting*, as in Figure 1.17(c), the slope visually appears to be 2.

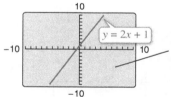

Using a *nonsquare setting*, you do *not* obtain a graph with a true geometric perspective. So, the slope does *not* visually appear to be 2.

(a) *Nonsquare setting*

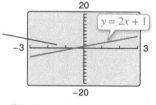

Using a *nonsquare setting*, you do *not* obtain a graph with a true geometric perspective. So, the slope does *not* visually appear to be 2.

(b) *Nonsquare setting*

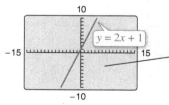

Using a *square setting*, you can obtain a graph with a true geometric perspective. So, the slope visually appears to be 2.

(c) *Square setting*
Figure 1.17

✓ *Checkpoint* ))) *Audio-video solution in English & Spanish at LarsonPrecalculus.com.*

Use a graphing utility to graph $y = 0.5x - 3$ using each viewing window. Describe the difference in the graphs.

a. Xmin = -5, Xmax = 10, Xscl = 1, Ymin = -1, Ymax = 10, Yscl = 1
b. Xmin = -2, Xmax = 10, Xscl = 1, Ymin = -4, Ymax = 1, Yscl = 1
c. Xmin = -5, Xmax = 10, Xscl = 1, Ymin = -7, Ymax = 3, Yscl = 1

Parallel and Perpendicular Lines

The slope of a line is a convenient tool for determining whether two lines are parallel or perpendicular.

Parallel Lines

Two distinct nonvertical lines are **parallel** if and only if their slopes are equal. That is, $m_1 = m_2$.

Explore the Concept

Graph the lines $y_1 = \frac{1}{2}x + 1$ and $y_2 = -2x + 1$ in the same viewing window. What do you observe?

Graph the lines $y_1 = 2x + 1$, $y_2 = 2x$, and $y_3 = 2x - 1$ in the same viewing window. What do you observe?

EXAMPLE 6   **Equations of Parallel Lines**

Find the slope-intercept form of the equation of the line that passes through the point $(2, -1)$ and is parallel to the line $2x - 3y = 5$.

Solution

Begin by writing the equation of the line in slope-intercept form.

$$2x - 3y = 5 \qquad \text{Write original equation.}$$

$$-2x + 3y = -5 \qquad \text{Multiply by } -1.$$

$$3y = 2x - 5 \qquad \text{Add } 2x \text{ to each side.}$$

$$y = \frac{2}{3}x - \frac{5}{3} \qquad \text{Write in slope-intercept form.}$$

Therefore, the given line has a slope of

$$m = \frac{2}{3}.$$

Any line parallel to the given line must also have a slope of $\frac{2}{3}$. So, the line through $(2, -1)$ has the following equation.

$$y - y_1 = m(x - x_1) \qquad \text{Point-slope form}$$

$$y - (-1) = \frac{2}{3}(x - 2) \qquad \text{Substitute for } y_1, m, \text{ and } x_1.$$

$$y + 1 = \frac{2}{3}x - \frac{4}{3} \qquad \text{Simplify.}$$

$$y = \frac{2}{3}x - \frac{7}{3} \qquad \text{Write in slope-intercept form.}$$

Notice the similarity between the slope-intercept form of the original equation and the slope-intercept form of the parallel equation. The graphs of both equations are shown in Figure 1.18.

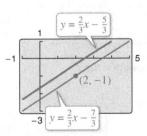

Figure 1.18

✓ **Checkpoint**  *Audio-video solution in English & Spanish at LarsonPrecalculus.com.*

Find the slope-intercept form of the equation of the line that passes through the point $(-4, 1)$ and is parallel to the line $5x - 3y = 8$. ■

Perpendicular Lines

Two nonvertical lines are **perpendicular** if and only if their slopes are negative reciprocals of each other. That is,

$$m_1 = -\frac{1}{m_2}.$$

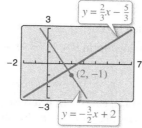

EXAMPLE 7   Equations of Perpendicular Lines

Find the slope-intercept form of the equation of the line that passes through the point $(2, -1)$ and is perpendicular to the line $2x - 3y = 5$.

Solution

From Example 6, you know that the equation can be written in the slope-intercept form $y = \frac{2}{3}x - \frac{5}{3}$. You can see that the line has a slope of $\frac{2}{3}$. So, any line perpendicular to this line must have a slope of $-\frac{3}{2}$ (because $-\frac{3}{2}$ is the negative reciprocal of $\frac{2}{3}$). So, the line through the point $(2, -1)$ has the following equation.

$y - (-1) = -\frac{3}{2}(x - 2)$ Write in point-slope form.

$y + 1 = -\frac{3}{2}x + 3$ Simplify.

$y = -\frac{3}{2}x + 2$ Write in slope-intercept form.

The graphs of both equations are shown in the figure.

✓ **Checkpoint** 🔊))) *Audio-video solution in English & Spanish at LarsonPrecalculus.com.*

Find the slope-intercept form of the equation of the line that passes through the point $(-4, 1)$ and is perpendicular to the line $5x - 3y = 8$.

EXAMPLE 8   Graphs of Perpendicular Lines

Use a graphing utility to graph the lines $y = x + 1$ and $y = -x + 3$ in the same viewing window. The lines are perpendicular (they have slopes of $m_1 = 1$ and $m_2 = -1$). Do they appear to be perpendicular on the display?

Solution

When the viewing window is nonsquare, as in Figure 1.19, the two lines will not appear perpendicular. When, however, the viewing window is square, as in Figure 1.20, the lines will appear perpendicular.

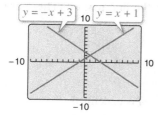

Figure 1.19

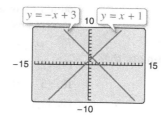

Figure 1.20

✓ **Checkpoint** 🔊))) *Audio-video solution in English & Spanish at LarsonPrecalculus.com.*

Identify any relationships that exist among the lines $y = 2x$, $y = -2x$, and $y = \frac{1}{2}x$. Then use a graphing utility to graph the three equations in the same viewing window. Adjust the viewing window so that each slope appears visually correct. Use the slopes of the lines to verify your results.

What's Wrong?

You use a graphing utility to graph $y_1 = 1.5x$ and $y_2 = -1.5x + 5$, as shown in the figure. You use the graph to conclude that the lines are perpendicular. What's wrong?

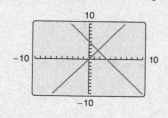

1.2 Exercises

See *CalcChat.com* for tutorial help and worked-out solutions to odd-numbered exercises.
For instructions on how to use a graphing utility, see Appendix A.

Vocabulary and Concept Check

1. Match each equation with its form.

(a) $Ax + By + C = 0$ (i)   vertical line
(b) $x = a$ (ii) slope-intercept form
(c) $y = b$ (iii) general form
(d) $y = mx + b$ (iv) point-slope form
(e) $y - y_1 = m(x - x_1)$ (v)   horizontal line

In Exercises 2 and 3, fill in the blank.

2. For a line, the ratio of the change in y to the change in x is called the _____ of the line.

3. Two lines are _____ if and only if their slopes are equal.

4. What is the relationship between two lines whose slopes are -3 and $\frac{1}{3}$?

5. What is the slope of a line that is perpendicular to the line represented by $x = 3$?

6. Give the coordinates of a point on the line whose equation in point-slope form is $y - (-1) = \frac{1}{4}(x - 8)$.

Procedures and Problem Solving

Using Slope   In Exercises 7 and 8, identify the line that has the indicated slope.

7. (a) $m = \frac{2}{3}$ (b) m is undefined.   (c) $m = -2$

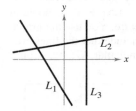

8. (a) $m = 0$ (b) $m = -\frac{3}{4}$ (c) $m = 1$

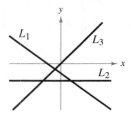

Estimating Slope   In Exercises 9 and 10, estimate the slope of the line.

9.

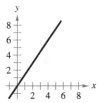

10.

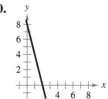

Sketching Lines   In Exercises 11 and 12, sketch the lines through the point with the indicated slopes on the same set of coordinate axes.

	Point		Slopes		
11.	$(2, 3)$	(a) 0	(b) 1	(c) 2	(d) -3
12.	$(-4, 1)$	(a) 4	(b) -2	(c) $\frac{1}{2}$	(d) Undefined

Finding the Slope of a Line   In Exercises 13–16, find the slope of the line passing through the pair of points. Then use a graphing utility to plot the points and use the *draw* feature to graph the line segment connecting the two points. (Use a *square setting*.)

13. $(0, -10), (-4, 0)$ **14.** $(2, 4), (4, -4)$
15. $(-6, -1), (-6, 4)$ **16.** $(4, 9), (6, 12)$

Using Slope   In Exercises 17–24, use the point on the line and the slope of the line to find three additional points through which the line passes. (There are many correct answers.)

	Point	Slope
17.	$(2, 1)$	$m = 0$
18.	$(3, -2)$	$m = 0$
19.	$(1, 5)$	m is undefined.
20.	$(-4, 1)$	m is undefined.
21.	$(0, -9)$	$m = -2$
22.	$(-5, 4)$	$m = 4$
23.	$(7, -2)$	$m = \frac{1}{2}$
24.	$(-1, -6)$	$m = -\frac{1}{3}$

The Point-Slope Form of the Equation of a Line   In Exercises 25–32, find an equation of the line that passes through the given point and has the indicated slope. Sketch the line by hand. Use a graphing utility to verify your sketch, if possible.

25. $(0, -2)$, $m = 3$ **26.** $(-3, 6)$, $m = -3$
27. $(2, -3)$, $m = -\frac{1}{2}$ **28.** $(-2, -5)$, $m = \frac{3}{4}$
29. $(6, -1)$, m is undefined.
30. $(-10, 4)$, m is undefined.
31. $\left(-\frac{1}{2}, \frac{3}{2}\right)$, $m = 0$
32. $(2.3, -8.5)$, $m = 0$

33. Finance   The median player salary for the New York Yankees was \$1.5 million in 2007 and \$1.7 million in 2013. Write a linear equation giving the median salary y in terms of the year x. Then use the equation to predict the median salary in 2020.

34. Finance   The median player salary for the Dallas Cowboys was \$348,000 in 2004 and \$555,000 in 2013. Write a linear equation giving the median salary y in terms of the year x. Then use the equation to predict the median salary in 2019.

Using the Slope-Intercept Form   In Exercises 35–42, determine the slope and y-intercept (if possible) of the linear equation. Then describe its graph.

35. $2x - 3y = 9$ **36.** $3x + 4y = 1$
37. $2x - 5y + 10 = 0$ **38.** $4x - 3y - 9 = 0$
39. $x = -6$ **40.** $y = 12$
41. $3y + 2 = 0$ **42.** $2x - 5 = 0$

Using the Slope-Intercept Form   In Exercises 43–48, (a) find the slope and y-intercept (if possible) of the equation of the line algebraically, and (b) sketch the line by hand. Use a graphing utility to verify your answers to parts (a) and (b).

43. $5x - y + 3 = 0$ **44.** $2x + 3y - 9 = 0$
45. $5x - 2 = 0$ **46.** $3x + 7 = 0$
47. $3y + 5 = 0$ **48.** $-11 - 4y = 0$

Finding the Slope-Intercept Form   In Exercises 49 and 50, find the slope-intercept form of the equation of the line shown.

49.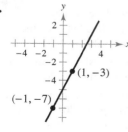

50.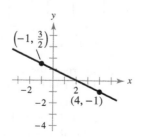

Finding the Slope-Intercept Form   In Exercises 51–60, write an equation of the line that passes through the points. Use the slope-intercept form (if possible). If not possible, explain why and use the general form. Use a graphing utility to graph the line (if possible).

51. $(5, -1), (-5, 5)$ **52.** $(4, 3), (-4, -4)$
53. $(-8, 1), (-8, 7)$ **54.** $(-1, 6), (5, 6)$
55. $\left(2, \frac{1}{2}\right), \left(\frac{1}{2}, \frac{5}{4}\right)$ **56.** $\left(1, 1\right), \left(6, -\frac{2}{3}\right)$
57. $\left(-\frac{1}{10}, -\frac{3}{5}\right), \left(\frac{9}{10}, -\frac{9}{5}\right)$ **58.** $\left(\frac{3}{4}, \frac{3}{2}\right), \left(-\frac{4}{3}, \frac{7}{4}\right)$
59. $(1, 0.6), (-2, -0.6)$ **60.** $(-8, 0.6), (2, -2.4)$

Different Viewing Windows   In Exercises 61 and 62, use a graphing utility to graph the equation using each viewing window. Describe the differences in the graphs.

61. $y = 0.25x - 2$

Xmin = -1	Xmin = -5	Xmin = -5
Xmax = 9	Xmax = 10	Xmax = 10
Xscl = 1	Xscl = 1	Xscl = 1
Ymin = -5	Ymin = -3	Ymin = -5
Ymax = 4	Ymax = 4	Ymax = 5
Yscl = 1	Yscl = 1	Yscl = 1

62. $y = -8x + 5$

Xmin = -5	Xmin = -5	Xmin = -5
Xmax = 5	Xmax = 10	Xmax = 13
Xscl = 1	Xscl = 1	Xscl = 1
Ymin = -10	Ymin = -80	Ymin = -2
Ymax = 10	Ymax = 80	Ymax = 10
Yscl = 1	Yscl = 20	Yscl = 1

Parallel and Perpendicular Lines   In Exercises 63–66, determine whether the lines L_1 and L_2 passing through the pairs of points are parallel, perpendicular, or neither.

63. L_1: $(0, -1), (5, 9)$ **64.** L_1: $(-2, -1), (1, 5)$
     L_2: $(0, 3), (4, 1)$ L_2: $(1, 3), (5, -5)$
65. L_1: $(3, 6), (-6, 0)$ **66.** L_1: $(4, 8), (-4, 2)$
     L_2: $(0, -1), \left(5, \frac{7}{3}\right)$ L_2: $(3, -5), \left(-1, \frac{1}{3}\right)$

Equations of Parallel and Perpendicular Lines   In Exercises 67–76, write the slope-intercept forms of the equations of the lines through the given point (a) parallel to the given line and (b) perpendicular to the given line.

67. $(2, 1)$, $4x - 2y = 3$ **68.** $(-3, 2)$, $x + y = 7$
69. $\left(-\frac{2}{3}, \frac{7}{8}\right)$, $3x + 4y = 7$ **70.** $\left(\frac{2}{5}, -1\right)$, $3x - 2y = 6$
71. $(-3.9, -1.4)$, $6x + 5y = 9$
72. $(-1.2, 2.4)$, $5x + 4y = 1$
73. $(3, -2)$, $x - 4 = 0$ **74.** $(3, -1)$, $y - 2 = 0$
75. $(-5, 1)$, $y + 2 = 0$ **76.** $(-2, 4)$, $x + 5 = 0$

Equations of Parallel Lines **In Exercises 77 and 78, the lines are parallel. Find the slope-intercept form of the equation of line y_2.**

77.
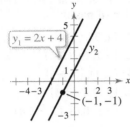

78.
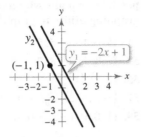

Equations of Perpendicular Lines **In Exercises 79 and 80, the lines are perpendicular. Find the slope-intercept form of the equation of line y_2.**

79.
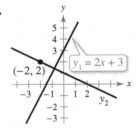

80.
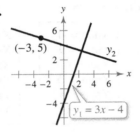

Graphs of Parallel and Perpendicular Lines **In Exercises 81–84, identify any relationships that exist among the lines, and then use a graphing utility to graph the three equations in the same viewing window. Adjust the viewing window so that each slope appears visually correct. Use the slopes of the lines to verify your results.**

81. (a) $y = 4x$ (b) $y = -4x$ (c) $y = \frac{1}{4}x$
82. (a) $y = \frac{2}{3}x$ (b) $y = -\frac{3}{2}x$ (c) $y = \frac{2}{3}x + 2$
83. (a) $y = -\frac{1}{2}x$ (b) $y = -\frac{1}{2}x + 3$ (c) $y = 2x - 4$
84. (a) $y = x - 8$ (b) $y = x + 1$ (c) $y = -x + 3$

85. **Architectural Design** The rise-to-run ratio of the roof of a house determines the steepness of the roof. The rise-to-run ratio of the roof in the figure is 3 to 4. Determine the maximum height in the attic of the house if the house is 32 feet wide.

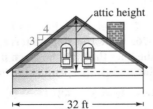

86. **Highway Engineering** When driving down a mountain road, you notice warning signs indicating that it is a "12% grade." This means that the slope of the road is $-\frac{12}{100}$. Approximate the amount of horizontal change in your position if you note from elevation markers that you have descended 2000 feet vertically.

87. **MODELING DATA**

The graph shows the sales y (in billions of dollars) of the Coca-Cola Company each year x from 2005 through 2012, where $x = 5$ represents 2005. (Source: Coca-Cola Company)

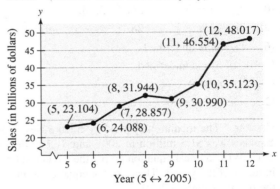

(a) Use the slopes to determine the years in which the sales showed the greatest increase and greatest decrease.

(b) Find the equation of the line between the years 2005 and 2012.

(c) Interpret the meaning of the slope of the line from part (b) in the context of the problem.

(d) Use the equation from part (b) to estimate the sales of the Coca-Cola Company in 2017. Do you think this is an accurate estimate? Explain.

88. **MODELING DATA**

The table shows the profits y (in millions of dollars) for Buffalo Wild Wings for each year x from 2007 through 2013, where $x = 7$ represents 2007. (Source: Buffalo Wild Wings, Inc.)

Year, x	Profits, y
7	19.7
8	24.4
9	30.7
10	38.4
11	50.4
12	57.3
13	71.6

Spreadsheet at LarsonPrecalculus.com

(a) Sketch a graph of the data.

(b) Use the slopes to determine the years in which the profits showed the greatest and least increases.

(c) Find the equation of the line between the years 2007 and 2013.

(d) Interpret the meaning of the slope of the line from part (c) in the context of the problem.

(e) Use the equation from part (c) to estimate the profit for Buffalo Wild Wings in 2017. Do you think this is an accurate estimate? Explain.

Using a Rate of Change to Write an Equation **In Exercises 89–92, you are given the dollar value of a product in 2015 and the rate at which the value of the product is expected to change during the next 5 years. Write a linear equation that gives the dollar value V of the product in terms of the year t. (Let $t = 15$ represent 2015.)**

2015 Value	Rate
89. $2540	$125 increase per year
90. $156	$5.50 increase per year
91. $20,400	$2000 decrease per year
92. $245,000	$5600 decrease per year

93. Accounting A school district purchases a high-volume printer, copier, and scanner for $25,000. After 10 years, the equipment will have to be replaced. Its value at that time is expected to be $2000.

(a) Write a linear equation giving the value V of the equipment for each year t during its 10 years of use.

(b) Use a graphing utility to graph the linear equation representing the depreciation of the equipment, and use the *value* or *trace* feature to complete the table. Verify your answers algebraically by using the equation you found in part (a).

t	0	1	2	3	4	5	6	7	8	9	10
V											

94. Meterology Recall that water freezes at 0°C (32°F) and boils at 100°C (212°F).

(a) Find an equation of the line that shows the relationship between the temperature in degrees Celsius C and degrees Fahrenheit F.

(b) Use the result of part (a) to complete the table.

C	−10°	10°			177°
F	0°		68°	90°	

95. Business A contractor purchases a bulldozer for $36,500. The bulldozer requires an average expenditure of $11.25 per hour for fuel and maintenance, and the operator is paid $19.50 per hour.

(a) Write a linear equation giving the total cost C of operating the bulldozer for t hours. (Include the purchase cost of the bulldozer.)

(b) Assuming that customers are charged $80 per hour of bulldozer use, write an equation for the revenue R derived from t hours of use.

(c) Use the profit formula ($P = R - C$) to write an equation for the profit gained from t hours of use.

(d) Use the result of part (c) to find the break-even point (the number of hours the bulldozer must be used to gain a profit of 0 dollars).

96. Real Estate A real estate office handles an apartment complex with 50 units. When the rent per unit is $580 per month, all 50 units are occupied. However, when the rent is $625 per month, the average number of occupied units drops to 47. Assume that the relationship between the monthly rent p and the demand x is linear.

(a) Write an equation of the line giving the demand x in terms of the rent p.

(b) Use a graphing utility to graph the demand equation and use the *trace* feature to estimate the number of units occupied when the rent is $655. Verify your answer algebraically.

(c) Use the demand equation to predict the number of units occupied when the rent is lowered to $595. Verify your answer graphically.

97. *Why you should learn it* (*p. 84*) In 1994, Penn State University had an enrollment of 73,500 students. By 2013, the enrollment had increased to 98,097. (Source: Penn State Fact Book)

(a) What was the average annual change in enrollment from 1994 to 2013?

(b) Use the average annual change in enrollment to estimate the enrollments in 1996, 2006, and 2011.

(c) Write an equation of a line that represents the given data. What is its slope? Interpret the slope in the context of the problem.

98. Writing Using the results of Exercise 97, write a short paragraph discussing the concepts of *slope* and *average rate of change*.

Conclusions

True or False? **In Exercises 99 and 100, determine whether the statement is true or false. Justify your answer.**

99. The line through $(-8, 2)$ and $(-1, 4)$ and the line through $(0, -4)$ and $(-7, 7)$ are parallel.

100. If the points $(10, -3)$ and $(2, -9)$ lie on the same line, then the point $\left(-12, -\frac{37}{2}\right)$ also lies on that line.

Exploration **In Exercises 101–104, use a graphing utility to graph the equation of the line in the form**

$$\frac{x}{a} + \frac{y}{b} = 1, \quad a \neq 0, b \neq 0.$$

Use the graphs to make a conjecture about what a and b represent. Verify your conjecture.

101. $\dfrac{x}{7} + \dfrac{y}{-3} = 1$ **102.** $\dfrac{x}{-6} + \dfrac{y}{2} = 1$

103. $\dfrac{x}{4} + \dfrac{y}{-\frac{2}{3}} = 1$ **104.** $\dfrac{x}{\frac{1}{2}} + \dfrac{y}{5} = 1$

Using Intercepts   **In Exercises 105–108, use the results of Exercises 101–104 to write an equation of the line that passes through the points.**

105. x-intercept: $(2, 0)$ **106.** x-intercept: $(-5, 0)$
    y-intercept: $(0, 9)$ y-intercept: $(0, -4)$

107. x-intercept: $\left(-\frac{1}{6}, 0\right)$ **108.** x-intercept: $\left(\frac{3}{4}, 0\right)$
    y-intercept: $\left(0, -\frac{2}{3}\right)$ y-intercept: $\left(0, \frac{4}{3}\right)$

Think About It   **In Exercises 109 and 110, determine which equation(s) may be represented by the graphs shown. (There may be more than one correct answer.)**

109. 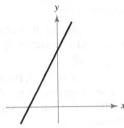   **110.**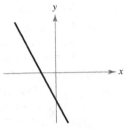

(a) $2x - y = -10$ (a) $2x + y = 5$
(b) $2x + y = 10$ (b) $2x + y = -5$
(c) $x - 2y = 10$ (c) $x - 2y = 5$
(d) $x + 2y = 10$ (d) $x - 2y = -5$

Think About It   **In Exercises 111 and 112, determine which pair of equations may be represented by the graphs shown.**

111. 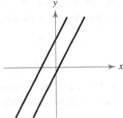   **112.**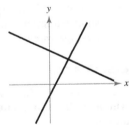

(a) $2x - y = 5$ (a) $2x - y = 2$
    $2x - y = 1$ $x + 2y = 12$
(b) $2x + y = -5$ (b) $x - y = 1$
    $2x + y = 1$ $x + y = 6$
(c) $2x - y = -5$ (c) $2x + y = 2$
    $2x - y = 1$ $x - 2y = 12$
(d) $x - 2y = -5$ (d) $x - 2y = 2$
    $x - 2y = -1$ $x + 2y = 12$

113. **Think About It**   Does every line have both an x-intercept and a y-intercept? Explain.

114. **Think About It**   Can every line be written in slope-intercept form? Explain.

115. **Think About It**   Does every line have an infinite number of lines that are parallel to it? Explain.

116. **HOW DO YOU SEE IT?**   Match the description with its graph. Determine the slope and y-intercept of each graph and interpret their meaning in the context of the problem. [The graphs are labeled (i), (ii), (iii), and (iv).]

(i) 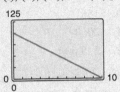   (ii)

(iii) 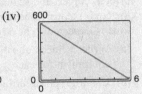   (iv)

(a) You are paying $10 per week to repay a $100 loan.
(b) An employee is paid $13.50 per hour plus $2 for each unit produced per hour.
(c) A sales representative receives $35 per day for food plus $0.50 for each mile traveled.
(d) A tablet computer that was purchased for $600 depreciates $100 per year.

Cumulative Mixed Review

Identifying Polynomials   **In Exercises 117–122, determine whether the expression is a polynomial. If it is, write the polynomial in standard form.**

117. $x + 20$ **118.** $3x - 10x^2 + 1$

119. $4x^2 + x^{-1} - 3$ **120.** $2x^2 - 2x^4 - x^3 + \sqrt{2}$

121. $\dfrac{x^2 + 3x + 4}{x^2 - 9}$ **122.** $\sqrt{x^2 + 7x + 6}$

Factoring Trinomials   **In Exercises 123–126, factor the trinomial.**

123. $x^2 - 6x - 27$ **124.** $x^2 + 11x + 28$

125. $2x^2 + 11x - 40$ **126.** $3x^2 - 16x + 5$

127. **Make a Decision**   To work an extended application analyzing the numbers of bachelor's degrees earned by women in the United States from 2001 through 2012, visit this textbook's website at *LarsonPrecalculus.com*. (Data Source: National Center for Education Statistics)

The *Make a Decision* exercise indicates a multipart exercise using large data sets. Visit this textbook's website at *LarsonPrecalculus.com*.

The Graph of a Quadratic Function

In this and the next section, you will study the graphs of polynomial functions.

Definition of Polynomial Function

Let n be a nonnegative integer and let $a_n, a_{n-1}, \ldots a_2, a_1, a_0$ be real numbers with $a_n \neq 0$. The function given by

$$f(x) = a_n x^n + a_{n-1} x^{n-1} + \cdots + a_2 x^2 + a_1 x + a_0$$

is called a **polynomial function of x with degree n.**

Polynomial functions are classified by degree. For instance, the polynomial function

$$f(x) = a, \quad a \neq 0 \qquad \text{Constant function}$$

has degree 0 and is called a **constant function.** In Chapter 1, you learned that the graph of this type of function is a horizontal line. The polynomial function

$$f(x) = mx + b, \quad m \neq 0 \qquad \text{Linear function}$$

has degree 1 and is called a **linear function.** You learned in Chapter 1 that the graph of $f(x) = mx + b$ is a line whose slope is m and whose y-intercept is $(0, b)$. In this section, you will study second-degree polynomial functions, which are called **quadratic functions.**

Definition of Quadratic Function

Let a, b, and c be real numbers with $a \neq 0$. The function given by

$$f(x) = ax^2 + bx + c \qquad \text{Quadratic function}$$

is called a **quadratic function.**

Often real-life data can be modeled by quadratic functions. For instance, the table at the right shows the height h (in feet) of a projectile fired from a height of 6 feet with an initial velocity of 256 feet per second at any time t (in seconds). A quadratic model for the data in the table is

$$h(t) = -16t^2 + 256t + 6 \quad \text{for} \quad 0 \leq t \leq 16.$$

The graph of a quadratic function is a special type of U-shaped curve called a **parabola.** Parabolas occur in many real-life applications, especially those involving reflective properties, such as satellite dishes or flashlight reflectors. You will study these properties in a later chapter.

All parabolas are symmetric with respect to a line called the **axis of symmetry,** or simply the **axis** of the parabola. The point where the axis intersects the parabola is called the **vertex** of the parabola. These and other basic characteristics of quadratic functions are summarized on the next page.

Time, (in seconds) t	Height, (in feet) h
0	6
2	454
4	774
6	966
8	1030
10	966
12	774
14	454
16	6

What you should learn
- Analyze graphs of quadratic functions.
- Write quadratic functions in standard form and use the results to sketch graphs of functions.
- Find minimum and maximum values of quadratic functions in real-life applications.

Why you should learn it

Quadratic functions can be used to model the design of a room. For instance, Exercise 63 on page 251 shows how the size of an indoor fitness room with a running track can be modeled.

Basic Characteristics of Quadratic Functions

Graph of $f(x) = ax^2, a > 0$
Domain: $(-\infty, \infty)$
Range: $[0, \infty)$
Intercept: $(0, 0)$
Decreasing on $(-\infty, 0)$
Increasing on $(0, \infty)$
Even function
Axis of symmetry: $x = 0$
Relative minimum or vertex: $(0, 0)$

Graph of $f(x) = ax^2, a < 0$
Domain: $(-\infty, \infty)$
Range: $(-\infty, 0]$
Intercept: $(0, 0)$
Increasing on $(-\infty, 0)$
Decreasing on $(0, \infty)$
Even function
Axis of symmetry: $x = 0$
Relative maximum or vertex: $(0, 0)$

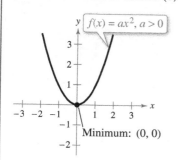

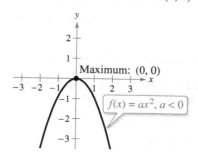

For the general quadratic form $f(x) = ax^2 + bx + c$, when the leading coefficient a is positive, the parabola opens upward; and when the leading coefficient a is negative, the parabola opens downward. Later in this section you will learn ways to find the coordinates of the vertex of a parabola.

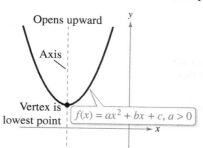

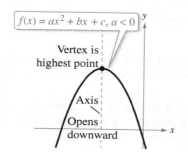

When sketching the graph of $f(x) = ax^2$, it is helpful to use the graph of $y = x^2$ as a reference, as discussed in Section 1.5. There you saw that when $a > 1$, the graph of $y = af(x)$ is a vertical stretch of the graph of $y = f(x)$. When $0 < a < 1$, the graph of $y = af(x)$ is a vertical shrink of the graph of $y = f(x)$. Notice in Figure 3.1 that the coefficient a determines how widely the parabola given by $f(x) = ax^2$ opens. When $|a|$ is small, the parabola opens more widely than when $|a|$ is large.

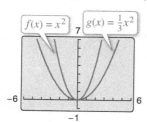

Vertical shrink
Figure 3.1

Vertical stretch

Library of Parent Functions: Quadratic Functions

The *parent quadratic function* is $f(x) = x^2$, also known as the *squaring function*. The basic characteristics of the parent quadratic function are summarized below and on the inside cover of this text.

Graph of $f(x) = x^2$

Domain: $(-\infty, \infty)$
Range: $[0, \infty)$
Intercept: $(0, 0)$
Decreasing on
Increasing on $(0, \infty)$
Even function
Axis of symmetry: $x = 0$
Relative minimum or vertex: $(0, 0)$

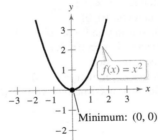

Recall from Section 1.5 that the graphs of $y = f(x \pm c)$, $y = f(x) \pm c$, $y = -f(x)$, and $y = f(-x)$ are rigid transformations of the graph of $y = f(x)$.

$y = f(x \pm c)$ Horizontal shift $y = -f(x)$ Reflection in *x*-axis

$y = f(x) \pm c$ Vertical shift $y = f(-x)$ Reflection in *y*-axis

EXAMPLE 1   Library of Parent Functions: $f(x) = x^2$

See LarsonPrecalculus.com for an interactive version of this type of example.

Sketch the graph of each function by hand and compare it with the graph of $f(x) = x^2$.

a. $g(x) = -x^2 + 1$ **b.** $h(x) = (x + 2)^2 - 3$

Solution

a. With respect to the graph of $f(x) = x^2$, the graph of g is obtained by a *reflection* in the *x*-axis and a vertical shift one unit *upward*, as shown in Figure 3.2. Confirm this with a graphing utility.

b. With respect to the graph of $f(x) = x^2$, the graph of h is obtained by a horizontal shift two units *to the left* and a vertical shift three units *downward*, as shown in Figure 3.3. Confirm this with a graphing utility.

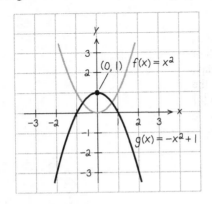

Figure 3.2

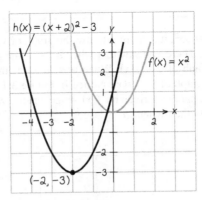

Figure 3.3

✓ *Checkpoint*))) *Audio-video solution in English & Spanish at LarsonPrecalculus.com.*

Sketch the graph of each function by hand and compare it with the graph of $f(x) = x^2$.

a. $g(x) = x^2 - 4$ **b.** $h(x) = (x - 3)^2 + 1$

The Standard Form of a Quadratic Function

The equation in Example 1(b) is written in the **standard form**

$$f(x) = a(x - h)^2 + k.$$

This form is especially convenient for sketching a parabola because it identifies the vertex of the parabola as (h, k).

> **Standard Form of a Quadratic Function**
>
> The quadratic function given by
>
> $$f(x) = a(x - h)^2 + k, \quad a \neq 0$$
>
> is in **standard form.** The graph of f is a parabola whose axis is the vertical line $x = h$ and whose vertex is the point (h, k). When $a > 0$, the parabola opens upward, and when $a < 0$, the parabola opens downward.

EXAMPLE 2   Identifying the Vertex of a Quadratic Function

Describe the graph of

$$f(x) = 2x^2 + 8x + 7$$

and identify the vertex.

Solution

Write the quadratic function in standard form by completing the square. Recall that the first step is to factor out any coefficient of x^2 that is not 1.

$f(x) = 2x^2 + 8x + 7$	Write original function.
$\quad = (2x^2 + 8x) + 7$	Group x-terms.
$\quad = 2(x^2 + 4x) + 7$	Factor 2 out of x-terms.
$\quad = 2(x^2 + 4x + 4 - 4) + 7$	Add and subtract $(4/2)^2 = 4$ within parentheses to complete the square.
$\qquad\qquad\quad (4/2)^2$	
$\quad = 2(x^2 + 4x + 4) - 2(4) + 7$	Regroup terms.
$\quad = 2(x + 2)^2 - 1$	Write in standard form.

From the standard form, you can see that the graph of f is a parabola that opens upward with vertex

$$(-2, -1)$$

as shown in the figure. This corresponds to a left shift of two units and a downward shift of one unit relative to the graph of

$$y = 2x^2.$$

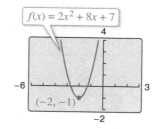

✓ **Checkpoint**  Audio-video solution in English & Spanish at LarsonPrecalculus.com.

Describe the graph of $f(x) = 3x^2 - 6x + 4$ and identify the vertex. ∎

To find the x-intercepts of the graph of $f(x) = ax^2 + bx + c$, solve the equation $ax^2 + bx + c = 0$. When $ax^2 + bx + c$ does not factor, you can use the Quadratic Formula to find the x-intercepts, or a graphing utility to approximate the x-intercepts. Remember, however, that a parabola may not have x-intercepts.

Explore the Concept

Use a graphing utility to graph $y = ax^2$ with $a = -2, -1, -0.5, 0.5, 1,$ and 2. How does changing the value of a affect the graph?

Use a graphing utility to graph $y = (x - h)^2$ with $h = -4, -2, 2,$ and 4. How does changing the value of h affect the graph?

Use a graphing utility to graph $y = x^2 + k$ with $k = -4, -2, 2,$ and 4. How does changing the value of k affect the graph?

EXAMPLE 3 Identifying *x*-Intercepts of a Quadratic Function

Describe the graph of $f(x) = -x^2 + 6x - 8$ and identify any *x*-intercepts.

Solution

$f(x) = -x^2 + 6x - 8$	Write original function.
$= -(x^2 - 6x) - 8$	Factor -1 out of *x*-terms.
$= -(x^2 - 6x + 9 - 9) - 8$	Add and subtract $(-6/2)^2 = 9$ within parentheses.

$$(-6/2)^2$$

$= -(x^2 - 6x + 9) - (-9) - 8$	Regroup terms.
$= -(x - 3)^2 + 1$	Write in standard form.

The graph of *f* is a parabola that opens downward with vertex $(3, 1)$, as shown in Figure 3.4. The *x*-intercepts are determined as follows.

$-(x^2 - 6x + 8) = 0$	Factor out -1.
$-(x - 2)(x - 4) = 0$	Factor.
$x - 2 = 0 \implies x = 2$	Set 1st factor equal to 0.
$x - 4 = 0 \implies x = 4$	Set 2nd factor equal to 0.

So, the *x*-intercepts are $(2, 0)$ and $(4, 0)$, as shown in Figure 3.4.

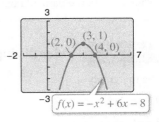

Figure 3.4

✓ **Checkpoint** ◀))) *Audio-video solution in English & Spanish at LarsonPrecalculus.com.*

Describe the graph of $f(x) = x^2 - 4x + 3$ and identify any *x*-intercepts.

EXAMPLE 4 Writing the Equation of a Parabola

Write the standard form of the equation of the parabola whose vertex is $(1, 2)$ and that passes through the point $(3, -6)$.

Solution

Because the vertex of the parabola is $(h, k) = (1, 2)$, the equation has the form

$$f(x) = a(x - 1)^2 + 2.$$
Substitute for *h* and *k* in standard form.

Because the parabola passes through the point $(3, -6)$, it follows that $f(3) = -6$. So, you obtain

$f(x) = a(x - 1)^2 + 2$	Write in standard form.
$-6 = a(3 - 1)^2 + 2$	Substitute -6 for $f(x)$ and 3 for *x*.
$-6 = 4a + 2$	Simplify.
$-8 = 4a$	Subtract 2 from each side.
$-2 = a.$	Divide each side by 4.

The equation in standard form is $f(x) = -2(x - 1)^2 + 2$. You can confirm this answer by graphing *f* with a graphing utility, as shown in Figure 3.5. Use the *zoom* and *trace* features or the *maximum* and *value* features to confirm that its vertex is $(1, 2)$ and that it passes through the point $(3, -6)$.

> **Remark**
>
> In Example 4, there are infinitely many different parabolas that have a vertex at $(1, 2)$. Of these, however, the only one that passes through the point $(3, -6)$ is the one given by
>
> $$f(x) = -2(x - 1)^2 + 2.$$

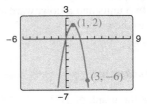

Figure 3.5

✓ **Checkpoint** ◀))) *Audio-video solution in English & Spanish at LarsonPrecalculus.com.*

Write the standard form of the equation of the parabola whose vertex is $(-4, 11)$ and that passes through the point $(-6, 15)$.

Finding Minimum and Maximum Values

Many applications involve finding the maximum or minimum value of a quadratic function. By completing the square of the quadratic function $f(x) = ax^2 + bx + c$, you can rewrite the function in standard form.

$$f(x) = a\left(x + \frac{b}{2a}\right)^2 + \left(c - \frac{b^2}{4a}\right) \qquad \text{Standard form}$$

So, the vertex of the graph of f is $\left(-\dfrac{b}{2a}, f\left(-\dfrac{b}{2a}\right)\right)$, which implies the following.

Minimum and Maximum Values of Quadratic Functions

Consider the function $f(x) = ax^2 + bx + c$ with vertex $\left(-\dfrac{b}{2a}, f\left(-\dfrac{b}{2a}\right)\right)$.

1. If $a > 0$, then f has a *minimum* at $x = -\dfrac{b}{2a}$.

 The minimum value is $f\left(-\dfrac{b}{2a}\right)$.

2. If $a < 0$, then f has a *maximum* at $x = -\dfrac{b}{2a}$.

 The maximum value is $f\left(-\dfrac{b}{2a}\right)$.

EXAMPLE 5   The Maximum Height of a Projectile

The path of a baseball is given by the function $f(x) = -0.0032x^2 + x + 3$, where $f(x)$ is the height of the baseball (in feet) and x is the horizontal distance from home plate (in feet). What is the maximum height reached by the baseball?

Algebraic Solution

For this quadratic function, you have

$$f(x) = ax^2 + bx + c = -0.0032x^2 + x + 3$$

which implies that $a = -0.0032$ and $b = 1$. Because the function has a maximum when $x = -b/(2a)$, you can conclude that the baseball reaches its maximum height when it is x feet from home plate, where x is

$$x = -\frac{b}{2a}$$

$$= -\frac{1}{2(-0.0032)}$$

$$= 156.25 \text{ feet.}$$

At this distance, the maximum height is

$$f(156.25) = -0.0032(156.25)^2 + 156.25 + 3$$

$$= 81.125 \text{ feet.}$$

Graphical Solution

The maximum height is $y \approx 81.125$ feet at $x \approx 156.25$ feet.

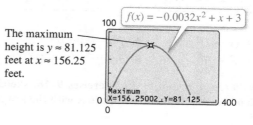

$f(x) = -0.0032x^2 + x + 3$

Maximum
X=156.25002 Y=81.125

✓ **Checkpoint**  *Audio-video solution in English & Spanish at LarsonPrecalculus.com.*

Rework Example 5 when the path of the baseball is given by the function

$$f(x) = -0.007x^2 + x + 4.$$

3.1 **Exercises**

See *CalcChat.com* for tutorial help and worked-out solutions to odd-numbered exercises.
For instructions on how to use a graphing utility, see Appendix A.

Vocabulary and Concept Check

In Exercises 1 and 2, fill in the blanks.

1. A polynomial function with degree n and leading coefficient a_n is a function of the form $f(x) = a_n x^n + a_{n-1} x^{n-1} + \cdots + a_2 x^2 + a_1 x + a_0$, $a_n \neq 0$, where n is a _____ and $a_n, a_{n-1}, \ldots, a_2, a_1, a_0$ are _____ numbers.

2. A _____ function is a second-degree polynomial function, and its graph is called a _____ .

3. Is the quadratic function $f(x) = (x - 2)^2 + 3$ written in standard form? Identify the vertex of the graph of f.

4. Does the graph of the quadratic function $f(x) = -3x^2 + 5x + 2$ have a relative minimum value at its vertex?

Procedures and Problem Solving

Graphs of Quadratic Functions **In Exercises 5–8, match the quadratic function with its graph. [The graphs are labeled (a), (b), (c), and (d).]**

(a)
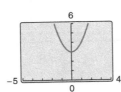

(b)

(c)
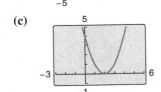

(d)
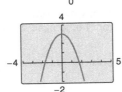

5. $f(x) = (x - 2)^2$
6. $f(x) = 3 - x^2$
7. $f(x) = x^2 + 3$
8. $f(x) = -(x - 4)^2$

Library of Parent Functions **In Exercises 9–16, sketch the graph of the function and compare it with the graph of $y = x^2$.**

9. $y = -x^2$
10. $y = x^2 - 1$
11. $y = (x + 3)^2$
12. $y = -(x + 3)^2 - 1$
13. $y = (x + 1)^2$
14. $y = -x^2 + 2$
15. $y = (x - 3)^2$
16. $y = -(x - 3)^2 + 1$

Identifying the Vertex of a Quadratic Function **In Exercises 17–30, describe the graph of the function and identify the vertex. Use a graphing utility to verify your results.**

17. $f(x) = 20 - x^2$
18. $f(x) = x^2 + 8$
19. $f(x) = \frac{1}{2}x^2 - 5$
20. $f(x) = -6 - \frac{1}{4}x^2$

21. $f(x) = (x + 3)^2 - 4$
22. $f(x) = (x - 7)^2 + 2$
23. $h(x) = x^2 - 2x + 1$
24. $g(x) = x^2 + 16x + 64$
25. $f(x) = x^2 - x + \frac{5}{4}$
26. $f(x) = x^2 + 3x + \frac{1}{4}$
27. $f(x) = -x^2 + 2x + 5$
28. $f(x) = -x^2 - 4x + 1$
29. $h(x) = 4x^2 - 4x + 21$
30. $f(x) = 2x^2 - x + 1$

Identifying x-Intercepts of a Quadratic Function **In Exercises 31–36, describe the graph of the quadratic function. Identify the vertex and x-intercept(s). Use a graphing utility to verify your results.**

31. $g(x) = x^2 + 8x + 11$
32. $f(x) = x^2 + 10x + 14$
33. $f(x) = -(x^2 - 2x - 15)$
34. $f(x) = -(x^2 + 3x - 4)$
35. $f(x) = -2x^2 + 16x - 31$
36. $f(x) = -4x^2 + 24x - 41$

Writing the Equation of a Parabola in Standard Form **In Exercises 37 and 38, write an equation of the parabola in standard form. Use a graphing utility to graph the equation and verify your result.**

37.

38.
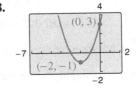

Writing the Equation of a Parabola in Standard Form In Exercises 39–44, write the standard form of the quadratic function that has the indicated vertex and whose graph passes through the given point. Use a graphing utility to verify your result.

39. Vertex: $(-2, 5)$;   Point: $(0, 9)$
40. Vertex: $(4, 1)$;   Point: $(6, -7)$
41. Vertex: $(1, -2)$;   Point: $(-1, 14)$
42. Vertex: $(-4, -1)$;   Point: $(-2, 4)$
43. Vertex: $\left(\frac{1}{2}, 1\right)$;   Point: $\left(-2, -\frac{21}{5}\right)$
44. Vertex: $\left(-\frac{1}{4}, -1\right)$;   Point: $\left(0, -\frac{17}{16}\right)$

Using a Graph to Identify x-Intercepts In Exercises 45–48, determine the x-intercept(s) of the graph visually. Then find the x-intercept(s) algebraically to verify your answer.

45.
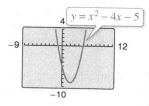
$y = x^2 - 4x - 5$

46.
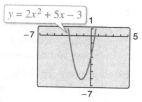
$y = 2x^2 + 5x - 3$

47.
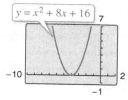
$y = x^2 + 8x + 16$

48.
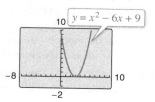
$y = x^2 - 6x + 9$

Graphing to Identify x-Intercepts In Exercises 49–54, use a graphing utility to graph the quadratic function and find the x-intercepts of the graph. Then find the x-intercepts algebraically to verify your answer.

49. $y = x^2 - 4x$
50. $y = -2x^2 + 10x$
51. $y = 2x^2 - 7x - 30$
52. $y = 4x^2 + 25x - 21$
53. $y = -\frac{1}{2}(x^2 - 6x - 7)$
54. $y = \frac{7}{10}(x^2 + 12x - 45)$

Using the x-Intercepts to Write Equations In Exercises 55–58, find two quadratic functions, one that opens upward and one that opens downward, whose graphs have the given x-intercepts. (There are many correct answers.)

55. $(-1, 0), (3, 0)$
56. $(0, 0), (10, 0)$
57. $(-3, 0), \left(-\frac{1}{2}, 0\right)$
58. $\left(-\frac{5}{2}, 0\right), (2, 0)$

Maximizing a Product of Two Numbers In Exercises 59–62, find the two positive real numbers with the given sum whose product is a maximum.

59. The sum is 110.
60. The sum is 66.

61. The sum of the first and twice the second is 24.
62. The sum of the first and three times the second is 42.

63. *Why you should learn it* (p. 244) An indoor physical fitness room consists of a rectangular region with a semicircle on each end. The perimeter of the room is to be a 200-meter single-lane running track.

(a) Draw a diagram that illustrates the problem. Let x and y represent the length and width of the rectangular region, respectively.

(b) Determine the radius of the semicircular ends of the track. Determine the distance, in terms of y, around the inside edge of the two semicircular parts of the track.

(c) Use the result of part (b) to write an equation, in terms of x and y, for the distance traveled in one lap around the track. Solve for y.

(d) Use the result of part (c) to write the area A of the rectangular region as a function of x.

(e) Use a graphing utility to graph the area function from part (d). Use the graph to approximate the dimensions that will produce a rectangle of maximum area.

64. Algebraic-Graphical-Numerical A child-care center has 200 feet of fencing to enclose two adjacent rectangular safe play areas (see figure). Use the following methods to determine the dimensions that will produce a maximum enclosed area.

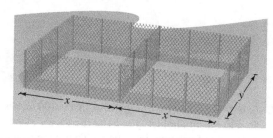

(a) Write the total area A of the play areas as a function of x.

(b) Use the *table* feature of a graphing utility to create a table showing possible values of x and the corresponding total area A of the play areas. Use the table to estimate the dimensions that will produce the maximum enclosed area.

(c) Use the graphing utility to graph the area function. Use the graph to approximate the dimensions that will produce the maximum enclosed area.

(d) Write the area function in standard form to find algebraically the dimensions that will produce the maximum enclosed area.

(e) Compare your results from parts (b), (c), and (d).

65. Height of a Projectile The height y (in feet) of a punted football is approximated by

$$y = -\frac{16}{2025}x^2 + \frac{9}{5}x + \frac{3}{2}$$

where x is the horizontal distance (in feet) from where the football is punted. (See figure.)

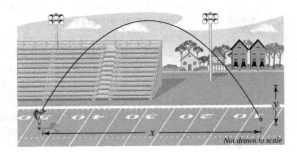

(a) Use a graphing utility to graph the path of the football.

(b) How high is the football when it is punted? (*Hint:* Find y when $x = 0$.)

(c) What is the maximum height of the football?

(d) How far from the punter does the football strike the ground?

66. Physics The path of a diver is approximated by

$$y = -\frac{4}{9}x^2 + \frac{24}{9}x + 12$$

where y is the height (in feet) and x is the horizontal distance (in feet) from the end of the diving board (see figure). What is the maximum height of the diver?

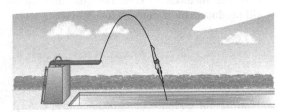

67. Geometry You have a steel wire that is 100 inches long. To make a sign holder, you bend the wire x inches from each end to form two right angles. To use the sign holder, you insert each end 6 inches into the ground. (See figure.)

(a) Write a function for the rectangular area A enclosed by the sign holder in terms of x.

(b) Use the *table* feature of a graphing utility to determine the value of x that maximizes the rectangular area enclosed by the sign holder.

68. Economics The monthly revenue R (in thousands of dollars) from the sales of a digital picture frame is approximated by $R(p) = -10p^2 + 1580p$, where p is the price per unit (in dollars).

(a) Find the monthly revenues for unit prices of $50, $70, and $90.

(b) Find the unit price that will yield a maximum monthly revenue.

(c) What is the maximum monthly revenue?

69. Public Health For selected years from 1955 through 2010, the annual per capita consumption C of cigarettes by Americans (ages 18 and older) can be modeled by

$$C(t) = -1.39t^2 + 36.5t + 3871, \quad 5 \le t \le 60$$

where t is the year, with $t = 5$ corresponding to 1955. (Sources: Centers for Disease Control and Prevention and U.S. Census Bureau)

(a) Use a graphing utility to graph the model.

(b) Use the graph of the model to approximate the year when the maximum annual consumption of cigarettes occurred. Approximate the maximum average annual consumption.

(c) Beginning in 1966, all cigarette packages were required by law to carry a health warning. Do you think the warning had any effect? Explain.

(d) In 2010, the U.S. population (ages 18 and older) was 234,564,000. Of those, about 45,271,000 were smokers. What was the average annual cigarette consumption *per smoker* in 2010? What was the average daily cigarette consumption *per smoker*?

70. Demography The population P of Germany (in thousands) from 2000 through 2013 can be modeled by

$$P(t) = -14.82t^2 + 95.9t + 82{,}276, \quad 0 \le t \le 13$$

where t is the year, with $t = 0$ corresponding to 2000. (Source: U.S. Census Bureau)

(a) According to the model, in what year did Germany have its greatest population? What was the population?

(b) According to the model, what will Germany's population be in the year 2075? Is this result reasonable? Explain.

Conclusions

True or False? In Exercises 71–74, determine whether the statement is true or false. Justify your answer.

71. The function $f(x) = -12x^2 - 1$ has no x-intercepts.

72. The function $f(x) = a(x - 5)^2$ has exactly one x-intercept for any nonzero value of a.

73. The functions $f(x) = 3x^2 + 6x + 7$ and $g(x) = 3x^2 + 6x - 1$ have the same vertex.

74. The graphs of $f(x) = -4x^2 - 10x + 7$ and $g(x) = 12x^2 + 30x + 1$ have the same axis of symmetry.

Library of Parent Functions In Exercises 75 and 76, determine which equation(s) may be represented by the graph shown. (There may be more than one correct answer.)

75. (a) $f(x) = -(x - 4)^2 + 2$
    (b) $f(x) = -(x + 2)^2 + 4$
    (c) $f(x) = -(x + 2)^2 - 4$
    (d) $f(x) = -x^2 - 4x - 8$
    (e) $f(x) = -(x - 2)^2 - 4$
    (f) $f(x) = -x^2 + 4x - 8$

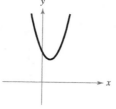

76. (a) $f(x) = (x - 1)^2 + 3$
    (b) $f(x) = (x + 1)^2 + 3$
    (c) $f(x) = (x - 3)^2 + 1$
    (d) $f(x) = x^2 + 2x + 4$
    (e) $f(x) = (x + 3)^2 + 1$
    (f) $f(x) = x^2 + 6x + 10$

Describing Parabolas In Exercises 77–80, let z represent a positive real number. Describe how the family of parabolas represented by the given function compares with the graph of $g(x) = x^2$.

77. $f(x) = (x - z)^2$ 78. $f(x) = x^2 - z$
79. $f(x) = z(x - 3)^2$ 80. $f(x) = zx^2 + 4$

Think About It In Exercises 81–84, find the value of b such that the function has the given maximum or minimum value.

81. $f(x) = -x^2 + bx - 75$; Maximum value: 25
82. $f(x) = -x^2 + bx - 16$; Maximum value: 48
83. $f(x) = x^2 + bx + 26$; Minimum value: 10
84. $f(x) = x^2 + bx - 25$; Minimum value: -50

85. **Proof** Let x and y be two positive real numbers whose sum is S. Show that the maximum product of x and y occurs when x and y are both equal to $S/2$.

86. **Proof** Assume that the function $f(x) = ax^2 + bx + c$, $a \neq 0$, has two real zeros. Show that the x-coordinate of the vertex of the graph is the average of the zeros of f. (*Hint:* Use the Quadratic Formula.)

87. **Writing** The parabola in the figure has an equation of the form $y = ax^2 + bx - 4$. Find the equation of this parabola two different ways, by hand and with technology. Write a paragraph describing the methods you used and comparing the results.

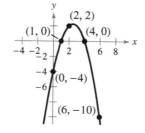

88. **HOW DO YOU SEE IT?** The graph shows a quadratic function of the form $R(t) = at^2 + bt + c$, which represents the yearly revenues for a company, where $R(t)$ is the revenue in year t.

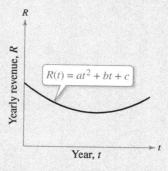

(a) Is the value of a positive, negative, or zero?

(b) Write an expression in terms of a and b that represents the year t when the company had the least revenue.

(c) The company made the same yearly revenues in 2004 and 2014. Estimate the year in which the company had the least revenue.

(d) Assume that the model is still valid today. Are the yearly revenues currently increasing, decreasing, or constant? Explain.

89. **Think About It** The annual profit P (in dollars) of a company is modeled by a function of the form $P = at^2 + bt + c$, where t represents the year. Discuss which of the following models the company might prefer.

(a) a is positive and $t \geq -b/(2a)$.
(b) a is positive and $t \leq -b/(2a)$.
(c) a is negative and $t \geq -b/(2a)$.
(d) a is negative and $t \leq -b/(2a)$.

Cumulative Mixed Review

Finding Points of Intersection In Exercises 90–93, determine algebraically any point(s) of intersection of the graphs of the equations. Verify your results using the *intersect* feature of a graphing utility.

90. $x + y = 8$
      $-\frac{2}{3}x + y = 6$

91. $y = 3x - 10$
      $y = \frac{1}{4}x + 1$

92. $y = 9 - x^2$
      $y = x + 3$

93. $y = x^3 + 2x - 1$
      $y = -2x + 15$

94. **Make a Decision** To work an extended application analyzing the heights of a softball after it has been dropped, visit this textbook's website at *LarsonPrecalculus.com*.

6.2 GRAPHICAL AND ALGEBRAIC METHODS FOR SOLVING TWO LINEAR EQUATIONS IN TWO VARIABLES

In this section, we will begin to look at methods for solving a system of simultaneous linear equations. Simultaneous linear equations are equations containing the same variables, such as

$$2x + y = 5$$
$$4x - y = 1$$

Our task in this section is to determine all the points, or ordered pairs, that these two equations have in common. We will begin by looking at a way to use graphing to help find these common points. Since we are looking for a common point of these two lines, this point will be where the two lines intersect if we graph each line. A graph of these two lines is shown in Figure 6.14.

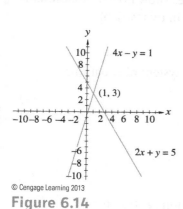

Figure 6.14

As you can see, the lines appear to meet at point (1, 3). A quick check of both equations will show that point (1, 3) is on both lines. To check, substitute $x = 1$ and $y = 3$ in the first equation. We obtain

$$2(1) + 3 = 2 + 3 = 5$$

Substituting $x = 1$ and $y = 3$ in the second equation produces

$$4(1) - 3 = 4 - 3 = 1$$

But, as we saw in Chapter 4, graphical methods are not always accurate ways to determine the roots to an equation. Graphical methods are also not very accurate ways to determine the common solutions of simultaneous equations. What we need are some algebraic methods for solving a system of equations. We will learn two methods in this section. Both methods involve solving for one of the variables by eliminating the other variable. These are called elimination methods.

SUBSTITUTION METHOD

The first elimination method involves elimination by substitution. It is generally called the substitution method.

SUBSTITUTION METHOD FOR SOLVING A SYSTEM OF LINEAR EQUATIONS

To use the substitution method to solve a system of linear equations:

1. Solve one equation for one of the variables.
2. Substitute the solution from Step 1 into the other equation and solve for the remaining variable.
3. Substitute the value from Step 2 into the equation from Step 1 and solve for the other variable.

In the substitution method, we change two equations in two variables into one equation in one variable. The next two examples show how to use the substitution method to solve systems of two equations in two variables.

EXAMPLE 6.16

Use the substitution method to solve the following system of equations.

$$\begin{cases} 2x + y = 5 & (1) \\ 4x - y = 1 & (2) \end{cases}$$

SOLUTION We will solve the first equation for y.

$$y = 5 - 2x \qquad (3)$$

Substitute this solution for y in equation (2). Equation (2) becomes

$$4x - (5 - 2x) = 1$$

Solve this equation for x.

$$4x - 5 + 2x = 1$$
$$6x = 6$$
$$x = 1$$

We then substitute this solution for x in equation (3) and find

$$y = 5 - 2(1)$$
$$y = 3$$

The solution is $(1, 3)$, which was the same answer we got by graphing.

EXAMPLE 6.17

Use the substitution method to solve the system of equations.

$$\begin{cases} -2x + 2y = 5 & (1) \\ x + 6y = 1 & (2) \end{cases}$$

SOLUTION This time we will solve equation (2) for x and get

$$x = 1 - 6y \qquad (3)$$

Substituting this value, $1 - 6y$, for x in equation (1) we get

$$-2(1 - 6y) + 2y = 5$$
$$-2 + 12y + 2y = 5$$
$$-2 + 14y = 5$$
$$14y = 7$$
$$y = \frac{7}{14} = \frac{1}{2}$$

Replacing the y in equation (3) with $\frac{1}{2}$ we get

$$x = 1 - 6\left(\frac{1}{2}\right)$$
$$x = 1 - 3$$
$$x = -2$$

The solution appears to be $\left(-2, \frac{1}{2}\right)$.

To be certain that we have the correct solution, we should substitute $\left(-2, \frac{1}{2}\right)$ into the original equations—equations (1) and (2)—and see if this solution satisfies both of these equations. It is very important that you always check your work by using the *original* equations. If you made any errors, you might not detect them unless you check your work in the original problem.

ADDITION METHOD

The second algebraic method for solving a system of linear equations is normally called the addition method. Technically, its name is the *elimination method by addition and subtraction*.

ADDITION METHOD FOR SOLVING A SYSTEM OF LINEAR EQUATIONS

To use the addition method to solve a system of linear equations:

Add or subtract the two equations in order to eliminate one of the variables.

It is sometimes necessary to multiply the original equations by a constant before it is possible to eliminate one of the variables by adding or subtracting the equations.

The next two examples will show how the addition method is used. These are the same examples that we worked with when using the substitution method.

EXAMPLE 6.18

Use the addition method to solve the following system.

$$\begin{cases} 2x + y = 5 & (1) \\ 4x - y = 1 & (2) \end{cases}$$

SOLUTION Equation (1) has a $(+y)$ term and equation (2) has a $(-y)$ term. If we add equations (1) and (2), the new equation will not have a y term.

$$
\begin{aligned}
2x + y &= 5 \\
4x - y &= 1 \\
\hline
\end{aligned}
$$

$$\text{adding} \quad 6x = 6 \qquad (1) + (2)$$

$$\text{or} \qquad x = 1 \qquad (3)$$

Substituting this value of x into equation (1) we get

$$2(1) + y = 5$$
$$y = 3$$

So, the solution is $x = 1$ and $y = 3$ or the ordered pair $(1, 3)$.

EXAMPLE 6.19

Use the addition method to solve the following system.

$$\begin{cases} -2x + 2y = 5 & (1) \\ x + 6y = 1 & (2) \end{cases}$$

SOLUTION Equations (1) and (2) do not have any terms that are equal so we will have to multiply at least one equation by a constant. If we multiply equation (2) by 2, the x-term will become $2x$, which is the additive inverse of the x term in equation (1). After multiplication, equation (2) becomes

$$2x + 12y = 2 \qquad (3)$$

and adding equations (1) and (3) we get

$$-2x + 2y = 5 \tag{1}$$

$$\underline{2x + 12y = 2} \tag{3}$$

adding $\quad 14y = 7 \tag{1} + (3)$

or $\quad y = \dfrac{1}{2} \tag{4}$

Substituting this value for y into equation (2) we get

$$x + 6\left(\tfrac{1}{2}\right) = 1$$

$$x + 3 = 1$$

$$x = -2$$

Thus, we have found $x = -2, y = \tfrac{1}{2}$, and the solution is $\left(-2, \tfrac{1}{2}\right)$, the same answer we got in Example 6.17.

You may get very strange-looking results when you attempt to solve a system of equations. For example, sometimes all the variables vanish. Consider the next example.

EXAMPLE 6.20

Use the addition method to solve the following system.

$$\begin{cases} 2x + 3y = 6 & (1) \\ 4x + 6y = 30 & (2) \end{cases}$$

SOLUTION If we multiply equation (1) by -2, the terms containing the variable x will be additive inverses of each other. This multiplication makes equation (1) into

$$-4x - 6y = -12 \tag{3}$$

and adding $\quad \underline{4x + 6y = 30} \tag{2}$

$$0 = 18 \tag{(3) + (2)}$$

Now we know that $0 \neq 18$, so something must be wrong. If we check our work, there do not appear to be any errors. Let's graph these equations. The graph in Figure 6.15 indicates the problem. The lines are parallel. They will never intersect, so there is no solution to this system of equations.

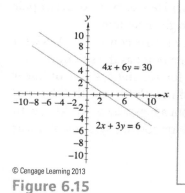

© Cengage Learning 2013

Figure 6.15

When two lines are parallel they will not intersect. Since there is no solution, the equations in the system are said to be **inconsistent**. When you try to solve a system of linear equations that is inconsistent, you will get an untrue equation. In Example 6.20, this equation was $0 = 18$.

In Example 6.21, we examine another kind of system of linear equations in which all the variables vanish.

EXAMPLE 6.21

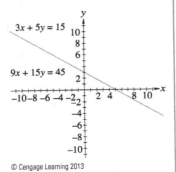

© Cengage Learning 2013

Figure 6.16

Solve the following system of linear equations.

$$\begin{cases} 3x + 5y = 15 & (1) \\ 9x + 15y = 45 & (2) \end{cases}$$

SOLUTION Multiplying equation (1) by -3, we get

$$-9x - 15y = -45 \qquad (3)$$

and adding this to equation (2) we have the following:

$$
\begin{aligned}
-9x - 15y &= -45 & (3) \\
9x + 15y &= \quad\ 45 & (2) \\
\hline
0 &= \quad\ 0 & (3) + (2)
\end{aligned}
$$

It is certainly true that $0 = 0$. But, how will that help us solve this system of equations? Once again, we will turn to graphing to help us solve this system. (See Figure 6.16.) The graphs of these two equations are exactly the same. Thus, there are an unlimited number of solutions to both equations. In fact, any ordered pair that satisfies one of the equations will satisfy the other.

If the graphs of two equations coincide, we say that the equations are **dependent**. In the case of dependent equations, every solution to one equation will be a solution to the other equation. When you try to solve a system of dependent equations, you will get an equality of two constants. In Example 6.21, this was $0 = 0$.

If we solve equation (1) in Example 6.21 for y, we get $y = -\frac{3}{5}x + 3$. (You get the same result if you solve equation (2) for y.) Hence, every ordered pair (a, b) of the form $(a, -\frac{3}{5}a + 3)$ is a solution of the given system.

Most of the systems of equations we will work with are consistent. A system of linear equations is **consistent** if it has exactly one point as the solution.

In this section, we looked at three methods for solving systems of linear equations—the graphical method, the substitution method, and the elimination method. In the next section, we will learn about a new way of working with numbers that will help us find an easier method for solving systems of linear equations.

EXERCISE SET 6.2

In Exercises 1–8, graphically solve each system of equations. Estimate each answer to the nearest tenth if necessary. Check your answers, but remember that your estimate may not check exactly.

1. $\begin{cases} x + y = 6 \\ x - y = 2 \end{cases}$

2. $\begin{cases} x + y = 8 \\ 2x - y = 1 \end{cases}$

3. $\begin{cases} 2x + 3y = 15 \\ 4x - 4y = 10 \end{cases}$

4. $\begin{cases} 3x + 2y = 2 \\ 2x - 6y = -39 \end{cases}$

5. $\begin{cases} 3x + 5y = 32 \\ 10x - 5y = -32 \end{cases}$

6. $\begin{cases} -5x + 11y = 11 \\ 5x + 2y = -11 \end{cases}$

7. $\begin{cases} 5x + 10y = 0 \\ 3x - 4y = 11 \end{cases}$

8. $\begin{cases} 4x + y = -8 \\ 3x + 2y = 0 \end{cases}$

In Exercises 9–20, use the substitution method to solve each system of equations.

9. $\begin{cases} y = 3x - 4 \\ x + y = 8 \end{cases}$

10. $\begin{cases} x = -2y + 12 \\ x + y = 5 \end{cases}$

11. $\begin{cases} y = -2x - 2 \\ 3x + 2y = 0 \end{cases}$

12. $\begin{cases} x = 7 + 2y \\ 3x + 4y = 1 \end{cases}$

13. $\begin{cases} 2x + 5y = 6 \\ x - y = 10 \end{cases}$

14. $\begin{cases} 3x - 2y = 5 \\ -7x + 4y = -7 \end{cases}$

15. $\begin{cases} 2x + 3y = 3 \\ 6x + 4y = 15 \end{cases}$

16. $\begin{cases} 2x + 2y = -3 \\ 4x + 9y = 5 \end{cases}$

17. $\begin{cases} 4.8x - 1.3y = 16.9 \\ -7.2x - 2.8y = -9.2 \end{cases}$

18. $\begin{cases} 2.3x + 1.7y = 8.5 \\ -6.7x + 3.7y = 38.4 \end{cases}$

19. $\begin{cases} 4.2x + 3.7y = 10.79 \\ 6.5x - 0.3y = -15.24 \end{cases}$

20. $\begin{cases} 0.75x + 1.5y = -0.225 \\ 3.13x + 1.74y = 13.073 \end{cases}$

In Exercises 21–30, use the addition method to solve each system of equations.

21. $\begin{cases} x + y = 9 \\ x - y = 5 \end{cases}$

22. $\begin{cases} 2x + 3y = 5 \\ -2x + 5y = 3 \end{cases}$

23. $\begin{cases} -x + 3y = 5 \\ 2x + 7y = 3 \end{cases}$

24. $\begin{cases} 3x - 2y = 8 \\ 5x + y = 9 \end{cases}$

25. $\begin{cases} 3x - 2y = -15 \\ 5x + 6y = 3 \end{cases}$

26. $\begin{cases} 2x - 3y = 11 \\ 6x - 5y = 13 \end{cases}$

27. $\begin{cases} 3x - 5y = 37 \\ 5x - 3y = 27 \end{cases}$

28. $\begin{cases} x + \frac{1}{2}y = 7 \\ 4x - 2y = 5 \end{cases}$

29. $\begin{cases} 6.4x - 1.7y = 66.7 \\ -4.2x + 5.1y = -62.1 \end{cases}$

30. $\begin{cases} 1.6x - 2.9y = -2.645 \\ 2.4x + 1.4y = 11.27 \end{cases}$

In Exercises 31–40, solve each system of equations by either the substitution method or the addition method. Graph each system of equations.

31. $\begin{cases} 2x + 3y = 5 \\ x - 2y = 6 \end{cases}$

32. $\begin{cases} 2x - 3y = -14 \\ 3x + 2y = 44 \end{cases}$

33. $\begin{cases} 8x + 3y = 13 \\ 3x + 2y = 11 \end{cases}$

34. $\begin{cases} 6x + 12y = 7 \\ 8x - 15y = -1 \end{cases}$

35. $\begin{cases} 10x - 9y = 18 \\ 6x + 2y = 1 \end{cases}$

36. $\begin{cases} 4x - 5y = 7 \\ -8x + 10y = -30 \end{cases}$

37. $\begin{cases} x - 9y = 0 \\ \frac{x}{3} = 2y + \frac{1}{3} \end{cases}$

38. $\begin{cases} 5x + 3y = 7 \\ \frac{3}{2}x - \frac{3}{4}y = 9\frac{1}{4} \end{cases}$

39. $\begin{cases} 4.9x + 1.7y = 10.6 \\ 3.6x - 1.2y = 14.4 \end{cases}$

40. $\begin{cases} 3.14x + 4.57y = -7.9 \\ 2.48x + 11.84y = 15.16 \end{cases}$

Solve Exercises 41–48.

41. *Land management* The perimeter of a rectangular field is 36 km. The length of the field is 8 km longer than the width. What are the length and width of the field? (Hint: To find the length and width of this rectangular field, you need to solve this system of linear equations where L represents the length of the field and w the width.)

$$\begin{cases} 2L + 2w = 36 \\ L = w + 8 \end{cases}$$

42. *Land management* The perimeter of a rectangular field is 72 mi. The length of the field is 9 mi longer that the width. What are the length and width of the field?

43. *Land management* The perimeter of a rectangular field is 45 km. The length is 3 times the width. What are the length and width of the field?

44. *Land management* The perimeter of a field in the shape of an isosceles triangle is 96 yd.

365

The length of each of the two equal sides is $1\frac{1}{2}$ times the length of the third side. What are the lengths of the three sides of this field?

45. **Petroleum technology** Two different gasohol mixtures are available. One mixture contains 5% alcohol and the other, 13% alcohol. In order to determine how much of each mixture should be used to get 10 000 L of gasohol containing 8% alcohol, you would solve the following equations:

$$\begin{cases} x+y=10\,000 \\ 0.05x+0.13y=(0.08)(10\,000) \end{cases}$$

where x is the number of liters of 5% gasohol mixture and y is the number of liters of 13% gasohol mixture. Determine the number of liters of each mixture that is needed.

46. **Petroleum technology** Two different gasohol mixtures are available. One mixture contains 4% alcohol and the other, 12% alcohol. How much of each mixture should be used to get 20 000 L of gasohol containing 9% alcohol?

In Exercises 49–51, use the following information.

The current that flows in each branch of a complex circuit can be found by applying **Kirchhoff's rules** to the circuit. The first rule applies to the junction of three or more wires as in Figure 6.18. The second applies to loops (circuits) or closed paths in the circuit.

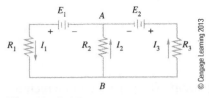

Figure 6.18

Rule 1: (Junction rule) The sum of the currents that flow into a junction is equal to the sum of the currents that flow out of the junction. In Figure 6.18, this means that $I_1 = I_2 + I_3$.

Rule 2: (Circuit rule) The sum of the voltages around any closed loop equals zero. In Figure 6.18, for the left loop this means that $E_1 = I_1R_1 + I_2R_2$ and for the right loop that $E_2 = R_2I_2 - R_3I_3$.

47. **Physics** Two forces are applied to the ends of a beam. The force on one end is 8 kg and the force at the other end is not known. The unknown force is 5 m from the centroid; we do not know the distance of the 8-kg force from the centroid. If an additional force of 4 kg is applied to the 8-kg force, the unknown force must be increased by 3.2 kg for equilibrium to be maintained. Find the unknown mass and distance. (See Figure 6.17.)

© Cengage Learning 2013

Figure 6.17

48. **Automotive technology** A 12-L cooling system is filled with 25% antifreeze. How many liters must be replaced with 100% antifreeze to raise the strength to 45% antifreeze?

49. **Electronics** Find the currents in the three resistors of the circuit shown in Figure 6.18, given that $E_1 = 8$ V, $E_2 = 5$ V, $R_1 = 3$ Ω, $R_2 = 5$ Ω, and $R_3 = 6$ Ω. [Use $E_1 = I_1R_1 + I_2R_2$ and $E_2 = R_2I_2 - R_3(I_1 - I_2)$.]

50. **Electronics** In Figure 6.18, if $E_1 = 10$ V, $E_2 = 15$ V, $R_1 = 2$ Ω, $R_2 = 4$ Ω, and $R_3 = 8$ Ω, find I_1, I_2, and I_3.

51. **Electronics** In Figure 6.19, we have $I_2 = I_1 + I_3$, $E_1 = R_1I_1 + R_2I_2$, and $E_2 = R_3I_3 + R_2I_2$. If $E_1 = 6$ V, $E_2 = 10$ V, $R_1 = 8$ Ω, $R_2 = 4$ Ω, and $R_3 = 7$ Ω, find I_1, I_2, and I_3.

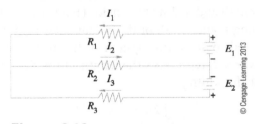

Figure 6.19

[IN YOUR WORDS]

52. Describe the advantages and disadvantages of the substitution method compared to the addition method.

53. Describe what it means for a system of equations to be consistent or inconsistent.

54. Describe how to use the substitution method for solving a system of linear equations.

6.3 ALGEBRAIC METHODS FOR SOLVING THREE LINEAR EQUATIONS IN THREE VARIABLES

In Section 6.2 we learned to solve a system of two linear equations in two variables by a graphical method and by two algebraic methods of elimination. In this section, we will expand these algebraic techniques to allow us to solve a system with three linear variables. These methods will be used later to allow us to solve n equations with n variables.

The graph of a linear equation in three variables is a plane. Graphing a system of three equations in three variables requires the ability to graph three planes and their intersections. We cannot graph three planes so that we can tell where they intersect. As a result, we will not consider graphical solutions to a system of three equations in three variables.

SUBSTITUTION METHOD

We will solve the same system of equations using both elimination methods. The first example uses the substitution method.

EXAMPLE 6.22

Solve this system of equations using the substitution method.

$$\begin{cases} x + 2y - 2z = 3 & (1) \\ 2x - y + 3z = -5 & (2) \\ 4x - 3y + z = 7 & (3) \end{cases}$$

SOLUTION If we solve equation (3) for z we get

$$z = 3y - 4x + 7 \qquad (4)$$

Substituting this value of z in equation (2) changes it to

$$2x - y + 3(3y - 4x + 7) = 2x - y + 9y - 12x + 21 = -5$$

Combining terms results in

$$-10x + 8y = -26 \qquad (5)$$

Solving equation (5) for y produces

$$8y = 10x - 26$$

$$\text{or} \quad y = \tfrac{5}{4}x - \tfrac{13}{4} \qquad (6)$$

EXAMPLE 6.22 (Cont.)

Substituting the value for z from equation (4) and the value for y from equation (6) in equation (1) we get

$$x + 2(\tfrac{5}{4}x - \tfrac{13}{4}) - 2(3y - 4x + 7) = 3$$
$$x + \tfrac{5}{2}x - \tfrac{13}{2} - 6y + 8x - 14 = 3$$
$$\tfrac{23}{2}x - 6y = \tfrac{47}{2} \tag{7}$$

Substituting the value of y from equation (6) into equation (7) results in

$$\tfrac{23}{2}x - 6(\tfrac{5}{4}x - \tfrac{13}{4}) = \tfrac{47}{2}$$
$$\tfrac{23}{2}x - \tfrac{15}{2}x + \tfrac{39}{2} = \tfrac{47}{2}$$
$$\tfrac{8}{2}x = \tfrac{8}{2}$$

or

$$x = 1$$

Using this value of $x = 1$ in equation (6) produces

$$y = \tfrac{5}{4} - \tfrac{13}{4} = -\tfrac{8}{4} = -2$$

Finally, using $x = 1$ and $y = -2$ in equation (4) we get

$$z = 3(-2) - 4(1) + 7 = -3$$

So, $x = 1$, $y = -2$, and $z = -3$.

ADDITION METHOD

There was no particular reason to begin by solving equation (3) for z in the previous example. We could just as easily have started by solving equation (1) for x or equation (2) for y or even equation (1) for y or z. Let's solve the same system of equations using the addition method.

EXAMPLE 6.23

Solve this system of equations using the addition method.

$$\begin{cases} x + 2y - 2z = 3 & (1) \\ 2x - y + 3z = -5 & (2) \\ 4x - 3y + z = 7 & (3) \end{cases}$$

SOLUTION We will begin by eliminating one of the variables. When this is done, we will have two equations with two variables. Let's start by eliminating the variable z. To do this, we multiply equation (3) by 2 and add this to equation (1).

$$8x - 6y + 2z = 14 \qquad \text{(3) multiplied by 2}$$
$$\underline{x + 2y - 2z = 3} \qquad (1)$$
$$9x - 4y \quad\quad = 17 \qquad \text{Adding to get equation (4)}$$

Next, we multiply equation (3) by 3 and subtract equation (2) from this new equation.

$$12x - 9y + 3z = 21 \qquad \text{(3) multiplied by 3}$$
$$\underline{2x - y + 3z = -5} \qquad (2)$$
$$10x - 8y \quad\quad = 26 \qquad \text{Subtracting to get equation (5)}$$

We now have two equations, (4) and (5), with two variables, x and y.

$$9x - 4y = 17 \qquad (4)$$

$$10x - 8y = 26 \qquad (5)$$

If we multiply equation (4) by -2 and add equation (5) to that equation, we will eliminate the variable y.

$$
\begin{array}{ll}
-18x + 8y = -34 & \text{(4) multiplied by } -2 \\
\underline{10x - 8y = 26} & (5) \\
-8x = -8 & \text{Adding to get (6)}
\end{array}
$$

Solving equation (6) for x, we get $x = 1$. Substituting this value in (4), we get $9 - 4y = 17$ or $-4y = 8$, which simplifies to $y = -2$. Then, if we substitute $x = 1$ and $y = -2$ in equation (3), we get $4 + 6 + z = 7$, or $z = -3$. Again, we get the solution $x = 1$, $y = -2$, and $z = -3$.

As you can see, the elimination method by addition and subtraction is often an easier method to use. We will use this method again in the next example.

 APPLICATION BUSINESS

EXAMPLE 6.24

By volume, one alloy is 70% copper, 20% zinc, and 10% nickel. A second alloy is 60% copper and 40% nickel. A third alloy is 30% copper, 30% nickel, and 40% zinc. How much of each must be mixed in order to get 1000 mm³ of a final alloy that is 50% copper, 18% zinc, and 32% nickel?

SOLUTION We must first determine the equations that are needed to solve this problem. If we let a represent the volume of the first alloy in the final alloy, b the volume of the second, and c the volume of the third, then we know that the total volume of the final alloy, 1000 mm³, is $a + b + c$.

We know that the final alloy contains 50% or 500 mm³ of copper and that this is $0.7a + 0.6b + 0.3c$. Also, 18% or 180 mm³ of the final solution is zinc, so $0.2a + 0.4c = 180$. This gives you a system of three linear equations in three variables.

$$
\begin{cases}
a + b + c = 1\,000 & (1) \\
0.7a + 0.6b + 0.3c = 500 & (2) \\
0.2a + 0.4c = 180 & (3)
\end{cases}
$$

We can also establish a fourth equation for the amount of nickel in the final solution, 32% or 320 mm³. This is

$$0.1a + 0.4b + 0.3c = 320 \qquad (4)$$

We do not need equation (4) to solve the problem, but we can use it to check our answers.

Since equation (3) does not contain variable b, we will combine equations (1) and (2) to eliminate this variable.

EXAMPLE 6.24 (Cont.)

$$0.7a + 0.6b + 0.3c = 500 \tag{2}$$
$$0.6a + 0.6b + 0.6c = 600 \qquad \text{(1) multiplied by 0.6}$$
$$0.1a \qquad\qquad -0.3c = -100 \qquad \text{Subtract to get (5).}$$

If we now multiply equation (5) by 2 and subtract this from equation (3), we will eliminate variable a.

$$0.2a + 0.4c = 180 \tag{3}$$
$$0.2a - 0.6c = -200 \qquad \text{(5) multiplied by 0.2}$$
$$c = 380 \qquad\qquad \text{Subtract to get } c.$$

So, alloy c is 380 mm³. Substituting this in (5) we get

$$0.1a - 0.3(380) = -100$$
$$0.1a - 114 = -100$$
$$0.1a = 14$$
$$a = 140$$

Then, substituting these values for a and c in equation (1) we get $140 + b + 380 = 1\,000$ or $b = 480$. The answer: we need 140 mm³ of alloy a, 480 mm³ of alloy b, and 380 mm³ of alloy c. If you put these values in equation (4) you will see that they check.

 APPLICATION BUSINESS

EXAMPLE 6.25

A trucking company has three sizes of trucks, large (L), medium (M), and small (S). The trucks are needed to move some packages, which come in three different shapes. We will call these three different shaped packages A, B, and C. From experience, the company knows that these trucks can hold the combination of packages as shown in this chart.

	Size of Truck		
	Large	Medium	Small
Package A	12	8	0
Package B	10	5	4
Package C	8	7	6

© Cengage Learning 2013

The company has to deliver a total of 64 A packages, 77 B packages, and 99 C packages. How many trucks of each size are needed, if each truck is fully loaded?

SOLUTION From the table we can see that the 64 A packages must be arranged with 12 on each large truck, 8 on each medium truck, and 0 on each small truck. We can write this as

$$12L + 8M = 64$$

Similarly, the B packages satisfy $10L + 5M + 4S = 77$ and the C packages satisfy $8L + 7M + 6S = 99$. Thus, we have the system

$$\begin{cases} 12L + 8M = 64 & (1) \\ 10L + 5M + 4S = 77 & (2) \\ 8L + 7M + 6S = 99 & (3) \end{cases}$$

Since equation (1) does not contain variable S, we will combine equations (2) and (3) to eliminate it.

$$\begin{array}{ll} 30L + 15M + 12S = 231 & \text{(2) multiplied by 3} \\ \underline{16L + 14M + 12S = 198} & \text{(3) multiplied by 2} \\ 14L + M = 33 & \text{Subtracting to get (4)} \end{array}$$

Now multiply equation (4) by 8 and subtract equation (1), and variable M is eliminated.

$$\begin{array}{ll} 112L + 8M = 264 & \text{(4) multiplied by 8} \\ \underline{12L + 8M = 64} & \text{(1)} \\ 100L = 200 & \text{Subtract.} \end{array}$$

So, $L = \dfrac{200}{100} = 2$. Substituting this in (1), we get

$$24 + 8M = 64$$
$$8M = 64 - 24$$
$$8M = 40$$
$$M = 5$$

And finally, substituting these values for L and M in (2), we obtain

$$10(2) + 5(5) + 4S = 77$$
$$20 + 25 + 4S = 77$$
$$4S = 77 - 45$$
$$= 32$$
$$S = 8$$

So, a total of 2 large, 5 medium, and 8 small trucks is needed.

As with a system of two equations in two variables, it is possible to have a system of three equations with three variables that is either inconsistent or dependent. If an elimination method results in an equation of the type $0x + 0y + 0z = c$, or $0 = c$, where $c \neq 0$, then the system is inconsistent and has no solutions. Graphically, this would mean that the plane of one equation was parallel to the plane of another equation or the planes intersect in three pairs of parallel lines.

If the elimination method results in an equation of the type $0x + 0y + 0z = 0$, or $0 = 0$, then two or more of the equations graph the same plane and the system is dependent.

EXAMPLE 6.26

Solve the system.

$$\begin{cases} 3x - y - z = 5 & (1) \\ x - 5y + z = 3 & (2) \\ x + 2y - z = 1 & (3) \end{cases}$$

EXAMPLE 6.26 (Cont.)

SOLUTION Adding equations (1) and (2) produces

$$4x - 6y = 8 \tag{4}$$

and adding equations (2) and (3) gives

$$2x - 3y = 4 \tag{5}$$

If we multiply equation (5) by 2 and subtract that result from equation (4), we obtain

$$0 = 0$$

Thus, we see that the given system of equations is dependent; and every ordered triple (a, b, c) of the form $(a, \frac{2}{3}a - \frac{4}{3}, \frac{7}{3}a - \frac{11}{3})$ is a solution of the given equation.

EXERCISE SET 6.3

In Exercises 1–4, use the substitution method to solve each system of equations.

1. $\begin{cases} 2x + y + z = 7 \\ x - y + 2z = 11 \\ 5x + y - 2z = 1 \end{cases}$ **2.** $\begin{cases} x + y + 2z = 0 \\ 2x - y + z = 6 \\ 4x + 2y + 2z = 0 \end{cases}$ **3.** $\begin{cases} 2x - y - z = -8 \\ x + y - z = -9 \\ x - y + 2z = 7 \end{cases}$ **4.** $\begin{cases} x + y + 5z = -10 \\ x - y - 5z = 11 \\ -x + y - 5z = 13 \end{cases}$

In Exercises 5–14, use the addition method to solve each system of equations. (Exercises 5–8 are the same as Exercises 1–4.)

5. $\begin{cases} 2x + y + z = 7 \\ x - y + 2z = 11 \\ 5x + y - 2z = 1 \end{cases}$ **8.** $\begin{cases} x + y + 5z = -10 \\ x - y - 5z = 11 \\ -x + y - 5z = 13 \end{cases}$ **11.** $\begin{cases} 3x - y - 2z = 11 \\ -x + 3y + 2z = -1 \\ 2x - 2y - 4z = 17 \end{cases}$ **13.** $\begin{cases} 2x + 3y + 3z = 9 \\ 5x - 2y + 8z = 6 \\ 4x - y + 5z = -1 \end{cases}$

6. $\begin{cases} x + y + 2z = 0 \\ 2x - y + z = 6 \\ 4x + 2y + 2z = 0 \end{cases}$ **9.** $\begin{cases} x + y + z = 2 \\ 8x - 2y + 4z = -3 \\ 6x - 4y - 3z = 3 \end{cases}$ **12.** $\begin{cases} x - 2y + z = -4 \\ 2x + y + 3z = 5 \\ 6x + 3y + 12z = 6 \end{cases}$ **14.** $\begin{cases} x + 2y + 3z = 4 \\ 2x - 3y - 4z = -1 \\ 3x - 4y + 5z = 6 \end{cases}$

7. $\begin{cases} 2x - y - z = -8 \\ x + y - z = -9 \\ x - y + 2z = 7 \end{cases}$ **10.** $\begin{cases} x + y - z = 7 \\ 8x + 4y + 2z = 21 \\ 4x + 3y + 6z = 2 \end{cases}$

Solve Exercises 15–22.

15. *Electronics* Kirchhoff's law for current states that the sum of the currents into and out of any point equals zero. Applying this to junction A in Figure 6.20 produces the equation $I_1 - I_2 + I_3 = 0$. Kirchhoff's voltage law states that the sum of the voltages around any closed loop equals zero. Applying this first to the left loop and then the right loop in Figure 6.20 results in the equations $6I_1 + 6I_2 = 18$ and $6I_2 + I_3 = 14$. What are the values of the currents I_1, I_2, and I_3? (Note that electromotive force E equals current I times resistance, or $E = IR$.)

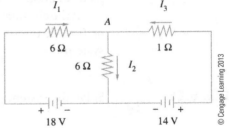

Figure 6.20

16. **Electronics** Applying Kirchhoff's laws to Figure 6.21 produces the following equations.

$$\begin{cases} I_1 + I_2 - I_3 = 0 \\ 3I_1 - 5I_2 - 10 = 0 \\ 5I_2 + 6I_3 - 5 = 0 \end{cases}$$

Find the currents associated with I_1, I_2, and I_3.

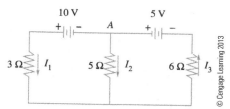

Figure 6.21

17. The standard equation for a circle is $x^2 + y^2 + ax + by + c = 0$. A circle passes through the points $P(5, 1)$, $Q(-2, -6)$, and $R(-1, -7)$. When the x- and y-coordinates for point P are put in the standard equation, it becomes $5^2 + 1^2 + a \cdot 5 + b \cdot 1 + c = 0$, or $5a + b + c + 26 = 0$. Use the coordinates of Q and R to obtain two more versions of the standard equation for this circle and then solve your system of equations for a, b, and c.

18. Another circle passes through the points $S(4, 16)$, $T(-6, -8)$, and $U(11, -1)$. Find the values of a, b, and c.

19. **Transportation** A trucking company has three sizes of trucks, large (L), medium (M), and small (S). Experience has shown that the large truck can carry 7 of container A, 6 of container B, and 4 of container C. The medium truck can carry 6 of A, 3 of B, and 2 of C, and the small truck can carry 8 of A, 1 of B, and 2 of C. How many trucks of the three sizes are needed to deliver 64 of container A, 33 of B, and 26 of C?

20. **Petroleum technology** Three crude oils are to be mixed and loaded aboard a supertanker that can carry 450 000 tonnes (metric tons, t). The crudes contain the following percentages of light-, medium-, and heavy-weight oils:

	Light	Medium	Heavy
Crude oil A	10%	20%	70%
Crude oil B	30%	40%	30%
Crude oil C	43%	44%	13%

© Cengage Learning 2013

How many tonnes of each crude should be mixed so that the new mixtures contain 24% light-, 32% medium-, and 44% heavy-weight oils?

21. **Landscape architecture** By weight, a 10-10-10 fertilizer contains 10% nitrogen, 10% phosphorous, and 10% potash. A 12-0-6 fertilizer contains 12% nitrogen, no phosphorous, and 6% potash. A landscaper has three types of fertilizer in stock: one is 10-12-15, a second is 10-0-5, and a third is 30-6-15. How much of each must be mixed in order to get 400 lb of fertilizer that is 16-3-9?

22. **Business** A company makes three types of patio furniture: chairs, tables, and recliners. Each requires the number of units of wood, plastic, and aluminum shown below:

	Wood	Plastic	Aluminum
Chair	1 unit	1 unit	2 units
Table	2 units	4 units	5 units
Recliner	1 unit	2 units	3 units

© Cengage Learning 2013

The company has in stock 500 units of wood, 900 units of plastic, and 1,300 units of aluminum. For its end-of-season production, the company wants to use all its stock. To do this, how many chairs, tables, and recliners should it make?

 [IN YOUR WORDS]

23. (a) Which do you find easier to use: the substitution method or the addition method?

    (b) Write an explanation defending your position.

24. Under what conditions is the substitution method easier than the addition method?

25. Explain what it means for a system of equations to be dependent.

19 MATRICES

Kirchhoff's laws can be used to write a system of linear equations. In Section 19.4, we will learn how to use matrices to solve this linear system and determine the currents in each electric circuit's path.

In Chapter 6, we studied systems of equations and we learned that determinants can be used to help solve systems of linear equations. In this chapter, another technique for solving systems of equations will be introduced. This technique uses matrices. The introduction of computers has led to increased applications of matrices in engineering, physics, biology, information science, transportation, and other technical areas. We will use calculators to help us work with matrices.

903

▼ Identify various types of arrays, vectors, and matrices, and recognize their dimensions.

▼ Write the transpose of a matrix.

▼ Add, subtract, and multiply matrices.

▼ Use technology to perform operations on matrices.

▼ Employ matrix operations to solve applications.

▼ Use technology to find the inverse of a nonsingular matrix.

19.1   MATRICES

DIMENSION

A **matrix** is a rectangular array of numbers arranged in rows and columns. A matrix with m rows and n columns is an $m \times n$ matrix. ($m \times n$ is read m by n.) The **dimensions** of a matrix are given in the form $m \times n$, where m represents the number of rows and n the number of columns.

A matrix is often used for presenting numerical data in a condensed form.

EXAMPLE 19.1

$\begin{bmatrix} 4 & 3 & 7 \\ 8 & 19 & -11 \end{bmatrix}$ is a matrix with dimension 2×3.

$\begin{bmatrix} 5 & 8 & -9 & 12 \\ 4 & 0 & -3 & 5.7 \\ 9 & 3 & 21 & -6 \end{bmatrix}$ is a 3×4 matrix.

$\begin{bmatrix} 2 & 4 & 6 & 8 & 9 \end{bmatrix}$ is a 1×5 matrix.

$\begin{bmatrix} 10 \\ 8 \\ 7 \\ 6 \\ 3 \end{bmatrix}$ is a 5×1 matrix.

Suppose a company makes two types of robots, C and S. Model C requires 78 h to assemble and contains 14 Type I computer chips, 7 Type II chips, and 16 m of wiring. Model S requires 65 h to assemble and contains 12 Type I chips, 9 Type II chips, and 11 m of wiring. The company makes a profit of $1,250 on each Model C it sells and $1,500 on each Model S. This information can be presented in a rectangular array or matrix like the following.

	Hours	Type I chip	Type II chip	Wiring (m)	Profit ($)
Model C	78	14	7	16	1,250
Model S	65	12	9	11	1,500

The numbers in the first row indicate the data for the Model C robot and those in the second row indicate the Model S data. This is a simple example of a matrix that has two rows and five columns.

ROW AND COLUMN VECTORS

A matrix of dimension $1 \times n$ is a row vector and a matrix of dimension $m \times 1$ is a column vector.

EXAMPLE 19.2

Some row vectors are:

$$\begin{bmatrix} 2 & 4 & 6 \end{bmatrix} \qquad \begin{bmatrix} 1 & -3 & 2 & 8 \end{bmatrix}$$
$$\begin{bmatrix} 4 & 6 & 0 & -7 & 0 \end{bmatrix} \qquad \begin{bmatrix} 9 \end{bmatrix}$$

Some column vectors are:

$$\begin{bmatrix} 2 \\ 4 \\ 6 \end{bmatrix} \quad \begin{bmatrix} 1 \\ -3 \\ 2 \\ 8 \end{bmatrix} \quad \begin{bmatrix} 4 \\ 6 \\ 0 \\ -7 \\ 0 \end{bmatrix} \quad \begin{bmatrix} 9 \end{bmatrix}$$

Notice that [9] is both a row vector and a column vector.

ZERO MATRIX

A matrix is a zero matrix if all the elements are zero. The matrix

$$\begin{bmatrix} 0 & 0 \\ 0 & 0 \\ 0 & 0 \end{bmatrix}$$

is a zero matrix of dimension 3×2.

SQUARE MATRIX

A matrix with the same number, n, of rows and columns is a square matrix of order n.

EXAMPLE 19.3

The matrix

$$\begin{bmatrix} 2 & 1 \\ 5 & 7 \end{bmatrix}$$

is a square matrix of order 2 and the matrix

$$\begin{bmatrix} 5 & -7 & 8 \\ 2 & -1 & 0 \\ 0 & 3 & 5 \end{bmatrix}$$

is a square matrix of order 3.

A double-subscript notation has been developed to allow us to refer to specific elements. The first numeral in the subscripts refers to the row in which the element lies and the second numeral refers to the column. An example of this notation is matrix A.

$$A = \begin{bmatrix} a_{11} & a_{12} & a_{13} & a_{14} \\ a_{21} & a_{22} & a_{23} & a_{24} \\ a_{31} & a_{32} & a_{33} & a_{34} \\ a_{41} & a_{42} & a_{43} & a_{44} \end{bmatrix}$$

The elements a_{11}, a_{22}, a_{33}, a_{44} are the *main diagonal* of this square matrix of order 4.

COEFFICIENT MATRIX

When working with a system of linear equations, a coefficient matrix can be formed from the coefficients of the equations. For example, the system

$$\begin{cases} 2x + 3y - 5z = 8 \\ 4x - 7y + 22z = 15 \end{cases}$$

has the coefficient matrix

$$\begin{bmatrix} 2 & 3 & -5 \\ 4 & -7 & 22 \end{bmatrix}$$

AUGMENTED MATRIX

If the column vector formed by the constants to the right of the equal symbols, $\begin{bmatrix} 8 \\ 15 \end{bmatrix}$, is adjoined to the right of the coefficient matrix, we get a new matrix called the augmented matrix of the system of linear equations. For example, for the system used previously,

$$\begin{cases} 2x + 3y - 5z = 8 \\ 4x - 7y + 22z = 15 \end{cases}$$

the augmented matrix would be

$$\begin{bmatrix} 2 & 3 & -5 & \vdots & 8 \\ 4 & -7 & 22 & \vdots & 15 \end{bmatrix}$$

The dashed line between columns 3 and 4 is not needed but is often used to indicate an augmented matrix.

Two matrices are *equal* if they have the same dimension and their corresponding elements are equal.

EXAMPLE 19.4

If $\begin{bmatrix} 6 & 4 & 3 & x \\ 2 & 9 & y & -3 \end{bmatrix} = \begin{bmatrix} z & 4 & 3 & -11 \\ 2 & w & 7 & -3 \end{bmatrix}$, then $x = -11, y = 7, z = 6$, and $w = 9$.

EXAMPLE 19.5

For the matrices $A = \begin{bmatrix} 1 & 2 & 6 \\ 7 & 8 & 9 \end{bmatrix}$, $B = \begin{bmatrix} 1 & 2 & 6 \\ 7 & 8 & 5 \end{bmatrix}$, and $C = \begin{bmatrix} 1 & 2 \\ 7 & 8 \end{bmatrix}$, $A \neq B$ because the corresponding elements $a_{23} = 9$ and $b_{23} = 5$ are not equal. $A \neq C$ because they have different dimensions.

ADDITION AND SUBTRACTION OF MATRICES

If A and B are two matrices, each of dimension $m \times n$, then their sum (or difference) is defined to be another matrix, C, also of dimension $m \times n$, where every element of C is the sum (or difference) of the corresponding elements A and B.

EXAMPLE 19.6

(a) $\begin{bmatrix} 2 & 3 & 5 \\ 6 & 7 & 8 \end{bmatrix} + \begin{bmatrix} 10 & 11 & 12 \\ 14 & 16 & 22 \end{bmatrix} = \begin{bmatrix} 2+10 & 3+11 & 5+12 \\ 6+14 & 7+16 & 8+22 \end{bmatrix}$

$= \begin{bmatrix} 12 & 14 & 17 \\ 20 & 23 & 30 \end{bmatrix}$

(b) $\begin{bmatrix} 4 & 9 \\ -2 & 8 \\ 6 & 1 \end{bmatrix} + \begin{bmatrix} 16 & 21 \\ 2 & -8 \\ 9 & 14 \end{bmatrix} = \begin{bmatrix} 4+16 & 9+21 \\ -2+2 & 8+(-8) \\ 6+9 & 1+14 \end{bmatrix}$

$= \begin{bmatrix} 20 & 30 \\ 0 & 0 \\ 15 & 15 \end{bmatrix}$

(c) $\begin{bmatrix} 1 & -5 \\ 4 & 3 \\ 2 & -1 \end{bmatrix} - \begin{bmatrix} 4 & -6 \\ 2 & 1 \\ -3 & 9 \end{bmatrix} = \begin{bmatrix} 1-4 & -5-(-6) \\ 4-2 & 3-1 \\ 2-(-3) & -1-9 \end{bmatrix}$

$= \begin{bmatrix} -3 & 1 \\ 2 & 2 \\ 5 & -10 \end{bmatrix}$

CAUTION You can only add or subtract two matrices if they have the same dimension.

EXAMPLE 19.7

If $A = \begin{bmatrix} 4 & 2 & 7 & 9 \\ 5 & 4 & 6 & 1 \end{bmatrix}$ and $B = \begin{bmatrix} 5 & 3 & 8 & 1 \\ 4 & 6 & 2 & 4 \end{bmatrix}$, then determine $A + B$, $A - B$, and $B - A$.

SOLUTIONS

$$A + B = \begin{bmatrix} 4+5 & 2+3 & 7+8 & 9+1 \\ 5+4 & 4+6 & 6+2 & 1+4 \end{bmatrix}$$

$$= \begin{bmatrix} 9 & 5 & 15 & 10 \\ 9 & 10 & 8 & 5 \end{bmatrix}$$

$$A - B = \begin{bmatrix} 4-5 & 2-3 & 7-8 & 9-1 \\ 5-4 & 4-6 & 6-2 & 1-4 \end{bmatrix}$$

$$= \begin{bmatrix} -1 & -1 & -1 & 8 \\ 1 & -2 & 4 & -3 \end{bmatrix}$$

$$B - A = \begin{bmatrix} 5-4 & 3-2 & 8-7 & 1-9 \\ 4-5 & 6-4 & 2-6 & 4-1 \end{bmatrix}$$

$$= \begin{bmatrix} 1 & 1 & 1 & -8 \\ -1 & 2 & -4 & 3 \end{bmatrix}$$

 APPLICATION HEALTHCARE

EXAMPLE 19.8

At the beginning of a laboratory experiment, two groups of four mice were timed to see how long it took them to go through a maze. The mice in the group that went through the maze at night took 8, 6, 5, and 7 sec. The mice in the group that went through the maze during the day took 22, 14, 18, and 12 sec. (a) Write a 2 × 4 matrix using this information.

A week later, the mice were sent through the maze again. They went in the same order as they did the week before. This time the night group completed the maze in 4, 3, 5, and 3 sec and the day group took 9, 8, 10, and 8 sec. (b) Write this information as a 2 × 4 matrix and use matrix subtraction to write a matrix that shows the amount of change each mouse made in its time to complete the maze.

SOLUTIONS

(a) We will put the night group in the top row and the day group of mice in the bottom row. The result is the following matrix:

$$\begin{array}{c} \text{Night group} \\ \text{Day group} \end{array} \begin{bmatrix} 8 & 6 & 5 & 7 \\ 22 & 14 & 18 & 12 \end{bmatrix}$$

(b) The matrix for the data at the end of the week is

$$\begin{array}{c} \text{Night group} \\ \text{Day group} \end{array} \begin{bmatrix} 4 & 3 & 5 & 3 \\ 9 & 8 & 10 & 8 \end{bmatrix}$$

To find the change in the amount of time each mouse took going through the maze, we subtract the last matrix from the matrix in (a).

$$\begin{array}{c} \text{Night group} \\ \text{Day group} \end{array} \begin{bmatrix} 8 & 6 & 5 & 7 \\ 22 & 14 & 18 & 12 \end{bmatrix} - \begin{bmatrix} 4 & 3 & 5 & 3 \\ 9 & 8 & 10 & 8 \end{bmatrix}$$

$$= \begin{bmatrix} 4 & 3 & 0 & 4 \\ 13 & 6 & 8 & 4 \end{bmatrix}$$

SCALAR MULTIPLICATION

If A is an $m \times n$ matrix and k a real number, then kA is an $m \times n$ matrix B, where $b_{ij} = ka_{ij}$ for each element of A. This is referred to as scalar multiplication and the real number k is called a scalar.

EXAMPLE 19.9

If $A = \begin{bmatrix} 3 & 5 \\ 9 & 2 \end{bmatrix}$ and $k = 4$, then

$$kA = 4 \begin{bmatrix} 3 & 5 \\ 9 & 2 \end{bmatrix} = \begin{bmatrix} 4 \cdot 3 & 4 \cdot 5 \\ 4 \cdot 9 & 4 \cdot 2 \end{bmatrix}$$

$$= \begin{bmatrix} 12 & 20 \\ 36 & 8 \end{bmatrix}$$

EXAMPLE 19.10

If $B = \begin{bmatrix} 2 & 4 \\ -3 & 7 \end{bmatrix}$ and $k = -\frac{1}{2}$, then

$$kB = -\frac{1}{2} \begin{bmatrix} 2 & 4 \\ -3 & 7 \end{bmatrix} = \begin{bmatrix} -\frac{1}{2} \cdot 2 & -\frac{1}{2} \cdot 4 \\ -\frac{1}{2}(-3) & -\frac{1}{2} \cdot 7 \end{bmatrix}$$

$$= \begin{bmatrix} -1 & -2 \\ \frac{3}{2} & -\frac{7}{2} \end{bmatrix}$$

These two examples help show that $A + A = 2A$, $B + B + B = 3B$, and so on.

APPLICATION BUSINESS

EXAMPLE 19.11

A computer retailer sells three types of computers: the personal computer (PC), the business computer (BC), and the industrial computer (IC). The retailer has two stores. The matrix below shows the number of each computer model in stock at each store.

EXAMPLE 19.11 (Cont.)

$$\begin{array}{c c c c} & \text{PC} & \text{BC} & \text{IC} \\ \text{Store A} & \begin{bmatrix} 6 & 18 & 12 \\ \text{Store B} & 10 & 22 & 28 \end{bmatrix} \end{array}$$

The store plans to have a sale in the near future. In order to have enough computers in stock at each store when the sale begins, it plans to order 1.5 times the current number. How many of each computer should be ordered for each store?

SOLUTION Here the scalar is 1.5, so we want to multiply each element of this matrix by 1.5. The result is

$$1.5 \left(\begin{array}{c c c c} & \text{PC} & \text{BC} & \text{IC} \\ \text{Store A} & \begin{bmatrix} 6 & 18 & 12 \\ \text{Store B} & 10 & 22 & 28 \end{bmatrix} \end{array} \right) = \begin{array}{c c c c} & \text{PC} & \text{BC} & \text{IC} \\ \text{Store A} & \begin{bmatrix} 9 & 27 & 18 \\ \text{Store B} & 15 & 33 & 42 \end{bmatrix} \end{array}$$

Thus, we see that the retailer needs to order 9 PCs for Store A and 15 for Store B, 27 BCs for Store A and 33 for Store B, and 18 ICs for Store A and 42 for Store B.

During this section we have used the following properties of matrices.

MATRIX PROPERTIES

If A, B, and C are three matrices, all of the same dimension, 0 is the zero matrix, and k is a real number, then

$A + B = B + A$ (commutative law)
$A + 0 = 0 + A = A$ (identity for addition)
$A + (B + C) = (A + B) + C$ (associative law)
$k(A + B) = kA + kB$

EXERCISE SET 19.1

Give the dimension of the matrices in Exercises 1–6. Solve Exercises 7–10.

1. $\begin{bmatrix} 2 & 4 & 5 \\ 3 & 2 & 1 \end{bmatrix}$

2. $\begin{bmatrix} 3 & 4 & 6 \\ 2 & 5 & 9 \\ 8 & 7 & 2 \end{bmatrix}$

3. $\begin{bmatrix} 2 & 1 & 0 & 7 & 9 & 6 \\ 3 & 2 & 4 & 8 & 7 & 2 \\ 9 & 6 & 4 & 5 & 0 & 2 \end{bmatrix}$

4. $\begin{bmatrix} 3 \\ 2 \\ 1 \\ 4 \end{bmatrix}$

5. $\begin{bmatrix} 3 & 2 \\ 4 & 1 \\ 5 & 3 \\ 7 & 9 \end{bmatrix}$

6. $\begin{bmatrix} 1 & 2 & 4 & 6 & 9 & 11 & 12 \end{bmatrix}$

7. Given matrix A, determine the values of elements a_{11}, a_{24}, a_{21}, and a_{32}.

$$A = \begin{bmatrix} 1 & 2 & 5 & 7 \\ 8 & 9 & 11 & 13 \\ 4 & 6 & 12 & 15 \end{bmatrix}$$

8. Given matrix B, determine the values of elements b_{12}, b_{21}, b_{23}, and b_{32}.

$$B = \begin{bmatrix} -5 & 0 & 2 \\ 4 & 7 & 9 \\ 5 & -8 & 11 \end{bmatrix}$$

9. Given that

$$\begin{bmatrix} 4 & 3 & 2 & x \\ 5 & 9 & 7 & 11 \\ y & 8 & 3 & 4 \end{bmatrix} = \begin{bmatrix} 4 & 3 & z & 12 \\ w & 9 & 7 & 11 \\ -6 & 8 & 3 & 4 \end{bmatrix},$$

determine the values of x, y, z, and w.

10. Given that

$$\begin{bmatrix} 3 & 2 & x-2 \\ 4 & y+5 & 9 \\ w+6 & 11 & 10 \end{bmatrix} = \begin{bmatrix} 3z & 2 & 7 \\ 4 & 3 & 9 \\ 7 & 11 & 2p \end{bmatrix},$$

determine the values of x, y, z, w, and p.

In Exercises 11–14, find the indicated sum or difference.

11. $\begin{bmatrix} 3 & 2 & 1 & -4 \\ 9 & 7 & 6 & -1 \\ 4 & 3 & 5 & 2 \end{bmatrix} + \begin{bmatrix} -6 & 4 & 5 & -4 \\ 3 & 2 & 11 & 1 \\ 5 & -3 & 0 & 8 \end{bmatrix}$

12. $\begin{bmatrix} 2 & 4 \\ -5 & 1 \\ 3 & 4 \end{bmatrix} + \begin{bmatrix} 5 & -6 \\ 2 & 9 \\ 8 & 2 \end{bmatrix}$

13. $\begin{bmatrix} 3 & 2 & -1 \\ 9 & 12 & 4 \end{bmatrix} - \begin{bmatrix} 1 & 3 & -5 \\ 4 & 3 & 6 \end{bmatrix}$

14. $\begin{bmatrix} 3 & 2 & -1 & 5 \\ 4 & 3 & 11 & 9 \\ 16 & 4 & 3 & -8 \\ 12 & 5 & 4 & 6 \\ 2 & 9 & 18 & 7 \end{bmatrix} - \begin{bmatrix} 1 & 2 & -4 & 2 \\ 1 & 3 & 2 & 8 \\ 2 & -4 & 3 & 6 \\ 2 & -5 & 2 & -4 \\ 2 & 3 & -5 & 3 \end{bmatrix}$

In Exercises 15–22, use matrices A, B, and C to determine the indicated matrix, where

$$A = \begin{bmatrix} 4 & 3 & 2 \\ 5 & 0 & 7 \end{bmatrix}, B = \begin{bmatrix} -5 & 4 & 2 \\ 3 & 1 & 8 \end{bmatrix}, \text{ and } C = \begin{bmatrix} 5 & 8 & 4 \\ 6 & -2 & 9 \end{bmatrix}.$$

15. $A + B$

16. $B - C$

17. $3A$

18. $4B$

19. $2B + C$

20. $4A - 3C$

21. $2B - 3A$

22. $4C + 2B$

In Exercises 23–30, use matrices D, E, and F to determine the indicated matrix, where

$$D = \begin{bmatrix} 4 \\ 2 \\ -1 \\ 5 \end{bmatrix}, E = \begin{bmatrix} 7 \\ 9 \\ -4 \\ 10 \end{bmatrix}, \text{ and } F = \begin{bmatrix} 14 \\ 18 \\ -8 \\ 5 \end{bmatrix}.$$

23. $D - E$

24. $E + F$

25. $3E$

26. $F - 2E$

27. $3D + 2E$

28. $2F - 7D$

29. $7D - 2F$

30. $5E - 2F$

Solve Exercises 31–36.

31. Business In keeping inventory records, a company uses a matrix. One storage location has 18 of computer chip *A*, 7 of computer chip *B*, 9 EPROMS, 7 keyboards, 11 motherboards, and 4 disk drives. This

is represented by the matrix $\begin{bmatrix} 18 & 7 & 9 \\ 7 & 11 & 4 \end{bmatrix}$. At a second storage point, the inventory is $\begin{bmatrix} 9 & 5 & 6 \\ 11 & 4 & 12 \end{bmatrix}$.

How many of each item are on hand?

32. Business Wrecker's Auto Supply Company has three stores, each of which carries five sizes of a certain tire model. The following matrix represents the present inventories:

Store	195/70SR-14	205/70SR-14	185/70SR-15	205/70SR-15	215/70SR-15
A	12	15	28	7	16
B	25	19	11	40	11
C	15	29	21	17	17

At the beginning of the next month, they would like to have the following inventory:

Store	195/70SR-14	205/70SR-14	185/70SR-15	205/70SR-15	215/70SR-15
A	20	48	60	24	44
B	36	64	24	40	32
C	44	72	48	60	40

Write a matrix that represents the number of each size of tire that must be ordered for each store, so as to achieve their goal. (Assume that no more tires are sold.)

33. Medical technology A drug company tested 400 patients to see if a new medicine is effective. Half of the patients received the new drug and half received a placebo. The results for the first 200 patients are shown in the following matrix:

	New drug	Placebo
Effective	70	40
Not effective	30	60

Using the same matrix format, the results for a second 200 patients were $\begin{bmatrix} 65 & 42 \\ 35 & 58 \end{bmatrix}$. What were the results for the entire test group?

34. Business A computer supply company has its inventory of four types of computer chips in three warehouses. At the beginning of the month it had the following inventory:

Chip type:	2 GHz	2.5 GHz	2.8 GHz	3.1 GHz
Warehouse A	1200	3200	4800	900
Warehouse B	1650	4580	7200	700
Warehouse C	1120	5100	6200	1200

The sales for the month were

Chip type:	2 GHz	2.5 GHz	2.8 GHz	3.1 GHz
Warehouse A	270	2130	3210	265
Warehouse B	1120	4230	3124	75
Warehouse C	320	3126	2743	1012

Write a matrix that shows the inventory at the end of the month.

35. Business The computer supply company in Exercise 34 expects sales to increase by 10% during the next month. What are next month's projected sales? (Round off any fractional answers.) Remember, last month the company sold

Chip type:	2 GHz	2.5 GHz	2.8 GHz	3.1 GHz
Warehouse A	270	2130	3210	265
Warehouse B	1120	4230	3124	75
Warehouse C	320	3126	2743	1012

36. Business The following matrix represents the normal monthly order of a retail store for three models of exercise suits in four different sizes:

	S	M	L	XL
Jogging	5	4	3	4
Sweating	7	12	15	7
Walking	4	8	12	14

During its spring sale, the store expects to do four times the usual volume of business. Determine the matrix that represents the store's order for the month of the sale.

 [IN YOUR WORDS]

37. Describe how to enter a matrix into your calculator. (Hint: Review the procedures in Section 6.4.)

38. Describe how to use your calculator to (**a**) add or subtract two matrices and (**b**) multiply a matrix by a scalar.

39. Explain what is needed for two matrices to be equal.

40. What is an augmented matrix?

19.2 MULTIPLICATION OF MATRICES

Learning to add and subtract matrices was straightforward. We had to be careful that each matrix had the same number of rows and the same number of columns. Multiplying matrices is more involved.

MULTIPLYING MATRICES

If A and B are two matrices, then in order to define the product AB, the number of columns in matrix A must be the same as the number of rows in matrix B. Thus, matrix A must be of dimension $m \times n$ and matrix B dimension $n \times p$. The product will have dimension $m \times p$.

We will begin by multiplying a row vector and a column vector.

 PRODUCT OF A ROW VECTOR AND A COLUMN VECTOR

If $A = \begin{bmatrix} a_{11} & a_{12} & a_{13} & \cdots & a_{1n} \end{bmatrix}$ is a row vector, and $B = \begin{bmatrix} b_{11} \\ b_{21} \\ b_{31} \\ \vdots \\ b_{n1} \end{bmatrix}$ is a

column vector, then

$$AB = [a_{11}b_{11} + a_{12}b_{21} + a_{13}b_{31} + \cdots + a_{1n}b_{n1}]$$

EXAMPLE 19.12

If $A = \begin{bmatrix} 3 & 4 \end{bmatrix}$ and $B = \begin{bmatrix} 5 \\ 1 \end{bmatrix}$, then

$$AB = \begin{bmatrix} 3 \cdot 5 + 4 \cdot 1 \end{bmatrix} = \begin{bmatrix} 15 + 4 \end{bmatrix} = \begin{bmatrix} 19 \end{bmatrix}$$

Since A is 1×2 and B is 2×1, the product AB is 1×1.

EXAMPLE 19.13

If $C = \begin{bmatrix} 1 & 2 & 3 & x \end{bmatrix}$, $D = \begin{bmatrix} 3 \\ -1 \\ 1 \\ 2 \end{bmatrix}$, and $CD = \begin{bmatrix} 22 \end{bmatrix}$, find x.

SOLUTION $CD = \begin{bmatrix} 1(3) + 2(-1) + 3(1) + 2x \end{bmatrix}$

$$= \begin{bmatrix} 3 - 2 + 3 + 2x \end{bmatrix}$$

$$= \begin{bmatrix} 4 + 2x \end{bmatrix} = \begin{bmatrix} 22 \end{bmatrix}$$

These two matrices are equal only if $4 + 2x = 22$ or $2x = 18$, so $x = 9$.

We will use the following method of multiplying a row vector and a column vector to multiply larger matrices.

MATRIX MULTIPLICATION

If A is an $m \times n$ matrix and B is an $n \times p$ matrix, then the product matrix $C = AB$ is an $m \times p$ matrix, where element c_{ij} in the ith row and jth column is formed by multiplying the elements in the ith row of A by the corresponding elements in the jth column of B and adding the results. Thus,

$$c_{ij} = a_{i1}b_{1j} + a_{i2}b_{2j} + \cdots + a_{in}b_{nj}$$

We will illustrate this definition by showing how you get an element in the following product. Suppose. $A = \begin{bmatrix} 1 & 2 & -1 & 0 \\ 3 & 5 & 2 & -3 \end{bmatrix}$ and $B = \begin{bmatrix} 2 & 1 & 3 \\ 0 & 4 & -2 \\ 1 & 2 & 0 \\ 1 & 3 & -2 \end{bmatrix}$.

You can see that A is a 2×4 matrix and B is a 4×3 matrix, so AB will have dimension 2×3. If we let $C = AB$, we will show how to find c_{12} or the element in row 1, column 2 of matrix C. To get this element, we multiply row 1 of matrix A and column 2 of matrix B. This is the same as multiplying a row vector and a column vector. Thus,

$$c_{12} = \begin{bmatrix} 1 & 2 & -1 & 0 \end{bmatrix} \begin{bmatrix} 1 \\ 4 \\ 2 \\ 3 \end{bmatrix}$$

$$= 1(1) + 2(4) - 1(2) + 0(3)$$

$$= 7$$

EXAMPLE 19.14

Multiply $\begin{bmatrix} 1 & 2 & -1 & 0 \\ 3 & 5 & 2 & -3 \end{bmatrix} \begin{bmatrix} 2 & 1 & 3 \\ 0 & 4 & -2 \\ 1 & 2 & 0 \\ 1 & 3 & -2 \end{bmatrix}$.

SOLUTION $\begin{bmatrix} 1 & 2 & -1 & 0 \\ 3 & 5 & 2 & -3 \end{bmatrix} \begin{bmatrix} 2 & 1 & 3 \\ 0 & 4 & -2 \\ 1 & 2 & 0 \\ 1 & 3 & -2 \end{bmatrix}$

$= \begin{bmatrix} 1(2) + 2(0) - 1(1) + 0(1) & 1(1) + 2(4) - 1(2) + 0(3) \\ 3(2) + 5(0) + 2(1) - 3(1) & 3(1) + 5(4) + 2(2) - 3(3) \end{bmatrix}$

$\qquad \begin{bmatrix} 1(3) + 2(-2) - 1(0) + 0(-2) \\ 3(3) + 5(-2) + 2(0) - 3(-2) \end{bmatrix}$

$= \begin{bmatrix} 2 + 0 - 1 + 0 & 1 + 8 - 2 + 0 & 3 - 4 - 0 + 0 \\ 6 + 0 + 2 - 3 & 3 + 20 + 4 - 9 & 9 - 10 + 0 + 6 \end{bmatrix}$

$= \begin{bmatrix} 1 & 7 & -1 \\ 5 & 18 & 5 \end{bmatrix}$

 NOTE In general, $AB \neq BA$. In fact, if AB is defined, then BA may not be defined. The only time that both AB and BA are defined is when both A and B are square matrices with the same dimensions. Thus, the commutative law does not hold for multiplication of matrices.

The following properties will hold, assuming that the dimensions of the matrices allow the products or sums to be defined.

$$A(BC) = (AB)C \qquad \text{associative law}$$
$$A(B + C) = AB + AC \qquad \text{left distributive law}$$
$$(B + C)A = BA + CA \qquad \text{right distributive law}$$

Because the commutative law does not hold, the left and right distributive laws usually give different results.

 APPLICATION **BUSINESS**

EXAMPLE 19.15

A computer supply company has its inventory of four types of computer chips in three warehouses. The sales of each chip from each warehouse are shown in matrix S.

Chip type:	286	386	486	586
Warehouse A	270	2130	3210	265
$S =$ Warehouse B	1120	4230	3124	75
Warehouse C	320	3126	2743	1012

EXAMPLE 19.15 (Cont.) | Matrix P below shows the selling price and the profit for each type of chip.

$$P = \begin{array}{c} \text{Chip} \\ 286 \\ 386 \\ 486 \\ 586 \end{array} \begin{array}{cc} \text{Selling Price} & \text{Profit} \\ \begin{bmatrix} 25 & 10 \\ 35 & 13 \\ 52 & 17 \\ 97 & 33 \end{bmatrix} \end{array}$$

(a) How much money in sales did each warehouse generate during this month?

(b) How much profit did each warehouse make?

SOLUTION Since matrix S is a 3×4 matrix and P is a 4×2, we can determine the solution from the 3×2 matrix that results when we multiply SP.

$$SP = \begin{bmatrix} 270 & 2130 & 3210 & 265 \\ 1120 & 4230 & 3124 & 75 \\ 320 & 3126 & 2743 & 1012 \end{bmatrix} \cdot \begin{bmatrix} 25 & 10 \\ 35 & 13 \\ 52 & 17 \\ 97 & 33 \end{bmatrix}$$

$$SP = \begin{array}{c} \\ \text{Warehouse A} \\ \text{Warehouse B} \\ \text{Warehouse C} \end{array} \begin{array}{cc} \text{Sales} & \text{Profit} \\ \begin{bmatrix} 273,925 & 93,705 \\ 345,773 & 121,773 \\ 358,210 & 123,865 \end{bmatrix} \end{array}$$

From this matrix we can see, for example, that Warehouse A sold \$273,925 in chips for a profit of \$93,705.

EXERCISE SET 19.2

In Exercises 1–10, find the indicated products.

1. $\begin{bmatrix} 2 & 3 \\ 1 & -4 \end{bmatrix} \begin{bmatrix} 4 & -3 \\ 6 & 5 \end{bmatrix}$

2. $\begin{bmatrix} 1 & -2 & 4 \end{bmatrix} \begin{bmatrix} 3 \\ 9 \\ -7 \end{bmatrix}$

3. $\begin{bmatrix} 5 & 1 & 6 & 2 \end{bmatrix} \begin{bmatrix} 2 \\ 9 \\ -8 \\ 3 \end{bmatrix}$

4. $\begin{bmatrix} 2 & 3 & 1 \\ -4 & 2 & 0 \end{bmatrix} \begin{bmatrix} 4 & 1 \\ -5 & 2 \\ 3 & 0 \end{bmatrix}$

5. $\begin{bmatrix} 1 & 2 & 4 \\ 2 & 3 & 6 \end{bmatrix} \begin{bmatrix} 5 & -7 & 4 \\ 4 & 6 & 0 \\ -4 & 2 & 1 \end{bmatrix}$

6. $\begin{bmatrix} 4 & 7 \\ 2 & 3 \\ 6 & 2 \\ 9 & 1 \end{bmatrix} \begin{bmatrix} 3 & 7 & 6 & 1 & -5 \\ 4 & -3 & 2 & 0 & 10 \end{bmatrix}$

7. $\begin{bmatrix} 1 & 2 & 3 \\ 6 & 5 & 4 \\ -1 & 0 & 2 \end{bmatrix} \begin{bmatrix} 9 & 8 & 7 \\ -2 & 3 & -1 \\ 0 & 1 & 0 \end{bmatrix}$

8. $\begin{bmatrix} 9 & 8 & 7 \\ -2 & 3 & -1 \\ 0 & 1 & 0 \end{bmatrix} \begin{bmatrix} 1 & 2 & 3 \\ 6 & 5 & 4 \\ -1 & 0 & 2 \end{bmatrix}$

9. $\begin{bmatrix} 3 & 4 & -2 \\ 7 & 8 & 10 \end{bmatrix} \begin{bmatrix} 0 & 4 & 1 \\ 1 & 0 & 2 \\ 8 & -1 & 0 \end{bmatrix}$

10. $\begin{bmatrix} 1 & 2 & -1 \\ 2 & -1 & 3 \end{bmatrix} \begin{bmatrix} 0 & 1 & 0 & 2 \\ 1 & 0 & 2 & -1 \\ 3 & 4 & -1 & 0 \end{bmatrix}$

In Exercises 11–20, use matrices A, B, and C to determine the indicated answer, where

$A = \begin{bmatrix} 1 & 2 \\ 3 & 4 \end{bmatrix}$, $B = \begin{bmatrix} 3 & 6 \\ 2 & 5 \end{bmatrix}$, *and* $C = \begin{bmatrix} 4 & -2 \\ -6 & 2 \end{bmatrix}$.

11. AB

12. BA

13. AC

14. BC

15. $A(BC)$

16. $(AB)C$

17. $A(B + C)$

18. $(B + C)A$

19. $(2A)(3B)$

20. $(2A + \frac{1}{2}C)B$

Solve Exercises 21–29.

21. Suppose $A = \begin{bmatrix} 2 & 10 \\ 3 & 15 \end{bmatrix}$ and $B = \begin{bmatrix} -10 & 25 \\ 2 & -5 \end{bmatrix}$. What is AB? Can you conclude that if $AB = 0$, then either $A = 0$ or $B = 0$?

22. If $\begin{bmatrix} 2 & x \\ y & 5 \end{bmatrix} \begin{bmatrix} 4 & 6 \\ 9 & -1 \end{bmatrix} = \begin{bmatrix} 35 & 9 \\ 49 & 1 \end{bmatrix}$, determine x and y.

23. *Business* A computer supply company has its inventory of four types of computer processors in three warehouses. One month it had the following sales:

Chip type:	2 GHz	2.5 GHz	2.8 GHz	3.1 GHz
Warehouse A	270	2,130	3,210	265
Warehouse B	1,120	4,230	3,124	75
Warehouse C	320	3,126	2,743	1,012

The 2-GHz processors sell for \$85, the 2.5-GHz processors sell for \$180, the 2.8-GHz processors sell for \$375, and the 3.1-GHz processors sell for \$725. How much money in sales did each warehouse generate during this month?

24. *Construction* A contractor builds three sizes of houses (ranch, bi-level, and two story) in two different models, A and B. The contractor plans to build 100 new homes in a subdivision. Matrix P shows the number of each type of house planned for the subdivision.

	Ranch	Bi-level	Two story
$P =$ Model A	30	20	15
Model B	10	10	15

The amounts of each type of exterior material needed for each house are shown in matrix A. Here, concrete is in cubic yards, lumber in 1,000 board feet, bricks in 1,000s, and shingles in units of 100 ft^2.

	Concrete	Lumber	Bricks	Shingles
Ranch	10	2	2	3
$A =$ Bi-level	15	3	4	4
Two story	25	5	6	3

The cost of each of the units for each kind of material is given by matrix C.

$$C = \begin{matrix} \text{Concrete} \\ \text{Lumber} \\ \text{Brick} \\ \text{Shingles} \end{matrix} \overset{\text{Cost per unit}}{\begin{bmatrix} 25 \\ 210 \\ 75 \\ 40 \end{bmatrix}}$$

(a) How much of each type of material will the contractor need for each house model?

(b) What will it cost to build each size of house?

(c) What will it cost to build each house model?

(d) What will it cost to build the entire subdivision?

25. **Physics** The *Pauli spin matrices* in quantum mechanics are $A = \begin{bmatrix} 0 & 1 \\ 1 & 0 \end{bmatrix}$, $B = \begin{bmatrix} 0 & -i \\ i & 0 \end{bmatrix}$, and $C = \begin{bmatrix} 1 & 0 \\ 0 & -1 \end{bmatrix}$, where $i = \sqrt{-1}$. Show that $A^2 = B^2 = C^2 = I$, where $I = \begin{bmatrix} 1 & 0 \\ 0 & 1 \end{bmatrix}$.

26. **Physics** Show that the Pauli spin matrices *anticommute*. That is, show that $AB = -BA$, $AC = -CA$, and $BC = -CB$.

27. **Physics** The *commutator* of two matrices P and Q is $PQ - QP$. For the Pauli spin matrices, show that **(a)** the commutator of A and B is $2iC$, **(b)** the commutator of A and C is $-2iB$, and **(c)** the commutator of B and C is $2iA$, where $i = \sqrt{-1}$.

28. Show, by multiplying the matrices, that the following equation represents an ellipse:

$$\begin{bmatrix} x & y \end{bmatrix} \begin{bmatrix} 5 & -7 \\ 7 & 3 \end{bmatrix} \begin{bmatrix} x \\ y \end{bmatrix} = \begin{bmatrix} 30 \end{bmatrix}$$

29. **Cartography** A figure defined by the four points $P_1(x_1, y_1)$, $P_2(x_2, y_2)$, $P_3(x_3, y_3)$, and $P_4(x_4, y_4)$ is rotated through an angle θ by using the product

$$\begin{bmatrix} x_1 & y_1 \\ x_2 & y_2 \\ x_3 & y_3 \\ x_4 & y_4 \end{bmatrix} \begin{bmatrix} \cos\theta & \sin\theta \\ -\sin\theta & \cos\theta \end{bmatrix}$$

(a) Find the resulting matrix if the points $P_1(1, 2)$, $P_2(5, 4)$, $P_3(-2, 7)$, and $P_4(-1, -5)$ are rotated through an angle $\theta = \pi$.

(b) Find the resulting matrix if the points $P_1(1, 2)$, $P_2(5, 4)$, $P_3(-2, 7)$, and $P_4(-1, -5)$ are rotated through an angle $\theta = \frac{\pi}{2}$.

(c) What product would be used if five points $P_1(x_1, y_1)$, $P_2(x_2, y_2)$, $P_3(x_3, y_3)$, $P_4(x_4, y_4)$, and $P_5(x_5, y_5)$ were rotated through an angle θ?

[IN YOUR WORDS]

30. The text states that the commutative law does not hold for the multiplication of matrices.

(a) If $A = \begin{bmatrix} 1 & 2 & 5 \\ 6 & 8 & 9 \end{bmatrix}$ and $B = \begin{bmatrix} 5 & 4 & 2 \\ 0 & 1 & 2 \\ 7 & 2 & 0 \end{bmatrix}$, does $AB = BA$? Explain why or why not.

(b) If $C = \begin{bmatrix} 2 & 5 \\ 3 & 4 \end{bmatrix}$ and $D = \begin{bmatrix} 5 & 4 \\ -2 & 0 \end{bmatrix}$, does $CD = DC$? Explain why or why not.

31. Describe how to multiply two matrices on your calculator.

19.3 INVERSES OF MATRICES

One use of matrices is to help solve a system of linear equations. For example, if you had the system of linear equations

$$\begin{cases} a_1 x_1 + a_2 x_2 + a_3 x_3 = k_1 \\ b_1 x_1 + b_2 x_2 + b_3 x_3 = k_2 \\ c_1 x_1 + c_2 x_2 + c_3 x_3 = k_3 \end{cases}$$

you could write these as the matrices:

$$\begin{bmatrix} a_1 & a_2 & a_3 \\ b_1 & b_2 & b_3 \\ c_1 & c_2 & c_3 \end{bmatrix} \begin{bmatrix} x_1 \\ x_2 \\ x_3 \end{bmatrix} = \begin{bmatrix} k_1 \\ k_2 \\ k_3 \end{bmatrix}$$

Another way to look at this would be to let the coefficients of the linear equations be represented by the matrix

$$A = \begin{bmatrix} a_1 & a_2 & a_3 \\ b_1 & b_2 & b_3 \\ c_1 & c_2 & c_3 \end{bmatrix}$$

If X represents the column vector of variables, and K represents the column vector of constants, you have

$$X = \begin{bmatrix} x_1 \\ x_2 \\ x_3 \end{bmatrix} \text{ and } K = \begin{bmatrix} k_1 \\ k_2 \\ k_3 \end{bmatrix}$$

and the system of equations could be represented by $AX = K$.

With normal equations you would divide both sides by A to get the values of X, but these are matrices and there is no commutative law for multiplication. We will return to this dilemma after we introduce a new matrix.

In Section 19.2, we introduced matrix multiplication. A square $n \times n$ matrix with a 1 in each position of the main diagonal and zeros elsewhere is called the $n \times n$ **identity matrix** and is denoted as I_n. Thus,

$$I_2 = \begin{bmatrix} 1 & 0 \\ 0 & 1 \end{bmatrix} \text{ and } I_3 = \begin{bmatrix} 1 & 0 & 0 \\ 0 & 1 & 0 \\ 0 & 0 & 1 \end{bmatrix}$$

are both identity matrices.

If the size of the identity matrix is understood, we simply write I.

Now, back to our problem of $AX = K$. What we need is a matrix A^{-1}, where $A^{-1}A = I$. We would then find that

$$X = A^{-1}K$$

When A is an $n \times n$ matrix, then A is an **invertible** or **nonsingular matrix**, if there exists another $n \times n$ matrix, A^{-1}, where

$$A^{-1}A = AA^{-1} = I$$

If A^{-1} exists, it is called the **inverse of matrix A**. A matrix is called a **singular matrix** if it does not have an inverse.

There are two procedures for finding the inverse of a matrix. The first method may be easier on 2×2 matrices.

STEPS FOR FINDING THE INVERSE OF A 2 × 2 MATRIX

If $A = \begin{bmatrix} a & b \\ c & d \end{bmatrix}$ is a 2 × 2 matrix, then use the following four steps to determine A^{-1}:

1. Interchange the elements on the main diagonal.
2. Change the signs of the elements that are not on the main diagonal.
3. Find the determinant of the original matrix.
4. Divide each element at the end of Step 2 by the determinant of the original matrix.

 NOTE Symbolically, we can summarize the four steps for finding the inverse of a 2 × 2 matrix as

$$A^{-1} = \frac{1}{ad - bc} \begin{bmatrix} d & -b \\ -c & a \end{bmatrix}$$

EXAMPLE 19.16 Find the inverse of the matrix $A = \begin{bmatrix} 1 & 2 \\ 4 & 10 \end{bmatrix}$.

SOLUTION

Step 1: $\begin{bmatrix} 10 & 2 \\ 4 & 1 \end{bmatrix}$ Interchange elements on main diagonal.

Step 2: $\begin{bmatrix} 10 & -2 \\ -4 & 1 \end{bmatrix}$ Change signs of elements not on main diagonal.

Step 3: $\begin{vmatrix} 1 & 2 \\ 4 & 10 \end{vmatrix} = 10 - 8 = 2$ Find the determinant of the original matrix.

Step 4: $\begin{bmatrix} \frac{10}{2} & \frac{-2}{2} \\ \frac{-4}{2} & \frac{1}{2} \end{bmatrix}$ Divide each element from Step 2 by the determinant (Step 3).

The inverse is $A^{-1} = \begin{bmatrix} 5 & -1 \\ -2 & \frac{1}{2} \end{bmatrix}$. Check your answer. Is $A^{-1}A = I$?

$$\begin{bmatrix} 5 & -1 \\ -2 & \frac{1}{2} \end{bmatrix} \begin{bmatrix} 1 & 2 \\ 4 & 10 \end{bmatrix} = \begin{bmatrix} 5-4 & 10-10 \\ -2+2 & -4+5 \end{bmatrix} = \begin{bmatrix} 1 & 0 \\ 0 & 1 \end{bmatrix} = I$$

The second method for determining the inverse of a matrix is slightly more complicated for a 2×2 matrix, but it will work for a matrix of any size.

With the second method, we are going to transform the given matrix into the identity matrix. At the same time, we will change an identity matrix into the inverse of the given matrix.

STEPS FOR FINDING THE INVERSE FOR ANY $n \times n$ MATRIX

The idea in this method for finding A^{-1} is to begin with the matrix $\begin{bmatrix} A & \vdots & I \end{bmatrix}$ and use the following two valid matrix operations as necessary to change it to $\begin{bmatrix} I & \vdots & A^{-1} \end{bmatrix}$.

1. Multiply or divide all elements in a row by a nonzero constant.

2. Add a constant multiple of the elements of one row to the corresponding elements of another row.

We demonstrate this method in Example 19.17 with the same matrix used in Example 19.16.

EXAMPLE 19.17   Find the inverse of $A = \begin{bmatrix} 1 & 2 \\ 4 & 10 \end{bmatrix}$.

SOLUTION First, we form the augmented matrix $\begin{bmatrix} A & \vdots & I \end{bmatrix}$.

$$\begin{bmatrix} 1 & 2 & \vdots & 1 & 0 \\ 4 & 10 & \vdots & 0 & 1 \end{bmatrix}$$

In the following demonstration, we let R_1 mean Row 1 and R_2 mean Row 2 for this 2×4 matrix. The arrows point to the row that we changed and that row

EXAMPLE 19.17 (Cont.) | is always listed last. Everything we do is designed to change the left half of the matrix to the identity matrix.

$$\left[\begin{array}{cc|cc} 1 & 2 & 1 & 0 \\ 4 & 10 & 0 & 1 \end{array}\right]$$

There is already a 1 in the a_{11} position. We need to get a 0 below it. First, multiply R_1 by -4 and add that to R_2 to get a new Row 2.

$$\left[\begin{array}{cc|cc} 1 & 2 & 1 & 0 \\ 0 & 2 & -4 & 1 \end{array}\right] \leftarrow -4R_1 + R_2$$

Now that the first column is $\begin{bmatrix} 1 \\ 0 \end{bmatrix}$, we move to the second column to get it in the form $\begin{bmatrix} 0 \\ 1 \end{bmatrix}$.

Next, multiply R_2 by -1 and add that to R_1. This is the new row 1.

$$\left[\begin{array}{cc|cc} 1 & 0 & 5 & -1 \\ 0 & 2 & -4 & 1 \end{array}\right] \leftarrow -R_2 + R_1$$

Now, all that is left is to divide Row 2 by 2 (or multiply it by $\frac{1}{2}$).

$$\left[\begin{array}{cc|cc} 1 & 0 & 5 & -1 \\ 0 & 1 & -2 & \frac{1}{2} \end{array}\right] \leftarrow \frac{1}{2}R_2$$

The left half of the matrix is the identity matrix and the right half is the inverse that we wanted.

$$A^{-1} = \begin{bmatrix} 5 & -1 \\ -2 & \frac{1}{2} \end{bmatrix}$$

This is the same answer we got for Example 19.16.

We will work another 2×2 example and then work a 3×3 example. Before beginning, you should always check to see if the matrix is invertible. It will not be invertible if every element in any row or column is zero. Thus

$$\begin{bmatrix} 1 & 2 & 3 \\ 0 & 0 & 0 \\ 4 & 5 & 6 \end{bmatrix} \text{ and } \begin{bmatrix} 1 & 2 & 0 \\ 4 & 5 & 0 \\ 7 & 8 & 0 \end{bmatrix}$$

cannot be inverted. A matrix cannot be inverted if every element in one row (or column) is a constant multiple of every corresponding element in another row (or column). Thus $\begin{bmatrix} 4 & 2 \\ 12 & 6 \end{bmatrix}$ cannot be inverted, because each element in row 2 is 3 times its corresponding element in row 1. Notice that a matrix that cannot be inverted has a determinant of 0.

EXAMPLE 19.18

Find the inverse of $B = \begin{bmatrix} 8 & 4 \\ 3 & 2 \end{bmatrix}$.

SOLUTION $\left[\begin{array}{cc|cc} 8 & 4 & 1 & 0 \\ 3 & 2 & 0 & 1 \end{array}\right]$

$\left[\begin{array}{cc|cc} 8 & 4 & 1 & 0 \\ 0 & 4 & -3 & 8 \end{array}\right] \leftarrow -3R_1 + 8R_2$

$\left[\begin{array}{cc|cc} 8 & 0 & 4 & -8 \\ 0 & 4 & -3 & 8 \end{array}\right] \leftarrow -R_2 + R_1$

$\left[\begin{array}{cc|cc} 1 & 0 & \frac{1}{2} & -1 \\ 0 & 1 & -\frac{3}{4} & 2 \end{array}\right] \begin{array}{l} \leftarrow R_1 \div 8 \\ \leftarrow R_2 \div 4 \end{array}$

The inverted matrix is $B^{-1} = \begin{bmatrix} \frac{1}{2} & -1 \\ -\frac{3}{4} & 2 \end{bmatrix}$.

EXAMPLE 19.19

Find the inverse of $C = \begin{bmatrix} 7 & -8 & 5 \\ -4 & 5 & -3 \\ 1 & -1 & 1 \end{bmatrix}$.

SOLUTION $\left[\begin{array}{ccc|ccc} 7 & -8 & 5 & 1 & 0 & 0 \\ -4 & 5 & -3 & 0 & 1 & 0 \\ 1 & -1 & 1 & 0 & 0 & 1 \end{array}\right]$

$\left[\begin{array}{ccc|ccc} 7 & -8 & 5 & 1 & 0 & 0 \\ -4 & 5 & -3 & 0 & 1 & 0 \\ 0 & -1 & -2 & 1 & 0 & -7 \end{array}\right] \leftarrow R_1 - 7R_3$

$\left[\begin{array}{ccc|ccc} 7 & -8 & 5 & 1 & 0 & 0 \\ 0 & 3 & -1 & 4 & 7 & 0 \\ 0 & -1 & -2 & 1 & 0 & -7 \end{array}\right] \leftarrow 4R_1 + 7R_2$

$\left[\begin{array}{ccc|ccc} 7 & -8 & 5 & 1 & 0 & 0 \\ 0 & 3 & -1 & 4 & 7 & 0 \\ 0 & 0 & -7 & 7 & 7 & -21 \end{array}\right] \leftarrow R_2 + 3R_3$

$\left[\begin{array}{ccc|ccc} 7 & -8 & 5 & 1 & 0 & 0 \\ 0 & -21 & 0 & -21 & -42 & -21 \\ 0 & 0 & -7 & 7 & 7 & -21 \end{array}\right] \leftarrow R_3 - 7R_2$

$\left[\begin{array}{ccc|ccc} 7 & -8 & 5 & 1 & 0 & 0 \\ 0 & 1 & 0 & 1 & 2 & 1 \\ 0 & 0 & 1 & -1 & -1 & 3 \end{array}\right] \begin{array}{l} \\ \leftarrow R_2 \div -21 \\ \leftarrow R_3 \div -7 \end{array}$

$\left[\begin{array}{ccc|ccc} 7 & -8 & 0 & 6 & 5 & -15 \\ 0 & 1 & 0 & 1 & 2 & 1 \\ 0 & 0 & 1 & -1 & -1 & 3 \end{array}\right] \leftarrow -5R_3 + R_1$

EXAMPLE 19.19 (Cont.)

$$\left[\begin{array}{ccc|ccc} 7 & 0 & 0 & 14 & 21 & -7 \\ 0 & 1 & 0 & 1 & 2 & 1 \\ 0 & 0 & 1 & -1 & -1 & 3 \end{array}\right] \leftarrow 8R_2 + R_1$$

$$\left[\begin{array}{ccc|ccc} 1 & 0 & 0 & 2 & 3 & -1 \\ 0 & 1 & 0 & 1 & 2 & 1 \\ 0 & 0 & 1 & -1 & -1 & 3 \end{array}\right] \leftarrow R_1 \div 7$$

The inverse of C is $C^{-1} = \begin{bmatrix} 2 & 3 & -1 \\ 1 & 2 & 1 \\ -1 & -1 & 3 \end{bmatrix}$.

INVERTING A MATRIX WITH A GRAPHING CALCULATOR

Using a graphing calculator to invert a matrix is much simpler than the process used in Examples 19.16 through 19.19.

USING A GRAPHING CALCULATOR TO INVERT A MATRIX

1. Define the matrix as described in Section 6.4
2. Enter the name of the matrix
3. Press x^{-1} **ENTER**

The next example shows how to find the inverse of a matrix by using a graphing calculator.

EXAMPLE 19.20

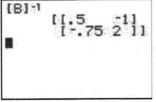

© Cengage Learning 2013

Figure 19.1a

Use a graphing calculator to find the inverse of $B = \begin{bmatrix} 8 & 4 \\ 3 & 2 \end{bmatrix}$.

SOLUTION Enter matrix B as described in the user's guide for your calculator, or as described in Section 6.4. Let this matrix be named B.

Quit the edit matrix mode and return to the home screen. Now press **2nd** **MATRIX** **2** x^{-1} **ENTER**. The result should be similar to the one shown in Figure 19.1a.

If your calculator can convert decimals to fractions, you might want to convert B^{-1} to fractional form. For example, on a TI-83 or TI-84, press the **▶Frac** key. The result, shown in Figure 19.1b, matches the result we got in Example 19.18.

© Cengage Learning 2013

Figure 19.1b

INVERSES OF MATRICES WITH A SPREADSHEET

EXAMPLE 19.21

Use a spreadsheet to find the inverse of $B = \begin{bmatrix} 8 & 4 \\ 3 & 2 \end{bmatrix}$.

SOLUTION Enter matrix B in Cells C1 through D2 as shown in Figure 19.2a.

In order to display each cell of the inverse matrix, Excel requires two functions. The MINVERSE function returns the inverse matrix as an array of numbers. The INDEX function returns the contents of the cell defined by rows and columns.

In Cell C4, enter =INDEX(MINVERSE(C1:D2),1,1). The C1:D2 portion of the formula identifies the matrix B in Cells C1 through D2. The 1, 1 portion of the formula identifies the ROW and COLUMN of the cell in the inverse matrix we want to write in this cell. (See Figure 19.2b.)

In Cell D4, enter =INDEX(MINVERSE(C1:D2),1,2). (See Figure 19.2c.)

The 1, 2 portion of the formula identifies the first row and second column as the cell in the inverse we wish to write. The process is repeated for the other two cells (see Figures 19.2d and 19.2e.)

To convert all the entries to fractions, select the array and, under Format, select Cells. Select the Number tab and select Fraction to convert the decimal representations to fractions. The result is shown in Figure 19.2f.

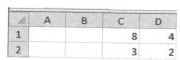

© Cengage Learning 2013

Figure 19.2a

f_x =INDEX(MINVERSE(C1:D2),1,1)

C	D	E	F	G
8	4			
3	2			
0.5				

© Cengage Learning 2013

Figure 19.2b

f_x =INDEX(MINVERSE(C1:D2),1,2)

C	D	E	F	G
8	4			
3	2			
0.5	-1			

© Cengage Learning 2013

Figure 19.2c

f_x =INDEX(MINVERSE(C1:D2),2,1)

C	D	E	F	G
8	4			
3	2			
0.5	-1			
-0.75				

© Cengage Learning 2013

Figure 19.2d

f_x =INDEX(MINVERSE(C1:D2),2,2)

C	D	E	F	G
8	4			
3	2			
0.5	-1			
-0.75	2			

© Cengage Learning 2013

Figure 19.2e

© Cengage Learning 2013

Figure 19.2f

EXERCISE SET 19.3

In Exercises 1–20, if the given matrix is invertible, find its inverse.

1. $\begin{bmatrix} 6 & 1 \\ 5 & 1 \end{bmatrix}$

2. $\begin{bmatrix} 5 & 1 \\ 9 & 2 \end{bmatrix}$

3. $\begin{bmatrix} 10 & 4 \\ 8 & 3 \end{bmatrix}$

4. $\begin{bmatrix} 9 & 6 \\ 4 & 3 \end{bmatrix}$

5. $\begin{bmatrix} 8 & -6 \\ -6 & 4 \end{bmatrix}$

6. $\begin{bmatrix} 12 & 9 \\ -9 & -7 \end{bmatrix}$

7. $\begin{bmatrix} 15 & 10 \\ 4 & 3 \end{bmatrix}$

8. $\begin{bmatrix} 15 & 10 \\ 3 & 4 \end{bmatrix}$

9. $\begin{bmatrix} 0 & -3 & 0 \\ 1 & 0 & 0 \\ 0 & 0 & 4 \end{bmatrix}$

10. $\begin{bmatrix} 1 & 0 & 0 \\ 0 & 4 & 0 \\ 0 & 0 & 2 \end{bmatrix}$

11. $\begin{bmatrix} 1 & 2 & 6 \\ 0 & 0 & 2 \\ -3 & -6 & -9 \end{bmatrix}$

12. $\begin{bmatrix} 4 & 5 & 1 \\ 1 & 0 & 1 \\ 4 & 5 & 1 \end{bmatrix}$

13. $\begin{bmatrix} 8 & 7 & -1 \\ -5 & -5 & 1 \\ -4 & -4 & 1 \end{bmatrix}$

14. $\begin{bmatrix} 1 & 2 & 3 \\ 2 & 5 & 7 \\ 1 & 1 & 1 \end{bmatrix}$

15. $\begin{bmatrix} 3 & -1 & 0 \\ -6 & 2 & 0 \\ 1 & 0 & 5 \end{bmatrix}$

16. $\begin{bmatrix} 1 & -1 & 1 \\ 7 & -8 & 5 \\ -4 & 5 & -3 \end{bmatrix}$

17. $\begin{bmatrix} 2 & 0 & 0 \\ 2 & 2 & 0 \\ 2 & 2 & 2 \end{bmatrix}$

18. $\begin{bmatrix} 3 & 1 & -1 \\ 1 & -2 & 0 \\ 0 & 3 & 1 \end{bmatrix}$

19. $\begin{bmatrix} 1 & -1 & 1 \\ 0 & 2 & -1 \\ 2 & 3 & 0 \end{bmatrix}$

20. $\begin{bmatrix} 1 & 2 & -1 \\ 2 & -2 & 1 \\ 6 & 4 & 3 \end{bmatrix}$

Solve Exercise 21.

21. Check your answers to 1–20 by multiplying the given matrix and its inverse. Remember, if the matrix in the problem is called A and your answer A^{-1}, then $AA^{-1} = I$.

 [IN YOUR WORDS]

22. Not all matrices have an inverse. List the conditions that will tell you if a matrix is not invertible.

23. If your calculator can work with complex numbers,
  (a) describe how to find the inverse of the matrix $A = \begin{bmatrix} i & 4+3i \\ 3 & 2-2i \end{bmatrix}$, and **(b)** compute A^{-1}.

19.4 MATRICES AND LINEAR EQUATIONS

Earlier in this chapter, we said that a system of equations could be represented by matrices. For example, the system

$$\begin{cases} 2x + 3y = 5 \\ 3x + 5y = 9 \end{cases}$$

would be represented by three matrices A, X, and K, where $AX = K$. To do this, let A be the matrix formed by the coefficients of the variables, let X be a column vector of the variables, and let K be a column vector of the constants. Thus, for this system, we have

$$A = \begin{bmatrix} 2 & 3 \\ 3 & 5 \end{bmatrix} \qquad X = \begin{bmatrix} x \\ y \end{bmatrix} \qquad K = \begin{bmatrix} 5 \\ 9 \end{bmatrix}$$

Now that we can invert a matrix, we can find A^{-1}. Since $A^{-1}A = I$ then $A^{-1}(AX) = (A^{-1}A)X = IX = X$. With this knowledge, we can find the solution to our system of equations.

$$AX = K$$
$$A^{-1}(AX) = A^{-1}K$$
$$X = A^{-1}K$$

EXAMPLE 19.22

Use the inverse of the coefficient matrix to solve the linear system

$$\begin{cases} 2x + 3y = 5 \\ 3x + 5y = 9 \end{cases}$$

SOLUTION We can think of this as the matrix equation $AX = K$, with $A = \begin{bmatrix} 2 & 3 \\ 3 & 5 \end{bmatrix}, X = \begin{bmatrix} x \\ y \end{bmatrix}$, and $K = \begin{bmatrix} 5 \\ 9 \end{bmatrix}$.

Using a calculator

On a TI-83 or TI-84 you cannot name a matrix K, so we will use C, for constant.

Figure 19.3a shows that the solution to this matrix is $X = A^{-1}C = \begin{bmatrix} -2 \\ 3 \end{bmatrix}$

Using a spreadsheet

We can think of this as the matrix equation $AX = K$ with $A = \begin{bmatrix} 2 & 3 \\ 3 & 5 \end{bmatrix}$, $X = \begin{bmatrix} x \\ y \end{bmatrix}$, and $K = \begin{bmatrix} 5 \\ 9 \end{bmatrix}$, as shown in Figure 19.3b.

To multiply two matrices, we use the MMULT function. The MMULT function returns an array (or list) of numbers, so again we must use the INDEX function to obtain each individual cell.

We know the result of the multiplication is a 2×1 matrix. So, move the cursor to Cell C7 and enter the appropriate function (see Figure 19.3c). Repeating this is Cell C8, we get the second value in the answer.

The result, shown in Figure 19.3d, means that $x = -2$ and $y = 3$.

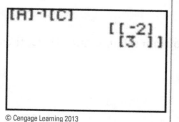

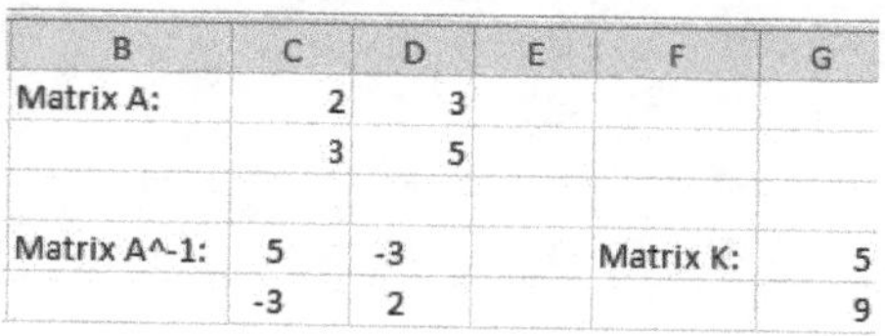

© Cengage Learning 2013

Figure 19.3a

B	C	D	E	F	G
Matrix A:	2	3			
	3	5			
Matrix A^-1:	5	-3		Matrix K:	5
	-3	2			9

© Cengage Learning 2013

Figure 19.3b

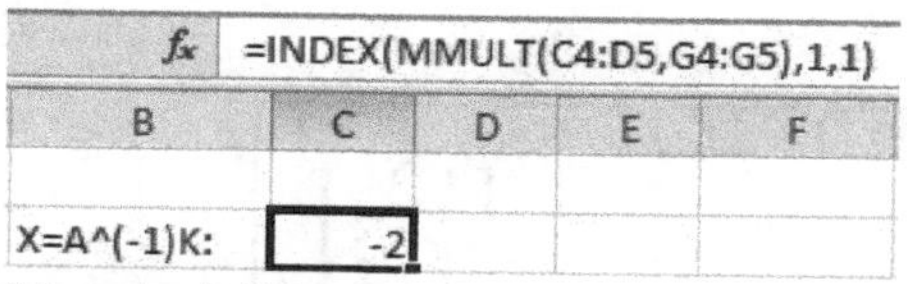

	f_x	=INDEX(MMULT(C4:D5,G4:G5),1,1)			
	B	C	D	E	F
X=A^(-1)K:		-2			

© Cengage Learning 2013

Figure 19.3c

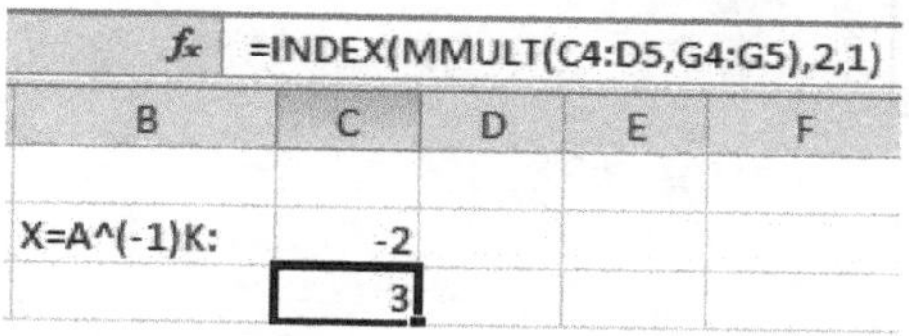

	f_x	=INDEX(MMULT(C4:D5,G4:G5),2,1)			
	B	C	D	E	F
X=A^(-1)K:		-2			
		3			

© Cengage Learning 2013

Figure 19.3d

Let's try this method for solving a system of linear equations on a system of three equations with three variables.

EXAMPLE 19.23

Use the inverse of the coefficient matrix to solve the linear system

$$\begin{cases} 7x - 8y + 5z = 18 \\ -4x + 5y - 3z = -11 \\ x - y + z = 1 \end{cases}$$

SOLUTION This linear system can be represented by the three matrices A, X, and K, where $AX = K$. Again, A is the matrix formed by the coefficients, X is the column vector of the variables, and K is the column vector of the constants. From this system we have

$$A = \begin{bmatrix} 7 & -8 & 5 \\ -4 & 5 & -3 \\ 1 & -1 & 1 \end{bmatrix} \qquad X = \begin{bmatrix} x \\ y \\ z \end{bmatrix} \qquad K = C \begin{bmatrix} 18 \\ -11 \\ 1 \end{bmatrix}$$

Using a calculator

We enter matrices A and C in the calculator. As you can see in Figure 19.4a, the solution to this equation is $X = A^{-1}C = \begin{bmatrix} 2 \\ -3 \\ -4 \end{bmatrix}$.

Using a spreadsheet

Figure 19.4b shows matrix A, X, and K.

(The dollar signs in the formula are used to "anchor" the cells from which we take the inverse [C1:E3] so that when the formula is copied from Cell C5 to the other eight cells, the reference will remain valid.)

The result, shown in Figure 19.4c, shows that $x = 2$, $y = -3$, and $z = -4$.

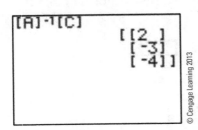

Figure 19.4a

© Cengage Learning 2013

	A	B	C	D	E	F	G	H
			C5		f_x	=INDEX(MINVERSE($C$1:$E$3),1,1)		
1		Matrix A:	7	-8	5			
2			-4	5	-3			
3			1	-1	1			
4								
5		Matrix A^-1:	2	3	-1		Matrix K:	18
6			1	2	1			-11
7			-1	-1	3			1

Figure 19.4b

© Cengage Learning 2013

	A	B	C	D	E	F	G	H	I
					f_x =INDEX(MMULT($C$5:$E$7,$H$5:$H$7),1,1)				
1		Matrix A:	7	-8	5				
2			-4	5	-3				
3			1	-1	1				
4									
5		Matrix A^-1:	2	3	-1		Matrix K:	18	
6			1	2	1			-11	
7			-1	-1	3			1	
8									
9		X=A^(-1)K:	2						
10			-3						
11			-4						

Figure 19.4c

APPLICATION ELECTRONICS

EXAMPLE 19.24

Apply Kirchhoff's laws to the circuit in Figure 19.5 and determine the currents I_1, I_2, and I_3.

SOLUTION If we apply Kirchhoff's laws to the circuit in Figure 19.5, we obtain the following system of linear equations:

$$\begin{cases} I_1 - I_2 + I_3 = 0 \\ 5I_1 + 8I_2 = 4 \\ 8I_2 + 2I_3 = 38 \end{cases}$$

The coefficient matrix for this system is $A = \begin{bmatrix} 1 & -1 & 1 \\ 5 & 8 & 0 \\ 0 & 8 & 2 \end{bmatrix}$. (Notice that the coefficients of the missing variables are 0.) If the constant matrix is

$$B = \begin{bmatrix} 0 \\ 4 \\ 38 \end{bmatrix} \text{ and } X = \begin{bmatrix} I_1 \\ I_2 \\ I_3 \end{bmatrix}, \text{ then}$$

$$X = A^{-1}B$$

As before, we enter matrices A and B in a calculator or spreadsheet. As you can see from the calculator screen in Figure 19.6, the solution to this equation is $X = A^{-1}B = \begin{bmatrix} -4 \\ 3 \\ 7 \end{bmatrix}$. (A spreadsheet gives the same result.) Thus, the three currents are $I_1 = -4$ A, $I_2 = 3$ A, and $I_3 = 7$ A.

Figure 19.5

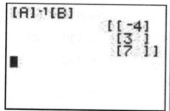

[A]⁻¹[B]
[[-4]
[3]
[7]]

Figure 19.6

EXERCISE SET 19.4

In Exercises 1–10, solve the given systems of equations by using the inverse of the coefficient matrix.

1. $\begin{cases} 6x + y = -4 \\ 5x + y = -3 \end{cases}$

2. $\begin{cases} 10x + 4y = 8 \\ 8x + 3y = 7 \end{cases}$

3. $\begin{cases} 8x - 6y = -27 \\ -6x + 4y = 19 \end{cases}$

4. $\begin{cases} 15x + 10y = -5 \\ 4x + 3y = 0 \end{cases}$

5. $\begin{cases} x + 2y + 6z = 12 \\ 2z = 2 \\ -3x - 6y - 9z = -27 \end{cases}$

6. $\begin{cases} 8x + 7x - z = 9 \\ -5x - 5y + z = -1 \\ -4x - 4y + z = 0 \end{cases}$

7. $\begin{cases} x + 2y + 3z = 4 \\ 2x + 5y + 7z = 7.5 \\ x + y + z = 1 \end{cases}$

8. $\begin{cases} x - y + z = -6.6 \\ 7x - 8y + 5z = -43 \\ -4x + 5y - 3z = 26.9 \end{cases}$

9. $\begin{cases} 2x = 11 \\ 2x + 2y = 4 \\ 2x + 2y + 2z = -9 \end{cases}$

10. $\begin{cases} x - y + z = 22 \\ 2y - z = -23 \\ 2x + 3y = -11.2 \end{cases}$

In Exercises 11–20, solve each system of equations by using the inverse of the coefficient matrix.

11. $\begin{cases} 2x + y = 1 \\ -3x + 2y = 16 \end{cases}$

12. $\begin{cases} 4x + 5y = 2 \\ 3x - 2y = 13 \end{cases}$

13. $\begin{cases} 2x + 2y = 4 \\ 4x + 3y = 1 \end{cases}$

14. $\begin{cases} 3x + y = -5 \\ 4x + 3y = 2 \end{cases}$

15. $\begin{cases} 1.5x + 2.5y = 0.3 \\ 3.2x + 2.6y = 7.2 \end{cases}$

16. $\begin{cases} 7x + 2y + z = 2 \\ 3x - 2y + 4z = 13 \\ 4x + 5y - z = 1 \end{cases}$

17. $\begin{cases} 5x + 2y + 3z = 1 \\ -3x + 2y - 8z = 6 \\ 4x - 2y + 9z = -7 \end{cases}$

18. $\begin{cases} 2x + 4y + z = 10 \\ 4x + 2y + z = 8 \\ 6x + 4y + 7z = -2 \end{cases}$

19. $\begin{cases} x + 2y + 4z = 7 \\ 3x + y + 4z = -2 \\ 2x + 9y - 2z = 10 \end{cases}$

20. $\begin{cases} 2x - y + z = 7 \\ 4x - 2y + z = 5 \\ 6x - 3y + 5z = -3 \end{cases}$

Solve Exercises 21–30.

21. *Electronics* If Kirchhoff's laws are applied to the circuit in Figure 19.7, the following equations are obtained. Determine the indicated currents.

$$I_A - I_B - I_C = 0$$
$$16I_A + 4I_C = 100$$
$$12I_B - 4I_C = 60$$

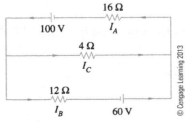

Figure 19.7

22. *Electronics* Applying Kirchhoff's laws to the circuit in Figure 19.8 results in the following equations. Determine the indicated currents.

$$I_3 - I_1 - I_2 = 0$$
$$20I_1 + 0.5I_1 - 15I_2 - 0.4I_2 = 120 - 80$$
$$15I_2 + 0.4I_2 + 10I_3 + 0.6I_3 = 140$$

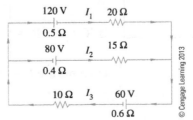

Figure 19.8

23. Electronics The currents through the resistors in Figure 19.9 produce the following equations. Determine the currents.

$$7.18I_1 - I_2 + 2.2I_3 = 10$$
$$-I_1 + 5.8I_2 + 1.5I_3 = 15$$
$$2.2I_1 + 1.5I_2 + 8.4I_3 = 20$$

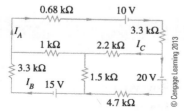

Figure 19.9

24. Business A company manufactures robotic controls. Its current models are the *RC*-1 and *RC*-2. Each *RC*-1 unit requires eight transistors and four integrated circuits. Each *RC*-2 unit uses nine transistors and five integrated circuits. Each day the company receives 1,596 transistors and 860 integrated circuits. How many units of each model can be made if all parts are used?

25. Metallurgy An alloy is composed of three metals, *A*, *B*, and *C*. The percentages of each metal are indicated by the following system of equations:

$$\begin{cases} A + B + C = 100 \\ A - 2B = 0 \\ -4A + C = 0 \end{cases}$$

Determine the percentage of each metal in the alloy.

26. Automotive technology A petroleum engineer was testing three different gasoline mixtures, *A*, *B*, and *C*, in the same car and under the same driving conditions. She noticed that the car traveled 90 km farther when it used mixture *B* than when it used mixture *A*. Using fuel *C*, the car traveled 130 km more than when it used fuel *B*. The total distance traveled was 1,900 km. Find the distance traveled on the three fuels.

27. Construction technology If three cables are joined at a point and three forces are applied so the system is in equilibrium, the following system of equations results.

$$\begin{cases} \frac{6}{7}F_B - \frac{2}{3}F_C = 2,000 \\ -F_A - \frac{3}{7}F_B + \frac{1}{3}F_C = 0 \\ \frac{2}{7}F_B + \frac{2}{3}F_C = 1,200 \end{cases}$$

Determine the three forces, F_A, F_B, and F_C, measured in newtons (N).

28. Environmental science To control ice and protect the environment, a certain city determines that the best mixture to be spread on roads consists of 5 units of salt, 6 units of sand, and 4 units of a chemical inhibiting agent. Three companies, *A*, *B*, and *C*, sell mixtures of these elements according to the following table:

	Salt	Sand	Inhibiting agent
Company A	2	1	1
Company B	2	2	2
Company C	1	5	1

© Cengage Learning 2013

(a) In what proportion should the city purchase from each company in order to spread the best mixture? (Assume that the city must buy, complete truckloads.)

(b) If the city expects to need 3,630,000 units for the winter, how many units should be bought from each company?

29. Automotive technology The relationship between the velocity, *v*, of a car (in mph) and the distance, *d* (in ft), required to bring it to a complete stop is known to be of the form $d = av^2 + bv + c$, where *a*, *b*, and *c* are constants. Use the following data to determine the values of *a*, *b*, and *c*. When $v = 20$, then $d = 40$; when $v = 55$, then $d = 206.25$; and when $v = 65$, then $d = 276.25$.

30. Metallurgy An alloy is composed of four metals, *A*, *B*, *C*, and *D*. The percentages of each metal are indicated by the following system of equations:

$$\begin{cases} A + B + C + D = 100 \\ A + B - C = 0 \\ -1.64A + D = 0 \\ 3A - 2C + 2D = -1 \end{cases}$$

Determine the percentage of each metal in the alloy.

[IN YOUR WORDS]

31. What conditions are necessary in order to use matrices to solve a system of equations?

32. Describe how to use your calculator to solve the system of linear equations $AX = K$, where A, X, and K are matrices.

CHAPTER 19   REVIEW

IMPORTANT TERMS AND CONCEPTS

Augmented matrix
Coefficient matrix
Column vector
Dimension
Identity matrix
Inverse of a matrix
Invertible matrix

Matrix
   Addition
   Multiplication
   Scalar multiplication
   Subtraction
Nonsingular matrix

Row vector
Scalar
Scalar multiplication
Singular matrix
Square matrix
Zero matrix

REVIEW EXERCISES

In Exercises 1–6, use the following matrices to determine the indicated matrix:

$$A = \begin{bmatrix} 4 & 3 & 2 & 5 \\ 6 & 7 & -1 & 4 \\ 9 & 10 & -8 & 3 \end{bmatrix} \quad B = \begin{bmatrix} 3 & -2 & 1 & 0 \\ 5 & -1 & 2 & 0 \\ 4 & 3 & -2 & 0 \end{bmatrix} \quad C = \begin{bmatrix} 0 & 1 & 0 & 2 \\ 3 & 0 & 4 & 0 \\ 0 & -5 & 0 & -6 \end{bmatrix}$$

1. $A + C$

2. $B + C$

3. $A - B$

4. $C - B$

5. $2A - 3C$

6. $4A + B - 2C$

In Exercises 7–10, find the indicated products.

7. $\begin{bmatrix} 3 & 2 \\ 4 & 5 \\ 1 & 0 \end{bmatrix} \begin{bmatrix} 1 & 2 \\ 0 & 1 \end{bmatrix}$

8. $\begin{bmatrix} 1 & -4 \\ 5 & 1 \end{bmatrix} \begin{bmatrix} 3 & 4 & 1 \\ 2 & 5 & 0 \end{bmatrix}$

9. $\begin{bmatrix} 3 \\ 2 \\ -1 \end{bmatrix} \begin{bmatrix} 4 & 5 & 1 \end{bmatrix}$

10. $\begin{bmatrix} 4 & 5 & 1 \end{bmatrix} \begin{bmatrix} -2 \\ 7 \\ -3 \end{bmatrix}$

In Exercises 11–14, if the given matrix is invertible, find its inverse.

11. $\begin{bmatrix} 2 & 3 \\ -4 & -5 \end{bmatrix}$

12. $\begin{bmatrix} 2 & -1 \\ 0 & 4 \end{bmatrix}$

13. $\begin{bmatrix} -2 & 1 & 0 \\ 0 & 4 & 0 \\ 1 & 0 & 1 \end{bmatrix}$

14. $\begin{bmatrix} 2 & 3 & -1 \\ 1 & 2 & 1 \\ -1 & -1 & 3 \end{bmatrix}$

In Exercises 15–18, solve the system of equations by using the inverse of the coefficient matrix.

15. $\begin{cases} 12x + 5y = -2 \\ 3x + y = 1.1 \end{cases}$

16. $\begin{cases} 4x + y = -4 \\ -3x + 2y = 14 \end{cases}$

17. $\begin{cases} 2x + 3y + 5z = 20 \\ -2x + 3y + 5z = 12 \\ 5x - 3y - 2z = 9 \end{cases}$

18. $\begin{cases} x + y + 6z = -3 \\ -2x + 2y + 4z = -2 \\ 3x + 2y + 4z = 14 \end{cases}$

Solve Exercises 19–24.

19. Physics Masses of 9 and 11 kg are attached to a cord that passes over a frictionless pulley. When the masses are released, the acceleration a of each mass, in meters per second squared (m/s²), and the tension T in the cord, in newtons (N), are related by the system

$$\begin{cases} T - 75.4 = 9a \\ 100.0 - T = 11a \end{cases}$$

Find a and T.

20. Business A computer company makes three types of computers—a personal computer (PC), a business computer (BC), and a technical computer (TC). There are three parts in each computer that it has difficulty getting: RAM chips, EPROMS, and transistors. The number of each part needed by each computer is shown in this table.

If the company is guaranteed 1,872 RAM chips, 771 EPROMS, and 1,770 transistors each week, how many of each computer can be made?

21. Given the equations

$$\begin{cases} x' = \frac{1}{2}(x + y\sqrt{3}) \\ y' = \frac{1}{2}(-x\sqrt{3} + y) \end{cases}$$

	RAM	EPROM	Transistor
PC	4	2	7
BC	8	3	6
TC	12	5	11

© Cengage Learning 2013

and

$$\begin{cases} x'' = \frac{1}{2}(-x' + y'\sqrt{3}) \\ y'' = -\frac{1}{2}(x'\sqrt{3} + y') \end{cases}$$

write each set as a matrix equation and solve for x'' and y'' in terms of x and y by multiplying matrices.

22. The equations in Exercise 21 represent rotations of axes in two directions. In Section 15.7, we found that, if the angle of rotation is θ, then

$$\begin{cases} x'' = x \cos \theta + y \sin \theta \\ y'' = -x \sin \theta + y \cos \theta \end{cases}$$

What was the rotation angle for the equations in Exercise 21?

23. Optics The following matrix product is used in discussing two thin lenses in air:

$$M = \begin{bmatrix} 1 & -\dfrac{1}{f_2} \\ 0 & 1 \end{bmatrix} \cdot \begin{bmatrix} 1 & 0 \\ d & 1 \end{bmatrix} \cdot \begin{bmatrix} 1 & -\dfrac{1}{f_1} \\ 0 & 1 \end{bmatrix}$$

where f_1 and f_2 are the focal lengths of the lenses and d is the distance between them. Evaluate M.

24. Optics In Exercise 23, element M_{12} of M is $-\dfrac{1}{f}$, where f is the focal length of the combination. Determine $\dfrac{1}{f}$.

CHAPTER 19 TEST

1. Given $A = \begin{bmatrix} 8 & 0 & -4 \\ 16 & -6 & 2 \end{bmatrix}$ and

$B = \begin{bmatrix} -1 & 5 & -3 \\ 3 & 0 & 4 \end{bmatrix}$, find

(a) $A + B$

(b) $3A - 2B$

2. Calculate the product $\begin{bmatrix} 1 & -2 & 3 \end{bmatrix} \begin{bmatrix} -4 \\ -6 \\ 8 \end{bmatrix}$.

3. If $C = \begin{bmatrix} 4 & 6 \\ -10 & 4 \end{bmatrix}$ and $D = \begin{bmatrix} \frac{1}{2} & 0 \\ -\frac{3}{2} & 4 \end{bmatrix}$, calculate (a) CD and (b) DC.

4. If $E = \begin{bmatrix} 2 & -3 \\ 7 & 9 \end{bmatrix}$, **(a)** find E^{-1}. **(b)** Use E^{-1} to

   solve $EX = F$, where $F = \begin{bmatrix} -31 \\ 28 \end{bmatrix}$.

5. Solve the following system of equations by using the inverse of the coefficient matrix:

$$\begin{cases} x + 3y + z = -2 \\ 2x + 5y + z = -5 \\ x + 2y + 3z = 6 \end{cases}$$

6. Three machine parts cost a total of $60. The first part costs as much as the other two together.

The cost of the second part is $3 more than twice the cost of the third part. How much does each part cost?

7. Find the currents of the system in Figure 19.10.

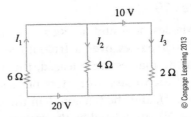

Figure 19.10

3.3 CIRCLES

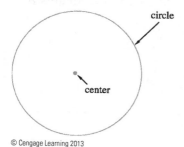

circle

center

© Cengage Learning 2013

Figure 3.40

Until now, the geometric figures we have studied have all been made of segments joined at their endpoints. A circle is a different type of geometric figure. Like the polygons, a circle is part of a plane. A circle is made up of the set of points that are all the same distance from a point called the center, as shown in Figure 3.40.

PARTS OF A CIRCLE

There are many parts to a circle. Some of them are shown in Figure 3.41. The radius is a segment with one endpoint at the center and the other on the circle. A chord is any segment with both endpoints on the circle. A diameter is a chord through the center of the circle. A secant is a line that intersects a circle twice, and a tangent intersects the circle in exactly one point. A tangent is perpendicular to the radius at its point of tangency. The circumference of a circle is the name for the perimeter and is equal to the distance around the circle.

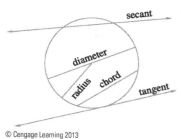

secant

diameter

radius   chord

tangent

© Cengage Learning 2013

Figure 3.41

Figure 3.42 shows a few more parts of the circle that will be used later. A central angle is an angle with a vertex at the center of the circle. An arc is a section of a circle and is often described in terms of the size of its central angle. Thus, we might refer to a 20° arc or an arc of $\frac{\pi}{9}$ rad. An arc with length equal to the radius is 1 rad.

A central angle divides a circle into a *minor arc* and a *major arc*. We also may refer to an arc by its endpoints. The minor arc in Figure 3.42 is identified as $\widehat{AB}$. The major arc is identified as ACB, where A and B are the endpoints and C is any other point on the major arc. The length of an arc is denoted by placing an m in front of the name of the arc. Thus, $m\,\widehat{AB}$ is the length of $\widehat{AB}$. A **sector** is the region inside the circle and is bounded by a central angle and an arc.

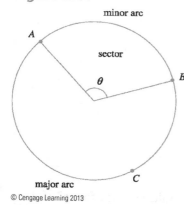

minor arc

A

sector

θ

B

major arc C

© Cengage Learning 2013

Figure 3.42

CIRCUMFERENCE AND AREA OF CIRCLES

The formulas for the circumference and area of a circle involve the use of the irrational number π. The circumference C of a circle is

$$C = \pi d \qquad \text{or} \qquad C = 2\pi r, \qquad (\text{where } d = 2r)$$

where d is the length of a diameter and r is the length of a radius.

The area of a circle is

$$A = \pi r^2$$

Some mechanics use the formula

$$A \approx 0.785d^2$$

Since $d = 2r$, you can see that $d^2 = 4r^2$ and so $r^2 = \dfrac{d^2}{4}$. The area of the circle can be written as $A = \pi\left(\dfrac{d^2}{4}\right) = \frac{\pi}{4}d^2$. Since $\frac{\pi}{4} \approx 0.785$, we have $A \approx 0.785d^2$.

CIRCUMFERENCE AND AREA OF A CIRCLE

A circle with radius r and diameter d has a circumference C and an area A where

$$C = 2\pi r = \pi d$$

$$\text{and } A = \pi r^2 = \frac{\pi}{4}d^2$$

EXAMPLE 3.15

Find the circumference and area of a circle with **(a)** diameter 7.00 in. and **(b)** radius 8.3 mm.

SOLUTIONS   (a) $d = 7.00\,\text{in.}$

$C = \pi d$

$= \pi(7)$

$\approx 21.99\,\text{in.}$

$A = \pi r^2$

$= \pi\left(\frac{7}{2}\right)^2$

$\approx 38.48\,\text{in.}^2$

(b) $r = 8.3\,\text{mm}$

$C = 2\pi r$

$= 2\pi(8.3)$

$\approx 52.2\,\text{mm}$

$A = \pi r^2$

$= \pi(8.3)^2$

$\approx 216.4\,\text{mm}^2$

This example raises a question. What value should you use for π? If you use 3.14 or $3\frac{1}{7}$, your answers may differ slightly from those shown. They were obtained using a value programmed into a calculator and recalled by pressing the π key, with the resulting display of 3.1415927. As you can see, $\pi \neq 3.14$. We use 3.14 as an approximation of π.

APPLICATION   ARCHITECTURE

EXAMPLE 3.16

The corporate headquarters of U.S. Xpress Enterprises, Inc. in Chattanooga, Tennessee, is shown in Figure 3.43. The building has a circular window in the

Figure 3.43

front of the building that has a diameter, including the frame, of $23'11\frac{1}{2}''$. What are the **(a)** circumference and **(b)** area of the window and frame together?

SOLUTIONS

In order to solve this problem we must first convert $23'11\frac{1}{2}''$ to feet. Using dimension analysis we see that $11\frac{1}{2}'' = 11.5'' = \dfrac{11.5 \text{ in.}}{1} \times \dfrac{1 \text{ ft}}{12 \text{ in.}} \approx 0.958\overline{3} \text{ ft}.$ Thus, the diameter is $23.958\overline{3}$ ft.

(a) To find the circumference we use the formula $C = \pi d$. For this window the circumference is $C = \pi \cdot 23.958\overline{3} \approx 75.27$ ft.

(b) For the area we will use the formula $A = \dfrac{\pi}{4}d^2$.

$$A = \frac{\pi}{4}d^2$$

$$= \frac{\pi}{4}(23.958\overline{3})^2$$

$$\approx 450.82$$

The area of this window and frame is about 450.82 ft^2.

ARC LENGTH

The arc length s is a direct result of the size of the angle that determines the arc. An angle of 2π rad is a complete revolution and has an arc length equal to the circumference, $2\pi r$. An angle of π rad is half a revolution, and so its arc length is πr. Similarly, an angle of 3 rad has an arc length of $3r$. In general, a central angle of θ rad has an arc length of θr. This gives us the following formula.

ARC LENGTH

An arc formed from a circle of radius r and central angle of θ rad has an arc length s, where

$$s = \theta r$$

Similarly, the area of a sector of a circle can be derived from the formula for the area of a circle. A complete circle has an angle of 2π rad and an area of $\pi r^2 = \frac{1}{2}(2\pi)r^2$. A semicircle, or half a circle, has an angle of π rad and an area of $\frac{1}{2}\pi r^2$. In general, a central angle of θ rad forms a sector with area $\frac{1}{2}\theta r^2 = \frac{1}{2}r^2\theta$.

AREA OF A SECTOR

A sector formed by a circular arc with radius r and a central angle of θ rad has an area, A, where

$$A = \frac{1}{2}r^2\theta$$

NOTE In both of the previous formulas, the central angle θ *must* be in radians.

APPLICATION ARCHITECTURE

EXAMPLE 3.17

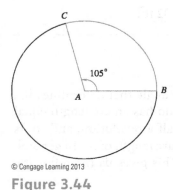

© Cengage Learning 2013

Figure 3.44

A landscaper is going to put some plastic edging around a pie-shaped flower bed. The flower bed is formed from a circle with radius 9.0 ft and a central angle of 105°. How much edging, in feet, will be needed?

SOLUTION A sketch of the flower bed is shown in Figure 3.44. The edging will go from C to A then to B and back to C around the arc of the circle. The length of edging needed is $CA + AB + m\widehat{BC} = 9.0 + 9.0 + m\widehat{BC} = 18.0 + m\widehat{BC}$. All we need to determine is the length of the arc $\widehat{BC}$.

To determine the length of the arc, we will use $s = \theta r$. Here, $r = 9.0$ and $\theta = 105°$. To use this formula, we must convert 105° to radians. Using the proportion $\dfrac{D}{180°} = \dfrac{R}{\pi}$, with $D = 105°$, we obtain $R = \dfrac{7\pi}{12}$. Thus,

$$m\,\widehat{BC} = r\theta$$

$$= 9.0\left(\frac{7\pi}{12}\right)$$

$$= \frac{21.0\pi}{4} \approx 16.5\,\text{ft}$$

So, the length of edging needed is $18.0 + 16.5 = 34.5$ ft.

APPLICATION MECHANICAL

EXAMPLE 3.18

A machine shop is installing two pulleys with radii 570 mm and 130 mm, respectively. The pulleys, as shown in Figure 3.45, are 1250 mm apart and the length AB is 1170 mm. If $\angle AOP = 70°$, what is the length of the driving belt?

SOLUTION To solve this problem we must add the lengths of the straight sections of the belt, AB and CD, and the two arc lengths, s_1 and s_2. We are given $AB = 1170$ mm. So, $CD = 1170$. To find s_1 we will use $s_1 = r\theta$. We are

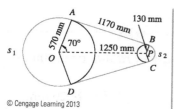

Figure 3.45

given $r = 570\,\text{mm}$, $\theta = 360° - \angle AOD = 360° - 140° = 220° \approx 3.84\,\text{rad}$. This means that

$$s_1 = r\theta$$
$$= 570(3.84)$$
$$= 2188.8\,\text{mm}$$

Now, $s_2 = r\theta$, where $r_2 = 130\,\text{mm}$ and $\theta_2 = 140° \approx 2.44\,\text{rad}$. So,

$$s_2 = r_2\theta_2$$
$$= (130)(2.44)$$
$$= 317.2\,\text{mm}$$

The length of the belt is $1170 + 317.2 + 1170 + 2188.8 = 4846\,\text{mm}$.

APPLICATION MECHANICAL

EXAMPLE 3.19

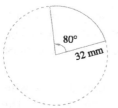

Figure 3.46

A pie-shaped piece is going to be cut out of a circular piece of metal. The radius of the circle is 32.00 mm and the central angle of the sector is 80°. What is the area of this sector? (See Figure 3.46.)

SOLUTION We will use the formula $A = \frac{1}{2}r^2\theta$. We are given $r = 32.00$ mm and $\theta = 80° \approx 1.396$ rad, so

$$A = \frac{1}{2}(32.0)^2(1.396) \approx 714.752$$

The area is about $714.8\,\text{mm}^2$.

APPLICATION BUSINESS

EXAMPLE 3.20

Two competing pizza companies sell pizza by the slice. At Checker's Pizza, a typical slice of pizza is a sector with a central angle of 60° formed from an 8″ radius pizza. A slice sells for \$1.75. Pizza Plus makes each slice from a 10″ radius pizza with a central angle of 45°. A slice sells for \$2.10. At which company do you get the most pizza for the price?

SOLUTION At Checker's, a sector with $\theta = 60° = \frac{\pi}{3}$ and $r = 8″$ has an area $A = \frac{1}{2}r^2\theta = \frac{1}{2}(8^2)\frac{\pi}{3} = \frac{32\pi}{3}\,\text{in.}^2$ At \$1.75 per slice, this is \$1.75 $\div \frac{32\pi}{3} \approx \$0.052/\text{in.}^2$

At Pizza Plus, a sector with $\theta = 45° = \frac{\pi}{4}$ and $r = 10″$ has an area $A = \frac{1}{2}r^2\theta = \frac{1}{2}(10^2)\frac{\pi}{4} = \frac{25\pi}{2}\,\text{in.}^2$ At \$2.10 per slice, this is \$2.10 $\div \frac{25\pi}{2} \approx \$0.053/\text{in.}^2$

Since the Checker's Pizza is \$0.052/in.² and the Pizza Plus slice cost \$0.053/in.², a slice from Checker's Pizza is the better bargain.

EXERCISE SET 3.3

Find the area and circumference of the circles in Exercises 1–8 with the given radius or diameter. (You may leave answers in terms of π.)

1. $r = 4$ cm

2. $d = 16$ in.

3. $r = 5$ in.

4. $d = 23$ mm

5. $r = 14.2$ mm

6. $r = 13\frac{1}{4}$ in.

7. $d = 24.20$ mm

8. $d = 23\frac{1}{2}$ in.

Solve Exercises 9–22.

9. *Interior design* **(a)** What is the area of a circular table top with a diameter of 48 in.? **(b)** How much metal edging would be needed to go around this table?

10. *Electricity* A coil of bell wire has 42 turns. The diameter of the coil is 0.5 m. How long is the wire on this coil?

11. *Industrial engineering* Two circular drums are to be riveted together, as shown in Figure 3.47, with the rivets spaced 75 mm apart. How many rivets will be needed?

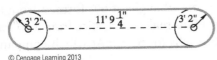

side view (cross-section)   end view

© Cengage Learning 2013

Figure 3.47

12. *Industrial design* Two pulleys each with a radius of $3'2''$ have their centers $11'9\frac{1}{4}''$ apart, as shown in Figure 3.48. What is the length of the belt needed for these pulleys?

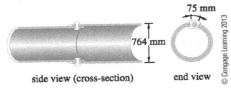

© Cengage Learning 2013

Figure 3.48

13. *Sheet metal technology* A sheet of copper has been cut in the shape of a sector of a circle. It is going to be rolled up to form a cone. **(a)** What is the arc length, $\overset{\frown}{AB}$, of the sector? **(b)** What is the area of this piece of copper? (See Figure 3.49.)

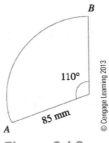

Figure 3.49

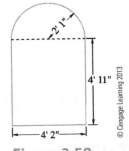

Figure 3.50

14. *Architecture* **(a)** Find the length of molding used around the window opening in Figure 3.50. **(b)** What is the area of the glass needed for this window?

15. *Architecture* The top of a stained glass window has the shape shown in Figure 3.51. The triangle is an equilateral triangle and the two arcs have their centers at the opposite vertices. That is, the arc from B to C is from a circle with center A. **(a)** What is the amount of molding

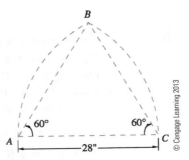

Figure 3.51

needed for this window? **(b)** What is the area of the glass needed for this window?

16. *Architecture* **(a)** Find the length of molding needed to go around the window molding in

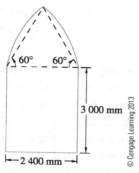

Figure 3.52

Figure 3.52. **(b)** What is the area of the glass needed for this window? (The radii for the arcs are 2 400 mm.)

17. **Industrial design** **(a)** What is the area of the table top in Figure 3.53? **(b)** How much metal edging would be required for this table?

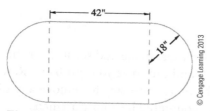

Figure 3.53

18. **Civil engineering** A cross-section of pipe is shown in Figure 3.54. What is the area of the cross-section?

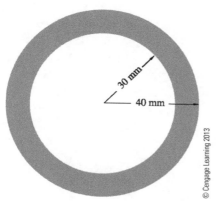

Figure 3.54

19. **Electronics** The resistance in a circuit can be reduced by 50% by replacing a wire with another wire that has twice the cross-sectional area. What is the diameter of a wire that will replace one that has a diameter of 8.42 mm?

20. **Space technology** A communications satellite is orbiting the earth at a fixed altitude above the equator. If the radius of the earth is 3,960 mi and the satellite is in direct communication with $\frac{1}{3}$ of the equator, what is the height h of the satellite? (See Figure 3.55.)

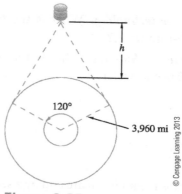

Figure 3.55

21. **(a)** What is the absolute error between $3\frac{1}{7}$ and π?

    (b) What is the percent error between $3\frac{1}{7}$ and π?

22. **(a)** What is the absolute error between 3.14 and π?

    (b) What is the percent error between 3.14 and π?

23. **Electricity** The outside diameter of an electrical conduit is $2\frac{1}{2}$ in. The conduit is 1/8 in. thick. What is the inside diameter of the conduit?

24. **Electricity** Juan is going to install some lights around a circular pond. If the lights are placed no more than 4 ft-3 in. apart and the pond has a diameter of 12 ft, how many lights will he need?

Figure 3.56 shows a 200-mm wafer placed on top of a 300- mm wafer. Notice that the term "200-mm wafer" refers to a wafer with a diameter of 200 mm. Use the figure to work Exercises 25–28.

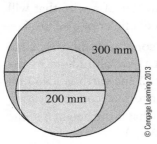

Figure 3.56

25. ***Semiconductor technology*** What is the total area of a 200-mm wafer?

26. ***Semiconductor technology*** What is the total area of a 300.0-mm wafer?

27. ***Semiconductor technology*** The entire surface of a wafer cannot be used to make chips. Each wafer has a border about 1.2 mm wide called the *exclusion area* that cannot be used. If the manufacturable area of a wafer is the total area with the exclusion area subtracted,

    (a) What is the manufacturable area on a 200.0-mm wafer?

    (b) What is the manufacturable area on a 300.0-mm wafer?

28. ***Semiconductor technology*** How much more manufacturability does a 300-mm wafer provide over a 200-mm wafer?

 [IN YOUR WORDS]

29. Explain what is meant by an arc and by a sector of a circle.

30. Write an application in your technology area of interest that requires you to use some of the circle concepts in this section. Give your problem to a classmate and see if he or she understands and can solve your problem. Rewrite the problem as necessary to remove any difficulties encountered by your classmate.

GEOMETRIC SOLIDS

The geometric figures we have looked at thus far have all been plane figures, that is, figures that can be drawn in two dimensions. But, we live in a three-dimensional world. Most of the objects we work with can be characterized as three-dimensional solids. The plane geometric figures we have studied are what the objects look like on one side when they are taken apart, or "sliced" into cross-sections.

CYLINDERS

A **cylinder** is a solid whose ends, or *bases*, are parallel congruent plane figures arranged in such a manner that the segments connecting corresponding points on the bases are parallel. Several cylinders are shown in Figure 3.69. A *circular* *cylinder* is a cylinder in which both bases are circles. A *right circular cylinder* is the most common type of cylinder and is formed when the bases are perpendicular to the elements. The *height* or *altitude* of a cylinder is a segment that is perpendicular to both bases.

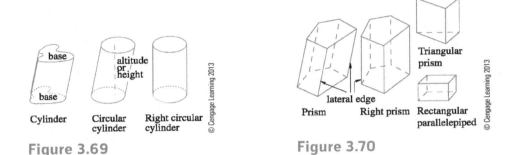

Figure 3.69

Figure 3.70

PRISMS

As shown in Figure 3.70, a **prism** is a solid with ends, or *bases*, that are parallel congruent polygons and with sides, called *faces* or *lateral faces*, that are parallelograms. The segments that form the intersections of the lateral faces are called the *lateral edges*. The height, or altitude, of a prism is the distance between the bases. A *right prism* has its bases perpendicular to its lateral edges; hence, its faces are rectangles.

Prisms get their names from their bases. If the bases are regular polygons, then the prism is a *regular prism*. A *triangular prism* has triangles for bases and a *rectangular prism* has rectangles for bases. The most common prisms are the right rectangular prisms, which are called *rectangular parallelepipeds*, and the right square prism, more commonly known as a *cube*.

There are two kinds of areas that are usually associated with any solid figure. The *lateral area* is the sum of the areas of all the sides. The **total surface area** is the lateral area plus the area of the bases. The volume of a cylinder or prism is the area of the base B times the height.

LATERAL AREA, TOTAL SURFACE AREA, AND VOLUME OF A CYLINDER OR PRISM

The lateral area, total surface area, and volume of a cylinder or prism are given by the following formulas

Solid	Lateral Area	Total Surface Area	Volume
	L	T	V
Prism	ph	$ph + 2B$	Bh
Cylinder	$2\pi rh$	$2\pi r(r + h)$	$\pi r^2 h$

where p is the perimeter of a base of the prism, h is the height, r is the radius of a base of the cylinder, and B is the area of a base.

EXAMPLE 3.25

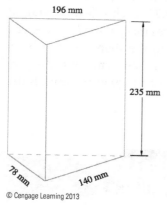

196 mm

235 mm

78 mm   140 mm

© Cengage Learning 2013

Figure 3.71

Find the (a) lateral area, (b) total surface area, and (c) volume of the triangular prism shown in Figure 3.71.

SOLUTIONS

(a) Lateral area $L = ph$, where p is the perimeter of the base and h the height of the prism. We are given $h = 235$ and add the lengths of the triangle's sides to obtain $p = 78 + 140 + 196 = 414$.

$$L = ph$$
$$= 414 \times 235$$
$$= 97\ 290$$

The lateral area is 97 290 mm^2.

(b) Total surface area $T = L + 2B$, where B is the area of a base. Using Hero's formula with $s = \dfrac{p}{2} = \dfrac{414}{2} = 207$, we get

$$B = \sqrt{s(s-a)(s-b)(s-c)}$$
$$= \sqrt{207(207-78)(207-140)(207-196)}$$
$$= \sqrt{207(129)(67)(11)}$$
$$= \sqrt{19\ 680\ 111}$$
$$\approx 4\ 436.23$$
$$T = 2B + L$$
$$= 2(4\ 436.23) + 97\ 290$$
$$= 8\ 872.46 + 97\ 290$$
$$= 106\ 162.46$$

The total surface area is 106 162.46 mm^2.

(c) Volume $V = Bh$

$$= 4\ 436.23 \times 235$$
$$= 1\ 042\ 514.1$$

The volume is 1 042 514.1 mm^3.

CONES

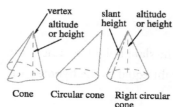

vertex
slant   altitude
altitude   height   or height
or height

Cone   Circular cone   Right circular
                        cone

© Cengage Learning 2013

Figure 3.72

A **cone** is formed by drawing segments from a plane figure, the *base*, to a point called the *vertex*. The vertex cannot be in the same plane as the base. The *altitude* is a segment from the vertex and perpendicular to the base. The most common cones are the *circular cone* and the *right circular cone*. Both have a base that is a circle. In a right circular cone, the altitude intersects the base at its center. The *slant height* of a right circular cone is a segment from the vertex to a point on the circumference. (See Figure 3.72.)

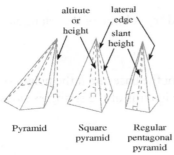

Pyramid   Square   Regular
           pyramid   pentagonal
                     pyramid

© Cengage Learning 2013

Figure 3.73

PYRAMIDS

A *pyramid* is a special type of cone, which has a base that is a polygon. A typical pyramid and some of its parts are shown in Figure 3.73. Each side of a pyramid is a triangle and is called a *lateral face*. The lateral faces meet at the *lateral edges*. As with prisms, pyramids are classified according to the shape of their base. A *regular pyramid* has a regular polygon for a base and an altitude that is perpendicular to the base at its center. The slant height of a regular pyramid is the altitude of any of the lateral faces.

LATERAL AREA, TOTAL SURFACE AREA, AND VOLUME OF CONES OR PYRAMIDS

The lateral area, total surface area, and volume of a right circular cone or regular pyramid are given by the following formulas

Solid	Lateral Area L	Total Surface Area T	Volume V
Pyramid	$\frac{1}{2}ps$	$\frac{1}{2}ps + B$	$\frac{1}{3}Bh$
Cone	πrs	$\pi r(r + s)$	$\frac{1}{3}\pi r^2 h$

where p is the perimeter of a base of the pyramid, h is the height or altitude, s is the slant height, r is the radius of a base of the cone, and B is the area of a base.

 APPLICATION MECHANICAL

EXAMPLE 3.26

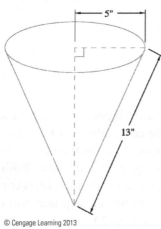

© Cengage Learning 2013

Figure 3.74

How many square inches of metal are needed to make a cone-shaped container like the one in Figure 3.74. What is the volume of this cone?

SOLUTION The amount of metal needed is the lateral area, L. We know that

$$L = \pi rs$$

where r is the radius of the base and s is the slant height of the cone.

$$L = \pi(5)(13)$$
$$= 65\pi \approx 204.2$$

It will take about 204.2 in.² of metal.

$V = \frac{1}{3}\pi r^2 h$, where h is the height of the cone. The slant height, a radius, and the altitude form a right triangle with the slant height equal to the hypotenuse. So, $h^2 + 5^2 = 13^2$ or $h = 12$.

$$V = \frac{1}{3}\pi(5)^2(12)$$
$$= 100\pi \approx 314.2$$

The volume is about 314.2 in.³

FRUSTUMS

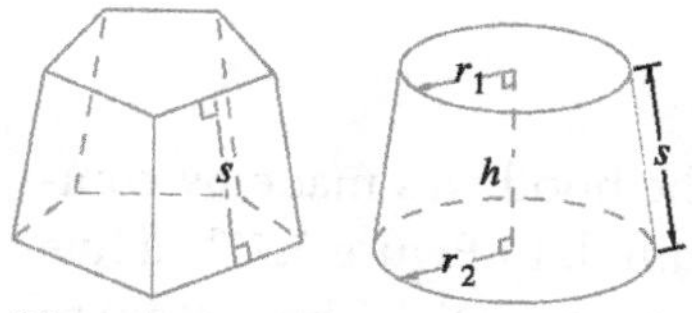

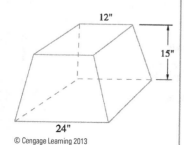

© Cengage Learning 2013

Figure 3.75

A **frustum** of a cone or a pyramid is formed by a plane parallel to the base that intersects the solid between the vertex and the base. We will limit our study to frustums of right circular cones or right regular pyramids, as shown in Figure 3.75. If the height of the frustum is h and the areas of the bases are B_1 and B_2 then the volume V is given by

$$V = \frac{h}{3}(B_1 + B_2 + \sqrt{B_1 B_2})$$

The lateral area L is given using p_1 and p_2 as the perimeter of the bases and s, the slant height:

$$L = \frac{s}{2}(p_1 + p_2)$$

For the frustum of a cone with bases of radii r_1 and r_2, p_1 and p_2 are actually the circumferences of the bases. Thus, $p_1 = 2\pi r_1$ and $p_2 = 2\pi r_2$ and the formula becomes $L = \frac{s}{2}(2\pi r_1 + 2\pi r_2)$ or

$$L = \pi s(r_1 + r_2)$$

APPLICATION CIVIL ENGINEERING

EXAMPLE 3.27

© Cengage Learning 2013

Figure 3.76

The concrete base of a light pole is constructed in the form of the frustum of a square pyramid, as shown in Figure 3.76. What is the volume of the base for the light pole?

SOLUTION The volume of a frustum of a square pyramid is given by the formula $V = \frac{h}{3}(B_1 + B_2 + \sqrt{B_1 B_2})$. We must first find the area of the bases. If B_1 is the area of the top base, then $B_1 = 12^2 = 144$ in.² and $B_2 = 24^2 = 576$ in.² So,

$$V = \frac{h}{3}(B_1 + B_2 + \sqrt{B_1 B_2})$$

$$= \frac{15}{3}(144 + 576 + \sqrt{144 \cdot 576})$$

$$= \frac{15}{3}(144 + 576 + 288)$$

$$= 5{,}040$$

The volume is 5,040 in.³

EXAMPLE 3.28

The photo in Figure 3.77a shows an oven hood. The hood was made by combining two prisms and the frustum of a square pyramid. In Figure 3.77b, a line drawing of the hood is shown with the measurements indicated. The bottom of the pyramid is 72 in. on each of the two longer sides and 36 in. on each of the two shorter sides. The top base measures 18 in. on each side. The slant height for the longer sides is 15 in. For the shorter sides, the slant height is 29.5 in. The top prism is 36 in. high and the bottom prism is 6 in. high. **(a)** How much metal will it take to form the outside of the part of the oven hood formed by the frustum of the pyramid? **(b)** How much metal will it take to form the outside of the entire oven hood?

© iStockphoto.com/Wayne Howard

Figure 3.77a

SOLUTIONS

(a) The amount of metal needed can be found by determining the lateral area L of this pyramid. Notice that this is a frustum of a rectangular pyramid and not of a square pyramid. This means that we cannot use the above formula for the lateral area of the frustum of a pyramid. Since we cannot use the formula, we will think of this frustum as if it were made of four trapezoids, as shown in Figure 3.77c. These four trapezoids are two pairs of congruent trapezoids, so we need only find the areas of the left two trapezoids, marked T_1 and T_2, and double their total area to get the lateral surface area of the frustum in the oven hood.

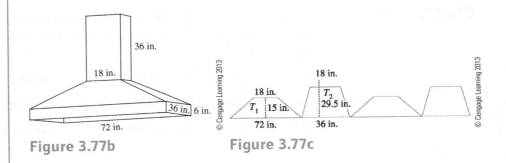

Figure 3.77b   **Figure 3.77c**

The left trapezoid T_1, has an area L_1 of

$$L_1 = \frac{1}{2}(b_1 + b_2)h$$

$$= \frac{1}{2}(18 + 72)15$$

$$= 675$$

Trapezoid T_2 has an area of $L_2 = \frac{1}{2}(36 + 18)(29.5) = 796.5\,\text{in.}^2$ The total lateral surface area for the frustum and hence the amount of metal it will take to make this portion of the oven hood is $2(675 + 796.5) = 2{,}943\,\text{in.}^2$

(b) To get the amount of metal it will take to form the outside of the entire oven hood, we add the answer to (a) to the lateral surface areas of the two prisms. The top prism has a square base that is 18 in. on each side and the prism is 36 in. high. So, it has a perimeter of $4 \times 18 = 72$ in. and its lateral area is $L_t = 36 \times 72 = 2{,}592$ in.^{2} The bottom prism is a rectangular prism with a perimeter of $72 + 36 + 72 + 36 = 216$ in. and a height of 6 in. Hence, its lateral surface area is $L_b = 6 \times 216 = 1{,}296$ in.^{2} The total amount of metal needed to form the outside of this oven hood is then $2{,}943 + 2{,}592 + 1{,}296 = 6{,}831$ in.^{2}

SPHERES

The final geometric solid that we will consider is the sphere. A *sphere* consists of all the points in space that are a fixed distance from some fixed point called the center. For a sphere with radius r, the volume and surface area are given by the following formulas.

SURFACE AREA AND VOLUME OF A SPHERE

A sphere with radius r has a surface area S and volume V where

$$S = 4\pi r^2$$

$$V = \frac{4}{3}\pi r^3$$

APPLICATION **CIVIL ENGINEERING**

EXAMPLE 3.29

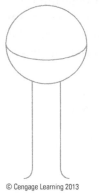

© Cengage Learning 2013

Figure 3.78

A water tower, like the one in Figure 3.78, is in the shape of a sphere on top of a cylinder. Most of the water is stored in the sphere, which has a radius of 30 ft. How much water can the tower hold?

SOLUTION We want to determine the volume of a sphere with a radius of 30 ft. The formula for the volume of a sphere is $V = \frac{4}{3}\pi r^3$. Since $r = 30$ ft, we have

$$V = \frac{4}{3}\pi(30)^3$$

$$= \frac{4}{3}\pi(27{,}000)$$

$$= 36{,}000\,\pi$$

$$\approx 113{,}097.34$$

The water tower will hold approximately $113{,}097$ ft^3 of water.

A summary of all the formulas for the areas and volumes of the solid figures is given in Table 3.1.

TABLE 3.1 Areas and Volumes of Solid Figures

Solid	Lateral Area (L)	Total Surface Area (T)	Volume (V)
Rectangular prism	$2h(l + w)$	$2lw + 2lh + 2hw$ $= 2(lw + lh + hw)$	lwh
Cube	$4s^2$	$6s^2$	s^3
Prism	ph	$ph + 2B$	Bh
Cylinder	$2\pi rh$	$2\pi r(r + h)$	$\pi r^2 h$
Pyramid	$\frac{1}{2}ps$	$\frac{1}{2}ps + B$	$\frac{1}{3}Bh$
Cone	πrs	$\pi r(r + s)$	$\frac{1}{3}\pi r^2 h$
Frustum of pyramid	$\frac{s}{2}(p_1 + p_2)$	$\frac{s}{2}(p_1 + p_2) + B_1 + B_2$	$\frac{h}{3}(B_1 + B_2 + \sqrt{B_1 B_2})$
Frustum of cone	$\pi s(r_1 + r_2)$	$\pi[r_1(r_1 + s) + r_2(r_2 + s)]$	$\frac{\pi h}{3}(r_1^2 + r_2^2 + r_1 r_2)$
Sphere	not applicable	$4\pi r^2$	$\frac{4}{3}\pi r^3$

© Cengage Learning 2013

VOLUMES OF IRREGULAR SHAPES

We can use the trapezoidal rule and Simpson's rule to approximate the volume of an irregular solid figure. Rather than find the length across the object at various places you need to find the cross-sectional area at several places. In Example 3.30 the cross-sectional areas are given, but you may need to calculate or approximate them.

 APPLICATION **CONSTRUCTION**

EXAMPLE 3.30

A road is going to be constructed through a hill. In order to determine the volume of material (soil, rock, etc.) that must be removed, a cross-section was surveyed every 100 feet and the area of each cross-section is given in the table below. Use the trapezoidal rule to determine the volume of material that has to be removed.

x(ft)	0	100	200	300	400	500	600	700	800
A(ft^2)	0	1681.0	2394.4	2525.6	2369.8	2107.4	1869.6	1713.8	1648.2

© Cengage Learning 2013

x(ft)	900	1000	1100	1200	1300	1400	1500	1600	1700
A(ft^2)	1682.4	1664.6	1640.0	1541.6	1320.2	975.8	565.8	180.4	0

© Cengage Learning 2013

SOLUTION The length of each interval is 100 ft, and so $h = 100$. We use the trapezoidal rule but change the ys to As since they represent area rather than length.

$$V_t \approx \frac{h}{2}(A_0 + 2A_1 + 2A_2 + 2A_3 + \cdots + 2A_{n-2} + 2A_{n-1} + A_n)$$

$$= \frac{100}{2}[0 + 2(1681.0) + 2(2394.4) + 2(2525.6) + 2(2369.8)$$

$$+ 2(2107.4) + 2(1869.6) + 2(1713.8) + 2(1648.2) + 2(1682.4)$$

$$+ 2(1664.6) + 2(1640.0) + 2(1541.6) + 2(1320.2) + 2(975.8)$$

$$+ 2(565.8) + 2(180.4) + 0]$$

$$= (50)(51{,}761.2)$$

$$= 2{,}588{,}060$$

According to the trapezoidal rule, about 2,588,060 ft³ of material must be removed to build this portion of the road.

EXERCISE SET 3.5

Find the lateral area, total surface area, and volume of each of the solids in Exercises 1–8.

1.

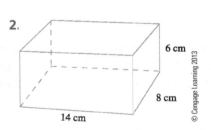

6"

18"

© Cengage Learning 2013

2.

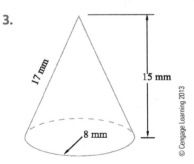

6 cm

8 cm

14 cm

© Cengage Learning 2013

3.

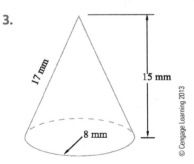

17 mm

15 mm

8 mm

© Cengage Learning 2013

4.

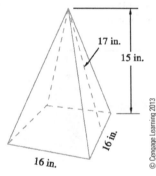

17 in.

15 in.

16 in.

16 in.

16 in.

© Cengage Learning 2013

5.

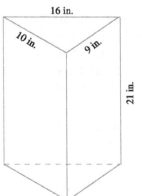

16 in.

10 in.

9 in.

21 in.

© Cengage Learning 2013

6.

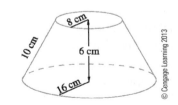

8 cm

6 cm

10 cm

16 cm

© Cengage Learning 2013

7.

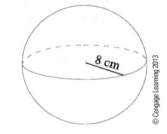

8 cm

© Cengage Learning 2013

8.

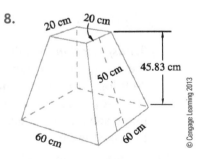

20 cm   20 cm

50 cm

45.83 cm

60 cm   60 cm

© Cengage Learning 2013

Solve Exercises 9–32.

9. Civil engineering The cross-section of a road is shown in Figure 3.79. Find the number of cubic yards of concrete it will take to pave 1 mi of this road. (There are 27 ft^3 in 1 yd^3 and 5,280 ft in 1 mi.)

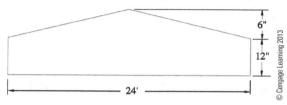

Figure 3.79

10. Civil engineering The cross-section of an I-beam is shown in Figure 3.80. **(a)** What is the volume of this beam if it is 10 m long? **(b)** How much paint, in cm^2, will be needed for this beam? **(c)** If 1 cm^3 of steel has a mass of 0.008 kg, what is the mass of this beam?

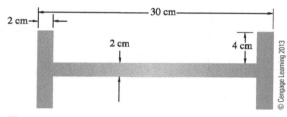

Figure 3.80

11. Transportation A railroad container car in the shape of a rectangular parallelepiped is 30 ft long, 10 ft wide, and 12 ft high. **(a)** How much can the container car hold? **(b)** How many square feet of aluminum were required to make the car?

12. Energy A cylindrical gas tank has a radius of 48 ft and a height of 140 ft. What are the volume and total surface area of the tank?

13. Product design A cylindrical soup can has a diameter of 66 mm and a height of 95 mm. **(a)** How much soup can the can hold (in mm^3)? **(b)** How many square millimeters of paper are needed for the label if the ends overlap 5 mm?

14. Mechanics A cross-section of pipe is shown in Figure 3.81. If the pipe is 2 m long, what is

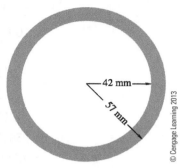

Figure 3.81

the volume of the material needed to make the pipe?

15. Energy A spherical fuel tank has a radius of 10 m. What is its volume?

16. Sheet metal technology A vent hood is made in the shape of a frustum of a square pyramid that is open at the top and bottom, as indicated in Figure 3.82. If the slant height is 730 mm, how much metal did it take to make this vent?

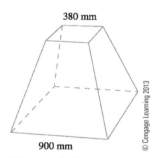

Figure 3.82

17. Civil engineering The concrete highway support in Figure 3.83 is 2 ft 6 in. thick. How many cubic yards of concrete are needed to make one support? (27 ft^3 = 1 yd^3.)

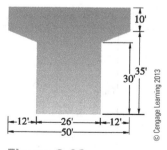

Figure 3.83

18. **Construction** How many cubic feet of dirt had to be excavated to dig a $\frac{1}{4}$-mi (1,320-ft) section of the river bed in Figure 3.84?

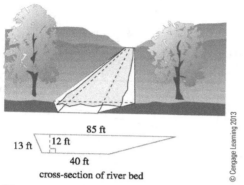

Figure 3.84

19. **Sheet metal technology** What is the volume of the cone that was made from the piece of copper in Figure 3.85?

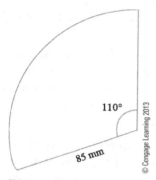

Figure 3.85

20. **Sheet metal technology** A manufacturer has an order for 500 tubs in the shape of a frustum of a cone that is 490 mm across at the top, 380 mm across at the bottom, and 260 mm deep. How much material will be needed for the sides of the tubs?

21. **Sheet metal technology** How many square inches of tin are required to make a funnel in the shape of a frustum of a cone that has a top and bottom with diameters of 3 in. and 8 in., respectively, and a slant height of 12 in.?

22. **Sheet metal technology** The funnel in Figure 3.86 has a diameter 3 cm at B and 1 cm at A. How much metal is needed to make this funnel?

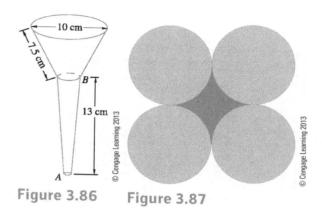

Figure 3.86   Figure 3.87

23. **Agricultural technology** Figure 3.87 shows the top view of four grain elevators. When the elevators are filled, the grain will overflow to fill the space in the middle. The radius of each elevator is 3 m and the height is 10 m. What is the total volume that can be held by the four elevators and the space in the middle if the grain is leveled at the top?

24. **Automotive technology** The piston displacement is the volume of the cylinder with a given bore (diameter) and piston stroke (height). **(a)** If the bore is 7 cm and the stroke is 8 cm, what is the displacement for this piston? **(b)** If this is a 6-cylinder engine, what is the total engine displacement?

25. **Construction** A pile of sand falls naturally into a cone. If a pile is 4 ft high and 12 ft in diameter, how many cubic feet of sand are there?

26. **Construction** A grain silo has the shape of a right circular cylinder topped by a hemisphere. The cylindrical part of the silo has a height of 40 ft and radius of 8 ft. What is the surface area of the silo?

27. **Sheet metal manufacturing** A tray for electronics parts is going to be made from the piece of sheet metal shown in Figure 3.88 by folding the metal on the dashed lines and welding the ends that meet.

(a) What is the name of the completed figure?

(b) What is the area of the bottom of this tray?

(c) What is the surface area of the tray? (Remember, the tray does not have a top.)

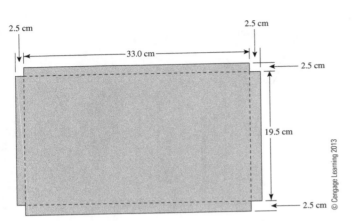

Figure 3.88

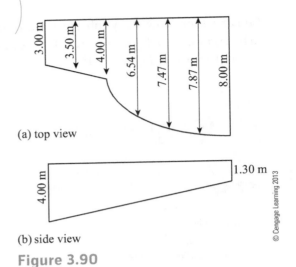

(a) top view

(b) side view

Figure 3.90

28. Electricity The core of a cylindrical electromagnet is 9.25 in. long with a radius of 15.4 in. If it is entirely covered with one layer of insulation paper, what is the area of the paper?

29. Construction A rectangular swimming pool, with a width of 6.4 m and a cross-section as shown in Figure 3.89, is to be lined with epoxy paint. Note that the entire sides of the pool including the portion above the water will need to be painted.

(a) What is the area of the surfaces that will need to be painted?

(b) If a minimum dry coat thickness of 3.0 mm is required and the paint will shrink 25% as it dries, how many liters of paint will be needed?

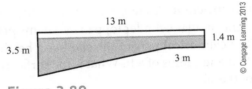

Figure 3.89

30. Recreation An automatic chlorination and purification system is being designed for the outdoor pool in Figure 3.90. The actual design of the system will depend on the volume of water in the pool. The width of the pool has been measured at 2-meter intervals. The walls of the pool are vertical.

(a) Use Simpson's rule to estimate the area of the pool.

(b) Use the trapezoidal rule to estimate the volume of water the pool will hold. Assume that the water will go to the top of the pool.

31. Construction A tunnel needs to be cut through a mountain. The cross-section of the tunnel will have an area of about 46.6 m², and its length will be 4327 m. How much rock will need to be removed?

32. Construction In Example 3.24 we used the trapezoidal rule to find the area of a parking lot at 10,856 yd². The lot is to be paved with asphalt. It will require an 8″ thick crushed rock base, 2″ of asphalt binder, and 1½″ of asphalt topping. The paving contractor measures the amount of material in "yards," where a yard is a square yard of material 2″ thick. A truck will hold around 20 tons of asphalt, which will be enough to cover about 200 yards.

(a) How many truck loads will be needed for the base?

(b) How many truck loads will be needed for the binder?

(c) How many truck loads will be needed for the topping?

33. **Construction** A pilaster is shown in Figure 3.91. Except for the very top and bottom portions the cross-sections of the pilaster are circles. Diameters of the post were measured every inch.

   (a) Use the diameters every two inches and the trapezpoidal rule to approximate the volume of this 22″ section of the pilaster.

   (b) Why can't you use these measures with Simpson's rule to get an estimate of the volume?

34. **Construction** A pilaster is shown in Figure 3.91. Except for the very top and bottom portions the cross-sections of the pilaster are circles. Diameters of the post were measured every inch.

   (a) Use the diameters every inch and the trapezoidal rule to approximate the volume of the 22″ section of the pilaster.

   (b) Use the diameters every inch and Simpson's rule to approximate the volume of the 22″ section of the pilaster.

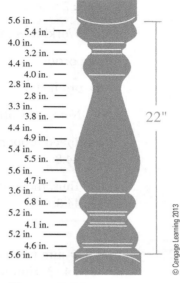

5.6 in.
5.4 in.
4.0 in.
3.2 in.
4.4 in.
4.0 in.
2.8 in.
2.8 in.
3.3 in.
3.8 in.
4.4 in.
4.9 in.
5.4 in.
5.5 in.
5.6 in.
4.7 in.
3.6 in.
6.8 in.
5.2 in.
4.1 in.
5.2 in.
4.6 in.
5.6 in.

22″

© Cengage Learning 2013

Figure 3.91

 [IN YOUR WORDS]

35. Describe how cylinders and prisms are alike and how they are different.

36. Describe how cylinders and cones are alike and how they are different.

3.6 SIMILAR GEOMETRIC SHAPES

In this section, we will examine similar triangles and other geometric figures. We begin with the concept of continued proportion.

CONTINUED PROPORTION

A **continued proportion** is a proportion that involves six or more quantities. If there are six quantities, a continued proportion is of the form $a : b : c = x : y : z$. This is a shorthand notation for writing $\dfrac{a}{x} = \dfrac{b}{y} = \dfrac{c}{z}$. We will use continued proportions when we study similar figures and later when we study trigonometry.

EXAMPLE 3.31

Solve the proportion $2 : 5 : 7 = x : 32 : z$.

SOLUTION We will solve this continued proportion in stages. Remember that $2 : 5 : 7 = x : 32 : z$ is a short way of writing $\dfrac{2}{x} = \dfrac{5}{32} = \dfrac{7}{z}$. We will first find x.

Working with the proportion from the two ratios on the left, we obtain the proportion $\dfrac{2}{x} = \dfrac{5}{32}$. The product of the extremes is $2 \times 32 = 64$ and is equal to the product of the means, $5x$. If $5x = 64$, then $x = 12.8$.

Next, we work with the proportion from the two ratios on the right of the continued proportion. This proportion is $\dfrac{5}{32} = \dfrac{7}{z}$ or $5z = 7(32) = 224$, and so $z = 44.8$.

Thus, the solution to the proportion $2 : 5 : 7 = x : 32 : z$ is $2 : 5 : 7 = 12.8 : 32 : 44.8$.

EXAMPLE 3.32

A 520-mm wire is to be cut into three pieces so that the ratio of the lengths is to be $6 : 4 : 3$. How long should each piece be?

SOLUTION The length of each piece is a multiple of some unknown length, x. If we represent the length of each piece by $6x$, $4x$, and $3x$, then we have the total length of $6x + 4x + 3x = 13x$. But the length of the wire is 520 mm. Thus,

$$13x = 520$$
$$x = 40$$

The lengths must then be $6(40) = 240$, $4(40) = 160$, and $3(40) = 120$. The proportion would be $6 : 4 : 3 = 240 : 160 : 120$.

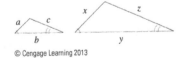

Figure 3.92

SIMILAR TRIANGLES

Two triangles that have the same shape are similar triangles. In similar triangles the corresponding angles are congruent and the corresponding sides are proportional. In Figure 3.92, since the triangles are similar, $\dfrac{a}{x} = \dfrac{b}{y} = \dfrac{c}{z}$ or $a : b : c = x : y : z$.

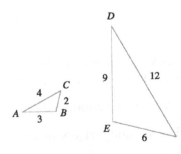

Figure 3.93

In Figure 3.93, $\angle A \cong \angle D$, $\angle B \cong \angle E$, and $\angle C \cong \angle F$. Since the corresponding angles are the same size, the triangles are similar. Congruent triangles are a special case of similar triangles in which the corresponding sides are the same length. In Figure 3.93, the sides of the larger triangle are three times as large as those of the smaller triangle. Thus, the ratios of the corresponding sides of the larger triangle to the smaller triangle are $\dfrac{12}{4} = \dfrac{9}{3} = \dfrac{6}{2} = \dfrac{3}{1}$.

APPLICATION CONSTRUCTION

EXAMPLE 3.33

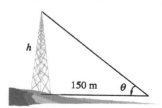

© Cengage Learning 2013

Figure 3.94

A television tower casts a shadow that is $15\bar{0}$ m long. At the same time, a vertical pole that is 1.60 m high casts a shadow 1.20 m long. How high is the television tower? (See Figure 3.94.)

SOLUTION We have two similar triangles, so the corresponding sides are proportional. If we call the unknown height h, then we have

$$\frac{h}{1.6} = \frac{150}{1.2}$$

$$h = \frac{150(1.6)}{1.2}$$

$$= 200$$

The height of the tower is 200 m.

EXAMPLE 3.34

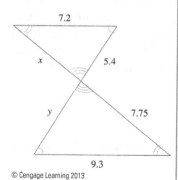

© Cengage Learning 2013

Figure 3.95

Find the lengths of the unknown sides of the similar triangles in Figure 3.95.

SOLUTION The corresponding sides of these triangles are proportional, thus $9.3 : 7.75 : y = 7.2 : x : 5.4$. Solving for x, produces

$$\frac{9.3}{7.2} = \frac{7.75}{x}$$

$$9.3x = (7.75)(7.2)$$

$$= 55.8$$

$$x = 6$$

Now, solving for y, we have the proportion

$$\frac{9.3}{7.2} = \frac{y}{5.4}$$

$$7.2y = (9.3)(5.4)$$

$$= 50.22$$

$$y = 6.975$$

OTHER SIMILAR FIGURES

Similar figures other than triangles can be more difficult to work with. If the corresponding angles of a triangle are congruent, we know that the triangles are similar. This is not true for other figures. But it is true that, for two similar figures, the distance between any two points on one figure is proportional to the distance between any two corresponding points on the other figure. This is true for any two similar figures whether they are plane figures or solid ones.

EXAMPLE 3.35

Figure 3.96 shows two similar frustums of cones. The radii of the bases of the smaller frustum are given as is the radius of the smaller base for the larger frustum. What is the radius of the bottom base of the larger frustum?

SOLUTION Since these are similar figures, we know that the ratios of the radius of the small base to the radius of the large base must be the same for each figure. Thus,

$$\frac{5.6}{8.4} = \frac{9.5}{x}$$

$$5.6x = (8.4)(9.5)$$

$$= 79.8$$

$$x = 14.25 \text{in.}$$

The radius of the bottom base of the larger frustum is 14.25 in.

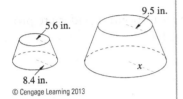

9.5 in.

5.6 in.

8.4 in.

© Cengage Learning 2013

Figure 3.96

If we know that two figures are similar, then it is easy to find the area or volume of one if we know the area or volume of the other.

AREAS OF SIMILAR FIGURES

Areas of similar figures are related to each other as the *squares* of any two corresponding dimensions. This is true for both plane and solid figures. It is also true for plane areas, lateral surface areas, total surface areas, or cross-sectional areas. For example, suppose two circles are similar. If one circle has a radius of r_1 and the other a radius of r_2, then the ratio of their areas is

$$\frac{A_1}{A_2} = \frac{\pi r_1^2}{\pi r_2^2} = \frac{r_1^2}{r_2^2}$$

Thus, the ratio of the areas of two circles is the same as the ratio of the squares of their radii.

EXAMPLE 3.36

The lateral surface area of the smaller frustum in Figure 3.96 is 220 in.^{2} What is the lateral surface area of the larger figure?

SOLUTION We will let L represent the lateral surface area that we are to find and use the proportion

$$\frac{220}{L} = \frac{5.6^2}{9.5^2}$$

$$5.6^2 L = (220)(9.5)^2$$

$$31.36\,L = 220(90.25)$$

$$= 19,855$$

$$L = 633.13138$$

The lateral surface area of the larger figure is about 633.13 in.^{2}

VOLUMES OF SIMILAR FIGURES

If two solid figures are similar, then their volumes are related to each other as the *cubes* of any two corresponding dimensions. Say two spheres are similar. If one sphere has a radius of r_1 and the other a radius of r_2, then the ratio of their volumes is

$$\frac{V_1}{V_2} = \frac{\frac{4}{3}\pi r_1^3}{\frac{4}{3}\pi r_2^3} = \frac{r_1^3}{r_2^3}$$

EXAMPLE 3.37

The volume of the smaller frustum in Figure 3.96 is 646.6 in.³ What is the volume of the larger figure?

SOLUTION We will let V represent the volume that we are to find and use the proportion

$$\frac{646.6}{V} = \frac{5.6^3}{9.5^3}$$

$$5.6^3 V = (646.6)(9.5)^3$$

$$175.616 V = 554{,}378.67$$

$$V = 3{,}156.7663$$

The volume of the larger frustum is about 3,156.77 in.³

SCALE DRAWINGS

Perhaps the most common use of similar figures applies when using scale drawings. Scale drawings are used in maps, blueprints, engineering drawings, and other figures. The ratio of distances on the drawing to corresponding distances on the actual object is called the scale of the drawing.

 APPLICATION **ARCHITECTURE**

EXAMPLE 3.38

A rectangular building 200′ × 145′ is drawn to a scale of $\frac{1}{4}'' = 1'0''$. What is the size of the rectangle that will represent this building on the blueprint?

SOLUTION This is the continuing proportion $\dfrac{\frac{1}{4}''}{1'0''} = \dfrac{x}{200'} = \dfrac{y}{145'}$. Solving each of these we get $x = 50''$ and $y = 36\frac{1}{4}''$.

The building will be represented by a rectangle that is $50'' \times 36\frac{1}{4}''$.

 APPLICATION **CIVIL ENGINEERING**

EXAMPLE 3.39

A map has a scale of 1 : 24 000. What is the actual distance of a map distance of 32 mm?

EXAMPLE 3.39 (Cont.)

SOLUTION We will use the proportion $\dfrac{1}{24\,000} = \dfrac{32\,\text{mm}}{x}$.

$$x = (32\,\text{mm})(24\,000) = 768\,000\,\text{mm}$$
$$= 768\,\text{m}$$

So, 32 mm on the map represents an actual distance of 768 m.

EXERCISE SET 3.6

The pairs of figures in each of Exercises 1–6 are similar. Find the lengths of the unknown sides.

1.
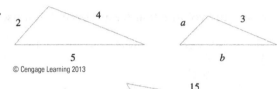
© Cengage Learning 2013

4.

© Cengage Learning 2013

2.
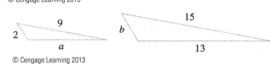
© Cengage Learning 2013

5.

© Cengage Learning 2013

3.
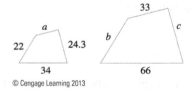
© Cengage Learning 2013

6.
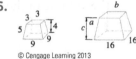
© Cengage Learning 2013

Solve each of the proportions in Exercises 7–10.

7. $2:5:9 = x:14:z$

8. $a:6:9 = 20:y:45$

9. $a:b:7.5 = 5.25:8.4:4.5$

10. $12.4:y:z = 15.5:52.75:84$

Solve Exercises 11–24.

11. *Architectural technology* The floor plan of a building has a scale of $\frac{1}{8}$ in. = 1 ft. One room of the floor plan has an area of 20 in.^{2} What is the actual room area in square inches? What is the area in square feet? (Hint: 144 in.^{2} = 1 ft^2)

12. *Wastewater technology* A pipe at a sewage treatment plant is 75 mm in diameter and discharges 2000 L of water in a given period of time. If a pipe is to discharge 3000 L in the same period of time, what is its diameter?

13. A square bar of steel, 38 mm on a side, has a mass of 22 kg. What is the mass of another bar of the same length that measures 19 mm on a side?

14. *Agricultural technology* It cost $982 to fence in a circular field that has an area of 652 ft^2. What will it cost to enclose another circular field with three times as much area?

15. *Construction* It requires 700 L to paint a spherical tank that has a radius of 20 m. How much paint will be needed to paint a tank with a radius of 35 m?

16. *Environmental technology* A water tank that is 12 m high has a volume of 20 kiloliters (kL) or 20 000 L. What is the volume of a similar tank that is 30 m high?

17. *Sheet metal technology* A cylinder has a capacity of 3 930 mm^3. Its diameter is 15 mm.

What is the volume of a similar container with a diameter of 5 mm?

18. *Sheet metal technology* A cylindrical container has a diameter of 4″ and a height of 5″. A similar container has a diameter of 2.5″. What is the height of the second container and the volume of each?

19. *Sheet metal technology* A sphere with a 10-cm radius has a volume of 4 188.79 cm³ and a surface area of 1 256.64 cm². Find **(a)** the surface area of a sphere with a radius of 2 cm and **(b)** the volume of a sphere with a radius of 2 cm.

20. *Product design* A cylindrical soup can has a diameter of 66.0 mm and a height of 95.0 mm, and holds about 325.013 5 cm³. The soup company wants to market a can that holds twice as much soup in a cylindrical can that is similar in size to the present can. What should be the dimensions of the new can?

21. *Broadcasting* The viewing size of a television screen refers to the length of a diagonal of the screen. The *aspect ratio* of a television screen is the ratio of the width to the height. A wide-screen TV has an aspect ratio of 16 : 9. What are the length and width of the screen of a 57″ wide-screen TV?

22. *Broadcasting* A traditional TV screen has an aspect ratio of 4 : 3. What are the length and width of the screen of a 57″ traditional TV?

23. *Nutrition* For a certain breakfast cereal, a serving size is 30 g and contains 130 mg of sodium and 14 g of dietary fiber. A box of this same cereal contains 453 g. How much sodium and how much dietary fiber is in a box of this cereal?

24. *Nutrition* For a certain brand of soup, a serving size is 240 g and contains 80 calories, 210 mg or 9% daily value of sodium, and 21 g or 7% daily value of carbohydrates. Based on a daily diet of 2000 calories, how many mg of sodium and how many grams of carbohydrates should a person have in his or her diet?

 [IN YOUR WORDS]

25. Describe how you would use similar figures to make a scale drawing.

26. **(a)** If the lengths of each side of a triangle are twice as long as the corresponding sides of a similar triangle, how are their areas related?

(b) If the lengths of each side of a triangle are three times as long as the corresponding sides of a similar triangle, how are their areas related?

(c) Describe how the areas between any two similar triangles are related to the lengths of their sides.

CHAPTER 3 REVIEW

IMPORTANT TERMS AND CONCEPTS

Adjacent angles
Altitude
Angle
   Acute
   Obtuse
   Right
   Straight

Arc
Arc length
Area
Central angle
Chord
Circumference
Complementary angles

Cone
Congruent angles
Congruent polygons
Congruent triangles
Continued proportion
Corresponding angles
Cylinder

Degree	Prism	Square
Diameter	Pythagorean theorem	Supplementary angles
Frustum	Quadrilateral	Tangent
Hero's formula	Radians	Total surface area
Hexagon	Radius	Transversal
Hypotenuse	Rectangle	Trapezoid
Isosceles trapezoid	Regular polygon	Trapezoidal rule
Lateral angle	Rhombus	Triangle
Line segment	Scale drawings	Acute
Octagon	Secant	Equilateral
Parallel lines	Similar figures	Isosceles
Parallelogram	Area	Obtuse
Pentagon	Volume	Right
Perimeter	Similar polygons	Scalene
Perpendicular lines	Similar triangles	Vertex
Polygon	Simpson's rule	

REVIEW EXERCISES

Convert each of the angle measures in Exercises 1–4 to either radians or degrees, without using a calculator. When you have finished, check your work by using a calculator.

1. $27°$

2. $212°$

3. 1.1π

4. 0.75

Solve Exercises 5 and 6.

5. What is the supplement of a $137°$ angle?

6. What is the complement of a $\frac{\pi}{6}$ angle?

Solve each of the proportions in Exercises 7–8.

7. $7 : 24.5 : x = 8 : y : 42$

8. $\dfrac{12.5}{x} = \dfrac{y}{47} = \dfrac{8}{5}$

Solve Exercise 9.

9. What is the distance from A to B in Figure 3.97, if lines ℓ_1, ℓ_2, and ℓ_3 are parallel?

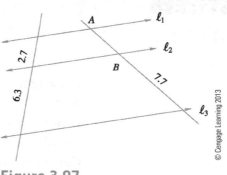

Figure 3.97

Find the variables indicated in Exercises 10 and 11.

10.

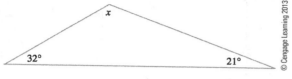

11.

Find the length of the missing side in the right triangles in Exercises 12 and 13.

12.

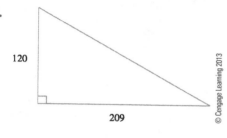

13.

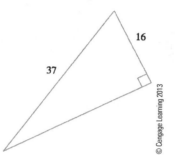

Find the area and perimeter or circumference of each of the figures in Exercises 14–21.

14.

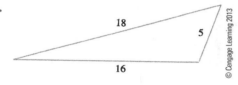

15.

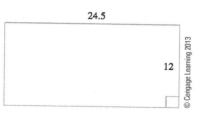

16.

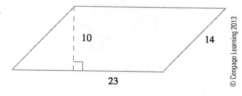

17.

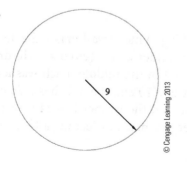

18.

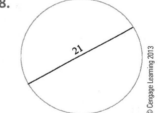

19.

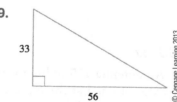

20.

21.

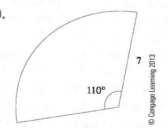

Find the lateral area, total surface area, and volume of each of the solid figures in Exercises 22–29.

22.
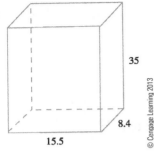

35
8.4
15.5

25.
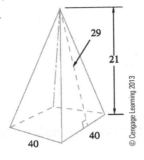

29
21
40   40

28.
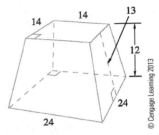

14   14   13
14   12
24
24

23.
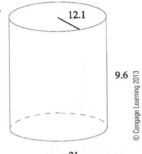

12.1
9.6

26.
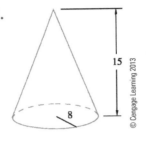

15
8

29.
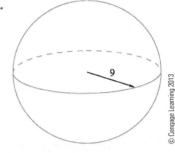

9

24.
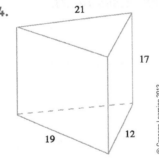

21
17
19   12

27.
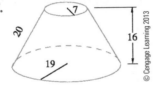

7
20
16
19

Solve Exercises 30–37.

30. *Construction* An antenna 175 m high is supported by cables positioned at three positions around the antenna. At each position, four cables go to various heights of the antenna. One set of cables is attached to the antenna 50 m above the ground, one set is attached 100 m above the ground, the third set is attached 150 m above the ground, and the fourth set is attached to the top of the antenna. If each of the three positions is located 75 m from the base of the antenna, what is the total length of all the cables used to support the antenna?

31. *Civil engineering* Find the distance across the lake in Figure 3.98.

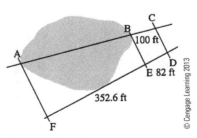

C
B   100 ft
A
D
E 82 ft
352.6 ft
F

Figure 3.98

32. *Metalworking* A metal washer is in the shape of a circular cylinder with a (circular cylindrical) hole punched in the middle. Each washer has a diameter of 3.20 cm, the hole has a diameter of 1.05 cm, and the washer is 0.240 cm thick. The washers are made by feeding a 1-m strip of metal that is the same width and thickness as a washer into a stamping machine. For safety reasons, the last 5 cm of each strip are not fed into the machine.

(a) How many strips of metal will be needed to make (stamp) 100,000 washers?

(b) How much actual metal is required for these washers?

(c) How much scrap metal is generated in the production of these washers?

33. *Electricity* The *turn ratio* in a transformer is the number of turns in the primary winding to the number of turns in the secondary winding. If the turn ratio for a transformer is 25, and there are 4,000 turns in the primary winding, how many turns are in the secondary winding?

34. The longest side of triangle A is 180 mm. Triangle B has sides of 4, 5, and 8 mm. Triangles A and B are similar. What are the lengths of the other two sides of triangle A?

35. *Physics* The theoretical mechanical advantage (TMA) of an inclined plane or ramp is equal to the ratio between its length and height. A ramp 90 ft long slopes down 5 ft to the edge of a lake. What is the TMA of the ramp?

36. *Machine technology* The efficiency of a machine is the ratio between its actual mechanical advantage (AMA) and its TMA. The AMA of the boat ramp in Exercise 35 is 16 because of the friction in a boat trailer's wheels. What is the efficiency of the ramp?

37. *Landscaping* The playing field of Oriole Park at Camden Yards in Baltimore, Maryland, is shown in Figure 3.99.

(a) Approximate the area of the playing field.

(b) Approximate the area of the portion of the field covered with grass.

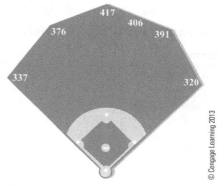

Figure 3.99

CHAPTER 3   TEST

1. Convert 35° to radians.

2. Convert $\frac{7\pi}{15}$ to degrees.

3. What is the supplement of a 76° angle?

4. Solve the proportion $6 : 8 : x = y : 14 : 24.5$.

5. Solve the proportion $\frac{a}{9} = \frac{b}{30} = \frac{75}{45}$.

6. In Figure 3.100, what is the length of $\overline{AB}$, if ℓ_1, ℓ_2, and ℓ_3 are parallel?

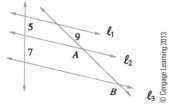

Figure 3.100

7. Determine the length of side a in Figure 3.101.

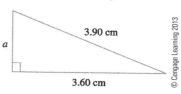

Figure 3.101

Find the perimeter of each of the figures in Exercises 8 and 9.

8.

9.
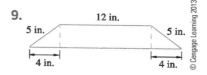

Find the area of each of the figures in Exercises 10 and 11.

10.

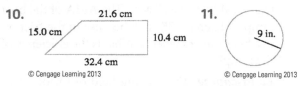

21.6 cm

15.0 cm   10.4 cm

32.4 cm

© Cengage Learning 2013

11.

9 in.

© Cengage Learning 2013

Solve Exercises 12–18.

12. A building casts a shadow of 120 m. At the same time, an antenna that is 14 m high casts a shadow of 11.6 m. How tall is the building?

13. An automobile tire has a diameter of 62 cm. How many revolutions must the tire make when the car travels 25 m in a straight line?

14. What is the volume of the box in Figure 3.102?

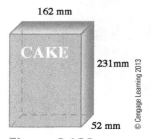

162 mm

CAKE

231 mm

52 mm

© Cengage Learning 2013

Figure 3.102

15. A spherical storage tank has a diameter of 35 ft. What is its volume?

16. The part of a cylindrical soup can that is covered by the label is 9.5 cm tall and has a diameter of 6.5 cm. What is the area of a label that covers the entire side of the can and that needs a 0.8-cm overlap to glue the ends of the label?

17. The perimeter of a rectangular solar panel is 540 cm. The ratio of the length to the width is 3 : 2. What are the length and width?

18. The area of a geometric figure varies directly as the square of any dimension. Two similar triangles have corresponding sides of length 12 m and 18 m. The smaller triangle has an area of 72 m². What is the area of the other triangle?

5.1   Angles and Their Measure

Angles

As derived from the Greek language, the word **trigonometry** means "measurement of triangles." Initially, trigonometry dealt with relationships among the sides and angles of triangles and was used in the development of astronomy, navigation, and surveying. With the development of calculus and the physical sciences in the seventeenth century, a different perspective arose—one that viewed the classic trigonometric relationships as *functions* with the set of real numbers as their domains. Consequently, the applications of trigonometry expanded to include a vast number of physical phenomena involving rotations and vibrations, including the following.

- sound waves
- light rays
- planetary orbits
- vibrating strings
- pendulums
- orbits of atomic particles

This text incorporates *both* perspectives, starting with angles and their measure.

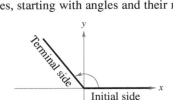

Figure 5.1   **Figure 5.2**

What you should learn
- ▶ Describe angles.
- ▶ Use degree measure.
- ▶ Use radian measure and convert between degrees and radians.
- ▶ Use angles to model and solve real-life problems.

Why you should learn it
Radian measures of angles are involved in numerous aspects of our daily lives. For instance, in Exercise 110 on page 407, you are asked to determine the measure of the angle generated as a skater performs an axel jump.

An **angle** is determined by rotating a ray (half-line) about its endpoint. The starting position of the ray is the **initial side** of the angle, and the position after rotation is the **terminal side,** as shown in Figure 5.1. The endpoint of the ray is the **vertex** of the angle. This perception of an angle fits a coordinate system in which the origin is the vertex and the initial side coincides with the positive *x*-axis. Such an angle is in **standard position,** as shown in Figure 5.2. **Positive angles** are generated by counterclockwise rotation, and **negative angles** by clockwise rotation, as shown in Figure 5.3. Angles are labeled with Greek letters such as α (alpha), β (beta), and θ (theta), as well as uppercase letters such as A, B, and C. In Figure 5.4, note that angles α and β have the same initial and terminal sides. Such angles are **coterminal.**

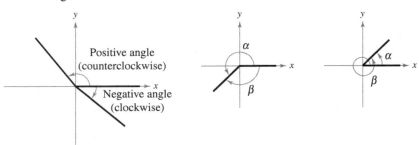

Figure 5.3   **Figure 5.4**

Degree Measure

The **measure of an angle** is determined by the amount of rotation from the initial side to the terminal side. The most common unit of angle measure is the **degree,** denoted by the symbol °. A measure of one degree (1°) is equivalent to a rotation of $\frac{1}{360}$ of a complete revolution about the vertex. To measure angles, it is convenient to mark degrees on the circumference of a circle, as shown in Figure 5.5. So, a full revolution (counterclockwise) corresponds to 360°, a half revolution to 180°, a quarter revolution to 90°, and so on.

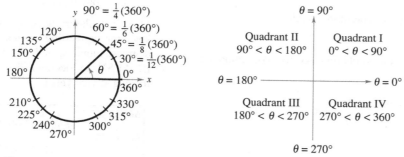

Figure 5.5   **Figure 5.6**

Recall that the four quadrants in a coordinate system are numbered I, II, III, and IV. Figure 5.6 shows which angles between 0° and 360° lie in each of the four quadrants. Figure 5.7 shows several common angles with their degree measures. Note that angles between 0° and 90° are **acute** and angles between 90° and 180° are **obtuse.**

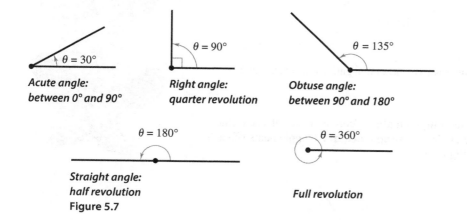

Figure 5.7

> ### Remark
>
> The phrase "the terminal side of θ lies in a quadrant" is often abbreviated by simply saying that "θ lies in a quadrant." The terminal sides of the "quadrant angles" 0°, 90°, 180°, and 270° do not lie within quadrants.

Two angles are coterminal when they have the same initial and terminal sides. For instance, the angles

0°   and   360°

are coterminal, as are the angles

30°   and   390°.

You can find an angle that is coterminal to a given angle θ by adding or subtracting 360° (one revolution), as demonstrated in Example 1 on the next page. A given angle θ has infinitely many coterminal angles. For instance, $\theta = 30°$ is coterminal with

30° + n(360°)

where n is an integer.

EXAMPLE 1   Finding Coterminal Angles

See LarsonPrecalculus.com for an interactive version of this type of example.

Find two coterminal angles (one positive and one negative) for (a) $\theta = 390°$ and (b) $\theta = -120°$.

Solution

a. For the positive angle $\theta = 390°$, subtract $360°$ to obtain a positive coterminal angle.

$$390° - 360° = 30° \qquad \text{See Figure 5.8.}$$

Subtract $2(360°) = 720°$ to obtain a negative coterminal angle.

$$390° - 720° = -330°$$

b. For the negative angle $\theta = -120°$, add $360°$ to obtain a positive coterminal angle.

$$-120° + 360° = 240° \qquad \text{See Figure 5.9.}$$

Subtract $360°$ to obtain a negative coterminal angle.

$$-120° - 360° = -480°$$

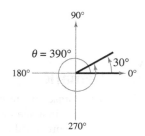

Figure 5.8   **Figure 5.9**

✓ *Checkpoint* 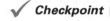 *Audio-video solution in English & Spanish at LarsonPrecalculus.com.*

Determine two coterminal angles (one positive and one negative) for each angle.

a. $\theta = 55°$ **b.** $\theta = -28°$

    Two positive angles α and β are **complementary** (complements of each other) when their sum is $90°$. Two positive angles are **supplementary** (supplements of each other) when their sum is $180°$. (See Figure 5.10.)

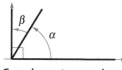   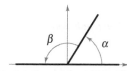

Complementary angles   *Supplementary angles*
Figure 5.10

EXAMPLE 2   Complementary and Supplementary Angles

a. The complement of $72°$ is $90° - 72° = 18°$.

    The supplement of $72°$ is $180° - 72° = 108°$.

b. Because $148°$ is greater than $90°$, $148°$ has no complement. (Remember that complements are *positive* angles.) The supplement is $180° - 148° = 32°$.

✓ *Checkpoint*  *Audio-video solution in English & Spanish at LarsonPrecalculus.com.*

If possible, find the complement and supplement of (a) $\theta = 23°$ and (b) $\theta = -28°$.

Technology Tip

Historically, fractional parts of degrees were expressed in *minutes* and *seconds*, using the prime (′) and double prime (″) notations, respectively. That is,

$$1' = \text{one minute} = \tfrac{1}{60}(1°)$$

$$1'' = \text{one second} = \tfrac{1}{3600}(1°).$$

Many calculators have special keys for converting angles in degrees, minutes, and seconds (D° M′S″) to decimal degree form, and vice versa.

Radian Measure

A second way to measure angles is in *radians*. This type of measure is especially useful in calculus. To define a radian, you can use a **central angle** of a circle, one whose vertex is the center of the circle, as shown in Figure 5.11.

Definition of Radian

One **radian** (rad) is the measure of a central angle θ that intercepts an arc s equal in length to the radius r of the circle. (See Figure 5.11.) Algebraically, this means that

$$\theta = \frac{s}{r}$$

where θ is measured in radians.

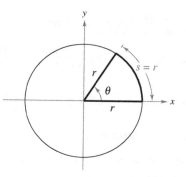

Arc length = radius when θ = 1 radian
Figure 5.11

Because the circumference of a circle is $2\pi r$ units, it follows that a central angle of one full revolution (counterclockwise) corresponds to an arc length of $s = 2\pi r$. Moreover, because $2\pi \approx 6.28$, there are just over six radius lengths in a full circle, as shown in Figure 5.12. Because the units of measure for s and r are the same, the ratio s/r has no units—it is simply a real number.

Because 2π radians corresponds to one complete revolution, degrees and radians are related by the equations

$$360° = 2\pi \text{ rad} \quad \text{and} \quad 180° = \pi \text{ rad}.$$

From the second equation, you obtain

$$1° = \frac{\pi}{180} \text{ rad} \quad \text{and} \quad 1 \text{ rad} = \frac{180°}{\pi}$$

which lead to the following conversion rules.

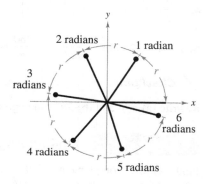

Figure 5.12

Conversions Between Degrees and Radians

1. To convert degrees to radians, multiply degrees by $\dfrac{\pi \text{ rad}}{180°}$.

2. To convert radians to degrees, multiply radians by $\dfrac{180°}{\pi \text{ rad}}$.

To apply these two conversion rules, use the basic relationship π rad $= 180°$. (See Figure 5.13.)

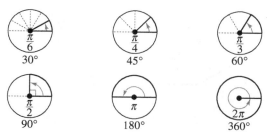

Figure 5.13

When no units of angle measure are specified, *radian measure is implied*. For instance, $\theta = 2$ implies that $\theta = 2$ radians.

EXAMPLE 3 Converting from Degrees to Radians

a. $135° = (135 \text{ deg}) \left(\dfrac{\pi \text{ rad}}{180 \text{ deg}} \right) = \dfrac{3\pi}{4} \text{ radians}$ Multiply by $\dfrac{\pi}{180}$.

b. $-270° = (-270 \text{ deg}) \left(\dfrac{\pi \text{ rad}}{180 \text{ deg}} \right) = -\dfrac{3\pi}{2} \text{ radians}$ Multiply by $\dfrac{\pi}{180}$.

✓ **Checkpoint** ◀))) *Audio-video solution in English & Spanish at LarsonPrecalculus.com.*

Rewrite (a) 60° and (b) 320° in radian measure as a multiple of π. (Do not use a calculator.) ◼

EXAMPLE 4 Converting from Radians to Degrees

a. $-\dfrac{\pi}{2} \text{ rad} = \left(-\dfrac{\pi}{2} \text{ rad} \right) \left(\dfrac{180 \text{ deg}}{\pi \text{ rad}} \right) = -90°$ Multiply by $\dfrac{180}{\pi}$.

b. $2 \text{ rad} = (2 \text{ rad}) \left(\dfrac{180 \text{ deg}}{\pi \text{ rad}} \right) = \dfrac{360}{\pi} \approx 114.59°$ Multiply by $\dfrac{180}{\pi}$.

✓ **Checkpoint** ◀))) *Audio-video solution in English & Spanish at LarsonPrecalculus.com.*

Rewrite (a) $\pi/6$ and (b) $5\pi/3$ in degree measure. (Do not use a calculator.) ◼

> **Technology Tip**
>
> Use a calculator with a "radian-to-degree" conversion key to verify the result shown in part (b) of Example 4.

EXAMPLE 5 Finding Angles

Find (a) the complement of $\theta = \pi/12$, (b) the supplement of $\theta = 5\pi/6$, and (c) a coterminal angle to $\theta = 17\pi/6$.

Solution

a. In radian measure, the complement of an angle is found by subtracting the angle from $\pi/2$ ($\pi/2 = 90°$). So, the complement of $\theta = \pi/12$ is

$$\frac{\pi}{2} - \frac{\pi}{12} = \frac{6\pi}{12} - \frac{\pi}{12} = \frac{5\pi}{12}.$$ See Figure 5.14.

b. In radian measure, the supplement of an angle is found by subtracting the angle from π ($\pi = 180°$). So, the supplement of $\theta = 5\pi/6$ is

$$\pi - \frac{5\pi}{6} = \frac{6\pi}{6} - \frac{5\pi}{6} = \frac{\pi}{6}.$$ See Figure 5.15.

c. In radian measure, a coterminal angle is found by adding or subtracting 2π ($2\pi = 360°$). For $\theta = 17\pi/6$, subtract 2π to obtain a coterminal angle.

$$\frac{17\pi}{6} - 2\pi = \frac{17\pi}{6} - \frac{12\pi}{6} = \frac{5\pi}{6}.$$ See Figure 5.16.

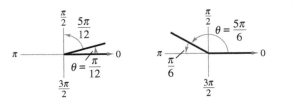

Figure 5.14   **Figure 5.15**   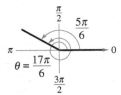 **Figure 5.16**

✓ **Checkpoint** ◀))) *Audio-video solution in English & Spanish at LarsonPrecalculus.com.*

Find (a) the complement of $\theta = 3\pi/16$, (b) the supplement of $\theta = 5\pi/12$, and (c) a coterminal angle to $\theta = -4\pi/3$. ◼

Linear and Angular Speed

The *radian measure* formula $\theta = s/r$ can be used to measure **arc length** along a circle.

Arc Length

For a circle of radius r, a central angle θ (in radian measure) intercepts an arc of length s given by

$s = r\theta$.   Length of circular arc

Note that if $r = 1$, then $s = \theta$, and the radian measure of θ equals the arc length.

EXAMPLE 6   **Finding Arc Length**

A circle has a radius of 4 inches. Find the length of the arc intercepted by a central angle of 240°, as shown in Figure 5.17.

Solution

To use the formula $s = r\theta$, first convert 240° to radian measure.

$$240° = (240 \text{ deg})\left(\frac{\pi \text{ rad}}{180 \text{ deg}}\right) = \frac{4\pi}{3} \text{ radians}$$

Then, using a radius of $r = 4$ inches, you can find the arc length to be

$s = r\theta$ Length of circular arc

$= 4\left(\dfrac{4\pi}{3}\right)$ Substitute for r and θ.

$= \dfrac{16\pi}{3}$ Simplify.

≈ 16.76 inches.   Use a calculator.

Note that the units for $r\theta$ are determined by the units for r because θ is given in radian measure and therefore has no units.

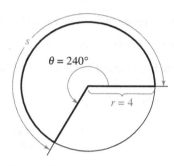

Figure 5.17

✓ **Checkpoint** 🔊))) *Audio-video solution in English & Spanish at LarsonPrecalculus.com.*

A circle has a radius of 27 inches. Find the length of the arc intercepted by a central angle of 160°. ◼

The formula for the length of a circular arc can be used to analyze the motion of a particle moving at a *constant speed* along a circular path.

Linear and Angular Speed

Consider a particle moving at a constant speed along a circular arc of radius r. If s is the length of the arc traveled in time t, then the **linear speed** of the particle is

$$\text{Linear speed} = \frac{\text{arc length}}{\text{time}} = \frac{s}{t}.$$

Moreover, if θ is the angle (in radian measure) corresponding to the arc length s, then the **angular speed** of the particle is

$$\text{Angular speed} = \frac{\text{central angle}}{\text{time}} = \frac{\theta}{t}.$$

Linear speed measures how fast the particle moves, and angular speed measures how fast the angle changes.

EXAMPLE 7 Finding Linear Speed

The second hand of a clock is 10.2 centimeters long, as shown in Figure 5.18. Find the linear speed of the tip of this second hand.

Solution

In one revolution, the arc length traveled is

$$s = 2\pi r$$

$$= 2\pi(10.2) \qquad \text{Substitute for } r.$$

$$= 20.4\pi \text{ centimeters.}$$

The time required for the second hand to travel this distance is

$$t = 1 \text{ minute} = 60 \text{ seconds.}$$

So, the linear speed of the tip of the second hand is

$$\text{Linear speed} = \frac{s}{t}$$

$$= \frac{20.4\pi \text{ centimeters}}{60 \text{ seconds}}$$

$$\approx 1.07 \text{ centimeters per second.}$$

Figure 5.18

✓ *Checkpoint* *Audio-video solution in English & Spanish at LarsonPrecalculus.com.*

The second hand of a clock is 8 centimeters long. Find the linear speed of the tip of this second hand as it passes around the clock face.

EXAMPLE 8 Finding Angular and Linear Speed

The blades of a wind turbine are 116 feet long (see Figure 5.19). The propeller rotates at 15 revolutions per minute.

a. Find the angular speed of the propeller in radians per minute.

b. Find the linear speed of the tips of the blades.

Solution

a. Because each revolution generates 2π radians, it follows that the propeller turns

$$(15)(2\pi) = 30\pi \text{ radians per minute.}$$

In other words, the angular speed is

$$\text{Angular speed} = \frac{\theta}{t} = \frac{30\pi \text{ radians}}{1 \text{ minute}} = 30\pi \text{ radians per minute.}$$

b. The linear speed is

$$\text{Linear speed} = \frac{s}{t} = \frac{r\theta}{t} = \frac{(116)(30\pi) \text{ feet}}{1 \text{ minute}} \approx 10{,}933 \text{ feet per minute.}$$

Figure 5.19

✓ *Checkpoint* *Audio-video solution in English & Spanish at LarsonPrecalculus.com.*

The circular blade on a saw rotates at 2400 revolutions per minute.

a. Find the angular speed of the blade in radians per minute.

b. The blade has a radius of 4 inches. Find the linear speed of a blade tip.

5.1   Exercises

See *CalcChat.com* for tutorial help and worked-out solutions to odd-numbered exercises. For instructions on how to use a graphing utility, see Appendix A.

Vocabulary and Concept Check

In Exercises 1–6, fill in the blank.

1. _____ means "measurement of triangles."

2. A(n) _____ is determined by rotating a ray about its endpoint.

3. An angle with its initial side coinciding with the positive x-axis and the origin as its vertex is said to be in _____ .

4. Two angles that have the same initial and terminal sides are _____ .

5. One _____ is the measure of a central angle that intercepts an arc equal in length to the radius of the circle.

6. The _____ speed of a particle is a ratio of the change in the central angle to the time.

7. Is one-half revolution of a circle equal to 90° or 180°?

8. What is the sum of two complementary angles in degrees? in radians?

9. Are the angles 315° and −225° coterminal?

10. Is the angle $\frac{2\pi}{3}$ acute or obtuse?

Procedures and Problem Solving

Estimating an Angle   In Exercises 11 and 12, estimate the number of degrees in the angle.

11.    12.

Determining Quadrants   In Exercises 13–18, determine the quadrant in which each angle lies.

13. (a) 55°   (b) 215°
14. (a) 121°   (b) 181°
15. (a) −150°   (b) 282°
16. (a) 87.9°   (b) −8.5°
17. (a) 132° 50′   (b) −336° 30′
18. (a) −245.25°   (b) 12.35°

Sketching Angles   In Exercises 19–24, sketch each angle in standard position.

19. (a) 45°   (b) 90°   20. (a) 60°   (b) 180°
21. (a) −30°   (b) 150°
22. (a) 270°   (b) −120°
23. (a) 405°   (b) −780°
24. (a) −450° (b) 600°

Finding Coterminal Angles   In Exercises 25–28, determine two coterminal angles in degree measure (one positive and one negative) for each angle. (There are many correct answers).

25. (a)   (b)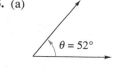

$\theta = 52°$ $\theta = -36°$

26. (a)   (b)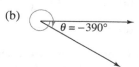

$\theta = 114°$ $\theta = -390°$

27. (a) 300°   (b) −740°
28. (a) −445°   (b) 230°

Converting to Decimal Degree Form   In Exercises 29–34, use the angle-conversion capabilities of a graphing utility to convert the angle measure to decimal degree form. Round your answer to three decimal places, if necessary.

29. 64° 45′   30. −124° 30′
31. 85° 18′30″   32. −408° 16′25″
33. −125° 36″   34. 330° 25″

Finding an Angle Difference   In Exercises 35–38, find the difference of the angles. Write your answer in D° M′S″ form.

35. 51° 22′30″ and 38° 17′15″
36. 120° 45′29″ and 12° 36′3″
37. 48° 18′ and 25° 16′59″
38. 36° 8′43″ and 81° 17″

Converting to D° M′S″ Form In Exercises 39–44, use the angle-conversion capabilities of a graphing utility to convert the angle measure to D° M′S″ form.

39. 280.6°

40. −115.8°

41. −345.12°

42. 490.75°

43. −20.34°

44. 45.063°

Complementary and Supplementary Angles In Exercises 45–48, find (if possible) the complement and supplement of the angle.

45. 24°

46. 129°

47. 87°

48. 167°

Estimating an Angle In Exercises 49 and 50, estimate the angle to the nearest one-half radian.

49.

50.

Determining Quadrants In Exercises 51–56, determine the quadrant in which each angle lies. (The angle measure is given in radians.)

51. (a) $\dfrac{\pi}{6}$ (b) $\dfrac{5\pi}{4}$ **52.** (a) $\dfrac{5\pi}{6}$ (b) $-\dfrac{5\pi}{3}$

53. (a) $\dfrac{7\pi}{4}$ (b) $\dfrac{11\pi}{4}$ **54.** (a) $-\dfrac{5\pi}{12}$ (b) $-\dfrac{13\pi}{9}$

55. (a) −1   (b) −2   **56.** (a) 3.5   (b) 2.25

Sketching Angles In Exercises 57–62, sketch each angle in standard position.

57. (a) $\dfrac{3\pi}{2}$ (b) $-\dfrac{\pi}{2}$ **58.** (a) $\dfrac{3\pi}{4}$ (b) $\dfrac{4\pi}{3}$

59. (a) $-\dfrac{7\pi}{4}$ (b) $-\dfrac{5\pi}{2}$ **60.** (a) $\dfrac{11\pi}{6}$ (b) $-\dfrac{2\pi}{3}$

61. (a) 5π (b) −4   **62.** (a) 2   (b) -3π

Converting From Degrees to Radians In Exercises 63–66, rewrite each angle in radian measure as a multiple of π. (Do not use a calculator.)

63. (a) 30°   (b) 150°

64. (a) 315°   (b) 120°

65. (a) 18°   (b) −240°

66. (a) −330°   (b) 144°

Converting From Radians to Degrees In Exercises 67–70, rewrite each angle in degree measure. (Do not use a calculator.)

67. (a) $\dfrac{3\pi}{2}$ (b) $-\dfrac{7\pi}{6}$

68. (a) -4π (b) 3π

69. (a) $\dfrac{7\pi}{3}$ (b) $-\dfrac{13\pi}{60}$

70. (a) $-\dfrac{15\pi}{6}$ (b) $\dfrac{28\pi}{15}$

Converting From Degrees to Radians In Exercises 71–76, convert the angle measure from degrees to radians. Round your answer to three decimal places.

71. 115°

72. 83.7°

73. −216.35°

74. −46.52°

75. −0.78°

76. 395°

Converting From Radians to Degrees In Exercises 77–82, convert the angle measure from radians to degrees. Round your answer to three decimal places.

77. $\dfrac{\pi}{7}$

78. $\dfrac{5\pi}{11}$

79. 6.5π

80. -4.2π

81. −2

82. −0.57

Finding Coterminal Angles In Exercises 83–86, determine two coterminal angles in radian measure (one positive and one negative) for each angle. (There are many correct answers).

83. (a) 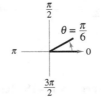   (b)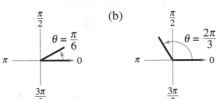

84. (a) 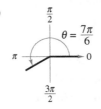   (b)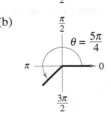

85. (a) $\dfrac{9\pi}{4}$ (b) $-\dfrac{2\pi}{15}$

86. (a) $-\dfrac{7\pi}{8}$ (b) $\dfrac{\pi}{12}$

Complementary and Supplementary Angles In Exercises 87–92, find (if possible) the complement and supplement of the angle.

87. $\dfrac{\pi}{3}$

88. $\dfrac{3\pi}{4}$

89. $\dfrac{2\pi}{3}$

90. $\dfrac{\pi}{6}$

91. $\dfrac{3\pi}{2}$

92. $\dfrac{12\pi}{5}$

Finding the Central Angle In Exercises 93–96, find the radian measure of the central angle of a circle of radius *r* that intercepts an arc of length *s*.

	Radius r	Arc Length s
93.	15 inches	8 inches
94.	22 feet	10 feet
95.	14.5 centimeters	35 centimeters
96.	80 kilometers	160 kilometers

Finding Arc Length In Exercises 97–100, find the length of the arc on a circle of radius *r* intercepted by a central angle *θ*.

	Radius r	Central Angle θ
97.	14 inches	π radians
98.	9 feet	$\dfrac{\pi}{3}$ radians
99.	27 meters	120°
100.	12 centimeters	135°

Finding the Radius In Exercises 101–104, find the radius *r* of a circle with an arc length *s* and a central angle *θ*.

	Arc Length s	Central Angle θ
101.	36 feet	$\dfrac{\pi}{2}$ radians
102.	3 meters	$\dfrac{4\pi}{3}$ radians
103.	82 miles	135°
104.	8 inches	330°

Earth-Space Science In Exercises 105 and 106, find the distance between the cities. Assume that Earth is a sphere of radius 4000 miles and the cities are on the same longitude (one city is due north of the other).

	City	Latitude
105.	Dallas, Texas	32° 47′39″N
	Omaha, Nebraska	41° 15′50″N
106.	San Francisco, California	37° 47′36″N
	Seattle, Washington	47° 37′18″N

107. Earth-Space Science Assuming that Earth is a sphere of radius 6378 kilometers, what is the difference in the latitudes of Syracuse, New York, and Annapolis, Maryland, where Syracuse is 450 kilometers due north of Annapolis?

108. Electrical Engineering A voltmeter's pointer is 6 centimeters in length (see figure). Find the number of degrees through which it rotates when it moves 2.5 centimeters on the scale.

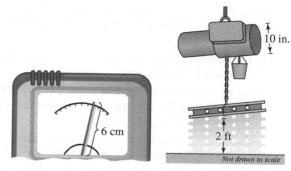

Figure for 108   Figure for 109

109. Mechanical Engineering An electric hoist is used to lift a piece of equipment 2 feet. The diameter of the drum on the hoist is 10 inches (see figure). Find the number of degrees through which the drum must rotate.

110. *Why you should learn it* (*p. 398*) The number of revolutions made by a figure skater for each type of axel jump is given. Determine the measure of the angle generated as the skater performs each jump. Give the answer in both degrees and radians.

(a) Single axel: $1\frac{1}{2}$ revolutions

(b) Double axel: $2\frac{1}{2}$ revolutions

(c) Triple axel: $3\frac{1}{2}$ revolutions

111. Linear Speed A satellite in a circular orbit 1250 kilometers above Earth makes one complete revolution every 110 minutes. What is its linear speed? Assume that Earth is a sphere of radius 6378 kilometers.

112. Mechanical Engineering The circular blade on a saw has a diameter of 7.25 inches and rotates at 4800 revolutions per minute.

(a) Find the angular speed of the blade in radians per minute.

(b) Find the linear speed of the saw teeth (in inches per minute) as they contact the wood being cut.

113. Mechanical Engineering A motorcycle wheel has a diameter of 19.5 inches (see figure) and rotates at 1050 revolutions per minute.

(a) Find the angular speed in radians per minute.

(b) Find the linear speed of the motorcycle (in inches per minute).

114. Angular Speed A computerized spin balance machine rotates a 25-inch diameter tire at 480 revolutions per minute.

(a) Find the road speed (in miles per hour) at which the tire is being balanced.

(b) At what rate should the spin balance machine be set so that the tire is being tested for 70 miles per hour?

115. Mechanical Engineering A Blu-ray disc is approximately 12 centimeters in diameter. The drive motor of the Blu-ray player is able to rotate up to 10,000 revolutions per minute, depending on what track is being read.

(a) Find the maximum angular speed (in radians per second) of a Blu-ray disc as it rotates.

(b) Find the maximum linear speed (in meters per second) of a point on the outermost track as the disc rotates.

116. MODELING DATA

The radii of the pedal sprocket, the wheel sprocket, and the wheel of the bicycle in the figure are 4 inches, 2 inches, and 14 inches, respectively. A cyclist is pedaling at a rate of 1 revolution per second.

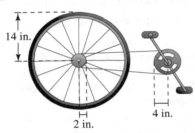

14 in.

4 in.

2 in.

(a) Find the speed of the bicycle in feet per second and miles per hour.

(b) Use your result from part (a) to write a function for the distance d (in miles) a cyclist travels in terms of the number n of revolutions of the pedal sprocket.

(c) Write a function for the distance d (in miles) a cyclist travels in terms of time t (in seconds). Compare this function with the function from part (b).

Conclusions

True or False? In Exercises 117–119, determine whether the statement is true or false. Justify your answer.

117. A degree is a larger unit of measure than a radian.

118. An angle that measures $-1260°$ lies in Quadrant III.

119. The angles of a triangle can have radian measures of $2\pi/3$, $\pi/4$, and $\pi/12$.

120. Proof Prove that the area of a circular sector of radius r with central angle θ is $A = \frac{1}{2}r^2\theta$, where θ is measured in radians.

Geometry In Exercises 121 and 122, use the result of Exercise 120 to find the area of the sector.

121.

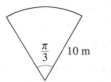

$\frac{\pi}{3}$ 10 m

122.

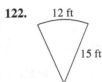

12 ft

15 ft

123. Think About It The formulas for the area of a circular sector and arc length are $A = \frac{1}{2}r^2\theta$ and $s = r\theta$, respectively. (r is the radius and θ is the angle measured in radians.)

(a) Let $\theta = 0.8$. Write the area and arc length as functions of r. What is the domain of each function? Use a graphing utility to graph the functions. Use the graphs to determine which function changes more rapidly as r increases. Explain.

(b) Let $r = 10$ centimeters. Write the area and arc length as functions of θ. What is the domain of each function? Use a graphing utility to graph and identify the functions.

124. HOW DO YOU SEE IT? Determine which angles in the figure are coterminal angles with angle A. Explain your reasoning.

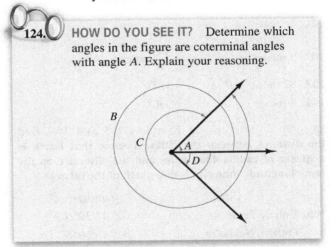

125. Writing In your own words, write a definition of 1 radian.

126. Writing In your own words, explain the difference between 1 radian and 1 degree.

Cumulative Mixed Review

Library of Parent Functions In Exercises 127–132, sketch the graph of $f(x) = x^3$ and the graph of the function g. Describe the transformation from f to g.

127. $g(x) = (x - 1)^3$

128. $g(x) = x^3 - 4$

129. $g(x) = 2 - x^3$

130. $g(x) = -(x + 3)^3$

131. $g(x) = (x + 1)^3 - 3$

132. $g(x) = (x - 5)^3 + 1$

5.4   Graphs of Sine and Cosine Functions

Basic Sine and Cosine Curves

In this section, you will study techniques for sketching the graphs of the sine and cosine functions. The graph of the sine function is a **sine curve.** In Figure 5.39, the black portion of the graph represents one period of the function and is called **one cycle** of the sine curve. The gray portion of the graph indicates that the basic sine wave repeats indefinitely to the right and left. The graph of the cosine function is shown in Figure 5.40. To produce these graphs with a graphing utility, make sure you set the graphing utility to *radian* mode.

Recall from Section 5.3 that the domain of the sine and cosine functions is the set of all real numbers. Moreover, the range of each function is the interval

$$[-1, 1]$$

and each function has a period of 2π. Do you see how this information is consistent with the basic graphs shown in Figures 5.39 and 5.40?

What you should learn
▶ Sketch the graphs of basic sine and cosine functions.
▶ Use amplitude and period to help sketch the graphs of sine and cosine functions.
▶ Sketch translations of graphs of sine and cosine functions.
▶ Use sine and cosine functions to model real-life data.

Why you should learn it
Sine and cosine functions are often used in scientific calculations. For instance, in Exercise 87 on page 441, you can use a trigonometric function to model the percent of the moon's face that is illuminated for any given day in 2016.

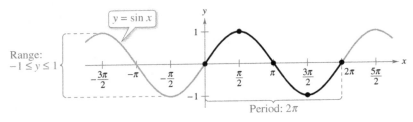

Figure 5.39

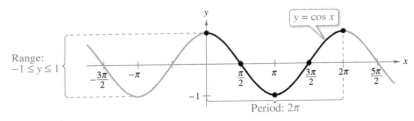

Figure 5.40

To sketch the graphs of the basic sine and cosine functions by hand, it helps to note five *key points* in one period of each graph: the *intercepts*, the *maximum points*, and the *minimum points*. The table below lists the five key points on the graphs of

$$y = \sin x \quad \text{and} \quad y = \cos x.$$

x	0	$\dfrac{\pi}{2}$	π	$\dfrac{3\pi}{2}$	2π
$\sin x$	0	1	0	-1	0
$\cos x$	1	0	-1	0	1

Note in Figures 5.39 and 5.40 that the sine curve is symmetric with respect to the *origin*, whereas the cosine curve is symmetric with respect to the *y-axis*. These properties of symmetry follow from the fact that the sine function is odd, whereas the cosine function is even.

Library of Parent Functions: Sine and Cosine Functions

The basic characteristics of the parent sine function and parent cosine function are listed below and summarized on the inside cover of this text.

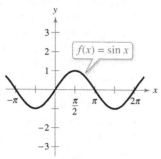

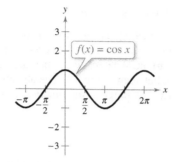

Domain: $(-\infty, \infty)$
Range: $[-1, 1]$
Period: 2π
x-intercepts: $(n\pi, 0)$
y-intercept: $(0, 0)$
Odd function
Origin symmetry

Domain: $(-\infty, \infty)$
Range: $[-1, 1]$
Period: 2π
x-intercepts: $(\pi/2 + n\pi, 0)$
y-intercept: $(0, 1)$
Even function
y-axis symmetry

EXAMPLE 1   Library of Parent Functions: $f(x) = \sin x$

See LarsonPrecalculus.com for an interactive version of this type of example.

Sketch the graph of $g(x) = 2 \sin x$ by hand on the interval $[-\pi, 4\pi]$.

Solution

Note that $g(x) = 2 \sin x = 2(\sin x)$ indicates that the y-values of the key points will have twice the magnitude of those on the graph of $f(x) = \sin x$. Divide the period 2π into four equal parts to get the key points

Intercept	*Maximum*	*Intercept*	*Minimum*		*Intercept*
$(0, 0),$	$(\pi/2, 2),$	$(\pi, 0),$	$(3\pi/2, -2),$	and	$(2\pi, 0).$

By connecting these key points with a smooth curve and extending the curve in both directions over the interval $[-\pi, 4\pi]$, you obtain the graph shown below. Use a graphing utility to confirm this graph. Be sure to set the graphing utility to *radian* mode.

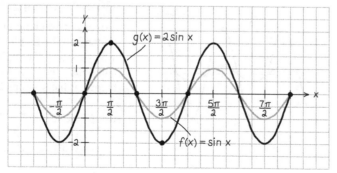

✓ *Checkpoint*)))) *Audio-video solution in English & Spanish at LarsonPrecalculus.com.*

Sketch the graph of $y = 2 \cos x$ by hand on the interval $[-\pi/2, 9\pi/2]$.   ■

Explore the Concept

Enter the Graphing a Sine Function Program, found at this textbook's *Companion Website*, into your graphing utility. This program simultaneously draws the unit circle and the corresponding points on the sine curve, as shown below. After the circle and sine curve are drawn, you can connect the points on the unit circle with their corresponding points on the sine curve by pressing [ENTER] . Discuss the relationship that is illustrated.

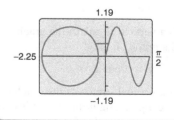

Amplitude and Period of Sine and Cosine Curves

In the rest of this section, you will study the graphic effect of each of the constants a, b, c, and d in equations of the forms

$$y = d + a \sin(bx - c) \quad \text{and} \quad y = d + a \cos(bx - c).$$

The constant factor a in $y = a \sin x$ acts as a *scaling factor*—a *vertical stretch* or *vertical shrink* of the basic sine curve. When $|a| > 1$, the basic sine curve is stretched, and when $|a| < 1$, the basic sine curve is shrunk. The result is that the graph of $y = a \sin x$ ranges between $-a$ and a instead of between -1 and 1. The absolute value of a is the **amplitude** of the function $y = a \sin x$. The range of the function $y = a \sin x$ for $a > 0$ is $-a \le y \le a$.

> **Definition of Amplitude of Sine and Cosine Curves**
>
> The **amplitude** of $y = a \sin x$ and $y = a \cos x$ represents half the distance between the maximum and minimum values of the function and is given by
>
> $$\text{Amplitude} = |a|.$$

EXAMPLE 2 **Scaling: Vertical Shrinking and Stretching**

On the same set of coordinate axes, sketch the graph of each function by hand.

a. $y = \frac{1}{2} \cos x$

b. $y = 3 \cos x$

Solution

a. Because the amplitude of $y = \frac{1}{2} \cos x$ is $\frac{1}{2}$, the maximum value is $\frac{1}{2}$ and the minimum value is $-\frac{1}{2}$. Divide one cycle, $0 \le x \le 2\pi$, into four equal parts to get the key points

Maximum	Intercept	Minimum	Intercept	Maximum
$\left(0, \frac{1}{2}\right),$	$\left(\frac{\pi}{2}, 0\right),$	$\left(\pi, -\frac{1}{2}\right),$	$\left(\frac{3\pi}{2}, 0\right),$ and	$\left(2\pi, \frac{1}{2}\right).$

b. A similar analysis shows that the amplitude of $y = 3 \cos x$ is 3, and the key points are

Maximum	Intercept	Minimum	Intercept	Maximum
$(0, 3),$	$\left(\frac{\pi}{2}, 0\right),$	$(\pi, -3),$	$\left(\frac{3\pi}{2}, 0\right),$ and	$(2\pi, 3).$

The graphs of these two functions are shown in the figure. Notice that the graph of

$$y = \frac{1}{2} \cos x$$

is a vertical shrink of the graph of $y = \cos x$ and the graph of

$$y = 3 \cos x$$

is a vertical stretch of the graph of $y = \cos x$. Use a graphing utility to confirm these graphs.

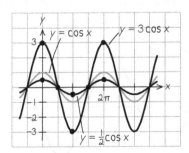

✓ **Checkpoint**)) *Audio-video solution in English & Spanish at LarsonPrecalculus.com.*

On the same set of coordinate axes, sketch the graph of each function by hand.

a. $y = \frac{1}{3} \sin x$ **b.** $y = 3 \sin x$

©Andresr/Shutterstock.com   ©Forster Forest/Shutterstock.com

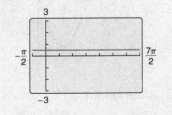

You know from Section 1.5 that the graph of $y = -f(x)$ is a *reflection* in the x-axis of the graph of $y = f(x)$. For instance, the graph of $y = -3 \cos x$ is a reflection of the graph of $y = 3 \cos x$, as shown in Figure 5.41.

Next, consider the effect of the *positive* real number b on the graphs of $y = a \sin bx$ and $y = a \cos bx$. Because $y = a \sin x$ completes one cycle from $x = 0$ to $x = 2\pi$, it follows that $y = a \sin bx$ completes one cycle from $x = 0$ to $x = 2\pi/b$.

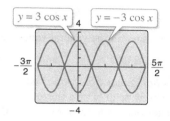

Figure 5.41

Period of Sine and Cosine Functions

Let b be a positive real number. The **period** of

$$y = a \sin\ bx \qquad \text{and} \qquad y = a \cos bx$$

is given by

$$\text{Period} = \frac{2\pi}{b}.$$

Note that when $0 < b < 1$, the period of $y = a \sin bx$ is greater than 2π and represents a *horizontal stretching* of the graph of $y = a \sin x$. Similarly, when $b > 1$, the period of $y = a \sin bx$ is less than 2π and represents a *horizontal shrinking* of the graph of $y = a \sin x$. When b is negative, the identities

$$\sin(-x) = -\sin x \qquad \text{and} \qquad \cos(-x) = \cos x$$

are used to rewrite the function.

EXAMPLE 3   Scaling: Horizontal Stretching

Sketch the graph of $y = \sin \dfrac{x}{2}$ by hand.

Solution

The amplitude is 1. Moreover, because $b = \frac{1}{2}$, the period is

$$\frac{2\pi}{b} = \frac{2\pi}{\frac{1}{2}} = 4\pi. \qquad \text{Substitute for } b.$$

Now, divide the period-interval $[0, 4\pi]$ into four equal parts using the values π, 2π, and 3π to obtain the key points on the graph

Intercept	Maximum	Intercept	Minimum		Intercept
$(0, 0),$	$(\pi, 1),$	$(2\pi, 0),$	$(3\pi, -1),$	and	$(4\pi, 0).$

The graph is shown below. Use a graphing utility to confirm this graph.

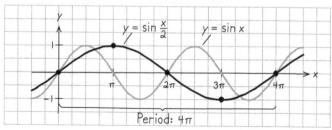

Sketch the graph of $y = \cos \dfrac{x}{3}$ by hand.

Remark

In general, to divide a period-interval into four equal parts, successively add "period/4," starting with the left endpoint of the interval. For instance, for the period-interval $[-\pi/6, \pi/2]$ of length $2\pi/3$, you would successively add

$$\frac{2\pi/3}{4} = \frac{\pi}{6}$$

to get $-\pi/6$, 0, $\pi/6$, $\pi/3$, and $\pi/2$ as the x-values of the key points on the graph.

Translations of Sine and Cosine Curves

The constant c in the general equations

$$y = a \sin(bx - c) \quad \text{and} \quad y = a \cos(bx - c)$$

creates *horizontal translations* (shifts) of the basic sine and cosine curves. Comparing $y = a \sin bx$ with $y = a \sin(bx - c)$, you find that the graph of $y = a \sin(bx - c)$ completes one cycle from $bx - c = 0$ to $bx - c = 2\pi$. By solving for x, you can find the interval for one cycle to be

Left endpoint   Right endpoint

$$\frac{c}{b} \leq x \leq \frac{c}{b} + \frac{2\pi}{b}.$$

Period

This implies that the period of $y = a \sin(bx - c)$ is $2\pi/b$, and the graph of $y = a \sin bx$ is shifted by an amount c/b. The number c/b is the **phase shift.**

Graphs of Sine and Cosine Functions

The graphs of $y = a \sin(bx - c)$ and $y = a \cos(bx - c)$ have the following characteristics. (Assume $b > 0$.)

$$\text{Amplitude} = |a| \qquad \text{Period} = \frac{2\pi}{b}$$

The left and right endpoints of a one-cycle interval can be determined by solving the equations $bx - c = 0$ and $bx - c = 2\pi$ for x.

EXAMPLE 4   Horizontal Translation

Analyze the graph of $y = \frac{1}{2} \sin\left(x - \frac{\pi}{3}\right)$.

Algebraic Solution

The amplitude is $\frac{1}{2}$ and the period is 2π. By solving the equations

$$x - \frac{\pi}{3} = 0 \quad \text{and} \quad x - \frac{\pi}{3} = 2\pi$$

$$x = \frac{\pi}{3} \qquad\qquad x = \frac{7\pi}{3}$$

you see that the interval

$$\left[\frac{\pi}{3}, \frac{7\pi}{3}\right]$$

corresponds to one cycle of the graph. Dividing this interval into four equal parts produces the key points

Intercept	Maximum	Intercept	Minimum	Intercept

$$\left(\frac{\pi}{3}, 0\right), \quad \left(\frac{5\pi}{6}, \frac{1}{2}\right), \quad \left(\frac{4\pi}{3}, 0\right), \quad \left(\frac{11\pi}{6}, -\frac{1}{2}\right), \quad \text{and} \quad \left(\frac{7\pi}{3}, 0\right).$$

Graphical Solution

Use a graphing utility set in *radian* mode to graph

$$y = \left(\frac{1}{2}\right) \sin\left(x - \frac{\pi}{3}\right)$$

as shown below. Use the *minimum*, *maximum*, and *zero* or *root* features of the graphing utility to approximate the key points $(1.05, 0)$, $(2.62, 0.5)$, $(4.19, 0)$, $(5.76, -0.5)$, and $(7.33, 0)$.

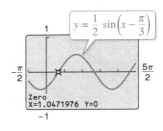

✓ **Checkpoint** ◀))) *Audio-video solution in English & Spanish at LarsonPrecalculus.com.*

Analyze the graph of $y = 2 \cos\left(x - \frac{\pi}{2}\right)$.

EXAMPLE 5   Horizontal Translation

Analyze the graph of $y = -3\cos(2\pi x + 4\pi)$.

Algebraic Solution

The amplitude is 3 and the period is

$$\frac{2\pi}{2\pi} = 1.$$

By solving the equations

$$2\pi x + 4\pi = 0 \qquad \text{and} \qquad 2\pi x + 4\pi = 2\pi$$

$$2\pi x = -4\pi \qquad\qquad\qquad 2\pi x = -2\pi$$

$$x = -2 \qquad\qquad\qquad\qquad x = -1$$

you see that the interval $[-2, -1]$ corresponds to one cycle of the graph. Dividing this interval into four equal parts produces the key points

Minimum	Intercept	Maximum	Intercept		Minimum
$(-2, -3)$,	$(-7/4, 0)$,	$(-3/2, 3)$,	$(-5/4, 0)$,	and	$(-1, -3)$.

✓ Checkpoint 🔊))) *Audio-video solution in English & Spanish at LarsonPrecalculus.com.*

Analyze the graph of $y = -\frac{1}{2}\sin(\pi x + \pi)$.

Graphical Solution

Use a graphing utility set in *radian* mode to graph $y = -3\cos(2\pi x + 4\pi)$, as shown below. Use the *minimum*, *maximum*, and *zero* or *root* features of the graphing utility to approximate the key points $(-2, -3)$, $(-1.75, 0)$, $(-1.5, 3)$, $(-1.25, 0)$, and $(-1, -3)$.

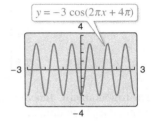

The final type of transformation is the *vertical translation* caused by the constant d in the equations $y = d + a\sin(bx - c)$ and $y = d + a\cos(bx - c)$. The shift is d units upward for $d > 0$ and d units downward for $d < 0$. In other words, the graph oscillates about the horizontal line $y = d$ instead of about the x-axis.

EXAMPLE 6   Vertical Translation

Use a graphing utility to analyze the graph of $y = 2 + 3\cos 2x$.

Solution

The amplitude is 3 and the period is π. The key points over the interval $[0, \pi]$ are

$$(0, 5), \qquad (\pi/4, 2), \qquad (\pi/2, -1), \qquad (3\pi/4, 2), \qquad \text{and} \qquad (\pi, 5).$$

The graph is shown in Figure 5.42. Compared with the graph of $f(x) = 3\cos 2x$, the graph of $y = 2 + 3\cos 2x$ is shifted upward two units.

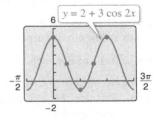

Figure 5.42

✓ Checkpoint 🔊))) *Audio-video solution in English & Spanish at LarsonPrecalculus.com.*

Use a graphing utility to analyze the graph of $y = 2\cos x - 5$.

EXAMPLE 7   Finding an Equation of a Graph

Find the amplitude, period, and phase shift of the function whose graph is shown in Figure 5.43. Write an equation of this graph in terms of a sine function.

Solution

The amplitude of this sine curve is 2. The period is 2π, and there is a right phase shift of $\pi/2$. So, you can write $y = 2\sin(x - \pi/2)$.

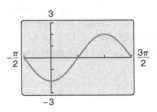

Figure 5.43

✓ Checkpoint 🔊))) *Audio-video solution in English & Spanish at LarsonPrecalculus.com.*

In Example 7, write an equation of the graph in terms of a cosine function.

Mathematical Modeling

Sine and cosine functions can be used to model many real-life situations, including electric currents, musical tones, radio waves, tides, and weather patterns.

EXAMPLE 8   Finding a Trigonometric Model

Throughout the day, the depth of the water at the end of a dock varies with the tides. The table shows the depths y (in feet) at various times during the morning.

Time	Depth, y
Midnight	3.4
2 A.M.	8.7
4 A.M.	11.3
6 A.M.	9.1
8 A.M.	3.8
10 A.M.	0.1
Noon	1.2

Spreadsheet at LarsonPrecalculus.com

a. Use a trigonometric function to model the data. Let t be the time, with $t = 0$ corresponding to midnight.

b. A boat needs at least 10 feet of water to moor at the dock. During what times in the afternoon can it safely dock?

Solution

a. Begin by graphing the data, as shown in Figure 5.44. You can use either a sine or cosine model. So, use a cosine model of the form

$$y = a\cos(bt - c) + d.$$

The difference between the maximum value and minimum value is twice the amplitude of the function. So, the amplitude is

$$a = \tfrac{1}{2}[(\text{maximum depth}) - (\text{minimum depth})] = \tfrac{1}{2}(11.3 - 0.1) = 5.6.$$

The cosine function completes one half of a cycle between the times at which the maximum and minimum depths occur. So, the period p is

$$p = 2[(\text{time of min. depth}) - (\text{time of max. depth})] = 2(10 - 4) = 12$$

which implies that $b = 2\pi/p \approx 0.524$. Because high tide occurs 4 hours after midnight, consider the left endpoint to be $c/b = 4$, so $c \approx 2.094$. Moreover, because the average depth is

$$\tfrac{1}{2}(11.3 + 0.1) = 5.7$$

it follows that $d = 5.7$. So, you can model the depth with the function

$$y = 5.6\cos(0.524t - 2.094) + 5.7.$$

b. Using a graphing utility, graph the model with the line $y = 10$. Using the *intersect* feature, you can determine that the depth is at least 10 feet between 2:42 P.M. ($t \approx 14.7$) and 5:18 P.M. ($t \approx 17.3$), as shown at the right.

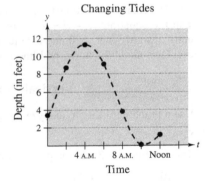

Changing Tides

Depth (in feet)

4 A.M.   8 A.M.   Noon

Time

Figure 5.44

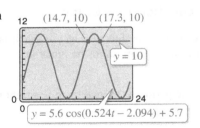

12   (14.7, 10)   (17.3, 10)

$y = 10$

0   24

$y = 5.6\cos(0.524t - 2.094) + 5.7$

 Checkpoint *Audio-video solution in English & Spanish at LarsonPrecalculus.com.*

Find a sine model for the data in Example 8.

5.4 Exercises

See *CalcChat.com* for tutorial help and worked-out solutions to odd-numbered exercises. For instructions on how to use a graphing utility, see Appendix A.

Vocabulary and Concept Check

In Exercises 1–4, fill in the blank.

1. The _____ of a sine or cosine curve represents half the distance between the maximum and minimum values of the function.
2. One period of a sine function is called _____ of the sine curve.
3. The period of a sine or cosine function is given by _____ .
4. For the equation $y = a \sin(bx - c)$, $\frac{c}{b}$ is the _____ of the graph of the equation.

5. What is the period of the sine function $y = \sin x$?
6. How do you find the period of a cosine function of the form $y = \cos bx$?
7. Describe the effect of the constant d on the graph of $y = \sin x + d$.
8. What is the amplitude of $y = -4.5 \sin x$?

Procedures and Problem Solving

Library of Parent Functions In Exercises 9 and 10, use the graph of the function to answer each question.

(a) **Find the x-intercepts of the graph of $y = f(x)$.**
(b) **Find the y-intercept of the graph of $y = f(x)$.**
(c) **Find the intervals on which the graph of $y = f(x)$ is increasing and the intervals on which the graph of $y = f(x)$ is decreasing.**
(d) **Find the relative extrema of the graph of $y = f(x)$.**

9. $f(x) = \sin x$

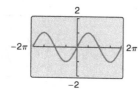

10. $f(x) = \cos x$

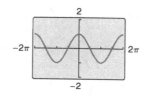

Finding the Period and Amplitude In Exercises 11–20, find the period and amplitude.

11. $y = 3 \sin 2x$

12. $y = 2 \cos 3x$

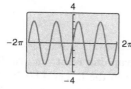

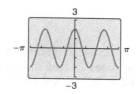

13. $y = 5 \cos \dfrac{x}{2}$

14. $y = -3 \sin \dfrac{x}{3}$

15. $y = \dfrac{2}{3} \sin \pi x$

16. $y = \dfrac{3}{2} \cos \dfrac{\pi x}{2}$

17. $y = -2 \sin x$

18. $y = -\cos \dfrac{2x}{5}$

19. $y = \dfrac{1}{4} \cos \dfrac{4x}{3}$

20. $y = \dfrac{5}{2} \cos \dfrac{x}{4}$

Describing the Relationship Between Graphs In Exercises 21–28, describe the relationship between the graphs of f and g. Consider amplitudes, periods, and shifts.

21. $f(x) = \sin x$
    $g(x) = \sin(x - \pi)$

22. $f(x) = \cos x$
    $g(x) = \cos(x + \pi)$

23. $f(x) = \cos 2x$
    $g(x) = -\cos 2x$

24. $f(x) = \sin 3x$
    $g(x) = \sin(-3x)$

25. $f(x) = \cos 2x$
    $g(x) = 3 + \cos 2x$

26. $f(x) = \cos 4x$
    $g(x) = -2 + \cos 4x$

27. $f(x) = \sin x$
    $g(x) = 5 \sin(-x)$

28. $f(x) = \sin x$
    $g(x) = -\frac{1}{2} \sin x$

Describing the Relationship Between Graphs In Exercises 29–32, describe the relationship between the graphs of f and g. Consider amplitudes, periods, and shifts.

29.

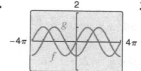

30.

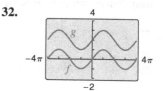

31.

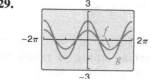

32.

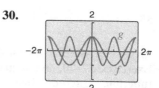

Sketching Graphs of Sine or Cosine Functions In Exercises 33–38, sketch the graphs of f and g in the same coordinate plane. (Include two full periods.)

33. $f(x) = \sin x$

     $g(x) = -4 \sin x$

34. $f(x) = \sin x$

     $g(x) = \sin \dfrac{x}{3}$

35. $f(x) = \cos \pi x$

     $g(x) = 1 + \cos \pi x$

36. $f(x) = 4 \sin x$

     $g(x) = 4 \sin x - 1$

37. $f(x) = -\dfrac{1}{2} \sin \dfrac{x}{2}$

     $g(x) = 2 \sin \dfrac{x}{4}$

38. $f(x) = 2 \cos 2x$

     $g(x) = -\cos 4x$

Using Graphs to Compare Functions In Exercises 39–42, use a graphing utility to graph f and g in the same viewing window. (Include two full periods.) Make a conjecture about the functions.

39. $f(x) = \sin x$

     $g(x) = \cos\left(x - \dfrac{\pi}{2}\right)$

40. $f(x) = \sin x$

     $g(x) = \cos\left(x + \dfrac{3\pi}{2}\right)$

41. $f(x) = \cos x$

     $g(x) = -\sin\left(x - \dfrac{\pi}{2}\right)$

42. $f(x) = \cos x$

     $g(x) = -\cos(x - \pi)$

Sketching a Sine or Cosine Function In Exercises 43–56, sketch the graph of the function. Use a graphing utility to verify your sketch. (Include two full periods.)

43. $y = 4 \sin x$

44. $y = 5 \sin x$

45. $y = \dfrac{1}{4} \cos x$

46. $y = \dfrac{3}{4} \cos x$

47. $y = \cos \dfrac{x}{2}$

48. $y = \sin \dfrac{x}{4}$

49. $y = \sin\left(x - \dfrac{\pi}{4}\right)$

50. $y = \sin(x - \pi)$

51. $y = -8 \cos(x + \pi)$

52. $y = 3 \cos\left(x + \dfrac{\pi}{2}\right)$

53. $y = 1 - \sin \dfrac{2\pi x}{3}$

54. $y = 2 \cos x - 3$

55. $y = \dfrac{2}{3} \cos\left(\dfrac{x}{2} - \dfrac{\pi}{4}\right)$

56. $y = -2 \cos(4\pi x + 1)$

Analyzing Graphs of Sine or Cosine Functions In Exercises 57–70, use a graphing utility to graph the function. (Include two full periods.) Identify the amplitude and period of the graph.

57. $y = -2 \sin \dfrac{2\pi x}{3}$

58. $y = -10 \cos \dfrac{\pi x}{6}$

59. $y = -4 + 5 \cos \dfrac{\pi t}{12}$

60. $y = 2 - 2 \sin \dfrac{2\pi x}{3}$

61. $y = -\dfrac{2}{3} \cos\left(\dfrac{x}{2} - \dfrac{\pi}{4}\right)$

62. $y = \dfrac{5}{2} \cos(6x + \pi)$

63. $y = -2 \sin(4x + \pi)$

64. $y = -4 \sin\left(\dfrac{2}{3}x - \dfrac{\pi}{3}\right)$

65. $y = \cos\left(2\pi x - \dfrac{\pi}{2}\right) + 1$

66. $y = 3 \cos\left(\dfrac{\pi x}{2} + \dfrac{\pi}{2}\right) - 2$

67. $y = 5 \sin(\pi - 2x) + 10$

68. $y = 5 \cos(\pi - 2x) + 6$

69. $y = \dfrac{1}{100} \sin 120\pi t$

70. $y = \dfrac{1}{100} \cos 50\pi t$

Finding an Equation of a Graph In Exercises 71–74, find a and d for the function $f(x) = a \cos x + d$ such that the graph of f matches the figure.

71.

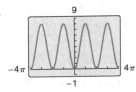

72.

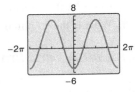

73.

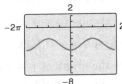

74.

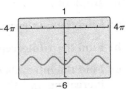

Finding an Equation of a Graph In Exercises 75–78, find a, b, and c for the function $f(x) = a \sin(bx - c)$ such that the graph of f matches the graph shown.

75.

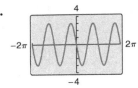

76.

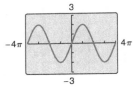

77.

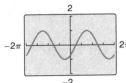

78.

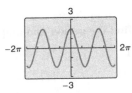

Solving a Trigonometric Equation Graphically In Exercises 79 and 80, use a graphing utility to graph y_1 and y_2 for all real numbers x in the interval $[-2\pi, 2\pi]$. Use the graphs to find the real numbers x such that $y_1 = y_2$.

79. $y_1 = \sin x$

     $y_2 = -\dfrac{1}{2}$

80. $y_1 = \cos x$

     $y_2 = \dfrac{1}{2}$

81. Health   The pressure P (in millimeters of mercury) against the walls of the blood vessels of a person is modeled by

$$P = 100 - 20 \cos \frac{8\pi t}{3}$$

where t is the time (in seconds). Use a graphing utility to graph the model. One cycle is equivalent to one heartbeat. What is the person's pulse rate in heartbeats per minute?

82. Health   For a person at rest, the velocity v (in liters per second) of air flow during a respiratory cycle (the time from the beginning of one breath to the beginning of the next) is given by

$$v = 0.85 \sin \frac{\pi t}{3}$$

where t is the time (in seconds). (Inhalation occurs when $v > 0$, and exhalation occurs when $v < 0$.)

(a) Use a graphing utility to graph v.

(b) Find the time for one full respiratory cycle.

(c) Find the number of cycles per minute.

(d) The model is for a person at rest. How might the model change for a person who is exercising? Explain.

83. Economics   A company that produces snowboards, which are seasonal products, forecasts monthly sales for one year to be

$$S = 74.50 + 43.75 \cos \frac{\pi t}{6}$$

where S is the sales in thousands of units and t is the time in months, with $t = 1$ corresponding to January.

(a) Use a graphing utility to graph the sales function over the one-year period.

(b) Use the graph in part (a) to determine the months of maximum and minimum sales.

84. Agriculture   The daily consumption C (in gallons) of diesel fuel on a farm is modeled by

$$C = 30.3 + 21.6 \sin\left(\frac{2\pi t}{365} + 10.9\right)$$

where t is the time in days, with $t = 1$ corresponding to January 1.

(a) What is the period of the model? Is it what you expected? Explain.

(b) What is the average daily fuel consumption? Which term of the model did you use? Explain.

(c) Use a graphing utility to graph the model. Use the graph to approximate the time of the year when consumption exceeds 40 gallons per day.

85. Physics   You are riding a Ferris wheel. Your height h (in feet) above the ground at any time t (in seconds) can be modeled by

$$h = 25 \sin \frac{\pi}{15}(t - 75) + 30.$$

The Ferris wheel turns for 135 seconds before it stops to let the first passengers off.

(a) Use a graphing utility to graph the model.

(b) What are the minimum and maximum heights above the ground?

86. Physics   The motion of an oscillating weight suspended from a spring was measured by a motion detector. The data were collected, and the approximate maximum displacements from equilibrium $(y = 2)$ are labeled in the figure. The distance y from the motion detector is measured in centimeters, and the time t is measured in seconds.

(a) Is y a function of t? Explain.

(b) Approximate the amplitude and period.

(c) Find a model for the data.

(d) Use a graphing utility to graph the model in part (c). Compare the result with the data in the figure.

87. _Why you should learn it_ (p. 432) The table shows the percent y (in decimal form) of the moon's face that is illuminated on day x of the year 2016, where $x = 1$ represents January 1. (Source: U.S. Naval Observatory)

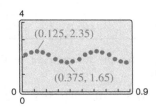

Day, x	Percent, y
10	0.0
16	0.5
24	1.0
32	0.5
39	0.0
46	0.5

Spreadsheet at LarsonPrecalculus.com

(a) Create a scatter plot of the data.

(b) Find a trigonometric model for the data.

(c) Add the graph of your model in part (b) to the scatter plot. How well does the model fit the data?

(d) What is the period of the model?

(e) Estimate the percent illumination of the moon on June 21, 2017. (Assume there are 366 days in 2016.)

88. MODELING DATA

The table shows the average daily high temperatures (in degrees Fahrenheit) for Quillayute, Washington, Q and Chicago, Illinois, C for month t, with $t = 1$ corresponding to January. (Source: U.S. Weather Bureau and the National Weather Service)

Month, t	Quillayute, Q	Chicago, C
1	47.1	31.0
2	49.1	35.3
3	51.4	46.6
4	54.8	59.0
5	59.5	70.0
6	63.1	79.7
7	67.4	84.1
8	68.6	81.9
9	66.2	74.8
10	58.2	62.3
11	50.3	48.2
12	46.0	34.8

Spreadsheet at LarsonPrecalculus.com

(a) A model for the temperature in Quillayute is given by

$$Q(t) = 57.5 + 10.6 \sin(0.566x - 2.568)$$

Find a trigonometric model for Chicago.

(b) Use a graphing utility to graph the data and the model for the temperatures in Quillayute in the same viewing window. How well does the model fit the data?

(c) Use the graphing utility to graph the data and the model for the temperatures in Chicago in the same viewing window. How well does the model fit the data?

(d) Use the models to estimate the average daily high temperature in each city. Which term of the models did you use? Explain.

(e) What is the period of each model? Are the periods what you expected? Explain.

(f) Which city has the greater variability in temperature throughout the year? Which factor of the models determines this variability? Explain.

Conclusions

True or False? In Exercises 89–92, determine whether the statement is true or false. Justify your answer.

89. The graph of the function given by $g(x) = \sin(x + 2\pi)$ translates the graph of $f(x) = \sin x$ one period to the right.

©Thomas Barrat/Shutterstock.com

90. The graph of $y = 6 - \dfrac{3}{4}\sin\dfrac{3x}{10}$ has a period of $\dfrac{20\pi}{3}$.

91. The function $y = \frac{1}{2}\cos 2x$ has an amplitude that is twice that of the function $y = \cos x$.

92. The graph of $y = -\cos x$ is a reflection of the graph of $y = \sin\left(x + \dfrac{\pi}{2}\right)$ in the x-axis.

93. **Writing** Sketch the graph of $y = \cos bx$ for $b = \frac{1}{2}, 2,$ and 3. How does the value of b affect the graph? How many complete cycles of the graph of y occur between 0 and 2π for each value of b?

94. **Writing** Use a graphing utility to graph the function given by $y = d + a\sin(bx - c)$ for several different values of $a, b, c,$ and d. Write a paragraph describing how the values of $a, b, c,$ and d affect the graph.

Library of Parent Functions In Exercises 95 and 96, determine which function is represented by the graph. Do not use a calculator.

95.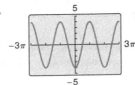

96.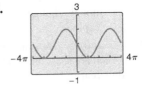

(a) $f(x) = 4\cos(x + \pi)$ (a) $f(x) = 1 + \sin\dfrac{x}{2}$

(b) $f(x) = 4\cos 4x$ (b) $f(x) = 1 + \cos\dfrac{x}{2}$

(c) $f(x) = 4\sin(x - \pi)$ (c) $f(x) = 1 - \sin\dfrac{x}{2}$

(d) $f(x) = -4\cos(x + \pi)$ (d) $f(x) = 1 - \cos 2x$

(e) $f(x) = 1 - \sin\dfrac{x}{2}$ (e) $f(x) = 1 - \sin 2x$

97. **Exploration** In Section 5.3, it was shown that $f(x) = \cos x$ is an even function and $g(x) = \sin x$ is an odd function. Use a graphing utility to graph h and use the graph to determine whether h is even, odd, or neither.

(a) $h(x) = \cos^2 x$

(b) $h(x) = \sin^2 x$

(c) $h(x) = \sin x \cos x$

98. **Conjecture** If f is an even function and g is an odd function, use the results of Exercise 97 to make a conjecture about whether h is even, odd, or neither.

(a) $h(x) = [f(x)]^2$

(b) $h(x) = [g(x)]^2$

(c) $h(x) = f(x)g(x)$

99. Exploration Use a graphing utility to explore the ratio $(\sin x)/x$, which appears in calculus.

(a) Complete the table. Round your results to four decimal places.

x	-1	-0.1	-0.01	-0.001
$\dfrac{\sin x}{x}$				

x	0	0.001	0.01	0.1	1
$\dfrac{\sin x}{x}$					

(b) Use the graphing utility to graph the function
$$f(x) = \frac{\sin x}{x}.$$
Use the *zoom* and *trace* features to describe the behavior of the graph as x approaches 0.

(c) Write a brief statement regarding the value of the ratio based on your results in parts (a) and (b).

100. Exploration Use a graphing utility to explore the ratio $(1 - \cos x)/x$, which appears in calculus.

(a) Complete the table. Round your results to four decimal places.

x	-1	-0.1	-0.01	-0.001
$\dfrac{1 - \cos x}{x}$				

x	0	0.001	0.01	0.1	1
$\dfrac{1 - \cos x}{x}$					

(b) Use the graphing utility to graph the function
$$f(x) = \frac{1 - \cos x}{x}.$$
Use the *zoom* and *trace* features to describe the behavior of the graph as x approaches 0.

(c) Write a brief statement regarding the value of the ratio based on your results in parts (a) and (b).

101. Exploration Using calculus, it can be shown that the sine and cosine functions can be approximated by the polynomials

$$\sin x \approx x - \frac{x^3}{3!} + \frac{x^5}{5!} \quad \text{and} \quad \cos x \approx 1 - \frac{x^2}{2!} + \frac{x^4}{4!}$$

where x is in radians.

(a) Use a graphing utility to graph the sine function and its polynomial approximation in the same viewing window. How do the graphs compare?

(b) Use the graphing utility to graph the cosine function and its polynomial approximation in the same viewing window. How do the graphs compare?

(c) Study the patterns in the polynomial approximations of the sine and cosine functions and predict the next term in each. Then repeat parts (a) and (b). How did the accuracy of the approximations change when an additional term was added?

102. HOW DO YOU SEE IT? The figure below shows the graph of $y = \sin(x - c)$ for

$$c = -\frac{\pi}{4}, \quad 0, \quad \text{and} \quad \frac{\pi}{4}.$$

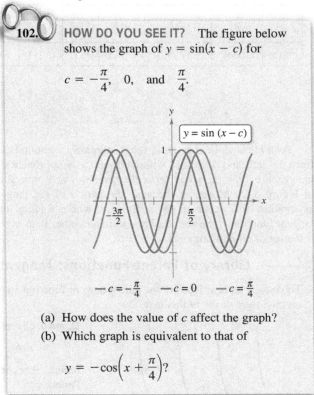

(a) How does the value of c affect the graph?

(b) Which graph is equivalent to that of

$$y = -\cos\!\left(x + \frac{\pi}{4}\right)?$$

Cumulative Mixed Review

Finding the Slope of a Line In Exercises 103 and 104, plot the points and find the slope of the line passing through the points.

103. $(0, 1), (2, 5)$ **104.** $(-1, 4), (3, -2)$

Converting from Radians to Degrees In Exercises 105 and 106, convert the angle measure from radians to degrees. Round your answer to three decimal places.

105. 8.5 **106.** -0.48

107. *Make a Decision* To work an extended application analyzing the mean monthly high temperature and normal precipitation in Cheyenne, Wyoming, visit this textbook's website at *LarsonPrecalculus.com*. (Data Source: NOAA)

5.5   Graphs of Other Trigonometric Functions

Graph of the Tangent Function

Recall that the tangent function is odd. That is, $\tan(-x) = -\tan x$. Consequently, the graph of $y = \tan x$ is symmetric with respect to the origin. You also know from the identity $\tan x = \sin x/\cos x$ that the tangent function is undefined when $\cos x = 0$. Two such values are $x = \pm\pi/2 \approx \pm 1.5708$.

x	$-\dfrac{\pi}{2}$	-1.57	-1.5	$-\dfrac{\pi}{4}$	0	$\dfrac{\pi}{4}$	1.5	1.57	$\dfrac{\pi}{2}$
$\tan x$	Undef.	-1255.8	-14.1	-1	0	1	14.1	1255.8	Undef.

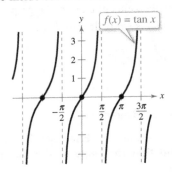

tan x approaches $-\infty$ as x approaches $-\pi/2$ from the right.

tan x approaches ∞ as x approaches $\pi/2$ from the left.

As indicated in the table, $\tan x$ increases without bound as x approaches $\pi/2$ from the left, and decreases without bound as x approaches $-\pi/2$ from the right. So, the graph of $y = \tan x$ has *vertical asymptotes* at $x = \pi/2$ and $x = -\pi/2$, as shown in Figure 5.45. Moreover, because the period of the tangent function is π, vertical asymptotes also occur at $x = \pi/2 + n\pi$, where n is an integer. The domain of the tangent function is the set of all real numbers other than $x = \pi/2 + n\pi$, and the range is the set of all real numbers.

Library of Parent Functions: Tangent Function

The basic characteristics of the parent tangent function are summarized below and on the inside cover of this text.

$f(x) = \tan x$

Domain: all real numbers x,

$$x \neq \frac{\pi}{2} + n\pi$$

Range: $(-\infty, \infty)$
Period: π
x-intercepts: $(n\pi, 0)$
y-intercept: $(0, 0)$

Vertical asymptotes: $x = \dfrac{\pi}{2} + n\pi$

Odd function
Origin symmetry

Figure 5.45

Sketching the graph of $y = a \tan(bx - c)$ is similar to sketching the graph of $y = a \sin(bx - c)$ in that you locate key points that identify the intercepts and asymptotes. Two consecutive asymptotes can be found by solving the equations $bx - c = -\pi/2$ and $bx - c = \pi/2$ for x. The midpoint between two consecutive asymptotes is an x-intercept of the graph. The period of the function $y = a \tan(bx - c)$ is the distance between two consecutive asymptotes. The amplitude of a tangent function is not defined. After plotting the asymptotes and the x-intercept, plot a few additional points between the two asymptotes and sketch one cycle. Finally, sketch one or two additional cycles to the left and right.

EXAMPLE 1   Library of Parent Functions: $f(x) = \tan x$

Sketch the graph of $y = \tan \dfrac{x}{2}$ by hand.

Solution

By solving the equations $x/2 = -\pi/2$ and $x/2 = \pi/2$, you can see that two consecutive asymptotes occur at $x = -\pi$ and $x = \pi$. Between these two asymptotes, plot a few points, including the x-intercept, as shown in the table. Three cycles of the graph are shown in Figure 5.46. Use a graphing utility to confirm this graph.

x	$-\pi$	$-\dfrac{\pi}{2}$	0	$\dfrac{\pi}{2}$	π
$\tan \dfrac{x}{2}$	Undef.	-1	0	1	Undef.

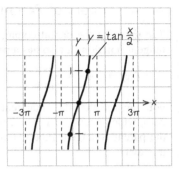

Figure 5.46

✓ **Checkpoint** 🔊))) *Audio-video solution in English & Spanish at LarsonPrecalculus.com.*

Sketch the graph of $y = \tan x/4$ by hand.

EXAMPLE 2   Library of Parent Functions: $f(x) = \tan x$

Sketch the graph of $y = -3 \tan 2x$ by hand.

Solution

By solving the equations $2x = -\pi/2$ and $2x = \pi/2$, you can see that two consecutive asymptotes occur at $x = -\pi/4$ and $x = \pi/4$. Between these two asymptotes, plot a few points, including the x-intercept, as shown in the table. Three cycles of the graph are shown in Figure 5.47. Use a graphing utility to confirm this graph, as shown in Figure 5.48.

x	$-\dfrac{\pi}{4}$	$-\dfrac{\pi}{8}$	0	$\dfrac{\pi}{8}$	$\dfrac{\pi}{4}$
$-3 \tan 2x$	Undef.	3	0	-3	Undef.

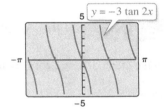

Figure 5.48

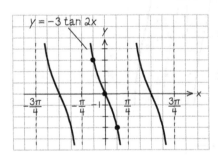

Figure 5.47

✓ **Checkpoint** 🔊))) *Audio-video solution in English & Spanish at LarsonPrecalculus.com.*

Sketch the graph of $y = \tan 2x$ by hand.

By comparing the graphs in Examples 1 and 2, you can see that the graph of $y = a \tan(bx - c)$ increases between consecutive vertical asymptotes when $a > 0$ and decreases between consecutive vertical asymptotes when $a < 0$. In other words, the graph for $a < 0$ is a reflection in the x-axis of the graph for $a > 0$.

Graph of the Cotangent Function

Library of Parent Functions: Cotangent Function

The graph of the parent cotangent function is similar to the graph of the parent tangent function. It also has a period of π. However, from the identity

$$f(x) = \cot x = \frac{\cos x}{\sin x}$$

you can see that the cotangent function has vertical asymptotes when $\sin x$ is zero, which occurs at $x = n\pi$, where n is an integer. The basic characteristics of the parent cotangent function are summarized below and on the inside cover of this text.

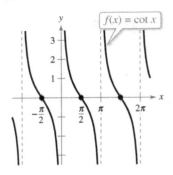

Domain: all real numbers x, $x \neq n\pi$
Range: $(-\infty, \infty)$
Period: π
x-intercepts: $\left(\dfrac{\pi}{2} + n\pi, 0\right)$
Vertical asymptotes: $x = n\pi$
Odd function
Origin symmetry

EXAMPLE 3   Library of Parent Functions: $f(x) = \cot x$

Sketch the graph of $y = 2 \cot \dfrac{x}{3}$ by hand.

Solution

To locate two consecutive vertical asymptotes of the graph, solve the equations $x/3 = 0$ and $x/3 = \pi$ to see that two consecutive asymptotes occur at $x = 0$ and $x = 3\pi$. Then, between these two asymptotes, plot a few points, including the x-intercept, as shown in the table. Three cycles of the graph are shown in the figure. Use a graphing utility to confirm this graph. [Enter the function as $y = 2/\tan(x/3)$.] Note that the period is 3π, the distance between consecutive asymptotes.

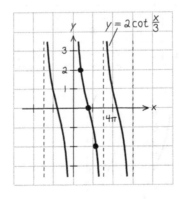

x	0	$\dfrac{3\pi}{4}$	$\dfrac{3\pi}{2}$	$\dfrac{9\pi}{4}$	3π
$2 \cot \dfrac{x}{3}$	Undef.	2	0	-2	Undef.

✓ **Checkpoint** 🔊))) *Audio-video solution in English & Spanish at LarsonPrecalculus.com.*

Sketch the graph of $y = \cot \dfrac{x}{4}$ by hand.

Graphs of the Reciprocal Functions

The graphs of the two remaining trigonometric functions can be obtained from the graphs of the sine and cosine functions using the reciprocal identities

$$\csc x = \frac{1}{\sin x} \quad \text{and} \quad \sec x = \frac{1}{\cos x}.$$

For instance, at a given value of x, the y-coordinate of $\sec x$ is the reciprocal of the y-coordinate of $\cos x$. Of course, when $\cos x = 0$, the reciprocal does not exist. Near such values of x, the behavior of the secant function is similar to that of the tangent function. In other words, the graphs of

$$\tan x = \frac{\sin x}{\cos x} \quad \text{and} \quad \sec x = \frac{1}{\cos x}$$

have vertical asymptotes where $\cos x = 0$—that is, at $x = \pi/2 + n\pi$, where n is an integer. Similarly,

$$\cot x = \frac{\cos x}{\sin x} \quad \text{and} \quad \csc x = \frac{1}{\sin x}$$

have vertical asymptotes where $\sin x = 0$—that is, at $x = n\pi$, where n is an integer.

To sketch the graph of a secant or cosecant function, you should first make a sketch of its reciprocal function. For instance, to sketch the graph of $y = \csc x$, first sketch the graph of $y = \sin x$. Then take the reciprocals of the y-coordinates to obtain points on the graph of $y = \csc x$. You can use this procedure to obtain the graphs shown in Figure 5.49.

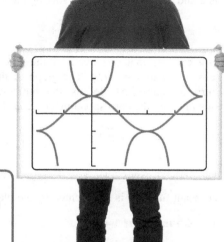

Library of Parent Functions: Cosecant and Secant Functions

The basic characteristics of the parent cosecant and secant functions are summarized below and on the inside cover of this text.

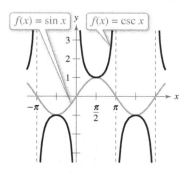

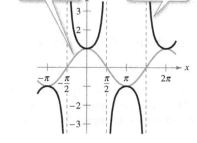

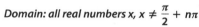

Domain: all real numbers x, x ≠ nπ

Range: $(-\infty, -1] \cup [1, \infty)$
Period: 2π
No intercepts

Vertical asymptotes: $x = n\pi$

Odd function
Origin symmetry

Figure 5.49

Domain: all real numbers x, $x \neq \dfrac{\pi}{2} + n\pi$

Range: $(-\infty, -1] \cup [1, \infty)$
Period: 2π
y-intercept: $(0, 1)$

Vertical asymptotes: $x = \dfrac{\pi}{2} + n\pi$

Even function
y-axis symmetry

In comparing the graphs of the cosecant and secant functions with those of the sine and cosine functions, note that the "hills" and "valleys" are interchanged. For instance, a hill (or maximum point) on the sine curve corresponds to a valley (a relative minimum) on the cosecant curve, and a valley (or minimum point) on the sine curve corresponds to a hill (a relative maximum) on the cosecant curve, as shown in Figure 5.50. Additionally, x-intercepts of the sine and cosine functions become vertical asymptotes of the cosecant and secant functions, respectively (see Figure 5.50).

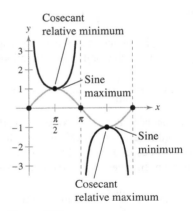

Figure 5.50

EXAMPLE 4   Library of Parent Functions: $f(x) = \csc x$

Sketch the graph of $y = 2\csc\left(x + \dfrac{\pi}{4}\right)$ by hand.

Solution

Begin by sketching the graph of $y = 2\sin\left(x + \dfrac{\pi}{4}\right)$. For this function, the amplitude is 2 and the period is 2π. By solving the equations

$$x + \frac{\pi}{4} = 0 \qquad \text{and} \qquad x + \frac{\pi}{4} = 2\pi$$

you can see that one cycle of the sine function corresponds to the interval from $x = -\pi/4$ to $x = 7\pi/4$. The graph of this sine function is represented by the gray curve in Figure 5.51. Because the sine function is zero at the midpoint and endpoints of this interval, the corresponding cosecant function

$$y = 2\csc\left(x + \frac{\pi}{4}\right) = 2\left(\frac{1}{\sin[x + (x/4)]}\right)$$

has vertical asymptotes at $x = -\dfrac{\pi}{4}$, $x = \dfrac{3\pi}{4}$, $x = \dfrac{7\pi}{4}$, and so on. The graph of the cosecant function is represented by the black curve in Figure 5.51.

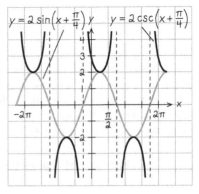

Figure 5.51

✓ **Checkpoint**))) *Audio-video solution in English & Spanish at LarsonPrecalculus.com.*

Sketch the graph of $y = 2\csc\left(x + \dfrac{\pi}{2}\right)$ by hand.

EXAMPLE 5   Library of Parent Functions: $f(x) = \sec x$

See LarsonPrecalculus.com for an interactive version of this type of example.

To sketch the graph of $y = \sec 2x$ by hand, begin by sketching the graph of $y = \cos 2x$, as indicated by the gray curve in Figure 5.52. Then, form the graph of $y = \sec 2x$, as indicated by the black curve in the figure. Note that the x-intercepts of $y = \cos 2x$

$$\left(-\frac{\pi}{4}, 0\right), \qquad \left(\frac{\pi}{4}, 0\right), \qquad \left(\frac{3\pi}{4}, 0\right), \dots$$

correspond to the vertical asymptotes

$$x = -\frac{\pi}{4}, \qquad x = \frac{\pi}{4}, \qquad x = \frac{3\pi}{4}, \dots$$

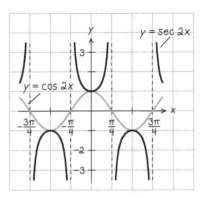

Figure 5.52

of the graph of $y = \sec 2x$. Moreover, notice that the period of $y = \cos 2x$ and $y = \sec 2x$ is π.

✓ **Checkpoint**))) *Audio-video solution in English & Spanish at LarsonPrecalculus.com.*

Sketch the graph of $y = \sec \dfrac{x}{2}$ by hand.

Damped Trigonometric Graphs

A *product* of two functions can be graphed using properties of the individual functions. For instance, consider the function

$$f(x) = x \sin x$$

as the product of the functions $y = x$ and $y = \sin x$. Using properties of absolute value and the fact that $|\sin x| \le 1$, you have $0 \le |x||\sin x| \le |x|$. Consequently,

$$-|x| \le x \sin x \le |x|$$

which means that the graph of $f(x) = x \sin x$ lies between the lines $y = -x$ and $y = x$. Furthermore, because

$$f(x) = x \sin x = \pm x \qquad \text{at} \qquad x = \frac{\pi}{2} + n\pi$$

and

$$f(x) = x \sin x = 0 \qquad \text{at} \qquad x = n\pi$$

where n is an integer, the graph of f touches the line $y = -x$ or the line $y = x$ at $x = \pi/2 + n\pi$ and has x-intercepts at $x = n\pi$. A sketch of f is shown in Figure 5.53. In the function $f(x) = x \sin x$, the factor x is called the **damping factor.**

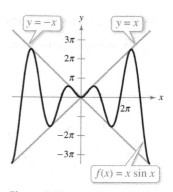

Figure 5.53

Remark

Do you see why the graph of $f(x) = x \sin x$ touches the lines $y = \pm x$ at $x = \pi/2 + n\pi$ and why the graph has x-intercepts at $x = n\pi$? Recall that the sine function is equal to ± 1 at $\pi/2, 3\pi/2, 5\pi/2, \ldots$ (odd multiples of $\pi/2$) and is equal to 0 at $\pi, 2\pi, 3\pi, \ldots$ (multiples of π).

EXAMPLE 6   Analyzing a Damped Sine Curve

Analyze the graph of $f(x) = e^{-x} \sin 3x$.

Solution

Consider $f(x)$ as the product of the two functions

$$y = e^{-x} \qquad \text{and} \qquad y = \sin 3x$$

each of which has the set of real numbers as its domain. For any real number x, you know that $e^{-x} > 0$ and $|\sin 3x| \le 1$. So, $e^{-x} |\sin 3x| \le e^{-x}$, which means that

$$-e^{-x} \le e^{-x} \sin 3x \le e^{-x}.$$

Furthermore, because

$$f(x) = e^{-x} \sin 3x = \pm e^{-x} \qquad \text{at} \qquad x = \frac{\pi}{6} + \frac{n\pi}{3}$$

and

$$f(x) = e^{-x} \sin 3x = 0 \qquad \text{at} \qquad x = \frac{n\pi}{3}$$

the graph of f touches the curves $y = -e^{-x}$ and $y = e^{-x}$ at $x = \pi/6 + n\pi/3$ and has intercepts at $x = n\pi/3$. The graph is shown below.

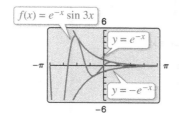

 **Checkpoint** ◀))) *Audio-video solution in English & Spanish at LarsonPrecalculus.com.*

Analyze the graph of $f(x) = e^x \sin 4x$.

Library of Parent Functions: Trigonometric Functions

Figure 5.54 summarizes the six basic trigonometric functions.

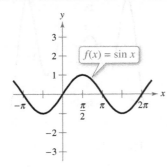

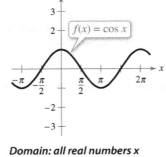

Domain: all real numbers x
Range: $[-1, 1]$
Period: 2π

Domain: all real numbers x
Range: $[-1, 1]$
Period: 2π

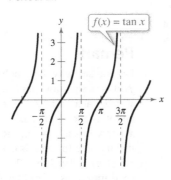

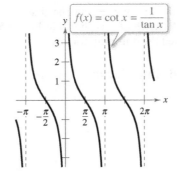

Domain: all real numbers x,
$$x \neq \frac{\pi}{2} + n\pi$$
Range: $(-\infty, \infty)$
Period: π

Domain: all real numbers x,
$$x \neq n\pi$$
Range: $(-\infty, \infty)$
Period: π

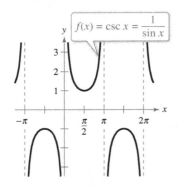

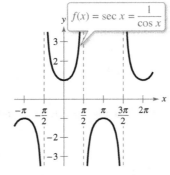

Domain: all real numbers x,
$$x \neq n\pi$$
Range: $(-\infty, -1] \cup [1, \infty)$
Period: 2π

Domain: all real numbers x,
$$x \neq \frac{\pi}{2} + n\pi$$
Range: $(-\infty, -1] \cup [1, \infty)$
Period: 2π

Figure 5.54

5.5   Exercises

See *CalcChat.com* for tutorial help and worked-out solutions to odd-numbered exercises.
For instructions on how to use a graphing utility, see Appendix A.

Vocabulary and Concept Check

In Exercises 1 and 2, fill in the blank.

1. The graphs of the tangent, cotangent, secant, and cosecant functions have _____ asymptotes.

2. To sketch the graph of a secant or cosecant function, first make a sketch of its _____ function.

3. Which two parent trigonometric functions have a period of π and a range that consists of the set of all real numbers?

4. What is the damping factor of the function $f(x) = e^{2x} \sin x$?

Procedures and Problem Solving

Library of Parent Functions   **In Exercises 5–8, use the graph of the function to answer each question.**

(a) Find any x-intercepts of the graph of $y = f(x)$.

(b) Find any y-intercepts of the graph of $y = f(x)$.

(c) Find the intervals on which the graph of $y = f(x)$ is increasing and the intervals on which the graph of $y = f(x)$ is decreasing.

(d) Find all relative extrema, if any, of the graph of $y = f(x)$.

(e) Find all vertical asymptotes, if any, of the graph of $y = f(x)$.

5. $f(x) = \tan x$ **6.** $f(x) = \cot x$

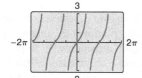   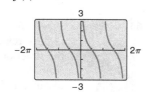

7. $f(x) = \sec x$ **8.** $f(x) = \csc x$

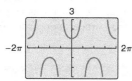   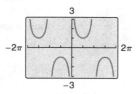

Library of Parent Functions   **In Exercises 9–28, sketch the graph of the function. (Include two full periods.) Use a graphing utility to verify your result.**

9. $y = \tan \dfrac{x}{5}$ **10.** $y = \tan 3x$

11. $y = -2 \tan 2x$ **12.** $y = -4 \tan \dfrac{x}{3}$

13. $y = \dfrac{1}{2} \cot \dfrac{x}{2}$ **14.** $y = 3 \cot \pi x$

15. $y = -\dfrac{1}{2} \sec x$ **16.** $y = \dfrac{1}{4} \sec x$

17. $y = 3 \csc \dfrac{x}{2}$ **18.** $y = -\csc \dfrac{x}{3}$

19. $y = \sec \pi x - 3$ **20.** $y = 2 \sec 4x + 2$

21. $y = 2 \tan \dfrac{\pi x}{4}$ **22.** $y = \dfrac{1}{2} \tan \pi x$

23. $y = -\csc(\pi - x)$ **24.** $y = -\sec(x + \pi)$

25. $y = \dfrac{1}{2} \sec(2x - \pi)$ **26.** $y = \csc(2x - \pi)$

27. $y = 2 \cot\left(x + \dfrac{\pi}{2}\right)$ **28.** $y = \dfrac{1}{4} \cot(x + \pi)$

Comparing Trigonometric Graphs   **In Exercises 29–34, use a graphing utility to graph the function (include two full periods). Graph the corresponding reciprocal function in the same viewing window. Describe and compare the graphs.**

29. $y = 2 \csc 3x$ **30.** $y = -\csc 4x$

31. $y = -2 \sec 4x$ **32.** $y = \dfrac{1}{4} \sec \pi x$

33. $y = \dfrac{1}{3} \sec\left(\dfrac{\pi x}{2} + \dfrac{\pi}{2}\right)$ **34.** $y = \dfrac{1}{2} \csc(2x - \pi)$

Solving a Trigonometric Equation Graphically   **In Exercises 35–40, use a graph of the function to approximate the solution of the equation on the interval $[-2\pi, 2\pi]$.**

35. $\tan x = 1$ **36.** $\cot x = -1$

37. $\sec x = 2$ **38.** $\csc x = \sqrt{2}$

39. $\cot x = -\sqrt{3}$ **40.** $\sec x = -\sqrt{2}$

Even and Odd Trigonometric Functions   **In Exercises 41–46, use the graph of the function to determine whether the function is even, odd, or neither.**

41. $f(x) = \sec x$ **42.** $f(x) = \tan x$

43. $f(x) = \csc 2x$ **44.** $f(x) = \cot 2x$

45. $f(x) = \tan\left(x - \dfrac{\pi}{2}\right)$ **46.** $f(x) = \sec(x + \pi)$

Using Graphs to Compare Functions **In Exercises 47–50, use a graphing utility to graph the two equations in the same viewing window. Use the graphs to determine whether the expressions are equivalent. Verify the results algebraically.**

47. $y_1 = \sin x \sec x, \quad y_2 = \tan x$

48. $y_1 = \dfrac{\cos x}{\sin x}, \quad y_2 = \cot x$

49. $y_1 = 1 + \cot^2 x, \quad y_2 = \csc^2 x$

50. $y_1 = \sec^2 x - 1, \quad y_2 = \tan^2 x$

Identifying Damped Trigonometric Graphs **In Exercises 51–54, match the function with its graph. Describe the behavior of the function as x approaches zero. [The graphs are labeled (a), (b), (c), and (d).]**

(a)

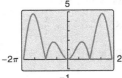

(b)

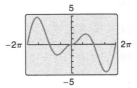

(c)

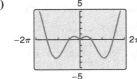

(d)

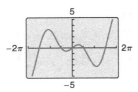

51. $f(x) = x \cos x$ **52.** $f(x) = |x \sin x|$

53. $g(x) = |x| \sin x$ **54.** $g(x) = |x| \cos x$

Analyzing a Damped Trigonometric Graph **In Exercises 55–58, use a graphing utility to graph the function and the damping factor of the function in the same viewing window. Then analyze the graph of the function using the method in Example 6.**

55. $f(x) = e^{-x} \cos x$ **56.** $f(x) = e^{-2x} \sin x$

57. $h(x) = 2^{-x^2/4} \sin x$ **58.** $g(x) = 2^{-x^2/2} \cos x$

Exploration **In Exercises 59 and 60, use a graphing utility to graph the function. Use the graph to determine the behavior of the function as $x \to c$.**

(a) $x \to \dfrac{\pi^+}{2} \left(\text{as } x \text{ approaches } \dfrac{\pi}{2} \text{ from the right}\right)$

(b) $x \to \dfrac{\pi^-}{2} \left(\text{as } x \text{ approaches } \dfrac{\pi}{2} \text{ from the left}\right)$

(c) $x \to -\dfrac{\pi^+}{2} \left(\text{as } x \text{ approaches } -\dfrac{\pi}{2} \text{ from the right}\right)$

(d) $x \to -\dfrac{\pi^-}{2} \left(\text{as } x \text{ approaches } -\dfrac{\pi}{2} \text{ from the left}\right)$

59. $f(x) = \tan x$ **60.** $f(x) = \sec x$

Exploration **In Exercises 61 and 62, use a graphing utility to graph the function. Use the graph to determine the behavior of the function as $x \to c$.**

(a) As $x \to 0^+$, the value of $f(x) \to$ ▨ .

(b) As $x \to 0^-$, the value of $f(x) \to$ ▨ .

(c) As $x \to \pi^+$, the value of $f(x) \to$ ▨ .

(d) As $x \to \pi^-$, the value of $f(x) \to$ ▨ .

61. $f(x) = \csc x$

62. $f(x) = \cot x$

63. Aviation A plane flying at an altitude of 7 miles over level ground will pass directly over a radar antenna. Let d be the ground distance from the antenna to the point directly under the plane and let x be the angle of elevation to the plane from the antenna (see figure). Write d as a function of x and graph the function over the interval $0 < x < \pi$. (Consider d as positive when the plane approaches the antenna.)

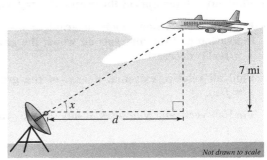

Not drawn to scale

64. *Why you should learn it* (p. 444) A television camera is on a reviewing platform 27 meters from the street on which a parade will be passing from left to right (see figure). Write the distance d from the camera to a particular unit in the parade as a function of the angle x, and graph the function over the interval $-\pi/2 < x < \pi/2$. (Consider x as negative when a unit in the parade approaches from the left.)

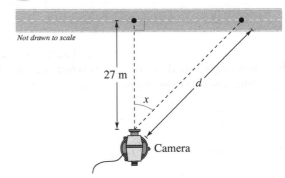

Not drawn to scale

65. Harmonic Motion   An object weighing W pounds is suspended from a ceiling by a steel spring. The weight is pulled downward (positive direction) from its equilibrium position and released (see figure). The resulting motion of the weight is described by the function $y = \frac{1}{2}e^{-t/4} \cos 4t$, where y is the distance in feet and t is the time in seconds ($t > 0$).

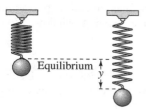

Equilibrium

(a) Use a graphing utility to graph the function.

(b) Describe the behavior of the displacement function for increasing values of time t.

66. Mechanical Engineering   A crossed belt connects a 10-centimeter pulley on an electric motor with a 20-centimeter pulley on a saw arbor (see figure). The electric motor runs at 1700 revolutions per minute.

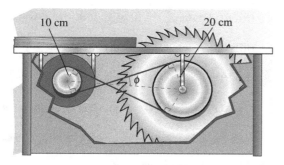

10 cm   20 cm

ϕ

(a) Determine the number of revolutions per minute of the saw.

(b) How does crossing the belt affect the saw in relation to the motor?

(c) Let L be the total length of the belt. Write L as a function of ϕ, where ϕ is measured in radians. What is the domain of the function? (*Hint:* Add the lengths of the straight sections of the belt and the length of the belt around each pulley.)

(d) Use a graphing utility to complete the table.

ϕ	0.3	0.6	0.9	1.2	1.5
L					

(e) As ϕ increases, do the lengths of the straight sections of the belt change faster or slower than the lengths of the belts around each pulley?

(f) Use the graphing utility to graph the function over the appropriate domain.

67. MODELING DATA

The motion of an oscillating weight suspended by a spring was measured by a motion detector. The data were collected, and the approximate maximum (positive and negative) displacements from equilibrium are shown in the graph. The displacement y is measured in centimeters and the time t is measured in seconds.

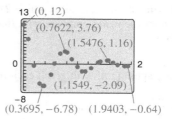

(a) Is y a function of t? Explain.

(b) Approximate the frequency of the oscillations.

(c) Fit a model of the form $y = ab^t \cos ct$ to the data. Use the result of part (b) to approximate c. Use the *regression* feature of a graphing utility to fit an exponential model to the positive maximum displacements of the weight.

(d) Rewrite the model in the form $y = ae^{kt} \cos ct$.

(e) Use the graphing utility to graph the model. Compare the result with the data in the graph above.

Conclusions

True or False?   In Exercises 68–71, determine whether the statement is true or false. Justify your answer.

68. The graph of $y = -\frac{1}{8}\tan\left(\frac{x}{2} + \pi\right)$ has an asymptote at $x = -7\pi$.

69. For the graph of $y = 2^x \sin x$, as x approaches $-\infty$, y approaches 0.

70. The graph of $y = \csc x$ can be obtained on a calculator by graphing the reciprocal of $y = \sin x$.

71. The graph of $y = \sec x$ can be obtained on a calculator by graphing a translation of the reciprocal of $y = \sin x$.

72. Exploration   Consider the functions

$$f(x) = 2 \sin x \qquad \text{and} \qquad g(x) = \tfrac{1}{2} \csc x$$

on the interval $(0, \pi)$.

(a) Use a graphing utility to graph f and g in the same viewing window.

(b) Approximate the interval in which $f(x) > g(x)$.

(c) Describe the behavior of each of the functions as x approaches π. How is the behavior of g related to the behavior of f as x approaches π?

73. Exploration Consider the functions given by

$$f(x) = \tan \frac{\pi x}{2} \quad \text{and} \quad g(x) = \frac{1}{2} \sec \frac{\pi x}{2}$$

on the interval $(-1, 1)$,

(a) Use a graphing utility to graph f and g in the same viewing window.

(b) Approximate the interval in which $f(x) < g(x)$.

(c) Approximate the interval in which $2f(x) < 2g(x)$. How does the result compare with that of part (b)? Explain.

74. Exploration

(a) Use a graphing utility to graph each function.

$$y_1 = \frac{4}{\pi}\left(\sin \pi x + \frac{1}{3}\sin 3\pi x\right)$$

$$y_2 = \frac{4}{\pi}\left(\sin \pi x + \frac{1}{3}\sin 3\pi x + \frac{1}{5}\sin 5\pi x\right)$$

(b) Identify the pattern in part (a) and find a function y_3 that continues the pattern one more term. Use the graphing utility to graph y_3.

(c) The graphs in parts (a) and (b) approximate the periodic function in the figure. Find a function y_4 that is a better approximation.

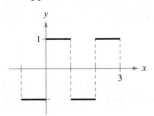

Exploration In Exercises 75 and 76, use a graphing utility to explore the ratio $f(x)$, which appears in calculus.

(a) **Complete the table. Round your results to four decimal places.**

x	-1	-0.1	-0.01	-0.001
$f(x)$				

x	0	0.001	0.01	0.1	1
$f(x)$					

(b) **Use the graphing utility to graph f. Use the *zoom* and *trace* features to describe the behavior of the graph as x approaches 0.**

(c) **Write a brief statement regarding the value of the ratio based on your results in parts (a) and (b).**

75. $f(x) = \dfrac{\tan x}{x}$ **76.** $f(x) = \dfrac{\tan 3x}{3x}$

77. Exploration Using calculus, it can be shown that the tangent function can be approximated by the polynomial

$$\tan x \approx x + \frac{2x^3}{3!} + \frac{16x^5}{5!}$$

where x is in radians. Use a graphing utility to graph the tangent function and its polynomial approximation in the same viewing window. How do the graphs compare?

78. **HOW DO YOU SEE IT?**   Determine which function is represented by each graph. Do not use a calculator.

(a) 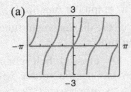 (b)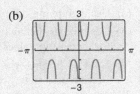

(i) $f(x) = \tan 2x$ (i) $f(x) = \sec 4x$

(ii) $f(x) = \tan \dfrac{x}{2}$ (ii) $f(x) = \csc 4x$

(iii) $f(x) = 2 \tan x$ (iii) $f(x) = \csc \dfrac{x}{4}$

(iv) $f(x) = -\tan 2x$ (iv) $f(x) = \sec \dfrac{x}{4}$

(v) $f(x) = -\tan \dfrac{x}{2}$ (v) $f(x) = \csc(4x - \pi)$

Cumulative Mixed Review

Properties of Real Numbers In Exercises 79–82, identify the rule of algebra illustrated by the statement.

79. $5(a - 9) = 5a - 45$

80. $7\left(\frac{1}{7}\right) = 1$

81. $(3 + x) + 0 = 3 + x$

82. $(a + b) + 10 = a + (b + 10)$

Finding an Inverse Function In Exercises 83–86, determine whether the function is one-to-one. If it is, find its inverse function.

83. $f(x) = -10$ **84.** $f(x) = (x - 7)^2 + 3$

85. $f(x) = \sqrt{3x - 14}$ **86.** $f(x) = \sqrt[4]{x - 5}$

Finding the Domain, Intercepts, and Asymptotes of a Function In Exercises 87–90, identify the domain, any intercepts, and any asymptotes of the function.

87. $y = x^2 + 3x - 4$ **88.** $y = \ln x^4$

89. $f(x) = 3^{x+1} + 2$ **90.** $f(x) = \dfrac{x - 7}{x^2 + 4x + 4}$

10.5   Polar Coordinates

Introduction

So far, you have been representing graphs of equations as collections of points (x, y) in the rectangular coordinate system, where x and y represent the directed distances from the coordinate axes to the point (x, y). In this section, you will study a second coordinate system called the **polar coordinate system.**

To form the polar coordinate system in the plane, fix a point O, called the **pole** (or **origin**), and construct from O an initial ray called the **polar axis,** as shown in the figure. Then each point P in the plane can be assigned **polar coordinates** (r, θ), as follows.

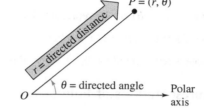

1. $r = $ *directed distance* from O to P

2. $\theta = $ *directed angle*, counterclockwise from the polar axis to segment $\overline{OP}$

EXAMPLE 1   **Plotting Points in the Polar Coordinate System**

Plot the points (a) $\left(2, \dfrac{\pi}{3}\right)$, (b) $\left(3, -\dfrac{\pi}{6}\right)$, and (c) $\left(3, \dfrac{11\pi}{6}\right)$ given in polar coordinates.

Solution

a. The point $(r, \theta) = \left(2, \dfrac{\pi}{3}\right)$ lies two units from the pole on the terminal side of the angle $\theta = \dfrac{\pi}{3}$, as shown in Figure 10.48.

b. The point $(r, \theta) = \left(3, -\dfrac{\pi}{6}\right)$ lies three units from the pole on the terminal side of the angle $\theta = -\dfrac{\pi}{6}$, as shown in Figure 10.49.

c. The point $(r, \theta) = \left(3, \dfrac{11\pi}{6}\right)$ coincides with the point $\left(3, -\dfrac{\pi}{6}\right)$, as shown in Figure 10.50.

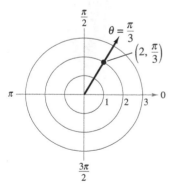

Figure 10.48

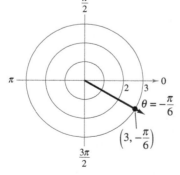

Figure 10.49

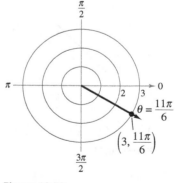

Figure 10.50

✓ **Checkpoint** 🔊))) *Audio-video solution in English & Spanish at LarsonPrecalculus.com.*

Plot the points (a) $\left(3, \dfrac{\pi}{4}\right)$, (b) $\left(2, -\dfrac{\pi}{3}\right)$, and (c) $\left(2, \dfrac{5\pi}{3}\right)$ given in polar coordinates. ■

In rectangular coordinates, each point (x, y) has a unique representation. This is not true for polar coordinates. For instance, the coordinates

$$(r, \theta) \quad \text{and} \quad (r, \theta + 2\pi)$$

represent the same point, as illustrated in Example 1. Another way to obtain multiple representations of a point is to use negative values for r. Because r is a *directed distance*, the coordinates

$$(r, \theta) \quad \text{and} \quad (-r, \theta + \pi)$$

represent the same point. In general, the point (r, θ) can be represented as

$$(r, \theta) = (r, \theta \pm 2n\pi) \quad \text{or} \quad (r, \theta) = (-r, \theta \pm (2n + 1)\pi)$$

where n is any integer. Moreover, the pole is represented by $(0, \theta)$, where θ is any angle.

EXAMPLE 2   Multiple Representations of Points

Plot the point

$$\left(3, -\frac{3\pi}{4}\right)$$

and find three additional polar representations of this point, using

$$-2\pi < \theta < 2\pi.$$

Solution

The point is shown in Figure 10.51. Three other representations are as follows.

$$\left(3, -\frac{3\pi}{4} + 2\pi\right) = \left(3, \frac{5\pi}{4}\right) \qquad \text{Add } 2\pi \text{ to } \theta.$$

$$\left(-3, -\frac{3\pi}{4} - \pi\right) = \left(-3, -\frac{7\pi}{4}\right) \qquad \text{Replace } r \text{ by } -r. \text{ subtract } \pi \text{ from } \theta.$$

$$\left(-3, -\frac{3\pi}{4} + \pi\right) = \left(-3, \frac{\pi}{4}\right) \qquad \text{Replace } r \text{ by } -r, \text{ add } \pi \text{ to } \theta.$$

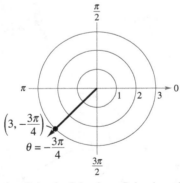

$$\left(3, -\tfrac{3\pi}{4}\right) = \left(3, \tfrac{5\pi}{4}\right) = \left(-3, -\tfrac{7\pi}{4}\right) = \left(-3, \tfrac{\pi}{4}\right) = \cdots$$

Figure 10.51

✓ **Checkpoint** 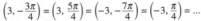 *Audio-video solution in English & Spanish at LarsonPrecalculus.com.*

Plot each point and find three additional polar representations of the point, using $-2\pi < \theta < 2\pi$.

a. $\left(3, \dfrac{4\pi}{3}\right)$ **b.** $\left(2, -\dfrac{5\pi}{6}\right)$ **c.** $\left(-1, \dfrac{3\pi}{4}\right)$

Explore the Concept

Set your graphing utility to *polar* mode. Then graph the equation $r = 3$. (Use a viewing window in which $0 \le \theta \le 2\pi$, $-6 \le x \le 6$, and $-4 \le y \le 4$.) You should obtain a circle of radius 3.

a. Use the *trace* feature to cursor around the circle. Can you locate the point $(3, 5\pi/4)$?

b. Can you locate other representations of the point $(3, 5\pi/4)$? If so, explain how you did it.

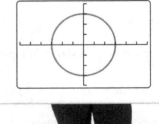

Coordinate Conversion

To establish the relationship between polar and rectangular coordinates, let the polar axis coincide with the positive *x*-axis and the pole with the origin, as shown in Figure 10.52. Because (x, y) lies on a circle of radius r, it follows that $r^2 = x^2 + y^2$. Moreover, for $r > 0$, the definitions of the trigonometric functions imply that

$$\tan \theta = \frac{y}{x}, \qquad \cos \theta = \frac{x}{r}, \qquad \text{and} \qquad \sin \theta = \frac{y}{r}.$$

You can show that the same relationships hold for $r < 0$.

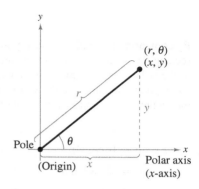

Figure 10.52

> **Coordinate Conversion**
>
> The polar coordinates (r, θ) are related to the rectangular coordinates (x, y), as follows.
>
> | *Polar-to-Rectangular* | *Rectangular-to-Polar* |
> |---|---|
> | $x = r \cos \theta$ | $\tan \theta = \dfrac{y}{x}$ |
> | $y = r \sin \theta$ | $r^2 = x^2 + y^2$ |

EXAMPLE 3   Polar-to-Rectangular Conversion

Convert the point $(2, \pi)$ to rectangular coordinates.

Solution

For the point $(r, \theta) = (2, \pi)$, you have the following.

$$x = r \cos \theta = 2 \cos \pi = -2$$
$$y = r \sin \theta = 2 \sin \pi = 0$$

The rectangular coordinates are $(x, y) = (-2, 0)$. (See Figure 10.53.)

✓ **Checkpoint**)))) *Audio-video solution in English & Spanish at LarsonPrecalculus.com.*

Convert the point $\left(4, \dfrac{\pi}{3}\right)$ to rectangular coordinates.

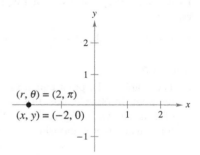

Figure 10.53

EXAMPLE 4   Rectangular-to-Polar Conversion

Convert the point $(-1, 1)$ to polar coordinates.

Solution

For the second-quadrant point $(x, y) = (-1, 1)$, you have

$$\tan \theta = \frac{y}{x} = \frac{1}{-1} = -1 \quad \Longrightarrow \quad \theta = \frac{3\pi}{4}.$$

Because θ lies in the same quadrant as (x, y), use positive r.

$$r = \sqrt{x^2 + y^2} = \sqrt{(-1)^2 + (1)^2} = \sqrt{2}$$

So, *one* set of polar coordinates is

$$(r, \theta) = \left(\sqrt{2}, \frac{3\pi}{4}\right). \qquad \text{See Figure 10.54}$$

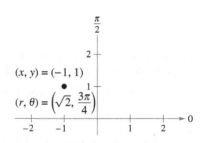

Figure 10.54

✓ **Checkpoint**)))) *Audio-video solution in English & Spanish at LarsonPrecalculus.com.*

Convert the point $(0, 2)$ to polar coordinates.

Equation Conversion

By comparing Examples 3 and 4, you can see that point conversion from the polar to the rectangular system is straightforward, whereas point conversion from the rectangular to the polar system is more involved. For equations, the opposite is true. To convert a rectangular equation to polar form, replace x by $r \cos \theta$ and y by $r \sin \theta$. For instance, the rectangular equation $y = x^2$ can be written in polar form, as follows.

$$y = x^2 \qquad \text{Rectangular equation}$$
$$r \sin \theta = (r \cos \theta)^2 \qquad \text{Polar equation}$$
$$r = \sec \theta \tan \theta \qquad \text{Simplest form}$$

On the other hand, converting a polar equation to rectangular form requires considerable ingenuity. Example 5 demonstrates several polar-to-rectangular conversions that enable you to sketch the graphs of some polar equations.

> **EXAMPLE 5** **Converting Polar Equations to Rectangular Form**
>
> *See LarsonPrecalculus.com for an interactive version of this type of example.*

Describe the graph of each polar equation and find the corresponding rectangular equation.

a. $r = 2$ **b.** $\theta = \dfrac{\pi}{3}$ **c.** $r = \sec \theta$

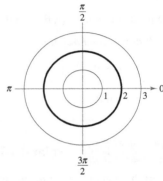

Figure 10.55

Solution

a. The graph of the polar equation $r = 2$ consists of all points that are two units from the pole. In other words, this graph is a circle centered at the origin with a radius of 2, as shown in Figure 10.55. You can confirm this by converting to rectangular form, using the relationship $r^2 = x^2 + y^2$.

$$r = 2 \implies r^2 = 2^2 \implies x^2 + y^2 = 2^2$$

$\underbrace{\text{Polar equation}} \qquad \underbrace{\text{Rectangular equation}}$

b. The graph of the polar equation

$$\theta = \frac{\pi}{3}$$

consists of all points on the line that makes an angle of $\pi/3$ with the positive x-axis, as shown in Figure 10.56. To convert to rectangular form, you make use of the relationship $\tan \theta = y/x$.

$$\theta = \frac{\pi}{3} \implies \tan \theta = \sqrt{3} \implies y = \sqrt{3}x$$

$\underbrace{\text{Polar equation}} \qquad \underbrace{\text{Rectangular equation}}$

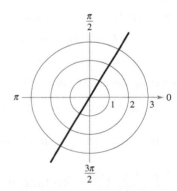

Figure 10.56

c. The graph of the polar equation $r = \sec \theta$ is not evident by simple inspection, so you convert to rectangular form by using the relationship $r \cos \theta = x$.

$$r = \sec \theta \implies r \cos \theta = 1 \implies x = 1$$

$\underbrace{\text{Polar equation}} \qquad \underbrace{\text{Rectangular equation}}$

Now you can see that the graph is a vertical line, as shown in Figure 10.57.

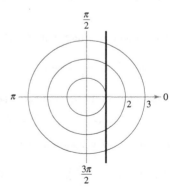

Figure 10.57

✓ **Checkpoint**  *Audio-video solution in English & Spanish at LarsonPrecalculus.com.*

Describe the graph of $r = 6 \sin \theta$ and find the corresponding rectangular equation. ∎

10.5 Exercises

See *CalcChat.com* for tutorial help and worked-out solutions to odd-numbered exercises. For instructions on how to use a graphing utility, see Appendix A.

Vocabulary and Concept Check

In Exercises 1 and 2, fill in the blank(s).

1. The origin of the polar coordinate system is called the _____ .

2. For the point (r, θ), r is the _____ from O to P and θ is the _____ counterclockwise from the polar axis to segment $\overline{OP}$.

3. How are the rectangular coordinates (x, y) related to the polar coordinates (r, θ)?

4. Do the polar coordinates $(1, \pi)$ and the rectangular coordinates $(-1, 0)$ represent the same point?

Procedures and Problem Solving

Matching Polar Coordinates **In Exercises 5–8, match the polar coordinates with the point on the graph. Then find the rectangular coordinates of the point.**

5. $\left(2, \dfrac{\pi}{2}\right)$

6. $\left(2, \dfrac{3\pi}{2}\right)$

7. $(0, 0)$

8. $\left(-2, \dfrac{5\pi}{4}\right)$

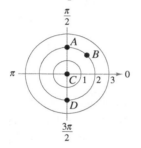

Plotting Points in the Polar Coordinate System **In Exercises 9–18, plot the point given in polar coordinates and find three additional polar representations of the point, using $-2\pi < \theta < 2\pi$.**

9. $\left(3, \dfrac{5\pi}{6}\right)$

10. $\left(2, \dfrac{3\pi}{4}\right)$

11. $\left(1, -\dfrac{\pi}{3}\right)$

12. $\left(3, -\dfrac{7\pi}{6}\right)$

13. $\left(-4, \dfrac{5\pi}{6}\right)$

14. $\left(-5, -\dfrac{11\pi}{6}\right)$

15. $\left(-\dfrac{3}{2}, -\dfrac{7\pi}{4}\right)$

16. $\left(-5\sqrt{2}, \dfrac{2\pi}{3}\right)$

17. $(0, -\pi/2)$

18. $(0, \pi/6)$

Polar-to-Rectangular Conversion **In Exercises 19–26, plot the point given in polar coordinates and find the corresponding rectangular coordinates for the point.**

19. $(3, \pi)$

20. $(2, 0)$

21. $\left(1, -\dfrac{3\pi}{4}\right)$

22. $\left(-16, \dfrac{5\pi}{2}\right)$

23. $\left(0, -\dfrac{7\pi}{6}\right)$

24. $\left(0, \dfrac{5\pi}{4}\right)$

25. $\left(-5, \dfrac{3\pi}{2}\right)$

26. $\left(-3, -\dfrac{\pi}{6}\right)$

Using a Graphing Utility to Find Rectangular Coordinates **In Exercises 27–32, use a graphing utility to find the rectangular coordinates of the point given in polar coordinates. Round your results to two decimal places.**

27. $(2, 2\pi/9)$

28. $(4, 11\pi/9)$

29. $(-4.5, 1.3)$

30. $(8.25, 3.5)$

31. $(1.5, -2.82)$

32. $(-5.3, -0.78)$

Rectangular-to-Polar Conversion **In Exercises 33–40, plot the point given in rectangular coordinates and find two sets of polar coordinates for the point for $0 \le \theta < 2\pi$.**

33. $(-7, 0)$

34. $(0, -5)$

35. $(1, 1)$

36. $(-3, -3)$

37. $\left(-\sqrt{3}, -\sqrt{3}\right)$

38. $\left(\sqrt{3}, -1\right)$

39. $(-3, 4)$

40. $(3, -1)$

Using a Graphing Utility to Find Polar Coordinates **In Exercises 41–46, use a graphing utility to find one set of polar coordinates for the point given in rectangular coordinates. (There are many correct answers.)**

41. $(3, -2)$

42. $(-5, 2)$

43. $\left(-\sqrt{3}, 2\right)$

44. $\left(3\sqrt{2}, 3\sqrt{2}\right)$

45. $\left(\dfrac{5}{2}, \dfrac{4}{3}\right)$

46. $\left(-\dfrac{7}{4}, -\dfrac{3}{2}\right)$

Converting a Rectangular Equation to Polar Form **In Exercises 47–64, convert the rectangular equation to polar form. Assume $a < 0$.**

47. $x^2 + y^2 = 9$

48. $x^2 + y^2 = 16$

49. $y = x$

50. $y = -\sqrt{3}x$

51. $y = a$

52. $x = a$

53. $3x - y + 2 = 0$

54. $3x + 5y - 2 = 0$

55. $xy = 4$

56. $2xy = 1$

57. $(x^2 + y^2)^2 = 9(x^2 - y^2)$

58. $y^2 - 8x - 16 = 0$

59. $x^2 + y^2 - 6x = 0$

60. $x^2 + y^2 - 8y = 0$

61. $x^2 + y^2 - 2ax = 0$

62. $x^2 + y^2 - 2ay = 0$

63. $y^2 = x^3$

64. $x^2 = y^3$

Converting a Polar Equation to Rectangular Form   In Exercises 65–80, convert the polar equation to rectangular form.

65. $r = 4 \sin \theta$

66. $r = 2 \cos \theta$

67. $\theta = \dfrac{5\pi}{6}$

68. $\theta = \dfrac{11\pi}{6}$

69. $\theta = \pi/2$

70. $\theta = \pi$

71. $r = -3 \csc \theta$

72. $r = 2 \sec \theta$

73. $r^2 = \cos \theta$

74. $r^2 = \sin 2\theta$

75. $r = 2 \sin 3\theta$

76. $r = -3 \cos 2\theta$

77. $r = \dfrac{1}{1 - \cos \theta}$

78. $r = \dfrac{2}{1 + \sin \theta}$

79. $r = \dfrac{6}{2 - 3 \sin \theta}$

80. $r = \dfrac{6}{2 \cos \theta - 3 \sin \theta}$

Converting a Polar Equation to Rectangular Form   In Exercises 81–86, describe the graph of the polar equation and find the corresponding rectangular equation. Sketch its graph.

81. $r = 6$

82. $r = 8$

83. $\theta = \dfrac{\pi}{4}$

84. $\theta = \dfrac{7\pi}{6}$

85. $r = 3 \sec \theta$

86. $r = 2 \csc \theta$

87. *Why you should learn it* (p. 813) The center of a  Ferris wheel lies at the pole of the polar coordinate system, where the distances are in feet. Passengers enter a car at $(30, -\pi/2)$. It takes 45 seconds for the wheel to complete one clockwise revolution.

 (a) Write a polar equation that models the possible positions of a passenger car.

 (b) Passengers enter a car. Find and interpret their coordinates after 15 seconds of rotation.

 (c) Convert the point in part (b) to rectangular coordinates. Interpret the coordinates.

88. **Ferris Wheel**   Repeat Exercise 87 when the distance from a passenger car to the center is 35 feet and it takes 60 seconds to complete one clockwise revolution.

Conclusions

True or False?   In Exercises 89 and 90, determine whether the statement is true or false. Justify your answer.

89. If (r_1, θ_1) and (r_2, θ_2) represent the same point in the polar coordinate system, then $|r_1| = |r_2|$.

90. If (r, θ_1) and (r, θ_2) represent the same point in the polar coordinate system, then $\theta_1 = \theta_2 + 2\pi n$ for some integer n.

91. **Think About It**

 (a) Show that the distance between the points (r_1, θ_1) and (r_2, θ_2) is $\sqrt{r_1^2 + r_2^2 - 2r_1 r_2 \cos(\theta_1 - \theta_2)}$.

 (b) Simplify the Distance Formula for $\theta_1 = \theta_2$. Is the simplification what you expected? Explain.

 (c) Simplify the Distance Formula for $\theta_1 - \theta_2 = 90°$. Is the simplification what you expected? Explain.

92. **HOW DO YOU SEE IT?**   Use the polar coordinate system shown below.

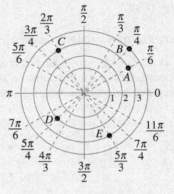

 (a) Identify the polar coordinates of the points.

 (b) Which points lie on the graph of $r = 3$?

 (c) Which points lie on the graph of $\theta = \pi/4$?

93. **Writing**   In the rectangular coordinate system, each point (x, y) has a unique representation. Explain why this is not true for a point (r, θ) in the polar coordinate system.

94. **Think About It**   Convert the polar equation $r = \cos \theta + 3 \sin \theta$ to rectangular form and identify the graph.

95. **Think About It**   Convert the polar equation $r = 2(h \cos \theta + k \sin \theta)$ to rectangular form and verify that it is the equation of a circle. Find the radius of the circle and the rectangular coordinates of the center of the circle.

Cumulative Mixed Review

Solving a Triangle Using the Law of Sines or Cosines   In Exercises 96–99, use the Law of Sines or the Law of Cosines to solve the triangle.

96. $a = 13, b = 19, c = 25$

97. $A = 24°, a = 10, b = 6$

98. $A = 56°, C = 38°, c = 12$

99. $B = 71°, a = 21, c = 29$

10.6   Graphs of Polar Equations

Introduction

In previous chapters, you sketched graphs in rectangular coordinate systems. You began with the basic point-plotting method. Then you used sketching aids such as a graphing utility, symmetry, intercepts, asymptotes, periods, and shifts to further investigate the natures of the graphs. This section approaches curve sketching in the polar coordinate system similarly.

EXAMPLE 1   **Graphing a Polar Equation by Point Plotting**

Sketch the graph of the polar equation $r = 4 \sin \theta$ by hand.

Solution

The sine function is periodic, so you can get a full range of r-values by considering values of θ in the interval $0 \le \theta \le 2\pi$, as shown in the table.

θ	0	$\dfrac{\pi}{6}$	$\dfrac{\pi}{3}$	$\dfrac{\pi}{2}$	$\dfrac{2\pi}{3}$	$\dfrac{5\pi}{6}$	π	$\dfrac{7\pi}{6}$	$\dfrac{3\pi}{2}$	$\dfrac{11\pi}{6}$	2π
r	0	2	$2\sqrt{3}$	4	$2\sqrt{3}$	2	0	-2	-4	-2	0

By plotting these points, as shown in the figure, it appears that the graph is a circle of radius 2 whose center is the point $(x, y) = (0, 2)$.

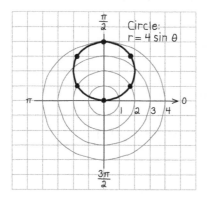

Circle: $r = 4 \sin \theta$

✓ **Checkpoint** ◀))) *Audio-video solution in English & Spanish at LarsonPrecalculus.com.*

Sketch the graph of the polar equation $r = 6 \cos \theta$.

You can confirm the graph found in Example 1 in three ways.

1. *Convert to Rectangular Form*   Multiply each side of the polar equation by r and convert the result to rectangular form.

2. *Use a Polar Coordinate Mode*   Set your graphing utility to *polar* mode and graph the polar equation. (Use $0 \le \theta \le \pi$, $-6 \le x \le 6$, and $-4 \le y \le 4$.)

3. *Use a Parametric Mode*   Set your graphing utility to *parametric* mode and graph $x = (4 \sin t) \cos t$ and $y = (4 \sin t) \sin t$.

Most graphing utilities have a *polar* graphing mode. If yours does not, you can rewrite the polar equation $r = f(\theta)$ in parametric form, using t as a parameter with the equations $x = f(t) \cos t$ and $y = f(t) \sin t$.

Symmetry and Zeros

In Example 1, note in the graph of $r = 4 \sin \theta$ that as θ increases from 0 to 2π, the graph is traced out twice. Moreover, note that the graph is *symmetric with respect to the line* $\theta = \pi/2$. Had you known about this symmetry and retracing ahead of time, you could have used fewer points. The three important types of symmetry to consider in polar curve sketching are shown in Figure 10.58.

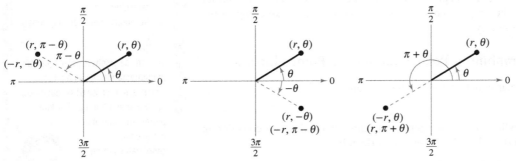

Symmetry with Respect to the Line $\theta = \dfrac{\pi}{2}$

Symmetry with Respect to the Polar Axis

Symmetry with Respect to the Pole

Figure 10.58

Testing for Symmetry in Polar Coordinates

The graph of a polar equation is symmetric with respect to the following when the given substitution yields an equivalent equation.

1. The line $\theta = \dfrac{\pi}{2}$:   Replace (r, θ) by $(r, \pi - \theta)$ or $(-r, -\theta)$.

2. The polar axis: Replace (r, θ) by $(r, -\theta)$ or $(-r, \pi - \theta)$.

3. The pole: Replace (r, θ) by $(r, \pi + \theta)$ or $(-r, \theta)$.

You can determine the symmetry of the graph of $r = 4 \sin \theta$ (see Example 1) as follows.

1. Replace (r, θ) by $(-r, -\theta)$:

$$-r = 4 \sin(-\theta)$$
$$r = -4 \sin(-\theta)$$
$$r = 4 \sin \theta$$

2. Replace (r, θ) by $(r, -\theta)$:

$$r = 4 \sin(-\theta)$$
$$r = -4 \sin \theta$$

3. Replace (r, θ) by $(-r, \theta)$:

$$-r = 4 \sin \theta$$
$$r = -4 \sin \theta$$

So, the graph of $r = 4 \sin \theta$ is symmetric with respect to the line $\theta = \pi/2$. Recall from Section 5.3 that the sine function is odd. That is,

$$\sin(-\theta) = -\sin \theta.$$

EXAMPLE 2   **Using Symmetry to Sketch a Polar Graph**

Use symmetry to sketch the graph of $r = 3 + 2 \cos \theta$.

Solution

Replacing (r, θ) by $(r, -\theta)$ produces

$$r = 3 + 2 \cos(-\theta) = 3 + 2 \cos \theta. \qquad \cos(-u) = \cos u$$

So, by using the even trigonometric identity, you can conclude that the curve is symmetric with respect to the polar axis. Plotting the points in the table and using polar axis symmetry, you obtain the graph shown in Figure 10.59. This graph is called a **limaçon.**

θ	0	$\dfrac{\pi}{6}$	$\dfrac{\pi}{3}$	$\dfrac{\pi}{2}$	$\dfrac{2\pi}{3}$	$\dfrac{5\pi}{6}$	π
r	5	$3 + \sqrt{3}$	4	3	2	$3 - \sqrt{3}$	1

Use a graphing utility to confirm this graph.

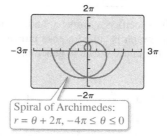

Figure 10.59

✓ ***Checkpoint*** 🔊))) *Audio-video solution in English & Spanish at LarsonPrecalculus.com.*

Use symmetry to sketch the graph of $r = 3 + 2 \sin \theta$.

The three tests for symmetry in polar coordinates on page 820 are sufficient to guarantee symmetry, but they are not necessary. For instance, the figure at the right shows the graph of

$$r = \theta + 2\pi. \qquad \text{Spiral of Archimedes}$$

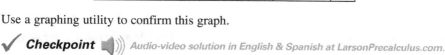

Spiral of Archimedes: $r = \theta + 2\pi, -4\pi \leq \theta \leq 0$

From the figure, you can see that the graph is symmetric with respect to the line $\theta = \pi/2$. Yet the tests on page 820 fail to indicate symmetry because neither of the following replacements yields an equivalent equation.

Original Equation	*Replacement*	*New Equation*
$r = \theta + 2\pi$	(r, θ) by $(-r, -\theta)$	$-r = -\theta + 2\pi$
$r = \theta + 2\pi$	(r, θ) by $(r, \pi - \theta)$	$r = -\theta + 3\pi$

The equations discussed in Examples 1 and 2 are of the form

$$r = f(\sin \theta) \qquad \text{Example 1}$$

and

$$r = g(\cos \theta). \qquad \text{Example 2}$$

The graph of the first equation is symmetric with respect to the line $\theta = \pi/2$, and the graph of the second equation is symmetric with respect to the polar axis. This observation can be generalized to yield the following *quick tests for symmetry.*

Quick Tests for Symmetry in Polar Coordinates

1. The graph of $r = f(\sin \theta)$ is symmetric with respect to the line $\theta = \dfrac{\pi}{2}$.

2. The graph of $r = g(\cos \theta)$ is symmetric with respect to the polar axis.

An additional aid to sketching graphs of polar equations involves knowing the θ-values for which $r = 0$. In Example 1, $r = 0$ when $\theta = 0$. Some curves reach their zeros at more than one point, as shown in Example 3.

EXAMPLE 3   Sketching a Polar Graph

See LarsonPrecalculus.com for an interactive version of this type of example.

Sketch the graph of

$r = 2 \cos 3\theta$.

Solution

Symmetry: With respect to the polar axis

Zeros of r: $r = 0$ when $3\theta = \dfrac{\pi}{2}, \dfrac{3\pi}{2}, \dfrac{5\pi}{2}$

or $\theta = \dfrac{\pi}{6}, \dfrac{\pi}{2}, \dfrac{5\pi}{6}$

θ	0	$\dfrac{\pi}{12}$	$\dfrac{\pi}{6}$	$\dfrac{\pi}{4}$	$\dfrac{\pi}{3}$	$\dfrac{5\pi}{12}$	$\dfrac{\pi}{2}$
r	2	$\sqrt{2}$	0	$-\sqrt{2}$	-2	$-\sqrt{2}$	0

By plotting these points and using the specified symmetry and zeros, you can obtain the graph shown in Figure 10.60. This graph is called a **rose curve,** and each loop on the graph is called a *petal.* Note how the entire curve is generated as θ increases from 0 to π.

Explore the Concept

Notice that the rose curve in Example 3 has three petals. How many petals do the rose curves $r = 2 \cos 4\theta$ and $r = 2 \sin 3\theta$ have? Determine the numbers of petals for the curves $r = 2 \cos n\theta$ and $r = 2 \sin n\theta$, where n is a positive integer.

$0 \le \theta \le \dfrac{\pi}{6}$

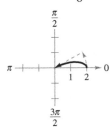

$0 \le \theta \le \dfrac{\pi}{3}$

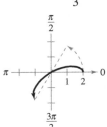

$0 \le \theta \le \dfrac{\pi}{2}$

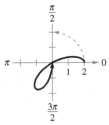

$0 \le \theta \le \dfrac{2\pi}{3}$

$0 \le \theta \le \dfrac{5\pi}{6}$

$0 \le \theta \le \pi$

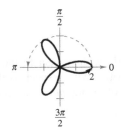

Figure 10.60

✓ **Checkpoint** 🔊))) *Audio-video solution in English & Spanish at LarsonPrecalculus.com.*

Sketch the graph of $r = 4 \sin 2\theta$.

Special Polar Graphs

Several important types of graphs have equations that are simpler in polar form than in rectangular form. For example, the circle

$$r = 4 \sin \theta$$

in Example 1 has the more complicated rectangular equation

$$x^2 + (y - 2)^2 = 4.$$

Several other types of graphs that have simple polar equations are shown below.

Limaçons

$r = a \pm b \cos \theta, r = a \pm b \sin \theta \quad (a > 0, b > 0)$

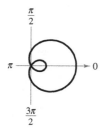   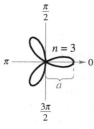   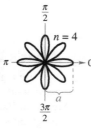   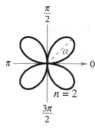

$\dfrac{a}{b} < 1$ $\dfrac{a}{b} = 1$ $1 < \dfrac{a}{b} < 2$ $\dfrac{a}{b} \geq 2$

Limaçon with inner loop   Cardioid (heart-shaped)   Dimpled limaçon   Convex limaçon

Rose Curves

n petals when n is odd, $2n$ petals when n is even $(n \geq 2)$

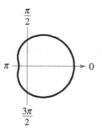   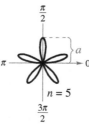   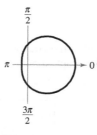   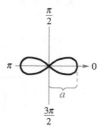

$r = a \cos n\theta$ $r = a \cos n\theta$ $r = a \sin n\theta$ $r = a \sin n\theta$

Circles and Lemniscates

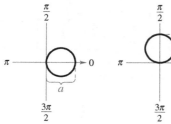   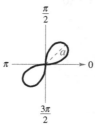

$r = a \cos \theta$ $r = a \sin \theta$ $r^2 = a^2 \sin 2\theta$ $r^2 = a^2 \cos 2\theta$

Circle   Circle   Lemniscate   Lemniscate

The quick tests for symmetry presented on page 821 are especially useful when graphing rose curves. Because rose curves have the form $r = f(\sin \theta)$ or the form $r = g(\cos \theta)$, you know that a rose curve will be either symmetric with respect to the line $\theta = \pi/2$ or symmetric with respect to the polar axis.

EXAMPLE 4 Graphing a Rose Curve

Use a graphing utility to graph $r = 3 \cos 2\theta$.

Solution

Type of curve: Rose curve with $2n = 4$ petals

Symmetry: With respect to the polar axis, the line $\theta = \dfrac{\pi}{2}$, and the pole

Zeros of r: $r = 0$ when $\theta = \dfrac{\pi}{4}, \dfrac{3\pi}{4}$

Using a graphing utility in *polar* mode, enter the equation, as shown in Figure 10.61 (with $0 \le \theta \le 2\pi$). You should obtain the graph shown in Figure 10.62.

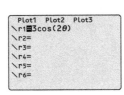

Figure 10.61

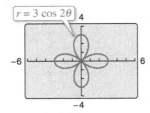

Figure 10.62

✓ **Checkpoint** 🔊 *Audio-video solution in English & Spanish at LarsonPrecalculus.com.*

Use a graphing utility to graph $r = 3 \sin 3\theta$.

EXAMPLE 5 Graphing a Lemniscate

Use a graphing utility to graph $r^2 = 9 \sin 2\theta$.

Solution

Type of curve: Lemniscate

Symmetry: With respect to the pole

Zeros of r: $r = 0$ when $\theta = 0, \dfrac{\pi}{2}$

Using a graphing utility in *polar* mode, enter the equation, as shown in Figure 10.63 (with $0 \le \theta \le 2\pi$). You should obtain the graph shown in Figure 10.64.

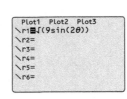

Figure 10.63

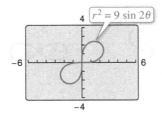

Figure 10.64

✓ **Checkpoint** 🔊 *Audio-video solution in English & Spanish at LarsonPrecalculus.com.*

Use a graphing utility to graph $r^2 = 4 \cos 2\theta$.

What's Wrong?

You use a graphing utility in *polar* mode to confirm the result in Example 5 and obtain the graph shown below (with $0 \le \theta \le 2\pi$). What's wrong?

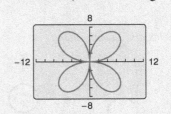

10.6   Exercises

See *CalcChat.com* for tutorial help and worked-out solutions to odd-numbered exercises. For instructions on how to use a graphing utility, see Appendix A.

Vocabulary and Concept Check

In Exercises 1–4, fill in the blank.

1. The equation $r = 2 + \cos \theta$ represents a _____ .

2. The equation $r = 2 \cos \theta$ represents a _____ .

3. The equation $r^2 = 4 \sin 2\theta$ represents a _____ .

4. The equation $r = 1 + \sin \theta$ represents a _____ .

5. How can you test whether the graph of a polar equation is symmetric with respect to the line $\theta = \frac{\pi}{2}$?

6. Is the graph of $r = 3 + 4 \cos \theta$ symmetric with respect to the line $\theta = \frac{\pi}{2}$ or to the polar axis?

Procedures and Problem Solving

Identifying Types of Polar Graphs   In Exercises 7–10, identify the type of polar graph.

7. $r = 3 \cos 2\theta$

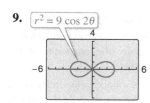

8. $r = 5 - 5 \sin \theta$

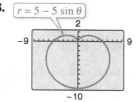

9. $r^2 = 9 \cos 2\theta$

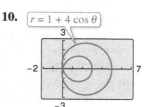

10. $r = 1 + 4 \cos \theta$

Finding the Equation of a Polar Curve   In Exercises 11–14, determine the equation of the polar curve whose graph is shown.

11.

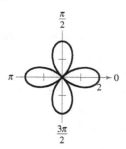

(a) $r = 2 \cos 4\theta$

(b) $r = \cos 4\theta$

(c) $r = 2 \cos 2\theta$

(d) $r = 2 \cos \frac{\theta}{2}$

12.

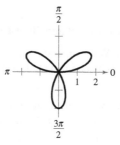

(a) $r = 2 \sin 6\theta$

(b) $r = 2 \cos\left(\frac{3\theta}{2}\right)$

(c) $r = 2 \sin\left(\frac{3\theta}{2}\right)$

(d) $r = 2 \sin 3\theta$

13.

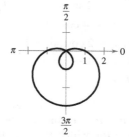

14.

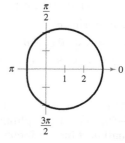

(a) $r = 1 - 2 \sin \theta$ (a) $r = 2 - \cos \theta$

(b) $r = 1 + 2 \sin \theta$ (b) $r = 2 - \sin \theta$

(c) $r = 1 + 2 \cos \theta$ (c) $r = 2 + \cos \theta$

(d) $r = 1 - 2 \cos \theta$ (d) $r = 2 + \sin \theta$

Testing for Symmetry   In Exercises 15–22, test for symmetry with respect to the line $\theta = \pi/2$, the polar axis, and the pole.

15. $r = 3$

16. $r = 5 + 4 \cos \theta$

17. $r = \dfrac{2}{1 - \cos \theta}$

18. $r = \dfrac{2}{1 + \sin \theta}$

19. $r = 6 \sin \theta$

20. $r = 4 \csc \theta \cos \theta$

21. $r^2 = 16 \sin 2\theta$

22. $r^2 = 36 \sin 2\theta$

Using Symmetry to Sketch a Polar Graph   In Exercises 23–30, use symmetry to sketch the graph of the polar equation. Use a graphing utility to verify your graph.

23. $r = 5$

24. $\theta = -5\pi/3$

25. $r = 3 \sin \theta$

26. $r = 2 \cos \theta$

27. $r = 3(1 - \cos \theta)$

28. $r = 4(1 + \sin \theta)$

29. $r = 4 + 5 \sin \theta$

30. $r = 3 + 6 \cos \theta$

Sketching a Polar Graph   In Exercises 31–36, identify and sketch the graph of the polar equation. Identify any symmetry and zeros of *r*. Use a graphing utility to verify your results.

31. $r = 5 \cos 3\theta$

32. $r = \sin 5\theta$

33. $r = -7 \sin 2\theta$

34. $r = 3 \cos 4\theta$

35. $r = 1 + 2 \sin \theta$

36. $r = \sqrt{3} - 2 \cos \theta$

Using a Graphing Utility to Graph a Polar Equation   In Exercises 37–50, use a graphing utility to graph the polar equation. Describe your viewing window.

37. $r = 8 \cos 2\theta$

38. $r = -\cos 2\theta$

39. $r = 2(5 - \sin \theta)$

40. $r = 6 - 4 \sin \theta$

41. $r = \dfrac{3}{\sin \theta - 2 \cos \theta}$

42. $r = \dfrac{6}{2 \sin \theta - 3 \cos \theta}$

43. $r^2 = \sin 2\theta$

44. $r^2 = 4 \cos 3\theta$

45. $r = 8 \sin \theta \cos^2 \theta$

46. $r = 2 \cos(3\theta - 2)$

47. $r = 2 \csc \theta + 6$

48. $r = 4 - \sec \theta$

49. $r = e^{\theta}$

50. $r = e^{\theta/2}$

Using a Graphing Utility to Find an Interval   In Exercises 51–56, use a graphing utility to graph the polar equation. Find an interval for θ for which the graph is traced *only once*.

51. $r = 3 - 4 \cos \theta$

52. $r = 2(1 - 2 \sin \theta)$

53. $r = 2 \cos \dfrac{3\theta}{2}$

54. $r = 3 \sin \dfrac{5\theta}{2}$

55. $r = 9 \sin \theta$

56. $r^2 = 25 \cos 2\theta$

Using a Graphing Utility to Graph a Polar Equation   In Exercises 57–60, use a graphing utility to graph the polar equation and show that the indicated line is an asymptote of the graph.

	Name of Graph	Polar Equation	Asymptote
57.	Conchoid	$r = 2 - \sec \theta$	$x = -1$
58.	Conchoid	$r = 2 + \csc \theta$	$y = 1$
59.	Hyperbolic spiral	$r = 3/\theta$	$y = 3$
60.	Strophoid	$r = 2 \cos 2\theta \sec \theta$	$x = -2$

61. *Why you should learn it* (p. 819) The sound pickup pattern of a microphone is modeled by the polar equation $r = 5 + 5 \cos \theta$, where $|r|$ measures how sensitive the microphone is to sounds coming from the angle θ.

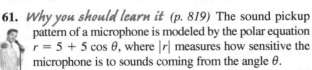

(a) Sketch the graph of the model and identify the type of polar graph.

(b) At what angle is the microphone most sensitive to sound?

62. Geometry   The area of the lemniscate $r^2 = a^2 \cos 2\theta$ is a^2. Sketch the graph of $r^2 = 16 \cos 2\theta$. Then find the area of one loop of the graph.

Conclusions

True or False?   In Exercises 63–65, determine whether the statement is true or false. Justify your answer.

63. The graph of $r = 6 \sin 5\theta$ is a rose curve with five petals.

64. The graph of $r = 4 + 2 \cos \theta$ is a dimpled limaçon.

65. A rose curve will always have symmetry with respect to the line $\theta = \pi/2$.

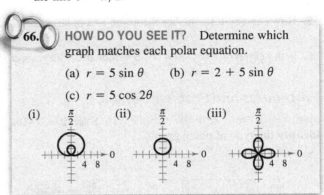

66.   **HOW DO YOU SEE IT?**   Determine which graph matches each polar equation.

(a) $r = 5 \sin \theta$ (b) $r = 2 + 5 \sin \theta$

(c) $r = 5 \cos 2\theta$

67. Exploration   The graph of $r = f(\theta)$ is rotated about the pole through an angle ϕ. Show that the equation of the rotated graph is $r = f(\theta - \phi)$.

68. Exploration   Consider the graph of $r = f(\sin \theta)$.

(a) Show that when the graph is rotated counterclockwise $\pi/2$ radians about the pole, the equation of the rotated graph is $r = f(-\cos \theta)$.

(b) Show that when the graph is rotated counterclockwise π radians about the pole, the equation of the rotated graph is $r = f(-\sin \theta)$.

(c) Show that when the graph is rotated counterclockwise $3\pi/2$ radians about the pole, the equation of the rotated graph is $r = f(\cos \theta)$.

Writing an Equation for Special Polar Graphs   In Exercises 69 and 70, use the results of Exercises 67 and 68.

69. Write an equation for the limaçon $r = 2 - \sin \theta$ after it has been rotated through each given angle.

(a) $\pi/4$ (b) $\pi/2$ (c) π (d) $3\pi/2$

70. Write an equation for the rose curve $r = 2 \sin 2\theta$ after it has been rotated through each given angle.

(a) $\pi/6$ (b) $\pi/2$ (c) $2\pi/3$ (d) π

Cumulative Mixed Review

Finding the Zeros of a Rational Function   In Exercises 71–74, find the zeros (if any) of the rational function.

71. $f(x) = \dfrac{x^2 - 9}{x + 1}$

72. $f(x) = 6 + \dfrac{4}{x^2 + 4}$

73. $f(x) = 5 - \dfrac{3}{x - 2}$

74. $f(x) = \dfrac{x^3 - 27}{x^2 + 4}$

ALTERNATING CURRENT

Alternating current electricity is produced in a coil of wire rotating in a magnetic field. This circular movement generates an ac current wave and an ac voltage wave in the wire, which behave like sine curves. The theory of alternating current is therefore linked to the mathematics of the sine function. The sine function is a periodic function that repeats its values after a certain number of degrees known as its period or cycle. Hence, ac current and ac voltage are periodic in nature. The fundamentals of ac electricity, including peak values, effective or root mean square values, frequency, period, and phase angles, are all studied in this chapter.

18.1 ALTERNATING CURRENT WAVES

Sine Curve

The graph of the sine function is generated by the movement of a point around a circle. Example 18.1 shows the basic sine curve using angles in degrees and radians. Radians, which are introduced in Section 16.1, are often used instead of degrees in electronic applications. Study Example 18.1 well. It is the basis for many ideas in this and subsequent chapters.

....
EXAMPLE 18.1
....

Graph $y = \sin \theta$ from $\theta = 0°$ to $\theta = 360°$.

Solution

To graph the basic sine function, you need to construct a table of values of θ and $y = \sin \theta$ using a convenient interval. The angle $30°$ ($\pi/6$ rad) is used as the interval because it is a common angle and provides enough points to sketch the graph. Using a calculator, find the values of $\sin \theta$ for each angle shown in the table below from $0°$ to $360°$. For example, to calculate the $\sin 210°$:

DAL: (sin) 210 (=) → -0.50

Not DAL: 210 (sin) → -0.50

In the following table, angles are shown in both degrees and radians in terms of π to help you become familiar with the radian values.

θ (deg)	0	30	60	90	120	150	180	210	240	270	300	330	360
θ (rad)	0	$\dfrac{\pi}{6}$	$\dfrac{\pi}{3}$	$\dfrac{\pi}{2}$	$\dfrac{2\pi}{3}$	$\dfrac{5\pi}{6}$	π	$\dfrac{7\pi}{6}$	$\dfrac{4\pi}{3}$	$\dfrac{3\pi}{2}$	$\dfrac{5\pi}{3}$	$\dfrac{11\pi}{6}$	2π
y = sin θ	0	0.50	0.87	1.0	0.87	0.50	0	−0.50	−0.87	−1.0	−0.87	−0.50	0

The graph of the sine function is shown in Figure 18-1 with points plotted every 30°. It illustrates how the sine curve is generated by the movement of a point in a circle. The radius of the circle $r = 1$, so $\sin \theta = y/r = y/1$ or simply $y = \sin \theta$. Therefore, *the height of the point on the circle for each angle θ equals the height of the sine curve.* By projecting these heights to the graph on the right as the radius revolves in a circle, you can see how the movement of the point around the circle produces the sine curve.

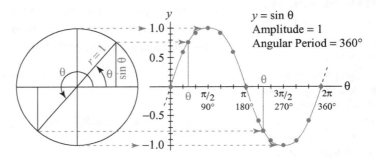

FIGURE 18-1 Sine curve showing projections of points on the unit circle for Example 18.1.

Observe that the sine curve begins at zero, reaches a maximum of 1 at 90° (π/2 rad), and returns to zero at 180° (π rad). The maximum value is called the *amplitude* of the curve. The sine becomes negative after 180°, reaches a minimum of −1 at 270° (3π/2 rad), and returns to zero at 360° (2π rad). The curve starts the same cycle again at 360° and repeats itself every 360°. The number of degrees in one cycle is called the *angular period* of the curve. The amplitude of the sine curve is therefore 1, and its angular period is 360°.

Cosine Curve

The cosine curve is essentially the same as the sine curve except for its position. Instead of beginning at zero, it begins and ends its cycle at the maximum value 1.

EXAMPLE 18.2

Graph $y = \cos \theta$ from $\theta = 0$ to $\theta = 360°$ for values of θ every 30°.

Solution

The table of values for θ and cos θ every 30° is:

θ (deg)	0	30	60	90	120	150	180	210	240	270	300	330	360
θ (rad)	0	$\frac{\pi}{6}$	$\frac{\pi}{3}$	$\frac{\pi}{2}$	$\frac{2\pi}{3}$	$\frac{5\pi}{6}$	π	$\frac{7\pi}{6}$	$\frac{4\pi}{3}$	$\frac{3\pi}{2}$	$\frac{5\pi}{3}$	$\frac{11\pi}{6}$	2π
y = cos θ	1.0	0.87	0.50	0	−0.50	−0.87	−1.0	−0.87	−0.50	0	0.50	0.87	1.0

Figure 18-2 shows the cosine curve with the sine curve superimposed in dashed lines for comparison.

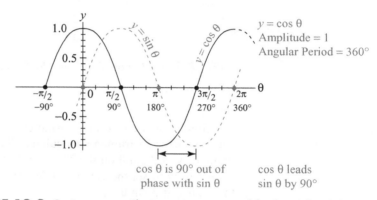

FIGURE 18-2 Cosine curve with sine curve compared for Example 18.2.

Both curves have an amplitude = 1 and an angular period = 360°. The cosine curve is extended back to −90° ($-\frac{\pi}{2}$ rad) where cos θ = 0. This point is equivalent to θ = 0° for the sine curve. If you move sin θ to the left 90°, both curves will match exactly. The difference is that *cos θ is 90° out of phase with sin θ.* Since cosine starts 90° before sine, *cos θ leads sin θ by 90°.* Because the sine and cosine curves are essentially the same, both are called *sinusoidal* curves.

You can change the amplitude of the sine or cosine curve by multiplying by a constant.

Definition   **Amplitude of Sine or Cosine**

The amplitude of $y = a \sin \theta$ or $y = a \cos \theta$ is $|a|$ **(18.1)**
$|a|$ = absolute or positive value.

EXAMPLE 18.3   Graph $y = 3 \sin \theta$ from $\theta = 0$ to $\theta = 2\pi$.

Solution

The values for $y = 3 \sin \theta$ are three times the values for $y = \sin \theta$ in Example 18.1. The curve looks the same except for its amplitude. See Figure 18-3. $y = 3 \sin \theta$ begins at 0, reaches a maximum of 3 at 90°, returns to 0 at 180°, reaches a minimum of −3 at 270°, and returns to 0 at 360°. The amplitude = |3| = 3 and the angular period = 360°.

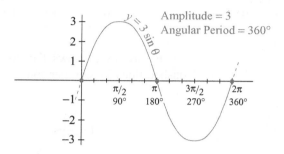

FIGURE 18-3 Graph of $y = \sin \theta$ for Example 18.3.

. . . .

Graphs of the sine and cosine curves can be done on a graphing calculator such as Texas Instruments calculators TI-83 to TI-86. For example, to draw the graph of $y = 3 \sin \theta$ on the TI-83 or TI-84, first press the $\boxed{\text{MODE}}$ key and then the down arrow to set the calculator for degrees. One set of keystrokes for the TI-83 to graph $y = 3 \sin \theta$ is:

$$\boxed{\text{ZOOM}} \; 7 \; \boxed{\text{Y=}} \; \boxed{\text{CLEAR}} \; 3 \; \boxed{\text{SIN}} \; \boxed{\text{X,T,}\theta} \; \boxed{\text{GRAPH}}$$

The keys $\boxed{\text{ZOOM}}$ 7 set the scale on the θ axis from $\theta = -360°$ to $\theta = 360°$ and the scale on the y axis from −4 to 4. You can set your own scale for x and y by pressing $\boxed{\text{WINDOW}}$. Appendix A shows some basic graphing functions on the TI-83 and TI-84.

Alternating Current

Alternating current behaves in the same way as a sinusoidal curve. It is produced in a coil of wire that rotates in a circle in a magnetic field. See Figure 18-4.

When the coil is in position (1) so it is perpendicular to the magnetic lines of force, there is no induced voltage and no current flow in the wire. As the coil turns and cuts the lines of force, there is an induced voltage that increases, and the current begins to flow in one direction. The voltage and current reach a maximum in position (2) when the coil has turned 90°. As the coil turns more, the induced voltage and current decrease. The voltage and current reach zero at position (3) after turning 180°. As the coil continues turning, there is an induced voltage of opposite polarity, and the current begins to move in the other direction. The voltage and current reach a maximum in the other direction at position (4) after turning 270°. As the coil continues to turn, the induced voltage again decreases, and the current decreases to zero at 360°, which is back to position (1). The cycle then repeats itself.

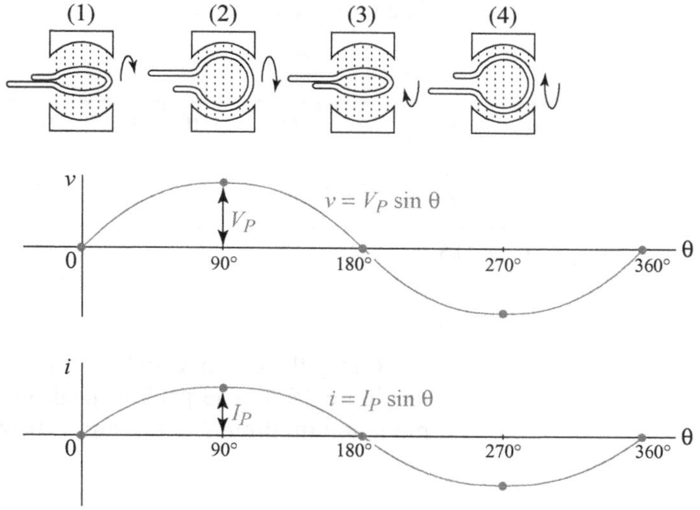

FIGURE 18-4 Induced ac voltage and ac current in a coil of wire.

The graph of the induced voltage and the induced current are both sine waves expressed by the following equations:

Formulas   **AC Voltage and Current Waves**

$$v = V_P \sin \theta \qquad\qquad i = I_P \sin \theta \qquad\qquad \textbf{(18.2)}$$

In formulas (18.2), v and i represent instantaneous values of the voltage and current. The amplitude or maximum value is called the *peak value* and is equal to V_P for the voltage and I_P for the current. The peak to peak value, V_{PP} or I_{PP}, is the difference between the maximum and minimum values and is twice the peak value. The number of degrees in one cycle or angular period is 360°.

CLOSE THE   **EXAMPLE 18.4**

CIRCUIT

Graph the ac voltage wave $v = 170 \sin \theta$ for one cycle. Give the peak value, the peak-to-peak value, and the angular period.

Solution

The peak value $V_P = 170$ V and the angular period $= 360°$. Construct the following table of values from 0° to 360° for angles every 30°. For example, when $\theta = 240°$ the value of v is found on the calculator as follows:

DAL: 170 [x] [sin] 240 [=] → −147 V

Not DAL: 240 [sin] [x] 170 [=] → −147 V

The table of values is:

θ (deg)	0	30	60	90	120	150	180	210	240	270	300	330	360
θ (rad)	0	$\dfrac{\pi}{6}$	$\dfrac{\pi}{3}$	$\dfrac{\pi}{2}$	$\dfrac{2\pi}{3}$	$\dfrac{5\pi}{6}$	π	$\dfrac{7\pi}{6}$	$\dfrac{4\pi}{3}$	$\dfrac{3\pi}{2}$	$\dfrac{5\pi}{3}$	$\dfrac{11\pi}{6}$	2π
v = 170 sin θ (V)	0	85	147	170	147	85	0	−85	−147	−170	−147	−85	0

Carefully set up a scale and plot the points to show the sine wave voltage as in Figure 18-5. The peak-to-peak value V_{PP} is the difference between the maximum and minimum values and is therefore equal to:

$$V_{PP} = 170 \text{ V} - (-170 \text{ V}) = 340 \text{ V}$$

or

$$V_{PP} = 2V_P = 2(170 \text{ V}) = 340 \text{ V}$$

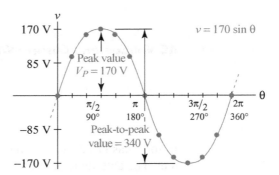

FIGURE 18-5 Sine wave voltage for Example 18.4.

To do Example 18.4 on the TI-83 or TI-84 graphing calculator, first press [WINDOW] to enter the range of values for θ (x) and y. Set x from 0° to 360° and y from −180 to 180. Then enter the following:

[Y=] [CLEAR] 170 [sin] [x,т,θ] [GRAPH]

In an ac circuit containing only a resistance, the sine wave current is *in phase* with the sine wave voltage, as shown in Figure 18-4. Both waves start at 0 and end at 360°. The sine wave current is graphed in the same way as the sine wave voltage. There are many other technical applications of sinusoidal curves such as sound waves, light waves, radio waves, water waves, and the mechanical vibration of a wire, spring, and beam.

In exercises 1 through 12 graph each sinusoidal curve from $\theta = 0$ to $\theta = 360°$ for θ every 30°. Give the amplitude and the angular period.

1. $y = 2 \sin \theta$
2. $y = 5 \sin \theta$
3. $y = 50 \sin \theta$
4. $y = 120 \sin \theta$
5. $y = 10 \sin \theta$
6. $y = 15 \sin \theta$

7. $y = 3 \cos \theta$
8. $y = 4 \cos \theta$
9. $y = 2.5 \cos \theta$
10. $y = 3.5 \cos \theta$
11. $y = 100 \cos \theta$
12. $y = 50 \cos \theta$

Applications to Electronics

In exercises 13 through 24 graph each ac voltage or current wave from $\theta = 0$ to $\theta = 360°$ for θ every 30°. Give the peak value, the peak-to-peak value, and the angular period.

13. $v = 100 \sin \theta$
14. $v = 60 \sin \theta$
15. $i = 20 \sin \theta$
16. $i = 30 \sin \theta$
17. $v = 300 \sin \theta$
18. $v = 150 \sin \theta$

19. $i = 1.5 \cos \theta$
20. $i = 1.2 \cos \theta$
21. $v = 12 \cos \theta$
22. $v = 3.6 \cos \theta$
23. $i = 6.0 \cos \theta$
24. $i = 0.50 \cos \theta$

In problems 25 through 28 solve each applied problem to two significant digits.

25. The current in an ac circuit containing an inductance is given by $i = 2.0 \sin \theta$, while the voltage is given by $v = 110 \cos \theta$. Sketch these two ac waves on the same graph to show that the current and the voltage are 90° out of phase. Use different scales for current and voltage.

26. The voltage in an ac circuit containing a capacitance is given by $v = 200 \sin \theta$, while the current is given by $i = 4.0 \cos \theta$. Sketch these two ac waves on the same graph to show that the voltage and the current are 90° out of phase. Use different scales for voltage and current.

27. The voltage in volts in an ac circuit containing a resistance is given by $v = 100 \sin \omega t$ where ω = angular velocity in rad/s, t = time in seconds, and ωt = angle in radians. If the angular velocity $\omega = 400$ rad/s,

    (a) Find v in volts when $t = 1.0$ ms.
    (b) Find the angle ωt in radians between 0 and 2π rad when $v = 50$ V.

28. The current in amps in an ac circuit containing a resistance is given by $i = 1.5 \sin \omega t$ where ω = angular velocity, t = time in seconds, and ωt = angle in radians. If the angular velocity $\omega = 300$ rad/s,

    (a) Find i in milliamps when $t = 2.0$ ms.
    (b) Find the angle ωt in radians between 0 and 2π rad when $i = 500$ mA.

18.2 ROOT MEAN SQUARE VALUES

The current and voltage in an ac circuit are continuously changing and assume different values every instant. However, we assign only one value to ac voltage or current, such as 120 V for ordinary household voltage, or 15 A for the current rating of an ac fuse. These values represent a type of mathematical "average" calculated over one cycle of the ac sine wave and are called the *root mean square* or *effective* values. The root mean square () value of an ac wave is equal to the value of a dc voltage or current that produces the same electrical energy as the ac voltage or current. For example, an ac voltage wave whose peak value is 170 V has an rms value of 120 V. When this ac source is connected to a certain resistance, it will dissipate the same amount of electrical energy as a dc voltage of 120 V connected to the same resistance. The name "root mean square" is used because of the way it is calculated. First, the instantaneous values of the voltage or current are squared. Second, the average or mean of these squared values is calculated. Third, the square root of this mean is computed. When this is done precisely, using the methods of calculus applied to a sine wave, it yields the following formulas:

Formulas **Root Mean Square Values**

$$V_{\text{rms}} = \left(\frac{1}{\sqrt{2}}\right) V_P \approx (0.707) \, V_P$$

$$I_{\text{rms}} = \left(\frac{1}{\sqrt{2}}\right) I_P \approx (0.707) \, I_P$$

(18.3)

EXAMPLE 18.5

Given $V_P = 170$ V and $I_P = 4.4$ A, find V_{PP}, I_{PP}, V_{rms}, and I_{rms}.

Solution

The peak-to-peak values are equal to twice the peak values:

$$V_{PP} = 2V_P = 2(170 \text{ V}) = 340 \text{ V}$$

$$I_{PP} = 2I_P = 2(4.4 \text{ A}) = 8.8 \text{ A}$$

To find the rms values, apply formulas (18.3):

$$V_{\text{rms}} = 0.707(170 \text{ V}) \approx 120 \text{ V}$$

$$I_{\text{rms}} = 0.707(4.4 \text{ A}) \approx 3.11 \text{ A}$$

Table 18-1 shows how an approximate calculation for the rms value of the voltage $v = 170 \sin \theta$ is done. Values of v and v^2 are calculated for θ every 15° from $\theta = 15°$ to $\theta = 180°$. The average of the v^2 values or mean square voltage is found from the total shown:

$$\text{Mean Square Voltage} = \frac{173{,}400}{12} = 14{,}450$$

The approximate rms voltage is then the square root of the mean square voltage:

$$V_{\text{rms}} \approx \sqrt{14{,}450} = 120.2 \text{ V}$$

Observe that this value agrees to four significant digits with that obtained using formula (18.3):

$$V_{\text{rms}} = 0.707(170 \text{ V}) = 120.2 \text{ V}$$

TABLE 18-1   ROOT MEAN SQUARE VALUE

Angle	Sine	v	v²
θ	$\mathrm{Sin}\ \theta$	$170\ \mathrm{sin}\ \theta$	$(170\ \mathrm{sin}\ \theta)^2$
15°	0.2588	44.0	1,936
30°	0.5000	85.0	7,225
45°	0.7071	120.2	14,450
60°	0.8660	147.2	21,675
75°	0.9659	164.2	26,964
90°	1.000	170.0	28,900
105°	0.9659	164.2	26,964
120°	0.8660	147.2	21,675
135°	0.7071	120.2	14,450
150°	0.5000	85.0	7,225
165°	0.2588	44.0	1,936
180°	0.0000	0.0	0
		Total	173,400

To find the peak values from the rms values, use formulas (18.3) solved for V_P and I_P:

Formulas   **Peak Values**

$$V_P = (\sqrt{2})\ V_{\mathrm{rms}} \approx (1.41)\ V_{\mathrm{rms}}$$
$$I_P = (\sqrt{2})\ I_{\mathrm{rms}} \approx (1.41)\ I_{\mathrm{rms}}$$

(18.4)

EXAMPLE 18.6   Given $V_{\mathrm{rms}} = 50$ V and $I_{\mathrm{rms}} = 1.5$ A, find V_P, I_P, V_{PP}, and I_{PP}.

Solution

Apply formulas (18.4) to find the peak values:

$$V_P = 1.41(50\ \mathrm{V}) \approx 70.5\ \mathrm{V}$$
$$I_P = 1.41(1.5\ \mathrm{A}) \approx 2.12\ \mathrm{A}$$

Double the peak values to find the peak-to-peak values:

$$V_{PP} = 2(70.5\ \mathrm{V}) = 141\ \mathrm{V}$$
$$I_{PP} = 2(2.12\ \mathrm{A}) = 4.24\ \mathrm{A}$$

Whenever voltage and current values are given for an ac circuit, they are always rms values unless stated otherwise. Since the rms value of an ac source provides the same power to a resistance as a dc source equal to the rms value, Ohm's law and the power formula can be applied to rms values in an ac circuit containing only resistances:

Formulas

Ohm's Law and Power Formula (Resistive circuit only)

$$I_{rms} = \frac{V_{rms}}{R}$$

$$P = (V_{rms})(I_{rms})$$

(18.5)

EXAMPLE 18.7

Given an ac series circuit with resistors $R_1 = 100\ \Omega$, $R_2 = 150\ \Omega$, and a source voltage $V = 120$ V:

(a) Find I_{rms}, I_P, V_1 = the voltage drop across R_1, and V_2 = the voltage drop across R_2.

(b) Find P_1 = the power dissipated in R_1, P_2 = the power dissipated in R_2, and P_T = total power.

Solution

(a) Since it is not indicated otherwise, the ac voltage given is the rms value: $V_{rms} = 120$ V. The total resistance $R_T = 100\ \Omega + 150\ \Omega = 250\ \Omega$. To find I_{rms}, apply Ohm's law (18.5):

$$I_{rms} = \frac{V_{rms}}{R_T} = \frac{120\text{ V}}{250\ \Omega} = 0.48\text{ A} = 480\text{ mA}$$

Apply (18.4) to find I_P:

$$I_P = 1.41(480\text{ mA}) \approx 680\text{ mA}$$

To find the voltage drops, apply Ohm's law:

$$V_1 = I_{rms}R_1 = (0.48\text{ A})(100\ \Omega) = 48\text{ V}$$

$$V_2 = I_{rms}R_2 = (0.48\text{ A})(150\ \Omega) = 72\text{ V}$$

(b) To find P_1, P_2, and P_T, apply the power formula (18.5) using the rms values:

$$P_1 = V_1 I_{rms} = (48\text{ V})(0.48\text{ A}) \approx 23\text{ W}$$
$$P_2 = V_2 I_{rms} = (72\text{ V})(0.48\text{ A}) \approx 35\text{ W}$$
$$P_T = V_{rms} I_{rms} = (120\text{ V})(0.48\text{ A}) \approx 58\text{ W}$$

EXERCISE 18.2

In all exercises, round answers to two significant digits.

In exercises 1 through 12 find the peak-to-peak and rms values of the ac voltage or current.

1. $V_P = 300$ V
2. $V_P = 160$ V
3. $I_P = 2.2$ A
4. $I_P = 5.6$ A
5. $V_P = 140$ V
6. $V_P = 100$ V

7. $I_P = 150$ mA
8. $I_P = 380$ mA
9. $I_P = 5.5$ A
10. $I_P = 38$ mA
11. $V_P = 200$ V
12. $V_P = 60$ V

In exercises 13 through 24 find the peak and peak-to-peak values of the ac voltage or current.

13. $V_{rms} = 110$ V
14. $V_{rms} = 230$ V
15. $I_{rms} = 1.2$ A
16. $I_{rms} = 3.3$ A
17. $I_{rms} = 600$ mA
18. $I_{rms} = 25$ mA
19. $V_{rms} = 75$ V
20. $V_{rms} = 36$ V
21. $I_{rms} = 80$ mA
22. $I_{rms} = 120$ mA
23. $V_{rms} = 12$ V
24. $V_{rms} = 9.0$ V

Applications to Electronics

25. An ac circuit contains a resistor $R = 50$ Ω connected to a voltage source $V = 110$ V. Find V_{rms}, V_P, I_{rms}, I_P, and the power P dissipated in the resistor.

26. A circuit contains a resistor $R = 5.1$ kΩ connected to an ac voltage source. If $I = 22$ mA, find V_{rms}, V_P, I_{rms}, I_P, and the power P dissipated in the resistor.

27. Given the ac series circuit in Figure 18-6 with $R_1 = 200$ Ω, $R_2 = 300$ Ω, $R_3 = 100$ Ω, and the current $I = 55$ mA, find:
    (a) The source voltage V and the voltage drops V_1, V_2, and V_3.

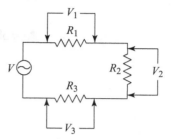

FIGURE 18-6 AC series circuit for problems 27 and 28.

(b) The power dissipated by each resistor P_1, P_2, P_3, and the total power P_T.

28. Given the ac series circuit in Figure 18-6 with $R_1 = 750$ Ω, $R_2 = 1.2$ kΩ, $R_3 = 1.6$ kΩ, and the source voltage $V = 100$ V, find:
    (a) The current I and the voltage drops V_1, V_2, and V_3.
    (b) The power dissipated by each resistor P_1, P_2, P_3, and the total power P_T.

29. Given the ac parallel circuit in Figure 18-7 with $R_1 = 1.2$ kΩ, $R_2 = 1.5$ kΩ, and $V = 80$ V, find:
    (a) I_1 and I_2, and the total current I_T.
    (b) The power dissipated in each resistance P_1 and P_2, and the total power P_T.

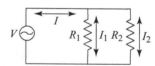

FIGURE 18-7 AC parallel circuit for problems 29 and 30.

30. Given the ac parallel circuit in Figure 18-7 with $R_1 = 620$ Ω, $R_2 = 510$ Ω, and $I_1 = 350$ mA, find:
    (a) The source voltage V, I_2 and I_T.
    (b) The power dissipated in each resistance P_1 and P_2, and the total power P_T.

18.3 FREQUENCY AND PERIOD

When alternating current is generated by revolving a coil of wire in a magnetic field, the speed of rotation is an important factor in the sine wave voltage and current. The speed of rotation ω (omega) is called the *angular velocity*. It is the rate of change of the angle θ with respect to time t and is measured in radians per second (rad/s):

Formula   **Angular Velocity (rad/s)**

$$\omega = \frac{\theta}{t} \text{ or } \theta = \omega t \tag{18.6}$$

EXAMPLE 18.8   Given the angular velocity of an ac wave $\omega = 120\pi$ rad/s, find the cycles per second of rotation.

Solution

Using 2π rad $= 1$ cycle, divided ω by 2π:

$$\frac{\omega}{2\pi} = \frac{120\pi}{2\pi} = 60 \text{ cycles per second}$$

Cycles per second is called the *frequency f* and the units for f are hertz (Hz). The frequency of the ac wave is therefore $f = 60$ Hz.

From Example 18.8 the relationship between frequency and angular velocity is:

Formula   **Frequency (Hz)**

$$f = \frac{\omega}{2\pi} \text{ or } \omega = 2\pi f \tag{18.7}$$

Substituting $2\pi f$ for ω in (18.6) gives you the relationship between the angle θ and the frequency:

Formula   **Angle (θ)**

$$\theta = \omega t = 2\pi ft \tag{18.8}$$

The equations for the sine wave voltage and current can then be written in terms of angular velocity ω or frequency f:

Formula   **AC Voltage and Current Waves**

$$\begin{aligned} v &= V_P \sin \omega t &\quad \text{or} \quad & v = V_P \sin 2\pi ft \\ i &= I_P \sin \omega t &\quad \text{or} \quad & i = I_P \sin 2\pi ft \end{aligned} \tag{18.9}$$

The *period T* of an ac wave in seconds is the time for one cycle and is the reciprocal of the frequency:

Formula **Period (seconds)**

$$T = \frac{1}{f} = \frac{2\pi}{\omega}$$ (18.10)

EXAMPLE 18.9

(a) Given $f = 60$ Hz for an ac wave, find the angular velocity ω and the period *T*.

(b) Given $f = 880$ kHz for an ac wave, find the angular velocity ω and the period *T*.

Solution

(a) Apply formulas (18.7) and (18.10):

$$\omega = 2\pi f = 2\pi(60) = 120\pi \text{ rad/s}$$

$$T \approx \frac{1}{f} = \frac{1}{60 \text{ Hz}} \approx 0.017 \text{ s} = 17 \text{ ms}$$

(b) Apply formulas (18.7) and (18.10) and change 880 kHz to Hz:

$$\omega = 2\pi f = 2\pi(880 \times 10^3) = 1.76\pi \times 10^6 \text{ rad/s}$$

$$T \approx \frac{1}{f} = \frac{1}{880 \times 10^3 \text{ Hz}} \approx 1.1 \times 10^{-6} \text{ s} = 1.1 \text{ } \mu\text{s}$$

Note that the period and the frequency are inversely proportional. As one increases the other decreases. Higher frequencies and smaller periods are encountered in circuits that transmit and receive radio waves.

EXAMPLE 18.10

Given the ac current wave $i = 3.0 \sin 500\pi t$:

(a) Find the angular velocity, frequency, and the period of the wave.

(b) Sketch the graph of current versus time for one cycle from $t = 0$.

Solution

(a) Apply formula (18.9) to find the angular velocity, which is the coefficient of *t*:

$$\omega = 500\pi \text{ rad/s}$$

Apply formula (18.7) to find the frequency:

$$f = \frac{\omega}{2\pi} = \frac{500\pi}{2\pi} = 250 \text{ Hz}$$

From formula (18.10), the period is the reciprocal of the frequency:

$$T = \frac{1}{250 \text{ Hz}} \text{ s} = 0.0040 \text{ s} = 4.0 \text{ ms}$$

(b) Since the period of the wave is given in units of time, the values of the current are plotted against time rather than radians. To sketch the sine wave you need to plot the maximum, minimum, and zero values. These values correspond to $\theta = 0$, $\pi/2(90°)$, $\pi(180°)$, $3\pi/2(270°)$, and 2π radians $(360°)$, and are enough to sketch the curve, since you know the shape is sinusoidal. For each of these values, first calculate t in milliseconds using formula (18.6) solved for t:

$$t = \frac{\theta}{\omega} = \frac{\theta}{500\pi}$$

For example, when $\theta = 3\pi/2$ rad:

$$t = \frac{3\pi}{2} \div 500\pi = \left(\frac{3\pi}{2}\right)\left(\frac{1}{500\pi}\right) = 0.003 \text{ s} = 3 \text{ ms}$$

The values of t that correspond to the five values of θ are then:

θ (rad)	0	$\frac{\pi}{2}$	π	$\frac{3\pi}{2}$	2π
t (ms)	0	1.0	2.0	3.0	4.0

Using the formula $i = 3.0 \sin 500\pi t$ and the values of t above, construct the table of values for current versus time:

t (ms)	0	1.0	2.0	3.0	4.0
i (A)	0	3.0	0.0	-3.0	0.0

Plot the values of i versus t and sketch the curve shown in Figure 18-8. See the Error Box for more information on ac waves.

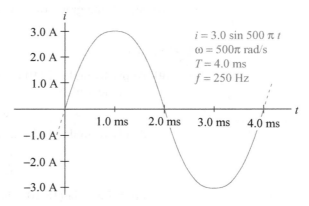

FIGURE 18-8 Frequency and period of ac sine wave for Example 18.10.

Error Box

A common error to watch out for when working with ac waves is not to confuse frequency, the angular period, which is number of *radians* in one cycle, and the time period T, which is the number of *seconds* in one cycle. For an ac wave $V_P \sin 2\pi ft$ or $I_P \sin 2\pi ft$, the angular period is 2π rad, but the time *period T* is not equal to 2π rad. It is equal to the value of t that makes the angle $2\pi ft$ equal to 2π. This is when $ft = 1$, which gives rise to the formula $T = \frac{1}{f}$. Using this information, see if you can do the practice problems correctly.

Practice Problems: For each ac wave, find the angular period, the frequency f, and the period T.

1. $170 \sin 120\pi t$
2. $170 \sin 377t$
3. $3 \sin 100\pi t$
4. $3 \sin 314t$
5. $80 \sin 150\pi t$
6. $80 \sin 471t$
7. $50 \sin 200\pi t$
8. $50 \sin 628t$
9. $1.5 \sin 50\pi t$
10. $1.5 \sin 157t$

EXAMPLE 18.11

Given the ac voltage wave $v = 160 \sin 100\pi t$, find to two significant digits:

(a) The value of v when $t = 5$ ms and $t = 13$ ms.

(b) The two values of t in the first cycle when $v = 50$ V.

Solution

(a) To find the value of v when $t = 5$ ms and 13 ms, substitute into the equation of the curve:

$$v = 160 \sin 100\pi(5 \times 10^{-3}) = 160 \sin(0.5\pi \text{ rad}) = 160 \text{ V}$$
$$v = 160 \sin 100\pi(13 \times 10^{-3}) = 160 \sin(1.3\pi \text{ rad}) \approx -130 \text{ V}$$

Note that 0.5π rad $= 90°$ and that 13π rad $= 234°$, which is in the third quadrant. This gives a negative value for the voltage. You need to set your calculator for radians or convert to degrees by letting $\pi = 180°$:

$$v = 160 \sin 100(180°)(5 \times 10^{-3}) = 160 \sin(90°) = 160 \text{ V}$$
$$v = 160 \sin 100(180°)(13 \times 10^{-3}) = 160 \sin 234° \approx -130 \text{ V}$$

(b) To find the values of t, you must use the $\sin^{-1}$ with radian measure. Substitute 50 V for v, solve for the sine of the angle, and then solve for the angle $100\pi t$:

$$50 = 160 \sin 100\pi t$$
$$\sin 100\pi t = \frac{50}{160} = 0.3125$$

The reference angle in radians is:

$$\sin^{-1}(0.3125) \approx 0.318 \text{ rad}$$

503

Since the value of the sine is positive, there are two solutions for the angle: one in the first quadrant, which is the reference angle:

$$\text{Quadrant I:} \quad 100\pi t \approx 0.318 \text{ rad}$$

and one in the second quadrant, which is the difference from π(1 80°) and the reference angle:

$$\text{Quadrant II:} \quad 100\pi t = \pi - 0.318 \text{ rad} \approx 2.82 \text{ rad}$$

Each value of the angle yields a value of t:

$$100\pi t = 0.318 \text{ rad} \Rightarrow t = \frac{0.318}{100\pi} \approx 1.0 \text{ ms}$$

$$100\pi t = 2.82 \text{ rad} \Rightarrow t = \frac{2.82}{100\pi} \approx 9.0 \text{ ms}$$

These solutions represent two points on the voltage wave that have the same value of v = 50 V, one when the curve is increasing and one when the curve is decreasing.

EXERCISE 18.3

Round all answers in the exercise to two significant digits.

In exercises 1 through 16 find the frequency f and the period T for each value of the angular velocity ω for an ac wave.

1. 110π rad/s
2. 130π rad/s
3. 140π rad/s
4. 100π rad/s
5. 380 rad/s
6. 370 rad/s
7. 100 rad/s
8. 400 rad/s
9. 300 rad/s
10. 320 rad/s
11. 50π rad/s
12. 200π rad/s
13. 5.3×10^6 rad/s
14. 600×10^3 rad/s
15. 75×10^3 rad/s
16. 8.8×10^6 rad/s

In exercises 17 through 28 find the period T and the angular velocity ω for each value of the frequency f for an ac wave.

17. 60 Hz
18. 50 Hz
19. 45 Hz
20. 75 Hz
21. 500 Hz
22. 100 Hz
23. 200 Hz
24. 150 Hz
25. 910 kHz
26. 60 kHz
27. 70 MHz
28. 100 MHz

In exercises 29 through 40 give the peak value, angular velocity ω, frequency f, and period T for each ac wave.

29. $i = 4.0 \sin 120\pi t$
30. $i = 1.0 \sin 100\pi t$
31. $v = 110 \sin 140\pi t$
32. $v = 90 \sin 150\pi t$
33. $v = 310 \sin 300t$
34. $v = 170 \sin 400t$
35. $i = 0.45 \sin 500t$
36. $i = 0.65 \sin 800t$
37. $i = 1.2 \sin 200\pi t$
38. $i = 2.5 \sin 50\pi t$
39. $v = 72 \sin (3.0 \times 10^6)t$
40. $i = 6.4 \sin (200 \times 10^6)t$
41. Find the angular velocity, frequency, and period for the ac voltage wave in Figure 18-9.

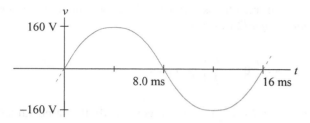

FIGURE 18-9   AC voltage wave for problem 41.

42. Find the angular velocity, frequency, and period for the ac current wave in Figure 18-10.

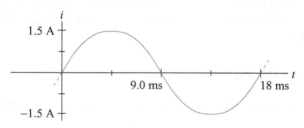

FIGURE 18-10   AC current wave for problem 42.

In exercises 43 through 50 write the equation of the ac sine wave having the given conditions.

43. $V_P = 180$ V, $f = 60$ Hz
44. $V_P = 90$ V, $f = 50$ Hz
45. $I_P = 2.5$ A, $f = 50$ Hz
46. $I_P = 330$ mA, $f = 60$ Hz
47. $I_P = 450$ mA, $T = 15$ ms
48. $I_P = 4.0$ A, $T = 20$ ms
49. $V_P = 160$ V, $T = 22$ ms
50. $V_P = 130$ V, $T = 18$ ms

In exercises 51 through 58 sketch each ac wave for one cycle plotting the maximum, minimum, and zero values. Give the angular velocity ω, the frequency f, and the period T.

51. $v = 340 \sin 100\pi t$
52. $v = 170 \sin 120\pi t$
53. $v = 170 \sin 377t$
54. $v = 340 \sin 314t$
55. $i = 2.5 \sin 120\pi t$
56. $i = 1.0 \sin 200\pi t$
57. $i = 12 \sin 1570t$
58. $i = 15 \sin 377t$

For problems 59 through 62 see Example 18.11.

59. Given the ac voltage wave $v = 160 \sin 120\pi t$, find:
    (a) The values of v when $t = 7.0$ ms and $t = 1.5$ ms.
    (b) The two values of t in the first cycle when $v = 100$ V.

60. Given the ac voltage wave $v = 300 \sin 100\pi t$, find:
    (a) The values of v when $t = 17$ ms and $t = 5.5$ ms.
    (b) The two values of t in the first cycle when $v = -100$ V.

61. Given the ac current wave $i = 2.0 \sin 100\pi t$, find:
    (a) The values of i when $t = 8.0$ ms and $t = 1.5$ ms.
    (b) The two values of t in the first cycle when $i = -1.0$ A.

62. Given the ac current wave $i = 3.0 \sin 120\pi t$, find:
    (a) The values of i when $t = 15$ ms and $t = 1.2$ ms.
    (b) The two values of t in the first cycle when $i = 2.0$ A.

18.4   PHASE ANGLE

Figure 18-2 compares the cosine curve with the sine curve. It shows that cos θ is 90° out of phase with sin θ and that cos θ *leads* sin θ by 90° (or sin θ *lags* cos θ by 90°). This is because cos θ is zero at −90° and therefore "starts" 90° before sin θ. Cos θ is already at the peak value when sin θ is just starting at 0°. If you

---

Answers to Error Box Problems, page 441:

1. 2π, 60 Hz, 17 ms **2.** 2π, 60 Hz, 17 ms **3.** 2π, 50 Hz, 20 ms **4.** 2π, 50 Hz, 20 ms
5. 2π, 75 Hz, 13 ms **6.** 2π, 75 Hz, 13 ms **7.** 2π, 100 Hz, 10 ms **8.** 2π, 100 Hz, 10 ms
9. 2π, 25 Hz, 40 ms **10.** 2π, 25 Hz, 40 ms

move sin θ to the left 90°, it will match cos θ exactly. This movement to the left is done by adding a *phase angle of π/2* to sin θ:

$$\sin\left(\theta + \frac{\pi}{2}\right) = \cos\theta$$

When you compute values of $\sin\left(\theta + \frac{\pi}{2}\right)$, you will get exactly the same values as cos θ. For example, when θ = 135°:

$$\text{Sin}\,(135° + 90°) = \sin\,(225°) = -0.707$$
$$\text{and } \cos 135° = -0.707$$

The concept of lead or lag for ac waves is important in the theory of alternating current. The equations of the ac voltage wave and ac current wave with a phase angle φ (phi) take the form:

Formulas | **AC Voltage and Current Waves**

$$v = V_P \sin(\omega t + \phi) \qquad i = I_P \sin(\omega t + \phi) \qquad \textbf{(18.11)}$$

Equations (18.11) use only the sine function since the cosine function is essentially the same function. The phase angle φ tells you how many degrees the wave leads a basic sine wave with the same frequency where the phase angle φ = 0. Phase angle differences can only apply to waves of the same frequency. Study the following examples, which illustrate the concept of phase angle in an ac circuit.

EXAMPLE 18.12

Given the ac wave $v = 180 \sin\left(130\pi t - \frac{\pi}{2}\right)$: Find the peak value, angular velocity, phase angle, frequency, and period.

Solution

Compare the equation of the curve to formula (18.11):

$$\text{Peak value} = V_p = 180\text{ V}$$

$$\text{Angular velocity} = \omega = 130\pi \text{ rad/s}$$

$$\text{Phase angle} = \phi = -\frac{\pi}{2}$$

Use formulas (18.7) and (18.10) to find the frequency and period:

$$f = \frac{\omega}{2\pi} = \frac{130\pi}{2\pi} = 65\text{ Hz}$$

$$T = \frac{1}{f} = \frac{1}{65\text{ Hz}} \approx 15\text{ ms}$$

EXAMPLE 18.13

In an ac circuit containing an inductance L, the current is given by $i = I_P \sin \omega t$ and the voltage across the inductance by:

$$v = V_P \sin\left(\omega t + \frac{\pi}{2}\right)$$

where the phase angle $\phi = \frac{\pi}{2}$. Given $f = 60$ Hz, $I_P = 2.0$ A, and $V_P = 100$ V:

(a) Write the equations for v and i and sketch each on the same graph for one cycle from $t = 0$.

(b) Determine the time difference between the two waves.

Solution

(a) Use formula (18.7) to express ω in terms of f:

$$\omega = 2\pi f = 2\pi(60) = 120\pi \text{ rad/s}$$

Write the current and voltage equations substituting the values for V_P, I_P, and ω:

$$i = 2.0 \sin 120\pi t$$

$$v = 100 \sin\left(120\pi t + \frac{\pi}{2}\right)$$

Find the period for both curves applying formula (18.10):

$$T = \frac{1}{f} = \frac{1}{60}s \approx 16.7 \text{ ms}$$

The current wave has a phase angle $\phi = 0$ rad and therefore starts at $t = 0$. The voltage wave has a phase angle $\phi = \pi/2$ rad and therefore *leads* the current wave by $\pi/2$ radians. It starts at $-\pi/2$ radians or a quarter of a period sooner, and reaches peak value at $t = 0$. Note that when the phase angle is *positive it shifts the curve to the left and vice versa*. The sketch of both sine waves is shown in Figure 18-11 with separate scales for i and v.

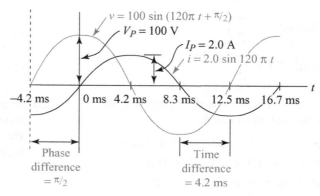

FIGURE 18-11 Voltage leads current in an ac inductive circuit for Example 18.13.

(b) To find the time difference between the two waves, you must convert the phase angle difference into time. Since $\theta = \omega t$, you have:

$$t = \frac{\theta}{\omega}$$

Therefore a phase angle difference of $\pi/2$ represents a time difference of:

$$t = \frac{(\pi/2)}{120\pi} = \frac{1}{240}\text{s} \approx 4.2 \text{ ms}$$

Observe that the phase angle difference is one-fourth of a period, which is $\frac{16.7}{4} \approx 4.2$ ms.

EXERCISE 18.4

Round all answers in the exercise to two significant digits.

In exercises 1 through 10 give the peak value, frequency, period, and phase angle for each ac wave.

1. $i = 1.5 \sin\left(100\pi t + \frac{\pi}{2}\right)$

2. $i = 2.3 \sin\left(120\pi t + \frac{\pi}{2}\right)$

3. $v = 300 \sin\left(200\pi t + \frac{\pi}{2}\right)$

4. $v = 170 \sin\left(110\pi t - \frac{\pi}{2}\right)$

5. $v = 60 \sin\left(377t - \frac{\pi}{2}\right)$

6. $v = 80 \sin\left(314t + \frac{\pi}{2}\right)$

7. $i = 18 \sin\left(314t + \frac{\pi}{2}\right)$

8. $i = 16 \sin\left(377t + \frac{\pi}{2}\right)$

9. $i = 5.5 \sin\left(628t - \frac{\pi}{2}\right)$

10. $i = 3.5 \sin\left(377t - \frac{\pi}{2}\right)$

In exercises 11 through 24 write the equation of the ac sine wave having the given conditions.

11. $I_P = 3.3$ A, $\omega = 120\pi$ rad/s, $\phi = \pi/2$ rad
12. $I_P = 7.5$ A, $\omega = 120\pi$ rad/s, $\phi = 0$ rad
13. $V_P = 400$ V, $\omega = 100\pi$ rad/s, $\phi = 0$ rad
14. $V_P = 380$ V, $\omega = 100\pi$ rad/s, $\phi = \pi/2$ rad
15. $V_P = 350$ V, $f = 50$ Hz, $\phi = \pi/2$ rad
16. $V_P = 150$ V, $f = 60$ Hz, $\phi = \pi/2$ rad
17. $I_P = 12$ A, $f = 60$ Hz, $\phi = 0$ rad
18. $I_P = 10$ A, $f = 50$ Hz, $\phi = 0$ rad
19. $V_P = 170$ V, $T = 18$ ms, $\phi = \pi/2$ rad
20. $V_P = 160$ V, $T = 16$ ms, $\phi = \pi/2$ rad
21. $V_P = 220$ V, $\omega = 380$ rad/s, $\phi = 0$ rad
22. $V_P = 240$ V, $\omega = 400$ rad/s, $\phi = \pi/2$ rad
23. $I_P = 500$ mA, $T = 20$ ms, $\phi = -\pi/2$ rad
24. $I_P = 800$ mA, $T = 25$ ms, $\phi = -\pi/2$ rad

Applications to Electronics

25. In an ac circuit containing a capacitance C, the current leads the voltage by $\pi/2$. The voltage across the capacitance and the current in the circuit are given by:

$$v = 200 \sin 120\pi t$$

$$i = 1.0 \sin\left(120\pi t + \frac{\pi}{2}\right)$$

   (a) Sketch each wave on the same graph for one cycle from $t = 0$.
   (b) Determine the time difference between the two waves. See Example 18.13.

26. In an ac circuit containing a resistance and an inductance in series (*RL* circuit), the voltage across the inductance, v_L, leads the voltage across the resistance, v_R, by $\pi/2$. The voltages are given by:

$$v_R = 100 \sin 100\pi t$$

$$v_L = 100 \sin\left(100\pi t + \frac{\pi}{2}\right)$$

(a) Sketch each wave on the same graph for one cycle from $t = 0$.

(b) Determine the time difference between the two waves. See Example 18.13.

27. For the ac waves in Figure 18-12 find:

(a) The frequency, period, and phase angle for each wave.

(b) The time difference. Tell whether v leads or lags i and the phase angle difference.

28. For the ac waves in Figure 18-13 find:

(a) The frequency, period, and phase angle for each wave.

(b) The time difference. Tell whether v leads or lags i and the phase angle difference.

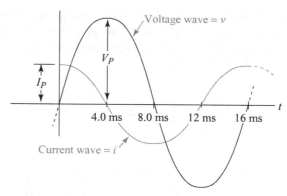

FIGURE 18-13 AC voltage and current waves for problem 28.

29. For the following current wave:

$$i = 3.1 \sin\left(120\pi t + \frac{\pi}{2}\right)$$

(a) Find i when $t = 6.0$ ms and $t = 14$ ms.

(b) Find the two positive values of t in the first cycle when $i = 0.0$ A.

Hint: Sketch the curve.

30. For the following voltage wave:

$$v = 200 \sin\left(100\pi t - \frac{\pi}{2}\right)$$

(a) Find v when $t = 5.0$ ms and $t = 17.5$ ms.

(b) Find the one positive value of t in the first cycle when $v = 200$ V.

Hint: Sketch the curve.

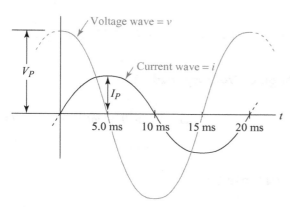

FIGURE 18-12 AC voltage and current waves for problem 27.

Chapter Highlights

18.1 ALTERNATING CURRENT WAVES

The cosine curve leads the sine curve by 90°(π/2 rad). See Figure 18-14. The number of degrees in one cycle or *angular period* = 360°.

Amplitude of Sine or Cosine

The amplitude of $y = a \sin \theta$ or
$y = a \cos \theta$ is $|a|$.   **(18.1)**
$|a|$ = absolute or positive value.

• • •

AC Voltage and Current Waves

$$v = V_P \sin \theta \qquad i = I_P \sin \theta \qquad \textbf{(18.2)}$$

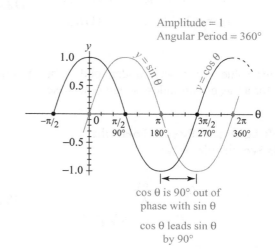

FIGURE 18-14 Key Example: Sine curve and cosine curve.

Key Example: Figure 18-15 shows the graph of the ac voltage wave $v = 170 \sin \theta$ for one cycle. The peak value $V_P = 170$ V and the peak-to-peak value $V_{PP} = 2V_P = 2(170 \text{ V}) = 340$ V.

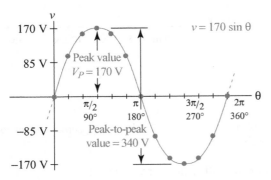

FIGURE 18-15 Key Example: Sine wave voltage.

18.2 ROOT MEAN SQUARE VALUES

The root mean square or effective value of an ac voltage wave or ac current wave is the dc value that produces the same electrical energy or heat dissipation in a resistance.

Root Mean Square Values

$$V_{\text{rms}} = \left(\frac{1}{\sqrt{2}}\right)V_P \approx (0.707)V_P$$

$$I_{\text{rms}} = \left(\frac{1}{\sqrt{2}}\right)I_P \approx (0.707)I_P$$

$$\text{(18.3)}$$

• • •

Peak Values

$$V_P = \left(\sqrt{2}\right)V_{\text{rms}} \approx (1.41)V_{\text{rms}}$$
$$I_P = \left(\sqrt{2}\right)I_{\text{rms}} \approx (1.41)I_{\text{rms}}$$

$$\text{(18.4)}$$

The rms values are always understood to be the ones given for an ac circuit unless stated otherwise.

Ohm's Law and Power Formula (Resistive circuit only)

$$I_{\text{rms}} = \frac{V_{\text{rms}}}{R}$$

$$P = (V_{\text{rms}})(I_{\text{rms}})$$

$$\text{(18.5)}$$

Key Example: In a series ac circuit with resistors $R_1 = 100 \ \Omega$, $R_2 = 150 \ \Omega$, and source voltage $V = 120$ V:

$$I_{\text{rms}} = \frac{V_{\text{rms}}}{R_T} = \frac{120 \text{ V}}{250 \ \Omega} = 0.48 \text{ A} = 480 \text{ mA}$$

$$I_p = 1.41(480 \text{ mA}) = 677 \text{ mA} \approx 680 \text{ mA}$$

$$V_1 = I_{\text{rms}} R_1 = (0.48 \text{ A})(100 \ \Omega) = 48 \text{ V}$$

$$V_2 = I_{\text{rms}} R_2 = (0.48 \text{ A})(150 \ \Omega) = 72 \text{ V}$$

$$P_1 = V_1 I_{\text{rms}} = (48 \text{ V})(0.48 \text{ A}) \approx 23 \text{ W}$$

$$P_2 = V_2 I_{\text{rms}} = (72 \text{ V})(0.48 \text{ A}) \approx 35 \text{ W}$$

$$P_T = V_{\text{rms}} I_{\text{rms}} = (120 \text{ V})(0.48 \text{ A}) \approx 58 \text{ W}$$

18.3 FREQUENCY AND PERIOD

Angular Velocity (rad/s)

$$\omega = \frac{\theta}{t} \text{ or } \theta = \omega t \qquad \text{(18.6)}$$

• • •

Frequency (Hz)

$$f = \frac{\omega}{2\pi} \text{ or } \omega = 2\pi f \qquad \text{(18.7)}$$

• • •

Angle (θ)

$$\theta = \omega t = 2\pi f t \qquad \text{(18.8)}$$

• • •

AC Voltage and Current Waves

$$v = V_P \sin \omega t \text{ or } v = V_P \sin 2\pi f t$$
$$i = I_P \sin \omega t \text{ or } i = I_P \sin 2\pi f t \qquad \text{(18.9)}$$

• • •

Period (seconds)

$$T = \frac{1}{f} = \frac{2\pi}{\omega} \qquad \text{(18.10)}$$

Key Example: For the ac current wave $i = 3.0 \sin 500\pi t$:

$$\omega = 500\pi$$

$$f = \frac{\omega}{2\pi} = \frac{500\pi}{2\pi} = 250 \text{ Hz}$$

$$T = \frac{1}{f} = \frac{1}{250 \text{ Hz}} = 0.004 \text{ s} = 4.0 \text{ ms}$$

18.4 PHASE ANGLE

AC Voltage and Current Waves

$$v = V_P \sin(\omega t + \phi) \quad i = I_P \sin(\omega t + \phi) \quad \textbf{(18.11)}$$

The phase angle ϕ tells you how many degrees the wave leads a sine wave with the same frequency whose phase angle is 0.

Key Example: For the wave:

$$v = 100 \sin\left(120\pi t + \frac{\pi}{2}\right):$$

$$\phi = \frac{\pi}{2}$$

$$\omega = 120\pi$$

$$f = \frac{\omega}{2\pi} = \frac{120\pi}{2\pi} = 60 \text{ Hz}$$

$$T = \frac{1}{f} = \frac{1}{60 \text{ Hz}} \approx 0.167 \text{ s} = 16.7 \text{ ms}$$

Review Exercises

Round all answers in the exercises to two significant digits.

In exercises 1 through 4 graph each ac wave from $\theta = 0$ to $\theta = 360°$ for θ every 30°. Give the peak value, the peak-to-peak value, and the angular period.

1. $v = 120 \sin \theta$
2. $v = 200 \sin \theta$
3. $i = 15 \sin \theta$
4. $i = 2.1 \sin \theta$

In exercises 5 through 16 give the peak value, rms value, angular velocity, frequency, period, and phase angle for each ac wave.

5. $v = 160 \sin 120\pi t$
6. $v = 100 \sin 150\pi t$
7. $i = 3.0 \sin 200\pi t$
8. $i = 11 \sin 100\pi t$
9. $v = 170 \sin 350t$
10. $v = 300 \sin 314t$
11. $i = 1.6 \sin 400t$
12. $i = 2.4 \sin 380t$
13. $i = 1.2 \sin\left(140\pi t + \dfrac{\pi}{2}\right)$
14. $i = 5.6 \sin\left(314t + \dfrac{\pi}{2}\right)$
15. $v = 320 \sin\left(377t + \dfrac{\pi}{2}\right)$
16. $v = 50 \sin\left(120\pi t - \dfrac{\pi}{2}\right)$

In exercises 17 through 28 write the equation of the ac sine wave having the given conditions.

17. $I_P = 2.4$ A, $f = 60$ Hz, $\phi = 0$ rad
18. $I_P = 5.5$ A, $\omega = 120\pi$ rad/s, $\phi = 0$ rad
19. $V_P = 110$ V, $\omega = 100\pi$ rad/s, $\phi = 0$ rad
20. $V_P = 50$ V, $f = 50$ Hz, $\phi = 0$ rad
21. $V_P = 120$ V, $T = 17$ ms, $\phi = 0$ rad
22. $I_P = 14$ A, $T = 19$ ms, $\phi = 0$ rad
23. $I_P = 1.3$ A, $T = 10$ ms, $\phi = 0$ rad
24. $V_P = 220$ V, $T = 20$ ms, $\phi = 0$ rad
25. $I_P = 14$ A, $\omega = 100\pi$ rad/s, $\phi = \pi/2$ rad
26. $V_P = 300$ V, $f = 50$ Hz, $\phi = \pi/2$ rad
27. $V_P = 220$ V, $f = 60$ Hz, $\phi = \pi/2$ rad
28. $I_P = 1.5$ A, $T = 40$ ms, $\phi = -\pi/2$ rad

Applications to Electronics

29. An ac circuit contains a resistor $R = 1.5$ kΩ connected to a voltage source. If the current $I = 50$ mA, find I_{rms}, I_P, V_{rms}, V_P, and the power dissipated by the resistor.

30. A series circuit contains two parallel resistors connected to an ac power supply of 120 V. If $R_1 = 30\ \Omega$ and $R_2 = 20\ \Omega$, find:

    (a) The total current I, I_P, V_P, and the current through each resistor, I_1 and I_2.

    (b) The power dissipated by each resistor P_1, P_2, and the total power P_T.

31. (a) An ac voltage wave takes 3 ms to go from 0 to peak value. What are the frequency, period, and angular velocity of the wave?

    (b) If the peak value of the voltage wave is 120 V and the phase angle = 0 rad, write the equation of the wave.

32. In Figure 18-16 find:

    (a) The frequency, period, and angular velocity of each ac wave.

    (b) The phase angle difference and time difference of the two ac waves.

33. Sketch the voltage wave $v = 90\sin 150\pi t$ for one cycle from $t = 0$. Give the peak value, frequency, and period of the wave.

34. An ac circuit contains a resistor and a capacitor in series (*RC* circuit). The voltage across the capacitor is given by $v_C = 200\sin 120\pi t$. The voltage across the resistor v_R leads the voltage across the capacitor by 90° and has the same peak value.

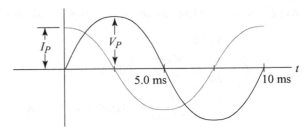

FIGURE 18-16 AC waves for problem 32.

   (a) Write the equation of the voltage wave v_R.

   (b) Sketch the two waves on the same graph for one cycle from $t = 0$, and find the time difference between the two waves.

35. Given the current wave $i = 0.50\sin 150\pi t$:

    (a) Find i when $t = 2.0$ ms and 10 ms.

    (b) Find the values of t in the first cycle when $i = 250$ mA.

    (c) Find the values of t in the first cycle when $i = 0$ mA.

36. Given the voltage wave $v = 400\sin(200\pi t + \frac{\pi}{2})$:

    (a) Find v when $t = 2.0$ ms and 5.5 ms.

    (b) At what value of t in the first cycle is $v = 400$ V?

21

TRIGONOMETRIC FORMULAS, IDENTITIES, AND EQUATIONS

Courtesy of Ruby Gold

A highway engineer is designing the curve at an intersection where two highways intersect at angle θ. In Section 21.3, we will learn how to use trigonometry to help design this curve.

In earlier chapters, we discussed the fundamental reciprocal and quotient identities of trigonometry. We also learned how to use trigonometry to solve both right and oblique triangles and how to graph trigonometric functions. In this chapter, we will return to the study of trigonometry, establishing the remaining standard trigonometric identities. Among these will be identities for the sums, differences, and multiples of angles. The identities you will learn in this chapter are used in advanced mathematics, particularly calculus, and in engineering, physics, and technical areas to simplify complicated expressions and to help solve equations that involve trigonometry.

OBJECTIVES

AFTER COMPLETING THIS CHAPTER, YOU WILL BE ABLE TO:

▼ Verify identities using the basic eight identities.

▼ Use sum, difference, double-angle, and half-angle formulas to simplify expressions and verify identities.

▼ Solve trigonometric equations using trigonometric identities.

21.1 BASIC IDENTITIES

An *identity* is an equation that is true for all values of the variable. In Section 5.2, we introduced two groups of trigonometric identities. One group was called **reciprocal identities** and consisted of

$$\csc \theta = \frac{1}{\sin \theta} \qquad \sec \theta = \frac{1}{\cos \theta} \qquad \cot \theta = \frac{1}{\tan \theta}$$

The second group was the **quotient identities**.

$$\tan \theta = \frac{\sin \theta}{\cos \theta} \qquad \cot \theta = \frac{\cos \theta}{\sin \theta}$$

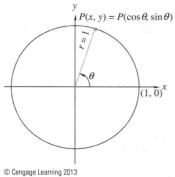

© Cengage Learning 2013

Figure 21.1

PYTHAGOREAN IDENTITY

Now, suppose that we have a unit circle as shown in Figure 21.1. (Remember, a unit circle is a circle with radius 1.) If this circle is centered at the origin and $P(x, y)$ is any point on the circle on the terminal side of an angle θ in standard position, then $x = \cos \theta$ and $y = \sin \theta$. By the Pythagorean theorem, $x^2 + y^2 = r^2$, and since $r = 1$, we get the first of the **Pythagorean identities**.

$$\sin^2 \theta + \cos^2 \theta = 1$$

 NOTE The term $\sin^2 \theta$ is an abbreviation for $(\sin \theta)^2$. Similarly, $\cos^2 \theta$ is an abbreviation for $(\cos \theta)^2$ and $\tan^2 \theta$ is an abbreviation for $(\tan \theta)^2$. While we write $\sin^2 \theta$, $\cos^2 \theta$, or $\tan^2 \theta$, you must enter them in a calculator as $(\sin \theta)^2$, $(\cos \theta)^2$, or $(\tan \theta)^2$.

If we divide both sides of this identity by $\cos^2 \theta$, we get

$$\frac{\sin^2 \theta}{\cos^2 \theta} + \frac{\cos^2 \theta}{\cos^2 \theta} = \frac{1}{\cos^2 \theta}$$

or
$$\tan^2 \theta + 1 = \sec^2 \theta$$

This is the second Pythagorean identity. The third, and last, Pythagorean identity is produced by dividing $\sin^2 \theta + \cos^2 \theta = 1$ by $\sin^2 \theta$, with the result

$$1 + \cot^2 \theta = \csc^2 \theta$$

Thus, there are three Pythagorean identities.

PYTHAGOREAN IDENTITIES

$$\sin^2 \theta + \cos^2 \theta = 1$$
$$\tan^2 \theta + 1 = \sec^2 \theta$$
$$1 + \cot^2 \theta = \csc^2 \theta$$

PROVING IDENTITIES

The eight basic identities, the reciprocal, quotient, and Pythagorean identities, can be used to develop and prove other identities. Your ability to prove an identity depends greatly on your familiarity with the eight basic identities.

To prove that an identity is true, you change either side, or both sides, until the sides are the same. Each side must be worked separately. Since you do not know that the two sides are equal (which is what you are trying to prove), you cannot transpose terms from one side to the other. Some people draw a vertical line between the two sides until they can show that the sides are equal. The vertical line acts as a reminder that you should work on each side separately.

EXAMPLE 21.1

Prove the identity $\csc \theta = \dfrac{\cot \theta}{\cos \theta}$.

SOLUTION We will change the right-hand side of the identity until it looks like the left-hand side.

$$
\begin{array}{c|ll}
\csc \theta & \dfrac{\cot \theta}{\cos \theta} & \\[2ex]
& \dfrac{\dfrac{\cos \theta}{\sin \theta}}{\cos \theta} & \text{Change } \cot \theta \text{ to } \dfrac{\cos \theta}{\sin \theta}. \\[3ex]
& \dfrac{\cos \theta}{\sin \theta} \cdot \dfrac{1}{\cos \theta} & \text{Change the division problem to a} \\
& & \quad \text{multiplication problem.} \\[2ex]
& \dfrac{1}{\sin \theta} & \text{Multiply.} \\[2ex]
& \csc \theta & \text{Reciprocal identity.}
\end{array}
$$

So, $\csc \theta = \dfrac{\cot \theta}{\cos \theta}$.

EXAMPLE 21.2

Prove the identity: $|\sin x| = \dfrac{|\tan x|}{\sqrt{1 + \tan^2 x}}$.

SOLUTION The right-hand side is more complicated than the left-hand side, so we will simplify the right-hand side until it matches the left-hand side.

$$|\sin x| \quad \left| \dfrac{|\tan|}{\sqrt{1 + \tan^2 x}} \right|$$

$$\left| \dfrac{|\tan x|}{\sqrt{\sec^2 x}} \right|$$

Use the Pythagorean identity to replace $1 + \tan^2 x$ with $\sec^2 x$.

$$\left| \dfrac{|\tan x|}{|\sec x|} \right|$$

Take the square root. Notice that $\sqrt{\sec^2 x} = |\sec x|$.

$$\left| \dfrac{\left|\dfrac{\sin x}{\cos x}\right|}{\left|\dfrac{1}{\cos x}\right|} \right|$$

Express $\tan x$ and $\sec x$ in terms of $\sin x$ and $\cos x$.

$$\left| \dfrac{\sin x}{\cos x} \cdot \dfrac{\cos x}{1} \right|$$

Change the division problem to a multiplication problem.

$$|\sin x|$$

Multiply.

Thus, we have shown that $|\sin x| = \dfrac{|\tan x|}{\sqrt{1 + \tan^2 x}}$.

Notice that we had to use the properties of absolute value to prove this identity.

EXAMPLE 21.3

Prove the identity $\sec \theta - \sec \theta \sin^2 \theta = \cos \theta$.

SOLUTION In this example, we start with the more complicated left-hand side and simplify it until it matches the right-hand side.

$$\sec \theta - \sec \theta \sin^2 \theta \quad | \quad \cos \theta$$
$$\sec \theta \,(1 - \sin^2 \theta) \qquad\qquad \text{Factor.}$$
$$\sec \theta \,(\cos^2 \theta) \qquad\qquad \text{Pythagorean identity.}$$
$$\dfrac{1}{\cos \theta}(\cos^2 \theta) \qquad\qquad \text{Reciprocal identity.}$$
$$\cos \theta \qquad\qquad \text{Multiply.}$$

And so, $\sec \theta - \sec \theta \sin^2 \theta = \cos \theta$.

In this example, we used a different version of a Pythagorean identity. We used the identity $\sin^2 \theta + \cos^2 \theta = 1$. You should also recognize the two variations of this identity: $\sin^2 \theta = 1 - \cos^2 \theta$ and $\cos^2 \theta = 1 - \sin^2 \theta$. There are two variations of each of the other Pythagorean identities.

EXAMPLE 21.4

Prove the identity: $\sec^2 \theta \csc^2 \theta = \sec^2 \theta + \csc^2 \theta$.

SOLUTION Here we simplify the right-hand side until it matches the left-hand side.

$\sec^2 \theta \csc^2 \theta$	$\sec^2 \theta + \csc^2 \theta$	
	$\dfrac{1}{\cos^2 \theta} + \dfrac{1}{\sin^2 \theta}$	Reciprocal identities.
	$\dfrac{\sin^2 \theta}{\cos^2 \theta \sin^2 \theta} + \dfrac{\cos^2 \theta}{\cos^2 \theta \sin^2 \theta}$	Rewrite with a common denominator.
	$\dfrac{\sin^2 \theta + \cos^2 \theta}{\cos^2 \theta \sin^2 \theta}$	Add.
	$\dfrac{1}{\cos^2 \theta \sin^2 \theta}$	Pythagorean identity.
	$\dfrac{1}{\cos^2 \theta} \cdot \dfrac{1}{\sin^2 \theta}$	Factor.
	$\sec^2 \theta \csc^2 \theta$	Reciprocal identities.

So, $\sec^2 \theta \csc^2 \theta = \sec^2 \theta + \csc^2 \theta$.

 APPLICATION GENERAL TECHNOLOGY

EXAMPLE 21.5

Malus's law concerns light incident on a polarizing plate and describes the amount of light transmitted, I, in terms of the angle of incidence, θ, and the, maximum intensity of light transmitted, M. Malus's law can be written as

$$I = M - M \tan^2 \theta \cos^2 \theta$$

Express the right-hand side of this equation in terms of $\cos \theta$.

SOLUTION We have

$$
\begin{aligned}
I &= M - M \tan^2 \theta \cos^2 \theta \\
&= M - M \left(\frac{\sin^2 \theta}{\cos^2 \theta} \right) \cos^2 \theta \\
&= M - M \sin^2 \theta \\
&= M(1 - \sin^2 \theta) \\
&= M \cos^2 \theta
\end{aligned}
$$

So, Malus's law can be more simply expressed as

$$I = M \cos^2 \theta$$

USING GRAPHS TO HELP VERIFY IDENTITIES

A graphing calculator, spreadsheet, or graphing software can also be used to prove or disprove an identity. With this technique you separately graph each side of the proposed identity over an interval that contains at least one complete period. If both graphs are identical, then you can conclude that the identity is true whenever the functions are defined. A major difficulty arises because neither calculators nor computers define the cot, sec, and csc functions.

EXAMPLE 21.6

Use a graphing calculator to "prove" the identity $\sec^2 \theta \csc^2 \theta = \sec^2 \theta + \csc^2 \theta$.

SOLUTION We know that this identity is true because it is the same identity that we proved in Example 21.4.

The graph of the left-hand side of this identity is shown in Figure 21.2a and the graph of the right-hand side is shown in Figure 21.2b. You can see that these two graphs are identical; hence this is a valid identity.

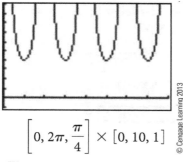

$$\left[0, 2\pi, \frac{\pi}{4}\right] \times [0, 10, 1]$$

© Cengage Learning 2013

Figure 21.2a

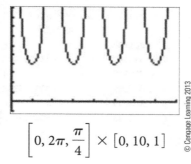

$$\left[0, 2\pi, \frac{\pi}{4}\right] \times [0, 10, 1]$$

© Cengage Learning 2013

Figure 21.2b

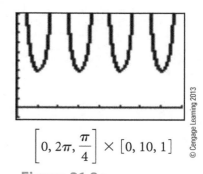

$$\left[0, 2\pi, \frac{\pi}{4}\right] \times [0, 10, 1]$$

© Cengage Learning 2013

Figure 21.2c

CAUTION In practice, when you graph the two sides of an identity, they both appear on the same screen. If you graph the second function using the calculator's "thick" style, as in Figure 21.2c, you can easily see if the new graph completely traces over the first function.

EXAMPLE 21.7

f_x	=A6*PI()/12

	A	B
1		t (theta)
2	0	0
3	1	0.261799
4	2	0.523599
5	3	0.785398
6	4	1.047198

© Cengage Learning 2013

Figure 21.3a

Use a spreadsheet to "prove" the identity $\sec^2 \theta \csc^2 \theta = \sec^2 \theta + \csc^2 \theta$.

SOLUTION We know that this identity is true because it is the same identity that we proved in Example 21.4.

Let's examine the graphs of the left- and right-hand sides. First, starting with Cell A2, enter 0 through 24 down Column A. This will be the multipliers for some fraction of π used in Column B. Enter =A2*pi()/12 in Cell B2 and copy this down Column B (see Figure 21.3a). This gives us values between 0 and 2π, covering at least one period of the functions.

In Cell C2, enter =(1/(COS(B2))^2)*(1/(SIN(B2))^2) and copy this formula down Column C.

EXAMPLE 21.7 (Cont.)

Next, in Cell D2, enter $= (1/(\text{COS}(B2))^{\wedge}2) + (1/(\text{SIN}(B2))^{\wedge}2)$ and copy this formula down Column D, as shown in Figure 21.3b.

It is obvious, from the table, that the values of each function are exactly the same. So, we expect the graphs to be the same, as shown in Figure 21.3c.

Looking at Figure 21.3c, we cannot tell that there are two graphs. A second way to use a spreadsheet to prove or disprove an identity is to subtract the two sides of the proposed identity and examine the difference. If the difference is zero over at least one period, then you can conclude that the identity is true whenever the functions are defined.

Column E of the spreadsheet contains the difference between the value in Column C and the value in Column D. We expect the values in this column to be zero. As you can see in Figure 21.2d, our expectations are fulfilled and we can conclude that the identity is "proved."

	f_x	=(1/COS(B8))^2+(1/SIN(B8))^2	
	A	B	C	D
		t (theta)	(sec t)^2*(csc t)^2	(sec t)^2+(csc t)^2
1				
2	0	0	#DIV/0!	#DIV/0!
3	1	0.261799	16	16
4	2	0.523599	5.333333333	5.333333333
5	3	0.785398	4	4
6	4	1.047198	5.333333333	5.333333333
7	5	1.308997	16	16
8	6	1.570796	2.66491E+32	2.66491E+32

© Cengage Learning 2013

Figure 21.3b

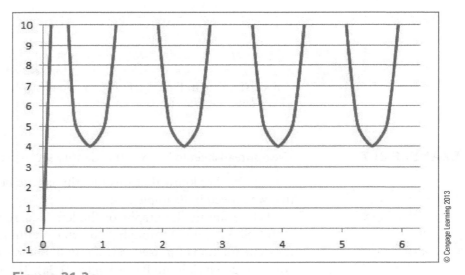

© Cengage Learning 2013

Figure 21.3c

	A	B	C	D	E
		t (theta)	(sec t)^2*(csc t)^2	(sec t)^2+(csc t)^2	Difference
1					
2	0	0	#DIV/0!	#DIV/0!	#DIV/0!
3	1	0.261799	16	16	0
4	2	0.523599	5.333333333	5.333333333	0
5	3	0.785398	4	4	0
6	4	1.047198	5.333333333	5.333333333	0
7	5	1.308997	16	16	0
8	6	1.570796	2.66491E+32	2.66491E+32	0

f_x =C8-D8

Figure 21.3d

EXERCISE SET 21.1

1. Prove the Pythagorean identity $1 + \cot^2 \theta = \csc^2 \theta$ from the identity $\sin^2 \theta + \cos^2 \theta = 1$.

Prove each of the identities in Exercises 2–26.

2. $\tan x \cot x = 1$

3. $\sin \theta \sec \theta = \tan \theta$

4. $\cos \theta(\tan \theta + \sec \theta) = \sin \theta + 1$

5. $\dfrac{\sin \theta}{\cot \theta} = \sec \theta - \cos \theta$

6. $\tan x = \dfrac{\sec x}{\csc x}$

7. $(1 - \sin^2 \theta)(1 + \tan^2 \theta) = 1$

8. $\dfrac{\sin A}{\csc A} + \dfrac{\cos A}{\sec A} = 1$

9. $1 - \dfrac{\sin A}{\csc A} = \cos^2 A$

10. $(1 + \tan \theta)(1 - \tan \theta) = 2 - \sec^2 \theta$

11. $(1 + \cos x)(1 - \cos x) = \sin^2 x$

12. $\sec^4 x - \sec^2 x = \tan^4 x + \tan^2 x$

13. $2 \csc \theta = \dfrac{\sin \theta}{1 + \cos \theta} + \dfrac{1 + \cos \theta}{\sin \theta}$

14. $\cos x = \sin x \cot x$

15. $(\sin \theta + \cos \theta)^2 = 1 + 2 \sin \theta \cos \theta$

16. $\csc^2 x(1 - \cos^2 x) = 1$

17. $\dfrac{\tan \theta + \cot \theta}{\tan \theta - \cot \theta} = \dfrac{\tan^2 \theta + 1}{\tan^2 \theta - 1}$

18. $\dfrac{1 - \sin x}{\cos x} = \dfrac{\cos x}{1 + \sin x}$

19. $\dfrac{\sec \theta - \csc \theta}{\sec \theta + \csc \theta} = \dfrac{\tan \theta - 1}{\tan \theta + 1}$

20. $(\sin A + \cos A)^2 + (\sin A - \cos A)^2 = 2$

21. $\tan^2 x \cos^2 x + \cot^2 x \sin^2 x = 1$

22. $\tan \theta + \dfrac{\cos \theta}{1 + \sin \theta} = \sec \theta$

23. $\sec^4 x - \sec^2 x = \tan^2 x \sec^2 x$

24. $\cos^2 A - \sin^2 A = 2 \cos^2 A - 1$

25. $\dfrac{\tan \theta - \sin \theta}{\sin^3 \theta} = \dfrac{\sec \theta}{1 + \cos \theta}$

26. $\dfrac{\sin x - \cos x + 1}{\sin x + \cos x - 1} = \dfrac{\sin x + 1}{\cos x}$

In Exercises 27–34, use your graphing calculator or a spreadsheet to prove or disprove each of the following identities.

27. $\tan^2 \theta \csc^2 \theta \cot^2 \theta \sin^2 \theta = 1$

28. $\tan x \sin x + \cos x = \sec x$

29. $\dfrac{\sec A + \csc A}{\tan A + \cot A} = \sin A + \cos A$

30. $\dfrac{\sin^3 x + \cos^3 x}{\sin x + \cos x} = 1 - \sin x \cos x$

31. $2 \csc 2x = \sec x \csc x$

32. $\cos 2x + 1 = 2 \cos^2 x$

33. $\sin \frac{1}{2}x = \frac{1}{2} \sin x$

34. $1 - \cos 2x = \sin^2 x$

To show that something is not an identity, all you need is one counterexample. A counterexample is an example that shows that something is not true. In Exercises 35–39, use the indicated angles as a counterexample to show that the relation is not an identity.

35. $2 \sin \theta \neq \sin 2\theta; \theta = 90°$

36. $\dfrac{\tan A}{2} \neq \tan\left(\dfrac{A}{2}\right); A = 60°$

37. $\cos(\theta^2) \neq (\cos \theta)^2; \theta = \pi$

38. $\sin(x - y) \neq \sin x - \sin y; x = 60°, y = 30°$

39. $\sin x \neq \dfrac{\tan x}{\sqrt{1 + \tan^2 x}}; x = 120°$

Solve Exercises 40–44.

40. In finding the rate of change of $\cot x$, you get the expression $\dfrac{(\sin x)(-\sin x) - (\cos x)(\cos x)}{\sin^2 x}$.
Show that this is equal to $-\csc^2 x$.

41. In finding the rate of change of $\cot^2 x$, you get the expression $-2 \cot x \csc^2 x$. Show that this is equal to $-2 \cos x \csc^3 x$.

42. In calculus, in order to determine the integral of $\sin^5 x$, we need to show that it is identical to $(1 - 2 \cos^2 x + \cos^4 x)\sin x$. Prove this identity.

43. *Electricity* In electric circuit theory, we use the expression

$$\dfrac{(1.2 \sin \omega t - 1.6 \cos \omega t)^2 + (1.6 \sin \omega t + 1.2 \cos \omega t)^2}{2L}$$

Show that this is identical to $\dfrac{2.0}{L}$.

44. *Physics* The range, R, of a projectile fired at an acute angle θ with the horizontal at an initial velocity v is given by

$$R = \dfrac{2v^2 \cos \theta \sin \theta}{g}$$

where g is the constant of gravitational acceleration. Rewrite the right-hand side using the sine function but not the cosine function.

 [IN YOUR WORDS]

45. Develop the other two Pythagorean identities from the identity $\sin^2 x + \cos^2 x = 1$.

46. Explain the process you use to prove an identity is true.

21.2 THE SUM AND DIFFERENCE IDENTITIES

We saw in Exercises 35 and 38 in Exercise Set 21.1 that $2 \sin \theta \neq \sin 2\theta$ and that $\sin(x - y) \neq \sin x - \sin y$. In this section, we will develop some identities for the sum and differences of the trigonometric functions. These identities are important for further studies in mathematics, such as in calculus. They are also important in wave mechanics, electric circuit theory, and in theory for other technical areas.

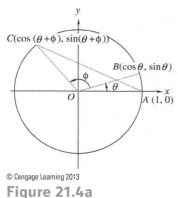

Figure 21.4a

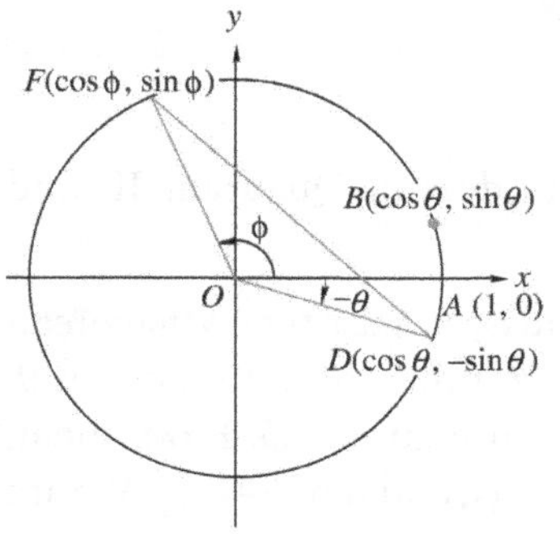

Figure 21.4b

$\cos(\theta + \phi)$

We will begin with a rather lengthy development of the identity for the $\cos(\theta + \phi)$. Even this lengthy proof does not include all cases, but it will serve our purposes.

In Figures 21.4a and 21.4b, we have drawn two unit circles. In Figure 21.4a, $\angle AOB$ is θ and $\angle BOC$ is ϕ, so $\angle AOC$ is $\theta + \phi$. The coordinates of A, B, and C are also given. Since A is on the x-axis, its coordinates are $(1, 0)$. The coordinates of B are given in terms of θ and those of C are given in terms of $\theta + \phi$.

In Figure 21.4b, we have rotated $\triangle AOC$ through the angle $-\theta$ to get $\triangle DOF$. The coordinates of D and F are given in terms of θ and ϕ. Now, since $\triangle AOC$ is congruent to $\triangle DOF$, the distance from A to C must be the same as the distance from D to F. According to the distance formula from Section 15.1, the distance from A to C is

$$d(A, C) = \sqrt{(\cos(\theta + \phi) - 1)^2 + (\sin(\theta + \phi) - 0)^2}$$

Squaring both sides, we get

$$[d(A, C)]^2 = (\cos(\theta + \phi) - 1)^2 + (\sin(\theta + \phi) - 0)^2$$
$$= \cos^2(\theta + \phi) - 2\cos(\theta + \phi) + 1 + \sin^2(\theta + \phi)$$
$$= 2 - 2\cos(\theta + \phi)$$

In a similar manner, the distance from D to F is

$$d(D, F) = \sqrt{(\cos\phi - \cos\theta)^2 + (\sin\phi + \sin\theta)^2}$$

Again, squaring both sides, we get

$$[d(D, F)^2] = (\cos\phi - \cos\theta)^2 + (\sin\phi + \sin\theta)^2$$
$$= \cos^2\phi - 2\cos\theta\cos\phi$$
$$\quad + \cos^2\theta + \sin^2\phi + 2\sin\theta\sin\phi + \sin^2\theta$$
$$= (\cos^2\phi + \sin^2\phi) + (\cos^2\theta + \sin^2\theta)$$
$$\quad - 2\cos\theta\cos\phi + 2\sin\theta\sin\phi$$
$$= 2 - 2\cos\theta\cos\phi + 2\sin\theta\sin\phi.$$

Since $d(A, C) = d(D, F)$, we have

$$2 - 2\cos(\theta + \phi) = 2 - 2\cos\theta\cos\phi + 2\sin\theta\sin\phi$$

or

$$\cos(\theta + \phi) = \cos\theta\cos\phi - \sin\theta\sin\phi$$

$\cos(\theta - \phi)$

If we substitute $-\phi$ for ϕ in the previous formula and remember the two identities $\cos(-\phi) = \cos\phi$ and $\sin(-\phi) = -\sin\phi$, we could show that

$$\cos(\theta - \phi) = \cos\theta\cos\phi + \sin\theta\sin\phi$$

Identities for the sum and difference of the sine and tangent functions can also be developed in a similar manner. The result is a total of six sum and difference identities.

SUM AND DIFFERENCE IDENTITIES

$$\sin(\theta + \phi) = \sin\theta\cos\phi + \cos\theta\sin\phi$$
$$\sin(\theta - \phi) = \sin\theta\cos\phi - \cos\theta\sin\phi$$
$$\cos(\theta + \phi) = \cos\theta\cos\phi - \sin\theta\sin\phi$$
$$\cos(\theta - \phi) = \cos\theta\cos\phi + \sin\theta\sin\phi$$
$$\tan(\theta + \phi) = \frac{\tan\theta + \tan\phi}{1 + \tan\theta\tan\phi}$$
$$\tan(\theta - \phi) = \frac{\tan\theta - \tan\phi}{1 + \tan\theta\tan\phi}$$

EXAMPLE 21.8

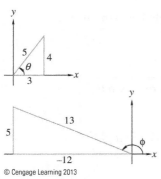

© Cengage Learning 2013

Figure 21.5

If $\sin\theta = \frac{4}{5}$, $\cos\phi = \frac{-12}{13}$, θ is in Quadrant I, and ϕ is in Quadrant II, find (a) $\sin(\theta + \phi)$, (b) $\cos(\theta - \phi)$, and (c) $\tan(\theta + \phi)$.

SOLUTIONS If we draw reference triangles for θ and ϕ, and use the Pythagorean theorem to determine the missing side, we can determine the values of $\cos\theta$, $\tan\theta$, $\sin\phi$, and $\tan\phi$. These triangles are shown in Figure 21.5. From them, we can determine that $\cos\theta = \frac{3}{5}$, $\tan\theta = \frac{4}{3}$, $\sin\phi = \frac{5}{13}$, and $\tan\phi = \frac{-5}{12}$. We are now ready to apply the formulas.

(a) $\sin(\theta + \phi) = \sin\theta\cos\phi + \cos\theta\sin\phi$

$$= \left(\frac{4}{5}\right)\left(\frac{-12}{13}\right) + \left(\frac{3}{5}\right)\left(\frac{5}{13}\right)$$

$$= \frac{-48}{65} + \frac{15}{65} = -\frac{33}{65}$$

(b) $\cos(\theta - \phi) = \cos\theta\cos\phi + \sin\theta\sin\phi$

$$= \left(\frac{3}{5}\right)\left(\frac{-12}{13}\right) + \left(\frac{4}{5}\right)\left(\frac{5}{13}\right)$$

$$= \frac{-36}{65} + \frac{20}{65} = -\frac{16}{65}$$

(c) $\tan(\theta + \phi) = \dfrac{\tan\theta + \tan\phi}{1 - \tan\theta\tan\phi}$

$$= \frac{\frac{4}{3} + \frac{-5}{12}}{1 - \left(\frac{4}{3}\right)\left(\frac{-5}{12}\right)}$$

$$= \frac{\frac{16}{12} - \frac{5}{12}}{\frac{56}{36}} = \frac{\frac{11}{12}}{\frac{56}{36}}$$

$$= \frac{11}{12} \cdot \frac{36}{56} = \frac{33}{56}$$

So, $\sin(\theta + \phi) = -\frac{33}{65}$, $\cos(\theta - \phi) = -\frac{16}{65}$, and $\tan(\theta + \phi) = \frac{33}{56}$. Since $\sin(\theta + \phi)$ is negative and $\tan(\theta + \phi)$ is positive, $\theta + \phi$ is in the third quadrant.

EXAMPLE 21.9

If $\sin \alpha = 0.25$ and $\cos \beta = 0.65$, α is in Quadrant II, and β is in Quadrant I, find (a) $\sin(\alpha - \beta)$ and (b) $\tan(\alpha + \beta)$.

SOLUTIONS Using the Pythagorean theorem and the fact that α is in Quadrant II, we determine that $\cos \alpha = -\sqrt{1 - 0.25^2} \approx -0.97$. Similarly, we find that $\sin \beta \approx 0.76$. We can now apply the formulas.

(a) $\sin(\alpha - \beta) = \sin \alpha \cos \beta - \cos \alpha \sin \beta$

$$\approx (0.25)(0.65) - (-0.97)(0.76)$$

$$= 0.1625 + 0.7372$$

$$= 0.8997$$

$$\approx 0.90$$

(b) $\tan(\alpha + \beta) = \dfrac{\tan \alpha + \tan \beta}{1 - \tan \alpha \tan \beta}$

$$\approx \frac{\dfrac{0.25}{-0.97} + \dfrac{0.76}{0.65}}{1 - \left(\dfrac{0.25}{-0.97}\right)\left(\dfrac{0.76}{0.65}\right)}$$

$$\approx \frac{-0.2577 + 1.1692}{1 - (-0.2577)(1.1692)}$$

$$\approx 0.7005$$

EXAMPLE 21.10

Find the exact value of $\sin 75°$ by using the trigonometric values for $30°$ and $45°$.

SOLUTION Since $75° = 30° + 45°$, we will use $\sin 75° = \sin(30° + 45°)$. Now $\sin 30° = \frac{1}{2}$, $\cos 30° = \dfrac{\sqrt{3}}{2}$, and $\sin 45° = \cos 45° = \dfrac{\sqrt{2}}{2}$. This gives

$$\sin 75° = \sin 30° \cos 45° + \cos 30° \sin 45°$$

$$= \frac{1}{2} \cdot \frac{\sqrt{2}}{2} + \frac{\sqrt{3}}{2} \cdot \frac{\sqrt{2}}{2}$$

$$= \frac{\sqrt{2}}{4} + \frac{\sqrt{6}}{4}$$

$$= \frac{\sqrt{2} + \sqrt{6}}{4}$$

NOTE We realize that the use of calculators makes it very unlikely that you will use such procedures to evaluate a given trigonometric value. We did these examples and have included exercises to give you practice using the sum and difference identities with numbers that you can verify on your calculator. This practice will also help you remember the identities later when you need them.

EXAMPLE 21.11

Simplify $\sin(x + \frac{\pi}{2})$.

SOLUTION $\sin\left(x + \dfrac{\pi}{2}\right) = \sin x \cos\dfrac{\pi}{2} + \cos x \sin\dfrac{\pi}{2}$

$$= \sin x \cdot 0 + \cos x \cdot 1$$

$$= \cos x$$

EXAMPLE 21.12

Verify that $\sin(\alpha + \beta) + \sin(\alpha - \beta) = 2\sin\alpha\cos\beta$.

SOLUTION

$\sin(\alpha + \beta) + \sin(\alpha - \beta)$	$2\sin\alpha\cos\beta$
$\sin\alpha\cos\beta + \cos\alpha\sin\beta$ $\quad + \sin\alpha\cos\beta - \cos\alpha\sin\beta$	Expand $\sin(\alpha + \beta)$ and $\sin(\alpha - \beta)$.
$2\sin\alpha\cos\beta$	Collect terms.

So, $\sin(\alpha + \beta) + \sin(\alpha - \beta) = 2\sin\alpha\cos\beta$.

 CAUTION Remember, $\sin(\alpha + \beta) \neq \sin\alpha + \sin\beta$. Make sure that you rewrite $\sin(\alpha + \beta)$ as $\sin\alpha\cos\beta + \cos\alpha\sin\beta$. In a similar way, you can show that $\cos(\alpha + \beta) \neq \cos\alpha + \cos\beta$ and $\tan(\alpha + \beta) \neq \tan\alpha + \tan\beta$.

 APPLICATION **GENERAL TECHNOLOGY**

EXAMPLE 21.13

The displacement d of an object oscillating in simple harmonic motion can be determined by the expression

$$d = a\sin 2\pi f t \cos\beta + a\cos 2\pi f t \sin\beta$$

Express the right-hand side as a single term.

SOLUTION If we factor an a out of both terms, then

$$d = a(\sin 2\pi f t \cos\beta + \cos 2\pi f t \sin\beta)$$

If we let $\alpha = 2\pi f t$, then the expression in parentheses is in the form $\sin\alpha\cos\beta + \cos\alpha\sin\beta = \sin(\alpha + \beta)$. So, the desired expression is

$$d = a\sin(2\pi f t + \beta)$$

EXERCISE SET 21.2

In Exercises 1–8, use the fact that $\sin 30° = \cos 60° = \frac{1}{2}$, $\sin 60° = \cos 30° = \dfrac{\sqrt{3}}{2}$, and $\sin 45° = \cos 45° = \dfrac{\sqrt{2}}{2}$, along with the other facts you know from trigonometry, to determine the following.

1. $\sin 15°$ **3.** $\sin 120°$ **5.** $\tan 15°$ **7.** $\sin 150°$

2. $\cos 75°$ **4.** $\cos(-15°)$ **6.** $\tan 135°$ **8.** $\cos 105°$

In Exercises 9–16, simplify the given expression.

9. $\sin(x + 90°)$ **11.** $\cos(x + \frac{\pi}{2})$ **13.** $\cos(\pi - x)$ **15.** $\sin(180° - x)$

10. $\cos(x + \pi)$ **12.** $\sin(\frac{\pi}{2} - x)$ **14.** $\tan(x - \frac{\pi}{4})$ **16.** $\tan(180° + x)$

If α and β are first-quadrant angles, $\sin \alpha = \frac{3}{4}$, and $\cos \beta = \frac{7}{8}$, evaluate the given expressions in Exercises 17–24.

17. $\sin(\alpha + \beta)$ **21.** $\cos(\alpha - \beta)$

18. $\cos(\alpha + \beta)$ **22.** $\tan(\alpha - \beta)$

19. $\tan(\alpha + \beta)$ **23.** In what quadrant is $\alpha + \beta$?

20. $\sin(\alpha - \beta)$ **24.** In what quadrant is $\alpha - \beta$?

If α is a second-quadrant angle, and β is a third-quadrant angle with $\sin \alpha = \frac{3}{4}$, and $\cos \beta = \frac{-7}{8}$, determine each of the given expressions in Exercises 25–32.

25. $\sin(\alpha + \beta)$ **29.** $\cos(\alpha - \beta)$

26. $\cos(\alpha + \beta)$ **30.** $\tan(\alpha - \beta)$

27. $\tan(\alpha + \beta)$ **31.** In what quadrant is $\alpha + \beta$?

28. $\sin(\alpha - \beta)$ **32.** In what quadrant is $\alpha - \beta$?

Simplify the given expression in Exercises 33–40.

33. $\sin 47° \cos 13° + \cos 47° \sin 13°$

34. $\sin 47° \sin 13° + \cos 47° \cos 13°$

35. $\cos 32° \cos 12° - \sin 32° \sin 12°$

36. $\dfrac{\tan 40° + \tan 15°}{1 - \tan 40° \tan 15°}$

37. $\cos(\alpha + \beta) \cos \beta + \sin(\alpha + \beta) \sin \beta$

38. $\sin(x - y) \cos y + \cos(x - y) \sin y$

39. $\cos(x + y) \cos(x - y) - \sin(x + y) \sin(x - y)$

40. $\sin A \cos(-B) + \cos A \sin(-B)$

Prove each of the identities in Exercises 41–46.

41. $\sin(x + y) \sin(x - y) = \sin^2 x - \sin^2 y$

42. $(\sin A \cos B - \cos A \sin B)^2 + (\cos A \cos B + \sin A \sin B)^2 = 1$

43. $\cos \theta = \sin(\theta + 30°) + \cos(\theta + 60°)$

44. $\dfrac{\sin(x + y)}{\cos(x - y)} = \dfrac{\tan x + \tan y}{1 + \tan x \tan y}$

45. $\tan x - \tan y = \dfrac{\sin(x - y)}{\cos x \cos y}$

46. $\cos(A + B) \cos(A - B) = 1 - \sin^2 A - \sin^2 B$

In Exercises 47–50, use a calculator or a spreadsheet to show that the statements are true.

47. $\sin(20° + 37°) = \sin 20° \cos 37° + \cos 20° \sin 37°$

48. $\cos(15° + 63°) = \cos 15° \cos 63° - \sin 15° \sin 63°$

49. $\tan(0.2 + 1.3) = \dfrac{\tan 0.2 + \tan 1.3}{1 - (\tan 0.2)(\tan 1.3)}$

50. $\sin(2.3 - 1.1) = (\sin 2.3)(\cos 1.1) - (\cos 2.3)(\sin 1.1)$

In Exercises 51–54, with the help of a calculator or a spreadsheet, use the given angles as a counterexample to show that each relation is not an identity.

51. $\sin(x + y) \neq \sin x + \sin y$; $x = 55°, y = 37°$

52. $\cos(x - y) \neq \cos x - \cos y$; $x = 68°, y = 24°$

53. $\cos(x + y) \neq \cos x + \cos y$; $x = 40°, y = 35°$

54. $\tan(x - y) \neq \tan x - \tan y$; $x = 76°, y = 37°$

Solve Exercises 55–60.

55. In Chapter 14, we learned that when two complex numbers are written in polar form their product is

$$[r_1(\cos \theta_1 + j \sin \theta_1)][r_2(\cos \theta_2 + j \sin \theta_2)]$$
$$= r_1 r_2[\cos(\theta_1 + \theta_2) + j \sin(\theta_1 + \theta_2)]$$

Prove this formula.

56. *Physics* A spring vibrating in harmonic motion described by the equation $y_1 = A_1 \cos(\omega t + \pi)$ is subjected to another harmonic motion described by $y_2 = A_2 \cos(\omega t - \pi)$. Show that

$$y_1 + y_2 = -(A_1 + A_2) \cos \omega t$$

57. *Optics* When a light beam passes from one medium through another medium and exists in a third medium of the same density as the first, the displacement d of the light beam is

$$d = \frac{h}{\cos \theta_r} \sin(\theta_i - \theta_r), \text{ where } \theta_r \text{ is the angle}$$

of refraction, θ_i is the angle of incidence, and h is the thickness of the medium. Show that $d = h(\sin \theta_i - \cos \theta_i \tan \theta_r)$.

58. *Electronics* The angle between voltage and current in an RC circuit is 45°. Develop an expression in terms of ω for $i(t)$ in milliamperes (mA) using $i(t) = I_p \sin(\theta - \omega t)$, if $I_p = 14.8$ mA.

59. *Meteorology* One way to measure cloud height at night is to place a light at point B so that the direction the light is pointing makes a 70° angle with the ground. An observer moves 1000 m away from the light to point A and measures the angle θ of elevation to the place where the light shines on the cloud, as shown in Figure 21.6. The height of the cloud is given by

$$h = \frac{1000}{\cot 70° + \cot \theta}$$

Show that this formula is identical to

$$h = \frac{1000 \sin 70° \sin \theta}{\sin(70° + \theta)}$$

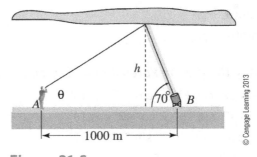

Figure 21.6

60. *Electronics* The potential difference in a certain three-phase alternator is given by

$$V = -E\left[\sin\left(2\pi f t - \frac{5\pi}{6}\right) + \sin\left(2\pi f t - \frac{7\pi}{6}\right)\right]$$

Show that $V = E\sqrt{3} \sin(2\pi f t)$.

[IN YOUR WORDS]

61. Describe how to develop $\sin(\theta - \phi)$ if you know that $\sin(\theta + \phi) = \sin\theta\cos\phi + \cos\theta\sin\phi$.

62. Describe how to develop the $\tan(\theta + \phi)$ identity from the identities for $\sin(\theta + \phi)$ and $\cos(\theta + \phi)$.

21.3 THE DOUBLE- AND HALF-ANGLE IDENTITIES

In Section 21.2, we studied the sum and difference identities. We can use these identities to develop double-angle identities. The double-angle identities can then be used to develop some half-angle identities.

DOUBLE-ANGLE IDENTITIES

The identity for $\sin(\theta + \phi)$ can be used to develop an identity for $\sin 2\theta$. To do this, calculate $\sin(\theta + \theta)$.

$$\begin{aligned} \sin 2\theta &= \sin(\theta + \theta) \\ &= \sin\theta\cos\theta + \cos\theta\sin\theta \\ &= 2\sin\theta\cos\theta \end{aligned}$$

In the same manner, we can develop $\cos 2\theta$.

$$\begin{aligned} \cos 2\theta &= \cos(\theta + \theta) \\ &= \cos\theta\cos\theta - \sin\theta\sin\theta \\ &= \cos^2\theta - \sin^2\theta \end{aligned}$$

This last identity has two other forms. If we use the Pythagorean identity, $\sin^2\theta + \cos^2\theta = 1$, we get

$$\begin{aligned} \cos 2\theta &= \cos^2\theta - \sin^2\theta \\ &= (1 - \sin^2\theta) - \sin^2\theta \\ &= 1 - 2\sin^2\theta \end{aligned}$$

We can replace $\sin^2\theta$ with $1 - \cos^2\theta$ and get a third version of this formula.

$$\begin{aligned} \cos 2\theta &= \cos^2\theta - \sin^2\theta \\ &= \cos^2\theta - (1 - \cos^2\theta) \\ &= 2\cos^2\theta - 1 \end{aligned}$$

Once again, if we evaluate $\tan(\theta + \theta)$, we get the third double-angle identity:

$$\begin{aligned} \tan 2\theta &= \tan(\theta + \theta) \\ &= \frac{\tan\theta + \tan\theta}{1 - \tan\theta\tan\theta} \\ &= \frac{2\tan\theta}{1 - \tan^2\theta} \end{aligned}$$

This completes the list of double-angle identities.

DOUBLE-ANGLE IDENTITIES

$$\sin 2\theta = 2\sin\theta\cos\theta$$

$$\cos 2\theta = \cos^2\theta - \sin^2\theta$$

$$= 2\cos^2\theta - 1$$

$$= 1 - 2\sin^2\theta$$

$$\tan 2\theta = \frac{2\tan\theta}{1 - \tan^2\theta}$$

EXAMPLE 21.14

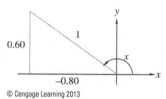

© Cengage Learning 2013

Figure 21.7

If $\sin x = 0.60$ and x is in the second quadrant, then determine (a) $\sin 2x$, (b) $\cos 2x$, and (c) $\tan 2x$.

SOLUTIONS We will first determine the value of $\cos x$. Since $\sin x = 0.60$, $\cos^2 x = 1 - \sin^2 x = 1 - (0.60)^2 = 0.64$ and $\cos x = \pm\sqrt{0.64} = \pm 0.80$. Since x is in Quadrant II (see Figure 21.7), $\cos x = -0.80$.

(a) $\sin 2x = 2\sin x\cos x$

$$= 2(0.60)(-0.80) = -0.96$$

(b) $\cos 2x = \cos^2 x - \sin^2 x$

$$= (-0.8)^2 - (0.6)^2$$

$$= 0.64 - 0.36 = 0.28$$

(c)   Since $\sin x = 0.60$, $\cos x = -0.8$, and $\tan x = \dfrac{\sin x}{\cos x}$, we have $\tan x = \dfrac{0.60}{-0.80} = -\frac{3}{4}$. Thus,

$$\tan 2x = \frac{2\tan x}{1 - \tan^2 x}$$

$$= \frac{2\left(-\frac{3}{4}\right)}{1 - \left(-\frac{3}{4}\right)^2}$$

$$= \frac{-\frac{3}{2}}{1 - \frac{9}{16}}$$

$$= \frac{-\frac{3}{2}}{\frac{7}{16}}$$

$$= \frac{-24}{7}$$

$$\approx -3.43$$

 CAUTION Don't forget that $\sin 2\alpha \neq 2\sin\alpha$ and $\cos 2\alpha \neq 2\cos\alpha$. We now know that

$$\sin 2\alpha = 2 \sin \alpha \cos \alpha$$

and that

$$\cos 2\alpha = \cos^2 \alpha - \sin^2 \alpha$$

EXAMPLE 21.15

Rewrite $\cos 4x$ in terms of $\cos x$.

SOLUTION Using the double-angle identity for $\cos 2\theta$, if we let $\theta = 2x$, then we get $\cos 4x = 2 \cos^2 2x - 1$. Now using the double-angle identity $\cos 2x = 2 \cos^2 x - 1$, we get

$$\cos 4x = 2(2 \cos^2 x - 1)^2 - 1$$
$$= 2(4 \cos^4 x - 4 \cos^2 x + 1) - 1$$
$$= 8 \cos^4 x - 8 \cos^2 x + 1$$

HALF-ANGLE IDENTITIES

If we solve $\cos 2x = 2 \cos^2 x - 1$ for the $\cos x$, we get another identity—a half-angle identity.

$$\cos 2x = 2 \cos^2 x - 1$$
$$\text{or} \qquad \cos^2 x = \frac{1 + \cos 2x}{2}$$

and, taking the square root of both sides,

$$\cos x = \pm \sqrt{\frac{1 + \cos 2x}{2}}$$

If we let $x = \dfrac{\theta}{2}$, then

$$\cos \frac{\theta}{2} = \pm \sqrt{\frac{1 + \cos \theta}{2}}$$

If we solve $\cos^2 x = 1 - 2 \sin^2 x$ for $\sin x$, we obtain

$$\sin^2 x = \frac{1 - \cos 2x}{2}$$
$$\text{or} \qquad \sin x = \pm \sqrt{\frac{1 - \cos 2x}{2}}$$

Again, if $x = \dfrac{\theta}{2}$, then

$$\sin \frac{\theta}{2} = \pm \sqrt{\frac{1 - \cos \theta}{2}}$$

Since $\tan x = \dfrac{\sin x}{\cos x}$, we can show that

$$\tan \frac{\theta}{2} = \pm \sqrt{\frac{1 - \cos\theta}{1 + \cos\theta}}$$

$$= \frac{\sin\theta}{1 + \cos\theta} = \frac{1 - \cos\theta}{\sin\theta}$$

We have developed the following three half-angle identities.

HALF-ANGLE IDENTITIES

$$\sin \frac{\theta}{2} = \pm \sqrt{\frac{1 - \cos\theta}{2}}$$

$$\cos \frac{\theta}{2} = \pm \sqrt{\frac{1 + \cos\theta}{2}}$$

$$\tan \frac{\theta}{2} = \pm \sqrt{\frac{1 - \cos\theta}{1 + \cos\theta}} = \frac{\sin\theta}{1 + \cos\theta}$$

$$= \frac{1 - \cos\theta}{\sin\theta}$$

EXAMPLE 21.16

If $\cos\theta = \frac{-5}{13}$ and θ is in the third quadrant, find the values of (a) $\sin \frac{\theta}{2}$, (b) $\cos \frac{\theta}{2}$, and (c) $\tan \frac{\theta}{2}$.

SOLUTIONS We need to determine which quadrant $\frac{\theta}{2}$ is in. We know θ is in Quadrant III, or $\pi < \theta < \frac{3\pi}{2}$, and so $\frac{\pi}{2} < \frac{\theta}{2} < \frac{1}{2}\left(\frac{3\pi}{2}\right)$ or $\frac{\pi}{2} < \frac{\theta}{2} < \frac{3\pi}{4}$. This means that $\frac{\theta}{2}$ is in Quadrant II. In Quadrant II, the sine is positive, cosine is negative, and tangent is negative.

(a) $\sin \dfrac{\theta}{2} = +\sqrt{\dfrac{1 - \cos\theta}{2}} = +\sqrt{\dfrac{1 - \left(-\frac{5}{13}\right)}{2}} = \sqrt{\dfrac{9}{13}} \approx 0.832$

(b) $\cos \dfrac{\theta}{2} = -\sqrt{\dfrac{1 + \cos\theta}{2}} = -\sqrt{\dfrac{1 + \left(-\frac{5}{13}\right)}{2}} = -\sqrt{\dfrac{4}{13}} \approx -0.555$

(c) $\tan \dfrac{\theta}{2} = -\sqrt{\dfrac{1 - \cos\theta}{1 + \cos\theta}} = -\sqrt{\dfrac{1 - \left(-\frac{5}{13}\right)}{1 + \left(-\frac{5}{13}\right)}} = -\sqrt{\dfrac{\frac{18}{13}}{\frac{8}{13}}} = -\sqrt{\dfrac{9}{4}}$

$$= -\frac{3}{2} = -1.500$$

We could have determined $\tan \dfrac{\theta}{2}$ by using $\dfrac{\sin \dfrac{\theta}{2}}{\cos \dfrac{\theta}{2}}$. With the values above, we would have gotten -1.499. The error of 0.001 was caused by the use of approximations in parts (a) and (b).

EXAMPLE 21.17

Prove the identity $2 \sin \dfrac{x}{2} \cos \dfrac{x}{2} = \sin x$.

SOLUTION

$2 \sin \dfrac{x}{2} \cos \dfrac{x}{2}$	$\sin x$
$2\left(\pm \sqrt{\dfrac{1 - \cos x}{2}} \right)\left(\pm \sqrt{\dfrac{1 + \cos x}{2}} \right)$	Replace with half-angle identities.
$2\sqrt{\dfrac{1 - \cos^2 x}{4}}$	Multiply.
$2\sqrt{\dfrac{\sin^2 x}{4}}$	Pythagorean identity.
$2\left(\dfrac{\sin x}{2} \right)$	Take the square root.
$\sin x$	Simplify.

 CAUTION Be careful when you use the double- and half-angle formulas. Begin by calculating the necessary values of θ, 2θ, and $\dfrac{\theta}{2}$ before they are substituted into the formula.

 APPLICATION **CIVIL ENGINEERING**

EXAMPLE 21.18

A highway engineer is designing the curve at an intersection like the one shown by the photograph in Figure 21.8a. These two highways intersect at an angle θ. The edge of the highway is to join the two points A and B with an arc or a circle that is tangent to the highways at these two points. Determine the relationship between the radius of the arc r, the distance d of A and B from the intersection, and angle θ.

SOLUTION We begin by noticing in Figure 21.8b, that $\angle BCA$ and θ are supplementary angles. So, $m\angle BCA = 180° - \theta$. If the center of the circle is at P, then

EXAMPLE 20.18 (Cont.)

$\overline{PA} \perp \overline{AC}$, because a tangent to a circle, in this case $\overline{AC}$, is perpendicular to a radius at the point of tangency. Now, $\overline{PC}$ bisects $\angle BCA$, so $m\angle PCA = \frac{1}{2} m\angle BCA$ $= 90° - \frac{\theta}{2}$. Since $\triangle PAC$ is a right triangle with right angle at A, $\tan \angle PCA = \frac{r}{d}$; so $d = \frac{r}{\tan \angle PCA} = r \cot \angle PCA = r \cot\left(90° - \frac{\theta}{2}\right) = r \tan \frac{\theta}{2}$. Thus, we have shown that $d = r \tan \frac{\theta}{2}$.

Figure 21.8a

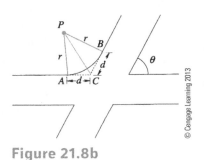

Figure 21.8b

 APPLICATION **CIVIL ENGINEERING**

EXAMPLE 21.19

Two highways meet at an angle of 34°. The curb is to join points A and B located 45 ft from the beginning of the intersection. (a) Approximate the radius of the arc joining A and B. (b) Determine the length of the arc.

SOLUTIONS   (a) From Example 21.18, we have the formula

$$d = r \tan \frac{\theta}{2}$$

In this example, $d = 45$ ft and $\theta = 34°$. We are to determine r.

$$r = \frac{d}{\tan \dfrac{\theta}{2}}$$

$$= \frac{45}{\tan \left(\frac{34}{2}\right)°}$$

$$= \frac{45}{\tan 17°}$$

$$\approx \frac{45}{0.3057}$$

$$\approx 147.19 \text{ ft}$$

(b) We want the length of the arc that forms the curb. As we saw in Section 5.6, the arc length s of a circle with radius r, formed by an angle θ, is

$$s = r\theta$$

provided that θ is in radians.

In this example, $\theta = 34° = \frac{34\pi}{180} = \frac{17\pi}{90}$ rad. So,

$$s = r\theta$$

$$= (147.19)\left(\frac{17\pi}{90}\right)$$

$$\approx 87.34 \text{ ft}$$

EXERCISE SET 21.3

In Exercises 1–14, if $\sin 30° = \cos 60° = \frac{1}{2}$, $\sin 60° = \cos 30° = \dfrac{\sqrt{3}}{2}$, and $\sin 45° = \cos 45° = \dfrac{\sqrt{2}}{2}$, determine the exact values of the given trigonometric function.

1. $\cos 15°$

2. $\sin 75°$

3. $\sin 15°$

4. $\cos 105°$

5. $\sin 105°$

6. $\cos 210°$

7. $\cos 7\frac{1}{2}°$

8. $\tan 15°$

9. $\tan 22\frac{1}{2}°$

10. $\cos 67\frac{1}{2}°$

11. $\cos 75°$

12. $\sin 37\frac{1}{2}°$

13. $\sin 127\frac{1}{2}°$

14. $\tan(-15°)$

Use the information given in each of Exercises 15–20 to determine $\sin 2x$, $\cos 2x$, $\tan 2x$, $\sin \dfrac{x}{2}$, $\cos \dfrac{x}{2}$, and $\tan \dfrac{x}{2}$.

15. $\sin x = \frac{7}{25}$, x in Quadrant II

16. $\cos x = \frac{8}{17}$, x in Quadrant IV

17. $\sec x = \frac{29}{20}$, x in Quadrant I

18. $\csc x = \frac{-41}{9}$, x in Quadrant III

19. $\tan x = \frac{35}{12}$, x in Quadrant III

20. $\cot x = \frac{-45}{28}$, x in Quadrant II

Prove the identities in Exercises 21–32 for all angles in the domains of the functions.

21. $\cos^2 x = \sin^2 x + \cos 2x$

22. $\cos^2 4x - \sin^2 4x = \cos 8x$

23. $\cos 4x = 1 - 8 \sin^2 x \cos^2 x$

24. $\cos 3x = 4 \cos^3 x - 3 \cos x$

25. $\dfrac{1 + \tan^2 \alpha}{1 - \tan^2 \alpha} = \sec 2\alpha$

26. $\sin 2x \cos 2x = \frac{1}{2} \sin 4x$

27. $1 - 2 \sin^2 3x = \cos 6x$

28. $\dfrac{2 \tan 3x}{1 - \tan^2 3x} = \tan 6x$

29. $\sin^2 x \cos^2 x = \frac{1}{4} \sin^2 2x$

30. $1 + \tan \beta \tan \dfrac{\beta}{2} = \dfrac{1}{\cos \beta}$

31. $\tan\left(\dfrac{\alpha + \beta}{2}\right) \cot\left(\dfrac{\alpha - \beta}{2}\right) = \dfrac{(\sin \alpha + \sin \beta)^2}{\sin^2 \alpha - \sin^2 \beta}$

32. $\cot \theta = \frac{1}{2}\left(\cot \dfrac{\theta}{2} - \tan \dfrac{\theta}{2}\right)$

In Exercises 33–36, use a calculator or a spreadsheet and the given angles as counterexamples to show that the following are not identities.

33. $\cos 2\theta \neq 2 \cos \theta;\ \theta = 45°$

34. $\tan\dfrac{\theta}{2} \neq \dfrac{\tan \theta}{2};\ \theta = 80°$

35. $\cot 2\alpha \neq 2 \cos \alpha;\ \alpha = 150°$

36. $\sin \dfrac{x}{2} \neq \dfrac{\sin x}{2};\ x = 210°$

Solve Exercises 37–42.

37. Optics The index of refraction n of a prism whose apex angle is α and whose angle of minimum deviation is ϕ is given by

$$n = \dfrac{\sin\left(\dfrac{\alpha + \phi}{2}\right)}{\sin \dfrac{\alpha}{2}} \text{ with } n > 0$$

Show that

$$n = \sqrt{\dfrac{1 - \cos \alpha \cos \phi + \sin \alpha \sin \phi}{1 - \cos \alpha}}$$

38. Optics Show that an equivalent expression for the index of refraction described in Exercise 37 is

$$n = \sqrt{\dfrac{1 + \cos \phi}{2}} + \left(\cot \dfrac{\alpha}{2}\right)\sqrt{\dfrac{1 - \cos \phi}{2}}$$

39. Electronics In an ac circuit containing reactance, the instantaneous power is given by

$$P = V_{max} I_{max} \cos \omega t \sin \omega t$$

Show that $P = \dfrac{V_{max} I_{max}}{2} \sin 2\omega t$.

40. Physics A cable vibrates with a decreased amplitude that is given by $A = \sqrt{e^{-2x}(1 + \sin 2x)}$. Show that $A = e^{-x}(\sin x + \cos x)$.

41. Transportation Engineers use the equation

$$x = 2r \sin^2\left(\dfrac{\theta}{2}\right)$$

to determine the width of the merging region of a highway. Solve for x in terms of $\cos \theta$ only.

42. Electronics The electron beam that forms the picture on a television or computer screen is controlled basically by a sawtooth function. This function can be approximated by sinusoidal curves of varying periods and amplitudes. A first approximation to the sawtooth curve is given by

$$y = \pi - 2 \sin(2x) - \sin(4x)$$

Show that this can be rewritten as

$$y = \pi - 4 \sin(2x) \cos^2 x$$

 [IN YOUR WORDS]

43. One of the identities for $\cos 2\theta$ is $\cos 2\theta = \cos^2 \theta - \sin^2 \theta$. There are two other identities for $\cos 2\theta$. Describe how you would develop each of them from the one above.

44. How would you establish the identity for $\tan 2\theta$?

45. The only difference between the formula for $\sin\dfrac{\theta}{2}$ and $\cos\dfrac{\theta}{2}$ is a + or − sign. Explain how you can tell which identity is for $\sin \dfrac{\theta}{2}$ and which is for $\cos \dfrac{\theta}{2}$.

46. The identities for $\sin \dfrac{\theta}{2}$ and $\cos \dfrac{\theta}{2}$ can both be developed from the identities for $\cos 2\theta$. Describe how you would do this.

21.4 TRIGONOMETRIC EQUATIONS

In Sections 21.1 through 21.3, we studied different types of trigonometric identities. Many people find proving and developing trigonometric identities to be very interesting. Our main interest in them, however, was to give you some skills for solving equations that involve trigonometric functions.

A trigonometric equation is an equation involving trigonometric functions of unknown angles. If these equations have been true for all angles, then we have called them identities. A trigonometric equation that is not an identity is a *conditional equation*. A conditional equation is true for some values for the angle and not true for others. To *solve* a conditional trigonometric equation means to find all values of the angle for which the equation is true. To solve a trigonometric equation, you must use both algebraic and trigonometric identities.

Solving a trigonometric equation of the type $2 \tan x = 1$ would produce an infinite number of answers. As you remember from our earlier study, the trigonometric functions are periodic. Thus, the solution to this equation would not only be true when $x = 26.565°$ but also for $x = 26.565° + 180°n$, where n is any integer. Usually, it is sufficient to give only the *primary solutions* or *principal values*, which are the solutions for x, where $0° \le x < 360°$ or $0 \le x < 2\pi$.

EXAMPLE 21.20

Solve $2 \tan x = 1$.

SOLUTION $2 \tan x = 1$

$$\tan x = \frac{1}{2}$$

We know that $x = \arctan \frac{1}{2} = \tan^{-1}\left(\frac{1}{2}\right)$. Using a calculator, we see that $x \approx 26.565°$. But, we know that the tangent function is also positive in Quadrant III, so $x = 26.565° + 180° = 206.565°$. The primary solutions are $26.565°$ and $206.565°$.

EXAMPLE 21.21

Solve $\cos 4x = \dfrac{\sqrt{2}}{2}$, where $0 \le x < 2\pi$.

SOLUTION   A natural way to proceed would be to use the double-angle identities to rewrite this as an equation in x.

A little foresight will save a lot of work. We will let $\theta = 4x$ and solve for θ.

EXAMPLE 21.21 (Cont.)

Once we have the value for θ we can then solve for x. But, since $x = \dfrac{\theta}{4}$ and $0 \leq x < 2\pi$, we must solve for $0 \leq \theta < 8\pi$.

$$\cos \theta = \frac{\sqrt{2}}{2}$$

$$\theta = \cos^{-1}\left(\frac{\sqrt{2}}{2}\right) = \frac{\pi}{4}$$

Since the cosine is also positive in Quadrant IV, we see that $\theta = \dfrac{7\pi}{4}$. If we keep adding 2π to each of these answers until we exceed 8π, we will get the other solutions for θ:

$$\frac{\pi}{4} + 2\pi = \frac{9\pi}{4}\ ,$$

$$\frac{\pi}{4} + 4\pi = \frac{17\pi}{4},$$

$$\frac{\pi}{4} + 6\pi = \frac{25\pi}{4};$$

and we also get

$$\frac{7\pi}{4} + 2\pi = \frac{15\pi}{4},$$

$$\frac{7\pi}{4} + 4\pi = \frac{23\pi}{4},$$

$$\text{and}\quad \frac{7\pi}{4} + 6\pi = \frac{31\pi}{4}$$

The solutions then for $0 \leq \theta < 8\pi$ are $4x = \theta = \frac{\pi}{4}, \frac{7\pi}{4}, \frac{9\pi}{4}, \frac{15\pi}{4}, \frac{17\pi}{4}, \frac{23\pi}{4}, \frac{25\pi}{4}$, and $\frac{31\pi}{4}$, and so the values of x are $x = \frac{\pi}{16}, \frac{7\pi}{16}, \frac{9\pi}{16}, \frac{15\pi}{16}, \frac{17\pi}{16}, \frac{23\pi}{16}, \frac{25\pi}{16}$, and $\frac{31\pi}{16}$.

EXAMPLE 21.22

Solve $\sin \theta \tan \theta = \sin \theta$ for $0 \leq \theta < 360°$.

SOLUTION We begin by collecting terms and factoring:

$$\sin \theta \tan \theta = \sin \theta$$

$$\sin \theta \tan \theta - \sin \theta = 0$$

$$\sin \theta(\tan \theta - 1) = 0$$

We now determine when each of these factors can be 0.

So $\sin \theta = 0$ or $\tan \theta - 1 = 0$

$\qquad\quad \sin \theta = 0 \qquad\qquad\qquad \tan \theta - 1 = 0$

$\qquad\quad \theta = 0°, 180° \qquad\qquad\quad \tan \theta = 1$

$\qquad\qquad\qquad\qquad\qquad\qquad\qquad \theta = 45°, 225°$

The solutions are 0°, 45°, 180°, and 225°.

GRAPHICAL SOLUTIONS TO TRIGONOMETRIC EQUATIONS

Earlier we used calculators and spreadsheets to help solve equations and inequalities. These techniques can also be applied to trigonometric equations. One of the major difficulties with using a TI-83 or TI-84 calculator is that it does not always give exact answers. We will rework Example 21.22 using a TI-84. Later we will use a spreadsheet to work Example 21.22.

USING A CALCULATOR TO SOLVE A TRIG EQUATION

EXAMPLE 21.23

Use a calculator to solve $\sin \theta \tan \theta = \sin \theta$ for $0 \le \theta < 360°$.

SOLUTION There are two ways in which use graphs to solve this equation. Both methods begin by letting $y_1 = \sin \theta \tan \theta$ and $y_2 = \sin \theta$. One method uses the `intersect` feature of the calculator and the other method uses the `zero` method discussed previously.

Using `Intersect`:

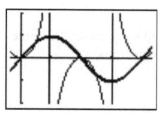

$[-30°, 390°, 90°] \times [-2, 2]$
© Cengage Learning 2013

Figure 21.9a

As you might be able to tell from the title, the intersect method locates where the two curves intersect. Figure 21.9a seems to indicate that the curves intersect in four points in the given interval. (The graph of $y_2 = \sin \theta$ is drawn using the "thick" style to make it easier to distinguish between the two graphs.)

Press `2nd` `CALC` `5` [5:intersect]. Move the cursor close to one of the points of intersection. We will select the second point from the left. Press `ENTER` twice. This tells the calculator which are the two curves that are intersecting. If there were more than two curves on the calculator screen, you could use ▲ or ▼ to move the cursor to the correct graphs. Make sure a cursor is near the point of intersection and press `ENTER`. After a few seconds you should see something like Figure 21.9b. This indicates that the two curves intersect near the point $(45°, 0.7071)$. Notice that this gives both the x- and y-values where the curves intersect.

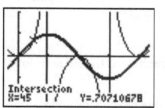

$[-30°, 390°, 90°] \times [-2, 2]$
© Cengage Learning 2013

Figure 21.9b

Repeat the procedure for each of the other three intersection points. You should get $(0°, 0)$, $(180°, 0)$, and $(225°, -0.7071)$.

Using `zero`:

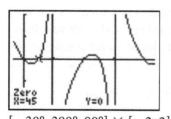

$[-30°, 390°, 90°] \times [-2, 2]$
© Cengage Learning 2013

Figure 21.9c

We have used the zero technique before. Graph $y_1 - y_2$ and determine where the curve crosses the x-axis. In Figure 21.9c we see that one solution is $x = 45°$. The other solutions are $x = 0°$, $x = 180°$, and $x = 225°$. Notice that the zero method does not give the y-values of the points of intersection.

EXAMPLE 21.24

Use a calculator to solve $2 \sin^2 x - \cos x - 1 = 0$ for $0 \le x < 2\pi$.

SOLUTION Since the right-hand side of this equation is zero, both the intersection method and the root method will produce the same result. From Figure 21.10a we see that one solution is $x \approx 1.0472$. (The actual value is $\frac{\pi}{3}$.)

EXAMPLE 21.24 (Cont.)

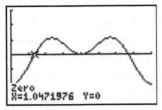

$\left[0, 2\pi, \frac{\pi}{4}\right] \times [-3, 3]$
© Cengage Learning 2013
Figure 21.10a

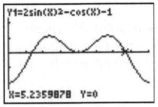

$\left[0, 2\pi, \frac{\pi}{4}\right] \times [-3, 3]$
© Cengage Learning 2013
Figure 21.10b

It looks as if the third solution (counting from the left) is approximately $2\pi - 1.0472$. We can verify that quickly by pressing 2 π – X, T, θ, n ENTER . Since the calculator automatically stores the root as x, you should get the result $x \approx 5.2360$, as in Figure 21.10b.

The second solution, the one in the middle, appears to be π. To verify this press π ENTER .

Thus, the solutions of $2 \sin^2 x - \cos x - 1 = 0$ for $0 \le x < 2\pi$ are $x \approx 1.0472$, $x = \pi$, and $x \approx 5.2360$.

SPREADSHEET SOLUTIONS FOR TRIGONOMETRIC EQUATIONS

Earlier, we used spreadsheets to help solve equations and inequalities. The same techniques used then can be applied to trigonometric equations.

EXAMPLE 21.25

Use a spreadsheet to solve $\sin \theta \tan \theta = \sin \theta$ for $0 \le \theta < 360°$.

SOLUTION There are two ways in which to use graphs to solve this equation. Both methods begin by letting $y_1 = \sin \theta \tan \theta$ and $y_2 = \sin \theta$.

Using a table and graph

Figure 21.11a shows a portion of the table and the graph used to find solutions to this equation.

Figures 21.11b to 21.11d show the portions of the table that identify close approximations of the four solutions.

Using Goal Seek

Figure 21.11e shows a portion of the table and the Goal Seek menu. Since the solutions to this equation were multiples of π, we were able to find exact solutions (in terms of π). However, Goal Seek may need to be employed on other equations.

EXAMPLE 21.26

Use a spreadsheet to solve $2 \sin^2 x - \cos x - 1 = 0$ for $0 \le x < 2\pi$.

SOLUTION We will use Goal Seek to solve this equation. The graph in Figure 21.12a shows there are at least three solutions between 0 and 2π.

The first solution, shown in Figure 21.12b, is 1.0472.

Figure 21.12c shows a second solution at 3.131. However, since the y-value isn't zero, even after another try with Goal Seek, we might want to try something else here. 3.131 is very close to π. Perhaps Excel just isn't accurate enough to get the solution using the process in Goal Seek for a curve shaped like this one. Place π in Cell A33 and see if we getter a value closer to zero. Figure 21.12d shows that π is a solution. Figure 21.12e shows the third solution.

The solutions are $x \approx 1.0472$, $x = \pi$, and $x \approx 5.2358$.

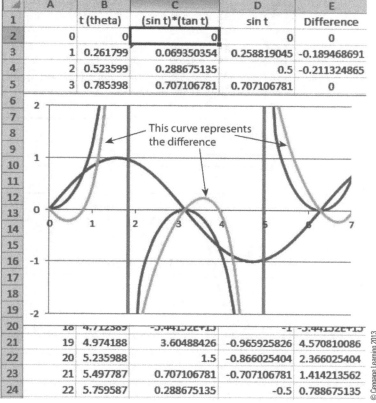

⊿	A	B	C	D	E
1		t (theta)	(sin t)*(tan t)	sin t	Difference
2	0	0	0	0	0
3	1	0.261799	0.069350354	0.258819045	-0.189468691
4	2	0.523599	0.288675135	0.5	-0.211324865
5	3	0.785398	0.707106781	0.707106781	0
20	18	4.712389	-3.44132E+15	-1	-3.44132E+15
21	19	4.974188	3.60488426	-0.965925826	4.570810086
22	20	5.235988	1.5	-0.866025404	2.366025404
23	21	5.497787	0.707106781	-0.707106781	1.414213562
24	22	5.759587	0.288675135	-0.5	0.788675135

This curve represents the difference

© Cengage Learning 2013

Figure 21.11a

	f_x	=A8*PI()/24			
⊿	A	B	C	D	E
8	6	0.785398	0.707106781	0.707106781	0

$$x = \frac{6\pi}{24} = \frac{\pi}{4} = 45°$$

© Cengage Learning 2013

Figure 21.11b

	f_x	=A26*PI()/24			
⊿	A	B	C	D	E
26	24	3.141593	-1.50099E-32	1.22515E-16	-1.22515E-16

$$x = \frac{24\pi}{24} = \pi = 180°$$

© Cengage Learning 2013

Figure 21.11c

	f_x	=A32*PI()/24			
⊿	A	B	C	D	E
32	30	3.926991	-0.707106781	-0.707106781	8.88178E-16

$$x = \frac{30\pi}{24} = \frac{5\pi}{4} = 225°$$

© Cengage Learning 2013

Figure 21.11d

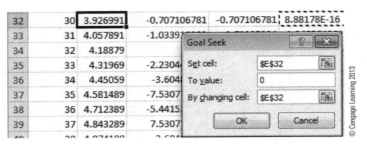

Figure 21.11e

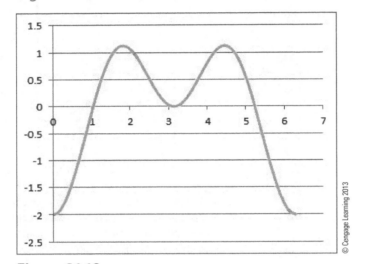

Figure 21.12a

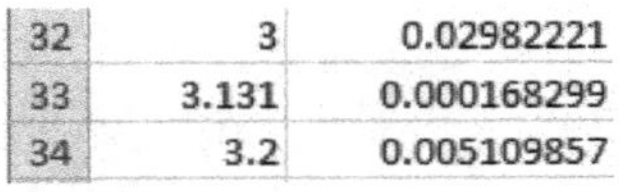

32	3	0.02982221
33	3.131	0.000168299
34	3.2	0.005109857

© Cengage Learning 2013

Figure 21.12c

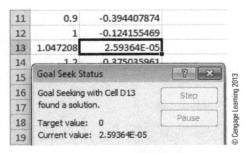

Figure 21.12b

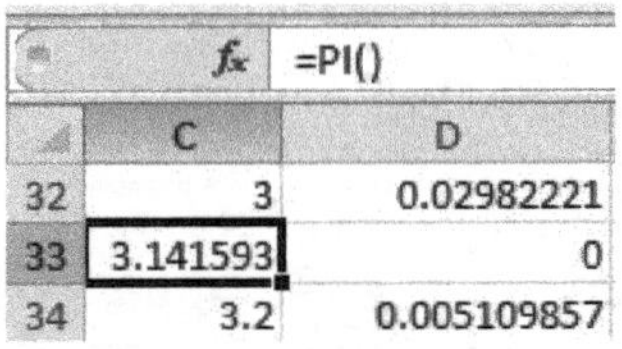

	f_x	=PI()
	C	D
32	3	0.02982221
33	3.141593	0
34	3.2	0.005109857

© Cengage Learning 2013

Figure 21.12d

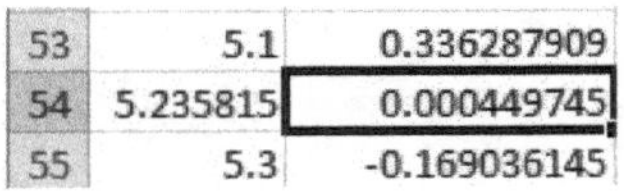

53	5.1	0.336287909
54	5.235815	0.000449745
55	5.3	-0.169036145

© Cengage Learning 2013

Figure 21.12e

APPLICATION GENERAL TECHNOLOGY

EXAMPLE 21.27

The range r of a projectile thrown at an angle of elevation θ at a velocity v is given by

$$r = \frac{2v^2 \cos\theta \sin\theta}{g}$$

EXAMPLE 21.27 (Cont.) If v is in ft/s, then g is 32 ft/s², and if v is in m/s, then g is 9.8 m/s². A projectile is fired with a velocity of 750 m/s with the purpose of hitting an object 20 000 m away. Determine the angle θ at which the projectile should be fired.

SOLUTION Here $v = 750$ m/s, $g = 9.8$ m/s², and $r = 20\,000$ m. Substituting these values in the given equation, we obtain

$$20\,000 = \frac{2(750)^2 \cos\theta \sin\theta}{9.8}$$

Now, $2\cos\theta \sin\theta = 2\sin\theta \cos\theta = \sin 2\theta$, and the equation becomes

$$20\,000 = \frac{(750)^2 \sin 2\theta}{9.8}$$

$$\text{or} \quad \sin 2\theta = \frac{20\,000(9.8)}{(750)^2}$$

$$\approx 0.3484$$

so

$$2\theta \approx 20.39° \text{ or } 159.61°$$

$$\text{and} \quad \theta \approx 10.195° \text{ or } 79.805°$$

So, the projectile should be fired at an angle of 10.195° or 79.805°.

EXERCISE SET 21.4

Solve each equation in Exercises 1–30 for nonnegative angles less than 360° or 2π. You may want to use a calculator or a spreadsheet.

1. $2\cos\theta = 0$

2. $2\sin\theta = -1$

3. $\sqrt{3}\tan x = 1$

4. $\sqrt{3}\sec x = -2$

5. $4\sin\theta = -3$

6. $2\cos x = 3$

7. $4\tan\alpha = 5$

8. $3\csc x = 1$

9. $\cos 2x = -1$

10. $\sin 2x = \frac{1}{2}$

11. $\tan\dfrac{\theta}{4} = 1$

12. $\cos\dfrac{\theta}{3} = -1$

13. $\sin^2\alpha = \sin\alpha$

14. $\cos^2\beta = \frac{1}{2}\cos\beta$

15. $\sin x \cos x = 0$

16. $\dfrac{\sec\theta}{\csc\theta} = -1$

17. $3\tan^2 x = 1$

18. $\sec^2\theta = 2$

19. $4\sin\alpha \cos\alpha = 1$

20. $\sin^2\beta = \frac{1}{2}\sin\beta$

21. $\sin\theta - \cos\theta = 0$

22. $\tan\theta = \csc\theta$

23. $\sin 6\theta + \sin 3\theta = 0$

24. $4\tan^2 x = 3\sec^2 x$

25. $2\cos^2 x - 3\cos 2x = 1$

26. $\sin^2 4\alpha = \sin 4\alpha + 2$

27. $\sec^2\theta + \tan\theta = 1$

28. $\tan 2x + \sec 2x = 1$

29. $\sin 2x = \cos x$

30. $\csc^2\theta - \cot\theta = 1$

Solve Exercises 31–36.

31. Optics The second law of refraction (Snell's law) states that as a light ray passes from one medium to a second, the ratio of the sine of the angle of incidence θ_i to the sine of the angle of refraction θ_r is a constant, μ, called the *index* of refraction, with respect to the two mediums (see Figure 21.13). Thus, we have

$$\frac{\sin\theta_i}{\sin\theta_r} = \mu$$

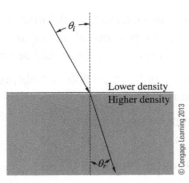

Figure 21.13

The index of refraction of general epoxy relative to air is $\mu = 1.61$. Determine the angle of refraction θ_r of a ray of light that strikes some general epoxy with an angle of incidence $\theta_i = 35°$.

32. Optics The index of refraction of glass silicone relative to air is 1.43. If the angle of incidence is 27°, what is the angle of refraction?

33. Electronics An oscillating signal voltage is given by $E = 125 \cos(\omega t - \phi)$ millivolts, where the angular frequency is $\omega = 120\pi$, phase angle is $\phi = \frac{\pi}{2}$, and t is time in seconds. The triggering mechanism of an oscilloscope starts the sweep when $E = 60$ mV. What is the smallest positive value of t for which the triggering occurs?

34. Agriculture As shown in Figure 21.14, an irrigation ditch has a cross-section in the shape of an isosceles trapezoid with the smaller base on the bottom. The area A of the trapezoid is given by

$$A = a \sin \theta (b + a \cos \theta)$$

If $a = 3$ m, $b = 3.4$ m, and $A = 10$ m^2, find θ to the nearest tenth of a degree if $\sin \theta \cos \theta \approx 0.4675$.

Figure 21.14

35. Automotive technology The displacement d of a piston is given by

$$d = \sin \omega t + \frac{1}{2} \sin 2\omega t$$

For what primary solutions of ωt less than 2π is $d = 0$?

36. Optics Refraction causes a submerged object in a liquid to appear closer to the surface than it actually is. The relation between the true depth a and the apparent depth b is

$$\frac{a}{b} = \sqrt{\frac{\mu^2 - \sin^2 \theta_i}{\cos^2 \theta_i}}$$

where μ is the index of refraction for the two media and θ_i is the angle of incidence. An object that is 14 ft under water appears to be only 10 ft under water. If the index of refraction of water is 1.333, what is the angle of incidence?

 [IN YOUR WORDS]

37. Equations with multiple angles have more than two solutions. Explain how you can determine that you have found all solutions.

38. Describe how you would use the methods for solving a trigonometric equation to solve a trigonometric inequality.

CHAPTER 21 REVIEW

IMPORTANT TERMS AND CONCEPTS

Double-angle identities
Half-angle identities
Pythagorean identities

Quotient identities
Reciprocal identities

Sum and difference identities
Trigonometric equations

REVIEW EXERCISES

Prove the identities in Exercises 1–10.

1. $\dfrac{\sin(x + y)}{\cos x \cos y} = \tan x + \tan y$

2. $(\sin x + \cos x)^2 = 1 + \sin 2x$

3. $\dfrac{\sin 3x}{\sin x} - \dfrac{\cos 3x}{\cos x} = 2$

4. $\cos(\theta + \phi)\cos(\theta - \phi) = \cos^2 \phi - \sin^2 \theta$

5. $\sin(\alpha - \beta)\cos \beta - \cos(\alpha + \beta)\sin \beta = \sin \alpha$

6. $\tan 2x = \dfrac{2 \cos x}{\csc x - 2 \sin x}$

7. $\cos^4 x - \sin^4 x = \cos 2x$

8. $\dfrac{\sin 2x - \sin x}{\cos 2x + \cos x} = \tan\dfrac{x}{2}$

9. $\sin 3\theta = 2 \sin \theta \cos 2\theta + \sin \theta$

10. $\dfrac{\cos 3x - \cos 5x}{\sin 3x + \sin 5x} = \tan x$

(Hint: Let $3x = 4x - x$ and $5x = 4x + x$.)

Solve the equations in Exercises 11–20 for nonnegative values less than 360° or 2π.

11. $2 \tan x = -\sqrt{3}$

12. $3 \sin x = -2$

13. $\cos 2x + \cos x = -1$

14. $\cos x - \sin 2x - \cos 3x = 0$

15. $\sin 4x - 2 \sin 2x = 0$

16. $\sin(30° + x) - \cos(60° + x) = -\dfrac{\sqrt{3}}{2}$

17. $2 \sin \theta = \sin 2\theta$

18. $\sin^2 \alpha + 5 \cos^2 \alpha = 3$

19. $\sin^2 x = 1 + \sin x$

20. $\sin \theta - 2 \csc \theta = -1$

In Exercises 21–24, use the facts that $\sin x = \frac{5}{13}$, $\cos x = -\frac{12}{13}$, and x is in Quadrant II to determine the exact value of the given function.

21. $\sin 2x$

22. $\cos \dfrac{x}{2}$

23. $\sin \dfrac{x}{2}$

24. $\tan 2x$

In Exercises 25–30, use the facts that x is in Quadrant III, $\sin x = \frac{-5}{13}$, and $\cos x = \frac{-12}{13}$, and y is in Quadrant II, $\sin y = \frac{8}{17}$, and $\cos y = \frac{-15}{17}$ to determine the exact value of the given function.

25. $\sin(x + y)$

26. $\cos(x - y)$

27. $\cos(x + y)$

28. $\tan(x + y)$

29. $\cos(y - x)$

30. $\sin(x - y)$

Solve Exercises 31–33.

31. *Automotive technology* The acceleration of a piston is given by

$$a = 5.0(\sin \omega t + \cos 2\omega t)$$

For what primary solutions of ωt does $a = 0$?

32. *Acoustical engineering* When two sinusoidal sound waves that are close together in frequency are superimposed, the resultant disturbance exhibits beats. The two waves are represented by $y_1 = A_1 \cos \omega_1 t$ and $y_2 = A_2 \cos(\omega_2 t$

$+ \phi$), where ω_2 is slightly larger than ω_1 and ϕ is a phase constant. If $\phi = 0$,

$$\alpha = \frac{\omega_1 + \omega_2}{2}, \text{ and } \beta = \frac{\omega_2 - \omega_1}{2}, \text{ show that}$$

$$y = y_1 + y_2 = A_1 \cos(\alpha - \beta)t + A_2 \cos(\alpha + \beta)t$$

33. *Mechanics* Consider a machine that is mounted on four springs with a known stiffness

and on four dampers with a known damping constant. If this system is initially at rest and a certain force is applied, then under certain conditions the system has a time-displacement equation of $x = 0.01e^{-6t}(\cos 8t + \sin 8t)$. Another version gives the time-displacement equation at $x = \frac{\sqrt{2}}{100}e^{-6t}\cos\left(8t - \frac{\pi}{4}\right)$. Show that these two equations are identical.

CHAPTER 21   TEST

In Exercises 1–8, use the fact that $\sin \alpha = \frac{4}{5}$ and α is in Quadrant II and that $\cos \beta = -\frac{12}{13}$, and β is in Quadrant III to determine the exact value of the given function.

1. $\sin(\alpha + \beta)$

2. $\cos(\alpha + \beta)$

3. $\sin(\alpha - \beta)$

4. $\cos(\alpha - \beta)$

5. $\sin 2\alpha$

6. $\cos 2\beta$

7. $\sin \dfrac{\alpha}{2}$

8. $\cos \dfrac{\beta}{2}$

Solve Exercises 9–13.

9. Write $8 \cos 6x \sin 6x$ using a single trigonometric function.

10. Prove the identity $\tan x = \dfrac{\sec x}{\csc x}$

11. Prove the identity $\dfrac{\sin x}{1 - \cos x} + \dfrac{\sin x}{1 + \cos x} = 2 \csc x$.

12. Solve $6 \cos^2 x + \cos x = 2$ for x with either $0° \le x < 360°$ or $0 \le x < 2\pi$.

13. The equation $x = 4r \sin^2\left(\dfrac{\theta}{2}\right)$ arises when engineers design the merging region for a rapid transit system. Solve this equation for x in terms of $\cos \theta$.

12.1 EXPONENTIAL FUNCTIONS

We will begin this section with the definition of an exponential function and with some examples of exponential functions.

EXPONENTIAL FUNCTION

An **exponential function** is any function of the form:

$$f(x) = b^x$$

where $b > 0$, $b \neq 1$, and x is any real number. The number b is called the *base*.

EXAMPLE 12.1

Some examples of exponential functions are: $f(x) = 2^x$, $g(x) = 3^x$, $h(x) = \pi^x$, $j(x) = 4.2^x$, and $k(x) = (\sqrt{3})^x$. The following exponential functions contain constants, represented by a and b: $y(x) = (5b)^{-x}$, $h(x) = (2a)^{x+1}$, and $k(x) = 3a^{x/3}$.

The functions $f(x) = (-2)^x$, $g(x) = 0^x$, and $h(x) = 1^x$ are not exponential functions. In $f(x) = (-2)^x$ the base, -2, is less than zero. Therefore, it is not an exponential function. We can see that if $x = \frac{1}{2}$, then $(-2)^{1/2} = \sqrt{-2}$ is not a real number. The function $g(x) = 0^x$ is not an exponential function, because the base is 0. Also, $h(x) = 1^x$ is not an exponential function, since the base is 1.

GRAPHING EXPONENTIAL FUNCTIONS; ASYMPTOTES

Graphing an exponential function is done in the same manner in which we have graphed other functions. We will choose values for x and determine the corresponding values for $f(x)$. We will then plot these points and connect them in order to get the graph. Notice that, since the base b of an exponential function is positive, all powers of that base are also positive. Thus, an exponential function is positive for all values of x.

EXAMPLE 12.2

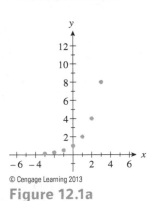

© Cengage Learning 2013

Figure 12.1a

Graph the exponential function $f(x) = 2^x$.

SOLUTION The following table gives integer values of x from -3 to 5:

x	-3	-2	-1	0	1	2	3	4	5
$f(x) = 2^x$	0.125	0.25	0.5	1	2	4	8	16	32

© Cengage Learning 2013

The first seven of these points are graphed in Figure 12.1a.

Notice that as x gets larger, $f(x)$ increases at a faster and faster rate. As x gets smaller, $f(x)$ keeps getting closer to 0, but never reaches 0.

The graph of $f(x) = 2^x$ is shown in Figure 12.1b. Notice how the curve keeps getting closer to the negative x-axis. As a curve approaches a line when a variable approaches a certain value, the curve is said to be asymptotic to the line. The line is an *asymptote* of the curve. In this example, $y = 2^x$ is asymptotic to the negative x-axis.

Either a calculator or a computer is helpful for finding values of an exponential function. On a calculator, you will use the ∧ key.

EXAMPLE 12.3

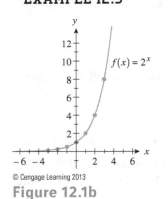

© Cengage Learning 2013

Figure 12.1b

Determine $f(4.5)$, when $f(x) = 2^x$.

SOLUTION

PRESS	DISPLAY
2 ∧ 4.5 **ENTER**	22.627417

The most common bases are those that are larger than 1. In fact, when the base is less than 1 (and greater than 0), you get an interesting effect, as shown in the next example.

EXAMPLE 12.4

Graph the exponential function $g(x) = \left(\frac{1}{2}\right)^x$.

SOLUTION Again, we will make a table of values:

x	-5	-4	-3	-2	-1	0	1	2	3
$g(x) = \left(\frac{1}{2}\right)^x$	32	16	8	4	2	1	0.5	0.25	0.125

© Cengage Learning 2013

The graph of the first seven of these points is shown in Figure 12.2a and the graph of the function is in Figure 12.2b. The graph of $g(x) = (\frac{1}{2})^x$ would be identical to the graph of $f(x) = 2^x$, if it were reflected over the y-axis.

Study the function again. Remember that $\frac{1}{2} = 2^{-1}$, so $(\frac{1}{2})^x = 2^{-x}$. These two examples show the differences between a function of the form b^x and one of the form b^{-x}. If $b > 1$, the graph of b^x rises and the graph of b^{-x} falls, as we move from left to right.

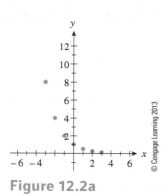

Figure 12.2a

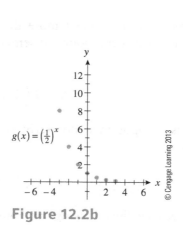

Figure 12.2b

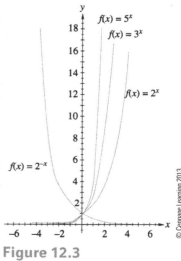

Figure 12.3

Figure 12.3 shows the graph of several exponential functions on the same set of coordinates. These functions, and all exponential functions, have the following three features in common.

COMMON FEATURES OF EXPONENTIAL FUNCTIONS

If $f(x) = b^x$, then

1. The y-intercept is 1.

2. If $b > 1$, the negative x-axis is an asymptote; if $b < 1$, the positive x-axis is an asymptote.

3. If $b > 1$, the curves all rise as the values of x increase; if $b < 1$, the curves all fall as the values of x increase.

 APPLICATION **BUSINESS**

One application of exponential functions has to do with money. When an amount of money P, called the principal, is invested and interest is compounded annually (once a year) at the interest rate of r per year, then the amount of money at the end of t years is given by the formula $S = P(1 + r)^t$. In this formula, r is expressed as a decimal. So, at 5% interest, $r = 0.05$ and at $6\frac{1}{4}$% interest, $r = 0.0625$.

EXAMPLE 12.5

If $800 is invested at 6% compounded annually, how much is the total value after 10 years?

SOLUTION Here $P = \$800$, $r = 0.06$, and $t = 10$. As a result we have

$$S = P(1 + r)^t$$
$$= 800(1 + 0.06)^{10}$$
$$\approx 800(1.790847697)$$
$$\approx 1{,}432.68$$

After 10 years, the total value of this investment is $1,432.68.

If interest is compounded more than once a year, then the formula is changed. If interest is compounded semiannually, or twice a year, the formula becomes

$$S = P\left(1 + \frac{r}{2}\right)^{2t}$$

If interest is compounded quarterly, or four times a year, the formula is changed to

$$S = P\left(1 + \frac{r}{4}\right)^{4t}$$

In general, we have the following compound interest formula.

COMPOUND INTEREST FORMULA

If an amount of money P is invested and interest is compounded k times a year at an interest rate of r per year, then the amount of money S at the end of t years is

$$S = P\left(1 + \frac{r}{k}\right)^{kt}$$

EXAMPLE 12.6

If $800 is invested in a savings account paying 6% interest compounded monthly, how much is this money worth after 10 years?

SOLUTION In this example, $P = \$800$, $r = 0.06$, $k = 12$, and $t = 10$, so

$$S = P\left(1 + \frac{r}{k}\right)^{kt}$$
$$= 800\left(1 + \frac{0.06}{12}\right)^{12\cdot10}$$
$$= 800(1.005)^{120}$$

$$\approx 800(1.819396734)$$

$$\approx 1455.52$$

Compare this to the result we obtained in Example 12.5. Compounding monthly increased the total by $22.84.

In Section 13.2, we will examine what happens if you compound interest daily or continuously. We will see that there is a limit to the amount of money you will receive.

MODELING WITH EXPONENTIAL FUNCTIONS

When you look at a graph of some data and it has the general shape of either of the graphs in Figures 12.1b and 12.2b, then the data may be modeled by an exponential function. Obtaining a regression formula is much the same as obtaining a linear, quadratic, or sinusoidal formula. The next example will outline the procedure and the one following will look at a variation.

 APPLICATION ENVIRONMENTAL SCIENCE

EXAMPLE 12.7

The population of the United States from 1900 to 2010 is given in Table 12.1.

(a) Determine the exponential regression function that best fits this data.

(b) Use the regression function to predict the U.S. population in 2020.

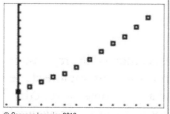
© Cengage Learning 2013

Figure 12.4a

TABLE 12.1 U.S. Population 1900–2010						
Year (t)	1900	1910	1920	1930	1940	1950
Population ($\times 10^6$)	76.0	92.0	105.7	122.8	131.7	151.3

Year (t)	1960	1970	1980	1990	2000	2010
Population ($\times 10^6$)	179.3	203.3	226.5	248.7	281.4	308.7

© Cengage Learning 2013

SOLUTIONS

(a) **Using a Calculator**

Enter the data into list L1 and L2 lists as before. However, in L1 enter the year after 1900, so instead of the values 1900, 1910, 1920, . . . , 2010, use 0, 10, 20, . . . , 110. A graph of these 12 points is in Figure 12.4a. If we ask the calculator to conduct an exponential regression using STAT ▶ 0 [ExpReg] ENTER , the result is $y \approx 80.9776 \times (1.0127)^x$. We can think of this as the function:

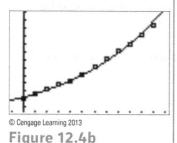
© Cengage Learning 2013

Figure 12.4b

$$P(t) \approx 80.9776(1.0127)^t$$

where P is the population of the United States in millions of people in year t after 1900. When this regression equation is graphed with the original data, we get the result shown in Figure 12.4b.

EXAMPLE 12.7 (Cont.) | **Using a spreadsheet**

The data is entered in two columns as in the table. However, instead of using the values 1900, 1910, 1920, ..., 2010, we use 0, 10, 20, ..., 110. The graph of these 12 points is shown in Figure 12.4c.

An exponential regression is performed on this data. The result is shown in Figure 12.4d. The regression equation is $y = 80.978e^{0.0126t}$. Recall that $(a^m)^n = a^{m \times n}$, so $y = 80.978(e^{0.0126})^t \approx 80.978(1.0126797)^t$. Thus

$$P(t) \approx 80.978(1.0127)^t$$

where P is the population of the United States in millions of people in year t since 1900.

(b) The estimated population for 2020 is $P(120) \approx 366.8$ million people.

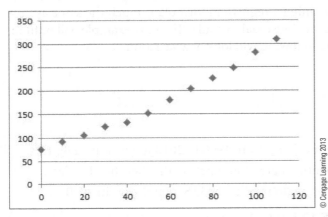

Figure 12.4c

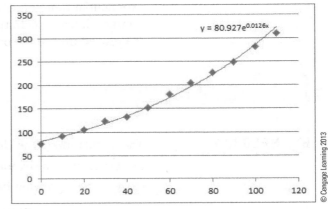

$y = 80.927e^{0.0126x}$

Figure 12.4d

© Cengage Learning 2013

Notice that both the calculator and the spreadsheet computed the regression formula $y = a * b^x$. This assumes that the data has a horizontal asymptote at the x-axis. This is not always the case. Just as the graph of a trigonometric function can have a vertical displacement (or vertical translation), so can an exponential function. Thus, if there is reason to believe that an exponential function has the line $y = c$ as a horizontal asymptote, then the regression formula would be

$$y = ab^x + c$$

The next example will show how this is accomplished with a calculator that does not take a vertical translation into account.

APPLICATION **GENERAL TECHNOLOGY**

EXAMPLE 12.8 | In a room with a temperature of 72°F, hot coffee is poured into a cup and temperature readings are taken every 10 s for $1\frac{1}{2}$ min. The results of the reading are in Table 12.2. Determine the exponential regression function that best fits this data.

TABLE 12.2 Temperature of Coffee, °F										
Time (s)	0	10	20	30	40	50	60	70	80	90
Temperature (°F)	180	164	153	141	130	121	116	111	106	102

© Cengage Learning 2013

SOLUTION

Using a Calculator

Enter the data into the L1 and L2 lists as before. A graph of these 10 points is in Figure 12.5a. The calculator produces the exponential regression $y \approx 172.9678(0.9937)^x$. When this regression equation is graphed with the original data, we get the result shown in Figure 12.5b.

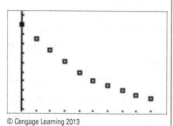

© Cengage Learning 2013

Figure 12.5a

While this does not look "too" bad, we can see that it is not realistic when we look at the same information for 180 s (3 min), as shown in Figure 12.5c. The graph of $y = 72$ has been added to the graph. Remember, the room was 72°F, so we would not expect the coffee to get cooler than 72°F. In fact, according to this regression formula, after 3 min the coffee has cooled to about 55.4°. This does not make sense and would seem to indicate that this is not a very good regression function.

What happened and how can we correct this? The exponential function produced by the calculator has a horizontal asymptote at the x-axis. If we want to use exponential regression with this data we will have to adjust the y-values so that they approach 0. In this case, we know that the coffee will never get below 72°F, so we will subtract 72 from each y-value and perform the exponential regression on the adjusted values.

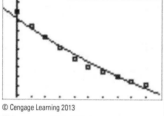

© Cengage Learning 2013

Figure 12.5b

Begin by saving the values in L2. Go the home screen, and press 2nd 2 [L2] STO▶ 2nd 3 [L3] ENTER. You should see

$$\{180\,164\,153\,141\ldots$$

on the screen. This copies all the values in L2 into L3.

To subtract 72 from each of the values in L2, press 2nd 2 [L2] − 72 STO▶ 2nd 2 [L2] ENTER. You should now see

$$\{108\,92\,81\,69\,58\ldots$$

on the screen. Now, compute the exponential regression by pressing STAT ▶ 0 [0:ExpReg] ENTER. The result is

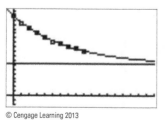

© Cengage Learning 2013

Figure 12.5c

$$y \approx 105.7977(0.9858)^x$$

This is *not* the final answer. Remember, this regression was performed on y-values that were 72 less than the values in Table 12.2. To get the regression equation we will add 72 to this equation and obtain the function:

$$T(t) \approx 105.7977(0.9858)^t + 72$$

When the function T is graphed with the original data (in L1 and L3) and the line $y = 72$, we get the graph in Figure 12.5d. Notice that this regression curve does not cross the line $y = 72$.

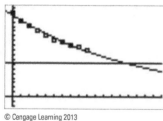

© Cengage Learning 2013

Figure 12.5d

EXAMPLE 12.8 (Cont.)

Using a Spreadsheet

Enter the data and produce a graph as we've done before (see Figure 12.5e).

When the regression equation is graphed with the original data, we get the result shown in Figure 12.5f.

While this does not look "too" bad, we can see that it is not realistic when we look at the same information for 180 s (3 min), as shown in Figure 12.5g. The graph of $y = 72$ has been added to this graph. Remember, the room was 72°F, so we would not expect the coffee to get cooler than 72°F. In fact, according to this regression formula, after 3 min, the coffee has cooled to about 55°F. This does not make sense and would seem to indicate that this is not a very good regression function.

What happened and how can we correct this? The exponential function produced has a horizontal asymptote at the x-axis. If we want to use exponential regression with this data, we will have to adjust the y-values so that they approach 0. In this case, we know the coffee will never get below 72°F,

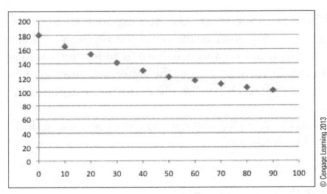

Figure 12.5e

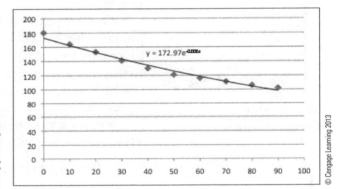

Figure 12.5f

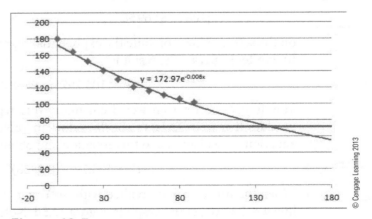

Figure 12.5g

so we will subtract 72 from each y-value and perform the exponential regression on the adjusted values. We first create a third column as shown in Figure 12.5h.

Now create a new scatter plot (see Figure 12.5i) and a new regression equation (see Figure 12.5j).

The regression equation is

$$\begin{aligned} y &= 105.8e^{-0.0143x} \\ &\approx 105.8(e^{-0.0143})^x \\ &\approx 105.8(0.9858)^x \end{aligned}$$

This is not the final answer. Recall that this regression was performed on y-values that were 72 less than the values in Table 12.2. To get a regression equation we will add 72 to this equation and obtain the function:

$$T(t) \approx 105.8(0.9858)^x + 72$$

When the function T is graphed with the original data, we get the graph in Figure 12.5k. Notice that this regression curve does not cross the line $y = 72$.

	A	B	C	D
1	Time	Temperature	Temp	
2	t	T	adjusted	
3	0	180	108	177.8
4	10	164	92	163.700944
5	20	153	81	151.480748
6	30	141	69	140.889032
7	40	130	58	131.708783
8	50	121	49	123.751907
9	60	116	44	116.855376
10	70	111	39	110.877885
11	80	106	34	105.696964
12	90	102	30	101.206459

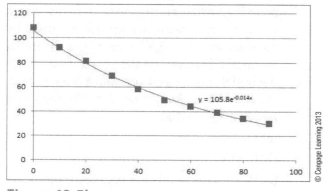

Figure 12.5h

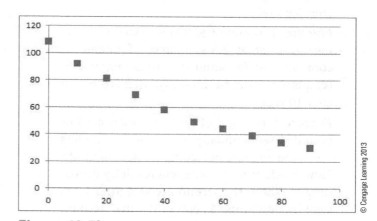

Figure 12.5i

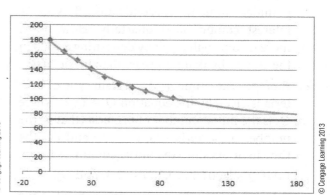

Figure 12.5j

Figure 12.5k

EXERCISE SET 12.1

In Exercises 1–6, use a calculator to approximate the given numbers. Round off each answer to four decimal places.

1. $3^{\sqrt{2}}$

2. 4^{π}

3. π^3

4. $(\sqrt{3})^{\pi}$

5. $(\sqrt{3})^{\sqrt{5}}$

6. $(\sqrt{4})^{4/3}$

In Exercises 7–16, make a table of values and draw the graph of each function.

7. $f(x) = 4^x$

8. $g(x) = 3^x$

9. $h(x) = 1.5^x$

10. $k(x) = 2.5^x$

11. $f(x) = 3^{-x}$

12. $g(x) = 5^{-x}$

13. $h(x) = 2.4^{-x}$

14. $k(x) = (\sqrt{3})^x$

15. $f(x) = 3^{(x + 1/2)}$

16. $g(x) = 2^{(x - 1/4)}$

Solve Exercises 17–34.

17. Finance The sum of \$1 000 is placed in a savings account at 6% interest. If interest is compounded **(a)** annually, **(b)** semiannually, **(c)** quarterly, and **(d)** monthly, what is the total after 5 years?

18. Finance The sum of \$2 000 is placed in a savings account at 3.5% interest. If interest is compounded **(a)** annually, **(b)** semiannually, **(c)** quarterly, and **(d)** monthly, what is the total after 10 years?

19. Finance One bank offers 4.1% interest compounded semiannually. A second bank offers the same interest but compounded monthly. How much more income will result by depositing \$1 000 in the second account for 5 years than by depositing \$1 000 in the first account for 5 years?

20. Finance A bank offers 3.25% interest compounded annually. A second bank offers 3.25% interest compounded quarterly. How much more income will result by depositing \$2 000 in the second bank for 10 years than in the first?

21. Biology The number of a certain type of bacteria is given by the equation $Q = Q_0 2^t$, where Q_0 is the initial number of bacteria (that is, the number of bacteria when $t = 0$) and t is the time in hours since the initial count was taken.

(a) If $Q = 200\,000$ when $t = 2.3$, find Q_0.

(b) Find the number of bacteria present at the end of 4 h.

(c) How long does it take for Q to become twice as large as Q_0?

(d) How long does it take for Q to become eight times as large as Q_0?

22. Medical technology A pharmaceutical company is growing an organism to be used in a vaccine. The organism's growth is given by the equation $Q = Q_0 3^t$, where Q_0 is the initial number of bacteria (that is, the number of bacteria when $t = 0$) and t is the time in hours since the initial count was taken. When $t = 1$, we know that $Q = 2760$.

(a) Find Q_0.

(b) What is the number of organisms at the end of 5 h?

(c) How long will it take for Q to become three times as large as Q_0?

23. Medical technology A pharmaceutical company is growing an organism to be used in a vaccine. The organism's growth is given by the equation $Q = Q_0 3^{kt}$, where Q_0 is the initial number of bacteria, t is the time in hours since the initial count was taken, and k is a constant. When $t = 0$, we know that $Q = 400$, and when $t = 2\frac{1}{2}$ h, $Q = 1,200$.

(a) Find Q_0.

(b) Find k.

(c) What is the number of organisms present at the end of 5 h?

24. **Ecology** In 1995, the world population was growing at the rate of approximately 1.8% per year. This can be expressed mathematically as $P = P_0(1.018)^t$, where $P_0 = 5.7 \times 10^9$ and P is the population t years after 1995.

    (a) What will the world's approximate population be in the year 2000?

    (b) What will the world's approximate population be in the year 2050?

    (c) Graph $P = P_0(1.018)^t = 5.7 \times 10^9(1.018)^t$.

    (d) Use the graph from (c) to approximate the year that the world's population will reach $10,000,000,000 = 10^{10}$.

25. **Lighting technology** Each 1-mm thickness of a certain translucent material reduces the intensity of a light beam passing through it by 12%. This means that the intensity, I, is a function of the thickness, T, of the material as given by $I = 0.88^T$.

    (a) What is the intensity when the thickness is 1.75 mm?

    (b) Graph I as a function of T.

    (c) Use the graph from (b) to approximate the thickness that produces an intensity of 0.50.

26. **Electronics** An important triode formula is

$$I_p + I_g = K\left(V_g + \frac{V_p}{\mu}\right)^{3/2}$$

    where I_p is the plate current in amperes, I_g is the grid current in amperes, V_p is the plate voltage, V_g is the grid voltage, and μ is an amplification

factor. Calculate $I_p + I_g$ if $K = 0.0005$, $V_p = 350$ V, $V_g = 8$ V, and $\mu = 14$.

27. **Medical technology** The amount D of medication, in mg, in the body t hours after taking a pill is given by $D(t) = 25(0.825^t)$.

    (a) What was the initial dose of the medication?

    (b) What percent of the medication leaves the body each hour?

    (c) How much of the medication will remain in the body after 10 h?

    (d) How long will it take before only 1 mg of the medication remains in the body?

28. **Meteorology** The relative humidity R is the ratio (expressed as a percent) of the amount of water vapor in the air to the maximum amount that the air can hold at a specific temperature and is given by the formula:

$$R = \left(10^{\left(\frac{37.5\,D - 6000}{1973.3 + 5\,D} - \frac{37.5\,T - 6000}{1973.3 + 5\,T}\right)}\right)100$$

    where T is the air temperature (in °F) and D is the dew point temperature (in °F).

    (a) Determine the relative humidity if the air temperature is 85°F and the dew point is 65°F.

    (b) Determine the relative humidity if the air temperature is 75°F and the dew point is 55°F.

    (c) What is the relative humidity if the air temperature and the dew point are the same?

29. **Sports management** Table 12.3 gives the average major league baseball player's salary on opening day each decade from 1970 through 2010.

TABLE 12.3 Average Major League Baseball Player's Salary					
Year, t	1970	1980	1990	2000	2010
Average salary, $S(t)$	29,303	143,756	597,537	1,895,630	3,014,572

© Cengage Learning 2013

(a) Assuming that the average salary is increasing exponentially, write a model, $S_e(t)$, that expresses the average salary t years after 1970.

(b) Write a quadratic model, $S_q(t)$, that describes the average salary t years after 1970.

(c) Use each model to estimate the average salary in 2010.

(d) What is the percent error for each of the estimates in (c)?

(e) Use the model with the lower percent error to estimate to three significant figures the average baseball salary in 2015.

(f) Use the model with the lower percent error to estimate to three significant figures the average baseball salary in 2020.

30. ***Communications*** Table 12.4 gives the number of billion text messages in December from 2003 through 2008.

TABLE 12.4 Number of Text Messages in December

Year, t	2003	2004	2005	2006	2007	2008
No. of text messages in billions, $M(t)$	2.1	4.7	9.8	18.7	48.1	110.4

© Cengage Learning 2013

(a) Assuming that the number of text messages is increasing exponentially, write a model, $M(t)$, for the number of billion text messages t years after 2000.

(b) Use your model to estimate the number of billion text messages in 2008.

(c) What is the percent error for the estimate in **(b)**?

(d) Use your model to predict the number of text messages in 2010.

(e) If possible, use the Internet to determine the actual number of text messages in 2010.

(f) Use your model to predict the number of text messages in 2015.

31. ***Thermodynamics*** In a room with a temperature of 22°C, boiling water is removed from a heat source and allowed to cool. Temperature readings are taken every minute. The results of the reading are in Table 12.5.

(a) Determine the exponential regression function that best fits this data.

(b) Estimate the temperature after 1 h.

(c) How long will it take for the water to reach 23.0°C?

TABLE 12.5 Water Temperature, °C

Time (min)	2	4	6	8	10	12	14	16
Temp (° C)	89.2	85.4	79.9	75.6	71.8	70.2	67.4	64.7

Time (min)	18	20	22	24	26	28	30
Temp (° C)	61.2	59.0	57.3	55.5	53.9	52.4	50.9

© Cengage Learning 2013

32. ***Finance*** Table 12.6 shows the amount of U.S. consumer credit outstanding from 1970 through 2005.

TABLE 12.6 U.S. Consumer Credit

Year, t	1970	1975	1980	1985	1990	1995	2000	2005
Credit (billion dollars), $C(t)$	134	208	349	593	824	1,096	1,741	2,321

© Cengage Learning 2013

(a) Fit an exponential model to the data.

(b) Use your model to predict the consumer credit in 2008.

(c) Use your model to predict the consumer credit in 2015.

33. ***Communications*** Table 12.7 shows the number of cell phone subscribers, in millions, in the United States from 2000 through 2009.

TABLE 12.7 U.S. Cell Phone Subscribers

Year, t	2000	2003	2004	2005	2006	2007	2008	2009
Subscribers (millions), $S(t)$	109	159	182	208	233	256		287

© Cengage Learning 2013

(a) Fit an exponential model to the data.

(b) Use your model to predict the number of million subscribers in 2008.

(c) If the actual number of subscribers in 2008 was 270 million, was the percent error with your prediction in (b)?

(d) Use your model to predict the number of million subscribers in 2015.

(e) Is your answer in (d) realistic? Explain your answer.

34. **Environmental science** The concentration of carbon dioxide (CO_2), in parts per million (ppm), at the Mauna Loa, Hawaii, observatory is given in Table 12.8.

TABLE 12.8 Carbon Dioxide at Mauna Loa, Hawaii, Observatory								
Year	1975	1980	1985	1990	1995	2000	2002	2005	2008
CO_2, $C(t)$	331	339	346	354	361	369	373	380	385

© Cengage Learning 2013

(a) Fit an exponential model to the data.

(b) Use your model to predict the concentration of carbon dioxide (CO_2), in ppm, at the Mauna Loa, Hawaii, observatory in 2010.

(c) If possible, test your prediction and calculate the percent error between your prediction and the actual value.

(d) Use your model to predict the concentration of carbon dioxide (CO_2), in ppm, at the Mauna Loa, Hawaii, observatory in 2015.

 [IN YOUR WORDS]

35. The text listed three common features of exponential functions. Without looking in the text, list each of these features. You may want to draw some graphs to help your explanation.

36. (a) Graph the two functions $f(x) = x^2$ and $g(x) = 2^x$ on your calculator.

(b) Explain how the two graphs are alike and how they are different.

(c) Describe how you would help someone learn which was the graph of $f(x) = x^2$ and which was the graph of $g(x) = 2^x$.

37. Write a paragraph that describes how the functions $f(x) = a^x$, where $a > 1$, and $g(x) = b^x$, where $0 < b < 1$, are alike and how they are different.

38. In the definition of an exponential function $f(x) = b^x$ it states that $b \neq 0$. Explain why this is not allowed.

12.2   THE EXPONENTIAL FUNCTION e^x

In Section 12.1, we were working with an equation that determined the amount of interest gathered in an account. A variation of that formula is $\left(1 + \dfrac{1}{n}\right)^n$. Let's examine the values of $\left(1 + \dfrac{1}{n}\right)^n$ as n gets larger. Use your calculator to check these numerical values.

n	$\left(1 + \dfrac{1}{n}\right)^n$
1	2
10	2.59374246
100	2.704813829
1,000	2.716923932
10,000	2.718145927
100,000	2.718268237
1,000,000	2.718280469
10,000,000	2.718281693
100,000,000	2.718281815
1,000,000,000	2.718281827

© Cengage Learning 2013

Mathematicians have been able to prove that as the value of n gets larger, the value of $\left(1 + \dfrac{1}{n}\right)^n$ also continues to get larger, but has a limit on how large it can get. This limit is such a special number that it has been given its own symbol, e. The first nine digits of e are the same ones that we got in the previous table, 2.71828182.

As we will see later in this section, the number e is a very important number. Some calculators have two special numbers marked on them—π and e. Later in this section, we will need to determine values for the exponential function $f(x) = e^x$. Both the calculator and the computer can be used to find these values.

FINDING e^x WITH A CALCULATOR

Some calculators have an $\boxed{e^x}$ key. If you want to determine e^5, use this method.

PRESS	DISPLAY
2nd $\boxed{e^x}$ 5 ENTER	148.4131591

FINDING e^x WITH A SPREADSHEET

On a spreadsheet, EXP() returns e raised to the power of the number in parentheses. For example, Figure 12.6 shows the value of e^5 in Cell A2.

	A
1	=exp(5)
2	148.4131591

© Cengage Learning 2013

Figure 12.6

BUSINESS AND FINANCE

Let's return to a problem involving compound interest. In Section 12.1, we learned that if a certain principal amount P is invested and interest is compounded k times a year at an interest rate of r, the amount after t year would be

$$S = P\left(1 + \frac{r}{k}\right)^{kt}$$

If we let $n = \frac{k}{r}$, then $k = nr$, and this formula becomes

$$S = P\left(1 + \frac{r}{nr}\right)^{nrt}$$

$$= P\left[\left(1 + \frac{1}{n}\right)^n\right]^{rt}$$

Now, if interest is compounded continuously, then the expression inside the brackets, $\left(1 + \dfrac{1}{n}\right)^n$, is equal to the number represented by e. So, the amount accumulated after t year at the interest rate of r would be

$$S = Pe^{rt}$$

CONTINUOUS INTEREST FORMULA

If an amount of money P is invested at an interest rate of r per year and interest is compounded continuously, then the amount of money S at the end of t years is

$$S = Pe^{rt}$$

APPLICATION BUSINESS

EXAMPLE 12.9

If $800 is invested in a savings account paying interest compounded continuously at 6%, how much has accumulated after 10 years?

SOLUTION Here $P = 800$, $r = 0.06$, and $t = 10$, so

$$
\begin{aligned}
S &= 800e^{(0.06)10} \\
&= 800e^{0.6} \\
&\approx 800(1.8221188) \\
&= 1\,457.70
\end{aligned}
$$

After 10 years, this $800 investment has increased to $1 457.70.

   When this is compared to the result in Example 12.6, we see that, after 10 years, continuous compounding of interest has provided an additional $2.18.

EXPONENTIAL GROWTH AND DECAY

The number represented by e is used in the two areas known as *exponential growth* and *exponential decay*.

   Exponential growth can be explained by letting y represent the size of a quantity at time t. If this quantity grows or decays exponentially, it obeys the exponential growth formula given here.

EXPONENTIAL GROWTH AND DECAY

The basic formula for the exponential growth or decay of a quantity is

$$y = ce^{kt}$$

where y represents the size of the quantity at time t, c is a positive real number constant, and k is a nonzero constant.
If $k > 0$, this is an *exponential growth* function.
If $k < 0$, this is an *exponential decay* function.

EXAMPLE 12.10

A culture of bacteria originally numbers 500. After 4 h, there are 8 000 bacteria in the culture. If we assume that these bacteria grow exponentially, how many will there be after 10 h?

SOLUTION Since the number of bacteria grows exponentially, their growth obeys the formula $y = ce^{kt}$. When $t = 0$, we are told that $y = 500$, and so $500 = ce^{k \cdot 0} = c$. (Remember, $k \cdot 0 = 0$, $e^{k \cdot 0} = e^0 = 1$.) The formula is now $y = 500e^{kt}$. When $t = 4$ h, we have $y = 8 000$ and from the formula,

$$8 000 = 500e^{k4}$$
$$16 = e^{k4}$$

However, the example asks us to determine y, when $t = 10$. It is possible to do this without determining k. (In Section 12.3, we will learn how to find the value of k.)

$$y = 500e^{k \cdot 10}$$
$$= 500(e^{k4})^{2.5}, \text{ since } 10 = (4)(2.5)$$
$$= 500(16)^{2.5}, \text{ since } e^{k4} = 16$$
$$= 500(1,024)$$
$$= 512 000$$

After 10 h, the number of bacteria increased from 500 to 512 000.

Exponential decay is seen most often in radioactive substances. A common measure of the rate of decay is the *half-life* of a substance. The half-life is the amount of time needed for a substance to diminish to one-half its original size.

For example, 1000 g of radioactive material would be reduced to 500 g after one half-life. After a second half-life there would be half of the 500 g (or 250 g) remaining. Each new half-life cuts the amount of radioactive material in half as outlined in Table 12.9.

TABLE 12.9 Amount of Radioactive Material Remaining After Each Half-Life

No. of half-lives, n	0	1	2	3	4	5	6	7
Amount remaining, g	1000	500	250	125	62.5	31.25	15.625	7.8125

EXAMPLE 12.11

The half-life of copper-67 is 62 h. How much of 100 g will remain after 15 days?

SOLUTION As in Example 12.10, we have some basic information. When $t = 0$, we know that $y = 100$ g, so

$$100 = ce^{k \cdot 0}$$

$$\text{or } 100 = c$$

and the exponential decay formula for copper-67 becomes

$$y = 100e^{kt}$$

Now, since the half-life is 62 h, we know that, when $t = 62$, there is only half as much copper-67, or $y = 50$ g, so

$$50 = 100e^{k(62)}$$

$$\tfrac{1}{2} = e^{k(62)}$$

We want to determine the amount when $t = 15$ days. Because the half-life is given in hours, we first convert 15 days to $15 \times 24 = 360$ h. Since $360 \div 62 \approx 5.8$, we can write the formula as

$$y = 100e^{k \cdot 360}$$

$$\approx 100\left(e^{k(62)}\right)^{5.8}$$

and since $e^{k(62)} = \tfrac{1}{2}$, we have

$$y \approx 100\left(\frac{1}{2}\right)^{5.8}$$

$$= 1.79 \text{ g}$$

So, of the original 100 g of copper-67, about 1.79 g remain after 15 days.

APPLICATION   ELECTRONICS

EXAMPLE 12.12

When a charged capacitor is discharged through a resistance, as in Figure 12.7, the charge Q in coulombs (C) is given by the formula

$$Q = Q_0 e^{-t/T}$$

where $Q_0 = CV$, the initial charge, $T = RC$, and C is the capacitance, V is (*) the battery voltage, and R is the resistance. The product RC is called the time constant of the circuit. If a 15-μF capacitor is charged by being connected to a 60-V battery through a circuit with a resistance of 12 000 Ω, what is the charge on the capacitor 9 s after the battery is disconnected?

SOLUTION   We are given $C = 15\ \mu\text{F} = 15 \times 10^{-6}$ F, $V = 60$ V, and $R = 12\,000\ \Omega$. Thus

$$Q_0 = CV$$

$$= 15 \times 10^{-6} \text{ F} \times 60 \text{ V}$$

$$= 900 \times 10^{-6} \text{ C}$$

$$= 9 \times 10^{-4} \text{ C}$$

$$\text{and} \quad T = RC$$

$$= 12\,000\Omega \times 15 \times 10^{-6} \text{ F}$$

© Cengage Learning 2013

Figure 12.7

EXAMPLE 12.12 (Cont.)

$$= 180\,000 \times 10^{-6}\,\text{s}$$

$$= 0.18\,\text{s}$$

Substituting these values for Q_0 and T into the formula $Q = Q_0 e^{-t/T}$, we obtain

$$Q = 9 \times 10^{-4}\,e^{-t/0.18}$$

We want to find the value of Q when $t = 9$ s, or

$$\frac{t}{T} = \frac{9\,\text{s}}{0.18\,\text{s}} = 50$$

Thus, returning to equation with $Q_0 = 9 \times 10^{-4}$ C and $\frac{t}{T} = 50$, we get

$$Q = 9 \times 10^{-4} e^{-50}\,\text{C}$$

$$= 1.74 \times 10^{-25}\,\text{C}$$

So, the charge is about 1.74×10^{-25} C, 9 s after the battery is disconnected.

EXERCISE SET 12.2

Use a calculator or a computer to evaluate each of the numbers in Exercises 1–8.

1. e^3 **3.** $e^{4.65}$ **5.** e^{-4} **7.** $e^{-2.75}$

2. e^7 **4.** $e^{5.375}$ **6.** e^{-9} **8.** $e^{-0.25}$

Make a table of values and graph each of the functions in Exercises 9–12 over the given domains of x.

9. $f(x) = 4e^x$, $\{x: -2 \leq x \leq 4\}$ **11.** $h(x) = 4e^{-x}$, $\{x: -4 \leq x \leq 2\}$

10. $g(x) = 3.5e^{5x}$, $\{x: -1 \leq x \leq 4\}$ **12.** $k(x) = 8.5e^{-6x}$, $\{x: -4 \leq x \leq 2\}$

Solve Exercises 13–30.

13. *Nuclear technology* The number of milligrams of a radioactive substance present after t year is given by $Q = 125e^{-0.375t}$. **(a)** How many milligrams were present at the beginning? **(b)** How many milligrams are present after 1 year? **(c)** How many milligrams are present after 16 years?

14. *Nuclear technology* Radium decays exponentially and has a half-life of 1 600 years. How much of 100 mg will be left after 2 000 years?

15. *Biology* The number of bacteria in a certain culture increases from 5 000 to 15 000 in 20 h. If we assume these bacteria grow exponentially, **(a)** how many will be there after 10 h? **(b)** How many can we expect after 30 h? **(c)** How many can we expect after 3 days?

16. *Finance* If $5 000 is invested in an account that pays 5% interest compounded continuously, how much can we expect to have after 10 years?

17. *Biology* The population of a certain city is increasing at the rate of 7% per year. The present population is 200 000. **(a)** What will be the population in 5 years? **(b)** What can the population be expected to reach in 10 years?

18. *Medical technology* A pharmaceutical company is growing an organism to be used in a vaccine. The organism grows at a rate of 4.5%

per hour. How many units of this organism must they begin with in order to have 1 000 units at the end of 7 days?

19. **Thermodynamics** According to *Newton's law of cooling*, the rate at which a hot object cools is proportional to the difference between its temperature and the temperature of its surroundings. The temperature T of the object after a period of time t is

$$T = T_m + (T_0 - T_m)e^{-kt}$$

where T_0 is the initial temperature and T_m is the temperature of the surrounding medium. An object cools from 180°F to 150°F in 20 min when surrounded by air at 60°F. What is the temperature at the end of 1 h of cooling?

20. **Thermodynamics** A piece of metal is heated to 150°C and is then placed in the outside air, which is 30°C. After 15 min the temperature of the metal is 90°C. What will its temperature be in another 15 min? (See Exercise 19.)

21. **Thermodynamics** You like your drinks at 45°F. When you arrive home from the store, the cans of drink you bought are 87°F. You place the cans in a refrigerator. The thermostat is set at 37°F. When you open the refrigerator 25 min later, the drinks are at 70°F. How long will it take for the drinks to get to 45°F? (See Exercise 19.)

22. **Electronics** The circuit in Figure 12.8 contains a resistance R, a voltage V, and an inductance L. The current I at t s after the switch is closed is given by

$$I = I_0\left(1 - e^{-t/T}\right)$$

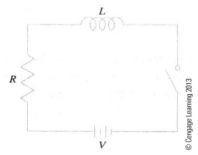

Figure 12.8

where I_0 is the steady state current $\dfrac{V}{R}$ and $T = \dfrac{L}{R}$. If a circuit has $V = 120$ V, $R = 40$ Ω, and $L = 3.0$ H (henrys), determine the current in the circuit (**a**) 0.01 s, (**b**) 0.1 s, and (**c**) 1.0 s after the connection is made.

23. **Electronics** A 130-μF capacitor is charged by being connected to a 120-V circuit. The resistance is 4 500 Ω. What is the charge on the capacitor 0.5 s after the circuit is disconnected?

24. **Nuclear technology** The half-life of tritium is 12.5 years. How much of 100 g will remain after 40 years?

25. **Medical technology** A radioactive material used in radiation therapy has a half-life of 5.4 days. This means that the radioactivity decreases by one-half each 5.4 days. A hospital gets a new supply that measures 1 200 microcuries (μCi). How much of this material will still be radioactive after 30 days?

26. **Medical technology** The average doubling time for a breast cancer cell is 100 days. It takes about 9 years before a lump can be seen on a mammogram and 10 years before a breast cancer is large enough to be felt as a lump. (Use 365.25 days = 1 year.)

   (**a**) How many cancer cells are in a lump that is just large enough to be seen on a mammogram?

   (**b**) How many cancer cells are in a lump that is just large enough to be felt?

   (**c**) If a lump must be approximately 1 cm in diameter before it can be felt, how large is each cancer cell? (Assume the lump is a perfect sphere.)

27. **Electronics** In a capacitive circuit, the equation for the current in amperes is given by

$$i = \frac{V}{R}e^{-t/RC}$$

where t is any elapsed time in seconds after the switch is closed, V is the impressed voltage, C is the capacitance of the circuit in F, and R is the circuit resistance in Ω. A capacitance of 500 μF in series with 1 kΩ is connected across a 50-V generator.

(a) What is the value of the current at the instant the switch is closed?

(b) What is the value of the current 0.02 s after the switch is closed?

(c) What is the value of the current 0.04 s after the switch is closed?

28. **Biology** The length L of a shark as a function of its age t can be predicted by the *von Bertalanffy growth function*, $L(t) = M - (M - b)e^{-kt}$ where M is the mean maximum length of this species of shark, b is the mean length at birth, k is a growth rate constant per year, and t is year since birth. For one species of shark $M = 3.0$ m, $b = 0.5$ m, and $k = 0.13863$/year. **(a)** Sketch the graph of L. **(b)** What is the length of this shark after 5 years? **(c)** What is the length of this shark after 10 years? **(d)** How many years does it take this shark to reach a length of 2.7 m?

29. **Medical technology** Hospitals use the radioactive substance iodine-131 in the diagnosis of conditions of the thyroid gland. The half-life of iodine-131 is 8 days. Suppose that it takes two days from the time an order is placed with the distributer until it arrives. If 20 units of iodine-131 are needed on a certain day, how much should be ordered?

30. The number e can be approximated by the infinite series:

$$e = 2 + \frac{1}{2} + \frac{1}{2 \cdot 3} + \frac{1}{2 \cdot 3 \cdot 4} + \frac{1}{2 \cdot 3 \cdot 4 \cdot 5} \cdots$$

$$= 2 + \frac{1}{2!} + \frac{1}{3!} + \frac{1}{4!} + \frac{1}{5!}$$

(Here $3! = 3 \cdot 2 \cdot 1 = 6$ and $4! = 4 \cdot 3 \cdot 2 \cdot 1 = 24$. In general, $n! = n \cdot (n - 1) \cdot (n - 2) \cdots 4 \cdot 3 \cdot 2 \cdot 1$. Some calculators have an $x!$ key. On a TI-83/84 the ! symbol is produced by pressing MATH ◄ [PRB] 4 [4: !]. On a TI-86 you get the ! symbol by pressing 2nd MATH F2 [PROB] F1 [!]. The symbols $n!$, $3!$, and $2!$ are read n factorial, 3 factorial, and 2 factorial.) Calculate e to four figures by adding the first six terms of this series.

 [IN YOUR WORDS]

31. Suppose that you are shown the graphs of $y = e^x$, $y = 2^x$, $y = x^2$, and $y = x^3$, but the graphs are not labeled. Explain how you would distinguish among the graphs.

32. Explain what is meant by the term "half-life."

12.3   LOGARITHMIC FUNCTIONS

If you look at the graphs of exponential functions, such as the ones in Figures 12.1b, 12.2b, and 12.3, you can see that they would pass the horizontal line test for the inverse of a function. The inverse of the exponential function $f(x) = b^x$, $b > 0$, $b \neq 1$, is called the **logarithmic function**. The symbol for the logarithmic function is $\log_b x$. So, if $f(x) = b^x$, we have

$$f^{-1}(x) = \log_b x, \quad b > 0, b \neq 1$$

which is read "log to the base b of x." This provides for the following definition.

LOGARITHMIC FUNCTION

A *logarithmic function* is any function of the form:

$$f(x) = \log_b x$$

where $x > 0$, $b > 0$, and $b \neq 1$. If $y = \log_b x$, then $x = b^y$. The number represented by b is called the *base*.

Since $y = \log_b x$ is equivalent to $b^y = x$, we can express each logarithm in exponential form.

EXAMPLE 12.13

Use the fact that $y = \log_b x$ is equivalent to $b^y = x$ to rewrite each logarithm in exponential form.

Logarithmic form	**Exponential form**
(a) $\log_5 125 = 3$	$5^3 = 125$
(b) $\log_7 49 = 2$	$7^2 = 49$
(c) $\log_2 128 = 7$	$2^7 = 128$
(d) $\log_5 \left(\frac{1}{25}\right) = -2$	$5^{-2} = \frac{1}{25}$
(e) $\log_2 0.125 = -3$	$2^{-3} = 0.125 = \frac{1}{8}$
(f) $\log_8 16 = \frac{4}{3}$	$8^{4/3} = 16$
(g) $\log_b 1 = 0$	$b^0 = 1$

Remember that for any function f, with an inverse f^{-1}, we have the following relationship:

$$f(f^{-1}(x)) = x \quad \text{and} \quad f^{-1}(f(x)) = x$$

This leads to the following important properties.

TWO PROPERTIES OF LOGARITHMS

If $f(x) = b^x$ and $f^{-1}(x) = \log_b x$, then we see that

$$b^{\log_b x} = x \quad \text{and} \quad \log_b b^x = x$$

Figure 12.9 shows the graph of $y = 2^x$. The line $y = x$ is shown as a dashed line. The reflection of $y = 2^x$ in the line $y = x$ is shown by the colored curve and is the graph of $y = \log_2 x = f^{-1}(2^x)$.

This is a rather awkward method to graph the curve of $y = \log_b x$. Let's find another way to evaluate $\log_b x$ so that we can set up a table of values and plot points, and to connect the points to sketch the graph.

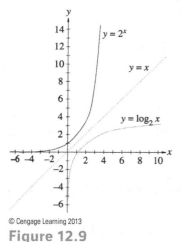

© Cengage Learning 2013

Figure 12.9

COMMON LOGS; NATURAL LOGS

There is another way to evaluate $\log_b x$, but the ease of doing it depends on the base of the logarithm. There are two bases that are used most often. These are 10 and e. Logarithms that have a base of 10 are called common logs and those with a base of e are called natural logs.

Because the bases 10 and e are used so often, they have special symbols. The symbol *log*, written with no indicated base, shows that common logs, or base 10 logs, are being used. If natural logs are involved, the symbol *ln* is used.

There are three major ways to find the values of a logarithm. These ways include a calculator, a computer, and a table. We will explain how to use a calculator and a spreadsheet to find the logarithm of a number. Tables are seldom used today. If, or when, you need to use a table of logarithms, you should carefully read the instructions for its use.

FINDING LOGS WITH A CALCULATOR

Look at your calculator. It probably has two keys on it that we have seldom used. One key is LOG , and the other is LN . Now, since $\log_{10} x$ means $\log x$, we can use the LOG key to determine $\log_{10} x$. Similarly, we can use the LN key to determine values of $\log_e x = \ln x$.

EXAMPLE 12.14

Use a calculator to evaluate (a) log 2, (b) log 100, (c) log 9.53, (d) ln 2, (e) ln 12.4, (f) ln 1, and (g) ln 32.4.

SOLUTIONS

	PRESS	DISPLAY
(a)	LOG 2 ENTER	0.3010299957
(b)	LOG 100 ENTER	2
(c)	LOG 9.53 ENTER	0.9790929006
(d)	LN 2 ENTER	0.6931471806
(e)	LN 12.4 ENTER	2.517696473
(f)	LN 1 ENTER	0
(g)	LN 32.4 ENTER	3.478158423

FINDING LOGS WITH A SPREADSHEET

On a spreadsheet, LOG() returns $\log_{10}$ and LN() returns $\log_e$ of the number in parentheses.

EXAMPLE 12.15

Use a spreadsheet to evaluate (a) log 2, (b) log 1000, (c) log 12.725, (d) ln 14.75, (e) ln 1, and (f) ln 2.71826.

SOLUTION The keystrokes and the results are shown in Figure 12.10.

⊿	A	B	C	D
1		Function	Enter	Result
2	(a)	log 2	=LOG(2)	0.30103
3	(b)	log 1000	=LOG(1000)	3
4	(c)	log 12.725	=LOG(12.725)	1.104658
5	(d)	ln 14.75	=LN(14.75)	2.691243
6	(e)	ln 1	=LN(1)	0
7	(f)	ln 2.71826	=LN(2.71826)	0.999992

Figure 12.10

LOGS OF DIFFERENT BASES

Now we see that we can use a calculator or spreadsheet to help us get values of ln x and log x. We can also use calculators and computers to help us find the value of $\log_b x$. To do this, we use the following relationship.

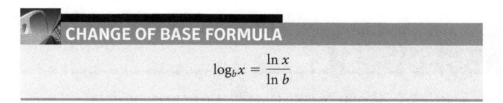

CHANGE OF BASE FORMULA

$$\log_b x = \frac{\ln x}{\ln b}$$

The relationship $\log_b x = \dfrac{\ln x}{\ln b}$ seems to be an unusual one. It uses some properties of logarithms that we will learn in Section 12.4. But, it works! In fact, it works for any base a of the logarithms on the right-hand side. So, it is true that $\log_b x = \dfrac{\log_a x}{\log_a b}$. Since $5^3 = 125$, we know $\log_5 125 = 3$. By this formula, $\log_5 125 = \dfrac{\ln 125}{\ln 5}$ should also be 3. Try it on your calculator.

PRESS	DISPLAY
125 LN	4.8283137
÷ 5 LN	1.6094379
=	3

With a spreadsheet LOG(a) returns $\log_{10} a$ and LOG(a, b) returns $\log_b a$.

EXAMPLE 12.16

Use a spreadsheet to evaluate (a) $\log_5 125$ and (b) $\log_9 12\,863.2$.

SOLUTION   The keystrokes and the results are shown in Figure 12.11.

⊿	A	B	C	D
1		Function	Enter	Result
2	(a)	log_5 125	=LOG(125,5)	3
3	(b)	lo_9 12,863.2	=LOG(12863.2,9)	4.306399

Figure 12.11

EXAMPLE 12.17

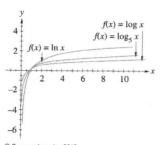

© Cengage Learning 2013

Figure 12.12

Plot the graphs of $\log x$, $\ln x$, and $\log_5 x$.

SOLUTION A table of values follows and the graphs of the functions are shown in Figure 12.12.

x	0.50	1	1.50	2.00	2.50	3.00	3.50	4.00	4.50	5.00	5.50	6.00
$\log x$	−0.30	0	0.18	0.30	0.40	0.48	0.54	0.60	0.65	0.70	0.74	0.78
$\ln x$	−0.69	0	0.41	0.69	0.92	1.10	1.25	1.39	1.50	1.61	1.70	1.79
$\log_5 x$	−0.43	0	0.25	0.43	0.57	0.68	0.78	0.86	0.93	1.00	1.06	1.11

© Cengage Learning 2013

Notice that all three curves cross the x-axis at the point (1, 0). If you look back at Example 12.14(f) or Example 12.15(e), you will see that $\log_b 1 = 0$. All logarithmic curves cross the x-axis at the point (1, 0).

EXERCISE SET 12.3

In Exercises 1–10, rewrite each logarithm in exponential form.

1. $\log_6 216 = 3$

2. $\log_9 6{,}561 = 4$

3. $\log_4 16 = 2$

4. $\log_7 16{,}807 = 5$

5. $\log_{1/7} \frac{1}{49} = 2$

6. $\log_{1/2} \frac{1}{64} = 6$

7. $\log_2 \frac{1}{32} = -5$

8. $\log_3 \frac{1}{243} = -5$

9. $\log_9 2{,}187 = \frac{7}{2}$

10. $\log_8 2{,}048 = \frac{11}{3}$

In Exercises 11–20, rewrite each exponential in logarithmic form.

11. $5^4 = 625$

12. $3^5 = 243$

13. $2^7 = 128$

14. $4^3 = 64$

15. $7^3 = 343$

16. $11^2 = 121$

17. $5^{-3} = \frac{1}{125}$

18. $3^{-5} = \frac{1}{243}$

19. $4^{7/2} = 128$

20. $125^{5/3} = 3{,}125$

In Exercises 21–32, use a calculator, spreadsheet, or computer to evaluate each of these logarithms.

21. $\ln 5$

22. $\ln 19$

23. $\ln 4.751$

24. $\ln 35.62$

25. $\log 4$

26. $\log 23$

27. $\log 12.67$

28. $\log 78.143$

29. $\log_5 8$

30. $\log_3 20$

31. $\log_{12} 16.4$

32. $\log_8 691.45$

In Exercises 33–39, make a table of values and sketch the graph of each function.

33. $f(x) = \ln x$

34. $g(x) = \log x$

35. $h(x) = \log_2 x$

36. $k(x) = \log_3 x$

37. $f(x) = \log_{12} x$

38. $g(x) = \log_{1/2} x$

39. $h(x) = \log_{1/4} x$

Solve Exercises 40–44.

40. Seismology The *Richter scale* used to be used to measure the magnitude of earthquakes. The formula for the Richter scale is $R = \log I$, where R is the Richter number, and I is the intensity of the earthquake. Express the Richter scale in exponential form.

41. Acoustical engineering The *decibel (dB) scale* is used for sound intensity. This scale is used because the response of the human ear to sound intensity is not proportional to the intensity. The intensity, $I_0 = 10^{-12}$ W/m² (watts/m²), is just audible and so is given a value of 0 dB. A sound 10 times more intense is given the value 10 dB; a sound $100 = 10^2$ times more intense than 0 dB is given the value 20 dB. Continuing in this manner gives the formula:

$$\beta = 10 \log \frac{I}{I_0}$$

where β is the intensity in decibels and I is the intensity in W/m². **(a)** Express the decibel scale in exponential notation. **(b)** What is the intensity in decibels of a sound that measures 10^{-7} W/m²? **(c)** What is the intensity of a heavy truck passing a pedestrian at the side of a road if the sound wave intensity of the truck I is 10^{-3} W/m²?

42. Land management To plan for the future needs of a city, the city engineer uses the function:

$$P(t) = 47,000 + 9,000 \ln (0.7t + 1)$$

to estimate the population t years from now.
(a) What is the city's current population?
(b) What is the expected population in 10 years?

(c) How long will it be until the population reaches 75 000?

43. Forestry The yield, Y, in total ft³/acre, of thinned stands of yellow poplar can be predicted by the equation:

$$\ln Y = 5.36437 - 101.16296 S^{-1} - 22.00048 A^{-1} + 0.97116 \ln BA$$

where S is the site index, A is the current age of the trees, and BA is the basal area. What is the predicted yield of a 40-year-old stand growing on a site with an index of 110 and a basal area of 90 ft² per acre?

44. Computer technology In designing a PC board, the impedance of a trace depends on the trace width, conductor thickness, and PC board material in a strip-line configuration, as shown by the equation:

$$Z_0 = \frac{87}{\sqrt{\varepsilon' + 1.4}} \ln \left(\frac{6H}{0.8W + t} \right)$$

Solve this equation for t.

45. Seismology The Richter scale described in Exercise 40 has been replaced with the moment magnitude scale (M_W) that is given by $M_W = \dfrac{\log E - 9}{1.5}$, where E is the energy, in joules, released by the earthquake. Express the moment magnitude scale in exponential form.

46. Seismology The 2010 earthquake in Haiti was a 7.0-magnitude quake. The 2011 earthquake in Japan measured 9.0. How much stronger was the earthquake in Japan than the one in Haiti?

 [IN YOUR WORDS]

47. Explain how the graph of a logarithmic function differs from that of an exponential function.

48. (a) What are common logarithms?

(b) What are natural logarithms?

(c) How are common logarithms and natural logarithms alike and how are they different?

12.4   PROPERTIES OF LOGARITHMS

In Section 12.3, we saw that logarithms were the inverses of exponentials. We also saw that we could write each logarithm as an exponential. It is not unexpected that the properties of logarithms must be related to the rules of exponents. We will examine three properties of logarithms and mention three others. These properties used to be very important in helping to calculate logarithms. Today, we use calculators and computers for these calculations, but the properties will be important later when we need to solve equations that involve logarithms or exponents.

PROPERTY 1

Let's consider two numbers, x and y, and consider $\log_b xy$. Suppose we know that $\log_b x = m$ and $\log_b y = n$, or, in exponential form, $b^m = x$ and $b^n = y$. Then,

$$xy = b^m b^n = b^{m+n}$$

Rewriting $xy = b^{m+n}$ in logarithmic form, we get $\log_b xy = m + n = \log_b x + \log_b y$. We have established the first property of logarithms.

LOGARITHMS: PROPERTY 1

If x and y are positive real numbers, $b > 0$, and $b \neq 1$, then

$$\log_b xy = \log_b x + \log_b y$$

EXAMPLE 12.18

Use the first property of logarithms to rewrite each of the following: (a) $\log_4 35$, (b) $\log 21$, (c) $\ln 18$, (d) $\log_3 5x$, (e) $\log_8 2 + \log_8 5$, (f) $\log 5 + \log 2 + \log 6$, (g) $\ln 3 + \ln 13$, and (h) $\log 5 + \log a$.

SOLUTIONS

(a) $\log_4 35 = \log_4 (5 \cdot 7) = \log_4 5 + \log_4 7$

(b) $\log 21 = \log (3 \cdot 7) = \log 3 + \log 7$

(c) $\ln 18 = \ln(2 \cdot 3 \cdot 3) = \ln 2 + \ln 3 + \ln 3$

(d) $\log_3 5x = \log_3 5 + \log_3 x$

(e) $\log_8 2 + \log_8 5 = \log_8 (2 \cdot 5) = \log_8 10$

(f) $\log 5 + \log 2 + \log 6 = \log (5 \cdot 2 \cdot 6) = \log 60$

(g) $\ln 3 + \ln 13 = \ln(3 \cdot 13) = \ln 39$

(h) $\log 5 + \log a = \log 5a$

PROPERTY 2

For the second property, let's consider $\log_b \dfrac{x}{y}$. Again, if we let $x = b^m$ and $y = b^n$, we have $\dfrac{x}{y} = \dfrac{b^m}{b^n} = b^{m-n}$. Now, $\log_b b^{m-n} = m - n = \log_b x - \log_b y$. This gives us the following property of logarithms.

LOGARITHMS: PROPERTY 2

If x and y are positive real numbers, $b > 0$, and $b \neq 1$, then

$$\log_b \frac{x}{y} = \log_b x - \log_b y$$

 CAUTION The symbol $\dfrac{\log_a x}{\log_b y}$ is not the same as $\log_b \dfrac{x}{y}$. In particular, $\dfrac{\log_b x}{\log_b y} \neq \log_b x - \log_b y$.

EXAMPLE 12.19

Use the second property of logarithms to rewrite each of the following: (a) $\log \frac{3}{5}$, (b) $\ln \frac{5}{4}$, (c) $\log_5 \dfrac{7}{x}$, (d) $\ln 8 - \ln 2$, (e) $\log_3 5 - \log_3 2$, and (f) $\log 8x^2 - \log 2x$.

SOLUTIONS

(a) $\log \frac{3}{5} = \log 3 - \log 5$

(b) $\ln \frac{5}{4} = \ln 5 - \ln 4$

(c) $\log_5 \dfrac{7}{x} = \log_5 7 - \log_5 x$

(d) $\ln 8 - \ln 2 = \ln \frac{8}{2} = \ln 4$

(e) $\log_3 5 - \log_3 2 = \log_3 \frac{5}{2}$

(f) $\log 8x^2 - \log 2x = \log \dfrac{8x^2}{2x} = \log 4x$

PROPERTY 3

Now let's consider x^p. If $m = \log_b x$, then $x = b^m$ and $x^p = (b^m)^p = b^{mp}$. So, if $x^p = b^{mp}$, then $\log_b x^p = mp$, and since $m = \log_b x$, we have the following third property of logarithms.

LOGARITHMS: PROPERTY 3

If x and y are positive real numbers, $b > 0$, and $b \neq 1$, then

$$\log_b x^p = p \log_b x.$$

EXAMPLE 12.20

Use the third property of logarithms to rewrite each of the following: (a) $\log 5^3$, (b) $\log_2 16^5$, (c) $\log 100^{3.4}$, (d) $\log \sqrt[3]{25}$, and (e) $2 \log 5 + 3 \log 4 - 4 \log 2$.

SOLUTIONS

(a) $\log 5^3 = 3 \log 5$

(b) $\log_2 16^5 = 5 \log_2 16$

(c) $\log 100^{3.4} = \log (10^2)^{3.4} = \log 10^{6.8} = 6.8 \log 10 = 6.8$

(d) $\log \sqrt[3]{25} = \log 25^{1/3} = \frac{1}{3} \log 25$

(e) $2 \log 5 + 3 \log 4 - 4 \log 2 = \log 5^2 + \log 4^3 - \log 2^4$

$$= \log 25 + \log 64 - \log 16$$

$$= \log \frac{25 \cdot 64}{16} = \log 100$$

$$= 2$$

PROPERTIES 4, 5, AND 6

In addition to these properties, there are three other properties of logarithms. These three properties are listed in the following box.

LOGARITHMS: PROPERTIES 4, 5, AND 6

If x and y are positive real numbers, $b > 0$, and $b \neq 1$, then

$\log_b 1 = 0$	Property 4
$\log_b b = 1$	Property 5
$\log_b b^n = n$	Property 6

The properties of logarithms allow us to simplify the logarithms of products, quotients, powers, and roots.

 CAUTION There is no way to simplify logarithms of sums or differences. You cannot change $\log_b (x + y)$ to $\log_b x + \log_b y$. This is very tempting, but do not make this error. Remember, $\log_b (x + y) \neq \log_b x + \log_b y$.

Logarithms were originally developed to help people compute. Slide rules were developed as a computational tool based on logarithms. At one time, every technician had, and knew how to use, a slide rule. Electronic calculators and the microcomputers have replaced slide rules and reduced the importance of logarithms as a help in computing.

However, logarithms are still an important tool in working many problems. In the remainder of this section, we will demonstrate the properties of logarithms. Values are sometimes obtained from a table of logarithms. We will not expect you to get values from tables. These exercises will prepare you for the next section where you will solve equations that involve logarithms.

EXAMPLE 12.21

If $\log 2 = 0.3010$, $\log 3 = 0.4771$, and $\log 5 = 0.6990$, determine each of the following: (a) $\log 6$, (b) $\log 81$, (c) $\log 1.5$, (d) $\log \sqrt{5}$, and (e) $\log 50$.

SOLUTIONS

(a) $\log 6 = \log (2 \cdot 3) = \log 2 + \log 3 = 0.3010 + 0.4771 = 0.7781$

(b) $\log 81 = \log 3^4 = 4 \log 3 = 4(0.4771) = 1.9084$

(c) $\log 1.5 = \log \frac{3}{2} = \log 3 - \log 2 = 0.4771 - 0.3010 = 0.1761$

(d) $\log \sqrt{5} = \log 5^{1/2} = \frac{1}{2} \log 5 = \frac{1}{2}(0.6990) = 0.3495$

(e) $\log 50 = \log(5 \cdot 10) = \log 5 + \log 10 = 0.6990 + 1 = 1.6990$

Use a calculator to check each of these answers.

EXERCISE SET 12.4

In Exercises 1–12, write each logarithm as the sum or difference of two or more logarithms.

1. $\log\frac{2}{3}$
2. $\log\frac{5}{4}$
3. $\log 14$
4. $\log 55$
5. $\log 12$
6. $\log 28$
7. $\log\frac{150}{7}$
8. $\log\dfrac{588}{5x}$
9. $\log 2x$
10. $\log\dfrac{1}{5x}$
11. $\log\dfrac{2ax}{3y}$
12. $\log\dfrac{4bc}{3xy}$

Express each of Exercises 13–24 as a single logarithm.

13. $\log 2 + \log 11$
14. $\log 3 + \log 13$
15. $\log 11 - \log 3$
16. $\log 17 - \log 23$
17. $\log 2 + \log 2 + \log 3$
18. $\log 3 + \log 3 + \log 5$
19. $\log 4 + \log x - \log y$
20. $\log 5 + \log 7 - \log 11$
21. $5 \log 2 + 3 \log 5$
22. $7 \log 3 - 2 \log 8$
23. $\log \frac{2}{3} + \log \frac{6}{7}$
24. $\log \frac{3}{24} + \log \frac{4}{7} - \log \frac{1}{3}$

If $\log 2 = 0.3010$, $\log 3 = 0.4771$, and $\log 5 = 0.6990$, determine the value of each logarithm in Exercises 25–36.

25. $\log 8$
26. $\log 9$
27. $\log 12$
28. $\log 36$
29. $\log 15$
30. $\log 30$
31. $\log\frac{75}{2}$
32. $\log\frac{45}{8}$
33. $\log 200$
34. $\log 150$
35. $\log 5\,000$
36. $\log 4\,500$

If $\log_b 2 = 0.3869$, $\log_b 3 = 0.6131$, and $\log_b 5 = 0.8982$, determine the value of each logarithm in Exercises 37–40.

37. $\log_b 16$ **38.** $\log_b 15$ **39.** $\log_b \frac{5}{3}$ **40.** $\log_b \frac{24}{5}$

Solve Exercises 41–44.

41. Use the change of base formula to determine the base for the logarithms in Exercises 37–40. (*Hint:* The answer is an integer. You may not get an integer, because the values have been rounded off to four decimal places.)

42. *Electronics* The gain or loss of power can be determined by the formula:

$$N = 20(\log I_1 - \log I_2) + 10(\log R_1 - \log R_2)$$

Simplify this formula.

43. *Acoustical engineering* Decibel gain or loss, Δ dB, can be computed by the formula:

$$\Delta dB = 20\left(\log I_2 + \frac{1}{2}\log R_2 - \log I_1 - \frac{1}{2}\log R_1 \right)$$

Simplify the right-hand side of this equation.

44. *Ecology* As a result of pollution, the population of fish in a certain river decreases according to the formula $\ln\left(\dfrac{P}{P_0}\right) = -0.0435t$, where P is the population after t years and P_0 is the original population.

(a) After how many years will there be only 50% of the original fish population remaining?

(b) After how many years will the original population be reduced by 90%?

(c) What percentage will die in the first year of pollution?

 [IN YOUR WORDS]

45. Explain Properties 4, 5, and 6 in your own words. Why do you think these three properties are especially useful?

46. (a) Explain the differences between $\log_b x - \log_b y$, $\log_b (x - y)$, and $\log_b x - y$.

(b) Graph $y_1 = \ln x - \ln 4x$, $y_2 = \ln (x - 4x)$, and $y_3 = \ln x - 4x$.

(c) Do your graphs in (b) support your explanations in (a)? If not, examine your work in both parts (a) and (b) and make any necessary changes.

12.5   EXPONENTIAL AND LOGARITHMIC EQUATIONS

We mentioned in Section 12.4 that logarithms were originally developed as an aid for computation. The wide use of electronic calculators decreased the importance of logarithms as a help for calculation. In this section, we will focus on ways we can use logarithms to help solve equations.

EXPONENTIAL EQUATIONS

We will start with an equation that is relatively easy. For one thing, we already know the answer. This will help us see that the method works.

EXPONENTIAL EQUATIONS

An **exponential equation** is any equation in which the variable is an exponent.

STEPS FOR SOLVING EXPONENTIAL EQUATIONS

In solving an exponential equation, you should:

1. Use the properties of exponents to rewrite each side of the equation in terms of exponents with the same base.
2. Use the fact that $x = b^y$ is equivalent to $\log_b x = y$ to rewrite the equation.
3. Solve the resulting equation.

EXAMPLE 12.22

Solve $3^x = 81$.

SOLUTION Since $3^4 = 81$ we know that $x = 4$. Now, let's see how we can solve this equation algebraically using techniques that we can use to solve more difficult problems.

To solve this equation, we will take the logarithm of both sides. We can use any base for the logarithm, but it is easiest to use one of the bases that is on a calculator. We will first use base 10 and then solve the same equation using base e to show that it will work either way:

$$3^x = 81$$
$$\log 3^x = \log 81$$

Since $\log 3^x = x \log 3$, we have

$$x \log 3 = \log 81$$
$$x = \frac{\log 81}{\log 3}$$
$$= 4$$

 NOTE Notice that $\log 81 \div \log 3 = \dfrac{\log 81}{\log 3} = 4$ and that $\log \frac{81}{3} = \log 81 - \log 3 \approx 1.431$. Since $4 \neq 1.431$, we see that $\log 81 \div \log 3 = \dfrac{\log 81}{\log 3} \neq \log \frac{81}{3}$.

Let's solve this same equation using natural logarithms:

$$3^x = 81$$

$\ln 3^x = \ln 81$	Take ln of both sides.
$x \ln 3 = \ln 81$	Use Property 3 of logs.
$x = \dfrac{\ln 81}{\ln 3} = 4$	Divide.

You could have used the properties of logarithms in the last step of Example 12.22 and the above comment. Thus, you could have solved Example 12.22 as

$$x = \frac{\log 81}{\log 3} = \frac{\log 3^4}{\log 3} = \frac{4 \log 3}{\log 3} = 4$$

or, using natural logarithms:

$$x = \frac{\ln 81}{\ln 3} = \frac{\ln 3^4}{\ln 3} = \frac{4 \ln 3}{\ln 3} = 4$$

EXAMPLE 12.23

Solve $5^{2x+1} = 25^{4x-1}$.

SOLUTION Notice that $25 = 5^2$, so we can write this equation as

$$5^{2x+1} = 25^{4x-1}$$
$$= \left(5^2\right)^{4x-1}$$
$$= 5^{8x-2}$$

Taking $\log_5$ of both sides produces

$$\log_5 \left(5^{2x+1}\right) = \log_5 \left(5^{8x-2}\right)$$
$$\text{or } (2x+1)\log_5 5 = (8x-2)\log_5 5$$

which simplifies to

$$2x + 1 = 8x - 2$$
$$3 = 6x$$
$$\tfrac{1}{2} = x$$

LOGARITHMIC EQUATIONS

Just as we used logarithms to solve equations that involved exponentials, we can use exponentials to solve problems that involve logarithms.

LOGARITHMIC EQUATIONS

A logarithmic equation is an equation that contains a logarithm of the variable.

STEPS FOR SOLVING LOGARITHMIC EQUATIONS

In solving a logarithmic equation, you should:

1. Use the properties of logarithms to combine all the logarithmic terms into one.
2. Use the fact that $\log_b x = y$ is equivalent to $x = b^y$ to rewrite the equation.
3. Solve the resulting equation.

EXAMPLE 12.24

Solve $\ln x = 7$.

SOLUTION The base in this equation is e, so $\ln x$ is the same as $\log_e x$ and this is equivalent to $\log_e x = 7$. Using the fact that $\log_e x = y$ is the same as $x = e^y$, we get

$$x = e^7$$
$$\approx 1{,}096.6$$

It is important that you remember to use the correct base when you solve a logarithmic equation. The next example will show you how to proceed with a more complicated situation. It also uses a different base; in this case, the base is 10.

EXAMPLE 12.25

Solve $\log(3x - 5) + 2 = \log 4x$.

SOLUTION We will first combine this into one logarithm:

$$\log(3x - 5) + 2 = \log 4x$$
$$\log(3x - 5) - \log 4x = -2$$
$$\log\left(\frac{3x - 5}{4x}\right) = -2$$

We will now use the fact that $\log_b x = y$ is equivalent to $x = b^y$. Since we are using common logarithms, the base is 10:

$$\frac{3x - 5}{4x} = 10^{-2}$$
$$\frac{3x - 5}{4x} = 0.01$$

We solve this as we would any fractional equation:

$$\frac{3x - 5}{4x} = 0.01$$
$$3x - 5 = 0.04x$$
$$2.96x = 5$$
$$x = \frac{5}{2.96} \approx 1.69$$

NOTE The approximate answer 1.69 does not check, but the exact answer $\frac{5}{2.96}$ does check.

BUSINESS AND FINANCE

An interesting equation results from the work with exponentials and we can use logarithms to solve it. If a certain amount of money P was invested at rate r compounded continuously, the investment would be worth

$$S = Pe^{rt}$$

after t years. How long does it take for the money to double?

If it doubles, then it is worth $2P$ and we have

$$2P = Pe^{rt}$$

or $$2 = e^{rt}$$

Taking the natural logarithm of both sides, we obtain

$$\ln 2 = \ln e^{rt}$$

or $$\ln 2 = rt$$

Solving for t results in

$$t = \frac{\ln 2}{r}$$

It will take $\dfrac{\ln 2}{r}$ year for the money to double. This same formula will apply

to anything that is growing or decaying at an exponential rate.

 APPLICATION BUSINESS

EXAMPLE 12.26

How long will it take for $1 000 to double at 5% compounded continuously?

SOLUTION We use the formula:

$$t = \frac{\ln 2}{r}$$

and since

$$r = 5\% = 0.05,$$
$$t = \frac{\ln 2}{0.05} \approx 13.86$$

 APPLICATION GENERAL TECHNOLOGY

EXAMPLE 12.27

What is the half-life of a radioactive material that decays at the rate of 1% per year?

SOLUTION The same formula will apply; only here $r = 1\% = 0.01$.

$$t = \frac{\ln 2}{0.01} \approx 69.31 \, \text{years}$$

EXERCISE SET 12.5

In Exercises 1–24, solve each equation for the indicated variable. You may want to use a calculator.

1. $5^x = 29$
2. $6^y = 32$
3. $4^{6x} = 119$
4. $3^{-7x} = 4$
5. $3^{y+5} = 16$
6. $2^{y-7} = 67$
7. $e^{2x-3} = 10$
8. $4^{3y+5} = 30$

9. $3^{4x+1} = 9^{3x-5}$
10. $2^{3-2x} = 8^{1+2x}$
11. $e^{3x-1} = 5e^{2x}$
12. $3^{2-5x} = 8(9^{x-1})$
13. $\log x = 2.3$
14. $\ln x = 5.4$
15. $\log (x - 5) = 17$
16. $\ln (y + 3) = 19$

17. $\ln 2x + \ln x = 9$
18. $2 \ln x = \ln 4$
19. $2 \ln 3x + \ln 2 = \ln x$
20. $2 \ln (x + 3) = \ln x + 4$
21. $\log (x - 1) = 2$
22. $\log (x - 4) = \log x - 4$
23. $2 \log (x - 4) = 2 \log x - 4$
24. $\ln x = 1 + 3 \ln x$

Solve Exercises 25–42.

25. **Finance** The amount of $5000 is placed in a savings account, where interest is compounded continuously at the rate of 6% per year. How long will it take for this amount to be doubled?

26. **Finance** How long will it take the money in Exercise 25 to double if the rate is 8% per year?

27. **Nuclear energy** A radioactive substance decays at the rate of 0.5% per year. What is the half-life of this substance?

28. **Nuclear energy** Another radioactive substance decays at the rate of 3% per year. What is its half-life?

29. **Nuclear energy** The half-life of tritium is 12.5 years. What is its annual rate of decay?

30. **Nuclear energy** The half-life of the sodium isotope $^{24}_{11}\text{Na}$ against beta decay is 15 h. What is the rate of decay?

31. **Finance** A person has some money to invest and would like to double the investment in 8.5 years. What annual rate of interest, compounded continuously, will be needed in order for this to be accomplished?

32. **Automotive technology** In a chrome-electroplating process, the mass m in grams of the chrome plating increases according to the formula $m = 200 - 2^{t/2}$, where t is the time in minutes. How long does it take to form 100 g of plating?

33. **Environmental science** In chemistry, the pH of a substance is defined by $\text{pH} = -\log [\text{H}^+]$, where $[\text{H}^+]$ is the concentration of hydrogen ions in the substance measured in moles per liter. The pH of distilled water is 7. A substance with a pH less than 7 is known as an *acid*. A substance with a pH greater than 7 is a *base*. Rain and snow have a natural concentration of $[\text{H}^+] = 2.5 \times 10^{-6}$ moles per liter. What is the natural pH of rain and snow?

34. **Environmental science** The pH of some acid rain is 5.3. What is the concentration of hydrogen ions in acid rain?

35. **Meteorology** The barometric equation,

$$H = (30T + 8{,}000) \ln \frac{P_0}{P}$$

relates the height H in meters above sea level, the air temperature T in degrees Celsius, the atmospheric pressure P_0 in centimeters of mercury at sea level, and the atmospheric pressure P in centimeters of mercury at height H. Atmospheric pressure at the summit of Mt. Whitney in California on a certain day is 43.29 cm of mercury. The average air temperature is $-5°$C and the atmospheric pressure at sea level is 76 cm of mercury. What is the height of Mt. Whitney?

36. **Environmental science** In Exercise Set 12.3, Exercise 41, we saw that the loudness in

decibels β of a noise is given by the formula $\beta = 10 \log \dfrac{I}{I_0}$, where $I_0 = 10^{-12}$ W/m^2, and I is the intensity of the noise in W/m^2. At takeoff, a certain jet plane has a noise level of 105 dB. What is the intensity I of the sound wave produced by this airplane?

37. **Electronics** The formula for the exponential decay of electric current is given by the formula $Q = Q_0 e^{-t/T}$, where $T = RC$. (See Example 12.12) If $Q_0 = 0.40$ A, $R = 500$ Ω, and $C = 100$ μF, what is t when $Q = 0.05$ A?

38. **Thermodynamics** The temperature T of an object after a period of time t is given by $T = T_0 + ce^{-kt}$, where T_0 is the temperature of the surrounding medium, and $c = T_I - T_0$, where T_I is the initial temperature of the object. A steel bar with a temperature of 1 200°C is placed in water with a temperature of 20°C. If the rate of cooling k is 8% per hour, how long will it take for the steel to reach a temperature of 40°C?

39. **Electronics** In an ac circuit, the current I at any time t, in seconds, is given by $I = I_0(1 - e^{-Rt/L})$, where I_0 is the maximum current, L is the inductance, and R the resistance. If a circuit has a 0.2-H inductor, a resistance of 4 Ω, and a maximum current of 1.5 A, at what instant does the current reach 1.4 A?

40. **Forestry** The yield, Y, in total ft^3/acre, of thinned stands of yellow poplar can be predicted by the equation:

$$\ln Y = 5.36437 - 101.16296\,S^{-1} - 22.00048\,A^{-1} + 0.97116 \ln BA$$

where S is the site index, A is the current age of the trees, and BA is the basal area. What is the basal area if the predicted yield of a 60-year-old stand growing on a site with an index of 110 is 4 720 ft^3/acre?

41. **Medical technology** An implantable pacemaker normally has a capacitive output. The amplitude of emitted pulses declines with time according to the equation:

$$E = \frac{U^2 C}{2}(1 - e^{-2t/RC})$$

where C is the capacitance of the pacemaker's output capacitor in farads (F), delivering the impulse to the heart, U is the pulse voltage in volts (V), E is the energy in joules (J), I is the pulse current in amperes (A), and t is the pulse duration in seconds (s). Solve this equation for t.

42. **Medical technology** In Exercise 41, the following formula was given for the amplitude of emitted pulses of an implantable pacemaker:

$$E = \frac{U^2 C}{2}(1 - e^{-2t/RC})$$

Solve this equation for R.

 [IN YOUR WORDS]

43. Without looking in the text, describe the steps for solving logarithmic equations.

44. Explain the difference between a logarithmic equation and an exponential equation.

Measures of Central Tendency

The Arithmetic Mean

Statistics involves the collection, organization, summarization, presentation, and interpretation of data. The branch of statistics that involves the collection, organization, summarization, and presentation of data is called **descriptive statistics**. The branch that interprets and draws conclusions from the data is called **inferential statistics**.

One of the most basic statistical concepts involves finding *measures of central tendency* of a set of numerical data. Here is a scenario in which it would be helpful to find numerical values that locate, in some sense, the *center* of a set of data. Elle is a senior at a university. In a few months she plans to graduate and start a career as a landscape architect. A survey of five landscape architects from last year's senior class shows that they received job offers with the following yearly salaries.

$43,750 $39,500 $38,000 $41,250 $44,000

Before Elle interviews for a job, she wishes to determine an *average* of these 5 salaries. This average should be a "central" number around which the salaries cluster. We will consider three types of averages, known as the *arithmetic mean*, the *median*, and the *mode*. Each of these averages is a **measure of central tendency** for numerical data.

The *arithmetic mean* is the most commonly used measure of central tendency. The arithmetic mean of a set of numbers is often referred to as simply the *mean*. To find the mean for a set of data, find the sum of the data values and divide by the number of data values. For instance, to find the mean of the 5 salaries listed above, Elle would divide the sum of the salaries by 5.

$$\text{Mean} = \frac{\$43,750 + \$39,500 + \$38,000 + \$41,250 + \$44,000}{5}$$

$$= \frac{\$206,500}{5} = \$41,300$$

The mean suggests that Elle can reasonably expect a job offer at a salary of about $41,300.

In statistics it is often necessary to find the sum of a set of numbers. The traditional symbol used to indicate a summation is the Greek letter *sigma*, Σ. Thus the notation Σx, called **summation notation**, denotes the sum of all the numbers in a given set. The use of summation notation enables us to define the mean as follows.

▼ **Mean**

The **mean** of n numbers is the sum of the numbers divided by n.

$$mean = \frac{\Sigma x}{n}$$

Statisticians often collect data from small portions of a large group in order to determine information about the group. In such situations the entire group under consideration is known as the **population**, and any subset of the population is called a **sample**. It is traditional to denote the mean of a *sample* by $\bar{x}$ (which is read as "*x* bar") and to denote the mean of a *population* by the Greek letter μ (lowercase mu).

▼ **example** **1** Find a Mean

Six friends in a biology class of 20 students received test grades of

92,   84,   65,   76,   88,   and   90

Find the mean of these test scores.

Solution

The 6 friends are a sample of the population of 20 students. Use $\bar{x}$ to represent the mean.

$$\bar{x} = \frac{\Sigma x}{n} = \frac{92 + 84 + 65 + 76 + 88 + 90}{6} = \frac{495}{6} = 82.5$$

The mean of these test scores is 82.5.

▼ **check your progress** **1** A patient had 4 separate blood tests to measure the patient's total blood cholesterol levels. The test results were

245,   235,   220,   and   210

Find the mean of the blood cholesterol levels.

Solution *See page S47.*

The Median

Another type of average is the *median*. Essentially, the median is the *middle number* or the *mean of the two middle numbers* in a list of numbers that have been arranged in numerical order from smallest to largest or from largest to smallest. Any list of numbers that is arranged in numerical order from smallest to largest or from largest to smallest is a **ranked list**.

POINT OF INTEREST

The average price of the homes in a neighborhood is often stated in terms of the median price of the homes that have been sold over a given time period. The median price, rather than the mean, is used because it is easy to calculate and is less sensitive to extreme prices. The median price of a home can vary dramatically, even for areas that are relatively close. For instance, in September 2010, the median sales price of a home in one ZIP code in Honolulu, Hawaii, was $1,203,000. In an adjacent ZIP code, the median sales price was $379,000. (*Source:* DQNews.com January 23, 2011)

> ▼ **Median**
>
> The median of a ranked list of n numbers is:
>
> - the middle number if n is odd.
> - the mean of the two middle numbers if n is even.

▼ **example** **2** Find a Median

Find the median for the data in the following lists.

a. 4, 8, 1, 14, 9, 21, 12   **b.** 46, 23, 92, 89, 77, 108

Solution

a. The list 4, 8, 1, 14, 9, 21, 12 contains 7 numbers. The median of a list with an odd number of numbers is found by ranking the numbers and finding the middle number. Ranking the numbers from smallest to largest gives

1, 4, 8, 9, 12, 14, 21

The middle number is 9. Thus 9 is the median.

b. The list 46, 23, 92, 89, 77, 108 contains 6 numbers. The median of a list of data with an even number of numbers is found by ranking the numbers and computing the mean of the two middle numbers. Ranking the numbers from smallest to largest gives

   23, 46, 77, 89, 92, 108

The two middle numbers are 77 and 89. The mean of 77 and 89 is 83. Thus 83 is the median of the data.

▼ **check your progress** **2**   Find the median for the data in the following lists.

a. 14, 27, 3, 82, 64, 34, 8, 51   **b.** 21.3, 37.4, 11.6, 82.5, 17.2

Solution   *See page S47.*

---

question   The median of the ranked list 3, 4, 7, 11, 17, 29, 37 is 11. If the maximum value 37 is increased to 55, what effect will this have on the median?

The Mode

A third type of average is the *mode*.

▼ **Mode**

The **mode** of a list of numbers is the number that occurs most frequently.

Some lists of numbers do not have a mode. For instance, in the list 1, 6, 8, 10, 32, 15, 49, each number occurs exactly once. Because no number occurs more often than the other numbers, there is no mode.

A list of numerical data can have more than one mode. For instance, in the list 4, 2, 6, 2, 7, 9, 2, 4, 9, 8, 9, 7, the number 2 occurs three times and the number 9 occurs three times. Each of the other numbers occurs less than three times. Thus 2 and 9 are both modes for the data.

▼ **example** **3**   Find a Mode

Find the mode for the data in the following lists.

a. 18, 15, 21, 16, 15, 14, 15, 21   **b.** 2, 5, 8, 9, 11, 4, 7, 23

Solution

a. In the list 18, 15, 21, 16, 15, 14, 15, 21, the number 15 occurs more often than the other numbers. Thus 15 is the mode.

b. Each number in the list 2, 5, 8, 9, 11, 4, 7, 23 occurs only once. Because no number occurs more often than the others, there is no mode.

▼ **check your progress** **3**   Find the mode for the data in the following lists.

a. 3, 3, 3, 3, 3, 4, 4, 5, 5, 5, 8   **b.** 12, 34, 12, 71, 48, 93, 71

Solution   *See page S47.*

---

answer   The median will remain the same because 11 will still be the middle number in the ranked list.

PRNewsFoto/Procter & Gamble; MLB

For professional sports teams, the salaries of a few very highly paid players can lead to large differences between the mean and the median salary. In 2008, when the mean salary of a Major League Baseball (MLB) player first hit $3 million, the median MLB player salary was about $1 million. In 2010, most MLB teams had mean salaries that were two, three, or four times the median salary. (*Source:* usatoday.com, mlb.com)

The mean, the median, and the mode are all averages; however, they are generally not equal. The mean of a set of data is the most sensitive of the averages. A change in any of the numbers changes the mean, and the mean can be changed drastically by changing an extreme value.

In contrast, the median and the mode of a set of data are usually not changed by changing an extreme value.

When a data set has one or more extreme values that are very different from the majority of data values, the mean will not necessarily be a good indicator of an average value. In the following example, we compare the mean, the median, and the mode for the salaries of 5 employees of a small company.

Salaries: $370,000 $60,000 $36,000 $20,000 $20,000

The sum of the 5 salaries is $506,000. Hence the mean is

$$\frac{506,000}{5} = 101,200$$

The median is the middle number, $36,000. Because the $20,000 salary occurs the most, the mode is $20,000. The data contain one extreme value that is much larger than the other values. This extreme value makes the mean considerably larger than the median. Most of the employees of this company would probably agree that the median of $36,000 better represents the average of the salaries than does either the mean or the mode.

MATHMATTERS   Average Rate for a Round Trip

Suppose you average 60 mph on a one-way trip of 60 mi. On the return trip you average 30 mph. You might be tempted to think that the average of 60 mph and 30 mph, which is 45 mph, is the average rate for the entire trip. However, this is not the case. Because you were traveling more slowly on the return trip, the return trip took longer than the time spent going to your destination. More time was spent traveling at the slower speed. Thus the average rate for the round trip is less than the average (mean) of 60 mph and 30 mph.

To find the actual average rate for the round trip, use the formula

$$\text{Average rate} = \frac{\text{total distance}}{\text{total time}}$$

The total round-trip distance is 120 mi. The time spent going to your destination was 1 h and the time spent on the return trip was 2 h. The total time for the round trip was 3 h. Thus

$$\text{Average rate} = \frac{\text{total distance}}{\text{total time}} = \frac{120}{3} = 40 \text{ mph}$$

The Weighted Mean

A value called the *weighted mean* is often used when some data values are more important than others. For instance, many professors determine a student's course grade from the student's tests and the final examination. Consider the situation in which a professor counts the final examination score as 2 test scores. To find the weighted mean of the student's scores, the professor first assigns a weight to each score. In this case the professor could assign each of the test scores a weight of 1 and the final exam score a weight of 2. A student with test scores of 65, 70, and 75 and a final examination score of 90 has a weighted mean of

$$\frac{(65 \times 1) + (70 \times 1) + (75 \times 1) + (90 \times 2)}{5} = \frac{390}{5} = 78$$

Note that the numerator of the weighted mean on the previous page is the sum of the products of each test score and its corresponding weight. The number 5 in the denominator is the sum of all the weights (1 + 1 + 1 + 2 = 5). The procedure on the previous page can be generalized as follows.

▼ **The Weighted Mean**

The **weighted mean** of the n numbers $x_1, x_2, x_3, \ldots, x_n$ with the respective assigned weights $w_1, w_2, w_3, \ldots, w_n$ is

$$\text{Weighted mean} = \frac{\Sigma(x \cdot w)}{\Sigma w}$$

where $\Sigma(x \cdot w)$ is the sum of the products formed by multiplying each number by its assigned weight, and Σw is the sum of all the weights.

Many colleges use the 4-point grading system:

$$A = 4, B = 3, C = 2, D = 1, F = 0$$

A student's grade point average (GPA) is calculated as a weighted mean, where the student's grade in each course is given a weight equal to the number of units (or credits) that course is worth. Use this 4-point grading system for Example 4 and Check Your Progress 4.

▼ **example 4** Find a Weighted Mean

Table 13.1 shows Dillon's fall semester course grades. Use the weighted mean formula to find Dillon's GPA for the fall semester.

Solution
The B is worth 3 points, with a weight of 4; the A is worth 4 points with a weight of 3; the D is worth 1 point, with a weight of 3; and the C is worth 2 points, with a weight of 4. The sum of all the weights is 4 + 3 + 3 + 4, or 14.

$$\text{Weighted mean} = \frac{(3 \times 4) + (4 \times 3) + (1 \times 3) + (2 \times 4)}{14}$$

$$= \frac{35}{14} = 2.5$$

Dillon's GPA for the fall semester is 2.5.

▼ **check your progress 4** Table 13.2 shows Janet's spring semester course grades. Use the weighted mean formula to find the Janet's GPA for the spring semester. Round to the nearest hundredth.

Solution *See page S48.*

Data that has not been organized or manipulated in any manner is called **raw data**. A large collection of raw data may not provide much pertinent information that can be readily observed. A **frequency distribution**, which is a table that lists observed events and the frequency of occurrence of each observed event, is often used to organize raw data. For instance, consider the following table, which lists the number of laptop computers owned by families in each of 40 homes in a subdivision.

TABLE 13.1

Dillon's Grades, Fall Semester

Course	Course grade	Course units
English	B	4
History	A	3
Chemistry	D	3
Algebra	C	4

TABLE 13.2

Janet's Grades, Fall Semester

Course	Course grade	Course units
Biology	A	4
Statistics	B	3
Business	C	3
Psychology	F	2
CAD	B	2

TABLE 13.3

Numbers of Laptop Computers per Household

2	0	3	1	2	1	0	4
2	1	1	7	2	0	1	1
0	2	2	1	3	2	2	1
1	4	2	5	2	3	1	2
2	1	2	1	5	0	2	5

The frequency distribution in Table 13.4 below was constructed using the data from Table 13.3. The first column of the frequency distribution consists of the numbers 0, 1, 2, 3, 4, 5, 6, and 7. The corresponding frequency of occurrence, f, of each of the numbers in the first column is listed in the second column.

TABLE 13.4

A Frequency Distribution for Table 13.3

Observed event Number of laptop computers, x	*Frequency* Number of households, f, with laptop computers
0	5
1	12
2	14
3	3
4	2
5	3
6	0
7	1
	40 total

This row indicates that there are 14 households with 2 laptop computers.

The formula for a weighted mean can be used to find the mean of the data in a frequency distribution. The only change is that the weights $w_1, w_2, w_3, \ldots, w_n$ are replaced with the frequencies $f_1, f_2, f_3, \ldots, f_n$. This procedure is illustrated in the next example.

▼ **example 5**   Find the Mean of Data Displayed in a Frequency Distribution

Find the mean of the data in Table 13.4.

Solution

The numbers in the right-hand column of Table 13.4 are the frequencies f for the numbers in the first column. The sum of all the frequencies is 40.

$$\text{Mean} = \frac{\Sigma(x \cdot f)}{\Sigma f}$$

$$= \frac{(0 \cdot 5) + (1 \cdot 12) + (2 \cdot 14) + (3 \cdot 3) + (4 \cdot 2) + (5 \cdot 3) + (6 \cdot 0) + (7 \cdot 1)}{40}$$

$$= \frac{79}{40}$$

$$= 1.975$$

The mean number of laptop computers per household for the homes in the subdivision is 1.975.

▼ check your progress 5   A housing division consists of 45 homes. The following frequency distribution shows the number of homes in the subdivision that are two-bedroom homes, the number that are three-bedroom homes, the number that are four-bedroom homes, and the number that are five-bedroom homes. Find the mean number of bedrooms for the 45 homes.

Observed event Number of bedrooms, x	*Frequency* Number of homes with x bedrooms
2	5
3	25
4	10
5	5
	45 total

Solution   *See page S48.*

EXCURSION

Linear Interpolation and Animation

Linear interpolation is a method used to find a particular number between two given numbers. For instance, if a table lists the two entries 0.3156 and 0.8248, then the value exactly halfway between the numbers is the mean of the numbers, which is 0.5702. To find the number that is 0.2 of the way from 0.3156 to 0.8248, compute 0.2 times the difference between the numbers and, because the first number is smaller than the second number, add this result to the smaller number.

$0.8248 - 0.3156 = 0.5092$ ◄──── Difference between the table entries

$0.2 \cdot (0.5902) = 0.10184$ ◄──── 0.2 of the above difference

$0.3156 + 0.10184 = 0.41744$ ◄──── Interpolated result, which is 0.2 of the way between the two table entries

The above linear interpolation process can be used to find an intermediate number that is any specified fraction of the difference between two given numbers.

EXCURSION EXERCISES

1. Use linear interpolation to find the number that is 0.7 of the way from 1.856 to 1.972.

2. Use linear interpolation to find the number that is 0.3 of the way from 0.8765 to 0.8652. Note that because 0.8765 is larger than 0.8652, three-tenths of the difference between 0.8765 and 0.8652 must be subtracted from 0.8765 to find the desired number.

3. A calculator shows that $\sqrt{2} \approx 1.414$ and $\sqrt{3} \approx 1.723$. Use linear interpolation to estimate $\sqrt{2.4}$. *Hint:* Find the number that is 0.4 of the difference between 1.414 and 1.732 and add this number to the smaller number, 1.414. Round your estimate to the nearest thousandth.

4. We know that $2^1 = 2$ and $2^2 = 4$. Use linear interpolation to estimate $2^{1.2}$.

5. At the present time, a football player weighs 325 lb. There are 90 days until the player needs to report to spring training at a weight of 290 lb. The player wants to lose weight at a constant rate. That is, the player wants to lose the same amount of weight each day of the 90 days. What weight, to the nearest tenth of a pound, should the player attain in 25 days?

Graphic artists use computer drawing programs, such as Adobe Illustrator, to draw the intermediate frames of an animation. For instance, in the following figure, the artist drew the small green apple on the left and the large ripe apple on the right. The drawing program used interpolation procedures to draw the five apples between the two apples drawn by the artist.

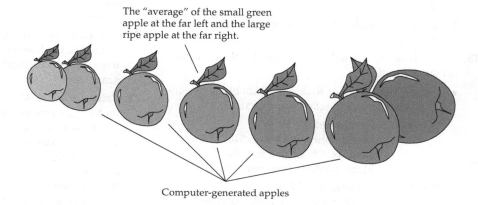

The "average" of the small green apple at the far left and the large ripe apple at the far right.

Computer-generated apples

EXERCISE SET 13.1

■ In Exercises 1 to 10, find the mean, the median, and the mode(s), if any, for the given data. Round noninteger means to the nearest tenth.

1. 2, 7, 5, 7, 14

2. 8, 3, 3, 17, 9, 22, 19

3. 11, 8, 2, 5, 17, 39, 52, 42

4. 101, 88, 74, 60, 12, 94, 74, 85

5. 2.1, 4.6, 8.2, 3.4, 5.6, 8.0, 9.4, 12.2, 56.1, 78.2

6. 5, 5, 5, 5, 5, 5, 5, 5, 5, 5, 5, 5, 5

7. 255, 178, 192, 145, 202, 188, 178, 201

8. 118, 105, 110, 118, 134, 155, 166, 166, 118

9. −12, −8, −5, −5, −3, 0, 4, 9, 21

10. −8.5, −2.2, 4.1, 4.1, 6.4, 8.3, 9.7

11. a. If exactly one number in a set of data is changed, will this necessarily change the mean of the set? Explain.

b. If exactly one number in a set of data is changed, will this necessarily change the median of the set? Explain.

12. If a set of data has a mode, then *must* the mode be one of the numbers in the set? Explain.

13. Academy Awards The following table displays the ages of female actors when they starred in their Oscar-winning Best Actor performances.

Ages of Best Female Actor Award Recipients, Academy Awards, 1975–2010

42	41	36	32	41	33	31	74	33	49	38	61
21	41	26	80	42	29	33	36	45	49	39	34
26	25	33	35	35	28	30	29	61	32	33	45

Find the mean and the median for the data in the table.

14.  **Academy Awards** The following table displays the ages of male actors when they starred in their Oscar-winning Best Actor performances.

Ages of Best Male Actor Award Recipients, Academy Awards, 1975–2010

56	38	60	30	40	42	37	76	39	53	45	36
62	43	51	32	42	54	52	37	38	32	45	60
46	40	36	47	29	43	37	38	45	50	48	60

a. Find the mean and the median for the data in the table.

b. How do the results of part a compare with the results of Exercise 13?

15. Dental Schools Dental schools provide urban statistics to their students.

a. Use the following data to decide which of the two cities you would pick to set up your practice in.

Cloverdale: Population, 18,250
Median price of a home, $167,000
Dentists, 12; median age, 49
Mean number of patients, 1294.5

Barnbridge: Population, 27,840
Median price of a home, $204,400
Dentists, 17.5; median age, 53
Mean number of patients, 1148.7

b. Explain how you made your decision.

16. Expense Reports A salesperson records the following daily expenditures during a 10-day trip.

$185.34 $234.55 $211.86 $147.65 $205.60
$216.74 $1345.75 $184.16 $320.45 $88.12

In your opinion, does the mean or the median of the expenditures best represent the salesperson's average daily expenditure? Explain your reasoning.

Grade Point Average In some 4.0 grading systems, a student's grade point average (GPA) is calculated by assigning letter grades the following numerical values.

A	= 4.00	B−	= 2.67	D+	= 1.33
A−	= 3.67	C+	= 2.33	D	= 1.00
B+	= 3.33	C	= 2.00	D−	= 0.67
B	= 3.00	C−	= 1.67	F	= 0.00

■ In Exercises 17 to 20, use this grading system to find each student's GPA. Round to the nearest hundredth.

17. Jerry's Grades, Fall Semester

Course	Course grade	Course units
English	A	3
Anthropology	A	3
Chemistry	B	4
French	C+	3
Theatre	B−	2

18. Rhonda's Grades, Spring Semester

Course	Course grade	Course units
English	C	3
History	D+	3
Computer science	B+	2
Calculus	B−	3
Photography	A−	1

19. Tessa's cumulative GPA for 3 semesters was 3.24 for 46 course units. Her fourth semester GPA was 3.86 for 12 course units. What is Tessa's cumulative GPA for all 4 semesters?

20. Richard's cumulative GPA for 3 semesters was 2.0 for 42 credits. His fourth semester GPA was 4.0 for 14 course units. What is Richard's cumulative GPA for all 4 semesters?

21. Calculate a Course Grade A professor grades students on 5 tests, a project, and a final examination. Each test counts as 10% of the course grade. The project counts as 20% of the course grade. The final examination counts as 30% of the course grade. Samantha has test scores of 70, 65, 82, 94, and 85. Samantha's project score is 92. Her final examination score is 80. Use the weighted mean formula to find Samantha's average for the course. *Hint:* The sum of all the weights is 100% = 1.

22. Calculate a Course Grade A professor grades students on 4 tests, a term paper, and a final examination. Each test counts as 15% of the course grade. The term paper counts as 20% of the course grade. The final examination counts as 20% of the course grade. Alan has test scores of 80, 78, 92, and 84. Alan received an 84 on his term paper. His final examination score was 88. Use the weighted mean formula to find Alan's average for the course. *Hint:* The sum of all the weights is 100% = 1.

 **Baseball** In baseball, a batter's *slugging average*, which measures the batter's power as a hitter, is a type of weighted mean. If s, d, t, and h represent the numbers of singles, doubles, triples, and home runs a player achieves in n times at bat, then the player's slugging average is $\dfrac{s + 2d + 3t + 4h}{n}$.

Mark Rucker/Transcendental Graphics, Getty Images

■ In Exercises 23 to 26, find the player's slugging average for the season or seasons described. Slugging averages are given to the nearest thousandth.

23. Babe Ruth, in his first season with the New York Yankees (1920), was at bat 458 times, resulting in 73 singles, 36 doubles, 9 triples, and 54 home runs. In this season, Babe Ruth achieved his highest slugging average, which stood as a major league record until 2001.

24. Babe Ruth, over his 22-year long career, was at bat 8399 times, resulting in 1517 singles, 506 doubles, 136 triples, and 714 home runs.

25. Albert Pujols, in his 2006 season with the St. Louis Cardinals, was at bat 535 times, resulting in 94 singles, 33 doubles, 1 triple, and 49 home runs.

26. Albert Pujols, during 10 years with the St. Louis Cardinals (2001-2010), was at bat 5733 times, resulting in 1051 singles, 426 doubles, 15 triples, and 408 home runs.

■ In Exercises 27 to 30, find the mean, the median, and all modes for the data in the given frequency distribution.

27. Points Scored by Lynn

Points scored in a basketball game	Frequency
2	6
4	5
5	6
9	3
10	1
14	2
19	1

28. Mystic Pizza Company

Hourly pay rates for employees	Frequency
$8.00	14
$11.50	9
$14.00	8
$16.00	5
$19.00	2
$22.50	1
$35.00	1

29. Quiz Scores

Scores on a biology quiz	Frequency
2	1
4	2
6	7
7	12
8	10
9	4
10	3

30. Ages of Science Fair Contestants

Age	Frequency
7	3
8	4
9	6
10	15
11	11
12	7
13	1

Meteorology In Exercises 31 to 34, use the following information about another measure of central tendency for a set of data, called the *midrange*. The **midrange** is defined as the value that is halfway between the minimum data value and the maximum data value. That is,

$$\text{Midrange} = \frac{\text{minimum value} + \text{maximum value}}{2}$$

The midrange is often stated as the *average* of a set of data in situations in which there are a large amount of data and the data are constantly changing. Many weather reports state the average daily temperature of a city as the midrange of the temperatures achieved during that day. For instance, if the minimum daily temperature of a city was 60° and the maximum daily temperature was 90°, then the midrange of the temperatures is $\frac{60° + 90°}{2} = 75°$.

31. Find the midrange of the following daily temperatures, which were recorded at 3-hour intervals.

52°, 65°, 71°, 74°, 76°, 75°, 68°, 57°, 54°

32. Find the midrange of the following daily temperatures, which were recorded at three-hour intervals.

−6°, 4°, 14°, 21°, 25°, 26°, 18°, 12°, 2°

33. During a 24-hour period on January 23–24, 1916, the temperature in Browning, Montana, decreased from a high of 44°F to a low of −56°F. Find the midrange of the temperatures during this 24-hour period. (*Source:* National Oceanic and Atmospheric Administration)

34. During a 2-minute period on January 22, 1943, the temperature in Spearfish, South Dakota, increased from a low of −4°F to a high of 45°F. Find the midrange of the temperatures during this 2-minute period. (*Source:* National Oceanic and Atmospheric Administration)

35. Test Scores After 6 biology tests, Ruben has a mean score of 78. What score does Ruben need on the next test to raise his average (mean) to 80?

36. Test Scores After 4 algebra tests, Alisa has a mean score of 82. One more 100-point test is to be given in this class. All of the test scores are of equal importance. Is it possible for Alisa to raise her average (mean) to 90? Explain.

37. Baseball For the first half of a baseball season, a player had 92 hits out of 274 times at bat. The player's batting average was $\frac{92}{274} \approx 0.336$. During the second half of the season, the player had 60 hits out of 282 times at bat. The player's batting average was $\frac{60}{282} \approx 0.213$.

    a. What is the average (mean) of 0.336 and 0.213?

    b. What is the player's batting average for the complete season?

    c. Does the answer in part a equal the average in part b?

38. Commuting Times Mark averaged 60 mph during the 30-mile trip to college. Because of heavy traffic he was able to average only 40 mph during the return trip. What was Mark's average speed for the round trip?

EXTENSIONS

Critical Thinking

39. The mean of 12 numbers is 48. Removing one of the numbers causes the mean to decrease to 45. What number was removed?

40. Find eight numbers such that the mean, the median, and the mode of the numbers are all 45, and no more than two of the numbers are the same.

41. The average rate for a trip is given by

$$\text{Average rate} = \frac{\text{total distance}}{\text{total time}}$$

If a person travels to a destination at an average rate of r_1 miles per hour and returns over the same route to the original starting point at an average rate of r_2 miles per hour, show that the average rate for the round trip is

$$r = \frac{2r_1 r_2}{r_1 + r_2}$$

42. Pick six numbers and compute the mean and the median of the numbers.

    a. Now add 12 to each of your original numbers and compute the mean and the median for this new set of numbers.

    b. How does the mean of the new set of data compare with the mean of the original set of data?

    c. How does the median of the new set of data compare with the median of the original set of data?

Cooperative Learning

Consider the data in the following table.

Summary of Yards Gained in Two Football Games

	Game 1	Game 2	Combined statistics for both games
Warren	12 yds on 4 carries Average: 3 yds/carry	78 yds on 16 carries Average: 4.875 yds/carry	90 yds on 20 carries Average: 4.5 yds/carry
Barry	120 yds on 30 carries Average: 4 yds/carry	100 yds on 20 carries Average: 5 yds/carry	220 yds on 50 carries Average: 4.4 yds/carry

- In the first game, Barry has the best average.
- In the second game, Barry has the best average.
- If the statistics for the games are combined, Warren has the best average.

You may be surprised by the above results. After all, how can it be that Barry has the best average in game 1 and game 2, but he does not have the best average for both games? In statistics, an example such as this is known as a **Simpson's paradox**.

■ Form groups of three or four students to work Exercises 43 to 45.

43. Consider the following data.

Batting Statistics for Two Baseball Players

	First month	**Second month**	**Both months**
Dawn	12 hits; 5 at-bats Average: ?	19 hits; 49 at-bats Average: ?	? hits; ? at-bats Average: ?
Joanne	29 hits; 73 at-bats Average: ?	31 hits; 80 at-bats Average: ?	? hits; ? at-bats Average: ?

Is this an example of a Simpson's paradox? Explain.

44. Consider the following data.

Test Scores for Two Students

	English	**History**	**English and history combined**
Wendy	84, 65, 72, 91, 99, 84 Average: ?	66, 84, 75, 77, 94, 96, 81 Average: ?	Average: ?
Sarah	90, 74 Average: ?	68, 78, 98, 76, 68, 92, 88, 86 Average: ?	Average: ?

Is this an example of a Simpson's paradox? Explain.

Explorations

45. Create your own example of a Simpson's paradox.

section 13.2 Measures of Dispersion

The Range

TABLE 13.5
Soda Dispensed (ounces)

Machine 1	**Machine 2**
9.52	8.01
6.41	7.99
10.07	7.95
5.85	8.03
8.15	8.02
$\bar{x} = 8.0$	$\bar{x} = 8.0$

In the preceding section we introduced three types of average values for a data set—the mean, the median, and the mode. Some characteristics of a set of data may not be evident from an examination of averages. For instance, consider a soft-drink dispensing machine that should dispense 8 oz of your selection into a cup. Table 13.5 shows data for two of these machines.

The mean data value for each machine is 8 oz. However, look at the variation in data values for Machine 1. The quantity of soda dispensed is very inconsistent—in some cases the soda overflows the cup, and in other cases too little soda is dispensed. The machine obviously needs adjustment. Machine 2, on the other hand, is working just fine. The quantity dispensed is very consistent, with little variation

This example shows that average values do not reflect the *spread* or *dispersion* of data. To measure the spread or dispersion of data, we must introduce statistical values known as the *range* and the *standard deviation*.

▼ **Range**

The **range** of a set of data values is the difference between the greatest data value and the least data value.

▼ example 1   Find a Range

Find the range of the numbers of ounces dispensed by Machine 1 in Table 13.5.

Solution

The greatest number of ounces dispensed is 10.07 and the least is 5.85. The range of the numbers of ounces dispensed is $10.07 - 5.85 = 4.22$ oz.

▼ check your progress 1   Find the range of the numbers of ounces dispensed by Machine 2 in Table 13.5.

Solution   *See page S48.*

MATH MATTERS   A World Record Range

Robert Wadlow

The tallest man for whom there is irrefutable evidence was Robert Pershing Wadlow. On June 27, 1940, Wadlow was 8 ft 11.1 in. tall. The shortest man for whom there is reliable evidence is Gul Mohammad. On July 19, 1990, he was 22.5 in. tall. (*Source:* Guinness World Records) The range of the heights of these men is $107.1 - 22.5 = 84.6$ in.

The Standard Deviation

TABLE 13.6
Machine 2:
Deviations from the Mean

x	$x - \bar{x}$
8.01	$8.01 - 8 = 0.01$
7.99	$7.99 - 8 = -0.01$
7.95	$7.95 - 8 = -0.05$
8.03	$8.03 - 8 = 0.03$
8.02	$8.02 - 8 = 0.02$
Sum of deviations $= 0$	

The range of a set of data is easy to compute, but it can be deceiving. The range is a measure that depends only on the two most extreme values, and as such it is very sensitive. A measure of dispersion that is less sensitive to extreme values is the *standard deviation*. The standard deviation of a set of numerical data makes use of the individual amount that each data value deviates from the mean. These deviations, represented by $(x - \bar{x})$, are positive when the data value x is greater than the mean $\bar{x}$ and are negative when x is less than the mean $\bar{x}$. The sum of all the deviations $(x - \bar{x})$ is 0 for all sets of data. This is shown in Table 13.6 for the Machine 2 data of Table 13.5.

Because the sum of all the deviations of the data values from the mean is *always* 0, we cannot use the sum of the deviations as a measure of dispersion for a set of data. Instead, the standard deviation uses the sum of the *squares* of the deviations.

You may question why a denominator of $n - 1$ is used instead of n when we compute a sample standard deviation. The reason is that a sample standard deviation is often used to estimate the population standard deviation, and it can be shown mathematically that the use of $n - 1$ tends to yield better estimates.

▼ Standard Deviations for Populations and Samples

If $x_1, x_2, x_3, \ldots, x_n$ is a *population* of n numbers with a mean of μ, then the **standard deviation** of the population is $\sigma = \sqrt{\dfrac{\Sigma(x - \mu)^2}{n}}$ (1).

If $x_1, x_2, x_3, \ldots, x_n$ is a *sample* of n numbers with a mean of $\bar{x}$, then the **standard deviation** of the sample is $s = \sqrt{\dfrac{\Sigma(x - \bar{x})^2}{n - 1}}$ (2).

Most statistical applications involve a sample rather than a population, which is the complete set of data values. Sample standard deviations are designated by the lowercase letter s. In those cases in which we *do* work with a population, we designate the standard deviation of the population by σ, which is the lowercase Greek letter sigma. To calculate the standard deviation of n numbers, it is helpful to use the following procedure.

▼ Procedure for Computing a Standard Deviation

1. Determine the mean of the n numbers.

2. For each number, calculate the deviation (difference) between the number and the mean of the numbers.

3. Calculate the square of each of the deviations and find the sum of these squared deviations.

4. If the data is a *population*, then divide the sum by n. If the data is a *sample*, then divide the sum by $n - 1$.

5. Find the square root of the quotient in Step 4.

▼ example 2   **Find the Standard Deviation**

The following numbers were obtained by sampling a population.

 2, 4, 7, 12, 15

Find the standard deviation of the sample.

Solution

Step 1: The mean of the numbers is

$$\bar{x} = \frac{2 + 4 + 7 + 12 + 15}{5} = \frac{40}{5} = 8$$

Step 2: For each number, calculate the deviation between the number and the mean.

Because the sum of the deviations is always 0, you can use this as a means to check your arithmetic. That is, if your deviations from the mean do not have a sum of 0, then you know you have made an error.

x	$x - \bar{x}$
2	$2 - 8 = -6$
4	$4 - 8 = -4$
7	$7 - 8 = -1$
12	$12 - 8 = 4$
15	$15 - 8 = 7$

Step 3: Calculate the square of each of the deviations in Step 2, and find the sum of these squared deviations.

x	$x - \bar{x}$	$(x - \bar{x})^2$
2	$2 - 8 = -6$	$(-6)^2 = 36$
4	$4 - 8 = -4$	$(-4)^2 = 16$
7	$7 - 8 = -1$	$(-1)^2 = 1$
12	$12 - 8 = 4$	$4^2 = 16$
15	$15 - 8 = 7$	$7^2 = 49$
		118

Sum of the squared deviations

Step 4: Because we have a sample of $n = 5$ values, divide the sum 118 by $n - 1$, which is 4.

$$\frac{118}{4} = 29.5$$

Step 5: The standard deviation of the sample is $s = \sqrt{29.5}$. To the nearest hundredth, the standard deviation is $s = 5.43$.

▼ **check your progress** **2** A student has the following quiz scores: 5, 8, 16, 17, 18, 20. Find the standard deviation for this population of quiz scores.

Solution *See page S48.*

In the next example we use standard deviations to determine which company produces batteries that are most consistent with regard to their life expectancy.

▼ **example** **3** Use Standard Deviations

A consumer group has tested a sample of 8 size-D batteries from each of 3 companies. The results of the tests are shown in the following table. According to these tests, which company produces batteries for which the values representing hours of constant use have the smallest standard deviation?

Company	Hours of constant use per battery
EverSoBright	6.2, 6.4, 7.1, 5.9, 8.3, 5.3, 7.5, 9.3
Dependable	6.8, 6.2, 7.2, 5.9, 7.0, 7.4, 7.3, 8.2
Beacon	6.1, 6.6, 7.3, 5.7, 7.1, 7.6, 7.1, 8.5

Solution
The mean for each sample of batteries is 7 h.
The batteries from EverSoBright have a standard deviation of

$$s_1 = \sqrt{\frac{(6.2 - 7)^2 + (6.4 - 7)^2 + \cdots + (9.3 - 7)^2}{7}}$$

$$= \sqrt{\frac{12.34}{7}} \approx 1.328 \text{ h}$$

The batteries from Dependable have a standard deviation of

$$s_2 = \sqrt{\frac{(6.8 - 7)^2 + (6.2 - 7)^2 + \cdots + (8.2 - 7)^2}{7}}$$

$$= \sqrt{\frac{3.62}{7}} \approx 0.719 \text{ h}$$

The batteries from Beacon have a standard deviation of

$$s_3 = \sqrt{\frac{(6.1 - 7)^2 + (6.6 - 7)^2 + \cdots + (8.5 - 7)^2}{7}}$$

$$= \sqrt{\frac{5.38}{7}} \approx 0.877 \text{ h}$$

The batteries from Dependable have the smallest standard deviation. According to these results, the Dependable company produces the most consistent batteries with regard to life expectancy under constant use.

▼ check your progress 3 A consumer testing agency has tested the strengths of 3 brands of $\frac{1}{8}$-inch rope. The results of the tests are shown in the following table. According to the sample test results, which company produces $\frac{1}{8}$-inch rope for which the breaking point has the smallest standard deviation?

Company	Breaking point of $\frac{1}{8}$-inch rope in pounds
Trustworthy	122, 141, 151, 114, 108, 149, 125
Brand X	128, 127, 148, 164, 97, 109, 137
NeverSnap	112, 121, 138, 131, 134, 139, 135

Solution *See page S48.*

Many calculators have built-in statistics features for calculating the mean and standard deviation of a set of numbers. The next example illustrates these features on a TI-83/84 graphing calculator.

▼ example 4   Use a Calculator to Find the Mean and Standard Deviation

 Use a graphing calculator to find the mean and standard deviation of the times in the following table. Because the table contains all the winning times for this race (up to the year 2008), the data set is a population.

Olympic Women's 400-Meter Dash Results, in Seconds, 1964–2008

52.0	52.0	51.08	49.29	48.88	48.83	48.65	48.83	48.25	49.11	49.41	49.62

Solution
On a TI-83/84 calculator, press [STAT] [ENTER] and then enter the above times into list L1. See the calculator display on the next page. Press [STAT] ▷ [ENTER] [ENTER]. The calculator displays the mean and standard deviations shown on the next page. Because we are working with a population, we are interested in the population standard deviation. From the calculator screen, $\bar{x} \approx 49.663$ seconds and $\sigma x \approx 1.240$ seconds.

Press Association via AP Images

Because the calculation of the population mean and the sample mean are the same, a graphing calculator uses the same symbol $\boxed{\overline{x}}$ for both. The symbols for the population standard deviation, $\boxed{\sigma x}$, and the sample standard deviation, $\boxed{s x}$, are different.

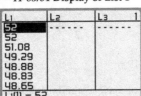

TI-83/84 **Display of List 1**

L₁	L₂	L₃	1
52	------	------	
52			
51.08			
49.29			
48.88			
48.83			
48.65			
L₁(1) = 52			

TI-83/84 **Display of $\overline{x}$, s, and σ**

```
1-Var Stats
  x̄=49.6625          ◄──── Mean
  Σx=595.95
  Σx²=29614.8323
  Sx=1.295636909    ◄──── Sample standard deviation
  σx=1.240477898    ◄──── Population standard deviation
  ↓n=12
```

▼ **check your progress** **4** Use a graphing calculator to find the mean and the population standard deviation of the race times in the following table.

Olympic Men's 400-Meter Dash Results, in Seconds, 1896–2008

54.2	49.4	49.2	53.2	50.0	48.2	49.6	47.6	47.8
46.2	46.5	46.2	45.9	46.7	44.9	45.1	43.8	44.66
44.26	44.60	44.27	43.87	43.50	43.49	43.84	44.00	43.75

Solution *See page S48.*

The Variance

A statistic known as the *variance* is also used as a measure of dispersion. The **variance** for a given set of data is the square of the standard deviation of the data. The following chart shows the mathematical notations that are used to denote standard deviations and variances.

> ▼ **Notations for Standard Deviation and Variance**
>
> σ is the standard deviation of a population.
>
> σ^2 is the variance of a population.
>
> s is the standard deviation of a sample.
>
> s^2 is the variance of a sample.

▼ **example** **5** **Find the Variance**

Find the variance for the sample given in Example 2.

Solution
In Example 2, we found $s = \sqrt{29.5}$. Variance is the square of the standard deviation. Thus the variance is $s^2 = \left(\sqrt{29.5}\right)^2 = 29.5$.

▼ **check your progress** **5** Find the variance for the population given in Check Your Progress 2.

Solution *See page S48.*

question Can the variance of a data set be less than the standard deviation of the data set?

Although the variance of a set of data is an important measure of dispersion, it has a disadvantage that is not shared by the standard deviation: the variance does not have the same unit of measure as the original data. For instance, if a set of data consists of times measured in hours, then the variance of the data will be measured in *square* hours. The standard deviation of this data set is the square root of the variance, and as such it is measured in hours, which is a more intuitive unit of measure.

---

answer Yes. The variance is less than the standard deviation whenever the standard deviation is less than 1.

EXCURSION

A Geometric View of Variance and Standard Deviation[1]

The following geometric explanation of the variance and standard deviation of a set of data is designed to provide you with a deeper understanding of these important concepts.

Consider the data $x_1, x_2, \ldots, x_n$ which are arranged in ascending order. The average, or mean, of these data is

$$\mu = \frac{\Sigma x_i}{n}$$

and the variance is

$$\sigma^2 = \frac{\Sigma(x_i - \mu)^2}{n}$$

TAKE NOTE

Up to this point we have used $\mu = \frac{\Sigma x_i}{n}$ as the formula for the mean. However, many statistics texts use the formula $\mu = \frac{\Sigma x_i}{n}$ for the mean. Letting the subscript i vary from 1 to n helps us to remember that we are finding the sum of all the numbers $x_1, x_2, x_3, \ldots, x_n$

In the last formula, each term $(x_i - \mu)^2$ can be pictured as the area of a square whose sides are of length $|x_i - \mu|$, the distance between the ith data value and the mean. We will refer to these squares as *tiles*, denoting by T_i the area of the tile associated with the data value x_i. Thus $\sigma^2 = \frac{\Sigma T_i}{n}$, which means that the variance may be thought of as the *area of the average-sized tile* and the standard deviation as the length of a side of this average-sized tile. By drawing the tiles associated with a data set, as shown below, you can visually estimate an average-sized tile, and thus you can roughly approximate the variance and standard deviation.

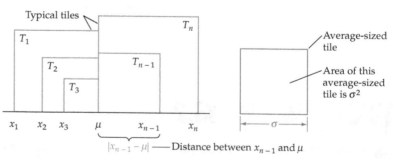

A typical data set, with its associated tiles and average-sized tile

---

[1] Adapted with permission from "Chebyshev's Theorem: A Geometric Approach," *The College Mathematics Journal*, Vol. 26, No. 2, March 1995. Article by Pat Touhey, College Misericordia, Dallas, PA 18612.

These geometric representations of variance and standard deviation enable us to see visually how these values are used as measures of the dispersion of a set of data. If all of the data are bunched up near the mean, it is clear that the average-sized tile will be small and, consequently, so will its side length, which represents the standard deviation. But if even a small portion of the data lies far from the mean, the average-sized tile may be rather large, and thus its side length will also be large.

EXCURSION EXERCISES

1. This exercise makes use of the geometric procedure just explained to calculate the variance and standard deviation of the population 2, 5, 7, 11, 15. The following figure shows the given set of data labeled on a number line, along with its mean, which is 8.

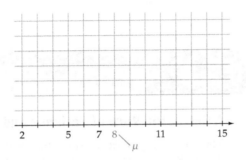
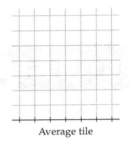

    a. Draw the tile associated with each of the five data values 2, 5, 7, 11, and 15.

    b. Label each tile with its area.

    c. Find the sum of the areas of all the tiles.

    d. Find the average (mean) of the areas of all 5 tiles.

    e. To the right of the above number line, draw a tile whose area is the average found in part d.

    f. What is the variance of the data? What geometric figure represents the variance?

    g. What is the standard deviation of the data? What geometric figure represents the standard deviation?

2. **a.** to **g.** Repeat all of the steps described in Excursion Exercise 1 for the data set

$$6, 8, 9, 11, 16$$

    h. Which of the data sets in these two Excursion exercises has the larger mean? Which data set has the larger standard deviation?

EXERCISE SET 13.2

1. **Meteorology** During a 12-hour period on December 24, 1924, the temperature in Fairfield, Montana, dropped from a high of 63°F to a low of −21°F. What was the range of the temperatures during this period? (*Source:* National Oceanic and Atmospheric Administration)

2. **Meteorology** During a 2-hour period on January 12, 1911, the temperature in Rapid City, South Dakota, dropped from a high of 49°F to a low of −13°F. What was the range of the temperatures during this period? (*Source:* National Oceanic and Atmospheric Administration)

■ In Exercises 3 to 12, find the range, the standard deviation, and the variance for the given *samples*. Round noninteger results to the nearest tenth.

3. 1, 2, 5, 7, 8, 19, 22

4. 3, 4, 7, 11, 12, 12, 15, 16

5. 2.1, 3.0, 1.9, 1.5, 4.8

6. 5.2, 11.7, 19.1, 3.7, 8.2, 16.3

7. 48, 91, 87, 93, 59, 68, 92, 100, 81

8. 93, 67, 49, 55, 92, 87, 77, 66, 73, 96, 54

9. 4, 4, 4, 4, 4, 4, 4, 4, 4, 4, 4, 4, 4, 4, 4, 4, 4

10. 8, 6, 8, 6, 8, 6, 8, 6, 8, 6, 8, 6, 8

11. −8, −5, −12, −1, 4, 7, 11

12. −23, −17, −19, −5, −4, −11, −31

13. **Mountain Climbing**   A mountain climber plans to buy some rope to use as a lifeline. Which of the following would be the better choice? Explain why you think your choice is the better choice.

Rope A: Mean breaking strength: 500 lb; standard deviation of 100 lb

Rope B: Mean breaking strength: 500 lb; standard deviation of 10 lb

14. **Lotteries**   Which would you expect to be the larger: the standard deviation of 5 random numbers picked from 1 to 47 in the California Super Lotto, or the standard deviation of 5 random numbers picked from 1 to 59 in the multistate PowerBall lottery?

15. **Weights of Students**   Which would you expect to be the larger standard deviation: the standard deviation of the weights of 25 students in a first-grade class, or the standard deviation of the weights of 25 students in a college statistics course?

16. Evaluate the accuracy of the following statement: When the mean of a data set is large, the standard deviation will be large.

Health   Exercises 17 and 18 refer to the following article about flu-related deaths in the United States.

> **IN THE NEWS**
> **Flu-Related Deaths: What's Average?**
>
> A newly released study by the Centers for Disease Control (CDC) lowers the average number of deaths per year due to the flu from the often-reported 36,000 to about 24,000. But the number of deaths has varied so much from year to year that the CDC now prefers *not* to state an average. Now the official word is that the number of flu-related deaths per year varies from about 3300 to 49,000.
> SOURCE: www.npr.org

17. The study described in the In the News article presented a data set listing the number of flu-related deaths in the United States each year for 31 years.

  a. Describe what the numbers 3300 and 49,000, given in the article, tell you about the data.

  b. The numbers 3300 and 49,000 given in the article were rounded off. The actual data values were 3349 deaths in the 1986–1987 flu season, and 48,614 deaths in the 2003–2004 flu season. Does this mean that the first year covered in the study was 1986–1987 and the last year in the study was 2003–2004? Explain.

  c. What statistic about the data set can you find using the exact values given in part b? Find this statistic.

18. The study described in the In the News article presented the data on flu-related deaths in several age categories. Here is the complete set of data for one category.

Number of Annual Flu-Related Deaths in People
Aged 0 to 19, United States, 1976/1977–2006/2007

136	197	136	108	123	57	146	168	156	120	97
106	161	120	87	111	131	102	102	117	134	105
117	114	107	151	117	135	147	130	102		

SOURCE: Centers for Disease Control and Prevention

Find the range, the mean, and the *population* standard deviation of the data. You may wish to use the statistics features of a graphing calculator.

 In Exercises 19 to 25, use the statistics features of a graphing calculator.

19. **Super Bowl**   The table on the next page lists the winning and losing scores for the Super Bowl games from 1967 through 2011.

AP Photo/Paul Spinelli

Super Bowl Results, 1967–2011

35–10	33–14	16–7	23–7	16–13
24–3	14–7	24–7	16–6	21–17
32–14	27–10	35–31	31–19	27–10
26–21	27–17	38–9	38–16	46–10
39–20	42–10	20–16	55–10	20–19
37–24	52–17	30–13	49–26	27–17
35–21	31–24	34–19	23–16	34–7
20–17	48–21	32–29	24–21	21–10
29–17	17–14	27–23	31–17	31–25

a. Find the mean and the *population* standard deviation of the winning scores. Round each result to the nearest tenth.

b. Find the mean and the *population* standard deviation of the losing scores. Round each result to the nearest tenth.

c. Which of the two data sets has the larger mean? Which of the two data sets has the larger standard deviation?

20. Academy Awards The following tables list the ages of female and male actors when they starred in their Oscar-winning Best Actor performances.

Ages of Best Female Actor Award Recipients,
Academy Awards, 1975–2010

42	41	36	32	41	33	31	74	33	49	38	61
21	41	26	80	42	29	33	36	45	49	39	34
26	25	33	35	35	28	30	29	61	32	33	45

Ages of Best Male Actor Award Recipients,
Academy Awards, 1975–2010

56	38	60	30	40	42	37	76	39	53	45	36
62	43	51	32	42	54	52	37	38	32	45	60
46	40	36	47	29	43	37	38	45	50	48	60

a. Find the mean and the *sample* standard deviation of the ages of the female recipients. Round each result to the nearest tenth.

b. Find the mean and the *sample* standard deviation of the ages of the male recipients. Round each result to the nearest tenth.

c. Which of the two data sets has the larger mean? Which of the two data sets has the larger standard deviation?

21. Baseball The following tables list the numbers of home runs hit by the leaders in the National and American Leagues from 1975 to 2010.

Home Run Leaders, 1975–2010

National League											
38	38	52	40	48	48	31	37	40	36	37	37
49	39	47	40	38	35	46	43	40	47	49	70
65	50	73	49	47	48	51	58	50	48	47	52

American League											
36	32	39	46	45	41	22	39	39	43	40	40
49	42	36	51	44	43	46	40	50	52	56	56
48	47	52	57	47	43	48	54	54	37	39	54

a. Find the mean and the *population* standard deviation of the number of home runs hit by the leaders in the National League. Round each result to the nearest tenth.

b. Find the mean and the *population* standard deviation of the number of home runs hit by the leaders in the American League. Round each result to the nearest tenth.

c. Which of the two data sets has the larger mean? Which of the two data sets has the larger standard deviation?

22. Triathlon The following table lists the winning times for the men's and women's Ironman Triathlon World Championships, held in Kailua-Kona, Hawaii.

Ironman Triathlon World Championships
(Winning times rounded to the nearest minute)

Men (1990–2010)			Women (1990–2010)		
8:28	8:33	8:33	9:14	9:32	9:50
8:19	8:24	8:14	9:08	9:24	9:10
8:09	8:17	8:12	8:55	9:13	9:19
8:08	8:21	8:19	8:58	9:26	9:09
8:20	8:31	8:18	9:20	9:29	9:06
8:21	8:30	8:23	9:17	9:08	8:54
8:04	8:23	8:11	9:07	9:12	8:58

a. Find the mean and the *population* standard deviation of the winning times of the male athletes. Round each result to the nearest tenth. *Hint:* You can work with just the number of minutes over 8 h and then add 8 h to your results.

b. Find the mean and the *population* standard deviation of the winning times of the female athletes. Round each result to the nearest tenth.

c. Which of the two data sets has the larger mean? Which of the two data sets has the larger standard deviation?

23.  **Political Science** The table on the following page lists the U.S. presidents and their ages at inauguration. President Cleveland has two entries because he served two nonconsecutive terms.

Washington	57	J. Adams	61
Jefferson	57	Madison	57
Monroe	58	J. Q. Adams	57
Jackson	61	Van Buren	54
W. H. Harrison	68	Tyler	51
Polk	49	Taylor	64
Fillmore	50	Pierce	48
Buchanan	65	Lincoln	52
A. Johnson	56	Grant	46
Hayes	54	Garfield	49
Arthur	50	Cleveland	47
B. Harrison	55	Cleveland	55
McKinley	54	T. Roosevelt	42
Taft	51	Wilson	56
Harding	55	Coolidge	51
Hoover	54	F. D. Roosevelt	51
Truman	60	Eisenhower	62
Kennedy	43	L. B. Johnson	55
Nixon	56	Ford	61
Carter	52	Reagan	69
G. H. W. Bush	64	Clinton	46
G. W. Bush	54	Obama	47

SOURCE: infoplease.com

Find the mean and the *population* standard deviation of the ages. Round each result to the nearest tenth.

24. **Biology** Some studies show that the mean normal human body temperature is actually somewhat lower than the commonly given value of 98.6°F. This is reflected in the following data set of body temperatures.

Body Temperatures (°F) of 30 Healthy Adults

97.1	97.8	98.0	98.7	99.5	96.3
98.4	98.5	98.0	100.8	98.6	98.2
99.0	99.3	98.8	97.6	97.4	99.0
97.4	96.4	98.0	98.1	97.8	98.5
98.7	98.8	98.2	97.6	98.2	98.8

a. Find the mean and *sample* standard deviation of the body temperatures. Round each result to the nearest hundredth.

b. Are there any temperatures in the data set that do not lie within 2 standard deviations of the mean? If so, list them.

25. **Recording Industry** Use the list of lengths of songs recorded by singer/songwriter Bruno Mars.

Lengths of Bruno Mars Songs (minutes:seconds)

3:42	3:40	3:50	3:17	3:15	3:37
2:27	3:01	3:47	3:49	4:02	3:30

SOURCE: itunes.apple.com

a. Find the mean and *sample* standard deviation of the song lengths. Round each result to the nearest second. *Hint:* Convert each data value into seconds.

b. Are there any song lengths in the data set that do not lie within 1 standard deviation of the mean? If so, list them.

E X T E N S I O N S

Critical Thinking

26. Pick five numbers and compute the *population* standard deviation of the numbers.

a. Add a nonzero constant c to each of your original numbers, and compute the standard deviation of this new population.

b. Use the results of part a and inductive reasoning to state what happens to the standard deviation of a population when a nonzero constant c is added to each data item.

27. Pick six numbers and compute the *population* standard deviation of the numbers.

a. Double each of your original numbers and compute the standard deviation of this new population.

b. Use the results of part a and inductive reasoning to state what happens to the standard deviation of a population when each data item is multiplied by a positive constant k.

28. a. All of the numbers in a sample are the same number. What is the standard deviation of the sample?

b. If the standard deviation of a sample is 0, must all of the numbers in the sample be the same number?

c. If two samples both have the same standard deviation, are the samples necessarily identical?

29. Under what condition would the variance of a sample be equal to the standard deviation of the sample?

Explorations

Before working on Exercises 30 and 31, you should complete Exercise 21 on page 824.

The *range rule of thumb* provides a rough estimate of the standard deviation of a data set based on the range of the data.

Range Rule of Thumb: The standard deviation of a data set is approximately the range of the data divided by 4:

$$s = \frac{\text{range}}{4}$$

30. a. Use the range rule of thumb to estimate the standard deviation of each data set in Exercise 21.

b. Compare the estimates you found in part a to the actual standard deviations of the data sets, as found in Exercise 21.

31. The range rule of thumb is based on the fact that for many data sets it is normal for about 95% of the data to lie within 2 standard deviations of the mean. So, given the mean $\bar{x}$ and standard deviation s of a data set, you can estimate minimum and maximum normal values:

$$\text{Minimum normal value} = \bar{x} - 2s$$
$$\text{Maximum normal value} = \bar{x} + 2s$$

a. Use the means and standard deviations that you found for the data sets in Exercise 21. Estimate the minimum and maximum normal values for each data set.

b. For each data set in Exercise 21, identify any data values that are outside the normal range.

Linear Regression and Correlation

Linear Regression

In many applications, scientists try to determine whether two variables are related. If they are related, the scientists then try to find an equation that can be used to *model* the relationship. For instance, the zoology professor R. McNeill Alexander wanted to determine whether the *stride length* of a dinosaur, as shown by its fossilized footprints, could be used to estimate the speed of the dinosaur. Stride length for an animal is defined as the distance x from a particular point on a footprint to that same point on the next footprint of the same foot. (See the figure at the left.) Because no dinosaurs were available, Alexander and fellow scientist A. S. Jayes carried out experiments with many types of animals, including adult men, dogs, camels, ostriches, and elephants. The results of these experiments tended to support the idea that the speed y of an animal is related to the animal's stride length x. To better understand this relationship, examine the data in Table 13.11, which are similar to, but less extensive than, the data collected by Alexander and Jayes.

TABLE 13.11   Speed for Selected Stride Lengths

a. Adult men

Stride length (m)	2.5	3.0	3.3	3.5	3.8	4.0	4.2	4.5
Speed (m/s)	3.4	4.9	5.5	6.6	7.0	7.7	8.3	8.7

b. Dogs

Stride length (m)	1.5	1.7	2.0	2.4	2.7	3.0	3.2	3.5
Speed (m/s)	3.7	4.4	4.8	7.1	7.7	9.1	8.8	9.9

c. Camels

Stride length (m)	2.5	3.0	3.2	3.4	3.5	3.8	4.0	4.2
Speed (m/s)	2.3	3.9	4.4	5.0	5.5	6.2	7.1	7.6

A graph of the ordered pairs in Table 13.11 is shown in Figure 13.15. In this graph, which is called a **scatter diagram** or **scatter plot**, the x-axis represents the stride lengths in meters and the y-axis represents the average speeds in meters per second. The scatter diagram seems to indicate that for each of the three species, a larger stride length generally produces a faster speed. Also note that for each species, a straight line can be drawn such that all of the points for that species lie on or very close to the line. Thus the relationship between speed and stride length appears to be a linear relationship.

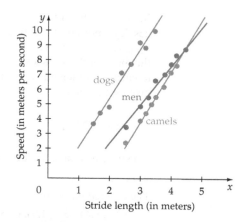

FIGURE 13.15 Scatter diagram for Table 13.11

After a relationship between paired data, which are referred to as **bivariate data**, has been discovered, a scientist tries to model the relationship with an equation. One method of determining a linear relationship for bivariate data is called **linear regression**. To see how linear regression is carried out, let us concentrate on the bivariate data for the dogs, which is shown by the green points in Figures 13.15 and 13.16. There are many lines that can be drawn such that the data points lie close to the line; however, scientists are generally interested in the line called the *line of best fit* or the *least-squares regression line*.

▼ The Least-Squares Regression Line

The **least-squares regression line** for a set of bivariate data is the line that minimizes the sum of the squares of the vertical deviations from each data point to the line.

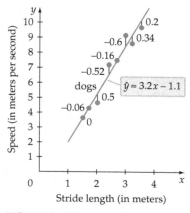

FIGURE 13.16 Vertical deviations

The least-squares regression line is also called the **least-squares line**. The approximate equation of the least-squares line for the bivariate data for the dogs is $\hat{y} = 3.2x - 1.1$. Figure 13.16 shows the graph of these data and the graph of $\hat{y} = 3.2x - 1.1$. In Figure 13.16, the vertical deviations from the ordered pairs to the graph of $\hat{y} = 3.2x - 1.1$ are 0, -0.06, 0.5, -0.52, -0.16, -0.6, 0.34 and 0.2.

It is traditional to use the symbol $\hat{y}$ (pronounced y-hat) in place of y in the equation of a least-squares line. This also helps us differentiate the line's y-values from the y-values of the given ordered pairs.

The next formula can be used to determine the equation of the least-squares line for a given set of ordered pairs.

▼ The Formula for the Least-Squares Line

The equation of the least-squares line for the n ordered pairs

$$(x_1, y_1), (x_2, y_2), (x_3, y_3), \ldots, (x_n, y_n)$$

is $\hat{y} = ax + b$, where

$$a = \frac{n\Sigma xy - (\Sigma x)(\Sigma y)}{n\Sigma x^2 - (\Sigma x)^2} \quad \text{and} \quad b = \bar{y} - a\bar{x}$$

In the formula for the least-squares regression line, Σx represents the sum of all the x values, Σy represents the sum of all the y values, and Σxy represents the sum of the n products $x_1y_1, x_2y_2, \ldots, x_ny_n$. The notation $\bar{x}$ represents the mean of the x values, and $\bar{y}$ represents the mean of the y values. The following example illustrates a procedure that can be used to calculate efficiently the sums needed to find the equation of the least-squares line for a given set of data.

▼ **example 1** Find the Equation of a Least-Squares Line

Find the equation of the least-squares line for the ordered pairs in Table 13.11a on page 850.

Solution
The ordered pairs are

$(2.5, 3.4), (3.0, 4.9), (3.3, 5.5), (3.5, 6.6), (3.8, 7.0), (4.0, 7.7), (4.2, 8.3), (4.5, 8.7)$

The number of ordered pairs is $n = 8$. Organize the data in four columns, as shown in Table 13.12. Then find the sum of each column.

TABLE 13.12

x	y	x^2	xy
2.5	3.4	6.25	8.50
3.0	4.9	9.00	14.70
3.3	5.5	10.89	18.15
3.5	6.6	12.25	23.10
3.8	7.0	14.44	26.60
4.0	7.7	16.00	30.80
4.2	8.3	17.64	34.86
4.5	8.7	20.25	39.15
$\Sigma x = 28.8$	$\Sigma y = 52.1$	$\Sigma x^2 = 106.72$	$\Sigma xy = 195.86$

TAKE NOTE

It can be proved that for any set of ordered pairs, the graph of the ordered pair $(\bar{x}, \bar{y})$ is a point on the least-squares line for the ordered pairs. This can serve as a check. If you have calculated the least-squares line for a set of ordered pairs and you find that, within rounding limits, $(\bar{x}, \bar{y})$ is not a point on your least-squares line, then you know that you have made an error.

Find the slope a.

$$a = \frac{n\Sigma xy - (\Sigma x)(\Sigma y)}{n\Sigma x^2 - (\Sigma x)^2}$$

$$= \frac{(8)(195.86) - (28.8)(52.1)}{(8)(106.72) - (28.8)^2}$$

$$\approx 2.7303$$

Find $\bar{x}$ and $\bar{y}$.

$$\bar{x} = \frac{\Sigma x}{n} = \frac{28.8}{8} = 3.6 \qquad \bar{y} = \frac{\Sigma y}{n} = \frac{52.1}{8} = 6.5125$$

Find the y-intercept b.

$$b = \bar{y} - a\bar{x}$$

$$\approx 6.5125 - (2.7303)(3.6)$$

$$= -3.31658$$

If a and b are each rounded to the nearest tenth, to reflect the accuracy of the original data, then we have as our equation of the least-squares line:

$$\hat{y} = ax + b$$

$$\hat{y} \approx 2.7x - 3.3$$

See Figure 13.17.

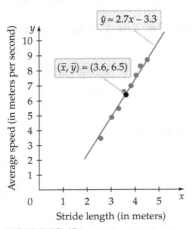

FIGURE 13.17 Least-squares line for speed versus stride length in adult men

▼ **check your progress 1** Find the equation of the least-squares line for the stride length and speed of camels given in Table 13.11c.

Solution *See page S50.*

Once the equation of the least-squares line is found, it can be used to make predictions. This procedure is illustrated in the next example.

▼ **example** **2**   Use a Least-Squares Line to Make a Prediction

Use the equation of the least-squares line from Example 1 to predict the average speed of an adult man for each of the following stride lengths. Round your results to the nearest tenth of a meter per second.

a. 2.8 m   **b.** 4.8 m

Solution

a. In Example 1, we found the equation of the least-squares line to be $\hat{y} = 2.7x - 3.3$. Substituting 2.8 for x gives

$$\hat{y} = 2.7(2.8) - 3.3 = 4.26$$

Rounding 4.26 to the nearest tenth produces 4.3. Thus 4.3 m/s is the predicted average speed for an adult man with a stride length of 2.8 m.

b. In Example 1, we found the equation of the least-squares line to be $\hat{y} = 2.7x - 3.3$. Substituting 4.8 for x gives

$$\hat{y} = 2.7(4.8) - 3.3 = 9.66$$

Rounding 9.66 to the nearest tenth produces 9.7. Thus 9.7 m/s is the predicted average speed for an adult man with a stride length of 4.8 m.

▼ **check your progress** **2**   Use the equation of the least-squares line from Check Your Progress 1 to predict the average speed of a camel for each of the following stride lengths. Round your results to the nearest tenth of a meter per second.

a. 2.7 m   **b.** 4.5 m

Solution   *See page S50.*

TAKE NOTE

Sometimes values predicted by extrapolation are not reasonable. For instance, if we wish to predict the speed of a man with a stride length of $x = 20$ m, the least-squares equation $\hat{y} = 2.7x - 3.3$ gives us a speed of 50.7 m/s. Because the maximum stride length of adult men is considerably less than 20 m, we should not trust this prediction.

The procedure in Example 2a made use of an equation to determine a point between given data points. This procedure is referred to as **interpolation**. In Example 2b, an equation was used to determine a point to the right of the given data points. The process of using an equation to determine a point to the right or left of given data points is referred to as **extrapolation**. See Figure 13.18.

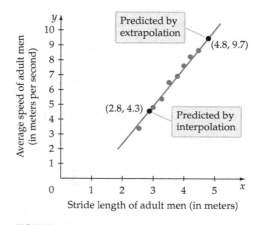

FIGURE 13.18 Interpolation and extrapolation

Linear Correlation Coefficient

To determine the strength of a linear relationship between two variables, statisticians use a statistic called the *linear correlation coefficient*, which is denoted by the variable r and is defined as follows.

▼ **Linear Correlation Coefficient**

For the n ordered pairs $(x_1, y_1), (x_2, y_2), (x_3, y_3), \dots, (x_n, y_n)$, the **linear correlation coefficient** r is given by

$$r = \frac{n(\Sigma xy) - (\Sigma x)(\Sigma y)}{\sqrt{n(\Sigma x^2) - (\Sigma x)^2} \cdot \sqrt{n(\Sigma y^2) - (\Sigma y)^2}}$$

HISTORICAL NOTE

Karl Pearson (pîr'sən) spent most of his career as a mathematics professor at University College, London. Some of his major contributions concerned the development of statistical procedures such as regression analysis and correlation. He was particularly interested in applying these statistical concepts to the study of heredity. The term *standard deviation* was invented by Pearson, and because of his work in the area of correlation, the formal name given to the linear correlation coefficient is the *Pearson product moment coefficient of correlation*. Pearson was a co-founder of the statistical journal *Biometrika*.

If the linear correlation coefficient r is positive, the relationship between the variables has a **positive correlation**. In this case, if one variable increases, the other variable also tends to increase. If r is negative, the linear relationship between the variables has a **negative correlation**. In this case, if one variable increases, the other variable tends to decrease.

Figure 13.19 shows some scatter diagrams along with the type of linear correlation that exists between the x and y variables. The closer $|r|$ is to 1, the stronger the linear relationship between the variables.

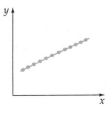

a. Perfect positive correlation, $r = 1$

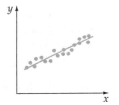

b. Strong positive correlation, $r \approx 0.8$

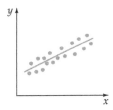

c. Positive correlation, $r \approx 0.6$

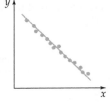

d. Strong negative correlation, $r \approx -0.9$

e. Negative correlation, $r \approx -0.5$

f. Little or no linear, correlation, $r \approx 0$

FIGURE 13.19 Linear correlation

▼ **example** **3** **Find a Linear Correlation Coefficient**

Find the linear correlation coefficient for stride length versus speed of an adult man. Use the data in Table 13.11a. Round your result to the nearest hundredth.

Solution

The ordered pairs are

$(2.5, 3.4), (3.0, 4.9), (3.3, 5.5), (3.5, 6.6), (3.8, 7.0), (4.0, 7.7), (4.2, 8.3), (4.5, 8.7)$

The number of ordered pairs is $n = 8$. In Table 13.12 on page 852 we found:

$\Sigma x = 28.8 \qquad \Sigma y = 52.1 \qquad \Sigma x^2 = 106.72 \qquad \Sigma xy = 195.86$

The only additional value that is needed is

$$\Sigma y^2 = 3.4^2 + 4.9^2 + 5.5^2 + 6.6^2 + 7.0^2 + 7.7^2 + 8.3^2 + 8.7^2$$
$$= 362.25$$

Substituting the above values into the equation for the linear correlation coefficient gives us

$$r = \frac{n(\Sigma xy) - (\Sigma x)(\Sigma y)}{\sqrt{n(\Sigma x^2) - (\Sigma x)^2} \cdot \sqrt{n(\Sigma y^2) - (\Sigma y)^2}}$$

$$= \frac{8(195.86) - (28.8)(52.1)}{\sqrt{8(106.72) - (28.8)^2} \cdot \sqrt{8(362.25) - (52.1)^2}}$$

$$\approx 0.993715$$

To the nearest hundredth, the linear correlation coefficient is 0.99.

▼**check your progress** **3**   Find the linear correlation coefficient for stride length versus speed of a camel as given in Table 13.11c. Round your result to the nearest hundredth.

Solution   *See page S50.*   ◄

question   What is the significance of the fact that the linear correlation coefficient is positive in Example 3?

The linear correlation coefficient indicates the strength of a linear relationship between two variables; however, it does not indicate the presence of a *cause-and-effect relationship*. For instance, the data in Table 13.13 show the hours per week that a student spent playing pool and the student's weekly algebra test scores for those same weeks.

TABLE 13.13

Algebra Test Scores vs. Hours Spent Playing Pool

Hours per week spent playing pool	4	5	7	8	10
Weekly algebra test score	52	60	72	79	83

The linear correlation coefficient for the ordered pairs in the table is $r \approx 0.98$. Thus there is a strong positive linear relationship between the student's algebra test scores and the time the student spent playing pool. This does not mean that the higher algebra test scores were caused by the increased time spent playing pool. The fact that the student's test scores increased with the increase in the stime spent playing pool could be due to many other factors or it could just be a coincidence.

In your work with applications that involve the linear correlation coefficient r, it is important to remember the following properties of r.

---

answer   It indicates a positive correlation between a man's stride length and his speed. That is, as a man's stride length increases, his speed also increases.

▼ **Properties of the Linear Correlation Coefficient**

1. The linear correlation coefficient r is always a real number between 1 and -1, inclusive. In the case in which

- all of the ordered pairs lie on a line with positive slope, r is 1.

- all of the ordered pairs lie on a line with negative slope, r is -1.

2. For any set of ordered pairs, the linear correlation coefficient r and the slope of the least-squares line both have the same sign.

3. Interchanging the variables in the ordered pairs does not change the value of r. Thus the value of r for the ordered pairs (x_1, y_1), (x_2, y_2), ..., (x_n, y_n) is the same as the value of r for the ordered pairs (y_1, x_1), (y_2, x_2), ..., (y_n, x_n).

4. The value of r does not depend on the units used. You can change the units of a variable from, for example, feet to inches and the value of r will remain the same.

MATHMATTERS — Use a Calculator to Find the Equation of the Least-Squares Line and the Linear Correlation Coefficient

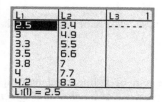

Calculators can be used to estimate the slope and y-intercept of the least-squares line for bivariate data. Many calculators will also estimate the linear correlation coefficient. A TI-83/84 calculator displays the linear correlation coefficient only if you have used the **DiagnosticOn** command, which is found in the **CATALOG** menu. Press [2nd] [CATALOG], scroll down to the **DiagnosticOn** command, and press [ENTER]. Using the data from Table 13.11a, enter the first components of the ordered pairs into list **L1** and the second components into list **L2**, as shown at the left (note that the last ordered pair of the table is not shown here). The key sequence [STAT] ▷ [4] [VARS] ▷ [ENTER] [ENTER] [ENTER] stores the equation for the least-squares line in **Y1** and produces the **LinReg** display in which **a** is the slope of the least-squares line, **b** is the y-intercept of the least-squares line, and **r** is the linear correlation coefficient.

LinReg($ax + b$) display

The equation of the least-squares line is stored in the Y= menu.

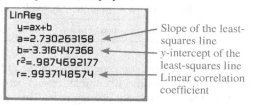

Slope of the least-squares line
y-intercept of the least-squares line
Linear correlation coefficient

To display a scatter diagram of the ordered pairs and a graph of the least-squares line, use the **WINDOW** menu to enter appropriate values for **Xmin**, **Xmax**, **Ymin**, and **Ymax**. Use the key sequence [2nd] [STAT PLOT] [ENTER] to display the **STAT PLOT** menu. Select the scatter diagram icon from the **Type** menu and enter **L1** to the right of **Xlist:** and **L2** to the right of **Ylist:**. Press the [GRAPH] key to display the scatter diagram of the data and the least-squares line.

Enter window settings.

Use the STAT PLOT menu to choose settings.

Press GRAPH to display the scatter diagram and least-squares line.

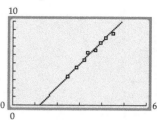

EXCURSION

An Application of Linear Regression

At this point, the work by Alexander and Jayes presented in this lesson cannot be used to estimate the speed of a dinosaur because for each animal species, we calculated a different least-squares regression line. Also, no dinosaurs are available to provide data for stride lengths and speeds. Motivated by a strong desire to find a mathematical model that could be used to estimate the speed of any animal from its stride length, Alexander came up with the idea of using *relative stride lengths*. A **relative stride length** is the number obtained by dividing the stride length of an animal by the animal's leg length. That is,

$$\text{Relative stride length} = \frac{\text{stride length}}{\text{leg length}} \quad \text{(I)}$$

Thus a person with a leg length of 0.9 m (distance from the hip to the ground) who runs steadily with a stride length of 4.5 m has a relative stride length of $(4.5 \text{ m}) \div (0.9 \text{ m}) = 5$. Note that a relative stride length is a dimensionless quantity.

Because Alexander found it helpful to convert stride length to a dimensionless quantity (relative stride length), it was somewhat natural for him also to convert speed to a dimensionless quantity. His definition of *dimensionless speed* is

$$\text{Dimensionless speed} = \frac{\text{speed}}{\sqrt{\text{leg length} \times g}} \quad \text{(II)}$$

where g is the gravitational acceleration constant of 9.8 m/s/s. At this point you may feel that things are getting a bit complicated and that you weren't really all that interested in the speed of a dinosaur anyway. However, once Alexander and Jayes converted stride lengths to *relative* stride lengths and speeds to *dimensionless* speeds, they discovered that many graphs of their data, even for different species, were nearly linear! To illustrate this concept, examine Table 13.14, in which the ordered pairs were formed by converting each ordered pair of Table 13.11 (page 850) from the form (stride length, speed) to the form (relative stride length, dimensionless speed). The conversions were calculated by using leg lengths of 0.8 m for the adult men, 0.5 m for the dogs, and 1.2 m for the camels.

TABLE 13.14 Dimensionless Speed for Relative Stride Lengths

a. Adult men

Relative stride length (x)	3.1	3.8	4.1	4.4	4.8	5.0	5.3	5.6
Dimensionless speed (y)	1.2	1.8	2.0	2.4	2.5	2.8	3.0	3.1

b. Dogs

Relative stride length (x)	3.0	3.4	4.0	4.8	5.4	6.0	6.4	7.0
Dimensionless speed (y)	1.7	2.0	2.2	3.2	3.5	4.1	4.0	4.5

c. Camels

Relative stride length (x)	2.1	2.5	2.7	2.8	2.9	3.2	3.3	3.5
Dimensionless speed (y)	0.7	1.1	1.3	1.5	1.6	1.8	2.1	2.2

A scatter diagram of the data in Table 13.14 is shown in Figure 13.20. The scatter diagram shows a strong linear correlation. (You didn't expect a perfect linear correlation, did you? After all, we are working with camels, dogs, and adult men.) Although we have considered only three species, Alexander and Jayes were able to show a strong linear correlation for several species.

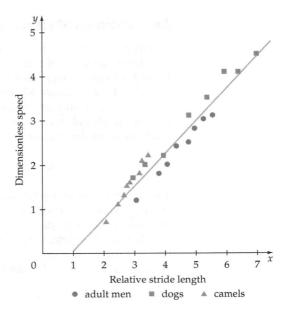

FIGURE 13.20

Finally it is time to estimate the speed of a dinosaur. Consider a large theropod with a leg length of 2.5 m. If the theropod's fossilized footprints show a stride length of 5 m, then its relative stride length is $\frac{5\,m}{2.5\,m} = 2$. The least-squares regression line in Figure 13.20 shows that a relative stride length of 2 has a dimensionless speed of about 0.8. If we use 2.5 m for the leg length and 0.8 for dimensionless speed and solve equation (II) (page 857) for speed, we get

$$\text{Speed} = (\text{dimensionless speed})\sqrt{\text{leg length} \times g}$$
$$= (0.8)\sqrt{2.5 \times 9.8}$$
$$\approx 4.0 \text{ m/s}$$

For more information about estimating the speeds of dinosaurs, consult the following article by Alexander and Jayes: "A dynamic similarity hypothesis for the gaits of quadrupedal mammals." *Journal of Zoology* 201:135–152, 1983.

EXCURSION EXERCISES

sauropod

pachycephalosaur

1. **a.** Use a calculator to find the equation of the least-squares regression line for *all* of the data in Table 13.14 on pages 857 and 858.

b. Find the linear correlation coefficient for the least-squares line in part a.

2. The photograph at the right shows a set of sauropod tracks and a set of tracks made by a carnivore. These tracks were discovered by Roland Bird in 1938 in the Paluxy River bed, near the town of Glen Rose, Texas. Measurements of the sauropod tracks indicate an average stride length of about 4.0 m. Assume that the sauropod that made the tracks had a leg length of 3.0 m. Use the equation of the least-squares regression line from Excursion Exercise 1 to estimate the speed of the sauropod that produced the tracks.

3. A pachycephalosaur has an estimated leg length of 1.4 m, and its footprints show a stride length of 3.1 m. Use the equation of the least-squares regression line from Excursion Exercise 1 to estimate the speed of this pachycephalosaur.

EXERCISE SET 13.5

1. Which of the scatter diagrams below suggests the

a. strongest positive linear correlation between the *x* and *y* variables?

b. strongest negative linear correlation between the *x* and *y* variables?

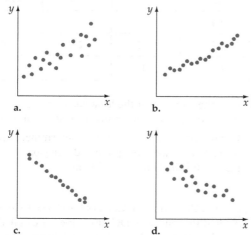

2. Which of the scatter diagrams below suggests

a. a near perfect positive linear correlation between the *x* and *y* variables?

b. little or no linear correlation between the *x* and *y* variables?

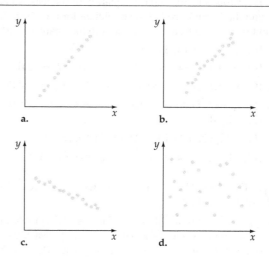

3. Given the bivariate data:

x	1	2	3	5	6
y	7	5	3	2	1

a. Draw a scatter diagram for the data.

b. Find n, Σx, Σy, Σx^2, $(\Sigma x)^2$, and Σxy.

c. Find a, the slope of the least-squares line, and b, the *y*-intercept of the least-squares line.

d. Draw the least-squares line on the scatter diagram from part a.

e. Is the point $(\overline{x}, \overline{y})$ on the least-squares line?

f. Use the equation of the least-squares line to predict the value of y when $x = 3.4$.

g. Find, to the nearest hundredth, the linear correlation coefficient.

4. Given the bivariate data:

x	3	4	5	6	7
y	2	3	3	5	5

a. Draw a scatter diagram for the data.

b. Find n, Σx, Σy, Σx^2, $(\Sigma x)^2$, and Σxy.

c. Find a, the slope of the least-squares line, and b, the y-intercept of the least-squares line.

d. Draw the least-squares line on the scatter diagram from part a.

e. Is the point $(\overline{x}, \overline{y})$ on the least-squares line?

f. Use the equation of the least-squares line to predict the value of y when $x = 7.3$.

g. Find, to the nearest hundredth, the linear correlation coefficient.

■ In Exercises 5 to 10, find the equation of the least-squares line and the linear correlation coefficient for the given data. Round the constants, a, b, and r, and to the nearest hundredth.

5. $\{(2, 6), (3, 6), (4, 8), (6, 11), (8, 18)\}$

6. $\{(2, -3), (3, -4), (4, -9), (5, -10), (7, -12)\}$

7. $\{(-3, 11.8), (-1, 9.5), (0, 8.6), (2, 8.7), (5, 5.4)\}$

8. $\{(-7, -11.7), (-5, -9.8), (-3, -8.1), (1, -5.9), (2, -5.7)\}$

9. $\{(1, 4.1), (2, 6.0), (4, 8.2), (6, 11.5), (8, 16.2)\}$

10. $\{(2, 5), (3, 7), (4, 8), (6, 11), (8, 18), (9, 21)\}$

In Exercises 11 to 19, use the statistics features of a graphing calculator.

11. **Value of a Corvette** The following table gives retail values of a 2010 Corvette for various odometer readings. (*Source:* Kelley Blue Book website)

Odometer reading	Retail value
13,000	$52,275
18,000	$51,525
20,000	$51,200
25,000	$50,275
29,000	$49,625
32,000	$49,075

a. Find the equation of the least-squares line for the data. Round constants to the nearest thousandth.

b. Use the equation from part a to predict the retail price of the model car with an odometer reading of 30,000.

c. Find the linear correlation coefficient for these data.

d. What is the significance of the fact that the linear correlation coefficient is negative for these data?

12. **Paleontology** The following table shows the length, in centimeters, of the humerus and the total wingspan, in centimeters, of several pterosaurs, which are extinct flying reptiles. (*Source:* Southwest Educational Development Laboratory)

Pterosaur Data

Humerus	Wingspan	Humerus	Wingspan
24	600	20	500
32	750	27	570
22	430	15	300
17	370	15	310
13	270	9	240
4.4	68	4.4	55
3.2	53	2.9	50
1.5	24		

a. Find the equation of the least-squares line for the data. Round constants to the nearest hundredth.

b. Use the equation from part a to determine, to the nearest centimeter, the projected wingspan of a pterosaur if its humerus is 54 cm.

13. **Health** The U.S. Centers for Disease Control and Prevention (CDC) use a measure called body mass index (BMI) to determine whether a person is overweight. A BMI between 25.0 and 29.9 is considered overweight and 30.0 or more is considered obese. The following table shows the percent of U.S. males 18 years old or older who were obese in the years indicated, judging on the basis of BMI. (*Source:* Centers for Disease Control and Prevention)

Year	Percent obese
2003	22.7
2004	23.9
2005	24.9
2006	25.3
2007	26.5
2008	26.6
2009	27.6

a. Using 3 for 2003, 4 for 2004, and so on, find the equation of the least-squares line for the data.

b. Use the equation from part a to predict the percent of overweight males in 2015.

14. ● **Health** The U.S. Centers for Disease Control and Prevention (CDC) use a measure called body mass index (BMI) to determine whether a person is overweight. A BMI between 25.0 and 29.9 is considered overweight, and 30.0 or more is considered obese. The following table shows the percent of U.S. females 18 years old or older who were overweight in the years indicated, judging on the basis of BMI. (*Source:* Centers for Disease Control and Prevention)

Year	Percent obese
2003	23.3
2004	23.7
2005	24.3
2006	25.6
2007	25.2
2008	27.6
2009	26.8

One Million Electric Cars by 2015?

In his 2011 State of the Union address, President Obama called for the United States to aim to have 1 million electric cars on the road by the year 2015. While current trends show reaching that goal to be a challenge, a goal of 1 million alternative fuel vehicles of all types is within reach.

Source: http://www.technologyreview.com

a. Using 3 for 2003, 4 for 2004, and so on, find the equation of the least-squares line for the data.

b. Use the equation from part a to predict the percent of overweight females in 2015.

15. ● **Wireless Phone** The following table shows the approximate number of wireless telephone subscriptions in the United States for recent years.

U.S. Wireless Telephone Subscriptions

Year	2005	2006	2007	2008	2009	2010
Subscriptions, in millions	194	220	243	263	277	293

Source: CTIA Semi-Annual Wireless Survey, Midyear 2010

a. Find the linear correlation coefficient for the data.

b. On the basis of the value of the linear correlation coefficient, would you conclude, at the $|r| > 0.9$ level, that the data can be reasonably modeled by a linear equation? Explain.

16. ● **Life Expectancy** The average remaining lifetimes for men in the United States are given in the following table. (*Source:* National Institutes of Health)

Average Remaining Lifetimes for Men

Age	Years	Age	Years
0	74.9	65	16.8
15	60.6	75	10.2
35	42.0		

Use the linear correlation coefficient to determine whether there is a strong correlation, at the level $|r| > 0.9$, between a man's age and the average remaining lifetime for that man.

17. ● **Alternative Fuel Vehicles** *Alternative fuel vehicles* run on fuel that is not petroleum based. Electric vehicles are one of a number of alternative fuel vehicles available. Read the article and use the table that follows the article.

Number of Alternative Fuel Vehicles in Use in the United States

Year	Electric vehicles	All alternative fuel vehicles
2004	49,536	565,492
2005	51,398	592,122
2006	53,526	634,559
2007	55,730	695,763
2008	56,901	775,664

Source: U.S. Department of Energy

a. Using 4 for 2004, 5 for 2005, and so on, find the equation of the least-squares line for the electric vehicles data and for the alternative fuel vehicles data.

b. Use your equations from part a to predict the number of electric vehicles and the number of alternative fuel vehicles that will be in use in the United States in 2015.

c. Is the procedure in part b an example of interpolation or extrapolation?

d. Do your results in part b support the statement made in the last sentence of the article? Explain.

18. **Life Expectancy** The average remaining lifetimes for women in the United States are given in the following table. (*Source:* National Institutes of Health)

Average Remaining Lifetimes for Women

Age	Years	Age	Years
0	79.9	65	19.5
15	65.6	75	12.1
35	46.2		

a. Find the equation of the least-squares line for the data.

b. Use the equation from part a to estimate the remaining lifetime of a woman of age 25.

c. Is the procedure in part b an example of interpolation or extrapolation?

19. **Fitness** An aerobic exercise instructor remembers the data given in the following table, which shows the recommended maximum exercise heart rates for individuals of the given ages.

Age (*x* years)	20	40	60
Maximum heart rate (*y* beats per minute)	170	153	136

a. Find the linear correlation coefficient for the data.

b. What is the significance of the value found in part a?

c. Find the equation of the least-squares line.

d. Use the equation from part c to predict the maximum exercise heart rate for a person who is 72.

e. Is the procedure in part d an example of interpolation or extrapolation?

EXTENSIONS

Critical Thinking

20. **Tuition** The following table shows the average annual tuition and fees of private and public 4-year colleges and universities for the school years 2003–2004 through 2008–2009. (*Source:* National Center for Education Statistics.)

Four-year Colleges and Universities Tuition and Fees

Year	Private	Public
2003–2004	17,763	4587
2004–2005	18,604	5027
2005–2006	19,292	5351
2006–2007	20,517	5666
2007–2008	21,979	5943
2008–2009	22,449	6319

a. Using 4 for 2003–2004, 5 for 2004–2005, and so on, find the linear correlation coefficient and the equation of the least-squares line for the tuition and fees at private 4-year colleges and universities, based on the year.

b. Using 4 for 2003–2004, 5 for 2004–2005, and so on, find the linear correlation coefficient and the equation of the least-squares line for the tuition and fees at public 4-year colleges and universities, based on the year.

c. Based on the linear correlation coefficients you found in parts a and b, are the equations you wrote in parts a and b good models of the growth in tuition and fees at 4-year colleges and universities?

d. The equation of a least-squares line is written in the form $\hat{y} = ax + b$. Explain the meaning of the *a* and *b* values for each equation you wrote in parts a and b.

Explorations

21. Another linear model that can be used to model data is called the *median-median* line. Use a statistics text or the Internet to read about the median-median line.

a. Find the equation of the median-median line for the data given in Exercise 13.

b. Explain the type of situation in which it would be better to model data using the median-median line than it would be to model the data using the least-squares line.

22.   Search for bivariate data (in a magazine, a newspaper, an almanac, or on the Internet) that can be closely modeled by a linear equation.

a. Draw a scatter diagram of the data.

b. Find the equation of the least-squares line and the linear correlation coefficient for the data.

c. Graph the least-squares line on the scatter diagram in part a.

d. Use the equation of the least-squares line to predict a range value for a specific domain value.

14 COMPLEX NUMBERS

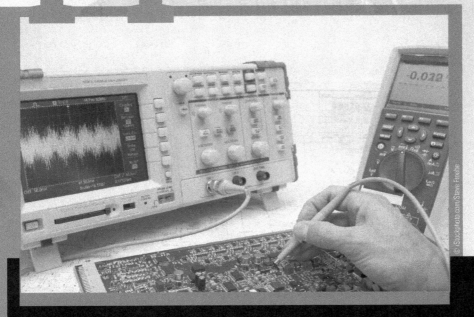

Complex numbers have many important applications in electronics. In Section 14.6, we will see how to use complex numbers to solve problems that involve alternating current.

All the numbers we have used until now have been real numbers. Several times in the history of mathematics, problems developed that people could not solve with the number system they had. These problems led to the invention of new numbers. The first time this happened was when the number 0 had to be invented. Later, negative numbers were needed. Each time, new numbers were invented to allow people to solve new kinds of problems. At last, the set of real numbers was developed, and with it we can solve many problems.

Not all problems, however, can be solved with the real numbers. People learned that they could take the cube root of -1 or -8. We know that $\sqrt[3]{-1} = -1$ because $(-1)^3 = -1$ and that $\sqrt[3]{-8} = -2$ because $(-2)^3 = -8$. But, there is no real number for the square root of -1, or -4, or for the square root of any negative number. People had problems that could be worked only if it were possible to take the square root of a

678

negative number. As a result, they invented the numbers we will begin using with this chapter—the complex numbers. Complex numbers have many important uses in technology. They make it much easier to work with vectors and problems that involve alternating current (ac). We will see many uses for complex numbers as we work through this chapter.

OBJECTIVES

AFTER COMPLETING THIS CHAPTER, YOU WILL BE ABLE TO:

▼ Simplify radicals with negative radicands.

▼ Write complex numbers in rectangular, polar, trigonometric, and exponential forms.

▼ Evaluate powers of j.

▼ Find sums, differences, products, quotients, powers, and roots of complex numbers.

▼ Solve quadratic equations that have complex solutions.

▼ Perform operations on complex numbers in polar form.

▼ Solve alternating current problems using complex numbers.

14.1   IMAGINARY AND COMPLEX NUMBERS

IMAGINARY UNIT

As we stated in the chapter introduction, the need for complex numbers arose because people had to solve problems that involved the square roots of negative numbers. In order to solve this dilemma, a new number was invented to correspond to the square root of -1. The name for this number is the imaginary unit, and it is represented by the symbol j. Thus, we have

$$j = \sqrt{-1}$$

Another popular name for the imaginary unit is the **j operator**.

 NOTE Many mathematics books use the symbol i instead of j. But, because i is used to represent electrical current, people in science and technology use j for the imaginary unit.

One of the basic steps we learn in working with imaginary numbers allows us to represent the square root of a negative number as the product of a real number and the imaginary unit, j. The square root of a negative number is called a **pure imaginary number** and is defined in the following box. Remember, if b is a real number, the symbol $\sqrt{b}$ represents the *principal square root* of b and is never negative. Thus, $\sqrt{9} = 3$, $\sqrt{25} = 5$, and $\sqrt{\frac{16}{9}} = \frac{4}{3}$.

PURE IMAGINARY NUMBER

If b is a real number and $b > 0$, then $\sqrt{-b}$ is a *pure imaginary number* and we have

$$\sqrt{-b} = \sqrt{(-1)b} = \sqrt{-1}\sqrt{b} = j\sqrt{b}$$

where $j = \sqrt{-1}$.

We call $j\sqrt{b}$ or $\sqrt{b}j$ the *standard form for a pure imaginary number.*

EXAMPLE 14.1

Simplify and express each of the following radicals in the standard form for a pure imaginary number: (a) $\sqrt{-9}$, (b) $\sqrt{-0.25}$, (c) $\sqrt{-3}$, (d) $-\sqrt{-18}$, and (e) $\sqrt{\dfrac{-4}{9}}$.

SOLUTIONS

(a) $\sqrt{-9} = \sqrt{9}\sqrt{-1} = 3j$

(b) $\sqrt{-0.25} = \sqrt{0.25}\sqrt{-1} = 0.5j$

(c) $\sqrt{-3} = \sqrt{3}\sqrt{-1} = \sqrt{3}j$

(d) $-\sqrt{-18} = -\sqrt{18}\sqrt{-1} = -\sqrt{9}\sqrt{2}\sqrt{-1} = -3\sqrt{2}j = -3j\sqrt{2}$

(e) $\sqrt{\frac{-4}{9}} = \sqrt{\frac{4}{9}}\sqrt{-1} = \dfrac{\sqrt{4}}{\sqrt{9}}\sqrt{-1} = \frac{2}{3}j$

NOTE Many people write the symbol j in front of a radical sign in order to reduce the danger of thinking that it is under the radical. Thus, you might prefer to write the answers to **(c)** and **(d)** as $j\sqrt{3}$ and $-3j\sqrt{2}$.

Since $j = \sqrt{-1}$, we have some interesting relationships.

$$j^2 = -1$$
$$j^3 = j^2 j = (-1)j = -j$$
$$j^4 = j^2 j^2 = (-1)(-1) = 1$$

Any larger power of j can be reduced to one of these basic four. Thus,

$$j^5 = j^{4+1} = j^4 j^1 = 1 \cdot j = j$$
$$j^{15} = j^{4+4+4+3} = j^4 j^4 j^4 j^3 = 1 \cdot 1 \cdot 1 \cdot (-j) = -j$$

NOTE The powers of j are cyclic, as can be seen above and in the table below.

$$1 = j^0 = j^4 = j^8 = j^{12} = \cdots$$
$$j = j^1 = j^5 = j^9 = j^{13} = \cdots$$
$$-1 = j^2 = j^6 = j^{10} = j^{14} = \cdots$$
$$-j = j^3 = j^7 = j^{11} = j^{15} = \cdots$$

This cyclic nature of imaginary numbers and of the trigonometric functions allow us to connect imaginary and complex numbers to cyclic applications, such as alternating electrical current.

We need to be careful when we work with imaginary numbers. Consider the problem $\sqrt{-9}\sqrt{-4}$. We know that $\sqrt{-9} = 3j$ and $\sqrt{-4} = 2j$, so $\sqrt{-9}\sqrt{-4} = (3j)(2j) = 6j^2 = -6$. But, we have gotten used to using the property $\sqrt{a}\sqrt{b} = \sqrt{ab}$. What if we tried to use it on this problem: $\sqrt{-9}\sqrt{-4} = \sqrt{(-9)(-4)} = \sqrt{36} = 6$? If we are going to have a successful set of numbers, we cannot get two different answers when we multiply imaginary numbers.

 CAUTION Remember that whenever you work with square roots of negative numbers, express each number in terms of j before you proceed.

Thus, the correct answer to $\sqrt{-9}\sqrt{-4}$ is -6.

 MULTIPLICATION OF RADICALS

If a and b are real numbers, then

$$\sqrt{a}\sqrt{b} = \sqrt{ab} \quad \text{if } a \geq 0 \text{ and } b \geq 0$$

If either $a < 0$ or $b < 0$ (or both a and b are negative), then convert the radical to "j form" before multiplying.

EXAMPLE 14.2

Simplify the following: (a) $(\sqrt{-4})^2$, (b) $\sqrt{-3}\sqrt{-12}$, (c) $\sqrt{2}\sqrt{-8}$, (d) $\sqrt{-0.5}\sqrt{-7}$, and (e) $(2\sqrt{-5})(\sqrt{-7})(3\sqrt{-14})$.

SOLUTIONS

(a) $(\sqrt{-4})^2 = (2j)^2$
$$= 4j^2$$
$$= -4$$

(b) $\sqrt{-3}\sqrt{-12} = (j\sqrt{3})(2j\sqrt{3})$
$$= 2j^2\sqrt{3^2}$$
$$= 2(-1)(3) = -6$$

(c) $\sqrt{2}\sqrt{-8} = (\sqrt{2})(j\sqrt{8})$
$$= j\sqrt{16}$$
$$= 4j$$

EXAMPLE 14.2 (Cont.)

(d) $\sqrt{-0.5}\sqrt{-7} = (j\sqrt{0.5})(j\sqrt{7})$
$= j^2\sqrt{(0.5)(7)}$
$= -\sqrt{3.5}$

(e) $(2\sqrt{-5})(\sqrt{-7})(3\sqrt{-14}) = (2j\sqrt{5})(j\sqrt{7})(3j\sqrt{14})$
$= 6j^3\sqrt{5 \cdot 7 \cdot 14}$
$= 42j^3\sqrt{10}$
$= -42j\sqrt{10}$

Note that $\sqrt{5 \cdot 7 \cdot 14} = 7\sqrt{10}$ and that $j^3 = -j$.

COMPLEX NUMBERS

When an imaginary number and a real number are added, we get a complex number. A **complex number** is of the form $a + bj$, where a and b are real numbers. When $a = 0$ and $b \neq 0$, we have a number of the form bj, which is a *pure imaginary number*. When $b = 0$, we get a number of the form a, which is a real number.

RECTANGULAR FORM OF A COMPLEX NUMBER

The form $a + bj$ is known as the **rectangular form** of a complex number, where a is the **real part** and b is the **imaginary part**.

Two complex numbers are equal if both the real parts are equal and the imaginary parts are equal. Symbolically, we express this as follows.

EQUALITY OF COMPLEX NUMBERS

If $a + bj$ and $c + dj$ are two complex numbers, then $a + bj = c + dj$, if and only if $a = c$ and $b = d$.

 HINT Two complex numbers, $a + bj$ and $c + dj$, are equal if the real parts are equal, that is, if $a = c$, **and** if the imaginary parts are equal, that is, if $b = d$.

EXAMPLE 14.3

Solve $4 + 3j = 7j + x + 2 + yj$ for x and y.

SOLUTION Here we need to determine both x and y. The best way is to rearrange the terms so that the known values are on one side of the equation and the variables are on the other.

$$4 + 3j = 7j + x + 2 + yj$$
$$4 + 3j - (2 + 7j) = x + yj$$
or $$x + yj = 4 + 3j - (2 + 7j)$$
$$x + yj = 2 - 4j$$

So, $x = 2$ and $y = -4$, since the real parts must be equal and the imaginary parts must also be equal.

EXAMPLE 14.4

Simplify and express in the form $a + bj$: (a) $7(3 + 2j)$, (b) $j(5 - 3j)$, and (c) $\dfrac{4 - \sqrt{-12}}{2}$.

SOLUTIONS

(a) $7(3 + 2j) = 21 + 14j$

(b) $j(5 - 3j) = 5j - 3j^2 = 5j - 3(-1) = 3 + 5j$

(c) $\dfrac{4 - \sqrt{-12}}{2} = \dfrac{4 - 2j\sqrt{3}}{2} = \dfrac{4}{2} - \dfrac{2j\sqrt{3}}{2} = 2 - j\sqrt{3}$

Notice that, in this last example, we had to divide *each* term of the numerator by 2 in order to get the final answer in the form $a + bj$.

CONJUGATES OF COMPLEX NUMBERS

Every complex number has a conjugate. As you will see in Section 14.2, conjugates are particularly useful when you are dividing by a complex number.

CONJUGATE OF A COMPLEX NUMBER

The **conjugate of a complex number** $a + bj$ is the complex number $a - bj$.

To form the conjugate of a complex number, you need to change only the sign of the imaginary part of the complex number.

EXAMPLE 14.5

(a) The conjugate of $3 + 4j$ is $3 - 4j$.

(b) The conjugate of $5 - 2j$ is $5 + 2j$.

(c) The conjugate of $-7j$ is $7j$, since $-7j = 0 - 7j$ and its conjugate is $0 + 7j = 7j$.

(d) The conjugate of 15 is 15, since $15 = 15 + 0j$ and its conjugate is $15 - 0j = 15$.

NOTE The conjugate of $a + bj$ is $a - bj$ and the conjugate of $a - bj$ is $a + bj$. Thus, each number is the conjugate of the other.

EXAMPLE 14.6

Use the quadratic formula to solve $x^2 + 2x + 10 = 0$.

SOLUTION The discriminant is $b^2 - 4ac$. Here $a = 1$, $b = 2$, and $c = 10$, so the discriminant is $2^2 - 4(1)(10) = 4 - 40 = -36$. Since the discriminant is negative, this trinomial has no real number roots.

The quadratic formula states that the solutions of $ax^2 + bx + c = 0$ are $x = \dfrac{-b \pm \sqrt{b^2 - 4ac}}{2a}$. Use the values of $a = 1$, $b = 2$, and $c = 10$ with the quadratic formula. From above we know that $b^2 - 4ac = -36$, so

$$x = \frac{-2 \pm \sqrt{-36}}{2}$$
$$= \frac{-2}{2} \pm \frac{\sqrt{36}}{2}j$$
$$= -1 \pm \frac{6}{2}j = -1 \pm 3j$$

Thus, the roots are $x = -1 + 3j$ and $x = -1 - 3j$. Notice that these roots are complex conjugates of each other.

EXAMPLE 14.7

Use the quadratic formula to solve $2x^2 + 3x + 5 = 0$.

SOLUTION Here $a = 2$, $b = 3$, and $c = 5$, and the discriminant is -31. Thus, this quadratic equation has no real number solutions. Using the quadratic formula, we obtain

$$x = \frac{-3 \pm \sqrt{-31}}{4} = \frac{-3 \pm j\sqrt{31}}{4}$$

Writing these in the form $a + bj$, we get $x = \dfrac{-3}{4} + \dfrac{\sqrt{31}}{4}j$ and $x = \dfrac{-3}{4} - \dfrac{\sqrt{31}}{4}j$.
As you can see, these roots are complex conjugates of each other.

APPLICATION ELECTRONICS

EXAMPLE 14.8

The susceptance, B, in siemens (S) of an ac circuit that contains R resistance and X reactance, both in Ω, is given by $B = \dfrac{X}{R^2 + X^2}$. Find the value of X when $B = 0.1$ S and $R = \sqrt{34} \approx 5.831\,\Omega$.

SOLUTION Substituting the values for B and R in the given equation, we get

$$0.1 = \frac{X}{(\sqrt{34})^2 + X^2} = \frac{X}{34 + X^2}$$

Multiplying both sides by the denominator produces the equation:

$$0.1(34 + X^2) = X$$
$$0.1(34 + X^2) - X = 0$$
$$3.4 + 0.1X^2 - X = 0$$
$$0.1X^2 - X + 3.4 = 0$$

This is a quadratic equation with $a = 0.1$, $b = -1$, and $c = 3.4$. Substituting these values in the quadratic formula, we obtain

$$X = \frac{-b \pm \sqrt{b^2 - 4ac}}{2a}$$
$$= \frac{-(-1) \pm \sqrt{(-1)^2 - 4(0.1)(3.4)}}{2(0.1)}$$
$$= \frac{1 \pm \sqrt{-0.36}}{0.2}$$
$$= \frac{1 \pm \sqrt{0.36}j}{0.2}$$
$$= \frac{1}{0.2} \pm \frac{\sqrt{0.36}j}{0.2}$$
$$= \frac{1}{0.2} \pm \frac{0.6j}{0.2}$$
$$= 5 \pm 3j$$

The reactance is either $5 + 3j\,\Omega$ or $5 - 3j\,\Omega$.

In Chapter 17, we will show that if a polynomial has only real number coefficients and has one complex root, then the conjugate of that complex number is also a root.

EXERCISE SET 14.1

In Exercises 1–12, simplify and express each radical in terms of j.

1. $\sqrt{-25}$
2. $\sqrt{-81}$
3. $\sqrt{-0.04}$

4. $\sqrt{-1.44}$
5. $\sqrt{-75}$
6. $-\sqrt{-72}$

7. $-3\sqrt{-20}$
8. $5\sqrt{-30}$
9. $\sqrt{-\frac{9}{16}}$

10. $\sqrt{-\frac{25}{36}}$
11. $-4\sqrt{-\frac{9}{16}}$
12. $-3\sqrt{-\frac{10}{81}}$

In Exercises 13–38, simplify each problem.

13. $(\sqrt{-11})^2$

22. $(-\sqrt{-7})(\sqrt{7})$

30. $\sqrt{-\frac{16}{81}}\sqrt{-\frac{9}{64}}$

14. $(\sqrt{-7})^2$

23. j^7

31. $(\sqrt{-0.5})(\sqrt{0.5})$

15. $(3\sqrt{-2})^2$

24. j^{26}

32. $(\sqrt{0.8})(\sqrt{-0.2})$

16. $(-2\sqrt{-3})^2$

25. $\sqrt{-\frac{1}{4}}\sqrt{\frac{16}{9}}$

33. $(-2\sqrt{2.7})(\sqrt{-3})$

17. $\sqrt{-4}\sqrt{-25}$

26. $\sqrt{\frac{4}{25}}\sqrt{-\frac{49}{9}}$

34. $(-4\sqrt{1.6})(2\sqrt{-0.4})$

18. $\sqrt{-9}\sqrt{-16}$

27. $\sqrt{-\frac{3}{25}}\sqrt{\frac{3}{16}}$

35. $(\sqrt{-5})(\sqrt{-6})(\sqrt{-2})$

19. $(\sqrt{-49})(2\sqrt{-9})$

28. $\sqrt{\frac{75}{36}}\sqrt{-\frac{49}{5}}$

36. $(\sqrt{-3})(\sqrt{-9})(\sqrt{-15})$

20. $(3\sqrt{-16})(\sqrt{-36})$

29. $\sqrt{-\frac{25}{36}}\sqrt{-\frac{9}{16}}$

37. $(-\sqrt{-7})^2(\sqrt{-2})^2j^3$

21. $(\sqrt{-5})(-\sqrt{5})$

38. $(\sqrt{-3})^2(\sqrt{-5})^2j^2(\sqrt{-2})$

In Exercises 39–48, solve each problem for the variables x and y.

39. $x + yj = 7 - 2j$

43. $x - 5j + 2 = 4 - 3j + yj$

47. $1.2x + 3 + yj = 7.2 - 4.3j$

40. $x + yj = -9 + 2j$

44. $2x - 4j = 6j + 4 - yj$

48. $3.7j - 1.5x = -4.8 + 2.4j + 0.5yj$

41. $x + 5 + yj = 15 - 3j$

45. $\frac{1}{2}x + \frac{3}{4}j = 2j - \frac{1}{4} + yj$

42. $6j - x + yj = 4 + 2j$

46. $\frac{2}{5}x - \frac{2}{3}j + 1 = 5 - \frac{4}{3}j - yj$

In Exercises 49–70, simplify each problem and express it in the form a + bj.

49. $2(4 + 5j)$

56. $-3j(2 - 5j)$

61. $\dfrac{6 + \sqrt{-18}}{3}$

65. $\frac{2}{3}(\frac{3}{4} - \frac{1}{3}j)$

50. $3(2 - 4j)$

57. $\frac{1}{2}(6 - 8j)$

66. $\frac{1}{2}(\frac{8}{5} + \frac{9}{4}j)$

51. $-5(2 + j)$

58. $\frac{2}{3}(6 + 9j)$

62. $\dfrac{7 - \sqrt{-98}}{7}$

67. $-\frac{5}{3}(-\frac{3}{8} + \frac{6}{15}j)$

52. $-3(4 + 7j)$

59. $\dfrac{5 - 10j}{5}$

63. $\dfrac{8 - \sqrt{-24}}{4}$

68. $-\frac{7}{4}(\frac{8}{21} - \frac{16}{35}j)$

53. $j(3 - 2j)$

69. $1.5(2.4 - 3j)$

54. $j(5 + 4j)$

60. $\dfrac{6 + 12j}{3}$

64. $\dfrac{9 + \sqrt{-27}}{6}$

70. $-7.2(-0.25 + 1.75j)$

55. $2j(4 + 3j)$

In Exercises 71–80, write the conjugate of the given numbers.

71. $7 + 2j$

74. $\frac{1}{2} - 9j$

77. $-8j$

80. $-4.5 - \sqrt{19}j$

72. $9 + \frac{1}{2}j$

75. 19

78. -11

73. $6 - 5j$

76. $7j$

79. $\sqrt{2} + 7.3j$

In Exercises 81–88, use the quadratic formula to solve each of the problems. Express your answers in the form a + bj.

81. $x^2 + x + 2.5 = 0$

83. $x^2 + 9 = 0$

85. $2x^2 + 3x + 7 = 0$

87. $5x^2 + 2x + 5 = 0$

82. $x^2 + 2x + 5 = 0$

84. $x^2 + 25 = 0$

86. $2x^2 + 7x + 9 = 0$

88. $3x^2 + 2x + 10 = 0$

Solve Exercises 89–92.

89. *Electronics* The susceptance, B, in siemens (S) of an ac circuit that contains R resistance and X reactance, both in Ω, is given by $B = \dfrac{X}{R^2 + X^2}$. Find the value of X when $B = 0.08$ S and $R = 50\ \Omega$.

90. *Electronics* The susceptance, B, in siemens (S) of an ac circuit that contains R resistance and X reactance, both in Ω, is given by $B = \dfrac{X}{R^2 + X^2}$. Find the value of X when $B = 0.05$ S and $R = 12\ \Omega$.

91. *Electronics* The susceptance, B, in siemens (S) of an ac circuit that contains R resistance and X reactance, both in Ω, is given by $B = \dfrac{X}{R^2 + X^2}$. Solve the equation for R.

92. *Electronics* The susceptance, B, in siemens (S) of an ac circuit that contains R resistance and X reactance, both in Ω, is given by $B = \dfrac{X}{R^2 + X^2}$. Find the general formula in terms of X.

 [IN YOUR WORDS]

93. Explain what it means for two complex numbers to be equal.

94. Describe how to determine the conjugate of a complex number.

14.2 OPERATIONS WITH COMPLEX NUMBERS

As with all number systems, we want to be able to perform the four basic operations of addition, subtraction, multiplication, and division. These operations are performed after all complex numbers have been expressed in terms of j.

ADDITION AND SUBTRACTION

We will begin by giving the definitions for addition and subtraction of complex numbers. After each definition, we will provide several examples showing how to use the definition.

ADDITION OF COMPLEX NUMBERS

If $a + bj$ and $c + dj$ are any two complex numbers, then their sum is defined as

$$(a + bj) + (c + dj) = (a + c) + (b + d)j$$

In words, this says to add the real parts of the complex numbers and add their imaginary parts.

EXAMPLE 14.9

Find each of these sums: (a) $(9 + 2j) + (8 + 6j)$, (b) $(6 + 3j) + (5 - 7j)$, (c) $(-2\sqrt{3} + 4j) + (5 - 6j)$, and (d) $(-4 + 3j) + (-1 - \sqrt{-4})$.

SOLUTIONS

(a) $(9 + 2j) + (8 + 6j) = (9 + 8) + (2 + 6)j$
$$= 17 + 8j$$

(b) $(6 + 3j) + (5 - 7j) = (6 + 5) + (3 - 7)j$
$$= 11 - 4j$$

(c) $(-2\sqrt{3} + 4j) + (5 - 6j) = (-2\sqrt{3} + 5) + (4 - 6)j$
$$= 5 - 2\sqrt{3} - 2j$$

Notice that the real part of this complex number is $5 - 2\sqrt{3}$ and the imaginary part is $-2j$.

(d) $(-4 + 3j) + (-1 - \sqrt{-4}) = (-4 + 3j) + (-1 - 2j)$
$$= (-4 - 1) + (3 - 2)j$$
$$= -5 + j$$

 APPLICATION ELECTRONICS

EXAMPLE 14.10

In an ac circuit, if two sections are connected in series and have the same current in each section, the voltage V is given by $V = V_1 + V_2$. Find the total voltage in a given circuit if the voltages in the individual sections are $8.9 - 2.4j$ and $11.2 + 6.3j$.

SOLUTION To find the total voltage in this circuit, we need to add the voltages in the individual sections.

$$V = V_1 + V_2$$
$$= (8.9 - 2.4j) + (11.2 + 6.3j)$$
$$= (8.9 + 11.2) + (-2.4 + 6.3)j$$
$$= 20.1 + 3.9j$$

The voltage in this circuit is $20.1 + 3.9j$ V.

 SUBTRACTION OF COMPLEX NUMBERS

If $a + bj$ and $c + dj$ are complex numbers, then their difference is defined as

$$(a + bj) - (c + dj) = (a - c) + (b - d)j$$

EXAMPLE 14.11

Find each of the following differences: (a) $(3 + 4j) - (2 + j)$, (b) $(5 + 7j) - (3 - 10j)$, (c) $(-8 + 4j) - (3 + 10j)$, and (d) $(9 + \sqrt{-18}) - (6 + \sqrt{-2})$.

SOLUTIONS

(a) $(3 + 4j) - (2 + j) = (3 - 2) + (4 - 1)j$
$$= 1 + 3j$$

(b) $(5 + 7j) - (3 - 10j) = (5 - 3) + [7 - (-10)]j$
$$= 2 + 17j$$

(c) $(-8 + 4j) - (3 + 10j) = (-8 - 3) + (4 - 10)j$
$$= -11 - 6j$$

(d) $(9 + \sqrt{-18}) - (6 + \sqrt{-2}) = (9 + 3j\sqrt{2}) - (6 + j\sqrt{2})$
$$= (9 - 6) + (3\sqrt{2} - \sqrt{2})j$$
$$= 3 + 2j\sqrt{2}$$

NOTE Notice that in Examples 14.9(d) and 14.11(d), we had to first write some of the numbers in the $a + bj$ form. In Example 14.9(d), we changed $\sqrt{-4}$ to $2j$, and in Example 14.11(d) we changed $\sqrt{-18}$ to $3j\sqrt{2}$ and $\sqrt{-2}$ to $j\sqrt{2}$. Do not overlook this step.

MULTIPLICATION

Multiplication of complex numbers uses the FOIL method, which was introduced in Chapter 2. As you can see, you will have to replace j^2 with -1 to obtain a simplified answer.

$$(a + bj)(c + dj) = ac + adj + bcj + bdj^2$$
$$= ac + adj + bcj - bd$$
$$= (ac - bd) + (ad + bc)j$$

MULTIPLICATION OF COMPLEX NUMBERS

If $a + bj$ and $c + dj$ are any two complex numbers, then their product $(a + bj)(c + dj)$ is defined as

$$(a + bj)(c + dj) = (ac - bd) + (ad + bc)j$$

EXAMPLE 14.12

Multiply and write each answer in the form $a + bj$: (a) $(2 + 5j)(3 - 4j)$, (b) $(5 + 3j)^2$, (c) $(7 + 3j)(7 - 3j)$, and (d) $(a + bj)(a - bj)$.

SOLUTIONS We have used the FOIL method rather than the definition to determine these products. By using the FOIL method, you do not have to remember the rule. However, remember that $j^2 = -1$.

EXAMPLE 14.12 (Cont.)

(a) $(2 + 5j)(3 - 4j) = 2 \cdot 3 + 2(-4)j + 5j(3) + 5(-4)j^2$
$$= 6 - 8j + 15j - 20(-1)$$
$$= 6 - 8j + 15j + 20$$
$$= 26 + 7j$$

(b) $(5 + 3j)^2 = (5 + 3j)(5 + 3j)$
$$= 5^2 + 2(5)(3)j + 9j^2$$
$$= 25 + 30j + 9(-1)$$
$$= 25 + 30j - 9$$
$$= 16 + 30j$$

(c) Here we can use the difference of squares.
$$(7 + 3j)(7 - 3j) = 7^2 - 3^2j^2$$
$$= 49 - 9(-1)$$
$$= 49 + 9$$
$$= 58$$

(d) $(a + bj)(a - bj) = a^2 + abj - abj - b^2j^2$
$$= a^2 - b^2j^2$$
$$= a^2 + b^2$$

APPLICATION ELECTRONICS

EXAMPLE 14.13

In an ac circuit, the formula $V = ZI$ relates the voltage V to impedance Z and current I. Find the voltage in a given circuit if the impedance is $8 - 2j\,\Omega$ and the current is $11 + 6j$ A.

SOLUTION To find the voltage, we need to multiply the given values of Z and I. As before, we will use the FOIL method.

$$V = ZI$$
$$= (8 - 2j)(11 + 6j)$$
$$= 8 \cdot 11 + 8(6j) + (-2j)(11) + (-2j)6j$$
$$= 88 + 48j - 22j + 12$$
$$= 100 + 26j$$

The voltage in this circuit is $100 + 26j$ V.

DIVISION

In Examples 14.12(c) and (d) we multiplied a complex number and its conjugate. The following note will be helpful when we divide complex numbers.

NOTE The product of a complex number and its conjugate is a real number.

DIVISION OF COMPLEX NUMBERS

If $a + bj$ and $c + dj$ are complex numbers, then the quotient

$$(a + bj) \div (c + dj) = \frac{a + bj}{c + dj} \text{ is defined as}$$

$$\frac{a + bj}{c + dj} = \frac{a + bj}{c + dj} \cdot \frac{c - dj}{c - dj} = \frac{(ac + bd) + (bc - ad)j}{c^2 + d^2}$$

$$= \frac{ac + bd}{c^2 + d^2} + \frac{bc - ad}{c^2 + d^2}j$$

This looks very complicated, but the following hint gives an important idea to remember whenever you divide by a complex number.

HINT In division of complex numbers, you multiply both the numerator and the denominator by the conjugate of the denominator.

The three problems in Example 14.14 show how to use the conjugate to divide.

EXAMPLE 14.14

Divide and express each answer in the form $a + bj$: (a) $\dfrac{8 + 6j}{2 - j}$, (b) $\dfrac{3 - 2j}{4 + 2j}$, and (c) $\dfrac{0.5 + j\sqrt{3}}{2.4j}$.

SOLUTIONS

(a) $\dfrac{8 + 6j}{2 - j} = \dfrac{8 + 6j}{2 - j} \cdot \dfrac{2 + j}{2 + j}$

$= \dfrac{16 + 8j + 12j + 6j^2}{4 + 1}$

$= \dfrac{16 + 8j + 12j - 6}{5}$

$= \dfrac{10 + 20j}{5} = 2 + 4j$

(b) $\dfrac{3 - 2j}{4 + 2j} = \dfrac{3 - 2j}{4 + 2j} \cdot \dfrac{4 - 2j}{4 - 2j}$

$= \dfrac{12 - 6j - 8j - 4}{16 + 4}$

$= \dfrac{8 - 14j}{20} = \dfrac{8}{20} - \dfrac{14}{20}j$

$= \dfrac{2}{5} - \dfrac{7}{10}j = 0.4 - 0.7j$

EXAMPLE 14.14 (Cont.)

(c) $\dfrac{0.5 + j\sqrt{3}}{2.4j} = \dfrac{0.5 + j\sqrt{3}}{2.4j} \cdot \dfrac{-2.4j}{-2.4j}$

$= \dfrac{(0.5)(-2.4j) + (j\sqrt{3})(-2.4j)}{(2.4j)(-2.4j)}$

$= \dfrac{-1.2j + 2.4\sqrt{3}}{5.76}$

$= \dfrac{2.4\sqrt{3} - 1.2j}{5.76}$

$= \dfrac{2.4\sqrt{3}}{5.76} - \dfrac{1.2}{5.76}j = \dfrac{\sqrt{3}}{2.4} - \dfrac{1}{4.8}j$

APPLICATION ELECTRONICS

EXAMPLE 14.15

In an ac circuit, use the formula $V = ZI$ to find the impedance in a given circuit if the voltage is $95 + 9j$ V and the current is $7 - 3j$ A.

SOLUTION We want to find the impedance Z, given V and I. Using the formula $V = ZI$, we see that $Z = \dfrac{V}{I}$.

$Z = \dfrac{V}{I}$

$= \dfrac{95 + 9j}{7 - 3j}$

$= \dfrac{95 + 9j}{7 - 3j} \cdot \dfrac{7 + 3j}{7 + 3j}$

$= \dfrac{95(7) + 95(3j) + (9j)7 + (9j)(3j)}{7^2 - (3j)^2}$

$= \dfrac{665 + 285j + 63j + 27j^2}{49 - 9j^2}$

$= \dfrac{638 + 348j}{58}$

$= 11 + 6j$

The impedance in this circuit is $11 + 6j\,\Omega$.

USING CALCULATORS WITH COMPLEX NUMBERS

A TI-83 or TI-84 has two modes for complex numbers. The rectangular complex mode displays numbers in the form $a + bi$, and we will use that form here. To put the calculator in the rectangular complex mode, press MODE and scroll down and over until $a + bi$ is highlighted, as in Figure 14.1a, press ENTER, and then press 2nd QUIT.

To enter a complex number in rectangular form, enter the value of a (the real component), press either ➕ or ➖, enter the value of b (the imaginary component), and press **2nd** **.** [i], as demonstrated in Figure 14.1b. Notice that the TI-83 and TI-84 calculators display the answers in the $a + bi$ from rather than $a + bj$.

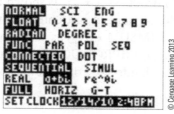

Figure 14.1a

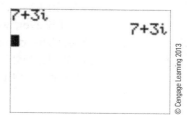

Figure 14.1b

EXAMPLE 14.16

Enter (a) $9 + 7j$ and (b) $12 - \frac{3}{4}j$ into a TI-84 calculator.

SOLUTIONS: First, make sure the calculator is in rectangular complex mode.

PRESS	DISPLAY
(a) 9 ➕ 7 **2nd** **.** [i]	$9 + 7i$
(b) 12 ➖ 3 ➗ 4 **2nd** **.** [i]	$12 - .75i$

Figure 14.2 shows these results as they appear on the screen of a TI-84 calculator.

```
9+7i
              9+7i
12-3/4i
            12-.75i
```

© Cengage Learning 2013

Figure 14.2

Calculations with a calculator are done in the same manner in which they are done with real numbers. The following example shows how each of these is done with a TI-83 or 84. However, other graphing calculators that allow computations with non-real complex numbers use similar procedures.

EXAMPLE 14.17

Use a calculator to perform each of the following: (a) $(3 + 5j) + (7 - 8j)$, (b) $(2 + j)(-6 - 3j)$, and (c) $\dfrac{10 - 4j}{1 + j}$.

SOLUTIONS

PRESS	DISPLAY
(a) (3 ➕ 5 **2nd** **.** [i])	
➕ (7 ➖ 8 **2nd** **.** [i]) **ENTER**	$10 - 3i$
(b) (2 ➕ **2nd** **.** [i])	
((−) 6 ➖ 3 **2nd** **.** [i]) **ENTER**	$-9 - 12i$
(c) (10 ➖ 4 **2nd** **.** [i]) ➗	
(1 ➕ **2nd** **.** [i]) **ENTER**	$3 - 7i$

Figure 14.3 shows these results as the appear on the screen of a TI-84 calculator.

```
(3+5i)+(7-8i)
             10-3i
(2+i)(-6-3i)
            -9-12i
(10-4i)/(1+i)
              3-7i
```

© Cengage Learning 2013

Figure 14.3

Figure 14.4a

© Cengage Learning 2013

USING SPREADSHEETS WITH COMPLEX NUMBERS

A complex number can be entered in a spreadsheet as either $a + bi$ or $a + bj$ by using the COMPLEX command. For example, Figure 14.4a shows that if you enter = COMPLEX (3, 4) you will get $3 + 4i$. On the other hand, entering = COMPLEX (5, 7, "j") produces $5 + 7j$, as shown in Figure 14.4b.

However, we seldom want to just enter a complex number into a spreadsheet. The command IMSUM (_, _) is used to add two complex numbers. Similarly, IMSUB (_, _), IMPRODUCT (_, _), and IMDIV (_, _) are used to subtract, multiply, and divide two complex numbers, respectively.

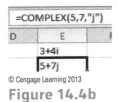

© Cengage Learning 2013

Figure 14.4b

EXAMPLE 14.18

Use a spreadsheet to calculate each of the following: (a) $(9 - 7j) + (14 + 6j)$, (b) $(8 - 7j) - (-2 + 5j)$, (c) $(2 + j)(-6 - 3j)$, and (d) $\dfrac{10 - 4j}{1 + j}$.

SOLUTIONS: The key strokes and results are shown in Figure 14.5. Notice that each complex number is placed between quotation marks.

	A	B	C	D
1		Operation	Enter	Result
2	(a)	(9-7j) + (14 +6j)	=IMSUM("9-7j","14+6j")	23-j
3	(b)	(8-7j)-(-2+5j)	=IMSUB("8-7j","-2+5j")	10-12j
4	(c)	(2+j)(-6-3j)	=IMPRODUCT("2+j","-6-3j")	-9-12j
5	(d)	(10-4j)/(1+j)	=IMDIV("10-4j","1+j")	3-7j

© Cengage Learning 2013

Figure 14.5

EXERCISE SET 14.2

In Exercises 1–48, perform the indicated operations. Express all answers in the form $a + bj$. If possible, use a calculator to check your answers.

1. $(5 + 2j) + (-6 + 5j)$

2. $(9 - 7j) + (6 - 8j)$

3. $(11 - 4j) + (-6 + 2j)$

4. $(21 + 3j) + (-7 - 6j)$

5. $(4 + \sqrt{-9}) + (3 - \sqrt{-16})$

6. $(-11 + \sqrt{-4}) + (9 + \sqrt{-36})$

7. $(2 + \sqrt{-9}) + (8j - \sqrt{5})$

8. $(3 + \sqrt{-8}) + (3 - \sqrt{8})$

9. $(14 + 3j) - (6 + j)$

10. $(-8 + 3j) - (4 - 3j)$

11. $(9 - \sqrt{-4}) - (\sqrt{-16} + 6)$

12. $(\sqrt{-25} - 3) - (3 - \sqrt{-25})$

13. $(4 + 2j) + j + (3 - 5j)$

14. $(2 - 3j) - j - (6 + \sqrt{-81})$

15. $(2 + j)3j$

16. $(5 - 3j)2j$

17. $(9 + 2j)(-5j)$

18. $(11 - 4j)(-3j)$

19. $(2 + j)(5 + 3j)$

20. $(3 - 2j)(4 + 5j)$

21. $(6 - 2j)(5 + 3j)$

22. $(4 - 2j)(7 - 3j)$

23. $(2\sqrt{-9} + 3)(5\sqrt{-16} - 2)$

24. $(6\sqrt{-25} - 4)(-3 - 2\sqrt{-49})$

25. $(\sqrt{-3})^4$

26. $(\sqrt{-9})^3$

27. $(1 + 2j)^2$

28. $(3 + 4j)^2$

29. $(7 - j)^2$

30. $(4 - 3j)^2$

31. $(5 + 2j)(5 - 2j)$

32. $(7 + 3j)(7 - 3j)$

33. $\dfrac{6 - 4j}{1 + j}$

34. $\dfrac{4 - 8j}{2 - 2j}$

35. $\dfrac{6 - 3j}{1 + 2j}$

36. $\dfrac{5 - 10j}{1 - 2j}$

37. $\dfrac{4 + 2j}{1 - 2j}$

38. $\dfrac{9 + 5j}{3 + j}$

39. $\dfrac{2j}{5 + j}$

40. $\dfrac{5j}{6 - j}$

41. $\dfrac{\sqrt{3} - \sqrt{-6}}{\sqrt{-3}}$

42. $\dfrac{\sqrt{5} + \sqrt{-10}}{\sqrt{-5}}$

43. $\dfrac{(5 + 2j)(3 - j)}{4 + j}$

44. $\dfrac{(6 - j)(2 + 3j)}{-1 + 3j}$

45. $(1 + j)^4$

46. $(1 - j)^4$

47. $\left(\dfrac{1}{2} + \dfrac{\sqrt{3}}{2}j\right)^2$

48. $\dfrac{4 + j}{(3 - 2j) + (4 - 3j)}$

Solve Exercises 49–63.

49. Show that the sum of a complex number and its conjugate is a real number.

50. Show that the difference of a complex number $a + bj$, with $b \neq 0$ and its conjugate, is a pure imaginary number.

51. Show that the product of a complex number and its conjugate is a real number.

52. *Electronics* In an ac circuit, if two sections are connected in series and have the same current in each section, the voltage V is given by $V = V_1 + V_2$. Find the total voltage in a given circuit if the voltages in the individual sections are $9.32 - 6.12j$ and $7.24 + 4.31j$.

53. *Electronics* Find the total voltage in an ac series circuit that has the same current in each section, if the voltages in the individual sections are $6.21 - 1.37j$ and $4.32 - 2.84j$.

54. *Electronics* If two sections of an ac series circuit have the same current in each section, what is the voltage in one section if the total voltage is $19.2 - 3.5j$ and the voltage in the other section is $12.4 + 1.3j$?

55. *Electronics* If two sections of an ac series circuit have the same current in each section, what is the voltage in one section if the total voltage is $7.42 + 1.15j$ and the voltage in the other section is $2.34 - 1.73j$?

56. *Electronics* The total impedance Z of an ac circuit containing two impedances Z_1 and Z_2 in series is $Z = Z_1 + Z_2$. If $Z_1 = 0.25 + 0.20j\,\Omega$ and $Z_2 = 0.15 - 0.25j\,\Omega$, what is Z?

57. *Electronics* If the total impedance of an ac series circuit containing two impedances is $Z = 9.13 - 4.27j\,\Omega$ and one of the impedances is $3.29 - 5.43j\,\Omega$, what is the impedance of the other circuit?

58. *Electronics* If an ac circuit contains two impedances Z_1 and Z_2 in parallel, then the total impedance Z is given by

$$Z = \dfrac{Z_1 Z_2}{Z_1 + Z_2}$$

What is Z when $Z_1 = 6\,\Omega$ and $Z_2 = 3j\,\Omega$?

59. *Electronics* What is the total impedance in an ac circuit that contains two impedances Z_1 and Z_2 in parallel, if $Z_1 = 20 + 10j\,\Omega$ and $Z_2 = 10 - 20j\,\Omega$?

60. *Electronics* In an ac circuit the voltage V, current I, and impedance Z are related by $V = IZ$. If $I = 12.3 + 4.6j$ A and $Z = 16.4 - 9.0j\,\Omega$, what is the voltage?

61. *Electronics* What is the current when $V = 5.2 + 3j$ V and $Z = 4 - 2j\,\Omega$? (See Exercise 60.)

62. *Electronics* What is the impedance when $V = 10.6 - 6.0j$ V and $I = 4 + j$ A?

63. *Programming* If your calculator cannot be used to calculate with complex numbers, write a program for your calculator that will **(a)** allow you to enter a complex number and **(b)** add, subtract, multiply, and divide two complex numbers.

[IN YOUR WORDS]

64. Describe how to multiply two complex numbers.

65. Describe how to divide two complex numbers.

66. If your calculator can be used to calculate with complex numbers, explain how to enter a complex number into your calculator and how to divide a complex number by another complex number. Give your explanation to a classmate and ask him or her to follow your directions.

Rewrite your directions to clarify places where your classmate had difficulty.

67. Describe how to enter a complex number into a spreadsheet and how to divide a complex number by another complex number. Give your explanation to a classmate and ask him or her to follow your directions. Rewrite your directions to clarify places where your classmate had difficulty.

14.3   GRAPHING COMPLEX NUMBERS; POLAR FORM OF A COMPLEX NUMBER

We have been able to graph real numbers since Chapter 4. It would be helpful if we could also represent complex numbers as points in a plane. The fact that each complex number has a real part and an imaginary part makes it possible to graph complex numbers.

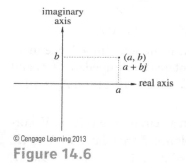

© Cengage Learning 2013

Figure 14.6

COMPLEX PLANE

Each complex number can be written in the form $a + bj$. We can represent this as the point (a, b) in the plane, as shown in Figure 14.6. Notice that the origin corresponds to the point $(0, 0)$, or $0 + 0j$. Since the points in the plane are representing complex numbers, this is called the complex plane. It is also referred to as the *Argand plane*, after the French mathematician Argand (1768–1822). In the complex plane, the horizontal axis acts as the real axis and the vertical axis as the *imaginary axis*.

EXAMPLE 14.19

Graph the following complex numbers: (a) $4 + 2j$, (b) $-3 + 5j$, (c) $-5 - 10j$, (d) $9 - 4j$, (e) 12, and (f) $-3j$.

SOLUTIONS   The solutions are shown in Figure 14.7.

The complex number $a + bj$ can also be represented in the plane by the position vector **OP** from the origin to the point $P(a, b)$. We now have three correct and interchangeable ways to refer to the complex number: $a + bj$, the point (a, b) on the complex (Argand) plane, and the vector $\mathbf{a} + \mathbf{bj}$ (see Figure 14.8.)

If we have two complex numbers on a graph, their sum or difference can be represented in the same way in which we add or subtract vectors. To add two complex numbers graphically, locate the point corresponding to one of them

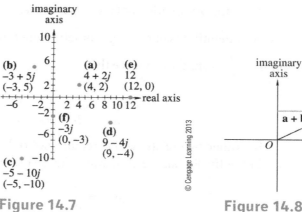

Figure 14.7

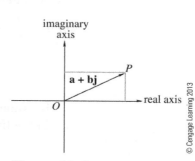

Figure 14.8

and draw the position vector for that point. Repeat the process for the second point. Finally, use the parallelogram method to add these two vectors. The sum will be the diagonal of the parallelogram that has the origin as an endpoint.

EXAMPLE 14.20

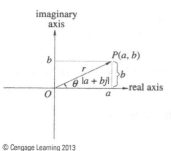

© Cengage Learning 2013

Figure 14.9

Graphically add the complex numbers $-9 + 5j$ and $4 - 7j$.

SOLUTION The solution is shown in Figure 14.9.

As you can see, the graphical solution agrees with the method given in Section 14.2.

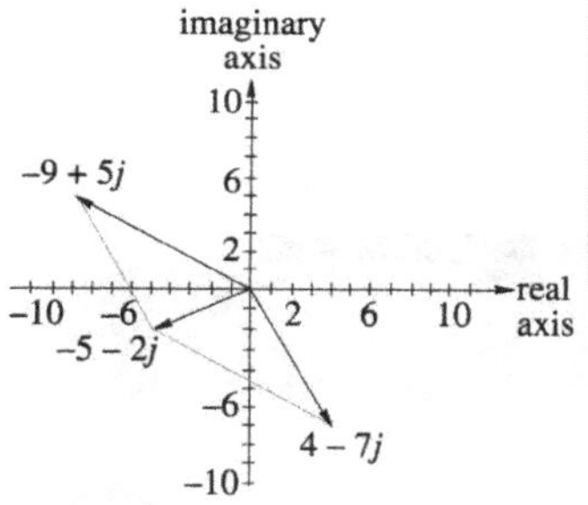

$$(-9 + 5j) + (4 - 7j) = (-9 + 4) + (5 - 7)j$$
$$= -5 - 2j$$

POLAR FORM OF A COMPLEX NUMBER

The rectangular form is not the only way to represent complex numbers. In Figure 14.10, the angle θ that the vector **OP** makes with the positive real axis is called the *argument* or *amplitude* of the complex number $a + bj$. The length r of **OP** is called the **absolute value** or *modulus* of $a + bj$. The absolute value is a real number and is never negative. The absolute value is always positive or 0. Using the Pythagorean theorem, we see that the length of r is $\sqrt{a^2 + b^2}$.

Since $a + bj$ can be considered a vector in the complex plane, $|a + bj|$ is the magnitude of the vector.

© Cengage Learning 2013

Figure 14.10

ABSOLUTE VALUE OF A COMPLEX NUMBER

The *absolute value of a complex number $a + bj$* is denoted $|a + bj|$ and has the value

$$|a + bj| = \sqrt{a^2 + b^2}$$

641

A careful examination of Figure 14.10 reveals four useful relationships. First, from our definitions of the trigonometric functions, we see that $\cos \theta = \dfrac{a}{r}$ and $\sin \theta = \dfrac{b}{r}$. From these, we see that

$$a = r \cos \theta \tag{1}$$

$$\text{and} \quad b = r \sin \theta \tag{2}$$

The other two relationships require not only our knowledge of trigonometry but of the Pythagorean theorem. These two relationships state that

$$\tan \theta = \dfrac{b}{a} \tag{3}$$

$$\text{and} \quad r = \sqrt{a^2 + b^2} \tag{4}$$

These four equations will be very valuable to us. From the first two, we see that

$$a + bj = r \cos \theta + jr \sin \theta = r(\cos \theta + j \sin \theta)$$

The expression $r(\cos \theta + j \sin \theta)$ is often abbreviated as $r \operatorname{cis} \theta$ or $r \underline{/\theta}$. In the abbreviation $r \operatorname{cis} \theta$, the c represents cosine, the s represents sine, and the i represents the mathematician's symbol for j. The symbol $r \underline{/\theta}$ is read "r at angle θ." The right-hand side of the previous equation, $r(\cos \theta + j \sin \theta)$, is called the *polar* or **trigonometric form** of a complex number.

CHANGING COMPLEX NUMBERS FROM POLAR TO RECTANGULAR FORM

A complex number written in **polar form** as

$$r \underline{/\theta} \qquad \text{or} \qquad r \operatorname{cis} \theta \qquad \text{or} \qquad r(\cos \theta + j \sin \theta)$$

has the rectangular coordinates $a + bj$, where

$$a = r \cos \theta \qquad \text{and} \qquad b = r \sin \theta$$

EXAMPLE 14.21

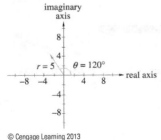

© Cengage Learning 2013

Figure 14.11

Locate the point $5(\cos 120° + j \sin 120°)$ in the complex plane and convert the number to rectangular form.

SOLUTION The graphical representation is given in Figure 14.11.
In this example, $r = 5$ and $\theta = 120°$, and so

$$a = r \cos \theta = 5 \cos 120° = 5(-0.5) = -2.5$$
$$b = r \sin \theta = 5 \sin 120° \approx 5(0.8660) = 4.3301$$

Thus, $5 \operatorname{cis} 120° \approx -2.5 + 4.3301j$.

The previous example was worked using a calculator. The exact value for b would have been represented by $\sin \theta = \frac{\sqrt{3}}{2}$, and so $b = \frac{5\sqrt{3}}{2}$. Even though a calculator gives values to more than four decimal places, we will give degrees to the nearest tenth and trigonometric functions to four decimal places.

 CAUTION Do not round off numbers until all calculations have been finished. Rounding off numbers before you complete the problem can make your final results differ from the degree of accuracy you are seeking.

EXAMPLE 14.22

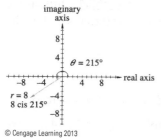

© Cengage Learning 2013

Figure 14.12

Locate the point $8 \underline{/215°}$ in the complex plane and convert the number to rectangular form.

SOLUTION The graphical representation is given in Figure 14.12.
In this example, $r = 8$ and $\theta = 215°$, so

$$a = r \cos \theta = 8 \cos 215° \approx 8(-0.8192) = -6.5532$$
$$b = r \sin \theta = 8 \sin 215° \approx 8(-0.5736) = -4.5886$$

Thus, $8 \underline{/215°} \approx -6.5532 - 4.5886j$.

CHANGING COMPLEX NUMBERS FROM RECTANGULAR TO POLAR FORM

A complex number written in rectangular form as

$$a + bj$$

has the polar coordinate forms

$$r \underline{/\theta}, \qquad r \operatorname{cis} \theta, \qquad \text{or} \qquad r(\cos \theta + j \sin \theta),$$

where

$$r = \sqrt{a^2 + b^2} \qquad \text{and} \qquad \tan \theta = \frac{b}{a}$$

 NOTE While there may be many values for θ that satisfy the given conditions, we will normally select the smallest *positive* value.

EXAMPLE 14.23

Represent $5 - 12j$ graphically and convert it to polar form.

SOLUTION Graphically, this point is shown as a vector in Figure 14.13.
Here $a = 5$ and $b = -12$, so

$$r = \sqrt{a^2 + b^2}$$
$$= \sqrt{5^2 + (-12)^2} = \sqrt{25 + 144}$$
$$= \sqrt{169} = 13$$

EXAMPLE 14.23 (Cont.)

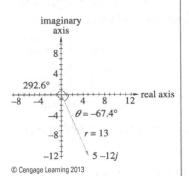

© Cengage Learning 2013

Figure 14.13

From the graph in Figure 14.13, we can see that this point is in Quadrant IV.

$$\tan \theta = \frac{b}{a}$$

$$= \frac{-12}{5}$$

$$\text{so} \qquad \theta = \tan^{-1}\left(\frac{-12}{5}\right)$$

$$\approx -67.4°$$

Notice that we used the arctan function. We can let θ be either $-67.4°$ or $-67.4° + 360° = 292.6°$. So, $5 - 12j \approx 13\ \underline{/292.6°} = 13\ \underline{/-67.4°}$. But, as we just stated, we will usually use the smallest positive value for θ that satisfies the given conditions. In this case, $\theta = 292.6°$.

EXAMPLE 14.24

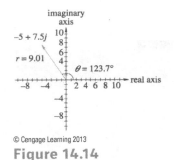

© Cengage Learning 2013

Figure 14.14

Locate the point $-5 + 7.5j$ in the complex plane and convert it to polar form.

SOLUTION The point $-5 + 7.5j$ is shown in the graph in Figure 14.14 and we see that it is in Quadrant II.

In this example $a = -5$ and $b = 7.5$, so

$$r = \sqrt{(-5)^2 + 7.5^2}$$

$$= \sqrt{25 + 56.25}$$

$$= \sqrt{81.25} \approx 9.01$$

$$\tan \theta = \frac{7.5}{-5} = -1.5$$

$$\text{so} \quad \theta \approx 123.7°$$

Thus, $-5 + 7.5j \approx 9.01\underline{/123.7°}$.

 CAUTION Remember that using a calculator to work with inverse trigonometric functions may not give the desired angle. You must determine which quadrant contains the point.

In Example 14.24, we had $\tan \theta = -1.5$. If you use a calculator (in degree mode) to determine $\theta = \tan^{-1}(-1.5)$, you get

PRESS	DISPLAY
2nd TAN (−) 1.5	−56.30993247

This value for θ, $-56.3°$, is an angle in the fourth quadrant. We can see, from Figure 14.14, that the point is in Quadrant II. So, $\theta = -56.3° + 180° = 123.7°$

The polar form of a real number or a pure imaginary number is on one of the axes. This makes finding them relatively easy, as shown in Example 14.25.

EXAMPLE 14.25

Express each of the following complex numbers in polar form: (a) 8, (b) −9, (c) 3j, and (d) −4j.

SOLUTIONS

(a) $8 = 8 + 0j$ lies on the positive real axis, so $\theta = 0°$ and $r = 8$; thus, $8 = 8(\cos 0° + j \sin 0°) = 8 \text{ cis } 0°$.

(b) $-9 = -9 + 0j$ lies on the negative real axis so, $\theta = 180°$ and $r = 9$; thus, $-9 = 9 \text{ cis } 180°$.

(c) $3j = 0 + 3j$ lies on the positive imaginary axis, so $\theta = 90°$ and $r = 3$; $3j = 3 \underline{/90°}$.

(d) $-4j = 0 - 4j$ lies on the negative imaginary axis, so $\theta = 270°$ and $r = 4$; $-4j = 4(\cos 270° + j \sin 270°) = 4 \text{ cis } 270°$.

NOTE Many graphing calculators can convert a complex number from polar form to rectangular form or from rectangular form to polar form. Since each make and model does this in a different way, consult the user's manual for your calculator to see how this is done.

APPLICATION **ELECTRONICS**

EXAMPLE 14.26

The voltage in an ac circuit is represented by the complex number $V = 28.4 - 65.7j$ V. Express this complex number in polar form.

SOLUTION First, we find r. Here, $a = 28.4$ and $b = -65.7$, so

$$r = \sqrt{28.4^2 + (-65.7)^2} = \sqrt{806.56 + 4{,}316.49} = \sqrt{5{,}123.05} \approx 71.58$$

Next, we find the angle θ.

$$\tan \theta = \frac{-65.7}{28.4}$$

$$\theta = \tan^{-1}\left(\frac{-65.7}{28.4}\right)$$

$$\theta \approx -66.6°$$

Since V is in the fourth quadrant, $\theta \approx -66.6°$. If we want to express θ as an angle in the interval $[0, 360°)$, then $\theta = -66.6° + 360° = 293.4°$.

So, in polar form, voltage $V = 28.4 - 65.7j \approx 71.6 \underline{/-66.6°} = 71.6 \underline{/293.4°}$ V.

APPLICATION **ELECTRONICS**

EXAMPLE 14.27

Express current $i = 4.5\underline{/40°}$ A in rectangular form.

SOLUTION Here, $r = 4.5$ and $\theta = 40°$, so $a = r\cos\theta = 4.5\cos 40° \approx 3.45$ and $b = r\sin\theta = 4.5\sin 40° \approx 2.89$. In rectangular form the current in amps, A, is $i = 4.5\underline{/40°} \approx 3.45 + 2.89j$.

EXERCISE SET 14.3

For each number in Exercises 1–16, locate the point in the complex plane and express the number in rectangular form.

1. $4(\cos 30° + j\sin 30°)$

2. $10(\cos 45° + j\sin 45°)$

3. $5(\cos 135° + j\sin 135°)$

4. $8(\cos 305° + j\sin 305°)$

5. 7 cis 260°

6. 3 cis 340°

7. 2 cis 115°

8. 5 cis 285°

9. $3\underline{/25°}$

10. $4\underline{/240°}$

11. $5\underline{/340°}$

12. $6\underline{/90°}$

13. $4.5\underline{/245°}$

14. $6.8\underline{/10°}$

15. $2.5\underline{/180°}$

16. $5.9\underline{/270°}$

For each number in Exercises 17–32, locate the point in the complex plane and express the number in polar form.

17. $5 + 5j$

18. $6 + 3j$

19. $4 - 8j$

20. $8 - 2j$

21. $-4 + 7j$

22. $-9 + 3j$

23. $-6 - 2j$

24. $-10 - 2j$

25. 6

26. $1.2 + 7.3j$

27. $4.2 - 6.3j$

28. $9j$

29. $-5.8 + 0.2j$

30. $-7j$

31. -2.7

32. $-4.7 - 1.1j$

In Exercises 33–40, perform the indicated operations graphically.

33. $(5 + j) + (3 + 2j)$

34. $(3 - 4j) + (4 - 2j)$

35. $(-4 + 2j) + (2 - 8j)$

36. $(8 - j) + (9 + 6j)$

37. $(-8 + 7j) + (-5 - 3j)$

38. $(4 + 2j) + (-3 - 9j)$

39. $(-5 + 3j) + (4 - 8j)$

40. $(-3 + 2j) + (-8 - 5j)$

Solve Exercises 41–46.

41. *Electronics* The current in amps, A, of an ac circuit is given by the complex number $4.7 - 6.5j$. Write this number in polar form.

42. *Electronics* The current in amps, A, of an ac circuit is given by the complex number $8.2 + 5.4j$. Write this number in polar form.

43. *Electronics* Convert the voltage given by $V = -110.4 + 46.1j$ V to polar form.

44. *Electronics* Convert the voltage given by $V = 108.5 - 57.6j$ V to polar form.

45. *Electronics* Express the current $i = 2.5\underline{/-50°}$ A in rectangular form.

46. *Electronics* Express the impedance $Z = 8.5\underline{/2\pi/3}$ Ω in rectangular form.

[IN YOUR WORDS]

47. (a) What is the absolute value or modulus of a complex number?

(b) What is the amplitude or argument of a complex number?

48. Describe how to change a complex number in rectangular form to its equivalent complex number in polar form.

49. Describe how to change a complex number in polar form to its equivalent complex number in rectangular form.

50. Explain how to use your calculator to change a complex number from rectangular form to polar form, or vice versa.

51. Consult the help menu for your spreadsheet and describe how to change a complex number from rectangular form to polar form, or vice versa. Give your explanation to a classmate and ask him or her to follow your directions. Rewrite your directions to clarify places where your classmate had difficulty.

14.4 EXPONENTIAL FORM OF A COMPLEX NUMBER

There is yet another way in which complex numbers are often represented. It is called the **exponential form of a complex number**, because it involves exponents of the number e. (Remember from Section 12.2 that $e \approx 2.718281828$.) If $z = r\underline{/\theta}$ is a complex number, then we know that $z = r(\cos \theta + j \sin \theta)$.

 EXPONENTIAL FORM OF A COMPLEX NUMBER

The *exponential form* of a complex number uses *Euler's formula*, $e^{j\theta} = \cos \theta + j \sin \theta$, and states that

$$z = re^{j\theta}$$

where θ is in radians.

While θ can have any value, we will express answers with $0 \leq \theta < 2\pi$.

 CAUTION When using the exponential form, you must remember that θ is in radians.

EXAMPLE 14.28

Write the complex number $6(\cos 180° + j \sin 180°)$ in exponential form.

SOLUTION In this example, $r = 6$ and $\theta = 180°$. The exponential form requires that θ be expressed in radians: $180° = \pi$ rad and so $\theta = \pi$. Thus $6(\cos 180° + j \sin 180°) = 6e^{j\pi}$.

EXAMPLE 14.29

Write the complex number $8\underline{/225°}$ in exponential form.

SOLUTION In this example, $r = 8$ and $\theta = 225° = \frac{5\pi}{4} \approx 3.927$ rad.

$$8\underline{/225°} = 8e^{\frac{5\pi}{4}j} = 8e^{5j\pi/4} \approx 8e^{3.927j}$$

All of the last three versions are correct. Because you will probably be using a calculator to convert from degrees to radians, the last version is the one that you will most likely use. But remember, $8e^{3.927j}$ is rounded off and therefore is the least accurate.

EXAMPLE 14.30

Express $-4 + 3j$ in exponential form.

SOLUTION This example is in the form $a + bj$. We must first determine r and θ. Now $r = \sqrt{a^2 + b^2} = \sqrt{(-4)^2 + 3^2} = 5$ and $\tan \theta = \frac{3}{-4} = -0.75$. With a graphing calculator in radian mode, we can determine θ.

PRESS	DISPLAY
2nd **tan** **(−)** $0.75 + \pi$ **ENTER**	2.498091545

The last two steps were needed because the arctan of a negative number produces an angle in Quadrant IV. The point $-4 + 3j$ is in Quadrant II, so we added π to the original answer. Thus, we can see that $\theta \approx 2.4981$ and $-4 + 3j \approx 5e^{2.4981j}$.

EXAMPLE 14.31

Express $-5 - 8j$ in exponential form.

SOLUTION $r = \sqrt{a^2 + b^2} = \sqrt{(-5)^2 + (-8)^2} = \sqrt{25 + 64} = \sqrt{89} \approx 9.4340$. $\tan \theta = \frac{-8}{-5} = 1.6$. Since $-5 - 8j$ is in Quadrant III, $\theta = \tan^{-1} 1.6 + \pi \approx 4.1538$. Thus, we see that $-5 - 8j = 9.4340e^{4.1538j}$.

EXAMPLE 14.32

Express $4.6e^{5.7j}$ in polar and rectangular form.

SOLUTION Here, $r = 4.6$ and $\theta = 5.7$, so we write the given expression in polar form as $4.6e^{5.7j} = 4.6(\cos 5.7 + j \sin 5.7)$. With a calculator in radian mode, we get

$$a = 4.6 \cos 5.7 \approx 3.8397$$
$$b = 4.6 \sin 5.7 \approx -2.5332$$

We have determined that $4.6e^{5.7j} = a + bj \approx 3.8397 - 2.5332j$.

 APPLICATION **ELECTRONICS**

EXAMPLE 14.33

The voltage in an ac circuit is represented by the complex number $V = -85.6 + 72.3j$ V. Express this complex number in exponential form.

SOLUTION First, we find r.

$$r = \sqrt{(-85.6)^2 + 72.3^2} = \sqrt{7327.36 + 5227.29} \approx 112.0$$

Next, we find the angle θ.

$$\tan \theta = \frac{72.3}{-85.6}$$

$$\theta \approx -0.70137$$

Since V is in the second quadrant, $\theta = -0.70137 + \pi \approx 2.4402$. So, in exponential form, we find that voltage $V = -85.6 + 72.3j \approx 112e^{2.4402j}$ V.

 APPLICATION ELECTRONICS

EXAMPLE 14.34

Express the current $I = 2.5\angle{-50°}$ A in exponential and rectangular forms.

SOLUTION Here, $r = 2.5$ and $\theta = -50° \approx -0.8727$ rad, so in exponential form we have $I = re^{j\theta} = 2.5e^{-0.8727j}$.

To convert the given number to rectangular form, we have $x = 2.5 \cos(-50°) \approx 1.6070$ and $y = 2.5 \sin(-50°) \approx -1.9151$. Thus, in rectangular form, the current is $I = 1.6070 - 1.9151j$ A.

MULTIPLYING AND DIVIDING IN EXPONENTIAL FORM

One advantage of using the exponential form for complex numbers is that complex numbers written in exponential form obey the laws of exponents. There are three properties of exponents that are of interest. These three properties concern multiplication, division, and powers, and all of them use four basic rules introduced in Section 1.4.

$$b^m b^n = b^{m+n}$$

$$\frac{b^m}{b^n} = b^{m-n}$$

$$(b^m)^n = b^{mn}$$

$$(ab)^m = a^m b^m$$

If we have two complex numbers $z_1 = r_1 e^{j\theta_1}$ and $z_2 = r_2 e^{j\theta_2}$, we can then multiply, divide, or take powers of them using the preceding rules. For example,

$$z_1 z_2 = \left(r_1 e^{j\theta_1}\right)\left(r_2 e^{j\theta_2}\right) = r_1 r_2 e^{j(\theta_1 + \theta_2)}$$

and

$$\frac{z_1}{z_2} = \frac{r_1 e^{j\theta_1}}{r_2 e^{j\theta_2}} = \frac{r_1}{r_2} e^{j(\theta_1 - \theta_2)}$$

EXAMPLE 14.35

Multiply $7e^{4.2j}$ and $2e^{1.5j}$.

SOLUTION $(7e^{4.2j})(2e^{1.5j}) = 7 \cdot 2e^{(4.2 + 1.5)j} = 14e^{5.7j}$

If we want to divide, then

$$\frac{z_1}{z_2} = \frac{r_1 e^{j\theta_1}}{r_2 e^{j\theta_2}} = \frac{r_1}{r_2} e^{j(\theta_1 - \theta_2)}$$

EXAMPLE 14.36

Divide $9e^{3.2j}$ by $2e^{4.3j}$.

SOLUTION $\dfrac{9e^{3.2j}}{2e^{4.3j}} = \tfrac{9}{2} e^{(3.2 - 4.3)j} = 4.5e^{-1.1j}$

If you want to express the angle in the answer between 0 and 2π ($0 \le \theta < 2\pi$), then let $\theta = 2\pi - 1.1$, or, using a calculator,

PRESS	DISPLAY
2 × π −	6.2831853
1.1 =	5.1831853

Thus, $4.5e^{-1.1j}$ could be expressed as $4.5e^{5.2j}$.

The last property involves raising a complex number to a power and the properties $(b^m)^n = b^{mn}$ and $(ab)^m = a^m b^m$.

$$z^n = (re^{j\theta})^n = r^n e^{jn\theta}$$

EXAMPLE 14.37

Calculate $(4e^{2.3j})^5$.

SOLUTION $(4e^{2.3j})^5 = 4^5 e^{5(2.3)j}$
$$= 1{,}024e^{11.5j}$$
$$\approx 1{,}024e^{5.2j}$$

Since 11.5 is greater than 2π, we subtracted 2π to get an angle of 5.2, which is between 0 and 2π.

 APPLICATION ELECTRONICS

EXAMPLE 14.38

Given that $I = 5.8e^{-0.4363j}$ A and $Z = 8.5e^{1.047j}$ Ω, calculate $V = IZ$.

SOLUTION Since $V = IZ$, we want to determine the product of the given numbers.
$$V = (5.8e^{-0.4363j})(8.5e^{1.047j}) = (5.8)(8.5)e^{-0.4363j + 1.047j}$$
$$= 49.3e^{0.6107j}$$

The voltage is $49.3e^{0.6107j}$ V.

APPLICATION **ELECTRONICS**

EXAMPLE 14.39

If $V_C = 78.3e^{-.3725j}$ V and $X_C = 87.0e^{-1.6500j}\,\Omega$, and $V_C = IX_C$, determine I.

SOLUTION Since $V_C = IX_C$, then $I = \dfrac{V_C}{X_C}$, and so we need to divide.

$$I = \frac{V_C}{X_C} = \frac{78.3e^{-.3725j}}{87.0e^{-1.6500j}}$$

$$= \frac{78.3}{87.0}e^{-.3725j-(-1.6500j)}$$

$$= 0.9e^{1.2775j}$$

So, we have determined that $I = 0.9e^{1.2775j}$ A.

EXERCISE SET 14.4

In Exercises 1–12, express each complex number in exponential form.

1. $3\left(\cos \frac{3\pi}{2} + j \sin \frac{3\pi}{2}\right)$

2. $7(\cos 1.4 + j \sin 1.4)$

3. $2(\cos 60° + j \sin 60°)$

4. $11(\cos 320° + j \sin 320°)$

5. $1.3(\cos 5.7 + j \sin 5.7)$

6. $9.5(\cos 2.1 + j \sin 2.1)$

7. $3.1(\cos 25° + j \sin 25°)$

8. $10.5(\cos 195° + j \sin 195°)$

9. $8 + 6j$

10. $12 - 5j$

11. $-9 + 12j$

12. $-8 - 12j$

In Exercises 13–16, express each number in rectangular and polar form.

13. $5e^{0.5j}$

14. $8e^{1.9j}$

15. $2.3e^{4.2j}$

16. $4.5e^{7j\pi/6}$

In Exercises 17–34, perform each of the indicated operations.

17. $2e^{3j} \cdot 6e^{2j}$

18. $3e^{j} \cdot 4e^{2j}$

19. $e^{1.3j} \cdot 2.4e^{4.6j}$

20. $1.5e^{4.1j} \cdot 0.2e^{1.7j}$

21. $7e^{4.3j} \cdot 4e^{5.7j}$

22. $3.6e^{5.4j} \cdot 2.5e^{6.1j}$

23. $8e^{3j} \div 2e^{j}$

24. $28e^{5j} \div 7e^{2j}$

25. $17e^{4.3j} \div 4e^{2.8j}$

26. $8.5e^{3.4j} \div 2e^{5.3j}$

27. $(3e^{2j})^4$

28. $(4e^{3j})^5$

29. $(2.5e^{1.5j})^4$

30. $(7.2e^{2.3j})^5$

31. $(4e^{6j})^{1/2}$

32. $(16e^{6j})^{1/4}$

33. $(6.25e^{4.2j})^{1/2}$

34. $(1.728e^{2.1j})^{1/3}$

Solve Exercises 35–44.

35. *Electronics* The voltage in an ac circuit is represented by the complex number $V = 56.5 + 24.1j$ V. Express this complex number in exponential form.

36. *Electronics* Express the current $I = 4.90 - 4.11j$ A in exponential form.

37. *Electronics* Express the impedance $Z = 135 \times \underline{/-52.5°}\,\Omega$ in exponential and rectangular forms.

38. *Electronics* Express the capacitive reactance $X_C = 40.5\underline{/-\pi/2}\,\Omega$ in exponential and rectangular forms.

39. *Electronics* Given that $I = 12.5e^{-0.7256j}$ A and $Z = 6.4e^{1.4285j}\,\Omega$, find $V = IZ$.

40. *Electronics* Given that $I = 4.24e^{0.5627j}$ A and $X_L = 28.5e^{-1.5708j}\,\Omega$, find $V_L = IX_L$.

41. *Electronics* If $V = 115e^{-0.2145j}$ V and $Z = 2.5e^{0.5792j}$ Ω, find I, given that $V = IZ$.

42. *Electronics* If $V_R = 35.1e^{1.3826j}$ V and $I = 0.78e^{1.3826j}$ A, find R, given that $V_R = IR$.

43. *Electronics* If $V = 122.4e^{0.2551j}$ V and $I = 36e^{-0.8189j}$ A, find Z, given that $V = IZ$.

44. *Electronics* If $V_L = IX_L$ with $V_L = 119.7e^{0.7254j}$ V and $I = 4.2e^{-0.1246j}$ A, find X_L.

 [IN YOUR WORDS]

45. Describe how to change a complex number in rectangular form to its equivalent complex number in exponential form.

46. Describe how to change a complex number in exponential form to its equivalent complex number in rectangular form.

14.5   OPERATIONS IN POLAR FORM; DeMOIVRE'S FORMULA

Multiplication, division, and powers of complex numbers are easily performed when the numbers are written in exponential form. They are just as easily performed when the numbers are in polar form. Remember the relationship between the exponential and polar forms.

$$re^{j\theta} = r(\cos \theta + j \sin \theta)$$

MULTIPLICATION

Again, we will let $z_1 = r_1e^{j\theta_1}$ and $z_2 = r_2e^{j\theta_2}$ be two complex numbers. We know that

$$z_1z_2 = r_1r_2e^{j(\theta_1 + \theta_2)}$$

so in polar form, this would be

$$r_1(\cos \theta_1 + j \sin \theta_1) \cdot r_2(\cos \theta_2 + j \sin \theta_2) = r_1r_2[\cos (\theta_1 + \theta_2) + j \sin(\theta_1 + \theta_2)]$$

Using the alternative way of writing the polar form of a complex number, we have

$$r_1\underline{/\theta_1} \cdot r_2\underline{/\theta_2} = r_1r_2 \underline{/\theta_1 + \theta_2}$$

Notice that the angles do not have to be written in radians. Angles can be in either degrees or radians.

 PRODUCT OF TWO COMPLEX NUMBERS

The product of two complex numbers $z_1 = r_1 \text{ cis } \theta_1 = r_1\underline{/\theta_1} = r_1e^{j\theta_1}$ and $z_2 = r_2 \text{ cis } \theta_2 = r_2\underline{/\theta_2} = r_2e^{j\theta_2}$ is

$$\begin{aligned} z_1z_2 &= (r_1 \text{ cis } \theta_1)(r_2 \text{ cis } \theta_2) = r_1r_2 \text{ cis}(\theta_1 + \theta_2) \\ &= r_1\underline{/\theta_1}r_2\underline{/\theta_2} = r_1r_2 \underline{/\theta_1 + \theta_2} \\ &= r_1r_2e^{j(\theta_1 + \theta_2)} \end{aligned}$$

EXAMPLE 14.40

Find each of the following products.

(a) $2(\cos 15° + j \sin 15°) \cdot 5(\cos 80° + j \sin 80°)$, (b) $6\,\underline{/30°} \cdot 3\,\underline{/60°}$,
(c) $4\,\underline{/2.3} \cdot 1.5\,\underline{/0.5}$, and (d) $(3e^{1.2j})(5e^{0.3j})$.

SOLUTIONS

(a) $2(\cos 15° + j \sin 15°) \cdot 5(\cos 80° + j \sin 80°)$

$$= 2 \cdot 5[\cos (15° + 80°) + j \sin (15° + 80°)]$$

$$= 10(\cos 95° + j \sin 95°)$$

(b) $6\,\underline{/30°} \cdot 3\,\underline{/60°} = 6 \cdot 3\,\underline{/30° + 60°} = 18\,\underline{/90°}$

$$= 18(\cos 90° + j \sin 90°)$$

$$= 18(0 + j \cdot 1) = 18j$$

(c) $4\,\underline{/2.3} \cdot 1.5\,\underline{/0.5} = 4(1.5)\,\underline{/2.3 + 0.5} = 6\,\underline{/2.8}$

(d) $(3e^{1.2j})(5e^{0.3j}) = 3(5)e^{(1.2 + 0.3)j} = 15e^{1.5j}$

 NOTE When complex numbers are written in exponential form, $z = re^{j\theta}$, you *must* have θ in radians. Complex numbers written in polar form, $z = r$ cis θ, may have θ in either degrees or radians.

DIVISION

Division uses a similar process. Again, we will use the exponential form from Section 14.4 to show that

$$\frac{z_1}{z_2} = \frac{r_1 e^{j\theta_1}}{r_2 e^{j\theta_2}} = \frac{r_1}{r_2} e^{j(\theta_1 - \theta_2)}$$

The results for both the exponential and polar forms are summarized as follows.

QUOTIENT OF TWO COMPLEX NUMBERS

The quotient of two complex numbers $z_1 = r_1$ cis $\theta_1 = r_1\,\underline{/\theta_1} = r_1 e^{j\theta_1}$ and $z_2 = r_2$ cis $\theta_2 = r_2\,\underline{/\theta_2} = r_2 e^{j\theta_2}$ is

$$\frac{z_1}{z_2} = \frac{r_1(\cos \theta_1 + j \sin \theta_1)}{r_2(\cos \theta_2 + j \sin \theta_2)}$$

$$= \frac{r_1}{r_2}[\cos (\theta_1 - \theta_2) + j \sin (\theta_1 - \theta_2)]$$

or $= \dfrac{r_1\,\underline{/\theta_1}}{r_2\,\underline{/\theta_2}}$

$= \dfrac{r_1}{r_2}\,\underline{/\theta_2 - \theta_2}$

or $= \dfrac{r_1 e^{j\theta_1}}{r_2 e^{j\theta_2}} = \dfrac{r_1}{r_2} e^{j(\theta_1 - \theta_2)}$

EXAMPLE 14.41

Find each of the following quotients.

(a) $\dfrac{12(\cos 45° + j \sin 45°)}{2(\cos 15° + j \sin 15°)}$, (b) $\dfrac{15\underline{/135°}}{3\underline{/75°}}$, and (c) $4e^{2.1j} \div 8e^{1.7j}$.

SOLUTIONS

(a) $\dfrac{12(\cos 45° + j \sin 45°)}{2(\cos 15° + j \sin 15°)} = \dfrac{12}{2}[\cos(45° - 15°) + j \sin(45° - 15°)]$

$$= 6(\cos 30° + j \sin 30°)$$

(b) $\dfrac{15\underline{/135°}}{3\underline{/75°}} = \dfrac{15}{3}\underline{/135° - 75°} = 5\underline{/60°}$

(c) $4e^{2.1j} \div 8e^{1.7j} = \frac{4}{8}e^{(2.1 - 1.7)j} = \frac{1}{2}e^{0.4j}$

APPLICATION ELECTRONICS

EXAMPLE 14.42

Ohm's law for ac circuits is $V = IZ$. If $V = 15\underline{/39°}$ V and $Z = 8\underline{/26°}$ Ω, what is the current?

SOLUTION Substituting the given values into the formula $V = IZ$, we obtain $15\underline{/39°} = I \cdot 8\underline{/26°}$. Solving for I produces

$$I = \frac{V}{Z}$$

$$= \frac{15\underline{/39°}}{8\underline{/26°}}$$

$$= \frac{15}{8}\underline{/39° - 26°}$$

$$= \frac{15}{8}\underline{/13°}$$

The current is $\frac{15}{8}\underline{/13°} = 1.875\underline{/13°}$ A.

POWERS, ROOTS, AND DeMOIVRE'S FORMULA

Finding powers of complex numbers in polar form also uses the same process we developed for powers in the exponential form.

DeMOIVRE'S FORMULA

For any complex number $z = r \operatorname{cis} \theta = r\underline{/\theta} = re^{j\theta}$

$$z^n = (re^{j\theta})^n = r^n e^{j\theta n} \text{ or } [r(\cos \theta + j \sin \theta)]^n = r^n(\cos n\theta + j \sin n\theta)$$

This formula is known as **DeMoivre's formula**.

EXAMPLE 14.43

Use DeMoivre's formula to find each of the following powers. Convert your answers to rectangular form.
(a) $[3(\cos 30° + j \sin 30°)]^6$, (b) $(2\underline{/135°})^5$, (c) $(16\underline{/225°})^{1/4}$, and (d) $(2e^{0.4j})^7$.

SOLUTIONS

(a) $[3(\cos 30° + j \sin 30°)]^6 = 3^6(\cos 6 \cdot 30° + j \sin 6 \cdot 30°)$
$$= 729(\cos 180° + j \sin 180°)$$
$$= -729$$

(b) $(2\underline{/135°})^5 = 2^5\underline{/5 \cdot 135°} = 32\underline{/675°}$
$$a = 32 \cos 675° \approx 22.6274$$
$$b = 32 \sin 675° \approx -22.6274$$
so, $(2\underline{/135°})^5 = 22.6274 - 22.6274j$

(c) $(16\underline{/225°})^{1/4} = 16^{1/4}\underline{/\frac{225°}{4}} = 2\underline{/56.25°}$
$$a = 2 \cos 56.25° \approx 1.1111$$
$$b = 2 \sin 56.25° = 1.6629$$
so, $(16\underline{/225°})^{1/4} \approx 1.1111 + 1.6629j$
There are three other fourth roots of $16\underline{/255°}$. We will soon see how to use DeMoivre's formula to find these other three roots.

(d) $(2e^{0.4j})^7 = (2)^7 e^{(0.4)7j} = 128e^{2.8j}$
$$\approx -120.6045 + 42.8785j$$

DeMoivre's formula can be used to help find all of the roots of a complex number. For example, the equation $z^3 = -1$ has three roots. One of the roots is -1. What are the other two? DeMoivre's formula can be used to find those roots.

First, we will write -1 in polar form.

$$-1 = 1(\cos 180° + j \sin 180°)$$

Using DeMoivre's formula with $n = \frac{1}{3}$, we get

$$(-1)^{1/3} = 1^{1/3}\left(\cos \frac{180°}{3} + j \sin \frac{180°}{3}\right)$$
$$= 1(\cos 60° + j \sin 60°)$$
$$= 0.5000 + \frac{\sqrt{3}}{2}j$$
$$\approx 0.5000 + 0.8660j$$

We can see that this is not -1, the answer that we had before. A check would verify that $(0.5 + 0.8660j)^3 = -1$. So, this is a correct answer.

Why did we get a different answer? If you divide any number between 0° and 1,080° (or 0 and 6π) by 3, you find an angle between 0° and 360° (or between 0 and 2π). Now, 180°, 540°, and 900° all have the same terminal side. So, we could have written -1 as $1(\cos 540° + j \sin 540°)$ or as $1(\cos 900° + j \sin 900°)$. Let's find the cube root of each of these numbers.

$$[1(\cos 540° + j \sin 540°)]^{1/3} = 1^{1/3}\left(\cos \frac{540°}{3} + j \sin \frac{540°}{3}\right)$$
$$= 1(\cos 180° + j \sin 180°)$$
$$= -1$$

$$[1(\cos 900° + j \sin 900°)]^{1/3} = 1^{1/3}\left(\cos \frac{900°}{3} + j \sin \frac{900°}{3}\right)$$
$$= 1(\cos 300° + j \sin 300°)$$
$$= 0.5000 - 0.8660j$$

We have found three different cube roots of -1. The first and last are conjugates of each other. We have also given an example of a process we can use to find all of the nth roots of a number, where n is a positive integer.

ROOTS OF A COMPLEX NUMBER

If $z = r(\cos \theta + j \sin \theta)$, then the nth roots of z are given by the formula

$$w_k = \sqrt[n]{r}\left[\cos\left(\frac{\theta}{n} + \frac{360° \cdot k}{n}\right) + j \sin\left(\frac{\theta}{n} + \frac{360° \cdot k}{n}\right)\right] \qquad (\ast)$$

where $k = 0, 1, 2, \ldots, n - 1$.

If θ is in radians, then substitute 2π for 360°.

EXAMPLE 14.44

Find the five fifth roots of $32j$.

SOLUTION The five fifth roots will be called w_0, w_1, w_2, w_3, and w_4. Using $32j = 32(\cos 90° + j \sin 90°)$ and applying formula ($\ast$), we obtain the following.

$$w_0 = \sqrt[5]{32}\left[\cos\left(\frac{90°}{5} + \frac{360° \cdot 0}{5}\right) + j \sin\left(\frac{90°}{5} + \frac{360° \cdot 0}{5}\right)\right]$$
$$= 2(\cos 18° + j \sin 18°)$$
$$\approx 1.9021 + 0.6180j$$
$$w_1 = \sqrt[5]{32}\left[\cos\left(\frac{90°}{5} + \frac{360° \cdot 1}{5}\right) + j \sin\left(\frac{90°}{5} + \frac{360° \cdot 1}{5}\right)\right]$$
$$= 2(\cos 90° + j \sin 90°)$$
$$= 2j$$

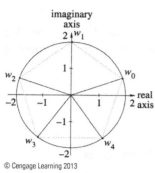

© Cengage Learning 2013

Figure 14.15

$$w_2 = \sqrt[5]{32}\left[\cos\left(\frac{90°}{5} + \frac{360° \cdot 2}{5}\right) + j\sin\left(\frac{90°}{5} + \frac{360° \cdot 2}{5}\right)\right]$$

$$= 2(\cos 162° + j\sin 162°)$$

$$\approx -1.9021 + 0.6180j$$

$$w_3 = \sqrt[5]{32}\left[\cos\left(\frac{90°}{5} + \frac{360° \cdot 3}{5}\right) + j\sin\left(\frac{90°}{5} + \frac{360° \cdot 3}{5}\right)\right]$$

$$= 2(\cos 234° + j\sin 234°)$$

$$\approx -1.1756 - 1.6180j$$

$$w_4 = \sqrt[5]{32}\left[\cos\left(\frac{90°}{5} + \frac{360° \cdot 4}{5}\right) + j\sin\left(\frac{90°}{5} + \frac{360° \cdot 4}{5}\right)\right]$$

$$= 2(\cos 306° + j\sin 306°)$$

$$\approx 1.1756 - 1.6180j$$

The five roots are shown in Figure 14.15. Notice the symmetry of these five roots around the circle. Any time you graph the n roots of a number, they should be equally spaced around a circle with the center at the origin in the complex plane.

EXAMPLE 14.45

Find the three cube roots of $2\sqrt{11} + 10j$.

SOLUTION   We first write this number in polar form. $r = \sqrt{(2\sqrt{11})^2 + 10^2} = \sqrt{144} = 12$ and $\tan\theta = \dfrac{10}{2\sqrt{11}} \approx 1.5075567$, so $\theta \approx 56.4°$. We will find the three cube roots w_0, w_1, and w_2.

$$w_0 = \sqrt[3]{12}\left[\cos\left(\frac{56.4°}{3} + \frac{360° \cdot 0}{3}\right) + j\sin\left(\frac{56.4°}{3} + \frac{360° \cdot 0}{3}\right)\right]$$

$$= \sqrt[3]{12}(\cos 18.8° + j\sin 18.8°)$$

$$\approx 2.1673 + 0.7378j$$

$$w_1 = \sqrt[3]{12}\left[\cos\left(\frac{56.4°}{3} + \frac{360° \cdot 1}{3}\right) + j\sin\left(\frac{56.4°}{3} + \frac{360° \cdot 1}{3}\right)\right]$$

$$= \sqrt[3]{12}(\cos 138.8° + j\sin 138.8°)$$

$$\approx -1.7230 + 1.5076j$$

$$w_2 = \sqrt[3]{12}\left[\cos\left(\frac{56.4°}{3} + \frac{360° \cdot 2}{3}\right) + j\sin\left(\frac{56.4°}{3} + \frac{360° \cdot 2}{3}\right)\right]$$

$$= \sqrt[3]{12}(\cos 258.8° + j\sin 258.8°)$$

$$\approx -0.4447 - 2.2459j$$

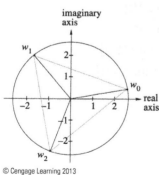

© Cengage Learning 2013

Figure 14.16

Geometrically, these three points are shown on the graph in Figure 14.16.

EXAMPLE 14.46

Find the three cube roots of $(-8)^5$.

SOLUTION   We first write -8 in polar form. Since $r = 8$ and $\theta = 180°$, we see that $-8 = 8$ cis $180°$. Using DeMoivre's formula to raise this to the fifth power, we obtain

$$(-8)^5 = 8^5 \text{ cis } (5 \cdot 180°)$$
$$= 32{,}768 \text{ cis } 900°$$
$$= 32{,}768 \text{ cis } 180°$$

We will find the three cube roots, w_0, w_1, and w_2, of 32,768 cis 180°.

$$w_0 = \sqrt[3]{32{,}768}\left[\cos\left(\frac{180°}{3} + \frac{360° \cdot 0}{3}\right) + j\sin\left(\frac{180°}{3} + \frac{360° \cdot 0}{3}\right)\right]$$
$$= 32(\cos 60° + j\sin 60°)$$
$$\approx 16 + 27.71j$$
$$w_1 = \sqrt[3]{32{,}768}\left[\cos\left(\frac{180°}{3} + \frac{360° \cdot 1}{3}\right) + j\sin\left(\frac{180°}{3} + \frac{360° \cdot 1}{3}\right)\right]$$
$$= 32(\cos 180° + j\sin 180°)$$
$$= -32$$
$$w_2 = \sqrt[3]{32{,}768}\left[\cos\left(\frac{180°}{3} + \frac{360° \cdot 2}{3}\right) + j\sin\left(\frac{180°}{3} + \frac{360° \cdot 2}{3}\right)\right]$$
$$= 32(\cos 300° + j\sin 300°)$$
$$\approx 16 - 27.71j$$

Thus, the three cube roots of $(-8)^5$ are $16 + 27.71j$, -32, and $16 - 27.71j$.

EXERCISE SET 14.5

In Exercises 1–20, perform the indicated operations and give the answers in polar form.

1. $3(\cos 46° + j\sin 46°) \cdot 5(\cos 23° + j\sin 23°)$

2. $4(\cos 135° + j\sin 135°) \cdot 5(\cos 63° + j\sin 63°)$

3. $2.5(\cos 1.43 + j\sin 1.43) \cdot 4(\cos 2.67 + j\sin 2.67)$

4. $6.4(\cos 0.25 + j\sin 0.25) \cdot 3.5(\cos 1.1 + j\sin 1.1)$

5. $\dfrac{8(\cos 85° + j\sin 85°)}{2(\cos 25° + j\sin 25°)}$

6. $\dfrac{6(\cos 273° + j\sin 273°)}{3(\cos 114° + j\sin 114°)}$

7. $\dfrac{9\,\underline{/137°}}{2\,\underline{/26°}}$

8. $\dfrac{18\,\underline{/3.52}}{5\,\underline{/2.14}}$

9. $(3\,\underline{/2.7})(4\,\underline{/5.3})$

10. $[3(\cos 20° + j\sin 20°)]^4$

11. $[5(\cos 84° + j\sin 84°)]^6$

12. $[2.5(\cos 118° + j\sin 118°)]^3$

13. $[10.4(\cos 3.42 + j\sin 3.42)]^3$

14. $(2\,\underline{/1.38})^5$

15. $(3.4\,\underline{/5.3})^4$

16. $(4.41\,\underline{/124°})^{1/2}$

17. $(4e^{2.1j})(3e^{1.7j})$

18. $6e^{1.5j} \div 4e^{0.9j}$

19. $(0.5e^{0.3j})^3$

20. $(0.0625e^{4.2j})^{1/2}$

In Exercises 21–28, use DeMoivre's formula to find the indicated roots. Give the answers in rectangular form.

21. cube roots of 1
22. cube roots of j
23. cube roots of $-8j$
24. fourth roots of -16
25. fourth roots of $-16j$
26. fourth roots of $1 - j$
27. fifth roots of $1 + j$
28. sixth roots of $-1 - j$

In Exercises 29–32, solve the given equations. Express your answers in rectangular form.

29. $x^3 = -j$
30. $x^3 = 125j$
31. $x^6 - 64j = 0$
32. $x^6 - 1 = j$

Solve Exercises 33–40.

33. **Electronics** Ohm's law for alternating current states that for a current with voltage V, current I, and impedance Z, $V = IZ$. If the current is $12\underline{/-23°}$ and the impedance is $9\underline{/42°}$, what is the voltage?

34. **Electronics** If an ac circuit has a voltage of $20\underline{/30°}$ and a current of $5\underline{/40°}$, what is the impedance?

35. **Electronics** The voltage divider rule in ac circuits is

$$V_x = \frac{Z_x E}{Z_T}$$

where V_x is the voltage across one or more elements in series that have total impedance Z_x, E is the total voltage appearing across the series circuit, and Z_T is the total impedance of the series circuit. Find the voltage across the element V_x given that $Z_x = 4\underline{/-90°}\,\Omega$, $E = 100\underline{/0°}\,V$, and $Z_T = 4\underline{/-90°} + 3\underline{/0°}\,\Omega$.

36. **Electronics** Use the voltage divider rule in ac circuits to find the voltage across the element V_x given that $Z_x = 6\underline{/0°}\,\Omega$, $E = 50\underline{/30°}\,V$, and $Z_T = 6\underline{/0°} + 9\underline{/90°} + 17\underline{/-90°}\,\Omega$.

37. **Electronics** The impedance in a series RLC circuit is given by

$$Z = \frac{(1 + j)^2(1 - j)^2}{(3 - 4j)^2}$$

Evaluate Z by changing the expression to polar form.

38. **Electronics** The admittance Y in an ac circuit is measured in siemens (S) and is given by $Y = Z^{-1}$, where Z is the impedance. If $Z = 12 - 5j$, find Y by using

(a) polar form and DeMoivre's formula. (Give the answer in polar form.)

(b) rectangular form.

39. **Electronics** The admittance, Y, in siemens (S) of an ac circuit is given by $Y = Z^{-1}$, where Z is the impedance. If $Z = 4.68\underline{/20.56°}\,\Omega$,

(a) find Y by using DeMoivre's formula. (Give the answer in polar form.)

(b) convert your answer in (a) to rectangular form.

40. **Electronics** The admittance Y in an ac circuit is given by $Y = Z^{-1}$, where Z is the impedance. If $Y = 0.087 - 0.034j$ S,

(a) find Z by using DeMoivre's formula. (Give the answer in polar form.)

(b) convert your answer in (a) to rectangular form.

 [IN YOUR WORDS]

41. Without looking in the text, describe how to multiply or divide two complex numbers in **(a)** exponential form and **(b)** polar form.

42. Explain how to use DeMoivre's formula to find all the n nth roots of the complex number z.

14.6   COMPLEX NUMBERS IN AC CIRCUITS

In direct current (dc) circuits, the basic relation between voltage and current is given by Ohm's law. If V is the voltage across a resistance R, and I is the current flowing through the resistor, then Ohm's law states that

$$V = IR$$

In alternating current (ac) circuits, there is a very similar equation. If V is the voltage across an impedance Z, and I is the current flowing through the impedance, then we have the relationship

$$V = IZ$$

The main difference in these equations is that the dc circuits are expressed as real numbers. Using complex numbers with the ac equations allows them to take the same simple form as the dc equations, except that all quantities are complex numbers. We will examine some of those relationships in this section.

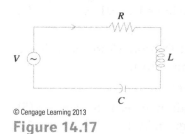

© Cengage Learning 2013

Figure 14.17

Impedance is the opposition to alternating current produced by a resistance R, an inductance L, a capacitance C, or any combination of these. When a sinusoidal voltage V of a given frequency f is applied to a circuit of constant resistance R, constant capacitance C, and constant inductance L, the circuit, like the one in Figure 14.17, is an *RLC* circuit.

In Figure 14.17, the opposition to the current produced by the inductance is called the *inductive reactance* X_L and the opposition to the current produced by the capacitance is the *capacitive reactance* X_C. The *reactance* X is a measure of how much the capacitance and inductance retard the flow of current in an ac circuit and is the difference between the capacitive reactance and the inductive reactance. Thus,

$$X = X_L - X_C$$

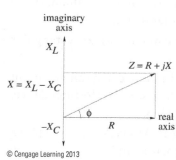

© Cengage Learning 2013

Figure 14.18

The impedance, resistance, and reactance can be represented by a *vector impedance triangle*. The angle ϕ between Z and R is the *phase angle*. In the complex plane, we can represent the resistance along the real axis and the reactance along the imaginary axis as shown in Figure 14.18 Thus,

$$Z = R + jX = R + j(X_L - X_C)$$

$$= Z\underline{/\phi}$$

From our study of complex numbers, you can see that the *magnitude* of the impedance is $|Z| = \sqrt{R^2 + X^2}$ and $\tan\phi = \dfrac{X}{R}$.

When the common circuit components of resistor, inductor, and capacitor are expressed as complex numbers they can be treated in much the same way as pure resistances are treated in Ohm's law. In such a case, Ohm's law is stated as $i = \dfrac{v}{Z}$ where i is the effective current, v is the applied voltage, and Z is the impedance. These circuit elements include normal resistance of a resistor, the "resistance" of a capacitor as it opposes the change in current, and the "resistance" of a capacitor as it opposes the change in voltage. The common circuit elements and their impedances are shown in Table 14.1.

TABLE 14.1				
Circuit Element	**Symbol and Units**	**Resistance or Reactance**	**Impedance Expressed in**	
			Rectangular Form	**Polar Form**
Resistor	$-\bigwedge\hspace{-1mm}\bigwedge\hspace{-1mm}\bigwedge-$ R (ohm)	Resistance: $R = R$	$Z_R = R = R + 0j$	$Z_R = R \underline{/0°}$
Inductor	$-\hspace{-1mm}\frown\hspace{-1mm}\frown\hspace{-1mm}\frown\hspace{-1mm}-$ L (henry)	Inductive reactance: $X_L = \omega L$	$Z_L = jX_L = 0 + jX_L$	$Z_L = X_L \underline{/90°}$
Capacitor	$-\hspace{-1mm})\hspace{-0.5mm}\|\hspace{-0.5mm}-$ C (farad)	Capacitive reactance: $X_C = \dfrac{1}{\omega C}$	$Z_C = -jX_C = 0 - jX_C$	$Z_C = X_C \underline{/-90°}$

© Cengage Learning 2013

APPLICATION ▪ ELECTRONICS

EXAMPLE 14.47

A circuit has a resistance of 8 Ω in series with a reactance of 5 Ω. What are the magnitude of the impedance and its phase angle?

SOLUTION   Using a vector impedance triangle, we can see that the impedance can be represented by

$$Z = 8 + 5j$$

The magnitude of the impedance is

$$|Z| = \sqrt{R^2 + X^2} = \sqrt{8^2 + 5^2} = \sqrt{89} \approx 9.43 \ \Omega$$

The phase angle ϕ is given by

$$\phi = \arctan \tfrac{5}{8} = 32° \text{ or } 0.56 \text{ rad}$$

APPLICATION ▪ ELECTRONICS

EXAMPLE 14.48

In the *RLC* circuit in Figure 14.18, $R = 60 \ \Omega$, $X_L = 75 \ \Omega$, $X_C = 30 \ \Omega$, and $I = 2.25$ A. Find (a) the magnitude and phase angle of Z, and (b) the voltage across the circuit.

EXAMPLE 14.48 (Cont.)   SOLUTIONS

(a) The reactance $X = X_L - X_C = 75 - 30 = 45\ \Omega$. The impedance $Z = 60 + 45j$, so the magnitude of the impedance is

$$|Z| = \sqrt{R^2 + X^2} = \sqrt{60^2 + 45^2} = 75\ \Omega$$

The phase angle ϕ is given by

$$\phi = \arctan \tfrac{45}{60} \approx 36.87° \text{ or } 0.64 \text{ rad}$$

(b) Since the current is 2.25 A and the impedance is 75 Ω, the voltage $V = IZ = (2.25)(75) = 168.75$ V, or approximately 169 V.

An alternating current is produced by a coil of wire rotating through a magnetic field. If the angular velocity of the wire is ω, the capacitive reactance X_C and the inductive reactance X_L are given by the formulas

$$X_C = \frac{1}{\omega C} \qquad \text{and} \qquad X_L = \omega L$$

Since $\omega = 2\pi f$, where f is the frequency of the current, these are also expressed as

$$X_C = \frac{1}{2\pi f C} \qquad \text{and} \qquad X_L = 2\pi f L$$

From these formulas you can see that if C, L, and either ω or f are known, the reactance of the circuit may be determined.

 APPLICATION ELECTRONICS

EXAMPLE 14.49   If $R = 40\ \Omega$, $L = 0.1$ H, $C = 50\ \mu F$, and $f = 60$ Hz, determine the impedance and phase difference between the current and voltage.

SOLUTION   Converting $C = 50\ \mu F$ to farads produces $C = 50 \times 10^{-6}$ F.

$$X_C = \frac{1}{2\pi f C} = \frac{1}{2\pi(60)(50 \times 10^{-6})} \approx 53\ \Omega$$

$$X_L = 2\pi f L = 2\pi(60)(0.1) \approx 38\ \Omega$$

$$Z = R + jX = R + j(X_L - X_C) = 40 + (38 - 53)j = 40 - 15j$$

$$|Z| = \sqrt{R^2 + X^2} = \sqrt{40^2 + (-15)^2} \approx 42.7\ \Omega$$

$$\phi = \arctan \tfrac{-15}{40} \approx -20.6°$$

So, the impedance is 42.7 Ω and the phase difference is $-20.6°$.

In the study of dc circuits, you learn that if several resistors are connected in series, their total resistance is the sum of the individual resistances. Thus, if two resistors R_1 and R_2 are connected in series, their total resistance, R, equals $R_1 + R_2$. If R_1, R_2, and R_3 are connected in series, then $R = R_1 + R_2 + R_3$.

If the resistors are connected in parallel, the relationship is more complicated. The total resistance is the reciprocal of the sum of the reciprocals of the resistances. What this means is that if two resistors R_1 and R_2 are connected in parallel, then the total resistance $R = \dfrac{1}{\dfrac{1}{R_1} + \dfrac{1}{R_2}}$. This can be simplified to $R = \dfrac{R_1 R_2}{R_1 + R_2}$. If three resistors, R_1, R_2, and R_3, are connected in parallel, then

$R = \dfrac{1}{\dfrac{1}{R_1} + \dfrac{1}{R_2} + \dfrac{1}{R_3}}$. This can be rewritten as $R = \dfrac{R_1 R_2 R_3}{R_1 R_2 + R_1 R_3 + R_2 R_3}$

Corresponding formulas hold for complex impedances. Thus, if two impedances Z_1 and Z_2 are connected in series, the total impedance is $Z = Z_1 + Z_2$. If there are three impedances in series, Z_1, Z_2, and Z_3, then $Z = Z_1 + Z_2 + Z_3$.

If complex impedances are connected in parallel, we then have the more complicated formulas. If two impedances are connected in parallel, then the total impedance $Z = \dfrac{1}{\dfrac{1}{Z_1} + \dfrac{1}{Z_2}} = \dfrac{Z_1 Z_2}{Z_1 + Z_2}$. If three impedances are connected in parallel, then the total impedance is $Z = \dfrac{1}{\dfrac{1}{Z_1} + \dfrac{1}{Z_2} + \dfrac{1}{Z_3}} = \dfrac{Z_1 Z_2 Z_3}{Z_1 Z_2 + Z_1 Z_3 + Z_2 Z_3}$.

 APPLICATION ELECTRONICS

EXAMPLE 14.50

If $Z_1 = 2 + 3j\,\Omega$ and $Z_2 = 1 - 6j\,\Omega$, what is the total impedance if these are connected (a) in series and (b) in parallel?

SOLUTIONS

(a) If they are connected in series,

$$Z = Z_1 + Z_2$$
$$= (2 + 3j) + (1 - 6j)$$
$$= 3 - 3j\,\Omega$$

EXAMPLE 14.50 (Cont.)

(b) If they are connected in parallel,

$$Z = \frac{1}{\dfrac{1}{Z_1} + \dfrac{1}{Z_2}} = \frac{Z_1 Z_2}{Z_1 + Z_2}$$

$$= \frac{(2 + 3j)(1 - 6j)}{(2 + 3j) + (1 - 6j)}$$

$$= \frac{20 - 9j}{3 - 3j} \qquad\qquad \text{multiply by } \frac{3 + 3j}{3 + 3j}$$

$$= \frac{87 + 33j}{18}$$

$$= \frac{87}{18} + \frac{33}{18}j\ \Omega = \frac{29}{6} + \frac{11}{6}j\ \Omega$$

APPLICATION ELECTRONICS

EXAMPLE 14.51

If $Z_1 = 3.16\underline{/18.4°}\ \Omega$ and $Z_2 = 4.47\underline{/63.4°}\ \Omega$, what is the total impedance if these are connected (a) in series and (b) in parallel?

SOLUTIONS

(a) If they are connected in series,

$$Z = Z_1 + Z_2$$

Since we cannot add complex numbers in polar form, we need to change these to rectangular form.

$$Z_1 = 3.16(\cos 18.4° + j \sin 18.4°) \approx 2.998 + 0.997j$$
$$Z_2 = 4.47(\cos 63.4° + j \sin 63.4°) \approx 2.001 + 3.997j$$
$$Z = (2.998 + 0.997j) + (2.001 + 3.997j)$$
$$= 4.999 + 4.994j\ \Omega$$
$$\approx 7.07\underline{/45.0°}\ \Omega$$

(b) If they are in parallel,

$$Z = \frac{Z_1 Z_2}{Z_1 + Z_2} = \frac{(3.16\underline{/18.4°})(4.47\underline{/63.4°})}{7.07\underline{/45.0°}}$$

Using our knowledge of multiplying and dividing complex numbers in polar form, we get

$$Z = \frac{(3.16)(4.47)}{7.07}\underline{/18.4° + 63.4° - 45.0°}$$

$$= 2.0\underline{/36.8°}\ \Omega$$

As you can see, some problems are easier to work if you use the rectangular form and some are easier if you use the polar form.

EXERCISE SET 14.6

In Exercises 1–12, find the total impedance if the given impedances are connected (a) in series and (b) in parallel.

1. $Z_1 = 2 + 3j, Z_2 = 1 - 5j$

2. $Z_1 = 4 - 7j, Z_2 = -3 + 4j$

3. $Z_1 = 1 - j, Z_2 = 3j$

4. $Z_1 = 2 + j, Z_2 = 4 - 3j$

5. $Z_1 = 2.19 / 18.4°, Z_2 = 5.16 / 67.3°$

6. $Z_1 = 2\sqrt{3} / 30°, Z_2 = 2 / 120°$

7. $Z_1 = 3\sqrt{5} / \frac{\pi}{7}, Z_2 = 1.5 / 0.45$

8. $Z_1 = 2.57 / 0.25, Z_2 = 1.63 / 1.38$

9. $Z_1 = 4 + 3j, Z_2 = 3 - 2j, Z_3 = 5 + 4j$

10. $Z_1 = 3 - 4j, Z_2 = 1 + 5j, Z_3 = -2j$

11. $Z_1 = 1.64 / 38.2°, Z_2 = 2.35 / 43.7°,$
$Z_3 = 4.67 / -39.6°$

12. $Z_1 = 0.15 / 0.95, Z_2 = 2.17 / 1.39,$
$Z_3 = 1.10 / 0.40$

In Exercises 13–18, use the formula $V = IZ$ to determine the missing unit.

13. $I = 4 - 3j$ A, $Z = 8 - 15j \Omega$

14. $V = 5 + 5j$ V, $I = 4 + 3j$ A

15. $Z = 1 - j \Omega, I = 1 + j$ A

16. $V = 3 + 4j$ V, $Z = 5 - 12j \Omega$

17. $V = 7 / 36.3°$ V, $I = 2.5 / 12.6°$ A

18. $V = 3 / 1.37$ V, $Z = 4 / 0.16 \Omega$

In Exercises 19–24, determine the inductive reactance, capacitive reactance, impedance, and phase difference between the current and voltage.

19. $R = 38 \Omega, L = 0.2$ H, $C = 40 \mu$F, and $f = 60$ Hz

20. $R = 35 \Omega, L = 0.15$ H, $C = 80 \mu$F, and $f = 60$ Hz

21. $R = 20 \Omega, L = 0.4$ H, $C = 60 \mu$F, and $f = 60$ Hz

22. $R = 12 \Omega, L = 0.3$ H, $C = 250 \mu$F, and $\omega = 80$ rad/s

23. $R = 28 \Omega, L = 0.25$ H, $C = 200 \mu$F, and $\omega = 50$ rad/s

24. $R = 2000 \Omega, L = 3.0$ H, $C = 0.5 \mu$F, and $\omega = 1000$ rad/s

In the RLC circuits in Exercises 25–28, find (a) the magnitude and phase angle of Z and (b) the voltage across the circuit.

25. $R = 75 \Omega, X_L = 60 \Omega, X_C = 40 \Omega$, and $I = 3.50$ A

26. $R = 40 \Omega, X_L = 30 \Omega, X_C = 60 \Omega$, and $I = 7.50$ A

27. $R = 3.0 \Omega, X_L = 6.0 \Omega, X_C = 5.0 \Omega$, and $I = 2.85$ A

28. $R = 12.0 \Omega, X_L = 11.4 \Omega, X_C = 2.4 \Omega$, and $I = 0.60$ A

Solve Exercises 29–34.

29. Electronics Figure 14.19 indicates part of an electrical circuit. Kirchhoff's law implies that $I_2 = I_1 + I_3$. If $I_1 = 7 + 2j$ A and $I_2 = 9 - 7j$ A, find I_3.

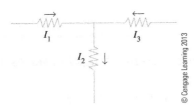

Figure 14.19

30. *Electronics* Resonance in an *RLC* circuit occurs when $X_L = X_C$. Under these conditions, the current and voltage are in phase. Resonance is required for the tuning of radio and television receivers. If $\omega = 100$ rad/s and $L = 0.500$ H, what is the value of C if the system is in resonance?

31. *Electronics* What is the frequency in hertz for a circuit in resonance if $L = 2.5$ H and $C = 20.0\ \mu$F?

32. *Electronics* The *admittance Y* is the reciprocal of the impedance. If $Z = 3 - 2j\ \Omega$, what is the admittance?

33. *Electronics* If the admittance is $4 + 3j\ \Omega$, what is the impedance?

34. *Electronics* The *susceptance B* of an ac circuit of reactance X and impedance Z is defined as $B = \dfrac{X}{Z^2}\ j$. If the reactance is 4 Ω and $Z = 8 + 7j$, what is the susceptance?

 [IN YOUR WORDS]

35. Write an electrical application that requires you to use complex numbers and some of the calculation techniques of this chapter. Give your problem to a classmate and see if he or she understands and can solve your problem. Rewrite the problem as necessary to remove any difficulties encountered by your classmate.

36. Suppose that you are applying for a job with an electronics company. One question on the application form asks you to explain how to perform a specific type of calculation involving complex numbers. It then asks you to give a specific example that uses this type of calculation. Write your answer using complete sentences.

CHAPTER 14   REVIEW

IMPORTANT TERMS AND CONCEPTS

Changing complex numbers from
    Polar form to rectangular form
    Rectangular form to polar form
Complex numbers
    Absolute value
    Addition

Conjugate
Division
Exponential form
Imaginary part
Multiplication
Polar form
Power
Real part
Rectangular form

Rectangular part
Roots
Subtraction
Trigonometric form
Complex plane
DeMoivre's formula
Imaginary unit
Pure imaginary number

REVIEW EXERCISES

In Exercises 1–6, simplify each number in terms of j.

1. $\sqrt{-49}$

2. $\sqrt{-36}$

3. $\sqrt{-54}$

4. $(2j^3)^3$

5. $\sqrt{-2}\sqrt{-18}$

6. $\sqrt{-9}\sqrt{-27}$

In Exercises 7–14, perform the indicated operation. Express each answer in the form a + bj.

7. $(2 - j) + (7 - 2j)$ **9.** $(5 + j) - (6 - 3j)$ **11.** $(6 + 2j)(-5 + 3j)$ **13.** $(4 - 3j)(4 + 3j)$

8. $(9 + j)(4 + 7j)$

10. $\dfrac{1}{11 - j}$ **12.** $\dfrac{2 - 5j}{6 + 3j}$ **14.** $\dfrac{-4}{\sqrt{3} + 2j}$

In Exercises 15–20, graph each complex number and change each number from rectangular form to polar form, or vice versa.

15. $9 - 6j$ **17.** $4 - 4j$ **19.** $6.5\underline{/2.3}$

16. $-8 + 2j$ **18.** 4 cis $60°$ **20.** $10\underline{/20°}$

In Exercises 21–28, perform the indicated operation and express each answer in rectangular form.

21. $(2$ cis $30°)(5$ cis $150°)$ **23.** $(3$ cis $\frac{5\pi}{4})^{14}$ **25.** $(3\underline{/\frac{\pi}{4}})(9\underline{/\frac{2\pi}{3}})$ **27.** $(2\underline{/\frac{\pi}{6}})^{12}$

22. $\dfrac{3 \text{ cis } 20°}{6 \text{ cis } 80°}$ **24.** $(324$ cis $225°)^{1/5}$ **26.** $44\underline{/125°} \div 4\underline{/97°}$ **28.** $(2048\underline{/330°})^{1/11}$

For Exercises 29–32, find all roots and express in rectangular form.

29. $\sqrt[3]{-j}$ **30.** $\sqrt[4]{16}$ **31.** $\sqrt{16 \text{ cis } 120°}$ **32.** $\sqrt[3]{27j}$

In Exercises 33–36, change each number to the exponential form and perform the indicated operation.

33. $(3 + 2j)(5 - j)$ **35.** $(5 + 3j)^5$ **36.** $(-7 - 2j)^{1/3}$

34. $\dfrac{4 - 7j}{3 + j}$

Solve Exercises 37–40.

37. *Physics* A force vector in the complex plane is given by $7.3 - 1.4j$. What is the magnitude and direction (argument) of this vector?

38. *Electronics* Given an *RLC* circuit with $R = 3.0\ \Omega$, $X_L = 7.0\ \Omega$, $X_C = 4.5\ \Omega$, and $I = 1.5$ A, **(a)** what is the magnitude and phase angle of Z, and **(b)** what is the voltage across the circuit?

39. *Electronics* What are the inductive reactance, capacitive reactance, impedance, and phase difference between the current and voltage, if $R = 55\ \Omega$, $L = 0.3$ H, $C = 50\ \mu$F, and $f = 60$ Hz?

40. *Electronics* If $Z_1 = 3 + 5j$ and $Z_2 = 6 - 3j$, then what is Z, if Z_1 and Z_2 are connected **(a)** in series and **(b)** in parallel?

CHAPTER 14   TEST

1. Write $\sqrt{-80}$ in terms of j.

2. Change $7 - 2j$ from rectangular form to polar form.

3. Change 8 cis $150°$ from polar form to rectangular form.

In Exercises 4–11, perform the indicated operation. Express each answer in the form a + bj.

4. $(5 + 2j) + (8 - 6j)$

5. $(-5 + 2j) - (8 - 6j)$

6. $(2 + 3j)(4 - 5j)$

7. $\dfrac{6 + 5j}{-3 - 4j}$

8. $(7 \text{ cis } 75°)(2 \text{ cis } 105°)$

9. $\dfrac{4 \text{ cis } 115°}{3 \text{ cis } 25°}$

10. $\left(9 \text{ cis } \frac{2\pi}{3}\right)^{5/2}$

11. $(27\underline{/129°})^{1/3}$

Solve Exercises 12–16.

12. Find all four roots of $\sqrt[4]{j}$.

13. If $Z_1 = 4 + 2j$ and $Z_2 = 5 - 3j$, what is Z, if Z_1 and Z_2 are connected in (a) series and (b) parallel?

14. The admittance, Y, in an ac circuit is given by $Y = Z^{-1}$, where Z is the impedance. If $Z = 9 - 3j\,\Omega$, what is the admittance?

15. The voltage in a certain ac circuit is $5 + 2j$ V and the current is $3 - 4j$ A. Use Ohm's law, $V = IZ$, to determine the impedance Z.

16. Two ac circuits with impedances Z_1 and Z_2 have total impedance Z, where $Z = Z_1 + Z_2$ if they are connected in series, and

$$Z = \dfrac{1}{\dfrac{1}{Z_1} + \dfrac{1}{Z_2}}$$ if they are connected in parallel.

If $Z_1 = 9 + 3j\,\Omega$ and $Z_2 = 7 - 2j\,\Omega$, determine the total impedance if they are connected (a) in series and (b) in parallel.

SERIES AC CIRCUITS

A lternating current electricity is introduced in Chapter 18, where ac circuits containing only resistors are studied. However, there are two other basic types of circuit components found in ac circuits: inductors and capacitors. Each of these tend to oppose the flow of current but in a different way than resistors. Their effect is called *reactance*. Resistance and reactance are two types of *impedances* found in ac circuits. Impedances can be combined in three basic ways to form a series ac circuit: a resistance-inductance or *RL* circuit, a resistance-capacitance or *RC* circuit, and a resistance-inductance-capacitance or *RLC* circuit. The mathematical relationships that apply to these circuits use complex phasors and the ideas studied in Chapter 20.

21.1 INDUCTIVE REACTANCE AND *RL* SERIES CIRCUITS

Inductive Reactance

An inductor is a coil of wire in an ac circuit. A voltage that opposes the applied voltage is induced in the coil by the ac current. The measure of the coil's capacity to produce voltage is called the inductance L, which is measured in henrys (H). The inductive reactance, X_L, is a measure of the inductor's effect on the applied voltage and current. X_L is measured in the same units as resistance, that is ohms, and is a function of the inductance L and the frequency f:

Formula

Inductive Reactance (Ω)

$$X_L = 2\pi f L \tag{21.1}$$

EXAMPLE 21.1

Given an inductance $L = 100$ mH in an ac circuit with a frequency $f = 2.0$ kHz: Find the inductive reactance.

Solution

Apply formula (21.1):

$$X_L = 2\pi(2.0 \text{ kHz})(100 \text{ mH}) \approx 1.3 \text{ k}\Omega$$

Formula (21.1) can also be used to find the frequency f, or the inductance L, given the other quantities, by solving the formula for f or L as follows.

EXAMPLE 21.2

Given an inductance $L = 70$ mH in an ac circuit whose inductive reactance $X_L = 500 \ \Omega$: Find the frequency of the current.

Solution

Solve formula (21.1) for the frequency by dividing both sides by $2\pi L$ and substitute the given values:

$$\frac{X_L}{2\pi L} = \frac{2\pi f L}{2\pi L}$$

$$f = \frac{X_L}{2\pi L} = \frac{500 \ \Omega}{2\pi(70 \text{ mH})} \approx 1.1 \text{ kHz}$$

One of the reasons X_L is measured in ohms is because Ohm's law applies to the reactance X_L, the voltage across the inductance V_L, and the current through the inductance I:

Law **Ohm's Law with X_L**

$$I = \frac{V_L}{X_L} \tag{21.2}$$

EXAMPLE 21.3

Figure 21-1 shows an ac source connected to an inductance. If $V_L = 10$ V and $X_L = 2.6 \text{ k}\Omega$, find the current in the circuit.

$X_L = 2\pi f L$

$I = \dfrac{V_L}{X_L}$

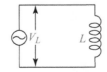

FIGURE 21-1 Inductive reactance for Example 21.3.

Solution

Apply Ohm's law (21.2):

$$I = \frac{V_L}{X_L} = \frac{10 \text{ V}}{2.6 \text{ k}\Omega} \approx 3.8 \text{ mA}$$

EXAMPLE 21.4

Given the inductive circuit in Figure 21-1 with $V_L = 55$ V, $f = 30$ kHz, and $I = 4.5$ mA: Find X_L and L.

Solution

Solve Ohm's law (21.2) for X_L and substitute the values:

$$X_L = \frac{V_L}{I} = \frac{55 \text{ V}}{4.5 \text{ mA}} = 12.22 \text{ k}\Omega \approx 12 \text{ k}\Omega$$

Then apply formula (21.1) solved for L:

$$L = \frac{X_L}{2\pi f} = \frac{12.22 \text{ k}\Omega}{2\pi(30 \text{ kHz})} \approx 65 \text{ mH}$$

RL Series Circuits

When a resistor and an inductor are connected in series to an ac source, the voltage across the inductor V_L is out of phase with both the current I and the voltage across the resistance V_R. The induced voltage in the inductor tends to oppose the current flow and the result is as follows: *V_L leads I and V_R by 90°*. Figure 21-2(a) shows the *RL* series circuit and the voltages. Figure 21-2(b) shows the three ac sine waves. The current I and the voltage V_R are sine waves with a phase angle of 0°. The voltage V_L is a sine wave with a phase angle of 90°. Therefore V_L leads I and V_R by 90°.

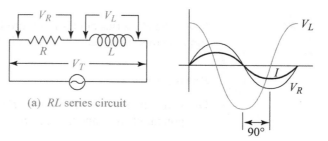

(a) *RL* series circuit

(b) Voltage and current waves: V_L leads I and V_R by 90°

FIGURE 21-2 *RL* series circuit for Examples 21.6 and 21.7.

Figure 21-3(a) shows the phasor diagram of the voltages and the current in the *RL* series circuit. The voltage V_R is the real component, and the voltage V_L is the imaginary component of the resultant or total voltage V_T. Applying formula (20.3) for converting from rectangular to polar form, V_T is given by:

Formula   **RL Series Voltage**

$$V_T = V_R + jV_L = \left(\sqrt{V_R^2 + V_L^2}\right) \angle \tan^{-1}\left(\frac{V_L}{V_R}\right) \tag{21.3}$$

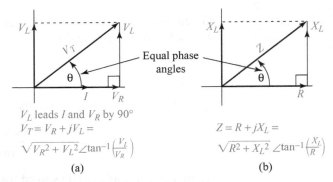

FIGURE 21-3 Phasor relationships in an *RL* series circuit.

The resistance R and the reactance X_L have the same phase relationship as the voltages V_R and V_L, respectively. R is the real component, and X_L is the imaginary component of the total impedance Z:

Formula

RL Series Impedance (Ω)

$$Z = R + jX_L = \left(\sqrt{R^2 + X_L^2}\right) \angle \tan^{-1}\left(\frac{X_L}{R}\right) \qquad \textbf{(21.4)}$$

Figure 21-3(b) shows the impedance triangle. Note that Z has the same phase angle as V_T.

EXAMPLE 21.5

Given the *RL* series circuit in Figure 21-2(a) with $R = 800\ \Omega$ and $X_L = 1.2\ k\Omega$: Find the total impedance Z of the circuit in rectangular and polar form.

Solution

Draw the impedance triangle with R as the real component and X_L as the imaginary component of the impedance Z. See Figure 21-4. Z in rectangular form is then:

$$Z = R + jX_L = 800 + j1200\ \Omega = 0.80 + j1.2\ k\Omega$$

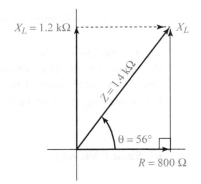

$$Z = 800 + j1200 = \sqrt{800^2 + 1200^2} \angle \tan^{-1}\left(\tfrac{1200}{800}\right) \approx 1.4 \angle 56°\ k\Omega$$

FIGURE 21-4 Impedance triangle for Example 21.5.

Apply formula (21.4) to find Z in polar form:

$$Z = \left(\sqrt{R^2 + X_L^2}\right) \angle \tan^{-1}\left(\frac{X_L}{R}\right) = \left(\sqrt{0.80^2 + 1.2^2}\right) \angle \tan^{-1}\left(\frac{1.2}{0.80}\right)$$

$$Z = \sqrt{2.08} \angle \tan^{-1}(1.5) \approx 1.4 \angle 56° \text{ k}\Omega$$

The magnitude of Z is 1.4 kΩ, and the phase angle is 56°. The calculation from rectangular to polar form, and vice versa, can be done on the calculator if you have the keys (R→P) and (P→R) or similar keys. Depending on your calculator, the key sequence may vary. For example, one way to change $800 + j1200$ to polar form on some TI calculators is:

$$\boxed{(}\; 0.80 \;\boxed{,}\; 1.2 \;\boxed{)}\; \boxed{\text{2nd}}\; \boxed{\text{INV}}\; \boxed{\text{P→R}}\; \boxed{=}\; \rightarrow \; (1.4 \angle 56°) \text{ k}\Omega$$

In ac circuits, impedance is analogous to resistance in dc circuits, and Ohm's law applies for both scalar *and* phasor quantities:

Law

Ohm's Law with *Z* (Scalar and Phasor)

$$I = \frac{V}{Z} \tag{21.5}$$

EXAMPLE 21.6

Given the total voltage in the *RL* series circuit of Example 21.5, $V_T = 15 \angle 56°$ V and the impedance $Z = 1.44 \angle 56°$ kΩ, find the magnitude and the phase angle of the current in polar form.

Solution

You can find I using scalars or phasors. Both methods are shown.

Scalars: Apply Ohm's law (21.5) to find the magnitude of I using the magnitudes of V_T and Z:

$$I = \frac{V_T}{Z} = \frac{15\,\text{V}}{1.44\,\text{k}\Omega} \approx 10\,\text{mA}$$

The phase angle of I is the same as V_R, which is 0°. Therefore $I = 10 \angle 0°$ mA.

Phasors: Apply Ohmís law (21.5) and divide the phasors in polar form:

$$I = \frac{V}{Z} = \frac{15 \angle 56° \text{ V}}{1.44 \angle 56° \text{ k}\Omega} = \frac{15}{1440} \angle (56° - 56°) \approx 0.010 \angle 0° \text{ A}$$

$$= 10 \angle 0° \text{ mA}$$

Remember, when you divide complex phasors you divide the magnitudes and subtract the angles. Observe that the phase angles of V_T and Z are the same, 56°, which verifies that the phase angle of I is 0°.

EXAMPLE 21.7

Given the *RL* series circuit in Figure 21-2(a) with $R = 15 \text{ k}\Omega$, $X_L = 11 \text{ k}\Omega$, and $I = 800 \text{ }\mu\text{A}$:

(a) Find V_R and V_L.

(b) Find the total voltage V_T and the impedance Z in polar form.

Solution

(a) Find the magnitudes of V_R and V_L by applying Ohm's law solved for V:

$$V_R = IR = (800 \text{ }\mu\text{A})(15 \text{ k}\Omega) = 12 \text{ V}$$

$$V_L = IX_L = (800 \text{ }\mu\text{A})(11 \text{ k}\Omega) = 8.8 \text{ V}$$

See Figure 21-5, which shows the voltage phasor diagram for the *RL* series circuit.

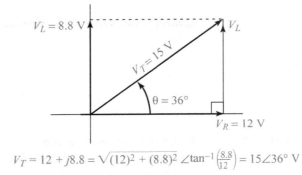

$$V_T = 12 + j8.8 = \sqrt{(12)^2 + (8.8)^2} \angle\tan^{-1}\left(\tfrac{8.8}{12}\right) = 15\angle 36° \text{ V}$$

FIGURE 21-5 Voltage phasors in an *RL* series circuit for Example 21.7.

(b) Apply formula (21.3) to find V_T:

$$V_T = V_R + jV_L = 12 + j8.8 \text{ V} = \sqrt{(12)^2 + (8.8)^2} \angle \tan^{-1}\left(\frac{8.8}{12}\right)$$
$$= \sqrt{221} \angle \tan^{-1}(0.733) \approx 15 \angle 36° \text{ V}$$

The magnitude of V_T is then 15 V, and the phase angle $\theta = 36°$.

Use Ohm's law (21.5) to find the impedance Z from the voltage and the current. In a series circuit, the phase angle of Z is the same as the phase angle of V_T. See Figure 21-3. Therefore, it is only necessary to calculate the magnitude of Z:

$$Z = \frac{V_T}{I} = \frac{15 \text{ V}}{800 \text{ }\mu\text{A}} = 19 \text{ k}\Omega$$

The impedance in polar form is then $Z = 19 \angle 36° \text{ k}\Omega$.

You can also find the impedance using the given values of R and X_L and formula (21.4):

$$Z = R + jX_L = 15 + j11 \text{ k}\Omega = \sqrt{15^2 + 11^2} \angle \tan^{-1}\left(\frac{11}{15}\right)$$

$$= \sqrt{346} \angle \tan^{-1}(0.733) \approx 19 \angle 36° \text{ k}\Omega$$

EXAMPLE 21.8 Given an *RL* series circuit with $L = 500$ mH, $f = 400$ Hz, $V_L = 6.5$ V, and $Z = 3.0$ kΩ:

(a) Find X_L and I.

(b) Find R and V_R.

(c) Find V_T and Z in rectangular and polar form.

Solution

(a) Apply formula (21.1) to find X_L:

$$X_L = 2\pi f L = 2\pi(400 \text{ Hz})(500 \text{ mH}) \approx 1.26 \text{ k}\Omega$$

Apply Ohm's law with X_L to find I:

$$I = \frac{V_L}{X_L} = \frac{6.5 \text{ V}}{1.26 \text{ k}\Omega} \approx 5.2 \text{ mA}$$

(b) Apply the Pythagorean theorem to the impedance triangle to find R:

$$R = \sqrt{Z^2 - X_L^2} = \sqrt{3.0^2 - 1.26^2} \approx 2.7 \text{ k}\Omega$$

V_R can then be found using Ohm's law:

$$V_R = IR = (5.2 \text{ mA})(2.7 \text{ k}\Omega) \approx 14 \text{ V}$$

(c) Apply (21.3) to find V_T in polar form:

$$V_T = V_R + jV_L = 14 + j6.5 \text{ k}\Omega$$

$$= \sqrt{14^2 + 6.5^2} \angle \tan^{-1}\left(\frac{6.5}{14}\right) \approx 15 \angle 25° \text{ V}$$

The phase angle of Z is the same as V_T, therefore $Z = 2.7 + j1.26 \text{ k}\Omega = 3.0 \angle 25° \text{ k}\Omega$.

EXERCISE 21.1

Round all answers in the exercise to two significant digits.

In exercises 1 through 14 using the given values for an inductance L, find the indicated quantity.

1. $L = 1.0$ H, $f = 600$ Hz; X_L
2. $L = 1.5$ H, $f = 500$ Hz; X_L
3. $L = 20$ mH, $f = 5.0$ kHz; X_L
4. $L = 100$ mH, $f = 6.0$ kHz; X_L
5. $L = 800$ mH, $f = 2.0$ kHz; X_L
6. $L = 700$ mH, $f = 1.0$ kHz; X_L
7. $X_L = 10$ kΩ, $f = 15$ kHz; L
8. $X_L = 15$ kΩ, $f = 20$ kHz; L
9. $X_L = 2.5$ kΩ, $f = 10$ kHz; L
10. $X_L = 2.7$ kΩ, $f = 15$ kHz; L
11. $X_L = 200$ Ω, $L = 50$ mH; f
12. $X_L = 330$ Ω, $L = 40$ mH; f
13. $X_L = 3.5$ kΩ, $L = 75$ mH; f
14. $X_L = 6.8$ kΩ, $L = 200$ mH; f

In exercises 15 through 22 using the given values for an ac circuit containing an inductance L, find the indicated quantity.

15. $V_L = 12$ V, $I = 15$ mA; X_L
16. $V_L = 4.5$ V, $I = 300$ μA; X_L
17. $V_L = 5.0$ V, $I = 3.5$ mA; X_L
18. $V_L = 18$ V, $I = 6.6$ mA; X_L
19. $X_L = 25$ kΩ, $I = 100$ μA; V_L
20. $X_L = 1.6$ kΩ, $I = 15$ mA; V_L
21. $X_L = 600$ Ω, $V_L = 1.5$ V; I
22. $X_L = 2.2$ kΩ, $V_L = 11$ V; I

In exercises 23 through 30 using the given values for an RL series circuit, find the impedance Z in rectangular and polar form.

23. $R = 750$ Ω, $X_L = 1.5$ kΩ
24. $R = 1.0$ kΩ, $X_L = 820$ Ω
25. $R = 3.3$ kΩ, $X_L = 4.5$ kΩ
26. $R = 6.8$ kΩ, $X_L = 3.9$ kΩ
27. $R = 2.0$ kΩ, $X_L = 1.2$ kΩ

28. $R = 1.5$ kΩ, $X_L = 1.5$ kΩ
29. $R = 910$ Ω, $X_L = 750$ Ω
30. $R = 620$ Ω, $X_L = 780$ Ω

In exercises 31 through 38 using the given values for an RL series circuit:

(a) Find V_R and V_L.
(b) Find V_T and Z in polar form.

31. $R = 620$ Ω, $X_L = 800$ Ω, $I = 20$ mA
32. $R = 680$ Ω, $X_L = 900$ Ω, $I = 50$ mA
33. $R = 1.0$ kΩ, $X_L = 1.5$ kΩ, $I = 5.0$ mA
34. $R = 5.6$ kΩ, $X_L = 3.3$ kΩ, $I = 3.6$ mA
35. $R = 22$ kΩ, $X_L = 18$ kΩ, $I = 750$ μA
36. $R = 16$ kΩ, $X_L = 16$ kΩ, $I = 820$ μA
37. $R = 2.7$ kΩ, $X_L = 2.2$ kΩ, $I = 15$ mA
38. $R = 2.7$ kΩ, $X_L = 880$ Ω, $I = 3.5$ mA

In exercises 39 through 46 using the given values for an RL series circuit:

(a) Find Z in polar form.
(b) Find I, V_R, and V_L.

39. $R = 620$ Ω, $X_L = 330$ Ω, $V_T = 15$ V
40. $R = 300$ Ω, $X_L = 500$ Ω, $V_T = 20$ V
41. $R = 3.0$ kΩ, $X_L = 1.0$ kΩ, $V_T = 12$ V
42. $R = 1.8$ kΩ, $X_L = 4.7$ kΩ, $V_T = 16$ V
43. $R = 4.3$ kΩ, $X_L = 2.4$ kΩ, $V_T = 60$ V
44. $R = 5.6$ kΩ, $X_L = 9.5$ kΩ, $V_T = 9.0$ V
45. $R = 11$ kΩ, $X_L = 11$ kΩ, $V_T = 50$ V
46. $R = 15$ kΩ, $X_L = 7.5$ kΩ, $V_T = 20$ V

47. Given an RL series circuit with $L = 150$ mH, $f = 1.5$ kHz, $V_L = 7.5$ V, and $Z = 2.3$ kΩ.

(a) Find X_L and I, R, and V_R. See Example 21.8.
(b) Find V_T in polar form.

48. Given an *RL* series circuit with $f = 800$ Hz, $R = 12$ kΩ, $V_R = 10$ V, and $X_L = 5.5$ kΩ.

(a) Find L, I, and V_L.
(b) Find V_T and Z in polar form.

49. Figure 21-6 shows a resistance in series with an inductance connected to a 120 V, 60 Hz generator. Given $R = 100 \ \Omega$ and $L = 750$ mH:

    (a) Find X_L, I, V_R, and V_L
    (b) Find Z in polar form.

50. In the circuit of Figure 21-6, the resistance $R = 150 \ \Omega$ and V_R is measured to be 50 V.

    (a) Find I, V_L, X_L, and L.

    Note: $V_L = \sqrt{V_T^2 - V_R^2}$

    (b) Find Z in polar form.

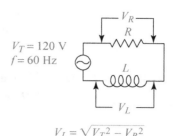

$V_T = 120$ V
$f = 60$ Hz

$V_L = \sqrt{V_T^2 - V_R^2}$

FIGURE 21-6 *RL* series circuit for problems 49 and 50.

21.2 CAPACITIVE REACTANCE AND *RC* SERIES CIRCUITS

Capacitive Reactance

A capacitor consists of two conductors separated by an insulator, or dielectric, and is capable of storing charge. See Figure 21-7 on page 498. The measure of the capacitor's ability to store charge is called capacitance C and is measured in farads (F). The capacitive reactance X_C is measured in ohms and depends on the capacitance C and the frequency f:

Formula

Capacitive Reactance (Ω)

$$X_C = \frac{1}{2\pi f C} \qquad (21.6)$$

EXAMPLE 21.9

Given a capacitance $C = 10$ nF in an ac circuit with a frequency $f = 5.0$ kHz: Find the capacitive reactance.

Solution

Apply formula (21.6):

$$X_C = \frac{1}{2\pi(5.0 \times 10^3 \ \text{Hz})(10 \times 10^{-9} \ \text{F})} \approx 3.2 \ \text{k}\Omega$$

This calculation can be done on the calculator using the reciprocal key:

DAL: 2 ⓧ π ⓧ 5 EE 3 ⓧ 10 EE (−) 9 = x⁻¹ =
        → 3.2×10^3 Hz

Not DAL: 2 ⓧ π ⓧ 5 EXP 3 ⓧ 10 EXP 9 +/− = 1/x =
        → 3.2×10^3 Hz

Formula (21.6) can also be used to find f or C, given the other quantities, by solving the formula for f or C as shown in the next examples.

EXAMPLE 21.10

Given a capacitance $C = 200$ nF in an ac circuit with a capacitive reactance $X_C = 750 \ \Omega$. Find the frequency of the current.

Solution

Solve formula (21.6) for f by multiplying both sides by f and dividing both sides by X_C. Then substitute the given values:

$$\left(\frac{f}{X_C}\right) X_C = \frac{1}{2\pi f C}\left(\frac{f}{X_C}\right)$$

$$f = \frac{1}{2\pi X_C C} = \frac{1}{2\pi(750 \ \Omega)(200 \times 10^{-9} = \text{F})} \approx 1.1 \ \text{kHz}$$

Ohm's law also applies to X_C, the current I and the voltage V_C across the capacitor:

Law   **Ohm's Law with X_c**

$$I = \frac{V_C}{X_C} \qquad\qquad \textbf{(21.7)}$$

EXAMPLE 21.11

In Figure 21-7, if the voltage across the capacitor $V_C = 14$ V, $f = 2.0$ kHz, and $I = 15$ mA, find X_C and C.

Solution

To find X_C, solve Ohm's law (21.7) for X_C and substitute:

$$X_C = \frac{V_C}{I} = \frac{14 \ \text{V}}{15 \ \text{mA}} \approx 930 \ \Omega$$

To find C, solve formula (21.6) for C by multiplying by C and dividing by X_C. Then substitute the given values:

$$\left(\frac{C}{X_C}\right) X_C = \frac{1}{2\pi f C}\left(\frac{C}{X_C}\right)$$

$$C = \frac{1}{2\pi f X_C} = \frac{1}{2\pi(2.0 \ \text{kHz})(933 \ \Omega)} \approx 85 \ \text{nF}$$

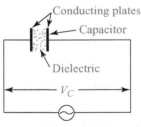

$C = $ Capacitance

$$X_C = \frac{1}{2\pi f C} \qquad X_C = \frac{V_C}{I}$$

FIGURE 21-7 Capacitor and capacitive reactance for Example 21.11.

RC Series Circuits

When a resistor and a capacitor are connected in series to an ac source, the voltage across the capacitor V_C is out of phase with both the current I and the voltage across the resistance V_R. The stored charge in the capacitor tends to oppose the applied voltage and the result is as follows: *I and V_R lead V_C by 90°*. Figure 21-8(a) shows the *RC* circuit and the voltages. Figure 21-8(b) shows the three ac sine waves. The current I and the voltage V_R are sine waves with a phase angle of 0°. The voltage V_C is a sine wave with a phase angle of −90°. Therefore, I and V_R lead V_C by 90°.

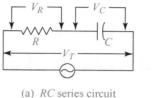

(a) *RC* series circuit

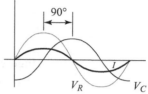

(b) Voltage and current waves: I and V_R lead V_C by 90°

FIGURE 21-8 *RC* series circuit for Examples 21.12 and 21.13.

A good way to remember the relationship between the current and voltage in *RL* and *RC* circuits is by the following mnemonic where *E* (electromotive force) is used for voltage: "***ELI*** the ***ICE*** man" {Voltage (*E*) in an inductive circuit (*L*) leads current (*I*)} *and* {Current (*I*) in a capacitive circuit (*C*) leads Voltage (*E*)}. In a dc circuit, *E* is often used for voltage.

Figure 21-9(a) shows the phasor diagram of the voltages and the current in the *RC* series circuit. The phasor V_R is the real component, and $-V_C$ is the negative imaginary component of the resultant or total voltage V_T:

Formula ·············

RC Series Voltage

$$V_T = V_R - jV_C = \left(\sqrt{V_R^2 + V_C^2}\right) \angle \tan^{-1}\left(\frac{-V_C}{V_R}\right) \tag{21.8}$$

Observe that the phasor V_C has a phase angle of −90°. As a result, the phase angle θ of V_T is a negative angle in the fourth quadrant.

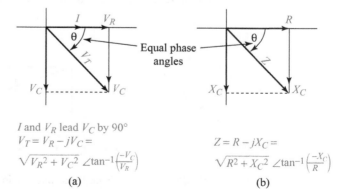

I and V_R lead V_C by 90°
$V_T = V_R - jV_C =$
$\sqrt{V_R^2 + V_C^2} \angle \tan^{-1}\left(\frac{-V_C}{V_R}\right)$

(a)

$Z = R - jX_C =$
$\sqrt{R^2 + X_C^2} \angle \tan^{-1}\left(\frac{-X_C}{R}\right)$

(b)

FIGURE 21-9 Phasor relationships in an *RC* series circuit.

The resistance and the reactance in an *RC* series circuit have the same phase relationship as V_R and V_C, respectively. The resistance *R* is the real component, and $-X_C$ is the negative imaginary component of the total impedance *Z*:

Formulas   **RC Series Impedance**

$$Z = R - jX_C = \left(\sqrt{R^2 + X_C^2}\right) \angle \tan^{-1}\left(\frac{-X_C}{R}\right) \qquad \text{(21.9)}$$

Figure 21-9(b) shows the impedance triangle. Note that *Z* has the same phase angle as V_T.

EXAMPLE 21.12   Given the *RC* circuit in Figure 21-8(a) with $R = 3.0 \text{ k}\Omega$ and $X_C = 1.0 \text{ k}\Omega$: Find the total impedance *Z* of the circuit in rectangular and polar form.

Solution

Draw the impedance triangle with *R* as the real component and $-X_C$ as the negative imaginary component of *Z*. See Figure 21-10. *Z* in rectangular form is then:

$$Z = R - jX_C = 3.0 - j1.0 \text{ k}\Omega$$

Apply formula (21.9) to find *Z* in polar form:

$$Z = \left(\sqrt{R^2 + X_C^2}\right) \angle \tan^{-1}\left(\frac{-X_C}{R}\right) = \sqrt{3.0^2 + 1.0^2} \ \angle \tan^{-1}\left(\frac{-1.0}{3.0}\right)$$

$$Z = \sqrt{10} \ \angle \tan^{-1}(-0.333) \approx 3.2 \ \angle -18° \text{ k}\Omega$$

The magnitude of *Z* is then 3.2 kΩ, and the phase angle is −18°.

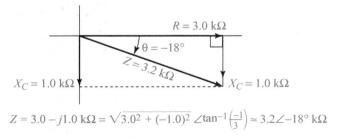

$$Z = 3.0 - j1.0 \text{ k}\Omega = \sqrt{3.0^2 + (-1.0)^2} \ \angle \tan^{-1}\left(\frac{-1}{3}\right) \approx 3.2\angle-18° \text{ k}\Omega$$

FIGURE 21-10 Impedance phasors for Example 21.12.

EXAMPLE 21.13

Given the *RC* circuit in Figure 21-8(a) with $R = 7.5$ kΩ, $C = 33$ nF, $f = 500$ Hz, and $V_T = 20$ V.

(a) Find X_C.

(b) Find Z in rectangular and polar form.

(c) Find I, V_C, and V_R.

Solution

(a) Apply formula (21.6) to find X_C:

$$X_C = \frac{1}{2\pi f C} = \frac{1}{2\pi(500 \text{ Hz})(33 \text{ nF})} \approx 9.65 \text{ k}\Omega$$

(b) Find Z by applying formula (21.9):

$$Z = 7.5 - j9.65 \text{ k}\Omega$$

$$= \sqrt{(7.5)^2 + (9.65)^2} \ \tan^{-1}\left(\frac{-9.65}{7.5}\right) \approx 12.2 \ \angle -52° \text{ k}\Omega$$

(c) Find the current I by applying Ohm's law with Z:

$$I = \frac{V_T}{Z} = \frac{20 \text{ V}}{12.2 \text{ k}\Omega} \approx 1.64 \text{ mA}$$

Now find V_C and V_R by applying Ohm's law using X_C and R:

$$V_C = IX_C = (1.64 \text{ mA})(9.65 \text{ k}\Omega) \approx 16 \text{ V}$$

$$V_R = IR = (1.64 \text{ mA})(7.5 \text{ k}\Omega) \approx 12 \text{ V}$$

Because of the many calculations in this example, results are calculated to three figures and then rounded to two figures for the voltages.

EXAMPLE 21.14

Given an *RC* series circuit with $R = 6.8$ kΩ, $I = 750$ μA, and $V_C = 8.5$ V.

(a) Find X_C and V_R.

(b) Find V_T and Z in polar form.

Solution

(a) Use Ohm's law to find X_C and V_R:

$$X_C = \frac{V_C}{I} = \frac{8.5 \text{ V}}{750 \text{ μA}} \approx 11.3 \text{ k}\Omega$$

$$V_R = IR = (750 \text{ μA})(6.8 \text{ k}\Omega) = 5.1 \text{ V}$$

(b) You can now find V_T and Z by applying formulas (21.8) and (21.9):

$$V_T = \sqrt{5.1^2 + 8.5^2} \; \angle\tan^{-1}\left(\frac{-8.5}{5.1}\right) \approx 9.9 \; \angle-59° \text{ V}$$

$$Z = \sqrt{6.8^2 + 11.3^2} \; \angle\tan^{-1}\left(\frac{-11.3}{6.8}\right) \approx 13 \; \angle-59° \text{ k}\Omega$$

You can also find the magnitude of V_T and Z by finding the phase angle first using $\tan^{-1}$, and then using the reference angle θ with sine and cosine functions. See Figure 21-11.

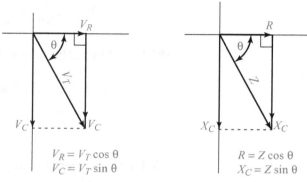

$$V_R = V_T \cos \theta$$
$$V_C = V_T \sin \theta$$

$$R = Z \cos \theta$$
$$X_C = Z \sin \theta$$

FIGURE 21-11 Phasor components for Example 21.14.

Using the components of V_T and Z given by:

$$V_C = V_T \sin \theta \text{ and } R = Z \cos \theta$$

It follows that:

$$V_T = \frac{V_C}{\sin \theta} = \frac{8.5 \text{ V}}{\sin 59°} \approx 9.9 \text{ V}$$

$$Z = \frac{R}{\cos \theta} = \frac{6.8 \text{ k}\Omega}{\cos 59°} \approx 13 \text{ k}\Omega$$

EXERCISE 21.2

Round answers to two significant digits.

In exercises 1 through 14 using the given values for a capacitance C, find the indicated quantity.

1. $C = 20$ nF, $f = 6.0$ kHz; X_C
2. $C = 50$ nF, $f = 5.0$ kHz; X_C
3. $C = 500$ pF, $f = 15$ kHz; X_C
4. $C = 400$ pF, $f = 20$ kHz; X_C

5. $C = 1.0$ μF, $f = 300$ Hz; X_C
6. $C = 2.0$ μF, $f = 200$ Hz; X_C
7. $X_C = 10$ kΩ, $f = 10$ kHz; C
8. $X_C = 16$ kΩ, $f = 12$ kHz; C
9. $X_C = 800$ Ω, $f = 2.0$ kHz; C
10. $X_C = 950$ Ω, $f = 3.0$ kHz; C

11. $X_C = 600\ \Omega, C = 200\ \text{nF}; f$

12. $X_C = 500\ \Omega, C = 100\ \text{nF}; f$

13. $X_C = 15\ \text{k}\Omega, C = 800\ \text{pF}; f$

14. $X_C = 5.6\ \text{k}\Omega, C = 400\ \text{pF}; f$

In exercises 15 through 22 using the given values for an ac circuit containing a capacitance C, find the indicated quantity.

15. $V_C = 20\ \text{V}, I = 12\ \text{mA}; X_C$

16. $V_C = 22\ \text{V}, I = 34\ \text{mA}; X_C$

17. $V_C = 12\ \text{V}, I = 1.5\ \text{mA}; X_C$

18. $V_C = 8.4\ \text{V}, I = 850\ \mu\text{A}; X_C$

19. $X_C = 6.2\ \text{k}\Omega, I = 780\ \mu\text{A}; V_C$

20. $X_C = 750\ \Omega, I = 7.5\ \text{mA}; V_C$

21. $X_C = 25\ \text{k}\Omega, V_C = 10\ \text{V}; I$

22. $X_C = 630\ \Omega, V_C = 14\ \text{V}; I$

In exercises 23 through 30 using the given values for an RC series circuit, find the impedance Z in rectangular and polar form.

23. $R = 1.6\ \text{k}\Omega, X_C = 1.2\ \text{k}\Omega$

24. $R = 8.2\ \text{k}\Omega, X_C = 16\ \text{k}\Omega$

25. $R = 680\ \Omega, X_C = 910\ \Omega$

26. $R = 3.3\ \text{k}\Omega, X_C = 2.2\ \text{k}\Omega$

27. $R = 550\ \Omega, X_C = 550\ \Omega$

28. $R = 1.5\ \text{k}\Omega, X_C = 750\ \Omega$

29. $R = 820\ \Omega, X_C = 1.0\ \text{k}\Omega$

30. $R = 710\ \Omega, X_C = 650\ \Omega$

In exercises 31 through 38 using the given values for an RC series circuit:

(a) Find V_R and V_C.

(b) Find V_T and Z in polar form.

31. $R = 7.5\ \text{k}\Omega, X_C = 4.0\ \text{k}\Omega, I = 3.2\ \text{mA}$

32. $R = 12\ \text{k}\Omega, X_C = 15\ \text{k}\Omega, I = 3.2\ \text{mA}$

33. $R = 10\ \text{k}\Omega, X_C = 25\ \text{k}\Omega, I = 500\ \mu\text{A}$

34. $R = 24\ \text{k}\Omega, X_C = 10\ \text{k}\Omega, I = 650\ \mu\text{A}$

35. $R = 500\ \Omega, X_C = 800\ \Omega, I = 4.0\ \text{mA}$

36. $R = 620\ \Omega, X_C = 480\ \Omega, I = 4.0\ \text{mA}$

37. $R = 4.3\ \text{k}\Omega, X_C = 2.7\ \text{k}\Omega, I = 6.5\ \text{mA}$

38. $R = 1.2\ \text{k}\Omega, X_C = 2.4\ \text{k}\Omega, I = 25\ \text{mA}$

In exercises 39 through 46 using the given values for an RC series circuit:

(a) Find Z in polar form.

(b) Find I, V_R, and V_C.

39. $R = 680\ \Omega, X_C = 620\ \Omega, V_T = 20\ \text{V}$

40. $R = 470\ \Omega, X_C = 620\ \Omega, V_T = 8.4\ \text{V}$

41. $R = 1.2\ \text{k}\Omega, X_C = 850\ \Omega, V_T = 24\ \text{V}$

42. $R = 5.6\ \text{k}\Omega, X_C = 6.2\ \text{k}\Omega, V_T = 24\ \text{V}$

43. $R = 8.2\ \text{k}\Omega, X_C = 13\ \text{k}\Omega, V_T = 12\ \text{V}$

44. $R = 20\ \text{k}\Omega, X_C = 30\ \text{k}\Omega, V_T = 10\ \text{V}$

45. $R = 750\ \Omega, X_C = 750\ \Omega, V_T = 9.7\ \text{V}$

46. $R = 470\ \Omega, X_C = 1.1\ \text{k}\Omega, V_T = 12\ \text{V}$

47. Given an *RC* series circuit with $R = 3.3\ \text{k}\Omega$, $C = 100\ \text{nF}, f = 1.0\ \text{kHz}$, and $V_T = 15\ \text{V}$.

(a) Find X_C, I, V_C, and V_R.

(b) Find Z in polar form.

48. Given an *RC* series circuit with $R = 820\ \Omega$, $I = 9.5\ \text{mA}$, and $V_C = 22\ \text{V}$.

(a) Find X_C and V_R.

(b) Find V_T and Z in polar form.

49. Figure 21-12 shows a resistor in series with a capacitor connected to a 120 V, 60 Hz generator. Given $R = 22\ \text{k}\Omega$ and $C = 150\ \text{nF}$:

(a) Find X_C, V_R, V_C, and I.

(b) Find Z in polar form.

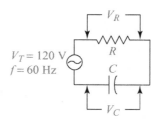

FIGURE 21-12 *RC* series circuit for problems 49 and 50.

50. In the circuit of Figure 21-12, given $X_C = 450\ \Omega$ and $V_C = 100\ \text{V}$.

(a) Find R, C, I, and V_R.

Note: $R = \sqrt{Z^2 - X_C^2}$

(b) Find Z in polar form.

21.3 *RLC* SERIES CIRCUITS AND RESONANCE

When an inductor and a capacitor are connected in series in an ac circuit, the reactances cancel each other because the phasors have opposite direction. Inductive reactance has a phase angle of 90°, while capacitive reactance has a phase angle of −90°. Consider the *RLC* series circuit in Figure 21-13 containing a resistor, an inductor, and a capacitor in series.

The total impedance of the *RLC* series circuit in rectangular form is:

Formula **RLC Series Impedance**

$$Z = R + j(X_L - X_C) = R \pm jX \quad X = |X_L - X_C| \qquad \textbf{(21.10)}$$

$$\text{Inductive } (+jX) \quad \text{Capacitive } (-jX)$$

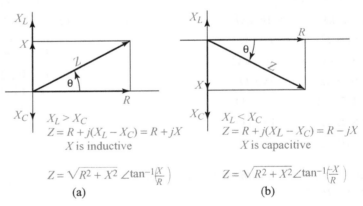

R V_X L C

X_L X_C

V_T

Net reactance $X = |X_L - X_C|$

FIGURE 21-13 *RLC* series circuit for Example 21.16.

where $X = |X_L - X_C|$ is the magnitude of the net reactance. When $X_L > X_C$, the net reactance X is inductive, and the imaginary term jX is positive. See Figure 21-14(a). When $X_L < X_C$, X is capacitive, and the imaginary term jX is negative, See Figure 21-14(b). To change Z to polar form, use formula (21.4) when X is inductive and use formula (21.9) when X is capacitive.

$X_L > X_C$
$Z = R + j(X_L - X_C) = R + jX$
X is inductive

$$Z = \sqrt{R^2 + X^2} \angle \tan^{-1}\left(\frac{X}{R}\right)$$

(a)

$X_L < X_C$
$Z = R + j(X_L - X_C) = R - jX$
X is capacitive

$$Z = \sqrt{R^2 + X^2} \angle \tan^{-1}\left(\frac{-X}{R}\right)$$

(b)

FIGURE 21-14 Impedance phasors in an *RLC* series circuit.

EXAMPLE 21.15

In the *RLC* series circuit in Figure 21-15(a), $R = 500 \ \Omega$, $X_L = 600 \ \Omega$, and $X_C = 1.0 \ \text{k}\Omega$.

(a) Find the net reactance X.

(b) Find the total impedance Z in rectangular and polar form.

Solution

(a) The magnitude of the net reactance is:

$$X = |X_L - X_C| = |600 - 1000| = 400 \ \Omega$$

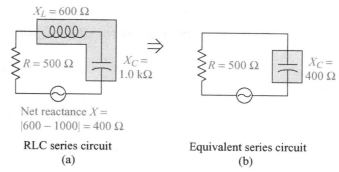

FIGURE 21-15 RLC series circuit and equivalent series circuit for Example 21.15.

The net reactance is capacitive since X_L is less than X_C. The circuit is equivalent to an RC series circuit where $R = 500$ Ω and $X_C = X = 400$ Ω. See Figure 21-15(b). This is called the *equivalent series circuit*.

(b) Apply formula (21.10) to find the total impedance in rectangular form:

$$Z = 500 + j(600 - 1000) \text{ Ω} = 500 - j400 \text{ Ω}$$

To find Z in polar form, apply formula (21.9) when X is capacitive. See Figure 21-14(b):

$$Z = 500 - j400 \text{ Ω}$$

$$= \left(\sqrt{500^2 + 400^2}\right) \angle \tan^{-1}\left(\frac{-400}{500}\right) \approx 640 \angle -39° \text{ Ω}$$

The total voltage of an RLC series circuit in rectangular form is:

RLC Series Voltage

$$V_T = V_R + j(V_L - V_C) = V_R \pm jV_X \quad V_X = |V_L - V_C| \quad \text{(21.11)}$$

where $V_X = |V_L - V_C|$ is the magnitude of the net reactive voltage. To change V_T to polar form, use formula (21.3) when the net reactance X is inductive and use formula (21.8) when X is capacitive. Study the next problem, which illustrates these concepts and others from Sections 21.1 and 21.2.

EXAMPLE 21.16

In the RLC series circuit in Figure 21-13, $R = 3.3$ kΩ, $L = 400$ mH, $C = 10$ nF. If the applied voltage $V_T = 14$ V with frequency $f = 3.0$ kHz:

(a) Find X_L and X_C. Find Z in rectangular and polar form.

(b) Find I, V_R, V_L, and V_C. Find V_T in rectangular and polar form.

Solution

(a) Find the reactances X_L and X_C using formulas (21.1) and (21.6):

$$X_L = 2\pi fL = 2\pi(3.0 \text{ kHz})(400 \text{ mH}) \approx 7.5 \text{ k}\Omega$$

$$X_C = \frac{1}{2\pi fC} = \frac{1}{2\pi(3.0 \text{ kHz})(10 \text{ nF})} \approx 5.3 \text{ k}\Omega$$

Apply formula (21.10) to find the total impedance in rectangular form:

$$Z = R + j(X_L - X_C) = 3.3 + j(7.5 - 5.3) \text{ k}\Omega = 3.3 + j2.2 \text{ k}\Omega$$

Since $X_L > X_C$, the term jX is positive. The net reactance X is inductive, and the equivalent series circuit is an RL series circuit with $R = 3.3$ kΩ and $X_L = X = 2.2$ kΩ. To change Z to polar form, apply formula (21.4):

$$Z = \left(\sqrt{R^2 + X_L^2}\right) \angle \tan^{-1}\left(\frac{X_L}{R}\right)$$

$$Z = \left(\sqrt{3.3^2 + 2.2^2}\right) \angle \tan^{-1}\left(\frac{2.2}{3.3}\right) \approx 4.0 \angle 34° \text{ k}\Omega$$

(b) To find I and the voltages across R, L and C, apply Ohm's law:

$$I = \frac{V}{Z} = \frac{14 \text{ V}}{4.0 \text{ kHz}} = 3.5 \text{ mA}$$

$$V_R = IR = (3.5 \text{ mA})(3.3 \text{ k}\Omega) \approx 11.6 \text{ V}$$

$$V_L = IX_L = (3.5 \text{ mA})(7.5 \text{ k}\Omega) \approx 26.3 \text{ V}$$

$$V_C = IX_C = (3.5 \text{ mA})(5.3 \text{ k}\Omega) \approx 18.6 \text{ V}$$

The voltage V_R, V_L, and V_C may appear to add up to more than the applied voltage 14 V. However, V_L tends to cancel V_C, and their phasor sum equals 14 V as follows. Apply (21.11) to find V_T in rectangular form:

$$V_T = 11.6 + j(26.3 - 18.6) \text{ V} = 11.6 + j7.7$$

The net reactive voltage $V_X = 7.74$ V. Since the circuit is inductive, apply formula (21.3) to change V_T to polar form where $V_L = V_X$:

$$V_T = \left(\sqrt{V_R^2 + V_L^2}\right) \angle \tan^{-1}\left(\frac{V_L}{V_R}\right)$$

$$V_T = \left(\sqrt{11.6^2 + 7.7^2}\right) \angle \tan^{-1}\left(\frac{7.7}{11.6}\right) \approx 14 \angle 34° \text{ V}$$

Error Box

A common error when working with *RLC* circuits is getting the wrong sign for the phase angle θ. The net reactance *X* is considered a positive quantity, however you must know if it is inductive or capacitive and supply the correct sign for θ. If X_L is greater than X_C, θ is positive. If X_L is less than X_C, θ is negative. When using the calculator, if you enter a positive value and press $\boxed{\tan^{-1}}$, you will get a positive angle. If you enter the *same* value with a negative sign and press $\boxed{\tan^{-1}}$, you will get the *same* angle with a negative sign. Therefore, if *X* is inductive, enter a positive value for $\frac{X}{R}$, and if *X* is capacitive, enter a negative value for $\frac{X}{R}$. See if you can get the correct angle in each of the practice problems.

Practice Problems: For each series *RLC* circuit, find the phase angle θ.

1. $R = 10\ \Omega$, $X_L = 20\ \Omega$, $X_C = 10\ \Omega$
2. $R = 10\ \Omega$, $X_L = 10\ \Omega$, $X_C = 20\ \Omega$
3. $R = 500\ \Omega$, $X_L = 600\ \Omega$, $X_C = 1.0\ k\Omega$
4. $R = 500\ \Omega$, $X_L = 2.7\ k\Omega$, $X_C = 2.4\ k\Omega$
5. $R = 100\ \Omega$, $X_L = 1.0\ \Omega$, $X_C = 1.0\ \Omega$
6. $R = 100\ \Omega$, $X_L = 500\ \Omega$, $X_C = 2.0\ k\Omega$
7. $R = 1.0\ k\Omega$, $X_L = 1.1\ k\Omega$, $X_C = 750\ \Omega$
8. $R = 1.0\ k\Omega$, $X_L = 500\ \Omega$, $X_C = 2.4\ k\Omega$

When an ac series circuit contains more than one resistor, you can add the resistances, as in a dc circuit, to obtain the total resistance. When an ac series circuit contains more than one inductor, or more than one capacitor, you can add the similar reactances to obtain the total inductive reactance and the total capacitive reactance:

$$X_{L_T} = X_{L_1} + X_{L_2} + X_{L_3} + \cdots$$

$$X_{C_T} = X_{C_1} + X_{C_2} + X_{C_3} + \cdots$$

You can therefore always reduce the circuit to an *RLC* series circuit with one resistor, one inductor, and one capacitor. Then, as in Example 21.16, you can find the equivalent *RL* or *RC* series circuit.

Power in an AC Circuit

There are three types of power in an ac circuit:

Formulas

True or Real Power (W)

$$P = I^2R = VI \cos \theta \tag{21.12a}$$

Reactive Power (VAR)

$$Q = VI \sin \theta \tag{21.12b}$$

Apparent Power (VA)

$$S = VI \qquad\qquad (21.12c)$$

The true power is the power dissipated by the resistance and is measured in watts (W). The reactive power is the power expended by the reactance and is measured in voltampere-reactive (VAR). The apparent power is the phasor sum of the true power and the reactive power: $S = \sqrt{P^2 + Q^2}$. It is measured in voltamperes (VA). The ratio $P/S = \cos\theta$ is called the power factor.

EXAMPLE 21.17 Find the true power, reactive power, apparent power, and the power factor for the circuit of Example 21.16.

Solution

Apply formulas (21.12) using $V = V_T = 14$ V, $I = 3.5$ mA and $\theta = 34°$:

$$\text{True power } P = (14 \text{ V})(3.5 \text{ mA}) \cos 34° \approx 41 \text{ mW}$$

$$\text{Reactive power } Q = (14 \text{ V})(3.5 \text{ mA}) \sin 34° \approx 27 \text{ mVAR}$$

$$\text{Apparent power } S = (14 \text{ V})(3.5 \text{ mA}) = 49 \text{ mVA}$$

$$\text{Power factor } = P/S = \cos\theta = \cos 34° \approx 0.829$$

Series Resonance

In an *RLC* circuit, the frequency at which the inductive reactance equals the capacitive reactance, that is, $X_L = X_C$, is called the *resonant frequency f_r*. At this frequency, the net reactance $X = 0$, and the circuit is purely resistive. That is, the total impedance $Z = R$, and the phase angle $\theta = 0°$. The true power is at a maximum because when $\theta = 0°$, $\cos\theta = 1$, and $P = VI$. Since $X_L = X_C$ at the resonant frequency F_r:

$$2\pi f_r L = \frac{1}{2\pi f_r C}$$

which leads to:

$$f_r^2 = \frac{1}{4\pi^2 LC}$$

Taking the square root of both sides, the formula for the resonant frequency f_r is:

Formula **Resonant Frequency (Hz)**

$$f_r = \frac{1}{2\pi\sqrt{LC}} \qquad\qquad (21.13)$$

EXAMPLE 21.18

Given $L = 50$ mH and $C = 20$ nF, find the resonant frequency.

Solution

Apply formula (21.13):

$$f_r = \frac{1}{2\pi\sqrt{(50 \text{ mH})(20 \text{ nF})}} \approx 5.0 \text{ kHz}$$

This calculation can be done by multiplying all the factors in the denominator and then taking the reciprocal:

DAL: 2 $\boxed{\times}$ $\boxed{\pi}$ $\boxed{\times}$ $\boxed{\sqrt{}}$ $\boxed{(}$ 50 $\boxed{\text{EE}}$ $\boxed{(-)}$ 3 $\boxed{\times}$ 20 $\boxed{\text{EE}}$ $\boxed{(-)}$ 9 $\boxed{)}$
$\boxed{=}$ $\boxed{x^{-1}}$ $\boxed{=}$ $\rightarrow 5.03 \times 10^3$

NOT DAL: 50 $\boxed{\text{EXP}}$ 3 $\boxed{+/-}$ $\boxed{\times}$ 20 $\boxed{\text{EXP}}$ 9 $\boxed{+/-}$ $\boxed{=}$ $\boxed{\sqrt{}}$ $\boxed{\times}$ 2 $\boxed{\times}$ $\boxed{\pi}$
$\boxed{=}$ $\boxed{x^{-1}}$ $\rightarrow 5.03 \times 10^3$

Resonance is important in tuning radio frequency (RF) circuits because at the resonant frequency the impedance Z is minimized. The current is at a maximum, the reactive power is zero, and the true power is at a maximum, and equal to the apparent power.

EXAMPLE 21.19

At a frequency of 4.0 kHz, how much inductance is required in series with a capacitance of 10 nF to obtain resonance?

Solution

You need to solve formula (21.13) for L. Square both sides:

$$f_r^2 = \frac{1}{4\pi^2 LC}$$

Multiply both sides by $\dfrac{L}{f_r^2}$:

$$\left(\frac{L}{f_r^2}\right)f_r^2 = \frac{1}{4\pi^2 \cancel{L}C}\left(\frac{\cancel{L}}{f_r^2}\right)$$

$$L = \frac{1}{4\pi^2 f_r^2 C}$$

Substitute the given values to find L:

$$L = \frac{1}{4\pi^2(4.0 \text{ kHz})^2(10 \text{ nF})} \approx 160 \text{ mH}$$

EXERCISE 21.3

Round all answers to two significant digits.

In exercises 1 through 10 using the given values for an RLC series circuit, find X and find Z in rectangular and polar form.

1. $R = 750 \ \Omega, X_L = 800 \ \Omega, X_C = 500 \ \Omega$

2. $R = 750 \ \Omega, X_L = 600 \ \Omega, X_C = 900 \ \Omega$

3. $R = 1.8 \ k\Omega, X_L = 3.3 \ k\Omega, X_C = 5.5 \ k\Omega$

4. $R = 3.0 \ k\Omega, X_L = 5.0 \ k\Omega, X_C = 3.0 \ k\Omega$

5. $R = 3.9 \ k\Omega, X_L = 11 \ k\Omega, X_C = 6.2 \ k\Omega$

6. $R = 5.1 \ k\Omega, X_L = 10 \ k\Omega, X_C = 16 \ k\Omega$

7. $R = 1.0 \ k\Omega, X_L = 750 \ \Omega, X_C = 1.2 \ \Omega$

8. $R = 680 \ \Omega, X_L = 1.3 \ k\Omega, X_C = 930 \ \Omega$

9. $R = 200 \ \Omega, X_L = 1.1 \ k\Omega, X_C = 750 \ \Omega$

10. $R = 200 \ \Omega, X_L = 880 \ \Omega, X_C = 1.5 \ k\Omega$

In exercises 11 through 18 using the given values for an RLC series circuit, find I, V_R, V_L, and V_C, and find V_T in polar form.

11. $R = 3.3 \ k\Omega, X_L = 1.2 \ , X_C = 4.7 \ k\Omega,$
    $V_T = 12 \ V$

12. $R = 3.0 \ k\Omega, X_L = 1.5, X_C = 1.2 \ k\Omega,$
    $V_T = 24 \ V$

13. $R = 270 \ \Omega, X_L = 510 \ \Omega, X_C = 450 \ \Omega,$
    $V_T = 20V$

14. $R = 680 \ \Omega, X_L = 660 \ \Omega, X_C = 780 \ \Omega,$
    $V_T = 15V$

15. $R = 910 \ \Omega, X_L = 4.3 \ k\Omega, X_C = 1.5 \ k\Omega,$
    $V_T = 14V$

16. $R = 11 \ k\Omega, X_L = 7.9 \ k\Omega, X_C = 12 \ k\Omega,$
    $V_T = 8.0V$

17. $R = 600 \ \Omega, X_L = 1.2 \ k\Omega, X_C = 840 \ \Omega,$
    $V_T = 30V$

18. $R = 500 \ \Omega, X_L = 920 \ \Omega, X_C = 1.0 \ k\Omega,$
    $V_T = 6.5V$

In exercises 19 through 26 using the given values for series resonance, find the indicated value.

19. $L = 100 \ mH, C = 20 \ nF; f_r$

20. $L = 50 \ mH, C = 100 \ nF; f_r$

21. $L = 40 \ mH, C = 800 \ pF; f_r$

22. $L = 350 \ mH, C = 100 \ pF; f_r$

23. $L = 400 \ \mu H, f_r = 6.5 \ kHz; C$

24. $L = 240 \ mH, f_r = 15 \ kHz; C$

25. $C = 1.0 \ \mu F, f_r = 600 \ Hz; L$

26. $C = 60 \ nF, f_r = 3.2 \ kHz; L$

27. Given an *RLC* series circuit with $R = 330 \ \Omega$, $L = 50 \ mH$, and $C = 100 \ nF$: If the applied voltage $V = 12 \ V$ with a frequency $f = 2.6 \ kHz$:
    (a) Find X_L and X_C. Find Z in rectangular and polar form.
    (b) Find I, V_R, V_L, and V_C. Find V_T in rectangular and polar form.

28. Given an *RLC* series circuit with $R = 1.0 \ k\Omega$, $L = 200 \ mH$, and $C = 40 \ nF$: If applied voltage $V = 24 \ V$ with a frequency $f = 1.5 \ kHz$:
    (a) Find X_L and X_C. Find Z in rectangular and polar form.
    (b) Find I, V_R, V_L, and V_C. Find V_T in rectangular and polar form.

29. Given an *RLC* series circuit with $R = 2.2 \ k\Omega$, $L = 500 \ mH$, and $C = 20 \ nF$: If the applied voltage $V = 20 \ V$ with a frequency $f = 1.2 \ kHz$:
    (a) Find X_L and X_C. Find, Z in rectangular and polar form.
    (b) Find I, V_R, V_L, and V_C. Find V_T in rectangular and polar form.

30. Given an *RLC* series circuit with $R = 500 \ \Omega$, $L = 200 \ mH$, and $C = 100 \ nF$: If the applied voltage $V = 10 \ V$ with a frequency $f = 1.6 \ kHz$:
    (a) Find X_L and X_C. Find Z in rectangular and polar form.
    (b) Find I, V_R, V_L, and V_C. Find V_T in rectangular and polar form.

Answers to Error Box Problems, page 507:

1. $45°$ **2.** $-45°$ **3.** $-39°$ **4.** $31°$ **5.** $0°$ **6.** $-86°$ **7.** $19°$ **8.** $-62°$

31. Figure 21-16 shows an *RLC* series circuit containing two inductors, a capacitor, and a resistor connected to a voltage source *V*. If $V = 20$ V, $R = 600$ Ω, $X_{L_1} = 500$ Ω, $X_{L_2} = 750$ Ω, and $X_C = 800$ Ω:

    (a) Find Z in rectangular and polar form.

    Note: $X_L = X_{L_1} + X_{L_2}$.

    (b) Find I, true power P, reactive power Q, apparent power S, and the power factor.

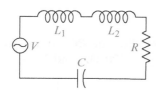

FIGURE 21-16 *RLC* series circuit for problems 31 and 32.

32. In the *RLC* series circuit in Figure 21-16, if $V = 10$ V, $R = 1.0$ kΩ, $X_{L_1} = 2.0$ kΩ, $X_{L_2} = 3.0$ kΩ, and $X_C = 7.5$ kΩ:

    (a) Find Z in rectangular and polar form.

    Note: $X_L = X_{L_1} + X_{L_2}$.

    (b) Find I, true power P, reactive power Q, apparent power S, and the power factor.

33. In an *RLC* series circuit, $R = 1.8$ kΩ, $X_L = 3.6$ kΩ, $X_C = 1.6$ kΩ, and $I = 10$ mA:

    (a) Find V_R, V_L, and V_C. Find V_T in rectangular and polar form.

    (b) Find Z in rectangular and polar form.

34. In an *RLC* series circuit, $R = 510$ Ω, $X_L = 360$ Ω, $X_C = 750$ Ω, and $V_R = 5.0$ V:

    (a) Find I, V_L, and V_C. Find V_T in rectangular and polar form.

    (b) Find Z in rectangular and polar form.

35. Given a series circuit containing two resistances $R_1 = 2.7$ kΩ and $R_2 = 1.2$ kΩ, an inductance $L = 300$ mH, and a capacitance $C = 50$ nF: If the applied voltage $V = 10$ V with $f = 1.0$ kHz:

    (a) Find X_L and X_C. Find Z in rectangular and polar form.

    (b) Find I, V_{R_1}, V_{R_2}, V_L, and V_C. Find V_T in rectangular and polar form.

36. In problem 35, given $R_1 = 330$ Ω, $R_2 = 180$ Ω, $L = 800$ μH, and $C = 800$ pF: If the applied voltage $V = 20$ V with $f = 130$ kHz:

    (a) Find X_L and X_C. Find Z in rectangular and polar form.

    (b) Find I, V_{R_1}, V_L, and V_C. Find V_T in rectangular and polar form.

Chapter Highlights

21.1 INDUCTIVE REACTANCE AND *RL* SERIES CIRCUITS

Inductive Reactance (Ω)

$$X_L = 2\pi f L \qquad \textbf{(21.1)}$$

• • •

Ohm's Law with X_L

$$I = \frac{V_L}{X_L} \qquad \textbf{(21.2)}$$

In an *RL* series circuit, V_L leads I and V_R by 90°, and the phase angle θ is positive.

RL Series Voltage

$$V_T = V_R + jV_L = \left(\sqrt{V_R^2 + V_L^2}\right) \angle \tan^{-1}\left(\frac{V_L}{V_R}\right) \textbf{(21.3)}$$

• • •

RL Series Impedance (Ω)

$$Z = R + jX_L = \left(\sqrt{R^2 + X_L^2}\right) \angle \tan^{-1}\left(\frac{X_L}{R}\right) \quad \textbf{(21.4)}$$

Key Example: For an *RL* series circuit with $L = 500$ mH, $f = 400$ Hz, $V_L = 6.5$ V, and $Z = 3.0$ kΩ:

$$X_L = 2\pi fL = 2\pi(400 \text{ Hz})(500 \text{ mH}) \approx 1.26 \text{ k}\Omega$$

$$I = \frac{V_L}{X_L} = \frac{6.5 \text{ V}}{1.26 \text{ k}\Omega} \approx 5.2 \text{ mA}$$

$$R = \sqrt{Z^2 - X_L^2} = \sqrt{3.0^2 - 1.26^2} \approx 2.7 \text{ k}\Omega$$

$$V_R = IR = (5.2 \text{ mA})(2.7 \text{ k}\Omega) \approx 14 \text{ V}$$

$$V_T = V_R + jV_L = 14 + j6.5$$

$$= \sqrt{14^2 + 6.5^2} \angle \tan^{-1}\left(\frac{6.5}{14}\right) \approx 15 \angle 25° \text{ V}$$

Ohm's Law with *Z* (Scalar and Phasor)

$$I = \frac{V}{Z} \qquad \textbf{(21.5)}$$

21.2 CAPACITIVE REACTANCE AND *RC* SERIES CIRCUITS

Capacitive Reactance (Ω)

$$X_C = \frac{1}{2\pi fC} \qquad \textbf{(21.6)}$$

• • •

Ohm's Law with X_c

$$I = \frac{V_C}{X_C} \qquad \textbf{(21.7)}$$

In an *RC* series circuit, *I* and V_R lead V_C by 90°, and the phase angle θ is negative.

RC Series Voltage

$$V_T = V_R - jV_C$$

$$= \left(\sqrt{V_R^2 + V_C^2}\right) \angle \tan^{-1}\left(\frac{-V_C}{V_R}\right) \quad \textbf{(21.8)}$$

Remember: "*ELI* the *ICE* man" {*E* (voltage) in *L* (inductor) leads *I*} *and* {*I* in *C* (capacitor) leads *E*}.

RC Series Impedance

$$Z = R - jX_C$$

$$= \left(\sqrt{R^2 + X_C^2}\right) \angle \tan^{-1}\left(\frac{X_C}{R}\right) \qquad \textbf{(21.9)}$$

Key Example: For an *RC* circuit with $R = 7.5$ kΩ, $C = 33$ nF, $f = 500$ Hz, and $V_T = 20$ V:

$$X_C = \frac{1}{2\pi fC} = \frac{1}{2\pi(500 \text{ Hz})(33 \text{ nF})} \approx 9.65 \text{ k}\Omega$$

$$Z = \sqrt{(7.5)^2 + (9.65)^2} \ \tan^{-1}\left(\frac{-9.65}{7.5}\right)$$

$$\approx 12.2 \angle {-52.1°} \text{ k}\Omega$$

$$I = \frac{V_T}{Z} = \frac{20 \text{ V}}{12.2 \text{ k}\Omega} \approx 1.64 \text{ mA}$$

$$V_C = IX_C = (1.64 \text{ mA})(9.65 \text{ k}\Omega) \approx 16 \text{ V}$$

$$V_R = IR = (1.64 \text{ mA})(7.5 \text{ k}\Omega) \approx 12 \text{ V}$$

21.3 *RLC* SERIES CIRCUITS AND RESONANCE

RLC Series Impedance

$$Z = R + j(X_L - X_C) = R \pm jX$$

$$X = |X_L - X_C| \qquad \textbf{(21.10)}$$

Inductive $(+jX)$ Capacitive $(-jX)$

When $X_L > X_C$, *X* is inductive, when $X_L < X_C$, *X* is capacitive. See Figure 21-14. To find *Z* in polar form, use formula (21.4) when *X* is inductive, and use formula (21.9) when *X* is capacitive.

RLC Series Voltage

$$V_T = V_R + j(V_L - V_C) = V_R \pm jV_X$$

$$V_X = |V_L - V_C| \qquad \textbf{(21.11)}$$

692

To find V_T in polar form, use formula (21.3) when X is inductive, and use formula (21.8) when X is capacitive.

Key Example: For an *RLC* series circuit with $R = 3.3$ kΩ, $L = 400$ mH, $C = 10$ nF, $V_T = 14$ V, and $f = 3.0$ kHz:

$$X_L = 2\pi fL = 2\pi(3.0 \text{ kHz})(400 \text{ mH}) \approx 7.5 \text{ k}\Omega$$

$$X_C = \frac{1}{2\pi fC} = \frac{1}{2\pi(3.0 \text{ kHz})(10 \text{ nF})} \approx 5.3 \text{ k}\Omega$$

$$Z = R + j(X_L - X_C) = 3.3 + j(7.5 - 5.3) \text{ k}\Omega$$

$$= 3.3 + j2.2 \text{ k}\Omega$$

$X_L > X_C$ and $X = 2.2$ kΩ is inductive. Use formula (21.4) for Z and formula (21.3) for V_T:

$$Z = \sqrt{3.3^2 + 2.2^2} \angle\tan^{-1}\left(\frac{2.2}{3.3}\right) \approx 4.0 \angle 34° \text{ k}\Omega$$

$$I = \frac{V}{Z} = \frac{14 \text{ V}}{4.0 \text{ kHz}} = 3.5 \text{ mA}$$

$$V_R = IR = (3.5 \text{ mA})(3.3 \text{ k}\Omega) \approx 11.6 \text{ V}$$

$$V_L = IX_L = (3.5 \text{ mA})(7.5 \text{ k}\Omega) \approx 26.3 \text{ V}$$

$$V_C = IX_C = (3.5 \text{ mA})(5.3 \text{ k}\Omega) \approx 18.6 \text{ V}$$

$$V_T = 11.6 + j(26.3 - 18.6) \text{ V} = 11.6 + j7.7$$

$$V_T = \sqrt{11.6^2 + 7.7^2} \angle\tan^{-1}\left(\frac{7.7}{11.6}\right) \approx 14 \angle 34° \text{ V}$$

True or Real Power (W)

$$P = I^2R = VI \cos\theta \qquad \textbf{(21.12a)}$$

Reactive Power (VAR)

$$Q = VI \sin\theta \qquad \textbf{(21.12b)}$$

Apparent Power (VA)

$$S = VI \qquad \textbf{(21.12c)}$$

Series resonance is when $X_L = X_C$, and the circuit is purely resistive with $Z = R$ and $\theta = 0°$. The current and true power are at a maximum.

Resonant Frequency (Hz)

$$f_r = \frac{1}{2\pi\sqrt{LC}} \qquad \textbf{(21.13)}$$

Review Exercises

Round all answers to two significant digits.

In exercises 1 through 10 using the given values for each series ac circuit, find the indicated quantity.

1. *RL* circuit: $L = 250$ mH, $f = 6.0$ kHz; X_L
2. *RL* circuit: $L = 750$ µH, $f = 55$ kHz; X_L
3. *RC* circuit: $C = 420$ nF, $f = 500$ Hz; X_C
4. *RC* circuit: $C = 700$ pF, $f = 100$ kHz; X_C
5. *RL* circuit: $X_L = 740$ Ω, $L = 60$ mH; f
6. *RL* circuit: $X_L = 1.1$ kΩ, $f = 900$ Hz; L
7. *RC* circuit: $X_C = 4.0$ kΩ, $f = 10$ kHz; C
8. *RC* circuit: $X_C = 850$ Ω, $C = 200$ nF; f
9. *RLC* circuit: $L = 200$ mH, $C = 500$ pF; f_r
10. *RLC* circuit: $L = 600$ mH, $C = 40$ pF; f_r

In exercises 11 through 22 using the given values for each series ac circuit, find the impedance Z in rectangular and polar form.

11. *RL* circuit: $R = 820$ Ω, $X_L = 1.0$ kΩ
12. *RL* circuit: $R = 3.3$ kΩ, $X_L = 1.8$ kΩ
13. *RL* circuit: $R = 150$ Ω, $X_L = 430$ Ω
14. *RL* circuit: $R = 1.0$ kΩ, $X_L = 640$ Ω
15. *RC* circuit: $R = 6.2$ kΩ, $X_C = 8.5$ kΩ
16. *RC* circuit: $R = 7.5$ kΩ, $X_C = 5.0$ kΩ
17. *RC* circuit: $R = 1.8$ kΩ, $X_C = 780$ Ω
18. *RC* circuit: $R = 330$ Ω, $X_C = 440$ Ω
19. *RLC* circuit: $R = 470$ Ω, $X_L = 910$ Ω, $X_C = 360$ Ω
20. *RLC* circuit: $R = 1.1$ kΩ, $X_L = 700$ Ω, $X_C = 1.3$ kΩ

21. *RLC* circuit: $R = 6.8$ kΩ, $X_L = 1.6$ kΩ, $X_C = 4.7$ kΩ

22. *RLC* circuit: $R = 560$ Ω, $X_L = 2.0$ kΩ, $X_C = 860$ Ω

In exercises 23 through 28 using the given values for a series ac circuit:

    (a) Find Z in polar form.
    (b) Find I and find V_T in rectangular and polar form.

23. *RL* circuit: $R = 390$ Ω, $X_L = 620$ Ω, $V_T = 15$ V

24. *RL* circuit: $R = 6.8$ kΩ, $X_L = 750$ Ω, $V_T = 14$ V

25. *RC* circuit: $R = 6.2$ kΩ, $X_C = 5.6$ kΩ, $V_T = 24$ V

26. *RC* circuit: $R = 4.3$ kΩ, $X_C = 13$ kΩ, $V_T = 8.5$ V

27. *RLC* circuit: $R = 3.3$ kΩ, $X_L = 4.7$ kΩ, $X_C = 1.2$ kΩ, $V_T = 12$ V

28. *RLC* circuit: $R = 820$ Ω, $X_L = 500$ Ω, $X_C = 1.1$ kΩ, $V_T = 36$ V

29. In an *RL* series circuit, $R = 1.8$ kΩ, $f = 900$ Hz, $L = 200$ mH, and $I = 10$ mA.

    (a) Find X_L, V_R, and V_L.
    (b) Find V_T and Z in polar and rectangular form.

30. In an *RL* series circuit, $R = 20$ kΩ, $f = 2.0$ kHz, $L = 1.6$ H, and $V_T = 10$ V.

    (a) Find X_L, V_R, V_L, and I.
    (b) Find V_T and Z in polar and rectangular form.

31. In an *RC* series circuit, $R = 3.3$ kΩ, $f = 2.3$ kHz, $C = 15$ nF, and $I = 800$ µA.

    (a) Find X_C, V_R, and V_C.
    (b) Find V_T and Z in polar and rectangular form.

32. In an *RC* series circuit, $R = 510$ Ω, $f = 250$ Hz, $C = 1.0$ µF, and $V_T = 10$ V.

    (a) Find X_C, V_R, V_C, and I.
    (b) Find V_T and Z in polar and rectangular form.

33. In an *RLC* series circuit, $R = 3.0$ kΩ, $L = 150$ mH, and $C = 10$ nF. The applied voltage $V_T = 32$ V with a frequency $f = 6.0$ kHz.

    (a) Find X_L, X_C, V_R, V_L, V_C, and I.
    (b) Find V_T and Z in rectangular and polar form.

34. In an *RLC* series circuit, $R = 6.2$ kΩ, $L = 50$ mH, and $C = 750$ pF. The current $I = 5.5$ mA with a frequency $f = 20$ kHz.

    (a) Find X_L, X_C, V_R, V_L, and V_C.
    (b) Find V_T and Z in rectangular and polar form.

35. In an *RLC* series circuit, $R = 750$ Ω, $L = 120$ mH, and $C = 7.5$ nF. The applied voltage $V_T = 30$ V with a frequency $f = 5.5$ kHz.

    (a) Find X_L, X_C, V_R, V_L, V_C, and I.
    (b) Find V_T and Z in rectangular and polar form.

36. In an *RCL* series circuit, $R = 3.9$ kΩ, $L = 10$ mH, and $C = 10$ nF. The current $I = 10$ mA with a frequency $f = 10$ kHz.

    (a) Find X_L, X_C, V_R, V_L, and V_C.
    (b) Find V_T and Z in rectangular and polar form.

37. Figure 21-17 shows an *RLC* series circuit containing two capacitors, an inductor, and a resistor connected to a voltage source. The applied voltage $V_T = 9.0$ V, $R = 680$ Ω, $X_{C_1} = 500$ Ω, $X_{C_2} = 1.6$ kΩ, and $X_L = 1.2$ kΩ.

    (a) Find Z in rectangular and polar form and find the current I.
        Note: $X_C = X_{C_1} + X_{C_2}$.
    (b) Find V_T in rectangular and polar form and find the true power P.

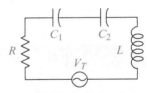

FIGURE 21-17 *RLC* series circuit for problems 37 and 38.

38. In the circuit in Figure 21-17, the current $I = 5.0$ mA, $R = 5.6$ kΩ, $X_{C_1} = 2.7$ kΩ, $X_{C_2} = 2.2$ kΩ, and $X_L = 8.2$ kΩ.

    (a) Find V_T and Z in polar and rectangular form.
    (b) Find the true power P.

2.6   Solving Inequalities Algebraically and Graphically

Properties of Inequalities

Simple inequalities were reviewed in Section P.1. There, the inequality symbols

$$<,\ \leq,\ >,\ \text{and}\ \geq \qquad \text{Inequality symbols}$$

were used to compare two numbers and to denote subsets of real numbers. For instance, the simple inequality $x \geq 3$ denotes all real numbers x that are greater than or equal to 3.

In this section, you will study inequalities that contain more involved statements such as

$$5x - 7 > 3x + 9$$

and

$$-3 \leq 6x - 1 < 3.$$

As with an equation, you **solve an inequality** in the variable x by finding all values of x for which the inequality is true. These values are **solutions** of the inequality and are said to **satisfy** the inequality. For instance, the number 9 is a solution of the first inequality listed above because

$$5(9) - 7 > 3(9) + 9$$
$$45 - 7 > 27 + 9$$
$$38 > 36.$$

On the other hand, the number 7 is not a solution because

$$5(7) - 7 \not> 3(7) + 9$$
$$35 - 7 \not> 21 + 9$$
$$28 \not> 30.$$

The set of all real numbers that are solutions of an inequality is the **solution set** of the inequality.

The set of all points on the real number line that represent the solution set is the **graph of the inequality.** Graphs of many types of inequalities consist of intervals on the real number line.

The procedures for solving linear inequalities in one variable are much like those for solving linear equations. To isolate the variable, you can make use of the **properties of inequalities.** These properties are similar to the properties of equality, but there are two important exceptions. When each side of an inequality is multiplied or divided by a negative number, *the direction of the inequality symbol must be reversed* in order to maintain a true statement. Here is an example.

$$-2 < 5 \qquad \text{Original inequality}$$
$$(-3)(-2) > (-3)(5) \qquad \text{Multiply each side by } -3 \text{ and reverse the inequality symbol.}$$
$$6 > -15 \qquad \text{Simplify.}$$

Two inequalities that have the same solution set are **equivalent inequalities.** instance, the inequalities

$$x + 2 < 5 \quad \text{and} \quad x < 3$$

are equivalent. To obtain the second inequality from the first, you can subtract 2 from each side of the inequality. The properties listed at the top of the next page describe operations that can be used to create equivalent inequalities.

Properties of Inequalities

Let a, b, c, and d be real numbers.

1. *Transitive Property*

$a < b$ and $b < c$ ⟹ $a < c$

2. *Addition of Inequalities*

$a < b$ and $c < d$ ⟹ $a + c < b + d$

3. *Addition of a Constant*

$a < b$ ⟹ $a + c < b + c$

4. *Multiplying by a Constant*

For $c > 0$, $a < b$ ⟹ $ac < bc$

For $c < 0$, $a < b$ ⟹ $ac > bc$ Reverse the inequality symbol.

Each of the properties above is true when the symbol $<$ is replaced by $\leq$ and $>$ is replaced by $\geq$. For instance, another form of Property 3 is as follows.

$a \leq b$ ⟹ $a + c \leq b + c$

The simplest type of inequality to solve is a **linear inequality** in one variable, such as $x + 3 > 4$. (For help with solving one-step linear inequalities, see Appendix D at this textbook's *Companion Website*.)

EXAMPLE 1   Solving a Linear Inequality

Solve $5x - 7 > 3x + 9$.

Solution

$5x - 7 > 3x + 9$	Write original inequality.
$2x - 7 > 9$	Subtract $3x$ from each side.
$2x > 16$	Add 7 to each side.
$x > 8$	Divide each side by 2.

The solution set is all real numbers that are greater than 8, which is denoted by $(8, \infty)$. The graph of this solution set is shown below. Note that a parenthesis at 8 on the real number line indicates that 8 is *not* part of the solution set.

Solution Interval: $(8, \infty)$

✓ **Checkpoint** 🔊))) *Audio-video solution in English & Spanish at LarsonPrecalculus.com.*

Solve $7x - 3 \leq 2x + 7$. Then graph the solution set.   ■

Note that the four inequalities forming the solution steps of Example 1 are all *equivalent* in the sense that each has the same solution set.

Checking the solution set of an inequality is not as simple as checking the solution(s) of an equation because there are simply too many x-values to substitute into the original inequality. However, you can get an indication of the validity of the solution set by substituting a few convenient values of x. For instance, in Example 1, try substituting $x = 6$ and $x = 10$ into the original inequality.

Explore the Concept

Use a graphing utility to graph $f(x) = 5x - 7$ and $g(x) = 3x + 9$ in the same viewing window. (Use $-1 \leq x \leq 15$ and $-5 \leq y \leq 50$.) For which values of x does the graph of f lie above the graph of g? Explain how the answer to this question can be used to solve the inequality in Example 1.

EXAMPLE 2   **Solving an Inequality**

Solve $1 - \frac{3}{2}x \geq x - 4$.

Algebraic Solution

$1 - \frac{3}{2}x \geq x - 4$	Write original inequality.
$2 - 3x \geq 2x - 8$	Multiply each side by the LCD.
$2 - 5x \geq -8$	Subtract $2x$ from each side.
$-5x \geq -10$	Subtract 2 from each side.
$x \leq 2$	Divide each side by -5 and reverse the inequality symbol.

The solution set is all real numbers that are less than or equal to 2, which is denoted by $(-\infty, 2]$. The graph of this solution set is shown below. Note that a bracket at 2 on the number line indicates that 2 *is* part of the solution set.

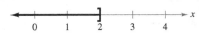

Solution Interval: $(-\infty, 2]$

Graphical Solution

Use a graphing utility to graph $y_1 = 1 - \frac{3}{2}x$ and $y_2 = x - 4$ in the same viewing window, as shown below.

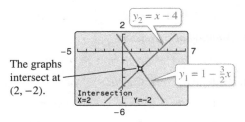

The graphs intersect at $(2, -2)$.

The graph of y_1 lies above the graph of y_2 to the left of their point of intersection, $(2, -2)$, which implies that $y_1 \geq y_2$ for all $x \leq 2$.

✓ **Checkpoint** *Audio-video solution in English & Spanish at LarsonPrecalculus.com.*

Solve $2 - \frac{5}{3}x > x - 6$ (a) algebraically and (b) graphically.

Sometimes it is possible to write two inequalities as a **double inequality,** as demonstrated in Example 3.

EXAMPLE 3   **Solving a Double Inequality**

Solve $-3 \leq 6x - 1$ and $6x - 1 < 3$.

Algebraic Solution

$-3 \leq 6x - 1 < 3$	Write as a double inequality.
$-3 + 1 \leq 6x - 1 + 1 < 3 + 1$	Add 1 to each part.
$-2 \leq 6x < 4$	Simplify.
$\dfrac{-2}{6} \leq \dfrac{6x}{6} < \dfrac{4}{6}$	Divide each part by 6.
$-\dfrac{1}{3} \leq x < \dfrac{2}{3}$	Simplify.

The solution set is all real numbers that are greater than or equal to $-\frac{1}{3}$ *and* less than $\frac{2}{3}$. The interval notation for this solution set is $\left[-\frac{1}{3}, \frac{2}{3}\right)$. The graph of this solution set is shown below.

Solution Interval: $\left[-\frac{1}{3}, \frac{2}{3}\right)$

Graphical Solution

Use a graphing utility to graph $y_1 = 6x - 1$, $y_2 = -3$, and $y_3 = 3$ in the same viewing window, as shown below.

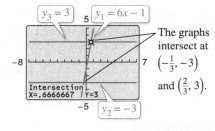

The graphs intersect at $\left(-\frac{1}{3}, -3\right)$ and $\left(\frac{2}{3}, 3\right)$.

The graph of y_1 lies above the graph of y_2 to the right of $\left(-\frac{1}{3}, -3\right)$ *and* the graph of y_1 lies below the graph of y_3 to the left of $\left(\frac{2}{3}, 3\right)$. This implies that $y_2 \leq y_1 < y_3$ when $-\frac{1}{3} \leq x < \frac{2}{3}$.

✓ **Checkpoint** *Audio-video solution in English & Spanish at LarsonPrecalculus.com.*

Solve $1 < 2x + 7 < 11$. Then graph the solution set.

Inequalities Involving Absolute Values

> **Solving an Absolute Value Inequality**
>
> Let x be a variable or an algebraic expression and let a be a positive real number.
>
> **1.** The solutions of $|x| < a$ are all values of x that lie between $-a$ and a.
>
> $|x| < a$ if and only if $-a < x < a$.   Double inequality
>
> **2.** The solutions of $|x| > a$ are all values of x that are less than $-a$ or greater than a.
>
> $|x| > a$ if and only if $x < -a$ or $x > a$.   Compound inequality
>
> These rules are also valid when $<$ is replaced by $\leq$ and $>$ is replaced by $\geq$.

EXAMPLE 4   **Solving Absolute Value Inequalities**

Solve each inequality.

a. $|x - 5| < 2$

b. $|x - 5| > 2$

Algebraic Solution

a. $|x - 5| < 2$ Write original inequality.

$\quad -2 < x - 5 < 2$ Write double inequality.

$\quad\quad 3 < x < 7$ Add 5 to each part.

The solution set is all real numbers that are greater than 3 *and* less than 7. The interval notation for this solution set is $(3, 7)$. The graph of this solution set is shown below.

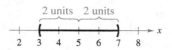

b. The absolute value inequality $|x - 5| > 2$ is equivalent to the following compound inequality: $x - 5 < -2$ *or* $x - 5 > 2$.

Solve first inequality: $x - 5 < -2$ Write first inequality.

$\quad\quad\quad\quad\quad x < 3$ Add 5 to each side.

Solve second inequality: $x - 5 > 2$ Write second inequality.

$\quad\quad\quad\quad\quad x > 7$ Add 5 to each side.

The solution set is all real numbers that are less than 3 *or* greater than 7. The interval notation for this solution set is $(-\infty, 3) \cup (7, \infty)$. The symbol $\cup$ is called a *union* symbol and is used to denote the combining of two sets. The graph of this solution set is shown below.

Graphical Solution

Use a graphing utility to graph

$$y_1 = |x - 5| \quad \text{and} \quad y_2 = 2$$

in the same viewing window, as shown below.

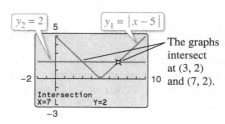

a. You can see that the graph of y_1 lies below the graph of y_2 when

$$3 < x < 7.$$

This implies that the solution set is all real numbers greater than 3 *and* less than 7.

b. You can see that the graph of y_1 lies above the graph of y_2 when

$$x < 3$$

or when

$$x > 7.$$

This implies that the solution set is all real numbers that are less than 3 *or* greater than 7.

✓ **Checkpoint** 🔊))) *Audio-video solution in English & Spanish at LarsonPrecalculus.com.*

Solve $|x - 20| \leq 4$. Then graph the solution set.

Polynomial Inequalities

To solve a polynomial inequality such as $x^2 - 2x - 3 < 0$, use the fact that a polynomial can change signs only at its zeros (the x-values that make the polynomial equal to zero). Between two consecutive zeros, a polynomial must be entirely positive or entirely negative. This means that when the real zeros of a polynomial are put in order, they divide the real number line into intervals in which the polynomial has no sign changes. These zeros are the **key numbers** of the inequality, and the resulting open intervals are the **test intervals** for the inequality. For instance, the polynomial above factors as $x^2 - 2x - 3 = (x + 1)(x - 3)$ and has two zeros, $x = -1$ and $x = 3$, which divide the real number line into three test intervals: $(-\infty, -1)$, $(-1, 3)$, and $(3, \infty)$. To solve the inequality $x^2 - 2x - 3 < 0$, you need to test only one value in each test interval.

> ### Finding Test Intervals for a Polynomial
>
> To determine the intervals on which the values of a polynomial are entirely negative or entirely positive, use the following steps.
>
> 1. Find all real zeros of the polynomial, and arrange the zeros in increasing order. These zeros are the key numbers of the polynomial.
>
> 2. Use the key numbers to determine the test intervals.
>
> 3. Choose one representative x-value in each test interval and evaluate the polynomial at that value. If the value of the polynomial is negative, then the polynomial will have negative values for *every* x-value in the interval. If the value of the polynomial is positive, then the polynomial will have positive values for *every* x-value in the interval.

EXAMPLE 5 Investigating Polynomial Behavior

To determine the intervals on which $x^2 - 3$ is entirely negative and those on which it is entirely positive, factor the quadratic as $x^2 - 3 = \left(x + \sqrt{3}\right)\left(x - \sqrt{3}\right)$. The key numbers occur at $x = -\sqrt{3}$ and $x = \sqrt{3}$. So, the test intervals for the quadratic are

$$\left(-\infty, -\sqrt{3}\right), \quad \left(-\sqrt{3}, \sqrt{3}\right), \quad \text{and} \quad \left(\sqrt{3}, \infty\right).$$

In each test interval, choose a representative x-value and evaluate the polynomial, shown in the table.

Interval	x-Value	Value of Polynomial	Sign of Polynomial
$\left(-\infty, -\sqrt{3}\right)$	$x = -3$	$(-3)^2 - 3 = 6$	Positive
$\left(-\sqrt{3}, \sqrt{3}\right)$	$x = 0$	$(0)^2 - 3 = -3$	Negative
$\left(\sqrt{3}, \infty\right)$	$x = 5$	$(5)^2 - 3 = 22$	Positive

The polynomial has negative values for every x in the interval $\left(-\sqrt{3}, \sqrt{3}\right)$ and positive values for every x in the intervals $\left(-\infty, -\sqrt{3}\right)$ and $\left(\sqrt{3}, \infty\right)$. In Figure 2.27, the graph of $y = x^2 - 3$ confirms this result.

✓ **Checkpoint**))) *Audio-video solution in English & Spanish at LarsonPrecalculus.com.*

Determine the intervals on which $x^2 - 2x - 3$ is entirely negative and those on which it is entirely positive.

Technology Tip

Some graphing utilities will produce graphs of inequalities. For instance, you can graph $2x^2 + 5x > 12$ by setting the graphing utility to *dot* mode and entering $y = 2x^2 + 5x > 12$. Using $-10 \le x \le 10$ and $-4 \le y \le 4$, your graph should look like the graph shown below. The solution appears to be $(-\infty, -4) \cup \left(\frac{3}{2}, \infty\right)$. See Example 6 for an algebraic solution and for an alternative graphical solution.

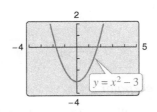

Figure 2.27

To determine the test intervals for a polynomial inequality, the inequality must first be written in general form with the polynomial on one side and zero on the other.

EXAMPLE 6 Solving a Polynomial Inequality

See LarsonPrecalculus.com for an interactive version of this type of example.

Solve $2x^2 + 5x > 12$.

Algebraic Solution

$$2x^2 + 5x - 12 > 0 \qquad \text{Write inequality in general form.}$$

$$(x + 4)(2x - 3) > 0 \qquad \text{Factor.}$$

Key Numbers: $x = -4, x = \frac{3}{2}$

Test Intervals: $(-\infty, -4), \left(-4, \frac{3}{2}\right), \left(\frac{3}{2}, \infty\right)$

Test: Is $(x + 4)(2x - 3) > 0$?

After testing these intervals, you can see that the polynomial $2x^2 + 5x - 12$ is positive on the open intervals $(-\infty, -4)$ and $\left(\frac{3}{2}, \infty\right)$. So, the solution set of the inequality is

$$(-\infty, -4) \cup \left(\frac{3}{2}, \infty\right).$$

Graphical Solution

First write the polynomial inequality $2x^2 + 5x > 12$ as $2x^2 + 5x - 12 > 0$. Then use a graphing utility to graph $y = 2x^2 + 5x - 12$. In the figure, you can see that the graph is *above* the x-axis when x is less than -4 *or* when x is greater than $\frac{3}{2}$. So, you can graphically approximate the solution set to be $(-\infty, -4) \cup \left(\frac{3}{2}, \infty\right)$.

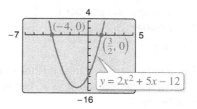

✓ **Checkpoint** ◀))) *Audio-video solution in English & Spanish at LarsonPrecalculus.com.*

Solve $2x^2 + 3x < 5$ (a) algebraically and (b) graphically.

EXAMPLE 7 Solving a Polynomial Inequality

$$2x^3 - 3x^2 - 32x + 48 > 0 \qquad \text{Original inequality}$$

$$x^2(2x - 3) - 16(2x - 3) > 0 \qquad \text{Factor by grouping.}$$

$$(x^2 - 16)(2x - 3) > 0 \qquad \text{Distributive Property}$$

$$(x - 4)(x + 4)(2x - 3) > 0 \qquad \text{Factor difference of two squares.}$$

The key numbers are $x = -4$, $x = \frac{3}{2}$, and $x = 4$; and the test intervals are $(-\infty, -4)$, $\left(-4, \frac{3}{2}\right)$, $\left(\frac{3}{2}, 4\right)$, and $(4, \infty)$.

Interval	x-Value	Polynomial Value	Conclusion
$(-\infty, -4)$	$x = -5$	$2(-5)^3 - 3(-5)^2 - 32(-5) + 48 = -117$	Negative
$\left(-4, \frac{3}{2}\right)$	$x = 0$	$2(0)^3 - 3(0)^2 - 32(0) + 48 = 48$	Positive
$\left(\frac{3}{2}, 4\right)$	$x = 2$	$2(2)^3 - 3(2)^2 - 32(2) + 48 = -12$	Negative
$(4, \infty)$	$x = 5$	$2(5)^3 - 3(5)^2 - 32(5) + 48 = 63$	Positive

From this you can conclude that the polynomial is positive on the open intervals $\left(-4, \frac{3}{2}\right)$ and $(4, \infty)$. So, the solution set is $\left(-4, \frac{3}{2}\right) \cup (4, \infty)$.

✓ **Checkpoint** ◀))) *Audio-video solution in English & Spanish at LarsonPrecalculus.com.*

Solve $3x^3 - x^2 - 12x > -4$. Then graph the solution set.

When solving a polynomial inequality, be sure to account for the particular type of inequality symbol given in the inequality. For instance, in Example 7, the original inequality contained a "greater than" symbol and the solution consisted of two open intervals. If the original inequality had been $2x^3 - 3x^2 - 32x + 48 \geq 0$, the solution would have consisted of the closed interval $\left[-4, \frac{3}{2}\right]$ and the interval $[4, \infty)$.

EXAMPLE 8   Unusual Solution Sets

a. The solution set of

$$x^2 + 2x + 4 > 0$$

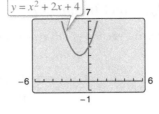

$y = x^2 + 2x + 4$

consists of the entire set of real numbers, $(-\infty, \infty)$. In other words, the value of the quadratic $x^2 + 2x + 4$ is positive for every real value of x, as shown in the figure at the right. (Note that this quadratic inequality has *no* key numbers. In such a case, there is only one test interval—the entire real number line.)

b. The solution set of

$$x^2 + 2x + 1 \leq 0$$

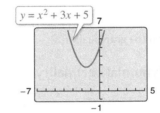

$y = x^2 + 2x + 1$

consists of the single real number $\{-1\}$, because the quadratic

$$x^2 + 2x + 1$$

has one key number, $x = -1$, and it is the only value that satisfies the inequality, as shown in the figure at the right.

c. The solution set of

$$x^2 + 3x + 5 < 0$$

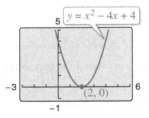

$y = x^2 + 3x + 5$

is empty. In other words, the quadratic

$$x^2 + 3x + 5$$

is not less than zero for any value of x, as shown in the figure at the right.

d. The solution set of

$$x^2 - 4x + 4 > 0$$

$y = x^2 - 4x + 4$

consists of all real numbers *except* the number 2. In interval notation, this solution set can be written as $(-\infty, 2) \cup (2, \infty)$. The graph of $y = x^2 - 4x + 4$ lies above the x-axis except at $x = 2$, where it touches the x-axis, as shown in the figure at the right.

✓ **Checkpoint**   *Audio-video solution in English & Spanish at LarsonPrecalculus.com.*

What is unusual about the solution set of each inequality?

a. $x^2 + 6x + 9 < 0$ **b.** $x^2 + 4x + 4 \leq 0$

c. $x^2 - 6x + 9 > 0$ **d.** $x^2 - 2x + 1 \geq 0$

Technology Tip

One of the advantages of technology is that you can solve complicated polynomial inequalities that might be difficult, or even impossible, to factor. For instance, you could use a graphing utility to approximate the solution of the inequality

$$x^3 - 0.2x^2 - 3.16x + 1.4 < 0.$$

Rational Inequalities

The concepts of key numbers and test intervals can be extended to inequalities involving rational expressions. To do this, use the fact that the value of a rational expression can change sign only at its *zeros* (the x-values for which its numerator is zero) and its *undefined values* (the x-values for which its denominator is zero). These two types of numbers make up the *key numbers* of a rational inequality. When solving a rational inequality, begin by writing the inequality in general form with the rational expression on one side and zero on the other.

EXAMPLE 9   Solving a Rational Inequality

Solve $\dfrac{2x - 7}{x - 5} \le 3$.

Algebraic Solution

$$\frac{2x - 7}{x - 5} - 3 \le 0 \qquad \text{Write in general form.}$$

$$\frac{2x - 7 - 3x + 15}{x - 5} \le 0 \qquad \text{Write as single fraction.}$$

$$\frac{-x + 8}{x - 5} \le 0 \qquad \text{Simplify.}$$

Now, in standard form you can see that the key numbers are $x = 5$ and $x = 8$, and you can proceed as follows.

Key Numbers: $x = 5, x = 8$

Test Intervals: $(-\infty, 5), (5, 8), (8, \infty)$

Test: Is $\dfrac{-x + 8}{x - 5} \le 0$?

Interval	x-Value	Polynomial Value	Conclusion
$(-\infty, 5)$	$x = 0$	$\dfrac{-0 + 8}{0 - 5} = -\dfrac{8}{5}$	Negative
$(5, 8)$	$x = 6$	$\dfrac{-6 + 8}{6 - 5} = 2$	Positive
$(8, \infty)$	$x = 9$	$\dfrac{-9 + 8}{9 - 5} = -\dfrac{1}{4}$	Negative

By testing these intervals, you can determine that the rational expression $(-x + 8)/(x - 5)$ is negative in the open intervals $(-\infty, 5)$ and $(8, \infty)$. Moreover, because

$$\frac{-x + 8}{x - 5} = 0$$

when $x = 8$, you can conclude that the solution set of the inequality is $(-\infty, 5) \cup [8, \infty)$.

Graphical Solution

Use a graphing utility to graph

$$y_1 = \frac{2x - 7}{x - 5} \quad \text{and} \quad y_2 = 3$$

in the same viewing window, as shown below.

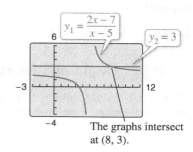

The graphs intersect at $(8, 3)$.

The graph of y_1 lies on or below the graph of y_2 on the intervals $(-\infty, 5)$ and $[8, \infty)$. So, you can graphically estimate the solution set to be all real numbers less than 5 *or* greater than or equal to 8.

✓ **Checkpoint**))) *Audio-video solution in English & Spanish at LarsonPrecalculus.com.*

Solve $\dfrac{4x - 1}{x - 6} > 3$.

Note in Example 9 that $x = 5$ is not included in the solution set because the inequality is undefined when $x = 5$.

Applications

In Section 1.3, you studied the *implied domain* of a function, the set of all x-values for which the function is defined. A common type of implied domain is used to avoid even roots of negative numbers, as shown in Example 10.

EXAMPLE 10   Finding the Domain of an Expression

Find the domain of $\sqrt{64 - 4x^2}$.

Solution

Because $\sqrt{64 - 4x^2}$ is defined only when $64 - 4x^2$ is nonnegative, the domain is given by $64 - 4x^2 \geq 0$.

$$64 - 4x^2 \geq 0 \qquad \text{Write in general form.}$$

$$16 - x^2 \geq 0 \qquad \text{Divide each side by 4.}$$

$$(4 - x)(4 + x) \geq 0 \qquad \text{Factor.}$$

The inequality has two key numbers: $x = -4$ and $x = 4$. A test shows that $64 - 4x^2 \geq 0$ in the *closed interval* $[-4, 4]$. The graph of $y = \sqrt{64 - 4x^2}$, shown in Figure 2.29, confirms that the domain is $[-4, 4]$.

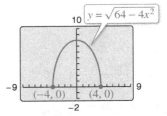

Figure 2.29

✓ **Checkpoint** 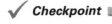 *Audio-video solution in English & Spanish at LarsonPrecalculus.com.*

Find the domain of $\sqrt{x^2 - 7x + 10}$.

EXAMPLE 11   Height of a Projectile

A projectile is fired straight upward from ground level with an initial velocity of 384 feet per second. During what time period will the height of the projectile exceed 2000 feet?

Solution

In Section 2.4, you saw that the position of an object moving vertically can be modeled by the *position equation*

$$s = -16t^2 + v_0 t + s_0$$

where s is the height in feet and t is the time in seconds. In this case, $s_0 = 0$ and $v_0 = 384$. So, you need to solve the inequality $-16t^2 + 384t > 2000$. Using a graphing utility, graph $y_1 = -16t^2 + 384t$ and $y_2 = 2000$, as shown in Figure 2.30. From the graph, you can determine that $-16t^2 + 384t > 2000$ for t between approximately 7.6 and 16.4. You can verify this result algebraically.

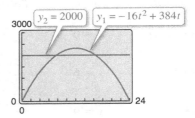

Figure 2.30

$$-16t^2 + 384t > 2000 \qquad \text{Write original inequality.}$$

$$t^2 - 24t < -125 \qquad \text{Divide by } -16 \text{ and reverse inequality symbol.}$$

$$t^2 - 24t + 125 < 0 \qquad \text{Write in general form.}$$

By the Quadratic Formula, the key numbers are $t = 12 - \sqrt{19}$ and $t = 12 + \sqrt{19}$, or approximately 7.64 and 16.36. A test will verify that the height of the projectile will exceed 2000 feet when $7.64 < t < 16.36$—that is, during the time interval $(7.64, 16.36)$ seconds.

✓ **Checkpoint**  *Audio-video solution in English & Spanish at LarsonPrecalculus.com.*

A projectile is fired straight upward from ground level with an initial velocity of 208 feet per second. During what time period will its height exceed 640 feet? ■

2.6 Exercises

See *CalcChat.com* for tutorial help and worked-out solutions to odd-numbered exercises.
For instructions on how to use a graphing utility, see Appendix A.

Vocabulary and Concept Check

In Exercises 1–4, fill in the blank(s).

1. It is sometimes possible to write two inequalities as one inequality, called a _____ inequality.
2. The solutions of $|x| \le a$ are those values of x such that _____ .
3. The solutions of $|x| \ge a$ are those values of x such that _____ or _____ .
4. The key numbers of a rational inequality are its _____ and its _____ .

5. Are the inequalities $x - 4 < 5$ and $x > 9$ equivalent?
6. Which property of inequalities is shown below?

   $a < b$ and $b < c$ $\Longrightarrow$ $a < c$

Procedures and Problem Solving

Matching an Inequality with Its Graph In Exercises 7–12, match the inequality with its graph. [The graphs are labeled (a), (b), (c), (d), (e), and (f).]

(a)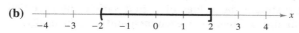

(b)

(c)

(d)

(e)

(f)

7. $x < 2$ 8. $x \le 2$
9. $-2 < x < 2$ 10. $-2 < x \le 2$
11. $-2 \le x < 2$ 12. $-2 \le x \le 2$

Determining Solutions of an Inequality In Exercises 13–16, determine whether each value of x is a solution of the inequality.

Inequality	Values
13. $5x - 12 > 0$	(a) $x = 3$ (b) $x = -3$
	(c) $x = \frac{5}{2}$ (d) $x = \frac{3}{2}$
14. $-5 < 2x - 1 \le 1$	(a) 2 (b) -2
	(c) 0 (d) $-\frac{1}{2}$
15. $-1 < \dfrac{3 - x}{2} \le 1$	(a) $x = -1$ (b) $x = \sqrt{5}$
	(c) $x = 1$ (d) $x = 5$
16. $|x - 10| \ge 3$	(a) $x = 13$ (b) $x = -1$
	(c) $x = 14$ (d) $x = 8$

Solving an Inequality In Exercises 17–30, solve the inequality and sketch the solution on the real number line. Use a graphing utility to verify your solution graphically.

17. $6x > 42$ 18. $-10x \le 40$
19. $4x + 7 < 3 + 2x$ 20. $3x + 1 \ge 2 + x$
21. $2(1 - x) < 3x + 7$ 22. $2x + 7 < 3(x - 4)$
23. $\frac{3}{4}x - 6 \le x - 7$ 24. $3 + \frac{2}{7}x > x - 2$
25. $1 \le 2x + 3 \le 9$
26. $-8 \le -3x + 5 < 13$
27. $-8 \le 1 - 3(x - 2) < 13$
28. $0 \le 2 - 3(x + 1) < 20$
29. $-4 < \dfrac{2x - 3}{3} < 4$
30. $0 \le \dfrac{x + 3}{2} < 5$

Approximating a Solution In Exercises 31–34, use a graphing utility to approximate the solution.

31. $5 - 2x \ge 1$
32. $20 < 6x - 1$
33. $3(x + 1) < x + 7$
34. $4(x - 3) > 8 - x$

Approximating Solutions In Exercises 35–38, use a graphing utility to graph the equation and graphically approximate the values of x that satisfy the specified inequalities. Then solve each inequality algebraically.

Equation	Inequalities
35. $y = 2x - 3$	(a) $y \ge 1$ (b) $y \le 0$
36. $y = \frac{2}{3}x + 1$	(a) $y \le 5$ (b) $y \ge 0$
37. $y = -3x + 8$	(a) $-1 \le y \le 3$ (b) $y \le 0$
38. $y = -\frac{1}{2}x + 2$	(a) $0 \le y \le 3$ (b) $y \ge 0$

Solving an Absolute Value Inequality In Exercises 39–46, solve the inequality and sketch the solution on the real number line. Use a graphing utility to verify your solutions graphically.

39. $|5x| > 10$

40. $\left|\dfrac{x}{2}\right| \le 1$

41. $|x - 7| \le 6$

42. $|x - 20| > 4$

43. $\left|\dfrac{x - 3}{2}\right| \ge 5$

44. $|x + 14| + 3 \ge 17$

45. $10|1 - x| < 5$

46. $3|4 - 5x| < 9$

Approximating Solutions In Exercises 47 and 48, use a graphing utility to graph the equation and graphically approximate the values of x that satisfy the specified inequalities. Then solve each inequality algebraically.

Equation	Inequalities	
47. $y = |x - 3|$	(a) $y \le 2$	(b) $y \ge 4$
48. $y = \left|\tfrac{1}{2}x + 1\right|$	(a) $y \le 4$	(b) $y \ge 1$

Using Absolute Value Notation In Exercises 49–56, use absolute value notation to define the interval (or pair of intervals) on the real number line.

49.

50.

51.

52.

53. All real numbers less than 10 units from 6

54. All real numbers no more than 8 units from -5

55. All real numbers more than 3 units from -1

56. All real numbers at least 5 units from 3

Investigating Polynomial Behavior In Exercises 57–62, determine the intervals on which the polynomial is entirely negative and those on which it is entirely positive.

57. $x^2 - 4x - 5$

58. $x^2 - 3x - 4$

59. $2x^2 - 4x - 3$

60. $-2x^2 + x + 5$

61. $-x^2 + 6x - 10$

62. $3x^2 + 8x + 6$

Solving a Polynomial Inequality In Exercises 63–76, solve the inequality and graph the solution on the real number line. Use a graphing utility to verify your solution graphically.

63. $x^2 + 4x + 4 \ge 9$

64. $x^2 - 6x + 9 < 16$

65. $(x + 2)^2 < 25$

66. $(x - 3)^2 \ge 1$

67. $x^3 - 4x^2 \ge 0$

68. $x^5 - 3x^4 \le 0$

69. $2x^3 + 5x^2 > 6x + 9$

70. $2x^3 + 3x^2 < 11x + 6$

71. $x^3 - 3x^2 - x > -3$

72. $2x^3 + 13x^2 - 8x - 46 \ge 6$

73. $3x^2 - 11x + 16 \le 0$ **74.** $4x^2 + 12x + 9 \le 0$

75. $4x^2 - 4x + 1 > 0$ **76.** $x^2 + 3x + 8 > 0$

Using Graphs to Find Solutions In Exercises 77 and 78, use the graph of the function to solve the equation or inequality.

(a) $f(x) = g(x)$ (b) $f(x) \ge g(x)$ (c) $f(x) > g(x)$

77.
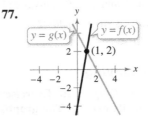

78.
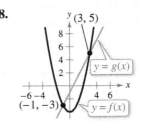

Approximating Solutions In Exercises 79 and 80, use a graphing utility to graph the equation and graphically approximate the values of x that satisfy the specified inequalities. Then solve each inequality algebraically.

Equation	Inequalities	
79. $y = -x^2 + 2x + 3$	(a) $y \le 0$	(b) $y \ge 3$
80. $y = x^3 - x^2 - 16x + 16$	(a) $y \le 0$	(b) $y \ge 36$

Solving a Rational Inequality In Exercises 81–84, solve the inequality and graph the solution on the real number line. Use a graphing utility to verify your solution graphically.

81. $\dfrac{1}{x} - x > 0$

82. $\dfrac{1}{x} - 4 < 0$

83. $\dfrac{x + 6}{x + 1} - 2 \le 0$

84. $\dfrac{x + 12}{x + 2} - 3 \ge 0$

Approximating Solutions In Exercises 85 and 86, use a graphing utility to graph the equation and graphically approximate the values of x that satisfy the specified inequalities. Then solve each inequality algebraically.

Equation	Inequalities	
85. $y = \dfrac{3x}{x - 2}$	(a) $y \le 0$	(b) $y \ge 6$
86. $y = \dfrac{5x}{x^2 + 4}$	(a) $y \ge 1$	(b) $y \le 0$

Finding the Domain of an Expression In Exercises **87–92, find the domain of x in the expression.**

87. $\sqrt{x - 5}$ **88.** $\sqrt{6x + 15}$

89. $\sqrt{-x^2 + x + 12}$ **90.** $\sqrt{2x^2 - 8}$

91. $\sqrt[4]{3x^2 - 20x - 7}$ **92.** $\sqrt[4]{2x^2 + 4x + 3}$

---

93. MODELING DATA

The graph models the population P (in thousands) of Sacramento, California, from 2003 through 2012, where t is the year, with $t = 3$ corresponding to 2003. Also shown is the line $y = 450$. Use the graphs of the model and the horizontal line to write an equation or an inequality that could be solved to answer the question. Then answer the question. (Source: U.S. Census Bureau)

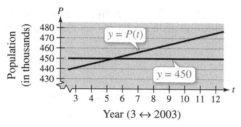

(a) In what year did the population of Sacramento reach 450,000?

(b) During what time period was the population of Sacramento less than 450,000? greater than 450,000?

---

94. MODELING DATA

The graph models the population P (in thousands) of Cleveland, Ohio, from 2003 through 2012, where t is the year, with $t = 3$ corresponding to 2003. Also shown is the line $y = 400$. Use the graphs of the model and the horizontal line to write an equation or an inequality that could be solved to answer the question. Then answer the question. (Source: U.S. Census Bureau)

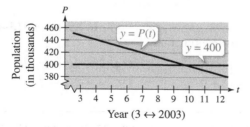

(a) In what year did the population of Cleveland reach 400,000?

(b) During what time period was the population of Cleveland less than 400,000? greater than 400,000?

---

95. Height of a Projectile A projectile is fired straight upward from ground level with an initial velocity of 160 feet per second.

(a) At what instant will it be back at ground level?

(b) When will the height exceed 384 feet?

96. Height of a Projectile A projectile is fired straight upward from ground level with an initial velocity of 128 feet per second.

(a) At what instant will it be back at ground level?

(b) When will the height be less than 128 feet?

---

97. MODELING DATA

The numbers D of doctorate degrees (in thousands) awarded to female students from 1991 through 2012 in the United States can be approximated by the model

$D = 0.0743t^2 + 0.628t + 42.61, \ 0 \le t \le 22$

where t is the year, with $t = 1$ corresponding to 1991. (Source: U.S. National Center for Education Statistics)

(a) Use a graphing utility to graph the model.

(b) Use the *zoom* and *trace* features to find when the number of degrees was between 50 and 60 thousand.

(c) Algebraically verify your results from part (b).

---

98. MODELING DATA

You want to determine whether there is a relationship between an athlete's weight x (in pounds) and the athlete's maximum bench-press weight y (in pounds). Sample data from 12 athletes are shown below. (*Spreadsheet at LarsonPrecalculus.com*)

 (165, 170), (184, 185), (150, 200), (210, 255), (196, 205), (240, 295), (202, 190), (170, 175), (185, 195), (190, 185), (230, 250), (160, 150)

(a) Use a graphing utility to plot the data.

(b) A model for the data is

$y = 1.3x - 36.$

Use the graphing utility to graph the equation in the same viewing window used in part (a).

(c) Use the graph to estimate the values of x that predict a maximum bench-press weight of at least 200 pounds.

(d) Use the graph to write a statement about the accuracy of the model. If you think the graph indicates that an athlete's weight is not a good indicator of the athlete's maximum bench-press weight, list other factors that might influence an individual's maximum bench-press weight.

Why you should learn it (*p. 210*)   In Exercises 99–102, use the models below, which approximate the numbers of Bed Bath & Beyond stores B and Williams-Sonoma stores W for the years 2000 through 2013, where t is the year, with $t = 0$ corresponding to 2000.   (Sources: Bed Bath & Beyond, Inc.; Williams-Sonoma, Inc.)

Bed Bath & Beyond:
$$B = 86.5t + 342, \quad 0 \le t \le 13$$

Williams-Sonoma:
$$W = -2.92t^2 + 52.0t + 381, \quad 0 \le t \le 13$$

99. Solve the inequality $B(t) \ge 900$. Explain what the solution of the inequality represents.

100. Solve the inequality $W(t) \le 600$. Explain what the solution of the inequality represents.

101. Solve the equation $B(t) = W(t)$. Explain what the solution of the equation represents.

102. Solve the inequality $B(t) \ge W(t)$. Explain what the solution of the inequality represents.

Music   In Exercises 103–106, use the following information. Michael Kasha, of Florida State University, used physics and mathematics to design a classical guitar. He used the model for the frequency of the vibrations on a circular plate

$$v = \frac{2.6t}{d^2} \sqrt{\frac{E}{\rho}}$$

where v is the frequency (in vibrations per second), t is the plate thickness (in millimeters), d is the diameter of the plate, E is the elasticity of the plate material, and ρ is the density of the plate material. For fixed values of d, E, and ρ, the graph of the equation is a line, as shown in the figure.

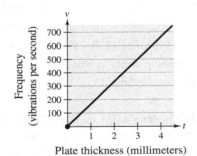

Plate thickness (millimeters)

103. Estimate the frequency when the plate thickness is 2 millimeters.

104. Estimate the plate thickness when the frequency is 600 vibrations per second.

105. Approximate the interval for the plate thickness when the frequency is between 200 and 400 vibrations per second.

106. Approximate the interval for the frequency when the plate thickness is less than 3 millimeters.

Conclusions

True or False?   In Exercises 107–109, determine whether the statement is true or false. Justify your answer.

107. If $-10 \le x \le 8$, then $-10 \ge -x$ and $-x \ge -8$.

108. The solution set of the inequality $\frac{3}{2}x^2 + 3x + 6 \ge 0$ is the entire set of real numbers.

109. The domain of $\sqrt[3]{6 - x}$ is $(-\infty, 6]$.

110. **Proof**   The arithmetic mean of a and b is given by $(a + b)/2$. Order the statements of the proof to show that if $a < b$, then $a < (a + b)/2 < b$.

    (i) $a < \dfrac{a + b}{2} < b$ (ii) $2a < 2b$

    (iii) $2a < a + b < 2b$ (iv) $a < b$

111. **Think About It**   Without performing any calculations, match the inequality with its solution. Explain your reasoning.

    (a) $2x \le -6$ (i) $x \le -8$ or $x \ge 4$

    (b) $-2x \le 6$ (ii) $x \ge -3$

    (c) $|x + 2| \le 6$ (iii) $-8 \le x \le 4$

    (d) $|x + 2| \ge 6$ (iv) $x \le -3$

112. **HOW DO YOU SEE IT?**   Consider the polynomial $(x - a)(x - b)$ and the real number line shown below.

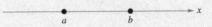

    (a) Identify the points on the line at which the polynomial is zero.

    (b) Determine the intervals on which the polynomial is entirely negative and those on which it is entirely positive. Explain your reasoning.

    (c) At what x-values does the polynomial change signs?

Cumulative Mixed Review

Finding the Inverse of a Function   In Exercises 113–116, find the inverse function.

113. $y = 12x$ 114. $y = 5x + 8$

115. $y = x^3 + 7$ 116. $y = \sqrt[3]{x - 7}$

117. *Make a Decision*   To work an extended application analyzing the number of lung transplants in the United States, visit this textbook's website at *LarsonPrecalculus.com*.   (Data Source: U.S. Department of Health and Human Services)

OBJECTIVES

AFTER COMPLETING THIS CHAPTER, YOU WILL BE ABLE TO:

▼ Use synthetic division to find roots of polynomials.

▼ Reduce a polynomial to linear and quadratic factors using synthetic division to find all the roots of a polynomial.

▼ Determine the possible rational roots and test them using synthetic division.

▼ Find irrational roots using a numerical method and technology, model applications with polynomial functions, and use the function to solve a problem.

▼ Find vertical and horizontal asymptotes of rational functions.

▼ Solve equations that involve rational functions.

17.1 THE REMAINDER AND FACTOR THEOREM

We will begin this section with the definition of a polynomial.

POLYNOMIAL

A **polynomial** is a function of the form

$$P(x) = a_n x^n + a_{n-1} x^{n-1} + \cdots + a_2 x^2 + a_1 x + a_0$$

where $a_0, a_1, a_2, \ldots, a_n$ are numbers, n is a nonnegative integer, and $a_n \neq 0$. This polynomial has *degree n*.

a_n is called the *leading coefficient* of the polynomial.

EXAMPLE 17.1

The following are some examples of polynomials:

$$P(x) = 3x^2 + 2x - 1 \text{ has degree 2.}$$

$$P(x) = 5x^6 + \frac{7}{3}x^3 - 4x + 1 \text{ has degree 6.}$$

$$P(x) = -\sqrt{7} \text{ has degree 0.}$$

$$P(x) = \frac{2}{3}x^4 - \frac{1}{2}x^3 + x^2 \text{ has degree 4.}$$

EXAMPLE 17.2

The following are not polynomials.

$P(x) = 4x^{5/2} + 2x^2 - 3$, because one of the exponents, $\frac{5}{2}$, is not an integer.

$P(x) = 5x^{-3}$, because the exponent is not positive.

The third polynomial in Example 17.1, $P(x) = -\sqrt{7}$, is an example of a constant polynomial.

CONSTANT AND ZERO POLYNOMIALS

A **constant polynomial** function is of the form $P(x) = c$, where c is a real number and $c \neq 0$. The degree of a constant polynomial function is zero.

$P(x) = 0$ is called the **zero polynomial**. It has no degree.

The roots, solutions, or zeros of a polynomial function $P(x)$ are the values of x for which $P(x) = 0$. In earlier chapters, we learned that if $P(x) = ax + b$, then $P(x) = 0$, when $x = \dfrac{-b}{a}$. We also learned the quadratic formula, which states that if $P(x)$ is of degree 2 and $P(x) = ax^2 + bx + c$, then $P(x) = 0$, when $x = \dfrac{-b \pm \sqrt{b^2 - 4ac}}{2a}$.

EXAMPLE 17.3

Find the roots of (a) $P(x) = 7x - \sqrt{2}$ and (b) $P(x) = 6x^2 - 3x - 5$.

SOLUTIONS

(a) The roots occur when $P(x) = 7x - \sqrt{2} = 0$. That is, when $7x = \sqrt{2}$ or $x = \frac{1}{7}\sqrt{2}$.

(b) Here, we want the solution of $6x^2 - 3x - 5 = 0$. Using the quadratic formula, we get

$$x = \frac{-(-3) \pm \sqrt{(-3)^2 - 4(6)(-5)}}{2(6)}$$

$$= \frac{3 \pm \sqrt{9 + 120}}{12} = \frac{3 \pm \sqrt{129}}{12}$$

The roots are $x = \frac{1}{4} + \frac{1}{12}\sqrt{129}$ and $x = \frac{1}{4} - \frac{1}{12}\sqrt{129}$.

We will now look at some ways we can solve polynomial functions of a degree larger than two.

REMAINDER THEOREM

Whenever we divide a polynomial $P(x)$ by $x - a$ we get a quotient $Q(x)$ that is a polynomial and a remainder R that is a constant. In fact, when $P(x)$ is divided by $x - a$, the remainder $R = P(a)$. This is the **remainder theorem**.

REMAINDER THEOREM

If a polynomial $P(x)$ is divided by $x - a$ until a remainder that does not contain x is obtained, then the remainder $R = P(a)$.

EXAMPLE 17.4

Determine the remainder when $P(x) = x^3 - 4x^2 + 2x + 5$ is divided by $x - 3$ and $x + 2$.

SOLUTION When $P(x) = x^3 - 4x^2 + 2x + 5$ is divided by $x - 3$, then $a = 3$. So, $P(3) = 3^3 - 4(3)^2 + 2(3) + 5 = 27 - 36 + 6 + 5 = 2$. When $P(x)$ is divided by $x - 3$, the remainder is 2.

When we divide $P(x)$ by $x + 2$, we have $a = -2$, so $P(-2) = (-2)^3 - 4(-2)^2 + 2(-2) + 5 = -23$. So, when $P(x)$ is divided by $x + 2$, the remainder is -23.

We can check to see if these are true by dividing $P(x)$ by $x - 3$ and by $x + 2$:

$$
\begin{array}{r}
x^2 - x - 1 \\
x - 3 \overline{)x^3 - 4x^2 + 2x + 5} \\
\underline{x^3 - 3x^2} \\
-x^2 + 2x + 5 \\
\underline{-x^2 + 3x} \\
-x + 5 \\
\underline{x + 3} \\
2
\end{array}
\qquad
\begin{array}{r}
x^2 - 6x - 14 \\
x + 2 \overline{)x^3 - 4x^2 + 2x + 5} \\
\underline{x^3 + 2x^2} \\
-6x^2 + 2x + 5 \\
\underline{-6x^2 - 12x} \\
14x + 5 \\
\underline{14x + 28} \\
-23
\end{array}
$$

From this we see that when $P(x) = x^3 - 4x^2 + 2x + 5$ is divided by $x - 3$, we get a quotient $Q(x) = x^2 - x - 1$ and a remainder of $R = 2$. When $P(x)$ is divided by $x + 2$, the quotient is $Q(x) = x^2 - 6x + 14$ with a remainder of $R = -23$. These remainders are the same ones we found in Example 17.4.

FACTOR THEOREM

In some cases, $R = 0$, and we see that $P(x) = Q(x)(x - a) + R$ can be rewritten as

$$P(x) = Q(x)(x - a)$$

That is, $x - a$ is a factor of $P(x)$. This leads to our second theorem for this section.

 FACTOR THEOREM

The **factor theorem** states that a polynomial $P(x)$ contains $x - a$ as a factor if and only if $P(a) = 0$.

The factor theorem means that a is a root of $P(x)$ if $x - a$ is a factor of $P(x)$.

EXAMPLE 17.5

Use the factor theorem to determine if $x + 1$ and $x - 2$ are factors of $P(x) = x^4 + x^3 - 3x^2 - 4x - 1$.

SOLUTION To see if $x + 1$ is a factor, we evaluate $P(x)$ at $x = -1$. Since $P(-1) = 0$, then $x + 1$ is a factor of P. [In fact, $P(x) = (x + 1)(x^3 + 3x - 1)$.]

To see if $x - 2$ is a factor of P, we evaluate $P(x)$ at $x = 2$. Since $P(2) = 3$, we know that $x + 2$ is not a factor of $x^4 + x^3 - 3x^2 - 4x - 1$.

SYNTHETIC DIVISION

What we need is a shorter method to determine the quotient and remainder of a polynomial. Both of the divisions we worked earlier took a lot of time and a lot of space. A process has been developed that allows us to shorten the division. This process is called synthetic division.

Consider the problem we worked earlier when $x^3 - 4x^2 + 2x + 5$ was divided by $x + 2$. We had the following work:

$$
\begin{array}{r}
x^2 - 6x + 14 \\
x + 2 \overline{)x^3 - 4x^2 + 2x + 5} \\
\underline{x^3 + 2x^2} \\
-6x^2 + 2x + 5 \\
\underline{-6x^2 - 12x} \\
14x + 5 \\
\underline{14x + 28} \\
-23
\end{array}
$$

In synthetic division, we do not write the x's and we do not repeat terms. So, if we erase all the x's and the terms that repeat, we get a group of coefficients that look like this:

$$
\begin{array}{r}
1 \quad -6 \quad 14 \\
2\overline{)1 \quad -4 \quad 2 \quad 5} \\
2 \\
\overline{-6} \\
-12 \\
\overline{14} \\
28 \\
\overline{-23}
\end{array}
$$

We can write all the numbers below the dividend in two lines and get

$$
\begin{array}{r}
1 \quad -6 \quad 14 \\
2\overline{)1 \quad -4 \quad 2 \quad 5} \\
2 \quad -12 \quad 28 \\
\overline{-6 \quad 14 \quad -23}
\end{array}
$$

If we repeat the leading coefficient on the bottom line, we see that the numbers on the third line represent the quotient and the remainder. Finally, we will change the sign of the divisor. Changing the sign of the divisor forces us to change the signs in the second row. This allows us to add the first two rows:

$$
\begin{array}{r|rrrr}
-2 & 1 & -4 & 2 & 5 \\
   &   & -2 & 12 & -28 \\
\hline
   & 1 & -6 & 14 & -23 \\
\end{array}
$$

$$\underbrace{}_{\text{quotient}} \qquad \underbrace{}_{\text{remainder}}$$

The next example shows you how to use synthetic division.

EXAMPLE 17.6

Use synthetic division to determine the quotient and remainder when $x^4 - 3x^2 + 10x - 5$ is divided by $x + 3$.

SOLUTION

$$
\begin{array}{r|rrrrr}
-3 & 1 & 0 & -3 & 10 & -5 \\
\end{array}
$$

Step 1: If the divisor is $x - a$, write a in the box. Arrange the coefficients of the dividend by descending powers of x. Use a zero coefficient when a power is missing. In this example, there is no x^3 term and $a = -3$.

$$
\begin{array}{r|rrrrr}
-3 & 1 & 0 & -3 & 10 & -5 \\
\hline
   & 1 \\
\end{array}
$$

Step 2: Copy the leading coefficient in the third row.

$$
\begin{array}{r|rrrrr}
-3 & 1 & 0 & -3 & 10 & -5 \\
   &   & -3 \\
\hline
   & 1 & -3 \\
\end{array}
$$

Step 3: Multiply the last entry in the third row by the number in the box and write the result in the second row under the second coefficient. Add the numbers in that column.

$$
\begin{array}{r|rrrrr}
-3 & 1 & 0 & -3 & 10 & -5 \\
   &   & -3 & 9 \\
\hline
   & 1 & -3 & 6 \\
\end{array}
$$

Step 4a: Repeat the process from Step 3, but write the results under the third coefficient.

$$
\begin{array}{r|rrrrr}
-3 & 1 & 0 & -3 & 10 & -5 \\
   &   & -3 & 9 & -18 & 24 \\
\hline
   & 1 & -3 & 6 & -8 & 19 \\
\end{array}
$$

$$\underbrace{}_{\text{quotient}} \qquad \underbrace{}_{\text{remainder}}$$

Step 4b: Repeat the process from Step 3 until there are as many entries in row 3 as there are in row 1. The last number in row 3 is the remainder. The other numbers are the coefficients of the quotient.

From this we see that the quotient is $Q(x) = x^3 - 3x^2 + 6x - 8$ and the remainder is $R = 19$.

EXAMPLE 17.7

Use synthetic division to determine the quotient and remainder when $2x^6 - 11x^4 + 17x^2 - 20$ is divided by $x - 2$.

SOLUTION Since there are no x^5, x^3, or x terms, we will replace them with 0 coefficients. The synthetic division looks like this:

$$
\begin{array}{r|rrrrrrr}
2 & 2 & 0 & -11 & 0 & 17 & 0 & -20 \\
  &   & 4 & 8 & -6 & -12 & 10 & 20 \\
\hline
  & 2 & 4 & -3 & -6 & 5 & 10 & 0
\end{array}
$$

$$\underbrace{\qquad\qquad\qquad}_{\text{quotient}} \qquad \underbrace{\quad}_{\text{remainder}}$$

The quotient is $2x^5 + 4x^4 - 3x^3 - 6x^2 + 5x + 10$ and the remainder is 0. So, $x - 2$ is a factor of the polynomial $2x^6 - 11x^4 + 17x^2 - 20$. In fact, this means that $2x^6 - 11x^4 + 17x^2 - 20 = (x - 2)(2x^5 + 4x^4 - 3x^3 - 6x^2 + 5x + 10)$.

EXAMPLE 17.8

Use synthetic division to determine if $3x - 2$ and $x - 1$ are factors of $18x^4 - 12x^3 - 45x^2 + 57x - 18$.

SOLUTION The remainder and factor theorems both refer to division by $x - a$. We are to check $3x - 2$. But $3x - 2 = 3(x - \frac{2}{3})$, and if $x - \frac{2}{3}$ divides the polynomial, then $3x - 2$ will also divide it. Our synthetic division follows:

$$
\begin{array}{r|rrrrr}
\frac{2}{3} & 18 & -12 & -45 & 57 & -18 \\
            &   & 12 & 0 & -30 & 18 \\
\hline
            & 18 & 0 & -45 & 27 & 0
\end{array}
$$

Since the remainder is zero, $3x - 2$ is a factor of $18x^4 - 12x^3 - 45x^2 - 57x - 18$. We will now see if $x - 1$ is a factor. Instead of checking the original equation, we will use the result from the synthetic division.

When we divided $18x^4 - 12x^3 - 45x^2 + 57x - 18$ by $x - \frac{2}{3}$, we got 18 0 −45 27 in the third row. This told us that $18x^4 - 12x^3 - 45x^2 + 57x - 18 = (x - \frac{2}{3})(18x^3 - 45x + 27)$. The factor $18x^3 - 45x + 27$ is called a **depressed equation** of the original equation. If $x - 1$ is a factor of the depressed equation $18x^3 - 45x + 27$, it is a factor of the original equation. Thus we can use the third row from our earlier synthetic division as the first row when we check $x - 1$.

$$
\begin{array}{rr|rrrrr}
 & \frac{2}{3} & 18 & -12 & -45 & 57 & -18 \\
 &   &   & 12 & 0 & -30 & 18 \\
1 & & 18 & 0 & -45 & 27 & 0 \\
 & &   & 18 & 18 & -27 & \\
\hline
 & & 18 & 18 & -27 & 0 &
\end{array}
$$

Thus, $x - 1$ is a factor of the depressed equation $18x^3 - 45x + 27$, so $x - 1$ is also a factor of $18x^4 - 12x^3 - 45x^2 + 57x - 18$.

EXAMPLE 17.8 (Cont.)

So,

$$18x^4 - 12x^3 - 45x^2 + 57x - 18$$

$$= \left(x - \frac{2}{3}\right)(x - 1)(18x^2 + 18x - 27)$$

$$= 9\left(x - \frac{2}{3}\right)(x - 1)(2x^2 + 2x - 3)$$

We can use the quadratic formula on the last depressed equation to find that the remaining roots are $x = \dfrac{-1 + \sqrt{7}}{2}$ and $x = \dfrac{-1 - \sqrt{7}}{2}$.

EXERCISE SET 17.1

In Exercises 1–8, find the value of P(x) for the given value of x.

1. $P(x) = 3x^2 - 2x + 1; x = 2$

2. $P(x) = 2x^3 - 4x + 5; x = -1$

3. $P(x) = x^4 + x^3 + x^2 - x + 1; x = -1$

4. $P(x) = x^4 - 2x^2 + x; x = -2$

5. $P(x) = 5x^3 - 4x + 7; x = 3$

6. $P(x) = 7x^4 - 5x^2 + x - 7; x = -2$

7. $P(x) = x^5 - x^4 + x^3 + x^2 - x + 1; x = -1$

8. $P(x) = 3x^5 + 4x^2 - 3; x = -3$

In Exercises 9–16, use the remainder theorem to find the remainder R, when P(x) is divided by x − a.

9. $P(x) = x^3 + 2x^2 - x - 2; x - 1$

10. $P(x) = x^3 + 2x^2 - 12x - 9; x - 3$

11. $P(x) = x^3 - 3x^2 + 2x + 5; x - 3$

12. $P(x) = x^3 - 9x^2 + 23x - 15; x - 1$

13. $P(x) = 4x^4 + 13x^3 - 13x^2 - 40x + 12; x + 2$

14. $P(x) = 2x^4 - 2x^3 - 6x^2 - 14x - 7; x - 7$

15. $P(x) = 3x^4 - 12x^3 - 60x + 4; x - 5$

16. $P(x) = 4x^3 - 4x^2 - 10x + 8; x - \frac{1}{2}$

In Exercises 17–24, use the factor theorem to determine whether or not the second factor is a factor of the first.

17. $x^3 + 2x^2 - 12x - 9; x - 3$

18. $x^4 - 9x^3 + 18x^2 - 3; x + 1$

19. $2x^5 - 6x^3 + x^2 + 4x - 1; x + 1$

20. $2x^5 - 6x^3 + x^2 + 4x - 1; x - 1$

21. $3x^5 + 3x^4 - 14x^3 + 4x^2 - 24x; x + 3$

22. $3x^5 + 3x^4 - 14x^3 + 4x^2 - 24x; x - 2$

23. $6x^4 - 15x^3 - 8x^2 + 20x; 2x - 5$

24. $20x^4 + 12x^3 + 10x + 9; 5x + 3$

In Exercises 25–32, use synthetic division to determine the quotient and remainder when each polynomial is divided by the given x − a.

25. $x^5 - 17x^3 + 75x + 9; x - 3$

26. $2x^5 - x^2 + 8x + 44; x + 2$

27. $5x^3 + 7x^2 + 9; x + 3$

28. $x^3 + 3x^2 - 2x - 4; x - 2$

29. $8x^5 - 4x^3 + 7x^2 - 2x; x - \frac{1}{2}$

30. $9x^5 + 3x^4 - 6x^3 - 2x^2 + 6x + 1; x + \frac{1}{3}$

31. $4x^4 - 12x^3 + 9x^2 - 8x + 12; 2x - 3$

32. $4x^3 + 7x^2 - 3x - 15; 4x - 5$

[IN YOUR WORDS]

33. Suppose that $P(x)$ is a polynomial and you determine that $P(3) = -5$. What does this mean?

34. Explain what it means for $P(r) = 0$ for some polynomial $P(x)$.

35. What precautions must you take when using synthetic division?

17.2 ROOTS OF AN EQUATION

In Section 17.1, we learned the factor theorem can help us determine if a number is a root of a polynomial. We also learned how to use synthetic division to quickly find the quotient and remainder when a polynomial is divided by a first-degree polynomial, $x - a$. In this section, we shall learn some theorems that determine the number of roots of the equation $P(x) = 0$.

In working with first-degree polynomials, we were always able to find one root. With second-degree polynomials, we could find two roots. At times, as in $P(x) = x^2 + 6x + 9$, both of these roots were the same. (Both roots of $x^2 + 6x + 9 = 0$ were -3.) As you might expect, every polynomial of degree n has exactly n roots. The **fundamental theorem of algebra** states that every polynomial equation of degree $n > 0$ has at least one (real or complex) root.

Combining the fundamental theorem of algebra with the factor theorem leads to the **linear factorization theorem**, which states the following:

LINEAR FACTORIZATION THEOREM

If $P(x)$ is a polynomial function of degree $n > 1$, then there is a non zero number a and there are numbers, $r_1, r_2, \ldots, r_n$, such that

$$P(x) = a(x - r_1)(x - r_2) \cdots (x - r_n)$$

The proof of this theorem is fairly easy. If $P(x)$ is a polynomial and $P(x) = 0$, then by the fundamental theorem there is a number r_1 such that $P(r_1) = 0$. From the factor theorem, we know $P(x) = (x - r_1)P_1(x)$, where $P_1(x)$ is a polynomial.

Again, the fundamental theorem states that there is a number r_2 such that $P_1(r_2) = 0$, so $P_1(x) = (x - r_2)P_2(x)$ and $P(x) = (x - r_1)(x - r_2)P_2(x)$.

We continue until one of the quotients is a constant a. At that time, we have

$$P(x) = a(x - r_1)(x - r_2) \cdots (x - r_n)$$

A linear factor appears each time a root is found. Since the degree of $P(x)$ is n, there are n linear factors and n roots. These roots are $r_1, r_2, r_3, \ldots, r_n$. Now, as we have seen, these roots may not all be different. Yet, even if they are not distinct, each root is counted.

The next example, Example 17.9, will apply the linear factorization theorem to a polynomial with distinct roots. The two examples after that, Examples 17.10 and 17.11, show how the theorem works when the roots are not all different.

EXAMPLE 17.9

Use the linear factorization theorem to determine the roots of the polynomial $P(x) = 3x^4 - 8x^3 - 11x^2 + 28x - 12$.

SOLUTION

$$
\begin{aligned}
3x^4 - 8x^3 - 11x^2 + 28x - 12 &= (x-1)(3x^3 - 5x^2 - 16x + 12) \\
&= (x-1)(x-3)(3x^2 + 4x - 4) \\
&= (x-1)(x-3)(x+2)(3x-2) \\
&= 3(x-1)(x-3)(x+2)\left(x - \frac{2}{3}\right)
\end{aligned}
$$

The roots are 1, 3, -2, and $\frac{2}{3}$.

Since $P(x)$ was of degree 4, it should have four roots. It does. Notice that the constant factor is the leading coefficient.

Just as it is not necessary that all roots be distinct, it is not necessary that all roots are real numbers. Remember that complex numbers can be roots to quadratic equations.

EXAMPLE 17.10

Determine the roots of $P(x) = x^2 + 6x + 25$.

SOLUTION Using the quadratic formula, we determine that $P(x) = x^2 + 6x + 25$ has the following roots:

$$
\begin{aligned}
x &= \frac{-6 \pm \sqrt{6^2 - 4(25)}}{2} \\
&= \frac{-6 \pm \sqrt{36 - 100}}{2} \\
&= \frac{-6 \pm \sqrt{-64}}{2} \\
&= \frac{-6 \pm 8j}{2} \\
&= -3 \pm 4j
\end{aligned}
$$

The roots are $r_1 = -3 + 4j$ and $r_2 = -3 - 4j$.

EXAMPLE 17.11

Determine the roots of $P(x) = (x-2)^3(x^2 + 6x + 25)$.

SOLUTION From the previous example we know that the roots of $x^2 + 6x + 25$ are $r_1 = -3 + 4j$ and $r_2 = -3 - 4j$. Thus, the roots of $P(x) = (x-2)^3(x^2 + 6x + 25)$ would be 2, 2, 2, $-3 + 4j$, and $-3 - 4j$. Notice that there are five roots, but three of them are the same.

One basic property of complex roots follows.

COMPLEX ROOTS THEOREM

If $P(x)$ is a polynomial with real coefficients and $a + bj$ is a root of $P(x)$, then its conjugate, $a - bj$, is also a root.

This would not be true if $P(x)$ was a polynomial with complex coefficients, but it is true when all the coefficients of P are real numbers.

 HINT Remember, when solving polynomials, if you find enough roots so the remaining factor is quadratic, you can always find the last two roots by using the quadratic formula.

EXAMPLE 17.12

Solve the equation $4x^3 - 9x^2 - 25x - 12$, given the fact that $-\frac{3}{4}$ is a root.

SOLUTION Using synthetic division, we get

$$
\begin{array}{r|rrrr}
-\frac{3}{4} & 4 & -9 & -25 & -12 \\
 & & -3 & 9 & 12 \\
\hline
 & 4 & -12 & -16 & 0
\end{array}
$$

© Cengage Learning 2013

So,

$$4x^3 - 9x^2 - 25x - 12 = \left(x + \frac{3}{4} \right)(4x^2 - 12x - 16)$$

$$= 4\left(x + \frac{3}{4} \right)(x^2 - 3x - 4)$$

We can factor $x^2 - 3x - 4$ as $(x - 4)(x + 1)$, and so

$$4x^3 - 9x^2 - 25x - 12 = 4\left(x + \frac{3}{4} \right)(x - 4)(x + 1)$$

The roots of $P(x) = 4x^3 - 9x^2 - 25x - 12$ are $-\frac{3}{4}$, 4, and -1.

EXAMPLE 17.13

Solve $P(x) = x^4 + 5x^3 + 10x^2 + 20x + 24$ if you know that $2j$ is a root.

SOLUTION Since $2j$ is a root and the coefficients of P are all real, its conjugate $-2j$ is also a root. So, two of the linear factors are $x - 2j$ and $x + 2j$. We can use synthetic division twice or divide the original polynomial by $(x - 2j)(x + 2j) = x^2 + 4$. We will use synthetic division twice:

$$
\begin{array}{r|rrrrr}
2j & 1 & 5 & 10 & 20 & 24 \\
 & & +2j & -4 + 10j & -20 + 12j & -24 \\
\hline
-2j & 1 & (5 + 2j) & (6 + 10j) & (0 + 12j) & 0 \\
 & & -2j & -10j & -12j & \\
\hline
 & 1 & 5 & 6 & 0 &
\end{array}
$$

© Cengage Learning 2013

EXAMPLE 17.13 (Cont.)   Thus,

$$x^4 + 5x^3 + 10x^2 + 20x + 24 = (x - 2j)(x + 2j)(x^2 + 5x + 6)$$
$$= (x - 2j)(x + 2j)(x + 3)(x + 2)$$

The four roots are $2j$, $-2j$, -3, and -2.

Notice that the second time we performed synthetic division it was done on the depressed equation that resulted from the first synthetic division.

EXAMPLE 17.14   Solve $2x^4 - 17x^3 + 49x^2 - 51x + 9$ if 3 is a double root.

SOLUTION   Since 3 is a double root, we know that two of the linear factors are $x - 3$ and $x - 3$. Using synthetic division twice, we get

$$
\begin{array}{r|rrrrr}
3 & 2 & -17 & 49 & -51 & 9 \\
  &   & 6   & -33 & 48 & -9 \\
\hline
3 & 2 & -11 & 16 & -3 & 0 \\
  &   & 6   & -15 & 3   &   \\
\hline
  & 2 & -5 & 1   & 0   &
\end{array}
$$

The last factor is $2x^2 - 5x + 1$. Using the quadratic formula, we see that its roots are

$$x = \frac{5 \pm \sqrt{(-5)^2 - 4(2)(1)}}{2(2)}$$
$$= \frac{5 \pm \sqrt{17}}{4}$$

Thus, the roots are 3, 3, $\dfrac{5 + \sqrt{17}}{4}$, and $\dfrac{5 - \sqrt{17}}{4}$.

EXERCISE SET 17.2

In Exercises 1–22, solve the equations using synthetic division and the given roots.

1. $5x^3 - 8x + 3$, $r_1 = 1$

2. $2x^3 + 5x^2 - 11x + 4$, $r_1 = -4$

3. $9x^3 - 3x^2 - 81x + 27$, $r_1 = \frac{1}{3}$

4. $10x^3 - 4x^2 - 40x + 16$, $r_1 = \frac{2}{5}$

5. $x^4 - 3x^2 - 4$, $r_1 = j$

6. $3x^4 + 6x^2 - 189$, $r_1 = -3j$

7. $x^4 + 2x^3 - 4x^2 - 18x - 45$, $r_1 = -1 + 2j$

8. $2x^4 + 4x^3 + 2x^2 - 16x - 40$, $r_1 = -1 - 2j$

9. $x^4 - 3x^3 - 3x^2 + 7x + 6$, $r_1 = 2$, $r_2 = 3$

10. $x^4 - 3x^3 - 12x^2 + 52x - 48$, $r_1 = 2$, $r_2 = -4$

11. $3x^4 + 12x^3 + 6x^2 - 12x - 9$, $r_1 = r_2 = -1$ (a double root)

12. $2x^4 + 6x^3 - 12x^2 - 24x + 16$, $r_1 = 2$, $r_2 = -2$

13. $6x^4 + 25x^3 + 33x^2 + x - 5$, $r_1 = -\frac{1}{2}$, $r_2 = \frac{1}{3}$

14. $12x^4 - 47x^3 + 55x^2 + 9x - 5$, $r_1 = \frac{1}{4}$, $r_2 = -\frac{1}{3}$

15. $3x^4 - 2x^3 - 3x + 2$, $r_1 = \frac{2}{3}$, $r_2 = 1$

16. $4x^4 + 3x^3 - 32x - 24$, $r_1 = 2$, $r_2 = -\frac{3}{4}$

17. $x^5 - x^4 + x^3 - 7x^2 + 10x - 4$, $r_1 = r_2 = r_3 = 1$ (a triple root)

18. $x^5 - 5x^4 + 7x^3 - 2x^2 + 4x - 8$, $r_1 = r_2 = r_3 = 2$

19. $3x^5 - 2x^4 - 24x^3 + x^2 + 28x - 12$, $r_1 = 3$, $r_2 = -2$, $r_3 = \frac{2}{3}$

20. $3x^5 - 4x^4 + 5x^3 - 18x^2 - 28x - 8$, $r_1 = -\frac{2}{3}$, $r_2 = 2j$

21. $x^6 - 6x^5 + 3x^4 - 60x^3 - 61x^2 - 54x - 63$, $r_1 = j$, $r_2 = -3j$

22. $6x^6 - 19x^5 + 63x^4 - 152x^3 + 216x^2 - 304x + 240$, $r_1 = r_2 = 2j$

 [IN YOUR WORDS]

23. The polynomial $P(x) = x^3 + ix^2 - 4x - 4i$ has two real roots, 2 and -2, and one nonreal complex root, i. Explain why this does not violate the complex roots theorem.

24. Explain how to create a polynomial if you know its leading coefficient and its roots.

17.3 FINDING ROOTS OF HIGHER-DEGREE EQUATIONS

In Section 17.2, we determined the number of roots of a polynomial. We also learned that complex roots come in pairs and that once we are able to reduce the nonlinear factor to degree 2, we can use the quadratic formula.

SOLVING EQUATIONS WITH A CALCULATOR

The TI-83 and TI-84 graphing calculators allow you to solve any polynomial of degrees 2–30. This is done by using the program `PlySmlt2`.[1] The following directions are for `PlySmlt2`.

To use this program, which TI refers to as an application, press **APPS** and use the ▼ to scroll down until the cursor is on `PlySmlt2` and press **ENTER** .[2] You will see a screen that shows the Texas Instruments logo and the name and version of the program. Press any key and you will get the MAIN MENU screen with several options. Select option 1 : PolyRootFinder

You will be presented with the heading "POLY ROOT FINDER MODE" and then several lines of options, and you should enter the degree (order) of the polynomial, whether you want real or complex roots, and if you want the roots as decimals (dec) or fractions (frac). Other options include representing numbers in normal, scientific, or engineering mode and the number of decimal points in the answer. The screen should look something like the one in Figure 17.1.

```
POLY ROOT FINDER MODE
ORDER    1 2 3 4 5 6 7 8 9 10
REAL     a+bi  re^(θi)
DEC      FRAC
NORMAL   SCI  ENG
FLOAT    0 1 2 3 4 5 6 7 8 9
RADIAN   DEGREE
MAIN              HELP NEXT
```
© Cengage Learning 2013

Figure 17.1

1 This is an updated version of the program PolySmlt and may need to be downloaded to your calculator. To download this software you need to go to the http://education.ti.com/ webpage. You must use TI™ Connect or TI-GRAPH LINK™ software and a TI-GRAPH LINK cable to install the application.

2 A faster method is to press **APPS** **ALPHA** **P** . This goes to all the apps that begin with the letter P. Then use the ▼ to scroll down until the cursor is on `PlySmlt2`.

Press the GRAPH button to advance to the next screen. You will then be asked to enter the coefficients starting with a_n, the coefficient of the x^n term, through a_0, the constant term. Then press the SOLVE by pressing the GRAPH button, and after a pause the n roots will be displayed. To solve another polynomial, press the Y= to select the MAIN option.

EXAMPLE 17.15

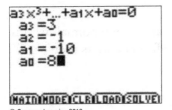

© Cengage Learning 2013

Figure 17.2a

Find all the roots of $P(x) = 3x^3 - x^2 - 10x + 8$.

SOLUTION   In this polynomial, $P(x) = 3x^3 - x^2 - 10x + 8$, $n = 3$, so the degree of the polynomial is 3. We also have $a_3 = 3$, $a_2 = -1$, $a_1 = -10$, and $a_0 = 8$. The data is entered as shown in Figure 17.2a and the solution looks like that in Figure 17.2b. From Figure 17.2b we see that the roots are $x_1 = -2$, $x_2 = 4/3 = \frac{4}{3}$, and $x_3 = 1$. If you want to save any of these solutions, access the STO (Store) feature by pressing the TRACE key and selecting from the options you are given.

The solutions are $x_1 = -2$, $x_2 = 4/3 = \frac{4}{3}$, and $x_3 = 1$, and using the factor theorem, we can write the polynomial as $P(x) = 3(x + 2)(x - \frac{4}{3})(x - 1)$.

EXAMPLE 17.16

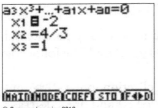

© Cengage Learning 2013

Figure 17.2b

Find all the roots of $P(x) = 4x^3 - 5x^2 - 2x + 3$.

SOLUTION   In this polynomial, $P(x) = 4x^3 - 5x^2 - 2x + 3$ with $n = 3$, so the order of the polynomial is 3. We also have $a_3 = 4$, $a_2 = -5$, $a_1 = -2$, and $a_0 = 3$. The data is entered as in Example 17.15 and the solution looks like that in Figure 17.3a, with $x_1 = 1$, $x_2 = 1$, and $x_3 = -\frac{3}{4}$.

If we look at the graph of this polynomial in the neighborhood of these roots we get Figure 17.3b. We can see that $x_1 = -\frac{3}{4} = -0.75$ is one place where the graph crosses the x-axis and it seems as if the graph just touches, but does not cross, the x-axis at $x = 1$. However, the resolution of the graphing calculator makes it difficult to tell whether the graph touches the x-axis.

We will check to see if $x = 1$ is a solution. Store 1 as x by pressing 1 STO▶ X,T,θ,n ENTER . Now, key in $4x^3 - 5x^2 - 2x + 3$ ENTER . The result is 0, which means that $P(1) = 0$. So, $x_1 = 1$ is a solution and so is $x_2 = 1$. Thus, 1 is a double root and this polynomial has three real roots. In factored form, $P(x) = (x + 0.75)(x - 1)^2 = (4x + 3)(x - 1)^2$.

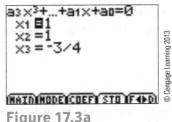

© Cengage Learning 2013

Figure 17.3a

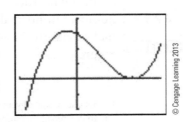

© Cengage Learning 2013

Figure 17.3b

EXAMPLE 17.17

Determine all the roots of $P(x) = 5x^6 - 4x^5 - 41x^4 + 32x^3 + 43x^2 - 28x - 7$.

SOLUTION In this polynomial $n = 6$. Entering the coefficients $a_6 = 5$, $a_5 = -4$, $a_4 = -41, \ldots, a_1 = -28$, and $a_0 = -7$ into the calculator, we get the following solutions:

$$x_1 = -2.645751311$$
$$x_2 = 2.645751311$$
$$x_3 = -1$$
$$x_4 = 1 + 3.844892716\text{E} - 7i$$
$$x_5 = 1 - 3.844892716\text{E} - 7i$$
$$x_6 = -0.2$$

All the roots seem to be between -2.7 and 2.7. If we graph P on this interval and use ZFIT, we obtain the graph in Figure 17.4. Here we can clearly see that there are real roots at $x_1 \approx -2.6458$, $x_2 \approx 2.6458$, $x_3 = -1$, and $x_6 = -0.2$. It appears that $x_4 = x_5 = 1$ is a double root, and if we check we see that these are the roots.

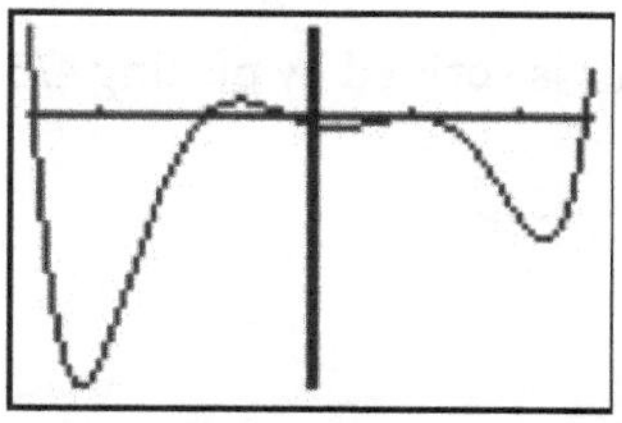

Thus,

$$P(x) \approx 5(x + 2.6458)(x - 2.6458)(x + 1)(x - 1)^2(x + 0.2)$$

© Cengage Learning 2013

Figure 17.4

In most technical areas the decimal approximations of x_1 and x_2 given by the calculator are sufficient. If you needed to determine the exact values of the roots $x_1 \approx -2.6458$ and $x_2 \approx 2.6458$ of the polynomial $P(x) = 5x^6 - 4x^5 - 41x^4 + 32x^3 + 43x^2 - 28x - 7$, you could use synthetic division using the first four roots and then use the quadratic formula on the resulting quadratic factor:

1	5	-4	-41	32	43	-28	-7
		5	1	-40	-8	35	7
1	5	1	-40	-8	35	7	0
		5	6	-34	-42	-7	
-1	5	6	-34	-42	-7	0	
		-5	-1	35	7		
-0.2	5	1	-35	-7	0		
		-1	0	7			
	5	0	-35	0			

© Cengage Learning 2013

Thus, we see that

$$P(x) = (x + 1)(x - 1)^2(x + 0.2)(5x^2 - 35)$$
$$= 5(x + 1)(x - 1)^2(x + 0.2)(x^2 - 7)$$

Since the solution to $x^2 - 7 = 0$ is $x = \pm\sqrt{7}$, we see that the exact values of x_1 and x_2 in Example 17.17 are $x_1 = -\sqrt{7}$ and $x_2 = \sqrt{7}$.

SOLVING EQUATIONS WITH A SPREADSHEET

To find the roots of a polynomial with a spreadsheet, it is best to sketch the curve first to get an approximation of the roots. A template like the one partially shown in Figure 17.5 can be constructed to make graphing polynomials easy. The polynomial is typed in Cell B5 and copied down Column B.

	A	B	C
1		Initial x:	-8
2		Increment for x:	1
3			
4	x	P(x)	
5	-8		
6	-7		
7	-6		
8	-5		

© Cengage Learning 2013

Figure 17.5

EXAMPLE 17.18

Find all the roots of $P(x) = 3x^3 - x^2 - 10x + 8$.

SOLUTION The degree of this polynomial is 3. The polynomial is entered in Cell B5 and a graph is constructed (see Figure 17.6a).

It appears that there are three real roots since the curve crosses the axis in three distinct places. The table of values identifies two roots since the values are integral (see Figure 17.6b). The two roots are $x = -2$ and $x = 1$. To find the third root, we will use Solver.

We copied a small portion of the table of values to another location where we'll keep track of the zeros we know. Figure 17.6c shows the two zeros we already know. Enter an estimate for the third root in Cell I7 (see Figure 17.6d). Place the cursor in Cell J7 and then use Solver. Change the value of Cell J7 to 0 by changing Cell I7. The result is shown in Figure 17.6e.

This third solution appears to actually be $\frac{4}{3}$ and this is verified by placing 4/3 in Cell I7 and seeing that Cell J7 has a value of 0.

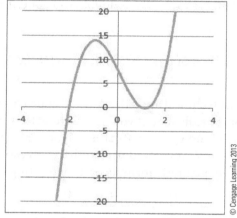

Figure 17.6a

4	x	P(x)
5	-3	-52
6	-2.5	-20.125
7	-2	0
8	-1.5	10.625
9	-1	14
10	-0.5	12.375
11	0	8
12	0.5	3.125
13	1	0
14	1.5	0.875
15	2	8

© Cengage Learning 2013

Figure 17.6b

	I	J
	ROOTS	
	x	P(x)
	-2	0
	1	0
		8

© Cengage Learning 2013

Figure 17.6c

	I	J
	ROOTS	
	x	P(x)
	-2	0
	1	0
	1.20	-0.256

© Cengage Learning 2013

Figure 17.6d

	I	J
	ROOTS	
	x	P(x)
	-2	0
	1	0
	1.333333	0.000000

© Cengage Learning 2013

Figure 17.6e

EXAMPLE 17.19

Find all the roots of $P(x) = 4x^3 - 5x^2 - 2x + 3$.

SOLUTION Construct a table of values using the template and then sketch the curve. The degree of the polynomial is 3. After adjusting the initial x and increment for x, a reasonable sketch is obtained (see Figures 17.7a and 17.7b).

The graph, supported by the table of values, identifies one root at $x = -0.75$ and a double root at $x = 1$.

We can verify that $x = 1$ is a double root and this polynomial has three real roots. In factored form $P(x) = (x + 0.75)(x - 1)^2 = (4x + 3)(x - 1)^2$.

◢	A	B	C
1		Initial x:	-1.5
2	Increment for x:		0.25
3			
4	x	P(x)	
5	-1.5	-18.75	
6	-1.25	-10.125	
7	-1	-4	
8	-0.75	0	
9	-0.5	2.25	
10	-0.25	3.125	
11	0	3	
12	0.25	2.25	
13	0.5	1.25	
14	0.75	0.375	
15	1	0	
16	1.25	0.5	

© Cengage Learning 2013

Figure 17.7a

© Cengage Learning 2013

Figure 17.7b

EXAMPLE 17.20

Determine all the roots of $P(x) = 5x^6 - 4x^5 - 41x^4 + 32x^3 + 43x^2 - 28x - 7$.

SOLUTION The degree of this polynomial is 6. A sketch (with the table of values) is shown in Figure 17.8a.

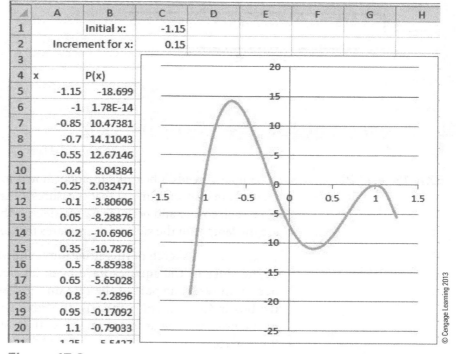

◢	A	B	C	D	E	F	G	H
1		Initial x:	-1.15					
2	Increment for x:		0.15					
3								
4	x	P(x)						
5	-1.15	-18.699						
6	-1	1.78E-14						
7	-0.85	10.47381						
8	-0.7	14.11043						
9	-0.55	12.67146						
10	-0.4	8.04384						
11	-0.25	2.032471						
12	-0.1	-3.80606						
13	0.05	-8.28876						
14	0.2	-10.6906						
15	0.35	-10.7876						
16	0.5	-8.85938						
17	0.65	-5.65028						
18	0.8	-2.2896						
19	0.95	-0.17092						
20	1.1	-0.79033						
21	1.25	5.5427						

© Cengage Learning 2013

Figure 17.8a

EXAMPLE 17.20 (Cont.)

K	L
ROOTS	
x	P(x)
-1	0
1	0
-0.2	0

© Cengage Learning 2013

Figure 17.8b

It appears that there are roots at $x = 1$ (a double root) and $x = -1$. These two roots are verified in Figure 17.8b. In addition, we are able to find (using Solver or trial and error) that -0.2 is a root. The other two roots must be found using synthetic division. Figure 17.8c shows the synthetic division using a spreadsheet template.

Thus, we see that

$$P(x) = (x + 1)(x - 1)^2(x + 0.2)(5x^2 - 35)$$
$$= 5(x + 1)(x - 1)^2(x + 0.2)(x^2 - 7)$$

Since the solution to $x^2 - 7 = 0$ is

$$x = \pm\sqrt{7}$$

we see that the exact values of the other two roots are

$$x_5 = \sqrt{7} \qquad \text{and} \qquad x_6 = -\sqrt{7}$$

This is verified in Figure 17.8d.

C3 f_x =$A$2*B4

▲	A	B	C	D	E	F	G	H
1								
2	1	5	-4	-41	32	43	-28	-7
3			5	1	-40	-8	35	7
4	1	5	1	-40	-8	35	7	0
5			5	6	-34	-42	-7	
6	-1	5	6	-34	-42	-7	0	
7			-5	-1	35	7		
8	-0.2	5	1	-35	-7	0		
9			-1	0	7			
10		5	0	-35	0			

Figure 17.8c

© Cengage Learning 2013

K	L
ROOTS	
x	P(x)
-1	0
1	0
-0.2	0
2.645751	2.13E-13
-2.64575	3.55E-13

© Cengage Learning 2013

Figure 17.8d

APPLICATION BUSINESS

EXAMPLE 17.21

A company needs a box like the one shown in Figure 17.9a. The box is to be made from a sheet of metal that measures 45 cm by 30 cm by cutting a square from each corner and bending up the sides. If the box is to hold 3 500 cm³, what are the lengths of the sides of the squares that are cut out of each corner?

SOLUTION A sketch of this situation is shown in Figure 17.9b. The lengths of the sides of the squares have been labeled x. Once these squares have been removed, the part of the remaining sheet that will form the length of the box is $45 - 2x$ cm. Similarly, the box's width is $30 - 2x$ cm. The width of the box must be at least 0 and less than 30 cm. So, $0 < 30 - 2x < 30$ or $0 < x < 15$.

When the metal is bent to form the sides of the box, a box like the one in Figure 17.9c is obtained. This box is a rectangular prism, so its volume is $V = (45 - 2x)(30 - 2x)x$. We are told that this box is to have a volume of 3500 cm^3, so

$$(45 - 2x)(30 - 2x)x = 3500$$

Multiplying the factors on the left-hand side produces

$$1350x - 150x^2 + 4x^3 = 3500$$
$$\text{or } 4x^3 - 150x^2 + 1350x - 3500 = 0$$

Using the PlySmlt2 feature of the calculator, we see that the solutions are

$$x_1 \approx 25.6873$$
$$x_2 \approx 6.8127$$
$$x_3 \approx 5$$

One of these possible solutions, $x \approx 25.7$ is too large since $x < 15$.

Thus, there are two possible ways to cut this metal to obtain a box with the desired volume. If $x = 5$ cm, the box has a length of $45 - 2(5) = 35$ cm and a width of $30 - 2(5) = 20$ cm. Checking, we see that $(35)(20)5 = 3500$.

If $x \approx 6.8127$ cm, the length is approximately 31.3746 cm and the width is about 16.3746 cm. Multiplying, we get a volume of $(31.3746)(16.3746)(6.8127)$ $= 3500.000952 \approx 3500$ cm^3.

This problem has two correct solutions. The solution the company uses will depend on other factors, such as which is easier (or less expensive) to make, which one does a better job of holding the product, and which shape is more appealing to the customer.

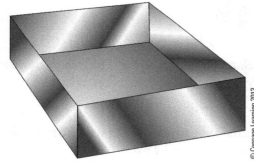

Figure 17.9a

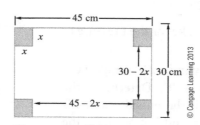

Figure 17.9b

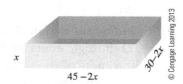

Figure 17.9c

© Cengage Learning 2013

APPLICATION **GENERAL TECHNOLOGY**

EXAMPLE 17.22

The stability of a molecule can be determined by solving its characteristic polynomial, $P(x)$. The roots of the equation $P(x) = 0$ determine the molecule's pi electrons. The characteristic polynomial of naphthalene $C_{10}H_8$ is

$$P(x) = x^{10} - 11x^8 + 41x^6 - 65x^4 + 43x^2 - 9$$

Determine the energies of naphthalene's 10 pi electrons.

EXAMPLE 17.22 (Cont.) | **SOLUTION** P is an even function and so it is symmetric about the y-axis. Thus, for each positive root, its additive inverse is also a root.

Using the PlySmlt2 feature of the calculator we obtain the roots, which are approximately ± 2.3028, ± 1.6180, ± 1.3028, ± 1, and ± 0.6180.

EXERCISE SET 17.3

In Exercises 1–16, find to four decimal places all rational and irrational roots of the given polynomial equation.

1. $x^3 + 5x - 3 = 0$

2. $x^3 - 3x + 1 = 0$

3. $x^4 + 2x^3 - 5x^2 + 1 = 0$

4. $x^4 - 5x^3 + 2x^2 + 1 = 0$

5. $x^3 + x^2 - 7x + 3 = 0$

6. $x^3 - 4x^2 - 7x + 3 = 0$

7. $x^4 - x - 2 = 0$

8. $x^5 - 2x^2 + 4 = 0$

9. $x^4 + x^3 - 2x^2 - 7x - 5 = 0$

10. $x^4 - 2x^3 - 3x + 4 = 0$

11. $2x^4 + 3x^3 - x^2 - 2x - 2 = 0$

12. $3x^4 + 3x^3 + x^2 + 4x + 3 = 0$

13. $2x^5 - 5x^3 + 2x^2 + 4x - 1 = 0$

14. $x^5 + 3x^4 - 5x^3 - 2x^2 + x + 2 = 0$

15. $8x^4 + 6x^3 - 15x^2 - 12x - 2 = 0$

16. $9x^4 + 15x^3 - 20x^2 - 20x + 16 = 0$

Solve Exercises 17–30.

17. **Petroleum engineering** The pressure drop P in pounds per square inch (psi) in a particular oil reservoir is a function of the number of years t that the reservoir has been in operation. The pressure drop is approximated by the equation:

$$P = 150t - 20t^2 + t^3$$

How many years will it take for the pressure to drop 400 psi?

18. **Industrial design** A cylindrical storage tank 12 ft high contains 674 ft³. Determine the thickness of the tank, if the outside radius is 4.5 ft and the sides, top, and bottom have the same thickness.

19. **Nuclear technology** A cylindrical container for storing radioactive waste is to be constructed from lead. The sides, top, and bottom of the cylinder of the container must be at least 15.5 cm thick. (**a**) If the volume of the outside cylinder is $1\,000\,000\,\pi$ cm³, and the height of the inside cylinder is twice the radius of the inside cylinder (as shown in Figure 17.10), determine the radius of the inside cylinder. (**b**) what is the volume of the inside cylinder?

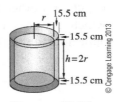

Figure 17.10

20. **Mechanical engineering** The characteristic polynomial for a certain material is

$$S^3 - 6S^2 - 78S + 108 = 0$$

Find the approximate value(s) of the stress that lies between 1 and 2 psi.

21. **Chemistry** The reference polynomial for a certain molecule is given by

$$R(x) = x^{10} - 11x^8 + 41x^6 - 61x^4 + 31x^2 - 3$$

Solve this reference polynomial.

22. **Medical technology** A pharmaceutical company is growing an organism to be used in a vaccine. The number of bacteria in millions at any given time t, in hours, is given by $Q(t) = -0.009t^5 + t^3 + 5.5$. Determine to the nearest tenth of a minute the value of t for which $Q(t) = 32.6$.

23. *Sheet metal technology* A rectangular sheet of metal was made from a box by cutting indentical squares from the four corners and bending up the sides. If the piece of sheet metal originally measured 8.0 in. by 10.0 in. and the volume of the box is 48 in.³, what was the length of each side of the squares that were removed?

24. *Drafting* A rectangular box is constructed so that its width is 2.5 cm longer than its height and the length is 4 cm longer than the width. If the box has a volume of 210 cm³, what are its dimensions?

25. *Agriculture* A grain silo has the shape of a right circular cylinder with a hemisphere on top, as shown in Figure 17.11. The total height of the silo is 34 ft. Determine the radius of the cylinder if the total volume is 2,511π ft³.

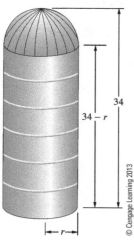

Figure 17.11

26. *Petroleum engineering* A propane gas storage tank is in the shape of a right circular cylinder

of height 6 m with a hemisphere attached at each end. Determine the radius r so that the volume of the tank is 18π m³.

27. *Electricity* Three electric resistors are connected in parallel. The second resistor is 4 Ω greater than the first and the third resistor is 1 Ω larger than the first. The total resistance is 1 Ω. In order to find the first resistance R, we must solve the equation:

$$\frac{1}{R} + \frac{1}{R + 4} + \frac{1}{R + 1} = 1$$

What are the values of the resistances?

28. *Electronics* Suppose that the resistors in Exercise 27 had been related such that the second was 4 Ω larger than the first and the third 9 Ω larger than the first. If the total resistance was 3 Ω, then

$$\frac{1}{R} + \frac{1}{R + 4} + \frac{1}{R + 9} = \frac{1}{3}$$

What are the values of these resistances?

29. *Industrial technology* A rectangular box is made from a piece of metal 12 cm by 19 cm by cutting a square from each corner and bending up the sides and welding the seams. If the volume of the box is 210 cm³, what is the size of the square that is cut from each corner?

30. *Architecture* The bending moment of a beam is given by $M(d) = 0.1d^4 - 2.2d^3 + 15.2d^2 - 32d$, where d is the distance in meters from one end. Find the values of d, where the bending moment is zero. (Hint: First multiply by 10 to eliminate the decimals.)

 [IN YOUR WORDS]

31. Some people think that the wording of Exercise 24 is not clear. Rewrite the exercise so that you think it is easier to understand. Hand it to a classmate for his or her comments. Did your classmate really think your wording was easier to understand than the wording in the textbook?

32. Without looking in the textbook or at your notes, write the hints for finding roots of polynomials.

SECTION II: Measurement

UNIT 7: PRECISION, ACCURACY, AND TOLERANCE

EXERCISE 7–4

1. a. 0.1″
   b. The range includes all numbers equal to or greater than 3.55″ and less than 3.65″.
3. a. 0.1 mm
   b. The range includes all numbers equal to or greater than 4.25 mm and less than 4.35 mm.
5. a. 0.001″
   b. The range includes all numbers equal to or greater than 15.8845″ and less than 15.8855″.
7. a. 0.001″
   b. The range includes all numbers equal to or greater than 12.0015″ and less than 12.0025″.
9. a. 0.01 mm
   b. The range includes all numbers equal to or greater than 7.005 mm and less than 7.015 mm.
11. a. 0.1 mm
   b. The range includes all numbers equal to or greater than 9.05 mm and less than 9.15 mm.

EXERCISE 7–5

1. 10.56 in.   **3.** 87.3 ft   **5.** 1472 mi   **7.** 8.001 in.   **9.** 61 gal   **11.** 0.01 sq in.

EXERCISE 7–6

1. 5   **3.** 5   **5.** 5   **7.** 5   **9.** 5   **11.** 2   **13.** 5   **15.** 3   **17.** 5   **19.** 4

EXERCISE 7–7

1. 5.05   **3.** 173   **5.** 123.0   **7.** 8.92   **9.** 70,108   **11.** 43.08   **13.** 0.0200   **15.** 818.0

EXERCISE 7–8

1. 44.8 mm   **3.** 170 ft   **5.** 7.6 mi   **7.** 0.006   **9.** 0.005   **11.** 10.378   **13.** 0.25   **15.** 755.0

EXERCISE 7–9

1. Absolute Error = 0.002 in.
   Relative Error = 0.0005
   Percent Error = 0.05%
3. Absolute Error = 0.2 lb
   Relative Error = 0.02
   Percent Error = 2%

5. Absolute Error = 0.14 cm
   Relative Error = 0.0059
   Percent Error = 0.59%
7. Absolute Error = 3 ohms
   Relative Error = 0.03
   Percent Error = 3%

9. Absolute Error = 0.010 m^2
   Relative Error = 0.01
   Percent Error = 1.0%
11. Absolute Error = 2.6 m
   Relative Error = 0.0014
   Percent Error = 0.14%

EXERCISE 7–10

1. Tolerance = $\dfrac{1}{32}$″
3. Minimum Limit = 16.74″

5. Tolerance = 0.0003″
7. Tolerance = 0.9 mm

9. 258.07 mm
11. 12.737 cm

EXERCISE 7–11

		Basic Dimension (inches)	Maximum Diameter (inches)	Minimum Diameter (inches)	Maximum Clearance (inches)	Minimum Clearance (inches)
1.	DIA A	1.4580	1.4580	1.4550	0.0090	0.0030
	DIA B	1.4610	1.4640	1.4610		
3.	DIA A	2.1053	2.1053	2.1023	0.0085	0.0025
	DIA B	2.1078	2.1108	2.1078		
5.	DIA A	0.9996	0.9996	0.9966	0.0071	0.0011
	DIA B	1.0007	1.0037	1.0007		

© Cengage Learning 2013

		Basic Dimension (millimetres)	Maximum Diameter (millimetres)	Minimum Diameter (millimetres)	Maximum Interference (millimetres)	Minimum Interference (millimetres)
7.	DIA A	32.07	32.09	32.05	0.10	0.02
	DIA B	32.01	32.03	31.99		
9.	DIA A	41.91	41.93	41.89	0.10	0.02
	DIA B	41.85	41.87	41.83		

© Cengage Learning 2013

UNIT EXERCISE AND PROBLEM REVIEW

1. a. 0.1 in.
  b. The range includes all numbers equal to or greater than 5.25 in. and less than 5.35 in.
3. a. 0.001 in.
  b. The range includes all numbers equal to or greater than 1.8335 in. and less than 1.8345 in.
5. a. 0.001 in.
  b. The range includes all numbers equal to or greater than 19.0005 in. and less than 19.0015 in.
7. a. 0.1 mm
  b. The range includes all numbers equal to or greater than 28.95 mm and less than 29.05 mm.

9. 20.917 mm
11. 2449 mi
13. 13.997 in.
15. 41 in.
17. 5
19. 5
21. 5
23. 6

25. 6.07
27. 48,070
29. 0.870
31. 3.0006
33. 14
35. 0.005
37. 360,000
39. 0.24

41. Absolute
  Error = 0.003 in.
  Relative Error = 0.0005
  Percent Error = 0.05%
43. Absolute Error = 58 lb
  Relative Error = 0.011
  Percent Error = 1.1%

45. Absolute Error = 0.0005 cm
  Relative Error = 0.0006
  Percent Error = 0.06%
47. Tolerance = $\dfrac{1''}{16}$
49. Maximum Limit = 2.781″
51. Tolerance = 0.6 mm
53. Minimum Limit = 78.66 mm

		Basic Dimension (inches)	Maximum Diameter (inches)	Minimum Diameter (inches)	Maximum Clearance (inches)	Minimum Clearance (inches)
55.	DIA A	1.7120	1.7120	1.7106	0.0044	0.0016
	DIA B	1.7136	1.7150	1.7136		
57.	DIA A	2.8064	2.8064	2.8050	0.0039	0.0011
	DIA B	2.8075	2.8089	2.8075		

© Cengage Learning 2013

		Basic Dimension (millimetres)	Maximum Diameter (millimetres)	Minimum Diameter (millimetres)	Maximum Interference (millimetres)	Minimum Interference (millimetres)
59.	DIA A	9.94	9.97	9.91	0.15	0.03
	DIA B	9.85	9.88	9.82		

© Cengage Learning 2013

61. Maximum value Length $A = 35\dfrac{23''}{32}$

  Minimum value Length $A = 35\dfrac{17''}{32}$

63. Maximum thickness = 2.82 mm
  Minimum thickness = 2.76 mm
65. Hole 5 is drilled out of tolerance.
  Hole 6 is drilled out of tolerance.

UNIT 8: CUSTOMARY MEASUREMENT UNITS

EXERCISE 8–2A
1. 4.25 ft   **3.** 7.083 yd   **5.** 1.2 mi   **7.** 3.70 ft   **9.** 18.9 yd   **11.** 0.675 mi

EXERCISE 8–2B
1. 6 ft 3 in.   **3.** 1 mi 660 yd   **5.** 10 ft $7\dfrac{1}{2}$ in.   **7.** 1 mi 165$\dfrac{1}{3}$ yd

EXERCISE 8–2C
1. 72 in.   **3.** 48.90 ft   **5.** 7128 ft   **7.** 12.8 ft   **9.** 1320 ft   **11.** 464 rd

EXERCISE 8–2D
1. 19 ft 6 in.   **3.** 158 yd 1.2 ft   **5.** 697 rd 3.3 yd   **7.** 2 ft 8.4 in.

EXERCISE 8–3A
1. 12 ft 9 in.
3. 19 ft $3\dfrac{1}{8}$ in.
5. 18 yd 2 ft
7. 23 yd 2 ft 3 in.
9. 5 rd 5 yd
11. 3 mi 115 rd
13. 4 ft 3 in.
15. 2 ft $4\dfrac{15}{16}$ in.
17. 3 yd 0.5 ft
19. 1 yd 2 ft 9.9 in.
21. 1 rd 1 yd 1 ft
23. 3 mi 250 rd

EXERCISE 8–3B

1. 14 ft 6 in. **7.** 19 yd 1 ft 6 in. **11.** 7 mi 294 rd **17.** $14\text{ yd }\dfrac{2}{3}\text{ ft}$ **21.** $13\text{ yd 1 ft }6\dfrac{1}{2}\text{ in.}$

3. 67 ft 4.5 in.   **13.** 3 ft 2 in.

5. 133 yd 1 ft **9.** $5\text{ yd 1 ft }4\dfrac{1}{2}\text{ in.}$ **15.** 4 ft 6.975 in. **19.** 7 yd 1 ft 3 in. **23.** 2 mi 100 rd

EXERCISE 8–4

1. A = 32′-1″   **3.** $52\text{ yd }2\dfrac{1}{4}\text{ ft}$ **5.** $1\text{ ft }11\dfrac{1}{2}\text{ in.}$ **7.** A = 30 ft **9.** $12.15

　B = 38′11″   B = 6 ft 1 in.

　C = 12′-9″   C = 4 ft 9 in.

　D = 8′-4″

EXERCISE 8–5

1. 1.36 sq ft **7.** 2.8 A **13.** 338 sq in. **19.** 93,650 sq ft

3. 5.09 sq yd **9.** 0.399 A **15.** 38.7 sq ft **21.** 165 sq yd

5. 2.5 sq mi **11.** 0.0312 sq mi **17.** 2436.8 A **23.** 697,000 sq ft

EXERCISE 8–6

1. 54 strips **3.** 8 gal **5.** 1320 tiles **7.** 59 panels

EXERCISE 8–7

1. 2.5 cu ft **5.** 7.47 cu ft **9.** 0.325 cu ft **13.** 443 cu ft **17.** 3062 cu ft

3. 4.33 cu yd **7.** 2.7 cu yd **11.** 2851 cu in. **15.** 472 cu in. **19.** 950 cu in.

EXERCISE 8–8

1. 12.30 cu ft **3.** 5.93 cu yd **5.** 3675 lb

EXERCISE 8–9

1. 3.26 qt **7.** 709 cu in. **11.** 1.9 qt

3. 37.0 qt **9.** 0.20 gal **13.** 51 oz

5. 8.8 gal

EXERCISE 8–10

1. 10 qt **3.** 30,700 gal **5.** 33 min **7.** 126 **9.** 25,100 gal

EXERCISE 8–11

1. 2.2 lb **3.** 5400 lb **5.** 2.7 short tons **7.** 2.72 lb **9.** 240 lb

EXERCISE 8–12

1. 108 lb **3.** 85 lb 3 oz **5.** 9500 lb **7.** 0.24 oz

EXERCISE 8–13A

1. 1.02 mi/min **3.** 35.8 rev/sec **5.** 936 ft/hr **7.** 320 lb/sq in.

EXERCISE 8–13B

1. 5.32 short tons/sq ft **3.** 29.0 cents/pt **5.** 133 cu ft/hr

EXERCISE 8–14

1. a. 4.4 short tons **3. a.** 304.3 ft³ **5.** 434 cu ft

　b. 3.9 long tons 　**b.** 59,300 lb **7. a.** 1.95 in.

　　　　　　　　　　　c. 25.62 hours or 　**b.** 0.374 in.

　　　　　　　　　　　　3 days, 1.62 hours 　**c.** 0.491 in.

　　　　　　　　　　　　(assuming an 8 hour day) 　**d.** 3.87 in.

　　　　　　　　　　　d. $4746.30 　**e.** 0.855 in.

UNIT EXERCISE AND PROBLEM REVIEW

1. 2.125 ft **19.** 26 ft 3 in. **41.** 0.4 cu yd **63.** 119 cu ft/hr

3. 0.75 mi **21.** 15 yd 1 ft 4 in. **43.** 61.2 qt **65.** A = 49′-6″

5. 15 yd 2 ft 　　　　　　　　　　**45.** 3.3 qt 　　B = 4′-0″

7. $24\dfrac{1}{2}\text{ ft}$ **23.** $3\text{ yd }2\dfrac{2}{3}\text{ ft}$ **47.** 240 cu in. 　　C = 26′-10″

　　　　　25. 3.50 sq ft **49.** 1.6 pt 　　D = 12′-10″

9. 81 in. **27.** 588 sq in. **51.** 2.1 lb **67.** 24 pieces

11. 146 yd 2 ft **29.** 5.000A **53.** 21.6 long tons **69.** 72 cu ft

13. 12 ft 3 in. **31.** 48.0 sq ft **55.** 1320 lb **71.** 7.9 cu yd

15. $10\text{ ft }1\dfrac{3}{4}\text{ in.}$ **33.** 104 sq in. **57.** 1170 lb/sq ft **73.** 25,600 gal

　　　　　35. 2.7 cu ft **59.** 2,220,000 cu ft/hr **75.** 189 sheets

17. $2\text{ yd }1\dfrac{1}{2}\text{ ft}$ **37.** 1230 cu in. **61.** 59.0 mi/hr

　　　　　39. 1026 cu in.

UNIT 9: METRIC MEASUREMENT UNITS

EXERCISE 9–1A

1. cm   **3.** m   **5.** cm   **7.** km

EXERCISE 9–1B

1. cm   **3.** cm   **5.** cm   **7.** m   **9.** mm

EXERCISE 9–2

1. 3.4 m   **5.** 0.335 m   **9.** 1050 m   **13.** 70 cm   **17.** 24 hm   **21.** 7.35 dm   **25.** 800 dm
3. 50 m   **7.** 84 m   **11.** 148 m   **15.** 50 mm   **19.** 31.06 m   **23.** 0.616 km   **27.** 600 cm

EXERCISE 9–4

1. 12 cm   **5.** Cost per piece: Cost per 2500 pieces:
3. 148.95 m   #105-AD: $0.1892   #105-AD: $544
                        #106-AD: $0.1428   #106-AD: $411
                        #107-AD: $0.2727   #107-AD: $784

EXERCISE 9–5

1. 5 cm^2 **5.** 1 dm^2 **9.** 800 dm^2 **13.** 208 cm^2
3. 49 dm^2 **7.** 0.35 m^2 **11.** 4800 cm^2 **15.** 4 400 000 dm^2

EXERCISE 9–7

1. 60 pieces   **3.** 120 t   **5.** 15 gaskets

EXERCISE 9–8

1. 2.7 cm^3 **5.** 0.048 dm^3 **9.** 0.07 dm^3 **13.** 800 000 cm^3 **17.** 1030 cm^3
3. 0.94 m^3 **7.** 150 m^3 **11.** 5000 cm^3 **15.** 5230 mm^3 **19.** 106 000 mm^3

EXERCISE 9–10

1. 2.5 m^3 **5.** 91.40% Magnesium
3. 8400 kg   8.29% Aluminum
                       0.13% Manganese
                       0.18% Zinc

EXERCISE 9–11

1. 3.67 L   **5.** 5.3 L   **9.** 83 L   **13.** 29 L
3. 23.6 cm^3 **7.** 80 L   **11.** 7.3 L

EXERCISE 9–12

1. 18 L   **3.** 32 198 000 L   **5.** 76 min   **7.** 36 L   **9.** 90 000 L

EXERCISE 9–13

1. 1720 mg   **3.** 2600 kg   **5.** 2.7 metric tons   **7.** 40 mg   **9.** 23 g

EXERCISE 9–14

1. 61.2 kg   **3.** 55 g   **5.** 62.8 kg/cm^2 **7.** 0.96 g/°C

EXERCISE 9–15A

1. 1.29 g/mm^2 **3.** 0.000128 m^3/sec   **5.** 0.0870 hp/cm^2 **7.** $0.00903/g

EXERCISE 9–15B

1. 19 m/sec   **3.** 0.7596 km/min   **5.** 0.477 cent/mL

EXERCISE 9–16

1. 5.3 metric tons   **5.** 20 m^3 **7. a.** 49.2 mm   **d.** 126 mm
3. 1100 kg   **b.** 13.6 mm   **e.** 26.4 mm
                                           c. 16.8 mm

EXERCISE 9–17A

1. 15.2 A   **5.** 8.2 Gb   **9.** 1.68×10^{12} b   **13.** 0.58 MHz
3. 0.75 kW   **7.** 0.38   **11.** 2.7×10^5 mW   **15.** $2.6 \times 10^6 \, \mu$A

EXERCISE 9–17B

1. 253 000 000 nm   **3.** 0.172 μg   **5.** 23 600 nL

EXERCISE 9–17C

1. 13.81 V   **5.** 3000 KHz   **9.** 135 Gb   **13.** 0.368 Gs   **17.** 0.038 mF
3. 38.6 mA   **7.** 71.5 Ω   **11.** 0.7 A   **15.** 40 s

EXERCISE 9–18A

1. 30.5 cm   **3.** 991 mm   **5.** 3.94 ft   **7.** 59.14 km   **9.** 10530 cm

EXERCISE 9–18B

1. 17 200 cm^2 **3.** 3.3 m^2 **5.** 160 acres   **7.** 201.8 ft^2

EXERCISE 9–18C

1. a. 4564 cm^3 **3.** 761.5 mL   **5.** 11.29 gal   **7.** 0.534 fl oz
   b. 4.564 L

EXERCISE 9–18D

1. 74.8 kg   **3.** 1241 g   **5.** 52.5 lb

UNIT EXERCISE AND PROBLEM REVIEW

1. cm	**19.** 2401.9 m	**37.** 4600 dm^3	**55.** 0.97 km/min	**73.** 1.864 in.
3. mm	**21.** 118.87 dm	**39.** 0.06 m^3	**57.** 320.4 Kg/dm^2	**75.** 19.7 m^2
5. cm	**23.** 5.32 cm^2	**41.** 1300 mL	**59.** 0.6348 km/min	**77.** 1.338 m^3
7. 80 mm	**25.** 1.466 m^2	**43.** 93.4 cm^3	**61.** 3.9 g/mm^2	**79.** 0.5096 qt
9. 2300 cm	**27.** 600 dm^2	**45.** 0.618 m^3	**63.** 0.094 kW	**81.** 282.0 kg
11. 800 m	**29.** 9000 m^2	**47.** 60 mL	**65.** 5×10^6 ns	**83.** 48 km
13. 122 mm	**31.** 0.028 m^2	**49.** 1.88 kg	**67.** 1.78×10^6 μA	**85.** 0.55 m^2
15. 76.6 mm	**33.** 2.4 cm^3	**51.** 2700 kg	**69.** 1.294 nm	**89.** 11.7 metric tons
17. 644.8 m	**35.** 7000 cm^3	**53.** 210 g	**71.** 3.744 m	

CHAPTER 4

Exercise 4.1

1. 4.26×10^{10}, 42.6×10^9
3. 9.30×10^{-4}, 930×10^{-6}
5. 1.05×10^7, 10.5×10^6
7. 4.56×10^1, 45.6×10^0
9. 2.35×10^0
11. 1.17×10^{-3}
13. 3.34×10^2, 334×10^0
15. 1.12×10^{-1}, 112×10^{-3}
17. 1×10^3
19. 1.62×10^5, 162×10^3
21. $56,400,000$, 5.64×10^7, 56.4×10^6
23. $1,200,000$, 1.2×10^6
25. 0.000000114, 1.14×10^{-7}, 114×10^{-9}
27. 52.8, 5.28×10^1, 52.8×10^0
29. 0.00569, 5.69×10^{-3}
31. $5,660,000$, 5.66×10^6
33. 0.000552, 5.52×10^{-4}, 552×10^{-6}
35. $26,400,000$, 2.64×10^7, 26.4×10^6
37. 0.00000390, 3.90×10^{-6}
39. 1.45, 1.45×10^0
41. 0.0101, 1.01×10^{-2}, 10.1×10^{-3}
43. $112,000$, 1.12×10^5, 112×10^3
45. 0.0000105, 1.05×10^{-5}, 10.5×10^{-6}

47. $871,000,000$, 8.71×10^8, 871×10^6
49. 1.23, 1.23×10^0
51. $125,000$, 1.25×10^5, 125×10^3
53. 0.503, 5.03×10^{-1}, 503×10^{-3}
55. 1.29×10^7, 12.9×10^6, $12,900,000$
57. 1.35×10^7, 13.5×10^6, $13,500,000$
59. 3.41×10^6, $3,410,000$
61. 7.18×10^{-8}, 71.8×10^{-9}, 0.0000000718
63. 1.49×10^5, 149×10^3, $149,000$
65. 9.42×10^{-3}
67. 7.88×10^{12}
69. 53.3×10^{-3}
71. 52.9×10^3
73. 7.28×10^{-9}
75. 57.0×10^0
77. 899×10^3
79. 5.00×10^{-6}
81. 40.0×10^6
83. 250×10^9
85. 1.5×10^9
87. $\$3490.57$
89. 2.40×10^{-6} m
91. 439×10^9 kWh
93. 183×10^{-3} V
95. 92.3×10^{-3} A
97. 5.41×10^3 Ω

ANSWERS FOR CHAPTER 2

Exercise Set 2.1

1. 4 is a constant; x and y are variables. **3.** 8 and π are constants; r is a variable. **5.** $3x^3$ and $4x$

7. $(2x^3)(5y)$, $\sqrt{3}ab$, and $-\dfrac{7a}{b}$ **9.** $-1, 5, x,$ and $\dfrac{1}{y}$

11. 47 **13.** $\dfrac{\pi a}{4}$, if a is a constant **15.** $3x^2y$ and $17x^2y$

17. $(x + y)^2$ and $5(x + y)^2$ **19.** $a + b - c$ and $-2(a + b - c)$ **21.** $11x$ **23.** $2z$ **25.** $6x + 9x^2$ or $9x^2 + 6x$ **27.** $10w - 7w^2$ or $-7w^2 + 10w$

29. $2ax^2 + a^2x$ **31.** $11xy^2 - 5x^2y$ **33.** $12b$

35. $2a^2 + 5b + 4a$ **37.** $2x^2 + 6x$ **39.** $12y^2 + 14x$

41. $-12b + 6c$ **43.** $7a + 7b$ **45.** $x + y$

47. $5a + 5b - c$ **49.** $6x + 6y$ **51.** $5a + 5b$

53. $6a - 2b + 4c$ **55.** $9x + 7y$ **57.** $-6x + 2y - 13z$

59. $-4x + 3y + 25z$ **61.** $6x + 2y$ **63.** $3y + z$

65. $x + 6y$ **67.** $a - 3b$ **69.** $-70a - 8b$

71. $\frac{13}{6}p = 2\frac{1}{6}p$ **73.** $\frac{1}{C_T} = \frac{C_2 + C_1}{C_1 C_2}$

75. **(a)** $N = W - (0.134W + 0.046W + 0.011W + 0.075W + 0.010W + 0.002W + 0.082W)$
    (b) $N = W - (0.36\,W) = 0.64\,W$

77. $42I_a^2 + 70I_b^2$

Exercise Set 2.2

1. a^3x^3 **3.** $6a^2x^3$ **5.** $-6x^3w^3z$ **7.** $-24ax^4b$

9. $10y - 12$ **11.** $35 - 20w$ **13.** $21xy + 12x$

15. $15t - 5t^2$ **17.** $2a^2 - a$ **19.** $6x^3 - 2x^2 + 8x$

21. $-20y^4 + 8y^3 - 20y^2 + 12y - 24$ **23.** $a^2 + ab + ac + bc$ **25.** $x^3 + 5x^2 + 6x + 30$ **27.** $6x^2 + xy - y^2$

29. $6a^2 - 7ab + 2b^2$ **31.** $2b^2 + 3b - 5$

33. $56a^4b^2 + 3a^2bc - 9c^2$ **35.** $x^2 - 16$ **37.** $p^2 - 36$

39. $a^2x^2 - 4$ **41.** $4r^4 - 9x^2$ **43.** $25a^4x^6 - 16d^2$

45. $\frac{9}{16}t^2b^6 - \frac{4}{9}p^2a^4f^2$ **47.** $x^2 + 2xy + y^2$

49. $x^2 - 10x + 25$ **51.** $a^2 + 6a + 9$

53. $4a^2 + 4ab + b^2$ **55.** $9x^2 - 12xy + 4y^2$

57. $12x^3 + 40x^2 - 32x$ **59.** $x^2 - y^2 - z^2 + 2yz$

61. $a^3 + 6a^2 + 12a + 8$ **63.** $2n^2 + 6n$

65. $\frac{1}{2}(y_2^2 - y_1^2) = \frac{1}{2}y_2^2 - \frac{1}{2}y_1^2$ **67.** $x = 3t^2 + 15t + 12$

69. $A = \frac{1}{2}(4 + x)[(6 + x) + (8 + x)] = x^2 + 11.0 + 28$

Exercise Set 2.3

1. x^4 **3.** $2x^2$ **5.** $3y^2$ **7.** $-3b$ **9.** $11y$ **11.** $-6ay$

13. $18c^2d^2$ **15.** $\frac{-3p}{5n^2}$ **17.** $\frac{4bcx}{7y}$ **19.** $2a^2 + a$

21. $4b^3 - 2b$ **23.** $6x^2 + 4x$ **25.** $2x^3 - 3$

27. $-6x^3 + 2x$ **29.** $5x + 5y$ **31.** $2x + 3y$

33. $ap - 2$ **35.** $a + 1$ **37.** $-3xy + z$

39. $-b^2x^2 - b^2$ **41.** $x + 1 - y$ **43.** $-\frac{3}{2}xy + 2y^2$

45. $x + 4$ **47.** $x - 1$ **49.** $x - 1$ **51.** $2a + 1$

53. $4y + 2$ **55.** $x - 2$ **57.** $2a - 1$

59. $2x^2 + x - 1 + \frac{3}{2x - 1}$ **61.** $r^2 - 3r + \frac{5}{r + 2}$

63. $x^3 + 3x^2 + 9x + 27$ **65.** $4x^3 - 3x^2 - x + 6$

67. $x + y$ **69.** $w^2 + wz + z^2$ **71.** $x^2 + y^2$

73. $c^2d^2 + 2cd + 4$ **75.** $x - y$ **77.** $p^2r - 2p + 3r^2$

79. $a + d + 4 + \frac{-4}{a - 3d - 1}$ **81.** af

83. $a + b - c$ **85.** $a^2 - a + 1$ **87.** $\frac{1}{R_1} + \frac{1}{R_2} + \frac{1}{R_3}$

89. $V_2 = \frac{V_1 T_2}{T_1}$ **91.** $8r - 5$

Exercise Set 2.4

1. 39 **3.** 12 **5.** -15 **7.** $\frac{9}{2}$ **9.** -8 **11.** $-\frac{2}{3}$

13. 15 **15.** -24 **17.** 2 **19.** -4 **21.** 4 **23.** 4

25. 7 **27.** $\frac{1}{2}$ **29.** $\frac{24}{5}$ **31.** 5 **33.** -6 **35.** 9

37. -6 **39.** $-\frac{40}{3}$ **41.** 6 **43.** 6 **45.** $\frac{13}{4}$

47. 14 **49.** -18 **51.** $\frac{24}{7}$ **53.** 78 **55.** $\frac{b}{2a}$

57. $-\frac{x}{x - 8}$ or $\frac{x}{8 - x}$ **59.** $\frac{7}{3}$ **61.** 1 **63.** -3

65. -15 **67.** -2 **69.** $a = -12$ **71.** $a = -2z$

73. $1.38 : 16$ **75.** $86 : 1$ **77.** $4.5 : 1$ **79.** $3.2857 : 1$

81. 28 **83.** 79 **85.** 4.267 **87.** 14

89. $C = \frac{5}{9}(F - 32)$

Exercise Set 2.6

1. 82 **3.** 60, since no score can be below 60

5. \$1150; \$230   **7.** \$6130   **9.** \$2200 at 7.5% and \$2300 at 6%   **11.** 7 hours   **13.** 266 miles   **15.** 320 km

17. 2.4 hours or 2 hours 24 minutes   **19.** $\frac{4}{3}$ hours or 1 hour 20 minutes   **21.** 57.5 mL   **23.** 468.75 kg of 75% copper; 281.25 kg of 35% copper

25. 350 lb; 8.235 feet from the 500 lb end   **27.** 4.5 ft from the left end   **29.** 6 in. from right end

31. 30 cc **33. (a)** $V = \sqrt{PR}$, where V is the voltage, P the power, and R the resistance **(b)** 23 Ω

35. (a) $Z = \sqrt{R^2 + X^2}$ **(b)** 8.9 Ω

ANSWERS FOR CHAPTER 7

Exercise Set 7.1

1. $3p + 3q$ 3. $15x - 3xy$ 5. $p^2 - q^2$
7. $4x^2 - 36p^2$ 9. $r^2 + 2rw + w^2$ 11. $4x^2 + 4xy + y^2$
13. $\frac{4}{9}x^2 + \frac{16}{3}xb + 16b^2$ 15. $4p^2 - 3pr + \frac{9}{16}r^2$
17. $a^2 + 5a + 6$ 19. $x^2 - 3x - 10$ 21. $6a^2 + 5ab + b^2$
23. $6x^2 - 7x - 20$ 25. $a^3 + 3a^2b + 3ab^2 + b^3$
27. $x^3 + 12x^2 + 48x + 64$ 29. $8a^3 - 12a^2b + 6ab^2 - b^3$
31. $27x^3 - 54x^2y + 36xy^2 - 8y^3$ 33. $m^3 + n^3$
35. $r^3 - t^3$ 37. $8x^3 + b^3$ 39. $27a^3 - d^3$
41. $3a^2 + 12a + 12$ 43. $5rt + 2r^2 + \frac{r^3}{5t}$
45. $x^4 - 36$ 47. $9x^4 - y^4$ 49. 0
51. $x^3 - 3x^2 - 9x + 27$ 53. $r^3 - 3r^2t + 3rt^2 - t^3$
55. $125 + 27x^3$ 57. $(x + y)^2 - 2(x + y)(w + z) + (w + z)^2$ 59. $(x + y)^2 - z^2 = x^2 + 2xy + y^2 - z^2$
61. $z^2 = R^2 + x_L^2 - 2x_Lx_C + x_C^2$
63. $a_c = \frac{(2t^2 - t)^2}{r} = \frac{4t^4 - 4t^3 + t^2}{r}$
65. $d = \left(\frac{P}{3EI}\right)(l_1^3 - l_2^3)$ 67. $L = L_0 + \alpha L_0 T$

Exercise Set 7.2

1. $6(x + 1)$ 3. $6(2a - 1)$ 5. $2(2x - y + 4)$
7. $5(x^2 + 2x + 3)$ 9. $5(2x^2 - 3)$ 11. $2x(2x + 3)$
13. $7b(by + 4)$ 15. $ax(3 + 6x - 2) = ax(1 + 6x)$
17. $2ap(2p + 3aq + 4q^2)$ 19. $(a - b)(a + b)$
21. $(x - 2)(x + 2)$ 23. $(y - 9)(y + 9)$
25. $(2x - 3)(2x + 3)$ 27. $(3a^2 - b)(3a^2 + b)$
29. $(5a - 7b)(5a + 7b)$ 31. $(12 - 5b^2)(12 + 5b^2)$
33. $5(a - 5)(a + 5)$ 35. $7(2a - 3b^2)(2a + 3b^2)$
37. $(a - 3)(a + 3)(a^2 + 9)$
39. $16(x - 2y)(x + 2y)(x^2 + 4y^2)$ 41. $2\pi r(r + h)$
43. $\frac{1}{2}d(v_2 - v_1)(v_2 + v_1)$ 45. $\frac{(\omega_f - \omega_0)(\omega_f + \omega_0)}{2\theta}$
47. $W = \frac{1}{2}I(\omega_2 - \omega_1)(\omega_2 + \omega_1)$
49. $\Delta A = 45\pi(2r + 45\pi)$

Exercise Set 7.3

1. $b^2 - 4ac = 113$; $\sqrt{113} \approx 10.6$; does not factor using rational numbers   3. $b^2 - 4ac = 196$; $\sqrt{196} = 14$; factors

5. $b^2 - 4ac = 169$; $\sqrt{169} = 13$; factors
7. $(x + 2)(x + 5)$ 9. $(x - 3)(x - 9)$
11. $(x - 2)(x - 25)$ 13. $(x - 2)(x + 1)$
15. $(x - 5)(x + 2)$ 17. $(r + 5)^2$ 19. $(a + 11)^2$
21. $(f - 15)^2$ 23. $(6y - 1)(y - 1)$
25. $(7t + 2)(t + 1)$ 27. $(7b + 1)(b - 5)$
29. $(4e - 1)(e + 5)$ 31. $(3u + 4)(u + 2)$
33. $(9t + 2)(t - 3)$ 35. $(3x - 1)(2x + 5)$
37. $(5a + 3)(3a - 5)$ 39. $(5e + 3)(3e + 5)$
41. $(5x - 2)(2x - 3)$ 43. $3(r - 7)(r + 1)$
45. $7t^2(7t - 1)(t - 2)$ 47. $(3x + 2y)(2x - 5y)$
49. $(2a + b)(4a - 9b)$ 51. $(a - b)(a^2 + ab + b^2)$
53. $(2x - 3)(4x^2 + 6x + 9)$
55. $i = 0.7(t^2 - 3t - 4) = 0.7(t - 4)(t + 1)$
57. $(0.009n^2 - 3)(n - 2000) = 0.0001(n^2 - 30,000)$ $(n - 2000)$
59. (a) $4x^2 + 32x - 36 = 0$; (b) $4(x + 9)(x - 1)$
61. $V = x(18 - 2x)(18 - 1.5x)$

Exercise Set 7.4

1. $\frac{35}{40}$ 3. $\frac{ax}{ay}$ 5. $\frac{3ax^3y}{3a^2x}$ 7. $\frac{4(x + y)}{x^2 - y^2} = \frac{4x + 4y}{x^2 - y^2}$
9. $\frac{(a + b)^2}{a^2 - b^2} = \frac{a^2 + 2ab + b^2}{a^2 - b^2}$ 11. $\frac{19}{12}$
13. $\frac{x}{4}$ 15. $\frac{4}{x - 3}$ 17. $\frac{x - 4}{x + 4}$ 19. $\frac{x}{3}$ 21. $\frac{x + 3}{x^2 + 5}$
23. $\frac{2m - m^2}{3 + 6m^2}$ 25. $\frac{x}{x - 3}$ 27. $\frac{2b}{3(b + 5)}$
29. $\frac{z + 3}{z - 3}$ 31. $\frac{x + 1}{x + 4}$ 33. $\frac{2x + 1}{x + 5}$ 35. $\frac{y(2y + 1)}{y - 1}$
37. $\frac{y^2 + xy + x^2}{2}$ 39. $x - y$ 41. $p = \frac{2wh}{s + 1}$
43. $\Delta V = \frac{V_1T_2}{T_1} + \frac{V_2T_1}{T_2} = \frac{V_1T_2^2 + V_2T_1^2}{T_1T_2}$

Exercise Set 7.5

1. $\frac{10}{xy}$ 3. $\frac{12x^2}{5y^3}$ 5. $\frac{3y}{7x}$ 7. $\frac{8x^3}{21y}$ 9. $\frac{5}{6xy}$ 11. $\frac{5a^3d}{2b}$
13. $\frac{8y^2}{25x^2}$ 15. $\frac{y^3}{5p^2}$ 17. $4y$ 19. $5(a - b)$

21. $\dfrac{3(x^2 - 100)}{4(x + 5)}$ **23.** $\dfrac{(2x - 1)(x + 3)}{-3x}$

25. $a + 2$ **27.** $\dfrac{1}{4a}$ **29.** $\dfrac{1}{x + 1}$ **31.** $\dfrac{4}{y}$

33. $\dfrac{x - 1}{3(x + 2)}$ **35.** $\dfrac{(x - 2y)(x - 5y)(x - 4y)}{(x + 4y)(x + 2y)(x - 7y)}$

37. $\dfrac{3x - 5}{x + 3}$ **39.** $\dfrac{x + y}{x - y}$ **41.** $\dfrac{x^3 + y^3}{4(x^3 - y^3)}$

43. $\dfrac{x + 5}{3x}$ **45.** $\dfrac{3}{x + 3}$ **47.** $\dfrac{a^2 + aa' + a'^2}{a(a + a')}$

49. $\dfrac{4\pi ne^2 wv}{(v - w^2)(mv^2 - \pi ne^2)}$

Exercise Set 7.6

1. 1 **3.** $\frac{2}{3}$ **5.** $\frac{5}{6}$ **7.** $\frac{2}{15}$ **9.** $\dfrac{6}{x}$ **11.** $\dfrac{1}{a}$ **13.** $\dfrac{5x}{y}$

15. $-\dfrac{3r}{2t}$ **17.** $\dfrac{3 + x}{x + 2}$ **19.** $\dfrac{t - 2}{t + 1}$ **21.** $\dfrac{2y}{x + 2}$

23. $\dfrac{7}{a + b}$ **25.** $\dfrac{2y + 3x}{xy}$ **27.** $\dfrac{ad - 4b}{bd}$

29. $\dfrac{7x - 3}{x(x^2 - 1)}$ **31.** $\dfrac{6 - 2x}{(x^2 - 1)(x + 1)}$

33. $\dfrac{x^2 + 8x - 10}{(x^2 - 36)(x - 5)}$ **35.** $\dfrac{11 - 3x}{(x - 3)(x^2 - 4)}$

37. $\dfrac{1 - x - 8x^2}{x(3x - 1)(x - 4)}$ **39.** $\dfrac{3x^2 - 8x - 5}{(x^2 - 1)(x + 4)}$

41. $\dfrac{6y + 13 - y^2}{(y - 2)(y + 1)(y + 4)}$

43. $\dfrac{2x^4 - x^3 + 13x^2 + 2x - 4}{(x^2 + 3)(x - 1)^2(x + 2)}$ **45.** $\dfrac{x + 2}{x - 3}$

47. $\dfrac{x(x - 1)}{x + 1}$ **49.** $\dfrac{x^2 - 2xy - y^2}{x^2 + y^2}$ **51.** $\dfrac{x + 3}{x + 2}$

53. $\dfrac{t(t - 1)}{t^2 + 1}$ **55.** $\dfrac{x^2 + y^2}{2x}$ **57.** $\dfrac{R_1 + R_2}{R_1 R_2}$

59. $\dfrac{C_1 C_2 + C_1 C_3 + C_2 C_3}{C_1 C_2 C_3}$ **61.** $P = \dfrac{Ak^2 r^2}{kr^2 + L^2}$

63. $\dfrac{V_1 R_2 R_3 + V_2 R_1 R_3 + V_3 R_1 R_2}{R_2 R_3 + R_1 R_3 + R_1 R_2}$

Review Exercises

1. $5x^2 - 5xy$ **3.** $x^3 - 6x^2 y + 12xy^2 - 8y^3$
5. $2x^2 - 9x - 18$ **7.** $x^4 - 25$ **9.** $8 + 12x + 6x^2 + x^3$
11. $9(1 + y)$ **13.** $7(x - 3)(x + 3)$ **15.** $(x - 6)(x - 5)$
17. $(x + 8)(x - 2)$ **19.** $(2x + 3)(x - 3)$

21. $\dfrac{x}{3y}$ **23.** $\dfrac{x - 3}{x + 3}$ **25.** $\dfrac{x^2 - xy + y^2}{x + y}$ **27.** $\dfrac{3xy}{7}$

29. $\dfrac{4}{x}$ **31.** $\dfrac{7x}{y}$ **33.** $\dfrac{7x^2 - 27x + 2}{(x + 2)^2(x - 5)^2}$

35. $\dfrac{-2x^2}{y^2 - x^2}$ **37.** $\dfrac{2(x^2 + 36)(x + 1)}{(x + 2)(x^2 - 36)}$ **39.** $\dfrac{(x - 6)^2}{(x + 6)^2}$

41. $\dfrac{y - x}{y + x}$ **43.** -1 **45.** $2x^2 - 1$

Chapter 7 Test

1. $x^2 + 2x - 15$ **3.** $-15x^3 + 6x^2 + 20x - 8$
5. $2(x - 8)(x + 8)$ **7.** $(5x - 7)(2x + 3)$
9. $\dfrac{x - 5}{x + 1}$ **11.** $\dfrac{3x(x - 1)}{(x + 2)^2} = \dfrac{3x^2 - 3x}{x^2 + 4x + 4}$

13. $\dfrac{x^2 - 2x + 6}{x - 5}$ **15.** $\dfrac{(x + 1)^2}{x(x + 2)}$ **17.** $\dfrac{2r_1 r_2}{r_1 + r_2}$

ANSWERS FOR　　**CHAPTER 9**

Exercise Set 9.1

1. 0.3　**3.** 10　**5.** $-\frac{1}{7}$　**7.** 9　**9.** -3　**11.** $\frac{15}{8}$

13. $\frac{9}{2}$　**15.** 15　**17.** -9　**19.** $\frac{2}{5}$　**21.** 1　**23.** $\frac{30}{37}$

25. $-\frac{3}{7}$　**27.** -6　**29.** 1　**31.** $\dfrac{rt}{r-t}$

33. $\dfrac{R_1 R_2 R_3}{R_1 R_2 + R_1 R_3 + R_2 R_3}$　**35.** $\dfrac{V - 2\pi r^2}{2\pi r}$

37. $\dfrac{R_1 f(n-1)}{R_1 - f(n-1)}$　**39.** $C = \dfrac{d R_1 R_2}{(9 \times 10^9)(R_1 - R_2)}$

41. $f = \dfrac{r_1 r_2}{(n-1)(r_2 - r_1)}$　**43.** $D = d + \dfrac{h}{2}$

45. $3\frac{3}{4}$ h or 3 h 45 min　**47.** 3 hours

49. $h = \frac{28}{5} = 5$ hours 36 minutes

51. 12 h　**53.** $f_a = \dfrac{f(V + V_L)}{V - V_s}$

55. $R_1 = \dfrac{R_2 R_3 (V_1 - V)}{V R_3 + V R_2 - V_2 R_3 - V_3 R_2}$

Exercise Set 9.2

1. $R = kl$　**3.** $A = kd^2$　**5.** $IN = k$

7. $r = kt, k = \frac{2}{3}$　**9.** $d = kr^2, k = \frac{1}{2}$

11. 9　**13.** 180 m/s　**15.** 435.6 neutrons

53. 2.25 inches wide, 7.5 inches deep, or 3.75 inches wide and 4.5 inches deep

55. $20   **57.** 1062.1 Ω   **59.** $\dfrac{-13 + 3\sqrt{46}}{2} \approx 3.67$ in.

61. 35.6 in.   **63.** 3.5 s

65. either 20 or 370 objects were sold

67. There are two possible answers. In one, each field is 300 ft $\times$ 450 ft; and in the other, each field measures 600 ft $\times$ 225 ft.

69. Answers will vary   **71. (a)** $-2, \frac{1}{3}$

Exercise Set 9.4

1. ± 3 **3.** $-3, 2$ **5.** $-1, 12$ **7.** $2, -4$ **9.** $0, 5$

11. $3, 4$ **13.** $-2, \frac{7}{2}$ **15.** $\frac{3}{2}, 4$ **17.** $3, -\frac{1}{3}$ **19.** $\frac{5}{2}, \frac{7}{2}$

21. $\frac{5}{3}, -\frac{7}{2}$ **23.** $\frac{1}{5}, \frac{3}{2}$ **25.** $-\frac{3}{2}, \frac{20}{3}$ **27.** $-1, 3$

29. $\frac{6}{5}, -\frac{2}{5}$ **31.** $2, -\frac{1}{2}$ **33.** $-12, 7$ **35.** $-3, 7$

37. $-1, 24$ **39.** $\frac{10}{7}, 5$ **41.** $7, 24$ **43.** $-\frac{1}{7}, 1.5$

45. 4 s   **47.** width 8 cm, length 13 cm   **49.** 5 m and 12 m   **51.** 3.00 in.   **53.** 12.0 m

55. Pipe A: 12 h, pipe B: 6 h   **57.** 15.00 in.

Exercise Set 9.5

1. $-2, -4$ **3.** -2 **5.** $\dfrac{3 \pm \sqrt{29}}{2}$

7. $-k \pm \sqrt{k^2 - c}$ **9.** $-4, 1$ **11.** $2, -\frac{1}{3}$

13. $-1, \frac{1}{7}$ **15.** $-1, \frac{7}{2}$ **17.** $-2, \frac{4}{3}$ **19.** $-\frac{2}{3}, -\frac{2}{3}$

21. $\dfrac{3 \pm \sqrt{17}}{4}$ **23.** $\dfrac{-5 \pm \sqrt{17}}{2}$ **25.** $\dfrac{-3 \pm \sqrt{15}}{2}$

27. $1 \pm \sqrt{8}$ **29.** $\pm \dfrac{\sqrt{6}}{2}$

31. no real roots because the discriminant is -48

33. no real roots because the discriminant is $-\frac{647}{81}$

35. $\dfrac{-0.2 \pm \sqrt{0.064}}{0.02}$ **37.** $5 \pm \sqrt{13}$

39. $\dfrac{2 \pm \sqrt{1.6}}{2.4}$ **41.** $\dfrac{-\sqrt{3} \pm \sqrt{87}}{6}$

43. no real root because the discriminant is negative

45. $\dfrac{-2 \pm \sqrt{13}}{3}$ **47.** Approximately 7.78 s

49. Approximately 11.86 s   **51.** approximately 16.38 cm wide and 24.57 cm long

ANSWERS FOR CHAPTER 11

Exercise Set 11.1

1. 5 **3.** 4 **5.** 1/5 **7.** 1/2 **9.** 9 **11.** 25

13. 1/8 **15.** −1/2 **17.** 1/2 **19.** 32 **21.** 3^7

23. 7^4 **25.** x^{10} **27.** y^2 **29.** 9^{10} **31.** x^{21}

33. $x^5 y^5$ **35.** $1/a^5 b^5$ **37.** x^8 **39.** $1/x^6$ **41.** x^2

43. $r^{7/4}$ **45.** $a^{5/6}$ **47.** $d^{5/12}$ **49.** b^3/a^3

51. r^2/s^3 **53.** y^6 **55.** a^5/b^{12}

57. $1/yb^{13/2} = \dfrac{1}{yb^{13/2}}$ **59.** p^3/x^2 **61.** $\dfrac{y^6}{z^2}$ **63.** $\dfrac{2y^2}{3x}$

65. $\dfrac{y^{19/15}}{x^{31/15}}$ **67.** $\dfrac{t^{11/6}x^{1/6}}{6}$ **69.** $\dfrac{4y^{11}}{27x^{10}}$

71. 4.0993852 **73.** 25.368006 **75.** 3.5162154

77. 4.5606226 **79.** −0.2253777406 **81.** 221.1125 m

≈ 221 m **83.** $p = 905\,146.3\,\text{N/m}^2\ T = 91\,238.747\,\text{K}$

85. $1 - \left(\dfrac{p_1}{p_2}\right)^{-7/2} = 1 - \left(\dfrac{p_2}{p_1}\right)^{7/2}$

Exercise Set 11.2

1. $2\sqrt[3]{2}$ **3.** $\sqrt[3]{5}$ **5.** y^4 **7.** $a\sqrt[5]{a^2}$ **9.** $xy^3\sqrt{y}$

11. $a\sqrt[4]{ab^3}$ **13.** $2x\sqrt[3]{x}$ **15.** $3x\sqrt{3xy}$ **17.** −2

19. ab^3 **21.** $pq^2r\sqrt[4]{r^3}$ **23.** $2x/3$ **25.** xy^2/z

27. $\dfrac{2x\sqrt[3]{2y^2}}{z^2}$ **29.** $8xy^2\sqrt{x}/3z^2p = \dfrac{8xy^2\sqrt{x}}{3z^2p}$

31. $4\sqrt{3}/3 = \dfrac{4\sqrt{3}}{3}$ **33.** $3\sqrt[3]{2}/2 = \dfrac{3\sqrt[3]{2}}{2}$

35. $5\sqrt{2x}/2x = \dfrac{5\sqrt{2x}}{2x}$ **37.** $3\sqrt[4]{8z}/4z = \dfrac{3\sqrt[4]{8z}}{4z}$

39. $2\sqrt[3]{2y}/x = \dfrac{2\sqrt[3]{2y}}{x}$ **41.** $-2x\sqrt[3]{by}/3bz =$

$\dfrac{-2x\sqrt[3]{by}}{3bz}$ **43.** $2 \times 10^2 = 2000$ **45.** $50\sqrt{10}$

47. $2\sqrt{10} \times 10^3 = 2000\sqrt{10}$ **49.** $\sqrt[3]{12.5} \times 10^3$

51. $\sqrt{\dfrac{x^2 + y^2}{xy}} = \dfrac{\sqrt{x^3y + xy^3}}{xy}$ **53.** $a + b$

55. $\sqrt{\dfrac{b + a^2}{a^2b}} = \dfrac{\sqrt{b^2 + a^2b}}{ab}$ **57.** $\sqrt[18]{27x^2}$

59. $\sqrt[21]{-624.2x^{15}y^{10}z}$ **61.** $f = \dfrac{\sqrt{T\mu}}{2L\mu} = \dfrac{1}{2L\mu}\sqrt{T\mu}$

63. $z = \dfrac{1}{\sqrt{\dfrac{R^2 + x^2}{R^2 x^2}}} = \sqrt{\dfrac{R^2 x^2}{R^2 + x^2}} = \dfrac{Rx\sqrt{R^2 + x^2}}{R^2 + x^2}$

$= \dfrac{Rx}{R^2 + x^2}\sqrt{R^2 + x^2}$ **65.** $1 + \dfrac{\sqrt{m^2 + 2h}}{m}$ or

$\dfrac{m + \sqrt{m^2 + 2h}}{m}$

Exercise Set 11.3

1. $7\sqrt{3}$ **3.** $5\sqrt[3]{9}$ **5.** $8\sqrt{3} + 4\sqrt{2}$ **7.** $3\sqrt{5}$

9. $-\sqrt{7}$ **11.** $5\sqrt{15}/3 = \frac{5}{3}\sqrt{15}$ **13.** $-\sqrt{2}$

15. $3x\sqrt{xy}$ **17.** $(2q + p^2)\sqrt[3]{3p^2 q}$ **19.** $\dfrac{x^2 - y^2}{x^2 y^2}\sqrt{xy}$

21. $2\sqrt{3ab}/3$ **23.** $\sqrt{40} = 2\sqrt{10}$ **25.** $x\sqrt{15}$

27. $8x\sqrt{x}$ **29.** $3/4$ **31.** $\sqrt{2x} + 2$ **33.** $x + 2$

$\sqrt{xy} + y$ **35.** $\dfrac{\sqrt[3]{5 \cdot 7^2}}{7} = \dfrac{\sqrt[3]{245}}{7}$ **37.** $a - b$

39. $\sqrt[6]{x^5}$ **41.** $\sqrt[12]{3^3 49^4 x^{11}} = \sqrt[12]{155{,}649{,}627 x^{11}}$ **43.** 4

45. $\sqrt[3]{2b}/2$ **47.** $\sqrt[6]{\dfrac{x^4}{3}} = \dfrac{\sqrt[6]{243 x^4}}{3}$

49. $2\sqrt{\dfrac{2a^5}{b^5}} = 2\dfrac{\sqrt{2a^5 b^7}}{b}$ **51.** $\sqrt[6]{2}$ **53.** $\cdot\dfrac{x - \sqrt{5}}{x^2 - 5}$

55. $\dfrac{(\sqrt{5} - \sqrt{3})^2}{2} = 4 - \sqrt{15}$

57. $2x\sqrt{x^2 - 1}/(x^2 - 1), x \neq \pm 1$

59. $-\dfrac{\sqrt{x^2 - y^2} + \sqrt{x^2 + xy}}{y}, y \neq 0$ **61.** $-\dfrac{b}{a}$

63. (a) $R = \dfrac{x^{3/2}}{x + 1}$, (b) $4.259\,\Omega$ **65.** $\dfrac{c}{a}$

ANSWERS FOR CHAPTER 3

Exercise Set 3.1

1. $\frac{\pi}{12} \approx 0.2617994$ 3. $\frac{7\pi}{6} \approx 3.6651914$

5. $\frac{427\pi}{900} \approx 1.4905112$ 7. $\frac{109\pi}{120} \approx 2.8536133$

9. $240°$ 11. $234°$ 13. $14.323945°$ 15. (a) $145°$
(b) $2.5307274 \approx \frac{29\pi}{36}$ 17. $70°$ 19. $x = 55°$,
$y = 70°$ 21. $x = y = 60°$ 23. $36.87°$

25. $A = 23.4 \text{ units}^2$; $P = 23.4 \text{ units}$ 27. $A =$
126 units^2; $P = 84 \text{ units}$ 29. $\frac{24}{5} = 4.8$ 31. $47.5°$

33. $120\pi \text{ rad/s}$ 35. $152°$ 37. (a) 133.3 m (b) 478.5 m^2

39. $\sqrt{200} = 10\sqrt{2} \text{ m} \approx 14.1421 \text{ m}$

41. $\sqrt{5869} \approx 76.6 \text{ ft}$ 43. (a) 5261.54 mm and
8123.08 mm (b) 9230.77 mm

45. $\sqrt{119} \approx 10.9 \text{ m}$ 47. (a) 212 m (b) 182.8 m

49. 73.4 m 51. (a) Yes (b) about 41 ft^2 53. 31.9 ft

Exercise Set 3.2

1. $P = 60 \text{ cm}$; $A = 225 \text{ cm}^2$ 3. $P = 96.5 \text{ in}$;
$A = 379.5 \text{ in.}^2$ 5. $P = 69 \text{ in}$; $A = 343.6 \text{ in.}^2$

7. $P = 44 \text{ cm}$; $A = 168 \text{ cm}^2$ 9. $P = 73.8 \text{ mm}$;
$A = 279.84 \text{ mm}^2$ 11. 444 ft^2 13. $10\,000 \text{ mm}^2$

15. $P = 3.031 \text{ in}$; $A = 0.663 \text{ in.}^2$ 17. (a) $A = 750 \text{ ft}^2$
(b) 94.76 ft 19. 2.1875 in.^2 or 2.19 in.^2

21. $18\,638 \text{ mm}^2$ 23. (a) 309 ft^2 (b) 2085.75
standard-size bricks (c) 1792.2 engineered/
oversize bricks (d) 1390.5 economy-size
bricks

ANSWERS FOR   **CHAPTER 5**

Exercise Set 5.1

1. 1.5705

3. 1.396

5. 2.70475

7. 3.75175

9. 114.592°

11. 85.944°

13. 60°

15. −45°

17. (c) 510°, −210°

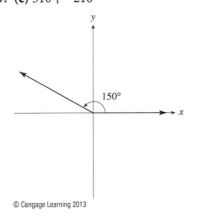

© Cengage Learning 2013

19. (c) −495°, 225°

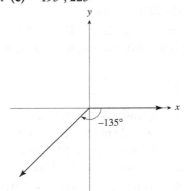

© Cengage Learning 2013

21. $\sin \theta = \frac{3}{5}$; $\cos \theta = \frac{4}{5}$; $\tan \theta = \frac{3}{4}$; $\csc \theta = \frac{5}{3}$; $\sec \theta \frac{5}{4}$; $\cot \theta = \frac{4}{3}$ **23.** $\sin \theta = \frac{-15}{17}$; $\cos \theta = \frac{8}{17}$; $\tan \theta = \frac{-15}{18}$; $\csc \theta = \frac{-17}{15}$; $\sec \theta = \frac{17}{8}$; $\cot \theta = \frac{-8}{15}$

25. $\sin \theta = \dfrac{2}{\sqrt{5}}$; $\cos \theta = \dfrac{1}{\sqrt{5}}$; $\tan \theta = 2$;

$\csc \theta = \dfrac{\sqrt{5}}{2}$; $\sec \theta = \sqrt{5}$; $\cot \theta = \frac{1}{2}$

27. $\sin \theta = -\dfrac{4}{\sqrt{41}}$; $\cos \theta = \dfrac{5}{\sqrt{41}}$; $\tan \theta = \frac{-4}{5}$;

$\csc \theta = -\dfrac{\sqrt{41}}{4}$; $\sec \theta = \dfrac{\sqrt{41}}{5}$; $\cot \theta = \frac{-5}{4}$

29. $\sin \theta = \frac{5}{6}$; $\cos \theta = \dfrac{\sqrt{11}}{6}$; $\tan \theta = \dfrac{5}{\sqrt{11}}$;

$\csc \theta = \frac{6}{5}$; $\sec \theta = \dfrac{6}{\sqrt{11}}$; $\cot \theta = \dfrac{\sqrt{11}}{5}$

31. $\sin \theta = 0$; $\cos \theta = 1$; $\tan \theta = 0$; $\csc \theta =$ Does not exist; $\sec \theta = 1$; $\cot \theta =$ Does not exist.

33. $\sin \theta = 0$; $\cos \theta = -1$; $\tan \theta = 0$; $\csc \theta =$ Does not exist; $\sec = -1$; $\cot \theta =$ Does not exist

35. $\sin \theta = \frac{4}{5}$; $\cos \theta = \frac{3}{5}$; $\tan \theta = \frac{4}{3}$; $\csc \theta = \frac{5}{4}$; $\sec \theta = \frac{5}{3}$; $\cot \theta = \frac{3}{4}$ **37.** $\sin \theta = \frac{21}{29}$; $\cos \theta = \frac{-20}{29}$; $\tan \theta = \frac{-21}{20}$; $\csc \theta = \frac{29}{21}$; $\sec \theta = \frac{-29}{20}$; $\cot \theta = \frac{-20}{21}$ **39.** $\sin \theta = -\dfrac{\sqrt{15}}{8}$; $\cos \theta = \frac{-7}{8}$; $\tan \theta = \dfrac{\sqrt{15}}{7}$; $\csc \theta = -\dfrac{8}{\sqrt{15}}$; $\sec \theta = \frac{-8}{7}$; $\cot \theta = \dfrac{7}{\sqrt{15}}$

Exercise Set 5.2

1. $\sin \theta = \frac{5}{13}$; $\cos \theta = \frac{12}{13}$; $\tan \theta = \frac{5}{12}$; $\csc \theta = \frac{13}{5}$; $\sec \theta = \frac{13}{12}$; $\cot \theta = \frac{12}{5}$ **3.** $\sin \theta = \frac{3}{5}$; $\cos \theta = \frac{4}{5}$; $\tan \theta = \frac{3}{4}$; $\csc \theta = \frac{5}{3}$; $\sec \theta = \frac{5}{4}$; $\cot \theta = \frac{4}{3}$

5. $\sin \theta = \dfrac{1.4}{\sqrt{7.25}}$; $\cos \theta = \dfrac{2.3}{\sqrt{7.25}}$;

$\tan \theta = \frac{14}{23}$; $\csc \theta = \dfrac{\sqrt{7.25}}{1.4}$; $\sec \theta = \dfrac{\sqrt{7.25}}{2.3}$;

$\cot \theta = \frac{23}{14}$ **7.** $\sin \theta = \frac{15}{17}$; $\cos \theta = \frac{8}{17}$; $\tan \theta = \frac{15}{8}$; $\csc \theta = \frac{17}{15}$; $\sec \theta = \frac{17}{8}$; $\cot \theta = \frac{8}{15}$ **9.** $\sin \theta = \frac{3}{5}$; $\cos \theta = \frac{4}{5}$; $\tan \theta = \frac{3}{4}$; $\csc \theta = \frac{5}{3}$; $\sec \theta = \frac{5}{4}$; $\cot \theta = \frac{4}{3}$ **11.** $\sin \theta = \frac{20}{29}$; $\cos \theta = \frac{21}{29}$; $\tan \theta = \frac{20}{21}$; $\csc \theta = \frac{29}{20}$; $\sec \theta = \frac{29}{21}$; $\cot \theta = \frac{21}{20}$ **13.** $\sin \theta = 0.866$; $\cos \theta = 0.5$; $\tan \theta = 1.732$; $\csc \theta = 1.155$; $\sec \theta = 2$; $\cot \theta = 0.577$ **15.** $\sin \theta = 0.085$; $\cos \theta = 0.996$; $\tan \theta = 0.085$; $\csc \theta = 11.765$; $\sec \theta = 1.004$; $\cot \theta = 11.718$ **17.** 0.3189593

19. 0.3307184 **21.** 4.1760011 **23.** 0.1298773
25. 0.247404 **27.** 0.7291147 **29.** 0.1417341
31. 4.7970857 **33.** $22.61\ m$ **35.** 4.92 V

Exercise Set 5.3

1. $47.05°$ **3.** $77.92°$ **5.** $32.97°$ **7.** $73.00°$
9. $61.68°$ **11.** $12.12°$

13. $B = 73.5°$, $b = 24.6$, $c = 25.7$
15. $B = 17.4°$, $a = 19.1$, $b = 5.9$
17. $B = 47°$, $a = 32.3$, $c = 47.3$
19. $B = 0.65$, $b = 4.9$, $c = 8.2$
21. $B = 1.42$, $a = 2.7$, $b = 17.8$
23. $B = 0.16$, $a = 246.6$, $c = 249.8$
25. $A = 0.54$, $B = 1.03$, $c = 17.5$
27. $A = 1.03$, $B = 0.54$, $a = 15.4$
29. $A = 0.73$, $B = 0.84$, $b = 22.4$ **31.** $32°$
33. 1147.3 m **35.** $F_y = 5$ N, $F_x = 8.7$ N
37. $9.62°$ **39.** 117.2 m from the intersection; 276.2 m from service station **41.** 61.56 ft
43. $23.9°$

Exercise Set 5.4

1. $87°$ **3.** $43°$ **5.** $\frac{\pi}{8}$ **7.** 1.36 **9.** $158°$
11. $209°$ **13.** 1.02 **15.** 4.11 **17.** Quadrant II
19. IV **21.** III **23.** II **25.** I, II **27.** II, IV
29. I, IV **31.** III, IV **33.** Quadrants I and II
35. Quadrants I and IV
37. IV **39.** positive **41.** positive **43.** negative
45. negative **47.** 0.6820 **49.** -2.3559 **51.** -0.2830
53. 0.6755 **55.** -0.1853 **57.** 4.9131 **59.** 0.8241
61. -0.0454 **63.** 0.9989 **65.** -1.8479
67. 0.9090 **69.** $30.0°; 150.0°$ **71.** $153.4°; 333.4°$
73. $76.6°; 283.4°$ **75.** $189.4°; 350.6°$ **77.** $0.85; 2.29$
79. $1.95; 5.09$ **81.** $0.23; 2.91$ **83.** $1.19; 5.09$
85. $57.1°$ **87.** $76.6°$ **89.** $18.7°$ **91.** $-32.6°$
93. 1.91 **95.** 1.28 rad **97.** 1.25 rad **99.** 0.24 rad
101. 24.26 mA **103.** 440.46 mm **105.** $4,546$ ft^2
107. -0.6898 rad $\approx -39.52°$ **109.** $43.57°$

Exercise Set 5.5

1. 861.525 m **3.** 2261.9 in/m or 37.7 in/s
5. 29.45 cm **7.** 220.80 cm^2 **9.** 0.168 m
11. $24\,776.5$ mm/min. or 412.9 mm/sec; $24\,776.5$ mm
13. $9.515°$; 657.66 miles **15.** 83 (The actual answer is 83.77, but this would be 83 bytes.) **17.** 5100
19. 8.80 m/sec **21.** 7393.3 km **23.** $30°$
25. (a) $\frac{\pi}{21600}$ rad/sec $\approx 0.000\,145\,444$ rad/s (b) about 2.175843801 mi/s
27. (a) about $3.54''$ (b) about $3.64''$

29. $B = \sin^{-1}\left(\dfrac{r \sin A}{C}\right)$

31. (a) 13 ft-9 in.

    (b) 22.5°

Review Exercises

1. $\frac{\pi}{3} \approx 1.047$ **3.** 5.672 **5.** -2.007 **7.** 135°

9. 123.19° **11.** $-246.94°$ **13.** (a) I (b) 60° (c) 420° and $-300°$ **15.** (a) IV (b) 35° (c) 685° and $-35°$

17. (a) III (b) 65° (c) 245° and $-475°$ **19.** (a) II (b) $\frac{\pi}{4}$ (c) $\frac{11\pi}{4}$ and $\dfrac{-5\pi}{4}$ **21.** (a) II, (b) 0.99, (c) 8.43 and -4.13 **23.** (a) II, (b) 1.17, (c) 1.97 and -10.59

25. $\sin\theta = -4/5$; $\cos\theta = 3/5$; $\tan\theta = -4/3$; $\csc\theta = -5/4$; $\sec\theta = 5/3$; $\cot\theta = -3/4$

27. $\sin\theta = 21/29$, $\cos\theta = -20/29$, $\tan\theta = -21/20$, $\csc\theta = 29/21$, $\sec\theta = -29/20$, $\cot\theta = -20/21$

29. $\sin\theta = 1/\sqrt{50}$, $\cos\theta = 7/\sqrt{50}$, $\tan\theta = 1/7$, $\csc\theta = \sqrt{50}$, $\sec\theta = \sqrt{50}/7$, $\cot\theta = 7$

31. $\sin\theta = 8/17$, $\cos\theta = 15/17$, $\tan\theta = 8/15$, $\csc\theta = 17/8$, $\sec\theta = 17/15$, $\cot\theta = 15/8$ **33.** $\sin\theta = 4/5$,

$\cos\theta = 3/5$, $\tan\theta = 4/3$, $\csc\theta = 5/4$, $\sec\theta = 5/3$, $\cot\theta = 3/4$ **35.** $\sin\theta = 84/91$, $\cos\theta = 35/91$, $\tan\theta = 84/35$, $\csc\theta|=|91/84$, $\sec\theta = 91/35$, $\cot\theta = 35/84$ **37.** $\cos\theta = 24/27.2$, $\tan\theta = 12.8/24$, $\csc\theta = 27.2/12.8$, $\sec\theta = 27.2/24$, $\cot\theta = 24/12.8$

39. $\sin\theta = 3.12/4$, $\cos\theta = 2.5/4$, $\tan\theta = 3.12; 2.5$, $\csc\theta = 4/3.12$, $\cot\theta = 2.5/3.12$ **41.** $\tan\theta = 0.577$, $\csc\theta = 2$, $\sec\theta = 1.155$, $\cot\theta = 1.732$

43. 0.7071 **45.** 0.6619 **47.** -0.6663 **49.** -0.0585

51. 30.0°; 150.0° **53.** 138.6°; 221.4° **55.** 2.09; 4.19

57. 2.38; 5.52 **59.** 60.0° **61.** $-45.0°$ **63.** 22.6°

65. 22.1° **67.** 6.3 A **69.** $\theta = 41.3°$; $V = 66.6$ V

71. 581.2 ft **73.** 66,705 miles/hr. **75.** 23.0°

77. 204.2 feet **79.** $F_y = 2891.3$ lb; $F_x = 1972.3$ lb.

Chapter 5 Test

1. $\frac{5\pi}{18} \approx 0.8725$ **3.** (a) III (b) 57°

5. (a) $\frac{9}{23.4} \approx 0.38462$ (b) $\frac{9}{21.6} \approx 0.41667$

7. (a) 0.79864 (b) 2.47509 (c) -1.66164 (d) -0.49026 **9.** 179.15 ft

ANSWERS FOR CHAPTER 8

Exercise Set 8.1

1.

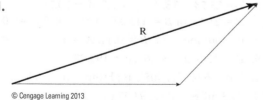

© Cengage Learning 2013

3.

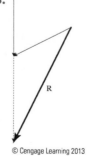

© Cengage Learning 2013

5.

© Cengage Learning 2013

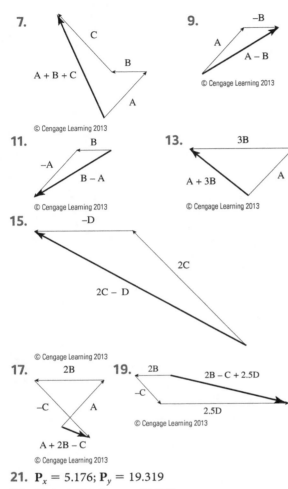

7.
A + B + C

© Cengage Learning 2013

9.
A − B

© Cengage Learning 2013

11.
−A
B − A

© Cengage Learning 2013

13.
3B
A + 3B

© Cengage Learning 2013

15.
−D
2C
2C − D

© Cengage Learning 2013

17.
2B
−C   A
A + 2B − C

© Cengage Learning 2013

19.
2B
−C
2B − C + 2.5D
2.5D

© Cengage Learning 2013

21. $\mathbf{P}_x = 5.176; \mathbf{P}_y = 19.319$

23. $\mathbf{P}_x = 4.688; \mathbf{P}_y = -17.793$

25. $\mathbf{V}_x = 9.372; \mathbf{V}_y = 2.687$ **27.** $A = 15$ **29.** $C = 17$

31. 13 km/h   **33.** $\mathbf{V}_x \approx 295$ N, $\mathbf{V}_x \approx 930$ N

35. parallel to the ramp ≈ 12.8 lb, perpendicular to the ramp ≈ 152.5 lb   **37.** $V = 17.5$ V, $\phi \approx 30.96°$

39. (a)   **(b)** velocity about 111.18 mph

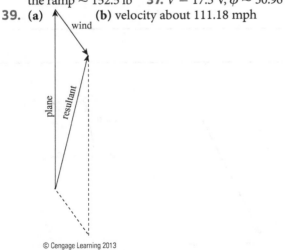

© Cengage Learning 2013

41. (a) $20\sqrt{101} \approx 201$ lb **(b)** $5.7°$

Exercise Set 8.2

1. $R = 12.5$, $\theta_R = 180°$ **3.** $R = 34.8$, $\theta_R = 270°$

5. $R = 73$, $\theta_R = 131.11°$ **7.** -89.7, $\theta_R = 24.79°$

9. $A = 65$, $\theta_A = 59.49°$ **11.** $C = 12.5$, $\theta_C = 20.61°$

13. $E = 6.5$, $\theta_E = 14.25°$ **15.** $G = 15.1$, $\theta_G = 56.31°$

17. $R = 12.33$, $\theta_R = 32.03°$ **19.** $R = 53$, $\theta_R = 178.11°$

21. $R = 88.50$, $\theta_R = 223.83°$ **23.** $R = 22.49$, $\theta_R = 349.18°$ **25.** $R = 13.04$, $\theta_R = 150.30°$

27. $R = 63.58$, $\theta_R = 4.6$ rad   **29.** $R = 13.13$, $\theta_R = 64.38°$

31. $A = 1213$ N, $B = 1832$ N, $C = 2107$ N

33. Tension in the cable: 390.5 lb, compression in the boom: 311.9 lb

35. ground speed ≈ 488.3 mph, course $\approx 68.2°$, drift angle $\approx 5.2°$

37. 324.9 V   **39. (a)** 46.8 mph **(b)** 220.1 mph

Exercise Set 8.3

1. $R = 114.50$, $\theta = 14.49°$ if 70-lb force has direction $0°$ **3. (a)** 20.48 lb **(b)** 14.34 lb **(c)** vertical $= 16.07$ horizontal $= 19.15$

5. 1616.8 N forward, 525.33 N sideward

7. 372.16 mi/hr in the compass direction $173.83°$

9. 1112.62 kg perpendicular, 449.53 kg parallel

11. 119.11 lb horizontal, 154.40 lb vertical

13. 6 A, $38.66°$ **15.** 10.68 A, $-59.46°$

17. 31.24 A, $\theta = -39.81°$ **19.** 55.84, $\theta = 6.52°$

21. 126.24 m/s at an angle of $-18.09°$

23. 43.1 in. $\times$ 13.5 in. or $3'7\frac{1}{10}'' \times 1'1\frac{1}{2}''$

Exercise Set 8.4

1. $a = 7.59$, $b = 22.77$, $C = 75.3°$ **3.** $A = 67.1°$, $C = 15.9°$, $c = 4.22$ **5.** $C = 73.31°$, $B = 20.37$, $b = 6.69$ **7.** no solution, not a triangle

9. $B = 57.31°$, $C = 77.69°$, $c = 22.5$; or $B = 122.69$, $C = 12.31°$, $c = 4.91$ **11.** $A = 148.8°$, $b = 20.17$, $c = 23.74$ **13.** $B = 64.62°$, $A = 79.78°$, $a = 21.13$; or $B = 115.38°$, $A = 29.02°$, $a = 10.42$

15. no solution   **17.** $B = 0.44$, $A = 1.33$, $a = 19.52$

19. $B = 1.35$, $a = 90.67$, $c = 193.98$

21. From B to C is 305.5 m; From A to C is 369.6 m

23. 34.3 miles   **25.** 294.77 m   **27.** 444 ft 4 in.

29. 8.49 cm   **31.** 79.50 mm

Exercise Set 8.5

1. $c = 11.31$, $A = 33.6°$, $B = 104.1°$

3. $b = 68.02$, $A = 40.1°$, $C = 26.2°$

5. $A = 45°$, $B = 23.2°$, $C = 111.8°$

7. $b = 103.25$, $A = 38.16°$, $C = 49.40°$

9. $A = 30.34°$, $B = 44.11°$, $C = 105.55°$

11. $c = 11.77$, $A = 0.56$, $B = 1.76$

13. $A = 0.70$ rad, $b = 74.52$, $C = 0.46$ rad

15. $A = 0.96$, $B = 0.59$, $C = 1.59$

17. $b = 68.56$, $A = 0.925$ rad, $C = 0.590$ rad

19. $A = 1.59$ rad, $B = 0.83$ rad, $C = 0.72$ rad

21. 5.61 in^2 **23.** 513.1 m^2 **25.** $10\,426$ km

27. 92.25 ft   **29.** 30.98 N, $\theta = 39.36°$

31. 76 kΩ **33.** downhill cable: 252.3 ft, uphill cable: 219.7 ft   **35.** $27{,}912$ ft$^2 \approx 0.64$ acre

Review Exercises

1.

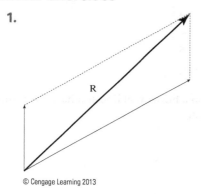

3.

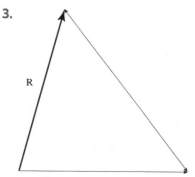

5. $P_x = -13.68$, $P_y = 32.22$

7. $P_x = -23.29$, $P_y = 3.09$

9. $R = 17.89$, $\theta_R = 333.43°$

11. $A_x = 36.71$, $A_y = 9.84$

13. $C_x = 6.12$, $C_y = 18.41$ **15.** $R = 50.41$, $\theta_R = 20.69°$

17. $R = 72.76$, $\theta_R = 3.13$ rad   **19.** $A = 25.7°$, $B = 97.5°$, $C = 56.8°$ **21.** $A = 145.93°$, $a = 146.17$, $C = 14.47°$ **23.** $B = 0.12$, $C = 2.90$, $c = 258.06$ **25.** $A = 0.52$, $B = 0.41$, $c = 109.27$

27. $2\,831.175$ kg at $83.97°$ **29.** 66.47 lb. parallel; 107.53 lb. perpendicular   **31.** 195.47 m

Chapter 8 Test

1. $V_x = -21.34$, $V_y = 41.88$ **3.** $R = 59.69$, $\theta_R = 93.86°$ **5.** $a = 9.38$ **7.** 49.59 in.

Exercise Set 4.3

1.
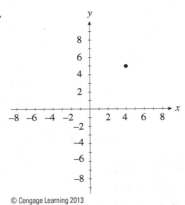
© Cengage Learning 2013

3.
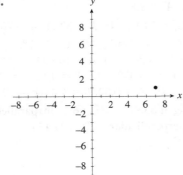
© Cengage Learning 2013

5.
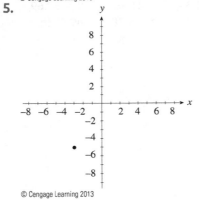
© Cengage Learning 2013

7.
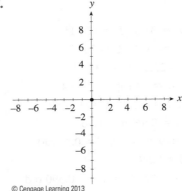
© Cengage Learning 2013

9.
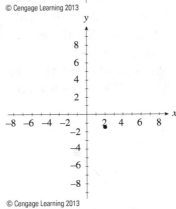
© Cengage Learning 2013

11. $(-1, -4)$

13. They are on a horizontal line and have the same y-coordinate.

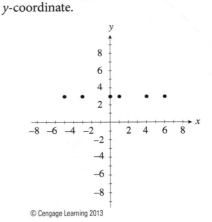
© Cengage Learning 2013

15. The points all lie on the same straight line.

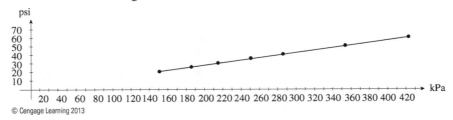
© Cengage Learning 2013

17. On the horizontal line through $y = -2$.

19. On the vertical line $x = -5$ **21.** To the right of the vertical line through $x = -3$. **23.** To the right of the line through the point $(1, 0)$ and below the horizontal line through the point $(0, -2)$.

25. (a)

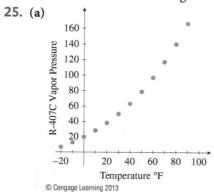

© Cengage Learning 2013

(b) about 70.9 psi (c) about 166 psi

27. (a)

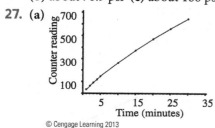

© Cengage Learning 2013

(b) Around 317 (c) Around 23.5 min

Section 1.2 (page 92)

1. (a) iii (b) i (c) v (d) ii (e) iv **3.** parallel

5. 0 **7.** (a) L_2 (b) L_3 (c) L_1 **9.** $\frac{3}{2}$

11.

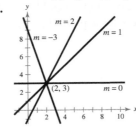

13. $m = -\frac{5}{2}$ **15.** m is undefined.

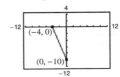 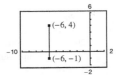

17. $(0, 1), (3, 1), (-1, 1)$ **19.** $(1, 4), (1, 6), (1, 9)$

21. $(-1, -7), (-2, -5), (-5, 1)$

23. $(3, -4), (5, -3), (9, -1)$

25. $y = 3x - 2$ **27.** $y = -\frac{1}{2}x - 2$

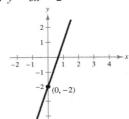 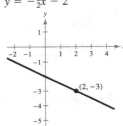

29. $x = 6$ **31.** $y = \frac{3}{2}$

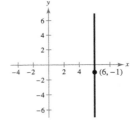 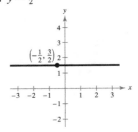

33. $y = \frac{1}{30}x + \frac{19}{15}$; about \$1.9 million

35. $m = \frac{2}{3}$; y-intercept: $(0, -3)$; a line that rises from left to right

37. $m = \frac{2}{5}$; y-intercept: $(0, 2)$; a line that rises from left to right

39. Slope is undefined; no y-intercept; a vertical line at $x = -6$

41. $m = 0$; y-intercept: $\left(0, -\frac{2}{3}\right)$; a horizontal line at $y = -\frac{2}{3}$

43. (a) $m = 5$;

     y-intercept: $(0, 3)$

  (b)

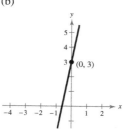

45. (a) Slope is undefined;

     there is no y-intercept.

  (b)

47. (a) $m = 0$;

     y-intercept: $\left(0, -\frac{5}{3}\right)$

  (b)

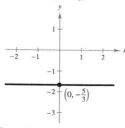

49. $y = 2x - 5$

51. $y = -\frac{3}{5}x + 2$

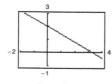

53. $x + 8 = 0$

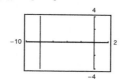

55. $y = -\frac{1}{2}x + \frac{3}{2}$

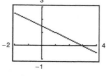

57. $y = -\frac{6}{5}x - \frac{18}{25}$

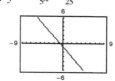

59. $y = \frac{2}{5}x + \frac{1}{5}$

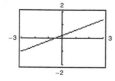

61.

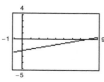

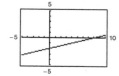

The first and second graphs do not give an accurate view of the slope. The third graph is best because it uses a square setting.

63. Perpendicular   **65.** Parallel

67. (a) $y = 2x - 3$ (b) $y = -\frac{1}{2}x + 2$

69. (a) $y = -\frac{3}{4}x + \frac{3}{8}$ (b) $y = \frac{4}{3}x + \frac{127}{72}$

71. (a) $y = -\frac{6}{5}x - 6.08$ (b) $y = \frac{5}{6}x + 1.85$

73. (a) $x = 3$ (b) $y = -2$

75. (a) $y = 1$ (b) $x = -5$

77. $y = 2x + 1$ **79.** $y = -\frac{1}{2}x + 1$

81. The lines $y = \frac{1}{4}x$ and $y = -4x$ are perpendicular.

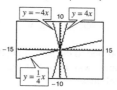

83. The lines $y = -\frac{1}{2}x$ and $y = -\frac{1}{2}x + 3$ are parallel. Both are perpendicular to $y = 2x - 4$.

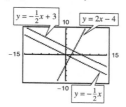

85. 12 ft

87. (a) The greatest increase was from 2010 to 2011, and the greatest decrease was from 2008 to 2009.

  (b) $y = 3.559x + 5.309$

  (c) There is an increase of about \$3.559 billion per year.

  (d) \$65.812 billion; Answers will vary.

89. $V = 125t + 665$ **91.** $V = -2000t + 50,400$

93. (a) $V = 25,000 - 2300t$

  (b)

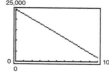

t	0	1	2	3	4
V	25,000	22,700	20,400	18,100	15,800

t	5	6	7	8	9	10
V	13,500	11,200	8900	6600	4300	2000

95. (a) $C = 30.75t + 36,500$

  (b) $R = 80t$

  (c) $P = 49.25t - 36,500$

  (d) $t \approx 741.1$ h

97. (a) Increase of about 1295 students per year

  (b) 76,090; 89,040; 95,515

  (c) $y = 1295x + 73,500$; where $x = 0$ corresponds to 1994; $m = 1295$; The slope determines the average increase in enrollment.

99. False. The slopes $\left(\frac{2}{7}\text{ and } -\frac{11}{7}\right)$ are not equal.

CHAPTER 1

101.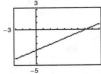

103.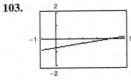

a and b represent the x- and y-intercepts.

a and b represent the x- and y-intercepts.

105. $9x + 2y - 18 = 0$ **107.** $12x + 3y + 2 = 0$

109. a   **111.** c

113. No. Answers will vary. Sample answer: The line $y = 2$ does not have an x-intercept.

115. Yes. Once a parallel line is established to the given line, there are an infinite number of distances away from that line, and thus an infinite number of parallel lines.

117. Yes; $x + 20$ **119.** No   **121.** No

123. $(x - 9)(x + 3)$ **125.** $(2x - 5)(x + 8)$

127. Answers will vary.

Chapter 3

Section 3.1   (page 250)

1. nonnegative integer, real   **3.** Yes; (2, 3)
5. c   **6.** d   **7.** b   **8.** a
9.

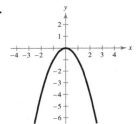

Reflection in the x-axis

11.

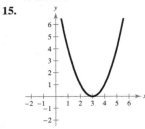

Horizontal shift three units to the left

13.

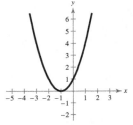

Horizontal shift one unit to the left

15.

Horizontal shift three units to the right

17. Parabola opening downward
    Vertex: (0, 20)
19. Parabola opening upward
    Vertex: (0, −5)
21. Parabola opening upward
    Vertex: (−3, −4)
23. Parabola opening upward
    Vertex: (1, 0)
25. Parabola opening upward
    Vertex: $\left(\frac{1}{2}, 1\right)$

27. Parabola opening downward
Vertex: $(1, 6)$

29. Parabola opening upward
Vertex: $\left(\frac{1}{2}, 20\right)$

31. Parabola opening upward
Vertex: $(-4, -5)$
x-intercepts: $\left(-4 \pm \sqrt{5}, 0\right)$

33. Parabola opening downward
Vertex: $(1, 16)$
x-intercepts: $(-3, 0), (5, 0)$

35. Parabola opening downward
Vertex: $(4, 1)$
x-intercepts: $\left(4 \pm \frac{1}{2}\sqrt{2}, 0\right)$

37. $y = -(x + 1)^2 + 4$ **39.** $f(x) = (x + 2)^2 + 5$

41. $y = 4(x - 1)^2 - 2$ **43.** $y = -\frac{104}{125}\left(x - \frac{1}{2}\right)^2 + 1$

45. $(5, 0), (-1, 0)$ **47.** $(-4, 0)$

49.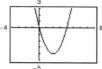

51.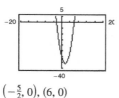

$(0, 0), (4, 0)$

$\left(-\frac{5}{2}, 0\right), (6, 0)$

53.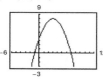

$(7, 0), (-1, 0)$

55. $f(x) = x^2 - 2x - 3$ **57.** $f(x) = 2x^2 + 7x + 3$
$g(x) = -x^2 + 2x + 3$ $g(x) = -2x^2 - 7x - 3$

59. $55, 55$ **61.** $12, 6$

63. (a)

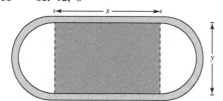

(b) $r = \frac{1}{2}y; \ d = y\pi$ (c) $y = \dfrac{200 - 2x}{\pi}$

(d) $A = x\left(\dfrac{200 - 2x}{\pi}\right)$

(e)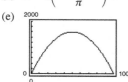

$x = 50 \text{ m}, \ y = \dfrac{100}{\pi} \text{ m}$

65. (a)

(b) $\frac{3}{2}$ ft

(c) About 104 ft (d) About 228.6 ft

67. (a) $A = -2x^2 + 112x - 600$ (b) $x = 28$ in.

69. (a)

(b) 1963; 4110 cigarettes

(c) Yes; Consumption began decreasing.

(d) 1057 cigarettes per year; about 3 cigarettes per day

71. True. The vertex is $(0, -1)$ and the parabola opens down.

73. False. The vertex of $f(x)$ is $(-1, 4)$ and the vertex of $g(x)$ is $(-1, -4)$.

75. c, d **77.** Horizontal shift z units to the right

79. Vertical stretch ($z > 1$) or shrink ($0 < z < 1$) and horizontal shift three units to the right

81. $b = \pm 20$ **83.** $b = \pm 8$ **85.** Proofs

87. $y = -x^2 + 5x - 4$; Answers will vary.

89. Model (a). The profits are positive and rising.

91. $(4, 2)$ **93.** $(2, 11)$

CHAPTER 3

Exercise Set 6.2

1. (4, 2)

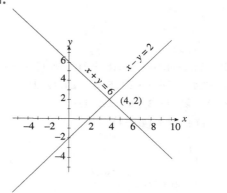

© Cengage Learning 2013

3.   (4.5, 2)

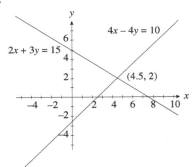

© Cengage Learning 2013

5. $(0, \frac{32}{5}) = (0, 6.4)$

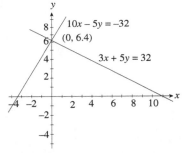

© Cengage Learning 2013

7.   (2.1, −1.1)

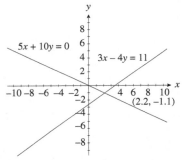

© Cengage Learning 2013

9. (3, 5)   **11.** (−4, 6)   **13.** (8, −2)   **15.** (3.3, −1.2)

17. (2.6, −3.4)   **19.** (−2.1, 5.3)   **21.** (7, 2)

23. (−2, 1)   **25.** (−3, 3)   **27.** (1.5, −6.5)

29. (9.2, −4.6)   **31.** (4, −1)

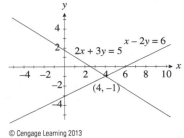

© Cengage Learning 2013

33. (−1, 7)

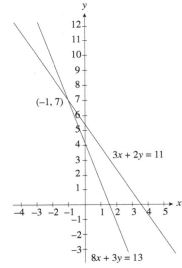

© Cengage Learning 2013

35. (0.608, −1.324)

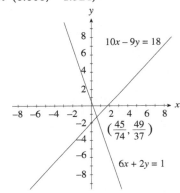

© Cengage Learning 2013

37. $(3, \frac{1}{3})$

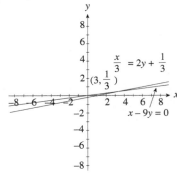

© Cengage Learning 2013

39. (3.1, −2.7)   **41.** length = 13 km, width = 5 km

43. length = 16.875 km, width = 5.625 km

45. 6 250 L of 5%; 3 750 L of 13% gasohol

47. 6.4 kg, 4 m   **49.** $I_1 = 1$ A, $I_2 = 1$ A, $I_3 = 0$ A

51. $I_1 = 0.224$ A, $I_2 = 1.052$ A, $I_3 = 0.828$ A

Exercise Set 6.3

1. $x = 2, y = -1, z = 4$ **3.** $x = -3, y = -2, z = 4$

5. $x = 2, y = -1, z = 4$ **7.** $x = -3, y = -2, z = 4$

9. $x = 1.3, y = 2.7, z = -2$ **11.** $x = 1.25, y = 3.75,$
$z = -5.5$ **13.** $x = -6, y = 2, z = 5$

15. $I_1 = 0.875$ A, $I_2 = 2.125$ A, $I_3 = 1.25$ A

17. $2a + 6b - c = 40; a + 7b - c = 50; a = -4,$
$b = 6, c = -12$ **19.** 4 large trucks, 2 medium,
3 small   **21.** 40 lb of the $10-12-15$ fertilizer,
240 lb of the $10-0-5$ fertilizer, and 120 lb of
the $30-6-15$ fertilizer

ANSWERS FOR   CHAPTER 19

Exercise Set 19.1

1. 2×3 **3.** 3×6 **5.** 4×2

7. $a_{11} = 1; a_{24} = 13; a_{21} = 8; a_{32} = 6$

9. $x = 12, y = -6, z = 2, w = 5$

11. $\begin{bmatrix} -3 & 6 & 6 & -8 \\ 12 & 9 & 17 & 0 \\ 9 & 0 & 5 & 10 \end{bmatrix}$ **13.** $\begin{bmatrix} 2 & -1 & 4 \\ 5 & 9 & -2 \end{bmatrix}$

15. $\begin{bmatrix} -1 & 7 & 4 \\ 8 & 1 & 15 \end{bmatrix}$ **17.** $\begin{bmatrix} 12 & 9 & 6 \\ 15 & 0 & 21 \end{bmatrix}$

19. $\begin{bmatrix} -5 & 16 & 8 \\ 12 & 0 & 25 \end{bmatrix}$ **21.** $\begin{bmatrix} -22 & -1 & -2 \\ -9 & 2 & -5 \end{bmatrix}$

23. $\begin{bmatrix} -3 \\ -7 \\ 3 \\ -5 \end{bmatrix}$ **25.** $\begin{bmatrix} 21 \\ 27 \\ -12 \\ 30 \end{bmatrix}$ **27.** $\begin{bmatrix} 26 \\ 24 \\ -11 \\ 35 \end{bmatrix}$

29. $\begin{bmatrix} 0 \\ -22 \\ 9 \\ 25 \end{bmatrix}$ **31.** $\begin{bmatrix} 27 & 12 & 15 \\ 18 & 15 & 16 \end{bmatrix}$

or 27 of computer chip A, 12 of computer chip B, 15 EPROMS, 18 keyboards, 15 motherboards, and 16 disk drives.

33. $\begin{bmatrix} 135 & 82 \\ 65 & 118 \end{bmatrix}$

35. Chip type:

	286	386	486	586
Warehouse A	297	2541	3531	292
Warehouse B	1232	4653	3436	83
Warehouse C	352	3439	3017	1113

Exercise Set 19.2

1. $\begin{bmatrix} 26 & 9 \\ -20 & -23 \end{bmatrix}$ **3.** $[-23]$

5. $\begin{bmatrix} -3 & 13 & 8 \\ -2 & 16 & 14 \end{bmatrix}$ **7.** $\begin{bmatrix} 5 & 17 & 5 \\ 44 & 67 & 37 \\ -9 & -6 & -7 \end{bmatrix}$

9. $\begin{bmatrix} -12 & 14 & 11 \\ 88 & 18 & 23 \end{bmatrix}$ **11.** $\begin{bmatrix} 7 & 16 \\ 17 & 38 \end{bmatrix}$

13. $\begin{bmatrix} -8 & 2 \\ -12 & 2 \end{bmatrix}$ **15.** $\begin{bmatrix} -68 & 18 \\ -160 & 42 \end{bmatrix}$

17. $\begin{bmatrix} -1 & 18 \\ 5 & 40 \end{bmatrix}$ **19.** $\begin{bmatrix} 42 & 96 \\ 102 & 228 \end{bmatrix}$ **21.** $\begin{bmatrix} 0 & 0 \\ 0 & 0 \end{bmatrix}$, No

23. Warehouse A: \$283,025, warehouse B: \$354,995, and warehouse C: \$364,415

25. $A^2 = \begin{bmatrix} 0 & 1 \\ 1 & 0 \end{bmatrix} \begin{bmatrix} 0 & 1 \\ 1 & 0 \end{bmatrix} = \begin{bmatrix} 0+1 & 0+0 \\ 0+0 & 1+0 \end{bmatrix}$

$= \begin{bmatrix} 1 & 0 \\ 0 & 1 \end{bmatrix} = I$. Similarly, $B^2 = C^2 = I$.

27. (a) The commutator of A and B is

$AB - BA = \begin{bmatrix} i & 0 \\ 0 & -i \end{bmatrix} - \begin{bmatrix} -i & 0 \\ 0 & i \end{bmatrix} = 2\begin{bmatrix} i & 0 \\ 0 & -i \end{bmatrix}$

$= 2i\begin{bmatrix} 1 & 0 \\ 0 & -1 \end{bmatrix} = 2iC$. Similar methods are used for

(b) and (c).

29. (a) $\begin{bmatrix} -1 & -2 \\ -5 & -4 \\ 2 & -7 \\ 1 & 5 \end{bmatrix}$ (b) $\begin{bmatrix} -2 & 1 \\ -4 & 5 \\ -7 & 2 \\ 5 & -1 \end{bmatrix}$

(c) $\begin{bmatrix} x_1 & y_1 \\ x_2 & y_2 \\ x_3 & y_3 \\ x_4 & y_4 \\ x_5 & y_5 \end{bmatrix} \begin{bmatrix} \cos\theta & \sin\theta \\ -\sin\theta & \cos\theta \end{bmatrix}$

Exercise Set 19.3

1. $\begin{bmatrix} 1 & -1 \\ -5 & 6 \end{bmatrix}$ **3.** $\begin{bmatrix} -1.5 & 2 \\ 4 & -5 \end{bmatrix}$

5. $\begin{bmatrix} -1 & -1.5 \\ -1.5 & -2 \end{bmatrix}$ **7.** $\begin{bmatrix} 0.6 & -2 \\ -0.8 & 3 \end{bmatrix}$

9. $\begin{bmatrix} 0 & 1 & 0 \\ -\frac{1}{3} & 0 & 0 \\ 0 & 0 & \frac{1}{4} \end{bmatrix}$ **11.** Singular matrix because

column 2 is twice column 1.

13. $\begin{bmatrix} 1 & 3 & -2 \\ -1 & -4 & 3 \\ 0 & -4 & 5 \end{bmatrix}$

15. Singular matrix because row 2 is -2 times row 1

17. $\begin{bmatrix} 0.5 & 0 & 0 \\ -0.5 & 0.5 & 0 \\ 0 & -0.5 & 0.5 \end{bmatrix}$ **19.** $\begin{bmatrix} 3 & 3 & -1 \\ -2 & -2 & 1 \\ -4 & -5 & 2 \end{bmatrix}$

21. All answers should check.

Exercise Set 19.4

1. $x = -1, y = 2$ **3.** $x = -1.5, y = 2.5$
5. No solution **7.** $x = 1.5, y = -4, z = 3.5$
9. $x = 5.5, y = -3.5, z = -6.5$
11. $x = -2, y = 5$ **13.** $x = -5, y = 7$
15. $x = 4.2, y = -2.4$ **17.** $x = -2, y = 4, z = 1$
19. $x = -3.4, y = 2.2, z = 1.5$
21. $I_1 = 6.05, I_2 = 5.26, I_3 = 0.79$
23. $I_1 = 1.22, I_2 = 2.37, I_3 = 1.64$
25. $A = \frac{200}{11} \approx 18.18, B = \frac{100}{11} \approx 9.09, C = \frac{800}{11} \approx 72.73$
27. $F_A = -1,000$ N, $F_B = 2,800$ N, and $F_C = 600$ N.
29. $a = 0.05, b = 1,$ and $c = 0$.

Review Exercises

1. $\begin{bmatrix} 4 & 4 & 2 & 7 \\ 9 & 7 & 3 & 4 \\ 9 & 5 & -8 & -3 \end{bmatrix}$ **3.** $\begin{bmatrix} 1 & 5 & 1 & 5 \\ 1 & 8 & -3 & 4 \\ 5 & 7 & -6 & 3 \end{bmatrix}$

5. $\begin{bmatrix} 8 & 3 & 4 & 4 \\ 3 & 14 & -14 & 8 \\ 18 & 35 & -16 & 24 \end{bmatrix}$ **7.** $\begin{bmatrix} 3 & 8 \\ 4 & 13 \\ 1 & 2 \end{bmatrix}$

9. $\begin{bmatrix} 12 & 15 & 3 \\ 8 & 10 & 2 \\ -4 & -5 & -1 \end{bmatrix}$ **11.** $\begin{bmatrix} -2.5 & -1.5 \\ 2 & 1 \end{bmatrix}$

13. $\begin{bmatrix} -0.5 & 0.125 & 0 \\ 0 & 0.25 & 0 \\ 0.5 & -0.125 & 1 \end{bmatrix}$ **15.** $x = 2.5, y = -6.4$

17. $x = 2, y = -3, z = 5$ **19.** $T = 86.47, a = 1.23$
21. $x'' = -x, y'' = -y$

23. $M = \begin{bmatrix} 1 - \dfrac{d}{f_2} & \dfrac{d}{f_1 f_2} - \dfrac{1}{f_1} - \dfrac{1}{f_2} \\ d & 1 - \dfrac{d}{f_1} \end{bmatrix}$

Chapter 19 Test

1. (a) $\begin{bmatrix} 7 & 5 & -7 \\ 19 & -6 & 6 \end{bmatrix}$ (b) $\begin{bmatrix} 26 & 10 & -6 \\ 42 & -18 & -2 \end{bmatrix}$

3. (a) $CD = \begin{bmatrix} -7 & 24 \\ -11 & 16 \end{bmatrix}$ (b) $DC = \begin{bmatrix} 2 & 3 \\ -46 & 7 \end{bmatrix}$

5. $x = 1, y = -2, z = 3$
7. $I_1 = \frac{20}{11}$ A, $I_2 = \frac{25}{11}$ A, $I_3 = -\frac{5}{11}$ A

Exercise Set 3.3

1. $A = 16\pi$ cm²; $C = 8\pi$ cm **3.** $A = 25\pi$ in.²; $C = 10\pi$ in **5.** $A = 201.64\pi$ mm²; $C = 28.4\pi$ mm

7. $A = 146.41\pi$ mm²; $C = 24.20\pi$ mm

9. (a) 576π in.² (b) $48\pi \approx 151$ in **11.** 32

13. (a) 163.2 mm (b) 6935.5 mm² **15.** (a) 86.643 in (b) 481.52 in.² **17.** (a) $A = 2529.876$ in.² (b) 197.1 in. **19.** 11.91 mm

21. (a) $3\frac{1}{7} - \pi \approx 0.00126$ (b) $\dfrac{3\frac{1}{7} - \pi}{\pi} \approx 0.040$

23. $2\frac{1}{4}$ in. **25.** $\approx 31\,420$ mm² **27.** (a) $\approx 30\,670$ mm² (b) $\approx 69\,560$ mm²

Exercise Set 3.5

1. $L = 216\pi \approx 678.6$ in.^{2}, $T = 288\pi \approx 904.8$ in.^{2}, $V = 648\pi \approx 2035.8$ in.^{3} 3. $L = 136\pi \approx 427.3$ mm^2, $T = 200\pi \approx 628.3$ mm^2, $V = 320\pi \approx 1005.3$ mm^3

5. $L = 735$ in.^{2}, $T = 816.8$ in.^{2}, $V = 859.1$ in.^{3}

7. A sphere has no lateral surface area, $T = 7256\pi \approx 804.26$ cm^2, $V = 682.7\pi \approx 2144.7$ cm^3

9. 5866.7 yd^3 11. (a) 3600 ft^3 (b) 1560 ft^2

13. (a) $103\,455\pi \approx 325\,013.5$ mm^3 (b) $20\,172.79$ mm^2 of paper   15. $1333.3\pi \approx 4188.8$ mm^3

17. 136.1 yd^3 19. $57\,172$ mm^3 21. $66\pi \approx 207.3$ in.^{2}

23. 1208.23 m^3 25. $48\pi \approx 150.8$ ft^3

27. (a) rectangular prism (b) 643.5 cm^2 (c) 906 cm^2

29. (a) 173.36 m^2 (b) 693.44 L   31. 46.6 m$^2 \times 4327$ m $= 201638$ m^3 33. (a) 364.7 in.^{3} (b) Simpson's rule requires that n be an even number. Here $n = 11$, so we cannot use Simpson's rule.

17. 145.56 mm^3 19. (a) 50.27 cm^2 (b) 33.51 cm^3

21. width: $49.68''$, height: $34.2''$ 23. sodium: 1963 mg, dietary fiber: 211.4 g

Exercise Set 3.6

1. $a = 1.5$, $b = 3.75$ 3. $a = 17$, $b = 42.71$, $c = 47.17$

5. $a = 2.55$, $b = 3.4$, $c = d = 4.25$ 7. $x = 5.6$, $z = 25.2$ 9. $a = 8.75$, $b = 14$ 11. $184,320$ in^2, 1280 ft^2 13. 5.5 kg   15. 2143.75 L

Chapter 5

Section 5.1   (page 405)

1. Trigonometry   **3.** standard position   **5.** radian

7. 180°   **9.** No   **11.** 210°

13. (a) Quadrant I   (b) Quadrant III

15. (a) Quadrant III   (b) Quadrant IV

17. (a) Quadrant II   (b) Quadrant I

19. (a)   (b)

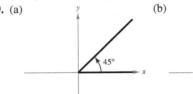

21. (a)   (b)

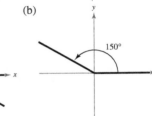

23. (a)   (b)

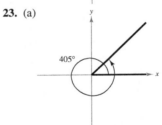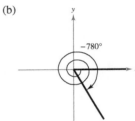

25. (a) 412°, −308°   (b) 324°, −396°

27. (a) 660°, −60°   (b) 340°, −380°

29. 64.75°   **31.** 85.308°   **33.** −125.01°

35. 13° 5′ 15″   **37.** 23° 1′ 1″   **39.** 280° 36′

41. −345° 7′ 12″   **43.** −20° 20′ 24″

45. Complement: 66°; supplement: 156°

47. Complement: none; supplement: 13°   **49.** 2

51. (a) Quadrant I   (b) Quadrant III

53. (a) Quadrant IV   (b) Quadrant II

55. (a) Quadrant IV   (b) Quadrant III

57. (a)   (b)

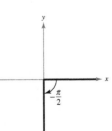

59. (a) 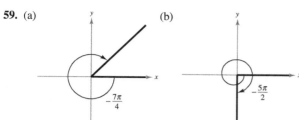   (b)

61. (a) 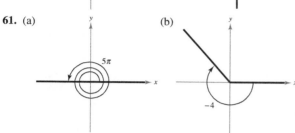   (b)

63. (a) $\dfrac{\pi}{6}$ (b) $\dfrac{5\pi}{6}$ **65.** (a) $\dfrac{\pi}{10}$ (b) $-\dfrac{4\pi}{3}$

67. (a) $270°$ (b) $-210°$ **69.** (a) $420°$ (b) $-39°$

71. 2.007 **73.** -3.776 **75.** -0.014 **77.** $25.714°$

79. $1170°$ **81.** $-114.592°$

83. (a) $\dfrac{13\pi}{6}, -\dfrac{11\pi}{6}$ (b) $\dfrac{8\pi}{3}, -\dfrac{4\pi}{3}$

85. (a) $\dfrac{\pi}{4}, -\dfrac{7\pi}{4}$ (b) $\dfrac{28\pi}{15}, -\dfrac{32\pi}{15}$

87. Complement: $\dfrac{\pi}{6}$; supplement: $\dfrac{2\pi}{3}$

89. Complement: none; supplement: $\dfrac{\pi}{3}$

91. Complement: none; supplement: none

93. $\dfrac{8}{15}$ rad   **95.** $\dfrac{70}{29}$ rad   **97.** 14π in.   **99.** 18π m

101. 22.92 ft   **103.** 34.80 mi   **105.** 591.32 mi

107. $4°\,2'\,33''$ **109.** $275.02°$ **111.** 435.71 km/min

113. (a) 2100π rad/min   (b) $64{,}324.1$ in./min

115. (a) $\dfrac{1000\pi}{3}$ rad/sec   (b) About 62.83 m/sec

117. False. A radian is larger: 1 rad $\approx 57.3°$.

119. True. The sum of the angles of a triangle must equal

$180° = \pi$ radians, and $\dfrac{2\pi}{3} + \dfrac{\pi}{4} + \dfrac{\pi}{12} = \pi$.

121. $\dfrac{50\pi}{3}$ m^2

123. (a) $A = 0.4r^2;\ r > 0;\ s = 0.8r,\ r > 0$

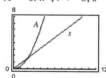

The area function changes more rapidly for $r > 1$ because it is quadratic and the arc length funciton is linear.

(b) $A = 50\theta,\ 0 < \theta < 2\pi;\ s = 10\theta,\ 0 < \theta < 2\pi$

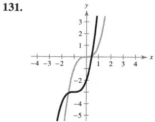

125. Answers will vary.

127.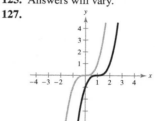

129.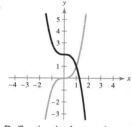

Horizontal shift one unit to the right

Reflection in the x-axis, vertical shift two units upward

131.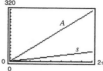

Horizontal shift one unit to the left, vertical shift three units downward

CHAPTER 5

27. g is a reflection of f in the y-axis and has five times the amplitude of f.

29. g has twice the amplitude of f.

31. g is a horizontal shift of f π units to the right.

33. 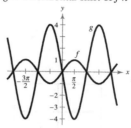   **35.**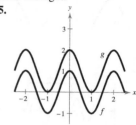

37.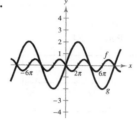

39. 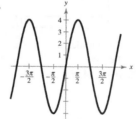   **41.**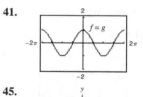

43. 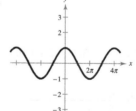   **45.**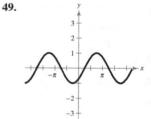

47. 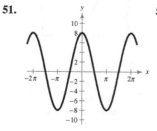   **49.**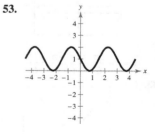

51.   **53.**

Section 5.4   (page 439)

1. amplitude   **3.** $\dfrac{2\pi}{b}$ **5.** 2π

7. It vertically shifts the graph d units.

9. (a) $x = -2\pi, -\pi, 0, \pi, 2\pi$ (b) $y = 0$

    (c) Increasing: $\left(-2\pi, -\dfrac{3\pi}{2}\right), \left(-\dfrac{\pi}{2}, \dfrac{\pi}{2}\right), \left(\dfrac{3\pi}{2}, 2\pi\right)$

    Decreasing: $\left(-\dfrac{3\pi}{2}, -\dfrac{\pi}{2}\right), \left(\dfrac{\pi}{2}, \dfrac{3\pi}{2}\right)$

    (d) Relative maxima: $\left(-\dfrac{3\pi}{2}, 1\right), \left(\dfrac{\pi}{2}, 1\right)$

    Relative minima: $\left(-\dfrac{\pi}{2}, -1\right), \left(\dfrac{3\pi}{2}, -1\right)$

11. Period: π **13.** Period: 4π

    Amplitude: 3   Amplitude: 5

15. Period: 2   **17.** Period: 2π

    Amplitude: $\dfrac{2}{3}$ Amplitude: 2

19. Period: $\dfrac{3\pi}{2}$

    Amplitude: $\dfrac{1}{4}$

21. g is a shift of f π units to the right.

23. g is a reflection of f in the x-axis.

25. g is a shift of f three units upward.

55.

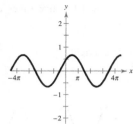

57.

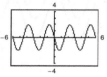

Amplitude: 2
Period: 3

59.

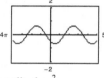

Amplitude: 5
Period: 24

61.

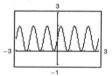

Amplitude: $\frac{2}{3}$

Period: 4π

63.

Amplitude: 2

Period: $\frac{\pi}{2}$

65.

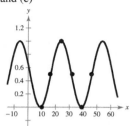

Amplitude: 1
Period: 1

67.

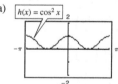

Amplitude: 5
Period: π

69.

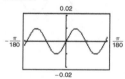

Amplitude: $\frac{1}{100}$
Period: $\frac{1}{60}$

71. $a = -4, d = 4$

73. $a = -1, d = -3$

75. $a = -3, b = 2, c = 0$

77. $a = 1, b = 1, c = \frac{\pi}{4}$

79.

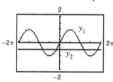

$x = -\frac{5\pi}{6}, -\frac{\pi}{6}, \frac{7\pi}{6}, \frac{11\pi}{6}$

81.

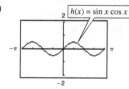

80 beats/min

83. (a)

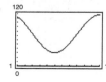

(b) Maximum sales:
   December
   Minimum sales: June

85. (a)

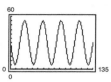

(b) Minimum height: 5 ft
   Maximum height: 55 ft

87. (a) and (c)

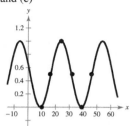

   The model fits the data well.
   (b) $y = 0.5 \sin(0.210x + 2.830) + 0.5$
   (d) About 30 days   (e) About 70.8%

89. True. The period of $\sin x$ is 2π. Adding 2π moves the graph one period to the right.

91. False. The function $y = \frac{1}{2}\cos 2x$ has an amplitude that is one-half that of the function $y = \cos x$.

93.

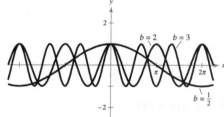

The value of b affects the period of the graph.
$b = \frac{1}{2} \rightarrow \frac{1}{2}$ cycle
$b = 2 \rightarrow 2$ cycles
$b = 3 \rightarrow 3$ cycles

95. a

97. (a)

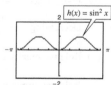

(b)

Even   Even

(c)

Odd

99. (a)

x	-1	-0.1	-0.01
$\dfrac{\sin x}{x}$	0.8415	0.9983	1.0000

x	-0.001	0	0.001
$\dfrac{\sin x}{x}$	1.0000	Undefined	1.0000

x	0.01	0.1	1
$\dfrac{\sin x}{x}$	1.0000	0.9983	0.8415

(b)

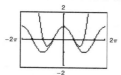

$f \to 1$ as $x \to 0$

(c) The ratio approaches 1 as x approaches 0.

101. (a)

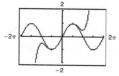

The polynomial function is a good approximation of the sine function when x is close to 0.

(b)

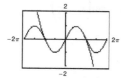

The polynomial function is a good approximation of the cosine function when x is close to 0.

(c) $\sin x \approx x - \dfrac{x^3}{3!} + \dfrac{x^5}{5!} - \dfrac{x^7}{7!}$

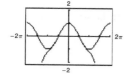

$\cos x \approx 1 - \dfrac{x^2}{2!} + \dfrac{x^4}{4!} - \dfrac{x^6}{6!}$

The accuracy increased.

103.

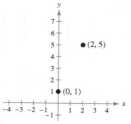

$m = 2$

105. 487.014°   **107.** Answers will vary.

Section 5.5   (page 451)

1. vertical   **3.** tangent, cotangent

5. (a) $x = -2\pi, -\pi, 0, \pi, 2\pi$ (b) $y = 0$

(c) Increasing on $\left(-2\pi, -\dfrac{3\pi}{2}\right), \left(-\dfrac{3\pi}{2}, -\dfrac{\pi}{2}\right), \left(-\dfrac{\pi}{2}, \dfrac{\pi}{2}\right),$
$\left(\dfrac{\pi}{2}, \dfrac{3\pi}{2}\right), \left(\dfrac{3\pi}{2}, 2\pi\right)$

(d) No relative extrema

(e) $x = -\dfrac{3\pi}{2}, -\dfrac{\pi}{2}, \dfrac{\pi}{2}, \dfrac{3\pi}{2}$

7. (a) No x-intercepts   (b) $y = 1$

(c) Increasing on $\left(-2\pi, -\dfrac{3\pi}{2}\right), \left(-\dfrac{3\pi}{2}, -\pi\right), \left(0, \dfrac{\pi}{2}\right), \left(\dfrac{\pi}{2}, \pi\right)$

Decreasing on $\left(-\pi, -\dfrac{\pi}{2}\right), \left(-\dfrac{\pi}{2}, 0\right), \left(\pi, \dfrac{3\pi}{2}\right), \left(\dfrac{3\pi}{2}, 2\pi\right)$

(d) Relative minima: $(-2\pi, 1), (0, 1), (2\pi, 1)$
Relative maxima: $(-\pi, -1), (\pi, -1)$

(e) $x = -\dfrac{3\pi}{2}, -\dfrac{\pi}{2}, \dfrac{\pi}{2}, \dfrac{3\pi}{2}$

9.

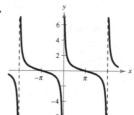

11.

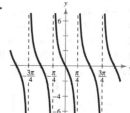

13.

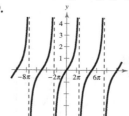

15.

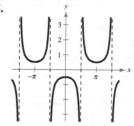

17.

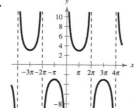

19.

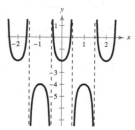

CHAPTER 5

21.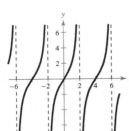

23.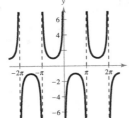

25.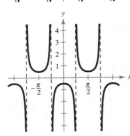

27.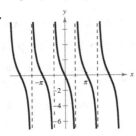

29.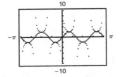

Answers will vary.

31.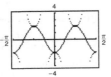

Answers will vary.

33.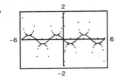

Answers will vary.

35. $-5.498, -2.356, 0.785, 3.927$

37. $-5.236, -1.047, 1.047, 5.236$

39. $-3.665, -0.524, 2.618, 5.760$

41. Even   **43.** Odd   **45.** Odd

47. 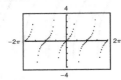   **49.**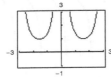

Equivalent   Equivalent

51. d; as x approaches 0, $f(x)$ approaches 0.

53. b; as x approaches 0, $g(x)$ approaches 0.

55.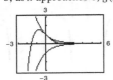

$-e^{-x} \le e^{-x} \cos x \le e^{-x}$

Touches $y = \pm e^{-x}$ at $x = n\pi$

Intercepts at $x = \dfrac{\pi}{2} + n\pi$

57.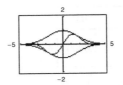

Touches $y = \pm 2^{-x^2/4}$ at $x = \dfrac{\pi}{2} + n\pi$

Intercepts at $x = n\pi$

59. (a) $f \to -\infty$ (b) $f \to \infty$ (c) $f \to -\infty$ (d) $f \to \infty$

61. (a) $f \to \infty$ (b) $f \to -\infty$ (c) $f \to -\infty$ (d) $f \to \infty$

63. $d = 7 \cot x$

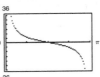

65. (a)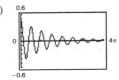

(b) Not periodic and damped; approaches 0 as t increases.

67. (a) Yes. To each t there corresponds one and only one value of y.

(b) 1.3 oscillations/sec

(c) $y = 12(0.221)^t \cos(8.2t)$

(d) $y = 12e^{-1.5t} \cos(8.2t)$

(e)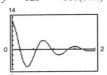

Answers will vary.

69. True. The sine function is damped.

71. True. $\sec x = \csc\left(x - \dfrac{\pi}{2}\right) = \dfrac{1}{\sin\left(x - \dfrac{\pi}{2}\right)}$

73. (a)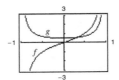

(b) $\left(-1, \dfrac{1}{3}\right)$

(c) $\left(-1, \dfrac{1}{3}\right)$; The intervals are the same.

75. (a)

x	-1	-0.1	-0.01
$\dfrac{\tan x}{x}$	1.5574	1.0033	1.0000

x	-0.001	0	0.001
$\dfrac{\tan x}{x}$	1.0000	Undefined	1.0000

x	0.01	0.1	1
$\dfrac{\tan x}{x}$	1.0000	1.0033	1.5574

(b)

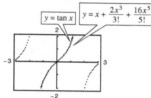

$f \to 1$ as $x \to 0$

(c) The ratio approaches 1 as x approaches 0.

77.

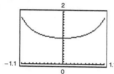

The polynomial function is a good approximation of the tangent function when x is close to 0.

79. Distributive Property   **81.** Additive Identity Property

83. Not one-to-one

85. One-to-one. $f^{-1}(x) = \dfrac{x^2 + 14}{3}, \ x \geq 0$

87. Domain: all real numbers x
Intercepts: $(-4, 0), (1, 0), (0, -4)$
No asymptotes

89. Domain: all real numbers x
Intercept: $(0, 5)$
Asymptote: $y = 2$

13.

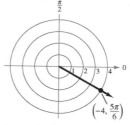

$$\left(4, \frac{11\pi}{6}\right), \left(-4, -\frac{7\pi}{6}\right), \left(4, -\frac{\pi}{6}\right)$$

15. 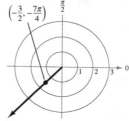   **17.**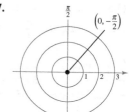

$$\left(-\frac{3}{2}, \frac{\pi}{4}\right), \left(\frac{3}{2}, \frac{5\pi}{4}\right), \left(\frac{3}{2}, -\frac{3\pi}{4}\right) \qquad \left(0, \frac{\pi}{2}\right), \left(0, \frac{3\pi}{2}\right), \left(0, -\frac{3\pi}{2}\right)$$

19. 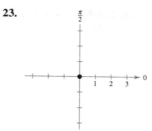   **21.**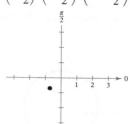

$$(-3, 0) \qquad\qquad \left(-\frac{\sqrt{2}}{2}, -\frac{\sqrt{2}}{2}\right)$$

23.    **25.**

$$(0, 0) \qquad\qquad (0, 5)$$

27. $(1.53, 1.29)$ **29.** $(-1.20, -4.34)$

31. $(-1.42, -0.47)$

33. 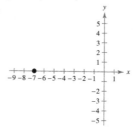   **35.**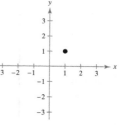

$$(7, \pi), (-7, 0) \qquad\qquad \left(\sqrt{2}, \frac{\pi}{4}\right), \left(-\sqrt{2}, \frac{5\pi}{4}\right)$$

Section 10.5   (page 817)

1. pole

3. $x = r\cos\theta, y = r\sin\theta$ and $\tan\theta = \frac{y}{x}, r^2 = x^2 + y^2$

5. $A; (0, 2)$ **6.** $D; (0, -2)$

7. $C; (0, 0)$ **8.** $B; (\sqrt{2}, \sqrt{2})$

9.

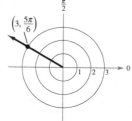

$$\left(3, -\frac{7\pi}{6}\right), \left(-3, \frac{11\pi}{6}\right), \left(-3, -\frac{\pi}{6}\right)$$

11.

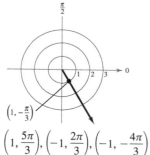

$$\left(1, \frac{5\pi}{3}\right), \left(-1, \frac{2\pi}{3}\right), \left(-1, -\frac{4\pi}{3}\right)$$

CHAPTER 10

37.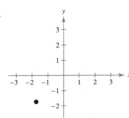

39.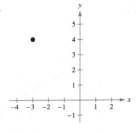

$\left(\sqrt{6}, \dfrac{5\pi}{4}\right), \left(-\sqrt{6}, \dfrac{\pi}{4}\right)$ $(5, 2.214), (-5, 5.356)$

41. $(3.61, -0.59)$ **43.** $(2.65, 2.28)$ **45.** $(2.83, 0.49)$

47. $r = 3$ **49.** $\theta = \dfrac{\pi}{4}$ **51.** $r = a \csc \theta$

53. $r = -\dfrac{2}{3\cos\theta - \sin\theta}$ **55.** $r^2 = 8\csc 2\theta$

57. $r^2 = 9\cos 2\theta$ **59.** $r = 6\cos\theta$ **61.** $r = 2a\cos\theta$

63. $r = \tan^2\theta \sec\theta$ **65.** $x^2 + y^2 - 4y = 0$

67. $y = -\dfrac{\sqrt{3}}{3}x$ **69.** $x = 0$ **71.** $y = -3$

73. $(x^2 + y^2)^3 = x^2$ **75.** $(x^2 + y^2)^2 = 6x^2y - 2y^3$

77. $y^2 = 2x + 1$ **79.** $4x^2 - 5y^2 = 36y + 36$

81. The graph is a circle centered at the origin with a radius of 6; $x^2 + y^2 = 36$.

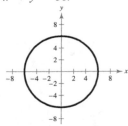

83. The graph consists of all points on the line that makes an angle of $\pi/4$ with the positive x-axis; $x - y = 0$.

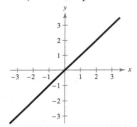

85. The graph is a vertical line through $(3, 0)$; $x - 3 = 0$.

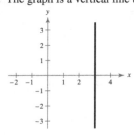

87. (a) $r = 30$
    (b) $(30, 5\pi/6)$; 30 represents the distance of the passenger car from the center, and $5\pi/6 = 150°$ represents the angle to which the car has rotated.
    (c) $(-25.98, 15)$; The car is about 25.98 feet to the left of the center and 15 feet above the center.

89. True. Because r is a directed distance, (r, θ) can be represented by $(-r, \theta \pm (2n + 1)\pi)$, so $|r| = |-r|$.

91. (a) Answers will vary.
    (b) $d = |r_1 - r_2|$; Answers will vary.
    (c) $d = \sqrt{r_1^2 + r_2^2}$; Answers will vary.

93. Answers will vary.

95. $(x - h)^2 + (y - k)^2 = h^2 + k^2$; radius $= \sqrt{h^2 + k^2}$; center: (h, k)

97. $B \approx 14.13°$ **99.** $A \approx 41.86°$
    $C \approx 141.87°$ $C \approx 67.14°$
    $c \approx 15.18$ $b \approx 29.76$

Section 10.6   (page 825)

1. convex limaçon   **3.** lemniscate

5. When (r, θ) can be replaced with $(r, \pi - \theta)$ or $(-r, -\theta)$ and yield an equivalent equation

7. Rose curve   **9.** Lemniscate   **11.** c   **13.** a

15. $\theta = \dfrac{\pi}{2}$, polar axis, pole   **17.** Polar axis   **19.** $\theta = \dfrac{\pi}{2}$

21. Pole

23.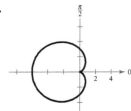

25.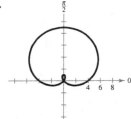

27.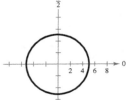

29.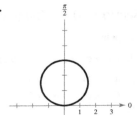

31.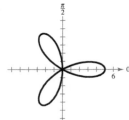

Symmetry: polar axis

Zeros: $\dfrac{\pi}{6}, \dfrac{\pi}{2}, \dfrac{5\pi}{6}$

w33.

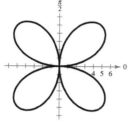

Symmetry: $\theta = \dfrac{\pi}{2}$, polar axis, pole

Zeros: $0, \dfrac{\pi}{2}, \pi, \dfrac{3\pi}{2}, 2\pi$

35.

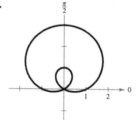

Symmetry: $\theta = \dfrac{\pi}{2}$

Zeros: $\dfrac{7\pi}{6}, \dfrac{11\pi}{6}$

37.

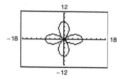

Answers will vary.

39.

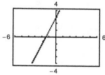

Answers will vary.

41.

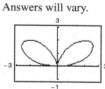

Answers will vary.

43.

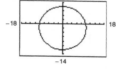

Answers will vary.

45.

Answers will vary.

47.

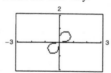

Answers will vary.

49.

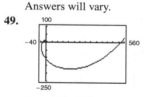

Answers will vary.

51.

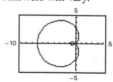

$0 \le \theta < 2\pi$

53.

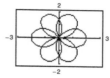

$0 \le \theta < 4\pi$

55.

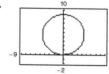

$0 \le \theta < \pi$

57.

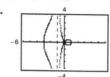

59.

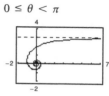

61. (a)

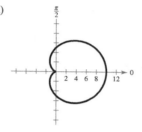

(b) 0 radians

Cardioid

63. True. $n = 5$

65. False. The rose curve $r = a\cos 3\theta$ is not symmetric with respect to the line $\theta = \pi/2$.

67. Answers will vary.

69. (a) $r = 2 - \sin\left(\theta - \dfrac{\pi}{4}\right)$ (b) $r = 2 + \cos\theta$

(c) $r = 2 + \sin\theta$ (d) $r = 2 - \cos\theta$

71. $x = -3, 3$ **73.** $x = \dfrac{13}{5}$

CHAPTER 10

CHAPTER 18

Exercise 18.1

1.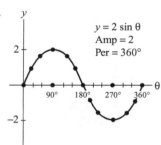

$y = 2 \sin \theta$
Amp = 2
Per = 360°

3.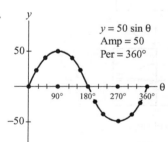

$y = 50 \sin \theta$
Amp = 50
Per = 360°

5.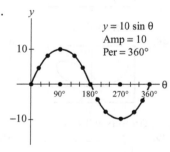

$y = 10 \sin \theta$
Amp = 10
Per = 360°

7.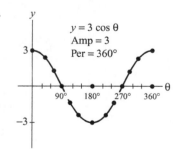

$y = 3 \cos \theta$
Amp = 3
Per = 360°

9.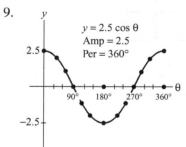

$y = 2.5 \cos \theta$
Amp = 2.5
Per = 360°

11.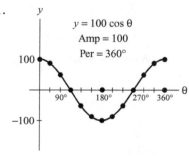

$y = 100 \cos \theta$
Amp = 100
Per = 360°

13.

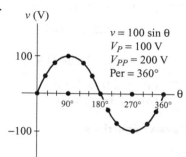

$v = 100 \sin \theta$
$V_P = 100 \text{ V}$
$V_{PP} = 200 \text{ V}$
Per $= 360°$

15.

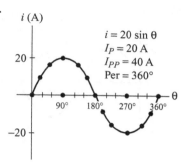

$i = 20 \sin \theta$
$I_P = 20 \text{ A}$
$I_{PP} = 40 \text{ A}$
Per $= 360°$

17.

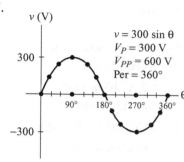

$v = 300 \sin \theta$
$V_P = 300 \text{ V}$
$V_{PP} = 600 \text{ V}$
Per $= 360°$

19.

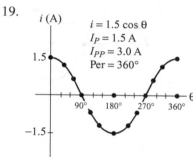

$i = 1.5 \cos \theta$
$I_P = 1.5 \text{ A}$
$I_{PP} = 3.0 \text{ A}$
Per $= 360°$

21.

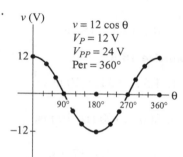

$v = 12 \cos \theta$
$V_P = 12 \text{ V}$
$V_{PP} = 24 \text{ V}$
Per $= 360°$

23.

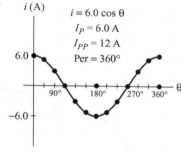

$i = 6.0 \cos \theta$
$I_P = 6.0 \text{ A}$
$I_{PP} = 12 \text{ A}$
Per $= 360°$

25.

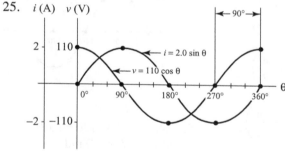

$i = 2.0 \sin \theta$
$v = 110 \cos \theta$

27. (a) 39 V
   (b) 0.52 rad, 2.6 rad

Exercise 18.2

1. 600 V, 210 V
3. 4.4 A, 1.6 A
5. 280 V, 99 V
7. 300 mA, 110 mA
9. 11 A, 4.0 A
11. 400 V, 140 V
13. 160 V, 320 V
15. 1.7 A, 3.4 A
17. 850 mA, 1.7 A
19. 110 V, 220 V

21. 110 mA, 220 mA
23. 17 V, 34 V
25. 110 V, 160 V, 2.2 A,
   3.1 A, 240 W
27. (a) 33 V, 11 V, 17 V, 5.5 V
   (b) 610 mW, 910 mW,
      300 mW, 1.8 W
29. (a) 67 mA, 53 mA, 120 mA
   (b) 5.3 W, 4.3 W, 9.6 W

Exercise 18.3

1. 55 Hz, 18 ms
3. 70 Hz, 14 ms
5. 60 Hz, 17 ms

7. 16 Hz, 63 ms
9. 48 Hz, 21 ms
11. 25 Hz, 40 ms
13. 840 kHz, 1.2 μs
15. 12 kHz, 84 μs
17. 17 ms, 120π rad/s
19. 22 ms, 90π rad/s
21. 2.0 ms, 1000π rad/s
23. 5.0 ms, 400π rad/s
25. 1.1 μs, 5.7×10^6 rad/s
27. 14 ns, 440×10^6 rad/s
29. 4.0 A, 120π rad/s, 60 Hz, 17 ms
31. 110 V, 140π rad/s,
   70 Hz, 14 ms

33. 310 V, 300 rad/s, 48 Hz, 21 ms

35. 450 mA, 500 rad/s, 80 Hz, 13 ms

37. 1.2 A, 200π rad/s, 100 Hz, 10 ms

39. 72 V, 3.0×10^6 rad/s, 480 kHz, 2.1 μs

41. 390 rad/s, 63 Hz, 16 ms

43. $v = 180 \sin 120\pi t$

45. $i = 2.5 \sin 100\pi t$

47. $i = 0.45 \sin 420t$

49. $v = 160 \sin 290t$

51.

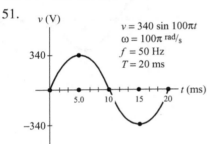

53.

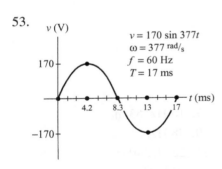

55.

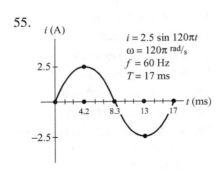

57.

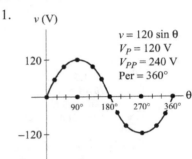

59. (a) 77 V, 86 V
    (b) 1.8 ms, 6.5 ms

61. (a) 1.2 A, −2.0 A
    (b) 12 ms, 18 ms

Exercise 18.4

1. 1.5 A, 50 Hz, 20 ms, $\frac{\pi}{2}$

3. 300 V, 100 Hz, 10 ms, $\frac{\pi}{2}$

5. 60 V, 60 Hz, 17 ms, $-\frac{\pi}{2}$

7. 18 A, 50 Hz, 20 ms, $\frac{\pi}{2}$

9. 5.5 A, 100 Hz, 10 ms, $-\frac{\pi}{2}$

11. $i = 3.3 \sin\left(120\pi t + \frac{\pi}{2}\right)$

13. $v = 400 \sin 100\pi t$

15. $v = 350 \sin\left(100\pi t + \frac{\pi}{2}\right)$

17. $i = 12 \sin 120\pi t$

19. $v = 170 \sin\left(350t + + \frac{\pi}{2}\right)$

21. $v = 220 \sin 380t$

23. $i = 0.50 \sin\left(100\pi t - \frac{\pi}{2}\right)$

25. (a)

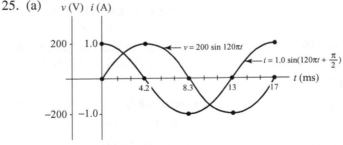

(b) t difference = 4.2 ms

27. (a) Both: 50 Hz, 20 ms; v: $\frac{\pi}{2}$ rad, i: 0 rad

    (b) 5 ms, v leads i by $\frac{\pi}{2}$

29. (a) − 2.0 A, 1.7 A
    (b) 4.2 ms, 13 ms

Review Exercises

1.

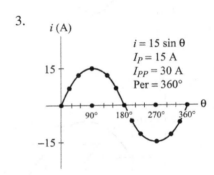

3.

5. 160 V, 113 V, 120π rad/s, 60 Hz, 17 ms, 0 rad

7. 3.0 A, 2.1 A, 200π rad/s, 100 Hz, 10 ms, 0 rad

9. 170 V, 120 V, 350 rad/s, 56 Hz, 18 ms, 0 rad

11. 1.6 A, 1.1 A, 400 rad/s, 64 Hz, 16 ms, 0 rad

13. 1.2 A, 850 mA, 140π rad/s,
    70 Hz, 14 ms, $\dfrac{\pi}{2}$

15. 320 V, 230 V, 377 rad/s, 60 Hz,
    17 ms, $\dfrac{\pi}{2}$

17. $i = 2.4 \sin 120\pi t$

19. $v = 110 \sin 100\pi t$

21. $v = 120 \sin 370t$

23. $i = 1.3 \sin 200\pi t$

25. $i = 14 \sin\left(100\pi t + \dfrac{\pi}{2}\right)$

27. $v = 220 \sin\left(120\pi t + \dfrac{\pi}{2}\right)$

29. 50 mA, 71 mA, 75 V, 110 V,
    3.8 W

31. (a) 83 Hz, 12 ms, 520 rad/s
    (b) $v = 120 \sin 520t$

33.

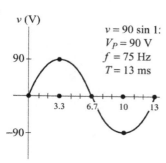

35. (a) 400 mA, -500 mA
    (b) 1.1 ms, 5.6 ms
    (c) 0 ms, 6.7 ms

ANSWERS FOR **CHAPTER 21**

Exercise Set 21.1

1-29. All answers are proofs and will not be displayed in this section.

31. This identity is true based on the graphs of $y = 2 \csc 2x$ and $y = \sec x \csc x$ shown below.

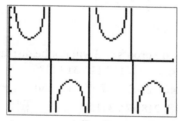

$y = 2 \csc 2x$

$$\left[0, 2\pi, \frac{\pi}{4}\right] \cdot [-5,5,1]$$

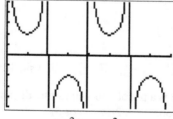

$y = 2 \sec x \csc 2x$

$$\left[0, 2\pi, \frac{\pi}{4}\right] \cdot [-5,5,1]$$

33. This identity is not true based on the graphs of $y = \sin \frac{1}{2} x$ and $y = \frac{1}{2} \sin x$ shown below.

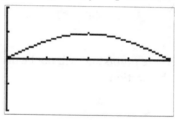

$y = \sin \frac{1}{2} x$

$$\left[0, 2\pi, \frac{\pi}{4}\right] \cdot [-2,2,1]$$

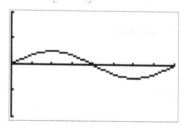

$y = \sin \frac{1}{2} x$

$$\left[0, 2\pi, \frac{\pi}{4}\right] \cdot [-2,2,1]$$

35-43. All answers are proofs and will not be displayed in this section.

Exercise Set 21.2

1. $\dfrac{\sqrt{6} - \sqrt{2}}{4}$ **3.** $\dfrac{\sqrt{3}}{2}$

5. $\dfrac{\sqrt{6} - \sqrt{2}}{\sqrt{6} + \sqrt{2}} = \dfrac{10 - 4\sqrt{3}}{4} = \dfrac{5 - 2\sqrt{3}}{2}$

7. $\frac{1}{2}$ **9.** $\cos x$ **11.** $-\sin x$ **13.** $-\cos x$

15. $\sin x$ **17.** $\dfrac{21 + \sqrt{105}}{32} \approx 0.97647$

19. $\dfrac{21 + \sqrt{105}}{7\sqrt{7} - 3\sqrt{15}} \approx 4.52768$

21. $\dfrac{7\sqrt{7} + 3\sqrt{15}}{32} \approx 0.94185$ **23.** I

25. $\dfrac{\sqrt{105} - 21}{32} \approx -0.33603$

27. $\dfrac{\sqrt{105} - 21}{7\sqrt{7} + 3\sqrt{15}} \approx -0.35678$

29. $\dfrac{7\sqrt{7} - 3\sqrt{15}}{32} \approx 0.21566$ **31.** IV

33. $\sin 60° = \dfrac{\sqrt{3}}{2}$ **35.** $\cos 44°$ **37.** $\cos \alpha$

39. $\cos^2 x - \sin^2 x$

41-59. All answers are proofs and will not be displayed in this section.

Exercise Set 21.3

1. $\sqrt{\dfrac{2 + \sqrt{3}}{4}} \approx x0.96593$

3. $\sqrt{\dfrac{2 - \sqrt{3}}{4}} \approx 0.25882$

5. $\sqrt{\dfrac{2 + \sqrt{3}}{4}} \approx 0.96593$

7. $\sqrt{\dfrac{1 + \sqrt{\frac{2+\sqrt{3}}{4}}}{2}} - 2 = \sqrt{\dfrac{2 + \sqrt{2 + \sqrt{3}}}{4}} \approx 0.99145$

9. $\dfrac{\sqrt{2}}{2} + \sqrt{2} \approx 0.41421$ **11.** $\sqrt{\dfrac{2 - \sqrt{3}}{4}} \approx 0.25882$

13. $\frac{1}{4}(\sqrt{3}\sqrt{2 + \sqrt{2 + \sqrt{3}}} - \sqrt{2 - \sqrt{2 + \sqrt{3}}}) \approx 0.79335$

15. $\sin 2x = -\dfrac{336}{625}$; $\cos 2x = \dfrac{527}{625}$; $\tan 2x = -\dfrac{336}{527}$;

$\sin \dfrac{x}{2} = \dfrac{7\sqrt{2}}{10}$; $\cos \dfrac{x}{2} = \dfrac{\sqrt{2}}{10}$; $\tan \dfrac{x}{2} = 7$

17. $\sin 2x = \dfrac{840}{841}$; $\cos 2x = -\dfrac{41}{841}$; $\tan 2x = -\dfrac{840}{41}$;

$\sin \frac{x}{2} = \sqrt{\dfrac{9}{58}}$; $\cos \frac{x}{2} = \sqrt{\dfrac{49}{58}}$; $\tan \dfrac{x}{2} = \dfrac{3}{7}$

19. $\sin 2x = \dfrac{840}{1369}$; $\cos 2x = \dfrac{-1081}{1369}$; $\tan 2x = -\dfrac{840}{1081}$; $\sin \dfrac{x}{2} = \sqrt{\dfrac{49}{74}}$; $\cos \dfrac{x}{2} = -\sqrt{\dfrac{25}{74}}$; $\tan \dfrac{x}{2} = -\dfrac{7}{5}$

21-41. All answers are proofs and will not be displayed in this section.

Exercise Set 21.4

1. $90°, 270°$ **3.** $30°, 210°$ **5.** $228.59°, 311.41°$

7. $51.34°, 231.34°$ **9.** $90°, 270°$ **11.** $180°$

13. $0°, 90°, 180°$ **15.** $0°, 90°, 180°, 270°$

17. $30°, 150°, 210°, 330°$ **19.** $15°, 75°, 195°, 255°$

21. $45°, 225°$ **23.** $0°, 40°, 60°, 80°, 120°, 160°, 180°, 200°, 240°, 280°, 300°, 320°$ **25.** $45°, 135°, 225°, 315°$

27. $0°, 135°, 180°, 315°$ **29.** $30°, 90°, 150°$

31. $20.87°$ **33.** $0.001\ 328\ s$ **35.** $0, \pi$

Review Exercises

1-9. All answers are proofs and will not be displayed in this section.   **11.** $139.11°, 319.11°$

13. $90°, 120°, 240°, 270°$ **15.** $0°, 90°, 180°, 270°$

17. $0°, 180°$ **19.** $218.17°, 321.83°$ **21.** $-\dfrac{120}{169}$

23. $\sqrt{25/26} \approx 0.98058$ **25.** $\dfrac{-21}{221} \approx -0.09502$

27. $\dfrac{220}{221} \approx 0.99548$ **29.** $\dfrac{140}{221} \approx 0.63348$

31. $90°, 210°, 330°$

Chapter 21 Test

1. $-\dfrac{33}{65}$ **3.** $-\dfrac{63}{65}$ **5.** $-\dfrac{24}{25}$ **7.** $\dfrac{2}{\sqrt{5}}$ **9.** $4 \sin 12x$

11. This answer is a proof and will not be displayed in this section.   **13.** $2r(1 - \cos \theta)$

ANSWERS FOR CHAPTER 12

Exercise Set 12.1

1. 4.7288 **3.** 5.6164 **5.** 3.4154

7.

x	-3	-2	-1	0	1	2	3	4	5
$f(x)$	$\frac{1}{64}$	$\frac{1}{16}$	$\frac{1}{4}$	1	4	16	64	256	1024

© Cengage Learning 2013

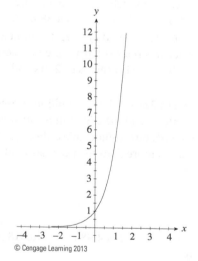

© Cengage Learning 2013

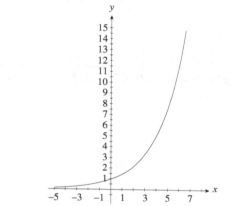

© Cengage Learning 2013

9.

x	-3	-2	-1	0	1	2	3	4	5
$h(x)$	$\frac{8}{27}$	$\frac{4}{9}$	$\frac{2}{3}$	1	1.5	2.25	3.375	5.0625	7.59375

© Cengage Learning 2013

11.

x	-3	-2	-1	0	1	2	3	4	5
$f(x)$	27	9	3	1	$\frac{1}{3}$	$\frac{1}{9}$	$\frac{1}{27}$	$\frac{1}{81}$	$\frac{1}{243}$

© Cengage Learning 2013

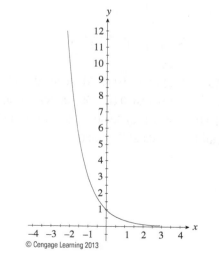

© Cengage Learning 2013

13.

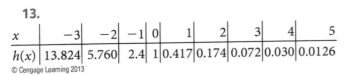

x	-3	-2	-1	0	1	2	3	4	5
$h(x)$	13.824	5.760	2.4	1	0.417	0.174	0.072	0.030	0.0126

© Cengage Learning 2013

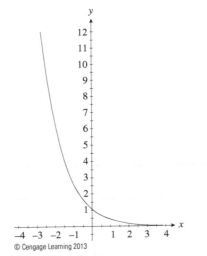

© Cengage Learning 2013

15.

x	-3	-2	-1	0	1	2	3	4
$f(x)$	0.064	0.192	0.577	1.732	5.196	15.588	46.765	140.296

© Cengage Learning 2013

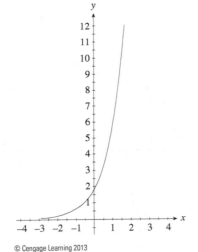

© Cengage Learning 2013

17. (a) \$1338.23 (b) \$1343.92 (c) \$1346.86 (d) \$1348.85

19. \$2.12 **21.** (a) 40,650 (b) 650,400 (c) 1 h (d) 3 h

23. (a) 400 (b) $\frac{2}{5} = 0.4$ (c) 3,600 **25.** (a) Here $T = 1.75$, and so $I = 0.88^{1.75} \approx 0.80$.

(b)

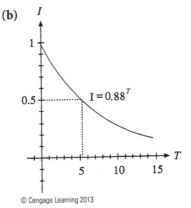

© Cengage Learning 2013

(c) Locate 0.50 on the I-axis. Draw a horizontal line from there until it intersects the graph of $I = 0.88^T$. From there draw a vertical line toward the T-axis. It intersects the T-axis near 5.42, and so we conclude that a thickness of 5.42 mm will produce an intensity of 0.50.

27. (a) $D(0) = 25$ mg (b) 17.5% (c) 3.65 mg (d) 16.73 hr. or about 16 hr 44 min

29. (a) $S_e(t) \approx 10.0299 \times 1.1258^t$ dollars, t years after 1970 (b) $S_q(t) \approx 2038.0643t^2 - 289627.4514t + 10286696.6571$ dollars, t years after 1970 (c) $S_e(110) \approx \$4,576,436$, $S_q(110) \approx \$3,088,255$, (d) Exponential model: 51.8%, Quadratic model: 2.4% (e) \$3,930,000 (f) \$4,880,000

31. (a) $T(t) = 69.3297(0.9703^t) + 22°C$ minutes after the water was removed from the heat source (b) 33.4°C (c) ≈ 141 minutes or 2 hrs and 21 min.

33. (a) $S(t) \approx 114.3245 \times 1.1177^t$ million subscribers t years after 2000 (b) 279 million subscribers (c) 3.3% (d) 607 million subscribers (e) No, because this is more than the population of the United States.

Exercise Set 12.2

1. 20.085 537 **3.** 104.584 986 **5.** 0.018 316

7. 0.063 928

9.

x	-2	-1	0	1	2	3	4
$f(x)$	0.5413	1.4715	4	10.8731	29.5562	80.3421	218.3926

© Cengage Learning 2013

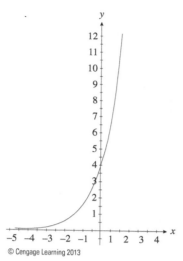
© Cengage Learning 2013

11.

x	-4	-3	-2	-1	0	1	2
$h(x)$	218.3926	80.3421	29.5562	10.8731	4	1.4715	0.5413

© Cengage Learning 2013

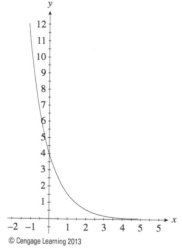
© Cengage Learning 2013

13. (a) 125 mg **(b)** 85.91 mg **(c)** 0.31 mg **15. (a)** 8660
(b) 25,981 **(c)** 260,980 **17. (a)** 280,510 **(b)** 393,430
19. 110.6°F **21.** 110.26 min or about 1 hour 50 minutes
23. 0.0066 C **25.** 25.5 μCi **27. (a)** 0.05 A **(b)** 0.048 A
(c) 0.046 A **29.** 23.8 units

Exercise Set 12.3

1. $6^3 = 216$ **3.** $4^2 = 16$ **5.** $(\frac{1}{7})^2 = \frac{1}{49}$
7. $2^{-5} = \frac{1}{32}$ **9.** $9^{7/2} = 2,187$ **11.** $\log_5 625 = 4$
13. $\log_2 128 = 7$ **15.** $\log_7 343 = 3$ **17.** $\log_5 \frac{1}{125} = -3$
19. $\log_4 128 = \frac{1}{128}$ **21.** 1.609 437 912

23. 1.558 355 122   **25.** 0.6020599913
27. 1.102776615
29. 1.292 029 674   **31.** 1.125 708 821
33.

x	0.1	0.5	1	2	4	6	8	10
$\ln x$	-2.30	-0.69	0	0.69	1.39	1.79	2.08	2.30

© Cengage Learning 2013

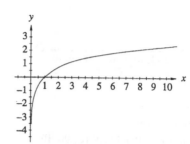
© Cengage Learning 2013

35.

x	0.1	0.5	1	2	4	6	8	10
$\log_2 x$	-3.32	-1	0	1	2	2.58	3	3.32

© Cengage Learning 2013

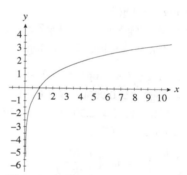
© Cengage Learning 2013

37.

x	0.1	0.5	1	2	4	6	8	10
$\log_{12} x$	-0.93	-0.28	0	0.28	0.56	0.72	0.84	0.93

© Cengage Learning 2013

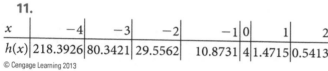
© Cengage Learning 2013

39.

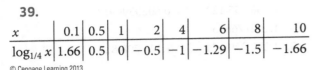

x	0.1	0.5	1	2	4	6	8	10
$\log_{1/4} x$	1.66	0.5	0	−0.5	−1	−1.29	−1.5	−1.66

© Cengage Learning 2013

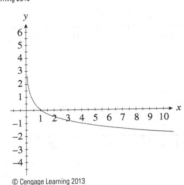

© Cengage Learning 2013

41. (a) $I = I_0\, 10^{\beta/10}$ (b) 50 dB (c) 90 dB

43. 3,884 ft³/acre **45.** $E = 10^{9+1.5M_w}$

Exercise Set 12.4

1. $\log 2 - \log 3$ **3.** $\log 2 + \log 7$

5. $\log 2 + \log 2 + \log 3$

7. $\log 2 + \log 3 + \log 5 + \log 5 - \log 7$ **9.** $\log 2 + \log x$

11. $\log 2ax - \log 3y$ **13.** $\log 22$ **15.** $\log \frac{11}{3}$

17. $\log 12$ **19.** $\log \frac{4x}{y}$ **21.** $\log (5^2 \cdot 5^3) = \log 4000$

23. $\log \frac{2}{3} \cdot \frac{6}{7} = \log \frac{4}{7}$ **25.** 0.9030 **27.** 1.0791

29. 1.1761 **31.** 1.5741 **33.** 2.3010 **35.** 3.6990

37. 1.5476 **39.** 0.2851 **41.** 6

43. $\log\left(\dfrac{I_2\sqrt{R_2}}{I_1\sqrt{R_1}}\right)^{20} = \log\left(\dfrac{I_2^{20}R_2^{10}}{I_1^{20}R_1^{10}}\right)$

Exercise Set 12.5

1. 2.0922 **3.** 0.5746 **5.** −2.4763 **7.** 2.6513

9. 5.5 **11.** 2.6094 **13.** $10^{2.3} \approx 199.53$ **15.** $10^{17} + 5$

17. $\sqrt{\frac{1}{2}e^9} = \dfrac{\sqrt{2}\,e^{4.5}}{2} \approx 63.6517$ **19.** $\frac{1}{18} \approx 0.056$

21. 101 **23.** 4.040404 **25.** 11.55 yr **27.** 138.63 yr

29. 5.5% **31.** 8.15% **33.** 5.6 **35.** 4418.07 m

37. 0.104 s **39.** 0.1354 seconds

41. $t = \dfrac{RC}{-2}\ln\left(1 - \dfrac{2E}{U^2C}\right)$

CHAPTER 13

▼ **check your progress 1**, *page 805*

The four tests are a complete population. Use μ to represent the mean.

$$\mu = \frac{\Sigma x}{n} = \frac{245 + 235 + 220 + 210}{4} = \frac{910}{4} = 227.5$$

The mean of the patient's blood cholesterol levels is 227.5.

▼ **check your progress 2**, *page 806*

a. The list 14, 27, 3, 82, 64, 34, 8, 51 contains 8 numbers. The median of a list of data with an even number of numbers is found by ranking the numbers and computing the mean of the two middle numbers. Ranking the numbers from smallest to largest gives 3, 8, 14, 27, 34, 51, 64, 82. The two middle numbers are 27 and 34. The mean of 27 and 34 is 30.5. Thus 30.5 is the median of the data.

b. The list 21.3, 37.4, 11.6, 82.5, 17.2 contains 5 numbers. The median of a list of data with an odd number of numbers is found by ranking the numbers and finding the middle number. Ranking the numbers from smallest to largest gives 11.6, 17.2, 21.3, 37.4, 82.5. The middle number is 21.3. Thus 21.3 is the median.

▼ **check your progress 3**, *page 806*

a. In the list 3, 3, 3, 3, 3, 4, 4, 5, 5, 5, 8, the number 3 occurs more often than the other numbers. Thus 3 is the mode.

b. In the list 12, 34, 12, 71, 48, 93, 71, the numbers 12 and 71 both occur twice and the other numbers occur only once. Thus 12 and 71 are both modes for the data.

▼ **check your progress 4**, *page 808*

The A is worth 4 points, with a weight of 4; the B in Statistics is worth 3 points, with a weight of 3; the C is worth 2 points, with a weight of 3; the F is worth 0 points, with a weight of 2; and the B in CAD is worth 3 points, with a weight of 2. The sum of all the weights is $4 + 3 + 3 + 2 + 2$, or 14.

$$\text{Weighted mean} = \frac{(4 \times 4) + (3 \times 3) + (2 \times 3) + (0 \times 2) + (3 \times 2)}{14}$$

$$= \frac{37}{14} \approx 2.64$$

Janet's GPA for the spring semester is approximately 2.64.

▼ **check your progress 5**, *page 810*

$$\text{Mean} = \frac{\Sigma(x \cdot f)}{\Sigma f}$$

$$= \frac{(2 \cdot 5) + (3 \cdot 25) + (4 \cdot 10) + (5 \cdot 5)}{45}$$

$$= \frac{150}{45}$$

$$= 3\frac{1}{3}$$

The mean number of bedrooms per household for the homes in the subdivision is $3\frac{1}{3}$.

SECTION 13.2

▼ **check your progress 1**, *page 816*

The greatest number of ounces dispensed is 8.03 and the least is 7.95. The range of the numbers of ounces is $8.03 - 7.95 = 0.08$ oz.

▼ **check your progress 2**, *page 818*

$$\mu = \frac{5 + 8 + 16 + 17 + 18 + 20}{6} = \frac{84}{6} = 14$$

x	$x - \mu$	$(x - \mu)^2$
5	$5 - 14 = -9$	$(-9)^2 = 81$
8	$8 - 14 = -6$	$(-6)^2 = 36$
16	$16 - 14 = 2$	$2^2 = 4$
17	$17 - 14 = 3$	$3^2 = 9$
18	$18 - 14 = 4$	$4^2 = 16$
20	$20 - 14 = 6$	$6^2 = 36$
		Sum: 182

$$\sigma = \sqrt{\frac{\Sigma(x - \mu)^2}{n}} = \sqrt{\frac{182}{6}} \approx \sqrt{30.33} \approx 5.51$$

The standard deviation for this population is approximately 5.51.

▼ **check your progress 3**, *page 819*

The rope from Trustworthy has a breaking point standard deviation of

$$s_1 = \sqrt{\frac{(122 - 130)^2 + (141 - 130)^2 + \cdots + (125 - 130)^2}{6}}$$

$$= \sqrt{\frac{1752}{6}} \approx 17.1 \text{ lb}$$

The rope from Brand X has a breaking point standard deviation of

$$s_2 = \sqrt{\frac{(128 - 130)^2 + (127 - 130)^2 + \cdots + (137 - 130)^2}{6}}$$

$$= \sqrt{\frac{3072}{6}} \approx 22.6 \text{ lb}$$

The rope from NeverSnap has a breaking point standard deviation of

$$s_3 = \sqrt{\frac{(112 - 130)^2 + (121 - 130)^2 + \cdots + (135 - 130)^2}{6}}$$

$$= \sqrt{\frac{592}{6}} \approx 9.9 \text{ lb}$$

The rope from NeverSnap has the lowest breaking point standard deviation.

▼ **check your progress 4**, *page 820*

The mean is approximately 46.472.

The population standard deviation is approximately 2.872.

L1	L2	L3	1
54.2	-----		
49.4			
49.2			
53.2			
50.0			
48.2			
49.6			

L1(1) = 54.2

```
1-Var Stats
x̄=46.47185185          ← Mean
Σx=1254.74
Σx²=58532.8412
Sx=2.926995095         ← Sample standard deviation
σx=2.872280082         ← Population standard deviation
↓n=27
```

▼ **check your progress 5**, *page 820*

In Check Your Progress 2, we found $\sigma \approx \sqrt{30.33}$. Variance is the square of the standard deviation. Thus the variance is $\sigma^2 \approx \left(\sqrt{30.33}\right)^2 = 30.33$.

▼ **check your progress 1**, *page 852*

x	y	x^2	xy
2.5	2.3	6.25	5.75
3.0	3.9	9.00	11.70
3.2	4.4	10.24	14.08
3.4	5.0	11.56	17.00
3.5	5.5	12.25	19.25
3.8	6.2	14.44	23.56
4.0	7.1	16.00	28.40
4.2	7.6	17.64	31.92
$\Sigma x = 27.6$	$\Sigma y = 42.0$	$\Sigma x^2 = 97.38$	$\Sigma xy = 151.66$

$n = 8$

$$a = \frac{n\Sigma xy - (\Sigma x)(\Sigma y)}{n\Sigma x^2 - (\Sigma x)^2}$$

$$= \frac{(8)(151.66) - (27.6)(42.0)}{(8)(97.38) - (27.6)^2}$$

$$\approx 3.1296$$

$$\bar{x} = \frac{\Sigma x}{n} = \frac{27.6}{8} = 3.45 \qquad \bar{y} = \frac{\Sigma y}{n} = \frac{42.0}{8} = 5.25$$

$$b = \bar{y} - a\bar{x}$$

$$= 5.25 - (3.1296)(3.45)$$

$$= -5.54712$$

$$\hat{y} = ax + b$$
$$\hat{y} \approx 3.1x - 5.5$$

▼ **check your progress 2**, *page 853*

a. $\hat{y} = 3.1x - 5.5$

$\hat{y} = 3.1(2.7) - 5.5 \approx 2.9$

The predicted average speed of a camel with a stride length of 2.7 m is approximately 2.9 m/s.

b. $\hat{y} = 3.1x - 5.5$

$\hat{y} = 3.1(4.5) - 5.5 \approx 8.5$

The predicted average speed of a camel with a stride length of 4.5 m is approximately 8.5 m/s.

▼ **check your progress 3**, *page 855*

From Check Your Progress 1:

$n = 8 \quad \Sigma x = 27.6 \quad \Sigma y = 42.0 \quad \Sigma x^2 = 97.38 \quad \Sigma xy = 151.66$

$\Sigma y^2 = 2.3^2 + 3.9^2 + 4.4^2 + 5.0^2 + 5.5^2 + 6.2^2 + 7.1^2 + 7.6^2$
$\quad\quad = 241.72$

$$r = \frac{n(\Sigma xy) - (\Sigma x)(\Sigma y)}{\sqrt{n(\Sigma x^2) - (\Sigma x)^2} \cdot \sqrt{n(\Sigma y^2) - (\Sigma y)^2}}$$

$$= \frac{8(151.66) - (27.6)(42.0)}{\sqrt{8(97.38) - (27.6)^2} \cdot \sqrt{8(241.72) - (42.0)^2}}$$

$$\approx 0.998498$$

The linear correlation coefficient, rounded to the nearest hundredth, is 1.00.

CHAPTER 13

EXERCISE SET 13.1 *page 811*

1. 7; 7; 7 **3.** 22; 14; no mode **5.** 18.8; 8.1; no mode **7.** 192.4; 190; 178 **9.** 0.1; −3; −5 **11. a.** Yes. The mean is computed by using the sum of all the data. **b.** No. The median is not affected unless the middle value, or one of the two middle values, in a data set is changed. **13.** ≈38.8 years; 35 years **15. a.** Answers will vary. **b.** Answers will vary. **17.** 3.22 **19.** 3.37 **21.** 82 **23.** 0.847 **25.** 0.671 **27.** ≈6.1 points; 5 points; 2 points and 5 points **29.** ≈7.2; 7; 7 **31.** 64° **33.** −6°F **35.** 92 **37. a.** ≈0.275 **b.** ≈0.273 **c.** No **39.** 81

41. $d_1 = d_2$

$$r_1 = \frac{d_1}{t_1} \qquad r_2 = \frac{d_2}{t_2} = \frac{d_1}{t_2}$$

$$t_1 = \frac{d_1}{r_1} \qquad t_2 = \frac{d_1}{r_2}$$

$$r = \frac{d_1 + d_2}{t_1 + t_2} = \frac{d_1 + d_1}{t_1 + t_2} = \frac{2d_1}{t_1 + t_2}$$

$$= \frac{2d_1}{\dfrac{d_1}{r_1} + \dfrac{d_1}{r_2}} = \frac{2d_1}{d_1\left(\dfrac{1}{r_1} + \dfrac{1}{r_2}\right)}$$

$$= \frac{2}{\dfrac{1}{r_1} + \dfrac{1}{r_2}} \cdot \left(\frac{r_1 r_2}{r_1 r_2}\right) = \frac{2r_1 r_2}{r_1 + r_2}$$

43. Yes. Joanne has a smaller average for the first month and the second month, but she has a larger average for both months combined.

EXERCISE SET 13.2 *page 822*

1. 84°F **3.** 21; 8.2; 67.1 **5.** 3.3; 1.3; 1.7 **7.** 52; 17.7; 311.6 **9.** 0; 0; 0 **11.** 23; 8.3; 69.6
13. Opinions will vary. However, many climbers would consider rope B to be safer because of its small standard deviation.
15. The students in the college statistics course because the range of weights is greater. **17. a.** The smallest data value is approximately 3300 deaths, and the largest data value is approximately 49,000 deaths. **b.** No; the smallest and largest data values are not necessarily the first and last data values when the data are listed in the order in which they were collected. The smallest and largest numbers of deaths could have occurred during any of the 31 years. **c.** The range; 45,265 deaths **19. a.** 30.2; 9.8 **b.** 15.6; 6.5 **c.** Winning scores; winning scores
21. a. 46.2 runs; 9.2 runs **b.** 44.6 runs; 7.5 runs **c.** National League; National League
23. 54.6 years; 6.2 years **25. a.** 210 s, or 3 min 30 s; 26 s **b.** Yes; 2:27, 3:01, 4:02 **27. a.** Answers will vary.
b. The standard deviation of the new data is k times the standard deviation of the original data. **29.** If the variance is 1 or 0 **31. a.** National League: minimum of 28 runs, maximum of 64 runs; American League: minimum of 30 runs, maximum of 59 runs **b.** National league: 65 runs, 70 runs, 73 runs; American League: 22 runs

EXERCISE SET 13.5 *page 859*

1. a. b   **b.** c   **3. a.**

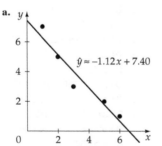

$\hat{y} \approx -1.12x + 7.40$

b. $n = 5, \Sigma x = 17, \Sigma y = 18, \Sigma x^2 = 75,$
$(\Sigma x)^2 = 289, \Sigma xy = 42$

c. $a = -\dfrac{48}{43} \approx -1.12, b = \dfrac{318}{43} \approx 7.40$

d. See the graph in part a.

e. Yes

f. $y \approx 3.6$

g. $r \approx -0.96$

5. $\hat{y} \approx 2.01x + 0.56; r \approx 0.96$ **7.** $\hat{y} \approx -0.72x + 9.23; r \approx -0.96$ **9.** $\hat{y} \approx 1.66x + 2.25; r \approx 0.99$
11. a. $\hat{y} \approx -0.170x + 54545.585$ **b.** $49,444   **c.** $r \approx -0.999$ **d.** As the number of miles the car is driven increases, the value of the car decreases.   **13. a.** $\hat{y} \approx 0.775x + 20.707$ **b.** $\approx 32.3\%$ **15. a.** $r \approx 0.99$ **b.** Yes, at least for the years 2005 to 2010. The correlation coefficient is very close to 1, which indicates a strong linear correlation.   **17. a.** Electric vehicles: $\hat{y} \approx 1906.2x + 41,981$; alternative feul vehicles: $\hat{y} \approx 52,398.5x + 338,329$ **b.** 70,574 electric vehicles; 1,124,307 alternative feul vehicles   **c.** Extrapolation   **d.** Yes. The estimated 70,574 electric vehicles is significantly lower than the desired amount of 1 million, indicating that given current trends, the goal will not be reached. The estimated 1,124,307 alternative fuel vehicles is over 1 million, indicating that given current trends, a goal of 1 million alternative fuel vehicles is reasonable.
19. a. $r = -1.00$ **b.** The graph of the least-squares line passes through all three data points   **c.** $\hat{y} = -0.85x + 187$
d. ≈ 126 beats per minute   **21. a.** $\hat{y} \approx 0.76x + 20.67$ **b.** In situations in which one or two of the y data values are suspected of being off by a considerable amount due to experimental error

ANSWERS FOR CHAPTER 14

Exercise Set 14.1

1. $5j$ **3.** $0.2j$ **5.** $5j\sqrt{3}$ **7.** $-6j\sqrt{5}$ **9.** $\frac{3}{4}j$

11. $-3j$ **13.** -11 **15.** -18 **17.** -10 **19.** -42

21. $-5j$ **23.** $-j$ **25.** $\frac{2}{3}j$ **27.** $\frac{3}{20}j$ **29.** $-\frac{5}{8}$

31. $0.5j$ **33.** $-2j\sqrt{8.1} = -6j\sqrt{0.9}$ **35.** $-2j\sqrt{15}$

37. $-14j$ **39.** $x = 7, y = -2$ **41.** $x = 10, y = -3$

43. $x = 2, y = -2$ **45.** $x = -\frac{1}{2}, y = -\frac{5}{4}$ **47.** $x = 3.5,$ $y = -4.3$ **49.** $8 + 10j$ **51.** $-10 - 5j$

53. $2 + 3j$ **55.** $-6 + 8j$ **57.** $3 - 4j$ **59.** $1 - 2j$

61. $2 + 3j\sqrt{2}$ **63.** $2 - \frac{1}{2}j\sqrt{6}$ **65.** $\frac{1}{2} - \frac{2}{9}j$

67. $\frac{5}{8} - \frac{2}{3}j$ **69.** $3.6 - 4.5j$ **71.** $7 - 2j$ **73.** $6 + 5j$

75. 19 **77.** $8j$ **79.** $\sqrt{2} - 7.3j$ **81.** $-\frac{1}{2} + \frac{3}{2}j,$ $-\frac{1}{2} - \frac{3}{2}j$ **83.** $3j, -3j$ **85.** $-\frac{3}{4} + \frac{j\sqrt{47}}{4},$ $-\frac{3}{4} - \frac{j\sqrt{47}}{4}$ **87.** $-\frac{1}{5} \pm \frac{2j\sqrt{6}}{5}, -\frac{1}{10} - \frac{j\sqrt{6}}{5}$

89. $6.25 + 49.61j\,\Omega$ or $6.25 - 49.61j\,\Omega$

91. $R = \pm\sqrt{\dfrac{X}{B} - X^2}$

Exercise Set 14.2

1. $-1 + 7j$ **3.** $5 - 2j$ **5.** $7 - j$

7. $2 - \sqrt{5} + 11j$ **9.** $8 + 2j$ **11.** $3 - 6j$

13. $7 - 2j$ **15.** $-3 + 6j$ **17.** $10 - 45j$

19. $7 + 11j$ **21.** $36 + 8j$ **23.** $-126 + 48j$

25. 9 **27.** $-3 + 4j$ **29.** $48 - 14j$ **31.** 29

33. $1 - 5j$ **35.** $-3j$ **37.** $2j$ **39.** $\frac{1}{13} + \frac{5}{13}j$

41. $-\sqrt{2} - j$ **43.** $4.059 - 0.765j$ **45.** -4

47. $-0.5 + \dfrac{j\sqrt{3}}{2}$ **49.** $(a + bj) + (a - bj) = 2a,$ which is a real number.   **51.** $(a + bj)(a - bj) = a^2 + b^2$, which is a real number.

53. $10.53 - 4.21j$ V   **55.** $5.08 + 2.88j$ V

57. $5.84 + 1.16j\,\Omega$ **59.** $0.4 - 0.3j\,\Omega$

61. $0.74 + 1.12j$ A

63. The following program will work on a TI-82 graphing calculator.

```
Disp "COMPLEX"
: ClrHome
: Disp "ENTER THE FIRST"
: Disp "NUMBER AS A + BJ"
: Prompt A, B
: ClrHome
: Disp "ENTER THE SECOND"
: Disp "NUMBER AS C + DJ"
: Prompt C, D
: ClrHome
: Disp "THE SUM IS"
: Disp "      REAL"
: Disp A + C
: Disp "      IMAGINARY"
: Disp B + D
: Disp " "
: Disp "PRESS <ENTER>"
: Pause
: ClrHome
: Disp "THE DIFFERENCE"
: Disp "IS REAL"
: Disp A — C
: Disp "      IMAGINARY"
: Disp B — D
: Disp " "
: Disp "PRESS <ENTER>"
: Pause
: ClrHome
: Disp "THE PRODUCT IS"
: Disp "      REAL"
: Disp AC — BD
: Disp "      IMAGINARY"
: Disp BC + AD
: Disp " "
: Disp "PRESS <ENTER>"
: Pause
: ClrHome
: Disp "THE QUOTIENT IS"
: Disp "      REAL"
: Disp (AC + BD) / (C² + D²)▶Frac
: Disp "      IMAGINARY"
: Disp (BC — AD) / (C² + D²)▶Frac
```

Exercise Set 14.3

1. $2\sqrt{3} + 2j$

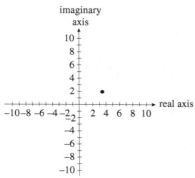

3. $-\dfrac{5\sqrt{2}}{2} + \dfrac{5j\sqrt{2}}{2} \approx -3.5355 + 3.5355\,j$

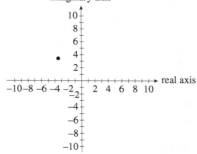

5. $-1.2155 - 6.8937\,j$

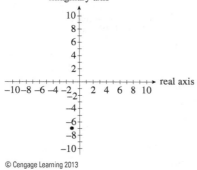

7. $-0.8452 + 1.8126\,j$

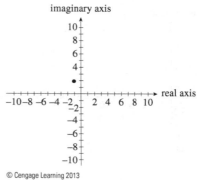

9. $2.7189 + 1.2679\,j$

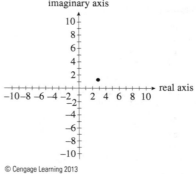

11. $4.6985 - 1.7101\,j$

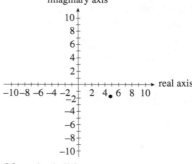

13. $-1.9018 - 4.0784\,j$

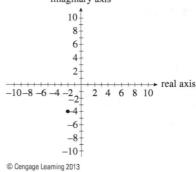

15. −2.5

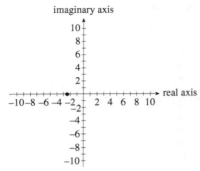

17. 7.071 $\underline{/45°}$

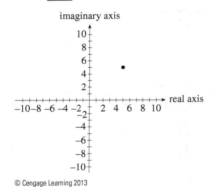

19. 8.944 $\underline{/296.6°}$

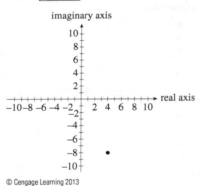

21. 8.0623 $\underline{/119.7°}$

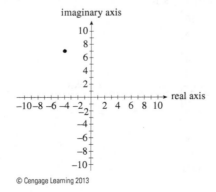

23. 6.3246 $\underline{/198.4°}$

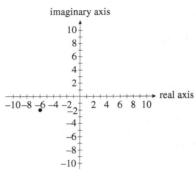

25. 6 $\underline{/0°}$

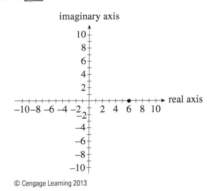

27. 7.5717 $\underline{/303.7°}$

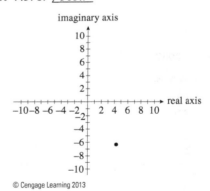

29. 5.8034 $\underline{/178.0°}$

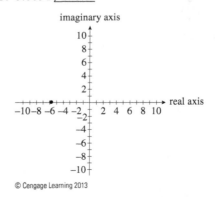

31. $2.7\ \underline{/180°}$

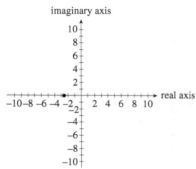

© Cengage Learning 2013

33.

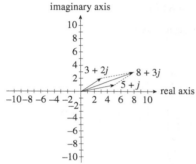

© Cengage Learning 2013

35.

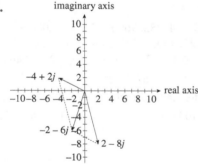

© Cengage Learning 2013

37.

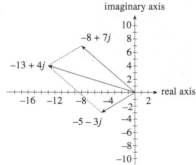

© Cengage Learning 2013

39.

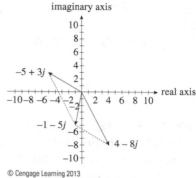

© Cengage Learning 2013

41. $8.0\ \underline{/-54.1°} = 8.0\ \underline{/305.9°}$ A

43. $119.6\ \underline{/157.3°}$ V   **45.** $1.61 - 1.92j$ A

Exercise Set 14.4

1. $3e^{3\pi/2\,j} \approx 3e^{4.7\,j}$ **3.** $2e^{1.05j}$ **5.** $1.3e^{5.7j}$

7. $3.1e^{0.44j}$ **9.** $10e^{0.64j}$ **11.** $15e^{2.21j}$

13. $5\ \text{cis}\ 0.5 = 4.3879 + 2.3971\,j$

15. $2.3\ \text{cis}\ 4.2 = -1.1276 - 2.0046\,j$

17. $12e^{5j}$ **19.** $2.4e^{5.9j}$ **21.** $28e^{3.72j}$ **23.** $4e^{2j}$

25. $4.25e^{1.5j}$ **27.** $81e^{8j}$ **29.** $39.0625e^{6j}$ **31.** $2e^{3j}$

33. $2.5e^{2.1j}$ **35.** $61.4e^{0.4031j}$ V

37. In exponential form $Z = 135e^{-0.9163j}\ \Omega$ or $135e^{5.37j}$; in rectangular form $Z = 82.2 - 107.1\,j\ \Omega$

39. $V = 80e^{0.7029j}$ V   **41.** $I = 46e^{-0.7937j}$ A

43. $3.4e^{1.074j}\ \Omega$

Exercise Set 14.5

1. $15(\cos 69° + j \sin 69°)$ **3.** $10(\cos 4.1 + j \sin 4.1)$

5. $4(\cos 60° + j \sin 60°)$ **7.** $4.5\ \underline{/111°}$ **9.** $12\ \underline{/8.0}$

11. $15625(\cos 144° + j \sin 144°)$

13. $1124.864\,(\cos 10.26 + j \sin 10.26)$

15. $3.4^4\ \underline{/21.2} = 113.6336$ **17.** $12e^{3.8j}$ **19.** $0.125e^{0.9j}$

21. $1, -0.5 + 0.866j, -0.5 - 0.866j$

23. $1.732 - j, 2j, -1.732 - j$

25. $1.8478 - 0.7654\,j, 0.7654 + 1.8478\,j, -1.8478 + 0.7654\,j, -0.7654 - 1.8478\,j$

27. $1.0586 + 0.1677\,j, 0.1677 + 1.0586\,j, -0.9550 + 0.5866\,j, -0.7579 - 0.7579\,j, 0.4866 - 0.9550\,j$

29. $0.866 - 0.5\,j, j, -0.866 - 0.5\,j$

31. $1.9319 + 0.5176\,j, 0.5176 + 1.9319\,j, -1.4142 + 1.4142\,j, -1.9319 - 0.5176\,j, -0.5176 - 1.9319\,j, 1.4142 - 1.4142\,j$ **33.** $108\ \underline{/19°}$

35. $80 \, \underline{/-36.87°} \, \text{V}$ **37.** $Z = -0.0448 + 0.1536 \, j = 0.16 \, \underline{/106.3°} \, \Omega$

39. **(a)** $0.2137 \, \underline{/-20.56°} \, \text{S}$ **(b)** about $0.200 - 0.075 \, j \, \text{S}$

Exercise Set 14.6

1. **(a)** $3 - 2j$ **(b)** $5 + j$ **3.** **(a)** $1 + 2j$ **(b)** $1.8 - 0.6 \, j$ **5.** **(a)** $6.803 \, \underline{/53.26°}$ **(b)** $1.6611 \, \underline{/32.44°}$

7. **(a)** $8.208 \, \underline{/0.449}$ **(b)** $1.226 \, \underline{/0.45}$ **9.** **(a)** $12 + 5 \, j$ **(b)** $1.9207 + 0.2387j$ **11.** **(a)** $6.595 \, \underline{/-2.95°}$ **(b)** $0.916 \, \underline{/29.32°}$ **13.** $-13 - 84 \, j \, \text{V}$ **15.** $2 \, \text{V}$

17. $2.8 \, \underline{/23.7°} \, \Omega$ **19.** $X_L = 75.40 \, \Omega$, $X_C = 66.31 \, \Omega$, $Z = 39.07 \, \Omega$, $\phi = 13.45°$ **21.** $X_L = 150.80 \, \Omega$, $X_C = 44.21 \, \Omega$, $Z = 108.45 \, \Omega$, $\phi = 79.37°$

23. $X_L = 12.5 \, \Omega$, $X_C = 100 \, \Omega$, $Z = 91.87 \, \Omega$, $\phi = -72.26°$ **25.** **(a)** $77.62 \, \underline{/14.93°}$ **(b)** $271.67 \, \text{V}$

27. **(a)** $\sqrt{10} \, \underline{/18.43°}$ **(b)** $9.01 \, \text{V}$ **29.** $2 - 9 \, j$

31. $22.51 \, \text{Hz}$ **33.** $0.16 - 0.12 \, j$

Review Exercises

1. $7j$ **3.** $3\sqrt{6}j$ or $3 \, j\sqrt{6}$ **5.** -6 **7.** $9 - 3j$

9. $-1 + 4j$ **11.** $-36 + 8 \, j$ **13.** 25

15. $10.82 \, \underline{/-33.69°}$

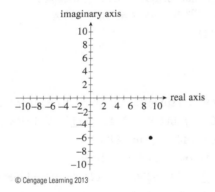

© Cengage Learning 2013

17. $5.657 \, \underline{/-45°}$

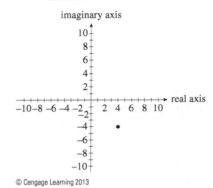

© Cengage Learning 2013

19. $-4.331 + 4.847 \, j$

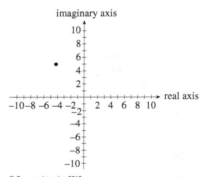

© Cengage Learning 2013

21. -10 **23.** $-4,782,969 \, j$ **25.** $-26.080 + 6.988 \, j$ **27.** 4096 **29.** $0.866 - 0.5 \, j, j, -0.866 - 0.5 \, j$ **31.** $2 + 3.464 \, j, -2 - 3.464 \, j$

33. $18.385e^{0.391j}$ **35.** $6740.6e^{2.702j}$

37. magnitude: 7.433, direction: $-10.86°$

39. $X_L = 113.10 \, \Omega$, $X_C = 53.05 \, \Omega$, $Z = 81.43$, $\phi = 47.51°$

Chapter 14 Test

1. $4j\sqrt{5}$ **3.** $-4\sqrt{3} + 4j$ **5.** $-13 + 8j$

7. $-\frac{38}{25} - \frac{9}{25}j = -1.52 + 0.36 \, j$ **9.** $\frac{4}{3}j$

11. $2.1941 + 2.0460 \, j$ **13.** **(a)** $9 - j \, \Omega$ **(b)** $\frac{118}{41} - \frac{4}{41}j \, \Omega \cong 2.878 + 0.098 \, j$

15. $0.28 + 1.04 \, j \, \Omega$

CHAPTER 21

Exercise 21.1

1. 3.8 kΩ

3. 630 Ω

5. 10 kΩ

7. 110 mH

9. 40 mH

11. 640 Hz

13. 7.4 kHz

15. 800 Ω

17. 1.4 kΩ

19. 2.5 V

21. 2.5 mA

23. $0.75 + j1.5$ kΩ
$= 1.7 \angle 63°$ kΩ

25. $3.3 + j4.5$ kΩ $= 5.6 \angle 54°$ Ω

27. $2 + j1.2$ kΩ $= 2.3 \angle 31°$ kΩ

29. $910 + j750$ Ω $= 1.2 \angle 39°$ kΩ

31. (a) $V_R = 12$ V, $V_L = 16$ V
(b) $V_T = 20 \angle 52°$ V,
$Z = 1.0 \angle 52°$ kΩ

33. (a) $V_R = 5$ V, $V_L = 7.5$ V
(b) $V_T = 9.0 \angle 56°$ V,
$Z = 1.8 \angle 56°$ kΩ

35. (a) $V_R = 17$ V, $V_L = 14$ V
    (b) $V_T = 21 \angle 39°$ V,
    $Z = 28 \angle 39°$ kΩ

37. (a) $V_R = 41$ V, $V_L = 33$ V
    (b) $V_T = 52 \angle 39°$ V,
    $Z = 3.5 \angle 39°$ kΩ

39. (a) $700 \angle 28°$ Ω
    (b) $I = 21$ mA, $V_R = 13$ V,
    $VL = 7.1$ V

41. (a) $3.2 \angle 18°$ kΩ
    (b) $I = 3.8$ mA, $V_R = 11$ V,
    $V_L = 3.8$ V

43. (a) $4.9 \angle 29°$ kΩ
    (b) $I = 12$ mA, $V_R = 52$ V,
    $V_L = 29$ V

45. (a) $16 \angle 45°$ kΩ
    (b) $I = 3.2$ mA, $V_R = 35$ V,
    $V_L = 35$ V

47. (a) $X_L = 1.4$ kΩ, $I = 5.3$ mA,
    $R = 1.8$ kΩ, $V_R = 9.6$ V
    (b) $V_T = 12 \angle 38°$ V

49. (a) $X_L = 280$ Ω, $I = 400$ mA,
    $VR = 40$ V, $V_L = 110$ V
    (b) $Z = 300 \angle 71°$ Ω

Exercise 21.2

1. 1.3 kΩ

3. 21 kΩ

5. 530 Ω

7. 1.6 nF

9. 99 nF

11. 1.3 kHz

13. 13 kHz

15. 1.7 kΩ

17. 8.0 kΩ

19. 4.8 V

21. 400 μA

23. $1.6 - j1.2$ kΩ $= 2.0 \angle -37°$ kΩ

25. $680 - j910$ Ω $= 1.1 \angle -53°$ kΩ

27. $550 - j550$ Ω $= 780 \angle -45°$ Ω

29. $0.82 - j1.0$ kΩ
    $= 1.3 \angle -51°$ kΩ

31. (a) $V_R = 24$ V, $V_C = 13$ V
    (b) $V_T = 27 \angle -28°$ V,
    $Z = 8.5 \angle -28°$ kΩ

33. (a) $V_R = 5.0$ V, $V_C = 13$ V
    (b) $V_T = 13 \angle -68°$ V,
    $Z = 27 \angle -68°$ kΩ

35. (a) $V_R = 2.0$ V, $V_C = 3.2$ V
    (b) $V_T = 3.8 \angle -58°$ V,
    $Z = 940 \angle -58°$ Ω

37. (a) $V_R = 28$ V, $V_C = 18$ V
    (b) $V_T = 33 \angle -32°$ V,
    $Z = 5.1 \angle -32°$ kΩ

39. (a) $Z = 920 \angle -42°$ Ω
    (b) $I = 22$ mA, $V_R = 15$ V,
    $V_C = 13$ V

41. (a) $Z = 1.5 \angle -35°$ Ω
    (b) $I = 16$ mA, $V_R = 20$ V,
    $V_C = 14$ V

43. (a) $Z = 15 \angle -58°$ kΩ
    (b) $I = 780$ μA, $V_R = 6.4$ V,
    $V_C = 10$ V

45. (a) $Z = 1.1 \angle -45°$ kΩ
    (b) $I = 9.1$ mA, $V_R = 6.9$ V,
    $V_C = 6.9$ V

47. (a) $X_C = 1.6$ kΩ, $I = 4.1$ mA,
    $V_C = 6.5$ V, $V_R = 14$ V
    (b) $Z = 3.7 \angle -26°$ kΩ

49. (a) $X_C = 18$ kΩ, $V_R = 94$ V,
    $V_C = 76$ V, $I = 4.3$ mA
    (b) $Z = 28 \angle -39°$ kΩ

Exercise 21.3

1. $X = 300$ Ω,
   $Z = 750 + j300$ Ω $= 810 \angle 22°$ Ω

3. $X = 2.2$ kΩ,
   $Z = 1.8 - j2.2$ kΩ $= 2.8 \angle -51°$ kΩ

5. $X = 4.8$ kΩ,
   $Z = 3.9 + j4.8$ kΩ $= 6.2 \angle 51°$ kΩ

7. $X = 450$ Ω,
   $Z = 1000 - j450$ Ω $= 1100 \angle -24°$ Ω

9. $X = 350$ Ω,
   $Z = 200 + j350$ Ω $= 400 \angle 60°$ Ω

11. $I = 2.5$ mA, $V_R = 8.3$ V,
    $V_L = 3.0$ V,
    $V_C = 12$ V, $V_T = 12 \angle -47°$ V

13. $I = 72$ mA, $V_R = 20$ V,
    $V_L = 37$ V, $V_C = 33$ V,
    $V_T = 20 \angle 13°$ V

15. $I = 4.8$ mA, $V_R = 4.3$ V,
    $V_L = 20$ V, $V_C = 7.1$ V,
    $V_T = 14 \angle 72°$ V

17. $I = 43$ mA, $V_R = 26$ V,
    $V_L = 51$ V, $V_C = 36$ V,
    $V_T = 30 \angle 31°$ V

19. 3.6 kHz

21. 28 kHz

23. 1.5 μF

25. 70 mH

27. (a) $X_L = 820$ Ω, $X_C = 610$ Ω,
    $Z = 330 + j210$ Ω $= 390 \angle 32°$ Ω
    (b) $I = 31$ mA, $V_R = 10$ V,
    $V_L = 25$ V, $V_C = 19$ V,
    $V_T = 10 + j6$ V $= 12 \angle 32°$ V

29. (a) $X_L = 3.8$ kΩ, $X_C = 6.6$ kΩ
    $Z = 2.2 - j2.9$ kΩ
    $= 36 \angle -52°$ kΩ
    (b) $I = 5.5$ mA,
    $V_C = 37$ V,
    $V_R = 12$ V, $V_L = 21$ V
    $V_T = 12 - j15.8$ V
    $= 20 \angle -j52°$ V

31. (a) $Z = 600 + j450$ Ω $= 750 -37°$ Ω
    (b) $I = 27$ mA, $P = 430$ mW,
    $Q = 320$ mVAR,
    $S = 540$ mVI, p.f. $= 0.80$

33. (a) $V_R = 18$ V, $V_L = 36$ V,
    $V_C = 16$ V, $V_T = 18 + j20$
    $V = 27 \angle 48°$ V
    (b) $Z = 1.8 + j2.0$ kΩ $= 2.7 \angle 48°$ kΩ

35. (a) $X_L = 1.9$ kΩ,
    $X_C = 3.2$ kΩ,
    $Z = 3.9 - j1.3$ kΩ $= 4.1 \angle -18°$ kΩ
    (b) $I = 2.4$ mA, $V_{R_1} = 6.6$ V,
    $V_{R_2} = 2.9$ V,
    $V_L = 4.6$ V,
    $V_C = 7.7$ V,
    $V_T = 9.5 - j3.2$ V $= 10 \angle -18°$ V

Review Exercises

1. 9.4 kΩ

3. 760 Ω

5. 2.0 kHz

7. 4.0 nF

9. 16 kHz

11. $820 + j1000$ Ω $= 1.3 \angle 51°$ kΩ

13. $150 + j430$ Ω $= 460 \angle 71°$ Ω

15. $6.2 - j8.5$ kΩ $= 11 \angle -54°$ kΩ

17. $1800 - j780$ Ω $= 2.0 \angle -23°$ kΩ

19. $470 + j550$ Ω $= 720 \angle 49°$ Ω

21. $6.8 - j3.1$ kΩ $= 7.5 \angle -25°$

23. (a) $Z = 730 \angle 58°$ Ω

   (b) $I = 20$ mA,
$V_T = 8.0 + j13$ V $= 15 \angle 58°$ V

25. (a) $Z = 8.4 \angle -42°$ Ω

   (b) $I = 2.9$ mA,
$V_T = 18 - j16$ V $= 24 \angle -42°$ V

27. (a) $Z = 4.8 \angle 47°$ kΩ

   (b) $I = 2.5$ mA,
$V_T = 8.2 + j8.7$ V $= 12 \angle 47°$ V

29. (a) $X_L = 1.1$ kΩ, $V_R = 18$ V, $V_L = 11$ V

   (b) $V_T = 18 + j11$ V $= 21 \angle 31°$ V,
$Z = 1.8 + j1.1$ kΩ $= 2.1 \angle 31°$ kΩ

31. (a) $X_C = 4.6$ kΩ, $V_R = 2.6$ V, $V_C = 3.7$ V

   (b) $V_T = 2.6 - j3.7$ V $= 4.5 \angle -54°$ V,
$Z = 3.3 - j4.6$ kΩ $= 5.7 \angle -54°$ kΩ

33. (a) $X_L = 5.7$ kΩ, $X_C = 2.7$ kΩ,
$V_R = 23$ V, $V_L = 43$ V,
$V_C = 20$ V, $I = 7.5$ mA

   (b) $V_T = 23 + j23$ V $= 32 \angle 45°$ V,
$Z = 3.0 + j3.0$ kΩ $= 4.2 \angle 45°$ kΩ

35. (a) $X_L = 4.1$ kΩ, $X_C = 3.9$ kΩ,
$V_R = 28$ V, $V_L = 155$ V,
$V_C = 145$ V, $I = 38$ mA

   (b) $V_T = 28 + j10$ V $= 29 \angle 20°$ V,
$Z = 750 + j280$ Ω $= 800 \angle 20°$ Ω

37. (a) $Z = 680 - j900$ Ω $= 1.1 \angle -53°$ Ω,
$I = 8.0$ mA

   (b) $V_T = 5.4 - j7.2$ V $= 9.0 \angle -53°$ V,
$P = 43$ mW

Section 2.6   (page 219)

1. double   **3.** $x \le -a, x \ge a$ **5.** No

7. d   **8.** a   **9.** f   **10.** b   **11.** e   **12.** c

13. (a) Yes   (b) No   (c) Yes   (d) No

15. (a) No   (b) Yes   (c) Yes   (d) No

17. $x > 7$

19. $x < -2$

21. $x > -1$

23. $x \ge 4$

25. $-1 \le x \le 3$

27. $-2 < x \le 5$

29. $-\frac{9}{2} < x < \frac{15}{2}$

31.

$x \le 2$

33.

$x < 2$

35.

(a) $x \ge 2$ (b) $x \le \frac{3}{2}$

37.

(a) $\frac{5}{3} \le x \le 3$ (b) $x \ge \frac{8}{3}$

39. $x < -2, x > 2$

41. $1 \le x \le 13$

43. $x \le -7, x \ge 13$

45. $\frac{1}{2} < x < \frac{3}{2}$

47.

(a) $1 \le x \le 5$ (b) $x \le -1, x \ge 7$

49. $|x| \le 3$ **51.** $|x + 1| \ge 4$ **53.** $|x - 6| < 10$

55. $|x + 1| > 3$

57. Positive on: $(-\infty, -1) \cup (5, \infty)$
Negative on: $(-1, 5)$

59. Positive on: 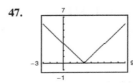 $\left(-\infty, \dfrac{2 - \sqrt{10}}{2}\right) \cup \left(\dfrac{2 + \sqrt{10}}{2}, \infty\right)$
Negative on: $\left(\dfrac{2 - \sqrt{10}}{2}, \dfrac{2 + \sqrt{10}}{2}\right)$

61. Negative on: $(-\infty, \infty)$

63. $(-\infty, -5], [1, \infty)$

65. $(-7, 3)$

67. $0, [4, \infty)$

69. $(-3, -1), \left(\frac{3}{2}, \infty\right)$

71. $(-1, 1), (3, \infty)$

73. No solution

75. $\left(-\infty, \frac{1}{2}\right), \left(\frac{1}{2}, \infty\right)$

77. (a) $x = 1$ (b) $x \geq 1$ (c) $x > 1$

79.

    (a) $x \leq -1, x \geq 3$ (b) $0 \leq x \leq 2$

81. $(-\infty, -1), (0, 1)$

83. $(-\infty, -1), [4, \infty)$

85.

    (a) $0 \leq x < 2$ (b) $2 < x \leq 4$

87. $[5, \infty)$ **89.** $[-3, 4]$ **91.** $\left(-\infty, -\frac{1}{3}\right], [7, \infty)$

93. (a) 2005   (b) $(2003, 2005); (2005, 2012)$

95. (a) 10 sec   (b) $(4, 6)$

97. (a)

    (b) $(1996, 2001)$
    (c) $6.605 < x < 11.646$

99. $t \geq 6.45$; In the year 2007, there were at least 900 Bed Bath & Beyond stores.

101. $t \approx 1.04$; In 2001, there were the same number of Bed Bath & Beyond stores as Williams-Sonoma stores.

103. $333\frac{1}{3}$ vibrations/sec   **105.** $1.2 < t < 2.4$

107. False. $10 \geq -x$

109. False. Cube roots have no restrictions on the domain.

111. (a) iv   (b) ii   (c) iii   (d) i

113. $y^{-1} = \dfrac{x}{12}$ **115.** $y^{-1} = \sqrt[3]{x - 7}$

117. Answers will vary.

CHAPTER 2

ANSWERS FOR **CHAPTER 17**

Exercise Set 17.1

1. 9 **3.** 3 **5.** 130 **7.** 0 **9.** 0 **11.** 11 **13.** 0

15. 79 **17.** yes **19.** yes **21.** yes **23.** yes

25. $Q(x) = x^4 + 3x^3 - 8x^2 - 24x + 3; R(x) = 18$

27. $Q(x) = 5x^2 - 8x + 24; R(x) = -63$

29. $Q(x) = 8x^4 + 4x^3 - 2x^2 + 6x + 1; R(x) = \frac{1}{2}$

31. $Q(x) = 2x^3 - 3x^2 - 4; R(x) = 0$

Exercise Set 17.2

1. $1, \dfrac{-5 + \sqrt{85}}{10}, \dfrac{-5 - \sqrt{85}}{10}$ **3.** $\frac{1}{3}, 3, -3$

5. $2, -2, j, -j$ **7.** $3, -3, -1 + 2j, -1 - 2j$

9. $-1, -1, 2, 3$ **11.** $-1, -1, -3, 1$

13. $-\frac{1}{2}, \frac{1}{3}, -2 + j, -2 - j$

15. $1, \frac{2}{3}, \dfrac{-1 + j\sqrt{3}}{2}, \dfrac{-1 - j\sqrt{3}}{2}$

17. $1, 1, 1, -1 + j\sqrt{3}, -1 - j\sqrt{3}$

19. $3, -2, \frac{2}{3}, \dfrac{-1 + \sqrt{5}}{2}, \dfrac{-1 - \sqrt{5}}{2}$

21. $j, -j, 3j, -3j, 7, -1$

Exercise Set 17.3

1. 0.5641

3. $x_1 = -3.4321$
$x_2 = 1.3315$
$x_3 = 0.520$
$x_4 = -0.4202$

5. $x_1 = -3.3539$
$x_2 = 1.8774$
$x_3 = 0.4765$

7. $x_1 = 1.3532$
$x_2 = -1$

9. $x_1 = 2.0946$
$x_2 = -1$

11. $x_1 = -1.6573$
$x_2 = 1$

13. $x_1 = -1$
$x_2 = -1.4333$
$x_3 = 0.2381$

15. $x_1 = 1.4142$
$x_2 = -1.4142$
$x_3 = -0.5$
$x_4 = -0.25$

17. 6.22731 years, or about 6 years 83 days

19. (a) 63.87006 cm (b) $521\,101\pi$ cm^3

21. The approximate roots are $\pm 0.3536, \pm 0.8654,$ $\pm 1.4639, \pm 1.7321,$ and ± 2.2323

23. 1 in. or 2 in. **25.** 9 feet **27.** $R = 2$ **29.** 3.5 cm